THE
BOOK
OF THE
STATES

**2006 EDITION
VOLUME 38**

ISBN 0-87292-832-2

9 780872 928329

**The Council of State Governments
Lexington, Kentucky**

Headquarters: (859) 244-8000
Fax: (859) 244-8001
Internet: www.csg.org

Sharing capitol ideas.

Headquarters:
Daniel M. Sprague, Executive Director
2760 Research Park Drive, P.O. Box 11910
Lexington, KY 40578-1910
Phone: (859) 244-8000
Internet: www.csg.org

Southern:
Colleen Cousineau, Director
P.O. Box 98129
Atlanta, GA 30359
Phone: (404) 633-1866
Internet: www.slcatlanta.org

Eastern:
Alan V. Sokolow, Director
40 Broad Street, 20th Floor
New York, NY 10004
Phone: (212) 482-2320
Internet: www.csgeast.org

Western:
Kent Briggs, Director
1107 9th Street, Suite 650
Sacramento, CA 95814
Phone: (916) 553-4423
Internet: www.csgwest.org

Midwestern:
Michael H. McCabe, Director
701 E. 22nd Street, Suite 110
Lombard, IL 60148
Phone: (630) 925-1922
Internet: www.csgmidwest.org

Washington, D.C.:
Jim Brown, General Counsel & Director
444 N. Capitol Street, NW, Suite 401
Washington, D.C. 20001
Phone: (202) 624-5460
Internet: www.csg-dc.org

Copyright 2006
The Council of State Governments
2760 Research Park Drive • P.O. Box 11910
Lexington, Kentucky 40578-1910

Manufactured in the United States of America

Publication Sales Department
1(800) 800-1910

Paperback Price: $99.00
ISBN # 0-87292-833-0

Hard Cover Price: $125.00
ISBN # 0-87292-832-2

Foreword

The major goal of The Council of State Governments is to provide state officials with the information and analysis of emerging trends and offer innovative state policy options and sound management tools, helping state officials deal with challenges they face. Other goals and objectives are to advocate multistate problem-solving, promote excellence in decision-making and champion state sovereignty within the U.S. federal system. Toward such goals, CSG conducts surveys and research and publishes a number of reports both annually and periodically. One of our primary and most renowned publications with the oldest history is *The Book of the States*.

I am pleased to offer another edition of the premier reference source. The 2006 edition of *The Book of the States* includes up-to-date information on state constitutional developments, the three branches of the states, commonwealths and territories, major agencies, finances, management and select state policies. This particular volume includes timely articles on recent trends and forecasts on some of the top issues for state policymakers: education, Medicaid and economic development. It also includes an article on a new leadership model for governors, legislators and others to consider.

This annual reference book contains nearly 200 tables with 50-state comparative data. Most tables have been updated, and new tables have been added thanks to state and federal officials, think tanks, academics and national organizations of state officials. For the convenience of readers, several tables have been rearranged by region and other categories.

We hope this new edition will be useful to state policymakers and managers for their work to improve management and service delivery for the benefit of their citizens. We will be delighted to know if this edition is used as a handy reference source by others as well. On behalf of The Council and the editorial staff, I would like to thank and acknowledge the article authors and others who have contributed to the production of this volume.

May 2006

Daniel M. Sprague
Executive Director
The Council of State Governments

The Book of the States 2006

Editor in Chief	Keon S. Chi
Project Manager	Audrey S. Wall
Associate Editor	Heather M. Perkins
Production Coordinators	Lisa K. Eads
	Susie D. Bush
Graphic Designer	Chris D. Pryor

Acknowledgements

The editorial and production staff members wish to thank the article authors who graciously shared their expertise and insights, the hundreds of individuals in the states who responded to national surveys conducted by The Council of State Governments, national organizations of state officials, federal agencies and think tank organizations who made their most recent data and information available for this volume.

Table of Contents

CONTENTS

Chapter Three
STATE LEGISLATIVE BRANCH 61

Chapter Four
STATE EXECUTIVE BRANCH 135

CONTENTS

CONTENTS

Chapter Seven
STATE FINANCE 331

Chapter Eight
STATE MANAGEMENT AND ADMINISTRATION **407**

CONTENTS

CONTENTS

Emerging Trends in State Governments: 2006 and Beyond

By Keon S. Chi

As we enter the second quarter of 2006, most state governments appear to be in much better shape—at least in their fiscal conditions—than they were in the past few years. After reviewing the State of the State addresses delivered by 40 governors early this year, Katherine Willoughby highlights major themes of the chief executives' speeches by saying: "Revenues are flowing more freely into state coffers; state governments are realizing surpluses. … Today's governors seem to have learned from periods of fiscal stringency. In fact, many are calling for measured approaches to budget making—emphasizing long-range planning, balance and good management to pursue the work of the states." Other observers of state finances, as cited below, agreed with this encouraging assessment.

A brighter fiscal picture notwithstanding, our states are faced with many challenges—stemming from both internal and external forces. The introduction section of the 2005 edition of *The Book of the States* cited global dynamics and terrorist threats, the potential elimination of some federal aid programs and federal encroachment upon state regulatory powers as external forces. Internal forces affecting states included partisan competition in legislative chambers as well as among the three branches of state government, structural deficits in budget-making and growing pressures from direct citizen control in many states. These forces continue to affect how states are operating this year and beyond. In some respects, we now see additional challenges in part due to actual cuts in federal funding for many domestic programs.

Some of these challenges and emerging trends state policymakers need to be aware of are included in the 2006 edition of *The Book of the States* under the usual headings: state constitutional development and the three branches, politics, administration and management and selected public policies. What follows is a summary of trends affecting state government this year and the next few years, based primarily on the 29 articles by knowledgeable observers included in this edition.

State Elections

2006 is an election year. Voters in most states are electing new leaders—legislators, governors, constitutional officers and judges. Approximately one-third of lawmakers will not return to their seats after the end of the year, while newly-elected or re-elected governors of 36 states will be inaugurated following the November elections. These state elections are in addition to midterm congressional elections and thousands of local races. Secretaries of state and other government election officials across the nation will be able to find out after the general election if reform measures put in place by the states in January under the Help America Vote Act of 2002 have worked.

This year's elections may affect partisan control in state legislatures and governors' offices, although no one can predict how many changes might take place. Following the 2005 elections, the map of partisan control in the states has remained very much the same as before. Republicans now control 20 state legislatures, and Democrats control 19. Currently, 28 states have Republican governors, and 22 have Democratic chief executives. The Republican Party has controlled both branches of state governments in the past two decades or so. It will be interesting to see if this trend changes after the November races. Partisan selection of judges adds another dimension to this year's elections. As David Rottman notes, "Politicizing the judiciary puts in jeopardy the checks and balances so carefully inserted into the federal and state constitutions."

In addition to choosing officers, voters in some states are likely to play a role in reshaping state policies through initiatives and referendums. It is interesting to note that voters approved only three of 20 measures on the ballot in 2005. In California, voters rejected all eight measures, including the governor's proposals on redistricting, budget and other controversial issues. Ohio voters rejected four measures designed for election reform. In Colorado, however, voters approved a constitutional amendment suspending the Taxpayer Bill of Rights Act to forgo the tax rebates they are due in the next five years. Overall, as John Matsusaka reports, voters in 10 states approved 21 of the 26 constitutional amendments proposed in 2005. Observers are predicting a much larger number of voter- or legislature-initiated ballot measures in the 2006 elections.

State-Federal Relations

The trend appears to be toward continued federal fiscal reductions and withdrawals from domestic programs. The president's 2007 budget proposal would reduce or cut more than 140 domestic discretionary programs by more than $12 billion, a 6.7 percent decline, while mandatory entitlement grants would increase by $6.4 billion. John Kincaid characterizes the current federal state relations as coercive federalism with three patterns: shifting aid from places to persons, using conditions of aid to achieve federal objectives that lie outside Congress's constitutionally enumerated powers, and increasing congressional earmarking.

State policymakers need to pay attention to protecting reserved powers of the states under the Constitution. Predicting future directions of the Roberts court, Kincaid says, "The Supreme Court is not enamored with state authority." The question is, what can states do to deal with the continuing trend of congressional pre-emption of state functions? Joseph Zimmerman offers an answer: "Protection of the reserved regulatory powers of the states against further congressional encroachment will necessitate enactment of new interstate regulatory compacts and/or uniform state laws."

Debates on state relations with the federal and local governments are likely to continue, especially in light of Hurricanes Katrina and Rita last year. As Beverly Bell observes, "Hurricane Katrina shone a bright light on the nation's level of preparedness. ... Debate continues on whether the federal government's focus on preparing for a terrorism incident has overlooked the more common threat of natural disasters. Adequate funding for all-hazards is a major concern for all state and local emergency managers, particularly since federal mandates in preparedness and response increase regularly, without matching federal funding."

State Finances and Policies

"Most state budgets were in very good shape at the end of fiscal year 2006, and election-year budgets for 2007 will lead to tax cuts," says Don Boyd. "But beyond 2007 states will face challenges, including the need to fund or constrain rapid Medicaid growth, pressures to strengthen pension funding and begin financing newly disclosed liabilities for retiree health care, and the need to respond to large cuts in federal grants."

In a nutshell, state policymakers will have to come up with new strategies to pick up their share in several policy areas as federal deficits are projected to continue as they have in the past five years or so.

Federal grants-in-aid to state and local governments amount to approximately 17 percent of the federal budget, and Medicaid accounts for more than 40 percent of federal grants. The federal-state joint health care program now is the largest budget item after education in most state budgets. According to the Center for Medicaid and State Operations, the modernized Medicaid system under the Deficit Reduction Act of 2005, which reflects the bipartisan recommendations of the National Governors Association, is expected to "give states greater flexibility with reduced administrative burden." The center was planning to send states new guidelines for the implementation of new provisions, including coverage for disabled children, toward the end of 2006 so changes can take effect in January 2007.

Some states are very likely to continue to ask for more funding for the No Child Left Behind Act. Critics of NCLB contend states needed billions of dollars more than the federal funding, which they say fell $36 billion short of the amount promised in the law's authorization. Connecticut and Utah openly resisted NCLB's implementation, while other states asked for more flexibility and lax standards. "As states anticipate the reauthorization of NCLB, scheduled for 2007 but ultimately likely to take place in 2008 or 2009, these issues will deserve much scrutiny," says Frederick Hess. "How NCLB ambitions fare through implementation, court challenges, and state resistance will have much to say about the feasibility of its authors' hopes."

Education accounts for the largest item in state budgets. It was the most frequently mentioned topic in the annual gubernatorial messages this and previous years. In addition to K–12 education, state policymakers also need to take a close look at how their budgets for higher education stack up. John Curtis reminds them of a relative decline in state funding for public higher education, now providing "a smaller percentage of institutional revenues than ever before." He observes: "Faced with a decline in state revenues, public institutions have raised tuition at an accelerated pace." Curtis also says that the maximum Pell grant has remained unchanged for several years and that many states have shifted funding for student financial aid programs from needs-based to merit-based awards.

In 2005, Congress reauthorized the welfare reform bill under the Deficit Reduction Act, substantially changing work participation requirements of the Temporary Assistance to Needy Families program. States will need to meet a 50 percent participation rate for all families receiving assistance. Sheila Zedlewski and Meghan Williamson predict this requirement could be a challenge to many states, since current work participation rates generally fall below the new rate. Also, many states have depleted their TANF reserve funds, leaving them little flexibility to develop new strategies to increase work among participants. The good news is that TANF caseloads have declined by 6 percent in the past two to three years.

When we review governors' State of the State addresses delivered this year, we find economic development listed as one of the top five topics mentioned, following education, health and Medicaid, taxes and natural resources and energy. Jeffrey Finkle reports: "While the country's economy ventures down the road to recovery, the push to foster economic development from coast to coast is no less pressing than it was when the country was in the throes of its most recent recession." As Katherine Willoughby noted, several governors are linking economic development to education and work force training programs.

In predicting future developments in the economic development field, state policymakers need to pay attention to the eminent domain issue and business incentive programs offered by states. This year, several states have passed legislation limiting government power of eminent domain to protect private property rights. Depending on how the Supreme Court deals with the pending *Cuno v. DaimlerChrysler* case and congressional action—the Economic Development Act of 2005—states will have to adjust their strategies to a new environment, as Adam Bruns explains.

On the international trade issue, Earl Fry updates U.S.-Canada trade relations, focusing on state-provincial activities. He says 12 of the state foreign offices are located in Canada, while the Canadian provincial governments are much more active than American states. "Many of the provincial governments have institutionalized their linkages to U.S. state governments through creation of bilateral or regional cross-border organizations and the signing of hundreds of memoranda, accords, or agreements with the U.S. states …," Fry says. "(M)ost state governments can do much more to build linkages with Canadian provincial governments and to encourage their business communities to export to Canada."

Separation of Power and Checks and Balances

Like the federal government, the principle of separation of power and checks and balances in state government is a long-held and well-respected tradition. Yet it is difficult to draw a pretty picture depicting harmonious or cooperative relationships among the three branches. This inter-branch issue becomes more complicated when the executive and legislative branches are controlled by different political parties as is the case in many states today.

On one hand, most state government observers agree that the legislative branch has gained more power over the other two branches in most states—especially in term-limited states—in the past 10 years. They say that in many states the balance of power has shifted to the governor, who has centralized the bureaucracy and expanded his or her policy staff. On the other hand, when one looks at gubernatorial fiscal power, the story is slightly different. Thad Beyle says the gubernatorial budgetary power actually declined from 1960 to 2005. He adds: "However, we must remember that during the same period, state legislatures were also undergoing considerable reform, and gaining more power to work on governor's proposed budget was one of those reforms sought. Hence, the increased legislative budgetary power more than balanced out any increases in gubernatorial budgetary power."

The legislative branch's relations with the judiciary branch are also disputed. The recent debate on the proper relationship between the two branches appears to be escalating in several states, including Arizona, Delaware, Florida, Kansas and Missouri. David Rottman argues: "Respect for the judicial branch was not evident in a number of states where legislatures and executive branch officials put traditional checks and balances in jeopardy," especially in judicial selection.

State Policymakers and Managers

Other than personnel, no drastic changes in elected statewide executive offices are expected in 2006. Many elected officials will not return to their jobs after this year's general elections. The beginning of the 21st century is a time of change in the governors' offices across the country, says Thad Beyle. In 2006, for example, 37 governors—74 percent—are serving in their first term. Recently, lieutenant governors in many states have expanded their roles and responsibilities, and this trend is likely to continue, as Julia Hurst reports. One major responsibility of secretaries of state is supervising the implementation of the Help America Vote Act aimed at reforming the way elections are administered. State attorneys general are working with their federal counterparts in the areas of antitrust, bankruptcy, consumer protection, criminal law and the environment. One issue they are concerned about is the potential impact of a decline in tobacco sales on the tobacco settlement agreements they handled. State auditors are implementing the new accounting and financial reporting standards for post-employment benefits, while treasurers are involved in cash management improvement and state investment.

State executive agencies continue to experiment with new approaches to improve productivity. As Marc Holzer and his colleagues suggest, state managers might want to consider replicating a new 311 system to open a new line of communication between governments and their citizens. State procurement officials regard "strategic sourcing" as a most significant trend in enhancing efficiency, according to John Adler and his co-authors. Pam Brinegar reports on a new trend in licensure: "State legislatures show signs of departing from their customary professional licensing approach as new professions gain state licensure without initiation by a profession or the public." Information technology outsourcing is likely to continue in the foreseeable future due to its efficiency and cost-effectiveness, as Mary Gay Whitmer predicts.

For state leaders and managers, new leadership styles and managerial skills are in constant demand. "State policymakers, like those in many other fields, are facing a crisis in leadership," Robert B. Denhardt and Janet V. Denhardt argue. They suggest state leaders consider a shared leadership model, which combines collective engagement, values and arts. They conclude: "Understanding shared leadership, the role of values in leadership, and the artistic side of leadership is a significant challenge, but one that will be important as state policymakers attempt to address the crises of leadership that they and others face today."

David Freel sees several emerging trends in ethics for state officials. One is "a fundamental re-examination of the core characteristics embodied within and mechanisms used to implement ethics oversight." Other trends include a shift toward mandatory ethics education for public officials, more efficient use of the Internet in education and outreach, resurgence in nepotism concerns and ethical issues involving gifts and gratuities provided by those with interests in government. He says, "With ethics questions related to gift and gratuities in the states and nationally continuing to unfold, there is no doubt that attention to, and reform of, the standards by which they are judged will continue as a leading ethics trend."

Looking Ahead

As the federal government is deeply involved in the war on terrorism and in Iraq, and as Uncle Sam continues to operate with deficit budgets with the largest debt in the nation's history, it is easy to foresee challenges that lie ahead for federal, as well as state and local, officials. One thing that seems certain is an increased burden on state governments to provide their citizens with services they expect—services such as education, health care and job creation, energy, natural resources and infrastructure and pubic safety.

State policymakers also face unprecedented pressures due to demographical and technological changes. We live in an era of aging, immigration, globalization, information revolution, scarce resources and polarized political environment. State leaders and managers should rethink how state government should work on a longer-term basis to better deal with emerging trends and transform some of the institutional characteristics that do not work, especially by addressing cross-cutting issues that transcend compartmentalized organizational jurisdictions. Now is the time for them to find more effective and efficient ways of managing state government in partnerships with non-governmental sectors and state and local agencies, and by adopting more innovations and best practices for the well-being of their citizens.

Keon S. Chi is editor in chief of *The Book of the States.*

Chapter One

STATE CONSTITUTIONS

"The 26 state constitutional amendments considered by voters in 2005 were all proposed by legislatures or through the constitutional initiative process."

—John Dinan

State Constitutional Developments in 2005
By John Dinan

Although relatively few state constitutional amendments were considered in 2005, several developments attracted significant attention, including the defeat of electoral-reform initiatives in Ohio and California, the passage of same-sex marriage bans in Kansas and Texas, the nationwide movement to respond to the U.S. Supreme Court's eminent domain ruling in Kelo v. City of New London *by considering additional statutory and constitutional protections for property rights, and the decision by Colorado voters to suspend for five years a Taxpayers' Bill of Rights (TABOR) provision that is the strictest tax and expenditure limitation in the country.*

As is usually the case with off-year elections, voters in 2005 considered and approved a relatively small number of state constitutional amendments. However, the infrequency of state constitutional change during the year was not indicative of a lack of public interest in the amendment and revision processes. Several developments were followed with much interest. First, voters in California and Ohio considered several amendments that sought to regulate various aspects of the electoral process, including bringing about more competitive elections. Although these measures were all soundly defeated, they attracted significant attention and generated much discussion. Second, two more same-sex marriage bans were approved in 2005, bringing to 19 the number of state constitutions containing such bans. With at least six states already scheduling votes on such bans in 2006, this number is likely to increase in the next few years. Additionally, the U.S. Supreme Court's June 2005 decision in *Kelo v. City of New London* to interpret the Fifth Amendment of the U.S. Constitution as not barring the use of eminent domain for economic development projects generated a significant public backlash and led state officials to propose statutes

and constitutional amendments to protect property owners against such proceedings. Although the ruling was issued too late in the year to permit votes to be taken on constitutional amendments in November 2005, at least one state has already scheduled a vote on an amendment in 2006, and other states are expected to follow suit. Also of interest was the decision of Colorado voters to narrowly approve a November referendum to suspend key aspects of the Taxpayers' Bill of Rights (TABOR) provision in the state constitution and thereby forego $3.7 billion in tax refunds over the next five years. The TABOR provision had been added to the Colorado Constitution in 1992 and is an especially stringent tax and expenditure limitation measure whose suspension is widely expected to have an impact on debates in other states where anti-tax advocates are pushing for adoption of similar provisions.

Constitutional Amendment and Revision Methods

Constitutional amendments were proposed in 2005 in only 11 states, far fewer than the 33 states that considered amendments in 2004, and slightly fewer

Table A: State Constitutional Changes by Method of Initiation: 2000–01, 2002–03 and 2004–05

Method of initiation	Number of states involved 2000–2001	Number of states involved 2002–2003	Number of states involved 2004–2005	Total proposals 2000–2001	Total proposals 2002–2003	Total proposals 2004–2005	Total adopted 2000–2001	Total adopted 2002–2003	Total adopted 2004–2005	Percentage adopted 2000–2001	Percentage adopted 2002–2003	Percentage adopted 2004–2005
All methods............................	40	38	40	212	232	166	154	164	112	72.0 (a)	70.6	67.5
Legislative proposal	38	36	38	180	208	127	141	155	95	91.0 (a)	74.5	74.8
Constitutional initiative........	10	11	13	32	24	39	13	9	17	40.6	37.5	43.6
Constitutional convention.....	...	...	...	...	...	...	...	...	...	...	...	...
Constitutional commission ...	...	...	...	...	...	...	...	...	...	...	...	...

Sources: Based on surveys conducted in previous years by Janice May and updated by John Dinan in January 2006.
Key:
... — Not applicable.
(a) — In calculating these percentages, the amendments adopted in Delaware (where proposals are not submitted to the voters) are excluded.

than the 13 states that considered amendments in 2003 (the most recent off-year election). All told in 2005, 26 amendments were proposed and 14 were approved. This compares with 2004, when 140 amendments were proposed and 98 were approved, and with 2003, when 57 amendments were proposed and 46 were approved.

Although in one sense the low number of amendments in 2005 could be seen as merely a continuation of a gradual recent decline in the pursuit of state constitutional change through formal amendment processes, this might also be understood as the product of strategic behavior by political actors who purposely delayed placing measures on the ballot until 2006 in an effort to boost turnout among particular voter groups and thereby influence the outcome of gubernatorial and congressional elections that year. For instance, the same-sex marriage bans placed on the ballot and easily approved in 11 states (including several battleground states) in the November 2004 election are believed to have boosted Republican voter turnout in the presidential election in those states. It is no surprise, then, that political strategists who had the option of qualifying ballot measures either in 2005 (an off-year election in every state but New Jersey and Virginia) or in 2006 (when all 435 U.S. representatives, plus 33 U.S. senators and 36 governors will be elected) occasionally chose to wait until 2006, with an eye toward gaining an electoral advantage in these elections. Thus Ohio Secretary of State Kenneth Blackwell, who is seeking the 2006 Republican gubernatorial nomination, opted to delay a planned 2005 tax and expenditure limitation measure in part from a desire to benefit in 2006 from the higher conservative turnout generally associated with such measures.[1] Conservative groups in other states are scheduling similar tax and expenditure limitation amendments, as well as additional same-sex marriage bans, in 2006, with an eye toward boosting turnout for Republican candidates. Liberal groups, meanwhile, are planning votes on minimum-wage and education-spending measures, some of which will take the form of constitutional amendments, in an effort to help Democratic candidates.

Legislative Proposal and Constitutional Initiative

The 26 state constitutional amendments considered by voters in 2005 were all proposed by legislatures or through the constitutional initiative process. Eighteen amendments were proposed by legislatures (a process in place in all 50 states which requires voter approval in every state but Delaware), and 14 of these

legislative-initiated amendments were approved, for a passage rate of 77.7 percent. Eight amendments were proposed by constitutional initiative (a process available in 18 states), but none of these initiative amendments was approved, a dramatic change from 2004, when 17 of 31 initiated amendments were approved.

Constitutional Conventions and Revision Commissions

Constitutional conventions were once called frequently, whether for the purpose of drafting constitutions for new states or making wholesale revisions or limited changes to existing constitutions. Conventions can be initiated by legislatures in all 50 states, with convention calls in most states requiring popular approval. Fourteen states also require the question of calling a convention be submitted to the people periodically, with the interval between required submissions ranging from nine to 20 years. However, in recent years legislatures have been reluctant to issue convention calls, and in cases where periodic convention questions have been submitted to the voters, such questions have been repeatedly rejected.

Although in 2005 no convention calls were approved by legislatures or submitted to the people, the question of whether to call a convention was considered in Alabama, New Jersey and Oklahoma. Constitutional reform has been on the political agenda in Alabama for half a decade now, dating back to the formation in 2000 of a public-interest group, Alabama Citizens for Constitutional Reform (ACCR), which has worked to build support for a constitutional convention to revise Alabama's 1901 Constitution, the longest and most frequently amended of any state. Although these efforts have been hindered by voters' defeat of Gov. Bob Riley's comprehensive constitutional reform amendment in September 2003 and by the death in November 2003 of ACCR founder and Chairman Bailey Thomson, ACCR continued its work in 2005 and collected 60,000 signatures (toward a goal of 100,000) on a petition urging the legislature to call a convention.[2]

In the last several years, New Jersey has considered calling a convention devoted to changing the structure of property taxes, which are the highest in the country. In fact, in May 2005 the New Jersey Assembly approved a measure calling for a vote on a convention to be held in the November 2005 general election, but the measure failed to emerge from the Senate. However, Jon Corzine, who was elected governor in November 2005, campaigned on the need to call a convention to address the issue of property

Table B: Substantive Changes in State Constitutions: Proposed and Adopted: 2000–01, 2002–03 and 2004–05

Subject matter	Total proposed			Total adopted			Percentage adopted		
	2000–01	2002–03	2004–05	2000–01	2002–03	2004–05	2000–01	2002–03	2004–05
Proposals of statewide applicability	162(a)	191	138(b)	114(b)	128	94(b)	70.3(a)(d)	67.0	68.1(b)(c)
Bill of Rights	4	12	16	1	8	15	25.0	66.6	93.8
Suffrage & elections	6	6	14	4	3	6	66.6	50.0	42.9
Legislative branch	37	24	14	27	17	6	72.9	70.8	42.8
Executive branch	9	8	5	7	4	4	77.7	50.0	80.0
Judicial branch	7(a)	19	10	8	11	5	100.0	57.8	50.0
Local government	9	5	4	6	5	3	66.6	100.0	75.0
Finance & taxation	38	65	33	25	39	23	65.5	60.0	69.7
State & local debt	5	10	7	5	5	6	100.0	50.0	85.7
State functions	24	16	14(b)	17	13	8(b)	70.8	81.2	57.1
Amendment & revision	3	3	1	0	3	1	0.0	100.0	100.0
General revision proposals	0	0	0	0	0	0	0.0	0.0	0.0
Miscellaneous proposals	20(c)	23(c)	20(c)	14	20(c)	17(c)	70.0	86.0	85.0
Local amendments	50	41	28	40	36	18	80.0	87.8	64.3

Sources: Based on surveys conducted in previous years by Janice May and updated by John Dinan in January 2006.
Key:
(a) — Excludes Delaware where proposals are not submitted to voters.
(b) — Includes Delaware.
(c) — Includes amendments that contain editorial revision.
(d) — Excludes one Oregon amendment not canvassed by court order.

taxes. After winning the election, he announced plans to call a special legislative session to deal with the property tax issue. He also urged the legislature to permit the people in November 2006 to vote on calling a convention to make necessary constitutional changes in this area.

Oklahoma also took a step in 2005 toward holding a convention, when the House of Representatives approved a measure that would submit to the people the question of whether to call a convention. The House resolution (which is pending in the Senate) takes note of the provision in the Oklahoma Constitution requiring a convention question to be submitted to the people at least once every 20 years—the last submission was in 1970—and then stipulates such a convention, if approved by the voters, would assemble in July 2007 and be comprised of the members of the state House and Senate.

Constitutional commissions have also been utilized throughout U.S. history, whether to propose amendments that are then considered by the legislature or to conduct research in preparation for a convention. In the last few decades, though, two additional types of commissions have been created. Florida has created two revision commissions with the unique power to refer amendments directly to the voters: a Constitutional Revision Commission (established in 1968) and a Taxation and Budget Reform Commission (established in 1988). In addition, the Utah Constitutional Revision Commission was created by the legislature in 1977 and is the only revision commission in the country that has a permanent charge to propose amendments that are then considered by the legislature. The Utah Revision Commission was the only one in effect in 2005, and commission members debated changes regarding gubernatorial succession and term limits, among other issues.

Constitutional Changes

Voters in 2005 were not asked to approve any new constitutions or wholesale revisions of existing constitutions. Rather, the proposed changes all took the form of constitutional amendments, which sought to add or revise provisions regarding elections, rights, governing institutions and various policies.

Elections

Voters in Ohio and California considered a number of amendments targeting the electoral process, and although these measures were all defeated, they attracted significant attention in the lead-up to the November 2005 election. The most far-reaching electoral reform measures were initiated amendments that sought to establish non-partisan redistricting panels that would create as many politically competitive districts as possible. In Ohio, the redistricting amendment was advocated by a coalition of liberal groups acting under the banner of Reform Ohio Now and would have created a five-member nonpartisan panel that would be selected in part by state judges and would be charged with drawing competitive congressional and state legislative districts (a five-member panel of elected officials currently draws state legislative districts, whereas congressional districting is now handled through the legislative process). The California redistricting amendment was a centerpiece of Gov. Arnold Schwarzenegger's reform package and would have established a three-member panel of retired federal or state judges. This panel would have been charged with immediately drawing up new congressional, state legislative and Board of Equalization districting plans, which would then be submitted to the voters, and, if approved, remain in effect through the next census.

The Ohio redistricting amendment was one of four electoral reform amendments supported by Reform Ohio Now and easily defeated at the polls. Another Ohio amendment would have taken election oversight authority from the secretary of state and vested the power in a newly created nine-member board of elections. The remaining amendments in the defeated reform package would have permitted voters to cast absentee ballots without providing a reason and reduced various contribution limits in state campaigns.

Electoral reform amendments of this sort can be expected to return to the ballot in coming years. States without legislative redistricting commissions are facing increasing pressure to boost the competitiveness of elections. And individuals are particularly apt to propose such commissions in states where the initiative process allows the minority party members to bypass the legislature and place the issue directly before the voters. In addition, in at least one state, the majority party views the constitutional amendment process as a vehicle for overcoming the veto power of a governor of the other party. Thus in Wisconsin, a Republican-controlled legislature has repeatedly approved a photo ID requirement for voters, which is a measure that has received much recent attention from Republican legislators around the country and has been opposed by Democrats and African-Americans. But the statute was vetoed three times by Democratic Gov. Jim Doyle. Given that constitutional amendments in Wisconsin can be proposed by a majority of legislators in successive sessions, with no requirement for gubernatorial approval, Republican legislators are currently seeking to overcome gubernatorial resistance to this reform by proposing the measure as a constitutional amendment. Such an amendment was approved by the Assembly in November, but has not yet been approved by the Senate. It could appear on the ballot in the future.[3]

Rights

The most prominent state constitutional changes concerning individual rights in 2005 were the approvals of same-sex marriage bans in Kansas and Texas, bringing to 19 the number of states with con-

stitutional provisions regulating same-sex marriage. Eighteen of these provisions ban same-sex marriage, while Hawaii's provision empowers the legislature to limit marriage to opposite-sex couples. Although four of these 19 provisions were adopted prior to the Massachusetts Supreme Judicial Court decision in *Goodridge v. Department of Public Health* (2003), which interpreted the Massachusetts Constitution as requiring the issuance of marriage licenses to same-sex couples, the remaining constitutional amendments were all enacted after Goodridge in an effort to prevent similar judicial rulings in other states. In every case, voters have approved the same-sex marriage bans by large margins—the closest vote was in Oregon in 2004, where the amendment was approved by a 56 to 44 percent margin—and this was also true in 2005 of the Kansas and Texas measures.

Amendments banning same-sex marriage are likely to attract continuing attention in the next few years. The constitutionality of existing amendments has already been challenged in several states—including Louisiana, where the state Supreme Court in January 2005 sustained the state's 2004 amendment against a constitutional challenge, and Nebraska, where a federal district judge in May 2005 ruled the state's sweeping 2000 amendment violated the federal constitution—and such challenges are likely to continue. Moreover, additional amendments have already been placed on the ballot in six states in 2006, with Alabama's vote scheduled for June, and votes in South Carolina, South Dakota, Tennessee, Virginia and Wisconsin scheduled for November. Voters in several other states could also vote on same-sex marriage bans in November 2006, including Arizona and Colorado, where same-sex marriage opponents are working to qualify amendments through the initiative process.[4]

Meanwhile, it was expected that voters in Massachusetts, the only state where same-sex marriage is now legal, would have a chance in November 2006 to vote on an amendment banning same-sex marriage but permitting civil unions; however, this vote will not take place. Such an amendment received the requisite first approval from a joint House-Senate legislative session in March 2004 by a 105-92 vote, but in September 2005 the measure failed to secure the requisite second legislative approval when it was defeated, 157-39. Opponents of the amendment in September 2005 were made up in part by legislators who opposed any constitutional restriction on same-sex marriage. But a number of legislative opponents, including many legislators who had supported the measure in March 2004, preferred a more stringent measure that would ban same-sex marriage and offer no support for civil unions. Supporters of this more stringent policy proceeded to secure the signatures necessary to place such an amendment on the ballot through the constitutional initiative process. In December 2005, the secretary of state certified that the petition-gatherers had met and exceeded the constitutional requirement—3 percent of voters in the last gubernatorial election. The next step in the Massachusetts constitutional initiative process is for the amendment to receive the approval of 25 percent of legislators in successive sessions, in which case the same-sex marriage ban would appear on the November 2008 ballot.

Two other rights-related amendments were on the ballot in 2005. California voters narrowly defeated an initiative amendment that would have required doctors to notify a parent or guardian 48 hours in advance of performing an abortion on a minor. And Texas voters approved an amendment permitting a judge to deny bail to an accused felon who violates the conditions of his release before trial.

Finally, although no amendments were enacted in 2005 regarding eminent domain, the U.S. Supreme Court's June 2005 *Kelo* decision led state officials to consider various statutory and constitutional means of limiting the use of eminent domain for economic development, and this will likely result in numerous amendments being considered in coming years. Michigan in December became the first state to approve the submission of such an amendment to the voters, and this measure will be on the November 2006 ballot. Up to this point, state legislatures have relied primarily on statutory means of strengthening protection for private property in the wake of the Court's decision, with Alabama, Delaware, Ohio and Texas having already enacted post-*Kelo* statutes. However, legislators in several of these states, as well as many others, have also introduced constitutional amendments to further strengthen state protections for property rights.[5]

Governing Institutions

The most significant constitutional change in state governance in 2005 was the decision of New Jersey voters in November to approve an amendment creating a lieutenant governor position. New Jersey had been one of eight states without such an office; in the event that the New Jersey governor resigned, as happened on two occasions in the past four years, the president of the Senate simply assumed the office and completed the term, while also retaining his Senate position. The amendment that was approved by New

Jersey voters in 2005 calls for a lieutenant governor to be elected on the same ticket with the governor, beginning in 2009.

Several other changes were made in 2005 in the structure of governing institutions. Amendments were passed in Texas and Washington to change the composition of the Commission on Judicial Conduct in those states: Texas added another member of the general public and a constitutional county court judge, and Washington made municipal court judges eligible to hold a position previously reserved solely for district court judges. In addition, voters in several states passed judgment on amendments to alter the term of office for various posts. In April, Wisconsin voters approved an amendment increasing from two to four years the term of office for many county officials. On the other hand, Texas voters rejected an amendment that would have permitted the legislature to increase from two to six years the terms of members of regional mobility authorities.

Policy

The most significant development in 2005 regarding state constitutional policy provisions was the decision of Colorado voters to narrowly approve a five-year suspension of key aspects of the state's Taxpayers' Bill of Rights (TABOR) provision. Colorado's TABOR provision was adopted in 1992 and is the country's strictest tax and expenditure limitation, in that it limits state spending to the previous year's spending, adjusted for inflation and population growth, and also requires that revenues in excess of this amount be refunded to the people. However, with the support of Democratic legislators and Republican Gov. Bill Owens, a one-time ardent supporter of TABOR, a measure was submitted to voters in November seeking to suspend these provisions for the next five years and thereby cancel an estimated $3.7 billion in tax refunds. The vote to suspend these TABOR provisions, which took place on Nov. 1, 2005, is significant not only for Colorado, but also for numerous other states considering adopting some version of TABOR, given that critics can now cite this vote as evidence of popular dissatisfaction with the policy's effects. Despite this setback for supporters of such provisions, tax and expenditure limitation amendments have already been placed on the November 2006 ballot in Maine and Ohio through the initiative process, and other states are considering similar amendments.[6]

Voters in California and New York in 2005 rejected amendments that would have also had significant effects on state budgeting policy. In California, voters easily defeated an initiative amendment promoted by Gov. Schwarzenegger that would have prevented state spending from exceeding the average of the previous three years' tax revenues and would have also empowered the governor to unilaterally reduce spending in certain circumstances. Meanwhile, New York voters handily defeated an amendment proposed by the legislature that would have shifted a significant amount of state budgeting power from the governor to the legislature, by providing that in the event of an executive-legislative deadlock the legislature would gain the power to prepare a budget.

A number of other policy amendments were considered in 2005. In the only amendment to pass in Ohio (out of five measures on the ballot), voters approved a $2 billion economic development package proposed by the legislature. Maine voters authorized the legislature to reduce taxes on waterfront property used for commercial fishing. New Jersey voters approved an amendment requiring certain motor vehicles to be outfitted with new emission-reducing equipment and stipulating that the new equipment be paid for from an existing business tax. Texas voters approved a number of policy amendments including the creation of a rail relocation and improvement fund, among other measures, but also defeated a proposal to remove interest-rate limits on commercial loans. Meanwhile, West Virginia voters in June rejected an amendment that would have authorized the issuance of $5.5 billion in bonds to finance the state's pension funds. And Oklahoma voters in September rejected an initiative amendment that would have increased gas and diesel taxes, earmarked this revenue for highway and bridge construction, and established a minimum level for annual state transportation spending.

About the Author

John Dinan is Zachary T. Smith Associate Professor of Political Science at Wake Forest University. He is the author of *The American State Constitutional Tradition* and *The Virginia State Constitution: A Reference Guide*, among other books and articles on state constitutional development.

Notes

[1] Robert Vitale, "Candidates Team with Issues; Ballot Initiatives Can Magnify Voter Support," *Columbus Dispatch*, October 3, 2005, 1C.

[2] Carla Crowder, "Pate: Iraq Leads Alabama on Constitution," *Birmingham News*, October 26, 2005, 6B.

[3] Anita Weier, "Assembly OKs Constitutional Change Requiring Photo Identification to Vote," *Capital Times*, November 2, 2005, 3A.

[4] Kavan Peterson, "Washington Gay Marriage Ruling Looms," *www.stateline.org*, November 23, 2005.

[5] Joyce Howard Price, "Michigan Lawmakers Adopt Property Rights," *Washington Times*, December 16, 2005 (netscape version).

[6] Kirk Johnson, "Colorado Cap on Spending Is Suspended," *New York Times*, November 3, 2005, A6.

Table 1.1
GENERAL INFORMATION ON STATE CONSTITUTIONS
(As of January 1, 2006)

State or other jurisdiction	Number of constitutions*	Dates of adoption	Effective date of present constitution	Estimated length (number of words)	Number of amendments Submitted to voters	Adopted
Alabama	6	1819, 1861, 1865, 1868, 1875, 1901	Nov. 28, 1901	340,136 (a)(b)(c)	1,063	766
Alaska	1	1956	Jan. 3, 1959	15,988 (b)	41	29
Arizona	1	1911	Feb. 14, 1912	28,876	246	136
Arkansas	5	1836, 1861, 1864, 1868, 1874	Oct. 30, 1874	59,500 (b)	189	91 (d)
California	2	1849, 1879	July 4, 1879	54,645	863	513
Colorado	1	1876	Aug. 1, 1876	74,522 (b)	304	145
Connecticut	4	1818 (f), 1965	Dec. 30, 1965	17,256 (b)	30	29
Delaware	4	1776, 1792, 1831, 1897	June 10, 1897	19,000	(e)	138
Florida	6	1839, 1861, 1865, 1868, 1886, 1968	Jan. 7, 1969	51,456 (b)	135	104
Georgia	10	1777, 1789, 1798, 1861, 1865, 1868, 1877, 1945, 1976, 1982	July 1,1983	39,526 (b)	83 (g)	63 (g)
Hawaii	1 (h)	1950	Aug. 21, 1959	20,774 (b)	123	104
Idaho	1	1889	July 3, 1890	24,232 (b)	204	117
Illinois	4	1818, 1848, 1870, 1970	July 1, 1971	16,510 (b)	17	11
Indiana	2	1816, 1851	Nov. 1, 1851	10,379 (b)	78	46
Iowa	2	1846, 1857	Sept. 3, 1857	12,616 (b)	57	52 (i)
Kansas	1	1859	Jan. 29, 1861	12,296 (b)	123	93 (i)
Kentucky	4	1792, 1799, 1850, 1891	Sept. 28, 1891	23,911 (b)	75	41
Louisiana	11	1812, 1845, 1852, 1861, 1864, 1868, 1879, 1898, 1913, 1921, 1974	Jan. 1, 1975	54,112 (b)	189	129
Maine	1	1819	March 15, 1820	16,276 (b)	202	170 (j)
Maryland	4	1776, 1851, 1864, 1867	Oct. 5, 1867	46,600 (b)	254	218 (k)
Massachusetts	1	1780	Oct. 25, 1780	36,700 (l)	148	120
Michigan	4	1835, 1850, 1908, 1963	Jan. 1, 1964	34,659 (b)	63	25
Minnesota	1	1857	May 11, 1858	11,547 (b)	213	118
Mississippi	4	1817, 1832, 1869, 1890	Nov. 1, 1890	24,323 (b)	158	123
Missouri	4	1820, 1865, 1875, 1945	March 30, 1945	42,600 (b)	165	105
Montana	2	1889, 1972	July 1, 1973	13,145 (b)	53	30
Nebraska	2	1866, 1875	Oct. 12, 1875	20,048	336 (m)	222 (m)
Nevada	1	1864	Oct. 31, 1864	31,377 (b)	220	132
New Hampshire	2	1776, 1784	June 2, 1784	9,200	285 (n)	143
New Jersey	3	1776, 1844, 1947	Jan. 1, 1948	22,956 (b)	71	38
New Mexico	1	1911	Jan. 6, 1912	27,200	280	151
New York	4	1777, 1822, 1846, 1894	Jan. 1, 1895	51,700	291	216
North Carolina	3	1776, 1868, 1970	July 1, 1971	16,532 (b)	42	34
North Dakota	1	1889	Nov. 2, 1889	19,130 (b)	258	145 (o)
Ohio	2	1802, 1851	Sept. 1, 1851	48,521 (b)	272	162
Oklahoma	1	1907	Nov. 16, 1907	74,075 (b)	336 (p)	171 (p)
Oregon	1	1857	Feb. 14, 1859	54,083 (b)	473 (q)	238 (q)
Pennsylvania	5	1776, 1790, 1838, 1873, 1968 (r)	1968 (r)	27,711 (b)	36 (r)	30 (r)
Rhode Island	3	1842 (f), 1986 (s)	Dec. 4, 1986	10,908 (b)	8 (s)	8 (s)
South Carolina	7	1776, 1778, 1790, 1861, 1865, 1868, 1895	Jan. 1, 1896	22,300	672 (t)	485 (t)
South Dakota	1	1889	Nov. 2, 1889	27,675 (b)	219	212
Tennessee	3	1796, 1835, 1870	Feb. 23, 1870	13,300	59	36
Texas	5 (u)	1845, 1861, 1866, 1869, 1876	Feb. 15, 1876	90,000	614 (v)	439
Utah	1	1895	Jan. 4, 1896	11,000	157	106
Vermont	3	1777, 1786, 1793	July 9, 1793	10,286 (b)	211	53
Virginia	6	1776, 1830, 1851, 1869, 1902, 1970	July 1, 1971	21,319 (b)	48	40
Washington	1	1889	Nov. 11, 1889	33,564 (b)	169	96
West Virginia	2	1863, 1872	April 9, 1872	26,000	121	71
Wisconsin	1	1848	May 29, 1848	14,392 (b)	182	134 (i)
Wyoming	1	1889	July 10, 1890	31,800	120	94
American Samoa	2	1960, 1967	July 1, 1967	6,000	14	7
No. Mariana Islands	1	1977	Jan. 9, 1978	11,000	55	51 (w)(x)
Puerto Rico	1	1952	July 25, 1952	9,281	6	6

See footnotes at end of table.

GENERAL INFORMATION ON STATE CONSTITUTIONS — Continued
(As of January 1, 2006)

Sources: Based on surveys conducted in previous years by Janice May and updated by John Dinan in January 2006.

*The constitutions referred to in this table include those Civil War documents customarily listed by the individual states.

(a) The Alabama constitution includes numerous local amendments that apply to only one county. An estimated 70 percent of all amendments are local. A 1982 amendment provides that after proposal by the legislature to which special procedures apply, only a local vote (with exceptions) is necessary to add them to the constitution.

(b) Computer word count.

(c) The total number of Alabama amendments includes one that is commonly overlooked.

(d) Eight of the approved amendments have been superseded and are not printed in the current edition of the constitution. The total adopted does not include five amendments proposed and adopted since statehood.

(e) Proposed amendments are not submitted to the voters in Delaware.

(f) Colonial charters with some alterations served as the first constitutions in Connecticut (1638, 1662) and in Rhode Island (1663).

(g) The Georgia constitution requires amendments to be of "general and uniform application throughout the state," thus eliminating local amendments that accounted for most of the amendments before 1982.

(h) As a kingdom and republic, Hawaii had five constitutions.

(i) The figure includes amendments approved by the voters and later nullified by the state supreme court in Iowa (three), Kansas (one), Nevada (six) and Wisconsin (two).

(j) The figure does not include one amendment approved by the voters in 1967 that is inoperative until implemented by legislation.

(k) Two sets of identical amendments were on the ballot and adopted in the 1992 Maryland election. The four amendments are counted as two in the table.

(l) The printed constitution includes many provisions that have been annulled. The length of effective provisions is an estimated 24,122 words

(12,400 annulled) in Massachusetts, and in Rhode Island before the "rewrite" of the constitution in 1986, it was 11,399 words (7,627 annulled).

(m) The 1998 and 2000 Nebraska ballots allowed the voters to vote separately on "parts" of propositions. In 1998, 10 of 18 separate propositions were adopted; in 2000, 6 of 9.

(n) The constitution of 1784 was extensively revised in 1792. Figure shows proposals and adoptions since the constitution was adopted in 1784.

(o) The figures do not include submission and approval of the constitution of 1889 itself and of Article XX; these are constitutional questions included in some counts of constitutional amendments and would add two to the figure in each column.

(p) The figures include five amendments submitted to and approved by the voters which were, by decisions of the Oklahoma or U.S. Supreme Courts, rendered inoperative or ruled invalid, unconstitutional, or illegally submitted.

(q) One Oregon amendment on the 2000 ballot was not counted as approved because canvassing was enjoined by the courts.

(r) Certain sections of the constitution were revised by the limited convention of 1967–68. Amendments proposed and adopted are since 1968.

(s) Following approval of the eight amendments and a "rewrite" of the Rhode Island Constitution in 1986, the constitution has been called the 1986 Constitution. Amendments since 1986 total eight proposed and eight adopted. Otherwise, the total is 106 proposals and 60 adopted.

(t) In 1981 approximately two-thirds of 626 proposed and four-fifths of the adopted amendments were local. Since then the amendments have been statewide propositions.

(u) The Constitution of the Republic of Texas preceded five state constitutions.

(v) The number of proposed amendments to the Texas Constitution excludes three proposed by the legislature but not placed on the ballot.

(w) By 1992, 49 amendments had been proposed and 47 adopted. Since then, one was proposed but rejected in 1994, all three proposals were ratified in 1996 and in 1998, of two proposals one was adopted.

(x) The total excludes one amendment ruled void by a federal district court.

Table 1.2
CONSTITUTIONAL AMENDMENT PROCEDURE: BY THE LEGISLATURE
Constitutional Provisions

State or other jurisdiction	Legislative vote required for proposal (a)	Consideration by two sessions required	Vote required for ratification	Limitation on the number of amendments submitted at one election
Alabama	3/5	No	Majority vote on amendment	None
Alaska	2/3	No	Majority vote on amendment	None
Arizona	Majority	No	Majority vote on amendment	None
Arkansas	Majority	No	Majority vote on amendment	3
California	2/3	No	Majority vote on amendment	None
Colorado	2/3	No	Majority vote on amendment	None (b)
Connecticut	(c)	(c)	Majority vote on amendment	None
Delaware	2/3	Yes	Not required	No referendum
Florida	3/5	No	Majority vote on amendment (d)	None
Georgia	2/3	No	Majority vote on amendment	None
Hawaii	(e)	(e)	Majority vote on amendment (f)	None
Idaho	2/3	No	Majority vote on amendment	None
Illinois	3/5	No	(g)	3 articles
Indiana	Majority	Yes	Majority vote on amendment	None
Iowa	Majority	Yes	Majority vote on amendment	None
Kansas	2/3	No	Majority vote on amendment	5
Kentucky	3/5	No	Majority vote on amendment	4
Louisiana	2/3	No	Majority vote on amendment (h)	None
Maine	2/3 (i)	No	Majority vote on amendment	None
Maryland	3/5	No	Majority vote on amendment	None
Massachusetts	Majority (j)	Yes	Majority vote on amendment	None
Michigan	2/3	No	Majority vote on amendment	None
Minnesota	Majority	No	Majority vote in election	None
Mississippi	2/3 (k)	No	Majority vote on amendment	None
Missouri	Majority	No	Majority vote on amendment	None
Montana	2/3 (i)	No	Majority vote on amendment	None
Nebraska	3/5	No	Majority vote on amendment (f)	None
Nevada	Majority	Yes	Majority vote on amendment	None
New Hampshire	3/5	No	2/3 vote on amendment	None
New Jersey	(l)	(l)	Majority vote on amendment	None (m)
New Mexico	Majority (n)	No	Majority vote on amendment (n)	None
New York	Majority	Yes	Majority vote on amendment	None
North Carolina	3/5	No	Majority vote on amendment	None
North Dakota	Majority	No	Majority vote on amendment	None
Ohio	3/5	No	Majority vote on amendment	None
Oklahoma	Majority	No	Majority vote on amendment	None
Oregon	(o)	No	Majority vote on amendment (p)	None
Pennsylvania	Majority (p)	Yes (p)	Majority vote on amendment	None
Rhode Island	Majority	No	Majority vote on amendment	None
South Carolina	2/3 (q)	Yes (q)	Majority vote on amendment	None
South Dakota	Majority	No	Majority vote on amendment	None
Tennessee	(r)	Yes (r)	Majority vote in election (s)	None
Texas	2/3	No	Majority vote on amendment	None
Utah	2/3	No	Majority vote on amendment	None
Vermont	(t)	Yes	Majority vote on amendment	None
Virginia	Majority	Yes	Majority vote on amendment	None
Washington	2/3	No	Majority vote on amendment	None
West Virginia	2/3	No	Majority vote on amendment	None
Wisconsin	Majority	Yes	Majority vote on amendment	None
Wyoming	2/3	No	Majority vote in election	None
American Samoa	2/3	No	Majority vote on amendment (u)	None
No. Mariana Islands	3/4	No	Majority vote on amendment	None
Puerto Rico	2/3 (v)	No	Majority vote on amendment	3

See footnotes at end of table.

CONSTITUTIONAL AMENDMENT PROCEDURE: BY THE LEGISLATURE — Continued
Constitutional Provisions

Sources: Surveys conducted in previous years by Janice May and updated by John Dinan in January 2006.

Key:

(a) In all states not otherwise noted, the figure shown in the column refers to the proportion of elected members in each house required for approval of proposed constitutional amendments.

(b) Legislature may not propose amendments to more than six articles of the constitution in the same legislative session.

(c) Three-fourths vote in each house at one session, or majority vote in each house in two sessions between which an election has intervened.

(d) Majority vote on amendment except amendment for "new state tax or fee" not in effect on Nov. 7, 1994 requires two-thirds of voters in the election.

(e) Two-thirds vote in each house at one session, or majority vote in each house in two sessions.

(f) Majority vote on amendment must be at least 50 percent of the total votes cast at the election (at least 35 percent in Nebraska); or, at a special election, a majority of the votes tallied which must be at least 30 percent of the total number of registered voters.

(g) Majority voting in election or three-fifths voting on amendment.

(h) If five or fewer political subdivisions of the state are affected, majority in state as a whole (and also in affected subdivisions) is required.

(i) Two-thirds of both houses.

(j) Majority of members elected sitting in joint session.

(k) The two-thirds must include not less than a majority elected to each house.

(l) Three-fifths of all members of each house at one session, or majority of all members of each house for two successive sessions.

(m) If a proposed amendment is not approved at the election when submitted, neither the same amendment nor one which would make substantially the same change for the constitution may be again submitted to the people before the third general election thereafter.

(n) Amendments concerning certain elective franchise and education matters require three-fourths vote of members elected and approval by three-fourths of electors voting in state and two-thirds of those voting in each county.

(o) Majority vote to amend constitution, two-thirds to revise ("revise" includes all or a part of the constitution).

(p) Emergency amendments may be passed by two-thirds vote of each house, followed by ratification by majority vote of electors in election held at least one month after legislative approval. There is an exception for an amendment containing a supermajority voting requirement, which must be ratified by an equal supermajority.

(q) Two-thirds of members of each house, first passage; majority of members of each house after popular ratification.

(r) Majority of members elected to both houses, first passage; two-thirds of members elected to both houses, second passage.

(s) Majority of all citizens voting for governor.

(t) Two-thirds vote senate, majority vote house, first passage; majority both houses, second passage. As of 1974, amendments may be submitted only every four years.

(u) Within 30 days after voter approval, governor must submit amendment(s) to U.S. Secretary of the Interior for approval.

(v) If approved by two-thirds of members of each house, amendment(s) submitted to voters at special referendum; if approved by not less than three-fourths of total members of each house, referendum may be held at next general election.

Table 1.3
CONSTITUTIONAL AMENDMENT PROCEDURE: BY INITIATIVE
Constitutional Provisions

State or other jurisdiction	Number of signatures required on initiative petition	Distribution of signatures	Referendum vote
Arizona	15% of total votes cast for all candidates for governor at last election.	None specified.	Majority vote on amendment.
Arkansas	10% of voters for governor at last election.	Must include 5% of voters for governor in each of 15 counties.	Majority vote on amendment.
California	8% of total voters for all candidates for governor at last election.	None specified.	Majority vote on amendment.
Colorado	5% of total legal votes for all candidates for secretary of state at last general election.	None specified.	Majority vote on amendment.
Florida	8% of total votes cast in the state in the last election for presidential electors.	8% of total votes cast in each of 1/2 of the congressional districts.	Majority vote on amendment except amendment for "new state tax or fee" not in effect Nov. 7, 1994 requires 2/3 of voters voting in election.
Illinois (a)	8% of total votes cast for candidates for governor at last election.	None specified.	Majority voting in election or 3/5 voting on amendment.
Massachusetts (b)	3% of total votes cast for governor at preceding biennial state election (not less than 25,000 qualified voters).	No more than 1/4 from any one county.	Majority vote on amendment which must be 30% of total ballots cast at election.
Michigan	10% of total voters for all candidates at last gubernatorial election.	None specified.	Majority vote on amendment.
Mississippi	12% of total votes for all candidates for governor in last election.	No more than 20% from any one congressional district.	Majority vote on amendment and not less than 40% of total vote cast at election.
Missouri	8% of legal voters for all candidates for governor at last election.	The 8% must be in each of 2/3 of the congressional districts in the state.	Majority vote on amendment.
Montana	10% of qualified electors, the number of qualified voters to be determined by number of votes cast for governor in preceding election in each county and in the state.	The 10% to include at least 10% of qualified voters in 1/2 of the counties.	Majority vote on amendment.
Nebraska	10% of total votes for governor at last election.	The 10% must include 5% in each of 2/5 of the counties.	Majority vote on amendment which must be at least 35% of total vote at the election.
Nevada	10% of voters who voted in entire state in last general election.	10% of total voters who voted in each of 75% of the counties.	Majority vote on amendment in two consecutive general elections.
North Dakota	4% of population of the state.	None specified.	Majority vote on amendment.
Ohio	10% of total number of electors who voted for governor in last election.	At least 5% of qualified electors in each of 1/2 of counties in the state.	Majority vote on amendment.
Oklahoma	15% of legal voters for state office receiving highest number of voters at last general state election.	None specified.	Majority vote on amendment.
Oregon	8% of total votes for all candidates for governor at last election at which governor was elected for four-year term.	None specified.	Majority vote on amendment except for supermajority equal to supermajority voting requirement contained in proposed amendment.
South Dakota	10% of total votes for governor in last election.	None specified.	Majority vote on amendment.
No. Mariana Islands	50% of qualified voters of commonwealth.	In addition, 25% of qualified voters in each senatorial district.	Majority vote on amendment if legislature approved it by majority vote; if not, at least 2/3 vote in each of two senatorial districts in addition to a majority vote.

Sources: Surveys conducted in previous years by Janice May and updated by John Dinan in January 2006.
Key:
(a) Only Article IV, the Legislature, may be amended by initiative petition.

(b) Before being submitted to the electorate for ratification, initiative measures must be approved at two sessions of a successively elected legislature by not less than one-fourth of all members elected, sitting in joint session.

Table 1.4
PROCEDURES FOR CALLING CONSTITUTIONAL CONVENTIONS
Constitutional Provisions

State or other jurisdiction	Provision for convention	Legislative vote for submission of convention question (a)	Popular vote to authorize convention	Periodic submission of convention question required (b)	Popular vote required for ratification of convention proposals
Alabama	Yes	Majority	ME	No	Not specified
Alaska	Yes	No provision (c)(d)	(c)	10 years (c)	Not specified (c)
Arizona	Yes	Majority	(e)	No	MP
Arkansas	No	No			
California	Yes	2/3	MP	No	MP
Colorado	Yes	2/3	MP	No	ME
Connecticut	Yes	2/3	MP	20 years (f)	MP
Delaware	Yes	2/3	MP	No	No provision
Florida	Yes	(g)	MP	No	Not specified
Georgia	Yes	(d)	No	No	MP
Hawaii	Yes	Not specified	MP	9 years	MP (h)
Idaho	Yes	2/3	MP	No	Not specified
Illinois	Yes	3/4	(i)	20 years; 1988	MP
Indiana	No	No			
Iowa	Yes	Majority	MP	10 years; 1970	MP
Kansas	Yes	2/3	MP	No	MP
Kentucky	Yes	Majority (j)	MP (k)	No	No provision
Louisiana	Yes	(d)	No	No	MP
Maine	Yes	(d)	No	No	No provision
Maryland	Yes	Majority	ME	20 years; 1970	MP
Massachusetts	No	No	No	Not specified	
Michigan	Yes	Majority	MP	16 years; 1978	MP
Minnesota	Yes	2/3	ME	No	3/5 voting on proposal
Mississippi	No	No			
Missouri	Yes	Majority	MP	20 years; 1962	Not specified (l)
Montana	Yes (m)	2/3	MP	20 years	MP
Nebraska	Yes	3/4	MP (o)	No	MP
Nevada	Yes	2/3	ME	No	No provision
New Hampshire	Yes	Majority	MP	10 years	2/3 voting on proposal
New Jersey	No	No			
New Mexico	Yes	2/3	MP	No	Not specified
New York	Yes	Majority	MP	20 years; 1957	MP
North Carolina	Yes	2/3	MP	No	MP
North Dakota	No	No			
Ohio	Yes	2/3	MP	20 years; 1932	MP
Oklahoma	Yes	Majority	(e)	20 years	MP
Oregon	Yes	Majority	(e)	No	No provision
Pennsylvania	No	No			
Rhode Island	Yes	Majority	MP	10 years	MP
South Carolina	Yes	(d)	ME	No	No provision
South Dakota	Yes	(d)	(d)	No	(p)
Tennessee	Yes (q)	Majority	MP	No	MP
Texas	No	No			
Utah	Yes	2/3	ME	No	MP
Vermont	No	No			
Virginia	Yes	(d)	No	No	MP
Washington	Yes	2/3	ME	No	Not specified
West Virginia	Yes	Majority	MP	No	Not specified
Wisconsin	Yes	Majority	MP	No	No provision
Wyoming	Yes	2/3	ME	No	Not specified
American Samoa	Yes	(r)	No	No	ME (s)
No. Mariana Islands	Yes	Majority (t)	2/3	No (u)	MP and at least 2/3 in each of 2 senatorial districts
Puerto Rico	Yes	2/3	MP	No	MP

See footnotes at end of table.

PROCEDURES FOR CALLING CONSTITUTIONAL CONVENTIONS — Continued
Constitutional Provisions

Sources: Surveys conducted in previous years by Janice May and updated by John Dinan in January 2006.

Key:

MP — Majority voting on the proposal.

ME — Majority voting in the election.

(a) In all states not otherwise noted, the entries in this column refer to the proportion of members elected to each house required to submit to the electorate the question of calling a constitutional convention.

(b) The number listed is the interval between required submissions on the question of calling a constitutional convention; where given, the date is that of the first required submission of the convention question.

(c) Unless provided otherwise by law, convention calls are to conform as nearly as possible to the act calling the 1955 convention, which provided for a legislative vote of a majority of members elected to each house and ratification by a majority vote on the proposals. The legislature may call a constitutional convention at any time.

(d) In these states, the legislature may call a convention without submitting the question to the people. The legislative vote required is two-thirds of the members elected to each house in Georgia, Louisiana, South Carolina and Virginia; two-thirds concurrent vote of both branches in Maine; three-fourths of all members of each house in South Dakota; and not specified in Alaska, but bills require majority vote of membership in each house. In South Dakota, the question of calling a convention may be initiated by the people in the same manner as an amendment to the constitution (see Table 1.3) and requires a majority vote on the question for approval.

(e) The law calling a convention must be approved by the people.

(f) The legislature shall submit the question 20 years after the last convention, or 20 years after the last vote on the question of calling a convention, whichever date is last.

(g) The power to call a convention is reserved to the people by petition.

(h) The majority must be 50 percent of the total votes cast at a general election or at a special election, a majority of the votes tallied which must be at least 30 percent of the total number of registered voters.

(i) Majority voting in the election, or three-fifths voting on the question.

(j) Must be approved during two legislative sessions.

(k) Majority must equal one-fourth of qualified voters at last general election.

(l) Majority of those voting on the proposal is assumed.

(m) The question of calling a constitutional convention may be submitted either by the legislature or by initiative petition to the secretary of state in the same manner as provided for initiated amendments (see Table 1.3).

(n) Two-thirds of all members of the legislature.

(o) Majority must be 35 percent of total votes cast at the election.

(p) Convention proposals are submitted to the electorate at a special election in a manner to be determined by the convention. Ratification by a majority of votes cast.

(q) Conventions may not be held more often than once in six years.

(r) Five years after effective date of constitutions, governor shall call a constitutional convention to consider changes proposed by a constitutional committee appointed by the governor. Delegates to the convention are to be elected by their county councils. A convention was held in 1972.

(s) If proposed amendments are approved by the voters, they must be submitted to the U.S. Secretary of the Interior for approval.

(t) The initiative may also be used to place a referendum convention call on the ballot. The petition must be signed by 25 percent of the qualified voters or at least 75 percent in a senatorial district.

(u) The legislature was required to submit the referendum no later than seven years after the effective date of the constitution. The convention was held in 1985; 45 amendments were submitted to the voters.

Table 1.5
STATE CONSTITUTIONAL CHANGES BY LEGISLATIVE PROPOSAL AND BY CONSTITUTIONAL INITIATIVE: 2005

	Legislative proposal			Constitutional initiative		
State	*Number of proposals*	*Number of adoptions*	*Percentage adopted*	*Number of proposals*	*Number of adoptions*	*Percentage adopted*
California	...	...	...	3	0	0.0%
Kansas	1	1	100.0%	...	...	...
Maine	1	1	100.0	...	...	...
New Jersey....................	2	2	100.0	...	...	...
New York	1	0	0.0	...	...	...
Ohio	1	1	100.0	4	0	0.0
Oklahoma	...	...	...	1	0	0.0
Texas	9	7	77.7	...	...	...
Washington...................	1	1	100.0	...	...	...
West Virginia................	1	0	0.0	...	...	...
Wisconsin......................	1	1	100.0	...	...	...
Total	**18**	**14**	**77.7**	**8**	**0**	**0.0**

Source: Survey conducted by John Dinan in January 2006.

Chapter Two

Federalism and Intergovernmental Relations

"Two events particularly marked recent state-federal relations: Hurricane Katrina and Supreme Court appointments."

—John Kincaid

"Protection of the reserved regulatory powers of the states against further congressional encroachment will necessitate enactment of new interstate regulatory compacts and or uniform state laws."

—Joseph F. Zimmerman

State-Federal Relations:
Federal Dollars Down, Federal Power Up
By John Kincaid

Most facets of coercive federalism—including federal aid shifted from places to persons, condi-tions and earmarks attached to federal aid, pre-emptions, limits on state taxation, federalization of criminal law, defunct intergovernmental political institutions, reduced federal-state cooperation in major programs, and federal-court litigation—remain vibrant. Only unfunded mandates and court orders requiring major state institutional change are less prevalent. State policy activism remains vigorous, but the Supreme Court is not enamored with state authority.

State-federal relations reflect long-term trends born in the late 1960s, and short-term trends triggered by current events. The long-term trends encompass coercive or regulatory federalism. These persist because Congress and the president feel politically and constitutionally uninhibited about displacing state powers.[1] The U.S. Supreme Court, which was state-friendly in the 1990s, is again less congenial.

A shorter term trend is one of fiscal constraint aris-ing from the costs of national defense and homeland security, social welfare, tax cuts, and federal deficits and debt.[2] Although state revenues have improved, states face rising costs for major programs such as Medicaid, which consumes 17 percent of states' gen-eral fund spending. Caught between rising social-welfare costs, reduced federal domestic spending and voter resistance to tax increases, states face daunting budget challenges.

Even so, states are touted for policy innovation. This activism, which began in the 1980s, reflects state governments' enhanced capacity produced by reforms that followed World War II, plus the demise by the mid-1970s of traditional boss rule, which removed a major obstacle to innovation. Additionally, President Richard Nixon's appointment of Warren Burger as chief justice of the Supreme Court in 1969 and Ronald Reagan's election in 1980 precipitated a federal-state partisan divide that generated liberal state activism in response to conservative federal policymaking.[3]

Legacies of 2005

Two events particularly marked recent state-federal relations: Hurricane Katrina and Supreme Court appointments.

Hurricane Katrina

Katrina struck the Gulf Coast Aug. 29, 2005, and became catastrophic in New Orleans when breached levees allowed Lake Pontchartrain to flood the city,

especially low-income neighborhoods. Katrina dis-placed about 1 million people, contributed to the deaths of more than 1,200 people, and produced damages of about $250 billion.

Katrina's destructiveness was made more deadly than necessary by the failure of all governments—city, parish, state and federal—to respond competently before, during and after the storm. Virtually all the responsible officials—elected and administrative—failed to identify and correct errors as the disaster unfolded, creating a dearth of leadership and initia-tive. Local and state officials bore heavy responsibility for pre-hurricane failures—from endemic corruption, a bloated city government and neglected levees to a failure to implement a timely evacuation of New Orleans. In turn, the initial post-disaster response of most federal agencies, especially the Department of Homeland Security (DHS), was non-existent.

This monumental intergovernmental failure was surprising in light of generally positive views of the principal federal response agency, the Federal Emer-gency Management Agency (FEMA). Columnist David Broder had recently noted that FEMA's "operations in the wake of hurricanes, tornadoes and other natural disasters are regarded as models of efficiency by state and local officials" and that the National Response Plan, unveiled in 2005 and developed in partnership with state and local officials, promised effective and cooperative intergovernmental responsiveness to disasters.[4]

Since Katrina, there have been calls for a massive increase in the federal role in disasters. The federal role certainly needs vast improvement, but the value of a predominant federal role is questionable because it would place too much reliance on only one gov-ernment to respond adequately. It would be more effective to have intergovernmental cooperation characterized by improved clarity of responsibilities, lines of authority, communication, coordination, and joint action achieved through better planning and training to enhance the fail-safe redundancies possible in a federal system. This approach is also suggested by the comparative success of the Emergency Management Assistance Compact (EMAC) in aiding the storm-devastated states. Many state and local officials prefer to work through EMAC than through FEMA when possible.

Supreme Court Appointments

Chief Justice William Rehnquist's death opened a Supreme Court seat that had been friendly to the states since 1976.[5] Sandra Day O'Connor's retirement opened the Court's most influential swing seat. O'Connor often joined Rehnquist in supporting the states. Hence, state-federal relations was an important issue in the selection of their successors.

John G. Roberts Jr. became the Court's 17th chief justice by a 78-22 vote. He appears unlikely to be as friendly as Rehnquist was to the states. In his first federalism case on the Court, Roberts joined his eight colleagues to deny 11th Amendment sovereign-immunity to Georgia by upholding the right of a paraplegic prisoner to sue Georgia under the Americans with Disability Act (ADA) for conduct that violated the 14th Amendment, not just the ADA.[6]

Roberts then dissented in a 6-3 ruling that upheld Oregon's Death With Dignity Act.[7] Former U.S. Attorney General John Ashcroft had declared that prescribing drugs to assist suicide is not a legitimate medical practice and that dispensing drugs for suicide violates the federal Controlled Substances Act (CSA). A majority of the Supreme Court held that the CSA does not permit the attorney general to prohibit doctors from prescribing controlled substances for physician-assisted suicide under Oregon's law. However, Roberts did dissent in a 5-4 ruling that upheld congressional authority to abrogate the sovereign immunity of states in bankruptcy proceedings.[8]

In contrast, Samuel A. Alito Jr., who was confirmed by a 58-42 vote, supported state powers in several cases during his service on the U.S. Court of Appeals. Alito dissented in a 1996 case involving a submachine gun manufactured in Pennsylvania and sold to a Pennsylvanian. He argued the gunmaker's federal firearms conviction was unconstitutional because, pursuant to the Supreme Court's 1995 *Lopez* ruling,[9] the federal law was unconstitutional because it overreached Congress's commerce power. In 1991, Alito voted to sustain a Pennsylvania law requiring married women seeking an abortion to first notify their husbands. Alito voted with the majority on the appeals court in 2000 to prohibit a state government employee from suing in federal court

for sick leave under the federal Family and Medical Leave Act. The Supreme Court rejected Alito's view on the 1991 and 2000 cases.

Enduring National Issues

The fiscal lifeblood of federalism will be defined by costs associated with national defense, aging, deficits and deconstruction of federal funding roles in many domestic programs.

Homeland Security

Having failed to respond competently to Hurricane Katrina, DHS is scrambling to enhance its disaster preparedness and move forward on other fronts. Grant funding was improved by exempting homeland security grants from the Cash Management Improvement Act of 1990—which requires grant funds to remain in the U.S. Treasury until state and local governments apply for reimbursement—and by creating a one-stop shop in DHS for its State Homeland Security Program, Urban Area Security Initiative, Law Enforcement Terrorism Prevention Program, Citizen Corps Program, Emergency Management Performance Grants and Metropolitan Medical Response System.

DHS also adopted a more risk-based eligibility formula for its FY 2006 Urban Areas Security Initiative grants. DHS identified 35 urban areas (compared to 50 in 2005) eligible for 2006 grants, and funding declined from $830 million in 2005 to $765 million in 2006. Another major change is that cities and counties in designated regions must submit a regional "investment justification" for funding. Some mayors and governors criticized the changes, arguing that in order to apply for funding, they will have to elicit cooperation from multiple jurisdictions in a very short time.

About 22 states have established "fusion centers," or "data integration centers," to assemble and share federal, state, regional, local and tribal law-enforcement and public-safety information. Also, big-city police chiefs are creating systems to gather and share information on terrorist threats independent of federal officials. Motorola has developed equipment to allow police chiefs to communicate directly with each other across the country and with counterparts outside the United States. Some big cities are stationing police abroad. New York, for instance, has officers in London, Lyon, Singapore, Tel Aviv and Toronto.

Aging

An aging population is the states' most formidable fiscal challenge. Federal aid will be constrained because the federal budget faces the same challenge.

Social Security, Medicare, Medicaid and other health spending will consume about 46 percent of the FY 2006 federal budget. In contrast, agriculture, commerce, community development, education, energy, environment, housing, job training, natural resources, social services and transportation jointly will consume only about 10 percent of the budget. Interest payments on the national debt will absorb 8 percent. The Medicare prescription drug benefit might cost more than $700 billion over 10 years. At the same time, senior citizens, many of whom live on fixed and time-limited incomes, will likely resist tax increases.

Federal Deficits

President Bush's proposed FY 2007 budget indicates that his planned tax cuts will cost $285 billion over the next five years. The budget projects a $354 billion deficit in FY 2007, compared to about $423 billion in FY 2006. Absent tax increases, deficits will induce rolling reductions in domestic spending.

The Deficit Reduction Act of 2005 cut $39.5 billion in federal spending—primarily from education and health, including Medicaid, Medicare, student loans and crop subsidies—over the next five years. A Medicaid reduction of $4.8 billion is expected to be achieved partly by increasing co-payments, allowing providers to refuse treatment to non-payers, reducing payments for pharmaceuticals, and increasing penalties for seniors who shift assets to qualify for Medicaid.

Federal-State Program Deconstruction

Federal fiscal reductions and withdrawals from domestic programs will continue for the foreseeable future. Yet, while state and local governments will pay more of the costs for domestic services, they also will be expected to comply with federal regulations.

The president's $2.77 trillion FY 2007 budget proposal would reduce or eliminate 141 domestic discretionary programs. Discretionary grants for state and local governments would decline by more than $12.1 billion (a 6.7 percent decline) while mandatory entitlement grants would increase by $6.4 billion (a 2.6 percent hike). Overall, grants-in-aid would decline by about 1.4 percent.[10]

Proposed cuts include reductions in crop subsidies, rural development, EPA's State and Tribal Assistance Grants, and the Clean Water State Revolving Fund. The Commodity Supplemental Food Program would also be eliminated. Education spending would decline by 3.8 percent and eliminate 42 programs, though spending would increase to improve K–12 math and science education. The budget would cut the Community Development Block Grant by 20 percent, Section

202 housing for low-income seniors by 26 percent, and Section 811 housing for low-income disabled persons by 50 percent. It terminates HOPE VI grants. A $1.1 billion cut in block grants for day care, job training and mental health is proposed, as is termination of the Preventive Health-Care Block Grant and the Community Services Block Grant. However, the three major entitlement programs—Social Security, Medicare and Medicaid, which will consume about 45 percent of federal spending—would increase by 8 percent, even though their growth would be slowed, with Social Security spending reduced by $2.2 billion, Medicare by $36 billion, and Medicaid by $13.5 billion over the next five years.

The largest spending increases would be 12.2 percent for the Department of State, 8 percent for Veterans, 6.9 percent for Defense, and 3.3 percent for Homeland Security.

The States' Fiscal Conditions

States closed a $264 billion budget gap as fiscal conditions "rebounded notably in fiscal 2005."[11] General fund spending rose by 6.5 percent in 2005. The increase reflected:

1. the final impact in 2005 of a $20 billion federal-aid package enacted in 2003, which provided $10 billion in Medicaid cost relief and $10 billion for states to use as a "flexible grant" for other budget relief;

2. restoration of funds to programs cut during the previous four lean years;

3. welfare needs, especially Medicaid; and

4. under-funded pension liabilities.

Total estimated state spending in 2005 was $1.3 trillion, of which 22.5 percent went to Medicaid, 21.9 percent to K–12 education, 10.8 percent to higher education, 8.1 percent to transportation, 3.4 percent to corrections, 2 percent to public assistance, and 31.3 percent to all other activities.

Onward Coercive Federalism

Although American federalism remains cooperative in many ways—especially in most areas of intergovernmental administration—the predominant political, fiscal, statutory, regulatory and judicial trends feature federal dictates on state and local governments.

Grants-in-Aid

Although Bush's FY 2007 budget proposes to reduce federal aid, that aid will still exhibit three significant characteristics of coercive federalism. First, aid has shifted substantially from places to people; almost two-thirds of federal aid is now dedicated for payments to individuals (i.e., social welfare).[12] Among the long-term consequences of this shift are that place-oriented aid for such things as infrastructure, economic development and education has declined sharply, increased aid for social welfare has locked state budgets into programs ripe for escalating federal regulation and matching state costs, and local governments have experienced a steep decline in federal aid. Medicaid, which accounts for almost 45 percent of all federal aid, is a prime example. Combined federal and state spending on Medicaid increased by 59 percent from 2000 to 2005.

A second characteristic of grants-in-aid under coercive federalism is the increased use of conditions of aid, now often mistakenly called "mandates" (unfunded or funded). These conditions of aid, a powerful tool for federal policymakers, are used to achieve federal objectives that lie outside Congress's constitutionally enumerated powers and to extract more state-local spending on federal objectives.

For example, in May 2005, the Supreme Court unanimously upheld the Religious Land Use and Institutionalized Persons Act (RLUIPA) of 2000, a congressional reaction to the Court's 1997 ruling which voided the Religious Freedom Restoration Act for states. RLUIPA prohibits government from burdening the exercise of religious beliefs unless the burdens meet a "compelling government interest." A state or local government that receives federal money for land development or prisons must comply with RLUIPA's "compelling interest" standard.[13]

Responding to the Court's 2005 ruling upholding municipal use of eminent domain for economic development,[14] Congress enacted a rider on an appropriations act prohibiting federal funds distributed under the act from being used to implement the Court's eminent domain ruling.

The No Child Left Behind Act (NCLB) of 2002 is the states' current *bête noir* because of the act's costly testing and performance requirements. The National Conference of State Legislatures blasted the NCLB as flawed, stifling of state innovation, and unconstitutional.[15] Although the U.S. Department of Education has taken a more flexible approach to enforcing NCLB, Bush wants to extend NCLB beyond the eighth grade to all public high schools. Other reformers urge more federal involvement, such as replacing the policy of "50 states, 50 standards and 50 tests" with "national standards, national tests and a national curriculum."[16]

The National Education Association and nine school districts sued the U.S. Department of Education, arguing that NCLB is an illegal unfunded mandate. When Connecticut's attorney general filed suit against the NCLB's testing provisions, however, some civil rights advocates defended the provisions, and Connecticut's NAACP sided with the U.S. Secretary of Education. Some groups fear that allowing states to not comply with allegedly unfunded portions of NCLB would open the door to non-compliance with unfunded civil rights mandates.

The Deficit Reduction Act of 2005 reauthorized welfare reform—Temporary Assistance for Needy Families (TANF)—for another five years at the FY 2004 level of $16.5 billion. The new law contains tougher work-participation rules, even though it keeps the previous 50 percent work-participation requirement. States also must establish and maintain work-verification procedures, and a 1–5 percent penalty can be imposed on a state's family-assistance grant for non-compliance.

The third notable change affecting federal aid has been increasing congressional earmarking (i.e., state or local pork-barrel projects), from 3,055 in 1996 to 14,211 in 2004.[17] For example, the 1981 highway authorization contained less than 10 earmarks; the 1987 law contained 121; the 1991 law had 538; the 1998 SAFETEA law contained 1,850; and the 2005 reauthorization was festooned with 6,371.

Otherwise, onerous conditions were blocked when Congress reauthorized surface transportation in the Safe, Accountable, Flexible, and Efficient Transportation Equity Act: A Legacy for Users (SAFETEA-LU). SAFETEA-LU provides $286.5 billion in new funding, and offers financial incentives for states that (1) recently enacted, or will enact within five years, a statute to fine drivers for failing to wear a seat belt even if they are not breaking other laws, and (2) enact more punitive laws for repeat DUI offenders.

A formula fight produced a compromise wherein donor states will by 2008 get back 92 cents (rather than the current 90.5 cents) for every dollar they contribute to the transportation program. Also, earmarked monies will be counted against the amount each state receives from the grant formula. At the same time, fast-growing states, mostly in the South and Southwest, will get more money.

An enduring characteristic of grants-in-aid has been the unwillingness of Congress and presidents to funnel substantial amounts of aid through block grants. The lion's share of aid, including Medicaid, flows through categorical grants.

Mandates

Mandates also characterize coercive federalism. However, the Unfunded Mandates Reform Act (UMRA) of 1995 cut mandate enactments, though it did not eliminate standing mandates. Only five intergovernmental mandates with costs above UMRA's threshold have been enacted since 1995.[18]

A sizable new mandate is the REAL ID Act of 2005. States argue that it is under-funded by Congress and could cost states $100 million in FY 2006 as they start producing licenses with digital photographs and machine-readable technology. States must get security clearances for motor vehicle workers, and motor vehicle offices must verify the authenticity of applicants' identification documents (e.g., birth certificates and passports). States, which must comply with REAL ID by 2008, can opt out of its rules, but then their licenses will not be accepted for any federal government purpose, including boarding an airplane, purchasing a firearm and entering a federal building.

Pre-emptions

With Republicans gaining four Senate seats and five House seats in 2004, the unprecedented levels of federal pre-emption of state powers characteristic of coercive federalism accelerated in 2005. This was symbolized by the Class Action Fairness Act, which moves from state to federal courts most class-action lawsuits involving at least 100 plaintiffs, two-thirds of whom live in different states, seeking $5 million or more in damages. Federal judges will apply state consumer protection laws, but federal procedural law will govern the cases.

The Protection of Lawful Commerce in Arms Act of 2005 prohibits civil liability lawsuits in state courts against firearm and ammunition manufacturers, distributors, dealers and importers when their products are used unlawfully by a third party. Existing lawsuits must be dismissed. Other pre-emptions enacted in 2005 included the Vaccine Liability Exemption Act, Patient Safety and Quality Improvement Act and the Energy Policy Act.

Pre-emption is frequently upheld by the Supreme Court. In fact, the former "Federalism Five" justices (Kennedy, O'Connor, Rehnquist, Scalia and Thomas) most often voted against the states in pre-emption cases.

Taxation

Another characteristic of coercive federalism is federal constraints on state taxation and borrowing. Federal judicial and statutory prohibitions of state taxation of Internet services and mail-order sales are among the most prominent constraints.

The President's Advisory Panel on Federal Tax Reform called for ending deductions for state and local taxes. This issue has a partisan electoral dimension because the average state and local tax payment in blue (Democratic) states was $7,487 in 2005 compared to $4,834 in red (Republican) states. State and local tax deductions equaled 5.9 percent of average income in the blue states and 3.7 percent in the red states.[19]

Federalization of Criminal Law

Another feature of coercive federalism is the federalization of state criminal law. There are now some 3,500 federal criminal offenses, more than half of which have been enacted since the mid-1960s. These laws cover a wide range of behavior from terrorism to carjacking, disrupting a rodeo, impersonating a 4-H Club member and carrying unlicensed dentures across state lines. Generally, federal criminal laws are tougher, including capital punishment, than comparable state laws.

Demise of Intergovernmental Institutions

Coercive federalism has been marked, too, by the demise of executive and congressional intergovernmental institutions established during the era of cooperative federalism. Most notable was the death of the U.S. Advisory Commission on Intergovernmental Relations (ACIR) in 1996 after 37 years of operation.

Decline of Political Cooperation

There also has been a decline in federal-state cooperation in major intergovernmental programs such as Medicaid and surface transportation, with Congress earmarking and altering programs more in response to national and regional interest groups than to elected state and local officials, who themselves are viewed as mere interest groups.

Indeed, a coalition led by Americans for Tax Reform (ATR) has petitioned Congress to terminate the exemption from federal lobbying rules of state and local government lobbyists. The ATR also is campaigning to remove funds from the National Governors Association, labeling it "another liberal lobbying group."[20]

Federal-Court Litigation

Coercive federalism also has been marked by unprecedented numbers of federal court orders and lawsuits filed against state and local governments. The extent to which such litigation might intrude into state affairs was illustrated by an age-discrimination lawsuit filed in federal court in 2005 by an 83-year-old justice of the Oklahoma Supreme Court against his eight colleagues because they declined to select him as chief justice.

Judicial consent decrees, some of which can last more than 20 years, often constrain state and local officials as well. Decrees have become a major means to guarantee state or local government compliance with federal rules in many intergovernmental policy areas (e.g., education, environmental protection and Medicaid). Bills introduced in Congress to allow state or local officials to seek judicial modifications of a decree four years after the agreement or after the election of a new governor or mayor appear unlikely to pass, in part because state and local officials are divided on the proposal.

Supreme Court's Federalism Fizzle

Since 2002, the Supreme Court has not advanced its state-friendly federalism initiated in 1991. In one of the most publicized federalism cases of 2005, the Court ruled 6-3 that the federal Controlled Substances Act pre-empts state laws allowing the possession and use of marijuana for medical purposes.[21] The Court in a 5-4 ruling struck down state laws that restricted or prohibited out-of-state wineries from selling directly to consumers while not imposing the same rules on in-state wineries.[22] The Court also refused to hear an appeal challenging application of the federal Endangered Species Act to six species of small insects that live in two Texas counties.[23]

Federalism and the Culture Wars

Federalism features prominently in the so-called culture wars, often producing strange political bedfellows and partisan flip-flops. Many liberals, traditionally champions of federal power, have become guardians of states' rights, seeking to protect assisted suicide, gay marriage, medicinal marijuana and state consumer-protection, environmental, labor and tort laws against federal pre-emption. Many conservatives, traditionally hostile to federal power, now champion federal power. Social conservatives seek to overturn state policies friendly to abortion, assisted suicide, gay rights, marijuana and the like; economic conservatives seek federal pre-emption of state regulations.

State Activism

A seemingly contrary characteristic of coercive federalism has been state policy activism, especially since the early 1980s. However, this activism has been both a response to coercive federalism as states have bucked federal policies and filled federal policy voids and a stimulant of coercive federalism as interest groups have sought federal tranquilization of hyperactive states.

State officials have pursued litigation and regulation in many policy areas, especially environmental and consumer protection. Connecticut Attorney General Richard Blumenthal expressed a leading justification for such activism: "Our action is the result of federal inaction."[24]

Conclusion

Although state activism generates a kind of competitive state-federal federalism, coercive federalism is the system's dominant motif.

Notes

[1] See, John Kincaid, "State-Federal Relations: Defense, Demography, Debt, and Deconstruction as Destiny," *The Book of the States* (Lexington, KY: The Council of State Governments, 2005), 25–30; "Trends in Federalism: Continuity, Change and Polarization," *The Book of the States* (Lexington, KY: The Council of State Governments, 2004), 21–7; "From Cooperation to Coercion in American Federalism: Housing, Fragmentation, and Pre-emption, 1780–1992," *Journal of Law and Politics* 9 (Winter 1993): 333–433.

[2] See, John Kincaid, "Trends in Federalism: Is Fiscal Federalism Fizzling?" *The Book of the States* (Lexington, KY: The Council of State Governments, 2003), 26–31.

[3] One of the first responses was the "new judicial federalism" initiated by state high courts. John Kincaid, "State Court Protections of Individual Rights Under State Constitutions: The New Judicial Federalism," *The Journal of State Government* 61 (September/October 1988): 163–69.

[4] David Broder, "Ridge left legacy of cooperation," *Express-Times* (Easton), January 14, 2005, A-6.

[5] *National League of Cities* v. *Usery*, 426 US 833 (1976).

[6] *United States* v. *Georgia*, No. 04-1203 (2006).

[7] *Gonzales* v. *Oregon*, No. 04-623 (2006).

[8] *Central Virginia Community College* v. *Katz*, No. 04-885 (2006).

[9] *United States* v. *Lopez*, 514 U.S. 549 (1995).

[10] Federal Funds Information for States, "President's FY 2007 Budget: Some New Twists on Old Themes," *Issue Brief 06-02* (Washington, D.C.: FFIS, February 10, 2006), Table 1.

[11] National Association of State Budget Officers, *Fiscal Survey of States* (Washington, D.C.: NASBO, December 2005), ix.

[12] For explication, see John Kincaid, "The State of U.S. Federalism, 2000–2001," *Publius: The Journal of Federalism* 31 (Summer 2001): 1–69.

[13] *Cutter* v. *Wilkinson*, 544 U.S. ____ (2005).

[14] *Kelo* v. *City of New London*, Connecticut, 125 S. Ct. 2655 (2005).

[15] Quoted in Sam Dillon, "Report From States Faults Bush's Education Initiative," *New York Times*, February 24, 2005, A18.

[16] Diane Ravitch, "Every State Left Behind," *New York Times*, November 7, 2005, A23.

[17] Jonathan Weisman and Charles R. Babcock, "'The Cur-

rency of Corruption'," *Washington Post National Weekly Edition*, February 6–12, 2006, 15.

[18] Congress of the United States, Congressional Budget Office, *A Review of CBO's Activities in 2004 Under the Unfunded Mandates Reform Act* (Washington, D.C.: Congressional Budget Office, March 2005).

[19] John Maggs, "Limping Toward Tax Reform," *National Journal* 37 (October 22, 2005): 3280.

[20] Peter J. Ferrara, "The NGA Should Pay Its Own Way," *Policy Brief* (Washington, D.C.: Americans for Tax Reform, 2005).

[21] *Gonzales* v. *Raich*, 543 U.S. ____ (2005).

[22] *Granholm* v. *Heald*, 543 U.S. ____ (2005).

[23] *GDF Realty Investments* v. *Norton*, 125 S. Ct. 2898 (2005).

[24] Quoted in Brooke A. Masters. "Who's Watching Out for the Consumer?" *Washington Post National Weekly Edition*, January 17, 2005, 30.

About the Author

John Kincaid is the Robert B. and Helen S. Meyner Professor of Government and Public Service and director of the Meyner Center for the Study of State and Local Government at Lafayette College, Easton, Pa. He is former editor of *Publius: The Journal of Federalism*; former executive director of the U.S. Advisory Commission on Intergovernmental Relations; and co-editor of *Constitutional Origins, Structure, and Change in Federal Countries* (2005).

Congressional Preemption and the States

By Joseph F. Zimmerman

National-state relations have undergone a major transformation since 1965, when Congress sharply increased the pace of enactment of regulatory preemption statutes including those in regulatory areas that had been the exclusive preserves of the states. Protection of the reserved regulatory powers of the states against further congressional encroachment will necessitate enactment of new interstate regulatory compacts and/or uniform state laws.

Ratification of the proposed U.S. Constitution by the requisite number of states in 1788 established the world's first federal system and created a Congress possessing broad powers exercisable to remove completely or partially the regulatory powers of the states.[1] It should be noted that Congress may devolve most of its regulatory powers upon the states. During its first session in 1789, Congress for the first time devolved a power (1 Stat. 54) to states by authorizing them to regulate marine port pilots.

In the same year, Congress exercised its powers of complete supersession of existing and prospective conflicting state laws by enacting the *Copyright Act* (1 Stat. 124) and the *Patent Act* (1 Stat. 109). A total of 535 complete or partial preemption statutes were enacted in the period 1789 to 2005 with 145 enacted since 1990. A number of these statutes contain preemptive provisions in two or more regulatory areas or amend earlier preemption statutes on the same subject. The importance and goal(s) effectiveness of the statutes vary greatly. Preemption statutes may include a sunset clause. The *Internet Tax Nondiscrimination Act of 2001* (115 Stat. 703) contained a Dec. 31, 2003 sunset date, but was renewed retroactively and prospectively by Congress (118 Stat. 2615), effective Dec. 4, 2004, for a period of three years.

The U.S. Constitution established the first federal system and thereby created potentially serious problems that do not exist in a unitary nation—non-uniform state statutes and conflicting national and state statutes. The problems were not serious ones until the post-Civil War period when industrialization and railroads made the market a national one and necessitated expanded national and state regulation.

Nature of Preemption

Section 8 of Article I of the Constitution and six constitutional amendments delegate to Congress, in very broad terms, latent powers that may be employed to remove regulatory powers from states completely or partially. The most commonly employed preemption power is based upon the authority of Congress to regulate interstate commerce and trade with foreign nations and the Indian tribes on reservations. Although the U.S. Supreme Court on a number of occasions urged Congress to exercise its delegated interstate commerce power, it is exercised on a discretionary basis by the national legislature which may not be forced to exercise this power.[2] The failure of Congress to employ this power until 1887 led to the term the "silence of Congress" as it relied upon the judicial system to protect the economic union from interstate trade barriers. Congressional preemption statutes are subject to court challenges alleging the statutes exceed the limits of delegated powers by encroaching, for example, upon the powers reserved to the states and the people by the 10th Amendment to the constitution.[3]

The delegated powers are supplemented by the necessary and proper clause (Art. I, §8) authorizing Congress to enact statutes necessary to effectuate the delegated powers, but the clause does not delegate a specific power to Congress. Similarly, the Constitution's supremacy of the laws clause (Art. VI) does not delegate a power to Congress, but simply provides for the displacement of a state law or any of its provisions directly conflicting with a provision of a national law as determined by a court.

Preemption Statutes

Congressional statutes superseding state statutes are classifiable as (1) complete, (2) partial, and (3) contingent. A complete preemption statute removes all regulatory powers in a given field, such as motor vehicle safety standards, from states. There are 18 subtypes of complete preemption statutes. A trade treaty validly entered into by the United States with a foreign nation, for example, is the supreme law of the land and is implemented by an act of Congress that negates all conflicting state constitutional and statutory provisions.[4] Several statutes, including the 1968 amendments (100 Stat. 3342) to the *Age Discrimination Act*, authorize the administering department or agency to enter into an agreement with individual states providing them with authority to enforce the provisions of the statutes. And the *Federal Railroad Safety Act of 1970* (84 Stat. 971) permits the administrative delegation of authority to states to perform railroad safety inspections utilizing federal standards.

The first of 12 types of partial preemption statutes invalidates only part of the regulatory powers of states in a specified field, thereby allowing states to continue to regulate the remainder of the field. The second type, minimum standards preemption, has had a major impact on national-state relations by generally fostering a cooperative national-state partnership to solve major problems such as air and water pollution. Congress employs this type by authorizing the concerned federal department or agency to promulgate minimum regulatory standards and to delegate regulatory primacy to states submitting a plan containing standards at least as stringent as the national ones and evidence that states possess the necessary qualified personnel and equipment. Regulatory primacy avoids dual regulation by the national government and state governments since only the latter regulate and the national agency is limited to monitoring state performance and revoking regulatory primacy if states fail to enforce their standards.

A contingent preemption statute is effective only if a specified condition(s) exists. Two such preemption statutes have been enacted: *Voting Rights Act of 1965* (79 Stat. 437) and *Gramm-Leach-Bliley Financial Modernization Act of 1999* (113 Stat. 1338). The latter act contains a provision threatening to establish a national licensing system for insurance agents if 26 states failed to develop a uniform licensing system by Nov. 12, 2002. Thirty-five states were certified on Sept. 10, 2002, as having uniform licensing statutes and preemption was avoided.

A preemption statute may be short and easily understood or several hundred pages in length and exceptionally complex as illustrated by the *Clean Air Act Amendments of 1990* (104 Stat. 2399). Numerous preemption statutes authorize the administering department or agency to promulgate administrative rules and regulations to implement the act fully. Such rules and regulations often are lengthy and technical in nature, and may invalidate conflicting state statutes and administrative rules and regulations.

An increasing trend is the inclusion of several preemption statutes in appropriations acts that are hundreds of pages in length. Examples include the *Commodities Futures Modernization Act of 2000* (114 Stat. 2763A-365) in the *Consolidated Appropriations Act for Fiscal Year 2001*, *Satellite Home Viewer Extension and Reauthorization Act of 2004* (117 Stat. 3393) in the *Consolidated Appropriations Act of 2005*, and the *Improved Security for Drivers' Licenses and Personal Identification Cards Acts of 2005* (119 Stat. 311) in the *Emergency Supplemental Appropriations Act for Defense, the Global War on Terror, and Tsunami Relief Act of 2005*.

Plaintiffs may request a state court or the U.S. District Court to interpret the provisions of a preemption statute or its implementing rules and regulations and determine whether there is a direct conflict triggering activation of the supremacy of the laws clause.[5]

Preemption Trends

Most preemption statutes are products of interest group lobbying. The motor vehicle industry, faced with differing air quality standards regulations promulgated by states, lobbied Congress to completely remove air quality regulatory authority from states by enacting the *Air Quality Act of 1967* (81 Stat. 485) in order to avoid the possibility that each manufacturer would have to develop 50 emission control systems to meet different states' standards. California's air quality standards were stricter than the proposed national standards contained in the bill. Those proposed standards would have been superseded and the state lobbied for an exemption that was incorporated in the act. On occasion, state officers request Congress to enact a preemption statute because of the failure of cooperative state efforts to solve the national problem such as commercial vehicle operators who continue to drive after revocation of their license(s) by one or more states. Governors requested enactment of the *Commercial Motor Vehicle Safety Act of 1986* (100 Stat. 3207) that makes it a federal crime for the operator of a commercial motor vehicle to hold a commercial operator's license issued by more than one state.

As noted, the first Congress enacted two preemption statutes and it appeared that such statutes might be enacted on a regular basis. Nevertheless, only 29 such statutes were enacted during the following 110 years. Subsequently, such statutes were enacted at the following pace: 14 (1900–09), 22 (1910–19), 17 (1920–29), 31 (1930–39), 16 (1940–49), 24 (1950–59), 47 (1960–69), 102 (1970–79), 93 (1980–89), 87 (1990–99), and 58 (2000–05).

The Republican-Controlled Congress

The Republican Party, often viewed as favoring states' rights, has controlled Congress since 1995. The pace of enactment of preemption statutes by the Republican-controlled Congress declined to 86 from 102 statutes enacted during the 11-year period ending in 1994.

Several trends are evident. Increased emphasis has been placed on protecting consumers as evidenced by the *Consumer Credit Reporting Act of 1996* (110 Stat. 3000-426), *Consumer Leasing Act Amendments of 1996* (110 Stat. 3009-471), *Consumer Reporting Employment Clarification Act of 1998* (112 Stat. 3208), *Securities Litigation Uniform Standards Act of 1998* (112 Stat. 3227), and *ATM Fee Reform Act of 1999* (113 Stat. 1601). In contrast, only two civil rights acts were enacted: *Age Discrimination in Employment Amendments of 1996* (110 Stat. 3009-23) and the *Religious Land Use and Institutionalized Persons Act of 2000* (114 Stat. 803).

Eight banking, commerce and finance preemption statutes were enacted: *Riegle-Neal Clarification Act of 1997* (111 Stat. 238), *Securities Litigation Uniform Standards Act of 1998* (112 Stat. 3227), *Gramm-Leach-Bliley Financial Modernization Act of 1999* (113 Stat. 1338), *Commodity Futures Modernization Act of 2000* (114 Stat. 2763A-65), *Public Company Accounting Reform and Corporate Responsibility Act of 2002* (116 Stat. 746), *Check Clearing for the 21st Century Act of 2003* (117 Stat. 1177), *Internet Tax Freedom Act of 2004* (118 Stat. 2615), and *Bankruptcy Abuse Prevention and Consumer Protection Act of 2005* (119 Stat. 23). The *Gramm-Leach-Bliley Act* is a particularly important one in that it removed many of the legal barriers, national and state, separating the banking and insurance industries established by the *Glass-Steagall Act of 1933* (48 Stat. 162). Nevertheless, banks have been slow to enter the insurance and investment banking areas. Insurance companies also have been slow to enter the banking and investment banking areas although MetLife—and State Farm—established subsidiary banks. The *Internet Tax Freedom Act of 2004* is of particular importance as it deprives states and local governments that levy a sales tax of revenues totaling in excess of an estimated $16 billion annually.

Congress enacted six free trade agreements with foreign nations since President George W. Bush assumed office in 2001. These agreements are part of the supreme law of the land and negate all conflicting state constitutional, statutory and administrative provisions of the states. Currently, the president is promoting a free trade agreement for all nations in the western hemisphere and a similar agreement with Mongolia.

The terrorists' assaults on the United States on Sept. 11, 2001, were responsible for the enactment of four important preemption statutes: *Uniting and Strengthening America by Providing Appropriate Tools Required to Intercept and Obstruct Terrorism Act of 2001* (USA Patriot Act) (115 Stat. 396), *Homeland Security Act of 2002* (116 Stat. 2135), *Terrorism Risk Insurance Act of 2002* (116 Stat. 2322), and *Improved Security for Drivers' Licenses and Personal identification Cards Act of 2005* (119 Stat. 311). The latter act in particular will be expensive for states to implement.

Eleven health and safety preemption statutes were enacted: *Food Quality Protection Act of 1996* (110 Stat. 1489), *Health Insurance Portability Act of 1996* (110 Stat. 1936), *Mental Health Parity Act of 1996* (110 Stat. 2945), *Newborn and Mother's Health Protection Act of 1996* (110 Stat. 2935), *Professional Boxing Safety Act of 1996* (110 Stat. 327), *Safe Drinking Water Amendments of 1996* (110 Stat. 1613), *Campus Sex Crimes Prevention Act of 2000* (114 Stat. 1537), *Violence Against Women Act of 2000* (114 Stat. 1491), *DNA Sexual Assault Justice Act of 2004* (118 Stat. 2271), *Food Allergen Labeling and Consumer Protection Act of 2004* (118 Stat. 905), and *Partial Birth Abortion Ban Act of 2004* (117 Stat. 1201).

Three preemption acts are designed to protect children and eliminate pornography: *Child Pornography Prevention Act of 1996* (110 Stat. 3009-26), *Controlling the Assault of Non-Solicited Pornography and Marketing Act of 2003* (117 Stat. 2699), and *Prosecutorial Remedies and Other Tools to End the Exploitation of Children Today Act of 2003* (117 Stat. 676).

Conclusions

The large number of congressional preemption statutes enacted in recent decades superficially suggests Congress is riding roughshod over the states. A closer inspection of national-state relations reveals they generally are good and the role of the states has increased since the terrorist attacks on Sept. 11, 2001. Congress is well aware the national government is incapable of solving all national problems, including terrorism, without the assistance of subnational governments. Minimum environmental standards acts in particular have fostered a close national-state partnership to solve problems.

Admittedly, certain preemption statutes have adverse consequences for many states in the form of loss of tax revenues attributable to the *Internet Tax*

Freedom Act of 2004 and implementation costs as illustrated by the *Clean Air Act* and the *Clean Water Act.* It should be noted, however, that Congress provides conditional grants-in-aid to assist states in achieving clean air and clean water goals. Forty-five states levying a corporate franchise or income tax also are concerned they may be faced with additional loss of tax revenues if Congress enacts the proposed *Business Activity Tax Simplification Act of 2005* (H.R. 1956) that would prohibit each state to tax the net income of an out-of-state business firm unless it has a physical nexus to the state as defined in the proposed act.

How effective are congressional preemption statutes? Not all have been examined in-depth, but the effectiveness of air and water quality statutes has been limited and has necessitated congressional extensions of the deadlines for achievement of the mandated quality standards. New York Attorney General Eliot Spitzer's investigations of large investment banking and other financial firms led to negotiated settlements and revealed the inadequacies of the U.S. Securities and Exchange Commission implementation of ten congressional regulatory securities acts. And the *Junk Fax Prevention Act of 2005* does little to prevent junk facsimile transmissions because business firms may send such transmissions to everyone with whom they have an "established business relationship."

On the other hand, the *Check Clearing for the 21st Century Act of 2003* has been implemented successfully with benefits accruing to banks in the form of reduced back-office processing costs and decreased processing time and to consumers in an improved flow of information and quicker access to deposited funds.

What do the trends since 1995 portend for future preemption statutes? A reasonable conclusion is that many of the most important laws will relate to banking, commerce, finance and taxation. The high business compliance costs associated with non-harmonious state tax laws will result in continued lobbying of Congress to establish tax jurisdictional standards and mandate the use of a common allocation and apportionment formula for state taxation of interstate commerce. The relative "silence of Congress" on this subject increasingly will be broken, thereby relieving the U.S. Supreme Court of the burden of conducting an original jurisdiction trial to settle interstate taxation disputes.

It is essential that states harmonize their regulatory tax statutes and administrative regulations if they wish to forestall additional congressional encroachment on their powers. Reciprocity statutes are helpful in removing discriminatory and nonhar-monious provisions, but are limited in scope. Interstate compacts and uniform state laws have a greater potential for promoting harmonized state regulatory and taxation statutes and administrative regulations. Congress should enact statutes, including contingent ones, encouraging states to draft and enact uniform state laws and regulatory interstate compacts. Congressional grants-in-aid to states to draft such compacts could pay large dividends to the states and the nation. States can obtain professional assistance in drafting compacts by contracting with the National Center for Interstate Compacts.

In sum, the federal system has undergone a major transformation since 1789 yet retains its major characteristic: a strong national Congress and strong states. The interactions between the two have become more entangled, kaleidoscopic and cooperative in nature. The reserved powers of the states continue to be vast and often are employed in an innovative manner to meet emerging challenges.

Notes

[1] Joseph F. Zimmerman, *Congressional Preemption: Regulatory Federalism* (Albany: State University of New York Press, 2005).

[2] Joseph F. Zimmerman, *Interstate Disputes: The Supreme Court's Original Jurisdiction* (Albany: State University of New York Press, 2006).

[3] An example is the U.S. Supreme Court's determination that the *Brady Handgun Violence Prevention Act of 1993* violated the Tenth Amendment. *Prinz v. United States*, 521 U.S. 898 at 935, 117 S.Ct. 2365 at 2384 (1997).

[4] See, for example, the *Dominican Republic-Central America-United States Free Trade Agreement Implementation Act of 2005*, 119 Stat. 462, 19 U.S.C. §4001.

[5] Timothy J. Conlan and Robert L. Dudley, "Janus-faced Federalism: State Sovereignty and Federal Preemption in the Rehnquist Court," *PS: Political Science and Politics* 38, July 2005, 363–66.

About the Author

Joseph F. Zimmerman is a professor of political science in Rockefeller College of the State University of New York at Albany. He is the author of numerous books including *Contemporary American Federalism: The Growth of National Power* (1992), *State-Local Relations* (1995), *Interstate Relations: The Neglected Dimension of Federalism* (1996), *Interstate Cooperation: Compacts and Administrative Agreements* (2002), *Interstate Economic Relations* (2004), and *Congressional Preemption: Regulatory Federalism* (2005).

Table 2.1
TOTAL FEDERAL GRANTS TO STATE AND LOCAL GOVERNMENTS BY STATE AND REGION: 1996–2004
(In millions of dollars)

State or other jurisdiction	2004	2003	2002	2001	2000	1999	1998	1997	1996
United States	$460,152	$441,038	$412,371	$338,977	$308,530	$294,469	$269,128	$229,778	$227,542
Eastern Region									
Connecticut..................	$5,556	$5,376	$5,279	$4,364	$4,033	$3,846	$3,653	$2,905	$3,080
Delaware......................	1,241	1,181	1,121	892	838	825	678	629	600
Maine...........................	2,758	2,610	2,270	1,905	1,770	1,664	1,602	1,378	1,389
Massachusetts	13,876	13,328	12,339	9,718	9,070	8,838	8,019	6,365	6,813
New Hampshire	1,879	1,865	1,632	1,288	1,238	1,120	1,042	842	890
New Jersey	11,333	11,481	10,822	8,478	7,876	7,262	7,108	6,602	6,506
New York.....................	50,009	47,575	42,461	32,897	31,564	28,870	28,066	24,384	24,560
Pennsylvania................	19,916	18,624	18,017	14,847	13,940	13,141	12,381	10,268	10,117
Rhode Island................	2,329	2,234	2,094	1,607	1,574	1,411	1,368	1,144	1,176
Vermont.......................	1,423	1,331	1,281	1,069	929	883	803	601	641
Region Total	110,320	105,605	97,316	77,065	72,832	67,860	64,720	55,118	55,772
Midwestern Region									
Illinois	$16,531	$15,720	$14,975	$11,883	$11,228	$10,586	$10,156	$9,296	$9,229
Indiana........................	7,436	7,313	6,969	5,850	5,108	4,706	4,152	3,539	3,657
Iowa............................	4,039	3,877	4,060	3,079	2,714	2,595	2,424	1,977	2,030
Kansas.........................	3,469	3,415	3,272	2,721	2,323	2,183	1,934	1,620	1,700
Michigan......................	13,227	12,970	13,279	10,887	10,107	9,764	8,618	7,237	7,194
Minnesota....................	7,209	6,914	6,492	5,260	4,753	4,499	4,199	3,952	3,535
Nebraska......................	2,531	2,512	2,342	2,054	1,720	1,651	1,511	1,227	1,232
North Dakota	1,515	1,537	1,425	1,284	1,101	1,009	1,067	1,074	734
Ohio............................	16,514	15,687	14,844	11,762	10,665	10,254	9,733	8,327	8,776
South Dakota	1,620	1,698	1,506	1,254	1,088	1,056	1,007	982	867
Wisconsin....................	7,484	7,544	7,255	5,843	5,254	4,842	4,697	3,617	3,679
Region Total	65,044	63,467	76,419	49,994	44,833	42,559	39,342	33,552	33,404
Southern Region									
Alabama.......................	$7,008	$6,649	$6,344	$5,298	$4,833	$4,632	$4,161	$3,483	$3,325
Arkansas	4,683	4,541	4,047	3,448	2,778	2,614	2,440	2,283	2,131
Florida	19,610	17,463	16,350	13,666	12,149	11,191	10,320	8,504	8,442
Georgia........................	11,759	10,561	10,500	7,929	7,520	6,752	6,233	5,469	5,359
Kentucky......................	6,743	6,634	6,346	5,100	4,687	4,395	4,236	3,702	3,355
Louisiana.....................	7,787	7,820	7,437	6,173	5,300	5,228	4,708	4,457	4,734
Maryland......................	8,837	8,632	6,312	7,586	6,911	5,744	5,022	3,950	3,544
Mississippi...................	5,379	5,318	5,046	4,246	3,517	3,387	3,025	2,626	2,754
Missouri.......................	8,734	8,655	8,429	6,865	5,939	5,478	5,065	4,231	4,091
North Carolina	12,574	11,613	10,939	9,122	8,518	7,608	7,133	6,284	5,227
Oklahoma	5,271	5,136	5,108	4,119	3,583	3,231	3,059	2,510	2,435
South Carolina	6,145	5,969	5,592	4,730	4,163	3,879	3,525	2,987	3,032
Tennessee.....................	9,863	9,057	8,658	7,027	6,372	5,900	5,510	4,555	4,476
Texas...........................	27,792	28,423	24,858	21,675	18,346	18,370	15,809	13,184	13,287
Virginia.......................	7,991	7,886	7,714	5,908	5,163	4,749	4,423	3,518	3,403
West Virginia	3,701	3,562	3,298	2,971	2,729	2,490	2,480	2,100	2,088
Region Total	96,287	94,251	136,978	115,863	102,508	95,648	87,149	73,843	71,683
Western Region									
Alaska.........................	$3,217	$3,022	$3,127	$2,314	$2,174	$1,929	$1,427	$1,303	$1,051
Arizona........................	8,364	7,235	6,664	5,190	4,704	4,537	4,147	3,355	3,095
California.....................	54,534	51,329	48,084	39,797	36,080	36,370	32,090	27,014	26,413
Colorado......................	5,643	6,014	4,740	3,916	3,591	3,446	3,048	2,444	2,410
Hawaii	2,158	1,911	1,835	1,514	1,348	1,335	1,190	1,184	1,126
Idaho...........................	1,995	1,858	1,837	1,505	1,270	1,177	1,055	936	887
Montana.......................	1,997	1,938	1,912	1,665	1,474	1,399	1,139	991	964
Nevada.........................	2,322	1,955	1,840	1,442	1,340	1,249	1,081	983	876
New Mexico	4,663	4,322	3,954	3,586	3,032	2,750	2,547	2,152	1,942
Oregon.........................	5,185	5,103	4,814	4,308	3,684	3,518	3,275	2,853	2,797
Utah............................	2,948	2,845	2,697	2,244	2,065	1,994	1,727	1,355	1,446
Washington	9,083	8,881	8,296	6,794	6,345	5,720	5,422	4,496	4,152
Wyoming......................	1,636	1,616	1,234	1,213	1,022	5,293	850	762	708
Region Total	103,745	98,029	91,034	75,488	68,129	70,717	58,998	49,828	47,867
Region Total without California	49,211	46,700	42,950	35,691	32,049	34,347	26,908	22,814	21,454
District of Columbia	$4,205	$4,310	$4,832	$4,020	$4,675	$933	$4,101	$2,740	$2,578
American Samoa...........	178	110	93	58	59	131	91	121	71
Fed. States of Micronesia	94	136	126	94	N.A.	N.A.	N.A.	N.A.	N.A.
Guam...........................	269	400	251	176	138	188	266	125	134
Marshall Islands............	56	66	58	48	N.A.	N.A.	N.A.	N.A.	N.A.
No. Mariana Islands.......	156	90	66	60	47	54	39	35	31
Palau...........................	47	51	41	35	N.A.	N.A.	N.A.	N.A.	N.A.
Puerto Rico	5,324	4,808	4,828	3,899	3,842	5,284	3,895	3,719	3,387
U.S. Virgin Islands.........	263	282	266	111	195	216	256	371	373
Undistributed...............	44	43	65	183	10	248	116	1,032	3,009

Source: U.S. Department of Commerce, Bureau of the Census, January 2004.
Released March 2006.

Table 2.2
SUMMARY OF STATE INTERGOVERNMENTAL PAYMENTS: (1944–2003)
(Amounts are in thousands of dollars and per capitas are in dollars)

				To local governments					
					For specified purposes				
	Total		To Federal government		For general local government				
Fiscal year	Amount	Per-capita	(a)	Total	support	Education	Public welfare	Highways	All other
1944	$1,842,000	$13.95	...	$1,842,000	$274,000	$861,000	$368,000	$298,000	$41,000
1946	2,092,000	15.03	...	2,092,000	357,000	953,000	376,000	339,000	67,000
1948	3,283,000	22.60	...	3,283,000	428,000	1,554,000	648,000	507,000	146,000
1950	4,217,000	28.13	...	4,217,000	482,000	2,054,000	792,000	610,000	279,000
1952	5,044,000	32.57	...	5,044,000	549,000	2,523,000	976,000	728,000	268,000
1953	5,384,000	34.20	...	5,384,000	592,000	2,737,000	981,000	803,000	271,000
1954	5,679,000	35.41	...	5,679,000	600,000	2,930,000	1,004,000	871,000	274,000
1955	5,986,000	36.61	...	5,986,000	591,000	3,150,000	1,046,000	911,000	288,000
1956	6,538,000	39.26	...	6,538,000	631,000	3,541,000	1,069,000	984,000	313,000
1957	7,440,000	43.87	...	7,440,000	668,000	4,212,000	1,136,000	1,082,000	342,000
1958	8,089,000	46.65	...	8,089,000	687,000	4,598,000	1,247,000	1,167,000	390,000
1959	8,689,000	49.26	...	8,689,000	725,000	4,957,000	1,409,000	1,207,000	391,000
1960	9,443,000	52.88	...	9,443,000	806,000	5,461,000	1,483,000	1,247,000	446,000
1962	10,906,000	58.97	...	10,906,000	839,000	6,474,000	1,777,000	1,327,000	489,000
1963	11,885,000	63.34	...	11,885,000	1,012,000	6,993,000	1,919,000	1,416,000	545,000
1964	12,968,000	68.15	...	12,968,000	1,053,000	7,664,000	2,108,000	1,524,000	619,000
1965	14,174,000	73.57	...	14,174,000	1,102,000	8,351,000	2,436,000	1,630,000	655,000
1966	16,928,000	86.94	...	16,928,000	1,361,000	10,177,000	2,882,000	1,725,000	783,000
1967	19,056,000	96.94	...	19,056,000	1,585,000	11,845,000	2,897,000	1,861,000	868,000
1968	21,950,000	110.56	...	21,950,000	1,993,000	13,321,000	3,527,000	2,029,000	1,080,000
1969	24,779,000	123.56	...	24,779,000	2,135,000	14,858,000	4,402,000	2,109,000	1,275,000
1970	28,892,000	142.64	...	28,892,000	2,958,000	17,085,000	5,003,000	2,439,000	1,407,000
1971	32,640,000	158.39	...	32,640,000	3,258,000	19,292,000	5,760,000	2,507,000	1,823,000
1972	36,759,246	176.27	...	36,759,246	3,752,327	21,195,345	6,943,634	2,633,417	2,234,523
1973	40,822,135	193.81	...	40,822,135	4,279,646	23,315,651	7,531,738	2,953,424	2,741,676
1974	45,941,111	216.07	$341,194	45,599,917	4,803,875	27,106,812	7,028,750	3,211,455	3,449,025
1975	51,978,324	242.03	974,780	51,003,544	5,129,333	31,110,237	7,136,104	3,224,861	4,403,009
1976	57,858,242	266.79	1,179,580	56,678,662	5,673,843	34,083,711	8,307,411	3,240,806	5,372,891
1977	62,459,903	285.10	1,386,237	61,073,666	6,372,543	36,964,306	8,756,717	3,631,108	5,348,992
1978	67,287,260	303.88	1,472,378	65,814,882	6,819,438	40,125,488	8,585,558	3,821,135	6,463,263
1979	75,962,980	339.25	1,493,215	74,469,765	8,224,338	46,195,698	8,675,473	4,148,573	7,225,683
1980	84,504,451	374.07	1,746,301	82,758,150	8,643,789	52,688,101	9,241,551	4,382,716	7,801,993
1981	93,179,549	406.89	1,872,980	91,306,569	9,570,248	57,257,373	11,025,445	4,751,449	8,702,054
1982	98,742,976	426.78	1,793,284	96,949,692	10,044,372	60,683,583	11,965,123	5,028,072	9,228,542
1983	100,886,902	431.77	1,764,821	99,122,081	10,364,144	63,118,351	10,919,847	5,277,447	9,442,292
1984	108,373,188	459.49	1,722,115	106,651,073	10,744,740	67,484,926	11,923,430	5,686,834	10,811,143
1985	121,571,151	510.56	1,963,468	119,607,683	12,319,623	74,936,970	12,673,123	6,019,069	13,658,898
1986	131,966,258	548.76	2,105,831	129,860,427	13,383,912	81,929,467	14,214,613	6,470,049	13,862,386
1987	141,278,672	581.88	2,455,362	138,823,310	14,245,089	88,253,298	14,753,727	6,784,699	14,786,497
1988	151,661,866	618.55	2,652,981	149,008,885	14,896,991	95,390,536	15,032,315	6,949,190	16,739,853
1989	165,415,415	667.98	2,929,622	162,485,793	15,749,681	104,601,291	16,697,915	7,376,173	18,060,733
1990	175,027,632	705.46	3,243,634	171,783,998	16,565,106	109,438,131	18,403,149	7,784,316	19,593,296
1991	186,398,234	740.91	3,464,364	182,933,870	16,977,032	116,179,860	20,903,400	8,126,477	20,747,101
1992	201,313,434	791.04	3,608,911	197,704,523	16,368,139	124,919,686	25,942,234	8,480,871	21,993,593
1993	214,094,882	832.00	3,625,051	210,469,831	17,690,986	131,179,517	31,339,777	9,298,624	20,960,927
1994	225,635,410	868.50	3,603,447	222,031,963	18,044,015	135,861,024	30,624,514	9,622,849	27,879,561
1995	240,978,128	919.10	3,616,831	237,361,297	18,996,435	148,160,436	30,772,525	10,481,616	28,926,886
1996	252,102,458	952.30	3,896,667	248,205,791	20,019,771	156,954,115	31,180,345	10,707,338	29,321,099
1997	264,207,209	989.10	3,839,942	260,367,267	21,808,828	164,147,715	35,754,024	11,431,270	27,225,430
1998	278,853,409	1,031.60	3,515,734	275,337,675	22,693,158	176,250,998	32,327,325	11,648,853	32,417,341
1999	304,933,250	1,120.40	3,801,667	301,131,583	25,495,396	192,416,987	35,161,151	12,075,195	39,784,521
2000	327,069,829	1,164.57	4,021,471	323,048,358	27,475,363	208,135,537	40,206,513	12,473,052	34,757,893
2001	350,326,546	1,230.32	4,290,764	346,035,782	31,693,016	222,092,587	41,926,990	12,350,136	37,973,053
2002	364,789,480	1,269.25	4,370,330	360,419,150	28,927,053	227,336,087	47,112,496	12,949,850	44,093,664
2003	382,781,397	1,318.89	4,391,095	378,390,302	30,766,480	240,788,692	49,302,737	13,337,114	44,195,279

Source: U.S. Department of Commerce, Bureau of the Census, 2004.
Released March 2006.
Key:
... —Not available
(a) Represents primarily state reimbursements for the supplemental security income program. This column also duplicates some funds listed under "Public welfare" and "All other" columns.

Table 2.3
INTERGOVERNMENTAL EXPENDITURES, BY STATE: (1997–2003)
(Amounts are in thousands of dollars and per capitas are in dollars)

State	Amount (in thousands)				Per capita amounts				Percentage change in per capita amounts		
									2002 to 2003	2001 to 2002	2000 to 2001
	2003	2002	2001	2000	2002	2001	2000	1999			
United States	$382,781,397	$364,789,480	$350,326,546	$327,069,829	$1,269.3	$1,269.3	$1,164.6	$1,120.4	25.5	19.6	11.5
Alabama	4,074,005	4,095,562	3,892,653	3,908,350	914.4	914.4	878.9	831.0	12.2	12.8	4.8
Alaska	1,091,391	1,055,596	986,921	1,026,962	1,646.8	1,646.8	1,637.9	1,659.5	6.1	2.6	2.8
Arizona	6,936,753	6,968,635	6,439,144	5,940,651	1,280.8	1,280.8	1,157.8	1,244.0	16.7	17.2	17.3
Arkansas.............	3,210,582	3,071,214	2,941,918	2,725,242	1,135.0	1,135.0	1,019.5	1,038.6	21.2	15.9	12.7
California	84,468,847	74,687,370	69,747,365	65,389,054	2,133.8	2,133.8	1,930.5	1,760.5	44.8	28.0	14.2
Colorado	4,666,350	4,295,239	3,909,362	3,702,849	954.3	954.3	860.9	867.8	32.6	22.0	16.0
Connecticut	3,030,485	3,734,962	3,252,917	3,362,551	1,079.8	1,079.8	987.2	856.5	7.8	32.9	11.1
Delaware..............	903,476	822,544	788,160	856,008	1,020.5	1,020.5	1,091.8	956.2	25.3	14.1	-3.9
Florida	14,460,722	14,053,858	15,010,631	14,073,445	842.0	842.0	880.6	889.3	7.6	4.6	-0.1
Georgia	9,016,458	8,644,827	8,383,261	7,179,698	1,011.8	1,011.8	877.1	857.3	35.0	29.5	20.4
Hawaii..................	125,434	130,387	124,448	157,902	105.1	105.1	130.3	129.3	-18.1	-14.9	-17.4
Idaho..................	1,449,076	1,407,058	1,363,445	1,277,688	1,047.7	1,047.7	987.4	969.2	19.4	16.0	10.1
Illinois.................	13,369,662	13,090,976	12,770,065	12,050,100	1,040.1	1,040.1	970.3	890.7	23.8	21.2	8.6
Indiana................	6,760,945	6,556,774	7,052,415	6,735,704	1,064.9	1,064.9	1,107.8	1,051.3	8.2	4.9	-2.7
Iowa	3,442,552	3,326,499	3,284,057	3,211,878	1,133.0	1,133.0	1,097.7	1,001.4	19.8	15.8	3.6
Kansas	2,925,220	2,971,413	2,953,527	2,853,333	1,095.7	1,095.7	1,061.5	1,057.3	4.2	5.9	4.1
Kentucky	3,693,634	3,559,669	3,620,278	3,280,144	870.3	870.3	811.5	820.3	13.7	9.6	8.5
Louisiana	4,329,053	4,168,290	3,800,785	3,721,576	931.3	931.3	832.8	833.7	18.8	14.4	12.0
Maine..................	1,051,164	1,009,582	976,233	912,376	779.6	779.6	715.6	684.9	22.5	17.6	10.7
Maryland	5,358,342	5,235,506	5,003,670	4,355,724	960.5	960.5	822.5	785.7	31.9	28.8	20.2
Massachusetts.......	6,435,841	6,283,972	6,886,054	6,240,692	978.5	978.5	982.9	1,093.4	-4.7	-6.9	0.7
Michigan..............	19,851,778	19,067,058	18,145,167	17,201,031	1,898.5	1,898.5	1,730.8	1,625.1	23.8	18.9	10.8
Minnesota	9,618,471	8,271,462	8,196,532	7,610,072	1,646.1	1,646.1	1,547.1	1,466.7	37.3	18.1	8.7
Mississippi	3,665,580	3,456,588	3,354,226	3,248,019	1,205.6	1,205.6	1,141.7	1,090.2	21.4	14.5	6.4
Missouri...............	5,159,094	5,073,185	4,802,371	4,528,746	894.7	894.7	809.4	812.3	16.2	14.2	12.0
Montana	938,000	910,845	863,553	760,511	1,000.9	1,000.9	843.1	802.1	32.4	28.6	19.8
Nebraska..............	1,784,749	1,820,137	1,684,159	1,585,847	1,053.3	1,053.3	926.9	892.7	20.0	22.4	14.8
Nevada	2,648,660	2,432,909	2,271,654	2,250,330	1,122.7	1,122.7	1,126.3	1,154.6	26.8	16.5	8.1
New Hampshire....	1,283,091	1,178,642	1,040,566	1,053,267	925.2	925.2	852.2	397.9	168.5	146.6	11.9
New Jersey...........	8,997,417	9,320,357	9,081,634	8,639,491	1,086.9	1,086.9	1,026.8	957.8	15.4	19.5	7.9
New Mexico	2,951,328	2,768,420	2,561,979	2,447,354	1,494.8	1,494.8	1,345.4	1,359.8	24.7	17.0	13.1
New York	40,874,514	38,982,253	34,712,602	31,273,000	2,037.3	2,037.3	1,648.0	1,669.7	34.5	28.3	24.7
North Carolina	10,356,152	9,450,766	9,309,537	9,301,095	1,137.8	1,137.8	1,155.6	1,116.5	21.2	10.6	1.6
North Dakota.......	1,190,923	585,521	569,034	589,807	923.5	923.5	918.7	878.9	113.7	5.1	-0.7
Ohio	15,249,395	15,052,078	14,594,220	12,932,081	1,319.3	1,319.3	1,139.1	1,067.4	26.9	25.3	16.4
Oklahoma	3,395,494	3,377,045	3,486,043	3,089,257	967.6	967.6	895.2	887.9	13.9	13.3	9.3
Oregon	4,071,501	4,212,673	4,027,505	3,919,771	1,196.8	1,196.8	1,145.8	1,107.5	10.9	14.7	7.5
Pennsylvania	11,943,470	12,787,590	13,120,752	11,369,795	1,037.2	1,037.2	925.8	912.8	9.1	16.8	12.5
Rhode Island	828,198	749,034	711,439	677,552	701.3	701.3	646.5	600.3	39.2	25.9	11.4
South Carolina	4,155,920	4,241,010	4,168,449	3,806,116	1,033.4	1,033.4	948.7	863.4	23.9	26.4	11.4
South Dakota.......	514,949	506,347	480,960	448,131	666.2	666.2	593.6	643.6	9.1	7.3	13.0
Tennessee.............	4,952,923	4,477,936	4,582,883	4,364,404	773.4	773.4	767.2	761.3	18.6	7.3	2.6
Texas	17,332,957	16,680,780	17,204,468	16,231,378	767.4	767.4	778.4	749.5	15.4	11.0	2.8
Utah	2,165,151	2,170,884	2,100,657	1,977,703	936.1	936.1	885.7	850.7	19.5	19.8	9.8
Vermont	938,085	918,858	919,865	931,604	1,491.7	1,491.7	1,529.7	1,177.2	34.2	31.4	-1.4
Virginia	8,352,635	8,369,313	7,869,121	7,132,350	1,148.4	1,148.4	1,007.5	945.7	28.5	28.8	17.3
Washington...........	6,785,341	6,806,350	6,576,757	6,370,710	1,121.9	1,121.9	1,080.9	1,062.7	10.9	11.3	6.8
West Virginia.......	1,544,758	1,453,707	988,322	1,359,668	805.4	805.4	752.0	872.9	-2.1	-7.8	6.9
Wisconsin.............	9,478,166	9,523,191	8,895,941	8,170,504	1,750.6	1,750.6	1,523.2	1,502.4	20.2	20.7	16.6
Wyoming..............	952,705	974,608	818,841	838,308	1,953.1	1,953.1	1,697.0	1,587.5	25.0	27.9	16.3

Source: U.S. Department of Commerce, Bureau of the Census, January 2003. Released March 2006.

Note: Includes payments to the federal government, primarily state reimbursements for the supplemental security income program.

Table 2.4
PER CAPITA STATE INTERGOVERNMENTAL EXPENDITURES, BY FUNCTION AND BY STATE: 2003
(Per capita amounts in dollars)

State	Total	General local government support	Education	Public welfare	Highways	Health	Miscellaneous and combined
				Specified functions			
United States	$1,318.9	$106.0	$829.6	$169.9	$46.0	$68.5	$98.9
Alabama	904.5	25.1	784.1	0.0	42.8	4.5	48.1
Alaska	1,684.2	33.7	1,099.4	184.4	14.0	77.4	275.3
Arizona	1,243.4	248.6	719.0	129.8	98.2	5.2	42.5
Arkansas..............	1,176.9	97.8	956.7	0.0	57.8	0.7	63.9
California	2,381.9	159.6	1,219.4	633.2	58.2	202.6	108.8
Colorado	1,026.0	5.0	669.8	196.8	59.9	10.8	83.7
Connecticut	869.1	53.2	648.4	20.3	4.6	29.2	113.5
Delaware..............	1,104.5	0.0	985.0	1.3	10.1	24.4	83.7
Florida	850.7	159.1	630.6	0.2	7.7	0.8	52.1
Georgia	1,039.2	43.4	851.7	61.1	0.6	39.8	42.7
Hawaii.................	100.4	61.9	0.0	1.0	0.0	17.5	20.1
Idaho...................	1,060.0	93.5	846.3	0.0	81.3	12.5	26.5
Illinois.................	1,057.0	99.8	631.7	137.5	53.7	10.9	123.3
Indiana................	1,090.5	250.9	666.9	54.1	56.0	17.0	45.6
Iowa	1,170.1	44.9	844.5	16.3	142.8	32.5	89.1
Kansas	1,073.5	26.4	901.6	5.5	60.1	13.7	66.2
Kentucky	896.9	0.0	745.8	11.5	29.7	31.4	78.4
Louisiana	963.3	38.8	737.8	17.2	21.7	0.1	147.7
Maine	803.0	97.3	622.5	37.0	17.1	0.4	28.7
Maryland..............	972.1	0.0	669.4	0.0	80.3	104.5	117.9
Massachusetts.......	1,002.5	117.3	535.2	46.8	19.5	1.9	281.8
Michigan..............	1,969.0	145.3	1,271.2	44.5	147.4	289.9	70.7
Minnesota	1,899.4	286.3	1,196.5	137.3	126.6	26.4	126.3
Mississippi	1,271.4	218.6	827.1	73.7	60.6	14.9	76.5
Missouri...............	902.1	0.8	734.8	18.5	49.9	3.5	94.6
Montana	1,021.4	143.9	745.8	19.0	18.2	19.4	75.5
Nebraska..............	1,027.5	165.6	624.2	9.3	0.0	155.0	73.3
Nevada	1,181.4	345.2	769.9	13.6	29.3	3.5	19.8
New Hampshire....	995.4	48.2	739.6	77.5	21.8	26.6	81.8
New Jersey...........	1,041.1	218.1	631.8	108.6	33.5	5.4	43.7
New Mexico	1,570.7	367.9	1,163.6	0.0	7.3	1.2	30.7
New York	2,127.6	56.7	1,007.7	561.0	1.8	193.2	307.2
North Carolina.....	1,229.8	76.2	881.6	148.6	17.0	41.3	65.0
North Dakota.......	1,881.4	191.7	1,249.3	6.8	203.8	51.3	178.6
Ohio	1,333.2	155.1	811.8	153.5	78.7	80.8	53.3
Oklahoma	968.5	23.1	771.7	13.2	75.0	25.9	59.6
Oregon	1,142.4	38.3	767.5	108.5	125.2	18.4	84.5
Pennsylvania	965.4	2.1	565.5	162.8	34.6	69.1	131.5
Rhode Island	769.7	69.3	665.9	27.9	0.0	0.0	6.6
South Carolina	1,001.7	214.1	686.5	3.0	18.0	18.7	61.4
South Dakota........	673.1	17.1	555.6	0.0	45.3	0.1	55.1
Tennessee	847.4	66.1	545.1	110.3	58.8	0.1	67.0
Texas	784.2	4.8	680.9	31.4	5.1	22.2	39.8
Utah	920.4	0.0	837.8	7.7	56.7	13.6	4.8
Vermont...............	1,515.5	20.9	1,360.7	0.4	100.2	0.0	33.2
Virginia................	1,134.1	118.0	696.7	83.9	37.4	32.5	165.6
Washington..........	1,106.7	14.0	900.4	5.3	92.4	29.3	65.4
West Virginia........	853.0	9.5	764.4	0.0	0.0	8.6	70.4
Wisconsin.............	1,731.5	340.9	976.5	189.6	81.9	59.7	82.9
Wyoming..............	1,897.8	347.9	1,263.9	1.8	12.0	88.2	184.0

Source: U.S. Department of Commerce, Bureau of the Census, January 2003. Released March 2006.

Note: Includes payments to the federal government, primarily state reimbursements for the supplemental security income program (under "public welfare").

Table 2.5
STATE INTERGOVERNMENTAL EXPENDITURES, BY FUNCTION AND BY STATE: 2003
(Amounts are in thousands of dollars)

State	Total	General local government support	Specified functions Education	Public welfare	Highways	Health	Miscellaneous and combined
United States	$382,781,397	$30,766,480	$240,788,692	$49,302,737	$13,337,114	$19,884,938	$28,701,436
Alabama	4,074,005	112,898	3,531,560	0	192,662	20,272	216,613
Alaska	1,091,391	21,849	712,386	119,501	9,069	50,177	178,409
Arizona	6,936,753	1,387,013	4,011,553	724,184	547,729	29,278	236,996
Arkansas..............	3,210,582	266,785	2,609,844	4	157,764	1,825	174,360
California	84,468,847	5,660,807	43,243,000	22,456,385	2,063,692	7,186,390	3,858,573
Colorado	4,666,350	22,558	3,046,164	895,197	272,585	49,304	380,542
Connecticut	3,030,485	185,365	2,261,036	70,753	15,936	101,739	395,656
Delaware	903,476	0	805,739	1,091	8,239	19,939	68,468
Florida	14,460,722	2,705,274	10,720,382	3,268	131,209	14,227	886,362
Georgia	9,016,458	376,515	7,389,085	529,818	5,371	345,338	370,331
Hawaii..................	125,434	77,251	0	1,215	0	21,835	25,133
Idaho...................	1,449,076	127,815	1,156,840	0	111,152	17,101	36,168
Illinois.................	13,369,662	1,262,928	7,989,840	1,739,140	679,627	138,312	1,559,815
Indiana.................	6,760,945	1,555,408	4,134,937	335,316	347,185	105,683	282,416
Iowa	3,442,552	131,975	2,484,619	47,917	420,161	95,733	262,147
Kansas	2,925,220	72,018	2,456,923	14,996	163,717	37,238	180,328
Kentucky	3,693,634	0	3,071,375	47,377	122,332	129,501	323,049
Louisiana	4,329,053	174,499	3,315,553	77,145	97,478	418	663,960
Maine	1,051,164	127,351	814,823	48,465	22,394	518	37,613
Maryland	5,358,342	0	3,689,625	23	442,751	576,191	649,752
Massachusetts.......	6,435,841	753,214	3,435,771	300,460	125,140	12,289	1,808,967
Michigan..............	19,851,778	1,464,637	12,815,989	448,909	1,486,420	2,922,973	712,850
Minnesota	9,618,471	1,449,709	6,059,104	695,325	640,943	133,698	639,692
Mississipp	i3,665,580	630,319	2,384,653	212,587	174,576	42,908	220,537
Missouri................	5,159,094	4,594	4,202,320	105,840	285,389	20,216	540,735
Montana	938,000	132,068	684,637	17,442	16,741	17,846	69,266
Nebraska..............	1,784,749	287,661	1,084,252	16,157	0	269,304	127,375
Nevada	2,648,660	773,968	1,726,160	30,585	65,800	7,777	44,370
New Hampshire....	1,283,091	62,173	953,302	99,881	28,113	34,234	105,388
New Jersey...........	8,997,417	1,885,031	5,460,085	938,522	289,638	46,857	377,284
New Mexico	2,951,328	691,375	2,186,467	0	13,725	2,169	57,592
New York	40,874,514	1,089,710	19,360,589	10,777,726	34,416	3,710,801	5,901,272
North Carolina	10,356,152	641,800	7,424,250	1,251,421	142,765	348,165	547,751
North Dakota........	1,190,923	121,318	790,783	4,290	129,035	32,451	113,046
Ohio	15,249,395	1,773,813	9,285,216	1,756,228	899,963	924,033	610,142
Oklahoma	3,395,494	80,962	2,705,722	46,166	263,069	90,656	208,919
Oregon	4,071,501	136,597	2,735,329	386,730	446,336	65,506	301,003
Pennsylvania	11,943,470	25,615	6,995,210	2,013,590	427,677	854,753	1,626,625
Rhode Island	828,198	74,582	716,523	30,002	0	0	7,091
South Carolina	4,155,920	888,397	2,848,157	12,447	74,822	77,516	254,581
South Dakota........	514,949	13,089	425,017	0	34,663	49	42,131
Tennessee	4,952,923	386,228	3,186,125	644,595	343,817	428	391,730
Texas	17,332,957	105,429	15,049,637	694,871	111,895	491,316	879,809
Utah	2,165,151	0	1,970,464	18,007	133,270	32,007	11,403
Vermont	938,085	12,914	842,303	271	62,039	0	20,558
Virginia.................	8,352,635	869,305	5,130,858	617,576	275,295	239,693	1,219,908
Washington...........	6,785,341	85,630	5,520,227	32,695	566,336	179,382	401,071
West Virginia........	1,544,758	17,227	1,384,376	0	0	15,611	127,544
Wisconsin.............	9,478,166	1,866,150	5,345,407	1,037,711	448,161	327,006	453,731
Wyoming...............	952,705	174,656	634,475	908	6,017	44,275	92,374

Source: U.S. Department of Commerce, Bureau of the Census, January 2003. Released March 2006.

Note: Detail may not add to total due to rounding.

Table 2.6
STATE INTERGOVERNMENTAL EXPENDITURES, BY TYPE OF RECEIVING GOVERNMENT AND BY STATE: 2003
(In thousands of dollars)

State	Total intergovernmental expenditure	Federal	School districts	Counties, municipalities, and townships	Special districts	Combined and unallocable
United States	$382,781,397	$4,391,095	$199,419,442	$161,424,123	$3,423,463	$14,123,274
Alabama	4,074,005	0	3,531,560	516,843	0	25,602
Alaska	1,091,391	0	0	840,693	0	250,698
Arizona	6,936,753	0	3,368,470	3,518,805	0	49,478
Arkansas..............	3,210,582	1,056	2,609,842	436,977	27,076	135,631
California	84,468,847	3,058,713	40,930,673	37,936,243	1,106,053	1,437,165
Colorado	4,666,350	2,747	3,037,908	1,598,015	27,680	0
Connecticut	3,030,485	0	21,640	2,836,060	0	172,785
Delaware..............	903,476	1,034	805,507	96,935	0	0
Florida	14,460,722	0	10,701,960	3,758,762	0	0
Georgia	9,016,458	0	7,389,085	1,495,219	44,541	87,613
Hawaii..................	125,434	1,215	0	100,671	0	23,548
Idaho....................	1,449,076	0	1,156,840	178,937	615	112,684
Illinois..................	13,369,662	3,152	7,964,002	4,079,765	575,815	746,928
Indiana.................	6,760,945	0	4,134,937	1,514,378	5,763	1,105,867
Iowa	3,442,552	45,834	2,484,619	691,788	0	220,311
Kansas	2,925,220	595	2,447,274	320,746	3,394	153,211
Kentucky	3,693,634	0	3,070,536	620,581	0	2,517
Louisiana	4,329,053	0	3,312,755	636,844	0	379,454
Maine...................	1,051,164	43,618	0	187,941	0	819,605
Maryland..............	5,358,342	0	0	5,285,832	0	72,510
Massachusetts.......	6,435,841	181,129	524,861	4,613,426	899,113	217,312
Michigan...............	19,851,778	54,921	12,815,989	6,684,238	713	295,917
Minnesota	9,618,471	0	6,038,015	3,250,751	174,729	154,976
Mississippi	3,665,580	0	2,370,493	1,280,210	0	14,877
Missouri................	5,159,094	3,536	4,202,178	604,463	34,488	314,429
Montana	938,000	1,147	684,637	213,935	0	38,281
Nebraska..............	1,784,749	15,956	1,084,147	201,346	34,120	449,180
Nevada	2,648,660	7,262	1,725,066	915,663	0	669
New Hampshire....	1,283,091	0	164	235,348	645	1,046,934
New Jersey............	8,997,417	71,328	3,959,781	4,937,206	0	29,102
New Mexico	2,951,328	0	2,186,462	764,866	0	0
New York	40,874,514	629,000	10,197,168	29,242,490	0	805,856
North Carolina	10,356,152	0	0	10,299,402	56,750	0
North Dakota........	1,190,923	0	790,451	383,855	15,708	909
Ohio	15,249,395	2,579	9,285,216	3,790,835	24,381	2,146,384
Oklahoma	3,395,494	41,083	2,705,722	469,750	6,717	172,222
Oregon	4,071,501	0	2,731,101	1,185,232	39,229	115,939
Pennsylvania	11,943,470	175,708	6,995,210	4,351,493	291,317	129,742
Rhode Island	828,198	27,156	39,369	755,673	0	6,000
South Carolina	4,155,920	0	2,766,121	1,385,674	1,150	2,975
South Dakota........	514,949	0	425,017	81,387	700	7,845
Tennessee	4,952,923	0	190,056	4,721,246	24,351	17,270
Texas	17,332,957	0	15,043,381	897,981	6,258	1,385,337
Utah	2,165,151	494	1,970,464	194,193	0	0
Vermont	938,085	271	842,303	95,511	0	0
Virginia.................	8,352,635	1,053	0	8,351,582	0	0
Washington...........	6,785,341	20,508	5,515,729	1,204,653	21,273	23,178
West Virginia........	1,544,758	0	1,384,376	143,905	190	16,287
Wisconsin..............	9,478,166	0	5,345,405	3,245,586	0	887,175
Wyoming...............	952,705	0	632,952	270,188	694	48,871

Source: U.S. Department of Commerce, Bureau of the Census, January 2003. Released March 2006.

Note: Detail may not add to total due to rounding.

Table 2.7
STATE INTERGOVERNMENTAL REVENUE FROM FEDERAL AND LOCAL GOVERNMENTS: 2003
(In thousands of dollars)

State	Total intergovernmental revenue	From federal government					From local governments				
		Total	Education	Public welfare	Health & hospitals	Highways	Total	Education	Public welfare	Health & hospitals	Highways
United States	$362,519,737	$344,190,331	$56,443,613	$197,386,194	$19,585,682	$29,691,144	$18,329,406	$1,678,036	$11,684,968	$503,248	$1,107,282
Alabama	6,668,784	6,115,367	1,260,295	3,347,684	269,150	587,754	553,417	12,732	501,068	16	12,357
Alaska	1,997,175	1,992,775	250,750	729,994	61,072	418,030	4,400	4,400	0	0	0
Arizona	6,092,557	5,652,650	1,045,260	3,625,794	107,604	447,406	439,907	21,140	300,469	49,679	30,443
Arkansas	3,685,249	3,661,996	573,783	1,945,881	77,043	447,530	23,253	13,572	0	892	0
California	48,245,951	45,530,883	8,871,979	24,833,543	2,165,152	2,610,299	2,715,068	132,969	1,659,422	5,735	216,288
Colorado	4,178,537	4,133,705	1,120,704	1,432,789	719,441	391,038	44,832	3,937	137	445	22,873
Connecticut	4,020,036	4,003,107	445,932	2,492,755	229,915	480,444	16,929	7,570	0	0	0
Delaware	994,952	959,517	119,660	494,054	70,002	112,097	35,435	32,555	0	0	0
Florida	12,850,982	12,746,716	1,064,926	7,000,502	1,388,184	1,747,322	104,266	21	0	66,364	0
Georgia	9,028,114	8,944,617	1,897,172	5,091,543	335,874	890,701	83,497	20,928	0	0	19,821
Hawaii	1,537,997	1,536,856	415,106	639,021	92,214	98,147	1,141	475	0	0	0
Idaho	1,455,705	1,449,188	236,742	674,764	132,442	213,852	6,517	137	638	1,238	4,503
Illinois	12,027,338	10,792,093	2,428,406	6,215,824	512,792	718,080	1,235,245	39,246	1,114,557	0	61,847
Indiana	6,346,679	6,191,193	1,004,020	3,730,032	171,395	552,664	155,486	13,755	58,617	4,998	54,064
Iowa	3,534,400	3,408,764	694,246	1,738,271	314,475	311,499	125,636	1,048	84,104	28,602	8,476
Kansas	3,266,719	3,235,973	804,032	1,244,838	166,568	388,079	30,746	5,266	0	0	25,480
Kentucky	5,330,212	5,307,649	891,484	3,238,697	182,643	479,832	22,563	14,672	0	0	0
Louisiana	6,501,978	6,425,520	1,045,544	3,965,502	257,608	508,981	76,458	9,682	0	3,094	7,401
Maine	2,062,560	2,053,319	203,019	1,318,623	61,563	177,884	9,241	0	0	8	0
Maryland	5,829,817	5,599,031	1,178,093	2,656,534	555,857	505,706	230,786	40,695	0	47,332	33,750
Massachusetts	5,130,127	4,794,237	867,449	1,646,825	810,733	436,481	335,890	6,123	7,675	0	165
Michigan	12,221,555	11,975,507	2,088,923	6,453,499	1,437,347	791,269	246,048	16,260	49,347	53,306	98,176
Minnesota	5,982,225	5,826,722	1,012,573	3,627,591	185,047	355,248	155,503	7,987	26,101	18,293	93,647
Mississippi	5,086,417	4,923,136	831,286	3,070,698	153,805	417,635	163,281	6,283	104,990	10	5,269
Missouri	7,172,806	7,020,669	975,740	4,279,088	361,375	768,849	152,137	3,707	87,996	8,697	37,479
Montana	1,582,665	1,571,804	258,917	615,007	94,230	311,984	10,861	2,380	7,346	0	786
Nebraska	2,139,810	2,126,239	125,157	1,534,181	96,431	213,956	13,571	1,310	2,426	94	7,885
Nevada	1,498,008	1,443,711	290,311	738,606	92,489	185,900	54,297	13,974	23,196	639	4,900
New Hampshire	1,464,454	1,300,545	177,403	568,743	34,311	144,260	163,909	1,877	143,048	0	9,814
New Jersey	9,064,614	8,657,999	1,259,262	4,588,236	589,899	1,029,245	406,615	248,876	30,000	0	934
New Mexico	3,220,765	3,108,257	640,978	1,813,580	146,415	307,306	112,508	45,878	0	64,855	0
New York	43,442,351	36,966,777	2,628,699	26,485,437	1,908,369	1,352,137	6,475,574	87,020	5,459,151	94	9,313
North Carolina	10,278,725	9,589,560	1,431,522	6,302,402	301,667	791,136	689,165	74,246	573,051	2,810	0
North Dakota	2,030,717	1,986,036	289,824	900,083	62,934	424,153	44,681	0	9,268	0	22,363
Ohio	14,058,065	13,697,045	1,700,174	8,953,182	804,181	905,410	361,020	54,199	72,978	23,566	57,507
Oklahoma	4,255,172	4,179,832	762,414	1,869,681	767,348	391,309	75,340	2,510	2,473	479	8,344
Oregon	4,215,696	4,202,491	926,991	2,116,830	283,404	353,152	13,205	9,202	0	0	0
Pennsylvania	14,466,919	14,339,237	2,256,096	8,997,139	384,436	1,370,295	127,682	81,322	0	4,708	21,246
Rhode Island	1,855,350	1,758,790	211,708	1,074,711	84,410	148,444	96,560	0	0	0	0
South Carolina	5,738,966	5,268,989	977,715	3,225,187	219,010	420,792	469,977	49,154	378,447	7,039	1,473

See footnotes at end of table.

STATE INTERGOVERNMENTAL REVENUE FROM FEDERAL AND LOCAL GOVERNMENTS: 2003 — Continued
(In thousands of dollars)

State	Total intergovernmental revenue	From federal government					From local governments				
		Total	Education	Public welfare	Health & hospitals	Highways	Total	Education	Public welfare	Health & hospitals	Highways
South Dakota......	1,111,450	1,088,407	152,587	493,911	50,228	210,441	23,043	5,188	0	9,919	6,798
Tennessee......	8,292,209	8,056,803	986,651	5,755,814	236,523	552,212	235,406	28,555	0	2,214	31,431
Texas......	24,349,595	23,616,336	4,744,692	12,304,632	1,036,336	2,812,548	733,259	316,873	382,148	32,452	0
Utah......	2,493,503	2,424,637	602,496	1,048,498	145,483	243,088	68,866	68,401	0	463	0
Vermont......	1,152,305	1,114,898	185,386	584,803	75,695	84,600	37,407	1,587	0	0	35,820
Virginia......	5,679,471	5,553,879	1,246,825	2,692,971	248,718	678,361	125,592	20,573	0	49,753	39,684
Washington......	7,012,389	6,859,972	1,465,598	3,421,655	763,436	612,930	152,417	73,137	0	0	47,896
West Virginia......	2,975,382	2,911,279	427,233	1,640,530	114,737	407,664	64,103	1,749	0	0	0
Wisconsin......	7,094,092	6,355,490	1,048,299	3,875,747	183,529	571,513	738,602	18,145	606,315	13,986	61,608
Wyoming......	1,798,192	1,730,128	319,551	290,282	42,162	311,481	68,064	56,720	0	1,562	7,441

Source: U.S. Department of Commerce, Bureau of the Census, January 2003. Released March 2006.
Note: Detail may not add to total due to rounding.

Table 2.8
SUMMARY OF FEDERAL GOVERNMENT EXPENDITURE, BY STATE AND OUTLYING AREA:
FISCAL YEAR 2004
(In millions of dollars)

State and outlying area	Total	Retirement and disability	Other direct payments	Grants	Procurement	Salaries and wages
United States	$2,161,948	$666,969	$469,544	$460,152	$339,681	$225,601
Alabama	39,047	12,930	8,017	7,008	7,600	3,492
Alaska	8,445	1,135	665	3,217	1,700	1,728
Arizona	41,979	12,942	7,269	8,364	9,797	3,608
Arkansas	19,489	7,404	5,045	4,683	848	1,509
California	232,387	64,078	51,492	54,534	40,254	22,029
Colorado	30,060	8,918	5,295	5,643	5,747	4,457
Connecticut	30,304	7,809	5,828	5,556	9,509	1,602
Delaware	5,253	2,085	1,168	1,241	265	494
Florida	121,934	48,050	32,432	19,610	11,447	10,395
Georgia	55,153	17,748	11,509	11,759	5,813	8,324
Hawaii	12,187	3,202	1,607	2,158	2,066	3,154
Idaho	8,968	3,053	1,649	1,995	1,373	898
Illinois	76,828	25,597	21,111	16,531	6,583	7,007
Indiana	37,918	14,019	10,004	7,436	4,002	2,457
Iowa	19,218	6,971	5,359	4,039	1,599	1,249
Kansas	19,131	6,412	4,801	3,469	2,242	2,208
Kentucky	31,714	10,579	6,523	6,743	4,637	3,231
Louisiana	32,954	9,981	8,950	7,787	3,418	2,818
Maine	10,865	3,587	1,852	2,758	1,711	957
Maryland	64,726	14,190	10,372	8,837	20,804	10,523
Massachusetts	53,120	14,186	12,374	13,876	9,127	3,557
Michigan	60,488	22,916	16,616	13,227	4,119	3,610
Minnesota	28,791	10,059	6,891	7,209	2,329	2,302
Mississippi	22,338	7,297	5,196	5,379	2,372	2,094
Missouri	45,730	14,071	10,892	8,734	7,991	4,042
Montana	7,494	2,394	1,629	1,997	587	886
Nebraska	11,795	4,070	3,199	2,531	697	1,298
Nevada	12,769	5,149	2,352	2,322	1,600	1,347
New Hampshire	7,959	3,028	1,412	1,879	985	654
New Jersey	55,264	18,922	14,549	11,333	6,132	4,328
New Mexico	19,864	4,681	2,476	4,663	5,973	2,072
New York	143,903	41,209	34,726	50,009	8,889	9,070
North Carolina	55,233	20,131	11,398	12,574	3,933	7,197
North Dakota	6,035	1,477	1,753	1,515	503	787
Ohio	73,195	26,251	17,918	16,514	6,936	5,576
Oklahoma	26,644	9,169	5,938	5,271	2,804	3,463
Oregon	21,871	8,452	5,048	5,185	1,283	1,903
Pennsylvania	94,900	33,147	25,917	19,916	9,311	6,609
Rhode Island	8,245	2,627	1,902	2,329	559	829
South Carolina	30,051	10,812	5,746	6,145	4,193	3,156
South Dakota	6,602	1,842	1,937	1,620	438	765
Tennessee	45,441	14,517	9,467	9,863	8,118	3,476
Texas	141,858	41,765	30,642	27,792	26,969	14,690
Utah	13,684	4,123	2,158	2,948	2,304	2,150
Vermont	4,633	1,417	847	1,423	541	405
Virginia	90,638	20,982	9,997	7,991	35,325	16,342
Washington	44,841	14,472	8,282	9,083	6,946	6,058
West Virginia	15,183	5,835	3,249	3,701	1,041	1,358
Wisconsin	31,554	12,065	7,469	7,484	2,641	1,895
Wyoming	4,393	1,192	641	1,636	403	521
Dist. of Columbia	37,630	1,882	2,670	4,205	13,347	15,526
American Samoa	262	44	14	178	17	9
Fed. States of Micronesia...	103	0		94	0	0
Guam	1,249	221	85	269	355	320
Marshall Islands	218	1		56	158	0
No. Mariana Islands	213	24	18	156	9	6
Palau	51	0		47		
Puerto Rico	15,479	5,668	2,999	5,324	462	1,026
Virgin Islands	592	155	86	263	21	66
Undistributed	23,075	26	89	44	18,851	4,065

Source: U.S. Department of Commerce, Bureau of the Census, Consolidated Federal Funds Report for Fiscal Year 2004, February 2006.

Table 2.9
FEDERAL GOVERNMENT EXPENDITURE FOR DIRECT PAYMENTS FOR INDIVIDUALS FOR RETIREMENT AND DISABILITY, FOR SELECTED PROGRAMS, BY STATE AND OUTLYING AREA: FISCAL YEAR 2004
(In thousands of dollars)

State and outlying area	Total	Social Security payments				Federal retirement and disability benefits		Veteran benefits		Other
		Retirement insurance payments	Survivors insurance payments	Disability insurance payments	Supplemental security income payments	Civilian	Military	Payments for service connected disability	Other benefit payments	
United States	$666,969,380	$315,780,113	$96,551,586	$80,439,028	$33,823,741	$53,358,037	$42,631,303	$22,145,959	$7,166,216	$15,073,398
Alabama	12,930,486	4,907,020	1,884,243	1,976,531	778,276	1,305,791	1,109,275	476,503	236,615	256,233
Alaska	1,135,323	371,558	126,327	118,864	46,223	172,624	174,285	99,197	9,268	16,977
Arizona	12,942,252	6,182,428	1,594,599	1,466,767	493,611	1,072,136	1,205,482	544,342	136,818	246,069
Arkansas	7,403,543	3,094,491	1,059,431	1,181,955	392,616	506,490	491,730	360,830	125,966	190,032
California	64,077,698	30,532,510	8,658,313	7,224,992	5,136,309	4,795,751	4,346,859	1,851,000	567,207	964,757
Colorado	8,917,674	3,787,661	1,128,109	880,809	263,350	966,157	1,183,267	410,973	99,151	198,197
Connecticut	7,809,446	4,690,016	1,132,363	855,482	279,232	328,571	218,175	157,126	38,056	110,423
Delaware	2,085,478	1,041,648	284,017	255,372	65,259	166,800	153,239	57,846	15,631	45,666
Florida	48,049,721	23,987,479	5,996,244	4,760,411	2,137,388	3,646,090	4,510,956	1,623,275	519,494	868,384
Georgia	17,747,906	7,179,098	2,435,158	2,385,352	937,443	1,653,185	1,780,211	711,101	273,155	393,202
Hawaii	3,202,245	1,449,376	315,726	239,702	110,650	544,952	357,679	124,352	26,297	33,510
Idaho	3,052,909	1,427,554	414,504	340,844	101,666	272,335	239,682	134,890	31,458	89,977
Illinois	25,596,955	13,481,722	4,264,312	2,907,895	1,413,874	1,379,792	676,572	454,617	165,125	853,047
Indiana	14,018,979	7,385,676	2,326,265	1,755,426	490,581	735,566	404,468	336,900	97,724	486,372
Iowa	6,971,457	3,861,177	1,186,565	713,591	197,986	418,158	184,530	167,315	61,731	180,404
Kansas	6,411,819	3,180,694	961,944	639,288	188,612	501,725	426,287	193,574	64,749	254,944
Kentucky	10,578,704	4,084,327	1,660,539	1,932,208	885,312	686,837	474,420	376,826	136,684	341,551
Louisiana	9,980,931	3,854,113	1,978,726	1,500,633	836,365	560,852	540,510	357,950	173,321	178,460
Maine	3,586,700	1,574,198	463,211	518,995	149,026	302,599	228,866	230,614	49,333	69,857
Maryland	14,190,244	5,306,641	1,631,456	1,150,222	474,168	3,537,402	1,170,120	368,397	107,169	444,669
Massachusetts	14,186,357	7,377,584	1,981,480	1,920,008	772,958	942,166	374,757	467,299	120,742	229,364
Michigan	22,915,679	12,196,837	3,925,055	3,255,794	1,163,890	874,475	460,816	451,609	159,960	427,243
Minnesota	10,059,091	5,450,438	1,549,564	1,083,264	357,576	549,693	285,145	360,894	91,975	330,543
Mississippi	7,296,543	2,804,267	1,090,855	1,262,014	603,519	522,735	507,740	252,384	120,073	132,955
Missouri	14,070,928	6,691,848	2,125,701	1,914,778	565,702	1,103,398	677,635	424,964	160,446	406,455
Montana	2,393,731	1,071,128	337,076	251,115	66,828	253,356	153,211	118,220	27,743	115,055
Nebraska	4,069,531	1,985,447	604,240	380,293	105,570	267,411	285,366	197,684	47,951	195,569
Nevada	5,149,411	2,397,212	569,754	567,242	160,307	468,007	617,235	216,269	57,958	95,426
New Hampshire	3,028,197	1,533,382	375,578	391,619	66,244	258,645	214,637	122,304	27,609	38,180
New Jersey	18,921,947	10,912,560	2,808,427	2,125,772	705,759	1,191,842	397,358	388,986	104,797	286,445

See footnotes at end of table.

FEDERAL GOVERNMENT EXPENDITURE FOR DIRECT PAYMENTS FOR INDIVIDUALS FOR RETIREMENT AND DISABILITY, FOR SELECTED PROGRAMS, BY STATE AND OUTLYING AREA: FISCAL YEAR 2004—Continued

State and outlying area	Total	Social Security payments			Supplemental security income payments	Federal retirement and disability benefits		Veteran benefits		Other
		Retirement insurance payments	Survivors insurance payments	Disability insurance payments		Civilian	Military	Payments for service connected disability	Other benefit payments	
New Mexico	4,680,750	1,790,396	580,951	515,307	245,398	575,176	484,927	310,452	65,883	108,260
New York	41,208,620	22,244,011	5,972,769	5,468,953	3,134,286	1,975,525	601,432	861,924	284,043	665,677
North Carolina	20,131,135	9,272,528	2,560,015	2,912,682	883,267	1,386,083	1,653,853	894,187	261,156	307,364
North Dakota	1,477,265	711,742	270,404	126,459	34,619	128,063	72,838	58,513	15,551	59,076
Ohio	26,251,410	13,072,842	4,731,633	2,937,551	1,332,197	1,558,668	827,999	636,565	251,530	902,425
Oklahoma	9,169,062	3,867,107	1,328,223	1,045,423	369,545	1,013,483	651,659	555,331	188,692	149,600
Oregon	8,452,069	4,285,328	1,156,601	921,560	292,481	687,089	434,335	389,510	108,621	176,543
Pennsylvania	33,146,850	16,987,377	5,370,410	3,666,130	1,607,229	2,231,626	911,518	751,174	287,795	1,333,593
Rhode Island	2,626,776	1,349,405	319,132	349,867	141,063	195,183	130,119	92,047	25,286	24,673
South Carolina	10,811,549	4,610,852	1,390,682	1,586,743	500,727	860,169	1,125,110	413,915	162,702	160,649
South Dakota	1,841,507	880,626	284,534	166,167	57,083	194,295	118,705	86,192	27,893	26,011
Tennessee	14,516,572	6,386,553	2,147,977	2,127,485	761,512	1,134,150	943,490	508,599	201,896	304,910
Texas	41,765,195	17,762,105	6,579,080	4,406,413	2,144,843	3,349,982	4,112,807	1,966,471	629,341	814,152
Utah	4,123,174	1,823,687	526,288	348,003	108,771	761,802	281,202	120,694	28,197	124,529
Vermont	1,416,964	736,134	203,693	182,185	53,849	87,007	64,734	52,523	13,707	23,131
Virginia	20,981,969	7,129,006	2,199,270	2,024,524	638,025	3,606,460	4,017,480	702,375	209,723	455,105
Washington	14,472,271	6,530,227	1,769,411	1,484,232	597,477	1,383,192	1,540,105	734,179	155,324	278,124
West Virginia	5,835,136	2,230,831	997,428	1,058,846	388,693	348,090	177,842	241,728	82,321	309,357
Wisconsin	12,064,717	6,816,175	1,901,050	1,355,653	445,116	535,352	303,702	374,460	101,168	232,042
Wyoming	1,192,428	555,200	162,105	115,814	25,623	120,542	91,612	49,775	10,635	61,122
Dist. of Columbia	1,882,456	419,234	132,172	129,962	111,566	934,262	69,280	37,971	18,301	29,708
American Samoa	43,973	11,191	11,580	9,905	0	1,756	4,022	4,376	1,076	66
Fed. States of Micronesia...	475	136	52	22	0	170	0	89	5	0
Guam	221,055	69,584	29,500	15,796	0	56,249	35,393	11,384	2,195	954
Marshall Islands...	1,162	741	291	91	0	21	0	9	7	2
No. Mariana Islands...	24,090	5,750	4,558	1,310	4,073	5,812	1,890	606	82	8
Palau...	450	167	87	13	0	143	0	8	32	0
Puerto Rico...	5,667,797	2,341,320	1,028,104	1,506,016	0	223,124	110,554	250,964	178,185	29,530
U.S. Virgin Islands...	155,075	89,762	23,803	18,678	0	14,908	4,824	1,698	659	744
Undistributed...	25,546	0	0	0	0	112	9,358	0	0	16,076

Source: U.S. Department of Commerce, Bureau of the Census, Consolidated Federal Funds Report for Fiscal Year 2004, February 2006.

Table 2.10
FEDERAL GOVERNMENT EXPENDITURE FOR DIRECT PAYMENTS OTHER THAN FOR RETIREMENT AND DISABILITY, FOR SELECTED PROGRAMS, BY STATE AND OUTLYING AREA: FISCAL YEAR 2004
(In thousands of dollars)

State and outlying area	Total	Medicare benefits		Excess earned income tax credits	Unemployment compensation	Food stamp payments	Housing assistance	Agricultural assistance	Federal employees life and health insurance	Other
		Hospital insurance	Supplementary medical insurance							
United States	$469,544,433	$165,968,515	$134,120,136	$34,454,758	$38,214,521	$24,696,715	$4,472,029	$16,795,129	$19,149,309	$31,673,319
Alabama	8,016,960	3,108,922	2,181,182	891,981	267,296	512,604	118,739	175,541	327,866	432,829
Alaska	665,018	138,700	93,482	50,657	142,317	64,405	9,093	11,221	1,629	153,514
Arizona	7,268,771	2,395,722	2,180,176	637,207	301,514	577,868	28,051	108,719	213,980	825,534
Arkansas	5,045,499	1,658,308	1,228,044	474,388	273,045	346,881	33,372	636,001	111,628	283,833
California	51,492,139	18,165,171	16,548,507	3,739,113	5,545,644	1,989,214	229,569	664,910	1,482,647	3,127,364
Colorado	5,294,717	1,657,279	1,373,591	368,132	481,549	252,942	28,658	370,211	291,257	471,098
Connecticut	5,827,902	2,407,108	1,913,774	231,332	649,150	197,530	70,682	17,639	122,116	218,572
Delaware	1,167,621	422,307	342,301	88,207	111,564	56,542	13,042	19,542	40,111	74,005
Florida	32,432,424	12,536,415	12,413,462	2,434,876	1,113,007	1,268,549	128,092	179,589	827,046	1,531,387
Georgia	11,509,304	3,867,564	2,937,164	1,475,470	671,573	923,815	122,479	357,212	446,003	708,023
Hawaii	1,606,602	491,416	466,121	118,148	122,952	151,809	14,356	5,893	157,232	78,675
Idaho	1,649,444	478,188	385,797	149,369	154,603	90,972	1,622	186,190	61,578	141,124
Illinois	21,110,712	7,546,821	5,581,114	1,323,323	2,306,458	1,211,362	318,858	1,302,001	483,877	1,036,898
Indiana	10,003,603	3,386,007	2,497,223	646,620	581,386	549,501	49,559	532,489	205,157	1,555,661
Iowa	5,359,100	1,458,764	1,344,514	236,538	340,512	176,334	7,702	1,311,256	144,884	338,597
Kansas	4,800,691	1,455,262	1,256,451	262,871	305,206	158,017	18,869	1,033,016	92,383	218,617
Kentucky	6,523,441	2,403,473	1,743,294	522,773	450,755	542,744	56,002	162,247	166,285	475,869
Louisiana	8,949,939	3,526,466	2,222,089	1,021,656	296,173	753,905	102,121	360,416	195,250	471,863
Maine	1,851,541	691,840	528,138	113,635	122,736	139,619	9,989	34,947	77,463	133,174
Maryland	10,371,837	3,003,914	2,533,503	517,671	469,056	286,695	105,776	65,622	2,886,285	503,315
Massachusetts	12,373,615	5,383,438	3,526,783	403,016	1,640,955	304,436	140,342	14,780	329,439	630,426
Michigan	16,616,037	5,939,648	5,223,537	974,216	2,182,233	896,140	71,683	267,153	256,856	804,571
Minnesota	6,890,961	2,175,764	1,697,492	341,316	755,206	256,580	57,368	878,567	231,100	497,569
Mississippi	5,196,060	1,834,931	1,232,403	715,183	166,546	360,952	31,991	373,315	139,451	341,287
Missouri	10,892,183	3,625,433	2,782,389	670,007	551,712	663,426	63,703	594,931	1,385,515	555,067
Montana	1,629,390	418,672	345,493	104,105	73,222	79,197	4,346	394,142	62,967	147,245
Nebraska	3,198,934	761,281	658,999	159,359	127,677	108,691	12,971	863,665	91,805	414,485
Nevada	2,351,616	781,645	699,544	239,156	280,135	119,520	15,659	18,294	76,413	121,250
New Hampshire	1,411,826	569,322	414,069	77,498	88,935	43,549	9,869	8,576	93,986	106,024
New Jersey	14,549,149	5,519,432	4,706,812	729,942	2,130,180	377,526	211,409	14,320	294,718	564,810
New Mexico	2,475,868	690,711	613,224	322,464	130,158	217,424	15,016	91,637	144,285	250,949
New York	34,726,294	13,235,956	10,819,230	2,181,059	2,778,505	1,876,078	1,040,005	101,337	615,452	2,078,672
North Carolina	11,397,621	3,914,633	2,906,209	1,241,212	1,011,574	753,200	110,269	369,870	297,482	793,173
North Dakota	1,752,999	332,999	279,184	54,951	37,398	40,286	2,675	820,407	37,499	147,599
Ohio	17,918,392	6,947,442	5,516,066	1,202,261	1,345,432	1,027,772	206,583	389,779	416,055	867,001

See footnotes at end of table.

FEDERAL GOVERNMENT EXPENDITURE FOR DIRECT PAYMENTS OTHER THAN FOR RETIREMENT AND DISABILITY, FOR SELECTED PROGRAMS, BY STATE AND OUTLYING AREA: FISCAL YEAR 2004 — Continued

State and outlying area	Total	Medicare benefits		Excess earned income tax credits	Unemployment compensation	Food stamp payments	Housing assistance	Agricultural assistance	Federal employees life and health insurance	Other
		Hospital insurance	Supplementary medical insurance							
Oklahoma	5,937,521	2,220,011	1,463,827	502,502	252,261	397,777	31,708	290,528	314,314	464,594
Oregon	5,048,156	1,513,218	1,338,760	315,176	784,582	430,542	19,157	131,498	200,244	314,979
Pennsylvania	25,917,388	10,401,546	7,994,982	1,118,578	2,557,152	933,274	288,690	143,691	1,170,610	1,308,866
Rhode Island	1,902,279	753,597	541,617	95,194	217,824	73,551	27,892	2,426	51,428	138,751
South Carolina	5,745,733	1,913,302	1,507,913	721,707	388,550	501,205	35,385	123,089	173,414	381,169
South Dakota	1,937,022	365,894	295,869	79,325	27,373	53,934	4,523	665,703	25,030	419,371
Tennessee	9,466,686	3,832,811	2,358,556	874,363	512,412	811,798	101,908	171,866	222,590	580,382
Texas	30,641,945	10,443,038	7,380,376	3,737,302	1,944,886	2,306,786	145,003	1,476,293	937,093	2,271,168
Utah	2,158,494	652,970	486,051	210,383	172,548	126,127	10,813	38,647	174,138	286,816
Vermont	846,747	296,254	207,162	46,362	82,274	47,076	3,160	16,927	23,608	123,923
Virginia	9,997,316	3,051,746	2,497,089	768,859	435,282	476,166	71,615	134,382	1,258,588	1,303,588
Washington	8,282,098	2,441,629	2,128,500	504,671	1,412,926	455,273	46,286	268,177	419,103	605,533
West Virginia	3,248,965	1,295,949	977,575	220,036	156,545	231,721	18,469	17,213	109,742	221,716
Wisconsin	7,469,165	2,544,911	2,097,250	408,958	894,421	269,439	28,233	393,016	192,614	640,323
Wyoming	641,467	216,041	161,534	48,410	40,803	24,381	1,023	47,756	35,083	65,835
Dist. of Columbia	2,669,812	461,260	382,698	79,580	93,126	97,508	49,459	86,467	942,721	476,993
American Samoa	14,073	0	0	0	0	5,500	0	24	0	8,449
Fed. States of Micronesia...	8,680	0	0	0	0	0	0	0	0	8,680
Guam	85,079	880	671	0	0	48,115	3,424	19	17,917	14,054
Marshall Islands	2,249	0	0	0	0	0	0	0	0	2,249
No. Mariana Islands	18,147	0	0	0	0	10,538	0	21	0	7,588
Palau	2,758	0	0	0	0	0	0	0	0	2,758
Puerto Rico	2,999,415	617,038	1,096,298	3,640	228,245	19,215	105,974	49,564	73,372	825,284
U.S. Virgin Islands	85,971	15,468	12,044	0	6,945	0	18,789	2,388	0	11,122
Undistributed	89,049	0	0	0	0	0	0	0	0	89,049

Source: U.S. Department of Commerce, Bureau of the Census, Consolidated Federal Funds Report for Fiscal Year 2004, February 2006.

Table 2.11
FEDERAL GOVERNMENT EXPENDITURE FOR GRANTS, BY AGENCY, BY STATE, AND OUTLYING AREA: FISCAL YEAR 2004
(In thousands of dollars)

State and outlying area	Total	Department of Agriculture	Appalachian Regional Commission	Department of Commerce	Corporation for National and Community Service	Corporation for Public Broadcasting	Department of Defense	Department of Education
United States	$460,152,282	$24,921,811	$65,702	$1,574,605	$707,511	$411,970	$4,537,556	$38,757,134
Alabama	7,007,819	396,308	6,257	15,290	5,192	2,582	69,772	618,145
Alaska	3,216,865	135,264	0	118,446	6,227	8,898	70,716	336,167
Arizona	8,363,600	443,707	0	6,599	9,633	4,118	136,443	842,604
Arkansas	4,682,798	287,349	0	5,585	7,079	1,722	37,948	391,889
California	54,534,048	3,016,896	0	119,325	115,478	41,919	565,788	4,723,920
Colorado	5,643,498	318,235	0	64,831	6,314	4,724	80,854	478,121
Connecticut	5,555,683	169,217	0	19,817	4,852	2,459	77,737	373,606
Delaware	1,241,092	67,357	0	10,805	2,050	1	24,137	115,962
Florida	19,609,519	1,082,251	0	66,117	31,917	13,314	133,382	1,843,862
Georgia	11,758,731	791,014	4,821	16,329	15,351	5,342	51,984	1,059,737
Hawaii	2,158,313	124,896	0	40,919	3,106	2,177	57,236	249,624
Idaho	1,994,706	140,582	0	11,115	5,352	2,281	33,730	179,965
Illinois	16,531,175	824,666	0	24,553	17,133	12,481	106,418	1,524,116
Indiana	7,436,310	393,574	0	3,642	8,218	6,626	92,038	642,599
Iowa	4,038,677	229,681	0	4,969	6,477	3,922	64,620	328,767
Kansas	3,468,608	294,720	0	3,596	6,371	2,867	91,360	380,600
Kentucky	6,743,285	362,886	6,740	17,334	7,524	4,664	18,199	574,246
Louisiana	7,786,693	492,383	0	50,204	8,356	3,483	111,676	711,018
Maine	2,757,942	90,887	0	19,145	4,719	1,652	46,174	174,385
Maryland	8,836,910	303,989	2,401	44,365	20,521	5,074	168,512	586,581
Massachusetts	13,876,126	348,936	30	60,752	19,906	14,133	251,119	805,137
Michigan	13,227,411	690,364	17	35,366	11,962	8,652	81,021	1,187,632
Minnesota	7,208,781	397,391	0	9,986	10,472	13,700	91,873	538,856
Mississippi	5,378,932	369,931	3,928	26,312	5,486	2,101	44,898	474,736
Missouri	8,734,296	447,244	0	11,011	10,793	4,988	84,996	655,606
Montana	1,997,362	139,441	0	3,811	9,360	1,113	58,647	215,546
Nebraska	2,530,936	225,610	0	4,776	4,592	4,065	35,510	242,153
Nevada	2,321,630	124,513	0	3,814	4,248	2,357	22,297	221,173
New Hampshire	1,878,737	65,068	0	64,002	4,219	1,954	38,136	142,390
New Jersey	11,333,180	441,016	0	37,120	12,251	3,567	98,928	927,276
New Mexico	4,662,536	258,942	0	11,758	4,737	3,498	48,135	532,553
New York	50,008,574	1,467,457	3,537	69,040	72,381	37,777	210,427	2,754,077
North Carolina	12,574,492	694,641	4,188	31,594	8,627	82,720	116,236	975,830
North Dakota	1,515,253	208,635	0	4,187	2,117	1,211	38,007	155,718
Ohio	16,513,740	695,346	5,655	33,323	15,071	11,168	114,915	1,267,074
Oklahoma	5,270,581	389,263	0	14,018	9,337	2,634	19,271	556,138
Oregon	5,184,929	266,644	0	62,179	11,425	4,810	38,120	456,573
Pennsylvania	19,915,826	711,687	8,800	27,375	19,440	11,741	232,139	1,349,422
Rhode Island	2,329,088	65,849	0	10,119	4,554	710	25,310	157,668
South Carolina	6,145,106	343,856	2,504	84,882	5,897	3,311	76,770	548,713
South Dakota	1,620,407	162,994	0	1,683	2,496	1,426	34,508	182,710
Tennessee	9,863,362	445,153	6,206	11,114	8,622	5,062	54,845	712,885
Texas	27,792,386	2,313,836	0	47,561	25,430	13,115	192,055	3,177,815
Utah	2,947,857	194,704	0	3,164	5,780	5,556	45,656	296,455
Vermont	1,423,455	71,054	0	2,646	2,259	1,714	36,319	109,905
Virginia	7,991,079	436,014	4,342	46,576	22,517	8,650	105,144	821,824
Washington	9,082,685	428,573	106	86,840	23,839	6,621	90,720	713,947
West Virginia	3,700,592	167,967	5,376	13,227	7,709	1,347	70,638	274,228
Wisconsin	7,483,990	367,835	0	27,943	11,038	6,900	55,860	619,511
Wyoming	1,635,620	53,454	0	2,441	1,675	836	1,985	118,905
Dist. of Columbia	4,204,862	70,002	793	42,367	50,469	6,351	43,193	348,230
American Samoa	178,059	7,823	0	1,806	492	427	0	39,976
Fed. States of Micronesia	93,914	2,670	0	0	0	0	0	10,411
Guam	268,701	21,698	0	1,726	495	665	0	50,101
Marshall Islands	56,384	1,112	0	0	0	0	0	4,492
No. Mariana Islands	156,107	12,211	0	1,632	0	0	0	29,402
Palau	47,403	149	0	0	0	0	0	3,055
Puerto Rico	5,323,856	1,820,770	0	13,431	5,280	3,647	37,190	903,225
Virgin Islands	263,364	20,051	0	2,037	661	609	3,964	39,871
Undistributed	44,412	6,046	0	0	0	2,528	0	0

Source: U.S. Department of Commerce, Bureau of the Census, February 2006.

FEDERAL GOVERNMENT EXPENDITURE FOR GRANTS, BY AGENCY, BY STATE, AND OUTLYING AREA: FISCAL YEAR 2004 — Continued

State and outlying area	Election Assistance Commission	Department of Energy	Environmental Protection Agency	Equal Employment Opportunity Commission	Department of Health and Human Services	Department of Homeland Security	Department of Housing and Urban Development	Institute of Museum and Library Services
United States	$1,333,855	$1,847,718	$4,116,198	$30,959	$267,189,711	$3,644,351	$33,848,541	$238,922
Alabama	35,867	34,795	52,581	0	3,842,686	196,475	391,143	3,495
Alaska	0	6,214	85,441	156	1,268,933	13,536	147,376	1,372
Arizona	0	15,219	53,534	477	4,974,829	16,202	447,625	3,021
Arkansas	21,599	3,366	42,043	0	2,705,421	51,594	251,547	1,711
California	94,559	229,234	329,222	2,984	33,194,283	110,664	4,378,192	21,709
Colorado	34,545	59,023	67,278	329	2,667,061	17,478	398,556	3,336
Connecticut	27,720	45,230	65,752	796	3,346,103	21,105	580,480	3,480
Delaware	4,150	9,008	29,684	327	626,906	9,048	92,862	861
Florida	47,417	25,558	133,905	1,598	11,278,983	850,333	1,246,989	11,806
Georgia	64,748	43,440	80,824	184	6,962,809	20,550	759,810	5,447
Hawaii	0	4,320	29,475	144	1,006,912	3,816	141,756	2,186
Idaho	11,597	14,145	49,525	303	994,872	7,910	82,193	1,626
Illinois	0	61,430	157,069	1,491	9,318,522	37,803	1,778,448	11,634
Indiana	48,545	37,327	71,274	546	4,321,705	45,671	527,817	6,181
Iowa	23,739	65,889	75,358	809	2,275,823	42,380	230,746	4,497
Kansas	7,662	11,537	42,449	327	1,770,890	20,711	199,849	2,025
Kentucky	32,899	13,834	59,971	202	4,053,926	68,730	450,887	3,370
Louisiana	35,068	9,852	58,652	38	4,790,508	38,236	486,638	3,230
Maine	4,150	5,793	37,581	225	1,806,184	14,378	187,212	1,799
Maryland	42,478	32,569	99,337	648	5,504,259	73,084	706,744	3,161
Massachusetts	52,222	141,440	128,340	1,674	8,582,655	35,191	1,685,156	8,100
Michigan	28,257	64,029	158,510	724	8,040,554	129,668	875,663	6,765
Minnesota	39,179	31,527	77,106	554	4,324,656	26,894	558,686	3,728
Mississippi	22,418	10,535	44,523	0	3,382,313	37,032	271,308	2,151
Missouri	44,915	13,114	88,676	766	5,481,317	27,759	542,818	4,261
Montana	4,150	6,632	36,197	267	831,614	8,108	108,635	1,468
Nebraska	4,920	5,738	31,482	567	1,355,822	22,172	143,383	1,623
Nevada	5,785	48,151	27,720	1,078	976,594	8,094	157,350	1,523
New Hampshire	11,597	6,390	28,113	110	983,258	7,615	145,953	1,230
New Jersey	24,358	38,732	82,368	531	6,381,963	71,943	1,292,431	6,222
New Mexico	14,280	62,227	47,761	287	2,540,713	19,981	167,670	2,118
New York	0	164,847	134,919	2,160	31,516,934	155,616	3,832,412	18,783
North Carolina	65,478	25,739	83,557	82	8,022,570	114,607	680,069	5,813
North Dakota	4,150	15,731	28,740	165	555,679	17,121	104,802	704
Ohio	90,993	40,443	157,598	1,923	10,696,462	87,879	1,348,263	9,250
Oklahoma	0	9,681	65,391	362	2,906,542	35,493	429,291	3,682
Oregon	9,962	16,176	75,372	519	2,808,885	44,178	349,489	2,221
Pennsylvania	100,579	98,062	164,126	2,014	12,493,067	114,766	1,543,558	12,165
Rhode Island	4,150	4,590	36,894	226	1,448,237	3,118	228,872	1,207
South Carolina	32,421	22,495	34,888	661	3,740,808	24,887	329,424	2,314
South Dakota	0	4,863	34,155	181	633,066	5,615	117,246	890
Tennessee	16,546	22,505	49,110	304	6,618,062	70,561	493,475	5,987
Texas	57,505	64,259	258,167	957	15,294,303	239,967	1,726,627	15,128
Utah	0	17,257	33,761	359	1,539,310	12,436	148,048	1,792
Vermont	11,597	5,645	30,340	60	799,357	7,509	79,660	775
Virginia	20,573	39,084	109,857	246	3,708,084	234,418	652,819	5,348
Washington	47,196	54,351	106,550	700	5,151,472	65,477	635,980	4,597
West Virginia	15,304	14,033	68,857	240	2,117,589	97,577	175,777	1,223
Wisconsin	43,064	39,250	119,357	1,099	4,379,926	39,835	482,733	3,867
Wyoming	11,597	6,540	22,005	92	386,998	5,059	36,589	865
Dist. of Columbia	11,597	23,792	82,334	100	1,624,807	16,208	321,134	4,499
American Samoa	2,319	460	3,279	0	20,226	36,564	1,241	147
Fed. States of Micronesia	0	0	0	0	10,120	16,650	0	0
Guam	0	400	4,874	0	41,944	13,905	38,173	114
Marshall Islands	0	0	0	0	5,597	100	0	56
No. Mariana Islands	0	230	5,693	0	14,580	29,598	3,525	151
Palau	0	0	0	0	5,319	0	0	0
Puerto Rico	0	745	28,728	367	1,006,031	99,201	624,581	2,102
Virgin Islands	0	248	5,896	8	50,660	2,117	27,604	104
Undistributed	0	0	0	0	0	0	1,226	0

See footnotes at end of table.

FEDERAL GOVERNMENT EXPENDITURE FOR GRANTS, BY AGENCY, BY STATE, AND OUTLYING AREA: FISCAL YEAR 2004 — Continued

State and outlying area	Department of the Interior	Department of Justice	Department of Labor	National Aeronautics and Space Administration	National Archives and Records Administration	National Endowment for the Arts	National Endowment for the Humanities	National Science Foundation
United States	$4,021,625	$7,155,656	$8,561,568	$1,084,871	$9,704	$96,057	$121,739	$5,232,033
Alabama	38,744	97,762	122,708	41,048	0	861	1,087	49,985
Alaska	99,445	73,382	54,312	5,569	78	742	854	35,380
Arizona	99,829	139,047	156,348	17,667	53	1,154	977	107,783
Arkansas	13,357	62,476	71,760	1,911	0	630	578	12,786
California	262,112	912,192	670,354	193,641	829	8,517	7,208	798,740
Colorado	149,231	127,252	113,475	48,493	0	2,421	1,467	274,527
Connecticut	8,407	80,040	107,155	9,117	203	1,521	3,477	45,574
Delaware	7,283	35,937	27,633	2,271	361	637	853	18,432
Florida	39,462	345,577	390,984	28,744	10	1,546	2,310	147,153
Georgia	21,960	222,873	172,887	21,857	82	2,523	3,269	110,184
Hawaii...............................	39,522	46,889	47,160	22,079	0	1,130	948	35,503
Idaho................................	57,687	48,470	55,188	3,515	10	809	628	10,684
Illinois..............................	21,220	219,871	420,744	16,821	387	3,303	6,617	244,015
Indiana..............................	14,782	100,256	139,572	6,885	22	941	1,670	90,939
Iowa	17,268	72,934	73,274	9,807	0	728	1,137	41,504
Kansas	15,765	63,827	61,055	6,281	20	981	677	29,775
Kentucky	46,420	107,194	125,919	2,783	99	994	811	32,130
Louisiana	60,400	117,022	105,195	6,215	0	1,264	769	39,932
Maine	19,313	49,389	54,097	5,160	199	1,040	1,492	19,002
Maryland...........................	17,874	147,039	191,664	101,155	276	2,615	2,371	120,385
Massachusetts....................	23,110	167,504	205,894	54,180	719	4,192	9,591	393,836
Michigan	39,456	169,540	346,446	17,102	111	1,646	3,186	144,009
Minnesota	35,726	111,433	133,860	4,832	87	3,489	3,283	73,483
Mississippi	22,578	59,466	89,123	17,553	0	801	1,190	27,108
Missouri	24,122	123,103	150,157	9,438	163	2,457	2,709	46,694
Montana	107,611	44,713	40,201	7,517	9	875	811	23,485
Nebraska...........................	14,042	65,415	36,901	2,248	56	712	802	27,872
Nevada..............................	231,602	83,292	59,443	1,979	20	659	519	13,246
New Hampshire..................	14,716	69,358	31,113	12,631	0	800	757	16,683
New Jersey.........................	13,329	188,682	239,348	12,977	445	1,303	2,381	108,354
New Mexico	435,457	91,174	61,602	4,972	71	1,449	1,538	39,720
New York	39,594	509,419	474,770	41,296	1,376	15,422	14,254	416,812
North Carolina	25,701	153,191	315,411	12,785	457	1,549	2,368	121,577
North Dakota.....................	51,996	42,909	24,315	2,218	47	635	749	11,433
Ohio	32,934	199,047	315,626	42,593	0	1,661	3,468	90,292
Oklahoma	30,867	82,389	78,151	9,934	147	675	653	28,518
Oregon	176,013	81,110	165,473	6,284	0	1,098	1,125	60,983
Pennsylvania	25,623	225,797	430,203	20,509	296	3,359	7,406	239,945
Rhode Island	6,514	40,431	33,822	5,322	0	1,061	1,324	34,453
South Carolina	14,207	111,901	114,521	5,081	227	1,009	792	30,410
South Dakota	85,202	45,238	32,524	1,897	0	664	549	10,720
Tennessee	25,330	114,582	164,220	8,195	131	1,184	2,138	55,627
Texas	66,188	408,316	584,069	73,098	271	2,801	4,009	166,710
Utah	136,931	54,610	71,650	3,951	0	1,066	966	40,639
Vermont	10,409	40,844	22,719	1,233	0	862	799	8,214
Virginia..............................	43,727	217,658	267,791	70,528	767	1,188	5,052	121,250
Washington........................	120,567	157,451	259,522	9,647	76	2,041	2,423	121,418
West Virginia......................	64,125	64,525	58,461	36,070	0	651	551	9,969
Wisconsin..........................	27,709	113,030	191,643	11,301	316	1,006	1,788	136,483
Wyoming............................	668,915	29,339	21,255	1,637	20	606	516	10,170
Dist. of Columbia	26,416	123,272	211,972	20,130	1,262	3,116	3,049	320,656
American Samoa	34,925	7,760	644	0	0	247	305	0
Fed. States of Micronesia	52,358	0	1,705	0	0	0	0	0
Guam	62,884	9,548	2,056	0	0	240	296	0
Marshall Islands.................	44,192	0	836	0	0	0	0	0
No. Mariana Islands	15,232	7,288	1,540	0	0	241	289	0
Palau	38,609	0	269	0	0	0	0	0
Puerto Rico........................	7,394	63,036	153,376	4,563	0	654	608	15,366
Virgin Islands....................	69,452	9,857	7,451	150	0	281	296	1,483
Undistributed	5,783	0	0	0	0	0	0	0

See footnotes at end of table.

FEDERAL GOVERNMENT EXPENDITURE FOR GRANTS, BY AGENCY, BY STATE, AND OUTLYING AREA: FISCAL YEAR 2004 — Continued

State and outlying area	Small Business Admin.	Social Security Admin.	Department of State	State Justice Institute	Tennessee Valley Authority (a)	Department of Transportation	Department of the Treasury (b)	Department of Veterans Affairs	Other
United States	$45,678	$11,016	$205,631	$1,767	$337,269	$48,496,756	$800,141	$654,107	$90,120
Alabama	2,085	0	805	2	80,958	887,492	151	13,231	312
Alaska	70	0	243	37	0	747,326	50	0	633
Arizona	372	0	3,199	6	0	873,747	2,738	5,853	815
Arkansas..........................	38	0	803	0	0	706,796	80	2,381	349
California	1,162	0	26,080	39	0	4,638,913	2,900	48,519	18,666
Colorado	0	0	3,700	184	0	710,868	78	8,748	2,369
Connecticut	0	0	2,623	0	0	549,112	236	8,647	1,217
Delaware..........................	0	0	850	1	0	149,234	52	3,729	659
Florida	1,153	0	5,908	2	0	1,860,100	5,001	11,751	2,386
Georgia	0	0	4,399	21	5,430	1,297,302	343	11,639	1,572
Hawaii..............................	0	0	935	8	0	276,835	119	20,006	612
Idaho................................	117	0	575	47	0	270,150	72	10,966	593
Illinois.............................	3,771	4,729	9,501	9	0	1,674,450	2,925	25,100	1,950
Indiana.............................	1,220	0	2,801	6	0	863,239	452	6,600	1,161
Iowa.................................	495	0	2,966	5	0	446,741	90	13,681	369
Kansas	307	0	1,327	6	0	438,043	58	14,829	694
Kentucky	0	0	1,575	20	27,193	711,514	319	10,554	350
Louisiana	235	0	2,455	0	0	623,269	100	30,395	99
Maine...............................	1,531	0	562	0	0	203,945	85	7,618	226
Maryland..........................	570	0	5,236	67	0	647,236	598	4,298	1,803
Massachusetts..................	44	3,449	12,205	1	0	834,230	1,388	25,933	5,061
Michigan..........................	479	2,838	4,355	203	0	1,159,870	1,127	17,252	606
Minnesota	602	0	4,287	39	0	697,540	152	14,208	1,154
Mississippi	0	0	875	0	18,704	429,788	176	13,646	251
Missouri...........................	1,327	0	3,662	0	0	924,927	349	25,717	1,204
Montana	3,386	0	1,127	0	0	338,929	32	3,318	361
Nebraska..........................	300	0	1,999	0	0	285,606	374	11,889	307
Nevada.............................	275	0	563	76	0	319,682	100	5,241	235
New Hampshire................	0	0	795	6	0	225,632	81	4,943	1,185
New Jersey.......................	433	0	3,189	19	0	1,323,741	2,937	16,578	755
New Mexico	981	0	1,759	20	0	305,088	44	3,127	873
New York	3,271	0	24,009	107	0	7,987,502	10,767	21,785	7,827
North Carolina	1,481	0	5,306	0	1,638	1,014,418	1,019	4,238	1,604
North Dakota....................	180	0	764	0	0	241,130	29	1,695	188
Ohio	553	0	5,090	16	0	1,224,484	1,880	16,732	3,999
Oklahoma	1,210	0	1,686	0	0	567,799	150	26,379	921
Oregon	1,647	0	3,223	0	0	536,715	731	2,915	1,060
Pennsylvania	4,321	0	8,319	22	0	2,028,265	406	31,198	1,214
Rhode Island	0	0	1,179	19	0	207,327	150	5,174	806
South Carolina	2,353	0	1,902	2	0	600,894	1,366	6,611	0
South Dakota....................	300	0	347	7	0	258,000	49	2,867	213
Tennessee	1,104	0	1,777	287	203,346	742,258	239	21,005	1,503
Texas	1,189	0	8,847	1	0	3,002,069	10,761	33,133	4,468
Utah	75	0	1,256	4	0	328,782	47	3,246	355
Vermont	0	0	986	26	0	173,083	167	3,187	2,085
Virginia............................	2,182	0	4,045	259	0	1,017,710	649	20,100	2,678
Washington.......................	0	0	4,432	48	0	975,161	397	11,728	807
West Virginia....................	1,187	0	321	44	0	431,228	70	1,785	514
Wisconsin.........................	1,520	0	2,787	32	0	760,754	197	36,092	1,112
Wyoming...........................	28	0	253	0	0	252,575	43	1,159	64
Dist. of Columbia	1,825	0	17,635	69	0	417,963	408,133 (c)	1,417	2,071
American Samoa................	300	0	0	0	0	19,119	0	0	0
Fed. States of Micronesia	0	0	0	0	0	0	0	0	0
Guam	0	0	0	0	0	19,583	0	0	0
Marshall Islands................	0	0	0	0	0	0	0	0	0
No. Mariana Islands	0	0	0	0	0	34,496	0	0	0
Palau	0	0	0	0	0	0	0	0	0
Puerto Rico.......................	0	0	107	0	0	191,962	339,634	1,265	593
Virgin Islands....................	0	0	0	0	0	20,516	50	0	0
Undistributed	0	0	0	0	0	21,619	0	0	7,210

Source: U.S. Department of Commerce, Bureau of the Census, Consolidated Federal Funds Report for Fiscal Year 2004, February 2006.

(a) Payments in lieu of taxes have been categorized as "grants."

(b) Includes distributions to state and local governments of seized cash and other assets.

(c) Also includes Treasury payments to recipients that are separate from the government of the District of Columbia and Washington Metropolitan Transit Authority (WMATA).

Table 2.12
FEDERAL GOVERNMENT EXPENDITURE FOR PROCUREMENT CONTRACTS, BY AGENCY, BY STATE AND OUTLYING AREA: FISCAL YEAR 2004
(In thousands of dollars)

State and outlying area	Total	Department of Defense						Nondefense agencies		
		Total	Army	Navy	Air Force	Army Corps of Engineers	Other defense	Total	Department of Agriculture	Department of Commerce
United States	$339,680,775	$211,538,185	$59,332,624	$59,586,122	$54,073,312	$3,304,576	$35,241,550	$128,142,590	$4,211,683	$1,678,062
Alabama	7,599,862	5,849,415	2,309,326	290,641	414,440	83,252	2,751,756	1,750,447	33,890	1,163
Alaska	1,699,744	1,262,270	659,026	52,142	355,224	46,938	148,941	437,474	44,841	42,809
Arizona	9,796,779	8,429,925	3,005,352	2,190,709	1,088,495	28,416	2,116,953	1,366,855	54,063	4,519
Arkansas...................	847,534	493,707	170,149	35,516	154,465	63,190	70,387	353,826	22,367	131
California	40,253,979	27,882,008	4,197,185	6,845,622	12,346,119	168,630	4,324,452	12,371,971	412,731	40,814
Colorado	5,747,033	3,151,275	622,817	143,424	1,919,786	26,066	439,182	2,595,759	113,034	38,542
Connecticut	9,508,964	8,958,624	1,673,515	5,068,128	1,926,510	5,756	284,715	550,340	8,576	3,409
Delaware	265,275	194,245	108,825	5,131	62,525	8,084	9,679	71,030	3,629	1,123
Florida	11,447,152	8,385,036	2,196,022	2,195,055	2,941,483	273,162	779,315	3,062,116	60,172	30,903
Georgia	5,812,510	3,905,793	1,413,601	388,941	1,750,770	103,051	249,430	1,906,717	47,980	12,703
Hawaii.......................	2,066,038	1,713,256	521,089	584,529	223,409	7,978	376,250	352,783	22,649	11,499
Idaho.........................	1,373,203	186,973	101,953	9,917	52,725	7,884	14,495	1,186,230	69,241	841
Illinois......................	6,582,810	3,007,055	1,014,867	492,774	743,968	170,374	585,072	3,575,755	164,636	8,957
Indiana......................	4,002,129	3,172,722	1,772,598	535,314	207,080	35,630	622,100	829,407	24,399	4,169
Iowa	1,599,246	733,831	224,471	145,644	268,350	19,324	76,043	865,414	141,030	773
Kansas	2,241,633	1,411,996	532,875	26,856	744,804	19,294	88,168	829,637	114,255	2,210
Kentucky	4,636,868	2,890,584	665,024	214,841	119,479	105,997	1,785,244	1,746,284	27,878	556
Louisiana	3,418,393	2,543,966	476,013	1,295,327	42,820	244,456	485,350	874,427	86,640	15,459
Maine	1,711,354	1,555,527	173,553	1,319,121	12,189	7,799	42,865	155,827	5,848	2,680
Maryland	20,803,835	9,214,124	3,038,038	946,829	981,848	42,463	2,074,945	11,589,711	74,745	376,806
Massachusetts............	9,127,096	6,962,816	2,121,918	2,041,062	2,184,608	63,873	551,355	2,164,279	7,747	56,754
Michigan	4,119,315	2,611,013	1,863,717	139,946	175,159	35,215	396,976	1,508,302	55,904	1,761
Minnesota	2,329,461	1,337,805	465,718	514,206	135,222	34,518	188,140	991,656	298,651	23,755
Mississippi	2,372,436	1,866,646	390,157	1,013,813	244,960	126,000	91,716	505,790	21,444	26,848
Missouri....................	7,991,155	6,502,161	894,516	3,467,324	1,689,706	144,781	305,835	1,488,993	221,955	6,130
Montana	587,088	206,883	86,540	2,285	78,900	15,891	23,268	380,205	39,698	402
Nebraska...................	697,175	401,287	93,321	5,719	261,505	24,364	16,378	295,888	54,016	3,206
Nevada......................	1,599,503	439,066	157,656	86,356	146,950	20,324	27,780	1,160,437	10,174	4,950
New Hampshire.........	985,478	715,932	290,102	161,972	205,226	3,797	54,834	269,546	1,341	5,899
New Jersey................	6,132,289	4,196,890	1,472,425	1,594,947	299,101	208,613	621,805	1,935,399	45,590	8,161
New Mexico	5,972,835	1,070,390	478,057	37,714	424,382	40,578	89,659	4,902,445	17,345	919
New York	8,888,842	5,058,181	1,043,886	2,646,254	709,308	89,561	569,172	3,830,661	39,380	10,943
North Carolina	3,933,055	2,212,804	824,092	717,759	255,071	54,704	361,178	1,720,251	51,971	32,940
North Dakota............	502,631	309,468	76,913	4,395	153,547	37,548	37,065	193,163	29,607	274
Ohio	6,935,685	4,636,529	1,551,633	327,210	1,657,398	61,451	1,038,838	2,299,156	77,350	2,515
Oklahoma	2,803,948	1,525,421	452,962	123,024	678,279	30,581	240,575	1,278,526	30,644	2,940
Oregon	1,282,768	529,634	282,292	103,529	19,801	80,029	43,983	753,135	176,852	9,216
Pennsylvania	9,311,177	6,202,651	3,072,896	1,425,830	542,202	66,197	1,095,526	3,108,526	50,702	86,217
Rhode Island	558,527	417,901	27,058	345,626	3,942	25,912	15,363	140,626		13,042
South Carolina	4,192,800	1,598,448	491,040	585,211	205,733	48,053	268,412	2,594,351	13,502	25,377
South Dakota............	437,779	236,224	60,967	28,090	40,684	7,112	99,371	201,555	26,599	319
Tennessee	8,118,171	2,117,272	436,565	84,682	1,238,147	63,131	294,747	6,000,900	78,056	447
Texas	26,968,708	21,050,237	4,874,679	5,611,111	8,152,438	172,556	2,239,453	5,918,472	208,450	22,506
Utah	2,303,926	1,877,903	348,335	126,337	1,306,938	6,716	89,577	426,023	50,353	1,505
Vermont	540,709	452,362	308,659	36,097	11,675	11,511	84,420	88,347	2,893	656
Virginia.....................	35,325,140	23,391,866	6,182,314	8,312,522	2,839,706	72,040	5,985,284	11,933,274	65,906	366,802
Washington...............	6,945,805	3,324,631	532,916	853,479	1,174,905	100,775	662,555	3,621,174	120,040	42,483
West Virginia............	1,040,791	279,595	51,905	45,511	30,782	89,162	62,236	761,196	19,524	844
Wisconsin..................	2,640,909	1,745,656	797,682	537,813	87,644	12,874	309,643	895,252	136,726	4,525
Wyoming...................	402,579	115,111	11,145	494	50,240	409	52,822	287,468	8,911	329
Dist. of Columbia	13,346,641	3,516,694	1,071,272	1,748,672	171,702	44,541	480,506	9,829,947	216,609	162,765
American Samoa.......	16,603	2,084	565	1,435	84	0	0	14,519	12,516	186
Fed. States of Micronesia	90	0	0	0	0	0	0	0	0	0
Guam	354,599	343,065	2,187	193,882	132,125	0	14,870	11,535	34	228
Marshall Islands........	158,014	158,014	158,014	0	0	0	0	0	0	0
No. Mariana Islands...	8,599	3,270	900	2,330	0	0	40	5,330	0	0
Palau	0	0	0	0	0	0	0	0	0	0
Puerto Rico...............	461,613	285,001	65,000	44,591	394	39,898	135,120	176,612	6,394	608
Virgin Islands	21,227	4,663	450	86	0	4,119	8	16,564	1,600	66
Undistributed (a)........	18,851,268	8,890,279	3,415,873	1,698,345	2,408,360	0	1,367,701	9,960,989	480,595	151,482

Source: U.S. Department of Commerce, Bureau of the Census, February 2006.

FEDERAL GOVERNMENT EXPENDITURE FOR PROCUREMENT CONTRACTS, BY AGENCY, BY STATE AND OUTLYING AREA: FISCAL YEAR 2004 — Continued

State and outlying area	Department of Education	Department of Energy	Environmental Protection Agency	General Services Administration	Department of Health and Human Services	Department of Homeland Security	Department of Housing and Urban Development	Department of the Interior	Department of Justice	Department of Labor
					Nondefense agencies—continued					
United States	$1,528,756	$22,160,730	$1,000,582	$13,718,993	$7,679,801	$6,074,213	$1,060,807	$4,825,789	$4,417,977	$1,616,315
Alabama	26	1,907	1,759	258,893	101,604	29,228	3,256	26,482	49,607	18,460
Alaska	0	1,281	0	48,798	34,610	33,647	0	91,499	6,653	3,448
Arizona	6,300	58,804	751	132,602	69,168	106,051	12,629	209,777	218,862	34,090
Arkansas...................	0	641	70	74,098	46,855	647	379	9,863	19,508	5,766
California	81,187	2,372,323	43,025	826,906	372,400	482,296	36,578	386,070	360,924	83,072
Colorado	4,492	999,845	29,971	269,886	33,689	18,306	83,572	228,973	31,986	10,230
Connecticut	78,065	4,137	1,526	27,719	10,852	26,778	2,548	5,501	36,989	10,437
Delaware...................	2	0	2,461	8,930	1,755	709	77	969	2,877	902
Florida	23	32,572	12,062	510,079	19,624	237,284	45,212	66,092	108,347	70,403
Georgia	55,326	14,153	35,833	420,030	363,953	154,208	75,726	31,225	34,171	50,272
Hawaii......................	4,237	37	0	92,121	6,402	52,112	31,569	25,138	4,003	10,547
Idaho........................	159	852,999	183	19,795	2,786	7,963	532	43,421	4,809	673
Illinois......................	28,348	921,760	32,425	183,918	95,260	10,196	34,796	32,979	54,580	19,544
Indiana.....................	0	2,490	490	57,894	40,113	14,534	942	14,583	22,871	19,232
Iowa	87,681	34,611	0	40,765	160,519	10,387	899	3,587	6,114	26,563
Kansas	945	328	9,789	57,401	5,754	23,064	215	7,934	7,303	7,351
Kentucky	0	36,713	3,647	116,095	8,531	8,034	133	21,370	22,908	41,040
Louisiana	0	119,051	230	148,810	13,050	50,992	223	31,982	26,056	16,687
Maine.......................	157	106	800	15,218	12,939	8,134	83	10,073	2,280	8,923
Maryland	572,584	258,139	82,873	1,028,718	3,168,554	455,485	92,622	263,054	255,867	129,854
Massachusetts...........	9,600	9,905	96,771	255,129	211,559	51,690	4,386	53,745	25,810	34,088
Michigan	117	492	32,496	527,197	71,399	17,376	689	27,343	24,012	24,999
Minnesota	675	2,462	5,557	69,847	81,241	4,806	142	14,617	26,504	13,154
Mississippi................	0	292	657	64,529	6,123	1,285	398	11,557	10,312	23,335
Missouri....................	876	482,104	23,192	187,676	26,619	5,209	286	22,467	22,305	29,163
Montana	316	18,285	367	23,928	126,247	1,518	97	42,507	7,397	7,158
Nebraska...................	1,042	779	0	66,431	17,018	189	0	5,984	4,566	455
Nevada	0	886,314	4,183	27,581	5,990	1,615	77	56,335	3,748	3,376
New Hampshire..........	8,811	193	9,249	78,933	1,979	1,310	16,159	2,480	9,970	0
New Jersey................	26,394	97,119	57,169	299,770	64,042	102,793	1,114	53,497	68,990	17,669
New Mexico	1	4,362,582	1,393	36,820	55,785	16,996	367	137,326	10,795	20,607
New York	32,567	752,043	22,410	367,414	117,066	44,771	86,427	41,919	118,311	51,426
North Carolina	28,362	127,211	61,766	146,182	303,853	59,178	9,341	19,265	65,252	13,741
North Dakota.............	0	8,083	582	30,756	8,064	160	3,043	11,481	27,500	10,931
Ohio	4,939	666,789	100,702	307,330	111,227	42,737	-993	34,365	20,907	39,239
Oklahoma	2,082	12,955	7,342	573,460	51,801	3,122	41,986	56,267	43,364	44,371
Oregon	7,743	3,537	3,687	133,746	11,610	11,615	50	83,610	10,644	19,215
Pennsylvania	17,894	541,497	34,724	269,894	99,071	22,666	21,078	101,504	101,533	65,166
Rhode Island	5,271	1,200	6,453	19,326	5,701	2,222	245	4,916	2,208	4,812
South Carolina	314	1,627,730	273	63,824	54,858	26,639	224	5,757	39,218	12,728
South Dakota.............	0	3,758	0	10,513	22,545	274	195	59,762	4,864	1,403
Tennessee	0	2,971,752	456	116,279	51,940	20,048	642	9,628	38,291	23,328
Texas	14,004	465,500	8,810	486,384	136,423	670,106	143,819	71,820	137,452	97,157
Utah	5	3,096	574	72,404	35,887	1,745	152	77,287	8,809	23,594
Vermont....................	254	2,500	-200	18,023	1,400	675	0	2,891	1,535	6,958
Virginia.....................	81,316	710,633	179,664	2,657,744	501,944	2,003,312	51,948	958,545	471,696	214,692
Washington...............	1,033	2,445,903	16,031	177,872	83,947	91,205	774	76,067	14,173	21,326
West Virginia.............	5,291	46,194	0	48,357	7,001	21,952	50,173	20,541	53,390	22,677
Wisconsin..................	0	2,264	1,069	61,692	76,286	4,154	83	21,154	63,249	1,332
Wyoming...................	0	1,374	0	6,722	7,488	2,947	16	49,081	1,312	0
Dist. of Columbia	356,355	68,488	32,938	2,010,549	356,660	734,152	198,692	569,808	1,083,616	160,647
American Samoa.......	0	0	0	0	0	680	0	13	0	0
Fed. States of Micronesia	0	0	0	0	0	0	0	0	0	0
Guam	0	0	0	7,244	63	423	0	313	381	0
Marshall Islands........	0	0	0	0	0	0	0	0	0	0
No. Mariana Islands...	0	0	0	487	0	66	0	4,238	328	0
Palau	0	0	0	0	0	0	0	0	0	0
Puerto Rico...............	0	0	0	24,003	830	7,078	242	336	8,494	21,487
Virgin Islands	0	0	0	1,860	197	764	190	2,548	2,404	1
Undistributed (a).......	3,964	125,799	34,373	130,408	397,521	366,682	6,775	604,265	607,720	18,585

See footnotes at end of table.

FEDERAL GOVERNMENT EXPENDITURE FOR PROCUREMENT CONTRACTS, BY AGENCY, BY STATE AND OUTLYING AREA: FISCAL YEAR 2004—Continued

State and outlying area	NASA	National Archives & Records Admin.	National Science Foundation	Postal Service	Small Bus. Admin.	Social Security Admin.	Dept. of State	Dept. of Transportation	Dept. of the Treasury	Dept. of Veterans Affairs	Other nondefense
						Nondefense agencies—continued					
United States	$12,545,284	$140,524	$56,914	$14,140,419	$49,500	$530,929	$1,656,725	$5,166,807	$4,041,389	$12,912,531	$6,927,861
Alabama	624,421	0	25	171,723	65	4,528	49,650	8,206	1,251	51,816	312,486
Alaska	24,115	0	0	36,226	0	113	11,096	31,631	15,532	10,985	189
Arizona	148,982	0	10	218,816	0	679	7,327	16,903	1,578	62,712	2,231
Arkansas.....................	1,355	210	0	110,965	0	60	27	1,495	1,087	58,175	127
California	3,848,597	1,312	1,291	1,488,099	1,499	9,545	68,020	323,985	371,321	736,640	23,334
Colorado	254,837	542	8,670	245,468	1,220	304	12,338	68,432	7,475	73,565	60,385
Connecticut	92,961	0	0	186,317	0	989	4,788	10,051	3,165	32,452	3,081
Delaware.....................	2,540	0	0	38,280	0	55	195	102	1,160	4,667	599
Florida	635,025	0	0	741,573	487	832	24,285	204,154	29,705	199,239	34,044
Georgia	21,724	1,624	3	370,016	55	5,171	7,558	17,088	41,782	100,417	45,699
Hawaii........................	8,371	0	0	47,722	0	43	96	13,254	38	22,095	849
Idaho..........................	2,580	0	0	49,495	0	19	1,024	3,792	76,223	49,328	368
Illinois	16,808	37	492	688,567	1,203	9,329	11,877	236,857	98,075	862,290	62,819
Indiana.......................	208,685	0	3	264,269	0	75	689	34,326	5,689	81,625	32,328
Iowa	8,282	640	0	156,865	992	267	120	14,036	147,837	12,874	10,573
Kansas	5,444	3,735	0	146,960	0	29	502	27,826	1,539	405,623	1,230
Kentucky	1,966	26	0	167,334	0	473	556	5,954	15,039	75,324	1,192,708
Louisiana	92,034	0	0	177,985	36	1,014	38	19,605	560	63,937	10,038
Maine	5,066	0	0	73,778	0	9	0	1,787	3	7,670	274
Maryland	2,153,135	86,089	7,457	289,861	3,014	304,510	97,249	1,051,646	599,323	132,069	106,058
Massachusetts............	216,414	3,273	1,463	381,827	324	3,862	29,516	301,279	136,084	263,760	9,292
Michigan	18,449	1,787	0	482,787	1,000	6,299	1,747	15,417	101,870	91,415	3,747
Minnesota	10,958	0	0	280,668	906	268	8,166	22,808	2,528	95,072	28,872
Mississippi	154,146	0	0	95,825	14	173	9	15,227	2,814	63,823	6,998
Missouri	12,381	2,553	175	328,456	303	12,403	15,464	46,697	8,111	32,112	2,355
Montana	10,586	0	0	45,751	0	151	805	43,264	5,023	6,437	269
Nebraska.....................	1,631	0	0	97,680	0	28	411	2,622	89	28,104	11,637
Nevada	5,280	0	0	88,172	0	99	33	8,738	1,832	51,358	581
New Hampshire........	24,753	491	3	73,099	139	34	16,762	10,714	604	3,785	2,838
New Jersey..................	97,218	0	131	536,141	0	6,501	7,285	334,213	34,939	50,572	26,092
New Mexico	117,579	0	0	71,045	260	312	0	21,085	380	30,280	568
New York	61,699	2,822	14	1,019,856	118	11,389	19,872	109,944	701,584	194,078	24,607
North Carolina	21,628	0	0	353,270	0	576	49,541	42,552	3,280	91,600	238,743
North Dakota.............	1,023	0	0	37,535	375	31	0	787	6,867	15,821	245
Ohio	159,849	245	0	546,825	3	1,192	5,442	28,409	7,773	130,033	12,277
Oklahoma...................	7,247	0	0	145,220	0	130	543	198,821	8,253	42,582	5,398
Oregon	14,565	0	0	145,519	0	55	1,204	28,244	182	90,544	1,299
Pennsylvania..............	265,938	1,649	124	666,073	5,586	20,830	4,299	62,442	29,670	311,457	328,514
Rhode Island	2,979	0	0	57,280	0	120	4	446	3,831	10,313	257
South Carolina	4,621	0	0	140,251	24	54	11,114	69,049	192	478,335	20,268
South Dakota.............	9,942	0	0	40,798	0	36	2,394	1,512	19	13,289	3,333
Tennessee	33,027	1,036	0	261,171	0	309	364	79,261	66,533	530,433	1,717,899
Texas	1,717,602	5,574	351	872,697	0	19,257	114,715	147,282	87,535	437,382	53,644
Utah	20,397	0	0	89,365	0	241	63	13,181	16,257	26,370	-15,261
Vermont	1,298	0	0	38,082	0	34	10	548	20	10,531	239
Virginia......................	848,285	5,484	31,277	354,860	5,742	32,039	508,801	679,689	370,347	387,546	445,000
Washington................	30,812	1,266	0	262,844	1	1,162	1,320	66,458	3,528	157,162	5,768
West Virginia.............	148,558	0	0	87,179	0	89	4,509	1,196	148,763	63,884	11,075
Wisconsin...................	22,578	0	0	253,204	0	308	1,087	13,112	851	224,410	7,169
Wyoming....................	1,146	0	0	22,842	0	33	0	27,918	4,666	11,965	140,716
Dist. of Columbia	262,874	6,323	1,311	103,263	20,192	18,188	482,494	460,528	741,938	283,678	1,497,881
American Samoa	0	0	0	166	0	0	0	959	0	0	0
Fed. States of Micronesia	0	0	0	0	0	0	90	0	0	0	0
Guam	20	0	0	2,004	0	0	0	825	0	0	0
Marshall Islands........	0	0	0	0	0	0	0	0	0	0	0
No. Mariana Islands...	0	0	0	182	0	0	0	23	5	0	0
Palau	0	0	0	0	0	0	0	0	0	0	0
Puerto Rico................	2,242	0	0	59,582	0	181	5	2,061	615	42,012	442
Virgin Islands............	150	0	0	4,158	0	0	0	2,497	3	16	9
Undistributed (a).......	80,481	13,804	4,114	424,420	5,944	56,504	71,223	215,867	126,021	5,598,771	435,668

Source: U.S. Department of Commerce, Bureau of the Census, Consolidated Federal Funds Report for Fiscal Year 2004, February 2006.

(a) For all agencies, this line includes contract awards under $25,000 and procurement purchases made using government-issued purchase cards.

Table 2.13
FEDERAL GOVERNMENT EXPENDITURE FOR SALARIES AND WAGES, BY AGENCY, BY STATE AND OUTLYING AREA: FISCAL YEAR 2004
(In thousands of dollars)

State and outlying area	Total	Nondefense civilian (a)	Department of Defense Total	Other defense civilian (b)	Military services Total	Active military	Inactive military	Civilian	Army Total	Army Active military
United States	$225,601,344	$136,618,955	$88,982,389	$4,783,642	$84,198,747	$50,932,566	$10,561,834	$22,704,347	$32,284,066	$15,944,870
Alabama	3,492,347	1,795,899	1,696,448	70,479	1,625,969	506,833	387,172	731,964	1,206,712	233,720
Alaska	1,728,440	714,139	1,014,301	13,439	1,000,862	812,168	27,748	160,946	402,247	306,600
Arizona	3,607,900	2,244,582	1,363,318	55,016	1,308,302	933,896	84,303	290,103	400,708	214,840
Arkansas.......................	1,509,449	937,219	572,230	4,066	568,164	222,660	235,919	109,585	301,513	9,720
California	22,029,304	12,100,523	9,928,781	393,688	9,535,093	6,497,680	645,750	2,391,663	1,061,356	313,120
Colorado	4,457,406	2,690,899	1,766,507	142,156	1,624,351	1,166,830	134,080	323,441	774,076	583,440
Connecticut	1,601,990	1,121,872	480,118	45,574	434,544	273,491	92,589	68,464	90,736	1,200
Delaware.......................	493,682	235,890	257,792	2,451	255,341	166,830	37,559	50,952	38,845	280
Florida	10,394,686	6,005,001	4,389,685	139,963	4,249,722	2,845,392	361,003	1,043,327	501,784	124,040
Georgia	8,324,460	3,887,526	4,436,934	98,842	4,338,092	2,924,648	329,491	1,083,953	2,687,103	2,088,840
Hawaii..........................	3,153,871	509,979	2,643,892	41,552	2,602,340	1,865,382	108,850	628,108	898,482	684,200
Idaho............................	897,942	614,668	283,274	1,859	281,415	182,164	51,785	47,466	67,536	1,480
Illinois..........................	7,006,708	4,878,485	2,128,223	77,026	2,051,197	1,286,383	315,437	449,377	528,364	24,560
Indiana.........................	2,457,431	1,661,645	795,786	161,265	634,521	55,673	327,960	250,888	369,879	19,120
Iowa	1,249,419	970,810	278,609	2,916	275,693	25,390	207,209	43,094	223,402	7,320
Kansas	2,207,926	1,189,624	1,018,302	14,678	1,003,624	675,828	152,876	174,920	777,917	521,640
Kentucky	3,231,244	1,482,706	1,748,538	43,259	1,705,279	1,417,239	129,109	158,931	1,649,920	1,388,560
Louisiana......................	2,818,104	1,581,530	1,236,574	17,668	1,218,906	746,384	252,348	220,174	706,404	382,240
Maine	957,014	490,845	466,169	15,135	451,034	137,016	65,853	248,165	69,740	7,680
Maryland	10,523,098	7,279,880	3,243,218	110,709	3,132,509	1,487,904	183,851	1,460,754	935,607	282,880
Massachusetts...............	3,557,251	2,906,164	651,087	76,337	574,750	153,443	178,293	243,014	243,409	10,200
Michigan	3,610,058	2,980,207	629,851	102,678	527,173	80,509	188,457	258,207	391,975	17,920
Minnesota	2,302,448	1,905,350	397,098	15,116	381,982	44,619	262,851	74,512	293,935	10,440
Mississippi	2,093,727	888,577	1,205,150	11,163	1,193,987	657,363	205,710	330,914	314,151	15,680
Missouri	4,041,576	2,721,617	1,319,959	99,842	1,220,117	619,075	378,522	222,520	872,450	367,880
Montana	885,996	646,948	239,048	1,514	237,534	140,182	55,616	41,736	65,642	1,080
Nebraska.......................	1,298,258	699,817	598,441	13,861	584,580	358,968	92,321	133,291	132,639	6,080
Nevada	1,347,252	814,126	533,126	6,496	526,630	407,761	44,353	74,516	51,126	3,880
New Hampshire.............	654,280	497,825	156,455	10,789	145,666	47,561	72,309	25,796	85,231	320
New Jersey	4,327,784	3,178,038	1,149,746	50,009	1,099,737	328,357	184,935	586,445	617,408	37,120
New Mexico	2,071,978	1,204,781	867,197	22,545	844,652	503,538	80,165	260,949	176,566	10,360
New York	9,070,246	7,385,357	1,684,889	85,757	1,599,132	860,036	416,633	322,463	1,202,644	630,920
North Carolina	7,197,116	2,500,687	4,696,429	77,604	4,618,825	3,761,793	358,097	498,935	2,213,901	1,714,400
North Dakota.................	786,652	374,453	412,199	2,873	409,326	280,630	69,429	59,267	73,571	880
Ohio	5,576,062	3,616,616	1,959,446	462,401	1,497,045	425,820	320,328	750,897	328,579	18,000
Oklahoma	3,462,800	1,380,544	2,082,256	57,630	2,024,626	988,368	196,481	839,777	784,311	484,600
Oregon	1,902,974	1,594,074	308,900	2,071	306,829	52,544	141,517	112,768	203,585	8,480
Pennsylvania	6,609,013	4,918,718	1,690,295	402,209	1,288,086	177,012	421,070	690,004	651,207	43,520
Rhode Island	828,541	379,795	448,746	4,667	444,079	149,145	59,856	235,078	60,436	4,120
South Carolina	3,155,983	1,074,994	2,080,989	47,686	2,033,303	1,489,952	242,593	300,758	716,266	428,200
South Dakota................	765,021	496,710	268,311	1,692	266,619	134,126	95,374	37,119	99,041	1,720
Tennessee	3,475,751	2,821,119	654,632	37,516	617,116	142,606	275,563	198,947	382,389	12,840
Texas	14,690,246	8,150,308	6,539,938	191,172	6,348,766	4,583,803	554,799	1,210,164	3,513,568	2,498,920
Utah	2,150,173	1,049,633	1,100,540	48,200	1,052,340	242,647	212,157	597,536	283,020	11,840
Vermont........................	405,058	335,487	69,571	2,642	66,929	8,738	41,914	16,277	48,491	800
Virginia	16,342,443	5,324,022	11,018,421	1,411,177	9,607,244	6,652,246	285,505	2,669,493	2,153,286	1,096,550
Washington...................	6,057,983	2,692,868	3,365,115	44,681	3,320,434	2,093,079	320,048	907,307	1,266,414	812,800
West Virginia	1,358,012	1,152,050	205,962	1,246	204,716	31,690	123,023	50,003	157,597	6,720
Wisconsin.....................	1,895,091	1,586,091	309,000	5,555	303,449	40,201	186,345	76,903	221,485	9,680
Wyoming.......................	521,214	317,657	203,557	1,124	202,433	139,427	25,618	37,388	29,137	160
Dist. of Columbia	15,525,884	13,891,484	1,634,400	20,640	1,613,760	721,566	81,751	810,443	530,614	319,080
American Samoa	9,225	5,071	4,154	0	4,154	0	4,104	50	4,154	0
Micronesia	0	0	0	0	0	0	0	0	0	0
Guam	319,996	38,776	281,220	4,494	276,726	206,570	20,533	49,623	14,957	1,560
Marshall Islands...........	0	0	0	0	0	0	0	0	0	0
No. Mariana Islands	6,264	6,253	11	0	11	0	0	11	11	0
Palau	0	0	0	0	0	0	0	0	0	0
Puerto Rico...................	1,025,908	726,455	299,453	8,514	290,939	22,818	225,045	43,076	242,357	7,440
Virgin Islands...............	66,108	53,278	12,830	0	12,830	1,382	9,563	1,885	10,982	0
Undistributed	4,064,549	3,909,285	155,264	0	155,264	155,200	64	0	155,200	155,200

Source: U.S. Department of Commerce, Bureau of the Census, February 2006.

FEDERAL GOVERNMENT EXPENDITURE FOR SALARIES AND WAGES, BY AGENCY, BY STATE AND OUTLYING AREA: FISCAL YEAR 2004 — Continued

State and outlying area	Army—continued Inactive military	Civilian	Navy Total	Active military	Inactive military	Civilian	Air Force Total	Active military	Inactive military	Civilian
United States	$9,364,146	$6,975,050	$29,304,761	$20,236,155	$565,618	$8,502,988	$22,609,920	$14,751,541	$632,070	$7,226,309
Alabama	356,112	616,880	39,200	29,428	7,917	1,855	380,057	243,685	23,143	113,229
Alaska	20,215	75,432	7,325	5,848	696	781	591,290	499,720	6,837	84,733
Arizona.......................	61,222	124,646	189,046	161,914	8,851	18,281	718,548	557,142	14,230	147,176
Arkansas.....................	218,229	73,564	4,085	1,940	1,846	299	262,566	211,000	15,844	35,722
California	524,533	223,703	6,911,875	5,187,504	78,035	1,646,336	1,561,862	997,056	43,182	521,624
Colorado	115,693	74,943	54,951	45,303	7,565	2,083	795,324	538,087	10,822	246,415
Connecticut	79,644	9,892	316,808	264,911	4,442	47,455	27,000	7,380	8,503	11,117
Delaware.....................	31,471	7,094	2,810	1,540	1,203	67	213,686	165,010	4,885	43,791
Florida........................	293,122	84,622	2,063,474	1,500,205	42,434	520,835	1,684,464	1,221,147	25,447	437,870
Georgia	284,049	314,214	500,436	328,791	17,587	154,058	1,150,553	507,017	27,855	615,681
Hawaii.........................	91,263	123,019	1,318,332	900,434	5,169	412,729	385,526	280,748	12,418	92,360
Idaho..........................	48,918	17,138	8,830	4,422	1,791	2,617	205,049	176,262	1,076	27,711
Illinois........................	278,141	225,663	1,012,586	928,084	20,712	63,790	510,247	333,739	16,584	159,924
Indiana........................	305,419	45,340	183,615	21,014	5,190	157,411	81,027	15,539	17,351	48,137
Iowa...........................	194,899	21,183	11,555	7,670	3,722	163	40,736	10,400	8,588	21,748
Kansas	131,115	125,162	8,665	6,673	1,967	25	217,042	147,515	19,794	49,733
Kentucky	122,987	138,373	27,602	11,956	4,060	11,586	27,757	16,723	2,062	8,972
Louisiana.....................	225,863	98,301	159,001	94,593	13,102	51,306	353,501	269,551	13,383	70,567
Maine..........................	56,159	5,901	358,798	120,777	6,638	231,383	22,496	8,559	3,056	10,881
Maryland.....................	174,552	478,175	1,617,463	738,561	4,674	874,228	579,439	466,463	4,625	108,351
Massachusetts..............	153,257	79,952	48,055	31,175	3,562	13,318	283,286	112,068	21,474	149,744
Michigan	170,178	203,877	46,446	38,222	7,325	899	88,752	24,367	10,954	53,431
Minnesota	240,904	42,591	27,849	18,812	8,406	631	60,198	15,367	13,541	31,290
Mississippi	194,676	103,795	428,625	312,401	4,898	111,326	451,211	329,282	6,136	115,793
Missouri......................	343,069	161,501	122,291	83,247	29,527	9,517	225,376	167,948	5,926	51,502
Montana	52,143	12,419	1,655	824	831	0	170,237	138,278	2,642	29,317
Nebraska......................	79,862	46,697	37,412	33,349	3,474	589	414,529	319,539	8,985	86,005
Nevada........................	38,281	8,965	64,739	49,734	3,246	11,759	410,765	354,147	2,826	53,792
New Hampshire............	69,132	15,779	40,663	36,575	1,370	2,718	19,772	10,666	1,807	7,299
New Jersey...................	173,644	406,644	176,207	57,778	4,589	113,840	306,122	233,459	6,702	65,961
New Mexico	68,347	97,859	15,729	10,983	2,881	1,865	652,357	482,195	8,937	161,225
New York.....................	365,371	206,353	179,580	150,431	22,382	6,767	216,908	78,685	28,880	109,343
North Carolina.............	333,055	166,446	1,915,892	1,623,465	11,257	281,170	489,032	423,928	13,785	51,319
North Dakota...............	60,909	11,782	1,500	809	590	101	334,255	278,941	7,930	47,384
Ohio...........................	274,166	36,413	53,106	32,333	17,570	3,203	1,115,360	375,487	28,592	711,281
Oklahoma....................	177,752	121,959	97,219	87,658	5,754	3,807	1,143,096	416,110	12,975	714,011
Oregon........................	121,446	73,659	28,145	21,690	5,636	819	75,099	22,374	14,435	38,290
Pennsylvania	374,645	233,042	506,890	98,588	19,871	388,431	129,989	34,904	26,554	68,531
Rhode Island	50,116	6,200	359,499	132,886	6,630	219,983	24,144	12,139	3,110	8,895
South Carolina.............	217,710	70,356	818,587	646,795	8,076	163,716	498,450	414,957	16,807	66,686
South Dakota...............	86,826	10,495	950	243	677	30	166,628	132,163	7,871	26,594
Tennessee	251,449	118,100	151,448	99,871	10,977	40,600	83,279	29,895	13,137	40,247
Texas	494,005	520,643	525,971	429,860	39,208	56,903	2,309,227	1,655,023	21,586	632,618
Utah	206,087	65,093	15,807	11,192	3,400	1,215	753,513	219,615	2,670	531,228
Vermont	40,048	7,643	1,941	1,653	259	29	16,497	6,285	1,607	8,605
Virginia.......................	238,188	818,548	6,187,056	4,574,966	34,121	1,577,963	1,266,902	980,730	13,190	272,982
Washington..................	282,977	170,637	1,626,286	950,771	19,259	656,256	427,734	329,508	17,812	80,414
West Virginia................	117,402	33,475	19,467	14,221	2,104	3,142	27,652	10,749	3,517	13,386
Wisconsin.....................	166,829	44,976	18,427	11,245	6,673	509	63,537	19,276	12,843	31,418
Wyoming......................	23,555	5,422	443	18	425	0	172,853	139,249	1,638	31,966
Dist. of Columbia	40,754	170,780	819,795	186,989	40,409	592,397	263,351	215,497	588	47,266
American Samoa..........	4,104	50	0	0	0	0	0	0	0	0
Micronesia	0	0	0	0	0	0	0	0	0	0
Guam	13,121	276	148,635	118,015	6	30,614	113,134	86,995	7,406	18,733
Marshall Islands...........	0	0	0	0	0	0	0	0	0	0
No. Mariana Islands	0	11	0	0	0	0	0	0	0	0
Palau	0	0	0	0	0	0	0	0	0	0
Puerto Rico..................	217,435	17,482	21,794	7,657	2,554	11,583	26,788	7,721	5,056	14,011
Virgin Islands...............	9,097	1,885	131	131	0	0	1,717	1,251	466	0
Undistributed	0	0	64	0	64	0	0	0	0	0

See footnotes at end of table.

FEDERAL GOVERNMENT EXPENDITURE FOR SALARIES AND WAGES, BY AGENCY, BY STATE AND OUTLYING AREA: FISCAL YEAR 2004 — Continued

State and outlying area	Total (a)	Dept. of Agriculture	Dept. of Commerce	Dept. of Education	Dept. of Energy	Environmental Protection Agency	Federal Deposit Insurance Corporation	General Services Admin.	Dept. of Health and Human Services
United States	$136,618,955	$5,707,828	$2,538,313	$364,676	$1,326,615	$1,494,644	$502,566	$936,686	$4,393,816
Alabama	1,795,899	71,131	6,105	84	0	3,199	2,537	3,415	3,477
Alaska	714,139	57,333	32,173	0	100	2,285	0	2,842	29,007
Arizona	2,244,582	107,299	9,867	0	16,869	421	1,902	3,894	192,144
Arkansas	937,219	114,410	2,932	0	2,432	0	1,975	1,350	25,195
California	12,100,523	467,971	60,915	14,478	41,679	77,689	29,026	68,299	85,623
Colorado	2,690,899	205,070	91,017	5,565	56,028	60,893	2,991	24,158	32,370
Connecticut	1,121,872	10,656	3,732	0	149	665	2,287	870	1,905
Delaware	235,890	12,899	457	0	0	0	978	188	670
Florida	6,005,001	101,044	54,213	335	109	6,875	5,546	6,958	17,235
Georgia	3,887,526	161,026	14,041	15,497	6,750	88,950	16,797	47,144	475,754
Hawaii	509,979	29,128	16,377	0	182	492	0	2,900	1,329
Idaho	614,668	148,557	7,224	0	32,554	1,837	0	1,162	2,532
Illinois	4,878,485	102,378	14,649	13,595	28,183	102,430	25,062	50,555	52,800
Indiana	1,661,645	51,912	57,167	107	0	123	3,237	2,423	2,339
Iowa	970,810	122,863	4,400	74	963	238	5,657	1,275	1,215
Kansas	1,189,624	63,122	10,167	0	0	41,636	6,876	979	11,339
Kentucky	1,482,706	66,825	6,547	0	2,008	220	4,537	1,073	1,085
Louisiana	1,581,530	170,432	9,737	0	6,686	1,056	3,972	2,870	11,553
Maine	490,845	17,189	5,061	0	0	0	0	457	1,392
Maryland	7,279,880	250,021	790,690	0	130,533	7,238	2,350	12,990	2,362,390
Massachusetts	2,906,164	25,884	35,739	7,157	1,542	60,117	17,686	18,699	39,636
Michigan	2,980,207	76,354	17,382	0	0	25,903	3,233	5,174	8,132
Minnesota	1,905,350	113,411	7,703	353	65	6,407	4,903	2,906	22,449
Mississippi	888,577	112,576	14,163	0	0	2,149	2,287	787	1,187
Missouri	2,721,617	261,736	30,525	7,680	8,274	821	15,930	56,799	29,739
Montana	646,948	172,933	7,187	0	9,918	2,716	1,041	1,259	49,678
Nebraska	699,817	90,441	5,403	0	1,319	92	3,181	1,066	4,599
Nevada	814,126	24,327	6,986	0	29,763	12,832	0	2,013	3,498
New Hampshire	497,825	21,520	2,109	0	147	0	1,933	1,320	659
New Jersey	3,178,038	30,849	15,839	0	1,582	18,665	3,910	13,696	11,687
New Mexico	1,204,781	92,963	4,651	0	75,293	162	1,498	2,722	135,845
New York	7,385,357	65,114	23,033	7,111	13,090	61,620	18,027	49,194	62,836
North Carolina	2,500,687	118,710	29,831	0	125	99,028	3,785	3,336	63,840
North Dakota	374,453	51,526	3,914	0	4,323	0	2,868	1,001	21,524
Ohio	3,616,616	57,267	9,361	2,364	10,627	45,361	2,374	7,353	39,914
Oklahoma	1,380,544	60,592	20,265	0	9,280	4,397	3,977	2,480	69,130
Oregon	1,594,074	253,399	20,239	0	108,883	9,728	1,505	2,691	11,302
Pennsylvania	4,918,718	99,905	14,527	8,034	30,926	70,964	5,471	40,531	64,717
Rhode Island	379,795	3,024	3,118	0	0	6,036	0	868	639
South Carolina	1,074,994	56,074	17,758	0	38,240	85	1,773	1,731	1,526
South Dakota	496,710	54,782	5,614	0	12,202	73	2,131	877	56,056
Tennessee	2,821,119	71,643	8,097	183	52,793	417	11,736	2,588	6,761
Texas	8,150,308	218,466	38,245	9,395	13,633	72,169	70,364	71,759	51,761
Utah	1,049,633	105,240	7,941	0	1,528	139	3,511	1,843	2,710
Vermont	335,487	18,156	2,324	0	0	82	0	337	577
Virginia	5,324,022	147,817	603,144	0	1,153	109,610	787	117,601	3,393
Washington	2,692,868	130,170	85,055	5,761	178,796	43,327	4,230	31,431	48,528
West Virginia	1,152,050	46,337	2,738	0	22,804	1,924	1,176	1,707	27,293
Wisconsin	1,586,091	103,695	7,030	0	59	153	5,670	1,769	3,553
Wyoming	317,657	49,338	3,680	0	4,577	0	0	810	4,537
Dist. of Columbia	13,891,484	606,268	281,857	266,492	370,448	439,650	191,070	252,608	227,312
American Samoa	5,071	384	1,068	0	0	0	0	0	0
Micronesia	0	0	0	0	0	0	0	0	0
Guam	38,776	3,453	1,889	0	0	59	0	0	0
Marshall Islands	0	0	0	0	0	0	0	0	0
No. Mariana Islands	6,253	498	0	0	0	80	0	0	47
Palau	0	0	0	0	0	0	0	0	0
Puerto Rico	726,455	30,927	2,427	411	0	3,523	779	1,825	7,365
Virgin Islands	53,278	783	0	0	0	108	0	103	32
Undistributed	3,909,285	0	0	0	0	0	0	0	0

See footnotes at end of table.

FEDERAL GOVERNMENT EXPENDITURE FOR SALARIES AND WAGES, BY AGENCY, BY STATE AND OUTLYING AREA: FISCAL YEAR 2004 — Continued

State and outlying area	Dept. of Homeland Security	Dept. of Housing and Urban Development	Dept. of the Interior	Dept. of Justice (c)	Dept. of Labor	National Aeronautics and Space Administration	National Archives and Records	National Science Foundation	United States Postal Service
				Nondefense agencies—continued					
United States	$10,291,135	$812,386	$4,126,443	$10,133,630	$1,242,288	$1,659,774	$143,471	$109,882	$52,030,998
Alabama	81,174	5,882	8,521	69,752	9,837	228,313	59	0	651,425
Alaska	151,770	2,952	134,268	12,541	1,007	0	218	214	137,423
Arizona........................	291,432	8,740	238,333	124,501	3,596	284	0	0	830,069
Arkansas......................	18,189	4,434	16,687	41,020	3,213	0	1,155	0	420,941
California	1,334,622	50,608	386,695	599,691	66,469	201,848	5,858	0	5,645,035
Colorado......................	114,902	27,180	473,094	137,221	29,666	585	2,082	0	931,173
Connecticut	101,551	5,210	3,317	50,747	5,283	84	0	0	706,784
Delaware......................	3,655	265	2,310	11,005	762	0	0	0	145,215
Florida	799,892	20,076	79,963	388,134	31,933	155,463	0	0	2,813,123
Georgia	293,221	31,352	61,692	177,805	39,056	0	4,062	0	1,403,640
Hawaii..........................	129,657	1,649	27,259	27,533	1,672	0	0	0	181,032
Idaho...........................	19,352	951	119,646	16,224	2,068	0	0	0	187,755
Illinois.........................	253,529	36,021	14,495	223,926	57,026	84	2,037	226	2,612,047
Indiana.........................	49,317	5,819	13,173	69,655	7,161	60	0	0	1,002,492
Iowa	16,399	2,489	7,224	19,095	2,364	0	933	0	595,061
Kansas	24,663	12,654	21,069	63,098	4,156	0	2,281	0	557,485
Kentucky	50,312	5,274	19,000	133,066	29,006	0	0	0	634,773
Louisiana	135,347	7,754	64,489	119,411	7,031	918	0	0	675,177
Maine	67,216	513	10,271	8,688	1,863	0	0	0	279,873
Maryland	241,642	9,911	45,054	295,056	6,653	263,401	59,370	0	1,099,574
Massachusetts...............	261,014	17,679	66,580	97,901	34,158	142	4,202	166	1,448,442
Michigan.......................	228,370	12,566	21,548	110,601	7,935	114	1,365	0	1,831,430
Minnesota	93,218	7,324	45,700	88,788	4,054	0	0	0	1,064,700
Mississippi	30,325	3,888	23,474	43,152	3,419	23,553	0	0	363,509
Missouri	94,404	9,184	46,033	98,981	28,723	77	26,673	0	1,245,983
Montana	37,513	701	109,713	13,023	1,901	107	0	0	173,554
Nebraska.......................	47,514	3,535	25,491	16,455	2,580	0	0	0	370,546
Nevada	70,955	2,238	108,924	37,697	2,013	0	0	0	334,478
New Hampshire.............	27,461	3,259	5,065	11,853	2,983	101	0	0	277,297
New Jersey....................	275,409	10,431	19,430	209,988	14,487	164	0	0	2,033,826
New Mexico	78,925	2,334	259,467	36,190	2,588	4,880	79	0	269,505
New York	626,711	40,932	52,414	371,252	51,056	2,565	2,009	0	3,868,775
North Carolina.............	177,219	8,169	30,754	114,249	5,294	0	0	61	1,340,112
North Dakota................	28,764	503	44,272	7,048	1,330	0	0	0	142,387
Ohio.............................	116,868	18,193	16,865	101,858	31,176	160,924	2,924	0	2,074,356
Oklahoma	35,158	10,054	55,203	82,508	3,585	0	0	0	550,887
Oregon	100,319	4,385	186,560	51,470	3,108	99	0	0	552,018
Pennsylvania	167,242	31,902	68,597	301,154	70,969	0	2,448	0	2,526,715
Rhode Island	47,738	2,163	3,282	9,716	1,808	0	0	0	217,288
South Carolina	72,844	5,538	11,735	74,306	2,886	0	0	0	532,036
South Dakota................	7,268	458	75,105	17,110	1,024	0	0	0	154,766
Tennessee	57,405	11,107	34,718	80,042	7,752	0	0	0	990,742
Texas	1,107,185	45,343	63,035	575,352	58,234	275,633	5,485	0	3,310,536
Utah	32,184	1,916	105,601	29,406	8,681	674	0	0	339,002
Vermont	98,360	424	3,319	7,418	415	0	0	0	144,461
Virginia........................	724,953	7,419	285,449	758,468	37,397	211,938	0	109,183	1,346,144
Washington...................	271,630	14,926	134,896	74,242	19,365	0	1,469	32	997,088
West Virginia................	21,616	1,853	43,951	216,473	33,822	3,005	0	0	330,708
Wisconsin.....................	45,958	5,371	35,809	49,107	7,172	108	0	0	960,517
Wyoming	4,711	318	91,182	8,219	1,227	0	0	0	86,651
Dist. of Columbia	955,969	282,113	291,230	1,630,167	478,703	124,650	18,762	0	391,722
American Samoa	884	0	888	0	0	0	0	0	628
Micronesia....................	0	0	0	0	0	0	0	0	0
Guam	14,006	64	1,110	5,468	53	0	0	0	7,603
Marshall Islands...........	0	0	0	0	0	0	0	0	0
No. Mariana Islands	2,731	0	764	944	104	0	0	0	691
Palau	0	0	0	0	0	0	0	0	0
Puerto Rico..................	128,491	6,362	6,958	63,614	2,464	0	0	0	226,023
Virgin Islands..............	19,877	0	4,761	8,474	0	0	0	0	15,772
Undistributed	2,094	0	0	2,142,770	0	0	0	0	0

See footnotes at end of table.

FEDERAL GOVERNMENT EXPENDITURE FOR SALARIES AND WAGES, BY AGENCY, BY STATE AND OUTLYING AREA: FISCAL YEAR 2004 — Continued

				Nondefense agencies—continued			
State and outlying area	*Small Business Admin.*	*Social Security Admin.*	*Dept. of State*	*Dept. of Transportation*	*Dept. of the Treasury*	*Dept. of Veterans Affairs*	*All other nondefense (d)*
United States	$255,926	$3,855,721	$1,111,956	$5,638,180	$6,835,610	$13,008,712	$8,097,699
Alabama	2,796	137,177	433	28,246	31,585	225,966	224,784
Alaska	1,204	2,823	66	113,384	6,857	24,796	875
Arizona	1,861	32,278	1,250	55,049	41,187	267,148	16,458
Arkansas......................	2,846	25,997	86	22,115	15,620	213,450	3,172
California	30,927	373,414	12,928	485,216	743,699	1,208,948	108,886
Colorado	9,258	42,051	632	135,992	105,429	167,999	35,543
Connecticut	1,679	23,453	1,201	22,741	46,922	128,269	4,366
Delaware......................	377	3,605	0	3,012	10,565	39,255	671
Florida	5,085	135,381	25,912	285,271	193,421	849,799	29,233
Georgia	12,610	96,708	1,583	246,382	318,410	316,288	58,758
Hawaii..........................	1,468	6,163	1,438	35,568	10,569	32,299	3,264
Idaho...........................	831	6,959	0	13,168	7,860	45,610	379
Illinois.........................	5,942	193,935	5,175	238,147	178,102	526,390	141,751
Indiana.........................	1,427	44,621	0	111,145	55,839	173,731	9,897
Iowa.............................	1,484	18,827	0	19,986	16,710	131,954	1,599
Kansas	1,161	19,553	126	100,616	100,339	143,104	5,200
Kentucky	2,147	45,602	189	39,445	213,366	158,892	69,339
Louisiana	1,566	47,796	4,528	34,210	41,104	227,168	8,725
Maine	1,291	10,709	72	17,322	8,873	59,325	729
Maryland......................	2,061	798,895	2,687	46,695	380,839	193,329	278,501
Massachusetts..............	3,315	70,045	3,443	123,750	212,979	319,422	36,466
Michigan.......................	2,319	78,629	528	76,912	137,048	320,530	14,134
Minnesota	1,822	27,371	199	111,617	54,809	237,680	9,870
Mississippi	1,017	34,004	139	16,576	15,593	178,431	18,348
Missouri	5,025	140,700	46	107,427	192,381	302,553	11,923
Montana	842	6,738	179	15,037	7,129	34,697	1,082
Nebraska......................	1,020	10,271	142	15,941	17,673	81,106	1,442
Nevada.........................	1,291	11,026	0	36,007	22,244	105,977	1,857
New Hampshire.............	1,146	7,940	4,919	78,882	13,323	35,185	723
New Jersey....................	2,770	60,098	1,152	162,592	95,622	186,126	9,716
New Mexico	1,068	41,733	509	71,269	11,618	109,006	2,476
New York	13,923	260,807	23,616	285,548	497,358	892,225	96,141
North Carolina..............	2,214	61,429	3,280	49,990	60,309	316,102	12,850
North Dakota................	1,136	5,599	0	12,884	5,967	39,026	381
Ohio	3,312	88,670	0	147,589	173,788	483,216	22,257
Oklahoma.....................	1,064	28,116	142	251,382	36,677	153,127	2,521
Oregon	1,689	26,249	0	28,826	34,096	195,002	2,506
Pennsylvania	5,475	229,152	3,728	92,932	421,678	568,279	93,373
Rhode Island	945	9,010	645	9,750	11,398	51,426	940
South Carolina.............	939	34,252	13,760	26,413	17,236	161,837	4,026
South Dakota................	822	5,598	0	8,053	6,034	88,031	706
Tennessee.....................	1,582	57,051	0	111,961	223,699	348,057	742,785
Texas	19,475	165,915	16,475	427,997	565,983	899,284	68,583
Utah	1,526	10,846	0	71,527	232,674	89,376	3,307
Vermont	1,090	3,574	0	8,141	5,172	41,318	319
Virginia	5,774	120,995	4,260	242,388	116,404	273,677	96,068
Washington...................	3,819	81,323	3,443	191,938	79,019	277,519	14,861
West Virginia................	977	26,226	0	15,057	162,704	188,745	2,934
Wisconsin.....................	1,819	38,997	0	27,890	39,361	245,350	6,703
Wyoming.......................	930	2,348	0	8,241	4,800	45,780	308
Dist. of Columbia	74,135	20,617	973,045	724,186	807,575	454,832	4,028,073
American Samoa..........	86	206	0	869	0	58	0
Micronesia	0	0	0	0	0	0	0
Guam	422	527	0	3,513	0	583	25
Marshall Islands...........	0	0	0	0	0	0	0
No. Mariana Islands	0	210	0	176	0	0	8
Palau	0	0	0	0	0	0	0
Puerto Rico..................	2,611	22,779	0	20,235	25,510	150,736	23,416
Virgin Islands...............	505	723	0	974	453	693	20
Undistributed	0	0	0	0	0	0	1,764,421

Source: U.S. Department of Commerce, Bureau of the Census, February 2006.

Note: Department of Defense data represent salaries, wages and compensation, such as housing allowances; distributions by state are based on duty station. State details for all other federal government agencies are estimates, based on place of employment.

(a) The "undistributed" amount includes the salary and wages data for the Federal Bureau of Investigation and for the Federal Judiciary that could not be geographically allocated.

(b) The "undistributed" amount represents Defense Logistics Agency salaries and wages that could not be geographically allocated.

(c) The "undistributed" amount includes the salaries and wages of the Federal Bureau of Investigation that could not be geographically allocated.

(d) The "undistributed" amount includes the salaries and wages for the Federal Judiciary that could not be geographically allocated.

Table 2.14
FEDERAL GOVERNMENT INSURANCE AND LOAN PROGRAMS, BY STATE AND OUTLYING AREA: FISCAL YEAR 2004
(In thousands of dollars)

State and outlying area	Direct loans by volume of assistance provided					Guaranteed loans by volume of coverage provided			
		Department of Agriculture						Federal	Veterans housing
	Total	Commodity loans— price supports	Other agriculture loans	Federal direct student loans	Other direct loans	Total	Mortgage insurance for homes	Family Education Loan program	guaranteed and insured loans— VA home loans
United States	$30,065,061	$2,771,370	$4,019,058	$22,072,946	$1,201,686	$228,779,115	$109,072,336	$45,097,174	$35,315,000
Alabama	934,471	360,805	66,273	501,604	5,789	2,909,379	1,245,827	669,600	603,665
Alaska	32,284	0	17,782	11,169	3,332	1,077,286	475,318	56,871	294,589
Arizona	547,083	3	35,775	509,431	1,875	8,775,014	3,693,177	2,724,189	1,642,498
Arkansas...................	169,253	0	113,189	54,786	1,277	1,990,458	819,609	414,438	277,770
California	2,924,512	458,900	219,615	2,025,121	220,876	16,012,010	5,938,035	3,648,825	1,966,460
Colorado...................	434,462	1,132	48,730	375,753	8,848	9,270,009	5,527,276	804,005	1,362,598
Connecticut	116,373	0	13,719	100,508	2,145	2,603,753	1,210,058	514,865	121,224
Delaware...................	68,232	0	19,871	44,267	4,094	636,702	289,724	83,656	156,278
Florida	659,440	0	69,887	457,756	131,796	12,632,586	5,621,421	2,497,149	2,742,847
Georgia	1,021,687	1	102,013	914,310	5,362	9,294,907	5,680,038	1,107,501	1,446,354
Hawaii.......................	21,104	0	20,196	668	240	601,631	149,822	120,743	100,623
Idaho........................	375,563	342	67,576	307,645	0	1,309,290	697,050	78,203	269,705
Illinois......................	1,386,263	0	106,798	1,230,438	49,027	10,260,918	5,412,151	2,233,512	893,705
Indiana......................	814,887	0	90,478	694,007	30,403	5,686,585	3,178,849	1,318,671	583,738
Iowa	923,422	7	116,928	798,339	8,148	1,609,590	451,048	420,127	184,853
Kansas	248,461	4,912	57,770	182,142	3,636	1,873,109	747,025	479,112	340,416
Kentucky	429,142	80,415	148,121	174,075	26,532	2,660,966	1,138,111	516,830	374,301
Louisiana	166,606	0	102,129	48,437	16,040	2,725,259	1,169,642	848,312	319,279
Maine........................	82,975	0	50,960	31,135	881	787,375	234,422	206,913	90,094
Maryland	563,279	0	37,041	459,153	67,086	7,535,946	4,477,207	497,696	1,632,411
Massachusetts............	928,697	0	33,000	891,098	4,598	3,495,177	1,477,336	1,158,566	153,766
Michigan	2,208,204	0	134,308	2,044,682	29,214	6,361,166	3,577,469	1,176,680	588,547
Minnesota	667,408	6	113,503	551,654	2,246	4,332,931	1,602,966	1,037,069	372,578
Mississippi	1,301,364	1,156,247	92,118	48,557	4,442	1,849,257	787,118	448,356	290,507
Missouri	479,863	0	94,907	346,382	38,574	4,688,908	2,038,865	1,183,176	680,196
Montana	117,980	486	41,407	71,642	4,445	835,926	310,042	171,711	103,863
Nebraska...................	246,220	433	77,985	154,190	13,612	1,602,579	603,997	319,790	383,323
Nevada......................	141,417	3	15,722	123,996	1,695	2,680,989	1,463,136	79,666	860,244
New Hampshire..........	63,249	0	32,097	28,587	2,565	836,850	271,281	272,621	93,140
New Jersey.................	451,765	0	37,749	375,201	38,815	6,291,918	4,308,482	582,567	385,130
New Mexico	169,734	0	34,617	134,773	343	1,623,561	907,831	155,561	419,865
New York	1,905,475	0	99,020	1,765,762	40,693	10,256,411	3,797,471	3,461,514	307,663
North Carolina...........	1,015,222	314,916	224,901	386,117	89,287	6,612,847	3,133,601	935,034	1,793,022
North Dakota.............	47,822	57	46,730	0	1,035	759,337	176,979	195,060	80,908
Ohio	1,881,693	0	105,443	1,724,026	52,224	8,028,767	4,143,894	1,605,874	1,058,209
Oklahoma..................	186,299	159	89,540	95,129	1,470	2,735,568	1,186,408	592,261	437,883
Oregon......................	821,413	0	78,209	742,177	1,027	2,714,452	1,325,005	473,524	544,238
Pennsylvania	254,313	0	122,494	93,564	38,255	7,402,576	2,489,193	3,311,412	759,797
Rhode Island	163,152	0	10,685	150,658	1,809	796,748	418,520	254,500	37,907
South Carolina...........	312,816	0	70,150	241,182	1,484	2,304,559	850,315	591,799	505,186
South Dakota.............	70,078	7	64,423	3,310	2,337	756,898	186,318	200,538	99,354
Tennessee	403,014	15,926	136,467	240,279	10,343	4,706,694	2,559,980	866,340	828,487
Texas	938,100	376,018	274,900	244,949	42,234	21,352,662	11,926,975	3,176,142	3,341,789
Utah	51,272	4	46,446	4,523	300	3,980,321	2,439,321	336,919	439,136
Vermont.....................	36,377	0	21,241	15,136	0	422,363	47,878	203,584	32,420
Virginia.....................	1,151,723	70	97,178	965,394	89,081	8,601,674	3,877,276	775,994	2,860,061
Washington................	755,676	463	75,818	659,327	20,069	6,154,475	2,929,210	605,030	1,776,193
West Virginia.............	533,703	0	47,174	468,827	17,702	562,262	238,345	122,575	92,478
Wisconsin..................	378,183	53	104,212	263,063	10,855	2,937,769	830,160	659,309	449,260
Wyoming....................	8,653	6	8,429	13	205	478,865	176,857	112,723	82,682
District of Columbia...	266,192	0	0	231,966	34,225	1,035,486	190,052	566,671	13,210
American Samoa........	7,513	0	0	0	7,513	38	0	0	0
Fed. States of Micronesia	2,064	0	1,773	0	291	0	0	0	0
Guam	5,930	0	960	2,081	2,889	30,352	1,224	3,960	2,837
Marshall Islands.........	1,685	0	1,685	0	0	0	0	0	0
No. Mariana Islands...	3,369	0	1,049	0	2,320	773	0	0	0
Palau	407	0	407	0	0	35,000	0	0	0
Puerto Rico................	159,365	0	71,170	82,122	6,074	1,248,709	640,323	219,423	37,234
Virgin Islands.............	8,152	0	6,288	1,833	32	11,473	2,699	2	479
Undistributed	0	0	0	0	0	0	0	0	0

See footnotes at end of table.

FEDERAL GOVERNMENT INSURANCE AND LOAN PROGRAMS, BY STATE AND OUTLYING AREA: FISCAL YEAR 2004—Continued

State and outlying area	Guaranteed loans by volume of coverage provided—continued			Insurance programs by volume of coverage provided					
	U.S.D.A. guaranteed loans	Small business loans	Other guaranteed loans	Total	Flood insurance	Crop insurance	Foreign Investment Insurance	Life Insurance for Veterans	Other insurance
United States	$12,303,320	$18,237,607	$1,634,451	$773,198,632	$722,811,352	$46,752,550	$1,279,824	$1,865,424	$489,481
Alabama	244,053	132,524	0	6,011,149	5,699,585	281,450	0	25,308	4,805
Alaska	134,101	23,056	0	408,402	399,394	546	0	2,560	5,902
Arizona	128,236	454,548	0	5,050,723	4,798,238	176,350	25,000	42,193	8,942
Arkansas......................	380,178	95,900	0	1,815,360	1,280,109	517,423	0	15,925	1,903
California	259,589	3,526,058	35,000	50,435,096	46,968,582	3,160,344	34,090	193,721	78,359
Colorado	393,169	504,354	0	3,327,343	2,657,932	606,102	883	29,866	32,560
Connecticut	23,476	448,489	63,553	5,516,296	5,249,687	76,984	158,150	29,881	1,593
Delaware.....................	43,011	59,842	0	3,322,296	3,121,411	52,508	141,800	5,822	755
Florida	474,988	768,593	6	309,479,746	306,582,634	2,668,739	9,360	172,441	46,572
Georgia	515,464	420,591	0	13,448,971	12,576,633	793,509	72	41,776	36,982
Hawaii.........................	70,441	40,778	0	6,436,137	6,321,889	93,867	0	15,979	4,402
Idaho..........................	152,253	109,171	0	1,509,403	931,489	508,485	60,000	8,138	1,292
Illinois	294,229	743,594	0	9,341,948	5,290,450	3,942,722	21,000	77,571	10,205
Indiana........................	370,093	181,797	0	4,892,213	2,831,007	2,028,611	0	28,083	4,512
Iowa............................	411,344	120,182	0	6,202,929	1,023,505	5,155,925	0	22,923	576
Kansas	187,966	112,901	0	3,090,385	1,016,179	2,034,337	10,782	18,523	10,564
Kentucky	431,834	152,040	0	2,445,375	1,987,898	436,858	0	18,352	2,267
Louisiana	290,907	81,647	0	52,929,954	52,451,732	410,144	20,060	22,126	25,891
Maine..........................	75,808	172,607	0	1,119,854	1,055,671	54,031	0	9,994	158
Maryland.....................	116,609	252,847	0	7,916,989	7,674,812	193,648	0	39,706	8,822
Massachusetts.............	37,701	517,041	0	7,101,746	6,996,266	46,969	7,200	50,114	1,197
Michigan.....................	468,728	361,643	0	4,066,748	3,113,725	898,124	0	50,882	4,017
Minnesota	613,295	408,788	0	4,828,383	1,138,473	3,649,111	0	38,287	2,511
Mississippi	217,723	104,301	0	5,553,703	5,049,874	484,623	360	13,323	5,523
Missouri......................	415,741	319,365	0	3,648,889	2,569,241	1,033,362	0	35,670	10,615
Montana	185,725	56,602	0	1,004,603	402,277	579,038	0	7,541	15,746
Nebraska.....................	212,682	81,097	0	4,632,969	1,461,707	3,155,584	0	13,814	1,864
Nevada........................	12,859	164,475	0	3,061,166	3,029,637	16,456	0	12,997	2,077
New Hampshire..........	29,885	117,003	0	747,841	727,970	10,069	0	9,802	0
New Jersey..................	16,492	571,238	1	32,225,292	32,078,618	71,795	2,519	64,600	7,760
New Mexico	65,173	62,331	0	1,469,257	1,372,734	80,476	0	14,018	2,029
New York	128,950	1,625,348	888,300	17,643,128	16,979,068	239,994	300,404	122,526	1,136
North Carolina	346,478	256,555	47,700	19,903,402	18,749,168	1,092,552	0	47,476	14,207
North Dakota..............	239,828	61,085	0	2,975,191	681,253	2,283,923	0	4,765	5,250
Ohio............................	395,058	578,158	83,701	5,291,116	3,828,680	1,374,919	0	69,281	18,237
Oklahoma	369,265	134,690	3,800	1,924,022	1,469,526	430,329	270	20,843	3,054
Oregon	115,161	213,153	0	4,902,181	4,291,181	584,585	0	23,794	2,621
Pennsylvania	228,883	519,306	13,750	8,079,362	7,617,076	282,162	76,225	96,822	7,097
Rhode Island	980	69,807	0	2,017,662	2,008,537	1,297	0	7,828	0
South Carolina	245,969	100,766	0	28,273,688	27,907,290	314,404	19,098	25,839	7,057
South Dakota..............	225,145	44,889	0	2,254,999	352,630	1,894,950	0	5,999	1,420
Tennessee	227,776	158,930	0	3,084,921	2,378,758	670,947	0	27,895	7,321
Texas	965,718	1,518,620	325,000	84,451,335	81,791,204	2,178,582	355,514	106,955	19,079
Utah	240,539	315,012	0	469,977	426,211	18,938	1,126	11,642	12,060
Vermont	47,274	77,956	5,460	386,375	365,110	16,903	0	4,362	0
Virginia.......................	155,103	330,189	100,685	14,015,983	13,588,841	339,890	14,951	54,650	17,651
Washington.................	140,318	396,382	0	5,388,072	4,474,312	860,955	1,180	41,151	10,474
West Virginia..............	80,058	28,578	0	1,740,278	1,714,766	14,539	0	10,265	707
Wisconsin....................	667,265	304,821	0	2,391,069	1,473,095	867,623	0	39,818	10,533
Wyoming.....................	71,611	34,517	0	365,558	292,967	66,869	0	3,536	2,187
District of Columbia...	0	176,650	67,497	141,558	114,336	0	19,780	3,444	3,999
American Samoa........	0	38	0	868	868	0	0	0	0
Fed. States of Micronesia	0	0	0	0	0	0	0	0	0
Guam	15,204	7,043	0	31,807	31,807	0	0	0	0
Marshall Islands.........	0	0	0	0	0	0	0	0	0
No. Mariana Islands...	63	710	0	73	73	0	0	0	0
Palau	35,000	0	0	0	0	0	0	0	0
Puerto Rico.................	83,856	116,641	0	4,135,383	4,131,212	0	0	4,171	0
Virgin Islands.............	4,062	2,864	0	289,231	283,816	0	0	426	4,989
Undistributed	0	0	0	210	210	0	0	0	0

Source: U.S. Department of Commerce, Bureau of the Census, Consolidated Federal Funds Report for Fiscal Year 2004, February 2006.

Note: Amounts represent dollar volume of direct loans made during the fiscal year.

Table 2.15
PER CAPITA AMOUNTS OF FEDERAL GOVERNMENT EXPENDITURE, BY MAJOR OBJECT CATEGORY, BY STATE AND OUTLYING AREA: FISCAL YEAR 2004
(In dollars)

State and outlying area	United States resident population— July 1, 2004 (a)	Total	Retirement and disability	Other direct payments	Grants	Procurement	Salaries and wages
United States	293,655,404	$7,222	$2,250	$1,588	$1,545	$1,089	$750
Alabama	4,530,182	8,619	2,854	1,770	1,547	1,678	771
Alaska	655,435	12,885	1,732	1,015	4,908	2,593	2,637
Arizona	5,743,834	7,309	2,253	1,265	1,456	1,706	628
Arkansas	2,752,629	7,080	2,690	1,833	1,701	308	548
California	35,893,799	6,474	1,785	1,435	1,519	1,121	614
Colorado	4,601,403	6,533	1,938	1,151	1,226	1,249	969
Connecticut	3,503,604	8,649	2,229	1,663	1,586	2,714	457
Delaware	830,364	6,326	2,512	1,406	1,495	319	595
Florida	17,397,161	7,009	2,762	1,864	1,127	658	597
Georgia	8,829,383	6,247	2,010	1,304	1,332	658	943
Hawaii	1,262,840	9,651	2,536	1,272	1,709	1,636	2,497
Idaho	1,393,262	6,437	2,191	1,184	1,432	986	644
Illinois	12,713,634	6,043	2,013	1,660	1,300	518	551
Indiana	6,237,569	6,079	2,248	1,604	1,192	642	394
Iowa	2,954,451	6,505	2,360	1,814	1,367	541	423
Kansas	2,735,502	6,993	2,344	1,755	1,268	819	807
Kentucky	4,145,922	7,649	2,552	1,573	1,626	1,118	779
Louisiana	4,515,770	7,298	2,210	1,982	1,724	757	624
Maine	1,317,253	8,248	2,723	1,406	2,094	1,299	727
Maryland	5,558,058	11,645	2,553	1,866	1,590	3,743	1,893
Massachusetts	6,416,505	8,279	2,211	1,928	2,163	1,422	554
Michigan	10,112,620	5,981	2,266	1,643	1,308	407	357
Minnesota	5,100,958	5,644	1,972	1,351	1,413	457	451
Mississippi	2,902,966	7,695	2,513	1,790	1,853	817	721
Missouri	5,754,618	7,947	2,445	1,893	1,518	1,389	702
Montana	926,865	8,085	2,583	1,758	2,155	633	956
Nebraska	1,747,214	6,751	2,329	1,831	1,449	399	743
Nevada	2,334,771	5,469	2,206	1,007	994	685	577
New Hampshire	1,299,500	6,124	2,330	1,086	1,446	758	503
New Jersey	8,698,879	6,353	2,175	1,673	1,303	705	498
New Mexico	1,903,289	10,437	2,459	1,301	2,450	3,138	1,089
New York	19,227,088	7,484	2,143	1,806	2,601	462	472
North Carolina	8,541,221	6,467	2,357	1,334	1,472	460	843
North Dakota	634,366	9,513	2,329	2,763	2,389	792	1,240
Ohio	11,459,011	6,388	2,291	1,564	1,441	605	487
Oklahoma	3,523,553	7,562	2,602	1,685	1,496	796	983
Oregon	3,594,586	6,084	2,351	1,404	1,442	357	529
Pennsylvania	12,406,292	7,649	2,672	2,089	1,605	751	533
Rhode Island	1,080,632	7,630	2,431	1,760	2,155	517	767
South Carolina	4,198,068	7,158	2,575	1,369	1,464	999	752
South Dakota	770,883	8,564	2,389	2,513	2,102	568	992
Tennessee	5,900,962	7,701	2,460	1,604	1,671	1,376	589
Texas	22,490,022	6,308	1,857	1,362	1,236	1,199	653
Utah	2,389,039	5,728	1,726	903	1,234	964	900
Vermont	621,394	7,456	2,280	1,363	2,291	870	652
Virginia	7,459,827	12,150	2,813	1,340	1,071	4,735	2,191
Washington	6,203,788	7,228	2,333	1,335	1,464	1,120	976
West Virginia	1,815,354	8,364	3,214	1,790	2,038	573	748
Wisconsin	5,509,026	5,728	2,190	1,356	1,358	479	344
Wyoming	506,529	8,673	2,354	1,266	3,229	795	1,029
District of Columbia	553,523	67,982	3,401	4,823	7,597	24,112	28,049
American Samoa	57,844	4,528	760	243	3,078	287	159
Fed. States of Micronesia	108,143	954	4	80	868	1	0
Guam	163,593	7,637	1,351	520	1,642	2,168	1,956
Marshall Islands	56,429	3,860	21	40	999	2,800	0
No. Mariana Islands	76,129	2,801	316	238	2,051	113	82
Palau	19,717	2,567	23	140	2,404	0	0
Puerto Rico	3,878,532	3,991	1,461	773	1,373	119	265
Virgin Islands	108,814	5,438	1,425	790	2,420	195	608

Source: U.S. Department of Commerce, Bureau of the Census, Consolidated Federal Funds Report for Fiscal Year 2004, February 2006.
Note: U.S. total population and per capita figures in the top row include only the 50 states and the District of Columbia; the U.S. Outlying Areas represented at the bottom of the table are excluded from this figure.
(a) All population figures represent resident population as of July 1, 2004.

Table 2.16
PERCENT DISTRIBUTION OF FEDERAL GOVERNMENT EXPENDITURE, BY MAJOR OBJECT CATEGORY, BY STATE AND OUTLYING AREA: FISCAL YEAR 2004
(In dollars)

State and outlying area	Percent distribution of United States resident population— July 1, 2004 (a)	Total	Retirement and disability	Other direct payments	Grants	Procurement	Salaries and wages
United States	100%	100%	100%	100%	100%	100%	100%
Alabama	1.5	1.8	1.9	1.7	1.5	2.2	1.5
Alaska	0.2	0.4	0.2	0.1	0.7	0.5	0.8
Arizona	2.0	1.9	1.9	1.5	1.8	2.9	1.6
Arkansas	0.9	0.9	1.1	1.1	1.0	0.2	0.7
California	12.2	10.7	9.6	11.0	11.9	11.9	9.8
Colorado	1.6	1.4	1.3	1.1	1.2	1.7	2.0
Connecticut	1.2	1.4	1.2	1.2	1.2	2.8	0.7
Delaware	0.3	0.2	0.3	0.2	0.3	0.1	0.2
Florida	5.9	5.6	7.2	6.9	4.3	3.4	4.6
Georgia	3.0	2.6	2.7	2.5	2.6	1.7	3.7
Hawaii	0.4	0.6	0.5	0.3	0.5	0.6	1.4
Idaho	0.5	0.4	0.5	0.4	0.4	0.4	0.4
Illinois	4.3	3.6	3.8	4.5	3.6	1.9	3.1
Indiana	2.1	1.8	2.1	2.1	1.6	1.2	1.1
Iowa	1.0	0.9	1.1	1.1	0.9	0.5	0.6
Kansas	0.9	0.9	1.0	1.0	0.8	0.7	1.0
Kentucky	1.4	1.5	1.6	1.4	1.5	1.4	1.4
Louisiana	1.5	1.5	1.5	1.9	1.7	1.0	1.2
Maine	0.4	0.5	0.5	0.4	0.6	0.5	0.4
Maryland	1.9	3.0	2.1	2.2	1.9	6.1	4.7
Massachusetts	2.2	2.5	2.1	2.6	3.0	2.7	1.6
Michigan	3.4	2.8	3.4	3.5	2.9	1.2	1.6
Minnesota	1.7	1.3	1.5	1.5	1.6	0.7	1.0
Mississippi	1.0	1.0	1.1	1.1	1.2	0.7	0.9
Missouri	2.0	2.1	2.1	2.3	1.9	2.4	1.8
Montana	0.3	0.3	0.4	0.3	0.4	0.2	0.4
Nebraska	0.6	0.5	0.6	0.7	0.6	0.2	0.6
Nevada	0.8	0.6	0.8	0.5	0.5	0.5	0.6
New Hampshire	0.4	0.4	0.5	0.3	0.4	0.3	0.3
New Jersey	3.0	2.6	2.8	3.1	2.5	1.8	1.9
New Mexico	0.6	0.9	0.7	0.5	1.0	1.8	0.9
New York	6.5	6.7	6.2	7.4	10.9	2.6	4.0
North Carolina	2.9	2.6	3.0	2.4	2.7	1.2	3.2
North Dakota	0.2	0.3	0.2	0.4	0.3	0.1	0.3
Ohio	3.9	3.4	3.9	3.8	3.6	2.0	2.5
Oklahoma	1.2	1.2	1.4	1.3	1.1	0.8	1.5
Oregon	1.2	1.0	1.3	1.1	1.1	0.4	0.8
Pennsylvania	4.2	4.4	5.0	5.5	4.3	2.7	2.9
Rhode Island	0.4	0.4	0.4	0.4	0.5	0.2	0.4
South Carolina	1.4	1.4	1.6	1.2	1.3	1.2	1.4
South Dakota	0.3	0.3	0.3	0.4	0.4	0.1	0.3
Tennessee	2.0	2.1	2.2	2.0	2.1	2.4	1.5
Texas	7.7	6.6	6.3	6.5	6.0	7.9	6.5
Utah	0.8	0.6	0.6	0.5	0.6	0.7	1.0
Vermont	0.2	0.2	0.2	0.2	0.3	0.2	0.2
Virginia	2.5	4.2	3.1	2.1	1.7	10.4	7.2
Washington	2.1	2.1	2.2	1.8	2.0	2.0	2.7
West Virginia	0.6	0.7	0.9	0.7	0.8	0.3	0.6
Wisconsin	1.9	1.5	1.8	1.6	1.6	0.8	0.8
Wyoming	0.2	0.2	0.2	0.1	0.4	0.1	0.2
District of Columbia	0.2	1.7	0.3	0.6	0.9	3.9	6.9
American Samoa	0.0	0.0	0.0	0.0	0.0	0.0	0.0
Fed. States of Micronesia	0.0	0.0	0.0	0.0	0.0	2.6	0.0
Guam	0.1	0.1	0.0	0.0	0.1	0.1	0.1
Marshall Islands	0.0	0.0	0.0	0.0	0.0	0.1	0.0
No. Mariana Islands	0.0	0.0	0.0	0.0	0.0	0.0	0.0
Palau	0.0	0.0	0.0	0.0	0.0	0.0	0.0
Puerto Rico	1.3	0.7	0.8	0.6	1.2	0.1	0.5
Virgin Islands	0.0	0.0	0.0	0.0	0.1	0.0	0.0
Undistributed	0.0	1.1	0.0	0.0	0.0	5.5	1.8

Source: U.S. Department of Commerce, Bureau of the Census, Consolidated Federal Funds Report for Fiscal Year 2004, February 2006.

Note: Values for the 50 states, the District of Columbia, and the U.S. Outlying Areas were used in calculating these distributions.

(a) All population figures represent resident population as of July 1, 2004.

Table 2.17
FEDERAL GOVERNMENT EXPENDITURE FOR DEFENSE DEPARTMENT AND ALL OTHER AGENCIES, BY STATE AND OUTLYING AREA: FISCAL YEAR 2004

State and outlying area	Federal expenditure (millions of dollars)		Per capita federal expenditure (dollars) (a)		Percent distribution of federal expenditure	
	Department of Defense	All other federal agencies	Department of Defense	All other federal agencies	Department of Defense	All other federal agencies
United States	347,689	1,814,259	1,147.75	6,074.00	100%	100%
Alabama	8,725	30,323	1,925.95	6,693.45	2.5	1.7
Alaska	2,522	5,924	3,847.17	9,037.99	0.7	0.3
Arizona	11,135	30,844	1,938.63	5,369.96	3.2	1.7
Arkansas............................	1,596	17,893	579.67	6,500.41	0.5	1
California	42,723	189,664	1,190.27	5,284.03	12.3	10.5
Colorado	6,182	23,878	1,343.48	5,189.38	1.8	1.3
Connecticut	9,735	20,569	2,778.47	5,870.91	2.8	1.1
Delaware............................	629	4,624	758	5,568.32	0.2	0.3
Florida	17,419	104,514	1,001.26	6,007.56	5	5.8
Georgia	10,175	44,978	1,152.39	5,094.13	2.9	2.5
Hawaii................................	4,772	7,415	3,778.83	5,871.69	1.4	0.4
Idaho..................................	744	8,225	533.75	5,903.09	0.2	0.5
Illinois	5,918	70,910	465.51	5,577.48	1.7	3.9
Indiana...............................	4,465	33,453	715.83	5,363.22	1.3	1.8
Iowa	1,262	17,956	427.01	6,077.71	0.4	1
Kansas	2,948	16,183	1,077.66	5,915.82	0.8	0.9
Kentucky	5,132	26,582	1,237.78	6,411.55	1.5	1.5
Louisiana	4,433	28,521	981.61	6,315.94	1.3	1.6
Maine.................................	2,297	8,568	1,743.58	6,504.30	0.7	0.5
Maryland	13,796	50,930	2,482.16	9,163.26	4	2.8
Massachusetts.....................	8,240	44,881	1,284.15	6,994.57	2.4	2.5
Michigan............................	3,783	56,706	374.06	5,607.43	1.1	3.1
Minnesota	2,112	26,679	414.02	5,230.16	0.6	1.5
Mississippi	3,624	18,713	1,248.53	6,446.26	1	1
Missouri	8,585	37,145	1,491.80	6,454.88	2.5	2
Montana	658	6,836	709.69	7,375.16	0.2	0.4
Nebraska............................	1,321	10,474	755.83	5,994.82	0.4	0.6
Nevada	1,612	11,158	690.31	4,778.92	0.5	0.6
New Hampshire...................	1,125	6,833	865.84	5,258.45	0.3	0.4
New Jersey..........................	5,843	49,421	671.69	5,681.36	1.7	2.7
New Mexico	2,471	17,393	1,298.09	9,138.56	0.7	1
New York	7,555	136,348	392.93	7,091.44	2.2	7.5
North Carolina	8,679	46,554	1,016.17	5,450.52	2.5	2.6
North Dakota......................	833	5,202	1,312.35	8,200.77	0.2	0.3
Ohio	7,539	65,656	657.9	5,729.67	2.2	3.6
Oklahoma	4,279	22,365	1,214.29	6,347.37	1.2	1.2
Oregon	1,311	20,560	364.71	5,719.69	0.4	1.1
Pennsylvania	9,037	85,864	728.39	6,920.98	2.6	4.7
Rhode Island	1,022	7,223	945.81	6,684.18	0.3	0.4
South Carolina	4,881	25,170	1,162.75	5,995.58	1.4	1.4
South Dakota......................	658	5,944	853.24	7,710.62	0.2	0.3
Tennessee	3,770	41,670	638.92	7,061.61	1.1	2.3
Texas	31,895	109,963	1,418.19	4,889.43	9.2	6.1
Utah	3,305	10,378	1,383.53	4,344.14	1	0.6
Vermont..............................	623	4,010	1,002.56	6,453.15	0.2	0.2
Virginia..............................	38,533	52,105	5,165.39	6,984.75	11.1	2.9
Washington.........................	8,321	36,520	1,341.21	5,886.77	2.4	2
West Virginia......................	734	14,449	404.35	7,959.58	0.2	0.8
Wisconsin...........................	2,414	29,140	438.23	5,289.44	0.7	1.6
Wyoming............................	412	3,981	813.9	7,859.46	0.1	0.2
District of Columbia	5,264	32,366	9,509.21	58,472.89	1.5	1.8
American Samoa	10	252	177.37	4,350.91	0	0
Fed. States of Micronesia...	0	103	0	953.91	0	0
Guam	660	590	4,032.43	3,605.00	0.2	0
Marshall Islands.................	158	60	2,800.23	1,059.64	0	0
No. Mariana Islands	5	208	67.92	2,732.69	0	0
Palau	0	51	0	2,566.87	0	0
Puerto Rico.........................	732	14,746	188.78	3,802.05	0.2	0.8
Virgin Islands	26	565	241.53	5,196.61	0	0
Undistributed	9,055	14,020	0	0	2.6	0.8

Source: U.S. Department of Commerce, Bureau of the Census, Consolidated Federal Funds Report for Fiscal Year 2004, February 2006.

(a) All population figures represent resident population as of July 1, 2004.

Table 2.18
STATE RANKINGS FOR PER CAPITA AMOUNTS
OF FEDERAL GOVERNMENT EXPENDITURE: FISCAL YEAR 2004

State	Total	Retirement and disability	Other direct payments	Grants	Procurement	Salaries and wages
Alabama	9	2	15	22	7	18
Alaska	1	49	48	1	5	1
Arizona	24	33	44	30	6	29
Arkansas	28	6	9	16	50	38
California	34	48	28	23	15	31
Colorado	32	46	46	46	13	11
Connecticut	8	35	21	21	4	45
Delaware	39	15	29	26	49	33
Florida	29	4	8	48	33	32
Georgia	41	44	40	39	32	13
Hawaii	5	13	42	15	8	2
Idaho	36	39	45	35	19	28
Illinois	45	43	22	42	40	37
Indiana	44	34	25	47	34	48
Iowa	33	21	11	37	39	47
Kansas	30	25	18	43	22	16
Kentucky	19	12	26	18	17	17
Louisiana	25	37	4	14	28	30
Maine	13	5	30	11	12	23
Maryland	3	11	7	20	2	4
Massachusetts	12	36	5	7	9	36
Michigan	46	32	23	40	46	49
Minnesota	49	45	36	36	45	46
Mississippi	17	14	13	13	23	24
Missouri	15	18	6	24	10	25
Montana	14	9	17	9	35	12
Nebraska	31	28	10	31	47	22
Nevada	50	38	49	50	31	35
New Hampshire	42	27	47	32	27	41
New Jersey	38	41	20	41	30	42
New Mexico	4	17	41	4	3	6
New York	22	42	12	3	43	44
North Carolina	35	22	39	27	44	15
North Dakota	6	29	1	5	26	5
Ohio	37	30	27	34	36	43
Oklahoma	21	8	19	25	24	9
Oregon	43	24	31	33	48	40
Pennsylvania	18	7	3	19	29	39
Rhode Island	20	19	16	8	41	19
South Carolina	27	10	32	29	18	20
South Dakota	10	20	2	10	38	8
Tennessee	16	16	24	17	11	34
Texas	40	47	34	44	14	26
Utah	48	50	50	45	20	14
Vermont	23	31	33	6	21	27
Virginia	2	3	37	49	1	3
Washington	26	26	38	28	16	10
West Virginia	11	1	14	12	37	21
Wisconsin	47	40	35	38	42	50
Wyoming	7	23	43	2	25	7

Source: U.S. Department of Commerce, Bureau of the Census, Consolidated Federal Funds Report for Fiscal Year 2004, February 2006.

Note: States are ranked from largest per capita amount of federal funds (1) to smallest per capita amount of federal funds (50). Rankings are based upon per capita amounts shown in Table 2.10. Federal funds for loans and insurance coverage are excluded from consideration in this table. Also excluded are per capita amounts from the District of Columbia and the U.S. Outlying Areas.

Chapter Three

STATE LEGISLATIVE BRANCH

"Following 2005 elections, the big picture of partisan control in states remains the same... Control of many legislative chambers will be in play in 2006 elections."

—Tim Storey

2005 Legislative Elections and Partisan Control
By Tim Storey

Following 2005 elections, the big picture of partisan control in states remains the same. Republicans control 20 state legislatures and Democrats are in charge of 19. Ten states have split control. The Nebraska legislature is unicameral and also nonpartisan. Even with Democrats retaining governors' mansions in the two off-year election states, they still lag substantially in control of governorships—28 Republicans to 22 Democrats.

State Political Control
Unchanged after Off-Year Elections

The legislative elections of 2005 were the smallest of the decade. With only two legislative chambers up for grabs, fewer seats were in play than in any November from 2000 redistricting to the 2010 census. Only the lower chambers in New Jersey and Virginia had regularly scheduled legislative elections in 2005. Voters in the Garden State and the Old Dominion endorsed the political status quo in 2005 off-year elections by returning the same party to run their lower chambers. Both states voted to leave the political landscape unchanged with Democrats controlling the New Jersey legislature, and Republicans holding the reigns in Virginia.

Both states also replaced outgoing Democratic governors with new Democratic governors. When all the votes were tallied, Democrats made ever so slight gains in New Jersey and Virginia, netting one seat in the New Jersey Assembly and two seats in the Virginia House of Delegates. Virginia Republicans still have a comfortable majority in the state House—with 57 Republicans, 40 Democrats and three Independents. In the New Jersey Assembly, the final partisan composition was 48 Democrats, 32 Republicans.

In Virginia, 64 of the 100 House races only had a candidate from one of the two major parties. In New Jersey, voters choose two Assembly members in each of the 40 districts. Only three Assembly districts were contested by candidates from only one of the two major parties. There were 23 third party candidates running for the New Jersey Assembly, although none

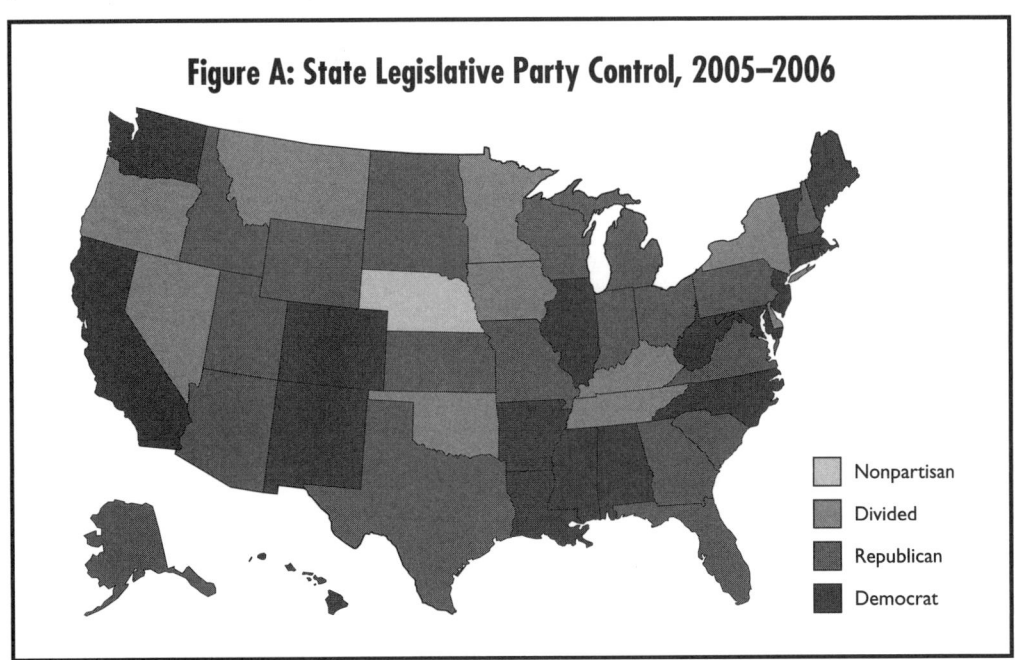

Figure A: State Legislative Party Control, 2005–2006

Nonpartisan
Divided
Republican
Democrat

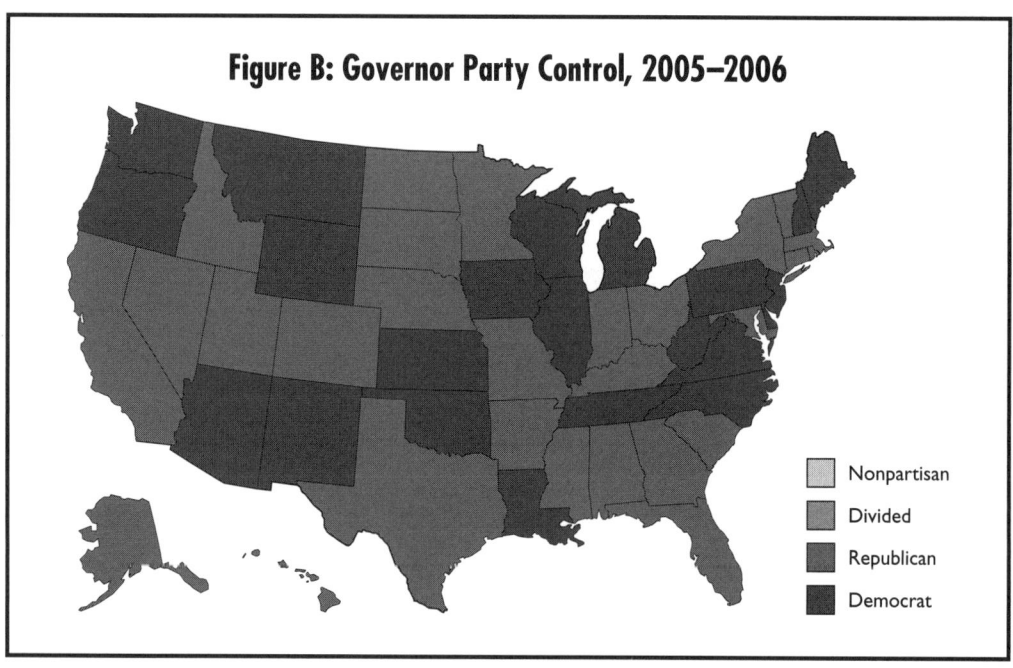

Figure B: Governor Party Control, 2005–2006

Nonpartisan
Divided
Republican
Democrat

were successful. Perhaps the most unusual third party challenge was in the 32nd New Jersey Assembly district where a candidate from the "Politicians are Crooks" party won only 2 percent of the vote.

2006 Party Control of States— The Big Picture

Following 2005 elections, the big picture of partisan control in states remains the same. Republicans control 20 state legislatures and Democrats are in charge in 19. Ten states have split control. The Nebraska legislature is unicameral and also nonpartisan. Even with Democrats retaining governors' mansions in the two off-year election states, they still lag substantially in control of governorships—28 Republicans to 22 Democrats. Democratic gains in November 2005 and in subsequent special elections give them the symbolic advantage of having more state legislative seats than the GOP by an infinitesimal 15-seat margin out of 7,382. That translates to an advantage in total legislative seats of less than one-fifth of 1 percent of all seats. The two parties remain essentially tied at the grassroots level of state legislative seats.

Redistricting Changes Soundly Defeated

Perhaps the biggest stories in 2005 legislative elections were the unsuccessful redistricting reform ballot issues in California and Ohio. Because redistricting is such a major factor in how legislative elections play out, the results of these efforts to dramatically alter the redistricting process in two major states could have influenced the outcome of legislative elections for years to come.

However, California and Ohio voters soundly rejected efforts to strip legislatures of their power to redraw political boundaries. In both states, voters overwhelmingly decided they preferred redistricting be done by accountable elected officials rather than a small number of non-elected commissioners. The California proposition that would have shifted redistricting authority to a three-member panel of retired judges failed 59.5 percent no to 40.5 percent yes. And in Ohio, a measure to give redistricting to an "independent" commission failed 70 percent no to 30 percent yes. In Ohio, legislative redistricting is already done by an independent commission, but the measure would have taken congressional redistricting and legislative line drawing and given it to a different commission constrained by strict criteria to draw competitive districts.

Current Partisan Composition and Control

2006 is shaping up to be a blockbuster election year at the state level. For the past several years, control of legislatures has teetered on a thin line between Democrats and Republicans with neither party gaining a strong upper hand. 2006 could be the year that one opens up a lead and begins an era of dominance.

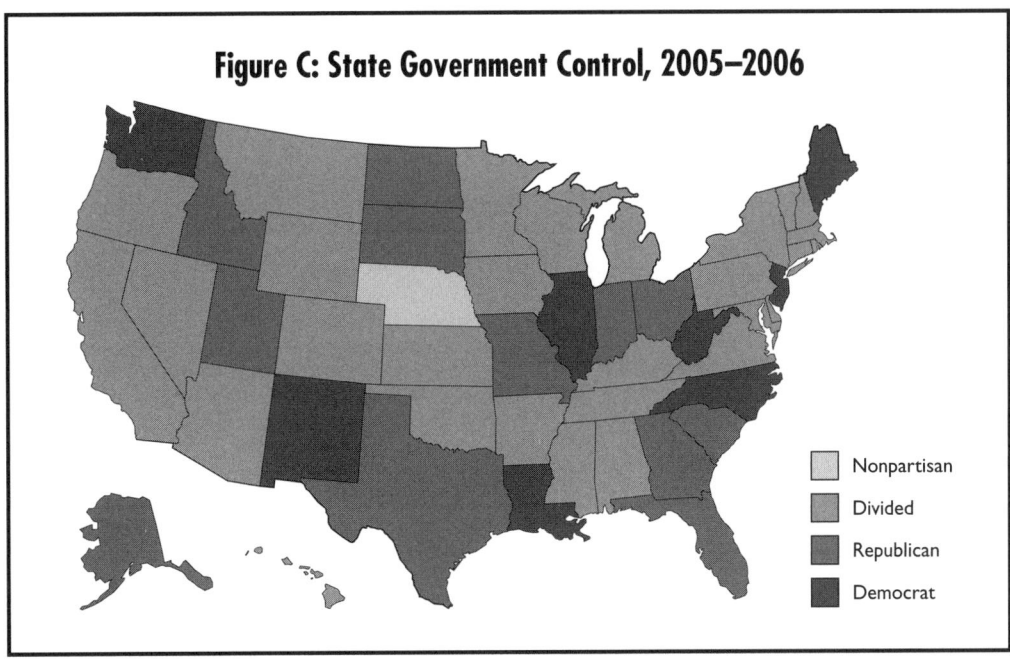

Figure C: State Government Control, 2005–2006

Nonpartisan
Divided
Republican
Democrat

Or it may be the year that establishes that the status quo of perpetual parity is here to stay. Just under 84 percent of all legislative seats are up for election in 2006, so the landscape is likely to change considerably in November. At least some, and in most cases all, of the legislative seats are up for grabs in 46 states. Louisiana, Mississippi, New Jersey and Virginia do not have legislative elections this year.

On average, 12 legislative chambers switch control in every two-year election cycle. The 2004 elections saw control switch in 12 chambers—right on average. It may be that fewer chambers will move in 2006 given that there is no race for the White House to drive up voter turnout. The elections in 2006 will also be the third in most states under district plans drawn using 2000 census data. That bodes for more stability, or fewer party control shifts, because the "X" factor of redistricting is fading in importance.

Heading into 2006 sessions, states are almost perfectly divided. Republicans control both chambers in 20 state legislatures, and Democrats boast only one less—19 states.

In 10 states, party control is divided. Democrats are coming off a strong showing in both 2004 and 2005 legislative elections and hold a symbolic edge in the total number of legislative seats. Heading into 2006 legislative sessions, there are 18 more Democratic legislators than GOP legislators, but out of 7,382 seats, that advantage is only a fraction of 1 percent. Democrats also had success in a handful of special elections in late 2005 and early 2006, boosting their optimism that 2006 will be a good year.

Many factors—such as strong candidates, good campaigns, redistricting and election funding— determine which party wins legislative races and thus can craft policies on critical issues that matter to Americans like immigration, education, environment, energy and transportation. One key factor in 2006 elections might actually be the popularity of President George W. Bush, even though he will not be on the ballot. Historically, the party of the president almost always loses seats in legislatures during mid-presidential term elections. That trend goes back to 1938. Bush became the first incumbent to break that losing legacy in the 2002 election netting a whopping 177 legislative seats. Will he be as successful in 2006 or will the grassroots races for state legislatures reflect a setback for the president?

Control of many legislative chambers will be in play in 2006 elections. There are 17 state senates where a shift of only three seats would alter partisan control. In 12 state houses, a shift of five or fewer seats will change the control. Key states to watch are Colorado, Delaware, Iowa, Maine, Michigan, Montana, Nevada, Oregon and Tennessee where both chambers are highly competitive. In all these states, recent elections have been impossible to predict with surprises being the norm.

Top-of-the-ticket races will also influence legislative elections. The governors' mansions in 36 states are up for grabs in 2006. Republicans have held a distinct edge in governors for several years, currently holding a 28-22 advantage. Of the 36 states holding 2006 gubernatorial elections, 22 have Republican governors and 14 have Democrats. Divided state government is the norm with 29 states having split control—neither party holding the state house, senate and governor's office. Republicans control everything in 12 states, and Democrats hold all the marbles in eight states. For roughly the past 10 years, divided government has been common in about 30 states, forcing the two parties to work together to accomplish any public policy goals.

Historic Partisan Control

During the last half of the 20th century, Democrats dominated control of state legislatures—reaching a high-water mark in the mid-1970s by holding nearly 70 percent of all legislative seats. Beginning in the early 1980s, the GOP started chipping away at the Democratic dominance making huge gains in the 1994 "realignment" election cycle. In the critical 2002 election after redistricting, the GOP surpassed Democrats in terms of total seats for the first time since 1952. Since then, Democrats have rebounded slightly to re-take the lead in overall control of seats.

2006 is clearly a pivotal year for both major parties. It will also be the election that sets the table for control of 2011 redistricting. In 44 states, legislatures are responsible for drawing congressional districts, and in 38 states, they craft their own lines. It is not too early to start thinking about the 2010 census and subsequent redistricting. Party strategists are well aware of this timing and will be focused on legislative races with renewed vigor.

About the Author

Tim Storey is a senior fellow in the Legislative Management Program of the National Conference of State Legislatures (NCSL) in Denver, Colo. He specializes in the areas of elections and redistricting as well as legislative staff organization and management. He has staffed NCSL's Redistricting Task Force since 1990 and authored many articles on the redistricting and elections process. Every two years, Storey leads NCSL's elections project tracking and analyzing the outcome of state legislative races and statewide ballot questions. He received his undergraduate degree from Mars Hill College and his master's degree from the Graduate School of Public Affairs of the University of Colorado.

Table 3.1
NAMES OF STATE LEGISLATIVE BODIES AND CONVENING PLACES

State or other jurisdiction	Both bodies	Upper house	Lower house	Convening place
Alabama	Legislature	Senate	House of Representatives	State House
Alaska	Legislature	Senate	House of Representatives	State Capitol
Arizona	Legislature	Senate	House of Representatives	State Capitol
Arkansas	General Assembly	Senate	House of Representatives	State Capitol
California	Legislature	Senate	Assembly	State Capitol
Colorado	General Assembly	Senate	House of Representatives	State Capitol
Connecticut	General Assembly	Senate	House of Representatives	State Capitol
Delaware	General Assembly	Senate	House of Representatives	Legislative Hall
Florida	Legislature	Senate	House of Representatives	The Capitol
Georgia	General Assembly	Senate	House of Representatives	State Capitol
Hawaii	Legislature	Senate	House of Representatives	State Capitol
Idaho	Legislature	Senate	House of Representatives	State Capitol
Illinois	General Assembly	Senate	House of Representatives	State House
Indiana	General Assembly	Senate	House of Representatives	State House
Iowa	General Assembly	Senate	House of Representatives	State Capitol
Kansas	Legislature	Senate	House of Representatives	State Capitol
Kentucky	General Assembly	Senate	House of Representatives	State Capitol
Louisiana	Legislature	Senate	House of Representatives	State Capitol
Maine	Legislature	Senate	House of Representatives	State House
Maryland	General Assembly	Senate	House of Delegates	State House
Massachusetts	General Court	Senate	House of Representatives	State House
Michigan	Legislature	Senate	House of Representatives	State Capitol
Minnesota	Legislature	Senate	House of Representatives	State Capitol
Mississippi	Legislature	Senate	House of Representatives	State Capitol
Missouri	General Assembly	Senate	House of Representatives	State Capitol
Montana	Legislature	Senate	House of Representatives	State Capitol
Nebraska	Legislature	(a)		State Capitol
Nevada	Legislature	Senate	Assembly	Legislative Building
New Hampshire	General Court	Senate	House of Representatives	State House
New Jersey	Legislature	Senate	General Assembly	State House
New Mexico	Legislature	Senate	House of Representatives	State Capitol
New York	Legislature	Senate	Assembly	State Capitol
North Carolina	General Assembly	Senate	House of Representatives	State Legislative Building
North Dakota	Legislative Assembly	Senate	House of Representatives	State Capitol
Ohio	General Assembly	Senate	House of Representatives	State House
Oklahoma	Legislature	Senate	House of Representatives	State Capitol
Oregon	Legislative Assembly	Senate	House of Representatives	State Capitol
Pennsylvania	General Assembly	Senate	House of Representatives	Main Capitol Building
Rhode Island	General Assembly	Senate	House of Representatives	State House
South Carolina	General Assembly	Senate	House of Representatives	State House
South Dakota	Legislature	Senate	House of Representatives	State Capitol
Tennessee	General Assembly	Senate	House of Representatives	State Capitol
Texas	Legislature	Senate	House of Representatives	State Capitol
Utah	Legislature	Senate	House of Representatives	State Capitol
Vermont	General Assembly	Senate	House of Representatives	State House
Virginia	General Assembly	Senate	House of Delegates	State Capitol
Washington	Legislature	Senate	House of Representatives	State Capitol
West Virginia	Legislature	Senate	House of Delegates	State Capitol
Wisconsin	Legislature	Senate	Assembly (b)	State Capitol
Wyoming	Legislature	Senate	House of Representatives	State Capitol
Dist. of Columbia	Council of the District of Columbia	(a)		Council Chamber
American Samoa	Legislature	Senate	House of Representatives	Maota Fono
Guam	Legislature	(a)		Congress Building
No. Mariana Islands	Legislature	Senate	House of Representatives	Civic Center Building
Puerto Rico	Legislative Assembly	Senate	House of Representatives	The Capitol
U.S. Virgin Islands	Legislature	(a)		Capitol Building

Source: The Council of State Governments, *Directory I—Elective Officials 2005.*

(a) Unicameral legislature. Except in Dist. of Columbia, members go by the title Senator.

(b) Members of the lower house go by the title Representative.

Table 3.2
LEGISLATIVE SESSIONS: LEGAL PROVISIONS

State or other jurisdiction	Regular sessions				Special sessions		
	Legislature convenes			Limitation on length of session (a)	Legislature may call	Legislature may determine subject	Limitation on length of session
	Year	Month	Day				
Alabama	Annual	Jan. Mar. Feb.	2nd Tues. (b) 1st Tues. (c)(d) 1st Tues. (e)	30 L in 105 C	No	Yes (f)	12 L in 30 C
Alaska	Annual	Jan.	2nd Mon.	121 C	By petition, 2/3 members, each house	Yes	30 C
Arizona	Annual	Jan.	2nd Mon.	(i)	By petition, 2/3 members, each house	Yes	None
Arkansas	Biennial–odd year	Jan.	2nd Mon.	60 C (h)	No	No (j)	None
California	(l)	Jan.	1st Mon. (d)	None	No	No	None
Colorado	Annual	Jan.	No later than 2nd Wed.	120 C	By petition, 2/3 members, each house	Yes	None
Connecticut	Annual	Jan. Feb.	Wed. after 1st Mon. (n) Wed. after 1st Mon. (o)	(p)	By petition, 2/3 members, each house (q) Joint call, presiding officers, both houses	Yes	None
Delaware	Annual	Jan.	2nd Tues.	June 30	Joint call, presiding officers, both houses	Yes	None
Florida	Annual	Mar.	1st Tues. after 1st Mon.(s)	60 C (h)	Joint call, presiding officers, toth houses or by petition	Yes	20 C (h)
Georgia	Annual	Jan.	2nd Mon.	40 L	By petition, 3/5 members, each house	No	40 L
Hawaii	Annual	Jan.	3rd Wed.	60 L (h)	By petition, 2/3 members, each house	Yes	30 L (h)
Idaho	Annual	Jan.	Mon. on or nearest 9th day	None	No	No	20 C
Illinois	Annual	Jan.	2nd Wed.	None (ll)	Joint call, presiding officers, both houses	Yes (g)	None
Indiana	Annual	Jan.	2nd Mon. (d)(t)	odd–61 C or Apr. 29; even–30 C or Mar. 14	No	Yes	30 L or 40 C
Iowa	Annual	Jan.	2nd Mon.	None	By petition, 2/3 members, each house	Yes	None
Kansas	Annual	Jan.	2nd Mon.	odd–None; even–90 C (h)	Petition to governor or 2/3 members, each house	Yes	None
Kentucky	Annual	Jan.	1st Tues after 1st Mon.	odd–30 L even–60 L	No	No	None
Louisiana	Annual	Mar. (o) Apr. (n)	last Mon. (o) last Mon. (n)	even–60 L in 85 C; odd–45 L in 60 C	By petition, majority, each house	Yes	30 C
Maine	(l)(m)	Dec. Jan.	1st Wed. (b) Wed. after 1st Tues. (o)	3rd Wed. of June 3rd Wed. of April	By petition, majority, each house	Yes	None
Maryland	Annual	Jan.	2nd Wed.	90 C	By petition, majority, each house	Yes	30 C
Massachusetts	Biennial	Jan.	1st Wed.	(w)	By petition (x)	Yes	None
Michigan	Annual	Jan.	2nd Wed.	None	No	No	None
Minnesota	(y)	Jan.	Tues. after 1st Mon. (n) 3rd Sat. in May (y)	120 L or 1st Mon. after	No	Yes	None

See footnotes at end of table.

LEGISLATIVE SESSIONS: LEGAL PROVISIONS—Continued

State or other jurisdiction	Regular sessions				Special sessions		
	Legislature convenes			Limitation on length of session (a)	Legislature may call	Legislature may determine subject	Limitation on length of session
	Year	Month	Day				
Mississippi	Annual	Jan.	Tues. after 1st Mon.	125 C (z); 90 C (z)	No	No	None
Missouri	Annual	Jan.	Wed. after 1st Mon.	May 30	By petition, 3/4 members, each house	Yes (g)	30 C (aa)
Montana	Biennial–odd year	Jan.	1st Mon.	90 L	By petition, majority, each house	Yes	None
Nebraska	Annual	Jan.	Wed. after 1st Mon.	odd–90 L; even–60 L	By petition, 2/3 members each house	Yes	None
Nevada	Biennial–odd year	Feb.	1st Mon.	120 C	No (oo)	No	None (k)
New Hampshire	Annual	Jan.	Wed. after 1st Tues.	45 L	By petition, 2/3 members, each house	Yes	15 L (r)
New Jersey	Annual (mm)	Jan.	2nd Tues. of even year	None	By petition, majority, each house (nn)	Yes	None
New Mexico	Annual	Jan.	3rd Tues.	odd–60 C; even–30 C	By petition, 3/5 members, each house	Yes (g)	30 C
New York	Annual	Jan. (kk)	Wed. after 1st Mon.	None	By petition, 2/3 members, each house	Yes (g)	None
North Carolina	(y)	Jan.	3rd Wed. after 2nd Mon. (n)	None	By petition, 3/5 members, each house	Yes	None
North Dakota	Biennial–odd year	Jan.	Tues. after Jan. 3, but not later than Jan. 11	80 L in the biennium	Yes (ff)	Yes	None (ff)
Ohio	Annual (mm)	Jan.	1st Mon. (ee)	None	Joint call, presiding officers, both houses	Yes	None
Oklahoma	Annual	Feb.	1st Mon.	last Fri. in May	By vote, 2/3 members, each house	Yes	None
Oregon	Biennial–odd year	Jan.	2nd Mon.	None	By petition, majority, each house	Yes	None
Pennsylvania	(dd)	Jan.	1st Tues.	None	Governor may call	No	None
Rhode Island	Annual	Jan.	1st. Tues.	None	Joint call, presiding officers, both houses	Yes	None
South Carolina	Biennial	Jan.	2nd Tues.	None	By vote, 2/3 members, each house	Yes	None
South Dakota	Annual	Jan.	2nd Tues.	odd–40 L; even–35 L	By petition, 2/3 members, each house	Yes	None
Tennessee	Annual (bb)	Jan.	2nd Tues.	90 L (u)	By petition, 2/3 members, each house	Yes	30 L (u)
Texas	Biennial–odd year	Jan.	2nd Tues.	140 C	No	No	30 C
Utah	Annual	Jan.	3rd. Mon.	45 C	No	No	30C
Vermont	Annual	Jan.	Wed. after 1st Mon.	None	No	Yes	None (gg)
Virginia	Annual	Jan.	2nd Wed.	odd–30 C (h); even–60 C (h)	By petition, 2/3 members, each house	Yes	None (gg)
Washington	Annual	Jan.	2nd Mon.	odd–105 C; even–60 C	By vote, 2/3 members, each house	Yes	30 C
West Virginia	Annual	Jan	2nd Wed.	60 C (h)	By petition, 3/5 members, each house	Yes (g)	None
Wisconsin	Biennial	Jan.	1st Mon.	None	By petition, majority members each house	Yes	None

See footnotes at end of table.

LEGISLATIVE SESSIONS: LEGAL PROVISIONS—Continued

State or other jurisdiction	Regular sessions				Special sessions		
	Legislature convenes			Limitation on length of session (a)	Legislature may call	Legislature may determine subject	Limitation on length of session
	Year	Month	Day				
Wyoming..............	Annual	Jan.(odd yrs.) Feb. (even yrs.)	2nd Tues.(odd yrs.) 2nd Mon. (even yrs.)	odd—40 L; even—20 L; biennium—60L	By petition, majority members each house	Yes	20 L
Dist. of Columbia	(hh)	Jan.	2nd day	None		No	None
American Samoa	Annual	Jan. July	2nd Mon. 2nd Mon.	45 L 45 L	No	No	None
Guam	Annual	Jan.	2nd Mon. (ii)	None	No	No	None
No. Mariana Islands	Annual	(jj)	(d)(jj)	90 L (jj)	Upon request of presiding officers, both houses	Yes (g)	10 C
Puerto Rico..............	Annual (v)	Jan. Aug.	2nd Mon. 3rd Mon.	5 mo. 4 mo.	No	No	20 C
U.S. Virgin Islands	Annual	Jan. (cc)	2nd Mon. (cc)	None	No, Governor calls	No	None

Source: The Council of State Governments' survey, December 2005.

Key:
C — Calendar day
L — Legislative day (in some states called a session day or workday; definition may vary slightly, however, generally refers to any day on which either house of legislature is in session).
(a) Applies to each year unless otherwise indicated.
(b) General election year (quadrennial election year).
(c) Year after quadrennial election.
(d) Legal provision for organizational session prior to stated convening date. Alabama—in the year after quadrennial election, second Tuesday in January for 10 C. California—in the even-numbered general election year, first Monday in December for an organizational session, recess until the first Monday in January of the odd-numbered year. Indiana—third Tuesday after first Monday in November. No. Mariana Islands—in year after general election, second Monday in January.
(e) Other years.
(f) By 2/3 vote each house.
(g) Only if legislature convenes itself. Special sessions (extraordinary sessions) called by the legislature are unlimited in scope in New Mexico.
(h) Session may be extended by vote of members in both houses. Arkansas—2/3 vote. Florida—3/5 vote, session may be extended by vote of members in each house. Hawaii—petition of 2/3 membership for maximum 15-day extension. Kansas—2/3 vote. Virginia—2/3 vote for 30 C extension. West Virginia—may be extended by the governor.
(i) No constitutional or statutory provision; however, by legislative rule regular sessions shall be adjourned sine die no later than Saturday of the week during which the 100th day from the beginning of each regular session falls. The Speaker/President may by declaration authorize the extension of the session for a period not to exceed seven additional days. Thereafter the session can be extended only by a majority vote of the House/Senate.
(j) After governor's business has been disposed of, members may remain in session up to 15 C by a 2/3 vote of both houses.
(k) No limit, however legislators are only paid up to 20 calendar days during a special session.
(l) Regular sessions begin after general election, in December of even-numbered year. In California, legislature meets in December for an organizational session, recesses until the first Monday in January of the odd-numbered year and continues in session until November 30 of next even-numbered year. In Maine, session which begins

in December of general election year runs into the following year (odd-numbered); second session begins in next even-numbered year.
(m) Second session limited to consideration of specific types of legislation. Maine—budgetary matters; legislation in the governor's call; emergency legislation; legislation referred to committees for study.
(n) Odd-numbered years
(o) Even-numbered years.
(p) Odd-numbered years—not later than Wednesday after first Monday in June; even-numbered years—not later than Wednesday after first Monday in May.
(q) Notice sent to secretary of state.
(r) Limitation is on payment of legislative pay and mileage.
(s) A regular session of the legislature shall convene on the first Tuesday after the first Monday of each odd-numbered year, and on the first Tuesday after the first Monday in March, or such other date as may be fixed by law, of each even-numbered year.
(t) Legislators may reconvene at any time after organizational meeting; however, second Monday in January is the final date by which regular session must be in process.
(u) 90 legislative days over a two-year period. During special sessions members will be paid up to 30 legislative days; further days will be without pay or per diem.
(v) Legislature meets twice a year. During general election years, the legislature only convenes on the January session.
(w) Legislative rules say formal business must be concluded by November 15th of the first session in the biennium, or by July 31st of the 2nd session for the biennium.
(x) Joint rules provide for the submission of a written statement requesting special session by a specified number of members of each chamber.
(y) Legal provision for session in odd-numbered year; however, legislature may divide, and in practice has divided, to meet in even-numbered years as well.
(z) 90 C sessions every year, except the first year of a gubernatorial administration during which the legislative session runs for 125 C.
(aa) 30 C if called by legislature; 60 C if called by governor.
(bb) Each General Assembly convenes for a First and Second Regular Session over a two-year period.
(cc) The legislature convenes in January on the second Monday, March, June and September, the third Wednesday.

LEGISLATIVE SESSIONS: LEGAL PROVISIONS — Continued

(dd) Sessions are two years and begin on the first Tuesday of January of the odd-numbered year. Session ends on November 30 of the even-numbered year. Each calendar year receives its own legislative number.

(ee) Unless Monday is a legal holiday; in second year, the General Assembly convenes on the same date.

(ff) Legislative Council may reconvene the Legislature assembly. However, a reconvened session may not exceed the number of days available (80) but not used by the last regular session.

(gg) No limitation, but the convening of the new General Assembly following an election would by operation end the special session.

(hh) Each Council period begins on January 2 of each odd-numbered year and ends on January 1 of the following odd-numbered year.

(ii) Legislature meets on the first Monday of each month following its initial session in January.

(jj) 60 L before April 1 and 30 L after July 31.

(kk) Session officially begins on the first Wednesday following the first Monday of the new legislative term (commencing the first of the year), and lasts until the legislature completes its business and adjourns sine die.

However, over the past several years, both houses have adopted the tactic of declaring a recess at the call of the leaders, in order to facilitate easy recall of the legislature to override vetoes, etc. Over time the custom has become to formally adjourn both houses just before the new session opens; in the case of 2005, on January 7th. This leads to the rather interesting convention that when the governor calls the legislature into session, it is considered "special" or "executive", even though the regular session is ongoing.

(ll) Constitution encourages adjournment by May 31.

(mm) Legislative session consists of two-year terms divided into annual sessions.

(nn) Governor may call legislature in certain cases.

(oo) Assembly Joint Resolution No. 13 from the 72nd Session (2003) passed during the 2005 Session. Therefore, the question of whether the Legislature should be able to call itself into special session will be on the 2006 General Election ballot for approval. If the voters approve the measure, a signed petition of 2/3 of the elected members in both houses would allow the legislature to call itself into a special session for specific business (to be specified in the petition) and for no more than 20 calendar days.

Table 3.3
THE LEGISLATORS: NUMBERS, TERMS, AND PARTY AFFILIATIONS: 2006

State or other jurisdiction	Senate						House/Assembly						Senate and House/Assembly totals
	Democrats	Republicans	Other	Vacancies	Total	Term	Democrats	Republicans	Other	Vacancies	Total	Term	
State and territory totals	1,002	983	13	3	2,068*	...	2,737	2,701	25	17	5,500*	...	7,568*
State totals	952	964	3	5	1,971*	...	2,703	2,676	15	17	5,411*	...	7,382*
Alabama	25	10	...	...	35	4	63	42	...	...	105	4	140
Alaska	8	12	...	...	20	4	14	26	...	...	40	2	60
Arizona	12	18	...	...	30	2	21	39	...	...	60	2	90
Arkansas.........................	27	8	...	...	35	4	72	28	...	...	100	2	135
California	25	15	...	...	40	4	48	32	...	...	80	2	120
Colorado.........................	18	17	...	...	35	2	35	30	...	...	65	2	100
Connecticut	24	12	...	...	36	2	99	52	...	...	151	2	187
Delaware.........................	13	8	...	...	21	4	15	25	1 (a)	...	41	2	62
Florida............................	14	26	...	...	40	4	36	84	...	...	120	2	160
Georgia	22	34	...	...	56	2	80	99	1 (a)	...	180	2	236
Hawaii.............................	20	5	...	...	25	4	41	10	...	...	51	2	76
Idaho..............................	7	28	...	...	35	2	13	57	...	...	70	2	105
Illinois............................	31	27	1 (a)	...	59	(b)	65	53	...	...	118	2	177
Indiana...........................	17	33	...	...	50	4	48	52	...	...	100	2	150
Iowa	25	25	...	...	50	4	49	51	...	...	100	2	150
Kansas	10	30	...	...	40	4	42	83	...	...	125	2	165
Kentucky	15	22	1 (a)	...	38	4	57	43	...	...	100	2	138
Louisiana	24	15	...	...	39	4	67	37	1 (a)	...	105	4	144
Maine..............................	19	16	...	...	35	2	76	73	2 (d)	...	151	2	186
Maryland	33	14	...	...	47	4	98	43	...	...	141	4	188
Massachusetts.................	34	6	...	...	40	2	138	21	...	1	160	2	200
Michigan	16	22	...	...	38	4	50	58	...	2	110	2	148
Minnesota	35 (c)	31	1 (a)	...	67	4	66 (c)	68	...	...	134	2	201
Mississippi	28	24	...	...	52	4	74	47	...	1	122	4	174
Missouri	11	22	...	1	34	4	64	96	...	3	163	2	197
Montana	27	23	...	...	50	4	50	50	...	...	100	2	150
Nebraska..........................	...............Nonpartisan election............				49	4	........................Unicameral........................						49
Nevada............................	9	12	...	...	21	4	26	15	...	1	42	2	63
New Hampshire...............	8	16	...	...	24	2	149	247	...	4	400	2	424
New Jersey	22	18	...	...	40	4 (e)	49	31	...	...	80	2	120
New Mexico	24	18	...	...	42	4	42	28	...	...	70	2	112
New York	27	35	...	...	62	2	104	46	...	...	150	2	212
North Carolina	29	21	...	...	50	2	63	57	...	...	120	2	170
North Dakota	15	32	...	...	47	4	27	67	...	...	94	4	141
Ohio	11	22	...	...	33	4	38	61	...	...	99	2	132
Oklahoma	26	22	...	...	48	4	44	57	...	...	101	2	149
Oregon	18	12	...	...	30	4	27	33	...	...	60	2	90
Pennsylvania	20	30	...	...	50	4	93	110	...	...	203	2	253
Rhode Island	33	5	...	...	38	2	60	15	...	...	75	2	113
South Carolina	20	26	...	...	46	4	49	74	...	1	124	2	170
South Dakota..................	10	25	...	...	35	2	19	51	...	...	70	2	105
Tennessee	15	17	...	1	33	4	53	46	...	...	99	2	132
Texas	12	19	...	...	31	4	62	87	...	1	150	2	181
Utah	8	21	...	...	29	4	19	56	...	...	75	2	104
Vermont	21	9	...	...	30	2	83	60	7 (f)	...	150	2	180
Virginia...........................	16	23	...	1	40	4	39	56	3 (a)	2	100	2	140
Washington.....................	26	23	...	...	49	4	55	43	...	...	98	2	147
West Virginia..................	21	13	...	...	34	4	68	32	...	...	100	2	134
Wisconsin........................	14	19	...	...	33 (p)	4	39	59	...	1	99 (p)	2	132
Wyoming.........................	7	23	...	...	30	4	14	46	...	...	60	2	90
Dist. of Columbia (g)......	11	1	1 (a)	...	13	4	........................Unicameral........................				20 (l)	2	13
American Samoa............	...............Nonpartisan election...........				18	4	...............Nonpartisan election...............						38
Guam	9	6	...	...	15	2	........................Unicameral........................						15
No. Mariana Islands	2	3	4 (m)	...	9	4	2	7	9 (n)	...	18	2	27
Puerto Rico.....................	17 (h)	9 (i)	1 (j)	...	27 (o)	4	32 (h)	18 (i)	1 (j)	...	51 (o)	4	78
U.S. Virgin Islands.........	11	...	4 (k)	...	15	2	........................Unicameral........................						15

See footnotes at end of table.

THE LEGISLATORS: NUMBERS, TERMS, AND PARTY AFFILIATIONS: 2006 — Continued

Source: The Council of State Governments, February 2006.

* *Note:* Senate and combined body (Senate and House/Assembly) totals include Unicameral legislatures.

Key:

. . . — Does not apply

(a) Independent.

(b) The entire Senate is up for election every 10 years, beginning in 1972. Senate districts are divided into three groups. One group elects senators for terms of four years, four years and two years; the second group for terms of four years, two years and four years; the third group for terms of two years, four years and four years.

(c) Democratic-Farmer-Labor.

(d) Unenrolled (1); Green Independent Party (1).

(e) All 40 Senate terms are on a 10-year cycle which is made up of a two-year term, followed by two consecutive four-year terms, beginning after the decennial census.

(f) Independent (1); Progressive (6).

(g) Council of the District of Columbia.

(h) New Progressive Party.

(i) Popular Democratic Party.

(j) Puerto Rico Independent Party.

(k) Independent (1); Independent Citizens Movement (3).

(l) Twenty-one seats; 20 are elected by popular vote and one is an appointed, non-voting delegate from Swains Island.

(m) Independent (1); Covenant (3).

(n) Covenant (7); Independent (2).

(o) An extra seat is granted to the opposition, if necessary, to limit any party's control to 2/3.

(p) All House seats contested in even-numbered years; in the Senate 17 seats contested in gubernatorial years; 16 seats contested in presidential years.

Table 3.3A
THE LEGISLATORS: NUMBERS, TERMS, AND PARTY AFFILIATIONS BY REGION: 2006

State	Senate						House/Assembly						Senate and House/Assembly totals
	Democrats	Republicans	Other	Vacancies	Total	Term	Democrats	Republicans	Other	Vacancies	Total	Term	
State totals	952	964	3	5	1,971*	...	2,703	2,676	15	17	5,411*	...	7,382*
Eastern Region													
Connecticut...........	24	12	...	...	36	2	99	52	...	...	151	2	187
Delaware...............	13	8	...	...	21	4	15	25	1 (a)	...	41	2	62
Maine....................	19	16	...	...	35	2	76	73	2 (d)	...	151	2	186
Massachusetts	34	6	...	...	40	2	138	21	...	1	160	2	200
New Hampshire	8	16	...	...	24	2	149	247	...	4	400	2	424
New Jersey	22	18	...	...	40	4 (e)	49	31	...	...	80	2	120
New York..............	27	35	...	...	62	2	104	46	...	...	150	2	212
Pennsylvania..........	20	30	...	...	50	4	93	110	...	...	203	2	253
Rhode Island..........	33	5	...	...	38	2	60	15	...	...	75	2	113
Vermont	21	9	...	...	30	2	83	60	7 (f)	...	150	2	180
Regional total	221	155	0	0	376	...	865	679	10	7	1,561	...	1,937
Midwestern Region													
Illinois	31	27	1 (a)	...	59	(b)	65	53	...	...	118	2	177
Indiana..................	17	33	...	...	50	4	48	52	...	...	100	2	150
Iowa......................	25	25	...	...	50	4	49	51	...	...	100	2	150
Kansas	10	30	...	...	40	4	42	83	...	...	125	2	165
Michigan...............	16	22	...	...	38	4	50	58	...	2	110	2	148
Minnesota	35 (c)	31	1 (a)	...	67	4	66 (c)	68	...	...	134	2	201
Nebraska................	............Nonpartisan election				49	4	............Unicameral............						49
North Dakota	15	32	...	...	47	4	27	67	...	...	94	4	141
Ohio......................	11	22	...	...	33	4	38	61	...	...	99	2	132
South Dakota	10	25	...	...	35	2	19	51	...	...	70	2	105
Wisconsin	14	19	...	...	33 (g)	4	39	59	...	1	99 (g)	2	132
Regional total	184	266	2	...	501	...	443	603	0	3	1,049	...	1,550
Southern Region													
Alabama.................	25	10	...	...	35	4	63	42	...	...	105	4	140
Arkansas	27	8	...	...	35	4	72	28	...	...	100	2	135
Florida	14	26	...	...	40	4	36	84	...	...	120	2	160
Georgia	22	34	...	...	56	2	80	99	1 (a)	...	180	2	236
Kentucky	15	22	1 (a)	...	38	4	57	43	...	...	100	2	138
Louisiana	24	15	...	...	39	4	67	37	1 (a)	...	105	4	144
Maryland	33	14	...	...	47	4	98	43	...	...	141	4	188
Mississippi.............	28	24	...	...	52	4	74	47	...	1	122	4	174
Missouri................	11	22	...	1	34	4	64	96	...	3	163	2	197
North Carolina	29	21	...	...	50	2	63	57	...	...	120	2	170
Oklahoma	26	22	...	...	48	4	44	57	...	...	101	2	149
South Carolina	20	26	...	...	46	4	49	74	...	1	124	2	170
Tennessee..............	15	17	...	1	33	4	53	46	...	...	99	2	132
Texas.....................	12	19	...	...	31	4	62	87	...	1	150	2	181
Virginia	16	23	...	1	40	4	39	56	3 (a)	2	100	2	140
West Virginia	21	13	...	...	34	4	68	32	...	...	100	2	134
Regional total	338	316	1	3	658	...	989	928	5	8	1,930	...	2,588
Western Region													
Alaska...................	8	12	...	...	20	4	14	26	...	...	40	2	60
Arizona.................	12	18	...	...	30	2	21	39	...	...	60	2	90
California..............	25	15	...	...	40	4	48	32	...	...	80	2	120
Colorado	18	17	...	...	35	4	35	30	...	...	65	2	100
Hawaii	20	5	...	...	25	4	41	10	...	...	51	2	76
Idaho....................	7	28	...	...	35	2	13	57	...	...	70	2	105
Montana...............	27	23	...	...	50	4	50	50	...	...	100	2	150
Nevada.................	9	12	...	...	21	4	26	15	...	1	42	2	63
New Mexico	24	18	...	...	42	4	42	28	...	...	70	2	112
Oregon..................	18	12	...	...	30	4	27	33	...	...	60	2	90
Utah......................	8	21	...	...	29	4	19	56	...	...	75	2	104
Washington	26	23	...	...	49	4	55	43	...	...	98	2	147
Wyoming	7	23	...	...	30	4	14	46	...	...	60	2	90
Regional total	209	227	0	0	436	...	405	465	0	1	871	...	1,307

Source: The Council of State Governments, February 2006.

* *Note:* Senate and combined body (Senate and House/Assembly) totals include Unicameral legislatures.

Key:

... — Does not apply

(a) Independent.

(b) The entire Senate is up for election every 10 years, beginning in 1972. Senate districts are divided into three groups. One group elects senators for terms of four years, four years and two years; the second group for terms of four years, two years and four years; the third group for terms of two years, four years and four years.

(c) Democratic-Farmer-Labor.

(d) Unenrolled (1); Green Independent Party (1).

(e) All 40 Senate terms are on a 10-year cycle which is made up of a two-year term, followed by two consecutive four-year terms, beginning after the decennial census.

(f) Independent (1); Progressive (6).

(g) All House seats contested in even-numbered years; in the Senate 17 seats contested in gubernatorial years; 16 seats contested in presidential years.

Table 3.4
MEMBERSHIP TURNOVER IN THE LEGISLATURES: 2005

State or other jurisdiction	Senate Total number of members	Senate Number of membership changes	Senate Percentage change of total	House/Assembly Total number of members	House/Assembly Number of membership changes	House/Assembly Percentage change of total
Alabama	35	0	0%	105	3	3%
Alaska	20	2	10	40	9	23
Arizona	30	0	0	60	0	0
Arkansas	35	0	0	100	0	0
California	40	0	0	80	1	1
Colorado	35	1	3	65	3	5
Connecticut	36	1	3	151	1	1
Delaware	21	0	0	41	0	0
Florida	40	0	0	120	0	0
Georgia	56	1	2	180	3	2
Hawaii	25	0	0	51	2	4
Idaho	35	1	3	70	1	1
Illinois	59	3	5	118	1	1
Indiana	50	3	6	100	6	6
Iowa	50	0	0	100	0	0
Kansas	40	0	0	125	6	5
Kentucky	38	0	0	100	0	0
Louisiana	39	4	10	105	5	5
Maine	35	0	0	151	2	1
Maryland	47	0	0	141	4	3
Massachusetts	40	1	3	160	3	2
Michigan	38	0	0	110	0	0
Minnesota	67	3	5	134	1	1
Mississippi	52	1	2	122	3	3
Missouri	34	3	9	163	2	1
Montana	50	1	2	100	0	0
Nebraska	49	0	0	·········· Unicameral ··········		
Nevada	21	0	0	42	0	0
New Hampshire	24	0	0	400	5	1
New Jersey	40	0	0	80	13	16
New Mexico	42	0	0	70	1	1
New York	62	2	3	150	20	13
North Carolina	50	2	4	120	4	3
North Dakota	47	0	0	94	0	0
Ohio	33	1	21	99	1	1
Oklahoma	48	1	2	101	1	1
Oregon	30	1	3	60	3	5
Pennsylvania	50	3	6	203	5	3
Rhode Island	38	0	0	75	1	1
South Carolina	46	0	0	124	3	2
South Dakota	35	0	0	70	1	1
Tennessee	33	1	3	99	4	4
Texas	31	0	0	150	2	1
Utah	29	3	10	75	3	4
Vermont	30	0	0	150	3	2
Virginia	40	0	0	100	18	18
Washington	49	0	0	98	1	1
West Virginia	34	2	6	100	6	6
Wisconsin	33	0	0	99	0	0
Wyoming	30	1	3	60	1	2
Dist. of Columbia	13	0	0	·········· Unicameral ··········		
American Samoa	18	10	56	21	0	0
Guam	15	6	40	·········· Unicameral ··········		
No. Mariana Islands	9	2	22	18	7	39
Puerto Rico	28	4	11	51	2	4
U.S. Virgin Islands	15	6	40	·········· Unicameral ··········		

Source: The Council of State Governments, February 2006.
Note: Turnover calculated after 2005 legislative elections.

Table 3.5
THE LEGISLATORS: QUALIFICATIONS FOR ELECTION

State or other jurisdiction	House/Assembly					Senate				
	Minimum age	U.S. citizen (years) (a)	State resident (years) (b)	District resident (years)	Qualified voter (years)	Minimum age	U.S. citizen (years) (a)	State resident (years) (b)	District resident (years)	Qualified voter (years)
Alabama	21	...	3 (c)	1	...	25	...	3 (c)	1	...
Alaska	21	★	3	1	★	25	...	3	1	★
Arizona	25	★	3	1	★	25	★	3	1	★
Arkansas	21	★	2	1	★	25	★	2	1	★
California	18	3	3	1	★	18	3	3	1	★
Colorado	25	★	1	1	...	25	★	1	1	...
Connecticut	18	★	★	★	★	18	★	★	★	★
Delaware	24	...	3	1	...	27	...	3	1	...
Florida	21	...	2	2	...	21	...	2	2	...
Georgia	21	...	2 (c)	1	★	25	...	2 (c)	1	★
Hawaii	18	★	3	(d)	★	18	★	3	(d)	★
Idaho	21	★	30 days	1	★	21	★	30 days	1	★
Illinois	21	★	2	2	★	21	★	2	2	★
Indiana	21	★	2	1	★	25	★	2	1	...
Iowa	21	★	1	60 days	...	25	★	1	...	...
Kansas	18	★	★ (c)	★	★	18	★	★ (c)	★	★
Kentucky	24	★	2 (c)	1	★	30	★	6 (c)	1	★
Louisiana	18	5	2	1	★	18	5	2	1	★
Maine	21	5	1	3 mo.	...	25	5	1	3 mo.	...
Maryland	21	★	1 (c)	6 mo. (f)	...	25	★	1 (c)	6 mo. (f)	...
Massachusetts	18	...	...	1	★	18	...	5	5	★
Michigan	21	★	★	(d)	★	21	★	★	(d)	★
Minnesota	18	★	1	6 mo.	★	21	...	1	6 mo.	★
Mississippi	21	...	4 (c)	2	★	25	...	4 (c)	2	★
Missouri	24	★	★	1	2	30	★	★	1	3
Montana	18	U	1	6 mo. (g)	U	18	...	1	6 mo. (g)	...
Nebraska	U	U	U	U	U	21	★	★ (c)	1	★
Nevada	21	★	1 (c)	30 days (l)	★	21	★	1 (c)	30 days (l)	★
New Hampshire	18	...	2 (c)	★	★	30	...	7 (c)	1	★
New Jersey	21	★	2 (c)	1	★	30	★	4 (c)	1	★
New Mexico	21	★	★	★	★	25	★	★	★	★
New York	18	★	5	1 (h)	...	18	★	5	1 (h)	...
North Carolina	21	...	1	1	★	25	...	2	1	★
North Dakota	18	...	1	1	★	18	...	1	1	★
Ohio	18	★	30 days	1	★	18	★	30 days	1	★
Oklahoma	21	★	★	★	★	25	★	★	★	★
Oregon	21	★	1	1	...	21	★	1	1	...
Pennsylvania	21	...	4 (c)	4	★	25	...	4 (c)	4	★
Rhode Island	18	★	30 days	30 days	★	18	★	30 days	30 days	★
South Carolina	21	...	...	★ (e)	...	25	...	...	★ (e)	...

See footnotes at end of table.

THE LEGISLATORS: QUALIFICATIONS FOR ELECTION—Continued

State or other jurisdiction	House/Assembly					Senate				
	Minimum age	U.S. citizen (years) (a)	State resident (years) (b)	District resident (years)	Qualified voter (years)	Minimum age	U.S. citizen (years) (a)	State resident (years) (b)	District resident (years)	Qualified voter (years)
South Dakota............	21	★	2	★	★	21	★	2	★	★
Tennessee................	21	★	3 (c)	1	★	30	★	3	1	★
Texas........................	21	★	2	1	★	26	★	5	1	★
Utah..........................	25	★	3 (c)	6 mo.	...	25	★	3 (c)	6 mo.	...
Vermont....................	18	★	2	1	...	18	★	2	1	...
Virginia....................	21	★	1	★	★(m)	21	★	1	★	★(m)
Washington..............	18	★	★	(d)	★	18	★	★	(d)	★
West Virginia...........	18	1	1 (c)	1	★	25	5	5 (c)	1	★
Wisconsin................	18	★	1	★(n)	★	18	★	1	★(n)	★
Wyoming..................	21	★	★(c)	1	★	25	★	★(c)	1	★
Dist. of Columbia....	U	U	U	U	U	18	...	1	★	★
American Samoa......	25	★(i)	5	1	...	30 (j)	★(i)	5	1	...
Guam........................	U	U	U	U	U	25	★	5	...	...
No. Mariana Islands	21	...	3	(d)	★	25	...	5	(d)	★
Puerto Rico	25	★	2	1 (k)	...	30	★	2	1 (k)	...
U.S. Virgin Islands...........	U	U	U	U	U	21	...	3 (c)	3	★

Source: The Council of State Governments' survey, December 2005.
Note: Many state constitutions have additional provisions disqualifying persons from holding office if they are convicted of a felony, bribery, perjury or other infamous crimes.

Key:
U — Unicameral legislature; members are called senators, except in District of Columbia.
★ — Formal provision; number of years not specified.
. . . — No formal provision.
(a) In some states candidate must be a U.S. citizen to be an elector, and must be an elector to run.
(b) In some states candidate must be a state resident to be an elector, and must be an elector to run.
(c) State citizenship requirement.
(d) Must be a qualified voter of the district; number of years not specified.
(e) At the time of filing.

(f) If the district was established for less than six months, residency is length of establishment of district.
(g) Shall be a resident of the county if it contains one or more districts or if the district contains all or parts of more than one county.
(h) Must have been a resident of the county in which the district is contained for one year immediately preceding election.
(i) Or U.S. national.
(j) Must be registered matai.
(k) The district legislator must live in the municipality he/she represents.
(l) 30 days prior to close of filing for declaration of candidacy.
(m) Qualified voters must be registered within 29 days of the election.
(n) Ten days prior to election.

Table 3.6
SENATE LEADERSHIP POSITIONS: METHODS OF SELECTION

State or other jurisdiction	President	President pro tem	Majority leader	Assistant majority leader	Majority floor leader	Assistant majority floor leader	Majority whip	Majority caucus chair	Minority leader	Assistant minority leader	Minority floor leader	Assistant minority floor leader	Minority whip	Minority caucus chair
Alabama	(a)	ES	AT	…	…	…	…	…	EC	…	…	…	EC	EC
Alaska	ES	ES	EC	…	…	…	EC	EC	EC	…	…	…	EC	EC
Arizona	(a)	AP	EC	…	…	…	EC	EC	EC	…	…	…	EC	EC
Arkansas	(a)	ES	EC	…	…	…	EC	EC	EC	…	…	…	EC	EC
California	ES (bb)	ES	EC	…	EC	…	EC	EC	EC	…	EC	…	EC	EC
Colorado	ES (bb)	ES (bb)	EC	EC	…	…	EC	EC (cc)	EC	EC	EC	…	EC	EC
Connecticut (b)	(a)	EC/ES	AP	AP	AP	…	AP	AP	EC	AL	AL	AL	AL	AL
Delaware	EC/ES	AP	EC	AL	AP or AL	…	EC	AP or A‑	EC	AL	EC	AL	EC	EC
Florida	EC/ES	AP	AP	AL	AP or AL	…	AP or AL	AP or AL	EC	…	AL	AL	AL	EC
Georgia	(a)	ES	EC	…	EC	…	EC	EC	EC	…	EC	…	EC	EC
Hawaii	ES	ES (f)	EC	EC	EC	…	EC	EC	EC	EC	EC	…	EC	EC
Idaho	(a)	ES	EC	EC	…	…	…	EC	EC	AL	…	…	AL	AL
Illinois	(a)	…	AP	AP	AT	…	AP	AP	EC	AL	EC	AL	(c)	EC
Indiana	(a)	…	EC	EC	AT	…	AT	EC	EC	EC	EC	(c)	(c)	EC
Iowa	ES	ES	EC	…	…	…	…	…	EC	…	…	…	EC	EC
Kansas	ES	ES (f)	EC	EC	EC	…	EC	EC	EC	EC	EC	…	EC	EC
Kentucky	ES	ES	EC	EC	EC	…	EC	EC	EC	AL	EC	AL	EC	AL
Louisiana	ES	ES	…	…	EC	…	AL	AP	EC	…	EC	…	…	EC
Maine	ES	AP	EC	…	(hh)	(hh)	(ii)	…	EC (bb)	…	(o)	(o)	(m)	…
Maryland	ES	ES	AP (n)	AP (n)	(n)	(n)	AP	EC	EC (bb)	…	(bb)	…	EC	EC
Massachusetts	EC	ES	AP	AP	EC	…	EC	(p)	EC	…	EC	…	EC	(p)
Michigan (aa)	(a)	ES	EC	EC	EC	…	EC	EC	EC	EC	EC	…	EC	EC
Minnesota	ES	ES	EC	EC	EC	…	AL	AP	EC	AL	EC	…	AL	AL
Mississippi	(a)	AP	…	…	EC	…	…	AP	EC	…	EC	…	…	EC
Missouri	(a)	ES	AP (n)	AP (n)	(n)	…	AP	EC	EC	…	EC	…	EC	…
Montana	ES	ES	…	…	ES	…	ES	…	…	…	ES	…	ES	…
Nebraska (U)	(a)	ES (g)	…	…	…	…	…	…	…	…	…	…	…	…
Nevada	(a)	ES	EC	AL/3	EC	…	EC	EC	EC	EC	EC	…	EC	EC
New Hampshire	ES	AP	AP	AP	EC	…	AP	AP	EC	AL	EC	…	AL	AL
New Jersey (h)	ES	ES	EC	EC	EC	…	EC	EC	EC	EC	EC	…	EC	EC
New Mexico	(a)	ES	EC (u)	EC	EC (u)	…	EC	EC (u)	EC (u)	AT	EC (u)	…	EC	EC
New York (v)	(a)	ES (i)	(i)	AT	…	…	AT	AT (j)	EC	AT	EC	EC	AL	AL (j)
North Carolina	(a)	ES	EC	EC	EC	…	EC	EC	EC	EC	EC	EC	AL	EC
North Dakota	(a)	ES	EC	EC	EC	…	EC	EC	EC	ES	ES	ES	ES	EC
Ohio (l)	ES (p)	ES	…	…	ES	…	ES (ff)	EC	ES (p)	…	ES	…	ES (gg)	EC
Oklahoma	(a)	ES	EC	EC	EC	…	EC	EC	EC	EC	EC	EC	EC	EC
Oregon	ES	ES	EC	AL/3	EC (p)	…	EC/1	(p)	EC (p)	EC/2	EC/1	EC	EC/1	AL (j)
Pennsylvania	ES	ES	EC	EC	EC	…	EC	(p)	EC	AL	EC	EC	EC	EC
Rhode Island (k)	ES	ES	EC	EC	EC	…	AL	…	EC	AL	EC	…	AL	(p)
South Carolina	(a)	ES	EC	…	…	…	…	…	EC	…	…	…	…	…

See footnotes at end of table.

SENATE LEADERSHIP POSITIONS: METHODS OF SELECTION—Continued

State or other jurisdiction	President	President pro tem	Majority leader	Assistant majority leader	Majority floor leader	Assistant majority floor leader	Majority whip	Majority caucus chair	Minority leader	Assistant minority leader	Minority floor leader	Assistant minority floor leader	Minority whip	Minority caucus chair
South Dakota	(a)	ES	EC	EC	...	...	EC	EC	EC	EC	...	...	EC	...
Tennessee	ES	AP	EC	...	EC	EC	EC	EC	EC	...	EC	EC	...	EC
Texas	(a)	ES	...	...	...	...	...	...	...	...	...	...	...	...
Utah (q)	ES	ES	EC	EC	EC (r)	EC (r)	EC (r)	EC (r)	EC	EC	EC (r)	EC (r)	EC (r)	EC (r)
Vermont	(a)	ES	EC	EC	EC	EC	EC (r)	EC (r)	EC	EC	EC (r)	EC (r)	EC (r)	EC (r)
Virginia	(a)	ES	EC (e)	...	EC (e)	...	EC	EC	EC	...	EC	...	...	EC
Washington (s)	ES	AP	EC	...	EC	...	EC	EC	EC	...	EC (t)	...	...	EC
West Virginia	ES (d)	EC	AP	...	EC	...	AP	EC	EC (t)	EC (t)	EC (t)	EC (t)	EC (t)	EC (t)
Wisconsin	ES	EC	EC	EC	EC	EC	EC	EC	EC	EC	EC	EC (t)	AL	EC
Wyoming	ES (f)	ES (f)	EC	...	EC	...	EC	EC	...	EC	EC	...	...	EC
Dist. of Columbia (U)	(w)	(x)	...	...	...	...	...	...	...	...	...	...	...	...
American Samoa	ES	ES	...	...	...	...	...	...	...	...	...	...	...	...
Guam (U)	ES (g)	ES (f)	EC	EC	...	...	EC	...	EC	EC	EC	...	EC	EC
No. Mariana Islands	ES (ee)	AS	(ee)	...	ES (y)	...	...	...	EC	EC	...	...	...	...
Puerto Rico	ES (p)	AS	AS	...	EC (z)	...	EC	(dd)	EC (p)	...	EC (z)	...	...	(p)
U.S. Virgin Islands (U)	ES	ES	ES	...	...	...	...	ES	ES	...	EC (z)	...	...	ES

Source: The Council of State Governments' survey, December 2005.

Note: In some states, the leadership positions in the Senate are not empowered by the law or by the rules of the chamber, but rather by the party members themselves. Entry following slash indicates number of individuals holding specified position.

Key:

ES — Elected or confirmed by all members of the Senate.
AP — Appointed by president.
AL — Appointed by party leader.
... — Position does not exist or is not selected on a regular basis.

EC — Elected by party caucus.
AT — Appointed by president pro tempore.
(U) — Unicameral legislative body.

(a) Lieutenant governor is president of the Senate by virtue of the office.
(b) Position titles are as follows: chief deputy president pro tem, two deputy presidents pro tem, a chief assistant president pro tem, three assistant presidents pro tem, three deputy majority leaders (AP); a minority leader pro tem, two chief deputy minority leaders, a deputy minority leader-at-large, and three deputy minority leaders (AL).
(c) Appointed by minority leader.
(d) Caucus nominee elected by whole membership.
(e) Minority party in Senate elects Caucus officers (vice-chair, secretary, and treasurer). The majority leader is also chair of the caucus. The majority floor leader is also vice-chair of the caucus.
(f) Official title is vice president. In Guam, vice speaker.
(g) Official title is speaker. In Tennessee, official also has the statutory title of "lieutenant governor."
(h) Additional positions include deputy majority leader (EC), two deputy assistant minority leaders (EC), and minority leader pro tem (EC).
(i) President pro tempore is also majority leader.
(j) Majority caucus chair: official title is majority conference chair. Minority caucus chair: official title is minority conference chair.
(k) Additional positions include deputy president pro tempore.
(l) While the entire membership actually votes on the election of leaders, selections generally have been made by the members of each party prior to the date of this formal election.
(m) Same position as assistant minority leader.
(n) Majority leader also serves as majority floor leader; deputy majority leader is official title and serves as assistant majority floor leader. There is also an assistant deputy majority leader; there is also a deputy majority whip and assistant deputy majority whips; minority leader also serves as minority floor leader.

(o) Same position as minority leader.
(p) President and minority floor leader are also caucus chairs. In Ohio and Puerto Rico, president and minority leader. In Oregon, majority leader and minority leader.
(q) Additional positions include majority whip (EC), assistant majority whip (EC), minority whip (EC), assistant minority whip (EC) and minority caucus leader (EC).
(r) Majority leader serves as majority floor leader and majority caucus chair. Assistant majority leader serves as assistant majority floor leader and majority whip. Minority leader serves as minority floor leader and minority caucus chair. Assistant minority leader serves as assistant minority floor leader and minority whip.
(s) Additional positions include vice president pro tem (ES), majority assistant whip (EC), and Republican assistant whip (EC).
(t) Customary title of minority party leaders is the party designation (Republican).
(u) Majority leader also serves as majority floor leader. Minority leader also serves as minority floor leader.
(v) Additional positions include vice president pro tem (AT), deputy majority leader for legislative operations (AT), majority conference vice-chair (AT), minority conference vice-chair (AL), majority conference secretary (AT), deputy majority whip (AT), majority steering committee chair (AT), minority conference secretary (AL), assistant majority whip (AT) and assistant minority whip (AL).
(w) Chair of the Council, which is an elected position.
(x) Appointed by the chair; official title is chair pro tem.
(y) Official title is floor leader.
(z) Office title is alternate floor leader.
(aa) Additional positions include assistant president, associate president pro tempore, assistant majority caucus chair, assistant minority caucus chair.
(bb) Minority leader also serves as the minority floor leader.
(cc) Official title is majority caucus leader.
(dd) Official title is caucus chairman.
(ee) Speaker also serves as majority leader.
(ff) Sixth ranking majority leadership position is assistant majority whip.
(gg) Fourth ranking minority leadership position is assistant minority whip.
(hh) Same position as majority leader.
(ii) Same position as assistant majority leader.

Table 3.7
HOUSE/ASSEMBLY LEADERSHIP POSITIONS: METHODS OF SELECTION

State or other jurisdiction	Speaker	Speaker pro tem	Majority leader	Assistant majority leader	Majority floor leader	Assistant majority floor leader	Majority whip	Majority caucus chair	Minority leader	Assistant minority leader	Minority floor leader	Assistant minority floor leader	Minority whip	Minority caucus chair
Alabama	EH	EH	EC						EC					
Alaska	EH	AS	EC				EC	EC	EC		EC		EC	EC
Arizona	EH	AS	EC				EC		EC				EC	EC
Arkansas	EH	AS	AS	AS			AS	EC	EC				EC	EC
California	EH	AS	AS	AS	AS		AS	EC	EC		EC		EC	EC
Colorado	EH (x)	AS	EC	EC			EC	EC	EC	EC	EC	EC	EC	EC
Connecticut	EC/EH	AS/4 (b)	EC	EC/4 (b)	AS (b)	AS (b)	AS (b)	AS (b)	EC	AL (b)	AL (b)	AL (b)	AL (b)	AL (b)
Delaware	EH	EH	AS	AS	AS	AS	AS	AS	EC	EC	AL	AL	EC	AL
Florida	EH	EH	AS	AS	AS		AS	AS	EC	EC	AL	AL	AL	AL
Georgia	EH	EH	EC				EC	EC	EC	EC	EC		EC	EC
Hawaii	EH	EH (a)	EC		EC	EC	EC	EC	EC	EC	EC	EC	EC	EC
Idaho	EH	EH	EC	EC	EC		EC	EC	EC	EC	EC		EC	EC
Illinois	EH	EH	AS	AS	AS	AS	EC	AS	AL	AL	AL	AL	AL	AL
Indiana	EH	AL	EC	AL	AL		AL	AL	EC	EC	EC	EC	AL	AL
Iowa	EH	EH	EC	EC	EC	EC	EC	EC	EC	EC	EC		EC	EC
Kansas (y)	EH	EH	EC	EC	EC	EC	EC	EC	EC	EC	EC	EC	EC	EC
Kentucky	EH	EH	EC (j)	EC (j)			(j)		EC (j)	EC (j)	EC		EC	EC
Louisiana	EH	AL	EC (e)	AS (e)			AS							
Maine	EH	AS (d)	EC (j)	EC (j)	(j)	(j)	(j)	(g)	EC (j)	EC (j)	(j)	(j)	(j)	(g)
Maryland	EH	EH (z)	AS (e)		(e)	AS	AS		ES (aa)	EC (j)			ES (aa)	
Massachusetts	EC		AS	AS	EC		EC	(h)	EC (h)	AL	EC	AL		(h)
Michigan	EH	EH	EC	EC			EC	EC	EC	EC	EC	EC	EC	EC
Minnesota	EH	AS	EC	EC	EC	EC	EC	EC	EC	AL	EC	AL	EC	EC
Mississippi	EH	EH	EC				EC	EC	EC		EC		EC	EC
Missouri	EH	EH		EC	EC	EC	EC	EC	EH (g)	EH	EH	EC	EH	EC
Montana	EH	EH			EH	EH	EH	(i)		EH	EH		EH	
Nevada	EH	EH	AS	AS	EC	EC	EC	AS	EC	AL (k)	EC	EC	EC	(k)
New Hampshire	EH	AS (a)	EC	AS (k)	EC	EC	AS (k)	EC (m)	AS (k)	EC	EC	EC	(k)	EC (m)
New Jersey (l)	EH	EH	EC	EC/3	EC	EC	EC	EC	EC	EC	EC	EC	EC	
New Mexico	EH	EH	EC	AS	EC (h)	EC	EC	EC	EC	AL	EC (h)	EC	EC	EC
New York (n)	EH	AS	AS	AS	AS	AS	AS	AS (o)	EC	AL	AL	AL	AL	AL (o)
North Carolina	EH	EH	EC	EC	EC	EC	EC	EC	EC	EC	EC	EC	EC	EC
North Dakota	EH		EC	EC	EC	EC	EC	EC	EC	EC	EC	EC	EH	EC
Ohio (p)	EH (g)	EH		EC	EH	EH	EH		EH (g)	EH	EH	EH	EH	
Oklahoma	EH	EH	AS	AS	AS	AS	AS	AS	EC	AL	EC	AS	EC	EC
Oregon	EH	EH	EC (q)	AL/7			EC	(q)	EC (q)	AL/5	EC	EC	EC/3	(q)
Pennsylvania	EH	EH	EC	EC	EC	EC	EC	EC	EC	EC	EC	EC	EC	EC
Rhode Island	EH	EH	EC	AL	EC	EC	AL		EC	AL	EH		AL	EC
South Carolina	EH	EH	EC						EC					

See footnotes at end of table.

HOUSE/ASSEMBLY LEADERSHIP POSITIONS: METHODS OF SELECTION—Continued

State or other jurisdiction	Speaker	Speaker pro tem	Majority leader	Assistant majority leader	Majority floor leader	Assistant majority floor leader	Majority whip	Majority caucus chair	Minority leader	Assistant minority leader	Minority floor leader	Assistant minority floor leader	Minority whip	Minority caucus chair
South Dakota	EH	EH	EC	EC	…	…	EC	…	EC	EC	…	…	EC	…
Tennessee	EH	EH	EC	EC	…	…	EC	EC	EC	EC	…	…	EC	EC
Texas	EH	AS	EC	EC (s)	…	…	EC	…	EC	EC (s)	…	…	…	…
Utah	EH	AS	EC	EC	…	…	EC	EC	EC	EC	…	…	EC	…
Vermont	EH	…	EC	…	(j)	(j)	(j)	(i)	EC	…	(j)	(j)	(i)	(i)
Virginia (f)	EH	EH	EC (h)	…	(c)	…	EC	EC	EC	…	EC	EC/2	AL	EC
Washington (o)	EH	EH	AS	AS	…	…	EC	EC (t)	EC	…	EC	…	EC	EC
West Virginia (r)	EH (r)	AS	AS	AS	…	…	AS	AS	EC	EC	EC	…	EC	EC
Wisconsin	EH	EH	EC	EC	…	…	EC	EC	EC	EC	…	…	EC	EC
Wyoming	EH	EH	…	EC	EH	…	EC	…	…	EC	EH	…	EC	EC
Dist. of Columbia	…	…	…	…	…	…	…	…	…	…	…	…	…	…
American Samoa	EH (a)	…	…	…	…	…	…	(i)	…	…	…	…	…	…
Guam	(u)	…	(u)	…	EH (v)	…	…	(i)	EC	…	EC (v)	…	…	…
No. Mariana Islands	EH (g)	EH (a)	EC	…	EC (w)	…	…	(i)	EC (g)	…	EC (w)	…	…	(g)
Puerto Rico	…	…	…	…	…	…	…	…	…	…	…	…	…	…
U.S. Virgin Islands	…	…	…	…	…	…	…	…	…	…	…	…	…	…

Source: The Council of State Governments' survey, December 2005.

Note: In some states, the leadership positions in the house are not empowered by the law or by the rules of the chamber, but rather by the party members themselves. Entry following slash indicates number of individuals holding specified position.

Key:
EH — Elected or confirmed by all members of the house.
EC — Elected by party caucus.
AS — Appointed by speaker.
AL — Appointed by party leader.
… — Position does not exist or is not selected on a regular basis.

(a) Official title is deputy speaker. In Hawaii, American Samoa and Puerto Rico, vice speaker.
(b) Official titles: speaker pro tem—deputy speaker; assistant majority leader—deputy majority leader.
(c) Selected by the minority leader with the approval of the Speaker.
(d) Each occurrence.
(e) Majority leader also serves as majority floor leader. Official title of assistant majority floor leader is deputy majority leader. There are also an assistant majority whip, chief deputy majority whips, and deputy majority whips.
(f) The majority caucus also has a secretary, who is appointed by the speaker, the minority caucus has 2 vice-chairs, 1 vice-chair/treasurer and an interim sergeant at arms.
(g) Speaker and minority leader are also caucus chair.
(h) Speaker and minority leader also serves as minority floor leader.
(i) Unicameral legislature; see entries in Table 3.6, "Senate Leadership Positions: Methods of Selection."
(j) Majority leader also serves as majority floor leader; minority leader also serves as assistant majority floor leader and majority whip; minority leader also serves as minority floor leader; assistant minority leader also serves as assistant minority floor leader and minority whip.
(k) Official titles: assistant majority leader is majority leader; majority whip is deputy majority whip; minority leader is Democratic leader and assistant minority leader is assistant Democratic leader; minority whip is Democratic Whip (2 positions); minority caucus chair is known as Director of Communications for Democratic Caucus.

(l) Additional positions include four deputy speakers (EC), three assistant majority whips (EC), majority budget officer (EC), minority leader pro tem (EC), and three deputy minority leaders (EC).
(m) Official titles: majority caucus chair is majority conference leader and minority caucus chair is conference chair.
(n) Additional positions: deputy speaker (AS), assistant speaker (AS), assistant speaker pro tem (AS), minority leader pro tem (AL), assistant minority leader pro tem (AL), deputy majority leader (AS), deputy minority leader (AL), deputy majority whip (AS), deputy minority whip (AL), assistant majority whip (AS), assistant minority whip (AL), majority conference vice-chair (AL), majority conference secretary (AS), minority conference vice-chair (AS), minority conference secretary (AL), majority steering committee chair (AS), majority steering committee vice-chair (AS), minority steering committee chair (AL), minority steering committee vice-chair (AL), majority program committee chair (AS), and minority program committee chair (AL).
(o) Official titles: majority caucus chair is majority conference chair; minority caucus chair is minority conference chair.
(p) While the entire membership actually votes on the election of leaders, selections generally have been made by the members of each party prior to the date of this formal election. Additional positions include assistant majority whip (EH) and assistant minority whip (EH).
(q) Majority leader also serves as majority caucus chair; minority leader also serves as minority caucus chair.
(r) Caucus nominee elected by whole membership.
(s) Assistant majority floor leader known as assistant majority whip, assistant minority floor leader known as assistant minority whip.
(t) Additional position is caucus vice-chair (EC).
(u) Speaker also serves as majority leader.
(v) Official title is floor leader.
(w) Official title is alternate floor leader.
(x) Selected informally by majority caucus shortly after November election.
(y) Additional positions include minority agenda chair (EC) and minority policy chair (EC).
(z) There is also a deputy speaker pro tem.
(aa) Minority leader also serves as the minority floor leader. There are also an assistant minority leader, a chief deputy minority whip, an assistant minority whip, and several deputy minority whips.

Table 3.8
METHOD OF SETTING LEGISLATIVE COMPENSATION

State or other jurisdiction	Constitution	Statute	Compensation commission	Legislators' salaries tied or related to state employees' salaries
Alabama	★	...	...	...
Alaska	...	★	★	...
Arizona	...	...	★(a)	...
Arkansas	★	★	...	...
California	★	...	★	...
Colorado	...	★	...	...
Connecticut	...	...	★(b)	...
Delaware	...	★	★(c)	...
Florida	...	★	...	Statute provides members same percentage increase as state employees.
Georgia	...	★	...	...
Hawaii	...	...	★(d)	...
Idaho	...	...	★	...
Illinois	...	★	★	Salaries are tied to employment cost index, wages and salaries for state and local government workers.
Indiana	...	★	...	...
Iowa	...	★	★	...
Kansas	...	★	...	...
Kentucky	...	...	★(e)	...
Louisiana	...	★	...	...
Maine	★	★(f)	★	...
Maryland	...	...	★(g)	...
Massachusetts	...	★(h)	...	...
Michigan	...	...	★(i)	...
Minnesota	...	★	★(j)	...
Mississippi	...	★	...	...
Missouri	★	★(k)	...	...
Montana	...	★	...	Tied to executive branch pay matrix.
Nebraska	★	★	...	...
Nevada	...	★	...	...
New Hampshire	★	...	...	...
New Jersey	★	★	★	...
New Mexico	★	★	...	...
New York	★	★	...	...
North Carolina	...	★	...	...
North Dakota	...	★	★	...
Ohio	★	★	...	...
Oklahoma	...	★	★	...
Oregon	...	★	...	...
Pennsylvania	...	★(l)	...	...
Rhode Island	★	...	...	...
South Carolina	...	★	...	...
South Dakota	★	★	...	...
Tennessee	★	★	...	...
Texas	★(m)	...	...	...
Utah	...	...	★	...
Vermont	...	★	...	...
Virginia	★	★(n)	...	...
Washington	★	★	★(o)	...
West Virginia	...	...	★(p)	...
Wisconsin	...	★	...	The Commission plan is approved by Joint Committee on Employment Relations and the governor. It is tied to state employer compensation.
Wyoming	...	★	...	...
Dist. of Columbia	...	★	...	...
U.S. Virgin Islands	...	★	...	...

See footnotes at end of table.

METHOD OF SETTING LEGISLATIVE COMPENSATION — Continued

Source: National Conference of State Legislatures, December 2005.

Key:

★ — Method used to set compensation.

. . . — Method not used to set compensation.

(a) Arizona commission recommendations are put on ballot for a vote of the people.

(b) The Connecticut General Assembly takes independent action pursuant to recommendations of a Compensation Committee.

(c) Are implemented automatically if not rejected by resolution.

(d) Commission recommendations take effect unless rejected by concurrent resolution or the governor. Any change in salary that becomes effective does not apply to the legislature to which the recommendation was submitted.

(e) The Kentucky committee has not met since 1995. The most recent pay raise was initiated and passed by the General Assembly.

(f) Presented to the legislature in the form of legislation, the legislature must enact and the governor must sign into law.

(g) Maryland commission meets before each four-year term of office and presents recommendations to the General Assembly for action. Recommendations may be reduced or rejected.

(h) In 1998, the voters passed a legislative referendum starting with the 2001 session, members will receive an automatic increase or decrease according to the median household income for the commonwealth for the preceding two-year period.

(i) If resolution is offered, it is put to legislative vote; if legislature does not vote recommendations down, the new salaries take effect January 1 of the new year.

(j) By May 1 in odd-numbered years the Council submits salary recommendations to the presiding officers.

(k) Recommendations are adjusted by legislature or governor if necessary.

(l) Each chamber receives a cost-of-living increase that is tied to the Consumer Price Index.

(m) In 1991 a constitutional amendment was approved by voters to allow the Ethics Commission to recommend the salaries of members. Any recommendations must be approved by voters to be effective. This provision has yet to be used.

(n) In 1998 the Joint Rules Committee created a Legislative Compensation Commission. It was composed of two former governors and citizens that made recommendations regarding salary, per diem and office expenses.

(o) Salary commission sets salaries of legislature and other state officials based on market study and input from citizens.

(p) Submits, by resolution and must be concurred by at least four members of the commission. The Legislature must enact the resolution into law and may reduce, but shall not increase, any item established in such resolution.

Table 3.9
LEGISLATIVE COMPENSATION: REGULAR SESSIONS

State or other jurisdiction	Salaries			Mileage cents per mile	Per diem living expenses
	Regular sessions				
	Per diem salary	Limit on days	Annual salary		
Alabama	$10 C	. . .	. . .	10/mile for a single roundtrip per session. 48.5/mile interim cmte. attendance.	$2,280/m plus $50/d for three days during each week that the legislature actually meets during any session (U).
Alaska	. . .	. . .	$24,012	40.5/mile for approved travel.	$156/d until May 1, 2006 then $200/d (U) tied to federal rate. Legislators who reside in the capitol area receive 75% of federal rate.
Arizona	. . .	. . .	$24,000	34.5/mile on actual miles.	$35/d for the 1st 120 days of regular session and for special session and $10/d thereafter. Members residing outside Maricopa County receive an additional $25/d for the 1st 120 days of regular session and for special session and an additional $10/d thereafter (V).
Arkansas	. . .	. . .	$14,067	48.5/mile until Dec. 31, 2005.	$110/d (V) plus mileage tied to federal rate.
California	. . .	. . .	$110,880	Members are provided a vehicle. Mileage is not reimbursed.	$138/d (V) by roll call. Maximum allowable per diem is paid regardless of actual expenses.
Colorado	. . .	. . .	$30,000	28/mile or 32/mile for 4wd. Actual miles paid.	$45/d for members living in the Denver metro area. $99/d for members living outside Denver (V). Per diem is determined by the legislature
Connecticut	. . .	. . .	$28,000	40.5/mile.	No per diem is paid.
Delaware	. . .	. . .	$39,785	30/mile set by statute.	No per diem is paid.
Florida	. . .	. . .	$29,916	29/mile for business travel.	$112/d (V) tied to the federal rate. Earned based on the number of days in session. Travel vouchers are filed to substantiate.
Georgia	. . .	. . .	$16,524	28/mile – set by legislature.	$128/d (U) set by the legislature.
Hawaii	. . .	. . .	$34,200	. . .	$80/d for members living outside Oahu; $10/d for members living on Oahu (V) set by the legislature.
Idaho	. . .	. . .	$15,646	One roundtrip per wk at state rate.	$99/d for members establishing second residence in Boise; $38/d if no second residence is established and up to $25/d travel (V) set by Compensation Commission.
Illinois	. . .	. . .	$57,619	40.5/mile, tied to federal rate.	$120/d (U) tied to federal rate.
Indiana	. . .	. . .	$11,600	40.5/mile.	$134/d (U) tied to federal rate.
Iowa	. . .	. . .	$21,380.54	29/mile.	$86/d (U). $65/d for Polk County legislators (U) set by the legislature. State mileage rates apply.
Kansas	$83.14 C	. . .	. . .	40/mile, set by Dept. of Administration.	$91/d (U) tied to federal rate.
Kentucky	$170.17 C	. . .	. . .	40.5/mile.	$100.10/d (U) tied to federal rate. (110% federal per diem rate.)
Louisiana	. . .	. . .	$16,800	40.5/mile, tied to federal rate.	$113/d (U) tied to federal rate. Additional $6,000/y (U) expense allowance.
Maine	. . .	. . .	$11,384 – 1st session $8,655 – 2nd session	34/mile.	$38/d housing or reimbursement for mileage and tolls in lieu of housing at the rate of .34/ mile up to $38/d.
Maryland	. . .	. . .	$40,500	34/mile, $500 allowance for indistrict travel as taxable income, members may decline.	Lodging $96/d; meals $39/d (V) tied to federal rate.
Massachusetts	. . .	. . .	$55,569.39	Between $10 and $100, determined by distance from State House.	From $10/d – $100/d, depending on distance from State House (V) set by the legislature.

See footnotes at end of table.

LEGISLATIVE COMPENSATION: REGULAR SESSIONS — Continued

State or other jurisdiction	Salaries			Mileage cents per mile	Per diem living expenses
	Regular sessions				
	Per diem salary	Limit on days	Annual salary		
Michigan......................	. . .	. . .	$79,650	41.5/mile.	$12,000 yearly expense allowance for session and interim (V) set by compensation commission.
Minnesota.....................	. . .	. . .	$31,140.90	Senate: a reasonable allowance. House: $75–$650 for indistict mileage.	Senators receive $66/d and Representatives receive $66/L (U) set by the legislature.
Mississippi....................	. . .	. . .	$10,000	40.5/mile, set by federal rate and legislature.	$91/d (U) tied to federal rate.
Missouri........................	. . .	. . .	$31,351	37.5/mile.	$76.80/d tied to federal rate.
Montana	$76.80 L	. . .	. . .	36/mile, rate is based on IRS rate. Reimbursement for actual mileage in connection with legislative business.	$90.31/d (U).
Nebraska.......................	. . .	. . .	$12,000	36/mile, tied to federal rate.	$91/d outside 50-mile radius from Capitol; $31/d if member resides within 50 miles of Capitol (V) tied to federal rate.
Nevada	$130/d	60 days	. . .	34.5/mile.	Federal rate for Capitol area (V). Legislators who live more than 50 miles from the capitol, if requiring lodging, will be paid Hud single room rate for Carson City area for each month of session.
New Hampshire............	. . .	2-yr. term	$200	Round trip home to State House at 38/mile for first 45 miles and 19/mile there-after; or members will be reimbursed for actual expenses and mileage will be paid at the IRS mileage rate.	No per diem is paid.
New Jersey....................	. . .	. . .	$49,000	. . .	No per diem is paid.
New Mexico	. . .	. . .	. . .	40.5/mile, tied to federal rate.	$141/d (V) tied to federal rate and the constitution.
New York	. . .	. . .	$79,500	34.5/mile.	Varies (V) tied to federal rate.
North Carolina.............	. . .	. . .	$13,951	29/mile, 1 rnd. trip/w during session; 1 rnd. trip for interim cmte. mtgs.	$104/d (U) set by statute. $559/m expense allowance.
North Dakota................	$125 C	. . .	. . .	37.5/mile, 1 rnd. trip/w during session.	Lodging reimbursement up to $900/m (V).
Ohio	. . .	. . .	$56,261	30/mile, 1 rnd. trip/w from home to Statehouse for legis-lators outside Franklin Co.	No per diem is paid.
Oklahoma	. . .	. . .	$38,400	40.5/mile, tied to federal rate.	$116/d (U) tied to federal rate.
Oregon	. . .	. . .	$16,284	40.5/mile.	$91/d (U) tied to federal rate.
Pennsylvania	. . .	. . .	$69,647	40.5/mile, tied to federal rate.	$128/d (V) tied to federal rate. Can receive actual expenses or per diem.
Rhode Island	. . .	. . .	$12,646	40.5/mile to and from session.	No per diem is paid.
South Carolina	. . .	. . .	$10,400	34.5/mile.	$95/d for meals and housing, for each state-wide session day and cmte. meeting (V) tied to federal rate.
South Dakota................	. . .	2-yr. term	$12,000	32/mile for 1 rnd. trip from Pierre to home each weekend. One trip is paid at 5/mile. 32/mile for interim cmte. mtgs.	$110/L (U) set by the legislature.
Tennessee	. . .	. . .	$16,500	35/mile.	$141/L (U) tied to the federal rate.

See footnotes at end of table.

LEGISLATIVE COMPENSATION: REGULAR SESSIONS — Continued

	Salaries				
	Regular sessions				
State or other jurisdiction	Per diem salary	Limit on days	Annual salary	Mileage cents per mile	Per diem living expenses
Texas	...	...	$7,200	35/mile set by General Approp. bill; an allowance for single, twin and turbo engines from 40/mile to $1/mile is given.	$128/d (U) set by Ethics Commission.
Utah	$120 C	...	...	40.5/mile, rnd. trip from home to capitol.	$79/d (U) lodging allotment for each calendar day, tied to federal rate. $39/d (U) meals.
Vermont	...	...	$589/w during session; $118/d special session or interim cmte. meetings.	40.5/mile, tied to federal rate and state employee reimbursement rate.	Federal per diem rate for Montpelier ($69/d for lodging and $35/d for meals for non-commuters; commuters receive $35/d for meals plus mileage.
Virginia	...	...	Senate – $18,000 House – $17,640	32.5/mile.	$117/d (U) tied to federal rate.
Washington	...	...	$34,227	40.5/mile.	$90/d (U) tied to federal rate (80% Olympia area).
West Virginia	...	...	$15,000	48.5/mile based on Dept. of Administration travel regs.	$115/d (U) during session set by compensation commission. $150 per diem salary for special sessions, extension of regular session, extraordinary session or attendance at interim meetings.
Wisconsin	...	...	$45,569	32.5/mile, one rnd. trip/w to capitol.	$88/d maximum (U) set by compensation commission (90% of federal rate).
Wyoming	$125 L	...	...	35/mile.	$85/d (V) set by the legislature, includes travel days for those outside of Cheyenne.

Source: National Conference of State Legislatures, December 2005.
Key:
C — Calendar day
L — Legislative day
(U) — Unvouchered
(V) — Vouchered
d — day
w — week
m — month
y — year
. . . — Not applicable
N.R.— Not reported

Table 3.10
LEGISLATIVE COMPENSATION: INTERIM PAYMENTS AND OTHER DIRECT PAYMENTS

State or other jurisdiction	Per diem compensation and living expenses for committee or official business during interim (2005)	Other direct payments or services to legislators (2005)
Alabama	$2,280/m (U); $50/d for committee meetings and $75/d attendance other legislative business. Not restricted to meals and lodging.	None.
Alaska	$150/d (V).	Senators receive $10,000/y and Representatives receive $8,000/y for postage, stationery and other legislative expenses. Staffing allowance determined by rules and presiding officers, depending on time of year.
Arizona	$35/d with prior approval of presiding officer (V) set by statute. Additional $25/d for those outside Maricopa County.	None.
Arkansas	$125/d plus mileage (V) tied to federal rate.	Legislators are entitled to receive a maximum reimbursement of $9,600/y for legislative expenses.
California	$138/d (V) tied to federal rate.	Senators are allowed staff according to the size of their districts. Assemblymen receive $264,000/y to cover non-specified salary expenses, travel costs, publications, printing, postage, etc.
Colorado	$99/d per diem plus actual expenses (V).	None.
Connecticut	None.	Senators receive $5,500/y and Representatives receive $4,500/y.
Delaware	None.	$6,728/y for office expenses.
Florida	$103/d.	$1,872/m for office expenses.
Georgia	$128/d (V) set by the Legislature. A committee roster is submitted with the members who attended the meeting. Those that did not attend do not get paid.	$7,000/y reimbursable expense account. If the member requests and provides receipts, the member is reimbursed for personal services, office equipment, rent, supplies, transportation, telecommunications, etc.
Hawaii	$10/d for official business on island of legal residence; $80/d for business on another island (V) set by the legislature.	House $5,000–$7,500/m for Jan.–April staffing. Senate varies between $350–$500/d for staffing allowance.
Idaho	Members are reimbursed for actual expenses (V).	$1,700/y for unvouchered constituent expense. No staffing allowance.
Illinois	No per diem is paid.	Senators receive $73,000/y and Representatives $66,483/y for office expenses, including district offices and staffing.
Indiana	$134/d (V) tied to federal rate.	40% of per diem for district offices during interim only. No staffing allowance.
Iowa	$86/d (U) set by the legislature. In addition, legislators may request reimbursement for meals, hotel/motel and air fare. State mileage rates apply.	$200/m to cover district constituency postage, travel, telephone and other expenses. No staffing allowance.
Kansas	During interim committee meetings, members receive $91/d tied to federal rate, plus round-trip tolls and mileage reimbursement at 40¢. All legislators receive $328.05 (U) for 20 pay periods ($6,561) considered taxable income.	$6,561/y which is taxable income to the legislators. Staffing allowances vary for leadership who have their own budget. Legislators provided with secretaries during the session only. This amount will increase to $332.10 in April 2006 (20 payments).
Kentucky	Vouchered only.	$1,617.09 for district expenses during interim.
Louisiana	$113/d (U) tied to federal rate.	$500/m. Representatives receive an additional $1,500 supplemental allowance for vouchered office expenses, rent, travel mileage in district. Senators and Representatives staff allowance $2,000/m starting salary up to $3,000 with annual increases paid directly to staff person.
Maine	Actual attendance reimbursed at: $55 per diem; actual meals and mileage/housing expense. Upon approval of committee chair or presiding officer.	None. Supplies for staff offices are provided and paid out of general legislative account.
Maryland	$96/d lodging; $39/d meals related to official business (V) tied to federal rate and compensation commission.	Members, $18,265/y for normal expenses of an office with limits on postage, telephone and publications. Members must document expenses. Legislators must use $5,800 for clerical services. Senators receive one administrative assistant and session secretary.

See footnotes at end of table.

LEGISLATIVE COMPENSATION: INTERIM PAYMENTS AND OTHER DIRECT PAYMENTS — Continued

State or other jurisdiction	Per diem compensation and living expenses for committee or official business during interim (2005)	Other direct payments or services to legislators (2005)
Massachusetts	None.	$7,200/y for office expenses.
Michigan	None.	$58,425/y majority senator for office budget; $58,425/y for minority senator for office budget.
Minnesota	Senators receive $66/d and Representatives receive $56/d per approval of committee chair or leadership (U) set by the legislature.	None.
Mississippi	$85/d for committee meetings (U) tied to federal rate. $1,500 allowance (U).	A total of $1,500 per month out of session.
Missouri	None.	$800/m to cover all reasonable and necessary business expenses.
Montana	In state rate for meals, receipt not required . In state rate for lodging and mileage, receipt required (V). Claim form required.	None.
Nebraska	None. Actual expense reimbursed with expense vouchers provided.	No allowance; however, each member is provided with two full-time capitol staff year-round.
Nevada	Statutory amount (V) maximum allowable per diem is paid regardless of actual expenses.	None.
New Hampshire	None.	None.
New Jersey	None.	$750 for supplies, equipment and furnishings supplied through a district office program. $110,000/y for district office personnel. State provides stationery for each legislator and 12,500 postage stamps.
New Mexico	$181/d (V) tied to federal rate.	Staff allowance set by majority leader for majority members and by minority leader for minority members. Staff allowance covers both district and capitol; geographic location; responsibilities will cause variations.
New York	Varies (V) tied to federal rate.	Non-leaders receive $6,708/y for any legislative expenses not otherwise provided. Full-time secretarial assistance is provided during session.
North Carolina	$104/d (V) set by statute.	None.
North Dakota	During interim committee meetings, members receive $100/d, $25/d meals (U); $50 plus tax/d lodging (V) plus round-trip mileage reimbursement at 37.5¢. All members receive a $350/m allowance for expenses during their term in office.	None.
Ohio	None.	$350/y for unvouched office supplies plus five rolls of stamps.
Oklahoma	$25/d (U) set by the legislature.	$2,635/session; interim allowance is $400–$750/m depending on geographic size of district. Staffing allowance of $4,134/m during session; $1,846/m during interim.
Oregon	$91/d committee and task force meetings (U) tied to federal rate.	Staffing is determined by leadership.
Pennsylvania	$128 (V) tied to federal rate. Can receive actual expenses or per diem.	None.
Rhode Island	None.	Senate $3,400/y for postage, stationery and telephone. House $1,800/y for telephone and $1,100/y for postage. Legislators also receive $1,000/m for in district expenses that are treated as income.
South Carolina	Member attending official meetings is eligible for $95/d subsistence and $35/d per diem (V) tied to the federal rate.	None.
South Dakota	$110 per diem for each day of a committee meeting (U). Meals and lodging expenses are paid at state rate.	$1,000/m for expenses in district and staff intrastate travel (U).
Tennessee	$141/d (U) tied to federal rate.	Approved allowance for staff salaries, supplies, stationery, postage, district office rental, telephone expense, etc.
Texas	$128/d.	

See footnotes at end of table.

LEGISLATIVE COMPENSATION: INTERIM PAYMENTS AND OTHER DIRECT PAYMENTS — Continued

State or other jurisdiction	Per diem compensation and living expenses for committee or official business during interim (2005)	Other direct payments or services to legislators (2005)
Utah	$39/d.	None.
Vermont	Actual cost plus mileage (U) set by the legislature.	None.
Virginia	$200/d additional compensation for committee meeting attendance. No per diem is paid.	Legislators receive $1,250/m; leadership receives $1,750/m office expense allowance. Legislators receive a staffing allowance of $33,537/y; leadership receives $50,305/y.
Washington	$90/d (V) tied to federal rate (80% Olympia area). Maximum allowable per diem is paid regardless of actual expenses.	$1,950/quarter for legislative expenses, for which the legislator has not been otherwise entitled to reimbursement. No staffing allowance.
West Virginia	$115/d (U) set by compensation commission.	None.
Wisconsin	Per diem is paid year-round up to $88/d (U) set by compensation commission (90% of federal rate).	$45,000 for two-year period for office expenses. $191,700 for two-year period for staffing allowance.
Wyoming	$80/d (V) set by the legislature. Includes travel for those where meetings are not in "hometown."	Up to $750 per quarter through constituent service allowance.
Puerto Rico	$93/d within 35 miles of the capitol; $103/d beyond the 35 miles limit (U) tied to CPI.	Senate receives $10,833/m for staffing. House members receive $17,000/m for staffing.

Source: National Conference of State Legislatures, December 2005.

Notes:

(i) For more information on legislative compensation, see the Chapter 3 table entitled "Legislative Compensation: Regular Sessions."

(ii) Although the official definition of "per diem" is daily expense allowance, it is also used in some states to refer to an interim salary that is taxed and reported as separate income from the annual salary.

Key:
(U) — Unvouchered
(V) — Vouchered
d — day
m — month
w — week
y — year
N.R. — Not reported

Table 3.11
ADDITIONAL COMPENSATION FOR SENATE LEADERS

State or other jurisdiction	Presiding officer	Majority leader	Minority leader	Other leaders
Alabama	$2/day plus $1,500/mo expense allowance	None	None	None
Alaska	$500	None	None	None
Arizona	None	None	None	None
Arkansas	$15,400 (a)	None	None	None
California	$113,850 (a)	$106,425 (a)	$106,425 (a)	None
Colorado	All leaders receive $99/day salary during interim when in attendance at committee or leadership meetings.			
Connecticut	$10,689	$8,835	$8,835	Dep. min. and maj. ldrs., $6,446/yr; asst. maj. and min. ldrs. and maj. and min. whips, $4,241/yr
Delaware	$19,983	$12,376	$12,376	Maj. and min. whips, $7,794
Florida	$11,568	None	None	None
Georgia	None	$200/mo	$200/mo	Pres. pro tem, $400/mo; admin. flr. ldr., $200/mo; asst. admin. flr. ldr., $100/mo
Hawaii	$7,500	None	None	None
Idaho	$3,000	None	None	None
Illinois	$23,388	$17,539	$23,388	Asst. maj. and min. ldr., $17,539; maj. and min. caucus chair, $17,539
Indiana	$6,500	$5,000	$5,500	Asst. pres. pro tem, $2,500; asst. maj. flr. ldr. and maj. caucus chair, $1,000; maj. caucus chair, $5,000; min. asst. flr. ldr. and min. caucus chair, $4,500; maj. and min. whips, $1,500; asst. min. caucus chair, $500
Iowa	$11,593	$11,593	$11,593	Pres. pro tem, $1,243
Kansas	$13,004.16/yr	$11,731.98/yr	$11,731.98/yr	Asst. maj., min. ldrs., vice pres., $6,637.28/yr
Kentucky	$42.82/day	$33.82/day	$33.82/day	Maj., min. caucus chairs and whips, $25.92/day
Louisiana	$32,000	None	None	Pres. pro tem, $24,500
Maine	150% of base salary	125% of base salary	112.5% of base salary	None
Maryland	$13,000/yr	None	None	None
Massachusetts	$35,000	$22,500	$22,500	Asst. maj. and min. ldr. (and 2nd and 3rd asst.), pres. pro tem, each $15,000
Michigan	$5,513	$26,000	$22,000	Maj. flr. ldr., $12,000; min. flr. ldr., $10,000
Minnesota	None	$43,596 (a)	$43,596 (a)	Asst. maj. ldr., $35,291 (a)
Mississippi	Lt. gov. – $60,000	None	None	Pres. pro tem, $15,000
Missouri	None	None	None	None
Montana	$5/day during session	None	None	None
Nebraska	None	None	None	None
Nevada	$900	$900	$900	Pres. pro tem, $900
New Hampshire	$50/two-yr term	None	None	None
New Jersey	1/3 above annual salary	None	None	None
New Mexico	None	None	None	None
New York	$41,500	None	$34,500	22 other leaders with compensation ranging from $13,000 to $34,000
North Carolina	$38,151 (a) and $16,956 expense allowance	$17,048 (a) and $7,992 expense allowance	$17,048 (a) and $7,992 expense allowance	Dep. pro tem: $21,739 (a) and $10,032 expense allowance

See footnotes at end of table.

ADDITIONAL COMPENSATION FOR SENATE LEADERS — Continued

State or other jurisdiction	Presiding officer	Majority leader	Minority leader	Other leaders
North Dakota (b).......	None	$10/day during session; $250/mo during term of office	$10/day during session; $250/mo during term of office	Asst. ldrs., $5/day during session
Ohio	$87,698 (a)	Pres. pro tem $80,016 (a)	$80,016 (a)	Compensation for cmte. leadership; maj.flr. ldr., $75,371; asst. maj. flr. ldr., $70,733; maj. whip, $66,094; asst. maj. whip, $61,452
Oklahoma	$17,932	$12,364	$12,364	None
Oregon	$16,284	None	None	None
Pennsylvania	$39, 076	$31,263	$31,263	Maj. and min. whip, $23,726; maj. and min. caucus chair, $14,793; maj. and min. caucus secretaries, $9,770; maj. and min. caucus admin., $9,770
Rhode Island	Double the base salary	None	None	None
South Carolina	Lt. gov. holds this position	None	None	Pres. pro tem, $11,000 (a)
South Dakota.............	None	None	None	None
Tennessee	$49,500 (a)	None	None	None
Texas	None	None	None	None
Utah	$2,500	$1,500	$1,500	Maj. whip, asst. maj. whip, min. whip and asst. min. whip, $1,500
Vermont	$593/wk during session. No add'l salary	None	None	None
Virginia......................	None	$200/day for interim business	$200/day for interim business	Pres. pro temp, $200/d for interim business
Washington................	Lt. gov. holds this position	$42,227 (a)	$42,227 (a)	None
West Virginia.............	$50/day during session	$25/day during session	$25/day during session	Up to 4 add'l people named by presiding officer receive $150 for a maximum of 30 days
Wisconsin...................	None	None	None	None
Wyoming....................	$3/day	None	None	None

Source: National Conference of State Legislatures, December 2005.
(a) Total annual salary for this leadership position.
(b) House and Senate majority and minority leaders each receive additional compensation of $250/mo during their term of office, pursuant to NDCC Section 54-03-20, in addition to other compensation amounts provided by law during legislative sessions.

Table 3.12
ADDITIONAL COMPENSATION FOR HOUSE LEADERS

State or other jurisdiction	Presiding officer	Majority leader	Minority leader	Other leaders
Alabama	$2/day plus $1,500/mo expense allowance	None	None	None
Alaska	$500	None	None	None
Arizona	None	None	None	None
Arkansas	$15,754 (a)	None	None	$2,400 spkr. designate
California	$113,850 (a)	$106,425 (a)	$106,425 (a)	None
Colorado	All leaders receive $99/day salary during interim when in attendance at committee or leadership matters.			
Connecticut	$10,689	$8,835	$8,835	Dep. spkr., dep. maj. and min. ldrs., $6,446/yr; asst. maj. and min. ldrs.; maj. and min. whips, $4,241/yr
Delaware	$16,893	$12,376	$12,376	Maj. and min. whips, $7,794
Florida	$11,568	None	None	None
Georgia	$6,462.32/mo	$200/mo	$200/mo	Governor's flr. ldr., $200/mo; asst. flr. ldr., $100/mo; spkr. pro tem, $400/mo
Hawaii	$7,500	None	None	None
Idaho	$3,000	None	None	None
Illinois	$23,388	$19,731	$23,388	Dep. maj. and min., $16,810; asst. maj. and asst. min., $15,346
Indiana	$6,500	$5,000	$5,500	Spkr. pro tem, $5,000; maj. caucus chair, $5,000; min. caucus chair, $4,500; asst. min. flr. ldr., $3,500; asst. maj. flr. ldr., $1,000; maj. whip, $3,500; min. whip, $1,500
Iowa	$11,593	$11,593	$11,593	Spkr. pro tem, $1,243
Kansas	$13,004.16/yr	$11,713.98/yr	$11,713.98/yr	Asst. maj. and min. ldrs., spkr. pro tem, $6,637.28/yr
Kentucky	$42.82/day	$33.82/day	$33.82/day	Maj. and min. caucus chairs and whips, $25.92/day
Louisiana	$32,000 (a)	None	None	Spkr. pro tem, $24,500 (a)
Maine	150% of base salary	125% of base salary	112.5% of base salary	None
Maryland	$13,000/yr	None	None	None
Massachusetts	$35,000	$22,500	$15,000	Asst. maj. and min. ldr. (and 2nd and 3rd asst.), and spkr. pro tem, $15,000
Michigan	$27,000	None	$22,000	Spkr. pro tem, $5,513; min. flr. ldr., $10,000; maj. flr. ldr., $12,000
Minnesota	140% of base salary	140% of base salary	140% of base salary	None
Mississippi	$60,000 (a)	None	None	Spkr. pro tem, $15,000
Missouri	$208.34/mo	$125/mo	$125/mo	None
Montana	$5/day during session	None	None	None
Nebraska	None	None	None	None
Nevada	$900	$900	$900	Spkr. pro tem, $900
New Hampshire	$50/two-year term	None	None	None
New Jersey	133% of base salary	None	None	None
New Mexico	None	None	None	None
New York	$41,500	$34,500	$34,500	31 leaders with compensation ranging from $9,000 to $25,000
North Carolina	$38,151 (a) and $16,956 expense allowance	$17,048 (a) and $7,992 expense allowance	$17,048 (a) and $7,992 expense allowance	Spkr. pro tem, $21,739 and $10,032 expense allowance
North Dakota (b)	$10/day during legislative session	$10/day during legislative session, $25/mo during term of office	$10/day during legislative session, $25/mo during term of office	Asst. ldrs., $5/day during legislative sessions

See footnotes at end of table.

ADDITIONAL COMPENSATION FOR HOUSE LEADERS — Continued

State or other jurisdiction	Presiding officer	Majority leader	Minority leader	Other leaders
Ohio	$87,698.58 (a)	None	$80,016 (a)	Spkr. pro tem, $80,016 (a); maj. flr. ldr., $75,371 (a); asst. maj. flr. ldr., $70,733 (a); maj. whip, $66,094 (a); asst. maj. whip, $61,452 (a)
Oklahoma	$17,932	$12,364	$12,364	Spkr. pro tem, $12,364
Oregon	$16,284	None	None	None
Pennsylvania	$39,076	$31,263	$31,263	Maj. and min. whips, $23,726; maj. and min. caucus chairs, $14,793; maj. and min. policy chairs, $9,770; maj. and min. caucus admin., $9,770; maj. and min. caucus secretaries, $9,770
Rhode Island	200% of base salary	None	None	None
South Carolina	$11,000/yr	None	None	Spkr. pro tem, $3,600/yr
South Dakota	None	None	None	None
Tennessee	$49,500 (a)	None	None	None
Texas	None	None	None	None
Utah	$2,500	$1,500	$1,500	Whips and asst. whips, $1,500
Vermont	$652/wk during session plus an additional $10,080 in salary	None	None	None
Virginia	$18,681	None	None	None
Washington	$42,227 (a)	None	$38,227 (a)	None
West Virginia	$50/day during session	$25/day during session	$25/day during session	Up to 4 add'l people named by presiding officer receive $150 for a maximum of 30 days
Wisconsin	$25/mo	None	None	None
Wyoming	$3/day	None	None	None

Source: National Conference of State Legislatures, December 2005.
(a) Total annual salary for this leadership position.
(b) House and Senate majority and minority leaders each receive additional compensation of $250/mo during their term of office, pursuant to NDCC Section 54-03-20, in addition to other compensation amounts provided by law during legislative sessions.

Table 3.13
STATE LEGISLATIVE RETIREMENT BENEFITS

State or other jurisdiction	Participation	Plan name	Requirements for regular retirement	Employee contribution rate	Benefit formula
Alabama	None available.				
Alaska	Optional Retirement System	Public Employees	Age 60 with 10 yrs.	Employee 6.75%	2% (first 10 yrs.); or 2.25% (second 10 yrs.); or 2.5% over 20 x average over 5 highest consecutive yrs. x yrs. of service.
Arizona	Mandatory–except that officials subject to term limits may opt out for a term of office.	Elected Officials Retirement System	Age 65, 5+ yrs. service: age 62, 10+ yrs. service;or 20 yrs. service; earlier retirement with an actuarial reduction of benefits. Vesting at 5 yrs.	Employee 7%	4% x years of credited service x highest 3-yr. average in the past 10 yrs. The benefit is capped at 80% of FAS. An elected official may elected position by buying it at an actuarially–determined amount. purchase service credit in the plan for service earned in a non-
Arkansas	Optional. Those elected before 7/1/99 may have service covered as a regular state employee but must have 5 years of regular service to do so.	Arkansas Public Employees Retirement System	Age 65, 10 yrs. service; or age 55, 12 yrs. service; or any age, 28 yrs. service; any age if serving in the General Assembly on 7/1/79; any age if in elected office on 7/1/79 with 17 and 1/2 yrs. of service. As a regular employee, age 65, 5 yrs. service, or any age and 28 yrs. Members of the contributory plan established in 2005 must have a minimum of 10 yrs. legislative service if they have only legislative state employment.	Non-contributory plan in effect for those elected before 2006. For those elected then and thereafter, a contributory plan that requires 5% of salary.	For service that began after 7/1/99: 2.07% x FAS x years of service. FAS based on three highest consecutive years or service. For service that began after 7/1/91, $35 x years of service equals monthly benefit. For contributory plan, 2% x FAS x years of service.
California	Legislators elected after 1990 are not eligible for retirement benefits for legislative service.				
Colorado	Mandatory	Either Public Employees' Retirement Association of State Defined Contribution Plan. A choice is not irrevocable.	PERA: age 65, 5 yrs. service; age 50, 30yrs. service; when age + service equals 80 or more (min. age of 55). DCP: no age requirement and vested immediately	Employee: 8%	PERA: 2.5% x FAS x yrs. of service, capped at 100% of FAS. DCP benefit depends upon contributions and investment returns.
Connecticut	Mandatory	State Employees Retirement System Tier IIA	Age 60, 25 yrs. credited service; age 62, 10–25 yrs. credited service; age 62, 5 yrs. actual state service. Reduced benefit available with earlier retirement ages.	2%	(.0133 x avg. annual salary) + (.005 x avg. annual salary in excess of "breakpoint" x credited service up to 35 years) 2003–$36,400 2004–$38,600 2005–$40,900 2006–$43,400 2007–$46,000 2008–$48,800 2009–$51,700 After 2009–increase breakpoint by 6% per year rounded to nearest $100.
Delaware	Mandatory	State Employees Pension Plan	Age 60, 5 yrs. credited service.	3% of total monthly compensation in excess of $6,000	2% x FAS x years of service before 1997 + 1.85% x FAS x years of service from 1997 on. FAS = average of highest 3 years.

See footnotes at end of table.

STATE LEGISLATIVE RETIREMENT BENEFITS — Continued

State or other jurisdiction	Participation	Plan name	Requirements for regular retirement	Employee contribution rate	Benefit formula
Florida	Optional. Elected officials may opt out and may choose between DB and DC plans.	Florida Retirement System	Vesting in DB plan, 6 years; in DC plan, 1 year. DB plan: age 62 with 6 years; 30 years at any age. DC plan: any age.	No employee contribution. Employer contribution for 2004–2005 for legislators is 12.49% of salary.	DB plan: 3% x years of creditable service x average final compensation (average of highest 5 yrs). DC plan: Dependent upon investment experience.
Georgia	Optional: Choice when first elected.	Georgia Legislative Retirement System	Vested after 8 yrs.; age 62, with 8 yrs. of service; age 60 with reduction for early retirement.	Employee rate 3.75% + $7 month	$36 month for each year of service.
Hawaii.............	Mandatory	Public Employees Retirement System; elected officials' plan	Age 55 with 5 years of service, any age with 10 years service. Vesting at 5 years.	Main plan is non-contributory; 7.8% for elected officials' plan for annuity.	3.5 x yrs. of service as elected official x highest average salary + annuity based on contributions as an elected official. Highest average salary = average of 3 highest 12-month periods as elected official.
Idaho.............	Mandatory	Public Employees Retirement System	Age 65 with 5 yrs. service; reduced benefit at age 55 with 5 yrs. of service.	6.97%	Avg. monthly salary for highest 42 consecutive months x 2% x months of credited service.
Illinois.............	Optional	General Assembly Retirement System	Age 55, 8 yrs. service; or age 62, 4 yrs. service.	8.5% for retirement; 2% for survivors; 1% for automatic increases; 11.5% total.	3% of each of 1st 4 yrs.; 3.5% for each of next 2 yrs.; 4% for each of next 2 yrs.; 4.5% for each of the next 4 yrs.; 5% for each yr. above 12.
Indiana.............	DB plan is optional for those serving on April 30, 1989. Defined contribution plan is optional for those serving on April 30, 1989 and mandatory for those elected or appointed since April 30, 1989.	Legislator's Retirement System and Defined Benefit (DB) Plan and Defined Contribution Plan (DC)	DB plan: vesting at 10 yrs. Age 65 with 10 yrs. of legislative service; or if no longer in the legislature, these options apply: at least 10 yrs. service; no state salary; at age 55+ Rule of 85 applies; or age 60 with 15 yrs. of service. Early retirement with reduced benefit. Immediate vesting in the DC plan.	DC plan: 5% employee, 20% state (of taxable income). DB plan and employer contributions funded by appropriation.	DB benefit plan monthly benefit: lesser of (a) $40 x years of General Assembly service completed before November 8, 1989 or (b) 1/12 of the average of the three highest consecutive years of General Assembly service salary. DC plan: numerous options for withdrawing accumulations in accord with IRS regulations. Loans are available. A participant in both plans may receive a benefit from both plans.
Iowa	Optional	Public Employees Retirement System	Age 65; age 62 with 20 yrs. service Rule of 88; reduced benefit at 55 with at least 4 years of service.	3.7% individual	2% x FAS x years of service for first 30 years, + 1% x FAS x years in excess of 30 but no more than 5 in excess of 30. FAS is average of 3 highest years.
Kansas	Optional	Public Employees Retirement System	Age 65, age 62 with 10 yrs. of service or age plus yrs. of service equals 85 pts.	4% of salary, (4% annualized salary for Legislators).	3 highest yrs. x 1.75% x yrs. service divided by 12.
Kentucky	Optional. Those who opt out are covered by the state employees' plan.	Kentucky Legislator's Retirement Plan	Age 65 with 5 years of service; any age with 30 years of service, and intermediate provisions. Early retirement with reduced benefits.	5% of creditable compensation, set by law at $27,500: not the same as actual salary. Revised to be payable on compensation reported on W-2 forms beginning in 2005.	2.75% of FAS (based on creditable compensation) x years of service. FAS is the average monthly earnings for the 60 months preceding retirement.
Louisiana	None available.				

See footnotes at end of table.

STATE LEGISLATIVE RETIREMENT BENEFITS—Continued

State or other jurisdiction	Participation	Plan name	Requirements for regular retirement	Employee contribution rate	Benefit formula
Maine.............	Mandatory	Maine State Retirement Plan	Age 60 (if 10 yrs. of service on 7/1/93) and age 62 (if less than 10 yrs. of service on 7/1/93). Reduced benefit available for earlier retirement.	7.65% legislators; employer contribution is actuarially determined.	2% of average final compensation (the average of the 3 high salary years) x years of service.
Maryland.............	Optional	State Legislator's Pension Plan	Age 60, with 8 yrs.; age 50, 8+ yrs creditable service (early reduced retirement).	5% of annual salary	3% of legislative salary for each yr of service up to a max. of 22 yrs. 3 months. Benefits are recalculated when legislative salaries are changed.
Massachusetts.............	Optional after each election or re-election to the General Court.	State Retirement System legislator's plan	Age 55 with 6 years service; unreduced benefit at 65. Vesting at 6 years. Reduced benefits for retirement before age 65.	9%. Some legislators are grandfathered at lower rates.	2.5 x years of service x FAS. FAS = average of highest 36 months. Service credit is allowed for membership in other Massachusetts retirement plans.
Michigan.............	Optional	Legislative Retirement System (DB) for legislators elected before 3/31/97. Others may join the state defined contribution plan.	Age 55, 5 yrs. or age plus service equals 70.	7% – 13% for DB plan. For the DC plan, the state contributes 4% of salary. Members may contribute up to 3% of salary. The state will match the member's contribution in addition to the state 4% contribution.	For DB plans, various provisions, depending on when service started. For the DC plan, benefits depend upon contributions and earnings.
Minnesota.............	Mandatory	Legislators Retirement Plan before 7/1/97; Defined Contribution Plan (DCP) since then.	LRP: age 62, 6 yrs. service and fully vested. DCP: age 55 and vested immediately. LRP members do not have Social Security coverage. DCP members have Social Security coverage.	LRP: 9% DCP: 4% from member, 6% from state.	2.7% x high 5-yr. avg. salary x length of service (yrs.). DCP benefit depends upon contributions and investment return.
Mississippi.............	Mandatory	Legislators' plan within the Public Employees' Retirement System	Age 60 with 4 or more years of service, or 25 years of service.	Regular: 7.25% state 9.75% to 10.75% effective July 1, 2005. Supplement for legislative service: 3%/6.33%.	Legislators who qualify for regular state retirement benefits also automatically qualify for the legislators' supplemental benefits. Regular: 2% x FAS x years of service up to and including 25 years of service + 2.5% x FAS x service in excess of 25 years. FAS is based on the high 4 years. Supplement: 1% x FAS x years of legislative service through 25 years, + 1.25% x FAS x years of service in excess of 25.
Missouri.............	Mandatory	Missouri State Employee Retirement System	Age 55; 3 full biennial assemblies (6 years) or Rule of 80. Vesting at 6 years of service.	Non-contributory	Monthly pay divided by 24 x years of creditable service, capped at 100% of salary. Benefit is adjusted by the percentage increase in pay for an active legislator.
Montana.............	Optional	Public Employees Retirement System. Either a DB or a DC plan is available.	Vesting at 5 years. Age 60 with at least 5 years service; age 65 regardless of years of service; or 30 years of service regardless of age	6.9% for DB plan. Employer contribution of 4.19% plus employee contribution of 6.9 % for DC plan.	DB plan: 1/56 years of service x FAS. Early retirement with reduced benefits is available. DC plan: employee contributions and earnings are immediately vested. Employer contributions and earnings are vested after 5 years.

See footnotes at end of table.

STATE LEGISLATIVE RETIREMENT BENEFITS—Continued

State or other jurisdiction	Participation	Plan name	Requirements for regular retirement	Employee contribution rate	Benefit formula
Nebraska............	None available.				
Nevada...............	Mandatory; but Chapter 380, Laws for 2005, allows legislators to withdraw from the system at will. The decision is final.	Legislator's Retirement System	Age 60, 10 yrs. service.	15% of session salary	Number of years x $25 = monthly allowance
New Hampshire..........	None available.				
New Jersey..........	Mandatory	Public Employees' Retirement System	Age 60; no minimum service requirement. Early retirement with no benefit reduction with 25 years of service. Vesting at 8 years.	5% of salary	3% x Final Average Salary x years of service. FAS = higher of three highest years or three final years. Benefit is capped at 2/3 of FAS. Other formulas apply if a legislator also has other service covered by the Public Employee Retirement System.
New Mexico..............	Optional	Legislative Retirement Plan	Plans 1A and 1B: age 65 with 5 years of service; 64/8; 63/11; 60/12; or any age with 14 years of service. Plan 2: 65 with 5 years of service or at any age with 10 years of service.	Plan 1A: $100 per year for service after 1959. Plan 1B: $200 per year (now closed to new enrollments). Plan 2: $500/year.	Plan 1A: $250 per year of service. Plan 1B: $500 per year of service after 1959. Plan 2: 11 percent of the IRS per diem rate in effect on December 31 of the year a legislator retires x 60 x the years of credited service. For a legislator who retired in 2003 the benefit would be $957 per year of credited service. Annual 3% COLA.
New York...............	Mandatory	New York State and Local Retirement System	Age 62 with 5 years of service; 55 with 30 years; reduced benefit available at 55/5. Vesting at 5 years.	3% for first 10 years of membership (Tier 4 provisions).	Tier 4: 2% x final average salary (average of 3 highest consecutive years) x years of service to 30 years; multiplier of 1.5% after 30 years. For members who retire with fewer than 20 years of service, the multiplier is 1.67.
North Carolina.........	Mandatory	Legislative Retirement System	Age 65 with 5 years of service; reduced benefit available at earlier ages.	7%	Highest annual compensation x 4.02% x years of service.
North Dakota............	None available.				
Ohio	Optional	Public Employees Retirement System	Age 60 with 5 years service or 55 with 25 years service or at any age with 30 years service.	8.5% of gross salary. A 10% contribution rate for legislators will be phased in over three years starting in 2006.	2.2% of final average salary x years of service up to and through 30 years of service. 2.5% starting with the 31st year of service and every year thereafter.
Oklahoma	Legislators may retain membership as regular public employees if they have that status when elected; one-time option to join Elected Officials' Plan.	Public Employee Retirement System, as regular member or elected official member. [Information here is for the Elected Officials' Plan.]	Elected Officials' Plan: age 60 with 6 years service. Vesting at 6 years.	Optional contribution of 4.5%, 6%, 7.5%, 8.5%, 9%, or 10% of total compensation.	Avg. participating salary x length of service x computation factor depending on optional contributions ranging from 1.9% for a 4.5% contribution to 4% for a 10% contribution.

See footnotes at end of table.

STATE LEGISLATIVE RETIREMENT BENEFITS—Continued

State or other jurisdiction	Participation	Plan name	Requirements for regular retirement	Employee contribution rate	Benefit formula
Oregon	Optional	Public Employee Retirement System legislator plan	Age 55, 30+ yrs. service, 5 years vesting.	16.317% of subject wages	1.67% x yrs. service and final avg. monthly salary.
Pennsylvania	Optional	State Employees' Retirement System	Age 50, 3 yrs. service; any age with 35 years of service; early retirement with reduced benefit.	7.5%	3% x final avg. salary x credited yrs. of service (x withdrawal factor if under regular retirement age–50 for legislators).
Rhode Island	Legislators elected after January 1995 are ineligible for retirement benefits based on legislative service. (a)				
South Carolina	Mandatory, but members may opt out 6 months after being sworn into office.	South Carolina Retirement System	Age 60, 8 yrs. service; 30 yrs. of service regardless of age.	10%	4.82% of annual compensation x yrs. service.
South Dakota	None available.				
Tennessee	Optional	Employee Retirement System: Elected Class Members	Age 55, 4 yrs. service.	5.43%	$70 per month x yrs. service with a $1,375 monthly cap.
Texas	Optional	Employee Retirement System: Elected Class Members	Age 60, 8 yrs. service; age 50, 12 yrs. service. Vesting at 8 years.	8%	2.3% x district judge's salary x length of service, with the monthly benefit capped at the level of a district judge's salary, and adjusted when such salaries are increased. Various annuity options are available. Military service credit may be purchased to add to elective class service membership. In July 2005, a district judge's salary was set at $125,000 a year.
Utah	Mandatory	Governors' and Legislators' Retirement Plan	Age 62 with 10 years and an actuarial reduction; age 65 with 4 years of service for full benefits.	Non-contributory	$24.80/month (as of July 2004) x years of service; adjusted semi-annually according to consumer price index up to a maximum increase of 2%.
Vermont	None available. Deferred compensation plan available.				
Virginia	Mandatory		Age 50, 30 yrs. service (unreduced); age 55, 5 yrs. service; age 50, 10 yrs. service (reduced).	8.91% of creditable compensation	1.7% of average final compensation x yrs. of service.
Washington	Optional. If before an election the legislator belonged to a state public retirement plan, he or she may continue in that by making contributions. Otherwise the new legislator may join PERS Plan 2 or Plan 3.	See column to left. PERS Plan 2 is a DB plan. PERS Plan 3 is a hybrid DB/DC plan.	PERS Plan 2: age 65 with 5 years of service credit. Plan 3: age 65 with 10 years of service credit for the DB side of the plan; immediate benefits (subject to federal restrictions) on the DC side of the plan. The member may choose various options for investment of contributions to the DC plan.	PERS Plan 2: employee contribution of 2.43% for 2002. Estimated at 3.33% for 2005–2007. Plan 3: no required member contribution for the DB component. The member may contribute from 5% to 15% of salary to the DC component.	PERS Plan 2: 2% x years of service credit x average final compensation. Plan 3: DB is 1% x service credit years x average final compensation. DC benefit depends upon the value of accumulations.
West Virginia	Optional		Age 55, if yrs. of service + age equal 80.	4.5% gross income	2% of final avg. salary x yrs. service. Final avg. salary is based on 3 highest yrs. out of last 10 yrs.

See footnotes at end of table.

STATE LEGISLATIVE RETIREMENT BENEFITS — Continued

State or other jurisdiction	Participation	Plan name	Requirements for regular retirement	Employee contribution rate	Benefit formula
Wisconsin..................	Mandatory		Age 62 normal; age 57 with 30 years of service.	2.6% of salary in 2003: adjusted annually.	Higher benefit of formula (2.165% x years of service x salary for service before 2000; 2% x years of service x salary for service 2000 and after) or money-purchase calculation.
Wyoming...................	None available.				
Dist. of Columbia	Mandatory		Age 62, 5 yrs. service; age 55, 30 yrs. service; age 60, 20 yrs. service.	Before 10/1/87, 7%; after 10/1/87, 5%	Multiply high 3 yrs. average pay by indicator under applicable yrs. months of service.
Puerto Rico..............	Optional	Retirement System of the Employees of the Government of Puerto Rico	After 1990, age 65 with 30 years of service.	8.28%	1.5% of average earnings multiplied by the number of years of accredited service.
Guam	Optional		Age 60, 30 yrs. service; age 55, 15 yrs. service.	5% or 8.5%	An amount equal to 2% of avg. annual salary for each of the first 10 yrs. of credited service and 2.5% of avg. annual salary for each yr. or part thereof of credited service over 10 yrs.
U.S. Virgin Islands........	Optional		Age 60, 10 yrs. service.	8%	At age 60 with at least 10 yrs. of service, at 2.5% for each yr. of service or at any time with at least 30 yrs. service

Source: National Conference of State Legislatures, January 2006.

Notes:
This table shows the retirement plans effective for state legislators elected in 2003, 2004 and thereafter. In general the table does not include information on closed plans, plans that continue in force for some legislators who entered the plans in previous years, but which have been closed to additional members.
   The information in this table was updated for all states and Puerto Rico in 2004 and updated for 2005 state legislation. Information for the District of Columbia, Guam and the Virgin Islands dates from 2002.

Key:
N.A. — Information not available.
None available. — No retirement benefit provided.
(a) Constitution has been amended effective 1/95. Any legislator elected after this date is not eligible to join the State Retirement System, but will be compensated for $10,000/yr. with cost-of-living increases to be adjusted annually.

Table 3.14
BILL PRE-FILING, REFERENCE AND CARRYOVER

State or other jurisdiction	Pre-filing of bills allowed (b)	Bills referred to committee by:		Bill referral restricted by rule (a)		Bill carryover allowed (c)
		Senate	House/Assembly	Senate	House/Assembly	
Alabama	★(d)	(e) (f)	Speaker	L	L	...
Alaska	★	President	Speaker	L, M	L, M	★
Arizona	★	President	Speaker	L	L	...
Arkansas	★	President	Speaker	L	L	...
California	★(w)	Rules Cmte.	Rules Cmte.	L	L	★(h)
Colorado	★	President	Speaker	L, M (i)	L (i)	...
Connecticut	★	Pres. Pro Tempore	Speaker	M	M	...
Delaware	★	Pres. Pro Tempore	Speaker	...	...	...
Florida	★	President	Speaker	L, M	M	...
Georgia	★	President (f)	Speaker	...	...	★
Hawaii	(j)	President	Speaker	...	...	★
Idaho	...	President (e)	Speaker	L	L	...
Illinois	★	Rules Cmte.	Rules Cmte.	(x)	(x)	★(y)
Indiana	★(o)	Pres. Pro Tempore	Speaker	(z)	...	...
Iowa	★	President	Speaker	M	M	★
Kansas	★	President	Speaker	L (aa)	L (aa)	★
Kentucky	★	Cmte. on Cmtes.	Cmte. on Cmtes.	L	L	...
Louisiana	★	President (l)	Speaker (l)	L	L	...
Maine	★	Secy. of Senate and Clerk of House		(bb)	(bb)	★(bb)
Maryland	★	President	Speaker	L	L	...
Massachusetts	★	Clerk	Clerk	M	M	★
Michigan	...	Majority Ldr.	Speaker	...	...	★
Minnesota	...	President	Speaker	L, M	L, M	★
Mississippi	★	President (e)	Speaker	L	L	...
Missouri	★	Pres. Pro Tempore	Speaker	L	L	...
Montana	★	President	Speaker	...	...	...
Nebraska	★	Reference Cmte. (dd)	U	L	U	★(p)
Nevada	★	(q)	(q)	L (t)	...	...
New Hampshire	★	President	Speaker	L	M	★
New Jersey	★(m)	President	Speaker	L	L	★(ee)
New Mexico	★(k)	(r)	Speaker	L, M (gg)	M (ff) (gg)	...
New York	★	Pres. Pro Tempore	Speaker	M	M	★(hh)
North Carolina	...	Rules Chair	Speaker	M	M	★
North Dakota	★	President (e)	Speaker	L	L	...
Ohio	★(ii)	Reference Cmte.	Rules & Reference Cmte.	L (jj)	L, M (kk)	★(ll)
Oklahoma	★	Majority Leader	Speaker	L	L	...
Oregon	★	President	Speaker	L	H	...
Pennsylvania	★	President Pro Tempore	Chief Clerk	M	M	...
Rhode Island	★	President	Speaker	M	M	...
South Carolina	★	President	Speaker	M	M	★(n)
South Dakota	★	President	Speaker	...	...	...
Tennessee	★	Speaker	Speaker	L, M	L, M	★(mm)
Texas	★	President	Speaker	L	L	...
Utah	★	President	Speaker	L	L	...
Vermont	(g)	President	Speaker	M	M	★
Virginia	★	Clerk	Clerk (u)	L, M (nn)	(oo)	★(cc)
Washington	★	(v)	(v)	...	...	★
West Virginia	★	President	Speaker	L, M	L, M	★(j)
Wisconsin	...	President	Speaker	...	...	★(s)
Wyoming	★	President	Speaker	M	M	...
Puerto Rico	...	President	Secretary	M	M	...
U.S. Virgin Islands	...	Senate President in Pro-Forma meeting	U	L	U	★

See footnotes at end of table.

BILL PRE-FILING, REFERENCE AND CARRYOVER — Continued

Source: The Council of State Governments survey, December 2005.
Key:
★ — Yes
. . . — No
L — Rules generally require all bills be referred to the appropriate committee of jurisdiction.
M — Rules require specific types of bills be referred to specific committees (e.g., appropriations, local bills).
U — Unicameral legislature
(a) Legislative rules specify all or certain bills go to committees of jurisdiction.
(b) Unless otherwise indicated by footnote, bills may be introduced prior to convening each session of the legislature. In this column only: ★ — pre-filing is allowed in both chambers (or in the case of Nebraska, in the unicameral legislature); . . . — pre-filing is not allowed in either chamber.
(c) Bills carry over from the first year of the legislature to the second (does not apply in Alabama, Arkansas, Montana, Nevada, North Dakota, Oregon and Texas, where legislatures meet biennially). Bills generally do not carry over after an intervening legislative election.
(d) Except between the end of the last regular session of the legislature in any quadrennium and the organizational session following the general election and special session.
(e) Lieutenant governor is the president of the Senate.
(f) Senate bills by president with concurrence of president pro tem; if no concurrence, by rules committee. House bills by president pro tem with concurrence of president; if no concurrence, by rules committee.
(g) Bills are drafted prior to session but released starting first day of session.
(h) Bills introduced in the first year of the regular session and passed by the house of origin on or before the January 31st constitutional deadline are carryover bills.
(i) In either house, state law requires any bill which affects the sentencing of criminal offenders and which would result in a net increase of imprisonment in state correctional facilities must be assigned to the appropriations committee of the house in which it was introduced. In the Senate, a bill must be referred to the Appropriations Committee if it contains an appropriation from the state treasury or the increase of any salary. Each bill which provides that any state revenue be devoted to any purpose other than that to which is devoted under existing law must be referred to the Finance Committee.
(j) House only in even-numbered years.
(k) In the House only.
(l) Subject to approval or disapproval. Louisiana – majority members present.
(m) Pre-filing occurs prior to convening of new legislative term, before first annual session only.
(n) Allowed during the first year of the two-year session.
(o) Only in the Senate.
(p) Bills can be carried over from the 90-day session beginning in the odd-numbered year to the 60-day session, which begins every even-numbered year. Bills not passing on the last day of the 60-day session are all indefinitely postponed by motion on the last day of the session. The odd-numbered year shall be carried forward to the even-numbered year.
(q) Motion for referral can be made by any member, but committee referrals are under the control of the majority floor leader.
(r) Senator introducing the bill endorses the name of the committee to which the bill is referred. If an objection is made, the Senate determines the committee to which the bill is referred.

(s) From odd-year to even-year, but not between biennial sessions.
(t) Suspension of rule by majority of elected members.
(u) Under the direction of the speaker.
(v) By the membership of the chamber.
(w) Bills drafted prior to session. Introduction on the first day.
(x) Rules Committees have considerable discretion in assigning bills to committees, especially in even-numbered years. Only fiscal bills, and bills considered important to state government, are to be assigned to substantive committees in even-numbered years.
(y) Although not forbidden, carryover of a bill from odd- to even-numbered year requires specific action by that house; bills not acted on by deadline in a year are automatically tabled.
(z) At the discretion of President Pro Tempore.
(aa) Appropriation bills are the only "specific type" mentioned in the rules to be referred to either House Appropriation Cmte. or Senate Ways and Means.
(bb) Maine Joint Rule 308 sections 1,2,3, " All bills and resolves must be referred to committee, except that this provision may be suspended by a majority vote in each chamber."
(cc) Even-numbered year session to odd-numbered year session.
(dd) The Nebraska Legislature's Executive Board serves as the Reference Committee.
(ee) Only in odd-numbered years.
(ff) Speaker refers bills to appropriate committee of jurisdiction.
(gg) Only appropriations bills are required by rule to specific (finance) committees.
(hh) From the first year of the term to the second year.
(ii) Senate Rule 33: Between the general election and the time for the next convening session, a holdover member or member-elect may file bills for introduction in the next session with the Clerk's office. Those bills shall be treated as if they were bills introduced on the first day of the session. House Rule 61: Bills introduced prior to the convening of the session shall be treated as if they were bills introduced on the first day of the session. Between the general election and the time for the next convening session, a member-elect may file bills for introduction in the next session with the Clerk's office. The clerk shall number such bills consecutively, in the order in which they are filed, beginning with the number "1."
(jj) Unless a motion or order to the contrary, bills are referred to the proper standing committee. All Senate bills and resolutions referred by the Committee on Reference on or before the first day of April in an even-numbered year shall be scheduled for a minimum of one public hearing.
(kk) All House bills and resolutions introduced on or before the fifteenth of May in an even-numbered year shall be scheduled for a minimum of one public hearing. All bills carrying an appropriation shall be referred to the Finance and Appropriations Committee for consideration and reported before considered the third time.
(ll) Bills carry over between the first and second year of each regular annual session, but not to the next biennial 2-year General Assembly.
(mm) Bills and resolutions introduced in the First Regular Session may carry over to the Second Regular Session (odd-numbered year to even-numbered year) only.
(nn) Jurisdiction of the committees by subject matter is listed in the Rules.
(oo) The House Rules establish jurisdictional committees. The speaker refers legislation to those committees as he deems appropriate.

Table 3.15
TIME LIMITS ON BILL INTRODUCTION

State or other jurisdiction	Time limit on introduction of bills	Procedures for granting exception to time limits
Alabama	House: no limit. Senate: 22nd day of regular session (a).	Unanimous vote to suspend rules.
Alaska	35th C day of 2nd regular session.	Introduction by committee or by suspension of operation of limiting rule.
Arizona	House: 29th day of regular session; 10th day of special session. Senate: 22nd day of regular session; 10th day of special session.	House: Permission of rules committee. Senate: Permission of rules committee.
Arkansas	55th day of regular session (50th day for appropriations bills).	2/3 vote of membership of each house.
California	Deadlines established by rules committee	House: Rules commitee grants exception with 3/4 vote of House. Senate: Approval of rules committee and 3/4 vote of membership.
Colorado	House: 22nd C day of regular session. Senate: 17th C day of regular session (b).	House and Senate: Committees on delayed bills may extend deadline.
Connecticut	10 days into session in odd-numbered years, 3 days into session in even-numbered years (c).	2/3 vote of members present.
Delaware	House: no limit. Senate: no limit.	
Florida	House: noon of the first day of regular session. Senate: noon first day of regular session (b)(e).	Existence of an emergency reasonably compelling consideration notwithstanding the deadline.
Georgia	Only for specific types of bills.	
Hawaii	Actual dates established during session.	Majority vote of membership.
Idaho	House: 20th day of session for personal bills (d); 36th day of session for all comittees (f). Senate: 12th day of session for personal bills (d); 36th day of session for all comittees (f).	House and Senate: Speaker/President Pro Tempore may designate any standing committee to serve as a privileged committee temporarily. (f)
Illinois	House: determined by speaker. Senate: determined by senate president.	House: rules governing limitations may not be suspended except for bills determined by a majority of members of the Rules Comm. to be an emergency bill. Senate: Rules may be suspended by a majority vote of members.
Indiana	House: mid-January. Senate: Date specific—set in rules, different for long and short session. Mid-January.	House: 2/3 vote. Senate: If date falls on weekend/Holiday—extended to next day. Sine die deadline set by statute, does not change.
Iowa	House: Friday of 6th week of 1st regular session; Friday of 2nd week of 2nd regular session. Senate: Friday of 7th week of 1st regular session; Friday of 2nd week of 2nd regular session.	Constitutional majority.
Kansas	Actual dates established during session. Actual dates established in the Joint Rules of the House and Senate every two years when the joint rules are adopted.	Resolution adopted by majority of members of either house may make specific exceptions to deadlines.
Kentucky	House: No introductions during the last 14 L day of odd-year session, during last 22 L days of even-year session. Senate: No introductions during the last 14L day of odd-year session, during last 22 L days of even-year session.	Can only be done through suspension of the Rules.
Louisiana	House: 10th C day of odd-year sessions and 23rd C day of even-year sessions. Senate: 10th C day of odd-year sessions and 23rd C day of even-year sessions.	None.
Maine	Cloture dates established by the Legislative Council. Cloture for 2nd session of 122nd legislature was October 7th.	Approval by Rules Committee. Senate: Appeals heard by Legislative Council. Six votes required to allow introduction of legislation.
Maryland	No introductions during last 35 C days of regular session.	2/3 vote of elected members of each house.
Massachusetts	1st Wednesday in December even-numbered years, 1st Wednesday in November odd-numbered years.	2/3 vote of members present and voting.
Michigan	No limit.	
Minnesota	No limit.	Must follow committee deadline process.
Mississippi	14th C day in 90-day session; 49th C day in 125-day session (h).	2/3 vote of members present and voting.
Missouri	House: 60th L day of regular session. Senate: March 1.	Majority vote of elected members of each house; governor's request for consideration of bill by special message.
Montana	General bills & resolutions: 10th L day; revenue bills: 17th L day; committee bills and resolutions: 36th L day; committee bills implementing provisions of a general appropriation act: 75th L day; committee revenue bills: 62nd L day; interim study resolutions: 75th L day (b)(i).	2/3 vote of members.

See footnotes at end of table.

TIME LIMITS ON BILL INTRODUCTION — Continued

State or other jurisdiction	Time limit on introduction of bills	Procedures for granting exception to time limits
Nebraska	10th L day of any session (g).	3/5 vote of elected membership.
Nevada	Actual dates established at start of session.	Waiver granted by Majority Leader of the Senate and Speaker of the Assembly acting jointly.
New Hampshire	Determined by rules.	2/3 vote of members present.
New Jersey	Assembly: No limit. Senate: No limit.	
New Mexico	House: 15 days in short session/even years, 30 days in long session/odd years. Senate: 15 days in short session/even years, 30 days in long session/odd years.	None. Statutory limit for legislators; governor not limited and can send bill with message.
New York	Assembly: for unlimited introduction of bills, 1st Tuesday in May; for introduction of 10 or fewer bills, last Tuesday in May. Senate: 1st Tuesday in March.	Unanimous consent.
North Carolina	Actual dates established during session.	Senate: 2/3 vote of membership present and voting shall be required.
North Dakota	Proposed limits for 2007 session; House: 9th L day. Senate: 14th L day.	2/3 vote or approval of majority of Committee on Delayed Bills.
Ohio	No limit.	
Oklahoma	Time limit set in rules.	2/3 vote of membership.
Oregon	House: 36th C day of session (k). Senate: 36th C day of session.	2/3 vote of membership.
Pennsylvania	No limit.	
Rhode Island	Second week of February for Public Bills.	Sponsor must give one legislative day's notice.
South Carolina	House: Prior to April 15 of the 2nd yr. of a 2-yr. legislative session; May 1 for bills first introduced in Senate. Senate: May 1 of regular session for bills originating in House.	House: 2/3 vote of members present and voting. Senate: 2/3 vote of membership.
South Dakota	40-day session: 15th L day; 35-day session: 10th L day.	2/3 vote of membership.
Tennessee	General bills, 10th L day of regular session (l).	Committee on Delayed Bills.
Texas	60th C day of regular session.	4/5 vote of members present and voting.
Utah	12:00 p.m. on 11th day of general session.	Motion for request must be approved by 2/3 vote of members.
Vermont	House: 1st session—last day of February; 2nd session—last day of January. Senate: 1st session—53 C day; 2nd session—25 C days before start of session.	Approval by Rules Committee.
Virginia	Set by joint procedural resolution adopted at the beginning of the session (usually the second Friday of the session is the last day to introduce legislation that does not have any earlier deadline).	As provided in the joint procedural resolution (usually unanimous consent or at written request of the Governor).
Washington	(Constitutional limit.) No introductions during final 10 days of regular session (j).	2/3 vote of elected members of each house.
West Virginia	House: 45th C day. Senate: 41st C day.	2/3 vote of members present.
Wisconsin	No limit.	
Wyoming	House: 15th L day of session. Senate: 12th L day of session.	2/3 vote of elected members.
Puerto Rico	1st session—within first 125 days; 2nd session—within first 60 days.	None.
U.S. Virgin Islands	None.	. . .

Source: The Council of State Governments' survey, December 2005.
Key:
C — Calendar
L — Legislative
(a) Not applicable to local bills, advertised or otherwise.
(b) Not applicable to appropriations bills. In West Virginia, supplementary appropriations bills or budget bills.
(c) Specific dates set in Joint Rules.
(d) Not applicable to standing committee bills.
(e) Not applicable to local bills and joint resolutions. Florida: not applicable to local bills (which have no deadline) or claim bills (deadline is August 1 of the year preceding consideration or within 60 days of a senator's election).
(f) Beyond 36th day for Privileged Cmtes. only. Privileged Committees—House: Appropriation, Education, Revenue and Tax, State Affairs, Ways and Means. Senate: Finance, Judiciary and Rules, State Affairs.
(g) Except appropriations bills and bills introduced at the request of the governor, bills can be introduced during the first 10 legislative days of the

session. Appropriation bills and bills introduced at the request of the governor can be introduced at any time during the session.
(h) Except Appropriation and Revenue bills (51st/86th C day) and Local & Private bills (83rd/118th C day).
(i) Only certain measures may be considered in the Short Session—primarily those relating to appropriations, finance, pensions and retirement and localities; certain legislation from the 2001 Session; and legislation proposed by study commissions.
(j) Not applicable to substitute bills reported by standing committees for bills pending before such committees.
(k) Not applicable to measures approved by Committee on Legislative Rules and Reorganization or by speaker; appropriation or fiscal measures sponsored by committees on Appropriations; true substitute measures sponsored by standing, special or joint committees; or measures drafted by legislative counsel.
(l) Not applicable to certain local bills.

Table 3.16
ENACTING LEGISLATION: VETO, VETO OVERRIDE AND EFFECTIVE DATE

State or other jurisdiction	Governor may item veto appropriation bills		Days allowed governor to consider bill (a)			Votes required in each house to pass bills or items over veto (c)	Effective date of enacted legislation (d)
	Amount	Other(b)	During session: Bill becomes law unless vetoed	After session: Bill becomes law unless vetoed	After session: Bill dies unless signed		
Alabama	...	...	6 (e)		10A	Majority elected	Date signed by governor
Alaska	★	...	15P	20P		2/3 elected (g)	90 days after enactment
Arizona	★	★	5	10A		2/3 elected (ll)	90 days after adjournment
Arkansas	★	★	5	20A		Majority elected	91st day after adjournment
California	(hh)	...	12	30A		2/3 elected	(j)
Colorado	★(ff)	...	10 (h)	30A (h)		2/3 elected	90 days after adjournment (k)
Connecticut	★	...	5	15P	(pp)	2/3 elected	Oct. 1 (gg)
Delaware	★	...	10P	10P	30A	3/5 elected	Immediately
Florida	...	★	7 (h)(p)	15P (h)		2/3 present	60 days after adjournment
Georgia	★	★	6	40A		2/3 elected	July 1 for generals, date signed by governor for locals
Hawaii (I)	★(f)	...	10 (o)(mm)	45A (o)(mm)	(mm)	2/3 elected	Immediately
Idaho	★	★	5	10P		2/3 present	July 1
Illinois	★(f)	...	60 (h)	60P (h)(nn)	(oo)	3/5 elected (g)	Ususally Jan. 1 of next year (n)
Indiana	...	★	7	7P		Majority elected	(q)
Iowa	★	★	3	30A	30A	2/3 elected	July 1 (n)
Kansas	★	★	10 (h)	10P		2/5 membership	Upon publication
Kentucky	★	★	10	10A		Majority elected	90 days after adjournment sine die. Unless the bill contains an emergency clause or special effective date.
Louisiana (I)	★	★	10 (h)	20P (h)	(qq)	2/3 elected	Aug. 15
Maine	★	★	10	10P		2/3 elected	90 days after adjournment unless enacted as an emergency.
Maryland	★	★	6	30P (m)		3/5 elected	June 1 (s)
Massachusetts	★	★	10	10P	10A	2/3 present	90 days after enactment
Michigan	★	★	14		14P	2/3 elected and serving	90 days after adjournment
Minnesota	★	(hh)	3	14A, 3P	3A, 14P	2/3 elected	Aug. 1 (t)
Mississippi	★	★	5	15P (m)		2/3 elected	July 1 unless specified otherwise
Missouri	★	...	15	45A		2/3 elected	Aug. 28 (u)
Montana (I)	★	★	10 (h)	25A (h)		2/3 present	Oct. 1 (t)
Nebraska	★	...	5	5A, 5P		3/5 elected	90 days following adjournment sine die
Nevada	...	...	5 (ss)	10A (ss)		2/3 elected	Oct. 1
New Hampshire	...	...	5	5P		2/3 present	60 days after enactment
New Jersey	★	★	45 (rr)		(w)	2/3 elected	July 4; other dates usually specified
New Mexico	★	★	3 (ee)		20A	2/3 present	90 days after adjournment
New York	★	...	10	(kk)	30A	2/3 elected	20 days after enactment
North Carolina	...	★	10	30A		3/5 elected	60 days after adjournment
North Dakota	★	★	3	15A		2/3 elected	(x)
Ohio	★	★	10	10P	10A	3/5 elected (ii)	91st day after filing with secretary of state (tt)

See footnotes at end of table.

ENACTING LEGISLATION: VETO, VETO OVERRIDE AND EFFECTIVE DATE—Continued

State or other jurisdiction	Governor may item veto appropriation bills		Days allowed governor to consider bill (a)			Votes required in each house to pass bills or items over veto (c)	Effective date of enacted legislation (d)
	Amount	Other(b)	During session — Bill becomes law unless vetoed	After session — Bill becomes law unless vetoed	After session — Bill dies unless signed		
Oklahoma	★	★	5	30A (o)	15A	2/3 elected (g)	90 days after adjournment
Oregon	★	★	5 (o)	30A, 10P		2/3 present	Jan. 1st of following year (jj)
Pennsylvania	★	★	30	10P (r)		majority	60 days after signed by governor
Rhode Island	…	…	6		(r)	3/5 present	Immediately (i)
South Carolina	★	…	5	(m)		2/3 elected	Date of signature
South Dakota.......	★	★	5 (uu)	15P (vv)		2/3 elected	July 1
Tennessee	★	…	10P	10A		Constitutional majority	40 days after enactment
Utah...................	★	…	10P	20A		2/3 elected	90 days after adjournment
Vermont	…	…	5P	60A	3A	2/3 present	60 days after adjournment
Virginia...............	★	★(ww)	7		30A	2/3 present (y)	July 1 (z)
Washington..........	★	★	5	20A		2/3 present	90 days after adjournment
West Virginia.......	…	(hh)	5P	15A (aa)		Majority elected	90 days after enactment
Wisconsin............	★	★	6	6P (xx)		2/3 present	Day after publication date unless otherwise specified
Wyoming.............	★	★	3	15A		2/3 elected	Specified in act
American Samoa...	★	…	10		30A	2/3 elected	60 days after adjournment (bb)
Guam	★	★	10		30P	2/3 elected	Immediately (cc)
No. Mariana Islands	★	…	40 (h)(dd)		30P	2/3 elected	Immediately
Puerto Rico..........	★	…	10		30A	2/3 elected	Specified in act
U.S. Virgin Islands	★(v)	★(v)	10	10P		2/3 elected	Immediately

See footnotes at end of table.

ENACTING LEGISLATION: VETO, VETO OVERRIDE AND EFFECTIVE DATE—Continued

Source: The Council of State Governments' survey, December 2005.

Key:
★ — Yes
. . . — No
A — Days after adjournment of legislature.
P — Days after presentation to governor.

(a) Sundays excluded, unless otherwise indicated.

(b) Includes language in appropriations bill.

(c) Bill returned to house of origin with governor's objections.

(d) Effective date may be established by the law itself or may be otherwise changed by vote of the legislature. Special or emergency acts are usually effective immediately.

(e) Except bills presented within five days of final adjournment.

(f) Governor can also reduce amounts in appropriations bills. In Hawaii, governor can reduce items in executive appropriations measures, but cannot reduce or item veto amounts appropriated for the judicial or legislative branches.

(g) Different number of votes required for revenue and appropriations bills. Alaska—3/4ths elected. Illinois—3/5ths members elected for bill to be totally enacted, or for vetoed item in appropriations bill. Majority of members elected for appropriations bill with reduction veto. Oklahoma—emergency bills, 3/4ths vote.

(h) Sundays included.

(i) Date signed, date received by Secretary of State if effective without signature, date that veto is overridden, or other specified date.

(j) For legislation enacted in regular sessions: January of the following year. Urgency legislation: immediately upon chaptering by Secretary of State. Legislation enacted in Special Session: 91st day after adjournment of the special session at which the bill was passed.

(k) An act takes effect on the date stated in the act, or if no date is stated in the act, then on its passage.

(l) Constitution withholds right to veto constitutional amendments.

(m) Bills vetoed after adjournment are returned to the legislature for reconsideration. Maryland—reconsidered at the next meeting of the same General Assembly. Mississippi—returned within three days after the beginning of the next session. South Carolina—within two days after the next meeting.

(n) Effective date for bills which become law on or after July 1. Illinois—Unless specified in the act. Exception: an act enacted by a bill passed after May 31 cannot take effect before June 1 of the following year unless it was passed by 3/5ths of the members elected to each house.

(o) Except Sundays and legal holidays. In Hawaii, except Saturdays, Sundays, holidays and any days in which the legislature is in recess prior to its adjournment. In Oregon, except Saturdays and Sundays.

(p) The governor must notify the legislature 10 days before the 45th day of his intent to veto a measure on that day. The legislature may convene on the 45th day after adjournment to consider the vetoed measures. If the legislature fails to reconvene, the bill does not become law. If the legislature reconvenes, it may pass the measure over the governor's veto or it may amend the law to meet the governor's objections. If the law is amended, the governor must sign the bill within 10 days after it is presented to him in order for it to become law.

(q) Varies with date of the veto.

(r) Bills become effective without signature if not signed or vetoed.

(s) Unless otherwise provided, June 1 is the effective date for bond bills, July 1 for budget, tax and revenue bills. By custom, October 1 is the usual effective date for legislation. For vetoed legislation, 30 days after the veto is overridden or on the date specified in the bill, whichever is later. If the bill is an emergency measure, it takes effect when enacted.

(t) Different date for fiscal legislation. Minnesota, Montana—July 1.

(u) If bill has an emergency clause, it becomes effective upon governor's signature.

(v) May item veto language or amounts in a bill that contains two or more appropriations.

(w) Bills passed between 45th and 10th day before the expiration of the two-year term become law unless vetoed before noon of the day prior to the expiration of the two-year term. A bill passed between the 10th and last day of the term becomes law only upon the governor's signature.

(x) August 1 after filing with the secretary of state. Appropriations and tax bills July 1 after filing with secretary of state, or date set in legislation by Legislative Assembly, or by date established by emergency clause.

(y) Must include majority of elected members.

(z) Special sessions—first day of fourth month after adjournment.

(aa) Five days for supplemental appropriation bills.

(bb) Laws required to be approved only by the governor. An act required to be approved by the U.S. Secretary of the Interior only after it is vetoed by the governor and so approved takes effect 40 days after it is returned to the governor by the secretary.

(cc) U.S. Congress may annul.

(dd) Twenty days for appropriations bills.

(ee) Except bills going up in the last three days of session, for which the governor has 20 days.

(ff) Must veto entire amount of any item; an item is an indivisible sum of money dedicated to a stated purpose.

(gg) Unless otherwise stated.

(hh) Line item veto.

(ii) The exception covers such matters as emergency measures and court bills that originally required a 2/3rds majority for passage. In those cases, the same extraordinary majority vote is required to override a veto.

(jj) Unless emergency declared or date specific in text of measure.

(kk) Following adjournment of the legislature, the governor has 30 days to sign or veto bills delivered to him. If no action is taken, the bill does not become law ("pocket veto").

(ll) Several specific requirements of 3/4 majority.

(mm) The governor must notify the legislature 10 days before the 45th day of his intent to veto a measure. The legislature may convene or the 45th day after adjournment to consider the vetoed measures. If the legislature fails to reconvene, the bill does not become law. If the legislature reconvenes, it may pass the measure over the governor's veto or it may amend the law to meet the governor's objections. If the law is amended, the governor must sign the bill within 10 days after it is presented to him in order for it to become law.

(nn) Legislature can up to 30 days after a bill's final passage to present it to the Governor.

(oo) Illinois has no "pocket veto."

(pp) Bill enacted if not signed/vetoed within time frames.

(qq) Bill becomes law unless the legislature by their adjournment prevents its return, in which case it shall have such force and effect, unless returned within 3 days after the next meeting of the same legislature which enacted the bill or resolution, the bill or resolution shall not be a law.

(rr) Or until house of origin returns.

(ss) The day of delivery and Sundays are not counted for purposes of calculating these periods.

(tt) Emergency, current appropriation, and tax legislation effective immediately. The General Assembly may also enact an uncodified section of law specifying a desired effective date that is after the constitutionally established effective date.

(uu) Excludes Saturdays, Sundays, and holidays.

(vv) Includes all calendar days.

(ww) If part of the item.

(xx) Six-day clock begins when governor calls for bills. If any bills are not called for by a fixed date, they are sent automatically.

Table 3.17
LEGISLATIVE APPROPRIATIONS PROCESS: BUDGET DOCUMENTS AND BILLS

State or other jurisdiction	Legal source of deadline		Budget document submission — Submission date relative to convening					Budget bill introduction		
	Constitutional	Statutory	Prior to session	Within one week	Within two weeks	Within one month	Over one month	Same time as budget document	Another time	Not until committee review of budget document
Alabama	★	★	...	★	...	...	...	★	...	...
Alaska	★	★	Dec. 15	(a)	...	...	...	★	...	...
Arizona	...	★	★	...	...	...	...	...	...	★
Arkansas	...	★	★	...	...	...	...	...	...	★
California	★	...	...	...	...	...	...	★	...	...
Colorado	...	★	★(b)	...	...	...	...	...	76th day by rule	...
Connecticut	...	★	...	...	...	(a)	...	★	...	...
Delaware	...	...	...	...	...	...	...	...	...	...
Florida	★	★	★	...	...	...	...	...	...	★
Georgia	★	...	...	(a)	...	...	...	★	...	...
Hawaii	...	★	30 days	...	...	...	...	...	★	...
Idaho	...	★	...	★	...	...	...	...	...	★
Illinois	...	★	...	...	...	...	★(v)	...	★(u)	...
Indiana	...	★	...	...	...	...	...	...	★	...
Iowa	...	★	...	...	...	(a)	...	...	...	★(c)
Kansas	...	★	...	...	★(e)	...	...	...	★	...
Kentucky	...	★	...	...	(a)	...	...	★	...	...
Louisiana	...	★	(f)	(f)	...	...	...	(g)	...	...
Maine	...	★	...	(a)	...	...	...	★	...	...
Maryland	★	...	...	★(e)	...	...	...	★(h)	...	...
Massachusetts	...	★	...	...	...	★	...	★	...	...
Michigan	...	★	...	...	...	★	...	★	...	...
Minnesota	...	★	...	...	...	★	...	★	...	...
Mississippi	...	★	★	...	...	...	...	...	★	...
Missouri	★	...	...	...	...	★	...	...	...	★
Montana	...	★	★	...	...	...	...	...	★	...
Nebraska	...	★	★	...	...	...	...	★(p)	...	...
Nevada	★	...	(a)	...	...	...	...	...	...	★
New Hampshire	...	★	...	...	...	...	(a)	★	...	...
New Jersey	...	★	...	...	...	...	★	...	...	★(p)
New Mexico	...	★	...	...	★	...	...	...	★	...
New York	★(l)	...	...	...	★(e)(o)	...	...	★(m)	...	...
North Carolina	...	...	...	...	...	...	...	★	...	...
North Dakota	...	★	(n)	...	...	...	...	...	...	★
Ohio	...	★	...	...	...	★(e)	...	★	...	...
Oklahoma	...	★	★	★	...	...	...	★	...	...
Oregon	...	★	Dec. 1 (e)	...	...	...	...	...	★(a)	...
Pennsylvania	★	...	...	...	...	★	...	...	★	★
Rhode Island	...	★	...	...	...	...	★	...	★	...
South Carolina	...	★	...	★	...	...	...	...	...	★(q)
South Dakota	...	★	...	...	...	...	★	...	★	...
Tennessee	...	★	...	...	★(a)(e)	★(a)(e)	...	★	...	...
Texas	...	★	...	6th day	...	...	...	...	★(t)	...
Utah	...	★	...	★(r)	...	...	...	...	★(s)	...
Vermont	...	...	...	(k)	...	...	...	...	...	★
Virginia	...	★	Dec. 20	...	...	...	...	★	...	...
Washington	...	★	Dec. 20 (d)	...	...	...	...	★	(i)	...
West Virginia	★	...	...	★	...	...	...	★	...	...
Wisconsin	...	★	...	...	...	★(j)	...	★	...	...
Wyoming	...	★	Dec. 1	...	...	...	...	...	...	★
No. Mariana Islands	...	★	(a)	...	...	...	...	...	(j)	★
Puerto Rico	...	★	...	...	...	★	...	...	...	★
U.S. Virgin Islands	...	★	May 30	...	...	...	...	...	★	...

See footnotes at end of table.

LEGISLATIVE APPROPRIATIONS PROCESS: BUDGET DOCUMENTS AND BILLS — Continued

Source: The Council of State Governments' survey, December 2005.
Key:
★ — Yes
. . . — No

(a) Specific time limitations: Alaska—4th legislative day; Connecticut—not later than the first session day following the 3rd day in February, in each odd-numbered year; Georgia—first five days of session; Iowa—no later than February 1; Kentucky—10th legislative day; Maine—by Friday following the first Monday in January; Nevada—no later than 14 days before commencement of regular session; New Hampshire—by February 15; Oregon—December 15 in even-numbered years; Tennessee—on or before February 1; No. Mariana Islands—no later than 6 months before the beginning of the fiscal year.

(b) Presented by November 1 to the Joint Budget Committee.

(c) Executive budget bill is introduced and used as a working tool for committee.

(d) For fiscal period other than biennium, 20 days prior to first day of session.

(e) Later for first session of a new governor; Kansas—21 days; Maryland—10 days after; New Jersey—February 15; New York—February 1; Ohio—by March 15; Oregon—February 1; Tennessee—March 1.

(f) The governor shall submit his executive budget to the Joint Legislative Committee on the budget no later than 45 days prior to each regular session; except that in the first year of each term, the executive budget shall be submitted no later than 30 days prior to the regular session. Copies shall be made available to the entire legislature on the first day of each regular session.

(g) Bills appropriating monies for the general operating budget and ancillary appropriations, bills appropriating funds for the expenses of the legislature and the judiciary must be submitted to the legislature for introduction no later than 45 days prior to each regular session, except that in the first year of each term, such appropriation bills shall be submitted no later than 30 days prior to the regular session.

(h) Appropriations bills other than the budget bill (supplementary) may be introduced at any time. They must provide their own tax source and may not be enacted until the budget bill is enacted.

(i) Even-numbered years.

(j) Last Tuesday in January. A later submission date may be requested by the governor.

(k) No official submission dates. Occurs by custom early in the session.

(l) The legislature must transmit to the Governor itemized estimates of its financial needs no later than December 1.

(m) Submission of the Governor's budget bills to the legislature occurs with submission of the executive budget. The bills, when passed by both houses, become law without further action by the Governor—with the exceptions of appropriations for the legislature, and separate items added to the Governor's bills, which require approval.

(n) Legislative Council's Budget Section receives budget during legislature's December organizational session.

(o) By enacting annual appropriations legislation.

(p) Governor's budget bill is introduced and serves as a working document for the Appropriations Committee. The Governor must submit the budget proposal by January 15 of each odd-numbered year. (Neb.Rev.Stat. sec. 81-125.) The statute extends this deadline to February 1 for a governor who is in his first year of office.

(q) The Ways and Means Committee introduces the Budget Bill within five days after the beginning of the session (S.C. Code 11-11-70).

(r) Must submit to the legislature no later than 3 days after session begins.

(s) Legislative rules require budget bills to be introduced by the 43rd day of the session.

(t) Within first 30 days of session.

(u) There is no constitutional or statutory deadline for introduction of budget bills. But deadlines set by the top leader in each house require bills, including appropriations bills, to be out of committee, passed by the first house, out of committee in the second house, etc. by specific dates.

(v) Third Wednesday in February.

Table 3.18
FISCAL NOTES: CONTENT AND DISTRIBUTION

State or other jurisdiction	Content						Distribution						
								Legislators					
										Appropriations Committee			
	Intent or purpose of bill	Cost involved	Projected future cost	Proposed source of revenue	Fiscal impact on local government	Other	All	Available on request	Bill sponsor	Members	Chair only	Fiscal staff	Executive budget staff
Alabama	★	★	...	★	★	★(a)	...	★	★	...	...	...	...
Alaska	...	★	★	★	...	...	(d)	...	...	...	...	...	...
Arizona	★	★	★	★	★	★	★	★	★	★	...	★	★
Arkansas (f)	...	★	★	...	★	★	★	...	...	...	...	...	...
California	★	★	★	★	★	...	★	★	★	...	...	★	★
Colorado	★	★	★	★	★	★	★	...	...	...	...	...	...
Connecticut	★	★	★	★	★	...	(i)	...	...	...	...	...	...
Delaware	...	★	★	...	...	...	★	...	...	...	...	★	★
Florida	★	★	★	★	★	★	★	...	...	...	...	★	...
Georgia	...	★	★	...	★	...	★	★	...	...	...	...	...
Hawaii	...	...	...	...	...	★	...	...	...	...	★	★	★
Idaho	★	★	★	★	★	...	★	...	...	...	...	(ee)	(ee)
Illinois	...	★	★	...	★	...	...	★	★	...	...	...	...
Indiana	★	★	★	★	★	...	★	...	...	...	...	★	★
Iowa	★	★	★	★	★	...	............................(b)............................						
Kansas	★	★	★	★	★	...	★	★	★	...	★(m)	★	★
Kentucky	★	★	★	★	★	★	...	★	★	★	...	★	...
Louisiana	...	★	★	...	★	...	★	★	...	...	★(o)	★	...
Maine	...	★	★	...	★	...	...	★	★	★	...	★	★
Maryland	...	★	★	★	★	★	...	...	★(y)	...	...	...	...
Massachusetts	...	★(q)	★	...	...	★	★	...	...	...	★	...	...
Michigan	★	★	★	★	★	★(r)	★	...	...	...	...	...	...
Minnesota	★	★	★	★	★	★	★	★	★	★	★	★	★
Mississippi	...	★	★	★	★	...	...	★(ff)	...	...	...	...	...
Missouri	★	★	★	★	★	...	...	★	★	...	...	...	★
Montana	...	★	★	...	★	★(k)	★	...	...	...	...	★	★
Nebraska	...	★	★	★	★	...	★	...	...	...	...	★	...
Nevada	...	★	★	★	★	★	★	...	...	...	...	...	...
New Hampshire	★	★	★	★	★	★	...	★	...	...	★	★	★
New Jersey	★	★	★	★	★	...	★	...	...	...	...	...	...
New Mexico	★	★	★	★	(t)	...	...	★	★	★	...	(v)	(v)
New York	...	★	★	...	★	...	...	★	★	★	...	★	...
North Carolina	...	★	★	...	★	★	(c)	...	...	...	...	...	...
North Dakota (w)	...	...	★(x)	★	★	★(n)	(gg)	★	...	...	...	★(z)	★
Ohio	★	★	★	★	★	...	(aa)	...	...	...	...	...	...
Oklahoma	★	★	★	★	...	...	...	★	★	...	★	★	...
Oregon	★	★	★	★	★	★(e)	★	...	...	...	...	...	...
Pennsylvania	...	★	★	★	★	...	...	...	...	★	★	★	...
Rhode Island	★	★	★	★	★	...	...	★	...	★	...	★	★
South Carolina	★	★	★	★	★	...	...	★	...	(j)	...	★	...
South Dakota	...	★	...	...	★	...	★	...	...	...	...	...	...
Tennessee	★	★	★	...	★	...	★(hh)	★	★	...	...	...	...
Texas	...	★	★	★	★	★(g)	★	★	★	★	...	...	★
Utah	...	★	★	★	★	★(u)	★	★	★	...	...	★	★
Vermont	...............(h)...............						...	★	...	★	...	...	...
Virginia	★	★	★	★	★	★(ii)	(bb)	...	★	...	★	★(s)	...
Washington	★	★	★	★	★	...	...	★	★(m)	...	★	★(cc)	...
West Virginia	...	★	★	★	★	...	...	...	...	★	...	...	...
Wisconsin	...	★	★	★	★	...	(l)	...	★	...	...	(l)	★
Wyoming	...	★	★	★	...	...	★(dd)	...	★	...	...	...	...
No. Mariana Islands	★	★	★	★	★	★	...	...	...	...	★	★	★
Puerto Rico	...............(p)...............												
U.S. Virgin Islands	★	★	...	★	...	...	★	...	...	...	...	...	...

See footnotes at end of table.

FISCAL NOTES: CONTENT AND DISTRIBUTION — Continued

Source: The Council of State Governments' survey, December 2005.

Note: A fiscal note is a summary of the fiscal effects of a bill on government revenues, expenditures and liabilities.

Key:

★ — Yes

. . .— No

(a) Fiscal notes are included in bills for final passage calendar.

(b) Fiscal notes are available to everyone.

(c) Fiscal notes are posted on the internet and available to all members.

(d) Fiscal notes are available online to anyone who wishes to review them. Formal copies go to the bill sponsor and each committee to which the bill is referred. A bill cannot be passed from committee without a fiscal note.

(e) Assumptions (methodology/explanation of fiscal figures).

(f) Only retirement, corrections and local government bills require fiscal notes.

(g) Equalized education funding impact statement and criminal justice policy impact statement.

(h) Fiscal notes are not mandatory and their content will vary.

(i) The fiscal notes are printed with the bills favorably reported by the committees.

(j) Fiscal impact statements on proposed legislation are prepared by the Office of State Budget and sent to the House or Senate standing committee that requested the impact. All fiscal impacts are posted on the OSB Web page.

(k) Mechanical defects in bill.

(l) The fiscal estimate is printed as an appendix to the bill; anyone that has a copy of the bill has a copy of the fiscal estimate.

(m) Or to the committee to which referred.

(n) Bills impacting workers' compensation benefits or premiums must have actuarial impact statement. Bills proposing changes in state and local government retirement system also must have an actuarial note.

(o) Prepared by the Legislative Fiscal Office when a state agency is involved and prepared by Legislative Auditor's office when a local board or commission is involved; copies sent to House and Senate staff offices respectively.

(p) The Legislature of Puerto Rico does not prepare fiscal notes, but upon request the economics unit could prepare one. The Department of Treasury has the duty to analyze and prepare fiscal notes.

(q) Fiscal notes are prepared only if cost exceeds $100,000 or matter has not been acted upon by the Joint Committee on Ways and Means.

(r) Other relevant data.

(s) Legislative budget directors.

(t) Occasionally.

(u) Fiscal notes are to include cost estimates on all proposed bills that anticipate direct expenditures by any Utah resident and the cost to the overall Utah resident population.

(v) Fiscal impact statements prepared by Legislative Finance Committee staff are available to anyone on request and on the legislature's Web site.

(w) Notes required only if impact is $5,000 or more.

(x) A four-year projection.

(y) And to the committee to which referred. After initial hard copy distribution to sponsor and committee, note is released to member computer system and thereafter to the legislative Web site.

(z) Only select fiscal staff.

(aa) Fiscal notes are prepared for bills before being voted on in any standing committee or floor session. Upon distribution to the legislators preparing to vote, the fiscal notes are made public.

(bb) Fiscal impact statements are widely available because they are also posted on the Internet shortly after they are distributed. The Joint Legislative Audit Review Commission (JLARC) also prepares a review of the fiscal impact statement if requested by a standing committee chair. The review statement is also available on the Internet.

(cc) Distributed to appropriate fiscal and policy staff.

(dd) Fiscal notes are included with the bill upon introduction.

(ee) Attached to bill, so available to both fiscal and executive budget staff.

(ff) And committee to which bill referred

(gg) Fiscal notes are available online to anyone from the legislative branch Web site.

(hh) Fiscal notes are available to anyone through our electronic system.

(ii) Technical amendments, if needed.

Table 3.19
BILL AND RESOLUTION INTRODUCTIONS AND ENACTMENTS:
2005 REGULAR SESSIONS

State or other jurisdiction	Duration of session**	Introductions		Enactments		Measures vetoed by governor	Length of session
		Bills	Resolutions*	Bills	Resolutions*		
Alabama	Feb. 1 – May 16, 2005	1,237	1,015	138	62	4 (a)	30L
Alaska	Jan. 10 – May 10, 2005	513	96	97	39	0	121C
Arizona	Jan. 10 – May 13, 2005	1,311	132	334	25	58 (c)	124C
Arkansas	Jan. 10 – May 13, 2005	3,176	174	2,325	112	3	97C
California	Dec. 6, 2004 – Sept. 9, 2005	2,892	214	729	145	232 (c)	123L (b)
Colorado	Jan. 12 – May 11, 2005	602	18	402	1	47	120C
Connecticut	Jan. 5 – June 8, 2005	3,391	265	304	206	9	155C
Delaware	Jan. 11 – June 30, 2005	546	146	222	64	0	44L
Florida	Mar. 8 – May 6, 2005	3,139	181	603	219	52 (c)(h)	60C
Georgia	Jan. 10 – Mar. 31, 2005	1,304	1,672	408	1,492	15	40C
Hawaii	Jan. 19 – May 5, 2005	3,680	905	250	245	26	60L
Idaho	Jan. 10 – Apr. 6, 2005	642	78	414	54	9	87C
Illinois	Jan. 12 – May 31, 2005	6,217	1,028	683	N.A.	30 (a)(c)	(b)
Indiana	Nov. 16, 2004 – Dec. 2004; Jan. 4 – Apr. 29, 2005	859	345	246	272	3	N.A.
Iowa	Jan. 10 – Apr. 29, 2005 (p)	2,182	154	184	N.A.	13	131C
Kansas	Jan. 10 – May 20, 2005	853	31	207	15	6 (c)	83C
Kentucky	Jan. 4 – Mar. 21, 2005	741	408	158	26	1 (c)	30L
Louisiana	Apr. 25 – June 23, 2005	1,243	678	513	619	5	60L
Maine	Dec. 1, 2004 – Mar. 30, 2005	1,693	40	463	36	1	30L
Maryland	Jan. 12 – Apr. 11, 2005	2,632	24	617	N.A.	209 (p)	90C
Massachusetts	Jan. 5, 2005 – July 31, 2006 (e)	5,400	250	223	N.A.	(r)	(f)
Michigan	Jan. 12 – Dec. 29, 2005	2,475	25	340	1	17 (c)	(b)
Minnesota	Jan. 4 – May 23, 2005	4,906	134	164	N.A.	5	66L
Mississippi	Jan. 4 – Apr. 6, 2005	2,950	456	396	260	0	N.A.
Missouri	Jan. 5 – May 30, 2005	1,528	100	289	17	2 (c)	77L
Montana	Jan. 2 – Apr. 20, 2005	1,441	87	693	78	8	108L
Nebraska	Jan. 5 – June 3, 2005	763 (n)	244	199	98	5 (n)	90L
Nevada	Feb. 7 – June 6, 2005	1,107	135	513	102	3	120C
New Hampshire	Jan. 5 – June 16, 2005	907	56	298	17	1	23L
New Jersey	Jan. 10, 2005 – Jan. 9, 2006 (q)	7,342	842	582	103	(c)	150
New Mexico	Jan. 18 – Mar. 19, 2005	2,182	50	420	7	69 (c)	60C
New York	Jan. 5, 2005 – Jan. 4, 2006	15,379	(i)	762	4,102	117 (g)	365C
North Carolina	Jan. 26 – Sept. 2, 2005	2,903	81 (d)	463	58 (d)	2	220C
North Dakota	Jan. 4 – Apr. 23, 2005	944	100	615	74	6	76C
Ohio	Jan. 3 – Dec. 29, 2005	709	70	64	21	1 (c)	(b)
Oklahoma	Feb. 7 – May 27, 2005	2,077	206	478	134	10 (c)	70L
Oregon	Jan. 10 – Aug. 8, 2005	2,957	131	843	46	4 (c)	208C
Pennsylvania	Jan. 4 – Nov. 30, 2005	3,423	756	96	375	2	76L
Rhode Island	Jan. 4 – July 15, 2005	2,914	N.A.	510	397	30	(b)
South Carolina	Jan. 11 – June 2, 2005	1,386	838	183	677	24 (a)(o)	66L
South Dakota	Jan. 11 – Mar. 12, 2005	491	33	284	26	7 (a)	40L
Tennessee	Jan. 11 – May 28, 2005	4,837	1,468	582	1,400 (m)	0	(b)
Texas	Jan. 11 – May 30, 2005	5,484	438	1,389	207	19	140C
Utah	Jan. 17 – Mar. 2, 2005	592	65	309	52	2 (c)	45C
Vermont	Jan. 5 – June 16, 2005	728	358	93	310	2	(j)
Virginia	Jan. 12 – Feb. 27, 2005	2,181	825	1,028	2	7	47C
Washington	Jan. 10 – Apr. 24, 2005	2,460	100	523	9	9	105C
West Virginia	Feb. 9 – Apr. 9, 2005	2,116	N.A.	265	N.A.	16	60C
Wisconsin	Jan. 3, 2005 – (k)	1,404	182	104	81	17 (c)	38L
Wyoming	Jan. 11 – Mar. 3, 2005	524	22	251	3	2 (c)	37L
U.S. Virgin Islands	(l)	131	N.A.	17	9	3 (a)	8C

See footnotes at end of table.

BILL AND RESOLUTION INTRODUCTIONS AND ENACTMENTS:
2005 REGULAR SESSIONS — Continued

Source: The Council of State Governments' survey of legislative agencies, January 2006.

*Includes Joint and Concurrent resolutions.

**Actual adjournment dates are listed regardless of constitutional or statutory limitations. For more information on provisions, see Table 3.2, "Legislative Sessions: Legal Provisions."

Key:

C — Calendar day.

L — Legislative day (in some states, called a session or workday; definition may vary slightly; however, it generally refers to any day on which either chamber of the legislature is in session).

N.A. — Not available.

(a) Number of vetoes overridden: Alabama – 4; Illinois – 8 vetoes and 6 amendatory vetoes; Rhode Island – 9; South Carolina – 22; South Dakota – 1; U.S. Virgin Islands – 1.

(b) Length of session: California – 123L for first year of session, 2005; Illinois – Senate 54L and House 63L; Michigan – Senate 113L and House 110L; Ohio – Senate 130L and House 122L; Rhode Island – Senate 61L and House 71L; Tennessee – Senate 47L and House 49L.

(c) Line-item or partial vetoes. Arizona – includes 3 line-item vetoes; California – 3 line-item vetoes; Illinois – plus 9 amendatory vetoes; Florida – 5 line-item vetoes; Kansas – includes 1 line-item veto; Kentucky – and 13 line-items; Michigan – 8 line-item vetoes; Missouri – 7 line-item appropriations; New Jersey – 1 line-item veto and 4 conditional vetoes; New Mexico – 3 partial vetoes; Ohio – budget bill contained line-item vetoes; Oklahoma – 2 item vetoes; Oregon – 1 line-item veto; Utah – 1 line-item veto; Wisconsin – 1 partial veto; Wyoming – 3 with line-item vetoes.

(d) Numbers include concurrent and joint resolutions only. For North Carolina, numbers only include joint resolutions.

(e) The Massachusetts legislative session convened January 5, 2005 and will adjourn July 31, 2006. Informal session will occur after July 31, 2006 until the end of 2006.

(f) Through the end of February 2006, 45 formal and 107 informal session days.

(g) As of January 27, 2006 there were still four bills remaining in the governor's hands. He has until the first week in February to take action on them.

(h) The legislature had until the end of the 2006 Regular Session to override a veto from the 2005 Regular Session.

(i) There are no official statistics for resolution introductions.

(j) Senate – 85 actual days, 181 calendar days; House – 86 actual days, 181 calendar days.

(k) All action carries over to even year.

(l) Session dates in 2005; January 10, February 10 through November, May 4 and 5 through June 2005, July 11, 2005 and August 12, 2005.

(m) Estimated. Tennessee does not track number of enacted resolutions.

(n) Bill introduction total does not include appropriation bills. Number of line-item vetoes by the Governor not specified. Three vetoes were overridden. No line-item vetoes were overridden.

(o) This number does not include appropriation bills. For the 2005–06 Appropriations Bill, H3716, Act 115, 149 measures were vetoed with the legislature overriding 139. The 2005 Capital Reserve Fund, H3717, Act 179, 14 measures were vetoed by the governor with the legislaure overriding 14.

(p) No veto overrides will occur until January of 2006 or if an earlier session is called. Override must be done at next session of the same General Assembly.

(q) New Jersey has a two-year legislative session. Information reflects numbers for January 10, 2005 through January 9, 2006.

(r) Total number of vetoes unavailable; however there were 100 vetoes, counting portions, overridden by the legislature as of February 2006.

Table 3.20
BILL AND RESOLUTION INTRODUCTIONS AND ENACTMENTS: 2005 SPECIAL SESSIONS

State or other jurisdiction	Duration of session**	Introductions		Enactments		Measures vetoed by governor	Length of session
		Bills	Resolutions*	Bills	Resolutions*		
Alabama	July 19 – July 26, 2005	240	187	54	72	6	5L
Alaska	May 11 – May 25, 2005	1	1	10	1	0	15C
Arizona	No special session in 2005						
Arkansas....................	No special session in 2005						
California	Jan. 6, 2005	13	1	0	2	0	46L
Colorado	No special session in 2005						
Connecticut	June 23 – June 29, 2005	7	5	7	5	0	7C
	Oct. 11 – Oct. 11, 2005	0	6	0	6	0	1C
	Oct 25, 2005 – (c)						
	Nov. 2, 2005 – (c)						
Delaware.....................	July 1, 2005	0	9	0	5	0	1C
Florida	Dec. 5 – Dec. 8, 2005	64	4	15	1	0	4C
Georgia	Sept. 6 – Sept. 10, 2005	3	83	2	80	0	5C
Hawaii.........................	July 12, 2005	0	5	12	5	0 (f)	1L
Idaho...........................	No special session in 2005						
Illinois........................	No special session in 2005						
Indiana........................	No special session in 2005						
Iowa	No special session in 2005						
Kansas	June 22 – July 6, 2005	29	12	3	2	4 (e)	15C
Kentucky	No special session in 2005						
Louisiana	No special session in 2005						
Maine	No special session in 2005						
Maryland	No special session in 2005						
Massachusetts.............	No special session in 2005						
Michigan	No special session in 2005						
Minnesota	May 24 – July 13, 2005	248	26	8	N.A.	0 (g)	23L
Mississippi	Mar. 12 – Mar. 13, 2005	7	1	2	1	0	2C
	May 18 – May 28, 2005	178	62	119	59	0	11C
	June 28 – July 2, 2005	9	43	1	35	0	5C
	July 15, 2005	2	7	1	6	0	1C
Missouri......................	Sept. 6 – Sept. 15, 2005	10	1	4	0	0	8L
Montana	Dec. 14 – Dec. 15, 2005	9	3	4	3	0	2L
Nebraska.....................	No special session in 2005						
Nevada	June 7, 2005	12	8	11	8	0	1C
New Hampshire..........	No special session in 2005						
New Jersey..................	No special session in 2005						
New Mexico	No special session in 2005						
New York	Dec. 21, 2005 (d)	2	0	2	0	0	1L
North Carolina	Oct. 12, 2005 (h)	0	1	0	1	1	1C
North Dakota..............	No special session in 2005						
Ohio	No special session in 2005						
Oklahoma	May 27 – Aug. 31, 2005	13	3	1	3	0	6C
Oregon	No special session in 2005						
Pennsylvania	Sept. 28, 2005 – (b)	113	5	0	4	0	(b)
Rhode Island	No special session in 2005						
South Carolina	No special session in 2005						
South Dakota..............	No special session in 2005						
Tennessee	No special session in 2005						
Texas	June 21 – July 20, 2005	202	50	3	20	0	30C
Utah	Apr. 20 – Apr. 21, 2005	15	1	14	1	0	2C
Vermont	June 16, 2005						1L
Virginia	No special session in 2005						
Washington.................	No special session in 2005						
West Virginia..............	Jan. 24 – Jan. 29, 2005	N.A.	N.A.	4	1	N.A.	6C
	Apr. 16, 2005	N.A.	N.A.	6	0	N.A.	1C
	May 16 – May 17, 2005	N.A.	N.A.	N.A.	N.A.	N.A.	2C
	Sept. 7 – Sept. 13, 2005	21	N.A.	N.A.	N.A.	N.A.	6C
Wisconsin....................	Jan. 12, 2005	2	0	1	0	0	1L
Wyoming.....................	No special session in 2005						
U.S. Virgin Islands	No special session in 2005						

See footnotes at end of table.

BILL AND RESOLUTION INTRODUCTIONS AND ENACTMENTS:
2005 SPECIAL SESSIONS — Continued

Source: The Council of State Governments' survey of state legislative agencies, December 2005 and January 2006.

*Includes Joint and Concurrrent resolutions.

**Actual adjournment dates are listed regardless of constitutional or statutory limitations. For more information on provisions, see Table 3.2, "Legislative Sessions: Legal Provisions."

Key:

N.A. — Not available.

C — Calendar day.

L — Legislative day (in some states, called a session or workday; definition may vary slightly; however, it generally refers to any day on which either chamber of the legislature is in session).

(a) Joint resolutions only.

(b) Still in session as of January 27, 2006.

(c) Connecticut is concurrently in two special sessions as of November, 16, 2005.

(d) New York has a year-round session. A special session, or extraordinary session, is a session called by the governor.

(e) All four were line-item vetoes.

(f) Twelve vetoes overridden by legislature.

(g) One line-item veto.

(h) This was a reconvened session to consider vetoed bills.

Table 3.21
STAFF FOR INDIVIDUAL LEGISLATORS

State or other jurisdiction	Senate Capitol Personal	Senate Capitol Shared	Senate District	House/Assembly Capitol Personal	House/Assembly Capitol Shared	House/Assembly District
Alabama	. . .	YR/2	(u)	. . .	YR/10	(u)
Alaska	YR/SO	. . .	YR	YR/SO	. . .	YR
Arizona	YR (a)	. . .	. . .	. . .	YR (a)	. . .
Arkansas	. . .	YR	. . .	. . .	YR	. . .
California	YR	. . .	YR	YR	. . .	YR
Colorado (b)	YR/5, SO/35	YR/5, SO/2	. . .	YR/5, SO/65	YR/2, SO/2	. . .
Connecticut (d)	YR/36	. . .	. . .	. . .	YR/38	. . .
Delaware	. . . . (v)					
Florida	YR (e)	. . .	YR (e)	YR (e)	. . .	YR (e)
Georgia	. . .	YR/3, SO/68	. . .	. . .	YR/25, SO/113	. . .
Hawaii	YR	. . .	. . .	YR	. . .	. . .
Idaho	. . .	SO, YR (x)	. . .	. . .	SO, YR (x)	. . .
Illinois	YR	YR (f)	YR (f)	YR	YR (f)	YR (f)
Indiana	. . .	YR/2 (g)	. . .	. . .	YR	. . .
Iowa	SO	. . .	. . .	SO	. . .	. . .
Kansas	SO	. . .	. . .	. . .	SO/3	. . .
Kentucky	. . .	YR (h)	. . .	. . .	YR (h)	. . .
Louisiana	(i)	YR (j)	YR (i)	(i)	YR (j)	YR (i)
Maine	YR, SO (y)	YR/27, SO/7	. . .	. . .	(l)	. . .
Maryland	YR, SO (t)	. . .	YR (t)	YR (t)	SO (t)	YR (t)
Massachusetts	YR	. . .	. . .	YR	. . .	. . .
Michigan	YR	. . .	. . .	YR	. . .	. . .
Minnesota	YR	. . .	. . .	YR	. . .	. . .
Mississippi	. . .	YR	. . .	. . .	YR	. . .
Missouri	YR	YR	. . .	YR	YR	. . .
Montana	. . .	SO	. . .	. . .	SO	. . .
Nebraska	YR	. . .	. . .	. . . . Unicameral		
Nevada	SO (c)	YR	. . .	SO (c)	YR	. . .
New Hampshire	. . .	YR	. . .	. . .	YR	. . .
New Jersey	YR (e)	. . .	(e)	YR (e)	. . .	(e)
New Mexico (k)	SO (m)	. . .	. . .	. . .	SO/2	. . .
New York	YR (aa)	. . .	YR (aa)	YR (aa)	. . .	YR (aa)
North Carolina	YR (w)	YR	. . .	YR (w)	YR	. . .
North Dakota	. . .	SO (c)	. . .	. . .	SO (c)	. . .
Ohio	YR	YR	(bb)	YR	YR	(bb)
Oklahoma	YR	. . .	. . .	. . .	YR	. . .
Oregon	YR	. . .	. . .	YR	. . .	YR
Pennsylvania	YR	. . .	YR	YR	. . .	YR
Rhode Island	. . .	YR (ee)	. . .	. . .	YR (ee)	. . .
South Carolina	. . .	YR (z)	. . .	YR	. . .	. . .
South Dakota	. . .	SO	. . .	. . .	SO	. . .
Tennessee	YR	. . .	. . .	(cc)	YR	. . .
Texas	YR	. . .	YR	YR	. . .	YR
Utah	(o)	SO	. . .	(o)	SO	. . .
Vermont	YR/1 (n)	. . .	. . .	YR/1 (n)	. . .	. . .
Virginia	SO (dd)	. . .	(dd)	SO (dd)	SO/2	(dd)
Washington	YR (p)	. . .	(q)	YR	. . .	. . .
West Virginia	SO	. . .	. . .	. . .	SO/17	. . .
Wisconsin	YR (r)	. . .	(r)	YR	. . .	(r)
Wyoming	. . .	. . .	. . .	. . .	. . .	. . .
No. Mariana Islands	YR (s)	(s)	. . .	YR (s)	(s)	(r)
Puerto Rico	YR (s)	. . .	. . .	YR (s)	. . .	. . .
U.S. Virgin Islands	YR (s)	. . .	. . .	. . . . Unicameral		

See footnotes at end of table.

STAFF FOR INDIVIDUAL LEGISLATORS — Continued

Source: The Council of State Governments' survey, December 2005.

Note: For entries under column heading "Shared," figures after slash indicate approximate number of legislators per staff person, where available.

Key:

. . . — Staff not provided for individual legislators.

YR — Year-round.

SO — Session only.

IO — Interim only.

(a) Representatives share a secretary with another legislator; however, House leadership and committee chairs usually have their own secretarial staff. All legislators share professional research staff.

(b) The number of year-round staff is comprised of leadership staff and caucus staff. Each caucus may also hire additional shared staff during the session. During the session, each legislator can hire an aide for a limited number of hours.

(c) Secretarial staff; in North Dakota, leadership only.

(d) The numbers are for staff assigned to specific legislators. There is additional staff working in the leadership offices that also supports the rank-and-file members.

(e) Personal and district staff are the same. In Florida, two out of the three district employees may travel to the capitol for sessions.

(f) The only staff working for individual rank-and-file legislators are (1) one secretary in the Capitol complex for each two members and (2) district staff, whom legislators select and pay from a separate allowance for that purpose. Partisan staffers help individual legislators with many issues in addition to staffing committees.

(g) Leadership has one legislative assistant. During session, college interns are hired to provide additional staff—one for every two members. Leadership has one intern.

(h) Leadership offices provide staff support year-round. Individual legislators have access to clerical support year-round, augmented during a session.

(i) Each legislator may hire as many assistants as desired, but pay from public funds ranges from $2,000 to $3,000 per month per legislator. Assistant(s) generally work in the district office but may also work at the capitol during the session.

(j) The six caucuses are assigned one full-time position each (potentially 24 legislators per one staff person).

(k) Speaker, pro tem and leadership have staff year-round.

(l) The House members do not have individual staff. There are 20 people who work year-round in the three partisan offices, 12 of whom are legislative aides who primarily work directly with legislators.

(m) Includes clerical plus attendant or analyst.

(n) No personal staff except one administrative assistant for the Speaker and one for the Senate Pro Tempore.

(o) Legislators are provided student interns during session.

(p) Leadership, caucus chair, and Ways and Means Committee chair have two full-time staff each. All other legislators have one full-time staff year-round and one additional staff session only.

(q) Full-time staff may move to the district office during interim period.

(r) Members may assign personal staff to work in the district office.

(s) Individual staffing and staff pool arrangements are at the discretion of the individual legislator.

(t) Senators have one year-round administrative aide and one session only secretary. Delegates have one part-time year-round administrative aide and a shared session only secretary. Legislators may increase staff and also hire student interns if their district office funds are used.

(u) Six counties have local delegation offices with shared staff.

(v) Staffers are a combination of full-time, part-time, shared, personal, etc. and their assignments change throughout the year.

(w) Part time during interim.

(x) Idaho has 2 full-time year-round, 3 part-time year-round employees and 32 session only employees in the Senate. The House has 2 full-time and 1 part-time person year-round and 37 additional people during session.

(y) President's office: 6 year-round; Majority office: 7 year-round, 1 session only; Minority office: 5 year-round, 1 session only; Secretary's office: 9 year-round, 5 session only.

(z) Senators that chair a committee do not share their staff.

(aa) House/party leaders determine allowances/funds for members once allocations are made. Members have considerable independence in hiring personal and committee staffs.

(bb) Some legislators maintain district offices at their own expense.

(cc) Several House members have year-round personal staff, depending on seniority and committee assignments.

(dd) Applies to secretarial staff provided to the members during the session by the Clerk's offices. Members also receive a set dollar allowance to hire additional staff (secretarial or legislative assistants) who may serve year-round.

(ee) The General Assembly has a total of 280 full-time positions, 267 full-time shared staff and additional 13 full-time positions for the House.

Table 3.22
STAFF FOR LEGISLATIVE STANDING COMMITTEES

State or other jurisdiction	Committee staff assistance				Source of staff services **							
	Senate		House/Assembly		Joint central agency (a)		Chamber agency (b)		Caucus or leadership		Committee or committee chair	
	Prof.	Cler.	Prof.	Cler.	Prof.	Cler.	Prof.	Cler.	Prof.	Cler.	Prof.	Cler.
Alabama	●	★	●	★	B	B	B	B	...	...	B	B
Alaska	★	●	★	●	B	B	...	...	B	B	...	...
Arizona	★	★	★	★	B	B	S, H	S, H	S, H	S, H	S, H	S, H
Arkansas	★	★	★	★	B	B	...	...	...	...	...	...
California	★	★	★	★	B	B	B	B	B	B	B	B
Colorado	★	...	★	...	B	...	B	B	B	B	...	...
Connecticut	...	★	...	★	B	...	...	...	...	B	...	B
Delaware	...	...	...	...	B	B	...	...	...	...	...	...
Florida	★	★	★	★	B	B	S, H	S, H	S, H	S, H	S, H	S, H
Georgia	●	★	●	★	B	B	B	B	B	B	B	...
Hawaii	●	★	★	★	B	B	S, H	S, H	S, H	S, H	S, H	S, H
Idaho	...	★	...	★	B (n)	B (n)	...	...	...	B (o)	...	...
Illinois	★	★	★	★	...	...	B	B	B	B	...	...
Indiana	★	...	●	...	...	...	S		S	...	...	...
Iowa	★	...	★	...	B	...	(d)	...	...	...	...	...
Kansas	★	★	★	★	B	B (e)	...	...	...	...	...	...
Kentucky	★	★	★	★	B	B	B	B	B (p)	B (p)	B	B
Louisiana	★(m)	★	★(m)	★	B	B	B	B	B	B	B (g)	B (g)
Maine	★(c)	★(c)	★(c)	★(c)	B	B	S, H	S, H	S, H	S, H	...	B
Maryland	★(h)	★(h)	★(h)	★(h)	B	B	...	...	...	...	...	...
Massachusetts	★	★	★	★	...	...	...	...	...	...	...	...
Michigan	★	★	★	★	B	...	...	H	B	...	...	S
Minnesota	★	★	★	★	...	...	B	...	H	H	B	B
Mississippi	●	★	●	★	...	...	B	B	...	...	B	B
Missouri	★	...	★	...	B	...	B, S, H	...	S	S	S, H	...
Montana	★	★	★	★	B	...	...	B	...	...	...	...
Nebraska	★	★	U	U	(q)	...	(q)	...	(q)	...	(q)	...
Nevada	★	★	★	★	B	...	...	B	...	...	...	...
New Hampshire	●	★	★	★	B	...	S, H	S, H	...	...	...	...
New Jersey	★	★	★	★	B (r)	B (r)	B (r)	B (r)	B (r)	B (r)	...	...
New Mexico	★	★	★	★	...	...	B (g)	B (g)	...	...	...	...
New York	★	★	★	★	...	...	B	B	B	B	B	B
North Carolina	★	★(i)	★	★(i)	B	...	...	...	...	...	...	B (i)
North Dakota	★(f)	★	★(f)	★	B	...	B	...	...	...	...	...
Ohio	★	★	★	★	B	...	...	...	...	...	B	B
Oklahoma	★	★	★	★	...	...	S, H	S, H	...	...	S, H	S, H
Oregon	★	★	★	★	B	B	...	...	...	...	B	B
Pennsylvania	★	★	★	★	B	B	B	B	B	B	B	B
Rhode Island	●	★	●	★	B	B	...	B	...	...	B	...
South Carolina	★	★	★	★	B	B	B	B	B	B	B	B
South Dakota	★	★	★	★	B (h)	...	...	...	...	...	...	...
Tennessee	★	★	★	★	B	...	B	B	...	...	...	B
Texas	★	★	★	★	B	B	B	...	...	...	B	B
Utah	★	★	★	★	B	...	...	B	...	...	...	...
Vermont	★	●	★	●	B	B	...	...	...	...	...	...
Virginia	★	★	★	★	B	...	B	B	...	...	(s)	(s)
Washington	★	★	★	★	...	...	...	...	B	B	B (k)	B (k)
West Virginia	★	★	★	★	B	B	B	B	B	B	B	B
Wisconsin	★	★	★	★	B	...	...	...	...	...	(t)	B
Wyoming	★(j)	★(j)	★(j)	★(j)	B	B	...	B	...	...	...	B
No. Mariana Islands	★	★	★	★	B (l)	B (p)	(l)	B (l)	B (l)	B (l)	B (l)	B (l)
Puerto Rico	★	★	★	★	B (l)	B (l)	B (l)	B (l)	B (l)	B (l)	B (l)	B (l)
U.S. Virgin Islands	★	★	U	U	S (l)	S (l)	S (l)	S (l)	S (l)	S (l)	S (l)	S (l)

See footnotes at end of table.

STAFF FOR LEGISLATIVE STANDING COMMITTEES — Continued

Source: The Council of State Governments' survey, December 2005.

** — Multiple entries reflect a combination of organizations and location of services.

Key:

★ — All committees

● — Some committees

. . . — Services not provided

B — Both chambers

H — House

S — Senate

U — Unicameral

(a) Includes legislative council or service agency or central management agency.

(b) Includes chamber management agency, office of clerk or secretary and House or Senate research office.

(c) Standing committees are joint House and Senate committees.

(d) The Senate secretary and House clerk maintain supervision of committee clerks.

(e) Senators select their secretaries and notify the central administrative services agency; all administrative employee matters handled by the agency.

(f) House and Senate Appropriations Committees have Legislative Council fiscal staff at their hearings.

(g) Staff are assigned to each committee but work under the direction of the chair.

(h) Committees hire additional staff on a contractual basis during session only under direction of chair.

(i) Member's personal secretary serves as a clerk to the committee or subcommittee that the member chairs.

(j) Nonpartisan professional staff from the Legislative Service Office staff joint interim committees and are available to a limited extent to provide some staffing services to standing committees during legislative sessions, but part-time session clerical staff primarily provide staffing support to the standing committees during legislative sessions.

(k) Each chamber has a nonpartisan research staff which provides support services to committees (including chair).

(l) In general, the legislative service agency provides legal and staff assistance for legislative meetings and provides associated materials. Individual legislators hire personal or committee staff as their budgets provide and at their own discretion.

(m) House Appropriations and Senate Finance Committees have Legislative Fiscal Office staff at their hearings.

(n) Professional staff and clerical support are provided via the Legislative Services Office, a nonpartisan office serving all members on a year-round basis.

(o) Leadership in each party hire their respective support staff.

(p) Most services are provided by centralized nonpartisan staff. Leadership offices are staffed by different means.

(q) Services not provided, except that the staff of the Legislative Fiscal Office serves the Appropriations Committee.

(r) Office of Legislative Services staff serve as primary aides to committees. Caucus (partisan) staff also serve as aides under "caucus leadership" staff and they serve their respective membership on a partisan basis.

(s) The House Appropriations Committee and the Senate Finance Committees have their own staff. The Staff members work under the direction of the chair.

(t) Standing committees are staffed by subject specialist from the Joint Legislative Council.

Table 3.23
STANDING COMMITTEES: APPOINTMENT AND NUMBER

State or other jurisdiction	Committee members appointed by:		Committee chairpersons appointed by:		Number of standing committees during regular 2005 session	
	Senate	House/Assembly	Senate	House/Assembly	Senate	House/Assembly
Alabama	CC	S	CC	S	24	24
Alaska	CC	CC	CC	CC	9	9
Arizona	P	S	P	S	13	18
Arkansas	(i)	(d)	(i)	S	10	10
California	CR	S	CR	S	23	29
Colorado	MjL, MnL	S, MnL	MjL	S	10 (a)	11 (a)
Connecticut	PT	S	PT	S	(e)	(e)
Delaware	PT	S	PT	S	26	27
Florida	P	S	P	S	20	18
Georgia	CC	S	CC	S	25	34
Hawaii	P (f)	(g)	P (f)	(g)	15	19
Idaho	PT (h)	S	PT	S	10	14
Illinois	P, MnL	S, MnL	P	S	22	37
Indiana	PT	S	PT	S	20	20
Iowa	MjL, MnL	S	MjL	S	16	17
Kansas	(j)	S	(j)	S	17	22
Kentucky	CC	CC	CC	CC	14	19
Louisiana	P	S (k)	P	S	17	17
Maine	P	S	P	S	17	6
Maryland	P	S	P	S	8	9
Massachusetts	P	S	P	S	5 (e)	8 (e)
Michigan	MjL	S	MjL	S	17	21
Minnesota	CR	S	MjL	S	14	26
Mississippi	P	S	P	S	39	47
Missouri	PT (l)	S	PT	S	35	35
Montana	CC	S	CC	S	17	17
Nebraska	CC	U	E	U	14	U
Nevada	MjL (m)	S (m)	MjL (m)	S (m)	9	10
New Hampshire	P (o)	S (o)	P (o)	S (o)	14	21
New Jersey	P	S	P	S	13 (c)	24 (c)
New Mexico	CC	S	CC	S	9 (aa)	15 (aa)
New York	PT (p)	S	PT (p)	S	33	37
North Carolina	PT	S	PT	S	22	32
North Dakota	CR	CC	MjL	MjL	11	12 (z)
Ohio	P (q)	S (q)	P (q)	S (q)	14	19
Oklahoma	PT, MnL	S	PT	S	19	26
Oregon	P	S	P	S	9 (n)	15 (n)
Pennsylvania	PT	S	PT	S	21	23
Rhode Island	P	S	P	S	11	9
South Carolina	(w)	S	(x)	E	15	11
South Dakota	PT, MnL	S	PT	S	13	13
Tennessee	S	S	S	S	13	16
Texas	P	S (r)	P	S	20	40
Utah	P	S	P	S	11	15
Vermont	CC	S	CC	S	11	14
Virginia	E	S	(s)	S	11	14
Washington	P (b)(t)	S (u)	CC	S (v)	15	21
West Virginia	P	S	P	S	18	15
Wisconsin	MjL	S	MjL	S	17	45
Wyoming	P	S	P	S	12	12
Dist. of Columbia	(y)	U	(y)	U	9	U
No. Mariana Islands	P	S	P	S	8	7
Puerto Rico	P	S	P	S	22	32
U.S. Virgin Islands	E	U	E	U	9	U

See footnotes at end of table.

STANDING COMMITTEES: APPOINTMENT AND NUMBER — Continued

Source: The Council of State Governments' survey, December 2005.

Key:
CC — Committee on Committees
CR — Committee on Rules
E — Election
MjL — Majority Leader
MnL — Minority Leader
P — President
PT — President pro tempore
S — Speaker
U — Unicameral Legislature

(a) Includes appropriations committee.

(b) Lieutenant governor is president of the senate.

(c) Also, joint standing committees. Colorado, 12; New Jersey, 4.

(d) Members of the standing committees shall be selected by House District Caucuses with each caucus selecting five members for each "A" standing committee and five members for each "B" standing committee.

(e) Substantive standing committees are joint committees. Connecticut, 18 (there are also three statutory and four select committees for the House and the Senate); Massachusetts, 26.

(f) President appoints committee members and chairs; minority members on committees are nominated by minority party caucus.

(g) By resolution, with members of majority party designating the chair, vice chairs and majority party members of committees, and members of minority party designating minority party members.

(h) Committee members appointed by the senate leadership under the direction of the president pro tempore, by and with the senate's consent.

(i) Selection process based on seniority.

(j) Committee on Organization, Calendar and Rules.

(k) Speaker appoints only 12 of the 19 members of the Committee on Appropriations.

(l) Senate minority committee members chosen by minority caucus, but appointed by president pro tempore.

(m) Committee composition and leadership usually determined by party caucus, with final decision by leader.

(n) Senate includes eight substantive committees and one procedural committee. House includes 12 substantive committees and three procedural committees.

(o) Senate president and house speaker consult with Democratic leaders.

(p) President pro tempore is also majority leader.

(q) The minority leader may recommend for consideration minority party members for each committee.

(r) For each standing substantive committee of the house, except for the appropriations committee, a maximum of one-half of the membership, exclusive of chair and vice chair, is determined by seniority; the remaining membership of the committee is determined by the speaker.

(s) Senior member of the majority party on the committee is the chair.

(t) Confirmed by the senate.

(u) By each party caucus.

(v) By majority caucus.

(w) Appointment based on seniority (Senate Rule 19D).

(x) Appointed by seniority which is determined by tenure within the committee rather than tenure within the Senate. Also, chair is based on the majority party within the committee (Senate Rule 19E).

(y) Chair of the Council.

(z) House had a constitutional revision committee; Senate did not.

(aa) Senate: includes eight substantive committees and one procedural committee. House: includes 12 substantive committees and three procedural committees.

Table 3.24
RULES ADOPTION AND STANDING COMMITTEES: PROCEDURE

State or other jurisdiction	Constitution permits each legislative body to determine its own rules	Committee meetings open to public*		Specific, advance notice provisions for committee meetings or hearings	Voting/roll call provisions to report a bill to floor
		Senate	House/ Assembly		
Alabama	★	★	★	Senate: 4 hours, if possible. House: 24 hours, except Rules & Local Legislations committees.	Senate: final vote on a bill is recorded. House: recorded vote if requested by member of committee and sustained by one additional committee member.
Alaska	. . .	★	★	For meetings, by 4:00 p.m. on the preceding Thurs.; for first hearings on bills, 5 days.	Roll call vote on any measure taken upon request by any member of either house.
Arizona	★	★	★	Senate: Written agenda for each regular and special meeting containing all bills, memorials and resolutions to be considered shall be distributed to each member of the committee and to the Secretary of the Senate at least five days prior to the committee meeting. House: The committee chair shall prepare an agenda and distribute copies to committee members, the Information Desk and the Chief Clerk's Office by 4 p.m. each Wednesday for all standing committees meeting on Monday of the following week and 4 p.m. each Thursday for all standing committees meeting on any day except Monday of the following week.	Senate: roll call vote. House: roll call vote.
Arkansas..................	★	★	★	Senate: 2 days. House: 24 hours.	Senate: roll call votes are recorded. House: report of committee recommendation signed by committee chair.
California	★	★	★	Senate: advance notice provisions exist. House: advance notice provisions exist.	Senate: roll call. House: roll call.
Colorado..................	★	★	★	Senate: final action on a measure is prohibited unless notice is posted one calendar day prior to its consideration (f). House: none.	Senate: final action by recorded roll call vote. House: final action by recorded roll call vote.
Connecticut	★	★	★	Senate: one day notice for meetings, five days notice for hearings. House: one day notice for meetings, five days notice for hearings.	Senate: roll call required. House: roll call required.
Delaware..................	★	★	★	Senate: agenda released the day before meetings. House: agenda for meetings released on last legislative day of preceding week.	Senate: results of any committee vote are recorded. House: results of any committee vote are recorded.
Florida	★	★	★	Senate: during session—3 hours notice for first 50 days, 4 hours thereafter. House: two days.	Senate: vote on final passage is recorded. House: vote on final passage is recorded.
Georgia	★	★	★	Senate: a list of committee meetings shall be posted by 10:00 a.m. the preceding Friday. House: none.	Senate: recorded roll call taken if one-third members sustain the call for yeas and nays. House: recorded roll call taken if one-fifth members sustain the call for yeas and nays.
Hawaii......................	★	★(a)	★(a)	Senate: 72 hours before 1st referral committee meetings, 48 hours before subsequent referral committee. House: 48 hours.	Senate: final vote is recorded. House: a record is made of a committee quorum and votes to report a bill out.
Idaho.......................	★	★(a)	★(a)	Senate: none. House: per rule; chair provides notice of next meeting dates and times to clerk to be read prior to adjournment each day or session.	Senate: bills can be voted out by voice vote or roll call. House: bills can be voted out by voice vote or roll call.
Illinois.....................	★	★	★	Senate: 6 days. House: 6 days.	Senate: votes on all legislative measures acted upon are recorded. House: votes on all legislative matters acted upon are recorded.

See footnotes at end of table.

RULES ADOPTION AND STANDING COMMITTEES: PROCEDURE — Continued

State or other jurisdiction	Constitution permits each legislative body to determine its own rules	Committee meetings open to public*		Specific, advance notice provisions for committee meetings or hearings	Voting/roll call provisions to report a bill to floor
		Senate	House/ Assembly		
Indiana......................	★	★	★	Senate: 48 hours. House: prior to adjournment or the meeting day next preceding the meeting or announced during session.	Senate: committee reports—do pass; do pass amended; reported out without recommendation. House: majority of quorum; vote can be by roll call or consent.
Iowa	★	★	★	Senate: none. House: none.	Senate: final action by roll call. House: committee reports include roll call on final disposition.
Kansas	★	★	★	Senate: none. House: none.	Senate: vote recorded upon request of member. House: the total for and against actions recorded.
Kentucky	★	★	★	Senate: none. House: none.	Senate: each member's vote recorded on each bill. House: each member's vote recorded on each bill.
Louisiana	★	★(a)	★(a)	Senate: no later than 1:00 p.m. the preceding day. House: no later than 4:00 p.m. the preceding day.	Senate: any motion to report an instrument is decided by a roll call vote. House: any motion to report an instrument is decided by a roll call vote.
Maine	★	★	★	Senate: must be advertised two weekends in advance. House: must be advertised two weekends in advance.	Senate: recorded vote is required to report a bill out of committee. House: recorded vote is required to report a bill out of committee.
Maryland	★	★	★	Senate: none (b). House: none (b).	Senate: the final vote on any bill is recorded. House: the final vote on any bill is recorded.
Massachusetts..........	★	★	★	Senate: 48 hours for public hearings. House: 48 hours for public hearings.	Senate: voice vote or recorded roll call vote at the request of 2 committee members. House: recorded vote upon request by a member.
Michigan..................	★	★	★	Senate and House: notice shall be published in the journal in advance of a hearing. Notice of a special meeting shall be posted at least 18 hours before a meeting. Special provisions for conference committees.	Senate: committee reports include the vote of each member on any bill. House: the daily journal reports the roll call on all motions to report bills.
Minnesota	★	★	★	Senate: 3 days. House: 3 days.	Senate: recorded vote upon request of one member. Upon the request of 3 members, the record of a roll call vote and committee report are printed in the journal. House: recorded roll call vote upon request by a member.
Mississippi	★	★	★	Senate: none. House: none.	Senate: bills are reported out by voice vote or recorded roll call vote. House: bills are reported out by voice vote or recorded roll call vote.
Missouri...................	★	★	★	Senate: 24 hours. House: 24 hours.	Senate: yeas and nays are reported in journal. House: bills are reported out by a recorded roll call vote.
Montana	★	★	★	Senate: 3 legislative days. House: none.	Senate: every vote of each member is recorded and made public. House: every vote of each member is recorded and made public.
Nebraska..................	★	★	U	Seven calendar days notice before hearing a bill.	In executive session, majority of the committee must vote in favor of the motion made.
Nevada	★	★	★	Senate: by rule—"adequate notice" shall be provided. House: by rule—"adequate notice" shall be provided.	Senate: recorded vote is taken upon final committee action on bills. House: recorded vote is taken upon final committee action on bills.
New Hampshire.......	★	★	★	Senate: 4 days. House: no less than 4 days.	Senate: committees may report a bill out by voice or recorded roll call vote. House: committees may report a bill out by voice or recorded roll call vote.
New Jersey...............	★	★	★	Senate: 5 days. House: 5 days.	Senate: the chair reports the vote of each member present on a motion to report a bill. House: the chair reports the vote of each member present on motions with respect to bills.

See footnotes at end of table.

RULES ADOPTION AND STANDING COMMITTEES: PROCEDURE — Continued

State or other jurisdiction	Constitution permits each legislative body to determine its own rules	Committee meetings open to public*		Specific, advance notice provisions for committee meetings or hearings	Voting/roll call provisions to report a bill to floor
		Senate	House/ Assembly		
New Mexico	★	★	★	Senate: none. House: none.	Senate: vote on the final report of the committee taken by yeas and nays. Roll call vote upon request. House: vote on the final report of the committee taken by yeas and nays. Roll call vote upon request.
New York	★	★	★	Senate: 1 week. House: 1 week for hearings, Thursday of prior week for meetings.	Senate: majority roll call vote requires to report. House: majority of committee members must be present for roll call vote; majority vote required to report. No proxy votes allowed.
North Carolina	(c)	★	★	Senate: none (e). House: none (e).	Senate: no roll call vote may be taken in any committee. House: roll call vote taken on any question when requested by member & sustained by one-fifth of members present.
North Dakota...........	★	★	★	Senate: hearing schedule printed Friday mornings. House: hearing schedule printed Friday mornings.	Senate: included with minutes from standing committee. House: included with minutes from standing committee.
Ohio	★	★	★	Senate: 2 days. In a case of necessity, the notice of hearing may be given in a shorter period by such reasonable method as prescribed by the Committee on Rules. House: 5 days. If an emergency requires consideration of a matter at a meeting not announced on notice, the chair may revise or supplement the notice at any time before or during the meeting to include the matter.	Senate: the affirmative votes of a majority of all members of a committee shall be necessary to report or to postpone further consideration of bills or resolutions. Every member present shall vote, unless excused by the chair. At discretion of chair, the roll call may be continued for a vote by any member who was present at the prior meeting, but no later than 10:00 a.m. of next calendar day. House: the affirmative votes of a majority of all members of a committee shall be necessary to report or to postpone further consideration of bills or resolutions. Every member present shall vote, unless excused by the chair. At discretion of chair, the roll call may be continued for a vote by any member who was present at the prior meeting, but no later than 12:00 noon one day following the meeting. Members must be present in order to vote on amendment.
Oklahoma	★	★	★	Senate: 3-day notice. House: 3-day notice.	Senate: roll call vote. House: roll call vote.
Oregon	★	★	★	Senate: 24 hours. House: 24 hours (d).	Senate: the vote on all official actions is recorded. House: motions on measures before a committee are by recorded roll call vote.
Pennsylvania	★	★	★	Senate: written notice to members containing date, time, place and agenda. House: written notice to members containing date, time, place and agenda.	Senate: a majority vote of committee members. House: a majority vote of committee members.
Rhode Island	★	★	★	Senate: notice required. House: notice required.	Senate: majority vote of the members present. House: majority vote of the members present.
South Carolina	★	★	★	Senate: 24 hours. House: 24 hours.	Senate: before the expiration of five days from the date of reference, any bill may be recalled from committee by the vote of three-fourths of the Senators present and voting. House: favorable report out of committee (majority of committee members voting in favor).
South Dakota...........	★	★	★	Senate and House: at least one legislative day must intervene between the date of posting and the date of consideration in both houses.	Senate and House: a majority vote of the members-elect taken by roll call is needed for final disposition on a bill. This applies to both houses.
Tennessee	★	★	★	Senate: 6 days. House: 72 hours when House is recessed or adjourned.	Senate: majority referral to Calendar and Rules Committee, majority of Calendar and Rules Committee referral to floor. House: majority referral to Calendar and Rules Committee, majority of Calendar and Rules Committee referral to floor.

See footnotes at end of table.

RULES ADOPTION AND STANDING COMMITTEES: PROCEDURE — Continued

State or other jurisdiction	Constitution permits each legislative body to determine its own rules	Committee meetings open to public*		Specific, advance notice provisions for committee meetings or hearings	Voting/roll call provisions to report a bill to floor
		Senate	House/ Assembly		
Texas	★	★	★	Senate: 24 hours. House: The House requires five calendar days notice before a public hearing at which testimony will be taken, and two hours notice or an announcement from the floor before a formal meeting (testimony cannot be taken at a formal meeting). 24-hour advance notice is required during special session.	Senate: bills are reported by recorded roll call vote. House: committee reports include the record vote by which the report was adopted, including the vote of each member.
Utah	★	★	★	Senate: 24 hours. House: 24 hours.	Senate: each member present votes on every question and all votes are recorded. House: each member present votes on every question and all votes are recorded.
Vermont	★	★	★	Senate: none. House: none.	Senate: vote is recorded for each committee member for every bill considered. House: vote is recorded for each committee member for every bill considered.
Virginia	★	★(a)	★(a)	Senate: none. House: none.	Senate: recorded vote, except resolutions that do not have a specific vote requirement under the Rules. In these cases, a voice vote is sufficient. House: vote of each member is taken and recorded for each measure.
Washington	★	★	★	Senate: 5 days. House: 5 days.	Senate: bills reported from a committee carry a majority report which must be signed by a majority of the committee. House: every vote to report a bill out of committee is by yeas and nays; the names of the members voting are recorded in the report.
West Virginia	★	★	★	Senate: none. House: none.	Senate: majority of committee members voting. House: majority of committee members voting.
Wisconsin	★	★	★	Senate: Monday noon of the preceding week. House: Monday noon of the preceding week.	Senate: number of ayes and noes, and members absent or not voting are reported. House: number of ayes and noes are recorded.
Wyoming	★	★	★	Senate: by 3:00 p.m. of previous day. House: by 3:00 p.m. of previous day.	Senate: bills are reported out by recorded roll call vote. House: bills are reported out by recorded roll call vote.
Puerto Rico	★	★	★	Senate: Must be notified every Thurs.,one week in advance. House: 24 hours advanced notice, no later than 4:00 p.m. previous day.	Senate: bills reported from a committee carry a majority vote. House: bills reported from a committee carry a majority vote by referendum or in an ordinary meeting.
U.S. Virgin Islands ...	★	★	U	Seven calendar days.	Bills must be reported to floor by Rules Committee.

Source: The Council of State Governments' survey, December 2005.
Key:
★ — Yes
* — Notice of committee meetings may also be subject to state open meetings laws; in some cases, listed times may be subject to suspension or enforceable only to the extent "feasible" or "whenever possible."
U — Unicameral
(a) Certain matters may be discussed in executive session. (Other states permit meetings to be closed for various reasons, but their rules do not specifically mention "executive session.")

(b) General directive in the Senate and House rules to the Department of Legislative Services to compile a list of the meetings and to arrange for distribution which in practice is done on a regular basis.
(c) Not referenced specifically, but each body publishes rules.
(d) May go to one-hour notice when president and speaker proclaim sine die imminent.
(e) If public hearing, five calendar days.
(f) The prohibition does not apply if the action receives a majority vote of the committee.

Table 3.25
LEGISLATIVE REVIEW OF ADMINISTRATIVE REGULATIONS: STRUCTURES AND PROCEDURES

State or other jurisdiction	Type of reviewing committee	Rules reviewed	Time limits in review process
Alabama	Joint bipartisan, standing committee	P, E (f)	35 days for action by committee.
Alaska	Legislative agency & Joint bipartisan	P, E	...
Arizona	Joint bipartisan	P, E	...
Arkansas.....................	Joint bipartisan	P, E	...
California		P, E	Regulation review conducted by independent executive branch agency.
Colorado	Joint bipartisan	E	Rules continue unless the annual legislative rule review bill discontinues a rule. The rule review bill is effective upon the Governor's signature.
Connecticut	Joint bipartisan, standing committee	P	Submittal of proposed regulation shall be on the first Tuesday of month; after first submittal, committee has 65 days after date of submission. Second submittal: 35 days for committee to review/take action on revised regulation.
Delaware....................		P	The Attorney General shall review any rule or regulation promulgated by any state agency and inform the issuing agency in writing as to the potential of the rule or regulation to result in a taking of private property before the rule or regulation may become effective.
Florida	Joint bipartisan	P, E	...
Georgia	Standing committee	P	The agency notifies the Legislative Counsel 30 days prior to the effective dates of proposed rules.
Hawaii........................	Legislative agency (c)	P, E	...
Idaho..........................	Germane joint subcommittees	P	Germane joint subcommittees vote to object or not object to a rule. They cannot reject a proposed rule directly, only advise an agency which may chose to adopt a rule subject to review by the full legislature. The legislature as a whole reviews rules during the first three weeks of session to determine if they comport with state law. The Senate and House may reject rules via resolution adopted by both. Rules imposing fees must be approved or are deemed approved unless rejected. Temporary rules expire at the end of session unless extended by concurrent resolution.
Illinois	Joint bipartisan	P, E	Joint Committee on Administrative Rules, during the 45-day "second notice period," can send objections to issuing agency. If it does, the agency has 90 days from then to withdraw, change, or refuse to change the proposed regulations. If the Joint Committee determines that proposed regulations would seriously threaten the public good, it can block their adoption. Within 180 days the Joint Committee, or both houses of the General Assembly, can "unblock" those regulations; if that does not happen, the regulations are dead.
Indiana.......................	Joint bipartisan	P	...
Iowa	Joint bipartisan	P, E	...
Kansas	Joint bipartisan	P	Agencies must give a 60-day notice to the public and the Joint Committee of their intent to adopt or amend specific rules and regulations, a copy of which must be provided to the committee. Within the 60-day comment period, the Joint Committee must review and comment, if it feels necessary, on the proposals. Final rules and regulations are resubmitted to the committee to determine whether further expression of concern is necessary.
Kentucky	Joint bipartisan statutory committee	P, E	45 days.
Louisiana (b)	Standing committee	P	All proposed rules and fees are submitted to designated standing committees of the legislature. If a rule or fee is unacceptable, the committee sends a written report to the governor. The governor has 10 days to disapprove the committee report. If both Senate and House committees fail to find the rule unacceptable, or if the governor disapproves the action of a committee within 10 days, the agency may adopt the rule change. (d)
Maine.........................	Joint bipartisan, standing committee	P	One legislative session.

See footnotes at end of table.

LEGISLATIVE REVIEW OF ADMINISTRATIVE REGULATIONS: STRUCTURES AND PROCEDURES — Continued

State or other jurisdiction	Type of reviewing committee	Rules reviewed	Time limits in review process
Maryland	Joint bipartisan	P, E	Proposed regulations are submitted for review at least 15 days before publication. Publication triggers 45-day review period which may be extended by the committee, but if agreement cannot be reached, the Governor may instruct the agency to modify or withdraw the regulation, or may approve its adoption.
Massachusetts (b)	Public hearing by agency	P	In Massachusetts, the General Court (Legislature) may by statute authorize an administrative agency to promulgate regulations. The promulgation of such regulations are then governed by Chapter 30A of the Massachusetts General Laws. Chapter 30A requires 21-day notice to the public of a public hearing on a proposed regulation. After public hearing, the proposed regulation is filed with the State Secretary who approves it if it is in conformity with Chapter 30A. The State Secretary maintains a register entitled "Massachusetts Register" and the regulation does not become effective until published in the register. The agency may promulgate amendments to the regulations following the same process.
Michigan	Joint bipartisan	P	Joint Committee on Administrative Rules (JCAR) has 15 days in which to consider the rule and to object to the rule by filing a notice of objection. If no objection is made, the rules may be filed and go into effect. If JCAR does formally object, bills to block the rules are introduced in both houses of the legislature simultaneously by the committee chair and placed directly on the Senate and House calendars for action. If the bills are not enacted by the legislature and presented to the governor within 15 session days, the rules may go into effect. Between legislative sessions the committee can meet and suspend rules promulgated during the interim between sessions.
Minnesota	Standing committee		
Mississippi	....(a)..		
Missouri	Joint bipartisan, standing committee	P, E	The committee must disapprove a final order of rulemaking within 30 days upon receipt or the order of rulemaking is deemed approved.
Montana	Germane joint bipartisan committees	P	Prior to adoption.
Nebraska	Standing committee	P	If an agency proposes to repeal, adopt or amend a rule or regulation, it is required to provide the Executive Board Chair with the proposal at least 30 days prior to the Public Hearing, as required by law. The Executive Board Chair shall provide to the appropriate standing committee of the Legislature, the agency proposal for comment.
Nevada	Ongoing statutory committee (Legislative Commission)	P	Proposed regulations are either reviewed at the Legislative Commission's next regularly scheduled meeting (if the regulation is received more than three working days before the meeting), or they are referred to the Commission's Subcommittee to Review Regulations. If there is no objection to the regulation, then the Commission will "promptly" file the approved regulation with the Secretary of State. If the Commission or its subcommittee objects to a regulation, then the Commission will "promptly" return the regulation to the agency for revision. Within 60 days of receiving the written notice of objection to the regulation, the agency must revise the regulation and return it to the Legislative Counsel. If the Commission or its subcommittee objects to the revised regulation, the agency shall continue to revise and resubmit it to the Commission or subcommittee within 30 days after receiving the written notice of objection to the revised regulation.
New Hampshire	Joint bipartisan	P	Under APA, for regular rulemaking, the joint committee of administrative rules has 45 days to review a final proposed rule from an agency, Otherwise the rule is automatically approved. If JLCAR makes a preliminary or revised objection, the agency has 45 days to respond, and JLCAR has another 50 days to decide to vote to sponsor a joint resolution, which suspends the adoption process. JLCAR may also, or instead, make a final objection, which shifts the burden of proof in court to the agency. There is no time limit on making a final objection. If no JLCAR action in the 50 days to vote to sponsor a joint resolution, the agency may adopt the rule.

See footnotes at end of table.

LEGISLATIVE REVIEW OF ADMINISTRATIVE REGULATIONS: STRUCTURES AND PROCEDURES — Continued

State or other jurisdiction	Type of reviewing committee	Rules reviewed	Time limits in review process
New Jersey	Chamber review	P, E	After initial review, if not consistent with the legislative intent, findings are transmitted to the Governor and the executive agency. The Legislature waits 30 days for the agency to withdraw or amend the regulation. If it is not withdrawn or amended, either house holds a public hearing on the invalidation or prohibition. The Legislature then adopts a concurrent resolution to invalidate or prohibit the regulation, no sooner than 20 calendar days after the public hearing transcript is placed on the desks.
New Mexico	....................(g)................		
New York	Joint bipartisan commission	P, E	Agencies must give public notice of a rule change, by publication in the State Register, 45 days prior to: (1) date of the rule change, if a hearing is not required; (2) if a hearing is required, date of first hearing. If the notice is only a description of the rule's subject, purpose and substance, and the full text is not available on an official Web site, the comment period is not less than 60 days after publication in the register. Notice expires unless continuation notice is published.
North Carolina	Rules Review Commission; Public membership appointed by Legislature	P, E	The Rules Review Commission must review a permanent rule submitted to it on or before the 20th of the month by the last day of the next month. The commission must review a permanent rule submitted to it after the 20th of the month by the last day of the second subsequent month.
North Dakota	Interim committee	E	The Administrative Rules Committee has 90 days from the time a rule is published to initially consider a rule and may carry over for one additional meeting its decision on whether to declare the rule void.
Ohio	Joint bipartisan	P, E (i)	The committee's jurisdiction is 65 days from date of original filing plus an additional 30 days from date of re-filing. Rules filed with no changes, pursuant to the five-year review, are under a 90-day jurisdiction.
Oklahoma	Standing committee (k)	P, E	The legislature has 30 legislative days to review proposed rules. A legislative day is any day on which both chambers convene and adjourn. However, the legislature may disapprove any rule at any time.
Oregon (h)	Joint bipartisan	E	. . .
Pennsylvania	Joint bipartisan, standing committee	E	Time limits decided by the President Pro Tempore and Speaker of the House.
Rhode Island	....................(a)................		
South Carolina	Standing committee (e)	P	General Assembly has 120 days to approve or disapprove. If not disapproved by joint resolution before 120 days, regulation is automatically approved. It can be approved during 120-day review period by joint resolution.
South Dakota	Joint bipartisan	P	Rules must be adopted within 75 days of the commencement of the public hearing; emergency rules must be adopted within 30 days of the date of the publication of the notice of intent.
Tennessee	Joint bipartisan	P	All permanent rules take effect 165 days after filing with the Secretary of State. Emergency rules take effect upon filing with the Secretary of State. Rules take effect regardless of whether they have been reviewed.
Texas	Standing committee	P	No time limit.
Utah	Joint bipartisan (j)	P, E	Each rule in effect on February 28 of each year expires May 1 of that year unless reauthorized by the legislature in annual legislation.
Vermont	Joint bipartisan	P	The Joint Legislative Committee Rules must review a proposed rule within 30 days of submission to the committee.
Virginia	Joint bipartisan, standing committee	P	Standing committees and the Joint Commission on Administrative Rules may object to a proposed or final adopted rule before it becomes effective. This delays the process for 21 days and the agency must respond to the objection.

See footnotes at end of table.

LEGISLATIVE REVIEW OF ADMINISTRATIVE REGULATIONS: STRUCTURES AND PROCEDURES — Continued

State or other jurisdiction	Type of reviewing committee	Rules reviewed	Time limits in review process
Washington (b)..........	Joint bipartisan	P, E	If the committee determines that a proposed rule does not comply with legislative intent, it notifies the agency, which must schedule a public hearing within 30 days of notification. The agency notifies the committee of its action within seven days after the hearing. If a hearing is not held or the agency does not amend the rule, the objection may be filed in the state register and referenced in the state code. The committee's powers, other than publication of its objections, are advisory.
West Virginia.............	Joint bipartisan		. . .
Wisconsin...................	Joint bipartisan, standing committee	P, E	The standing committee in each house has 30 days to conduct its review for a proposed rule. If either objects, the Joint Committee for the Review of Administrative Rules has 30 days to introduce legislation in each house overturning the rules. After 40 days, the bills are placed on the calendar. If either bill passes, the rules are overturned. If they fail to pass, the rules go into effect.
Wyoming....................	Joint bipartisan	P, E	An agency shall submit copies of adopted, amended or repealed rules to the legislative service office for review within five days after the date of the agency's final action adopting, amending or repealing those rules. The legislature makes its recommendations to the governor who within 15 days after receiving any recommendation, shall either order that the rule be amended or rescinded in accordance with the recommendation or file in writing his objections to the recommendation.
Puerto Rico...............	....(a)...		
U.S. Virgin Islands	....(a)...		

Source: The Council of State Governments' survey, December 2005.
Key:
P — Proposed rules
E — Existing rules
. . . — No formal time limits
(a) No formal rule review is performed by both legislative and executive branches.
(b) Review of rules is performed by both legislative and executive branches.
(c) In Hawaii, the legislative reference bureau assists agencies to comply with a uniform format of style. This does not affect the status of rules.
(d) If the committees of both houses fail to find a fee unacceptable, it can be adopted. Committee action on proposed rules must be taken within 5 to 30 days after the agency reports to the committee on its public hearing (if any) and whether it is making changes on proposed rules.

(e) Submitted by General Assembly for approval.
(f) Existing rules prior to 1982.
(g) No formal review is performed by legislature. Periodic review and report to legislative finance committee is required of certain agencies.
(h) Oregon created a second kind of review. An executive department agency must submit a proposed rule to a member or committee of the legislative assembly (the recipient differs depending upon the rule) and then, if requested, a standing or interim committee must review the rule and return its comments to the adopting agency.
(i) The Committee participates in a five-year review of every rule.
(j) Created by statute.
(k) House only by standing committee. In the Senate, rules are sent to standing committee which deals with that specific agency.

Table 3.26
LEGISLATIVE REVIEW OF ADMINISTRATIVE RULES/REGULATIONS: POWERS

State or other jurisdiction	Reviewing committee's powers			Legislative powers
	Advisory powers only (a)	No objection constitutes approval of proposed rule	Committee may suspend rule	Method of legislative veto of rules
Alabama	...	★	★	Joint resolution (b)
Alaska	★	...	(c)	Statute
Arizona	★	N.A.	N.A.	N.A.
Arkansas.....................	★	...	...	...
California	...	★	★	...
Colorado	...	★	...	(f)
Connecticut	...	★	...	Statute CGS 4-170 (d) and 4-171; see footnote (g)
Delaware.....................	(h)	N.A.	N.A.	N.A.
Florida	★	...	...	Statute
Georgia	...	★	...	Resolution (j)
Hawaii........................	★	...	...	...
Idaho..........................	...	★	...	Concurrent resolution (k)
Illinois.......................	...	...	★	(i)
Indiana.......................	★	...	...	(m)
Iowa	...	...	(p)	E-mail legislation
Kansas	★	...	...	Statute
Kentucky	...	★	★	(t)
Louisiana	...	★	(n)	Concurrent resolution to suspend, amend or repeal adopted rules or fees. For proposed rules and emergency rules, see footnote (n).
Maine	...	★	...	(o)
Maryland	★(l)	...	...	...
Massachusetts............	...	...	...	The legislature may pass a bill which would supersede a regulation if signed into law by the governor.
Michigan....................	...	...	(q)	Joint Committee on Rules has 15 days to approve the filing of a notice of objection. The filing of the notice of objection starts another 15-day session period that stays the rules and causes committee members to introduce legislation in both houses of the legislature for enactment and presentment to the governor. Any member of the legislature, pursuant to statute, can introduce a bill at a session, which in effect amends or rescinds a rule.
Minnesota	★	...	...	(s)
Mississippi			(e)	
Missouri.....................	...	★	★	Concurrent resolution passed by both houses of the General Assembly.
Montana	...	...	★(b)	Statute
Nebraska....................	★(d)	★	...	(d)
Nevada	...	★	★	Proposed regulations are either reviewed at the Legislative Commission's next regularly scheduled meeting (if the regulation is received more than three working days before the meeting), or they are referred to the Commission's Subcommittee to Review Regulations. If there is no objection to the regulation, then the Commission will "promptly" file the approved regulation with the Secretary of State. If the Commission or its subcommittee objects to a regulation, then the Commission will "promptly" return the regulation to the agency for revision. Within 60 days of receiving the written notice of objection to the regulation, the agency must revise the regulation and return it to the Legislative Counsel. If the Commission or its subcommittee objects to the revised regulation, the agency shall continue to revise and resubmit it to the Commission or subcommittee within 30 days after receiving the written notice of objection to the revised regulation.

See footnotes at end of table.

LEGISLATIVE REVIEW OF ADMINISTRATIVE RULES/REGULATIONS: POWERS — Continued

State or other jurisdiction	Reviewing committee's powers			Legislative powers
	Advisory powers only (a)	No objection constitutes approval of proposed rule	Committee may suspend rule	Method of legislative veto of rules
New Hampshire.........	★	(u)	. . .	(v)
New Jersey................				(w) ....
New Mexico				(e) ....
New York	★	. . .	. . .	The legislature may pass a bill which would supersede a regulation if signed into law by the governor.
North Carolina	★	. . .	. . .	Any member of the General Assembly may introduce a bill during first 30 days to disapprove a controversial rule that has been approved by the commission and that has not become effective or has become effective by executive order. (x)
North Dakota.............	. . .	★(y)	. . .	The Administrative Rules Committee can void a rule.
Ohio	★	. . .	. . .	Concurrent resolution. Committee recommends to the General Assembly that a rule be invalidated. The General Assembly invalidates a rule through adoption of concurrent resolution.
Oklahoma	★	★(d)	★(d)	The legislature may veto proposed rules by concurrent or joint resolution. A concurrent resolution soes not require the governor's signature. Existing rules may be disapproved by joint resolution. A committee may not disapprove; only the full legislature may do so. Failure of the legislature to disapprove constitutes approval.
Oregon	★	N.A.	N.A.	(bb)
Pennsylvania	. . .	★	★	Written or oral
Rhode Island				(e) ....
South Carolina	. . .	★	. . .	. . .
South Dakota.............	. . .	★	★	The Interim Rules Review Committee may, by statute, suspend rules that have not become effective yet by an affirmative vote of the majority of the committee.
Tennessee	. . .	. . .	★	Bill approved by Constitutional majority of both houses declaring rule invalid.
Texas	★	. . .	. . .	N.A.
Utah	★	. . .	. . .	All rules must be reauthorized by the legislature annually.
Vermont		(ee)		Statute
Virginia......................	. . .	. . .	(dd)	The General Assembly must pass a bill enacted into law to directly negate the administrative rule.
Washington................	★(cc)	N.A.	(aa)	N.A.
West Virginia.............	★	. . .	. . .	(z)
Wisconsin..................	. . .	★	★	The standing committee in each house has 30 days to conduct its review for a proposed rule. If either objects, the Joint Committee for the Review of Administrative Rules has 30 days to introduce legislation in each house overturning the rules. After 40 days, the bills are placed on the calendar. If either bill passes, the rules are overturned. If they fail to pass, the rules go into effect.
Wyoming....................	(r)	. . .	. . .	Action must be taken by legislative order adopted by both houses before the end of the next succeeding legislative session to nullify a rule.
U.S. Virgin Islands....				(e) ....

See footnotes at end of table.

LEGISLATIVE REVIEW OF ADMINISTRATIVE RULES/REGULATIONS: POWERS — Continued

Source: The Council of State Governments' survey, December 2005.
Key:
★ — Yes
. . . — No
N.A. — Not applicable

(a) This column is defined by those legislatures or legislative committees that can only recommend changes to rules but have no power to enforce a change.

(b) A rule disapproved by the reviewing committee is reinstated at the end of the next session if a joint resolution in the legislature fails to sustain committee action.

(c) Authorized, although constitutionally questionable.

(d) If an agency proposes to repeal, adopt or amend a rule or regulation, it is required to provide the Executive Board Chairperson with the proposal at least 30 days prior to the Public Hearing, as required by law. The Executive Board Chairperson shall provide to the appropriate standing committee of the Legislature, the agency proposal for comment. No method of legislative veto exists for veto of rules.

(e) No formal mechanism for legislative review of administrative rules. In Virginia, legislative review is optional.

(f) A bill is introduced that includes rules the Committee on Legal Services has determined should be discontinued. The bill must be enacted for the rules to be discontinued.

(g) Disapproval of proposed regulations may be sustained, or reversed by action of the General Assembly in the ensuing session. The General Assembly may by resolution sustain or reverse a vote of disapproval.

(h) During the legislative interim, July 1 and the second Tuesday in January, the chairperson of a standing committee of either house may, by majority vote, draft a committee report setting forth its suggestions and recommendations and requesting the president pro tempore of the Senate or the speaker of the House to call a special session to consider the committee's recommendations. Each committee report shall be forwarded to the Sunset Committee.

(i) Joint Committee on Administrative Rules, during the 45-day "second notice period," can send objections to issuing agency. If it does, the agency has 90 days from then to withdraw, change, or refuse to change the proposed regulations. If the Joint Committee determines that proposed regulations would seriously threaten the public good, it can block their adoption. Within 180 days the Joint Committee, or both houses of the General Assembly, can "unblock" those regulations; if that does not happen, the regulations are dead.

(j) The reviewing committee must introduce a resolution to override a rule within the first 30 days of the next regular session of the General Assembly. If the resolution passes by less than a two-thirds majority of either house, the governor has final authority to affirm or veto the resolution.

(k) All rules are terminated one year after adoption unless the legislature reauthorizes the rule.

(l) Except for emergency regulations which require committee approval for adoption.

(m) None—except by passing statute.

(n) If the committee determines that a proposed rule is unacceptable, it submits a report to the governor who then has 10 days to accept or reject the report. If the governor rejects the report, the rule change may be adopted by the agency. If the governor accepts the report, the agency may not adopt the rule. Emergency rules become effective upon adoption or up to 60 days after adoption as provided in the rule, but a standing committee or governor may void the rule by finding it unacceptable within 2 to 61 days after adoption and reporting such finding to agency within 4 days.

(o) No veto allowed. Legislation must be enacted to prohibit agency from adopting objectionable rules.

(p) Committee may delay rules.

(q) Committee can suspend rules during interim.

(r) Legislative Management Council can recommend action be taken by the full legislature.

(s) The Legislative Commission to Review Administrative Rules (LCRAR) ceased operating, effective July 1, 1996. The Legislative Coordinating Commission (LCC) may perform the statutory functions of the LCRAR as it deems necessary. Contact the LCC for more information.

(t) Enacting legislation to void.

(u) Failure to object or approve within 45 days of agency filing of final proposal constitutes approval.

(v) The legislature may permanently block rules through legislation. The vote to sponsor a joint resolution suspends the adoption of a proposed rule for a limited time so that the full legislature may act on the resolution, which would then be subject to governor's veto and override.

(w) Article V, Section IV of the Constitution, as amended in 1992, says the legislature may review any rule or regulation to determine whether the rule or regulation is consistent with legislative intent. The legislature transmits its objections to existing or proposed rules or regulations to the governor and relevant agency via concurrent resolutions. The legislature may invalidate or prohibit an existing or proposed rule from taking effect by a majority vote of the authorized membership of each house.

(x) If a rule approved by the commission is noncontroversial, it is not subject to legislative disapproval.

(y) Unless formal objections are made or the rule is declared void, rules are considered approved.

(z) State agencies have no power to promulgate rules without first submitting proposed rules to the legislature which must enact a statute authorizing the agency to promulgate the rule. If the legislature during a regular session disapproves all or part of any legislative rule, the agency may not issue the rule nor take action to implement all or part of the rule unless authorized to do so. However, the agency may resubmit the same or a similar proposed rule to the committee.

(aa) By a majority vote of the committee members, the committee may request the governor to approve suspension of a rule. If the governor approves, the suspension is effective until 90 days after the end of the next regular session.

(bb) The committee reports to the legislature during each regular session on the review of rules by the committee.

(cc) Objections are published in the Washington State Register.

(dd) With the concurrence of the governor. The Joint Commission on Administrative Rules may also suspend regulations with the concurrence of the rules.

(ee) JLCAR may recommend that an agency amend or withdraw a proposal. A vote opposing a rule does not prohibit its adoption but assigns the burden of proof in any legal challenge to the agency.

Table 3.27
SUMMARY OF SUNSET LEGISLATION

State	Scope	Preliminary evaluation conducted by	Other legislative review	Other oversight mechanisms in bill	Phase-out period	Life of each agency (in years)	Other provisions
Alabama	C	Dept. of Examiners of Public Accounts	Standing Cmte.	Perf. audit	No later than Oct. 1 of the year following the regular session or a time as may be specified in the Sunset bill.	(usually 4)	Schedules of licensing boards and other enumerated agencies are repealed according to specified time tables.
Alaska	C	Budget & Audit Cmte.	...	...	1/y	...	...
Arizona	C	Legislative staff	Joint Cmte.	...	6/m	10	...
Arkansas	D	...	...	...	...	...	...
California	S	St. Legis. Sunset Review Cmte. (a)	...	...	...	Varies	...
Colorado	R	Dept. of Regulatory Agencies	Legis. Cmtes. of reference	(b)	1/y	up to 15	State law provides certain criteria that are used to determine whether a public need exists for an entity or function to continue and that its regulation is the least restrictive regulation consistent with the public interest.
Connecticut	S	Legis. Program Review & Investigations Cmte.	...	...	1/y (o)	5 years	...
Delaware	C	Agencies under review submit reports to Del. Sunset Comm. based on criteria for review and set forth in statute. Comm. staff conducts separate review.	...	Perf. audit	Dec. 31 of next succeeding calendar year	4	Yearly sunset review schedules must include at least nine agencies. If the number automatically scheduled for review or added by the General Assembly is less than a full schedule, additional agencies shall be added in order of their appearance in the Del. Code to complete the review schedule.
Florida	C	Cmte. charged with oversight of the subject area.	Jt. cmte. charged with oversight of the subject area.	...	4-6/y	10	...
Georgia	R	Dept. of Audits	Standing Cmtes.	Perf. audit	...	...	A performance audit of each regulatory agency must be conducted upon the request of the Senate or House standing committee to which an agency has been assigned for oversight and review. (e)
Hawaii	R	Legis. Auditor	Standing Cmtes.	Perf. eval.	None	Established by the legislature	Schedules various professional and vocational licensing programs for repeal. Proposed new regulatory measures must be referred to the Auditor for sunrise analysis.
Idaho	(f)	...	...	...	...	...	...
Illinois	R	Governor's Office of Mgmt. & Budget	Cmte. charged with re-enacting law.	(t)	...	10 (max.)	Automatic repeal if legislature fails to re-enact regulatory authority before sunset.
Indiana	S	Nonpartisan staff units	Interim cmte. formed to review.	...	...	...	Smaller program review process now in place after about a dozen years of formal sunset program.
Iowa		.... No program					
Kansas	(g)	...	...	...	...	...	...

See footnotes at end of table.

SUMMARY OF SUNSET LEGISLATION — Continued

State	Scope	Preliminary evaluation conducted by	Other legislative review	Other oversight mechanisms in bill	Phase-out period	Life of each agency (in years)	Other provisions
Kentucky	R	Administrative Regulation Review Subcommittee	Joint committee with subject matter jurisdiction.	...	...	...	...
Louisiana	C	Standing cmtes. of the two houses with subject matter jurisdiction.	...	Perf. eval.	1/y	Up to 6	Act provides for termination of a department and all offices in a department. Also permits committees to select particular agencies or offices for more extensive evaluation. Provides for review by Jt. Legis. Cmte. on Budget of programs that were not funded during the prior fiscal year for possible repeal.
Maine	S	Joint standing cmte. of jurisdiction.	Office of Program Evaluation & Government Accountability (not yet established)	...	...	Generally 10	...
Maryland	R	Dept. of Legislative Services	Standing Cmtes.	Perf. eval.	...	Varies (usually 10)	...
Massachusetts				.... No program			
Michigan	(f)	...	...	...	...	...	...
Minnesota	(f)	...	...	...	...	...	...
Mississippi	(h)	...	...	...	...	...	...
Missouri	R	Oversight Division of Cmte. on Legislative Research	...	...	...	6, not to exceed total of 12	...
Montana	(f)	...	...	...	...	...	...
Nebraska	D(f)(u)	...	...	...	...	...	...
Nevada	(f)	...	...	...	...	...	...
New Hampshire	(i)	...	...	...	...	...	...
New Jersey	(f)	...	...	...	...	...	...
New Mexico	R	Legis. Finance Cmte.	...	Perf. eval., Progress	(j)	6	...
New York	(f)	...	...	...	...	...	...
North Carolina	(k)	...	...	...	...	...	...
North Dakota				.... No program			
Ohio	C (s)	Sunset Review Cmte.	Appropriations & Budget Cmte.	...	(l)	4	...
Oklahoma	S, D	Jt. Cmtes. with jurisdiction over sunset bills	...	...	1/y	6	...
Oregon	(m)	...	(m)	...	...	...	...
Pennsylvania	R	Leadership Cmte.	...	...	...	Varies	...
Rhode Island	(p)	...	...	...	...	...	...
South Carolina	(n)	...	...	...	...	...	...
South Dakota	(q)	...	...	...	...	...	...

See footnotes at end of table.

SUMMARY OF SUNSET LEGISLATION — Continued

State	Scope	Preliminary evaluation conducted by	Other legislative review	Other oversight mechanisms in bill	Phase-out period	Life of each agency (in years)	Other provisions
Tennessee	C	Office of the Comptroller	Government Operations Committees	...	1/y	up to 6 years	...
Texas	S	Sunset Advisory Commission staff	...	...	1/y	12	...
Utah	C	Legislative staff and committee members	Periodic interim committee review	...	...	...	...
Vermont	(c)	Legis. Council staff	Senate and House Government Operations Cmtes.	...	...	...	...
Virginia	S (f)	...	...	...	...	...	Sunset provisions vary in length. The only standard sunset required by law is on bills that create a new advisory board or commission in the executive branch of government. The legislation introduced for these boards and commissions must contain a sunset provision to expire the entity after three years.
Washington	C	Jt. Legis. Audit & Review Cmte.	Standing Cmtes.	...	1/y	Varies	...
West Virginia	S	Jt. Cmte. on Govt. Operations	Performance Evaluation and Research Division	Perf. audit	1/y	6	Jt. Cmte. on Govt. Operations composed of five House members, five Senate members and five citizens appointed by governor. Agencies may be reviewed more frequently.
Wisconsin	(f)	...	...	...	...	...	...
Wyoming	(r)	...	...	...	...	...	...

Source: The Council of State Governments' survey, December 2005.

Key:
C — Comprehensive
R — Regulatory
S — Selective
D — Discretionary
d — day
m — month
y — year
... — Not applicable

(a) Review by the Jt. Legislative Sunset Review Cmte. of professional and vocational licensing boards terminated on January 1, 2004. Sunset clauses are included in other selected programs and legislation.

(b) Bills need adoption by the legislature.

(c) Sunsets are at the legislature's discretion. Their structure will vary on an individual basis.

(d) July 1 of the year next succeeding the year of termination.

(e) The automatic sunsetting of an agency every six years was eliminated in 1992. The legislature must pass a bill in order to sunset a specific agency.

(f) While they have not enacted sunset legislation in the same sense as the other states with detailed information in this table, the legislatures in Idaho, Michigan, Minnesota, Montana, Nebraska, Nevada, New Jersey, New York, Virginia and Wisconsin have included sunset clauses in selected programs or legislation.

(g) Sunset legislation terminated July 1992. Legislative oversight of designated state agencies, consisting of audit, review and evaluation, continues.

(h) Sunset Act terminated December 31, 1984.

(i) New Hampshire's Sunset Committee was repealed July 1, 1986.

(j) Agency termination is scheduled on July 1 of the year prior to the scheduled termination of statutory authority for that agency.

(k) North Carolina's sunset law terminated on July 30, 1981. Successor vehicle, the Legislative Committee on Agency Review, operated until June 30, 1983.

(l) Authority for latest review (HB 548 of the 123rd General Assembly) expired December 31, 2004. H.B. 516 of the 125th General Assembly re-establishes the Sunset Review Committee, but postpones its operation until the 128th General Assembly. The bill terminates the Sunset Review Law on December 31, 2010.

(m) Sunset legislation was repealed in 1993. Joint Legislative Audit Committee still serves as legislative review body.

(n) Law repealed by 1998 Act 419.

(o) Upon termination a program shall continue for one year to conclude its affairs.

(p) No standing sunset statutes or procedures at this time.

(q) South Dakota suspended sunset legislation in 1979. Under current law, the Executive Board of the Legislative Research Council is directed to establish one or more interim committees each year to review state agencies so that each state agency is reviewed once every 10 years.

(r) Wyoming repealed sunset legislation in 1988.

(s) There are statutory exceptions.

(t) Governor is to read GOMB report and make recommendations to the General Assembly every even-numbered year.

(u) Sunset legislation is discretionary, meaning that senators are free to offer sunset legislation or attach termination dates to legislative proposals. There is no formal sunset commission. Nebraska Revised Statutes section 50-1303 directs the Legislature's Government, Military and Veteran's Committee to conduct an evaluation of any board, commission, or similar state entity. The review must include, among other things, a recommendation as to whether the board, commission, or entity should be terminated, continued or modified.

Chapter Four

STATE EXECUTIVE BRANCH

66*This year, though, state chief executives find themselves in a different fiscal environment–their budget and policy agendas vary marginally from those that they have been relaying to citizens in the recent past.*99

—Katherine Willoughby

66*Governors remain in the forefront of activity as we move into the 21st century.*99

—Thad Beyle

66*The office of the lieutenant governor is growing in power and prominence.*99

—Julia Hurst

66*Secretaries of state make decisions every day that affect the lives of their constituents.*99

—George A. Munro

66*As the chief legal officers of the states, commonwealths and territories of the United States, attorneys general serve as counselors to state government agencies and legislatures, and as representatives of the public interest.*99

—Angelita Plemmer

66*State treasurers are vital players in the healthy management of state budgets and federal policy.*99

—National Association of State Treasurers

66*State financial officers have long been interested in increasing the efficiency and effectiveness of their operations and of financial management across state government.*99

—R. Thomas Wagner, Jr.

The State of the States: Governors Consider the Long View

By Katherine Willoughby

Governors did seem to concentrate heavily on their education budgets this year, and then on the budgets of other activities that are primary to the mission of state government. Yet threaded through these addresses is a stronger consideration of a multi-pronged and multi-year view of government operations—understanding state education services on a continuum from pre-kindergarten to work force retraining, for instance. Governors are aware of the federal government's slowing financial support as well as its poor reaction to Katrina and what this means for state coffers.

Governors have spent the last few years lamenting the poor fiscal climate that settled across the United States, explaining the necessity of pulling state governments back to their primary missions, especially education. This year, however, while state chief executives find themselves in a different fiscal environment, their budget and policy agendas vary marginally from those they have been relaying to citizens in the recent past. That is, revenues are flowing more freely into state coffers; state governments are realizing surpluses.

While revenue growth fuels a common gubernatorial mantra to cut taxes, it has not necessarily opened the floodgates to different spending initiatives. Today's governors seem to have learned from periods of fiscal stringency. In fact, many are calling for measured approaches to budget making—emphasizing long-range planning, balance and good management to pursue the work of the states.[1]

The Politics

Governors seemed to take a calculated approach in their State of the State addresses, most likely because 2006 is an election year. The Republican stronghold at the national and state levels is under fire. In the 28 states with Republican governors, 22 will hold gubernatorial elections this year. The governors in Arkansas, Colorado, Florida, Nevada and Ohio cannot run again. Three more Republican governors—in Idaho, Massachusetts and New York—have said they will not run again. In the 22 states with Democratic governors (New Jersey elected Democrat John Corzine as governor in 2005), 14 will hold elections for the chief executive spot in 2006. Of these 14 governors, only one, Tom Vilsack of Iowa, has said he will not seek re-election.[2] Quite a few of these state-level chief executives are actively seeking the nation's top spot, or at least are being considered as likely presidential candidates. Vilsack, Philip Bredesen of Tennessee, Mike Easley of North Carolina, Mark Warner of Virginia (2002–2006), and Bill Richardson of New Mexico

are some of the Democratic governors considering or mentioned as possible candidates for president. Haley Barbour of Mississippi, Mike Huckabee of Arkansas, Bill Owens of Colorado, George Pataki of New York and Mitt Romney of Massachusetts, are some of the Republican governors who also have been mentioned as possible presidential candidates.[3]

With the upcoming elections, governors understand the need for strategic political maneuvering to hold onto or gain political power in their states. The party advantage in state legislatures just slightly favors Republicans. The GOP controls both houses in 20 states, while Democrats control both houses in 19 states. Legislatures in 10 states are split between the two parties, while Nebraska's legislature is unicameral and nonpartisan. Therefore, it is expected that elected officials are tempering discussions of their budget and policy agendas. This year, governors want to focus attention on the taxing and spending interests of constituents, but they seem more cognizant of the difficulties experienced when unable to deliver on promises made.

California Gov. Arnold Schwarzenegger's mea culpa is just one example of a more considered approach to policymaking and problem-solving:

"Now what a difference a year makes—a year ago USC and I were #1—what happened? … I've thought a lot about the last year and the mistakes I made and the lessons I've learned. Now it's true that I was in too much of a hurry. I didn't hear the majority of Californians when they were telling me they didn't like the special election. I barreled ahead anyway when I should have listened. I have absorbed my defeat and I have learned my lesson. And the people, who always have the last word, sent a clear message—cut the warfare, cool the rhetoric, find common ground and fix the problems together. So to my fellow Californians, I say—message received."

This year, Schwarzenegger suggested using "bonding capacity more wisely ... to attract other resources—like federal funding, more local funding and more private investment." Yet, he does call on legislators, civil servants and citizens to come forward with their ideas and innovations, to help come up with ways to solve the state's problems.

Revenues, Expenditures and Balance

Governors and legislators are surely breathing a sigh of relief that the revenue picture is brighter. Nonetheless, this picture is just slightly off-center. Revenue actions in the states in 2006 realized a net increase of $2.5 billion in state treasuries; this is the lowest positive change to revenues in the last three years.[4] These revenue actions garnered increases in all taxes and fees noted below in Table A.[5] However, cuts to state personal income taxes led to the decrease in this revenue tax source by $739 million.

Table A: Net Increase from 2006 State Revenue Actions (In millions of dollars)

Revenue source	Net increase
Cigarette/tobacco	$1,249
Sales	995
Fees	686
Other taxes	142
Corporate income	120
Motor fuel	81
Alcohol	36

Source: NASBO, *The Fiscal Survey of the States*, 2005.

On the other hand, because of the upturn in the economy, collections from sales taxes and personal and corporate income taxes are expected to increase in 2006 when compared to the previous fiscal year. States have been able to continue shoring up resources as evidenced by examining budget stabilization funds—states with these funds realized $12.1 billion in 2004, $14.9 billion in 2005, and $16.3 billion by 2006.

In real terms, state spending grew by 3.2 percent in 2005 and is expected to rise about the same (by 3 percent) in 2006.[6] The rosier budget picture is further evidenced when considering that by 2005, just six states had to go back and cut the budget as passed, whereas three quarters of states made such cuts in 2002 and 2003. Also, in spite of federal reductions

in support, states illustrate continued commitment to human welfare enhancement—while a few states increased cash assistance levels to families, "no state will decrease benefit levels."[7] On the other hand, states are falling short in terms of getting a handle on Medicaid spending. In spite of attempts to contain costs, more than half (26) the states expect their Medicaid spending to exceed their 2005 budgets.[8]

A clearer indication of the budget trend in the states is evidenced by looking at total balances as a percent of expenditures. While these balances rebounded by 2005, they quickly deflated by 2006. In fiscal 2000, total balances swelled to $48.8 billion (10.4 percent of expenditures). By 2006, total balances as a percent of expenditures are expected to be 4.6. Figure A illustrates the trend in end of year balances of states for the last 25 years. Note that the increase in total balances in 2005 is not expected to be sustained in 2006. The soaring costs associated with activities like Medicaid will continue to swallow much of any new and increased revenues flowing into states.

What's on the Agenda?

An assessment of the content of the 40 State of the State addresses this year yields interesting results. Table B illustrates different topics addressed and the number and proportion of governors mentioning such topics in their 2006 speech. Clearly, governors are keeping conversations to the primary expenditures of state government. Virtually every governor providing an address this year discussed his or her agenda regarding education. Yet, a multiyear approach to education is often evidenced. Illinois's chief executive, Rod Blagojevich, believes the new revenue environment will support his kindergarten to college initiative. Similarly, Oregon Gov. Ted Kulongoski describes this continuum as the "Education Enterprise" that moves "Oregonians seamlessly from pre-K/Head Start to K through 12, to post-secondary institutions, to workforce training—and retraining." Kulongoski asked for "big changes" in managing and funding education that involves guaranteed percentage increases in future funding, and for the creation of a "stability fund" as a safety measure when the revenue flow slows.

The focus of health care initiatives swirls around Medicaid reforms, prescription drug plans, avian flu and even personal responsibility. For example, Idaho Gov. Dirk Kempthorne talks of a proactive approach to modernizing the [Medicaid] system that focuses on results and outcomes. "My common sense plan will simplify the system, reduce costs, and turn our attention to prevention, wellness and personal responsibil-

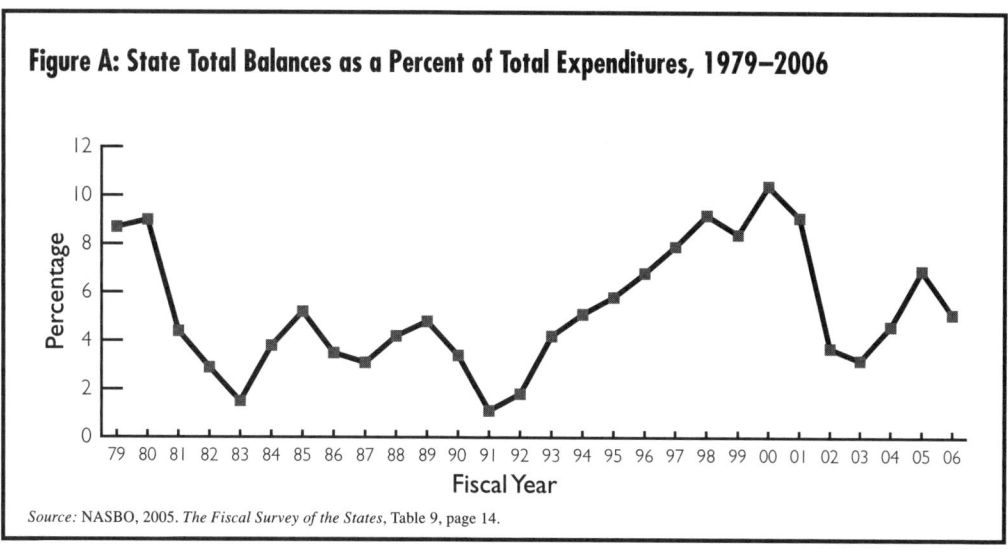

Figure A: State Total Balances as a Percent of Total Expenditures, 1979–2006

Percentage

Fiscal Year

Source: NASBO, 2005. *The Fiscal Survey of the States*, Table 9, page 14.

ity," said Kempthorne. Indiana Gov. Mitch Daniels and Tennessee Gov. Phil Bredesen also harp on basic wellness programs as a means to lasso health care costs. Blagojevich, who boasts that Illinois is the only one that "guarantees access to affordable, comprehensive health care for every single child," seeks to extend access to comprehensive health care to veterans. He suggested better coordination with the federal prescription drug plan to help contain health care costs.

Several chief executives also allotted time to a possible avian flu pandemic and plans are underway to prepare for such a calamity. Utah Gov. Jon Huntsman Jr., for example, explained the state is "better prepared than ever before for any such catastrophic event. I have already spoken with Health and Human Services Secretary Mike Leavitt about hosting, in collaboration with our Department of Health, a Governor's Summit in March to prepare for any possible avian flu pandemic. On this important issue, we in Utah will lead out, rather than stand back and react." Interpretations of government response to Katrina undoubtedly influenced many of the governors' statements about state response to possible health or other crises.

Aside from taxes, the governors addressed other important topics, including natural resources—particularly discussions of energy costs, sources and relief. Hawaii Gov. Linda Lingle was most graphic in her request for approval of the state's Department of Land and Natural Resources budget, one "that is unprecedented in scope and scale. Residents and visitors alike expect and deserve better than broken or filthy restrooms." Vilsack asked legislators and citizens in Iowa to "dedicate our work this year to making E85 and soy diesel the future fuel for Iowa and for all of America." South Dakota Gov. Mike Rounds talked of power plants, pollution control and renewable energy. And Gov. Don Carcieri of Rhode Island discussed a multi-pronged approach to energy policy including conservation, increasing LNG

Table B: Issues Considered in 2006 State of the State Addresses (n=40)

Issues	Number of governors mentioning topic	Percent of addresses where topic is mentioned
Education	40	100%
Health/medicaid	39	98
Taxes	37	93
Natural resources/energy	33	83
Economic development	31	78
Corrections	26	65
National guard/military	26	65
Transportation	24	60
Terrorism/security	19	48
Methamphetamine	18	45
Rainy day fund	12	30
Pensions	7	18
Illegal immigrants	5	13

Source: Content analysis of 2006 State of State Addresses, Katherine Willoughby.

supplies without building in populated areas, support to the most vulnerable, pursuit of renewable energy sources, and reform of "the unfair electricity pricing system in New England."

Discussions about transportation fed into talk of economic development. Good roads support efficiency of work, both within and across states. Stem cell research, technology investment, collaboration between industry and agriculture in other countries, and regional cooperation agreements were all mentioned as avenues toward increasing job creation and productivity. Several governors also linked work force training and other education services and programs to economic development programs in their states.

Most governors also thanked their military personnel and National Guard members for work in and out of the United States. While fewer than half the governors mentioned the war in Iraq or security specifically, many did recognize the crises of Katrina and/or Iraq when discussing state work in the last year. Few governors, however, waded into the quagmire of immigration in the United States—a topic of debate in many state legislatures as well as in Congress. Finally, the conversations about corrections focused primarily on generating deterrents to methamphetamine use—mentioned specifically by 18 governors—as well as building more prisons and locking up sexual predators.

The relatively few governors who brought up rainy day funds and/or pensions were pointed in their comments. Lingle, of Hawaii, seeks to double her state's rainy day fund to shore up resources for lean times. West Virginia Gov. Joe Manchin also asked to increase the state's rainy day fund. He kept the state's pension woes front and center by discussing a new long view of state finances. "For the very first time in West Virginia's history, I am providing the legislature with a five-year forecast of our revenues and expenditures. Never before has this been done, but if, as I've pledged, we're going to run this state like a business, then this is a vitally important component of that effort. Our state's traditional shortsightedness has to end. We must ensure that the decisions we make today are right for tomorrow as well, and this five-year forecast gives us the tools we all need to do just that," he said.

Pennsylvania Gov. Ed Rendell said, "In the near future, the state budget and local taxpayers will be expected to increase school funding annually simply to meet growing pension obligations. This could impair our ability to fund the cost of educating our students. We must work together to address the growing pension obligations of our school districts."

Where is the Money?

As expected, the current swell of revenues has encouraged governors to continue whittling away at tax structures, whether these structures are reasonably balanced or not. The Government Performance Project examined states' abilities to balance ongoing revenues with expenditures. Of the eight states scoring well on "structural balance," only Minnesota Gov. Tim Pawlenty did not give a State of the State address this year. The tax changes considered by some of the others are interesting.[9] For example, Vermont Gov. James Douglas is going after that state's significant property tax. Vermont has one of the highest tax burdens in the country (9.2 percent compared to the national average of 6.8 percent as measured by total taxes as a percent of personal income).[10] Though sales taxes are the primary tax source in this state (approximately 35 percent of total tax sources come from general and selective sales taxes in Vermont), it also receives considerable revenues from property and individual income taxes (these make up approximately 27 and 25 percent of total tax sources in the state). Douglas explains while property tax revenues have multiplied to keep up with state spending, he believes the burden of the tax is unsustainable. In his speech, Douglas called for a significant restructuring of the property tax. With an eye toward the long-term effects of such reform, however, he emphasized that to avert added stress to the education budget from reduced revenues, instead of adding "more pre-kindergarten grades to the already stressed K–12 education system and putting taxpayers on the hook to fund it. … We need to find ways to assist our private pre-school providers."

Delaware's tax burden is also high compared to most states at 8.5 percent, though its tax structure has been termed "recession proof" given its ability to sustain the state fiscally through rough waters.[11] Gov. Ruth Ann Minner proposed to "modernize Delaware's bank franchise tax" to hold on to present business and further grow the banking industry. On the other hand, Pennsylvania's Gov. Edward Rendell called for property tax relief in his 2006 budget address—asking the Pennsylvania legislature to honor a compact that originally linked property tax relief with gaming funds. In his budget address, Rendell proposed:

- Accelerating phase out of capital stock and franchise tax;
- Increasing tax credit for research and development;
- Uncapping net operating losses (NOLs)—and, "should future revenues permit us to continue to uncap these losses, it is my intention to propose

each year additional increases in the NOL cap until the limit is completely removed";

- Lowering the rate and also closing loopholes of the corporate income tax; and
- Adopting a single sales factor.

Pennsylvania's tax burden ranks closer to the bottom than the top—total taxes as a percent of personal income is 6.4 percent, just under the state average of 6.8 percent.[12]

Virginia's tax burden is lower than Pennsylvania's at 5.7 percent. Virginia also underwent significant tax code reforms under Gov. Mark Warner to achieve stronger structural balance. So it is not surprising that the state's new governor, Timothy Kaine, urged a calculated approach to any tax changes—"we shouldn't race to the bottom in taxes and jeopardize our ability to fund the critical services that our citizens demand. … But, we must always examine the way we tax and watch for opportunities to make our tax code fairer." He focused attention on the property tax—by not passing unfunded mandates to local governments that would necessitate property tax increases, by providing taxpayers with more information about tax assessments and rates, and through creation of a homestead exemption.

Governors in states not scoring as well on structural balance by the GPP also had many ideas regarding taxes. Wisconsin has a higher than average tax burden (7.5 percent) and the state's weakest component of money management as scored by the GPP was structural balance.[13] In his address, Wisconsin Gov. Jim Doyle said "no to higher sales taxes, no to higher income taxes, no to higher excise taxes. … And, in fact we've cut taxes for veterans, for businesses, for manufacturers … repealed automatic increases in gas taxes, expanded middle class tax deductions for health care, for college. And next year, the tax on Social Security benefits will be history." Hawaii has the highest tax burden in the country (10.1 percent) if measured by total taxes as a percent of personal income. The state also maintains a strong dependence on federal dollars that weakens its ability to weather economic downturns. Lingle outlined her tax relief package, including:

- Raising the standard deduction to 75 percent of the federal level;
- Widening income tax brackets;
- Allowing a $100 per person tax credit to households earning $50,000 or less a year; and
- Imposing a one-time tax refund of $150 per exemption for all but the highest income residents.

Alabama's strict earmarking of revenues to education means that it constantly grapples with fueling

most other activities in the general fund. Gov. Bob Riley called for a "historic tax reduction package" in his 2006 address, despite the state's weak score in structural balance by the GPP and the low tax burden (total taxes make up 5.9 percent of personal income) compared to the rest of the country. His effort to provide for a more equitable tax structure crashed in 2003. Now he wants every citizen who pays income taxes to get a tax cut. "Over the next five years, taxpayers will keep more than $200 million to meet the needs of their families," Riley said. The plan includes an increase to the tax deduction for dependents; an increase in the personal tax exemption, and an increase in the threshold where income is taxed. Riley also asked for a state sales tax holiday.

In the past, Michigan's strong dependence on one-time revenues has hampered budget balancing in that state. The state had a weak grade on structural balance by the GPP, and has a high tax burden of 7.7 percent. Gov. Jennifer Granholm called attention to a $600 million tax-cut package recently passed by the legislature "that will fight the outsourcing of our existing jobs and encourage the insourcing of new ones." She said she "signed 51 tax cuts into law, both for individuals and to help businesses create jobs, without leaving gaping holes in our budget. I've also made it clear that I will not support business tax breaks that would shift the burden to everyday citizens or force cuts to education and health care." On the other hand, in New Hampshire, a tough anti-tax ethos has weakened the structural balance yet resulted in the state's position as having the lowest tax burden in the country—total taxes comprise just 4.4 percent of personal income. New Hampshire depends heavily on the property tax for revenue (approximately 26 percent of total tax collections are from the state property tax; selective sales taxes comprise 32 percent of tax collections while corporate income taxes comprise about 20 percent of these collections). In 2006, Gov. John Lynch seeks to eliminate the statewide property tax "once and for all."

Conclusion

Governors did seem to concentrate heavily on their education budgets this year, and then on the budgets of other activities that are primary to the mission of state government. Yet threaded through these addresses is a stronger consideration of a multi-pronged and multi-year view of government operations—understanding state education services on a continuum from pre-kindergarten to work force retraining, for instance. Governors are aware of the federal government's slowing financial support as well as its poor reaction to Katrina and what this means for state coffers. And, the U.S. Supreme Court's consideration of the tax credit and exemption package by the State of Ohio to DaimlerChrysler has governors alert to the ramifications on state governments' ability to use tax concessions as economic development. Most importantly, perhaps, the last year has generated interest in examining the balance between state revenues and expenditures. Case in point, Wyoming Gov. Dave Freudenthal talked about creating a budget that is structurally sound, of limiting ongoing obligations, and spending one-time revenues more logically.

Finally, it is interesting that governors seem more determined to place advancing responsibility for state operations with citizens, albeit indirectly. Ultimately, control of government spending lies with citizens, although control can be approached several ways. David Walker, the comptroller general of the United States, noted recently that citizens must be more active and vocal in holding elected officials accountable to spending prudently and responsibly. "In our republic, ultimate accountability for government rests with each of us," he said. "It's no accident that our Constitution begins with the words, 'We the people.'" [14] On the other hand, governors are calling on individuals to take active responsibility for solving problems themselves and in turn, reducing state responsibility (costs). Tennessee's governor extolled a "matter of values"—the personal responsibility required of parents to teach their children the values of education, hard work and respect and that required of every individual regarding personal health and fitness. "Government can't solve every problem, but government can and should be a partner to help our citizens solve more problems themselves," Bredesen said.

Notes

[1] Chief executives of state governments report annually or biennially to their legislatures regarding the fiscal condition of their state, commonwealth or territory. Governors often use their address to lay out their policy and budget agendas for their upcoming or continuing administration. The 2006 state of the state addresses were accessed from January through March 1, 2006 at *www.stateline.org*, *www.nga.org*, or at the state government homepage. This research considers those 40 states with transcripts available at these sites as of March 1, 2006. Although both Virginia's outgoing and newly elected governors gave state speeches, only that of the newly elected Gov. Timothy Kaine (D) is assessed here. Speeches not available by March 1, 2006 included those from Florida, Louisiana, Massachusetts and Minnesota. Also in 2006 in six states, governors did not give state of state addresses, including: Arkansas, Montana, Nevada, North Carolina, North Dakota and Texas. All quotes and

data presented here are from the addresses accessed at these Web sites, unless otherwise noted.

[2] A summary of 2006 gubernatorial elections is available at *www.nga.org* and accessing the "Governors" link at the top of this Web site.

[3] Linda Feldmann, "Governors Line Up for Oval Office," *The Christian Science Monitor*, (March 1, 2005) at: *http://www.cbsnews.com/stories/2005/03/01/politics/main677300.shtml*.

[4] NASBO, *The Fiscal Survey of the States*, The National Governors Association, December 2005, Table 6, page 8.

[5] NASBO, *The Fiscal Survey of the States*, The National Governors Association, December 2005, Table 7, page 9.

[6] NASBO, 2005, Table 2, p. 3.

[7] NASBO, 2005, p. ix.

[8] Ibid.

[9] The Government Performance Project (GPP) is a periodic survey conducted of state government management practices in the areas of human resources, budget and finance, infrastructure and information. The project is sponsored by The Pew Charitable Trusts and involves both academic and journalist partners. Results from the most recent survey are available at *www.results.gpponline.org*. The eight states indicating strong structural balance in the 2005 survey include: Delaware, Kansas, Minnesota, Pennsylvania, South Dakota, Utah, Vermont and Virginia. Scores for structural balance required examination of state revenue structures, use of one-time or windfall revenues, cash and risk management activities as well as use of counter-cyclical or contingency planning, particularly in periods of economic decline.

[10] Federation of Tax Administrators, 2004. State Tax Collections, 2004 State Revenues Per Capita and as Percent of Personal Income accessed February 22, 2006 at *http://www.taxadmin.org/fta/rate/burden.html*.

[11] See Delaware's scores for Money and Structural Balance at *www.results.gpponline.org*.

[12] Federation of Tax Administrators, 2004.

[13] See Wisconsin's scores for Money and Structural Balance at *www.results.gpponline.org*.

[14] David Walker, Comptroller General of the United States Government Accountability Office, Lecturer at Getzen Lecture Series on Government Accountability at the University of Georgia, Athens, Georgia, on February 8, 2006.

About the Author

Katherine Willoughby is professor of Public Administration and Urban Studies in the Andrew Young School of Policy Studies at Georgia State University in Atlanta. Her research concentrates on state and local government budgeting and financial management, public policy development and public organization theory. She has conducted extensive research in the area of state budgeting practices, with a concentration on performance measurement applicability at this level of government in the United States.

Gubernatorial Elections, Campaign Costs and Powers
By Thad Beyle

Only two governorships were contested and decided in the elections of 2005—those in New Jersey and Virginia. In both political situations the races seemed very close in the campaign "horse-race" polls, yet in the final vote count, the Democratic candidates won by nearly nine points in New Jersey and by nearly six points in Virginia. This continued the Democratic Party's control over these two gubernatorial chairs and left the 50 states split with 28 Republican governors and 22 Democratic governors holding office in 2006.

Governors remain in the forefront of activity as we move into the 21st century. With Republican governors across the country serving as his major supporters and guides, Texas Gov. George W. Bush sought and won the presidency in the 2000 election. He became the fourth of the last five presidents who had served as governor just prior to seeking and winning the presidency.[1] When George H. W. Bush, a non-governor, won the 1988 presidential election, he beat a governor, Michael Dukakis (D-Mass., 1975–1979 and 1983–1991). Clearly, governors have been key players in presidential politics in the three decades following the Watergate scandal.

Additionally, the demands on governors to propose state budgets and then keep them in balance during the two recessions of the early 1990s and now in the early 2000s have made the governor's chair a "hot seat" in more ways than one.[2] In the current downturn, governors have moved from the half-decade of economic boom of the late 1990s, in which they could propose tax cuts and program increases, to an economic downturn period in which there is increasing demand for program support while state tax revenues fell off significantly. Proposed and adopted budgets fell victim to severe revenue shortfalls in most states. As we entered 2006, signs of an upturn in the economy eased some of the budgetary problems that governors have faced.

2005 Gubernatorial Politics

Only two governorships were contested and decided in the elections of 2005—those in New Jersey and Virginia. In both political situations the races seemed very close in the campaign "horse-race" polls, yet in the final vote count, the Democratic candidates won by nearly nine points in New Jersey and by nearly six points in Virginia. This continued the Democratic Party's control over these two gubernatorial chairs and left the 50 states split with 28 Republican governors and 22 Democratic governors holding office in 2006.

Incumbents did not seek another term in these races as Virginia only allows a governor to serve a single term and New Jersey's acting Gov. Richard Codey, a Democrat, opted not to seek election to a full term. Codey, as president of the New Jersey Senate, had ascended to the governorship in 2004 when Democratic Gov. Jim McGreevey stepped down for personal reasons. Both races were for an open seat, which U.S. Sen. Jon Corzine, a Democrat, won in New Jersey and Democratic Lt. Gov. Timothy Kaine won in Virginia.

One other new governor was sworn in Jan. 21, 2005—Nebraska Republican Dave Heineman. As lieutenant governor, he ascended to the governorship upon the resignation of incumbent Republican Gov. Mike Johanns, who was appointed by President Bush and sworn in as U.S. Secretary of Agriculture. In March 2006, Gov. Dirk Kempthorne, (R-Idaho), was appointed U.S. Interior Secretary by President George W. Bush. Upon his confirmation by the U.S. Senate and resignation as governor, Republican Lt. Gov. Jim Risch will be sworn in as Idaho's 31st governor to fill out the rest of the last year of Kempthorne's term.

Gubernatorial Elections

As can be seen in Table A, in the 483 gubernatorial elections held between 1970 and 2005, incumbents were eligible to seek another term in 368 (76 percent) of the contests. Of the 286 (78 percent) eligible incumbents seeking re-election, 211 succeeded (74 percent). Those who were defeated for re-election were more likely to lose in the general election than in their own party primary by a 2.9-to-1 ratio, although two of the four incumbent losses in 2004 were tied to party primaries. Not since 1994 had an incumbent governor been defeated in his party's primary.

Democratic candidates held a winning edge in the elections held between 1970 and 2005 (55 percent). In 195 races (40 percent), the results led to a party shift in which a candidate other than the incumbent

Table A: Gubernatorial Elections: 1970–2005

| | | Democratic winner | | Number of incumbent governors | | | | | | | | | |
| | | | | Eligible to run | | Actually ran | | Won | | Lost | | | |
Year	Number of races	Number	Percent	Number	Percent	Number	Percent	Number	Percent	Number	Percent	In primary	In general election
1970	35	22	63	29	83	24	83	16	67	8	33	1 (a)	7 (b)
1971	3	3	100	0	...	...	...	...	...	...	...	...	...
1972	18	11	61	15	83	11	73	7	64	4	36	2 (c)	2 (d)
1973	2	1	50	1	50	1	100	...	...	1	100	1 (e)	...
1974	35	27 (f)	77	29	83	22	76	17	77	5	23	1 (g)	4 (h)
1975	3	3	100	2	66	2	100	2	100	...	...	...	...
1976	14	9	64	12	86	8	67	5	63	3	38	1 (i)	2 (j)
1977	2	1	50	1	50	1	100	1	100	...	...	...	...
1978	36	21	58	29	81	23	79	16	70	7	30	2 (k)	5 (l)
1979	3	2	67	0	...	...	...	...	...	...	...	...	...
1980	13	6	46	12	92	12	100	7	58	5	42	2 (m)	3 (n)
1981	2	1	50	0	...	...	...	...	...	...	...	...	...
1982	36	27	75	33	92	25	76	19	76	6	24	1 (o)	5 (p)
1983	3	3	100	1	33	1	100	...	...	1	100	1 (q)	...
1984	13	5	38	9	69	6	67	4	67	2	33	...	2 (r)
1985	2	1	50	1	50	1	100	1	100	...	...	...	...
1986	36	19	53	24	67	18	75	15	83	3	17	1 (s)	2 (t)
1987	3	3	100	2	67	1	50	...	...	1	100	1 (u)	...
1988	12	5	42	9	75	9	100	8	89	1	11	...	1 (v)
1989	2	2	100	0	...	...	...	...	...	...	...	...	...
1990	36	19 (w)	53	33	92	23	70	17	74	6	26	...	6 (x)
1991	3	2	67	2	67	2	100	...	...	2	100	1 (y)	1 (z)
1992	12	8	67	9	75	4	44	4	100	...	...	...	...
1993	2	0	0	1	50	1	100	...	...	1	100	...	1 (aa)
1994	36	11 (bb)	31	30	83	23	77	17	74	6	26	2 (cc)	4 (dd)
1995	3	1	33	2	67	1	50	1	100	...	...	...	...
1996	11	7	36	9	82	7	78	7	100	...	...	...	...
1997	2	0	0	1	50	1	100	1	100	...	...	...	...
1998	36	11 (ee)	31	27	75	25	93	23	92	2	8	...	2 (ff)
1999	3	2	67	2	67	2	100	2	100	...	...	...	...
2000	11	8	73	7	88	6	86	5	83	1	17	...	1 (gg)
2001	2	2	100	0	...	...	...	...	...	...	...	...	...
2002	36	14	39	22	61	16	73	12	75	4	25	...	4 (hh)
2003	4 (ii)	1	25	2	50	2	100	...	...	2	100	...	2 (jj)
2004	11	6	55	11	100	8	73	4	50	4	50	2 (kk)	2 (ll)
2005	2	2	100	1	50	...	...	...	...	...	...	...	...
Totals:													
Number	483	266		368		286		211		75		19	56
Percent	100	55.1		76.2		77.7		73.8		26.2		25.3	74.7

Source: The Council of State Governments, *The Book of the States, 2005,* (Lexington, KY: The Council of State Governments, 2005), 192, updated.

Key:

(a) Albert Brewer, D-Ala.

(b) Keith Miller, R-Alaska; Winthrop Rockefeller, R-Ark.; Claude Kirk, R-Fla.; Don Samuelson, R-Idaho; Norbert Tieman, R-Neb.; Dewey Bartlett, R-Okla.; Frank Farrar, R-S.D.

(c) Walter Peterson, R-N.H.; Preston Smith, D-Texas.

(d) Russell Peterson, R-Del.; Richard Ogilvie, R-Ill.

(e) William Cahill, R-N.J.

(f) One independent candidate won: James Longley of Maine.

(g) David Hall, D-Okla.

(h) John Vanderhoof, R-Colo.; Francis Sargent, R-Mass.; Malcolm Wilson, R-N.Y.; John Gilligan, D-Ohio.

(i) Dan Walker, D-Ill.

(j) Sherman Tribbitt, D-Del.; Christopher 'Kit' Bond, R-Mo.

(k) Michael Dukakis, D-Mass.; Dolph Briscoe, D-Texas.

(l) Robert F. Bennett, R-Kan.; Rudolph G. Perpich, D-Minn.; Meldrim Thompson, R-N.H.; Robert Straub, D-Oreg.; Martin J. Schreiber, D-Wis.

(m) Thomas L. Judge, D-Mont.; Dixy Lee Ray, D-Wash.

(n) Bill Clinton, D-Ark.; Joseph P. Teasdale, D-Mo.; Arthur J. Link, D-N.D.

(o) Edward J. King, D-Mass.

(p) Frank D. White, R-Ark.; Charles Thone, R-Neb.; Robert F. List, R-Nev.; Hugh J. Gallen, D-N.H.; William P. Clements, R-Texas.

(q) David Treen, R-La.

(r) Allen I. Olson, R-N.D.; John D. Spellman, R-Wash.

(s) Bill Sheffield, D-Alaska.

(t) Mark White, D-Texas; Anthony S. Earl, D-Wis.

(u) Edwin Edwards, D-La.

(v) Arch A. Moore, R-W.Va.

(w) Two Independent candidates won: Walter Hickel (Alaska) and Lowell Weiker (Conn.). Both were former statewide Republican office holders.

(x) Bob Martinez, R-Fla.; Mike Hayden, R-Kan.; James Blanchard, D-Mich.; Rudy Perpich, DFL-Minn.; Kay Orr, R-Neb.; Edward DiPrete, R-R.I.

(y) Buddy Roemer, R-La.

(z) Ray Mabus, D-Miss.

(aa) James Florio, D-N.J.

(bb) One Independent candidate won: Angus King of Maine.

(cc) Bruce Sundlun, D-R.I.; Walter Dean Miller, R-S.D.

(dd) James E. Folsom Jr., D-Ala.; Bruce King, D-N.M.; Mario Cuomo, D-N.Y.; Ann Richards, D-Texas.

(ee) Two Independent candidates won: Angus King of Maine and Jesse Ventura of Minnesota.

(ff) Fob James, R-Ala.; David Beasley, R-S.C.

(gg) Cecil Underwood, R-W.Va.

(hh) Don Siegelman, D-Ala.; Roy Barnes, D-Ga., Jim Hodges, D-S.C.; and Scott McCallum, R-Wis.

(ii) The California recall election and replacement vote of 2003 is included in the 2003 election totals and as a general election for the last column.

(jj) Gray Davis, D-Calif., Ronnie Musgrove, D-Miss.

(kk) Bob Holden, D-Mo.; Olene Walker, R-Utah, lost in the pre-primary convention.

(ll) Joe Kernan, D-Ind.; Craig Benson, R-N.H.

won. These party shifts have evened out over the years so that neither of the two major parties has an edge. In three of the five party shifts in the 2004 elections, a Democrat won the seat for the first time since the 1984 election (Montana), and two Republicans also won the seat for the first time since the 1984 elections (Indiana and Missouri). But there have been some interesting patterns in these shifts over the past 35 years of gubernatorial elections.

Between 1970 and 1992, Democrats won 200 of the 324 races for governor (62 percent). From 1993 to date, Republicans leveled the playing field by winning 94 of the 159 races for governor (59 percent). Despite this Republican trend, Democratic candidates did win eight of the 11 gubernatorial races in 2000, when Gov. Bush won the presidency in a very close race, and six of the 11 when Bush won his second term in 2004. But since the 1994 elections there have been more Republicans than Democrats serving as governor each year.

Another factor in determining how many governors have served in the states is the number of newly-elected governors who are truly new to the office and the number who are returning after complying with constitutional term limits or holding other positions. Looking at the number of actual new governors taking office over a decade, the average number of new governors elected dropped from 2.3 new governors per state in the 1950s to 1.9 in the 1970s and to 1.1 in the 1980s. In the 1990s, the rate began to move up a bit to 1.4 new governors per state.

As we move through the first decade of the 21st century, we continue to find new faces in the governors' offices. New governors were elected in 45 of 66 elections held between 2000 and 2005 (68 percent). And, two other governors ascended to the office during 2004 and one in 2005. In 2006, 37 of the incumbent governors will be serving in their first term (74 percent). The beginning of the 21st century has certainly proved to be a time of change in the governors' offices across the 50 states.

The New Governors

Over the 2002–2005 cycle of gubernatorial elections and resignations, there were several different routes to the governor's chair by the elected governors and those who have ascended to the office. First were the 12 new governors who had previously held statewide office. These include: four attorneys general—Janet Napolitano (D-Ariz.), Jennifer Granholm (D-Mich.), Christine Gregoire (D-Wash.) and Jim Doyle (R-Wisc.); four lieutenant governors—M. Jodi Rell (R-Conn.), Kathleen Blanco (D-La.), Dave

Heineman (R-Neb.) and Timothy Kaine (D-Va.); two secretaries of state—Matt Blunt (R-Mo.) and Joe Manchin (D-W.Va.); one state insurance commissioner—Kathleen Sebelius (D-Kan.); and one state treasurer—James Douglas (R-Vt.).

Second were the nine members or former members of Congress who returned to work within their state. These included U.S. Sens. Frank Murkowski (R-Alaska) and Jon Corzine (D-N. J.), and Congressmen Bob Riley (R-Ala.), Rod Blagojevich (D-Ill.), Ernie Fletcher (R-Ky.), John Baldacci (D-Maine), Robert Ehrlich (R-Md.), and Mark Sanford (R-S.C.). Former Congressman Bill Richardson (D-N.M.) had also served as an administrator in the Clinton administration. And Brian Schweitzer (D-Mont.), who had unsuccessfully sought a U.S. Senate seat in 2000 as the Democratic candidate, turned that around to win the governorship in 2004.

Third were the five legislators or former legislators who moved up from a district to a statewide office. These included Sonny Perdue (a Republican from the Georgia Senate), Tim Pawlenty (a Republican from the Minnesota House), Brad Henry (a Democrat from the Oklahoma Senate), Mike Rounds (a Republican from the South Dakota Senate), and as noted earlier Richard Codey (a Democrat from the New Jersey Senate).

Fourth were four from the business sector: Craig Benson (R-N.H., 2002), John Lynch (D-N.H., 2004), Don Carcieri (R-R.I.) and John Huntsman Jr. (R-Utah).

Fifth were the three mayors or former mayors: Linda Lingle (R-Maui, Hawaii), Ed Rendell (D-Philadelphia, Pa.) and Phil Bredesen (D-Nashville, Tenn.).

Finally, were the six new governors who followed a unique path compared to their counterparts: actor-businessman Arnold Schwarzenegger (R-Calif.), former head of the Federal Office of Management and Budget Mitch Daniels (R-Ind.), the 2000 Winter Olympics Chairman Mitt Romney (R-Mass.), former Republican Party National Chairman Haley Barbour (R-Miss.), former state Supreme Court Justice Ted Kulongoski (D-Ore.) and former U.S. Attorney Dave Freudenthal (D-Wyo.).

In the 373 gubernatorial races between 1977 and 2005, among the candidates were 101 lieutenant governors (29 won), 84 attorneys general (21 won), 27 secretaries of state (seven won), 22 state treasurers (six won) and 14 state auditors, auditors general or comptrollers (three won). Looking at these numbers from a bettor's point of view, the odds of a lieutenant governor winning were 3.5-to-1, an attorney general 4.0-to-1, a secretary of state 3.9-to-1, a state treasurer 3.7-to-1 and a state auditor 4.7-to-1.

Table B: Total Cost of Gubernatorial Elections: 1977–2004
(in thousands of dollars)

Year	Number of races	Total campaign costs		Average cost per state (2004$)	Percent change in similar elections (b)
		Actual $	*2004$ (a)*		
1977	2	12,312	38,840	19,420	N.A.
1978	36	102,342	300,125	8,337	N.A. (c)
1979	3	32,744	86,167	28,722	N.A.
1980	13	35,634	82,677	6,360	N.A.
1981	2	24,648	51,782	25,891	+33
1982	36	181,832	360,064	10,002	+20 (d)
1983	3	39,966	76,710	25,570	-11
1984	13	47,156	86,683	6,668	+5
1985	2	18,859	33,497	16,748	-35
1986	36	270,605	471,438	13,095	+31
1987	3	40,212	67,583	22,528	-12
1988	12 (e)	52,208	84,343	7,029	-3
1989	2	47,902	73,809	36,905	+120
1990	36	345,493	505,107	14,031	+7
1991	3	34,564	48,477	16,159	-28
1992	12	60,278	82,011	6,834	-3
1993	2	36,195	47,814	23,907	-35
1994	36	417,873	538,496	14,958	+7
1995	3	35,693	44,728	14,909	-8
1996	11 (f)	68,610	85,019	7,729	+4
1997	2	44,823	53,045	26,522	+11
1998	36	470,326	548,166	15,227	+2
1999	3	16,277	18,666	6,222	-58
2000	11	97,098	107,647	9,786	+27
2001	2	70,400	75,944	37,972	+43
2002	36	839,650	891,348	24,760	+63
2003	3	69,939	72,626	24,209	+289
2004	11	112,625	112,625	10,239	+4.6

Source: Thad Beyle.

(a) Developed from the Table, "Historical Consumer Price Index for All Urban Consumers (CPI-U)," Bureau of Labor Statistics, U.S. Department of Labor. Each year's actual expenditures are converted to the 2004$ value of the dollar to control for the effect of inflation over the period.

(b) This represents the percent increase or decrease in 2004$ over the last bank of similar elections, i.e., 1977 v. 1981, 1978 v. 1982, 1979 v. 1983, etc.

(c) The data for 1978 are a particular problem as the two sources compiling data on this year's elections did so in differing ways that excluded some candidates. The result is that the numbers for 1978 under-represent the actual costs of these elections by some unknown amount. The sources are: Rhodes Cook and Stacy West, "1978 Advantage," *CQ Weekly Report*, (1979): 1757–1758, and *The Great Louisiana Spendathon* (Baton Rouge: Public Affairs Research Council, March 1980).

(d) This particular comparison with 1978 is not what it would appear to be for the reasons given in note (c). The amount spent in 1978 was more than indicated here so the increase is really not as great as it appears.

(e) As of the 1986 election, Arkansas switched to a four-year term for the governor, hence the drop from 13 to 12 for this off-year.

(f) As of the 1994 election, Rhode Island switched to a four-year term for the governor, hence the drop from 12 to 11 for this off-year.

One other unique aspect about the current governors is that there will be eight women serving as governor in 2006—one less than the nine women serving as governor in the last half of 2004, which was the all-time high for women governors serving at the same time. Seven are women elected in their own right: Janet Napolitano (D-Ariz.), Ruth Ann Minner (D-Del.), Linda Lingle (R-Hawaii), Kathleen Sebelius (D-Kan.), Kathleen Blanco (D-La.), Jennifer Granholm (D-Mich.) and Christine Gregoire (D-Wash.). The other is M. Jodi Rell of Connecticut, who became governor upon the resignation of Gov. John Rowland. While gubernatorial politics continues to be volatile, women continue to hold their own in these races. In the 2002–2005 gubernatorial races, seven of the 12 women running either as the incumbent or as the candidate of a major party won—a 58 percent success rate. There will be more soon.[3]

Timing of Gubernatorial Elections

The election cycle for governors has settled into a regular pattern. Over the past few decades, many states have moved their elections to the off-presidential election years to decouple the state and national campaigns. Now, only 11 states hold their gubernatorial elections in the same year as a presidential election. Two of these states—New Hampshire and Vermont—still have two-year terms for their governor so their elections alternate between presidential and the even non-presidential years.

As can be seen in Table A, the year following a presidential election has only two states with gubernatorial elections.[4] Then in the even years between presidential elections, 36 states hold their gubernatorial elections, and in the year before a presidential election, three Southern states hold their gubernatorial elections.[5]

Cost of Gubernatorial Elections

Table C presents data on the costs of the most recent elections. There is a wide range in how much these races cost, from the all-time most expensive race recorded in New York in 2002 ($155.8 million in 2004 dollars) to the low-cost 2004 race in Vermont ($1,201,530 in 2004 dollars). Both the New York and the Vermont races saw an incumbent Republican governor successfully win re-election.

But if we look at how much was spent by all the candidates per general election vote, a slightly different picture evolves. In 2004, the West Virginia governor's race was the most expensive at $15.52 per vote, followed by the Indiana race at $13.08 per vote. Both of these races were for an open seat. The most expensive governor's race per vote in the 2001–2004 cycle was in New Hampshire's 2002 race when the candidates spent $45.41 per vote in 2004 dollars. The least expensive race during the same cycle was in Minnesota's 2002 race when the candidates spent only $2.81 per vote.

In Figure A, by converting the actual dollars spent each year into the equivalent 2004 dollars, we see how the cost of these elections has increased over time. Since 1981, we have been able to compare the costs of each four-year cycle of elections with the previous cycle of elections.

In the 54 elections held between 1977 and 1980, the total expenditures were $507.8 million in equivalent 2004 dollars. In the 53 elections held between 2001 and 2004—just over two decades later—the total expenditures were a bit over $1.14 billion in 2004 dollars, an increase of 125 percent. The greatest increases in expenditures were between the 1977–1980 and the 1987–1990 cycles, when there was a 43.9 percent

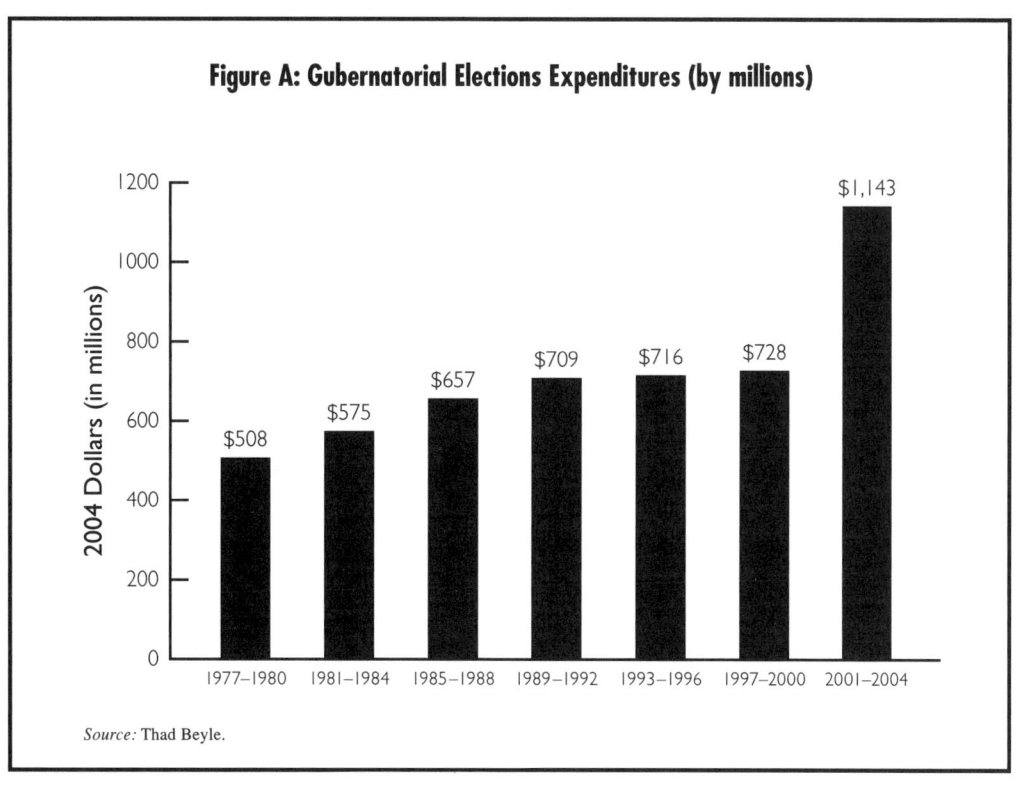

Figure A: Gubernatorial Elections Expenditures (by millions)

Source: Thad Beyle.

Table C: Cost of Gubernatorial Campaigns, Most Recent Elections, 2000–2004

State	Year	Winner	Point margin	All candidates (2004$)	Cost per vote (2004$)	Winner Spent (2004$)	Winner Percent of all expenditures	Winner Vote percent
Alabama	2002	R★★★	+0.3	$33,512,464	24.51	$14,700,611	43.9	49.2
Alaska	2002	R#	+15	5,672,033	25.01	1,835,582	32.4	55.9
Arizona	2002	D#	+1	8,085,414	6.59	2,439,470	30.2	46.2
Arkansas..............	2002	R★	+6	4,790,362	5.94	2,898,362	60.5	53.0
California	2002	D★	+4.9	116,314,901	15.56	68,169,007	58.6	47.3
Colorado	2002	R★	+29	6,426,516	4.55	5,116,110	79.6	62.6
Connecticut	2002	R★	+12	8,353,753	8.17	6,493,702	77.7	56.1
Delaware..............	2004	D★	+5.1	2,645,766	7.25	1,764,586	66.7	50.9
Florida	2002	R#	+13	18,216,101	3.57	8,094,338	44.4	56.0
Georgia	2002	R★★★	+5	25,752,306	12.70	3,880,257	15.1	51.4
Hawaii.................	2002	R#	+4	10,041,642	26.28	5,741,536	57.2	51.1
Idaho..................	2002	R★	+14	2,374,205	5.77	1,181,847	49.8	56.3
Illinois................	2002	D#	+8	51,768,316	14.63	23,789,347	46.0	52.2
Indiana................	2004	R★★★	+5.3	32,028,028	13.08	16,829,092	52.5	50.8
Iowa	2002	D★	+8	13,958,685	13.61	6,424,202	46.0	52.7
Kansas	2002	D#	+8	16,201,626	19.39	4,631,042	28.6	52.9
Kentucky	2003	R#	+10	11,877,641	10.96	5,917,266	49.8	55.0
Louisiana	2003	D#	+3.8	40,427,109	28.72	6,871,733	17.0	51.9
Maine..................	2002	D#	+5.6	4,595,672	9.10	1,681,932	36.6	47.1
Maryland	2002	R#	+3.9	5,452,542	3.20	2,689,846	49.3	51.6
Massachusetts.......	2002	R#	+5	32,486,102	14.63	9,937,370	30.6	49.8
Michigan..............	2002	D★★★	+4	16,228,800	5.11	9,336,445	57.5	51.4
Minnesota	2002	R#	+8	6,334,174	2.81	2,681,285	42.3	44.4
Mississippi	2003	R★★★	+7	20,326,276	22.72	11,721,105	57.7	52.6
Missouri	2004	R★★	+2.9	15,526,723	5.71	4,287,730	31.1	50.8
Montana	2004	D#	+4.4	3,790,902	8.50	1,726,951	45.6	50.4
Nebraska..............	2002	R★	+41	1,697,424	3.53	1,287,850	75.9	68.7
Nevada	2002	R★	+46	2,883,964	5.72	2,806,829	97.3	68.1
New Hampshire....	2004	D★★★	+2.1	5,735,434	8.61	2,977,714	51.9	51.0
New Jersey...........	2001	D#	+15	39,452,688	17.71	16,414,420	41.6	56.4
New Mexico	2002	D#	+15	10,639,323	21.97	7,777,598	73.1	55.5
New York	2002	R★	+16	155,787,222	33.21	46,909,872	30.1	48.2
North Carolina.....	2004	D★	+13	18,178,511	5.21	8,227,561	45.3	55.6
North Dakota.......	2004	R★	+44	1,395,649	8.82	1,245,918	48.7	55.0
Ohio	2002	R★	+20	15,362,890	4.76	13,623,911	88.7	57.8
Oklahoma	2002	D#	+0.7	11,912,260	11.50	3,430,690	28.8	43.3
Oregon	2002	D#	+2.8	16,041,053	12.73	4,424,201	27.6	49.0
Pennsylvania	2002	D#	+9	69,151,599	19.31	41,574,906	60.1	53.4
Rhode Island	2002	R#	+10	7,350,029	22.15	2,592,029	35.3	54.8
South Carolina	2002	R★★★	+6	31,432,056	28.58	7,597,776	24.2	52.8
South Dakota........	2002	R#	+15	9,833,246	29.39	1,724,149	17.5	56.8
Tennessee	2002	D#	+3	18,255,080	11.04	10,364,483	56.8	50.6
Texas	2002	R★	+18	112,055,236	24.61	29,617,542	26.4	57.8
Utah	2004	R★★	+16	6,298,295	6.85	3,276,294	52.0	57.7
Vermont	2004	R★	+21	1,201,530	3.88	681,662	56.7	58.7
Virginia	2001	D#	+5	36,491,411	19.34	21,555,447	59.1	52.2
Washington..........	2004	D#	+0.005	14,270,735	5.08	6,210,217	43.5	48.9
West Virginia.......	2004	D#	+29.6	11,553,283	15.52	3,540,719	30.6	63.5
Wisconsin............	2002	D★★★	+3.7	18,158,028	10.23	5,866,573	32.3	45.1
Wyoming..............	2002	D#	+2.1	2,735,552	14.75	781,845	29.0	50.0

Source: Thad Beyle.

Note: 2004$–Using the November 2004 CPI Index which was 1.910 of the 1982–84 Index = 1,000, the actual 2000 expenditures were based on a 1.722 value or .901 of the 2004$ index, the actual 2001 expenditures were based on a 1.771 index value or .927 of the 2004$ index, the actual 2002 expenditures were based on a 1.799 index value or .942 of the 2004$ index, and the 2003 expenditures were based on a 1.840 index value or .963 of the 2004$ index. Then the actual expenditures of each state's governor's race were divided by the .9 value for that year to get the equivalent 2004$ value of those expenditures.

Key:
D — Democrat
I — Independent
R — Republican
— Open seat
★ — Incumbent ran and won.
★★ — Incumbent ran and lost in party primary.
★★★ — Incumbent ran and lost in general election.

increase, and between the 1992–1995 and the 2001–2004 cycles when there was a 60.3 percent increase.

These increases reflect the new style of campaigning for governor—with the candidates developing their own personal party by using outside consultants, opinion polls, media ads and buys, and extensive fundraising efforts to pay for it all. This style has now reached almost every state. Few states will be surprised by a high-price, high-tech campaign; they are commonplace now. The "air-war" campaigns have replaced the "ground-war" campaigns across the states.

Another factor has been the increasing number of candidates who are either wealthy or who have access to wealth and are willing to spend some of this money to become governor. For some, spending a lot of money leads to winning the governor's chair. In 2002, Gov. Gray Davis spent $68.2 million in 2004 dollars in his successful bid for re-election in California, while Gov. George Pataki spent $46.9 million in 2004 dollars to win his third term in New York. However, spending that amount of money and winning re-election did not deter those wanting to have Davis recalled from office less than a year later.

But spending a lot doesn't always lead to a win. For example, in the 2002 New York election, Thomas Golisano spent $81 million in 2004 dollars in his unsuccessful campaign for governor as an independent candidate. And in Texas, Tony Sanchez also spent $81 million in 2004 dollars as the unsuccessful Democratic candidate. In California's 1998 gubernatorial election, three candidates spent $126 million in 2004 dollars in their campaigns. Two of these candidates won their party's nomination and faced off in November, with Democrat Gray Davis at $43.9 million in 2004 dollars the winner over Republican Dan Lundgren at $36.8 million in 2004 dollars. The largest spender at $45.4 million in 2004 dollars, Al Checci wasn't even able to win the Democratic nomination.

Gubernatorial Forced Exits[6]

The 2003 California gubernatorial recall and replacement votes highlighted the fact that some elected governors faced situations in which they could lose their office without being beaten by a challenger at the ballot box, becoming ill or dying. In 2004, two other governors resigned from office, John Rowland (R-Conn.), facing the threat of a potential impeachment move, and Jim McGreevey (D-N.J.), due to personal reasons.

However, 2005 has been rather quiet on this type of situation and no governor has been driven or recalled from office. Several governors have been facing some difficult times in terms of things that have happened while they served and their job approval ratings in state level polls indicate many are not happy with their performance.

Gubernatorial Powers[7]

One way to view the changes that have been occurring in gubernatorial powers is to look at the "Index of Formal Powers of the Governorship" first developed by Joseph Schlesinger in the 1960s,[8] which this author has continued to update.[9] The index used here consists of six different indices of gubernatorial power as seen in 1960 and 2005. These indices include the number and importance of separately elected executive branch officials, the tenure potential of governors, the appointment powers of governors for administrative and board positions in the executive branch, the governor's budgetary power, the governor's veto power and the governor's party control in the legislature. Each of the individual indices is set in a five-point scale, with five being the most power and one being the least.

During the four and a half decades between 1960 and 2005, the overall institutional powers of the nation's governors increased by 12.5 percent. The greatest increase among the individual gubernatorial powers was in their veto power (plus 61 percent) as more governors gained an item veto, and in 1996 North Carolina voters were finally able to vote on a constitutional amendment giving their governor veto power. Voters approved it by a 3-to-1 ratio.

The indices measuring the governor's tenure potential (length of term and ability to seek an additional term or terms) and the number of separately elected executive branch officials showed identical 28 percent increases in favor of the governor. The governors' appointment power over specific functional area executive branch officials increased by only 7 percent. In addition, the states continue to hold to the concept of the multiple executive in terms of how many statewide elected officials there are. In 2004, there were 308 separately elected executive officials covering 12 major offices in the states.[10] This compares to 709 elected officials in 1955.[11] Ten states also have multimember boards, commissions or councils with members selected by statewide or district election.

The gubernatorial budgetary power actually declined over the period (minus 14 percent). However, we must remember that during the same period, state legislatures were also undergoing considerable reform, and gaining more power to work on the governor's proposed budget was one of those reforms sought. Hence, the increased legislative budgetary power more than balanced out any increases in gubernatorial budgetary power.

There has also been a drop in the gubernatorial party control in state legislatures over the period (minus 17 percent). Much of this can be attributed to the major partisan shifts occurring in the Southern states as the region has been moving from one-party dominance to a very competitive two-party system.[12] In 1960, 13 of the 14 governors were Democrats, and all 28 state legislative chambers were under Democratic control. In 2005, Republicans controlled eight governorships to the Democrats' six, while the Democrats held a 15-to-13 edge in control of the legislative chambers. Four Southern governors face a legislature completely controlled by the other party,[13] while three others face a legislature with split partisan control.[14]

Notes

[1] The former governors winning the presidency over the past three decades were Jimmy Carter (D-Ga., 1971–1975) in 1976, Ronald Reagan (R-Calif., 1967–1975) in 1980 and 1984, Bill Clinton (D-Ark., 1979–1981 and 1983–1992) in 1992 and 1996, and George W. Bush (R-Texas, 1995–2001) in 2000.

[2] For an analysis of governors trying to handle the impact of the early 1990s economic downturn, see Thad Beyle, ed., *Governors in Hard Times* (Washington, D.C.: CQ Press, 1994).

[3] For more detail on this topic check "Table D: Women Governors" and accompanying text "A Shift to More Women Governors" in *The Book of the States, 2005* (Lexington, KY: The Council of State Governments, 2005): 197, 199.

[4] New Jersey and Virginia.

[5] Kentucky, Louisiana and Mississippi.

[6] For more detail on this topic check "Table E: Impeachments and Removals of Governors" and accompanying text "Gubernatorial Forced Exits" in *The Book of the States, 2005* (Lexington, KY: The Council of State Governments, 2005): 198–200.

[7] For more detail on this topic check "Table F: Governors' Institutional Powers, 1960 v. 2005," in *The Book of the States, 2005* (Lexington, KY: The Council of State Governments, 2005): 200.

[8] Joseph A. Schlesinger, "The Politics of the Executive," *Politics in the American States*, 1st and 2nd ed, Herbert Jacob and Kenneth N. Vines, eds., (Boston: Little Brown, 1965 and 1971).

[9] Thad L. Beyle, "The Governors," *Politics in the American States* 8th ed, Virginia Gray and Russell L. Hanson, eds., (Washington, D.C.: CQ Press, 2003). Earlier versions of this index by the author appeared in the 4th edition (1983), the 5th edition (1990), the 6th edition (1996), and the 7th edition (1999).

[10] Kendra Hovey and Harold Hovey, "D-12—Number of

Statewide Elected Officials, 2004," *CQ's State Fact Finder, 2005* (Washington, D.C.: CQ Press, 2005): 113.

[11] *The Book of the States, 1984–85* (Lexington, KY: The Council of State Governments, 1984), 44.

[12] The following states are included in this definition of the South: Alabama, Arkansas, Florida, Georgia, Kentucky, Louisiana, Mississippi, North Carolina, Oklahoma, South Carolina, Tennessee, Texas, Virginia and West Virginia.

[13] Republicans Bob Riley in Ala., Mike Huckabee in Ark. and Haley Barbour in Miss., and Democrat Mark Warner in Va.

[14] Republican Ernie Fletcher in Ky., and Democrats Brad Henry in Okla. and Phil Bredesen in Tenn.

About the Author

Thad Beyle is professor of Political Science at the University of North Carolina at Chapel Hill. A Syracuse University AB and Am, he received his Ph.D. at the University of Illinois. He spent a year in the North Carolina governor's office in the mid-1960s and has worked with the National Governors Association in several capacities on gubernatorial transitions.

Table 4.1
THE GOVERNORS, 2006

State or other jurisdiction	Name and party	Length of regular term in years	Date of first service	Present term ends	Number of previous terms	Maximum consecutive terms allowed by constitution	Joint election of governor and lieutenant governor (a)	Official who succeeds governor	Birthdate	Birthplace
Alabama	Bob Riley (R)	4	1/03	1/07	...	2 (d)	No	LG	10/3/1944	AL
Alaska	Frank H. Murkowski (R)	4	12/02	12/06	...	2	Yes	LG	3/28/1933	WA
Arizona	Janet Napolitano (D)	4	1/03	1/07	...	2	(k)	SS	11/29/1957	NY
Arkansas	Mike Huckabee (R)	4	7/96 (b)	1/07	2 (b)	2	No	LG	8/24/1955	AR
California	Arnold Schwarzenegger (R)	4	11/03 (c)	1/07	...	2	No	LG	7/30/1947	Aus.
Colorado	Bill Owens (R)	4	1/99	1/07	1	2	Yes	LG	10/22/1950	TX
Connecticut	M. Jodi Rell (R)	4	7/04 (o)	1/07	...	...	Yes	LG	6/16/1946	VA
Delaware	Ruth Ann Minner (D)	4	1/01	1/09	1	2	No	LG	1/17/1935	DE
Florida	Jeb Bush (R)	4	1/99	1/07	1	2 (d)	Yes	LG	2/11/1953	TX
Georgia	Sonny Perdue (R)	4	1/03	1/07	...	2	No	LG	12/20/1946	GA
Hawaii	Linda Lingle (R)	4	12/02	12/06	...	2	Yes	LG	6/4/1953	MO
Idaho	Dirk Kempthorne (R) (q)	4	1/99	1/07	1	...	No	LG	10/29/1951	CA
Illinois	Rod R. Blagojevich (D)	4	1/03	1/07	...	...	Yes	LG	12/10/1956	IL
Indiana	Mitch Daniels (R)	4	1/05	1/09	...	2 (f)	Yes	LG	4/7/1949	PA
Iowa	Thomas J. Vilsack (D)	4	1/99	1/07	1	2	Yes	LG	12/13/1950	PA
Kansas	Kathleen Sebelius (D)	4	1/03	1/07	...	2	Yes	LG	5/15/1948	OH
Kentucky	Ernie Fletcher (R)	4	12/03	12/07	...	2	Yes	LG	11/12/1952	KY
Louisiana	Kathleen Babineaux Blanco (D)	4	1/04	1/08	...	2	No	LG	12/15/1942	LA
Maine	John Baldacci (D)	4	1/03	1/07	...	2	(k)	PS	1/30/1955	ME
Maryland	Robert L. Ehrlich Jr. (R)	4	1/03	1/07	...	2	Yes	LG	11/25/1957	MD
Massachusetts	Mitt Romney (R)	4	1/03	1/07	...	...	Yes	LG	3/12/1947	MI
Michigan	Jennifer Granholm (D)	4	1/03	1/07	...	2	Yes	LG	2/5/1959	BC
Minnesota	Tim Pawlenty (R)	4	1/03	1/07	...	...	Yes	LG	11/27/1960	MN
Mississippi	Haley Barbour (R)	4	1/04	1/08	...	2	No	LG	10/22/1947	MS
Missouri	Matt Blunt (R)	4	1/05	1/09	...	2	No	LG	11/20/1970	MO
Montana	Brian Schweitzer (D)	4	1/05	1/09	...	2 (g)	Yes	LG	9/4/1955	MT
Nebraska	Dave Heineman (R)	4	1/05 (e)	1/07	...	2	Yes	LG	5/12/1948	NE
Nevada	Kenny Guinn (R)	4	1/99	1/07	1	2	No	LG	8/24/1936	AR
New Hampshire	John Lynch (D)	2	1/05	1/07	...	...	(k)	PS	11/25/1952	MA
New Jersey	Jon Corzine (D)	4	1/06	1/10	...	2	(i)	(i)	1/1/1947	IL
New Mexico	Bill Richardson (D)	4	1/03	1/07	...	2	Yes	LG	11/15/1947	CA
New York	George E. Pataki (R)	4	1/95	1/07	2	...	Yes	LG	6/24/1945	NY
North Carolina	Michael F. Easley (D)	4	1/01	1/09	1	2 (f)	No	LG	3/23/1950	NC
North Dakota	John Hoeven (R)	4	12/00	12/08	1	...	Yes	LG	3/13/1957	ND
Ohio	Bob Taft (R)	4	1/99	1/07	1	2 (f)	Yes	LG	1/8/1942	OH
Oklahoma	Brad Henry (D)	4	1/03	1/07	...	2	No	LG	6/10/1963	OK
Oregon	Ted Kulongoski (D)	4	1/03	1/07	...	2	(k)	SS	11/5/1940	MO
Pennsylvania	Edward G. Rendell (D)	4	1/03	1/07	...	2	Yes	LG	1/5/1944	NY
Rhode Island	Don Carcieri (R)	4	1/03	1/07	...	2	No	LG	12/16/1942	RI
South Carolina	Mark Sanford (R)	4	1/03	1/07	...	2	No	LG	5/28/1960	FL

See footnotes at end of table.

THE GOVERNORS, 2006 — Continued

State or other jurisdiction	Name and party	Length of regular term in years	Date of first service	Present term ends	Number of previous terms	Maximum consecutive terms allowed by constitution	Joint election of governor and lieutenant governor (a)	Official who succeeds governor	Birthdate	Birthplace
South Dakota	Mike Rounds (R)	4	1/03	1/07	…	2	Yes	LG	10/24/1954	SD
Tennessee	Phil Bredesen (D)	4	1/03	1/07	…	2	No	SpS (l)	11/21/1943	NJ
Texas	Rick Perry (R)	4	12/00 (h)	1/07	1	…	No	LG	3/4/1950	TX
Utah	Jon M. Huntsman Jr. (R)	4	1/05	1/09	…	…	Yes	LG	3/26/1960	CA
Vermont	Jim Douglas (R)	2	1/03	1/07	1	…	No	LG	6/21/1951	MA
Virginia	Tim Kaine (D)	4	1/06	1/10	…	(j)	No	LG	2/26/1958	MN
Washington	Christine Gregoire (D)	4	1/05	1/09	…	…	No	LG	3/24/1957	WA
West Virginia	Joe Manchin III (D)	4	1/05	1/09	…	2	(k)	PS	8/24/1947	WV
Wisconsin	Jim Doyle (D)	4	1/03	1/07	…	…	Yes	LG	11/23/1945	D.C.
Wyoming	Dave Freudenthal (D)	4	1/03	1/07	…	2 (g)	(k)	SS	10/12/1950	WY
American Samoa	Togiola Tulafono (D)	4	4/03 (m)	1/09	1	2	Yes	LG	2/28/1947	AS
Guam	Felix P. Camacho (R)	4	1/03	1/07	…	2	Yes	LG	10/30/1957	GU
No. Mariana Islands	Benigno Fitial (C)	4	1/06	1/10	…	2 (n)	Yes	LG	11/27/1945	CNMI
Puerto Rico	Anibal Acevedo-Vila (PDP)	4	1/05	1/09	…	(k)	(k)	(p)	2/13/1963	PR
U.S. Virgin Islands	Charles W. Turnbull (D)	4	1/99	1/07	1	(f)	Yes	LG	2/5/1935	VI

Source: The Council of State Governments' survey, January 2006.

Key:
C — Covenant
D — Democrat
PDP — Popular Democratic Party
R — Republican
LG — Lieutenant Governor
SS — Secretary of the Senate
PS — President of the Senate
SpS — Speaker of the Senate
… — Not applicable

(a) The following also choose candidates for governor and lieutenant governor through a joint nomination process: Florida, Kansas, Maryland, Minnesota, Montana, North Dakota, Ohio, Utah, American Samoa, Guam, No. Mariana Islands and U.S. Virgin Islands.

(b) Governor Huckabee, as lieutenant governor, became Governor in July 1996 after Governor Jim Guy Tucker resigned. He was elected to a full four-year term in November 1998 and November 2002.

(c) Governor Schwarzenegger was sworn in on November 17, 2003 after defeating Governor Gray Davis in a recall election.

(d) Limited to eight consecutive years in office.

(e) Governor Heineman, as lieutenant governor, was sworn in as Nebraska's governor on Friday, January 21, 2005 after Governor Johanns resigned on January 20, 2005 upon being confirmed as the United States Secretary of Agriculture.

(f) After two consecutive terms as Governor, the candidate must wait four years before becoming eligible to run again.

(g) Absolute limit of eight years of service out of every 16 years.

(h) Lt. Gov. Perry was sworn in on December 21, 2000 to complete President George W. Bush's term as governor of Texas.

(i) New Jersey will elect a lieutenant governor in 2009. The governor and lieutenant governor will be elected jointly. In the event of a permanent vacancy in the office before the inauguration date of the first lieutenant governor, the president of the senate, followed by the speaker of the General Assembly, would become governor, rather than acting governor.

(j) Governor cannot serve immediate successive terms.

(k) No lieutenant governor.

(l) Official bears the additional title of "lieutenant governor."

(m) Governor Tulafono, as lieutenant governor, became Governor in April 2003 after Governor Sunia's death.

(n) Absolute two-term limitation, but terms need not be consecutive.

(o) Lieutenant Governor Rell was sworn in as governor on July 1, 2004 after Governor John Rowland resigned.

(p) Secretary of State succeeds the Governor.

(q) When this publication went to press, Governor Kempthorne had been appointed Secretary of the Interior. Confirmation hearings are scheduled to begin May 2006. If Kempthorne is confirmed, Lt. Gov. Jim Risch will fill the office until the inauguration in January 2007.

Table 4.2
THE GOVERNORS: QUALIFICATIONS FOR OFFICE

State or other jurisdiction	Minimum age	State citizen (years)	U.S. citizen (years) (a)	State resident (years) (b)	Qualified voter (years)
Alabama	30	7	10	...	★
Alaska	30	7	7	7	★
Arizona	25	5	10	...	...
Arkansas	30	★	★	7	...
California	18	...	5	5	★
Colorado	30	...	★	2	...
Connecticut	30	...	★	★	★
Delaware	30	...	12	6	...
Florida	30	...	★	7	★
Georgia	30	...	15	6	★
Hawaii	30	...	...	5	★
Idaho	30	...	★	2	...
Illinois	25	3	★	3	★
Indiana	30	...	5	5	★
Iowa	30	...	2	2	...
Kansas	...	...	...	...	...
Kentucky	30	6	...	6	...
Louisiana	25	5	5	5	★
Maine	30	...	15	5	...
Maryland	30	...	(c)	5	5
Massachusetts	...	...	...	7	...
Michigan	30	...	★	★	4
Minnesota	25	...	★	1	★
Mississippi	30	...	20	5	★
Missouri	30	...	15	10	...
Montana	25	★	★	★	...
Nebraska	30	5	5	5	...
Nevada	25	2	2	2	★
New Hampshire	30	...	...	7	...
New Jersey	30	...	20	7	...
New Mexico	30	...	★	5	★
New York	25	★	★	1	...
North Carolina	30	...	5	2	★
North Dakota	30	...	★	5	★
Ohio	18	...	★	★	★
Oklahoma	31	...	...	...	★
Oregon	30	...	★	3	★
Pennsylvania	30	...	★	7	...
Rhode Island	18	30 days	★	30 days	★
South Carolina	30	5	5	5	...
South Dakota	21	...	★	2	...
Tennessee	30	7	★	...	...
Texas	30	...	★	5	...
Utah	30	5	★	5	★
Vermont	18	1	...	4	★
Virginia	30	...	★	5	5
Washington	18	...	★	★	★
West Virginia	30	5	★	1	★
Wisconsin	18	...	★	★	★
Wyoming	30	★	★	5	...
American Samoa	35	...	★	5	...
Guam	30	...	5	5	★
No. Mariana Islands	35	...	★	10	★
Puerto Rico	35	5	5	5	...
U.S. Virgin Islands	30	...	5	5	★

Source: The Council of State Governments' survey of governor's offices, January 2006.

Key:

★ — Formal provision; number of years not specified.

... — No formal provision.

(a) In some states you must be a U.S. citizen to be an elector, and must be an elector to run.

(b) In some states you must be a state resident to be an elector, and must be an elector to run.

(c) *Crosse v. Board of Supervisors of Elections* 243 Md. 555, 221A.2d431 (1966)—opinion rendered indicated that U.S. citizenship was, by necessity, a requirement for office.

Table 4.3
THE GOVERNORS: COMPENSATION, STAFF, TRAVEL AND RESIDENCE

State or other jurisdiction	Salary	Governor's office staff (a)	Access to state transportation			Travel allowance	Official residence
			Automobile	Airplane	Helicopter		
Alabama	$96,361	43	★	★	★	(b)	★
Alaska	125,000	70	★	★	...	(k)	★
Arizona	95,000	39	★	★	...	(b)	...
Arkansas	77,028	55	★	★	★	★	★
California	175,000 (m)	185	★	...	...	(c)	(d)
Colorado	90,000	39	★	★	...	(e)	★
Connecticut	150,000	30	★	★	★	(e)	★
Delaware	132,500	32	★	...	...	...	★
Florida	129,060	278	★	★	...	(b)	★
Georgia	131,481	87	★	★	★	(e)	★
Hawaii	94,780	67	★	★	★	★	★
Idaho	98,500	24	★	★	...	★(e)	(o)
Illinois	154,100	130	★	★	★	(b)	★
Indiana	95,000	34	★	★	★	(b)	★
Iowa	130,000	19	★	...	...	(b)	★
Kansas	98,331	24	★	★	...	(b)	★
Kentucky	130,705	80	★	★	★	(b)	★
Louisiana	95,000	123 (l)	★	★	★	(b)	★
Maine	70,000	19	★	★	★	(b)	★
Maryland	150,000	84	★	★	★	(e)	★
Massachusetts	135,000 (j)	78	★	...	★	(b)	...
Michigan	177,000	56	★	★	...	(e)	★
Minnesota	120,303	45	★	★	★	(e)	★
Mississippi	122,160	29	★	★	★	(e)	★
Missouri	120,087	38	★	★	...	(c)	★
Montana	96,462	18	★	★	★	(b)	★
Nebraska	85,000	9	★	★	...	(b)	★
Nevada	117,000	(g)	★	★	...	(c)	★
New Hampshire	96,060	23	★	...	...	(e)	★(f)
New Jersey	157,000	156	★	...	★	$61,000	★
New Mexico	110,000	27	★	★	★	$79,200 (c)	★
New York	179,000	180	★	★	★	(b)	★
North Carolina	123,819	76	★	★	★	$11,500	★
North Dakota	88,926	17	★	★	...	(b)	★
Ohio	130,291	60	★	★	★	(f)	★
Oklahoma	110,299	34	★	★	...	(b)	★
Oregon	93,600	29	★	...	...	(e)	★
Pennsylvania	161,173	68	★	★	...	(b)	★
Rhode Island	105,194	49	★	...	...	N.A.	...
South Carolina	106,078	22	★	★	...	(b)	★
South Dakota	105,544	23	★	★	...	(b)	★
Tennessee	85,000	36	★	★	★	(e)	★
Texas	115,345	266	★	★	★	(b)	★
Utah	104,100	16.5	★	★	★	$76,000	★
Vermont	138,465	14	★	...	...	★	...
Virginia	124,855	45	★	★	★	(b)	★
Washington	148,035	36	★	★	...	(e)	★
West Virginia	95,000	56	★	★	★	(h)	★
Wisconsin	131,768 (n)	39.75	★	★	...	(e)	★
Wyoming	105,000	8	★	★	...	(b)	★
American Samoa	50,000	23	★	...	...	$105,000 (c)	★
Guam	90,000	42	★	...	...	$218/day	★
No. Mariana Islands	70,000	16	★	...	...	(e)(i)	★
Puerto Rico	70,000	370	★	...	...	...	★
U.S. Virgin Islands	80,000	86	★	...	...	(b)	★

See footnotes at end of table.

THE GOVERNORS: COMPENSATION, STAFF, TRAVEL AND RESIDENCE — Continued

Source: The Council of State Governments' survey, January 2006.
Key:
★ — Yes
. . . — No
N.A. — Not available.
(a) Definitions of "governor's office staff" vary across the states—from general office support to staffing for various operations within the executive office.
(b) Reimbursed for travel expenses. Alabama—reimbursed for travel expenses. Arizona—receives up to $38/day for meals based on location; receives per diem for lodging out-of-state; default $28/day for meals and $50/day lodging in-state. Florida—reimbursed at same rate as other state officials: in-state, choice between $50 per diem or actual expenses; out-of-state, actual expenses. Indiana—statute allows $12,000 but due to budget cuts the amount has been reduced to $9,800 and reimbursed for actual expenses for travel/lodging. Illinois—no set allowance. Iowa—reimbursed for expenses, limit set in annual office budget. Kentucky—mileage at same rate as other state officials. Kansas—reimbursed for actual expenses. Louisiana—reimbursed for actual expenses. Massachusetts—as necessary. Montana—reimbursed for actual and necessary expenses. Nebraska—reimbursed for travel expenses. New York—reimbursed for actual and necessary expenses. North Dakota—reimbursed at state rate. Oklahoma—reimbursed for actual expenses. Pennsylvania—reimbursed for reasonable expenses. Texas—full reimbursement. South Dakota—reimbursed at state rate. Virginia—reimbursed for travel related to the duties of office. Wyoming—$85/day or actual. U.S. Virgin Islands—reimbursed 100 percent.

(c) Amount includes travel allowance for entire staff. Missouri amount not available. California—$145,000 in-state; $36,000 out-of-state. Nevada—these figures include travel expenses for governor and staff, $22,254 in-state; $16,596 out-of-state. New Mexico—$79,200 (in-state $45,600, out-of-state $33,600).
(d) In California—provided by Governor's Residence Foundation, a non-profit organization which provides a residence for the governor of California. No rent is charged; maintenance and operational costs are provided by California Department of General Services.
(e) Travel allowance included in office budget.
(f) The current governor does not occupy the official residence.
(g) Nineteen active and 25 authorized staff.
(h) Included in general expense account.
(i) Governor has a "contingency account" that can be used for travel expenses and expenses in other departments or other projects.
(j) Governor Romney waives his salary.
(k) Travel allowance—Alaska—$42/day per diem plus actual lodging expenses.
(l) Figure does not include 39 part-time employees.
(m) Governor Schwarzenegger waives his salary.
(n) Governor Doyle remits a portion of his salary to the state.
(o) J.R. and Esther Simplot donated their home to the state of Idaho in December 2004 for use as future Governor's residence. Efforts are under way to raise private monies for renovation, with projected completion in August 2006.

Table 4.4
THE GOVERNORS: POWERS

State or other jurisdiction	Budget making power		Item veto power					Authorization for reorganization through executive order (a)
	Full responsibility	Shares responsibility	Governor has item veto power on all bills	Governor has item veto power on appropriations only	Governor has no item veto power	Item veto—2/3 legislators present or 3/5 elected to override	Item veto—majority legislators elected to override	
Alabama					★(m)			★
Alaska	★		★				★	★
Arizona	★(b)			★		★		
Arkansas		★		★		★		
California	★(b)		★			★		★(g)
Colorado	★		★			★		
Connecticut		★	★			★		★
Delaware	★(b)		★			★		
Florida	★			★(d)		★		★
Georgia		★		★		★		
Hawaii	★		★			★		
Idaho	★		★			★		
Illinois	★			★		★		★(f)
Indiana	★				★			★
Iowa	★		★			★		★
Kansas	★			★		★		★
Kentucky	★(b)			★		★(k)		★★
Louisiana	★★			★★		★		★(l)
Maine	★★				★★		★	★
Maryland	★★		★			★		★
Massachusetts	★		★			★(k)		★(g)
Michigan		★	★			★		★
Minnesota	★(b)			★		★(k)		★
Mississippi		★		★		★(k)		★
Missouri	★(b)			★		★		★
Montana	★		(j)			★		(e)
Nebraska	★		★★			★★		
Nevada	★				★			
New Hampshire	★(b)				★			
New Jersey	★		★			★		★
New Mexico	★			★		★		
New York		★	★★			★★		
North Carolina	★★			★		★		
North Dakota	★★			★★		★★		★★
Ohio	★			★		★		
Oklahoma	★(b)			★			★	
Oregon	★		★★			★★		
Pennsylvania	★(b)			★★		★★		★★
Rhode Island					★			
South Carolina	★(b)		★			★		★

See footnotes at end of table.

THE GOVERNORS: POWERS — Continued

State or other jurisdiction	Budget making power		Governor has item veto power on all bills	Item veto power				Authorization for reorganization through executive order (a)
	Full responsibility	Shares responsibility		Governor has item veto power on appropriations only	Governor has no item veto power	Item veto—2/3 legislators present or 3/5 elected to override	Item veto—majority legislators elected to override	
South Dakota............	...	★	...	★	...	★	...	★
Tennessee	...	★	...	★	...	...	★	★
Texas	...	...	...	★	...	★	...	...
Utah	★	...	...	...	...	★	...	★
Vermont	★	...	...	...	★	...	...	★
Virginia..................	★	...	...	★	...	★	...	★
Washington.............	★	...	★(h)	★	...	★	...	...
West Virginia...........	★	...	...	★	...	★	...	...
Wisconsin................	★(b)	...	...	★(i)	...	★	...	...
Wyoming.................	...	★	★	...	...	★	...	...
American Samoa.......	...	★	...	...	...	...	...	★
Guam	★	...	...	...	...	...	...	★
No. Mariana Islands	...	★	...	★	...	★	...	...
Puerto Rico..............	★(b)	...	...	★	...	★	...	(n)
U.S. Virgin Islands......	★	...	...	★	...	...	...	★

Source: The Council of State Governments' survey of governor's offices, January 2006.

Key:

★ — Yes; provision for.

. . . — No; not applicable.

(a) For additional information on executive orders, see Table 4.5.

(b) Full responsibility to propose; legislature adopts or revises and governor signs or vetoes.

(c) Includes only executive branch officials who are popularly elected either on a constitutional or statutory basis (elected members of state boards of education, public utilities commissions, university regents, or other state boards or commissions are also included); the number of agencies involving theses officials is also listed.

(d) Governor may only veto a specific appropriation within a general appropriation bill or an entire bill. Two-thirds of both houses can override.

(e) Statutory.

(f) Limited. Sole authority to grant clemency after recommendation of Iowa Board of Parole.

(g) Authorization for reorganization provided for in state constitution.

(h) Governor has veto power of selections for nonappropriations and item veto in appropriations.

(i) In Wisconsin, governor has "partial" veto over appropriation bills. The partial veto is broader than item veto.

(j) Amendatory veto while legislature is in session.

(k) Two-thirds of elected legislators of each house to override.

(l) Only for agencies and offices within the Governor's Office.

(m) Governor may amend one or more provisions of any bill, but legislature may override by a majority vote.

(n) There is a scope of administrative reorganization that can be made by executive order which does not include the authority to suppress or merge existing agencies.

Table 4.5
GUBERNATORIAL EXECUTIVE ORDERS: AUTHORIZATION, PROVISIONS, PROCEDURES

State or other jurisdiction	Authorization for executive orders	Civil defense disasters, public emergencies	Energy emergencies and conservation	Other emergencies	Executive branch reorganization plans and agency creation	Create advisory, coordinating, study or investigative committees/commissions	Respond to federal programs and requirements	State personnel administration	Other administration	Filing and publication procedures	Subject to administrative procedure act	Subject to legislative review
Alabama	S,I (b)	★	★	★	★	★	★	★	★	(pp)	…	…
Alaska	C	★(a)	…	★	★	★	…	…	…	★	…	★
Arizona	I	★(a)	★(a)	★(a)	…	★	…	…	…	★(c)	…	…
Arkansas	C	★	★	★	★	★	★	★	★	…	…	★
California	I	★	★	★	…	★	★	…	★	…	★	…
Colorado	S,I	★	★	★(f)	★	★	★	★	…	…	…	…
Connecticut	S	★	★	★	…	★	★	…	★(gg)	…	…	…
Delaware	C	★	★	★	★	★	★	★	…	★(c)	…	…
Florida	C,S	★(mm)	★	★(h)	★	★	★	★(nm)	★(i)(j)(ll)	★(c)	★	★
Georgia	S,I (qq)	★	★	★	★	★	★	★	★	★	…	…
Hawaii	S	★	I	I	★	I	I	…	★	(rr)	…	…
Idaho	S	★	I	I	★	I	I	…	★	★	…	★
Illinois	C,S	★	★	★	★	★	★	★	…	…	★	★
Indiana	C,S, Case Law	★	I	I	★(limited)	I	I	…	…	…	…	…
Iowa	(ll)	★	★	★	…	★	★	★	★	★(l)	★	★
Kansas	C,S	★	★	★(m)	★	★	★	★	★(n)(o)(p)	★(c)	★	(ee)
Kentucky	C,S	★	★	★	★	★	★	★	★	★(l)	…	★(w)
Louisiana	C,S (g)	★	★	★	★	★	★	★	★	★	★	★(v)
Maine	(u)	★	…	…	…	…	…	…	…	…	…	…
Maryland	C,S	★	★	★	(s)	★	★	★	★(v)	★	★	★(w)
Massachusetts	C,S	★	★	★	★	★	★	★	★	★	★	★
Michigan	C	★	★(x)	★	★	★	★	★	★(y)	★(c)(l)	★	★(w)
Minnesota	S	★	★(x)	I	★	★	I	★	★(y)	★	★	★
Mississippi	C	★	I	I	…	I	I	…	★	★(l)	★	★
Missouri	C,S, Common Law	★	I	I	S,C	★	★	★	I	★(w)	★	★
Montana	S	★	★	★	★	★	★	★	I	★(c)	★	…
Nebraska	C,S	★	★	★	★	★	★	★	★(o)	★	★	…
Nevada	S,I	★	S	I	(dd)	I	…	…	★(aa)	★	…	★(w)(bb)
New Hampshire	S	★	★(a)	★(cc)	★	★	★	S	I	★	…	…
New Jersey	C,S,I	★	S	S	S,C	I	S	S	I	…	…	…
New Mexico	C	★	★	★	…	★	★	★	★(o)	★(c)	★	…
New York	C,S	★	★	★	★	★	★	★	(y)	★	★	★(w)
North Carolina	S,I	S	S	S	S,C	I	S	S	S,C	S	★	★
North Dakota	S,I	★	★	★	★	★	★	…	★(aa)	…	★	★
Ohio	S,I (z)	★	★	★	★	★	★	…	(j)(p)(q)(r)(y)(aa)	★	…	★(w)(bb)

See footnotes at end of table.

GUBERNATORIAL EXECUTIVE ORDERS: AUTHORIZATION, PROVISIONS, PROCEDURES—Continued

State or other jurisdiction	Authorization for executive orders	Provisions								Procedures		
		Civil defense, disasters, public emergencies	Energy emergencies and conservation	Other emergencies	Executive branch reorganization plans and agency creation	Create advisory, coordinating, study or investigative committees/commissions	Respond to federal programs and requirements	State personnel administration	Other administration	Filing and publication procedures	Subject to administrative procedure act	Subject to legislative review
Oklahoma	C	★	★		★	★	★	★	★	★(c)		
Oregon	C,S	★	★		★					★(c)		
Pennsylvania	C,S	★		★(l)(t)(v)(ff)				★(k)	★(ff)	★(c)(l)		
Rhode Island	S (a)	★	★(a)		★(a)	★	★		★			
South Carolina	S	★	★	★		★	★	★	★	★		★
South Dakota	C	★	★	★	★	★	★	★				
Tennessee	S	★	★	★	★	★	★	★	★	★(c)		
Texas	I	★	★	★	★	★	★	★				
Utah	S	★	★			★	★	★	★			
Vermont	S,I	★	★	★	★(ii)	★	★	★				★(jj)
Virginia	S,I	★	★	★(g)	★(kk)	★	★	★		★(c)		
Washington	S	★	★					★				
West Virginia	C,S	★	★	★		★	★	★	★			
Wisconsin	C,S	★					★	★	★(o)(aa)(dd)	★(c)		
Wyoming	(e)		★	★	★	★	★	★		★		
American Samoa	C,S	★	★	★	★	★	★	★	★	★(oo)	★(oo)	
Guam	C	★	I		(hh)	S,I	S	★	★	S	I	
No. Mariana Islands	C	★	★	★	C				★			
Puerto Rico	C	★	★	★	★	★	★	★	★	★(d)		
U.S. Virgin Islands	C	★	★	★	★	★	★	★	★	★		

See footnotes at end of table.

GUBERNATORIAL EXECUTIVE ORDERS: AUTHORIZATION, PROVISIONS, PROCEDURES — Continued

Sources: The Council of State Governments' survey, December 2004.

Key:

C — Constitutional
S — Statutory
I — Implied
★ — Formal provision.
. . . — No formal provision.

(a) Broad interpretation of gubernatorial authority.
(b) Authorization for executive orders granted by constitution, statute, case law, common law, and implied.
(c) Executive orders must be filed with secretary of state or other designated officer. In Idaho, must also be published in state general circulation newspaper.
(d) Governor signs and then sends to the Secretary of State to be signed. It is then posted, executive number is registered and then published.
(e) No specific authorization granted, general authority only.
(f) To regulate distribution of necessities during shortages.
(g) Broad grant of authority.
(h) Local financial emergency, shore erosion, polluted discharge and energy shortage.
(i) To reassign state attorneys and public defenders.
(j) To suspend certain officials and/or other civil actions.
(k) To transfer allocated funds.
(l) Filing.
(m) To give immediate effect to state regulation in emergencies.
(n) To control administration of state contracts and procedures.
(o) To impound or freeze certain state matching funds.
(p) To reduce state expenditures in revenue shortfall.
(q) To designate game and wildlife areas or other public areas.
(r) Appointive powers.
(s) Executive Orders generally may issue with respect to both emergent and non-emergent matters falling within the Executive Branch.
(t) For fire emergencies.

(u) Authority implied statutorily and by course of practice.
(v) To control procedures for dealing with public.
(w) Reorganization plans and agency creation.
(x) If an energy emergency is declared by the state's Executive Council or legislature.
(y) To assign duties to lieutenant governor, issue writ of special election.
(z) Executive authority implied except for emergencies which are established by statute.
(aa) To administer and govern the armed forces of the state.
(bb) Reorganization plans and agency creation and for meeting federal program requirements.
(cc) To declare air pollution emergencies.
(dd) Relating to local governments.
(ee) Only for EROs.
(ff) To transfer funds in an emergency.
(gg) Matters relating to the enforcement and administration of Connecticut law.
(hh) Can reorganize, but not create.
(ii) Subject to legislative approval.
(jj) Only if reorganization order filed with the legislature.
(kk) To shift agencies between secretarial offices; all other reorganizations require legislative approval.
(ll) By executive order, governor may also suspend collection of fines and forfeitures, grant reprieves not exceeding 60 days and with approval of three cabinet members, grant full or conditional pardons, restore civil rights, commute punishment and remit fines and forfeiture for offenses.
(mm) Governor may also delineate an interjurisdictional area to prepare, plan, mitigate or respond to emergency.
(nn) Governor may also declare an office vacant.
(oo) If executive order fits definition of rule.
(pp) The Secretary of State also signs. Notices are sent to both houses of the legislature and a number of other state officials.
(qq) Governor customarily exercises powers via executive order; authorization implied via selected statutes.
(rr) Some implied.
(ss) Subject to judicial review.

Table 4.6
STATE CABINET SYSTEMS

State or other jurisdiction	Authorization for cabinet system				Criteria for membership			Number of members in cabinet (including governor)	Frequency of cabinet meetings	Open cabinet meetings
	State statute	State constitution	Governor created	Tradition in state	Appointed to specific office (a)	Elected to specified office (a)	Gubernatorial appointment regardless of office			
Alabama	★	...	...	...	...	...	★	29	Monthly	★
Alaska	...	...	★	...	★	...	...	18	Gov.'s discretion	★(b)
Arizona	...	...	★	...	★	...	★	38	Monthly	...
Arkansas	...	...	...	★	★	...	...	46	Monthly	...
California	★	...	★	...	★	...	★	11	Every two weeks	...
Colorado	...	★	...	...	★	...	...	21	Gov.'s discretion	★
Connecticut	...	★	...	...	★	...	...	27	Gov.'s discretion	...
Delaware	★	...	...	...	★	...	★	19	Gov.'s discretion	...
Florida	...	★	...	...	...	★	...	4	Every two weeks	★
Georgia	......................................(d)..									
Hawaii	★	★	...	...	★	...	★	25	Monthly	...
Idaho	...............(d)...............							22	Gov.'s discretion	...
Illinois	★	...	...	...	...	...	★	18	N.A.	...
Indiana	...	...	★	...	...	...	★	16	Bi-monthly	...
Iowa	★	...	...	...	★	...	...	32	Quarterly	...
Kansas	★	...	...	...	...	...	★	14	Bi-weekly	...
Kentucky	★	...	★	...	★	...	★	10	Weekly	...
Louisiana	★	...	★	★	★	...	...	14	Monthly	...
Maine	...	...	...	(g)	...	...	★	21	Weekly	...
Maryland	★	...	...	...	★	...	...	28	Every other week	...
Massachusetts	★	...	...	...	★	...	...	10	Bi-weekly	...
Michigan	...	...	★	★	...	...	★	24	Monthly	...
Minnesota	...	...	★	...	★	...	...	25	Regularly	...
Mississippi	......................................(d)..									
Missouri	...	★	...	★	★	...	...	17	Gov.'s discretion	...
Montana	★	...	★	...	★	...	...	17	Gov.'s discretion	★
Nebraska	...	...	★	★	★	...	★	29	Monthly	...
Nevada	...............(d)...............							23	At call of the governor	...
New Hampshire	......................................(d)..									
New Jersey	★	★	...	...	★	...	...	19	Gov.'s discretion	...
New Mexico	★	...	...	★	★	...	...	17	Weekly	...
New York	...	...	...	★	...	...	★	75	Gov.'s discretion	...
North Carolina (e)	★	★	★	...	...	...	★	10	Monthly	...
North Dakota	...	...	★	...	...	...	★	18	Monthly	★
Ohio	★	...	...	...	★	...	...	24	Gov.'s discretion	★
Oklahoma	★	...	...	...	...	...	★	10–15	Monthly	...
Oregon	......................................(d)..									
Pennsylvania	★	★	★	...	★(c)	...	★	19	Gov.'s discretion	★
Rhode Island	...............(d)...............							14	Gov.'s discretion	Gov.'s discretion
South Carolina	★	...	...	...	★(c)	...	...	15	Monthly	★
South Dakota	★	★	...	...	★	...	...	19	Monthly	★
Tennessee	★	...	...	...	★	...	...	28	Monthly	...
Texas	......................................(d)..									
Utah	★	...	★	(f)	★	...	...	31	Monthly	...
Vermont	★	...	...	...	★	...	...	7	Gov.'s discretion	...
Virginia	★	...	...	...	★	...	...	13	Weekly	...
Washington	...	...	★	...	★	...	...	28	Bi-weekly, weekly during legislative session	...
West Virginia	...	...	★	★	★	...	...	10	Weekly	...
Wisconsin	★	...	...	...	★	...	...	16	Gov.'s discretion	★
Wyoming	★	...	...	...	...	...	★	20	Monthly	...
American Samoa	★	★	...	...	★	...	★	16	Gov.'s discretion	★
Guam	...	...	★	...	★	...	...	55	Bi-monthly	...
No. Mariana Islands	...	★	...	...	★	...	...	16	Gov.'s discretion	★
Puerto Rico	★	★	...	...	★	...	★	18	Every 2 months	...
U.S. Virgin Islands	...	★	...	...	★	...	...	21	Monthly	★

See footnotes at end of table.

STATE CABINET SYSTEMS — Continued

Source: The Council of State Governments' survey, January 2006.
Key:
★ — Yes
. . . — No
N.A. — Not available
(a) Individual is a member by virtue of election or appointment to a cabinet-level position.
(b) Except when in executive session.
(c) With the consent of the senate.
(d) No formal cabinet system. In Idaho, however, sub-cabinets have been formed, by executive order; the chairs report to the governor.

(e) Constitution provides for a Council of State made up of elective state administrative officials, which makes policy decisions for the state while the cabinet acts more in an advisory capacity.
(f) In Utah, department heads serve as cabinet; meet at discretion of governor, but when first appointed, department heads also require advice and consent of Senate.
(g) Cabinet consists of agencies, created by legislation; directors of agencies appointed by the governor.
(h) Authority implied statutorily and by course of practice. Some of those department heads along with other officials compose the Governor's Cabinet.

Table 4.7
THE GOVERNORS: PROVISIONS AND PROCEDURES FOR TRANSITION

State or other jurisdiction	Legislation pertaining to gubernatorial transition	Appropriation available to gov-elect ($)	Provision for:					
			Gov-elect's participation in state budget for coming fiscal year	Gov-elect to hire staff to assist during transition	State personnel to be made available to assist gov-elect	Office space in buildings to be made available to gov-elect	Acquainting gov-elect staff with office procedures and routing office functions	Transfer of information (files,) (records, etc.)
Alabama	...	...	★	●	●	●	●	●
Alaska	●	★(l)	...	●	●	●	●	★
Arizona	...	...	★	...	●	●	●	●
Arkansas	●	30,000	...	●	...	●	●	●
California	★	450,000	★	★	★	★	●	●
Colorado	★	10,000	...	★	★	★	★	★
Connecticut	★	0	...	★	...	★	●	★
Delaware	★	30,000	●	★	●	●	●	●
Florida	...	300,000	★	★	●	●	●	●
Georgia	★	50,000	★	★	★	★	★	★
Hawaii	★	50,000	★	★	★	★	●	●
Idaho	★	15,000	★	★	★	★	★	★
Illinois	...	...	...	★	...	★	★	★
Indiana	★	40,000	...	...	...	★	★	★
Iowa	★(d)	10,000	★	★	●(i)	●	●	★
Kansas	★	150,000 (g)	★	★	★	★	★	★
Kentucky	★	200,000	★	★	★	★	★	★
Louisiana	★	65,000	★	★	★(f)	★(h)	...	●(c)
Maine	●	5,000	...	●	●	★	●	●
Maryland	★	●	...	★	★	★	★	★
Massachusetts	●	●	●	...	●	●	●	★
Michigan	...	1,200,000	...	★	...	...	★	★
Minnesota	★	0	★	...	★	★	●	★
Mississippi	★	60,000	★	★	★	★	★	★
Missouri	★	100,000	★	★	●	★	●	●(i)
Montana	★	50,000	★	★	★	★	★	★
Nebraska	★	60,879	★	★	★	★	★	★
Nevada	★	Reasonable amount	★	●	●	●	●	★(d)
New Hampshire	★	75,000	★	★	★	★	★	...
New Jersey	★	Unspecified	★	★	★	★	●	★
New Mexico	★	(b)	★	★	●	★	●	●
New York	...	...	...	...	★	★	★	★
North Carolina	★	80,000 (j)	●(k)	★	★	★	●	●
North Dakota	●	10,000	(m)	(a)	●	...	●	★
Ohio	★	Unspecified (e)	●	★	●	...	●	★
Oklahoma	...	30,000	★	...	...	...	...	...
Oregon	★	...	★	★	★	★	★	★
Pennsylvania	★	100,000	...	★	●	●	●	●
Rhode Island	...	●	●	●(a)	●	●	●	●
South Carolina	...	●	●	●	●	●	●	●
South Dakota	●	●	●	●	●	●	●	●
Tennessee	★	★	●	★	★	★	●	●
Texas	●	●	●	●	●	●	●	●
Utah	...	●(Varies)	●	●	●	●	●	●
Vermont	...	(p)	★	●	●	●	●	...
Virginia	...	●	...	●	★(i)	★(i)	●	★
Washington	★	★	●	★	●	★	●	★
West Virginia	...	●	...	●	...	●	●	●
Wisconsin	★	Unspecified	★	★	★	★	★	★
Wyoming	...	●	...	●	●	●	●	●
American Samoa	...	Unspecified	★(n)	★	●	●	★	●
Guam	★	(o)	...	...	★	★	★	...
No. Mariana Islands	★	Unspecified	...	★	★	★	★	★
Puerto Rico	...	600,000 (j)	...	★	★	★	★	★
U.S. Virgin Islands	★	100,000	...	★	★	★	★	★

See footnotes at end of table.

THE GOVERNORS: PROVISIONS AND PROCEDURES FOR TRANSITION — Continued

Source: The Council of State Governments' survey, January 2006.

Key:

. . . — No provisions or procedures.

★ — Formal provisions or procedures.

● — No formal provisions, occurs informally.

N.A. — Not applicable.

(a) Governor usually hires several incoming key staff during transition.

(b) Legislature required to make appropriation; no dollar amount stated in legislation.

(c) In Louisiana–statute directs the records and associated historical records of any governor to be transferred to the custody of the state archivist.

(d) Pertains only to funds.

(e) Determined in budget.

(f) No unclassified employees are made available; however, a list of civil service employees is made available within 60 days.

(g) Transition funds are used by both the incoming and outgoing administrations.

(h) The $65,000 may be used to rent space.

(i) Activity is traditional and routine, although there is no specific statutory provision.

(j) Inaugural expenses are not paid from this amount.

(k) New governor can submit supplemental budget.

(l) Varies.

(m) Responsible for submitting budget for coming biennium.

(n) Can submit reprogramming or supplemental appropriation measure for current fiscal year.

(o) Appropriations given upon the request of governor-elect.

(p) Governor-elect entitled to 70 percent of Governor's salary.

Table 4.8
IMPEACHMENT PROVISIONS IN THE STATES

State or other jurisdiction	Governor and other state executive and judicial officers subject to impeachment	Legislative body which holds power of impeachment	Vote required for impeachment	Legislative body which conducts impeachment trial	Chief justice presides at impeachment trial (a)	Vote required for conviction	Official who serves as acting governor if governor impeached (b)	Legislature may call special session for impeachment
Alabama	★	H	maj. mbrs.	S	...	Majority of elected mbrs.	LG	★
Alaska	★	S	2/3 mbrs.	H	(c)	2/3 mbrs.	LG	★
Arizona	★(d)	H	maj. mbrs.	S	★(e)	2/3 mbrs.	SS	★
Arkansas	★	H	maj. mbrs.	S	★	2/3 mbrs.	LG	...
California	★	H	...	S	...	2/3 mbrs.	LG	...
Colorado	★	H	maj. mbrs.	S	★	2/3 mbrs.	LG	...
Connecticut	★	H	...	S	★	2/3 mbrs.	LG	...
Delaware	★	H	2/3 mbrs.	S	★(f)	2/3 mbrs.	LG	...
Florida	★	H	2/3 mbrs.	S	★(e)	2/3 mbrs.	LG	★
Georgia	★	H	...	S	★(e)	2/3 mbrs.	LG	★(g)
Hawaii	★	H	maj. mbrs.	S	...	2/3 mbrs.	LG	...
Idaho	★	H	2/3 mbrs.	S	★	2/3 mbrs.	LG	...
Illinois	★	H	2/3 mbrs.	S	★	2/3 mbrs.	LG	★
Indiana	★(u)	H	2/3 mbrs.	S	...	2/3 mbrs.	LG	...
Iowa	★	H	2/3 mbrs.	S	...	2/3 mbrs.	LG	...
Kansas	★	H	... (m)	S	...	2/3 mbrs.	LG	...
Kentucky	★	H	...	S	★	2/3 mbrs. present	LG	...
Louisiana	★	H	2/3 mbrs. elected	S	...	2/3 mbrs. elected	LG	★(h)
Maine	★	H	maj. mbrs.	S	★	2/3 mbrs. present	PS	...
Maryland	★	H	maj. mbrs.	S	...	2/3 mbrs.	LG	...
Massachusetts	★	H	maj. mbrs.	S	...	...	LG	★
Michigan	★	H	maj. mbrs.	S (i)	★	2/3 mbrs.	LG	...
Minnesota	★	H	maj. mbrs.	S	...	2/3 mbrs. present	LG	...
Mississippi	★	H	2/3 mbrs. present	S	★	2/3 mbrs. present	LG	...
Missouri	★	H	...	S (j)	(j)	(j)	LG	...
Montana	★	H	2/3 mbrs.	S	(l)	2/3 mbrs.	LG	★
Nebraska	★(d)	S (k)	maj. mbrs.	(l)	(l)	2/3 mbrs. of sup. court	LG	...
Nevada	★(d)	H	maj. mbrs.	S	★	2/3 mbrs.	LG	...
New Hampshire	★	H	...	S	★	...	PS	...
New Jersey	★	H	maj. mbrs.	S	★	2/3 mbrs.	PS	★
New Mexico	★	H	maj. mbrs.	S	★	2/3 mbrs.	LG	★
New York	★	H	maj. mbrs.	S	★	2/3 mbrs. present	LG	★
North Carolina	★(d)	H	...	S	★(e)	2/3 mbrs. present	LG	★
North Dakota	★(d)	H	maj. mbrs.	S	★	2/3 mbrs.	LG	...
Ohio	★(d)	H	maj. mbrs.	S	...	2/3 mbrs. present	LG	...
Oklahoma	★(n)	H	maj. mbrs.	S	★	2/3 mbrs. present	SS	★
Oregon	...	...	...	(o)	...	...	...	...
Pennsylvania	★	H	1/4 mbrs. (p)	S	...	2/3 mbrs. present	LG	★
Rhode Island	★	H	...	S	★	2/3 mbrs.	LG	...
South Carolina	★	H	2/3 mbrs.	S	★	2/3 mbrs.	LG	...

See footnotes at end of table.

IMPEACHMENT PROVISIONS IN THE STATES — Continued

State or other jurisdiction	Governor and other state executive and judicial officers subject to impeachment	Legislative body which holds power of impeachment	Vote required for impeachment	Legislative body which conducts impeachment trial	Chief justice presides at impeachment trial (a)	Vote required for conviction	Official who serves as acting governor if governor impeached (b)	Legislature may call special session for impeachment
South Dakota	★(d)	H	maj. mbrs.	S	★	2/3 mbrs.	LG	★
Tennessee	★	H	maj. mbrs.	S	★	2/3 mbrs. (q)	PS	★
Texas	★	H	maj. mbrs.	S	...	2/3 mbrs. present	LG	...
Utah	★(d)	H	2/3 mbrs.	S	★	2/3 mbrs.	LG	★
Vermont	★	H	2/3 mbrs.	S	...	2/3 mbrs. present	LG	...
Virginia	★	H	...	S	...	2/3 mbrs. present	LG	★
Washington	★(d)	H	maj. mbrs.	S	★	2/3 mbrs.	LG	★
West Virginia	★	H	...	S	★	2/3 mbrs.	PS	★
Wisconsin	★	H	maj. mbrs.	S	...	2/3 mbrs.	LG	...
Wyoming	★	H	2/3 mbrs.	S	★	2/3 mbrs.	SS	...
Dist. of Columbia	.... (r)							
American Samoa	(s)	H	2/3 mbrs.	S	★	2/3 mbrs.	...	...
Guam	.... (r)							
No. Mariana Islands	★	H	2/3 mbrs.	S	...	2/3 mbrs.	LG	...
Puerto Rico	(t)	H	2/3 mbrs.	S	★	3/4 mbrs.	SS	★
U.S. Virgin Islands	.... (r)							

Source: The Council of State Governments' survey, January 2006.

Key:
★ — Yes; provision for.
. . . — Not specified, or no provision for.
H — House or Assembly (lower chamber)
S — Senate
LG — Lieutenant Governor
PS — President or Speaker of the Senate
SS — Secretary of State

(a) Presiding justice of state court of last resort. In many states, provision indicates that chief justice presides only on occasion of impeachment of governor.

(b) For provisions on official next in line of succession if governor is convicted and removed from office, refer to Chapter 4, "The Governors."

(c) An appointed Supreme Court justice presides.

(d) With exception of certain judicial officers. In Arizona and Washington—justices of courts not of record. In Nevada and Utah—justices of the peace. In North Dakota and South Dakota—county judges, justices of the peace, and police magistrates. In Oklahoma—all judicial officers not serving on the Supreme Court.

(e) Should the Chief Justice be on trial, or otherwise disqualified, the Senate shall elect a judge of the Supreme Court to preside.

(f) Except in a trial of the chief justice, in which case the governor shall preside.

(g) Special sessions of the General Assembly shall be limited to a period of 40 days unless extended by 3/5 vote of each house and approved by the Governor or unless at the expiration of such period an impeachment trial of some officer of state government is pending, in which event the House shall adjourn and the Senate shall remain in session until such trial is completed.

(h) In Louisiana—not specified; both the governor and the legislature appear to have authority to call a special session for impeachment.

(i) House elects three members to prosecute impeachment.

(j) All impeachments are tried before the state Supreme Court, except that the governor or a member of the Supreme Court is tried by a special commission of seven eminent jurists to be elected by the Senate. A vote of 5/7 of the court of special commission is necessary to convict.

(k) Unicameral legislature; members use the title "senator."

(l) Court of impeachment is composed of chief justice and supreme court. A vote of 2/3 of the court is necessary to convict.

(m) No statute, simple majority is the assumption.

(n) Includes justices of Supreme Court. Other judicial officers not subject to impeachment.

(o) No provision for impeachment. Public officers may be tried for incompetence, corruption, malfeasance, or delinquency in office in same manner as criminal offenses.

(p) Vote of 2/3 members required for an impeachment of the governor.

(q) Vote of 2/3 of members sworn to try the officer impeached.

(r) Removal of elected officials by recall procedure only.

(s) Governor, lieutenant governor.

(t) Governor and Supreme Court justices.

(u) Judges not included.

Table 4.9
CONSTITUTIONAL AND STATUTORY PROVISIONS FOR
NUMBER OF CONSECUTIVE TERMS OF ELECTED STATE OFFICIALS
(All terms last four years unless otherwise noted)

State or other jurisdiction	Governor	Lt. Governor	Secretary of state	Attorney general	Treasurer	Auditor	Comptroller	Education	Agriculture	Labor	Insurance
Alabama	2	2	(b)	2	2	...	...	...	2	...	...
Alaska	2	2	(b)	...	(w)	...	...	...	...	...	...
Arizona	2	(e)	2	2	2	...	...	2	...	...	...
Arkansas	2	2	2	2	2	...	...	...	...	...	...
California	2	2	2	2	2	...	2	2	...	...	...
Colorado	2	2	2	2	2	...	...	...	...	...	...
Connecticut	N	N	N	N	N	...	N	...	...	...	...
Delaware	2 (f)	2	...	N	N	N	...	...	...	...	N
Florida	2	2	...	2	2 (g)	...	2	N	N	...	(g)
Georgia	2 (a)	N	N	N	...	...	...	N	N	N	N
Hawaii	2	2	(b)	...	...	...	...	...	...	...	...
Idaho	N	N	N	N	N	...	2	N	...	...	...
Illinois	N	N	N	N	N	...	N	...	...	...	...
Indiana	(h)	2	2	...	(h)	...	2 (i)	...	...	...	...
Iowa	N	N	N	N	N	N	...	...	...	...	...
Kansas	2	N	N	N	...	...	...	...	...	...	...
Kentucky	2	2	2	2	2	2	...	...	2	2	...
Louisiana	2 (a)	N	N	N	N	...	...	N	N	...	N
Maine	2 (a)	(k)	...	(j)	...	...	...	...	...	...	...
Maryland	2 (a)	2	...	N	...	...	N	...	...	...	...
Massachusetts	N	N	N	2	N	N	...	...	...	...	...
Michigan	2	2	2	2	...	...	...	...	...	...	...
Minnesota	N	N	N	N	(l)	N	...	...	...	...	(m)
Mississippi	2 (f)	2 (a)	N	N	N	N	...	...	...	...	...
Missouri	2 (f)	N	N	N	2 (f)	N	...	...	...	...	...
Montana	2 (n)	2 (n)	2 (n)	2 (n)	...	N	...	2 (n)	...	...	...
Nebraska	2 (a)	2 (a)	N	N	2 (a)	N	...	...	...	...	...
Nevada	2	2	2	2	2	...	2	...	...	...	...
New Hampshire	(o)	(k)	...	...	...	...	...	...	...	...	...
New Jersey	2 (a)	(k)	...	...	...	...	...	...	...	...	...
New Mexico	2 (a)	2 (a)	2 (a)	2 (a)	2 (a)	2 (a)	...	...	...	...	...
New York	N	N	...	N	...	N (c)	N	...	...	...	...
North Carolina	2 (a)	2	N	N	N	N	...	N	N	N	N
North Dakota	N	N	N (q)	N (q)	N	N	...	N	N (q)(r)	N (q)	N
Ohio	2 (a)	2	2	2	2	2	...	...	...	...	...
Oklahoma	2 (a)	N	...	N	N	N	...	2 (a)	...	2 (a)	N
Oregon	(h)	(d)	(h)	N	(h)	...	...	...	...	...	...
Pennsylvania	2	2	...	2 (a)	2 (s)	2 (a)	...	...	...	...	...
Rhode Island	2	2 (a)	2 (a)	2 (a)	2 (a)	...	...	...	...	...	...
South Carolina	2 (a)	2	N	N	N	...	N	N	N	...	...
South Dakota	2 (a)	2 (a)	2 (a)	2 (a)	2 (a)	...	2	...	...	...	...
Tennessee	2 (a)	(k)	...	(y)	...	...	...	...	...	...	...
Texas	N	N	...	N	(c)	...	N	...	...	...	...
Utah	N	N	(b)	N	N	N	...	...	...	...	...
Vermont	(o)	(o)	(o)	(o)	(o)	(o)	...	...	...	...	...
Virginia	(t)	(u)	...	(u)	...	...	...	...	...	...	...
Washington	N	N	N	N	N	N	...	N	...	...	...
West Virginia	2	N (k)	N	N	N	...	N	...	N	...	...
Wisconsin	N	N	N	N	N	...	...	N	...	...	...
Wyoming	2 (n)	(d)	N	...	2	...	2	N	...	...	...
Dist. of Columbia	N (v)	2	...	...	...	...	...	...	...	...	...
American Samoa	2	2	(b)	...	...	...	(p)	...	...	...	...
Guam	2 (a)	2	(b)	...	...	2	(x)	...	...	...	...
No. Mariana Islands	(h)	N	...	...	...	...	(p)	...	...	...	(m)
Puerto Rico	N	(e)	...	...	...	1	...	...	...	...	...
U.S. Virgin Islands	2 (a)	2	(c)	...	(e)	...	(e)	...	...	...	(b)

See footnotes at end of table.

CONSTITUTIONAL AND STATUTORY PROVISIONS FOR
NUMBER OF CONSECUTIVE TERMS OF ELECTED STATE OFFICIALS — Continued
(All terms last four years unless otherwise noted)

Sources: The Council of State Governments' survey January 2006 and state constitutions and statutes, December 2004.

Note: All terms last four years unless otherwise noted. Footnotes specify if a position's functions are performed by an appointed official under a different title.

Key:

N — No provision specifying number of terms allowed.

. . . — Position is appointed or elected by governmental entity (not chosen by the electorate).

(a) After two consecutive terms, must wait four years and/or one full term before being eligible again.

(b) Lieutenant Governor performs this function.

(c) Comptroller performs this function.

(d) Secretary of State is next in line to the governorship.

(e) Finance Administrator performs function.

(f) Absolute two-term limitation, but not necessarily consecutive.

(g) Chief Financial Officer performs this function as of January 2003.

(h) Eligible for eight out of any period of twelve years.

(i) State auditor performs this function.

(j) Serves two-year term and is eligible to serve four terms.

(k) President or Speaker of the Senate is next in line of succession to the governorship. In Tennessee, Speaker of the Senate has the statutory title "Lieutenant Governor."

(l) Office of the State Treasurer was abolished on the first Monday in January 2003.

(m) Commerce administrator performs this function.

(n) Eligible for eight out of sixteen years.

(o) Serves two-year term, no provision specifying the number of terms allowed.

(p) State treasurer performs this function.

(q) The terms of the office of the elected officials are four years, except that in 2004 the agricultural commissioner, attorney general, secretary of state and the tax commissioner are elected to a term of two years.

(r) Constitution provides for a secretary of agriculture and labor. However, the legislature was given constitutional authority to provide for (and has provided for) a department of labor distinct from agriculture, and a commissioner of labor distinct from the commissioner of agriculture.

(s) Treasurer must wait four years before being eligible for the office of auditor general.

(t) Cannot serve consecutive terms, but after four-year respite can seek re-election.

(u) Provision specifying individual may hold office for an unlimited number of terms.

(v) Mayor.

(w) Deputy Commissioner of Department of Revenue performs function.

(x) General services administrator performs function.

(y) Term is for eight years and official is appointed by judges of the State Supreme Court.

Table 4.10
SELECTED STATE ADMINISTRATIVE OFFICIALS: METHODS OF SELECTION

State or other jurisdiction	Governor	Lieutenant governor	Secretary of state	Attorney general	Treasurer	Adjutant general	Administration	Agriculture	Auditor	Banking
Alabama	CE	CE	CE	CE	CE	GS	G	SE	CE	GS
Alaska	CE	CE	(a-1)	GB	AG	GB	GB	AG	L	AG
Arizona	CE	(a-2)	CE	CE	CE	GS	GS	GS	L	GS
Arkansas	CE	CE	CE	CE	CE	G	G	G	CE	GS
California	CE	CE	CE	CE	CE	GS	...	G	GB	GS
Colorado	CE	CE	CE	CE	CE	GS	GS	GS	L	CS
Connecticut	CE	CE	CE	CE	CE	GE	GE	GE	L	GE
Delaware	CE	CE	GS	CE	CE	GS	(ee)	GS	CE	GS
Florida	CE	CE	GS	CE	CE (dd)	G	GS	CE	L	CE (dd)
Georgia	CE	CE	CE	CE	G	G	G	CE	(i)	G
Hawaii	CE	CE	(a-1)	GS	GS	GS	(x)	GS	CL	AG
Idaho	CE	CE	CE	CE	CE	GS	GS	GS	...	GS
Illinois	CE	CE	CE	CE	CE	GS	GS	GS	SL	B
Indiana	CE	CE	CE	SE	CE	G	G	LG	CE	G
Iowa	CE	CE	CE	CE	CE	GS	GS	CE	CE	GS
Kansas	CE	CE	CE	CE	SE	GS	GS	GS	LS	GS
Kentucky	CE	CE	CE	CE	CE	G	CG	CE	CE	G
Louisiana	CE	CE	CE	CE	CE	GS	GS	CE	L	GLS
Maine	CE	(o)	CL	CL	CL	G	G	G	N.A.	G
Maryland	CE	CE	GS	CE	CL	G	GS (a-16)	GS	LS	AG
Massachusetts	CE	CE	CE	CE	CE	G	G	CG	CE	G
Michigan	CE	CE	CE	CE	GS	GS	GS	B	CL	GS
Minnesota	CE	CE	CE	CE	(mm)	GS	GS	GS	CE	A
Mississippi	CE	CE	CE	CE	CE	GE	GS	SE	CE	GS
Missouri	CE	CE	CE	CE	CE	G	GS	GS	CE	AGS
Montana	CE	CE	CE	CE	GS (a-5)	GS	GS	G	CE	A
Nebraska	CE	CE	CE	CE	CE	GS	GS	GS	CE	GS
Nevada	CE	CE	CE	CE	CE	G	G	BA	...	A
New Hampshire	CE	(o)	CL	GC	CL	GC	GC	GC	N.A.	GC
New Jersey	CE	(o)	GS	GS	GS	GS	...	BG	(t)	GS
New Mexico	CE	CE	CE	CE	CE	G	GS (a-16)	B	CE	G
New York	CE	CE	GS	CE	A	G	...	GS	CE (a-9)	GS
North Carolina	CE	CE	SE	CE	CE	A	G	CE	CE	G
North Dakota	CE	CE	CE	CE	CE	G	...	CE	CE	GS
Ohio	SE	SE	CE	SE	SE	(d)	GS	GS	SE	GS (a-7)
Oklahoma	CE	CE	A	CE	CE	GS	GS	GS	CE	GS
Oregon	CE	(a-2)	CE	SE	CE	G	GS	GS	SS	...
Pennsylvania	CE	CE	GS	CE	CE	GS	G	GS	CE	GS
Rhode Island	SE	SE	CE	SE	SE	GB	GB	CS	LS	CS
South Carolina	CE	CE	CE	CE	CE	CE	B	CE	B	A
South Dakota	CE	CE	CE	CE	CE	GS	GS	GS	CE	(a-26)
Tennessee	CE	(o) (y)	CL	CT	CL	G	G	G	SL (a-9)	G
Texas	CE	CE	G	CE	CE (a-9)	G	A	SE	L	B
Utah	CE	CE	CE (a-1)	CE	CE	G	GS	GS	CE	GS
Vermont	CE	CE	CE	CE	CE	CL	G	G	CE	G
Virginia	CE	CE	GB	CE	GB	GB	GB	GB	SL	SL
Washington	CE	CE	CE	CE	CE	GS	GS	GS	CE	GS
West Virginia	CE	(o)	CE	CE	CE	GS	GS	CE	CE	GS
Wisconsin	CE	CE	CE	CE	CE	G	GS	GS	LS	A
Wyoming	CE	(a-2)	CE	CE	G	CE	G	GS	GS	CE	A
American Samoa	CE	CE	(a-1)	GB	GB	N.A.	GB	GB	N.A.	N.A.
Guam	CE	CE	...	CE	CS	GS	GS	GS	N.A.	GS
No. Mariana Islands	CE	CE	...	GS	CS	...	G	...	GB	C
U.S. Virgin Islands	SE	SE	SE (a-1)	GS	GS	GS	GS	GS	GS	LG

Sources: The Council of State Governments' survey of state personnel agencies, January 2005 and January 2006.

Note: The chief administrative officials responsible for each function were determined from information given by the states for the same function as listed in *State Administrative Officials Classified by Function*, 2005, published by The Council of State Governments.

Key:
N.A. — Not available.
... — No specific chief administrative official or agency in charge of function.
CE — Constitutional, elected by public.
CL — Constitutional, elected by legislature.
SE — Statutory, elected by public.
SL — Statutory, elected by legislature.
L — Selected by legislature or one of its organs.
CT — Constitutional, elected by state court of last resort.
CP — Competitve process.

Appointed by:
G — Governor
GS — Governor — Senate (in Nebraska, unicameral legislature)
GB — Governor — Both houses
GE — Governor — Either house
GC — Governor — Council
GD — Governor — Departmental board
GLS — Governor — Appropriate legislative committee & Senate
GOC — Governor & Council or cabinet
LG — Lieutenant Governor
LGS — Lieutenant Governor — Senate
AT — Attorney General
SS — Secretary of State
C — Cabinet Secretary
CG — Cabinet Secretary — Governor

SELECTED STATE ADMINISTRATIVE OFFICIALS: METHODS OF SELECTION — Continued

State or other jurisdiction	Budget	Civil rights	Commerce	Community affairs	Comptroller	Consumer affairs	Corrections	Economic development	Education	Election administration
Alabama	CS	...	G	G	CS	CS	G	G (a-8)	B	CS
Alaska	G	GB	GB	...	AG	...	GB	...	GD	AG
Arizona	L	AT	GS	GS (a-7)	A	AT	GS	GS (a-7)	CE	CE (a-2)
Arkansas	A	...	GS	GS	G	A	B	GS	BG	CE (a-2)
California	G (a-15)	...	...	GS	CE	G	GS	...	CE	N.A.
Colorado	G	CS	G	GS	C	CE	GS	G	AB	CS
Connecticut	CS	GE	GE	GE	CE	GE	GE	GE	BG	CS
Delaware	GS	CG	GS (a-2)	...	CG	AT	GS	GS	GS	GS
Florida	G	AB	...	A	CE (dd)	A	GS	(a-28)	GS	A
Georgia	G	G	BG	BG	CE	G	GD	N.A.	CE	A
Hawaii	GS	B	GS	...	GS	A	GS	GS	B	CL
Idaho	GS	B	GS	A	CE	CE (a-3)	B	A	CE	CE
Illinois	G	GS	GS	GS (a-7)	CE	CE (a-3)	GS	GS (a-7)	B	B
Indiana	G	G	LG	G	CE	AT	G	LG	CE	(k)
Iowa	GS	GS	...	GS	...	GS	GS	GS	GS	A
Kansas	G	GS	GS	A	C	AT	GS	(m)	B	(n)
Kentucky	G	B	G	G	CG	CE (a-3)	G	GC	B	B
Louisiana	A	A	GS	A	GS	AG	GS	GS	BG	GS
Maine	C	BA	G (a-11)	...	C	C	G	G	G	SS
Maryland	GS	G	GS	A	CE	A	AGS	GS	B	B
Massachusetts	CG	G	G	G	G	G	CG	G	B	SS
Michigan	GS	GS	GS	N.A.	CS	N.A.	GS	N.A.	B	(s)
Minnesota	(mm)	GS	GS	GS (a-11)	(mm)	A	GS	GS	GS	CE (a-2)
Mississippi	GS	...	SE	A	GS	A	GS	GS	BS	A (nn)
Missouri	AGS	AGS	GS (a-11)	(d)	A	CE (a-3)	GS	GS	BG	SS
Montana	G	CP	GS	CP	CP	CP	GS	G	CE	SS
Nebraska	A	B	GS (a-11)	A	A	CE (a-3)	GS	GS	B	A
Nevada	(a-5)	CS	G	...	CE	A	G	GD	B	(z)
New Hampshire	GC	CS	GC	G	AGC	AGC	GC	AGC	B	CL (a-2)
New Jersey	GS	A	GS	GS	GS (a-6)	A	GS	G	GS	A
New Mexico	G	G	GS (a-11)	G	...	G	GS	GS	B	G
New York	G	GS	GS	GS (a-2)	CE	GS	GS	GS	B	B
North Carolina	G (a-15)	A	G	A	G	(d)	G	A	CE	G
North Dakota	(r)	G	G	CE	(e)	AT	G	G	CE	SS
Ohio	GS	AG	GS	GS	N.A.	GS	GS	GS	GS	SE
Oklahoma	A	B	G	G	A	B	B	G	CE	L
Oregon	A	A	GS	G	A	GS	GS	GS	SE	A
Pennsylvania	G	B	GS	AG	G	AT	GS	GS	GS	C
Rhode Island	AG	B	G (a-11)	CS	CS	SE (a-3)	GB	G	B	F
South Carolina	A	B	GS	N.A.	CE	B	GS	GS (a-7)	CE	B
South Dakota	(a-15)	A	(a-26)	(a-11)	(a-23)	A	GS	(a-28)	GS	SS
Tennessee	A	G	G (a-11)	G (a-11)	SL	A	G	G	G	N.A.
Texas	G	B	G	G	CE	CE (a-3)	B	G (a-7)	B	(cc)
Utah	G	A	GS	GS	A	A	GS	A	B	A
Vermont	G (a-15)	A	G	G	G (a-15)	A	G	G	G	CE (a-2)
Virginia	GB	GB	GB	GB	GB	A	GB	B	GB	GB
Washington	GS	B	GS	G	CE (a-4)	AT	GS	GS	CE	A
West Virginia	CS	GS	GS	B	CE (a-31)	AT	GS	B (a-8)	B	CE (a-2)
Wisconsin	A	A	GS	A	A	A	GS	CS	CE	B
Wyoming	A	A	GS	G	A	A	GS	G	CE	A
American Samoa	GB	N.A.	GB	(a-7)	(a-4)	(a-3)	A	(a-7)	GB	G
Guam	GS	...	GS	...	CS	CS	GS	B	B	GS
No. Mariana Islands	G	A	GS	GS	C	GS	C	C	B	B
U.S. Virgin Islands	GS	GS	GS	GS	GS (a-15)	GS	GS	GS	GS	B

Appointed by:
A — Agency head
AB — Agency head
AG — Agency head
AGC — Agency head
AGS — Agency head
ALS — Agency head
ASH — Agency head
B — Board or commission
BG — Board
BGS — Board
BS — Board or commission
BA — Board or commission
CS — Civil Service
LS — Legislative Committee

Approved by:
Board
Governor
Governor & Council
Senate
Appropriate legislative committee
Senate president & House speaker
Governor
Governor & Senate
Senate
Agency head
Senate

(a) Chief administrative official or agency in charge of function:
(a-1) Lieutenant Governor

(a-2) Secretary of state
(a-3) Attorney general
(a-4) Treasurer
(a-5) Administration
(a-6) Budget
(a-7) Commerce
(a-8) Community affairs
(a-9) Comptroller
(a-10) Consumer affairs
(a-11) Economic development
(a-12) Education (chief state school officer)
(a-13) Energy
(a-14) Environmental protection
(a-15) Finance
(a-16) General services
(a-17) Highways
(a-18) Labor

SELECTED STATE ADMINISTRATIVE OFFICIALS: METHODS OF SELECTION—Continued

State or other jurisdiction	Emergency management	Employment services	Energy	Environmental protection	Finance	Fish & wildlife	General services	Health	Higher education	Highways
Alabama	G	CS	CS	B	G	CS	CS	B	B	G (a-29)
Alaska	AG	AG	B	GB	AG	GB	...	AG	B	GB
Arizona	G	A	...	GS	A	B	A	GS	B	A
Arkansas	GS	G	A	BG/BS	G	(d)	A	BG	BG	BS (a-29)
California	GS	GS	G	GS	G	G	GS	GS	B	GS (a-29)
Colorado	CS	GS	G	CS	CS	AB	GS	GS	GS	GS (a-29)
Connecticut	GE	A	A	GE	GE	CS (bb)	GE	GE	BG	GE (a-29)
Delaware	CG	CG	A	GS (a-19)	GS	CG	CG	CG	B	GS (a-29)
Florida	A	GS	A	GS	CE (dd)	GS	GS	GS	N.A.	GOC
Georgia	G	A	G	B	G	A	A	A	B	B (a-29)
Hawaii	A	CS	CS	CS	GS	CS	GS (a-9)	GS	B	CS
Idaho	A	GS	A	GS	GS	B	...	GS	B	B (a-29)
Illinois	GS	GS	GS (a-7)	GS	G (a-6)	GS (a-19)	GS (a-5)	GS	B	GS (a-29)
Indiana	G	G	LG	G	G (a-6)	A	G (a-5)	G	G	G (a-29)
Iowa	GS	GS	...	A	A	A	A	A	...	A
Kansas	CS	GS	B	C	...	CS	GS	C	B	GS (a-29)
Kentucky	AG	AG	AG	G	G	G	CG (a-5)	CG	B	CG
Louisiana	A	A	A	GS	GS	GS	GS	GS	B	GS (a-29)
Maine	C	N.A.	G	G	G (a-5)	G	C	G	B	G (a-29)
Maryland	AG	A	G	GS	GS	A	GS	GS	G	AG
Massachusetts	G	CG	CG	CG	G (a-5)	CG	G (a-5)	CG	B	G
Michigan	CS	GS	...	GS	GS (a-6)	(l)	N.A.	GS	CS	GS (a-29)
Minnesota	GS	A	A	GS	(mm)	A	GS (a-5)	GS (aa)	B	CE (u)
Mississippi	GS	GS	A	GS	GS	GS	N.A.	BS	BS	B (a-29)
Missouri	A	A	...	A	AGS	(w)	A	GS	B	B (a-29)
Montana	CP	CP	CP	GS	CP	GS	CP	GS (a-27)	CP	GS (a-29)
Nebraska	A	A	A	GS	(ff)	(gg)	A	GS	B	GS (a-29)
Nevada	A	A	A	A	...	A	...	AG	B	...
New Hampshire	G	GC	G	GC	GC (a-5)	BGC	GC	AGC	B	GC (a-29)
New Jersey	GS	A	A	GS	A	B	(oo)	GS	B	A
New Mexico	G	GS (a-18)	GS	GS	GS	G	GS	GS	B	GS (a-29)
New York	G	GS (a-18)	B	GS	CE (a-9)	GS	G	GS	B (a-12)	GS (a-29)
North Carolina	G	G	A	G	G	G	G	G	B	A
North Dakota	A	G	...	A	A	G	G	G	B	G (a-29)
Ohio	A	GS	N.A.	GS	GS	AG	AG	GS	B	GS
Oklahoma	GS	B	GS	B	GS	B	GS (a-5)	(d)	(d)	B (a-29)
Oregon	G	GS	G	B	CE (a-4)	B	GS (a-5)	A	B	A
Pennsylvania	G	AG	AG	AG	G	B	GS	GS	AG	AG
Rhode Island	G	G	CS	GB	AG (a-6)	GB (bb)	GB	GB	B	GB (a-29)
South Carolina	A	B	A	B	B	B	A	GS	B	B (a-29)
South Dakota	CG	(a-21)	A	(a-19)	GS	CG	GS (a-5)	GS	B	GS (a-32)
Tennessee	A	G	A	G	G	B	G	G	B	G (a-29)
Texas	A	B	B	B	CE (a-9)	B	B	BG	B	B (a-29)
Utah	A	GS	A	GS	A	A	A	GS	B	GS (a-29)
Vermont	A	G	G	G	G	G	G	G	N.A.	G (a-29)
Virginia	GB	GB	GB	GB	GB	B	GB	GB	B	GB
Washington	A	A	A	GS	GS	B	GS (a-5)	GS	B	B (a-29)
West Virginia	GS	GS	GS	GS (a-13)	GS (a-5)	CS	C	GS	B	GS (a-29)
Wisconsin	A	A	A	A	A	A	GS (a-5)	A	N.A.	A
Wyoming	G	GS	A	GS	CE	CS	A	GS	B	GS (a-29)
American Samoa	G	A	GB	GB	(a-4)	GB	G	GB	(a-12)	GB (a-29)
Guam	GS	GS	G	GS	GS	GS	CS	GS	B	GS
No. Mariana Islands	G	C	C	G	GS	C	GS	GS	B	C
U.S. Virgin Islands	GS	GS	GS	GS	GS	GS	GS	GS	GS	GS

(a-19) Natural Resources
(a-20) Parks and recreation
(a-21) Personnel
(a-22) Post-audit
(a-23) Pre-audit
(a-24) Public utility regulation
(a-25) Purchasing
(a-26) Revenue
(a-27) Social services
(a-28) Tourism
(a-29) Transportation
(a-30) Welfare
(a-31) Auditor
(a-32) Emergency Management
(a-33) Fish and Wildlife
   (b) Responsibilities shared between Commissioner of Mental Health (GE) and Commissioner of Retardation (GE).

   (c) Responsibilities shared between Section Manager–Central Account Service Manager (A) and Team Leader Audit Services (CS).
   (d) Method not specified.
   (e) Responsibilities shared between Director of Fiscal Management (A) and Director of Management and Budget (G).
   (f) Responsibilities shared between Director, Division of Substance Abuse and Mental Health Department of Health and Social Services (CG); and Director, Division of Developmental Disabilities Services, same department (CG).
   (g) Responsibilities shared between Secretary of Health and Social Services (GS); and Secretary, Department of Services of Children, Youth and their Families (GS).
   (h) Responsibilities shared between Director, Division of Licensing, Department of State (SS); and Secretary, Department of Professional Regulation (N.A.).
   (i) The State Auditor is appointed by the House and approved by the Senate.
   (j) Responsibilities shared between Deputy Director of Mental Health (G) and Deputy Director of Retardation (G).

SELECTED STATE ADMINISTRATIVE OFFICIALS: METHODS OF SELECTION — Continued

State or other jurisdiction	Information systems	Insurance	Labor	Licensing	Mental health & retardation	Natural resources	Parks & recreation	Personnel	Planning	Post audit
Alabama	G	G	G	...	G	G	CS	B	G (a-8)	LS
Alaska	AG	AG	GB	AG	AG	GB	AG	AG	...	B
Arizona	A	GS	B	...	A	GS	B	A	L (a-6)	(d)
Arkansas	GS	GS	GS	...	A	A	GS	A	...	L
California	...	CE	AG	G	GS	GS	GS	GS	...	(d)
Colorado	G	GS	GS	GS	GS	GS	C	GS	G	L
Connecticut	GE	GE	GE	CS	GE (b)	CS	CS	GE	A	L (a-31)
Delaware	GS	CE	CE	GS	CG (f)	GS	CG	CG	CG	CE (a-31)
Florida	G	CE (dd)	N.A.	(h)	A	(a-14)	(a-14)	A	GS	CE
Georgia	CE	CE	CE	A	A	B	A	GS	G	(i)
Hawaii	CS	AG	GS	CS	(j)	GS	CS	GS	CS	CS
Idaho	GS (a-5)	GS	GS	GS	...	B	B	GS	...	CE (a-9)
Illinois	GS (a-5)	GS	GS	GS	GS (a-27)	GS	GS (a-19)	GS (a-5)	...	SL
Indiana	G	G	G	G	A	G	A	G	...	G
Iowa	A	GS	GS	...	A	GS	A	A	...	...
Kansas	C	SE	GS	B	C	GS	CS	C	BG	L
Kentucky	G	G	G	...	CG	G	G	G	G	CE
Louisiana	A	CE	GS	...	GS	GS	LGS	B	A	CL
Maine	C	G	G	C	G	G	C	C	G	CL
Maryland	A	GS	GS	A	A (p)	GS	A	A	GS	N.A.
Massachusetts	C	G	G	G	CG (q)	CG	CG	CG	...	G
Michigan	GS	GS	GS (a-7)	CS	CS	GS	CS	CS	N.A.	CL
Minnesota	GS	A	GS	A	GS (aa)	GS	A	GS	N.A.	CE (a-31)
Mississippi	BS	SE	...	...	B	GS (a-14)	GS	B	A	CE (a-31)
Missouri	A	GS	GS	A	A	GS	A	G	...	CE (a-31)
Montana	A	GS	GS	CP	CP	GS	CP	CP	G	L
Nebraska	A	GS	GS	A	A	GS	B	A	GS	CE (a-31)
Nevada	G	A	G	...	GD	G	A	G	...	...
New Hampshire	GC (a-5)	GC	GC	...	AGC	GC	AGC	AGC	G	AGC (a-9)
New Jersey	A	GS	GS	A	A (pp)	A	A	GS	A	L (a-31)
New Mexico	G	G	GS	G	G	GS	G	G	...	CE (a-31)
New York	G	GS	GS	(jj)	(kk)	GS (a-14)	GS	GS	GS (a-11)	CE (a-9)
North Carolina	G	CE	CE	...	A	G	A	G	G	CE (a-31)
North Dakota	G	CE	G	CE (a-2)	A	A	G	A	...	SE
Ohio	A	G	A	A	...	GS	AG	AG	N.A.	SE
Oklahoma	A	CE	CE	...	B	B (a-28)	B (a-28)	GS	...	...
Oregon	A	GS	SE	GS	A	GOC	B	A	...	SS
Pennsylvania	G	GS	GS	G	AG	GS	A	G	G	CE (a-31)
Rhode Island	CS	CS	AGS	CS	GB	GB (a-14)	CS	CS	CS	CS
South Carolina	A	GS	GS	GS (a-18)	B (rr)	B	GS	A	AB	B (ss)
South Dakota	GS	GS	GS	CG	GS	GS	(a-33)	GS	(a-15)	(a-31)
Tennessee	A	G	G	A	G	G	A	G	G (a-6)	SL (a-9)
Texas	B	G	B	B	B	B	B	A	G (a-6)	L
Utah	A	GS	A	AG	AB	GS	AG	GS	G	CE (a-31)
Vermont	G	G	G	A	G	G	G	G	...	CE (a-31)
Virginia	GB	SL	GB	GB	GB	GB	GB	GB	GB	SL (a-31)
Washington	GS	CE	GS	GS	A	CE	B	GS	GS (a-15)	CE
West Virginia	C	GS	GS	...	GS	GS	GS	C	GS (a-5)	LS
Wisconsin	A	GS	GS	A	A	GS	A	GS	...	CE (a-31)
Wyoming	A	G	A	GS	A	G	GS	A	G	CE
American Samoa	(a-29)	G	N.A.	N.A.	(a-27)	AG	GB	A	(a-7)	G
Guam	GS	GS	GS	GS	GS (qq)	GS	GS	GS	GS	CE
No. Mariana Islands	C	CS	C	B	C	GS	C	GS	G	GS
U.S. Virgin Islands	G	SE	GS	GS	GS	GS	GS	GS	G	L

(k) Responsibilities shared between Co-Directors in Election Commission (G); appointed by the Governor, subject to approval by the Chairs of the State Republican/Democratic parties.

(l) Responsibilities shared between Director (GS), Chief of Fisheries (CS) and Chief of Wildlife (CS).

(m) Responsibilities shared between Lieutenant Governor (CE), Director Business Development Division (C) and President Kansas Inc.(BG).

(n) Responsibilities shared between Secretary of State (CE); and Deputy Assistant for Elections (SS).

(o) In Maine, New Hampshire, New Jersey, Tennessee and West Virginia, the Presidents (or Speakers) of the Senate are next in line of succession to the Governorship. In Tennessee, the Speaker of the Senate bears the statutory title of Lieutenant Governor.

(p) Responsibilities shared between Director, Mental Hygiene Administration (A); and Director, Developmental Disabilities Administration, Department of Health and Mental Hygiene (A).

(q) Responsibilities shared between Commissioner, Department of Mental Retardation (CG); and Commissioner, Department of Mental Health, Executive Office of Human Services (CG).

(r) Responsibilities shared between Assistant Executive Budget Analyst (A) and Director or Management and Budget (G).

(s) Responsibilities shared between Secretary of State (CE); and Director, Bureau of Elections (CS).

(t) The auditor is a Constitutional office, but it is appointed by the Senate and General Assembly in joint meeting as mandated in the New Jersey Constitution.

(u) The Lieutenant Governor currently serves as the agency head of the Department of Transportation.

(v) Responsibilities shared between the five Public Utility Commissioners (G).

(w) Responsibilities shared between Administrator, Division of Fisheries, Department of Conservation; Administrator, Division of Wildlife, same department (AB).

(x) Responsibilities shared between Director of Budget and Finance, (GS): Director of Human Resource Development, (GS) and the Comptroller, (GS).

SELECTED STATE ADMINISTRATIVE OFFICIALS: METHODS OF SELECTION — Continued

State or other jurisdiction	Pre-audit	Public library development	Public utility regulation	Purchasing	Revenue	Social services	Solid waste mgmt.	State police	Tourism	Transportation	Welfare
Alabama	CS (a-9)	B	SE	CS	G	B	CS	G	G	G (a-17)	B (a-27)
Alaska	...	AG	GB	AG	GB	GB	...	AG	AG	GB	AG
Arizona	A (a-9)	B	B	A	GS	A	A	GS	GS	GS	A
Arkansas	A	B	A	A	A	GS	A	G	GS	BS (1-17)	GS
California	CE (a-9)	GS	GS	GS	BS	GS	G	GS	N.A.	GS	AG
Colorado	C (a-9)	A	CS	CS	GS	GS	CS	CS	CS	GS (a-17)	CS
Connecticut	CE (a-9)	CS	GB	CS	GE	GE	CS	GE	GE	GE (a-17)	GE
Delaware	CE (a-31)	CG	CG	(a-16)	CG	GS (g)	B	CG	CG	GS (a-17)	CG
Florida	CE	A	L	A	GOC	GS	A	A	G	GS	A
Georgia	(i)	AB	CE	A	G	GD	A	B	A	B (a-17)	A
Hawaii	CS	B	GS	GS	GS	GS	CS	...	B	GS	CS
Idaho	CE (a-9)	B	GS	A	GS	GS	...	GS	A	B (a-17)	A
Illinois	CE (a-9)	SS	GS	GS (a-5)	GS	GS	GS (a-14)	GS	GS (a-7)	GS (a-17)	GS
Indiana	CE	G	G	A	G	N.A.	A	G	LG	G (a-17)	A
Iowa	A	A	GS	A	GS	GS	A	A	A	GS	...
Kansas	(c)	GS	GS	C	GS	GS	C	GS	A	GS (a-17)	C
Kentucky	G (a-15)	G	G	G	G	G	AG	G	G	G	CG
Louisiana	A	BGS	BS	A	GS	GS	GS	GS	LGS	GS (a-17)	GS
Maine	C	B	G	CS	C	G	CS	G	C	G (a-17)	C
Maryland	A	A	GS	A	A	GS	A	GS	A	GS	GS (a-27)
Massachusetts	G (a-9)	B	G	CG	CG	CG	CG	CG	CG	CG	CG
Michigan	...	CL	GS	CS	CS	GS	CS	GS	(d)	GS (a-17)	GS (a-27)
Minnesota	CE (a-31)	N.A.	G (v)	A	GS	GS	GS	A	A	CE (u)	GS (aa)
Mississippi	CE (a-31)	B	GS	A	GS	GS	A	GS	A	B (a-17)	GS
Missouri	A	B	GS	A	GS	GS	A	GS	A	B (a-17)	A
Montana	L	B	CE	CP	GS	GS	GS	A	CP	GS	GS (a-27)
Nebraska	A	B	B	A	GS	GS	A	GS	A	GS (a-17)	GS
Nevada	...	G	G	A	G	G	...	A	GD	BG	AG
New Hampshire	AGC (a-9)	AGC	GC	CS	GC	GC	AGC	AGC	AGC	GC (a-17)	AGC
New Jersey	...	...	GS	GS	A	GS	A	GS	A	GS	A
New Mexico	G	G	CE	G	GS	...	A	GS	GS	GS (a-17)	GS
New York	CE (a-9)	B (a-12)	GS	G (a-16)	GS	GS	GS (a-14)	G	GS (a-11)	GS (a-17)	GS (a-27)
North Carolina	CE (a-31)	A	G	A	G	A	A	G	A	G	A
North Dakota	A	A	CE	A	CE	G	A	G	G	G (a-17)	G
Ohio	SE	B	N.A.	A	CS	G	A	GS	...	GS	GS
Oklahoma	A (a-9)	B	(hh)	A	GS	GS	A	GS	B	B (a-17)	GS
Oregon	A (a-6)	B	GS	A	GS	GS	B	GS	A	GS	GS
Pennsylvania	CE (a-4)	G	GS	A	GS	AG	A	GS	G	GS	GS
Rhode Island	CS (a-9)	G	(ll)	CS	CS	CS	CS	GB	A	GB (a-17)	CS
South Carolina	CE (a-9)	B	B	A	GS	GS	A	GS	GS	B (a-17)	GS
South Dakota	CE	CG	CE	(a-5)	GS	G	CG	(a-32)	GS	GS (a-17)	GS (a-27)
Tennessee	A	A	SE	A	G	G	A	G	G	G (a-17)	G
Texas	CE (a-9)	A	B	B	CE (a-9)	G	A	B	A	B (a-17)	BG
Utah	A	A	A	A	BS	GS	A	A	A	GS (a-17)	GS
Vermont	G (a-15)	G	G	A	G	G	A	A	G	G (a-17)	G
Virginia	GB (a-9)	B	SL	GB (a-16)	GB	GB	GB (a-14)	GB	GB	GB	GB (a-27)
Washington	CE (a-4)	B	GS	A	GS	GS	A	GS	A	B (a-17)	GS (a-27)
West Virginia	GS (a-31)	B	GS	CS	GS	C	B	GS	GS	GS (a-17)	GS
Wisconsin	A	A	GS	A	GS	A	A	A	GS	GS	A
Wyoming	CE	A	A	G	A	GS	A	A	A	GS	GS
American Samoa	(a-4)	(a-12)	N.A.	A	(a-4)	GB	GB	GB	(a-7)	GB (a-17)	N.A.
Guam	GS	(d)	(ii)	GS	GS	GS	GS	GS	B	GS	GS
No. Mariana Islands	G	B	B	C	C	C	A	GS	GB	CS	A
U.S. Virgin Islands	GS	GS	GS	GS	GS	GS	GS	GS	GS	GS	GS

(y) Elected to the Senate by the public and elected Lieutenant Governor by the Senate (CL).

(z) Responsibilities shared between Secretary of State (CE); Deputy Secretary of State for Elections, Office of Secretary of State (SS); and Chief Deputy Secretary of State, same office (A).

(aa) Human/Social Services, Mental Health and Retardation and Welfare are under the Commissioner of Human Services (GS).

(bb) Responsibilities shared between Director of Wildlife, Director of Inland Fisheries and Director of Marine Fisheries.

(cc) Responsibilities shared between Secretary of State (G); and Division Director of Elections, Elections Division, Secretary of State (A).

(dd) Effective Jan. 1, 2003, the positions of Commissioner & Treasurer and Comptroller will merge into one Chief Financial Officer.

(ee) Department abolished 7/1/05; responsibilities transferred to Office of Management and Budget, General Services and Department of State.

(ff) Responsibilities shared between State Tax Commissioner, Department of Revenue (GS); Administrator, Budget Division (A) and the Auditor of Public Accounts (CE).

(gg) Responsibilities shared between Director, Game and Parks Commission (B), Division Administrator, Wildlife Division, Game & Parks Commission (A) and Assistant Director of Fish and Wildlife (A).

(hh) Responsibilities shared between Director, Public Utility Division, Corporation Commission (A); and 3 Commissioners, Corporation Commission (CE).

(ii) Responsibilities shared between Public Utility Regulation (GS) and Chair, Consolidated Commission on Utilities (GS).

(jj) Responsibilities shared between Secretary of State (GS) and Commissioner of State Education Department (B).

(kk) Responsibilities shared between Commissioner, Office of Mental Health, and Commissioner, Office of Mental Retardation and Developmental Disabilities, both (GS).

(ll) Responsibilities shared between Administrator Thomas Ahearn (G) and Chairman Elia Germani (B).

SELECTED STATE ADMINISTRATIVE OFFICIALS: METHODS OF SELECTION — Continued

(mm) Effective Jan. 6, 2003, the offices of State Treasurer, State Budget Director and Commerce will be abolished and the duties will be transferred to the Commissioner of Finance, (GS), in the Department of Finance.

(nn) Responsibilities shared between the Assistant Secretary of State (A) and the Senior Counsel for Elections (A).

(oo) Responsibilities shared between Director, Division of Purchasing, Department of the Treasury (GS), and Director, Division of Property and Management, Department of the Treasury (A).

(pp) Responsibilities shared between Director, Division of Mental Health Services, Dept of Human Services (A) and Director, Division of Developmental Disabilities, Department of Human Services (A).

(qq) Responsibilities shared between Director, Mental Health and Substance Abuse (GS) and Director, Department of Integrated Services for Individuals with Disabilities (GS).

(rr) Responsibilities shared between Director Stan Butkus (B) and State Director John Connery (B).

(ss) Responsibilities shared between Director George Schroeder (B) and State Auditor Thomas Wagner (B).

Table 4.11
SELECTED STATE ADMINISTRATIVE OFFICIALS: ANNUAL SALARIES BY REGION

State or other jurisdiction	Governor	Lieutenant governor	Secretary of state	Attorney general	Treasurer	Adjutant general	Administration	Agriculture	Auditor	Banking
Eastern Region										
Connecticut....................	$150,000	$110,000	$110,000	$110,000	$110,000	$148,816	$144,200	$110,000	(mm)	$121,200
Delaware........................	132,500	73,100	119,700	136,600	106,200	114,300	. . .	111,700	101,600	104,300
Maine............................	70,000	(s)	N.A.	78,062	71,032	91,208	91,208	87,692	84,302	85,758
Massachusetts	135,000 (jj)	120,000 (jj)	120,000	122,500	120,000	132,091	150,000	99,617	120,000	108,105
New Hampshire	102,704	(s)	89,128	99,317	89,128	89,128	99,317	84,232	N.A.	89,128
New Jersey	175,000	(s)	141,000	141,000	141,000	141,000	. . .	141,000	132,000	141,000
New York.......................	179,000	151,500	120,800	151,500	109,190	120,800	120,800	120,800	151,500	127,000
Pennsylvania.................	161,173	135,383	116,045	134,096	134,096	116,045	136,255	116,045	134,096	116,045
Rhode Island.................	105,194	88,584	88,584	94,121	88,584	85,067	110,321	54,864	137,418	77,867
Vermont	138,465	58,760	87,796	105,102	87,796	81,348	125,320	106,246	87,796	93,537
Regional average	134,904	73,733	99,305	117,230	105,703	111,980	97,742	103,220	115,171	106,394
Midwestern Region										
Illinois	154,100	117,800	135,900	135,900	117,800	100,400	123,600	115,700	115,100	123,600
Indiana..........................	95,000	76,000	66,000	79,400	66,000	106,723	96,915	102,004	66,000	93,210
Iowa..............................	130,000	103,212	103,212	123,669	103,212	119,357	129,205	103,212	103,212	89,872
Kansas...........................	98,331	111,523	76,389	76,389	76,389	91,232	91,350	91,362	96,804	80,185
Michigan........................	177,000	123,900	124,900	124,900	118,616	136,333	129,842	129,842	145,230	112,199
Minnesota	120,303	78,197	90,227	114,288	(v)	136,200	108,388	108,388	102,257	82,852
Nebraska........................	85,000	60,000	65,000	75,000	60,000	83,679	111,792	90,124	60,000	87,549
North Dakota	88,926	69,035	70,739	77,655	66,805	125,112	. . .	72,669	70,739	76,968
Ohio..............................	130,291	130,020	105,185	105,185	105,185	N.A.	126,006	107,827	105,185	112,320
South Dakota	105,544	14,399 (ee)	71,713	89,618	71,713	86,269	90,227	99,874	90,000	(a-26)
Wisconsin	131,768	69,579	62,549	127,868	62,549	98,217	131,767	111,094	113,516	96,163
Regional average	119,660	86,697	88,347	102,716	86,969	98,502	103,554	102,918	97,095	95,634
Southern Region										
Alabama.........................	96,361	48,966	71,500	153,927	71,500	80,916	103,880	71,003	71,500	139,920
Arkansas	77,028	37,229	48,182	64,189	48,182	93,223	124,402	80,091	48,182	110,730
Florida	129,060	123,688	119,000	127,771	127,771	136,184	124,320	127,771	143,424	(a-4)
Georgia..........................	131,481	86,442	116,664	130,020	121,882	136,184	121,882	114,701	129,132	124,950
Kentucky	130,705	95,815	95,815	95,815	95,815	130,705	N.A.	95,815	95,815	90,000
Louisiana	95,000	85,008	85,000	85,000	85,000	153,795	185,744	85,000	120,000	103,901
Maryland	150,000	125,000	87,500	125,000	125,000	94,367 (b)	101,633 (b)	101,633 (b)	. . .	53,236 (b)
Mississippi....................	122,160	60,000	90,000	108,960	90,000	111,400	108,000	90,000	90,000	127,179
Missouri........................	120,087	77,184	96,455	104,332	96,455	81,672	112,356	97,044	96,455	. . .
North Carolina	123,819	109,279	109,279	109,279	109,279	91,946	106,765	109,279	109,279	109,279
Oklahoma	110,299	85,500	90,000	103,109	87,875	132,091	76,100	78,100	N.A.	130,704
South Carolina	106,078	46,545	92,007	92,007	92,007	92,007	146,076	92,007	101,794	89,168
Tennessee......................	85,000	49,500 (s)	139,116	129,948	139,116	98,004	139,116	98,004	139,116	98,004
Texas.............................	115,345	115,345	117,546	125,000	(a-9)	105,000	N.A.	92,217	180,000	135,951
Virginia	124,855	36,321	135,311	110,667	118,644	103,285	135,311	135,311	141,612	136,796
West Virginia	95,000	(s)	70,000	85,000	75,000	75,000	75,000	75,000	75,000	60,000
Regional average	113,267	73,864	97,711	109,377	98,484	107,236	103,780	96,436	96,332	102,349
Western Region										
Alaska...........................	125,000	100,000	(a-1)	124,752	100,476	124,752	124,752	73,404	87,800	100,476
Arizona	95,000	(a-2)	70,000	90,000	70,000	103,175	140,000	97,632	120,080	93,000
California.......................	175,000	131,250	131,250	148,750	140,000	177,366	. . .	131,412	131,412	123,255
Colorado	90,000	68,500	68,500	80,000	68,500	133,575	134,823	143,823	132,079	103,428
Hawaii	94,780	90,041	(a-1)	107,100	(a-6)	181,525	. . .	91,800	102,000	84,552
Idaho.............................	98,500	26,750	82,500	91,500	82,500	120,162	84,552	86,778	. . .	86,278
Montana.........................	96,462	74,173	76,539	85,762	(a-5)	86,870	86,870	86,870	76,579	82,468
Nevada...........................	117,000	50,000	80,000	110,000	80,000	106,080	115,770	97,410	. . .	88,740
New Mexico	110,000	85,000	85,000	95,000	85,000	101,000	99,000	131,560	85,000	80,956
Oregon..........................	93,600	(a-2)	72,000	77,200	72,000	126,240	126,000	103,884	101,844	N.A.
Utah..............................	104,100	81,000	(a-1)	98,895	81,000	88,385	99,012	88,385	83,500	88,385
Washington	148,035	77,382	103,736	134,577	103,736	115,000	115,000	115,000	103,736	115,000
Wyoming	105,000	(a-2)	92,000	100,776	92,000	103,000	91,764	78,000	92,000	75,684
Regional Average...........	111,729	78,315	87,120	103,409	89,545	120,548	93,657	101,997	85,848	86,325
Regional Average without California......	106,456	73,904	83,443	99,630	85,340	115,814	101,462	99,546	82,052	83,247
Guam	90,000	85,000	. . .	90,000	58,199	68,152	74,096	60,850	82,025	74,096
No. Mariana Islands.......	70,000	65,000	. . .	80,000	40,800 (b)	. . .	54,000	40,800 (b)	80,000	40,800 (b)
U.S. Virgin Islands.........	80,000	75,000	75,000 (a-1)	76,500	76,500	85,000	76,500	76,500	76,500	75,000

Sources: The Council of State Governments' survey of state personnel agencies, January 2005 and January 2006.

Note: The chief administrative officials responsible for each function were determined from information given by the states for the same function as listed in State Administrative Officials Classified by Function, 2005, published by The Council of State Governments.

Key:
N.A. — Not available.
. . . — No specific chief administrative official or agency in charge of function.
(a) Chief administrative official or agency in charge of function:
(a-1) Lieutenant governor.
(a-2) Secretary of state.

SELECTED OFFICIALS: ANNUAL SALARIES — Continued

State or other jurisdiction	Budget	Civil rights	Commerce	Community affairs	Comptroller	Consumer affairs	Corrections	Economic development	Education	Election administration
Eastern Region										
Connecticut.................	$153,787	$117,420	$135,457	$150,000	$110,000	$121,199	$153,281	$135,457	$148,525	$116,868
Delaware	138,600	69,000	(a-2)	...	138,532	99,024	138,600	119,700	150,700	75,500
Maine	80,267	61,672	(a-11)	N.A.	80,267	75,171	91,208	91,208	91,208	67,330
Massachusetts	95,000	127,307	(a-11)	50,000	137,500	108,000	132,667	150,000	181,640	(a-2)
New Hampshire	99,317	61,913	96,461	69,322	75,806	82,504	99,317	77,255	85,753	(a-2)
New Jersey	125,950	114,970	141,000	141,000	125,950	122,400	141,000	155,000	141,000	112,801
New York....................	165,998	109,800	120,800	120,800	151,500	101,600	136,000	120,800	170,165	109,800
Pennsylvania...............	155,404	110,768	122,490	106,093	128,627	103,003	128,938	122,490	128,938	76,167
Rhode Island...............	106,679	N.A.	N.A.	N.A.	95,874	(a-3)	118,914	N.A.	135,516	N.A.
Vermont	(a-15)	84,406	99,028	77,022	(a-15)	84,406	95,721	82,513	117,104	(a-2)
Regional average.........	120,811	85,726	102,905	71,424	113,117	99,143	123,565	105,442	135,055	85,140
Midwestern Region										
Illinois........................	125,839	100,400	123,600	(a-7)	117,800	(a-3)	130,500	(a-7)	142,500	108,204
Indiana	112,203	102,004	1	86,716	(a-23)	N.A.	104,052	1	79,400	66,000
Iowa...........................	127,630	84,250	...	84,594	...	119,107	119,107	140,000	123,900	70,242
Kansas........................	86,528	39,354	(a-1)	64,349	79,590	70,410	93,887	(o)	137,280	(p)
Michigan	135,252	129,842	128,250	...	112,734	...	135,252	...	168,300	(e)
Minnesota...................	(v)	108,388	108,388	(a-11)	(v)	82,434	108,388	108,388	108,388	(a-2)
Nebraska	(a-5)	65,000	(a-11)	83,011	99,669	(a-3)	106,606	94,621	151,276	66,023
North Dakota	(tt)	60,000	112,008	72,669	(kk)	74,196	70,008	77,988	80,532	28,200
Ohio	114,738	57,798	112,320	130,020	N.A.	105,185	124,852	130,020	209,456	(a-2)
South Dakota	(a-15)	N.A.	(a-26)	(a-28)	(a-23)	N.A.	92,740	(a-28)	147,444	N.A.
Wisconsin...................	109,933	69,971	107,102	...	101,615	75,933	118,481	87,126	N.A.	105,576
Regional average.........	108,512	74,273	80,304	78,024	81,213	67,106	109,443	88,705	122,589	77,734
Southern Region										
Alabama	153,678	...	137,800	80,916	126,056	69,628	100,700	(a-8)	164,300	52,915
Arkansas.....................	102,168	...	(a-11)	(a-27)	124,402	80,767	118,700	111,172	122,295	53,218
Florida........................	134,680	123,578	...	119,140	(a-4)	92,953	124,320	(a-28)	225,000	104,118
Georgia.......................	125,000	N.A.	150,000	137,700	N.A.	106,182	124,032	(a-7)	117,332	88,464
Kentucky	155,000	96,600	130,038	N.A.	100,253	(a-3)	101,130	225,000	200,744	104,108
Louisiana....................	140,000	71,053	(a-11)	N.A.	(a-5)	80,000	N.A.	223,600	202,259	100,000
Maryland	117,952(b)	81,414(b)	117,952(b)	...	125,000	73,795(b)	87,642(b)	117,952(b)	175,000	75,647(b)
Mississippi..................	108,000	...	90,000	59,328	108,000	75,000	108,400	5,000(j)	292,500	(q)
Missouri	92,064	68,268	97,032	N.A.	86,364	(a-3)	97,044	97,032	154,128	59,088
North Carolina	(a-15)	67,678	106,765	84,598	135,997	N.A.	106,765	104,550	109,279	92,892
Oklahoma...................	98,000	61,320	107,060	N.A.	83,700	58,416	110,000	N.A.	95,898	76,057
South Carolina	116,034	89,739	(c)	N.A.	92,007	96,545	132,934	(a-7)(c)	92,007	82,349
Tennessee	100,500	78,540	104,304	(a-11)	139,116	65,784	108,000	104,304	104,304	N.A.
Texas..........................	139,526	78,324	N.A.	117,516	92,217	99,289	165,000	N.A.	164,748	(ff)
Virginia......................	123,197	76,240	135,311	104,867	110,469	95,130	130,466	198,284	135,311	76,355
West Virginia..............	88,548	45,000	90,000	85,908	75,000	99,406	75,000	(a-8)	146,100	70,000
Regional average.........	121,387	58,610	114,360	63,918	107,006	86,203	105,633	108,011	156,325	77,632
Western Region										
Alaska	125,004	104,496	124,752	...	90,324	...	124,752	...	124,752	78,660
Arizona.......................	104,192	122,803	125,091	(a-7)	99,666	106,270	138,312	(a-7)	85,000	(a-2)
California	(a-15)	...	...	108,753	140,000	123,255	131,412	...	148,750	123,996
Colorado.....................	124,836	103,428	N.A.	129,285	111,240	(a-3)	131,078	128,580	171,032	91,704
Hawaii........................	102,000	86,041	100,000	...	102,000	84,552	91,800	96,900	150,000	79,866
Idaho	88,962	65,728	94,910	57,491	82,500	91,500	115,523	57,491	82,500	82,500
Montana	91,599	61,082	86,870	67,935	74,660	50,232	88,173	96,461	89,472	49,680
Nevada	(a-5)	79,560	115,770	...	80,000	88,740	115,770	106,080	112,200	(oo)
New Mexico	79,135	76,964	106,835	74,158	...	86,543	101,000	106,835	138,002	66,136
Oregon	94,284	74,028	N.A.	103,884	103,884	114,516	126,000	N.A.	72,000	103,884
Utah	98,365	72,696	88,385	95,121	83,500	88,385	102,792	128,523	168,168	65,208
Washington.................	150,000	103,200	115,000	106,128	(a-4)	134,577	135,000	135,000	105,861	103,736
Wyoming....................	84,864	60,972	146,580	146,580	92,000	146,580	114,576	146,580	92,000	70,000
Regional average.........	106,956	77,769	84,938	78,033	89,501	91,935	116,630	86,734	118,441	84,591
Regional average without California	104,918	84,250	92,016	75,473	85,293	89,325	115,398	93,962	115,916	81,776
Guam	88,915	...	75,208	...	68,152	46,596	67,150	82,025	98,430	61,939
No. Mariana Islands	54,000	49,000	52,000	52,000	40,800(b)	52,000	40,800(b)	45,000	80,000	53,000
U.S. Virgin Islands.......	76,500	60,000	76,500	(hh)	76,500	76,500	76,500	85,000	76,500	76,500

(a-3) Attorney general.
(a-4) Treasurer.
(a-5) Administration.
(a-6) Budget.
(a-7) Commerce.
(a-8) Community affairs.
(a-9) Comptroller.

(a-10) Consumer affairs.
(a-11) Economic development.
(a-12) Education (chief state school officer).
(a-13) Energy.
(a-14) Environmental protection.
(a-15) Finance.
(a-16) General services.

SELECTED OFFICIALS: ANNUAL SALARIES — Continued

State or other jurisdiction	Emergency management	Employment services	Energy	Environmental protection	Finance	Fish & wildlife	General services	Health	Higher education	Highways
Eastern Region										
Connecticut.....................	$123,600	$121,200	$110,865	$127,250	$150,000	(rr)	$144,200	$148,816	$160,000	$153,281
Delaware	76,800	89,700	52,790	(a-19)	138,600	92,100	(a-5)	154,100	85,900	(a-29)
Maine	64,667	N.A.	80,267	91,208	(a-5)	91,208	80,267	91,208	N.A.	(a-29)
Massachusetts..................	82,559	100,913	99,162	117,678	150,000(a-5)	106,358	105,000	119,125	180,000	110,000
New Hampshire	71,482	89,128	70,005	96,461	(a-5)	84,232	99,317	77,255	66,779	(a-29)
New Jersey	126,000	120,000	108,018	141,000	120,554	101,704	(pp)	141,000	121,900	120,000
New York	124,705	(a-18)	120,800	136,000(ss)	(a-9)	136,000(ss)	136,000	136,000	170,165	(a-29)
Pennsylvania....................	115,013	113,233	108,362	109,927	155,404	103,707	122,490	128,938	99,247	123,032
Rhode Island...................	68,311	108,460	77,867	108,460	(a-6)	108,460	N.A.	110,321	134,639	(a-29)
Vermont	74,859	99,028	93,537	82,513	87,110	77,022	90,459	116,729	...	(a-29)
Regional average..............	92,800	96,866	92,167	113,020	125,037	104,122	99,353	122,349	101,863	118,602
Midwestern Region										
Illinois	100,400	123,600	(a-7)	115,700	(a-6)	(a-19)	(a-5)	130,500	182,000	(a-29)
Indiana	(m)	91,806	N.A.	97,929	(a-6)	98,260	(a-5)	(m)	144,939	(a-29)
Iowa	78,315	126,000	...	106,122	105,643	92,222	106,122	128,856	...	135,595
Kansas.............................	57,948	92,086	47,789	86,525	...	46,509	(a-5)	80,000	149,025	(a-29)
Michigan	100,617	105,647	...	140,452	(a-6)	(w)	...	135,252	100,617	(a-29)
Minnesota........................	108,388	95,192	106,759	108,388	108,388(v)	99,180	(a-5)	(t)	261,494	(a-1)
Nebraska	73,574	81,505	67,091	101,419	(z)	(aa)	78,252	105,587	146,160	102,954
North Dakota	63,600	75,408	...	74,988	87,360	84,996	97,760	137,904	183,750	(a-29)
Ohio	94,640	94,484	N.A.	111,358	105,185	92,638	98,592	149,864	220,480	117,884
South Dakota	86,269	(a-21)	N.A.	(a-19)	104,170	99,874	(a-5)	99,874	201,151	(n)
Wisconsin........................	92,217	N.A.	90,782	114,262	109,933	114,262	131,767	118,481	320,000	114,262
Regional average..............	77,815	88,846	39,638	105,183	96,990	94,712	92,998	108,610	173,601	108,711
Southern Region										
Alabama	132,500	82,677	86,918	128,199	80,916	100,888	73,135	207,059	162,136	80,916
Arkansas..........................	75,000	117,219	95,110	103,526	(a-9)	105,531	110,224	176,077	125,679	(a-29)
Florida.............................	112,835	124,320	61,198	124,320	(a-4)	125,660	124,320	155,000	N.A.	134,726
Georgia............................	N.A.	87,869	109,884	124,032	124,032	100,572	94,109	153,000	425,000	(a-29)
Kentucky	88,200	N.A.	74,383	98,000	130,038	121,958	N.A.	151,470	233,000	120,155
Louisiana.........................	N.A.	96,200	100,172	124,100	(a-5)	111,758	(a-5)	208,000	283,896	(a-29)
Maryland	81,414(b)	81,414(b)	69,109(b)	109,476(b)	117,952(b)	N.A.	(a-5)	117,952(b)	109,476(b)	152,250
Mississippi.......................	83,000	104,150	85,951	122,250	108,000	104,000	...	188,057	325,000	(a-29)
Missouri	73,872	N.A.	...	86,200	90,317	(y)	82,380	103,224	135,000	(a-29)
North Carolina	86,292	108,986	82,179	91,452	126,960	102,764	106,765	144,868	425,000	138,161
Oklahoma	70,000	88,752	N.A.	89,450	98,000	96,511	75,920	182,100	N.A.	(a-29)
South Carolina	86,477	120,510	96,548	144,817	146,076	118,466	108,000	130,043	N.A.	(a-29)
Tennessee	85,380	115,932	97,332	98,004	139,116	98,004	98,004	144,720	165,228	98,004
Texas...............................	124,000	131,000	N.A.	128,004	(a-9)	130,000	N.A.	175,000	150,000	(a-29)
Virginia...........................	92,269	110,469	123,534	134,280	135,311	111,865	122,801	155,636	134,310	156,636
West Virginia...................	45,000	82,620	85,000	(a-13)	(a-5)	74,304	75,000	90,000	180,000	(a-29)
Regional average..............	77,265	90,757	72,957	111,944	118,866	98,701	89,743	155,138	178,358	132,535
Western Region										
Alaska	93,576	84,036	168,000	124,752	97,080	124,752	...	124,752	128,257	100,476
Arizona............................	86,394	105,148	...	127,634	72,774(b)	121,000	115,938	127,125	160,000	111,000
California	114,191	123,255	123,000	131,412	131,412	129,418	129,418	123,255	(gg)	(a-29)
Colorado..........................	103,428	134,823	121,200	116,700	N.A.	126,768	134,823	134,823	134,823	134,823
Hawaii.............................	79,866	68,628(b)	75,012(b)	68,628(b)	(vv)	68,628(b)	(a-9)	102,000	341,256	75,012(b)
Idaho	57,179	94,910	71,469	84,510	86,278	107,016	...	104,978	104,686	(a-29)
Montana	69,500	80,169	80,498	86,870	74,660	86,870	74,362	(a-27)	150,075	(a-29)
Nevada	79,560	115,770	61,200	112,200	...	106,080	...	106,080	23,600(nn)	(a-29)
New Mexico	104,998	100,000	101,695	99,998	120,000	95,000	99,000	111,925	102,000	105,000
Oregon	103,884	114,516	94,284	103,884	(a-4)	103,884	(a-5)	114,516	219,504	94,284
Utah	56,950	112,459	74,692	102,792	95,368	97,988	95,368	112,892	179,469	(a-29)
Washington......................	89,352	135,000	115,000	135,000	150,000	135,000	(a-5)	135,000	105,861	(a-29)
Wyoming..........................	63,648	90,168	62,124	95,470	92,000	105,000	70,000	175,000	90,120	(a-29)
Regional average..............	84,810	104,529	88,321	106,912	85,398	108,262	81,685	119,940	145,953	111,186
Regional average without California	82,361	102,969	85,431	104,870	81,858	106,499	77,708	119,663	144,971	110,181
Guam	68,152	73,020	55,303	60,850	88,915	60,850	47,918	74,096	160,000	88,915
No. Mariana Islands	45,000	40,800(b)	45,000	58,000	54,000	40,800(b)	54,000	80,000	80,000	40,800(b)
U.S. Virgin Islands	71,250	76,500	69,350	76,500	76,500	76,500	76,500	76,500	76,500	65,000

(a-17) Highways.
(a-18) Labor.
(a-19) Natural resources.
(a-20) Parks and recreation.
(a-21) Personnel.
(a-22) Post audit.
(a-23) Pre-audit.

(a-24) Public utility regulation.
(a-25) Purchasing.
(a-26) Revenue.
(a-27) Social services.
(a-28) Tourism.
(a-29) Transportation.
(a-30) Welfare.

SELECTED OFFICIALS: ANNUAL SALARIES — Continued

State or other jurisdiction	Information systems	Insurance	Labor	Licensing	Mental health & retardation	Natural resources	Parks & recreation	Personnel	Planning	Post audit
Eastern Region										
Connecticut......................	$145,000	$121,200	$135,456	$96,047	(d)	$126,401	$116,868	$144,200	$110,865	(a-31)
Delaware	150,700	101,600	111,700	91,300	(f)	119,700	92,700	105,000	88,836	(a-31)
Maine	82,451	91,208	91,208	75,171	91,208	91,208	40,134	80,267	80,267	82,659
Massachusetts	129,708	N.A.	108,000	102,599	(u)	99,617	115,595	127,307	(a-5)	(a-31)
New Hampshire	95,000	84,670	80,213	. . .	81,191	96,461	64,036	75,806	69,322	(a-9)
New Jersey	122,801	141,000	141,000	122,400	(qq)	120,000	112,410	141,000	93,636	132,000
New York.........................	143,500	127,000	127,000	(bb)	(ii)	(a-14)	127,000	120,800	(a-11)	(a-9)
Pennsylvania....................	113,252	116,045	128,938	95,062	110,866	122,490	110,768	128,979	125,204	(a-31)
Rhode Island....................	85,067	N.A.	N.A.	N.A.	N.A.	108,460	68,311	95,874	68,311	N.A.
Vermont	78,873	93,537	99,028	69,992	116,729	99,028	77,022	83,033	. . .	(a-31)
Regional average..............	114,635	87,626	102,254	85,776	117,319	111,937	92,484	110,227	90,724	104,454
Midwestern Region										
Illinois.............................	(a-5)	(a-32)	107,800	(a-32)	(a-27)	115,700	(a-19)	(a-5)	. . .	(a-31)
Indiana	93,853	90,129	94,867	84,162	86,716	98,260	98,260	91,806	. . .	97,929
Iowa.................................	142,563	92,000	96,500	. . .	116,563	119,107	92,277	105,643	. . .	. . .
Kansas..............................	96,425	76,389	92,086	63,665	N.A.	94,311	51,272	72,100	N.A.	98,254
Michigan	146,017	112,199	128,250	113,173	118,616	135,252	103,020	139,077	. . .	145,230
Minnesota.........................	119,997	89,387	108,388	95,985	(t)	108,388	104,588	108,388	N.A.	(a-31)
Nebraska	111,243	85,792	82,470	88,525	97,001	94,270	96,524	87,859	111,792	(a-31)
North Dakota	N.A.	70,059	60,000	(a-2)	72,684	71,532	72,281	72,936	. . .	. . .
Ohio.................................	109,226	124,800	94,484	96,850	. . .	124,852	94,640	103,818	N.A.	105,185
South Dakota	119,604	N.A.	97,053	N.A.	93,300	99,874	99,874	91,580	N.A.	(a-31)
Wisconsin.........................	97,366	97,366	91,495	92,310	101,940	114,262	99,479	95,252	. . .	(a-31)
Regional average..............	105,445	87,429	95,763	75,364	84,155	106,892	93,447	99,278	10,163	84,316
Southern Region										
Alabama...........................	139,131	80,916	80,916	. . .	129,178	80,916	78,720	129,178	(a-8)	161,444
Arkansas...........................	112,371	103,989	102,396	. . .	89,348	88,484	97,007	87,862	. . .	127,238
Florida.............................	(h)	(a-4)	111,718(ss)	101,000	(i)	(a-14)	(a-14)	90,000	119,140	(a-4)
Georgia............................	134,232	114,070	114,714	89,776	121,992	124,032	106,054	145,000	125,000	(a-31)
Kentucky..........................	111,353	100,942	107,048	N.A.	100,000	107,047	N.A.	130,038	130,038	95,815
Louisiana.........................	114,275	85,000	120,203	. . .	102,128	116,876	100,402	97,822	104,141	123,735
Maryland..........................	101,633(b)	101,633(b)	101,633(b)	81,414(b)	136,784(b)	109,476(b)	64,729(b)	94,367(b)	101,633(b)	N.A.
Mississippi.......................	140,000	90,000	. . .	. . .	142,561	122,250	104,000	102,450	77,385	(a-31)
Missouri...........................	109,344	97,104	97,044	74,000	94,128	97,044	84,876	82,380	. . .	(a-31)
North Carolina	135,915	109,279	109,279	. . .	119,787	106,765	82,772	106,765	N.A.	(a-31)
Oklahoma.........................	94,500	99,875	80,750	. . .	124,987	82,000	82,000	76,100	. . .	. . .
South Carolina	129,000	100,000	111,320	(a-18)	(dd)	118,466	109,803	1,308,665	85,214	(uu)
Tennessee	127,308	98,004	115,932	60,000	104,304	98,004	75,000	98,004	N.A.	(a-9)
Texas...............................	135,000	163,800	131,000	112,500	141,000	128,004	130,000	N.A.	112,000	180,000
Virginia............................	155,636	136,796	111,371	94,166	155,636	135,311	113,359	122,171	(a-6)	141,612
West Virginia....................	109,999	60,000	60,000	. . .	90,000	70,000	74,964	82,632	(a-8)	80,400
Regional average..............	119,781	104,503	97,208	45,261	118,806	106,812	89,250	172,090	71,536	106,053
Western Region										
Alaska..............................	78,660	93,576	124,752	93,576	87,192	124,752	78,660	90,324	. . .	93,576
Arizona............................	111,027	109,650	134,999	. . .	105,462	114,450	123,053	109,836	(a-6)	N.A.
California	N.A.	140,000	131,412	123,255	(ww)	131,412	123,255	123,255	. . .	. . .
Colorado..........................	117,000	105,576	134,823	124,836	103,428	133,575	126,768	134,823	124,836	132,079
Hawaii..............................	68,628(b)	89,148	96,900	65,364(b)	(k)	96,900	68,628(b)	91,800	72,828(b)	68,628(b)
Idaho	84,552	83,304	94,910	58,802	. . .	88,234	88,816	82,098	. . .	(a-9)
Montana	100,000	76,579	86,870	78,594	89,944	86,870	64,168	76,390	96,461	112,719
Nevada	112,200	106,080	88,740	. . .	112,200	115,770	. . .	97,410	. . .	. . .
New Mexico	95,000	91,425	100,000	97,678	81,401	101,695	84,594	86,488	. . .	85,000
Oregon.............................	N.A.	114,516	72,000	74,028	109,128	103,884	103,884	94,284	. . .	103,884
Utah	112,898	88,385	88,385	88,550	90,334	99,994	92,810	102,792	(a-6)	83,500
Washington.......................	135,000	103,736	135,000	115,000	150,000	105,861	111,000	135,000	(a-15)	150,000
Wyoming..........................	81,468	81,156	74,616	61,000	136,000	37,572	83,280	76,884	79,560	(a-9)
Regional average..............	84,341	98,702	104,877	75,437	98,287	103,151	88,378	100,106	55,865	77,222
Regional average without California	91,369	95,261	102,666	71,452	96,367	100,796	85,472	98,177	60,520	83,657
Guam	74,096	74,096	73,020	74,096	67,150	60,850	60,850	74,096	75,208	82,025
No. Mariana Islands	45000	40,800(b)	45,000	45,360	40,800(b)	52,000	40,800(b)	60,000	45,000	80,000
U.S. Virgin Islands............	71,250	75,000	76,500	76,500	70,000	76,500	76,500	76,500	76,500	55,000

(a-31) Auditor.
(a-32) Banking.

(b) Salary ranges and top figure in ranges follow: Arizona: Finance, $123,057; Welfare, $123,057. Hawaii: Employment Services, $101,544; Energy, $110,952; Environmental Protection, $101,544; Fish and Wildlife, $101,544; Highways, $110,952; Information Systems, $101,544; Licensing, $96,708; Parks and Recreation, $101,544; Planning, $107,736; Post-Audit,

$101,544; Pre-Audit, $101,544; Solid Waste Management, $96,708; Welfare, $101,544. Maryland: Minimum figure in range: top of range follows: Adjutant general, $126,542; Administration, $136,305; Agriculture, $136,305; Banking, $82,542; Budget, $158,232; Civil rights, $109,134; Commerce, $158,232; Consumer affairs, $114,905; Corrections, $117,503; Economic development, $158,232; Election administration, $101,387; Emergency management, $109,134; Employment services, $109,134; Energy, $107,525; Environmental

SELECTED OFFICIALS: ANNUAL SALARIES — Continued

State or other jurisdiction	Pre-audit	Public library development	Public utility regulation	Purchasing	Revenue	Social services	Solid waste management	State police	Tourism	Transportation	Welfare
Eastern Region											
Connecticut................	(a-9)	$103,890	$149,307	$101,372	$153,281	$153,281	$109,872	$149,350	$122,004	$153,281	153,281
Delaware	(a-31)	78,000	89,700	(a-16)	116,900	(g)	155,397	141,600	59,000	129,600	107,700
Maine	(a-9)	77,438	101,420	69,326	85,758	91,208	58,573	80,267	69,326	91,208	73,590
Massachusetts	(a-31)	73,918	99,162	(a-16)	132,026	128,555	(a-14)	133,976	100,883	120,000	124,970
New Hampshire	(a-9)	77,255	94,024	53,586	99,317	102,704	75,806	89,128	77,255	99,317	89,321
New Jersey	. . .	. . .	141,000	120,702	110,269	141,000	98,246	126,000	96,300	141,000	118,154
New York	(a-9)	(a-12)	127,000	(a-16)	127,000	136,000	(a-14)	127,000	(a-11)	136,000	136,000
Pennsylvania.............	(a-4)	97,663	124,990	100,499	122,490	N.A.	92,871	122,490	104,431	128,938	128,938
Rhode Island.............	(a-9)	85,067	106,679	99,471	110,278	110,321	68,311	124,114	N.A.	117,337	. . .
Vermont	(a-15)	83,075	113,360	90,459	86,715	98,009	82,513	99,028	76,939	106,246	98,009
Regional average........	95,625	84,647	114,664	95,642	114,403	111,307	99,527	119,295	82,694	122,293	102,996
Midwestern Region											
Illinois.....................	(a-9)	84,972	117,000	(a-5)	123,600	130,500	(a-14)	115,100	(a-7)	130,500	123,600
Indiana	90,792	64,818	94,848	97,929	97,929	110,175	N.A.	120,179	N.A.	97,929	91,806
Iowa	79,331	106,413	99,521	92,227	130,000	132,483	92,227	111,238	90,397	128,232	. . .
Kansas.....................	(r)	77,557	81,200	80,000	91,350	94,856	75,795	82,215	60,900	91,350	72,000
Michigan	. . .	127,296	113,612	114,000	111,726	130,050	118,616	129,842	. . .	140,000	(a-27)
Minnesota	(a-31)	N.A.	(l)	95,985	108,388	(t)	108,388	94,774	106,759	(a-1)	(t)
Nebraska	99,669	83,275	97,897	78,252	95,106	105,583	59,320	94,760	63,500	102,954	105,583
North Dakota	87,360	68,952	72,669	58,728	76,774	110,820	61,164	70,950	73,188	100,880	110,820
Ohio	105,185	N.A.	N.A.	90,038	N.A.	122,512	79,872	118,300	. . .	121,108	122,512
South Dakota	71,713	N.A.	93,634	90,227 (a-5)	97,053	97,053	N.A.	(n)	104,915	99,957	(a-27)
Wisconsin.................	(a-31)	102,356	112,000	85,682	114,262	118,481	99,479	93,139	94,196	114,262	89,972
Regional average........	83,000	65,058	88,308	91,515	95,108	114,627	73,687	101,524	65,223	109,579	95,617
Southern Region											
Alabama	(a-9)	91,224	86,801	117,029	80,916	147,669	91,379	80,916	80,916	(a-17)	(a-27)
Arkansas...................	59,596	86,941	96,577	87,862	94,110	128,417	51,153	94,260	97,007	130,290	(a-27)
Florida.....................	(a-4)	96,762	128,605	99,425	128,537	134,680	90,000	125,980	116,446	145,040	111,888
Georgia....................	(a-31)	124,500	109,884	125,000	129,132	N.A.	96,891	124,032	110,000	180,132	127,000
Kentucky	(a-15)	99,826	98,826	85,000	111,353	105,000	102,868	100,494	114,694	130,038	105,000
Louisiana	97,552	88,400	93,000	90,022	112,528	113,256	100,838	115,481	100,693	142,165	91,482
Maryland	87,642(b)	81,414(b)	116,880	75,647(b)	87,642(b)	109,476(b)	81,414(b)	109,476(b)	87,642(b)	117,952(b)	109,476(b)
Mississippi................	(a-31)	80,500	107,350	70,818	118,935	126,500	64,253	110,600	87,062	137,635	126,500
Missouri	86,364	76,200	80,000	82,380	103,224	103,224	N.A.	92,748	74,200	(a-17)	88,188
North Carolina	(a-31)	90,211	121,701	94,612	106,765	103,952	89,589	102,137	90,211	106,765	N.A.
Oklahoma	(a-9)	74,100	(cc)	71,700	98,400	155,000	88,374	88,400	82,000	112,100	155,000
South Carolina	(a-9)	82,182	140,000	92,544	115,113	138,036	144,817	98,913	109,803	142,381	138,036
Tennessee	99,258	100,668	98,004	65,508	98,004	98,004	81,888	98,004	98,004	98,004	98,004
Texas	(a-9)	88,500	105,000	81,808	(a-9)	N.A.	N.A.	15,000	N.A.	130,000	200,000
Virginia	(a-9)	117,686	136,796(ll)	(a-16)	125,031	139,019	(a-14)	126,841	150,000	135,311	(a-27)
West Virginia.............	(a-31)	66,996	75,000	94,836	75,000	85,908	74,784	75,000	70,000	N.A.	90,000
Regional average........	99,799	90,382	101,922	92,090	105,951	105,244	80,741	96,587	92,069	120,052	116,414
Western Region											
Alaska	. . .	93,576	84,036	93,852	124,752	124,752	. . .	93,576	96,984	124,752	91,200
Arizona....................	(a-9)	114,946	100,124	86,445	134,224	137,295	90,000	104,253	110,853	130,000	72,774(b)
California	133,333	108,744	117,818	. . .	123,255	123,255	117,818	131,412	N.A.	123,255	131,412
Colorado..................	(a-9)	100,730	107,424	97,248	134,823	134,823	103,428	125,868	70,041	134,823	N.A.
Hawaii.....................	68,628(b)	115,000	79,866	79,866	102,000	96,900	65,364(b)	. . .	240,000	102,000	68,628(b)
Idaho	(a-9)	82,992	82,740	70,845	71,708	104,978	. . .	87,214	73,819	130,000	78,000
Montana	112,719	75,152	77,418	53,948	86,870	86,870	86,870	79,384	67,699	86,871	(a-29)
Nevada	. . .	(x)	112,200	88,740	115,770	115,770	(a-14)	115,770	106,080	115,770	106,080
New Mexico	87,210	67,704	N.A.	83,943	104,713	N.A.	. . .	104,998	97,608	105,000	122,938
Oregon	(a-6)	94,284	109,080	81,504	114,516	N.A.	103,884	120,040	N.A.	N.A.	N.A.
Utah	(a-15)	95,368	76,773	95,368	95,004	112,898	97,988	95,368	91,915	112,459	112,898
Washington...............	(a-4)	89,004	115,000	115,000	135,000	150,000	135,000	135,000	135,000	153,472	(a-27)
Wyoming..................	(a-9)	75,636	91,000	66,000	89,000	90,000	82,803	89,736	92,292	103,000	(a-27)
Regional average........	83,130	93,425	88,729	77,905	110,126	98,272	76,566	98,663	90,945	109,339	85,446
Regional average without California ..	78,946	92,247	86,305	84,397	109,032	96,191	73,128	95,934	98,524	108,179	81,616
Guam	74,096	55,303	12,000	74,096	74,096	74,096	88,915	74,096	74,000	74,096	74,096
No. Mariana Islands ...	54,000	45,000	80,000	40,800(b)	45,000	40,800(b)	54,000	54,000	70,000	40,800(b)	52,000
U.S. Virgin Islands.....	76,500	53,350	54,500	76,500	76,500	76,500	76,500	76,500	76,500	65,000	76,500

protection, $146,845; Finance, $158,232; General Services, $136,305; Health, $158,232; Higher education, $146,845; Information systems, $136,305; Insurance, $136,305; Labor, $136,305; Licensing, $109,134; Mental Health, $218,415; Natural resources, $146,845; Parks and recreation, $100,636; Personnel, $126,542; Planning, $136,305; Pre-audit, $117,503; Public library development, $109,134; Purchasing, $101,387; Revenue, $117,503; Social services,

$146,845; Solid waste management, $109,134; Police, $146,845; Tourism, $117,503; Transportation, $158,232; Welfare, $146,845. Northern Mariana Islands: $49,266 top of range applies to the following positions: Treasurer, Banking, Comptroller, Corrections, Employment Services, Fish and Wildlife, Highways, Insurance, Mental Health and Retardation, Parks and Recreation, Purchasing, Social/Human Services, Transportation.

SELECTED OFFICIALS: ANNUAL SALARIES — Continued

(c) The present Secretary of Commerce forgoes regular salary and receives $1 in compensation.

(d) Responsibilities shared between Commissioner Thomas Kirk, Mental Health: $153,281 and Commissioner Peter O'Meara, Retardation: $153,281.

(e) Responsibilities shared between Secretary of State, $124,900 and Bureau Director, $107,291.

(f) Responsibilities shared between Director, Division of Substance Abuse and Mental Health, Department of Health and Social Services, $132,800 and Director, Division of Developmental Disabilities Service, same department, $107,600.

(g) Function split between two cabinet positions: Secretary, Dept. of Health and Social Services: $138,600 (if incumbent holds a medical license, amount is increased by $12,000) and Secretary, Dept. of Services for Children, Youth and their Families, $124,700; if a Board-certified physician, a supplement of $3,000 is added.

(h) Position is vacant at press time. Salary range is $66,800–$275,059.

(i) Responsibilities shared between, Director of Mental Health, Department of Children and Family Services, $102,564; and Director, Substance Abuse, same department, $102,500.

(j) Maximum salary available is $183,240; incumbent has requested a reduced salary.

(k) Responsibilities shared between Deputy Director of Mental Health, $93,840 and Deputy Director of Retardation, $93,840.

(l) Responsibilities shared between five commissioners with salaries of $88,448 each.

(m) Contractual.

(n) Under Emergency Management, $86,269.

(o) Responsibilities shared between Lieutenant Governor, $111,523; Director, Business Development Division, same department, $86,275; and President, Kansas Inc., salary unavailable.

(p) Responsibilities shared between Secretary of State, $76,389 and Deputy Secretary of State, $62,301.

(q) Responsibilities shared between Assistant Secretary of State, $80,000 and Senior Counsel for Elections, $60,000.

(r) Responsibilities shared between Central Account Service Manager, Division of Accounts & Reports, Department of Administration, $70,428; and Team Leader, Audit Services, same division and department, $57,948.

(s) In Maine, New Hampshire, New Jersey, Tennessee and West Virginia, the presidents (or speakers) of the Senate are next in line of succession to the governorship. In Tennessee, the speaker of the Senate bears the statutory title of lieutenant governor.

(t) Commissioner of Health and Human Services also oversees Mental Health and Retardation and Welfare (Human Services), $108,388.

(u) Responsibilities shared between Commissioner, Department of Mental Retardation, $182,831; and Commissioner, Department of Mental Health, $126,871.

(v) State Treasurer Position was abolished in January 2003. Functions now served by The Department of Finance, Commissioner, $108,388.

(w) Responsibilities shared between Director, Dept. of Natural Resources, $135,200, and Chief, Fish, $107,291, and Chief, Wildlife, $92,257.

(x) Responsibilities shared between Director, Department of Cultural Affairs, $106,080 and Division Administrator, Library and Archives, $88,740.

(y) Responsibilities shared between Administrator, Department of Conservation, $82,800; Administration, Division of Protection, same department, $92,832.

(z) Responsibilities shared between, State Auditor – $60,000; Director of Administration – $111,792 and State Tax Administrator – $95,106.

(aa) Responsibilities shared between Game & Parks Director – $96,524; Game & Parks Assistant Director – Fish & Wildlife – $74,461; Wildlife Division Administrator – $68,313.

(bb) Responsibilities shared between Commissioner, State Education Department, $170,165; Secretary of State, Department of State, $120,800.

(cc) Responsibilities shared between three Commissioners, $87,875, $87,875, and $89,875, and Director, $77,805.

(dd) Responsibilities shared between Director for Mental Retardation, $150,367 and Director of Mental Health, $131,235.

(ee) Annual salary for duties as presiding officer of the Senate.

(ff) Responsibilities shared between Secretary of State, $117,546; and Division Director, $104,656.

(gg) Responsibilities shared between Chancellor of California Community Colleges, $185,484 and California Post Secondary Education Commission $130,000.

(hh) Responsibilities for St. Thomas, $74,400; St. Croix, $76,500; St. John, $74,400.

(ii) Responsibilities shared between Commissioner of Mental Health, $136,000 and Commissioner of Mental Retardation, $136,000.

(jj) Governor Romney and Lieutenant Governor Healey waive their salaries.

(kk) Responsibilities shared between Director of Fiscal Management, $87,360 and Director of Management and Budget, $97,760.

(ll) Banking has this responsibility.

(mm) Responsibilities shared between Kevin Johnston, $159,083 and Robert Jaekle, $159,083.

(nn) James Rogers, the Interim Chancellor, only accepts the minimum amount of pay permitted through FLSA, $23,660.

(oo) Responsibilities shared between Secretary of State, $80,000; Deputy Secretary of State for Elections, $97,410; and Chief Deputy Secretary of State, $106,080.

(pp) Responsibilities shared between Director, Division of Purchasing, Dept. of the Treasury, $120,702 and Director, Division of Property and Management, Dept. of the Treasury, $114,444.

(qq) Responsibilities shared between Director, Division of Mental Health Services, Dept. of Human Services, $113,566 and Director, Division of Developmental Disabilities, Dept. of Human Services, $117,565.

(rr) Responsibilities shared between Director of Wildlife, $116,868, Director of Inland Fisheries, $110,593 and Director of Marine Fisheries, $121,212.

(ss) This is the statutory salary. The current incumbent's salary is less than this amount.

(tt) Responsibilities shared between Assistant Executive Budget Analyst, $67,908 and Director of Management and Budget, $97,760.

(uu) Responsibilities shared between Director George Schroeder, $93,429 and State Auditor Thomas Wagner, $107,469.

(vv) Responsibilities shared between Director of Budget and Finance, $102,000 and Comptroller, $102,000.

(ww) Responsibilities shared between Director of Mental Health, $123,255 and Director of Developmental Services, $123,255.

Lieutenant Governors: Significant and Visible
By Julia Hurst

Forty-five states now have an officeholder using the title "lieutenant governor." The experience and profile of the candidates for the office have grown for two years, and that trend continues in the 2006 elections. The duties of the office are also increasing: USA Today *newspaper reported in August 2005 that the office of lieutenant governor is a significant, visible and often controversial office. As the office gains attention, future trends indicate state officials will examine the most effective uses of the office.*

Introduction

In the November 2005 elections, New Jersey voters changed the state constitution creating an office of lieutenant governor. The first New Jersey lieutenant governor will be elected on a ticket with the governor in 2009. Forty-three states have a statewide elected lieutenant governor. In Tennessee and West Virginia, the Senate president is first in line of gubernatorial succession and both officeholders are statutorily empowered to use the title "lieutenant governor" in recognition of that vital function. In Arizona, Oregon, and Wyoming, the secretary of state is first in line of gubernatorial succession. In New Hampshire and Maine, the Senate presidents hold that role.

Candidate Qualifications

The office continues to draw experienced and high-profile candidates. Virginia elected Bill Bolling lieutenant governor in 2005. Lieutenant Governor-elect Bill Bolling had served 2½ terms as a state senator, where he chaired the Subcommittee on Health Care. Prior to state service, he was chairman of a County Board of Supervisors and served on regional commissions.

This background in public service is consistent with recent candidates for the office. In 2004, Utah elected Gary Herbert to the office after he served 14 years on County Commission, nine as chairman. The same year, Missourians elected Senate President Peter Kinder as lieutenant governor and Montana elected two-term state Sen. John Bohlinger.

Thirty-two states will hold elections in 2006. At this writing, at least 10 states will elect new lieutenant governors. Among the contenders are high-profile candidates with some celebrity in state government or nationally. For example, Ralph Reed is a candidate for lieutenant governor in Georgia. Named one of the top 10 political newsmakers in the nation by *Newsweek* magazine, Reed is most known for his role as head of the Christian Coalition from 1989–1997.

Likewise, Alabama and South Carolina may have showdowns of famous political families within the states through the office of lieutenant governor. In Alabama, George Wallace Jr., son of an Alabama governor, is expected to face Jim Folsom Jr., son of a two-term Alabama governor, for election to the office of lieutenant governor. In South Carolina, incumbent Lt. Gov. Andre Bauer is being challenged in a primary by Mike Campbell, son of the late and former Gov. Carroll Campbell. In addition, Michael Hollings, son of South Carolina U.S. Sen. Fritz Hollings, is fundraising to run for lieutenant governor.

Job Duties

Perhaps it was the increase in statutory duties in the South Carolina office of lieutenant governor that gained the attention of so many high-profile candidates. In July 2004, the lieutenant governor assumed direction of the State Bureau of Senior Services. The trend to increase duties in the office is traced to the beginning of 2002.

With new homeland security issues on the plate for states, and a downturn in budgets, states and territories looked to do more with less. Several lieutenant governors were tapped to lead homeland security, including those in Nebraska and Indiana. The Indiana lieutenant governor, in fact, has 42 statutory duties and more duties assigned by the governor. The Departments of Commerce and Agriculture, the Office of Tourism Development and the Office of Rural Affairs, the Counter-Terrorism and Security Council, the Housing and Community Development Authority, and the Indiana Energy Group all report to the lieutenant governor in that state. The lieutenant governor also presides over the state Senate.

States continued this trend increasing duties in 2005. In Utah, the lieutenant governor has overseen elections since 1980 when the state voted to abolish the Office of Secretary of State, giving those duties that year to the newly created position of lieutenant governor. Under current Gov. Jon Huntsman, Lt. Gov. Gary Herbert has retained his elections duties but has also been appointed to lead the administration's efforts in the issue areas of water, transportation, and rural affairs. The lieutenant governor has also been made head of the Utah Homeland Security Executive Board and he sits on the Utah Sports Commission.

Missouri and Montana, like Utah, elected new lieutenant governors who took office in 2005. Missouri Lt. Gov. Peter Kinder retained the statutory duty as "Elder Advocate" for the state and he presides over the state Senate. He also retained the office's membership on the Missouri Tourism Commission, where he was subsequently elected vice-chair, and he chairs the Missouri Senior Rx Commission. The lieutenant governor also serves on eight other commissions. During his 2005 tenure, the lieutenant governor also added duties, becoming chair of the Veterans Affairs Advisory Council and being named a member of the Missouri State Government Review Commission. Likewise, the Montana lieutenant governor broke barriers crossing parties to run on a team ticket with a governor of the opposite party.

"Far from being a ceremonial office, the lieutenant governor often presides as President of the Senate chairs and sits on commissions" and works on major issues, according to the State and Local Government on the Net Web site. This was true of the lieutenant governors of Louisiana and Mississippi who appeared on many national news outlets after Hurricane Katrina. Mississippi Lt. Gov. Amy Tuck is chair of the Joint Legislative Budget Commission and is leading the state's new budget writing process. Louisiana Lt. Gov. Mitch Landrieu heads tourism, a key component of the economy. He is also exhibiting statewide leadership calling on the governor and New Orleans mayor to merge rebuilding commissions and calling on all officials to support a merge of the area's various levee boards.

Higher Office

Virginia Lt. Gov. Tim Kaine won his bid for governor in November 2005, and, as of this writing, one in every five officials holding the title of "lieutenant governor" is running for higher office in 2006 or 2008. The members are running for governor, U.S. Representative, U.S. Senator, and Insurance Commissioner. Six current Congressmen were once lieutenant governor, as follows: U.S. Rep. Mike Castle of Delaware, U.S. Rep. Butch Otter of Idaho, U.S. Rep. Denny Rehberg of Montana, U.S. Rep. Madeleine Bordallo of Guam, and U.S. Senators Mike DeWine of Ohio and John Kerry of Massachusetts.

Future Trends

"Lieutenants Rise in Rank: States' second in command take on new responsibilities" said a July 24, 2005, *USA Today* headline. "Lieutenant governors, once the fifth wheels of U.S. politics, are playing an increasingly significant, visible and controversial role in state government. Their importance has been underscored six times over the past two years, as governors died or resigned." On August 7, 2005, the *Washington Post* noted, "The job (of lieutenant governor) groomed two of last year's leading Democratic presidential candidates: Sen. John Kerry and former Vermont Governor Howard Dean. It helped launch several current governors, including those of Louisiana, Utah, Indiana, Arkansas and Delaware."

With greater attention, high-profile and experienced candidates, and continually growing job duties, the office will come under renewed scrutiny. Part of that scrutiny is likely to result in more job duties as legislators come to the conclusion that the office is an excellent position from which to lead various initiatives. In addition, the nature of the office as successor to governor makes it an office eligible for any topic or issue in state or territorial government.

Legislators and the press are also likely to examine the structure of the office in regard to how to ensure its most effective functioning for the state. Twenty-four lieutenant governors are elected on a team ticket with the governor while 18 are elected statewide separately from the governor. Separate elections can result in the governor and lieutenant governor being of opposite parties. Both methods have strengths. For teams, a strong partnership with the governor is likely to continue while governing. A lieutenant governor may have a role in the budget process, a voice in vetoes, or may lead key policy. If elected separately, the lieutenant governor has the independent strength of statewide election to lead on key issues, sometimes providing an alternate view.

At this writing, consideration of changing the method of election from separate to team was highlighted in Pennsylvania, Rhode Island and South Carolina. In Pennsylvania, legislation passed the House and is pending in the Senate. In South Carolina, at least one candidate for the office in 2006 as part of their platform is endorsing that future elections be team elections.

The conclusion is that the office of lieutenant governor is growing in power and prominence. The candidates seeking the office generally have significant backgrounds. Those in the office are seeking higher office in growing numbers and are succeeding in same. Lieutenant governors received significant press attention in 2005 both in the course of their duties and for the office. These trends are likely to continue.

About the Author

Julia Hurst is executive director of the National Lieutenant Governors Association. Hurst's nearly 15 years of state government experience include time as chief operating officer of The Council of State Governments, four sessions as a legislative chief of staff, and time as a multistate lobbyist.

Table 4.12
THE LIEUTENANT GOVERNORS, 2006

State or other jurisdiction	Name and party	Method of selection	Length of regular term in years	Date of first service	Present term ends	Number of previous terms	Maximum consecutive terms allowed by constitution
Alabama	Lucy Baxley (D)	CE	4	1/03	1/07	. . .	2
Alaska	Loren Leman (R)	CE	4	12/02	12/06	. . .	2
Arizona	....(a)..						
Arkansas....................	Winthrop Rockefeller (R)	CE	4	1/96 (b)	1/07	1.5 (b)	2
California	Cruz Bustamante (D)	CE	4	1/98	1/06	1	2
Colorado	Jane E. Norton (R)	CE	4	1/03	1/07	. . .	2
Connecticut	Kevin Sullivan (D)	CE	4	7/04 (g)	1/07	. . .	. . .
Delaware...................	John Carney (D)	CE	4	1/01	1/09	. . .	2
Florida	Toni Jennings (R)	CE	4	3/03	1/07	. . .	2
Georgia	Mark Taylor (D)	CE	4	1/99	1/07	1	. . .
Hawaii......................	James Aiona (R)	CE	4	12/02	12/06	. . .	2
Idaho........................	Jim Risch (R) (i)	CE	4	1/03	1/07	. . .	. . .
Illinois......................	Patrick Quinn (D)	CE	4	1/03	1/07	. . .	. . .
Indiana......................	Becky Skillman (R)	CE	4	1/05	1/09	. . .	2
Iowa	Sally Pederson (D)	CE	4	1/99	1/07	1	. . .
Kansas	John E. Moore (D)	CE	4	1/03	1/07	. . .	. . .
Kentucky	Stephen Pence (R)	CE	4	12/03	12/07	. . .	2
Louisiana	Mitch Landrieu (D)	CE	4	1/04	1/08	. . .	. . .
Maine	....(a)..						
Maryland	Michael Steele (R)	CE	4	1/03	1/07	. . .	2
Massachusetts............	Kerry Healey (R)	CE	4	1/03	1/07	. . .	. . .
Michigan...................	John D. Cherry (D)	CE	4	1/03	1/07	. . .	2
Minnesota	Carol Molnau (R)	CE	4	1/03	1/07	. . .	. . .
Mississippi................	Amy Tuck (R)	CE	4	1/00	1/08	1	2
Missouri....................	Peter Kinder (R)	CE	4	1/05	1/09	. . .	. . .
Montana	John Bohlinger (R)	CE	4	1/05	1/09	. . .	2 (c)
Nebraska...................	Rick Sheehy (R)	CE	4	1/05 (e)	1/07	. . .	2
Nevada	Lorraine Hunt (R)	CE	4	1/99	1/07	1	2
New Hampshire........	....(a)..						
New Jersey................	Beginning with the November 3, 2009 general election this office will be filled.						
New Mexico	Diane Denish (D)	CE	4	1/03	1/07	. . .	2
New York	Mary Donohue (R)	CE	4	1/99	1/07	1	. . .
North Carolina	Beverly Purdue (D)	CE	4	1/01	1/09	1	2
North Dakota.............	Jack Dalrymple (R)	CE	4	12/00	12/08	. . .	. . .
Ohio	Bruce Johnson (R)	SE	4	1/03	1/07	. . .	2
Oklahoma	Mary Fallin (R)	CE	4	1/95	1/07	2	. . .
Oregon	....(a)..						
Pennsylvania	Catherine Baker Knoll (D)	CE	4	1/03	1/07	. . .	2
Rhode Island	Charles J. Fogarty (D)	SE	4	1/99	1/07	1	2
South Carolina	R. Andre Bauer (R)	CE	4	1/03	1/07	. . .	2
South Dakota.............	Dennis Daugaard (R)	CE	4	1/03	1/07	. . .	2
Tennessee..................	....(a)..						
Texas	David Dewhurst (R)	CE	4	1/03	1/07	. . .	. . .
Utah	Gary Herbert (R)	CE	4	1/05	1/09	. . .	. . .
Vermont	Brian Dubie (R)	CE	2	1/03	1/07	1	. . .
Virginia.....................	William T. Bolling (R)	CE	4	1/06	1/10	. . .	2
Washington................	Brad Owen (D)	CE	4	1/97	1/09	2	. . .
West Virginia (d).......	Earl Ray Tomblin (D)	(d)	2	1/95	1/07	6	. . .
Wisconsin..................	Barbara Lawton (D)	CE	4	1/03	1/07	. . .	. . .
Wyoming...................	....(a)..						
American Samoa.......	Ipulasi Aitofele Sunia (D)	CE	4	4/03 (f)	1/09	(f)	2
Guam	Kaleo Moylan (R)	CE	4	1/03	1/07	. . .	2
No. Mariana Islands...	Timothy Villagomez (h)	CE	4	1/06	1/10	. . .	2
Puerto Rico...............	....(a)..						
U.S. Virgin Islands	Vargrave Richards (D)	SE	4	1/03	1/07	. . .	2

See footnotes at end of table.

THE LIEUTENANT GOVERNORS, 2006 — Continued

Sources: The Council of State Governments and the National Lieutenant Governors Association, January 2006.

Key:

CE — Constitutional, elected by public

. . . — Not applicable

SE — Statutory, elected by public

(a) No lieutenant governor. In Tennessee, the Speaker of the Senate John Wilder (D), elected from Senate membership, has statutory title of "lieutenant governor."

(b) Elected in November 1996 in a special election when Mike Huckabee assumed the office of governor after Governor Jim Guy Tucker's resignation on July 15, 1996.

(c) Eligible for eight out of 16 years.

(d) In West Virginia, the President of the Senate and the Lieutenant Governor are one in the same. The legislature provided in statute the title of Lieutenant Governor upon the Senate President. The Senate President serves two-year terms, elected by the Senate on the first day of the first session of each two-year legislative term.

(e) Lt. Governor Sheehy was appointed to the position of Lieutenant Governor January 24, 2005 by Governor Heineman.

(f) Lt. Governor Sunia was appointed to the position of Lieutenant Governor in April 2003 by Governor Togiola Tulafono.

(g) Senate President pro Tempore Sullivan took office after Lieutenant Governor Rell was sworn in as governor on July 1, 2004 after Governor John Rowland resigned.

(h) Covenant Party.

(i) When this publication went to press, Governor Kempthorne had been appointed Secretary of the Interior. Confirmation hearings are scheduled to begin May 2006. If Kempthorne is confirmed, Lt. Gov. Jim Risch will fill the office until the inauguration in January 2007.

Table 4.13
LIEUTENANT GOVERNORS: QUALIFICATIONS AND TERMS

State or other jurisdiction	Minimum age	State citizen (years)	U.S. citizen (years) (a)	State resident (years) (b)	Qualified voter (years)	Length of term (years)	Maximum consecutive terms allowed
Alabama	30	7	10	7	★	4	2
Alaska	30	...	7	7	★	4	2
Arizona				(c)			
Arkansas	30	7	★	7	...	4	2
California	18	★	★	5	★	4	2
Colorado	30	...	★	2	★	4	2
Connecticut	...	★	★	★	★	4	...
Delaware	30	★	12	16	★	4	2
Florida	30	★	★	7	★	4	2
Georgia	30	★	15	6	★	4	...
Hawaii	30	5	★	5	★	4	2
Idaho	30	...	★	2	...	4	...
Illinois	25	...	★	3	...	4	...
Indiana	30	5	5	5	...	4	2
Iowa	30	...	2	2	...	4	...
Kansas	...	...	...	...	...	4	...
Kentucky	30	6	...	6	...	4	2
Louisiana	25	5	5	5	...	4	...
Maine				(c)			
Maryland	30	...	(d)	5	5	4	2
Massachusetts	...	★	★	★	★	4	...
Michigan	30	(h)	(h)	4	4	4	2
Minnesota	25	★	★	1	...	4	...
Mississippi	30	★	20	5	★	4	2
Missouri	30	...	15	10	★	4	...
Montana	25	2	★	2	★	4	2 (e)
Nebraska	30	5	5	5	...	4	2
Nevada	25	2	★	2	★	4	2
New Hampshire				(c)			
New Jersey				(c)			
New Mexico	30	★	★	5	★	4	2
New York	30	★	★	5	★	4	...
North Carolina	30	...	5	2	★	4	2
North Dakota	30	...	★	5	★	4	...
Ohio	18	...	★	★	★	4	2
Oklahoma	31	★	★	★	10	4	...
Oregon				(c)			
Pennsylvania	30	★	★	7	★	4	2
Rhode Island	18	★	★	★	30 days	4	2
South Carolina	30	5	5	5	★	4	2
South Dakota	21	...	★	2	...	4	2
Tennessee				(c)			
Texas	30	...	★	5	...	4	...
Utah	30	5	★	5	★	4	...
Vermont	...	...	...	4	...	2	...
Virginia	30	...	★	5	5	4	...
Washington	18	★	★	★	★	4	...
West Virginia (f)	25	1	1	1	★	2	...
Wisconsin	18	★	★	★	★	4	...
Wyoming				(c)			
American Samoa	35	(g)	★	5	★	4	2
Guam	30	...	5	5	★	4	2
No. Mariana Islands	35	...	★	10	★	4	...
Puerto Rico				(c)			
U.S. Virgin Islands	30	...	5	5	5	4	2

Sources: The Council of State Government's survey, January 2006 and state constitutions, statutes and secretaries of state Web sites, January 2005.

Note: This table includes constitutional and statutory qualifications.

Key:

★ — Formal provision; number of years not specified.

... — No formal provision.

(a) In some states you must be a U.S. citizen to be an elector, and must be an elector to run.

(b) In some states you must be a state resident to be an elector, and must be an elector to run.

(c) No lieutenant governor. In Tennessee, the speaker of the Senate, elected from Senate membership, has statutory title of "lieutenant governor."

(d) *Crosse v. Board of Supervisors of Elections* 243 Md. 555, 221A.2d431 (1966)—opinion rendered indicated that U.S. citizenship was, by necessity, a requirement for office.

(e) Eligible for eight out of 16 years.

(f) In West Virginia, the President of the Senate and the Lieutenant Governor are one in the same. The legislature provided in statute the title of Lieutenant Governor upon the Senate President. The Senate President serves two-year terms, elected by the Senate on the first day of the first session of each two-year legislative term.

(g) Must be a U.S. national.

(h) In order to be a qualified voter in the state (which is a requirement for office) one must be a U.S. Citizen and a resident of the State of Michigan.

Table 4.14
LIEUTENANT GOVERNORS: POWERS AND DUTIES

State or other jurisdiction	Presides over Senate	Appoints committees	Breaks roll-call ties	Assigns bills	Authority for governor to assign duties	Member of governor's cabinet or advisory body	Serves as acting governor when governor out of state
Alabama	★	★(p)	★	★(p)	...	...	...
Alaska (q)	...	...	...	...	★	★	...
Arizona	......................(b)......................						
Arkansas	★	...	★	...	...	...	★
California	...	...	★	...	...	...	★
Colorado	...	...	...	...	★	★	★
Connecticut	★	...	★	...	★	★	★
Delaware	★	...	★	...	...	...	★
Florida	...	...	...	...	★	...	★
Georgia	★	...	...	...	★	...	...
Hawaii (r)	...	...	...	...	★	...	★
Idaho	★	...	★	★	★	...	★
Illinois	...	...	...	...	★	★	...
Indiana	★	...	★	...	...	★	...
Iowa	...	(a)	...	...	★	(g)	(f)
Kansas	...	...	...	...	...	★	...
Kentucky	...	...	...	...	★	★	...
Louisiana	...	...	...	...	★	★	★
Maine	......................(c)......................						
Maryland	...	...	...	...	★	★	★
Massachusetts	...	★	★	...	★	★	★
Michigan	★	...	★	...	★	★	★
Minnesota	...	...	...	...	★	★	★
Mississippi	★	★	★	★	...	...	★
Missouri	★	...	★	...	★	★	★
Montana	...	...	...	...	★	★	★
Nebraska	★(d)	...	★	...	★	...	★
Nevada	★	...	★(e)	...	...	...	★
New Hampshire	......................(c)......................						
New Jersey	......................(c)......................						
New Mexico	★	...	★	...	...	★	★
New York	★	...	★(o)	...	★	★	★
North Carolina	★	...	★	...	...	...	★
North Dakota	★	...	★	...	...	★	★
Ohio	...	...	...	...	★	★	...
Oklahoma	★(n)	...	★	...	★	★	★
Oregon	......................(b)......................						
Pennsylvania	★	...	★	...	...	...	...
Rhode Island (j)	...	...	...	...	...	...	...
South Carolina	★	...	★	★	★	...	(i)
South Dakota	★	(h)	★	★	★	(m)	...
Tennessee	......................(c)......................						
Texas	★	★	★	★	...	...	★
Utah	...	...	...	...	★	★	...
Vermont	★	★(a)	★	...	...	...	★
Virginia	★	...	★	...	...	...	...
Washington	★	★	★	...	...	...	★
West Virginia (l)	★	★	...	★	...	...	...
Wisconsin	...	...	...	...	★	...	...
Wyoming	......................(b)......................						
American Samoa	...	...	...	...	★	★	★
Guam	(d)	...	...	...	★	★	★
No. Mariana Islands	...	...	...	...	★	(k)	★
Puerto Rico	......................(b)......................						
U.S. Virgin Islands	...	...	...	...	★(g)	★	★

See footnotes at end of table.

LIEUTENANT GOVERNORS: POWERS AND DUTIES — Continued

Sources: The Council of State Governments' survey, January 2006 and state constitutions and statutes.

Key:

★ — Provision for responsibility.

. . . — No provision for responsibility.

(a) Appoints all standing committees. Iowa—appoints some special committees; Vermont—appoints all committees as one of three members of Senate Committee on Committees.

(b) No lieutenant governor; secretary of state is next in line of succession to governorship.

(c) No lieutenant governor; senate president or speaker is next in line of succession to governorship. In Tennessee, speaker of the senate bears the additional statutory title of "lieutenant governor."

(d) Unicameral legislative body. In Guam, that body elects own presiding officer.

(e) Except on final passage of bills and joint resolutions.

(f) Only in emergency situations.

(g) Presides over cabinet meetings in absence of governor.

(h) Conference committees.

(i) As directed by the governor.

(j) Under state law, responsible for overseeing a number of policy areas in state government through councils and committees, which he chairs.

(k) The Lieutenant Governor is an automatic member of the Governor's cabinet.

(l) In West Virginia, the President of the Senate and the Lieutenant Governor are one in the same. The legislature provided in statute the title of Lieutenant Governor upon the Senate President. The Senate President serves two-year terms, elected by the Senate on the first day of the first session of each two-year legislative term.

(m) If assigned.

(n) Only for joint sessions.

(o) With respect to procedural matters, not legislation.

(p) The Lieutenant Governor serves on the Assignment Committee (five members) and in such capacity has input in the appointment of committees and assigning of bills.

(q) The Lieutenant Governor oversees the Division of Elections; signs and files administrative regulations; publishes Administrative Code and Online Public Notice System; regulates use of State Seal; presides during the organization of first session of each legislature; certifies ballot measures and writes ballot summaries; authenticates supplements to Alaska Statutes; chairs the Alaska Historical Commission; serves on the Alaska Workforce Board; distributes legislative joint resolutions.

(r) Serves as Secretary of State.

Secretaries of State: Trends and Issues

By George A. Munro

Secretaries of state make decisions every day that affect the lives of their constituents. While the decisions may sometimes seem small, they often affect how business is conducted or how government officials are selected. This piece highlights the varying roles of the secretaries of state and looks at issues that secretaries may soon be addressing, and how their decisions will affect their constituents.

Overview

Since 2000, secretaries of state have been widely recognized for supervising elections, but they are responsible for a whole host of duties—each of them vital to the successful functioning of state government. While some might think of them as quiet partners in state government, the services they provide, from conducting elections to protecting their constituents from fraud, affect all citizens every day. The duties and responsibilities performed by a secretary vary greatly from state to state. One of the only constants in the position is that the officeholder possesses specialized skills and knowledge, and a willingness to modify policies and procedures as technology continues to advance.

The differences in the position begin with how a secretary of state is selected to serve. Thirty-nine secretaries are elected, nine are appointed by their state's governor, and three are chosen by their state legislature. In most states, the secretary of state is third in line to assume the office of governor upon death or resignation of the incumbent, after the lieutenant governor. Three states do not have a secretary of state. In those states, the lieutenant governor assumes responsibilities that would otherwise be handled by a secretary.[1]

The secretaries are as diverse as their job descriptions. Because of the variety of duties and responsibilities of secretaries of state, their unique backgrounds and interests often help them achieve success in public service.

At 33, Kentucky Secretary of State Trey Grayson, a Harvard graduate, is currently the youngest secretary of state in the country.[2] The youngest secretary to date was Vermont's Jim Douglas, who was elected in 1980 at age 29.[3] New Mexico Secretary of State Rebecca Vigil-Giron is the highest ranking elected Latino woman state official in the United States and was the first Latino president of the National Association of Secretaries of State (NASS) in 2004.[4]

Missouri's Secretary of State Robin Carnahan is continuing her family's tradition of public service.

Her father served as Missouri's governor, her mother served as Missouri's United States senator and her grandfather served as a U.S. ambassador.[5] The Carnahan family isn't the only Missouri family with a rich history in politics. Missouri Gov. Matt Blunt served as secretary of that state before being elected governor. Blunt's father, Roy Blunt, is a United States congressman and former Missouri secretary of state.

Many secretaries served in public office for long periods of time before they took that office. Washington Secretary of State and current NASS President Sam Reed served five terms as Thurston County auditor before being elected secretary of state.[6] Prior to his election, Wyoming Secretary of State Joe Meyer served as Wyoming's attorney general for almost 10 years.[7]

Not every secretary of state started their career in government. Alabama Secretary of State Nancy Worley and Iowa Secretary of State Chet Culver were both high school teachers before being elected to the office. Cathy Cox, the first woman to serve as Georgia's secretary of state, began her career as a newspaper reporter.[8] Prior to serving in public office, Oregon Secretary of State Bill Bradbury worked as a television news reporter, director and producer.[9]

Several secretaries of state have experienced considerable career longevity. Thirty-nine secretaries have served terms of 20 or more years, including New Hampshire's current Secretary of State William Gardner, who was first elected in 1976. The longest-serving secretary of state was Thad Eure of North Carolina, who served for 52 years from 1936 to 1989.[10]

Many secretaries have gone on to higher office. United States Attorney General Alberto Gonzales served as Texas' 100th secretary of state from 1997 to 1999. Current governors Matt Blunt of Missouri, Jim Douglas of Vermont and Bob Taft of Ohio all served as secretary of state before being elected governor. There are currently seven members of Congress who served as secretaries of state: Sen. Evan Bayh, D-Ind., Rep. Roy Blunt, R-Mo., Rep. Sherrod Brown, D-Ohio, Rep. Tom Cole, R-Okla., Rep.

Katherine Harris, R-Fla., Rep. Jim Langevin, D-R.I., and Rep. Candice Miller, R-Mich. In NASS' history, 28 secretaries have become governors, and six have been elected to the U.S. Senate.[11]

Duties and Responsibilities

Before the 2000 election, secretaries of state were relatively low-profile statewide public officials. That changed in 2000, when all eyes focused on the presidential election and how votes were counted in Florida. It was during the aftermath of that election that the general public learned much more about the role of a secretary of state.

In 2002, NASS conducted its Office and Duties Survey (updated in 2004) to further educate the public about the role its members play in their states. The results demonstrated that secretaries across the country play a variety of roles in their states' governments, which include administering elections, promoting civic engagement, managing and improving the relationship between corporations and state government and record-keeping, as well as various other duties.

Elections

The secretaries of state are probably best known for running elections. Thirty-nine secretaries of state serve as chief state election officials. The Help America Vote Act (HAVA), which passed in 2002, gave these secretaries additional election responsibilities, including developing and maintaining statewide voter registration databases, establishing provisional balloting processes, and modernizing voting equipment. Secretaries with election duties are also responsible for supplying voter registration materials, certifying elections, authorizing ballot measures, and tracking campaign contributions and expenditures. Some secretaries are also in charge of their states' voter outreach efforts, which may include public service campaigns and youth outreach.[12]

Registration, Filing and Licensing

General business duties are the most common area of responsibility among NASS members. Forty-nine of the 50 secretaries handle business-related filings; 42 register trademarks; 39 register corporations; 10 handle securities regulation; 24 register charitable organizations; and 45 process professional licensing applications.[13] In some states, the secretary of state even serves as the head of the state boxing commission. With technology constantly advancing, secretaries with business registration, filing and licensing duties continue to look for new ways to make it easier for their citizens to complete business transactions with the state.

Custodial and Publishing Duties

Forty secretaries serve as their states' chief notaries.[14] These secretaries are exploring ways to make the notarization process easier, including electronic notarization. Many secretaries also oversee their states' archives, the publication of their agencies' rules and regulations, Uniform Commercial Code filings, and state land record and charters. Twenty-two secretaries are in charge of publishing a directory of their states' elected officials; 19 publish their states' blue books; and 26 publish their states' constitutions.[15]

Additional Duties

While the majority of secretaries are responsible for the duties listed above, there are some important responsibilities that only a few secretaries have. The secretaries of state in Illinois, Maine and Michigan are in charge of their states' Departments of Motor Vehicles. Some secretaries are responsible for convening their state legislatures.[16] Six secretaries oversee their states' libraries and four are charged with maintaining their states' Capitol grounds.[17]

The National Association of Secretaries of State

All the secretaries are members of the National Association of Secretaries of State. As the oldest professional, nonpartisan organization of public officials in the United States, NASS serves as a forum for the exchange of information among secretaries of state, members of Congress, federal and state government agencies, special interest groups and the general public. NASS hosts biannual conferences that allow secretaries to share ideas and discuss common issues that affect them. Throughout the year, NASS works with its members to collect data on important issues that affect the secretaries and represents them around the country at various forums, conferences and symposiums.

Trends for the Future

Improving the Election Process

In 2002, Congress passed the Help America Vote Act (HAVA), which gave states until Jan. 1, 2006, to comply with key federal election mandates. HAVA authorized $3.9 billion for states to replace outdated voting equipment and improve their overall election administration. Many states used a portion of this money to replace punch card and lever voting machines with equipment that met new federal requirements, such as notifying voters if they overvote, producing a permanent paper record with a manual audit capability, and accessibility. HAVA also requires states to implement a statewide voter registration database that includes the name and registration information for every voter in the state, and assigns a unique identifier to each one. The implementation of these databases will allow every state and local election official to immediately access the information from anywhere in the state. Finally, HAVA guarantees that anyone who says they are eligible to vote will be given a ballot on Election Day.

The federal elections of 2006 will allow states to showcase the election improvements they have worked so hard to implement. In a 2005 NASS survey on the HAVA implementation process, 95 percent of the respondents said their state would be fully compliant with HAVA mandates before their states' first federal elections in 2006. [18]

Making Every Vote Count

NASS continues to support the restructuring of the presidential primary/caucus calendar and in 1999 introduced the NASS Presidential Primary/Caucus Plan. This plan outlines a system of rotating regional primaries and caucuses designed to help avoid the problematic front-loading phenomenon and give every state an opportunity to take center stage.

Under the NASS Rotating Regional Primary/Caucus Plan, primaries and caucuses would be held the first Tuesday of the months of February, March, April and May. The country would be divided into regions and the regions would rotate the order in which they voted every presidential election. The NASS plan also maintains the first caucus spot for Iowa and the first primary for New Hampshire.

The NASS plan provides a fair opportunity for every vote to count. It has been endorsed by the Carter-Baker Commission on Federal Election Reform. NASS must win support of both the Democratic and Republican political parties and secure its passage by all 50 state legislatures before the plan can take effect.

Encouraging Civic Engagement

NASS and its members are active in the effort to get more young people registered to vote and to the polls to cast their votes. In 1998, NASS established the New Millennium Young Voters Project to identify the new and creative ways in which states are reaching out to young Americans. Ninety-eight percent of states surveyed by NASS have developed some sort of youth outreach program.[19] These states use various methods, including partnering with national voter outreach groups, educating students of all grade levels of the importance of civic engagement, and hiring poll workers under age 18.

With the upcoming federal election in 2006 and the presidential election in 2008, NASS, its members and its partner organizations will continue working hard to educate young people on the importance of civic engagement. In 2006, NASS will release its annual Civic Vacation Guide, which gives parents ideas for family vacations around the country that can be both fun and educational for their children. NASS also plans to develop a poll worker recruitment kit to help secretaries recruit poll workers ages 18 to 24.

Connecting Businesses with Their Government

According to the NASS E-Gov Primer for Secretaries of State, more states are allowing transactions previously handled in person to be conducted online. Two-thirds of the survey respondents allow businesses to make their UCC filings online. While every state's online progress is different, all the states that responded to the survey are constantly working to improve their technology to benefit their citizens, while keeping the process secure.

More states are passing some form of the Uniform Electronic Transactions Act, which describes what an electronic signature is and gives electronic contracts and signatures the same legal validity as their paper counterparts. The secretaries responsible for notaries public must decide how to implement the law. Colorado and Arizona have already passed laws that define how electronic notarization can be used. Other states are in the process of drafting similar legislation.

Because of the rapid advancements in electronic notarization, NASS passed a resolution in July 2005 which "affirms the role of the secretary of state or other state notary commissioning entity as the sole authority to establish standards enabling electronic notarizations that will protect signature credibility, avoid identity fraud and provide accountability to the public in order to promote secure electronic commerce."[20]

Continuing to Develop International Relations

Over the past quarter century, countries around the world have opened up their borders and more states conduct a significant amount of international trade. As relationships have developed between the 50 states and countries around the world, the secretaries have had a significant role in the process. In some states, secretaries serve as their states' lead protocol officers and host visiting delegations of dignitaries from around the world. Secretaries also often lead delegations of business leaders from their state overseas to promote trade and travel.

In 2005, as part of his role as chief protocol officer for Nebraska, Secretary of State John Gale hosted an international relations conference to highlight the state's international appeal. Forty-two dignitaries from 33 countries, including consul generals, businesspeople and academics, attended the conference. State officials have decided to make the conference an annual one because of the success of the initial one.

The District of Columbia has a unique program that takes advantage of the numerous embassies located there. The city's Adopt-an-Embassy Program matches a sixth grade class with one of 42 participating foreign embassies. The students learn about the history and culture of the countries they adopt and present the information they have learned to the countries' ambassadors at the end of the program. In the process, they also gain a greater understanding of the importance of international relations.

Summary

Every secretary of state's office has many unique features, from the method used to select the secretary to the duties and responsibilities of the office. Even with these many differences, the commitment to service is a constant in every office. The secretaries are sworn to perform their duties in a manner that serves their constituents while maintaining the integrity and reliability of the office. At the same time, a successful secretary of state is always looking for new ways to improve services offered by their office. Their methods may be different, but their goal is always the same—to satisfy the needs of their constituents.

Notes

[1] National Association of Secretaries of State. "Fact Sheet: Secretaries of State Office and Duties," August 5, 2005, *http://www.nass.org/Office%20and%20Duties.pdf*, (November 3, 2005).

[2] Kentucky Secretary of State. "Biography," November 16, 2005, *http://sos.ky.gov/secdesk/biography.htm*, (November 18, 2005).

[3] Vermont Governor. "About the Governor," 2003, *http://www.vermont.gov/governor/*, (December 15, 2005).

[4] New Mexico Secretary of State. "Rebecca Vigil-Giron," *http://www.sos.state.nm.us/bio.htm*, (November 18, 2005).

[5] Missouri Secretary of State. "Robin Carnahan's Biography," *http://www.sos.mo.gov/sosbio.asp*, (November 18, 2005).

[6] Washington Secretary of State. "About Sam Reed," *http://www.secstate.wa.gov/office/sam_reed.aspx*, (November 18, 2005).

[7] Wyoming Secretary of State. "Biography of Secretary of State Joe Meyer," July 5, 2005, *http://soswy.state.wy.us/bio.htm*, (November 18, 2005).

[8] Secretary of State Cathy Cox. "About Cathy," *http://www.sos.state.ga.us/misc/cathybio.htm*, (November 18, 2005).

[9] Oregon Secretary of State. "About Bill Bradbury," *http://www.sos.state.or.us/executive/who/bill.htm*, (November 18, 2005).

[10] Bill Gardner. "Statistics about Secretaries of State," *Pillars of Public Service* (Hobblebush Books, 2004), 205–206.

[11] Bill Gardner. "Statistics about Secretaries of State," *Pillars of Public Service* (Hobblebush Books, 2004), 213–214.

[12] National Association of Secretaries of State. "General Election Responsibilities," March 11, 2004, *http://www.nass.org/sos/duties_survey/table3.1_generalelection.pdf*, (November 3, 2005).

[13] National Association of Secretaries of State. "General Business Duties," March 11, 2004, *http://www.nass.org/sos/duties_survey/table4.1_generalbiz.pdf*, (November 3, 2005).

[14] National Association of Secretaries of State. "Registration of Charitable Organizations, Notaries Public, Trademarks, Securities & Other Entities," March 11, 2004, *http://www.nass.org/sos/duties_survey/table4.3_regofcharities.notaries.other.pdf*, (November 3, 2005).

[15] National Association of Secretaries of State. "Election Related Publishing Duties," March 11, 2004, *http://www.nass.org/sos/duties_survey/table5.2_electionpublish.pdf*, (November 3, 2005).

[16] National Association of Secretaries of State. "General Legislative Duties," March 11, 2004, *http://www.nass.org/sos/duties_survey/table7.1_genlegislative.pdf*, (November 3, 2005).

[17] National Association of Secretaries of State. "Additional Duties and Responsibilities," March 11, 2004, *http://www.nass.org/sos/duties_survey/table8.1_additional.duties.pdf*, (November 3, 2005).

[18] National Association of Secretaries of State. "Implementing HAVA," December 21, 2005, *http://www.nass.org/Implementing%20HAVA.pdf*, (December 21, 2005).

[19] National Association of Secretaries of State. "New Millennium State Practices Survey," August 2005, *http://www.stateofthevote.org/New%20Mill%20Survey%20Update.pdf*, (November 3, 2005).

[20] National Association of Secretaries of State. "Electronic Notarization Resolution," July 24, 2005, *http://www.nass.org/Electronic%20Notarization%20Resolution.pdf*, (November 3, 2005).

About the Author

George A. Munro is the press secretary for the National Association of Secretaries of State. During his career, he has worked in the political, business, government and non-profit sectors. He has also volunteered in numerous voter outreach efforts, coordinating events for different organizations including Rock the Vote and WWE's Smackdown Your Vote.

Table 4.15
THE SECRETARIES OF STATE, 2006

State or other jurisdiction	Name and party	Method of selection	Length of regular term in years	Date of first service	Present term ends	Number of previous terms	Maximum consecutive terms allowed by constitution
Alabama	Nancy Worley (D)	E	4	1/03	1/07	0	2
Alaska	. . . . (a)						
Arizona	Jan Brewer (R)	E	4	1/03	1/07	0	2
Arkansas	Charlie Daniels (D)	E	4	1/03	1/07	0	2
California	Bruce McPherson (R)	E (i)	4	3/05 (i)	1/07	0	2
Colorado	Gigi Dennis (R)	E	4	8/05 (b)	1/07	0 (b)	2
Connecticut	Susan Bysiewicz (D)	E	4	1/99	1/07	1	. . .
Delaware	Harriet Smith Windsor (D)	A	. . .	1/01	. . .	0	. . .
Florida	Sue Cobb (R)	A	. . .	11/05 (j)	. . .	0	. . .
Georgia	Cathy Cox (D)	E	4	1/99	1/07	1	. . .
Hawaii	. . . . (a)						
Idaho	Ben Ysursa (R)	E	4	1/03	1/07	0	. . .
Illinois	Jesse White (D)	E	4	1/99	1/07	1	. . .
Indiana	Todd Rokita (R)	E	4	1/03	1/07	0	2
Iowa	Chet Culver (D)	E	4	1/99	1/07	1	. . .
Kansas	Ron Thornburgh (R)	E	4	1/95	1/07	2	. . .
Kentucky	Trey Grayson (R)	E	4	12/03	12/07	0	2
Louisiana	Al Ater (R)	E (k)	4	7/05	1/08 (k)	4	. . .
Maine	Matthew Dunlap (D)	L	2	1/05	1/07	0	. . .
Maryland	Mary Kane (R)	A	. . .	8/05	. . .	0	. . .
Massachusetts	William Francis Galvin (D)	E	4	1/95	1/07	2	. . .
Michigan	Terri Lynn Land (R)	E	4	1/03	1/07	0	2
Minnesota	Mary Kiffmeyer (R)	E	4	1/99	1/07	1	. . .
Mississippi	Eric Clark (D)	E	4	1/96	1/08	2	. . .
Missouri	Robin Carnahan (D)	E	4	1/05	1/09	0	. . .
Montana	Brad Johnson (R)	E	4	1/05	1/09	0	(c)
Nebraska	John Gale (R)	E	4	12/00 (d)	1/07	(d)	. . .
Nevada	Dean Heller (R)	E	4	1/95	1/07	2	2 (f)
New Hampshire	William Gardner (D)	L	2	12/76	12/06	14	. . .
New Jersey	Nina Mitchell Wells	A	. . .	1/06	1/10	0	. . .
New Mexico	Rebecca Vigil-Giron (D)	E	4	1/87 (g)	1/07	2	2
New York	Frank P. Milano (l)	A	. . .	(l)	(l)	0	. . .
North Carolina	Elaine Marshall (D)	E	4	1/97	1/09	2	. . .
North Dakota	Alvin Jaeger (R)	E	4 (h)	1/93	1/07 (h)	2	. . .
Ohio	J. Kenneth Blackwell (R)	E	4	1/99	1/07	1	2
Oklahoma	M. Susan Savage (D)	A	4	1/03	1/07	0	. . .
Oregon	Bill Bradbury (D)	E	4	1/99 (e)	1/09	(e)	2
Pennsylvania	Pedro A. Cortes (D)	A	. . .	5/03	. . .	0	. . .
Rhode Island	Matthew Brown (D)	E	4	1/03	1/07	0	2
South Carolina	Mark Hammond (R)	E	4	1/03	1/07	0	. . .
South Dakota	Chris Nelson (R)	E	4	1/03	1/07	0	2
Tennessee	Riley Darnell (D)	L	4	1/93	1/09	3	. . .
Texas	Roger Williams (R)	A	. . .	2/05	. . .	0	. . .
Utah	. . . . (a)						
Vermont	Deb Markowitz (D)	E	2	1/99	1/07	3	. . .
Virginia	Katherine K. Hanley (D)	A	. . .	3/06	. . .	0	. . .
Washington	Sam Reed (R)	E	4	1/01	1/09	1	. . .
West Virginia	Betty Ireland (R)	E	4	1/05	1/09	0	. . .
Wisconsin	Douglas LaFollette (D)	E	4	1/99	1/07	1	. . .
Wyoming	Joe Meyer (R)	E	4	1/99	1/07	1	. . .
American Samoa	. . . . (a)						
Guam	. . . . (a)						
No. Mariana Islands	. . . . (a)						
Puerto Rico	Fernando J. Bonilla	A	. . .	N.A.	. . .	. . .	. . .
U.S. Virgin Islands	. . . . (a)						

See footnotes at end of table.

THE SECRETARIES OF STATE, 2006—Continued

Source: The Council of State Governments' survey, December 2005.
Key:
E — Elected by voters
L — Elected by legislature
A — Appointed by governor
. . . — No provision for
(a) No secretary of state.
(b) Appointed August 29, 2005, to finish Secretary Donetta Davidson's term after she resigned to accept a federal appointment.
(c) Eligible for eight out of 16 years.
(d) Secretary Gale was appointed by Gov. Mike Johanns in December 2000 upon the resignation of Scott Moore. He was elected to a full four-year term in November 2002.
(e) Secretary Bradbury was appointed Secretary of State in November 1999 and was elected to a four-year term in November 2000 and 2004.

(f) Term limits were not effective until Secretary Heller's second term in office. His second term counts as his first.
(g) Secretary Vigil-Giron served from 1987–1991. She was elected again in 1998 and in 2002.
(h) Because of a constitutional change approved by voters in 2000, the term for the secretary elected in 2004 will be only two years. It will revert to a four-year term in 2007.
(i) Appointed in March 2005 upon the resignation of Kevin Shelley.
(j) Became acting Secretary after Glenda Hood resigned from office in November 2005.
(k) After the death of W. Fox McKeithen in July 2005, First Deputy Secretary Al Ater assumed the duties of Secretary of State. A special election will be held to fill the unexpired term on September 30, 2006, with a runoff, if necessary, scheduled for November 7, 2006. The regular term of office was until October 20, 2007.
(l) Randy Daniels resigned effective September 23, 2005. As of December 2005, Frank Milano is serving as Acting Secretary of State.

Table 4.16
SECRETARIES OF STATE: QUALIFICATIONS FOR OFFICE

State or other jurisdiction	Minimum age	U.S. citizen (years) (a)	State resident (years) (b)	Qualified voter (years)	Method of selection to office
Alabama	25	7	5	★	E
Alaska	......................................(c)......................................				
Arizona	25	10	5	. . .	E
Arkansas	18	★	★	★	E
California	18	★	★	★	E
Colorado	25	★	2	. . .	E
Connecticut	18	★	★	★	E
Delaware	. . .	. . .	★	. . .	A
Florida	......................................(f)......................................				
Georgia	25	10	4	★	E
Hawaii	......................................(c)......................................				
Idaho	25	★	2	★	E
Illinois	25	★	3	. . .	E
Indiana	. . .	. . .	★	. . .	E
Iowa	18	. . .	. . .	. . .	E
Kansas	. . .	. . .	. . .	. . .	E
Kentucky	30	★	★	★	E
Louisiana	25	5	5	★	E
Maine	. . .	. . .	. . .	. . .	(e)
Maryland	. . .	. . .	. . .	. . .	A
Massachusetts	18	★	5	★	E
Michigan	18	★	★	★	E
Minnesota	21	★	★	★	E
Mississippi	25	★	5 (d)	★	E
Missouri	. . .	★	★	2	E
Montana	25	★	2	★	E
Nebraska	. . .	★	★	★	E
Nevada	25	2	2	. . .	E
New Hampshire	18	★	★	★	(e)
New Jersey	18	★	★	★	A
New Mexico	30	★	5	★	E
New York	18	★	★	. . .	A
North Carolina	21	. . .	. . .	★	E
North Dakota	25	★	5	★	E
Ohio	18	★	★	★	E
Oklahoma	31	★	10	★	A
Oregon	18	. . .	★	★	E
Pennsylvania	. . .	. . .	. . .	. . .	A
Rhode Island	18	★	30 days	★	E
South Carolina	18	★	★	★	E
South Dakota	. . .	. . .	. . .	. . .	E
Tennessee	. . .	. . .	. . .	. . .	(e)
Texas	18	★	. . .	. . .	A
Utah	......................................(c)......................................				
Vermont	. . .	★	★	★	E
Virginia	. . .	. . .	. . .	. . .	A
Washington	18	★	★	★	E
West Virginia	. . .	★	★	★	E
Wisconsin	18	★	★	★	E
Wyoming	25	★	1	★	E
American Samoa	......................................(c)......................................				
Guam	......................................(c)......................................				
No. Mariana Islands	......................................(c)......................................				
Puerto Rico	. . .	5	5	. . .	A
U.S. Virgin Islands	......................................(c)......................................				

Source: The Council of State Governments' survey of secretaries of state, December 2005.

Key:

★ — Formal provision; number of years not specified.

. . . — No formal provision.

A — Appointed by governor

E — Elected by voters

(a) In some states you must be a U.S. citizen to be an elector, and must be an elector to run.

(b) In some states you must be a state resident to be an elector, and must be an elector to run.

(c) No secretary of state.

(d) State citizenship requirement.

(e) Chosen by joint ballot of state senators and representatives. In Maine and New Hampshire, every two years. In Tennessee, every four years.

(f) As of January 1, 2003, the office of Secretary of State shall be an appointed position (appointed by the governor). It will no longer be a cabinet position, but an agency head and the Department of State shall be an agency under the governor's office.

Table 4.17
SECRETARIES OF STATE: ELECTION AND REGISTRATION DUTIES

State or other jurisdiction	Election								Registration				
	Chief election officer	Determines ballot eligibility of political parties	Receives initiative and/or referendum petition	Files certificate of nomination or election	Supplies election ballots or materials to local officials	Files candidates' expense papers	Files other campaign reports	Conducts voter education programs	Registers charitable organizations	Registers corporations (a)	Processes and/or commissions notaries public	Registers securities	Registers trade names/marks
Alabama	★	★	·	★	...	★	★	★	★	★	★	...	★
Alaska (b)	★	★	★	★	★	...	...	★	...	...	★	...	★
Arizona	★	★	★	★	...	★	★	★	...	...	★	...	★
Arkansas	★	★	★	★	...	★	★	★	★	★	★	...	★
California	★	★	★	★	...	★	★	★	...	★	★	...	★
Colorado	★	★	★	★	...	★	★	★	★	★	★	...	★
Connecticut	★	★	...	★	★	★	★	★	★	★	★	...	★
Delaware	...	...	...	(c)	...	...	(d)	...	★(e)	★	★	...	★
Florida	★	★	★	★	...	★	★	...	★	★	...	...	★
Georgia	★	★	...	★	★	★	★	★	★	★	...	★	★
Hawaii (b)	...	...	...	...	...	...	...	...	...	...	...	...	...
Idaho	★	★	★	★	★	★	★	★	...	★	★	...	★
Illinois	...	...	★	(h)	...	★	★	★	★	★	★	★	★
Indiana	★	★	...	★	★	★	★	★	★	★	★	★	★
Iowa	★	★	...	★	...	...	...	★	★	★	★	...	★
Kansas	★	★	...	★	...	★	★	★	★	★	...	...	★
Kentucky	★	★	...	★	...	...	...	★	★	★	★	...	★
Louisiana	★	...	...	...	★	...	...	...	★	★	★	★	★
Maine	★	★	★	★	★	...	...	★	...	★	★	...	★
Maryland	...	★	...	★	...	...	...	...	★	★	★	...	★
Massachusetts	★	★	★	★	★	(d)	(d)	★	...	★	★	★	★
Michigan	★	★	★	★	...	★	★	★	...	★	★	...	★
Minnesota	★	★	★	★	...	...	...	★	★	★	...	...	★
Mississippi	★	★	★	★	★	★	★	★	★	★	★	★	★
Missouri	★	★	★	★	★	...	...	★	★	★	★	★	★
Montana	★	★	★	★	★	...	...	★	★	★	★	...	★
Nebraska	★	★	★	★	★	...	...	★	★	★	★	★	★
Nevada	★	★	★	★	★	★	★	★	...	★	★	★	★
New Hampshire	★	★	...	★	★	★	★	...	★	★	★	★	★
New Jersey	...	...	...	...	...	...	...	...	...	...	...	...	...
New Mexico	★	★	★	★	★	★	★	★	...	...	★	...	★
New York	...	...	...	...	...	...	...	...	...	★	★	★	★
North Carolina	...	...	...	...	...	...	...	...	★	★	★	★	★
North Dakota	★	★	★	★	★	★	★	★	★	★	★	...	★
Ohio	★	★	★	★	★	...	...	★	...	★	★	...	★
Oklahoma	...	...	★	★(f)	...	...	...	...	★	★	★	...	★
Oregon	★	★	★	★	★	★	★	★	★	★	★	★	★
Pennsylvania	★	★	...	★	...	★	★	★	★	★	★	...	★
Rhode Island	★	★	...	★	★	...	...	★	★	★	★	...	★
South Carolina	...	...	...	...	...	...	...	...	★	★	★	...	★
South Dakota	★	★	★	★	...	★	★	★	...	★	★	...	★
Tennessee	...	★	...	★	★	...	...	★	★	★	★	...	★
Texas	★	★	...	★	★	...	...	★	★	★	★	...	★
Utah (b)	★	★	★	★	★	★	★	★	...	...	...	...	★
Vermont	★	★	...	★	★	★	★	★	...	★	★	...	★
Virginia	...	...	...	...	...	...	...	...	...	...	...	...	...
Washington	★	★	★	★	...	...	...	★	★	★	...	★	★
West Virginia	★	★	...	★	...	★	★	★	★	★	★	...	★
Wisconsin	...	...	...	...	...	...	...	...	★	...	★	...	★
Wyoming	★	★	★	★	(i)	★	★	★	★	★	★	★	★
American Samoa (b)	...	...	...	★	...	★	★	★	★	★	★	...	...
Guam (b)	...	...	...	...	...	...	...	...	...	...	...	...	...
Puerto Rico	...	...	...	...	...	...	...	...	★	★	★	★	★
U.S. Virgin Islands (b)	...	...	...	...	...	...	...	...	★	★(g)	★	...	★

Source: The Council of State Governments' survey of secretaries of state, December 2005.

Key:

★ — Responsible for activity.   . . . — Not responsible for activity.

(a) Unless otherwise indicated, office registers domestic, foreign and nonprofit corporations.

(b) No secretary of state. Duties indicated are performed by lieutenant governor. In Hawaii, election-related responsibilities have been transferred to an independent Chief Election Officer.

(c) Files certificates of election for publication purposes only; does not file certificates of nomination.

(d) Federal candidates only.

(e) Incorporated organizations only.

(f) Files certificates of congressional and judicial retention elections only; does not file certificates of nomination.

(g) Both domestic and foreign profit; but only domestic nonprofit.

(h) Office issues document, but does not receive it.

(i) Materials not ballots.

Table 4.18
SECRETARIES OF STATE: CUSTODIAL, PUBLICATION AND LEGISLATIVE DUTIES

State or other jurisdiction	Custodial				Publication					Legislative			
	Archives state records and regulations	Files state agency rules and regulations	Administers uniform commercial code provisions	Files other corporate documents	State manual or directory	Session laws	State constitution	Statutes	Administrative rules and regulations	Opens legislative sessions (a)	Enrolls or engrosses bills	Retains copies of bills	Registers lobbyists
Alabama	...	...	★	★	...	★	...	★	...	...	★	★	...
Alaska (b)	...	★	...	...	...	...	★	...	★	★	...	★	...
Arizona	★	★	★	...	...	...	★	...	★	...	...	★	★
Arkansas	★	★	★	★	...	★	★	...	★	...	...	★	★
California	★	...	★	★	...	...	...	...	...	...	...	...	★
Colorado	...	★	★	★	...	...	★	...	★	...	...	★	★
Connecticut	★(c)	★	★	★	★	...	...	...	...	S	...	★	...
Delaware	★	★	★	★	...	...	...	...	★	...	...	...	...
Florida	★	★	...	★	...	★	★	★	★	...	...	...	...
Georgia	★	★	...	...	★	...	★	...	★	...	...	...	...
Hawaii (b)	...	★	...	...	...	...	...	★	...	...	...	★	...
Idaho	...	...	★	...	★	★	★	...	...	...	...	★	★
Illinois	★	★	★	★	★	★	★	...	★	H	...	★	★
Indiana	★	★	★	★	...	...	...	...	...	...	...	★	...
Iowa	★	...	★	★	...	...	...	★	...	...	...	★	...
Kansas	...	★	★	★	...	★	...	...	★	★	...	★	★
Kentucky	★	★	★	★	...	...	...	...	...	...	★	★	...
Louisiana	★	...	★	★	★	...	...	★	...	...	...	★	...
Maine	★	★	★	★	...	...	★	★	★	...	...	...	...
Maryland	...	...	...	...	...	...	...	...	(d)	...	...	★	...
Massachusetts	★	★	★	★	★	★	★	★	★	...	...	★	★
Michigan	★	★	★	...	...	★	★	★	★	...	...	...	★
Minnesota	★	★	★	★	★	★	★	★	...	H	...	★	...
Mississippi	★	★	★	★	★	★	★	★	★	H	★	★	★
Missouri	★	★	★	★	★	...	★	...	★	H	★	★	...
Montana	★	★	★	★	...	...	★	...	★	H	★	★	...
Nebraska	★	★	★	★	...	...	...	...	...	...	...	★	...
Nevada	★	★	★	★	...	...	...	...	...	...	...	★	...
New Hampshire	★	...	★	★	★	...	...	★	...	...	...	★	★
New Jersey	★	...	...	...	...	...	...	★	...	...	...	...	...
New Mexico	...	...	★	...	★	★	★	★	...	H	...	★	...
New York	...	★	★	...	★	...	★	...	★	...	...	...	...
North Carolina	★	★	★	★	★	★	★	...	...	...	...	...	★
North Dakota	...	...	★	★	...	...	...	...	...	...	...	★	★
Ohio	...	★	★	★	★	★	★	...	...	...	...	★	★
Oklahoma	...	★	...	★	...	★	★	★	★	...	...	★	...
Oregon	★	★	★	★	★	...	★	...	...	...	...	★	...
Pennsylvania	...	...	★	★	...	...	★	...	...	...	★	★	★
Rhode Island	★	★	★	★	★	...	★	...	★	...	...	★	★
South Carolina	...	...	★	★	...	...	★	...	...	...	...	★	...
South Dakota	★	★	★	★	★	...	★	...	...	H	...	★	★
Tennessee	★	★	★	★	★	★	★	...	★	...	...	★	...
Texas	★	★	★	★	...	★	...	...	★	...	...	★	...
Utah (b)	...	...	...	...	...	...	...	...	...	...	...	★	★
Vermont	★	★	★	★	★	★	★	...	★	H	...	★	★
Virginia	...	...	...	...	★	...	...	...	...	...	...	...	★
Washington	★	...	...	★	★	...	...	...	...	...	...	★	...
West Virginia	★	★	★	★	...	...	...	...	★	...	...	...	...
Wisconsin	...	...	...	...	...	...	...	...	...	...	...	...	...
Wyoming	★	★	★	★	★	...	★	...	...	H	...	★	★
American Samoa (b)	...	★	...	★	...	★	★	★	★	...	...	...	...
Guam (b)	...	...	...	...	...	...	...	...	...	...	...	...	...
Puerto Rico	...	★	★	★	...	★	★	★	★	...	...	...	...
U.S. Virgin Islands (b)	...	★	★	★	...	...	...	★	...	...	★	★	...

Source: The Council of State Governments survey of secretaries of state, December 2005.

Key:
★ — Responsible for activity.
... — Not responsible for activity.

(a) In this column only: ★ — Both houses; H — House; S — Senate.
(b) No secretary of state. Duties indicated are performed by lieutenant governor.
(c) The secretary of state is keeper of public records, but the state archives is a department of the Connecticut State Library.
(d) Code of Maryland regulations.

Attorneys General: Trends and Issues
By Angelita Plemmer

As the chief legal officers of the states, commonwealths and territories of the United States, attorneys general serve as counselors to state government agencies and legislatures, and as representatives of the public interest. In many areas traditionally considered the exclusive responsibility of the federal government, attorneys general now share enforcement authority and enjoy cooperative working relationships with their federal counterparts, particularly in the areas of antitrust, bankruptcy, consumer protection, criminal law and cybercrime and the environment.

Antitrust

During the past decade, the trend in state antitrust enforcement has been toward multistate litigation filed by a number of the attorneys general on cases with national impact. Multistate litigation typically includes cost-sharing arrangements among the attorneys general and may also include deputization of staff attorneys from one state to act as assistant attorneys general in other states for investigation and litigation. Some examples of successful multistate coordination in antitrust cases include vertical price fixing cases in the agricultural chemical, shoe and music industries. Recently, attorneys general have concentrated on the pharmaceutical industry, challenging tying arrangements and attempted monopolization, as well as anticompetitive activities designed to delay entry by generic competitors.

Attorneys general also use federal and state antitrust laws to challenge anticompetitive activity within a single state. For example, the attorney general of New York successfully challenged an arrangement between two hospitals through which they negotiated jointly with third-party payers and allocated services between themselves. The California attorney general reached a settlement with a ferry company accused of forcing customers to purchase tickets for other cruises in order to obtain tickets to its most popular destination, Alcatraz Island.

As the enforcers of state and federal antitrust laws and as the chief legal officers of their respective states, the attorneys general have a substantial interest in ensuring that antitrust laws are applied in a manner that is consistent with underlying Congressional policy and federal judicial precedent.

Appellate Advocacy

A continuing trend in the management of state attorney general offices is the increasing use of state solicitors to oversee the offices' respective appellate practices. On the criminal law side, most attorney general offices exclusively (or almost exclusively) engage in appellate work. More than half the states now have a state solicitor (or a person with a different title who serves that role), whose responsibility is to oversee the office's civil appellate work to ensure high quality and consistency of the state's position. See generally James R. Layton, *The Evolving Role of the State Solicitor: Toward the Federal Model?*, 3 J. App. Prac. & Process 533 (2001) (chart showing which offices have state solicitors).[1]

Attorney general offices continue to play a major role in the United States Supreme Court. During the court's 2005 term, attorney general offices served as counsel in 30 of the 76 cases set for argument. These cases cover the spectrum of issues. On the civil side, the court held that the U.S. attorney general cannot override Oregon's assisted suicide law, vacated a First Circuit opinion striking down New Hampshire's parental-notification-of-abortion statute on its face, and will resolve whether a state can place limits on campaign expenditures. On the criminal law side, the court will resolve the constitutionality of Kansas' death penalty statute, whether police may conduct searches without suspicion of parolees, and whether police may search a house when it has the consent of one occupant to enter the house but another occupant objects.

This marks the second straight term in which state attorney general offices have been extremely active in the court. During the 2004 term, attorney general offices served as counsel in 33 of the 75 argued cases.

Bankruptcy

As with pre-emption generally, bankruptcy is a federal law and affects the ability of attorneys general to collect a vast array of debts owed to the states, ranging from traditional contracts with private parties and student loans, to enforcing domestic support obligations owed to dependent spouses and children. Whenever states seek to collect restitution for amounts owed to victims in consumer protection and antitrust cases, or to require cleanup of environmentally contaminated facilities, or to order a party to cease and desist from unlawful activities, they may find that the defendant will file bankruptcy to resist those enforcement efforts.

The Bankruptcy Code allows many, but not all, of the states' enforcement activities to continue, despite the bankruptcy filing, and also limits the state's ability to deny licenses, grants and permits to those who have filed bankruptcy. States have both special rights and responsibilities under the Code to deal with debtors. Moreover, since bankruptcies have a national scope, states have frequently chosen to work together, often with the assistance of the National Association of Attorneys General (NAAG), to present a common front in the bankruptcy case to resolve common issues. The most important bankruptcy development over the last year was the final passage of a major bankruptcy overhaul under consideration since 1997. The new bill will primarily impact individual bankruptcies but has a number of provisions of particular interest to the states, including a number of provisions to better ensure taxes are properly reported and paid, and other provisions that will assist states in collecting on domestic support obligations owed to its citizens and to the states themselves.

Consumer Protection

The consumer protection programs administered by the state attorneys general are multifaceted. State attorneys general have primary responsibility in their states for the enforcement of their state's consumer protection laws. Every state has a consumer protection statute prohibiting deceptive acts and practices. These broad general statutes are supplemented in all jurisdictions by laws that address specific industries or practices.

Attorneys general have varied tools and authority to address abuses and illegalities in the market place. These include civil and criminal litigation, mediation, public and business education, creating and commenting on state and federal legislative proposals, and cooperative enforcement ventures with state, local and federal enforcement agencies. The consumer protection work of state attorneys general over the past year has run the gamut from telemarketing to telecommunications and from prescription drugs and privacy to price-gouging.

Earlier this year, state attorneys general and financial regulators announced that Ameriquest Mortgage Company, the nation's largest sub-prime lender, agreed to pay $295 million to consumers and make sweeping reforms of practices states alleged amounted to predatory lending. Ameriquest also agreed to pay

$30 million to the 49 states and District of Columbia that are participants in the settlement.

The $325 million nationwide total Ameriquest payment ranks as the second-largest state or federal consumer protection settlement in history, after the $484 million predatory lending agreement reached in 2002 between most states and Household Finance Corporation.

In the agreement, Ameriquest denied all the allegations raised by the states, but the company agreed to be bound by a battery of new standards to prevent what the states alleged were unfair and deceptive practices.

This settlement is an excellent example of a significant and continuing trend in state consumer protection enforcement—the increasing reliance on cooperative enforcement efforts. Interstate cooperation has greatly enhanced the enforcement work of attorneys general in stopping practices found in more than one jurisdiction.

Criminal Law

In many states, methamphetamine has become the number one drug threat facing state and local law enforcement. A powerfully addictive central nervous system stimulant, methamphetamine has been identified by an increasing number of state and local law enforcement agencies as the drug that most contributes to violence and property crimes. It can be easily manufactured in clandestine laboratories using simple instructions, and many ingredients necessary to make methamphetamine, including the pseudoephedrine contained in many over-the-counter medicines, are cheap and easily accessible. The impact of these labs on local communities is devastating, threatening the safety of law enforcement and first responder personnel, damaging the environment, and, tragically, endangering a rapidly growing number of children.

Attorneys general are working cooperatively to address the methamphetamine crisis that pervades cities and towns across the country. In an effort to put an end to this scourge, 53 attorneys general adopted a resolution in June 2005 outlining the dangers that methamphetamine brings and encouraging action on state and federal levels. The resolution encourages the federal government to increase efforts to disrupt the flow of methamphetamine and the precursor chemicals used in the manufacturing process. It also calls on Congress to enact federal legislation to combat the manufacture, trafficking and abuse of methamphetamine without precluding the ability of states and territorial jurisdictions to respond to unique circumstances within their own jurisdictions; and to assist state, local and territorial law enforcement by providing additional resources to combat issues related to methamphetamine.

Cybercrime

As personal computers and the Internet have become an integral part of life, criminal activity has become more sophisticated, making it more difficult to investigate crimes and prosecute perpetrators. The difficulty is compounded when computers and other high-tech tools are used to commit crimes across jurisdictional boundaries. The majority of attorneys general have either established cybercrime units or dedicated resources to address this growing problem. NAAG, through a partnership with the National Center for Justice and the Rule of Law (NCJRL), provides technical assistance to other states in developing or enhancing their own cybercrime units or cybercrime capability.

As attorney general enforcement efforts continue to expand in this area, attorneys general have launched a number of new initiatives designed to increase public awareness and public safety. Many of these new programs include cyber tiplines, online sex offender registries featuring live data, high-tech child ID cards, AMBER Alert e-mail plans, Internet safety programs for adults and youths, and advocacy for more stringent legislation in the areas of phishing, ID theft, child predators and fraudulent online charitable solicitations.

Data Security

Another area of concern for attorneys general is data security. Recent incidences of security breaches have exposed millions of consumers to harm, including potential identity theft. Forty-eight attorneys general submitted a letter to Congress in November 2005 encouraging members to enact a strong national security breach notification and security freeze law, which would provide critical assistance to identity theft victims throughout the nation.

The public has become aware of the numerous incidences of security breaches as a result of California's security breach notification laws, which went into effect July 1, 2003. These laws require businesses and California public institutions to notify the public about any breach of the security of their computer information system where unencrypted personal information was, or is reasonably believed to have been, acquired by an unauthorized person. The public has become so concerned about security breaches and their potential role in the increased incidence of identity theft that at least 22 states enacted security breach legislation in 2005.[2]

Environment

The state attorney general is the primary enforcer of laws protecting the environment and natural resources. As a general rule, attorneys general are responsible for enforcing federal environmental statutes when enforcement of those laws devolves to the states, as well as responsibility for state-specific environmental protection laws.

As environmental enforcement practice has matured, many attorneys general have integrated air, water and waste disposal issues into largely standardized initiatives. New practice areas have focused on three emerging sets of issues. Regional or geographically linked questions include: water issues in the West, downwind air pollution questions and coastal issues such as cruise ship pollution, invasive species and coastal zone management. In the context of cleanup statutes and broad principles of tort law, attorneys general are pursuing natural resource damage claims that are the conclusion of long-standing cleanup efforts. Finally, state attorneys general continue to litigate the limits of federal environmental authority in a variety of contexts. For example, various aspects of the definition of "waters of the United States" have been repeatedly litigated in the last 10 years, and the Supreme Court is slated to hear two cases touching on that definition in its 2006 term. Other legal questions about the boundaries between state and federal authority include the discretionary—or ministerial—responsibility of the federal government to promulgate regulations on specific subjects, and the scope of federal facilities' responsibility to comply with environmental statutes.

Legislation

NAAG takes positions on federal legislation in several ways. NAAG policies are created either by members voting on resolutions at full-member conferences or by signing onto letters as a group. Generally, resolutions and sign-on letters are limited to those matters that diminish or enhance the powers, duties and responsibilities of state attorneys general or those that pre-empt state law.

Frequently, attorneys general across the country are asked by Congress, media, business organizations and constituents for their views on pending bills in Congress that affect the powers and duties of attorneys general. Often, such legislation seeks to pre-empt state law in the areas of consumer protection, environment, antitrust, bankruptcy, securities, criminal law and many other areas within the jurisdiction of state attorneys general.

Attorneys general from around the country have come to Capitol Hill to testify before both House and Senate committees on issues affecting the states. State attorneys general have testified often on behalf of consumers regarding fair credit, online pharmaceuticals, identity theft, data security, banking issues and predatory lending. In addition, attorneys general have testified before Congress on environmental bills, legislation affecting criminal laws, securities and many other issues.

Tobacco

Cigarette consumption nationally in 2005 fell by almost 4 percent compared to 2004, one of the largest declines since the landmark 1998 tobacco Master Settlement Agreement (MSA) went into effect. Since 1997, the year before the MSA was executed, cigarette consumption in the United States has fallen by 20 percent. The decline in cigarette consumption in the years following the MSA is unprecedented and represents a sharp break from the pattern of the early and mid-1990s, during which nationwide cigarette consumption was essentially static.

Tobacco companies paid more than $7.3 billion to the states under the MSA and the four separate state settlements,[3] a record amount. States successfully defended the MSA against attacks on its constitutionality and its validity under the antitrust laws in federal court actions in Kentucky, Tennessee, Oklahoma, Louisiana, California and Kansas. All these decisions are currently on appeal and similar litigation remains pending in other states.

Seven more states passed legislation in 2005 strengthening statutes that require companies outside the MSA to make escrow deposits on cigarette sales made in the state. All but two of the MSA states have enacted this legislation.

Attorneys general took numerous actions in the past year to enforce and extend the public health provisions of the MSA. Attorneys general reached agreements with several major owners of retail chain stores, including ConocoPhillips, 7-Eleven and CVS, embodying the adoption of specific tobacco retailing "best practices" aimed at reducing sales to minors.

Armed with a new study that demonstrates that "exposure to movie smoking has a strong association with smoking initiation" by adolescents, a coalition of attorneys general has challenged Hollywood movie studios to reduce smoking depictions in movies and to include an anti-smoking public service announcement on all videos and DVDs with movies that depict smoking.

Attorneys general concluded an agreement with Time, Inc. (which publishes *Time*, *People* and *Sports Illustrated*), and Newsweek, Inc. (which publishes *Newsweek*) to eliminate tobacco advertising from school library editions of those four major magazines, which have significant youth readerships.

A group of attorneys general obtained a commitment by several major credit card companies and carriers that they would not provide their services in connection with the illegal sale of cigarettes over the Internet. Attorneys general entered into a Protocol with Philip Morris, the largest manufacturer of cigarettes in the United States, that would combat the illegal sales of its cigarettes over the Internet by having Philip Morris suspend shipments to, or incentive programs with, its distributors or retailers found to be engaging in illegal Internet sales or selling to those who make such sales.

After multistate investigations, the attorneys general brought two actions to enforce the Master Settlement Agreement and Smokeless Tobacco Master Settlement Agreement: (1) Vermont sued R.J. Reynolds Tobacco Company alleging material misrepresentations of fact by making express and implied health claims in its advertising for "Eclipse" cigarettes; and (2) California sued U.S. Smokeless Tobacco Company for various violations of the Brand Name Sponsorship limitations in its "Skoal Racing" sponsorship in the National Hot Rod Association.

As advocates for the public interest, or interpreters of the law, attorneys general are faced with increasingly complex issues that intersect the law and public policy.

Notes

[1] Subsequent to the publication of the article, the Alabama, California, Nebraska and North Carolina attorney general offices instated their first state solicitors.

[2] Arkansas, Connecticut, Delaware, Florida, Georgia, Illinois, Indiana, Louisiana, Maine, Minnesota, Montana, Nevada, New Jersey, New York, North Carolina, North Dakota, Ohio, Pennsylvania, Rhode Island, Tennessee, Texas and Washington.

[3] Florida, Minnesota, Mississippi and Texas.

About the Author

This article was compiled and edited by **Angelita Plemmer**, director of communications for the National Association of Attorneys General. A former newspaper journalist, Plemmer joined the association staff in 2001. She formerly worked as the public information officer for the city of Roanoke, Va., and as the assistant city manager for public information for the city of Alexandria, Va. She holds a master's degree in journalism from Columbia University and a bachelor of arts degree in rhetoric and communications studies from the University of Virginia.

Table 4.19
THE ATTORNEYS GENERAL, 2006

State or other jurisdiction	Name and party	Method of selection	Length of regular term in years	Date of first service	Present term ends	Number of previous terms	Maximum consecutive terms allowed
Alabama	Troy King (R)	E	4	3/04 (i)	1/07	0	2
Alaska	David W. Marquez (R)	A	...	3/05	...	0	...
Arizona	Terry Goddard (D)	E	4	1/03	1/07	0	2 (a)
Arkansas	Mike Beebe (D)	E	4	1/03	1/07	0	2
California	Bill Lockyer (D)	E	4	1/99	1/07	1	2
Colorado	John W. Suthers (R)	E	4	1/05 (m)	1/07	0	2
Connecticut	Richard Blumenthal (D)	E	4	1/91	1/07	3	★
Delaware	Carl Danberg (D) (o)	E	4	12/05 (o)	1/07	0	★
Florida	Charlie Crist (R)	E	4	1/03	1/07	0	2
Georgia	Thurbert E. Baker (D)	E	4	6/97 (j)	1/07	1 (j)	★
Hawaii	Mark J. Bennett (R)	A	4 (k)	12/02	12/06	0	...
Idaho	Lawrence Wasden (R)	E	4	1/03	1/07	0	★
Illinois	Lisa Madigan (D)	E	4	1/03	1/07	0	★
Indiana	Steve Carter (R)	E	4	1/01	1/09	1	...
Iowa	Tom Miller (D)	E	4	1/79	1/07	4	★
Kansas	Phill Kline (R)	E	4	1/03	1/07	0	★
Kentucky	Greg Stumbo (D)	E	4	1/04	12/07	0	2
Louisiana	Charles C. Foti Jr. (D)	E	4	1/04	1/08	0	★
Maine	G. Steven Rowe (D)	(b)	2	1/01	1/07	1	4
Maryland	J. Joseph Curran Jr. (D)	E	4	1/87	1/07	4	★
Massachusetts	Tom Reilly (D)	E	4	1/99	1/07	1	2
Michigan	Mike Cox (R)	E	4	1/03	1/07	0	2
Minnesota	Mike Hatch (D)	E	4	1/99	1/07	1	★
Mississippi	Jim Hood (D)	E	4	1/04	1/08	0	★
Missouri	Jeremiah W. Nixon (D)	E	4	1/93	1/09	3	★
Montana	Mike McGrath (D)	E	4	1/01	1/09	1	2 (c)
Nebraska	Jon Bruning (R)	E	4	1/03	1/07	0	★
Nevada	George J. Chanos (R)	E (n)	4	11/05 (n)	1/07	0	2
New Hampshire	Kelly Ayotte (R)	A	...	7/04	11/06	0	...
New Jersey	Zulima Farber (D)	A	...	1/06	...	0	...
New Mexico	Patricia A. Madrid (D)	E	4	1/99	1/07	1	2 (a)
New York	Eliot Spitzer (D)	E	4	1/99	1/07	1	★
North Carolina	Roy Cooper (D)	E	4	1/01	1/09	1	★
North Dakota	Wayne Stenehjem (R)	E	4 (d)	12/00	12/06	1	★ (d)
Ohio	Jim Petro (R)	E	4	1/03	1/07	0	2
Oklahoma	W.A. Drew Edmondson (D)	E	4	1/95	1/07	2	★
Oregon	Hardy Myers (D)	E	4	1/97	1/09	2	★
Pennsylvania	Tom Corbett (R)	E	4	1/05	1/09	0	2 (a)
Rhode Island	Patrick Lynch (D)	E	4	1/03	1/07	0	2 (a)
South Carolina	Henry McMaster (R)	E	4	1/03	1/07	0	★
South Dakota	Larry Long (R)	E	4	1/03	1/07	0	2 (a)
Tennessee	Paul G. Summers (D)	(f)	8	1/99	1/07	0	...
Texas	Greg Abbott (R)	E	4	1/03	1/07	0	★
Utah	Mark Shurtleff (R)	E	4	1/01	1/09	1	★
Vermont	William H. Sorrell (D)	E	2	5/97 (e)	1/07	3 (e)	★
Virginia	Robert F. McDonnell (R)	E	4	1/06	1/10	0	(g)
Washington	Rob McKenna (R)	E	4	1/05	1/09	0	★
West Virginia	Darrell Vivian McGraw Jr. (D)	E	4	1/93	1/09	3	★
Wisconsin	Peg Lautenschlager (D)	E	4	1/03	1/07	0	★
Wyoming	Pat Crank (D)	A (h)	...	1/03	1/07	0	...
Dist. of Columbia	Robert Spanoletti (D)	A	...	6/03	...	0	...
American Samoa	Malaetasi M. Togafau	A	4	2/05	...	0	...
Guam	Douglas Moylan	E	4	1/03	1/07	0	...
No. Mariana Islands	Matt Gregory	A	4	N.A.	N.A.	N.A.	...
Puerto Rico	Roberto J. Sanchez-Ramos	A	4	N.A.	...	0	...
U.S. Virgin Islands	Kerry Drue	A	4	9/05	...	0	...

See footnotes at end of table.

THE ATTORNEYS GENERAL, 2006 — Continued

Source: The Council of State Governments' survey of attorneys general, January 2006.

Key:

★ — No provision specifying number of terms allowed.

. . . — No formal provision, position is appointed or elected by governmental entity (not chosen by the electorate).

A — Appointed by the governor

E — Elected by the voters

L — Elected by the legislature

(a) After two consecutive terms, must wait four years and/or one full term before being eligible again.

(b) Chosen biennially by joint ballot of state senators and representatives.

(c) Eligible for eight out of 16 years.

(d) The term of the office of the elected official is four years, except that in 2004 the attorney general was elected for a term of two years.

(e) Appointed to fill unexpired term in May 1997. He was elected in 1998 to his first full term.

(f) Appointed by judges of state Supreme Court.

(g) Provision specifying individual may hold office for an unlimited number of terms.

(h) Must be confirmed by the Senate.

(i) Appointed to fill unexpired term in March 2004.

(j) Appointed to fill unexpired term in June 1997. He was elected in 1998 to his first full term.

(k) Term runs concurrently with the Governor.

(l) Appointed to fill unexpired term in February 2004.

(m) Appointed to fill unexpired term in January 2005.

(n) George Chanos was appointed to fill the unexpired term of Brian Sandoval after he resigned to accept a federal district judgeship on November 2, 2005.

(o) Appointed to fill the unexpired term of M. Jane Brady on December 7, 2005 when she resigned to become a Superior Court judge.

Table 4.20
ATTORNEYS GENERAL: QUALIFICATIONS FOR OFFICE

State or other jurisdiction	Minimum age	U.S. citizen (years) (a)	State resident (years) (b)	Qualified voter (years)	Licensed attorney (years)	Membership in the state bar (years)	Method of selection to office
Alabama	25	7	5	★	...	...	E
Alaska	...	★	...	...	...	...	A
Arizona	25	10	5	...	5	5	E
Arkansas	...	...	★	★	...	...	E
California	18	★	★	★	(c)	(c)	E
Colorado	25	★	2	...	★	(d)	E
Connecticut	18	★	★	★	10	10	E
Delaware	...	...	...	...	...	...	E
Florida	30	★	7	★	★	5	E
Georgia	25	10	4	★	★	7	E
Hawaii	...	1	1	...	★	(e)	A
Idaho	30	★	2	...	★	★	E
Illinois	25	★	3	★	★	...	E
Indiana	...	2	2	★	5	...	E
Iowa	18	★	★	...	...	...	E
Kansas	...	...	...	...	...	...	E
Kentucky	30	...	2 (f)	...	8	2	E
Louisiana	25	5	5 (f)	★	5	5	E
Maine	...	...	...	...	...	...	(g)
Maryland	...	★(h)	★	★	★	10	E
Massachusetts	18	...	5	★	...	★	E
Michigan	18	★	★	...	★	★	E
Minnesota	21	★	30 days	★	...	...	E
Mississippi	26	★	5	★	5	★	E
Missouri	...	★	1	...	...	...	E
Montana	25	★	2	...	5	★	E
Nebraska	...	...	...	...	...	...	E
Nevada	25	★	2 (f)	★	...	...	E
New Hampshire	18	...	...	★	★	★	A
New Jersey	18	...	★	...	...	...	A
New Mexico	30	★	5	★	★	...	E
New York	30	★	5	...	(i)	...	E
North Carolina	21	★	★	★	★	(i)	E
North Dakota	25	★	5	★	★	★	E
Ohio	18	★	★	★	...	...	E
Oklahoma	31	★	10	10	...	...	E
Oregon	18	★	★	★	...	...	E
Pennsylvania	30	★	7	...	★	★	E
Rhode Island	18	★	30 days (f)	★	...	...	E
South Carolina	...	★	30 days	★	...	...	E
South Dakota	18	★	★	★	(i)	(i)	E
Tennessee	...	...	...	...	...	...	(j)
Texas	...	...	★	...	(i)	(i)	E
Utah	25	★	5 (f)	★	★	★	E
Vermont	18	★	★	★	...	...	E
Virginia	30	★	1 (k)	★	...	5 (k)	E
Washington	18	★	★	★	★	★	E
West Virginia	25	...	5	★	...	...	E
Wisconsin	...	★	★	...	...	...	E
Wyoming	...	★	★	★	4	4	A (l)
Dist. of Columbia	...	...	★	...	★	★	A
American Samoa	...	...	(c)	...	(i)	(i)	A
Guam	...	...	...	...	...	...	A
No. Mariana Islands	...	...	3	...	5	...	A
Puerto Rico	...	★	...	...	★	★	A
U.S. Virgin Islands	...	...	★	★	★	★	A

Sources: The Council of State Governments' survey of attorneys general, December 2005 and state constitutions and statutes, February 2005.

Key:

★ — Formal provision; number of years not specified.

. . . — No formal provision.

A — Appointed by governor

E — Elected by voters

(a) In some states you must be a U.S. citizen to be an elector, and must be an elector to run.

(b) In some states you must be a state resident to be an elector, and must be an elector to run.

(c) No statute specifically requires this, but the State Bar Act can be interpreted as making this a qualification.

(d) Licensed attorneys are not required to belong to the bar association.

(e) No period specified, all licensed attorneys are members of the state bar.

(f) State citizenship requirement.

(g) Chosen biennially by joint ballot of state senators and representatives.

(h) *Crosse v. Board of Supervisors of Elections* 243 Md. 555, 221A.2d431 (1966)—opinion rendered indicated that U.S. citizenship was, by necessity, a requirement for office.

(i) Implied.

(j) Appointed by judges of state Supreme Court.

(k) Same as qualifications of a judge of a court of record.

(l) Must be confirmed by the Senate.

Table 4.21
ATTORNEYS GENERAL: PROSECUTORIAL AND ADVISORY DUTIES

State or other jurisdiction	Authority in local prosecutions: Authority to initiate local prosecutions	May intervene in local prosecutions	May assist local prosecutor	May supersede local prosecutor	Issues advisory opinions: To state executive officials	To legislators	To local prosecutors	On the constitutionality of bills or ordinances	Reviews legislation: Prior to passage	Before signing
Alabama	A	A,D	A,D	A	★	★	★	. . .	★	. . .
Alaska	(a)	(a)	(a)	(a)	★	★	. . .	★	★	★
Arizona	A,B,C,D,F	B,D	B,D	B	★	★	★	. . .	. . .	. . .
Arkansas	. . .	. . .	D	. . .	★	★	★	★	. . .	. . .
California	A,B,C,D,E	A,B,C,D,E	A,B,C,D,E	A,B,C,D,E	★	★	★	. . .	. . .	. . .
Colorado	B,F	B	D,F (b)	B	★	★	★	★	★	★
Connecticut	. . .	. . .	. . .	. . .	★	(c)	. . .	★	(e)	(e)
Delaware	A (j)	(j)	(j)	(j)	★	★	. . .	★	★(o)	★(o)
Florida	F	. . .	D	. . .	★	★	★	. . .	. . .	. . .
Georgia	B,D,E,F,G	B,D,G	A,B,D,E,F,G	. . .	★	★	★	. . .	. . .	. . .
Hawaii	A,B,C,D,E	A,B,C,D,E	A,B,C,D,E	A,B,C,D,E	★	★	. . .	★(k)	★	★
Idaho	B,D,F	. . .	D	. . .	★	★	★	★	★	★
Illinois	D,F	D,G	D	G	★	★	★	. . .	. . .	. . .
Indiana	F	. . .	D	. . .	★	★	★	★	. . .	. . .
Iowa	D,F	D,F	D,F	D,E,F	★	★	★	. . .	(p)	(p)
Kansas	A,B,C,D,F	A,D	D	A,F	★	★	★	. . .	. . .	(g)
Kentucky	D,F,G	B,D,G	D	B	★	★	★	★	. . .	. . .
Louisiana	A,D,G	A,D,G	D	G	★	★	★	★	★	★
Maine	A	A	A	A	★	★	. . .	★	★	★
Maryland	B,F	D	D	. . .	★	★	★	★	★	★
Massachusetts	A	A	A,D	A	★	★(h)	★	★	(g)	(g)
Michigan	A	A	D	(b)	★	★	★	★	. . .	. . .
Minnesota	B,F	B,D,G	A,B,D,G	B	★	★(h)	★	. . .	. . .	(g)
Mississippi	A,D,F	D,F	A,D,F	D,F	★	★	★	. . .	. . .	. . .
Missouri	F,G	. . .	B,F	G	★	★	★	. . .	(g)	(g)
Montana	D,F	A,B,D	A,B,D	A	★	★(i)	★	. . .	(t)	. . .
Nebraska	A	A	A	A	★	★	★	★	. . .	. . .
Nevada	D,F,G	D	. . .	. . .	★	. . .	★	★	. . .	. . .
New Hampshire	A	A	A	A	★	★	★	★	(q)	(q)
New Jersey	A	A,B,D,G	A,D	A,B,D,G	★	★	★	★	★	★
New Mexico	B,D,E,F	D,E,F	A,B,D,E,F	D,E,F,G	★	★	★	★	★	★
New York	B,F	B,D,F	D	B	★	★(h)	★	★	★	★
North Carolina	. . .	D	D	. . .	★	★	★	. . .	★	. . .
North Dakota	A,D,E,F,G	A,D,G	A,B,D,E,F,G	A,G	★	★	★	. . .	(f)	(g)
Ohio	F	D	D	F	★	(i)	★	. . .	. . .	. . .
Oklahoma	A,B,C,E,F	A,B,C,E,F	A,B,C,E	E	★	★	★	. . .	(r)	(r)
Oregon	B,D,F	B,D	B,D	. . .	★	★	★	. . .	. . .	★
Pennsylvania	D,F,G	. . .	. . .	G	★	. . .	. . .	★	. . .	. . .
Rhode Island	A	A	. . .	. . .	★	★	★	. . .	. . .	. . .
South Carolina	A,D,E,F (b)	A,B,C,D,E,F	A,D	A,E	★	(l)	★	★	★(m)	★(g)
South Dakota	A,B,D,E,F (b)	D,G (b)	A,B,D,E	D,F	★	★	★	. . .	★	. . .
Tennessee	D,F,G (b)	D,G (b)	D	. . .	★	★	★	★	. . .	. . .
Texas	F	. . .	D	. . .	★(d)	★(d)	★(d)	★(d)	(n)	(n)
Utah	A,B,D,E,F,G	E,G	D,E	E	★	★(l)	★	★	★(g)	★(g)
Vermont	A	A	A	G	★	★	★	★	★	★
Virginia	B,F	B,D,F	B,D,F	B	★	★	★	★	★	★
Washington	B,D	D	D	. . .	★	★	★	. . .	(g)	(g)
West Virginia	. . .	. . .	. . .	. . .	★	★	★	★	. . .	. . .
Wisconsin	B,C,F	B,C,D	D	B	★	★	★	★(k)	(e)	(e)
Wyoming	B,D,F	B,D	B,D	G	★	★	★	★(k)	. . .	. . .
Dist. of Columbia	F	D	D	F	★	★	(s)	. . .	★	★
American Samoa	A (j)	(j)	(j)	(j)	★	. . .	(j)	(e)	(g)	(g)
Guam	A	A	A	A	★	★	★	★	(g)	B
No. Mariana Islands	A (j)	(j)	(j)	(j)	★	★	★	★	. . .	. . .
Puerto Rico	A	(j)	(j)	(j)	★	★	. . .	. . .	★	★
U.S. Virgin Islands	A (j)	(j)	(j)	(j)	★	. . .	. . .	★	★	★

See footnotes at end of table.

ATTORNEYS GENERAL: PROSECUTORIAL AND ADVISORY DUTIES — Continued

Source: The Council of State Governments' survey of attorneys general, December 2005.

Key:

A — On own initiative.

B — On request of governor.

C — On request of legislature.

D — On request of local prosecutor.

E — When in state's interest.

F — Under certain statutes for specific crimes.

G — On authorization of court or other body.

★ — Has authority in area.

. . . — Does not have authority in area.

(a) Local prosecutors serve at pleasure of attorney general.

(b) Certain statutes provide for concurrent jurisdiction with local prosecutors.

(c) To legislative leadership.

(d) Only upon request by a statutorily authorized requestor.

(e) Informally reviews bills or does so upon request.

(f) Opinion may be issued to officers of either branch of General Assembly or to chairman or minority spokesman of committees or commissions thereof.

(g) Only when requested by governor or legislature.

(h) To legislature as a whole, not individual legislators.

(i) To either house of legislature, not individual legislators.

(j) The attorney general functions as the local prosecutor.

(k) Bills, not ordinances.

(l) Only when requested by legislature.

(m) Has concurrent jurisdiction with states' attorneys.

(n) Official opinions, when requested, regarding proper construction or constitutionality of proposed or enacted legislation.

(o) Also at the request of agency or legislature.

(p) No requirements for review.

(q) When legislation impacts the office or upon request.

(r) If required by legislature; may assist in drafting.

(s) The office of attorney general prosecutes local crimes to an extent. The office's Legal Counsel Division may issue legal advice to the office's prosecutorial arm. Otherwise, the office does not usually advise the OUSA, the district's other local prosecutor.

(t) If requested by a legislator.

Table 4.22
ATTORNEYS GENERAL: CONSUMER PROTECTION ACTIVITIES, SUBPOENA POWERS AND ANTITRUST DUTIES

State or other jurisdiction	May commence civil proceedings	May commence criminal proceedings	Represents the state before regulatory agencies (a)	Administers consumer protection programs	Handles consumer complaints	Subpoena powers (b)	Antitrust duties
Alabama	★	★	★	★	★	●	A,B,C
Alaska	★	★	★	★	★	★	A,B,C
Arizona	★	...	...	★	★	(n)	A,B,C,D
Arkansas	★	...	★	★	★	●	A,B
California	★	★	...	★	★	★	A,B,C
Colorado	★	★	★	★	★	★	A,B,C,D
Connecticut	★	(l)	★	★	★	●	A,B,D
Delaware	★	★	★	★	★	★	A,B,C,D
Florida	★	...	...	★	★	★	A,B,D
Georgia	★	★	★	...	...	●	...
Hawaii	★	★	...	★	★	●	A,B,C,D
Idaho	★	...	★	★	★	★	A,B,D
Illinois	★	★(n)	★	★	★	●	A,B,C
Indiana	★	...	★	★	★	★	A,B
Iowa	★	★	★	★	★	★	B,C
Kansas	★	★	★	★	★	★	A,B
Kentucky	★	★	★	★	★	★	A,B,C,D
Louisiana	★	★	★	★	★	★	A,B,D
Maine	★	★	★	★	★	★	A,B,C
Maryland	★	★(f)	...	★	★	★	B,C,D
Massachusetts	★	★	★	★	★	★	A,B,C,D
Michigan	★	★	★	★	★	★	A,B,C,D
Minnesota	★	...	★	★	★	●	A,B,C
Mississippi	★	★	...	★	★	★	A,B,C,D
Missouri	★	★	★	★	★	★	A,B,C
Montana (h)	...	...	...	...	...	...	A,B
Nebraska	★	★	★	★	★	★	A,B,C,D
Nevada	★	★	★	★	★(m)	★	A,B,C,D
New Hampshire	★	★	★	★	★	★	A,B,C
New Jersey	★	★	★	★	★	★	A,B,C,D
New Mexico	★	★	★	★	★	★	A,B,C (p)
New York	★	★	★	★	★	★	A,B,C,D
North Carolina	★	★(e)	★	★	★	★	A,B,C,D
North Dakota	★	...	★	★	★	★	A,B,D
Ohio	★	★	★	★	★	★	A,B,C,D
Oklahoma	★	★	★	★	★	★	A,B,C,D
Oregon	★	★(e)	★	★	★	●	A,B,C
Pennsylvania	★	★	...	★	★	★	A,B,C,D
Rhode Island	★	★	...	★	★	●	B,C
South Carolina	★(a)	★(c)	★	...	★(m)	●	A,B,C,D
South Dakota	★	★	★	★	★	★	A,B,C
Tennessee	★	(e)(f)	(e)	...	...	★	B,C,D
Texas	★	★(j)	★	★	★	●	A,B,D
Utah	★(d)	★	★(d)	...	★(g)	●	A (i),B,C,D (i)
Vermont	★	★	★	★	★	★	A,B,C
Virginia	★	(e)	★	★(g)	★(g)	●	A,B,C,D
Washington	★	...	(k)	★	★	★	A,B,D
West Virginia	★	...	★	★	★	★	A,B,D
Wisconsin	★	★	★	★	★	●	A,B,C (p)
Wyoming	★	...	★	★	★	●	A,B
Dist. of Columbia	★	★(o)	★	★	★	★	A,B,C,D
American Samoa	★	★	★	★	★	...	...
Guam	★	★	★	★	★	●	A,B,C,D
No. Mariana Islands	★	★	★	★	★	★	A,B
Puerto Rico	★	★	...	...	...	★	A,B,C,D
U.S. Virgin Islands	★	★	★	★	★	●	A

See footnotes at end of table.

ATTORNEYS GENERAL: CONSUMER PROTECTION ACTIVITIES, SUBPOENA POWERS AND ANTITRUST DUTIES — Continued

Source: The Council of State Governments' survey of attorneys general, January 2006.

Key:

A — Has parens patriae authority to commence suits on behalf of consumers in state antitrust damage actions in state courts.

B — May initiate damage actions on behalf of state in state courts.

C — May commence criminal proceedings.

D — May represent cities, counties and other governmental entities in recovering civil damages under federal or state law.

★ — Has authority in area.

. . . — Does not have authority in area.

(a) May represent state on behalf of: the "people" of the state; an agency of the state; or the state before a federal regulatory agency.

(b) In this column only: ★ broad powers and ● limited powers.

(c) When permitted to intervene.

(d) Attorney general has exclusive authority.

(e) To a limited extent.

(f) May commence criminal proceedings with local district attorney.

(g) Attorney general handles legal matters only with no administrative handling of complaints.

(h) Exercise consumer protection authority only in cooperation with the state department of administration.

(i) Opinion only, since there are no controlling precedents.

(j) Under specific statutes for specific crimes.

(k) The Public Counsel Unit appears and represents the public before the Utilities & Transportation Commission.

(l) In certain cases only.

(m) On a limited basis because the state has a separate consumer affairs department.

(n) Antitrust only.

(o) In antitrust not criminal proceedings.

(p) May represent other governmental entities in recovering civil damages under federal or state law.

Table 4.23
ATTORNEYS GENERAL: DUTIES TO ADMINISTRATIVE AGENCIES AND OTHER RESPONSIBILITIES

State or other jurisdiction	Serves as counsel for state	Appears for state in criminal appeals	Issues official advice	Interprets statutes or regulations	Conducts litigation: On behalf of agency	Conducts litigation: Against agency	Prepares or reviews legal documents	Represents the public before the agency	Involved in rule-making	Reviews rules for legality
Alabama	A,B,C	★(a)	★	★	★	★	★	(b)	(b)	★
Alaska	A,B,C	★	★	★	★	★	★	...	★	★
Arizona	A,B,C	★	★	★	★	...	★	...	★	★
Arkansas	A,B,C	★	★	★	★	★	★	★	...	...
California	A,B,C	★	★	★	★	...	★	...	...	...
Colorado	A,B,C	★(a)	★	★	★	★	★	(e)	★	★
Connecticut	A,B,C	(b)	★	★	★	★	★	★	★	★
Delaware	A,B,C	★	★	★	★	★(i)	★	★	★	★
Florida	A,B,C	★	★	★	★	...	★	...	...	...
Georgia	A,B,C	★	★	★	★	...	★	...	...	★
Hawaii	A,B,C	★	★	★	★	★	★	★	★	★
Idaho	A,B,C	★(a)	★	★	★	★	★	★	★	★
Illinois	A,B,C	★	...	★	★	...	★	...	...	...
Indiana	A,B,C	★	★	★	★	...	★	...	★	★
Iowa	A,B,C	★	★	★	★	★	★	★	★	★
Kansas	A,B,C	★	★	★	★	★	★	...	★	★
Kentucky	A,B,C	★	★	★	★	...	...	★	...	...
Louisiana	A,B,C	(h)	★	★	★	...	★	...	★	...
Maine	A,B,C	★	★	★	★	...	★	...	...	★
Maryland	A,B,C	★	★	★	★	(b)	★	★	★	★
Massachusetts	A,B,C	(b)(c)(d)	★	★	★	★	★	★	★	★
Michigan	A,B,C	★	★	★	★	...	★	★	★	★
Minnesota	A,B,C	(c)(d)	★	★	(a)	★	★	★	★	★
Mississippi	A,B,C	...	★	★	★	...	★	...	...	...
Missouri	A,B,C	★	★	★	★	...	★	★	★	...
Montana	A,B,C	★	★	★	★	★	★	...	★	★
Nebraska	A,B,C	★	★	★	★	★	★	...	★	★
Nevada	A,B,C	★	★	★	★	...	★	...	★	★
New Hampshire	A,B,C	★	★	★	★	★	★	★	(f)	(f)
New Jersey	A,B,C	★	★	★	★	★	★	...	★	★
New Mexico	A,B,C	★	★	★	★	★	★	★	★	★
New York	A,B,C	(b)	...	★	★	(b)	★	(b)	...	...
North Carolina	A,B,C	★	★	★	★	★	★	(b)	★	★
North Dakota	A,B,C	(b)	★	★	★	★	★	...	★	★
Ohio	A,B,C	★	★	...	★	...	★	...	...	...
Oklahoma	A,B,C	★	★	★	★	★	★	★	(b)	★
Oregon	A,B	★	★	★	★	...	★	...	★	★
Pennsylvania	A,B	...	★	★	★	...	★	...	★	★
Rhode Island	A,B,C	★	★	★	★	★	★	...	...	...
South Carolina	A,B,C	★(d)	(a)	★	★	(b)	★	...	★	★
South Dakota	A,B,C	★	★	★	★	★	★	...	...	★
Tennessee	A,B,C	★(a)	★	★	★	...	★	(e)	(e)	★
Texas	A,B,C	★(g)	★	★	★	★	★	...	★	...
Utah	A,B,C	★(a)	★	★	★	★	★	(b)	★	★
Vermont	A,B,C	★	★	★	★	★	★	★	★	★
Virginia	A,B,C	★	★	★	★	★	★	★	★	★
Washington	A,B	★	★	★	★	★	★	★	★	★
West Virginia	A,B,C	★	★	★	★	★	★	...	...	...
Wisconsin	A,B,C	★	★	★	★	(b)	(b)	(b)	(b)	(b)
Wyoming	A,B,C	★	★	★	★	★	★	...	★	★
Dist. of Columbia	A,B	★(j)	★	★	★	...	★	...	★	★
American Samoa	A,B,C	★(a)	★	★	★	...	★	...	★	★
Guam	A,B,C	★	★	★	(d)	★	★	(b)	★	★
No. Mariana Islands	A,B,C	★	★	★	★	★	★	...	★	★
Puerto Rico	A,B,C	★	★	★	★	...	★	...	★	★
U.S. Virgin Islands	A,B	★	★	★	★	★	★	★	...	★

See footnotes at end of table.

ATTORNEYS GENERAL: DUTIES TO ADMINISTRATIVE AGENCIES AND OTHER RESPONSIBILITIES — Continued

Source: The Council of State Governments' survey of attorneys general, January 2006.

Key:

A — Defend state law when challenged on federal constitutional grounds.
B — Conduct litigation on behalf of state in federal and other states' courts.
C — Prosecute actions against another state in U.S. Supreme Court.
★ — Has authority in area.
. . . — Does not have authority in area.
(a) Attorney general has exclusive jurisdiction.
(b) In certain cases only.
(c) When assisting local prosecutor in the appeal.
(d) Can appear on own discretion.
(e) Consumer Advocate Division represents the public in utility rate-making hearings and rule-making proceedings.
(f) Limited.
(g) Primarily federal habeas corpus appeals only.
(h) Upon DA recusal.
(i) Rarely.
(j) However, OUSA handles felony cases and most major misdemeanors.

State Treasurers: Guardians of the Public's Purse

By The National Association of State Treasurers

The roles and responsibilities of state treasurers are countless and critically important to the fiscal well-being of their states. Sound and profitable investments made by state treasurers make it possible for budgets to be balanced, for taxpayer-supported programs to be maintained and grown, and for a positive and equitable level of investment growth for public funds to be achieved.

State treasurers are chief financial officers whose duty is to assure the absolute safety of all state taxpayer dollars as well as guarantee the prudent use of public resources to fund vital government programs. In several states, treasurers also improve the financial security of citizens by providing college savings opportunities and financial education, as well as returning unclaimed property.

The role of the state treasurer is integral to the sound financial operation of the state. Financial stewardship in the complex modern economy is significantly impacted by the status of the state budget, shaping the financial health of the state as a whole. From times of profound budget shortfalls to the current budget surpluses many states are experiencing, state treasurers must decide the appropriate use of an unexpected windfall or determine the least harmful targets for budget reductions.

Policy Leaders

State treasurers are vital players in the healthy management of state budgets and federal policy. The state treasurers play a unique role in policy setting at both the state and federal levels. On issues ranging from corporate governance to accounting standards, state treasurers are at the forefront of policy discussions and initiatives that attempt to safeguard investments made by and on behalf of the residents of their states.

State treasurers commit substantial time and resources to proactive interactions with Congress, the federal government and other organizations representing state government. They have had a lasting and substantive impact on federal actions and activities impacting the investment and management of state and local government funds, debt management, financial education, and a wide range of other fiscal issues. In this respect, treasurers partner with the federal government to affect public policy to enhance state financial well-being.

Through this fiscal oversight and policy setting, state treasurers work daily to protect and benefit their individual states and the nation as a whole.

Selection and Term of Service

State treasurers are elected by the people in 37 states, elected by the legislature in four states and appointed by the governor in nine states. Forty state treasurers serve four-year terms in office, while the state treasurers of Maine, New Hampshire, Tennessee and Vermont serve two-year terms. The remaining state treasurers serve at the discretion and pleasure of the state official making the appointment, which usually is the governor.

Responsibilities of State Treasurers

All state treasurers are responsible for cash management, a fundamental duty of the states' chief financial officers. All but three state treasurers are responsible for banking services and in 35 states, state treasurers are responsible for some aspect of debt management—issuance, service or both. Thirty-three state treasurers are administrators of unclaimed property programs.

All 50 state treasurers are involved in either the oversight or investment of their state's retirement or trust funds. Retirement funds for public employees are scattered in literally thousands of public pension plans. Sound investment of these funds is critical to the successful operation of public pension funds. Twenty-four state treasurers sit on the oversight board for their individual state's investment plan.

Several examples—though certainly not an exhaustive listing—are included and touch on the wide array of state treasurer responsibilities.

Cash management and banking services

It is especially important for treasurers to diligently allocate every state dollar for which they are responsible. Treasurers effectively employ innovative cash management practices to increase capital and contribute to a state's solid financial reputation in national and world markets. Managing shortfalls in state budgets, while largely viewed by the public as an issue for their state's governor and state legislature, also relies heavily on the guidance of the state's treasurer.

Forty-five states forecast cash flow using two methods: float analysis in the collection and disbursement processes or an automated system for cash flow forecasting. Both methods allow for the efficient use of funds in the demand deposit during the disbursement float period. All but one state treasury use in-house sources to develop their cash flow forecasting method. Nearly 2,500 different banking institutions are utilized by the states to serve as their depositories for distribution of demand deposits.

State treasurers are also responsible for managing states' short- and long-term investment portfolios, depositing public funds in financial institutions and protecting public funds, collecting various fees from all state agencies, and ensuring that the state's financial obligations are paid on a daily basis. These activities encompass but are not limited to lock boxes, wire transfers, bank drafts and zero balance accounts.

Twenty-three state treasurers host collection services of some type, whether performed "in-house" or through a banking partner. Twenty-four states offer controlled disbursement programs, while all 50 states utilize an automated clearinghouse. All but nine states engage in account reconciliation services and 30 state treasuries conduct data transfer services.

Debt management

Tax-exempt municipal bonds are the basic tools used by states and local governments to fund the capital improvements necessary to provide utilities, roads and bridges, airports, health care, education, housing and other public services. The ability to sell debt with interest exempt from federal income taxes has been a significant benefit to state and local government borrowers, directly reducing the tax burdens that citizens would otherwise have to shoulder to finance essential public services. The practical effect of this lower borrowing cost is a direct reduction of the tax burdens that citizens would otherwise have to shoulder to finance essential public services.

Debt management is a critical component of state financial operations. To pay for a state's essential capital and public infrastructure needs, many times the state treasury must borrow money by issuing state debt, usually in the form of bonds. That money is often used to fund school and road improvements, airports, water and waste systems, housing and other vital services. The most recently collected statistics show that state treasurers issued $13,285,296,405 in general obligation bonds and $5,111,065,053 in taxable bonds in Fiscal Year 2004.

All but four states issue debt, and of the 46 states that do issue debt, all the state treasurers are involved in the oversight of debt issuance. State treasurers in two states are solely responsible for the authorization of a state's short-term debt. In seven states, the treasurer shares this responsibility usually with a board, the legislature or the governor. Six state treasurers share the responsibility of issuing general obligation bonds, while four state treasurers share investment responsibility on the issuance of revenue bonds. However, only Michigan's treasury shares authority to issue taxable bonds. Treasurers in Maine, Michigan, Montana and Oregon have the ability to authorize taxable debt. Only Florida, Kansas, Kentucky and Utah state treasuries have the authority to issue foreign currency as denominated debt.

Investment of state funds

Management and oversight of state investment functions is a key function of the state treasurers. Earnings from investments are an important source of revenue for state governments. These earnings are used to fund vital public services, cover public employee retirement obligations, and fund beneficial economic development programs, among other uses. In contemporary financial markets, maximizing this source of revenue is a complex and time-consuming undertaking. To make the best use of investment for eligible public funds, public investors like the state treasurers must try to earn the best returns possible without sacrificing the safety of their funds or subjecting their portfolios to undue risks. State treasurers and other public investors must achieve this goal within the constraints of applicable state and federal laws, and state treasurers must make their decisions within the overriding principles of safety, liquidity and yields.

While the task of investing available state funds may seem fairly straightforward to the public, the process is quite complex and requires specialized knowledge and skill. Treasurers must invest using the safest, most efficient methods available while earning the highest possible return. State treasurers' performance and record of investment income critically affects the bottom line of the states' fiscal fitness, which in turn can have a measurable effect on the well-being of the states' budgetary status in any given year.

The state treasurers, who collectively have fiduciary responsibility for more than $1 trillion in public funds, contend that greater corporate responsibility is vital, since the business practices of U.S. corporations have a profound effect on public monies ranging from pension funds to state tax revenue investments. State treasurers, in particular, have fiduciary responsibility not only for pension plans, trust funds and general state funds, but also for other investment vehicles, such as state college savings plans.

Repurchase agreements and U.S. Treasury or agency obligations are the most common types of investments states are allowed to use. Forty-seven states choose to optimize their investment return with repurchase agreements, while 46 states invest with U.S. Treasury or agency obligations. Only seven states utilize real estate as an allowable investment, while nine states use derivatives in their investment portfolio. Eleven state treasurers invest in foreign corporate stocks, and three states opt to put their money into venture capital and private equity enterprises. All but five state treasurers invest in commercial paper. In comparison, 33 states invest in mortgage backed securities.

Treasurers in Alabama, Alaska, Michigan, Mississippi, North Carolina, Vermont and West Virginia are the sole fiduciaries for their state's investments. Twenty-seven states have some type of investment board, committee or council that determines investment policy. Treasurers sit on 24 of these boards.

Fifteen state treasurers are considered administrators for their state's "Rainy Day" funds. While these funds come with a variety of titles, they all serve as a state's reserve or budget stabilization source. Treasurers, auditors and comptrollers are responsible for the safe investment and appropriate draw down of these reserve funds, which total more than $5 billion in assets.

College Savings Plans

State college savings plans have existed since 1988, offering many attractive benefits not included in other savings options. In establishing college savings plans, the states leveraged their experience as major institutional investors to establish low-cost, low-fee college savings investment options for their residents. Thanks to the states' involvement, families now have access to a savings plan that does not require the services of a financial intermediary and does not charge a sale load or commission. These plans provide an easy, affordable and dedicated way for the average American family to save for college. All 50 states and the District of Columbia have college savings plans. Without this state involvement, college savings plans would not be able to meet the needs of all Americans.

College savings plans are often called 529 plans, in reference to the Internal Revenue Service Code Section 529 and the resulting federal tax break. Section 529 plans are offered in two forms—prepaid tuition programs and savings plans. The prepaid tuition program offers families a method to prepay tuition based on current college tuition rates and provides a guarantee to keep pace with tuition inflation. The savings plans offer dedicated qualified state college savings accounts, which provide families a variable rate of return in a tax advantaged college savings account.

More than 8.2 million children across the country have been enrolled in state college tuition or savings plans. Participants in both types of programs receive a federal tax exemption on the investment earnings of the accounts, when the funds are used to pay for qualified higher education expenses, which include tuition, room and board, books and fees, and any other expenses that students are required to pay to attend any accredited college or university in the United States.

The state treasurer plays a vital role in the administration of the programs, including oversight of all program operations and serving as the board chairman or board member, investment manager or committee member.

Unclaimed Property

State treasurers are responsible for the administration of unclaimed property programs in 33 states and the District of Columbia. Unclaimed property refers to accounts in financial institutions and companies that have had no activity generated or contact with the owner for one year or a longer period. Common forms of unclaimed property include savings or checking accounts, stocks, uncashed dividends or payroll checks, refunds, traveler's checks, trust distributions, unredeemed money orders or gift certificates, insurance payments and life insurance policies, annuities, certificates of deposit, customer overpayments, utility security deposits, mineral royalty payments and contents of safe deposit boxes.

Each state has enacted—in the best interest of consumers—an unclaimed property statute that keeps funds from reverting back to the company if it has lost contact with the owner. These laws instruct companies to turn forgotten funds over to state officials, who utilize a variety of public outreach efforts to find and return record amounts of property to the owners or their heirs. By capitalizing on proactive outreach to missing owners, state unclaimed property programs returned nearly $1 billion to citizens last year alone. States will continue to make these committed efforts toward public outreach, and their goal is to increase the amount of returned property in the future.

In addition to the free searchable databases available on the Internet, state officials utilize a variety of resources to promote their return efforts, such as publishing extensive lists of missing owners in newspapers and employing staff to find and return lost accounts. Most states hold lost funds until owners are found, returning them at no cost or for a nominal handling fee upon filing a claim form and verification of identity.

Financial Literacy Initiatives

For the entire year of 2005, America's personal savings rate was in the negative, a first since the Great Depression. At a time when credit is readily accessible and so many households are spending far more than they save, it is imperative for individuals to learn and employ strong financial management skills. Many state treasurers are working toward this goal.

Over the past few decades, state treasurers have taken an active role in promoting financial literacy. State treasurers operate financial education programs for the benefit of their citizens, drawing upon their substantial expertise in the financial management of both personal and public funds to provide opportunities to educate the citizens of the states on savings, from birth to retirement.

Thirty-five state treasurers offer some type of program, ranging from "Bank at School" programs designed to teach students basic monetary concepts to women's conferences that help adults gain control of their personal finances.

Conclusion

The roles and responsibilities of state treasurers are countless and critically important to the fiscal well-being of their states. Sound and profitable investments made by state treasurers make it possible for budgets to be balanced, for taxpayer-supported programs to be maintained and grown, and for a positive and equitable level of investment growth for public funds to be achieved.

About the Author

The **National Association of State Treasurers**, an organization of state financial leaders, encourages the highest ethical standards, promotes education and the exchange of ideas, builds professional relationships, develops standards of excellence and influences public policy for the benefit of the citizens of the states. NAST is composed of all state treasurers, or state financial officials with comparable responsibilities from the United States, its commonwealths, territories and the District of Columbia.

Table 4.24
THE TREASURERS, 2006

State or other jurisdiction	Name and party	Method of selection	Length of regular term in years	Date of first service	Present term ends	Maximum consecutive terms allowed by constitution
Alabama	Kay Ivey (R)	E	4	1/03	1/07	2
Alaska (a).....................	Tom Boutin	A	4	2/05	. . .	. . .
Arizona	David Petersen (R)	E	4	1/03	1/07	2
Arkansas....................	Gus Wingfield (D)	E	4	1/03	1/07	2
California	Philip Angelides (D)	E	4	1/99	1/07	2
Colorado	Mark Coffman (R)	E	4	1/99	1/07	2
Connecticut	Denise Nappier (D)	E	4	1/99	1/07	★
Delaware....................	Jack Markell (D)	E	4	1/99	1/07	★
Florida (b)	Tom Gallagher (R)	E	4	1/88	1/07	2
Georgia	W. Daniel Ebersole	A	Pleasure of the Board	11/97	. . .	. . .
Hawaii (c)	Georgina Kawamura	A	4	12/02	. . .	. . .
Idaho.........................	Ron Crane (R)	E	4	1/99	1/07	★
Illinois.......................	Judy Baar Topinka (R)	E	4	1/95	1/07	★
Indiana......................	Tim Berry (R)	E	4	2/99	2/07	(d)
Iowa	Michael Fitzgerald (D)	E	4	1/83	1/07	★
Kansas	Lynn Jenkins (R)	E	4	1/03	1/07	★
Kentucky	Jonathan Miller (D)	E	4	1/00	12/07	2
Louisiana	John Kennedy (D)	E	4	1/00	1/08	★
Maine	David Lemoine (D)	L	2	1/05	1/07	4
Maryland	Nancy Kopp (D)	L	4	2/02	1/07	★
Massachusetts............	Timothy Cahill (D)	E	4	1/03	1/07	★
Michigan....................	Robert J. Kleine	A	Governor's discretion	4/06	. . .	. . .
Minnesota (e).............	Peggy Ingison	A	. . .	2/04	. . .	. . .
Mississippi	Tate Reeves (R)	E	4	1/04	1/08	★
Missouri.....................	Sarah Steelman (R)	E	4	1/05	1/09	2
Montana	Janet Kelly	A	4	1/05	. . .	. . .
Nebraska....................	Ron Ross (R)	E	4	12/03	1/07	2
Nevada	Brian Krolicki (R)	E	4	1/99	1/07	2
New Hampshire.........	Michael Ablowich	L	2	3/02	12/06	★
New Jersey	Bradley I. Abelow	A	Governor's discretion	1/06	. . .	. . .
New Mexico	Douglas Brown (R) (acting)	E	4	11/05	1/07	2
New York	Aida Brewer	A	Governor's discretion	2/02	. . .	. . .
North Carolina	Richard Moore (D)	E	4	1/01	1/09	★
North Dakota.............	Kelly Schmidt (R)	E	4	1/05	1/09	★
Ohio	Jennette Bradley (R)	E	4	1/05	1/07	2
Oklahoma	Scott Meacham (D)	E	4	6/05	1/07	★
Oregon	Randall Edwards (D)	E	4	1/01	1/09	2
Pennsylvania	Robert Casey Jr. (D)	E	4	1/05	1/09	2
Rhode Island	Paul Tavares (D)	E	4	1/99	1/07	2
South Carolina	Grady Patterson Jr. (D)	E	4	1/66	1/07	★
South Dakota.............	Vernon L. Larson (R)	E	4	1/03	1/07	2
Tennessee	Dale Sims	L	2	10/03	1/07	. . .
Texas (f)	Carole Keeton Strayhorn (R)	E	4	1/99	1/07	★
Utah	Edward Alter (R)	E	4	1/81	1/09	★
Vermont	Jeb Spaulding (D)	E	2	1/03	1/07	★
Virginia......................	Braxton Powell	A	Governor's discretion	1/06	. . .	. . .
Washington................	Michael Murphy (D)	E	4	1/97	1/09	★
West Virginia.............	John Perdue (D)	E	4	1/97	1/09	★
Wisconsin...................	Jack Voight (R)	E	4	1/95	1/07	★
Wyoming....................	Cynthia Lummis (R)	E	4	1/99	1/07	2
American Samoa.......	Velega Savali Jr.	A	4	N.A.	N.A.	. . .
Dist. of Columbia	Lasana Mack	A	Pleasure of CFO	8/05	N.A.	. . .
Guam	Yasela Pereira	CS	. . .	10/96	. . .	. . .
No. Mariana Islands...	Antoinette S. Calvo	A	4	N.A.	N.A.	. . .
Puerto Rico................	Juan Carlos Méndez Torres	N.A.	4	N.A.	N.A.	. . .
U.S. Virgin Islands	Bernice A. Turnbull	A	4	N.A.	N.A.	. . .

Source: National Association of State Treasurers, April 2006.

Key:

★ — No provision specifying number of terms allowed.

. . . — No formal provision, position is appointed or elected by governmental entity (not chosen by the electorate).

A — Appointed by the governor. (In the District of Columbia, the Treasurer is appointed by the Chief Financial Officer. In Georgia, position is appointed by the State Depository Board.)

E — Elected by the voters

L — Elected by the legislature

CS — Civil Service

(a) The Deputy Commissioner of Department of Revenue performs this function.

(b) The official title of the office of state treasurer is Chief Financial Officer.

(c) The Director of Finance performs this function.

(d) Eligible for eight out of any period of 12 years.

(e) The Commissioner of Finance performs this function.

(f) The Comptroller of Public Accounts performs this function.

Table 4.25
TREASURERS: QUALIFICATIONS FOR OFFICE

State or other jurisdiction	Minimum age	U.S. citizen (years)	State resident (years)	Qualified voter (years)
Alabama	25	7	5	...
Alaska	...	...	★	...
Arizona	25	10	5	...
Arkansas	21	★	★	...
California	18	★	★	★
Colorado	25	★	★	★
Connecticut	...	★	★	★
Delaware	18	★	★	★
Florida	30	★	7	★
Georgia	...	...	...	...
Hawaii	...	★	★	...
Idaho	25	★	2	...
Illinois	25	★	★	...
Indiana	...	★	★	★
Iowa	18	...	...	...
Kansas	...	...	...	...
Kentucky	30	★	6	★
Louisiana	25	(a)	(c)	(c)
Maine	...	★	★	...
Maryland	...	...	...	...
Massachusetts	...	...	★	...
Michigan	...	...	...	...
Minnesota	...	...	...	...
Mississippi	25	★	1	★
Missouri	...	★	5	★
Montana	...	...	...	...
Nebraska	19	★	★	★
Nevada	25	★	★	★
New Hampshire	...	...	...	...
New Jersey	...	...	★	...
New Mexico	30	★	★	★
New York	...	★	★	N.A.
North Carolina	21	★	1	★
North Dakota	25	★	5	★
Ohio	18	★	★	★
Oklahoma	31	★	★	(e)
Oregon	18	...	★	...
Pennsylvania	...	...	...	...
Rhode Island	(d)	★	★	★
South Carolina	...	★	★	★
South Dakota	...	...	...	...
Tennessee	...	...	...	...
Texas	18	★	★	...
Utah	25	★	5	★
Vermont	18	★	2	...
Virginia	...	...	...	...
Washington	18	★	...	★
West Virginia	18	(b)	(b)	★
Wisconsin	18	★	★	★
Wyoming	25	★	1	★
District of Columbia	...	...	...	...

Source: National Association of State Treasurers, January 2006.
Key:
★ — Formal provision; number of years not specified.
... — No formal provision.

(a) Five years immediately preceding the date of election.
(b) Five years prior to taking office.
(c) Five years immediately preceding the date of qualification for office.
(d) Must be qualified elector.
(e) Must be able to vote for at least 10 years immediately preceding election.

Table 4.26
TREASURERS: DUTIES OF OFFICE

State or other jurisdiction	Cash management and banking services	Investment of general funds	Investment of retirement and/or trust funds	Oversight of retirement funds	Oversight/ management of debt issuance	Unclaimed property	Link deposit program	College Savings/ Prepaid Tuition Programs
Alabama	★	★	...	★	★	★	★	★
Alaska	★	...	★	★	★	★	...	...
Arizona	★	...	★	★	...	...	...	★
Arkansas	★	...	★	★	...	...	...	★
California	★	★	★	★	★	...	...	★
Colorado	★	...	...	★	...	★	★	★
Connecticut	★	★	★	★	★	★	★	★
Delaware	★	★	...	★	★	...	...	★
Florida	★	★	★	★	★	★	...	...
Georgia	★	...	...	★	★	...	...	...
Hawaii	★	...	★	★	...	★	...	★
Idaho	★	...	...	★	...	...	...	★
Illinois	★	...	★	★	★	★	★	★
Indiana	★	...	★	★	...	...	...	★
Iowa	★	...	★	★	★	★	★	★
Kansas	★	...	...	★	...	★	★	★
Kentucky	★	...	...	★	...	★	★	★
Louisiana	★	...	★	★	★	★	★	★
Maine	★	...	★	★	★	★	★	★
Maryland	★	★	...	★	★	...	★	★
Massachusetts	★	...	★	★	★	★	★	...
Michigan	★	...	★	★	★	★	...	★
Minnesota	★	★	...	★	★	...	...	★
Mississippi	★	★	★	★	★	★	...	★
Missouri	★	...	★	★	...	★	★	★
Montana	★	★	...	★	★	...	★	...
Nebraska	★	...	...	★	...	★	...	★
Nevada	★	...	★	★	★	★	...	★
New Hampshire	★	★	★	★	★	★	...	★
New Jersey	★	...	★	★	★	★	...	★
New Mexico	★	...	...	★	...	...	...	...
New York	★	...	...	★	★	...	★	★
North Carolina	★	...	★	★	★	★	...	★
North Dakota	★	★	★	★	...	...	★	...
Ohio	★	...	★	★	★	...	...	...
Oklahoma	★	★	★	★	★	★	★	★
Oregon	★	...	★	★	★	...	...	★
Pennsylvania	★	...	★	★	★	★	★	★
Rhode Island	★	...	★	★	★	★	...	★
South Carolina	★	...	★	★	★	★	...	★
South Dakota	★	...	★	★	...	★	...	★
Tennessee	★	...	★	★	...	★	...	...
Texas	★	★	★	★	...	...	★	★
Utah	★	★	★	★	★	★	...	★
Vermont	★	...	★	★	★	★	...	★
Virginia	★	...	★	...	★	★	...	★
Washington	★	...	★	★	★	...	★	★
West Virginia	★	...	...	★	★	★	★	★
Wisconsin	★	...	...	★	...	★	...	★
Wyoming	★	...	★	★	★	★	...	★
District of Columbia	★	★	★	...	★	★	★	...

Source: National Association of State Treasurers, March 2006.
Key:
★ — Responsible for activity.
... — Not responsible for activity.

Table 4.27
STATE INVESTMENT BOARD MEMBERSHIP

State or other jurisdiction	Name of board	Governor	Lt. Governor	Treasurer	Auditor	Comptroller	Attorney General	Secretary of State	Secretary/ Director of Finance	Gubernatorial Appointments	Other
Alabama	N.A.	...	...	...	...	...	...	...	...	...	(a)
Alaska	N.A.	...	...	...	...	...	...	...	...	...	(a)
Arizona	Arizona State Board of Investment	...	...	Yes	...	...	...	...	...	...	(b)
Arkansas	State Board of Finance	Yes	...	Yes	Yes	...	...	...	Yes	1	(c)
California	Pooled Money Investment Board	...	...	Yes	...	Yes	...	...	Yes	...	...
Colorado	Investment Advisory Board	...	...	Yes	...	...	...	...	...	...	(d)
Connecticut	...	...	...	...	...	...	...	...	...	...	(f)
Delaware	Cash Management Policy Board	...	...	Yes	...	Yes	...	Yes	Yes	5	...
Florida	N.A.	...	...	...	...	...	...	...	...	...	(f)
Georgia	State Depository Board	Yes	...	Yes	Yes	...	...	...	Yes	...	(e)
Hawaii	N.A.	...	...	...	...	...	...	...	...	...	(f)
Idaho	N.A.	...	...	...	...	...	...	...	...	...	(f)
Illinois	N.A.	...	...	...	...	...	...	...	...	...	(f)
Indiana	N.A.	...	...	...	...	...	...	...	...	...	(f)
Iowa	Treasurer's Investment Committee	...	...	Yes	...	...	...	...	...	...	(g)
Kansas	Pooled Money Investment Board	...	...	Yes	...	...	...	...	...	4	...
Kentucky	Kentucky State Investment Commission	Yes	...	Yes	...	...	...	...	Yes	2	...
Louisiana	N.A.	...	...	...	...	...	...	...	...	...	(f)
Maine	Trust Committee	...	...	Yes	...	...	Yes	...	Yes	...	(h)
Maryland	N.A.	...	...	...	...	...	...	...	...	...	(f)
Massachusetts	Investment Advisory Council	...	...	Yes	...	...	...	...	...	2	(i)
Michigan	N.A.	...	...	Yes	...	...	...	...	...	...	(a)
Minnesota	Minnesota State Board of Investment	Yes	...	...	Yes	...	Yes	Yes	...	...	...
Mississippi	N.A.	...	...	...	...	...	...	...	...	...	(a)
Missouri	N.A.	...	...	...	...	...	...	...	...	...	(f)
Montana	Montana Board of Investments	...	...	...	...	...	...	...	...	9	...
Nebraska	Nebraska Investment Council	...	...	Yes	...	...	...	...	...	5	(j)
Nevada	State Board of Finance	Yes	...	Yes	...	Yes	...	...	...	2	...
New Hampshire	N.A.	...	...	...	...	...	...	...	...	...	(f)
New Jersey	State Investment Council	...	...	Yes	...	...	...	...	...	6	(k)
New Mexico	State Board of Finance	Yes	Yes	...	...	...	...	...	Yes	4 to 5	...
New York	N.A.	...	...	...	...	...	...	...	...	...	(f)
North Carolina	N.A.	...	...	...	...	...	...	...	...	...	(a)
North Dakota	State Investment Board	...	Yes	Yes	...	...	...	...	...	...	(l)
Ohio	N.A.	...	...	...	...	...	...	...	...	...	...
Oklahoma	Cash Management and Investment Oversight Commission	...	...	...	...	...	...	...	Yes	1	(m)
Oregon	Oregon Investment Council	...	...	Yes	...	...	...	...	...	...	(n)
Pennsylvania	N.A.	...	...	...	...	...	...	...	...	...	(f)
Rhode Island	State Investment Commission	...	...	Yes	...	...	...	...	...	3	...
South Carolina	N.A.	...	...	...	...	...	...	...	...	...	(f)
South Dakota	South Dakota Investment Council	...	...	Yes	...	...	...	...	...	...	(o)
Tennessee	State Pooled Investment Fund	Yes	...	Yes	...	Yes	...	Yes	Yes	...	...
Texas	N.A.	...	...	...	...	...	...	...	...	...	(f)
Utah	N.A.	...	...	...	...	...	...	...	...	...	(f)
Vermont	N.A.	...	...	...	...	...	...	...	...	...	(a)
Virginia	Virginia Treasury Board	...	...	Yes	...	Yes	...	...	...	4	(p)
Washington	N.A.	...	...	Yes	...	...	...	...	...	...	(a)
West Virginia	WV Investment Management Board	Yes	...	Yes	Yes	...	...	...	...	10	...
Wisconsin	State of Wisconsin Investment Board	...	...	...	...	...	...	...	...	5	...
Wyoming	Wyoming State Loan and Investment Board	Yes	...	Yes	Yes	...	...	Yes	...	...	(q)
District of Columbia	N.A.	...	...	...	...	...	...	...	...	...	(f)

See footnotes at end of table.

STATE INVESTMENT BOARD MEMBERSHIP — Continued

Source: National Association of State Treasurers.

Notes:

(a) State treasurer is sole fiduciary.

(b) Director of the Department of Administration, State Banking Superintendent. Two individuals appointed by treasurer.

(c) Bank Commissioner.

(d) Deputy Treasurer and a representative from the Land Board, Department of Labor. Three investment officers and nine public investment professionals from private sector.

(e) Insurance Commissioner, Transportation Commissioner, Banking and Finance Commissioner, Revenue Commissioner.

(f) Does not have an investment board.

(g) Deputy Treasurers and Chief Investment Officer.

(h) Commissioner of Education.

(i) Two Treasury appointees. Executive Director of both state and teacher's retirement system.

(j) Public Employees Retirement System Director.

(k) Five representatives of Pension Fund Boards.

(l) Commissioner of University and School Lands. Director of Worker's Compensation. Commissioner of Insurance.

(m) Senate appoint. President Pro Tempore Appoint.

(n) Executive Director, Oregon Public Employees Retirement System (non-voting).

(o) Commissionary of School and Public Lands. State Retirement Director and five others appointed by state legislature.

(p) Tax Commissioner.

(q) Superintendent of Public Instruction.

State Auditors and Comptrollers: Trends and Issues

By R. Thomas Wagner Jr.

If there is one thing the past year has taught us, it is to expect the unexpected. No one could have foreseen some of the events our nation has experienced during calendar year 2005—events that have had tremendous impact on citizens and, by default, also on governments. Uncertainty spawned by unpreventable natural occurrences, coupled with longstanding issues faced by state governments, has made this year an interesting one, to say the least. However, state governments continue working to learn from the past and make informed decisions for the future.

The Road Behind—and Ahead

Disaster Planning and Recovery

When disasters strike, such as the natural disasters that slammed southern portions of the country in 2005, "business as usual" is not an option. Hurricanes Katrina and Rita forced the nation to revisit the concepts of disaster planning and recovery. At first impact during a disaster, citizens are not worried about the delivery of government services—they are consumed with addressing immediate dangers and ensuring that they and their loved ones find safe harbor from threat. Too soon afterwards, however, reliance upon government systems, which have most likely also been impacted by the same threat, becomes a reality.

We tend to think of government as an abstract ideal, forgetting that "government" is essentially a cumulative effort by citizens who have chosen to make the successful operation of the "business of the people" their lifework. In the cases of this year's hurricanes, government services were, and still are, being coordinated by citizens who are not only responding to, but also experiencing, the crisis. It is essential for government leaders to recognize the potential for disaster in advance and have action plans in place to address an endless list of possible scenarios. It is also essential for government financial management leaders to ensure that "disaster" mentalities do not override processes embedded to ensure accountability and transparency.

Disasters can and will strike. This is a reality that must be accepted. It is up to government leaders, however, to continually assess the operational successes and failures that follow in the wake of disasters to fine-tune and improve systems nationwide. What does this mean for state auditors, comptrollers and treasurers? First and foremost, it means we must support our professional colleagues and aid them in responding to disasters that have directly impacted their jobs and lives. It also means that in areas affected by disaster, we must closely scrutinize and work to improve government accounting and auditing processes and test

their capacity to withstand pressures resulting from extreme circumstances. And finally, it means we must take this information, apply it to possible scenarios for our own jurisdictions, and use it to plan accordingly for the future well-being of each state.

Accounting and Financial Reporting

Conversations about "change" in government must include discussion about changes in accounting and financial reporting. State and local governments are now preparing for implementation of new accounting and financial reporting standards for other post-employment benefits (OPEB), promulgated by the Governmental Accounting Standards Board in 2004. OPEB plans include post-employment benefits other than pensions; the largest of these by far is the post-employment health care benefit offered by many state governments. The new standards would treat OPEB plans much like pension plans. Instead of the traditional pay-as-you-go system, governments will be required to report the assets and liabilities for their OPEB plans in their financial statements.

Since the OPEB liabilities are expected to be quite large, states have started to engage actuarial services and otherwise estimate their OPEB obligations, so that their governments might consider options for managing the new and significant liability on their balance sheets. Some are considering legislation curtailing OPEB benefits for current employees and/or not offering these benefits to new hires. Others will establish funds similar to pension funds to which they make annual contributions. OPEB will first appear in states' annual financial reports in fiscal year 2007.

Benchmarking and Best Practices

State financial officers have long been interested in increasing the efficiency and effectiveness of their operations and of financial management across state government. They are now starting to use a proven tool to measure and assess performance. Benchmarking has been used extensively in the private sector for more than a decade. There, it has been proven to be a very effective way to improve processes and find the kinds of elusive cost-cutting efficiencies government leaders are always seeking. States are taking the initiative to address change by using this proven method to improve government processes.

In 2005, the National Association of State Auditors, Comptrollers and Treasurers (NASACT) expanded on a 2004 pilot to launch its state government benchmarking project. As of August 2005, states may contract through NASACT to receive benchmarking services in four areas—finance, HR/payroll, procurement and information technology. The purpose of the project is to help state governments identify areas where they can benefit from best practices, target processes that are inefficient, and prioritize areas to make process improvements through standardization and simplification. By comparing states to other states, agencies within states and agencies/states to the private sector, state governments will be in a better position to make informed decisions about the deployment of resources and also about how best to implement new ERP or other systems.

Technology and Government

Technology issues pervade each layer of the business of government. From physical network infrastructures to the more ethereal world of wireless capabilities to complicated security and authentication issues, governments address technology-oriented concerns every day at every level. Old ways of maintaining control over finances have been abandoned, and new methods have been adopted to maintain accuracy and accountability. These new methods present new challenges, including maintaining privacy and ensuring the integrity of electronic data.

The authentication of electronic credentials remains a technological challenge for both government and the private sector. Through the Electronic Authentication Partnership, or EAP, state government finance officials are working to address the challenge. The EAP, which includes representatives from both the public and private sectors, is embarking on its first pilot project. The pilot aims to use EAP rules to support a single card for federated logical and physical access authentication to commercial and government facilities. The success of this project should aid the partnership in meeting its mission to promote the interoperability of digital identity credentials and should open the way for further application of standard credentialing methods.

In the continued search for ways to streamline processes, states are still looking to enterprise resource planning as a means to an end. Technology has enabled a clearer view toward business process re-engineering, data retrieval, reporting and effective system interfacing. States that have not implemented ERP systems are learning from those that have. States that already have ERP systems are learning to evolve within the sphere of their new processes and capabilities.

Increased concern about data security and integrity within the private sector has inevitably spilled over into the public domain. States are regulated by the federal government via privacy and data management laws and also by new payment card industry data security standards from the major credit card companies. From managing the physical lock-down of desktop workstations to ensuring the encryption of data transmitted over wireless networks, IT staff within state governments are stepping up to meet extreme challenges, tackling complicated technical problems in jobs that are often not competitive in terms of salaries found within the private sector.

Investing in technology is essential for state government. Technology is not just a concern for chief information officers or IT managers; it is a concern for *every* state government employee, from administrative assistants to the highest leadership ranks. Technology makes our jobs easier. At the same time, technology complicates processes that may once have seemed "simple" by embedding a layer of high-tech reliance into everything we do. State auditors, comptrollers and treasurers *must* remain aware of technology changes and potential and *must* seek to hire and retain the brightest and best IT employees to continue offering expanded and improved services to citizens.

Even with a heightened awareness of our reliance on technology, state government leaders must ensure that the key concepts of "what we do" and "why" do not become lost in the tangle of wires. When the technologies that we rely on are not available, for whatever reason, we must have contingency plans in place to ensure that operations and service to citizens can continue in a reasonable manner.

Corporate Governance and Accountability

Today's economy necessitates a tie between government and the private sector; thus, state government leaders are closely attuned to corporate governance and its effects on the business of the states. Our interest is two-pronged. As investors in U.S. and foreign corporations, states are shareholders with a responsibility to monitor the financial well-being of companies in which they invest. As entities that are also held to established measures of accountability and integrity, states also have an obligation to examine corporate governance models and study how they may apply to government.

The Sarbanes-Oxley Act, while applicable only to the private sector, has generated new interest in strengthening internal control in state government. Many projects have recently been implemented, from the creation of an Office of the Inspector General to new emphasis on internal control across all agencies. More intensive training about internal control is being offered to state agencies, and reviews and self-assessments of internal controls are being required of the agencies. There is increased emphasis on risk-based analysis, and much attention is given to building controls into new ERP or other financial management systems.

There is no present requirement for states to implement Sarbanes-Oxley, but governments are under pressure to be held to the same standards as private sector companies. A recent survey on the extent to which Sarbanes-Oxley-type provisions have been implemented in state and local government shows that some governments are voluntarily implementing certain provisions. Although there are some obvious benefits to the implementation of Sarbanes-Oxley for government, there are also some cons to consider. For example, the cost-benefit of Sarbanes-Oxley has not been proven and the risks and objectives of a governmental entity are clearly different from those of a private sector corporation.

Assuring that state funds are not being used to support terrorism in any manner also remains an important challenge facing the states. At least one state has taken proactive measures to assure payments being made are not to individuals listed on U.S. Treasury's Office of Foreign Asset Control's list of Specially Designated Nationals. Fiscal officials continue to seek information from the federal government regarding companies with business ties to sanctioned countries. Information from the federal government is essential, as it is credible, and institutional investors are not in the position to determine whether companies compromise national security through the business they conduct.

Corporate governance and accountability are issues fiscal officials have always monitored closely and will continue to watch.

Additional Challenges that Lie Ahead

States continue to face significant challenges in hiring and maintaining a qualified work force, particularly qualified finance professionals. With a majority of the work force at or near retirement, states are struggling to hire qualified professionals with education in accounting and finance. Governmental accounting classes are no longer being offered in many universities and more and more accounting degree candidates are turning instead to the business side to secure successful careers. The passage of Sarbanes-Oxley has further exacerbated the problem, as existing professionals and financial degree candidates are lured away by the private sector with appealing compensation packages. Unfortunately, state governments can no longer rely on the appeal of plush benefit packages to attain desirable workers, as pension plans are under attack and are targeted for change in many states.

Although slowly emerging from very difficult financial times, states continue to face troubling budget problems. Perhaps the biggest crisis is the rapidly rising cost of health care. Across the country, Medicaid continues to be the largest and fastest-growing component of state budgets, and there appears to be no end in sight.

States continue to experience difficulties in fully maximizing the potential for credit card acceptance for payments. Although citizens are accustomed to the convenience of using credits cards for payments of all types, credit card interchange fees often make it cost prohibitive for states to offer credit cards as a payment option for large payments (i.e., for tax payments, etc.). In some states, passing costs on to consumers for fees, such as interchange fees, is even prohibited by statute. Although an alliance of states through NASACT is working to negotiate with major credit companies to address the issue, no resolution has been reached. States will continue efforts to find a resolution that takes into account the unique, low-risk circumstances surrounding the acceptance of credit cards for payments by government.

Conclusions and Perspectives

Every year the same conclusion is reached—"state government is different today than it was yesterday." That conclusion still holds true. The challenge for state financial leaders, then, is to continue to meet changing conditions head-on, with a firm grasp on the reality that change is inevitable.

Partnership is essential as state fiscal leaders work to address old problems and new challenges. Technology has become a common bond for government leaders at all levels—comptrollers, treasurers, auditors, chief information officers, chief strategy officials ... the list goes on and on. Technology will be the enabler of new efficiencies and innovations that will usher in a new era of service and convenience to citizens. When disasters strike, we may falter momentarily, but we will use each setback as a learning experience to aid us and our peers in future planning and improvement efforts.

About the Author

R. Thomas Wagner Jr. is the auditor of accounts of Delaware and president of the National Association of State Auditors, Comptrollers and Treasurers. He is the past president of the National State Auditors Association and past chairman of the Mid-Atlantic Audit Forum. Wagner has worked as a bank examiner, a staff member for the Delaware House of Representatives, and as a two-term mayor of Camden, Del. He is a certified fraud examiner and a certified government financial manager.

Table 4.28
THE STATE AUDITORS, 2006

State or other jurisdiction	State Agency	Agency head	Title	Legal basis for office	Method of selection	Term of office	U.S. citizen	State resident	Maximum consecutive terms allowed
Alabama	Dept. of Examiners of Public Accounts	Ronald L. Jones	Chief Examiner	S	L	7 yrs.	★	★	None
Alaska	Division of Legislative Audit	Pat Davidson	Legislative Auditor	C, S	L	(a)	...	...	None
Arizona	Auditor General	Debra K. Davenport	Auditor General	S	LC	5 yrs.	...	...	None
Arkansas	Legislative Auditor	Charles L. Robinson	Legislative Auditor	N.A.	L	N.A.	★	...	
California	Bureau of State Audits	Elaine Howle	State Auditor	S	G	4 yrs.	★	...	None
Colorado	State Auditor	Joanne Hill	State Auditor	C	L	5 yrs.	★	...	None
Connecticut	Auditors of Public Accounts	Kevin P. Johnston, Robert G. Jaekle	State Auditors	C	L	4 yrs.	...	...	None
Delaware	Auditor of Accounts	R. Thomas Wagner Jr.	Auditor of Accounts	C, S	E	4 yrs.	★	★	None
Florida	Auditor General	William O. Monroe	Auditor General	C, S	L	(a)	...	...	None
Georgia	Dept. of Audits and Accounts	Russell W. Hinton	State Auditor	S	L	Indefinite	...	...	None
Hawaii	Office of the Auditor	Marion M. Higa	State Auditor	C, S	LC	8 yrs.	...	★	None
Idaho	Legislative Services Office– Legislative Audits	Raymond Ineck	Supervisor of Legislative Audits	S	LC	Indefinite	...	★	None
Illinois	Auditor General	William G. Holland	Auditor General	C, S	L	10 yrs.	...	...	None
Indiana	State Board of Accounts	Bruce Hartman	State Examiner	S	G	4 yrs.	...	★	None
Iowa	Auditor of State	David A. Vaudt	Auditor of State	C, S	E	4 yrs.	★	★	None
Kansas	Legislative Division of Post Audit	Barbara J. Hinton	Legislative Post Auditor	S	LC	(b)	...	★	None
Kentucky	Auditor of Public Accounts	Crit Luallen	Auditor of Public Accounts	C, S	E	4 yrs.	★	★	2
Louisiana	Legislative Auditor	Steve J. Theriot	Legislative Auditor	C, S	L	(a)	★	★	None
Maine	State Auditor	Neria Douglas	State Auditor				...	...	
Maryland	Office of Legislative Audits	Bruce A. Myers	Legislative Auditor	S	ED	Indefinite	★	...	None
Massachusetts	State Auditor	A. Joseph DeNucci	Auditor of the Commonwealth	C, S	E	4 yrs.	★	★	None
Michigan	Auditor General	Thomas H. McTavish	Auditor General	C	L	8 yrs.	...	★	None
Minnesota	Legislative Auditor	James R. Nobles	Legislative Auditor	S	LC	6 yrs.	...	★	None
Mississippi	State Auditor	Patricia Anderson	State Auditor	C	E	4 yrs.	★	★	None
Missouri	State Auditor	Phil Bryant	State Auditor	C, S	E	4 yrs.	★	★	None
	State Auditor	Claire McCaskill	State Auditor	C, S	E	4 yrs.	★	★	None
Montana	Legislative Audit Division, Legislative Branch	Scott A. Seacat	Legislative Auditor	C, S	LC	2 yrs.	...	...	None
Nebraska	Auditor of Public Accounts	Kate Witek	Auditor of Public Accounts	C, S	E	4 yrs.	★	★	None
Nevada	Legislative Auditor	Paul Townsend	Legislative Auditor	S	LC	Indefinite	...	...	None
New Hampshire	Legislative Budget Assistant	Michael L. Buckley	Legislative Budget Assistant	S	LC	2 yrs.	...	...	None
New Jersey	State Auditor	Richard L. Fair	State Auditor	C, S	L	5 yr. term and until successor is appointed	...	...	N.A.
New Mexico	State Auditor	Domingo Martinez	State Auditor	C	E	4 yrs.	★	★	None
New York	Office of the State Comptroller, State Audit Services	Alan G. Hevesi	Deputy Comptroller– State Audit Services	C, S	E	4 yrs.	★	★	2
North Carolina	State Auditor	Leslie W. Merritt Jr.	State Auditor	C, S	E	4 yrs.	★	★	None
North Dakota	State Auditor	Robert R. Petersen	State Auditor	C, S	E	4 yrs.	...	★	None
Ohio	Auditor of State	Betty D. Montgomery	Auditor of State	C	E	4 yrs.	★	★	2

See footnotes at end of table.

THE STATE AUDITORS, 2006 — Continued

State or other jurisdiction	State Agency	Agency head	Title	Legal basis for office	Method of selection	Term of office	U.S. citizen	State resident	Maximum consecutive terms allowed
Oklahoma	State Auditor and Inspector	Jeff McMahan	State Auditor and Inspector	C, S	E	4 yrs.	★	★	None
Oregon	Secretary of State, Audits Division	Charles Hibner	State Auditor	C	SS	(c)	. . .	. . .	N.A.
Pennsylvania	Auditor General	Jack Wagner	Auditor General	C	E	4 yrs.	. . .	. . .	2
Rhode Island	Legislative Finance and Budget	Philip R. Durgin	Executive Director	S	LC	(b)	. . .	. . .	None
	Auditor General	Ernest A. Almonte	Auditor General	S	LC	(b)	. . .	. . .	None
South Carolina	Legislative Audit Council	George L. Schroeder	Director	S	LC	4 yrs.	. . .	. . .	None
	State Auditor	Thomas L. Wagner Jr.	State Auditor	S	SB	Indefinite	. . .	. . .	N.A.
South Dakota	Dept. of Legislative Audit	Martin L. Guindon	Auditor General	C	E	8 yrs.	. . .	. . .	None
Tennessee	Comptroller of the Treasury, Dept. of Audit	John G. Morgan	Comptroller of the Treasury	C, S	L	2 yrs.	. . .	. . .	No
Texas	State Auditor	John Keel, CPA	State Auditor	S	LC	(b)	★	★	None
Utah	State Auditor	Auston G. Johnson	State Auditor	C, S	E	4 yrs.	★	★	None
Vermont	State Auditor	Randy Brock	State Auditor	C, S	E	2 yrs.	★	★	None
Virginia	Auditor of Public Accounts	Walter J. Kucharski	Auditor of Public Accounts	C	L	4 yrs.	. . .	. . .	None
Washington	Office of the State Auditor	Brian Sonntag	State Auditor	C, S	E	4 yrs.	★	★	None
West Virginia	Legislative Auditor	Aaron Allred	Legislative Auditor			Indefinite	. . .	. . .	
Wisconsin	Legislative Audit Bureau	Janice Mueller	State Auditor	C, S	LC	Indefinite	. . .	. . .	None
Wyoming	Dept. of Audit	Michael Geesey	Director	S	GC	6 yrs.	. . .	★	None
Guam	Office of the Public Auditor	Doris Flores Brooks	Public Auditor		E	4 yrs.	★	★	2
Puerto Rico	Office of the Comptroller of Puerto Rico	Manuel Diaz Saldana	Comptroller of Puerto Rico	C, S	GL	10 yrs.	★	. . .	1

Source: Auditing in the States: A Summary, 2003 Edition, The National Association of Auditors, Comptrollers and Treasurers, updated January 2006.

Key:
★ — Provision for
. . . — No provision
E — Elected by the public.
L — Appointed by the legislature.
G — Appointed by the governor.
SS — Appointed by the secretary of state.
LC — Selected by legislative committee, commission or council.

ED — Appointed by the executive director of legislative services.
GC — Appointed by governor, secretary of state and treasurer.
GL — Appointed by the governor and confirmed by both chambers of the legislature.
SB — Appointed by state budget and control board.
C — Constitutional
S — Statutory
N.A. — Not available.
(a) Serves at the pleasure of the legislature.
(b) Serves at the pleasure of a legislative committee.
(c) Serves at the pleasure of the secretary of state.

Table 4.29
STATE AUDITORS: SCOPE OF AGENCY AUTHORITY

State or other jurisdiction	Authority to audit all state agencies	Authority to audit local governments	Authority to obtain information	Authority to issue subpoenas	Authority to specify accounting principles for local governments	Investigations Agency investigates fraud, waste, abuse, and/or illegal acts	Agency operates a hotline
Alabama	★	★	★	★	★(q)	★	...
Alaska	★	...	★	...	...	★	...
Arizona	★	★	★	...	★(r)	★	...
Arkansas	N.A.	N.A.	N.A.	N.A.	N.A.	N.A.	N.A.
California	★	★	★	★	...	★	★
Colorado	★	★	★	★	★	★	...
Connecticut	★	...	★	...	...	★	★
Delaware	★	★	★	★	...	★	★
Florida	(a)	★	★	...	...	★	...
Georgia	★	(g)	★	★	★	★	...
Hawaii	(a)	★	★	★	...	★	...
Idaho	★	★	★	★	...	★	...
Illinois	★	★	★	★	...	★	...
Indiana	★	★	★	★	★	★	...
Iowa	★	★	★	★	...	★	...
Kansas	★	★	★	★	...	★	...
Kentucky	(b)	★	★	★	...	★	★
Louisiana	★	(h)	★	★	★	★	...
Maine	N.A.	N.A.	N.A.	N.A.	N.A.	N.A.	N.A.
Maryland	(a)	★	★	★	...	★	★
Massachusetts	★	★	★	...	...	★	★
Michigan	★	...	★	★	...	★	...
Minnesota							
Legislative Auditor	★	(i)	★	★	...	★	...
State Auditor	(c)	★	★	★	★	★	...
Mississippi	★	★(j)	★	...	★	★	★
Missouri	★	★	★	★	...	★	★
Montana	★	...	★	...	...	★	★
Nebraska	★	★	★	...	★	★	★
Nevada	★	...	★	...	...	★	...
New Hampshire	★	...	★	...	...	★	...
New Jersey	★	(k)	★	...	...	★	...
New Mexico	★(d)	★	★	...	...	★	...
New York	★	★	★	★	★	★	...
North Carolina	★	...	★	★	...	★	★
North Dakota	★	★	★	...	★	★	...
Ohio	★	★	★	★	★	★	★
Oklahoma	★(e)	(l)	★	★	...	★	★
Oregon	★	★	★	★	★	★	★
Pennsylvania							
Auditor General	(b)	...	★	★	...	★	★
Legislative Budget and Finance Cmte.	★	...	★	★	...	...	...
Rhode Island	★	(m)	★	★	★	★	...
South Carolina							
Legislative Audit Council	★	(n)	★	...	...	★	...
State Auditor	(s)	...	★	...	...	★	...
South Dakota	★	★	★	★	★	★	...
Tennessee	★	★	★	★	★	★	★
Texas	★	...	★	★	★(o)	★	★
Utah							
Legislative Auditor	★	★	★	★	...	★	...
State Auditor	(f)	★	★	★	★	...	...
Vermont	★	...	★	★	★	★	...
Virginia	★	...	★	...	★	★	...
Washington	★	★	★	★	★	★	...
West Virginia	N.A.	N.A.	N.A.	N.A.	N.A.	N.A.	N.A.
Wisconsin	★	★	★	★	...	★	...
Wyoming	★	★	★	★	(p)	★	...
Guam	...	★	★	★	★	★	★
Puerto Rico	★	★	★	★	★	★	★

See footnotes at end of table.

STATE AUDITORS: SCOPE OF AGENCY AUTHORITY — Continued

Source: Auditing in the States, 2003 Edition, The National Association of State Auditors, Comptrollers and Treasurers updated January 2006.

Key:

★ — Provision for responsibility.

. . . — No provision for responsibility.

N.A. — Not available.

(a) The legislature or legislative branch is excluded from audit authority.

(b) The legislative and judicial branches are excluded from audit authority.

(c) State agencies are audited by the Office of Legislative Auditor.

(d) The Gaming Commission, Mortgage Finance Authority, State Lottery Commission, Student Loan Guarantee Corporation are excluded from audit authority.

(e) Higher education and most public trusts are only audited upon request by various authorities. Commissioners of the Land Office are excluded since the State Auditor and Inspector serve on this commission.

(f) State Retirement and Worker's Compensation Fund are excluded from audit authority.

(g) All local governments are excluded from audit authority, except Public School Systems and Regional and Local Libraries.

(h) Performs only investigative audits of local governments.

(i) Financial audits of local governments are excluded from audit authority.

(j) All local governments excluded but municipalities.

(k) Entities not receiving state aid or state grants and school districts receiving less than 80% funding from the state are excluded from audit authority.

(l) The State Auditor and Inspector have the authority to audit counties. Generally, cities, towns, school districts, fire protection districts, rural water districts can be audited upon request by citizen petition or various authorities.

(m) No local governments are specifically excluded, but the agency goes in on orders from the Joint Committee and Legislative Services.

(n) County, school districts, special purpose districts are excluded from audit authority.

(o) Comptroller prescribes guidelines but SAO has responsibility to review and comment.

(p) Set by statute.

(q) Municipalities not covered.

(r) Except for cities and towns, and certain special taxing districts.

(s) Ports Authority, Public Service Authority, Research Authority and 16 technical colleges are excluded from audit authority.

Table 4.30
STATE AUDITORS: TYPES OF AUDITS

State or other jurisdiction	Financial statement	Single audit	Financial related	Compliance only	Economy and efficiency	Program	Sunset	Performance measures	IT	Accounting and review sources	Agreed upon procedures	Other audits
Alabama	★	★	★	...	★	★	...	★	★	...	...	...
Alaska	★	★	★	★	★	★	★	★	...	...	...	...
Arizona	★	★	★	★	★	★	★	★	...	★	★	(a)
Arkansas	N.A.	N.A.	N.A.	N.A.	N.A.	N.A.	N.A.	N.A.	N.A.	N.A.	N.A.	N.A.
California	★	★	★	★	★	★	★	★	★	★	★	(b)
Colorado	★	★	★	...	★	★	★	...	★	...	★	...
Connecticut	★	★	★	★	★	★	...	★	★	...	★	...
Delaware	★	★	★	★	★	★	...	★	★	...	★	...
Florida	★	★	★	★	★	★	★	...	★	★	...	...
Georgia	★	★	★	...	★	★	★	★	★	★	★	(c)
Hawaii	...	...	...	...	★	★	★	★	★	...	...	...
Idaho	★	...	★	...	★	★	...	...	★	...	★	(b)
Illinois	★	★	★	★	★	★	...	★	★	...	★	(d)
Indiana	★	★	...	...	★	★	...	★	★	...	★	...
Iowa	★	★	★	...	...	★	...	★	★	...	★	...
Kansas	★	★	...	...	★	★	...	★	★	...	★	...
Kentucky	★	★	★	...	★	...	...	★	★	★	★	...
Louisiana	★	★	★	...	★	★	...	★	★	...	★	...
Maine	N.A.	N.A.	N.A.	N.A.	N.A.	N.A.	N.A.	N.A.	N.A.	N.A.	N.A.	...
Maryland	★	...	★	★	★	★	★	★	★	...	...	(e)
Massachusetts	★	★	★	★	★	★	...	★	★	★	★	(f)
Michigan	★	★	★	...	★	★	...	★	★	...	★	...
Minnesota — Legislative Auditor	★	★	★	...	...	...	...	...	★	...	...	...
Minnesota — State Auditor	★	★	...	★	...	★	...	...	...	★	★	(g)
Mississippi	★	★	★	★	★	★	...	...	★	...	★	(h)
Missouri	★	★	★	★	★	★	...	★	★	★	...	...
Montana	★	★	★	★	★	★	...	★	★	...	★	...
Nebraska	★	★	★	★	★	★	...	★	★	...	★	...
Nevada	...	...	★	★	★	★	...	★★	★	★	...	...
New Hampshire	★	...	...	★	★	★	...	...	★	...	...	...
New Jersey	★	★	★	★	★	...	...	★	★	...	...	...
New Mexico	★	★	★	★	★	★	...	★	★	...	★	...
New York	★	...	★	...	★	★	...	...	★	...	★	...
North Carolina	★	★	★	...	★	★	...	...	★	★	★	...
North Dakota	★	★	...	...	★	...	...	...	★	★	...	(i)
Ohio	★	★	★	★	★	★	...	★	★	★	★	...

See footnotes at end of table.

STATE AUDITORS: TYPES OF AUDITS — Continued

State or other jurisdiction	Financial statement	Single audit	Financial related	Compliance only	Economy and efficiency	Program	Sunset	Performance measures	IT	Accounting and review sources	Agreed upon procedures	Other audits
Oklahoma	★	★	★	★	★	★	...	...	★	...	★	(j)
Oregon	★	★	★	★	★	★	...	...	★	★	★	(k)
Pennsylvania												
Auditor General	★	★	★	★	★	...	...	★	★	...	...	(l)
Legislative Budget and Finance Cmte.	...	...	...	...	...	...	...	...	...	...	...	...
Rhode Island	...	★	...	★	★	★	...	...	★	...	...	...
South Carolina												
Legislative Audit Council	★	...	...	...	★	★	...	...	...	...	...	...
State Auditor	★	★	★	...	★	★	...	...	...	...	★	...
South Dakota	★	★	★	...	...	...	...	...	...	...	★	...
Tennessee	★	★	★	★	★	★	★	...	★	★	★	(m)
Texas	★	★	★	★	★	★	...	★	★	★	★	(n)
Utah												
Legislative Auditor	...	...	...	...	★	★	★	★	...	...	★	...
State Auditor	★	★	★	★	★	★	...	★	★	★	★	(o)
Vermont	★	...	★	...	★	★	...	...	★	...	★	...
Virginia	★	★	★	...	...	...	...	★	★	...	★	...
Washington	★	★	★	...	★	★	N.A.	★	N.A.	...	★	...
West Virginia	N.A.	N.A.	N.A.	N.A.	N.A.	N.A.	N.A.	N.A.	N.A.	N.A.	N.A.	N.A.
Wisconsin	★	★	★	...	★	★	...	...	★	...	★	...
Wyoming	...	...	★	★	★	★	...	★	★	...	★	...
Guam	...	★	...	★	★	★	...	...	★	...	...	(b)
Puerto Rico	...	...	...	...	★	★	...	...	...	...	...	...

Sources: Auditing in the States: A Summary, 2003 edition. The National Association of State Auditors, Comptrollers and Treasurers, updated January 2006.

Note: Government audits are divided into two types, financial and performance audits. Financial audits include financial statement audits and financial-related audits. Performance audits include economy and efficiency audits and program audits. In addition, government auditors perform a number of other audit-related functions that do not fall into one of these categories. State audit agencies must make certain that audit coverage is broad enough to fulfill the needs of potential audit report users.

Key:
★ — Provision for responsibility.
. . . — No provision for responsibility.
N.A.— Not available.
(a) Fraud, special audits, studies, and program evaluations.
(b) Investigations.
(c) Attestation engagements.

(d) Sunset analyses, mandatory health insurance analyses.
(e) Federal grant audits.
(f) Special requests and follow-up reviews.
(g) Special investigation reviews.
(h) Investigations and best practices reviews.
(i) Performance reviews.
(j) Internal control reviews: studies.
(k) Quality assurance reviews.
(l) Fraud investigations.
(m) Informational reports, including referrals or investigation or fraud.
(n) Special investigations.
(o) Internal controls review, investigative, management advisory, training and other educational services.
(p) Special projects, consulting, feasibility studies.

Table 4.31
THE STATE COMPTROLLERS, 2006

State	Agency or office	Name	Title	Legal basis for office	Method of selection	Approval or confirmation, if necessary	Date of first service	Present term ends	Consecutive time in office	Length of term	Elected comptroller's maximum consecutive terms	Civil service or merit system employee
Alabama	Office of the State Comptroller	Robert L. Childree	State Comptroller	S	(c)	AG	5/1987	(b)	18 yrs.	(b)	...	★
Alaska	Division of Finance	Kim J. Gamero	Director of Finance	S	(d)	AG	8/1999	(a)	6 yrs.	(a)	...	...
Arizona	Financial Services Division	D. Clark Partridge	State Comptroller	S	(d)	AG	4/2002	N.A.	4 yrs.	...	...	...
Arkansas	Dept. of Finance and Administration	Richard A. Weiss	Director	S	G	...	5/2002	(a)	4 yrs.	(a)	...	...
California	Office of the State Controller	Steve Westly (D)	State Controller	C	E	...	1/2003	1/2006	3 yrs.	(b)	2 terms	...
Colorado	Office of the State Controller	Leslie Shenefelt	State Controller	S	E	...	7/2004	(b)	1.5 yrs.	(b)	...	★
Connecticut	Office of the Comptroller	Nancy Wyman (D)	Comptroller	C	E	...	1/1995	1/2007	11 yrs.	4 yrs.	unlimited	...
Delaware	Dept. of Finance	Richard S. Cordrey	Secretary of Finance	C,S	G	AS	2/2005	(a)	1 yr.	(a)	...	...
Florida	Dept. of Financial Services	Tom Gallagher (R)	Chief Financial Officer	C	E	...	1/2003	12/2006	3 yrs.	4 yrs.	2 terms	...
Georgia (l)	State Accounting Office	Lynn H. Vellinga	State Accounting Officer	S	G	...	10/2004	(a)	1 yr.	(a)	...	...
Hawaii	Dept. of Accounting and General Services	Russ K. Satio	State Comptroller	S	G	AS	12/2002	12/2006	3 yrs.	(a)	...	...
Idaho	Office of State Controller	Keith Johnson (R)	State Controller	C,S	E	...	1/2003	12/2006	2 yrs.	4 yrs.	2 terms	★
Illinois	Office of the Comptroller	Daniel W. Hynes (D)	State Comptroller	C	E	...	11/1999	1/2007	7 yrs.	4 yrs.	unlimited	...
Indiana	Office of the Auditor of State	Connie Kay Nass (R)	Auditor of State	C	E	...	1/1999	12/2006	7 yrs.	4 yrs.	2 terms	...
Iowa	State Accounting Enterprise	Calvin McKelvogue	Chief Operating Officer	S	G	AS	7/2004	N.A.	1.5 yrs.	(a)	...	★
Kansas	Division of Accounts and Reports	Robert Mackey	Director	S	(d)	...	1/2006	(b)	6 mos.	(b)	...	★
Kentucky	Office of the Controller	Edgar C. Ross	Controller	S	(f)	AG	6/1975	N.A.	31 yrs.	(i)	...	...
Louisiana	Division of Administration	Jerry Luke LeBlanc	Commissioner of Administration	S	G	...	1/2004	1/2008	2 yrs.	(a)	...	...
Maine	Office of the State Controller	Edward Karass	State Controller	S	(f)	AG	4/2003	1/2007	3 yrs.	(b)	...	...
Maryland	Office of the Comptroller of the Treasury	William Donald Schaefer (D)	State Comptroller	C,S	E	...	1/1999	1/2007	7 yrs.	4 yrs.	unlimited	...
Massachusetts	Office of the Comptroller	Martin J. Benison	State Comptroller	S	G	...	1/1999	1/2007	7 yrs.	(j)	...	...
Michigan	Office of Financial Management	Michael J. Moody	Director	S	SBD	SBD	8/2002	8/2006	3 yrs.	(k)	...	★
Minnesota	Department of Finance	Peggy Ingison	Commissioner	S	G	AS	2/2004	1/2007	2 yrs.	(a)	...	...
Mississippi	Department of Finance and Administration	J.K. Stringer Jr.	State Fiscal Officer	S	G	AS	1/2004	1/2008	2 yrs.	(a)	...	...
Missouri	Division of Accounting	Thomas Sadowski	Director of Accounting	C,S	(d)	...	2/2005	N.A.	1 yr.	(g)	...	...
Montana	Administrative Financial Services Division	Paul Christofferson	Administrator	S	(m)	...	6/2004	N.A.	1.5 yrs.	(b)	...	★
Nebraska	Accounting Division	Paul Carlson	State Accounting Administrator	S	(d)	...	11/2000	N.A.	5 yrs.	(g)	...	...
Nevada	Office of the State Controller	Kathy Augustine (R)	State Controller	C	E	...	1/1999	12/2006	6 yrs.	(j)	2 terms	...
New Hampshire	Division of Accounting Services	Sheri Rockburn	Comptroller	S	G	...	8/2004	6/2008	1 yr.	(a)	...	...
New Jersey	Office of Management and Budget	Charlene M. Holzbaur	Director/State Controller	S	G	AS	10/1999	(b)	6 yrs.	(a)	...	...
New Mexico	Department of Finance and Administration, Financial Control Division	Anthony I. Armijo	State Controller and Director	S	G	...	1/1991	(b)	15 yrs.	(a)	...	★

See footnotes at end of table.

THE STATE COMPTROLLERS, 2006 — Continued

State	Agency or office	Name	Title	Legal basis for office	Method of selection	Approval or confirmation, if necessary	Date of first service	Present term ends	Consecutive time in office	Length of term	Elected comptroller's maximum consecutive terms	Civil service or merit system employee
New York	Office of the State Comptroller	Alan G. Hevesi (D)	State Comptroller	C,S	E	…	1/2003	12/2006	3 yrs.	4 yrs.	unlimited	…
North Carolina	Office of the State Controller	Robert L. Powell	State Controller	S	G	GA	7/2001	7/2008	4.5 yrs.	7 yrs.	…	…
North Dakota	Office of Management and Budget	Pam Sharp	Director	S	G	…	1/2003	(a)	3 yrs.	(a)	…	…
Ohio	Office of Budget and Management	Thomas W. Johnson	Director	S	G	AS	1/1999	1/2007	7 yrs.	(a)	…	…
Oklahoma	Office of State Finance	Brenda Bolander	State Comptroller	S	(e)	…	12/2001	(b)	4 yrs.	(h)	…	…
Oregon	State Controller's Division	John J. Radford	State Controller	S	(d)	AG	11/1989	(b)	16 yrs.	(g)	…	…
Pennsylvania	Comptroller Operations	Harvey C. Eckert	Commonwealth Comptroller	S	G	…	3/1983	(b)	23 yrs.	(a)	…	…
Rhode Island	Office of Accounts and Control	Lawrence C. Franklin Jr.	State Controller	S	CS	…	8/1986	N.A.	19 yrs.	(b)	…	★
South Carolina	Office of the Comptroller General	Richard Eckstrom (R)	Comptroller General	C,S	E	…	1/2003	1/2007	3 yrs.	4 yrs.	unlimited	…
South Dakota	Office of the State Auditor	Richard L. Sattgast (R)	State Auditor	C	E	…	1/2003	1/2007	3 yrs.	4 yrs.	2 terms	…
Tennessee	Division of Accounts	Jan I. Sylvis	Chief of Accounts	C,S	(f)	…	12/1995	N.A.	10 yrs.	(b)	…	…
Texas	Office of the Comptroller of Public Accounts	Carole Keeton Strayhorn (R)	Comptroller of Public Accounts	C,S	E	…	1/1999	1/2007	7 yrs.	4 yrs.	unlimited	…
Utah	Division of Finance	John Reidhead	Director	S	(d)	AG	7/2005	N.A.	8 mos.	(g)	…	★
Vermont	Department of Finance and Management	James Reardon	Commissioner	S	G	AS	2/2005	2/2007	1 yr.	(a)	…	…
Virginia	Department of Accounts	David A. Von Moll	State Comptroller	S	G	GA	11/2001	(a)	1 yr.	(a)	…	★
Washington	Office of Financial Management	Victor Moore	Director	C,S	G	…	1/2005	N.A.	1 yr.	(a)	…	…
West Virginia	Office of the State Auditor	Glen B. Gainier III (D)	State Auditor	C,S	E	…	1/1992	1/2008	14 yrs.	4 yrs.	unlimited	…
	Finance Division, Office of the State Comptroller	Ross Taylor	Acting State Comptroller and Finance Director	S	(d)	AG	10/2005	(a)	4 mos.	(g)	…	…
Wisconsin	State Controller's Office	William J. Rafferty	State Controller	S	CS	…	12/1988	N.A.	17 yrs.	(b)	…	★
Wyoming	Office of the State Auditor	Max Maxfield (R)	State Auditor	C,S	E	…	1/1999	12/2006	7 yrs.	4 yrs.	2 terms	…

Sources: Comptrollers: *Technical Activities and Functions, 2005 Edition,* National Association of State Auditors, Comptrollers and Treasurers, 2005 and January 31, 2006.

Key:
… — No provision for.
C — Constitutional
S — Statutory
N.A. — Not applicable.
E — Elected by the public.
G — Appointed by the Governor.
CS — Civil Service
AS — Approved/confirmed by the Senate.
AG — Approved by the governor.
SBD — Approved by State Budget Director.
GA — Confirmed by the General Assembly.
SDB — Confirmed by State Depository Board.

(a) Serves at the pleasure of the governor.
(b) Indefinite.
(c) Appointed by the Director of the Dept. of Finance (merit system position).
(d) Appointed by the head of the department of administration or administrative services.
(e) Appointed by the head of finance department or agency.
(f) Appointed by the head of financial and administrative services.
(g) Serves at the pleasure of the head of the department of administration or administrative services.
(h) Serves at the pleasure of the head of the finance department or agency.
(i) Serves at the pleasure of the head of the financial and administrative services.
(j) Two full terms coterminous with the governor.
(k) Two-year renewable contractual term; classified executive service.
(l) As of July 1, 2005, the responsibility for accounting and financial reporting in Gerogia was transferred to the newly-created State Accounting Office.
(m) Classified position.

Table 4.32
STATE COMPTROLLERS: QUALIFICATIONS FOR OFFICE

State or other jurisdiction	Minimum age	U.S. citizen (years)	State resident (years) (b)	Education years or degree	Professional experience and years	Professional certification and years	Other qualifications	No specific qualifications for office
Alabama	★	★	★	★, B.S.	★, 6 yrs.	...	...	...
Alaska	...	...	...	...	...	...	...	★
Arizona	...	★, 1 yr.	★, 1 yr.	★, B.S.	★, 7–10 yrs.	★(a)	...	...
Arkansas	30	...	...	...	★	...	...	...
California	★	...	...	...	...	...	(b)	...
Colorado	...	...	★	★(i)	★, 6 yrs.	★, CPA	...	...
Connecticut	...	...	★	...	...	...	...	...
Delaware	...	...	...	...	...	...	...	★
Florida	★	...	★, 7 yrs.	...	...	...	...	...
Georgia	...	...	...	...	...	...	...	★
Hawaii	...	...	...	...	...	...	...	★
Idaho	★	★(j)	★, 2 yrs.	...	...	...	...	...
Illinois	25	★	★, 3 yrs.	...	...	...	...	...
Indiana	...	...	★(j)	...	...	...	...	...
Iowa	...	...	...	...	...	...	...	★
Kansas	...	...	...	...	...	...	...	★
Kentucky	...	...	...	...	...	...	(c)	★
Louisiana	...	...	...	...	...	...	...	★
Maine	...	...	...	...	...	...	(d)	★
Maryland	18	★	★	...	...	...	...	...
Massachusetts	...	...	...	★(k)	★, 7 yrs.	...	...	...
Michigan	...	...	...	★(l)	★, 5 yrs.	(l)	(l)	...
Minnesota	...	...	...	...	...	...	...	★
Mississippi	...	...	...	★(k)	★, 10 yrs.	★, CPA	(e)	...
Missouri	...	...	...	...	...	...	...	★
Montana	...	...	...	★(p)	★, 5 yrs.	★, CPA	...	★
Nebraska	...	...	...	★(m)	★(n)	★, CPA	...	...
Nevada	25	★	★	...	...	...	...	...
New Hampshire	...	...	...	...	...	...	(f)	★
New Jersey	...	...	...	...	...	...	...	★
New Mexico	30	★	5	N.A.	N.A.	N.A.	N.A.	N.A.
New York	★	★	★, 5 yrs.	...	...	...	...	...
North Carolina	...	...	...	★	★	...	(g)	...
North Dakota	...	...	...	...	...	...	...	★
Ohio	...	...	...	...	...	...	...	...
Oklahoma	...	★	★	★(q)	★, 5 yrs.	...	...	★
Oregon	...	...	...	...	...	...	...	★
Pennsylvania	...	...	...	...	...	...	...	★
Rhode Island	...	★	★	★(h)	★, 5 yrs.	★, CPA	...	...
South Carolina	18	★	★	...	...	...	...	...
South Dakota	★	★	★, 1 yr.	...	...	...	...	...
Tennessee	...	...	...	★	★, 7 yrs.	★, CPA	...	...
Texas	18	★(j)	★, 1 yr.	...	...	...	...	...
Utah	...	...	...	★	★, 6 yrs.	★, CPA	...	...
Vermont	...	...	...	...	...	...	...	★
Virginia	...	...	...	...	...	...	...	★
Washington	★	★, Whole life	★	★(o)	★	★, J.D.	...	...
West Virginia								
Office of State Auditor	...	★	★	...	...	...	...	...
Division of Finance, Office of State Comptroller	...	★	★	★, B.S.B.A.	★, 7 yrs.	...	...	...
Wisconsin	...	...	...	★(p)	...	★, CPA	...	...
Wyoming	★	★	★	...	...	...	...	...

Sources: Comptrollers: Technical Activities and Functions, 2003 Edition, The National Association of State Auditors, Comptrollers and Treasurers, 2005 and January 2006.

Key:
★ — Formal provision.
... — No formal provision.
(a) Any of those mentioned or CFE, CPM, etc.
(b) 18 yrs. At time of election or appointment and a citizen of the state.
(c) The Kentucky Revised Statutes state that "The state controller shall be a person qualified by education and experience for the position and held in high esteem in the accounting community."
(d) There are no educational or professional mandates, yet the appointed official is generally qualified by a combination of experience and education.
(e) At least 5 yrs. experience in high level management.
(f) Education and relevant experience.

(g) Qualified by education and experience for the position.
(h) Master's degree in accounting, finance or business management or public administration.
(i) 5 yrs. or college degree.
(j) Years not specified.
(k) Master's degree.
(l) Bachelor's degree, no professional certification required, but CPA certification is considered desirable. Financial management experience, knowledge of GAAP and good communication skills are other qualifications.
(m) 4 yrs. with major in accounting.
(n) 3 yrs. directing the work of others.
(o) 7 yrs. and law degree.
(p) Bachelor's degree in accounting.
(q) Bachelor's degree.

Table 4.33
STATE COMPTROLLERS: DUTIES AND RESPONSIBILITIES

State	Appropriation control	Budgetary reporting	Comprehensive annual financial report (CAFR)	Disbursement of state funds	Maintenance of the general ledger and chart of accounts	Payroll processing	Pre-auditing of payments	Post-audit	Operation of statewide financial management system	Management of state travel policies
Alabama	★	★	★	★(a)	★	★	★	…	★	★
Alaska	★	…	★	★	★	★	…	…	★	★
Arizona	★	…	★	★	★	★	★	★	★	★
Arkansas	★	…	★	…	…	…	★	★	…	…
California	★	★	★	★	★	★	★	★	★	…
Colorado	★	…	★	★	★	★	…	…	★	…
Connecticut	…	…	★	…	★	★	…	★	★	…
Delaware	★	…	★	★(b)	★	★	★	★	★(c)	★
Florida	★	…	★	★	★	★	★	★	★	★
Georgia	…	…	★	…	★	★	…	…	★	★(aa)
Hawaii	★(e)	…	★	★	★	★	★(d)	N.A.	★	★
Idaho	★	★	★	★(f)	★	★	★(g)	★	…	★
Illinois	★	…	★	★	★	★	★	★	★	★
Indiana	★	★	★	★	★	★	…	…	★	…
Iowa	★	★	★	★	★	★	★	★	★	★
Kansas	★	…	★	★	★	★	★	★	★	★
Kentucky	★	…	★	★	★	★	…	…	★	★
Louisiana	★	★	★	…	★	★	…	…	★	…
Maine	★	…	★	…	★	★	★(h)	★(i)	★	…
Maryland	★	★	★	★(a)	★	★	★	★(j)	★	…
Massachusetts	…	…	★	…	★	★	★	…	★	…
Michigan	…	★	★	★	★	★	…	…	★	…
Minnesota	…	★	★	★	★	★	★	★(k)	★	★
Mississippi	★	…	★	★	★	★	★	★	★	…
Missouri	★	★	★	★	★	★	★	★	★	…
Montana	…	…	★	★	★	★	…	…	★	…
Nebraska	…	★(l)	★	★	★	★	★	★	★	★
Nevada	★	★	★	★	★	★	…	…	★	★
New Hampshire	★	…	★	…	★	★	★	…	★	…
New Jersey	★	★	★	★	★	★	★	★	★	★
New Mexico	★(m)	★	★	…	★	★	★	★	★	★
New York	★(o)	★	★	…	★	★	★(m)	★	…	★
North Carolina	★	★	★	★	★	★	…	★	★	…
North Dakota	★	…	★	★	★	★	…	…	★	★
Ohio	★	★	★	★	★	…	★	★	★	★
Oklahoma	★	★	★	★	★	★	★	★	★	★
Oregon	…	★(p)	★	…	★	★	★(a)	★	★	★
Pennsylvania	…	…	★	…	★	★	…	…	★	★
Rhode Island	★	…	★	…	★	★	★(a)	★	★	★
South Carolina	★	★	★	★(q)	★	…	★	…	…	★

See footnotes at end of table.

STATE COMPTROLLERS: DUTIES AND RESPONSIBILITIES — Continued

State	Appropriation control	Budgetary reporting	Comprehensive annual financial report (CAFR)	Disbursement of state funds	Maintenance of the general ledger and chart of accounts	Payroll processing	Pre-auditing of payments	Post-audit	Operation of statewide financial management system	Management of state travel policies
South Dakota	...	...	...	★	...	★	★	...	...	...
Tennessee	...	...	★	★	★	★	★(r)	★(s)	★	★
Texas	★	★	★	★	★	★	★	★	★	...
Utah	★	...	★	★	★	★	★(t)	★	★	★
Vermont	★	★	★	...	★	...	★	★	★	★
Virginia	★(u)	...	★	★	★	★	★	★(v)	★	★
Washington	★	★(w)	★	...	★	...	...	...	★	★
West Virginia										
Office of State Auditor	★(x)	★(y)	...	★	...	★	★	...	...	...
Division of Finance, Office of State Comptroller	★(x)	...	★	...	★	...	★(z)	...	★	★
Wisconsin	★	★	★	...	★	★	★	★	...	★
Wyoming	★	...	★	...	★	★	★	★	★	★

Sources: Comptrollers: Technical Activities and Functions, 2003 Edition, The National Association of State Auditors, Comptrollers and Treasurers 2005 and January 2006.

Key:

★ — Formal provision.

... — No formal provision; number of years not specified.

A — Appointed by governor.

(a) Responsibilities shared between Comptroller and Treasury.
(b) Responsibilities shared between Department of Finance and State Treasurer's Office.
(c) Responsibilities shared between Department of Finance and the Auditor of Accounts.
(d) Except for various autonomous agencies.
(e) Responsibilities shared between Office of State Controller and the Division of Financial Management.
(f) Responsibilities shared between Office of the State Controller and the State Treasurer's Office.
(g) Responsibilities shared between state agencies and the Office of the State Comptroller.
(h) Responsibilities shared between agencies and the Office of the State Controller.
(i) Responsibilities shared between Office of the State Controller and the State Auditor.
(j) Responsibilities shared between Office of the State Comptroller and the Legislative Auditor.
(k) Responsibilities shared between Dept. of Finance and the Office of the Legislative Auditor.
(l) Responsibilities shared between Accounting Division and the Dept. of Administrative Services.
(m) Responsibilities shared between Comptroller and Budget Director.

(n) Responsibilities shared between office of the State Comptroller with delegation to state agencies and universities.
(o) Responsibilities shared between shared Comptroller and Office of State Budget and Management.
(p) Responsibilities shared between State Controller and the Dept. of Administrative Services.
(q) Responsibilities shared, Comptroller General issues warrants, Treasurer issues checks, colleges maintain their own systems and write their own checks.
(r) Responsible for all departments that have not been authorized to do their own based own excellent performance.
(s) Responsibilities shared between Division of Audits and Department of Audit.
(t) Responsibilities shared between various agencies and the Division of Finance.
(u) Responsibilities shared between Comptroller and Dept. of Planning and Budget.
(v) Responsibilities shared between Comptroller and Auditor.
(w) Responsibilities shared between Office of Financial Management and all state agencies.
(x) Responsibilities shared between State Budget Office within the Office of the State Comptroller and the Office of the State Auditor.
(y) Responsibilities shared between State Budget Office and the Office of the State Auditor.
(z) Responsibilities delegated to state agencies by the State Controller's Office.
(aa) State travel policies are managed in cooperation with the Office of Planning and Budget.

Chapter Five

STATE JUDICIAL BRANCH

"Politicizing the judiciary puts in jeopardy the checks and balances so carefully inserted into the federal and state constitutions."

—David Rottman

The State Courts in 2005: A Year of Living Dangerously
By David Rottman

Court security proved to be a danger that could bring the branches of government together. A series of summits brought together officials from all three branches of government at the local, state and federal levels. The result was A National Strategic Plan for Judicial Branch Security. *Other dangers were not adequately addressed, especially those resulting from efforts for politicize the judiciary in ways that pose fundamental threats to longstanding checks and balances among the branches of state government.*

Introduction

For the nation's courts, 2005 was a year of living dangerously. High profile national news stories tell part of the story. February: In Chicago, a federal judge, recently the target of an assassination plot by a white supremacist, returned home to find her husband and mother murdered by a litigant whose medical malpractice claim had been dismissed.[1] March: In an Atlanta courthouse, a defendant on trial for rape and other violent felonies grabbed the gun of a sheriff's deputy while being escorted to the courtroom, and then killed the judge and court reporter. April: A Florida trial judge was "vilified, bombarded with harassing letters and e-mails, and even threatened with death by people who disagree with his rulings in the (Terri) Schiavo case."[2]

The other part of the story emerges from efforts in many states to politicize the judiciary as a way to leverage political party advantage or to promote the agendas of specific social or economic interests. State legislators in 2005 sought to remove court jurisdiction over entire categories of cases, to make judicial selection more political, and to assume authority over court rules. Federal courthouses also proved to be dangerous places for the state courts, especially the 39 states that elect some or all of their judges. Litigation in several U.S. circuits and individual states (notably Alaska, Kentucky, North Dakota, and, still pending, in Indiana) eliminated basic steps states have taken for decades to keep judicial elections different from those for political office. As a result, judicial candidates in many states now can personally solicit campaign funds from lawyers or litigants and can engage in partisan political activities—and also render fair and impartial justice in actuality and appearance.[3]

The consequences of such politicized arrangements emerged in another national news story. Texas: The indictment of former House Majority Leader Tom Delay led to a scramble to find a trial judge acceptable to both the defense and the prosecu-

tion in a state where judges are elected on a partisan ticket and often personally contribute to the funding of partisan causes.[4]

Checks and Balances

Court security proved to be a danger that could bring the branches of government together. One response to the year of living dangerously was a series of summits—one in April and a follow-up in November—that brought together officials from all three branches of government at the local, state and federal levels. The result was *A National Strategic Plan for Judicial Branch Security*, containing eight recommended strategies.[5]

For the most part, however, 2005 posed some fundamental threats to preserving the checks and balances among the branches of government. Politicizing the judiciary puts in jeopardy the checks and balances so carefully inserted into the federal and state constitutions.

"Court stripping" is one way those checks and balances can become misaligned. It is also "one of the words we will not be able to live without next year in 2006," according to those who compiled the *Oxford American Dictionary*. "Court stripping is when legislatures try to remove powers from the courts, usually federal but often state, so that the courts can't rule on laws they've passed."[6] In the *Schiavo* case, Congress sought to strip the Florida state courts of their final jurisdiction over a state court matter by superimposing federal court jurisdiction, and by ordering the federal courts to consider the claims of Schiavo's parents, contrary to fundamental constitutional principles. The state court decision ultimately stood.

At the state level, bills were introduced to eliminate the jurisdiction of any state court to hear and decide school funding challenges (e.g., Kansas, Missouri), and shift the power to write court rules from the state supreme court to the legislature (e.g., Arizona, Florida).[7] The Delaware legislature, fully informed of the dubious constitutionality of its action, in January passed legislation overturning the state Supreme Court's 2004 ruling interpreting the meaning of "life imprisonment with the possibility of parole." The state Supreme Court subsequently granted the state attorney general's motion for re-argument of the case, an action that, to one commentator, "demonstrates respect for the other branches of government."[8]

Respect for the judicial branch was not evident in a number of states where legislatures and executive branch officials put traditional checks and balances in jeopardy. Some of the more striking examples are described in the next section, which deals with trends in judicial selection.

Judicial Elections

The fate of judges at election time increasingly is caught up in state politics, even where the court is on the sidelines of the controversy. In Pennsylvania, the immediate target of public anger was the legislature because of a pay raise they granted themselves, buried in an amendment to an unrelated bill passed at 2 a.m. The state Supreme Court upheld the legislature's action. Solely because of that, vigorous campaigns were mounted against the two Supreme Court justices up for retention election, in which the public is asked whether a sitting judge shall be retained in office. Both justices received atypically low "yes" votes; Justice Russell Nigro, with 49 percent of the vote, lost his seat. A political analyst commented: "This election has been a proxy for the reformers to send a message to Harrisburg."[9]

Federal courts in 2005 increased the likelihood state courts would be driven deeper into state politics. The Supreme Court on Jan. 23, 2006, refused to grant a writ of certiorari to review the 8th Circuit Court of Appeal's decision in *Dimick v. Republican Party of Minnesota* (previously known as the *White* case) that struck down significant portions of the state's code of judicial conduct. Rules limiting judges' and judicial candidates' participation in partisan political activities and banning certain direct solicitation of campaign contributions were deemed unconstitutional. The attorney who litigated the challenge to the Minnesota rules concluded, "It's becoming clear the First Amendment has a broad application to judicial elections and that the original foundation for the regulation of judicial elections has been pretty well destroyed."[10]

North Dakota offers an example of the consequences of such federal court decisions. The state's canons of judicial conduct were challenged in U.S. District Court two years ago and ruled unconstitu-

tional in 2005. Under the existing canons, judicial candidates were permitted to discuss their backgrounds and qualifications, but were barred from making statements "that commit or appear to commit the candidate with respect to cases, controversies or issues that are likely to come before the court."[11] The new rules, released in January, 2006, allow candidates to respond "with caution" to questions about their opinion on issues and to make clear their commitment to keeping an open mind while on the bench, regardless of their own personal views.

In a number of states, considerable legislative effort was also expended on making judicial elections more partisan. Arizona is a prime example. About 35 bills were introduced to alter the long-standing relationship between the legislature and the courts, and the courts and the public. Many proposed pieces of legislation targeted the states' tradition of merit selection of judges, replacing them with contested elections. None of these bills became law, but the onslaught has been unrelenting, leading retired U.S. Supreme Court Justice Sandra Day O'Connor to urge a group of female lawyers in her native state to fight "attacks on an independent judiciary." "If you don't know about it, find out about it because it's real, it is very serious and, unless all of us take it seriously and do what we can to make the public understand, then an activist judge is a judge who gets up in the morning and goes to work."[12]

Kansas and Missouri also offer examples. In Kansas, two controversial state Supreme Court rulings—one striking down the death penalty and the other ruling that implementation of school funding was not proceeding according to the law—led to proposed constitutional amendments. One amendment would substitute contested elections for the current (since 1958) merit selection of Supreme Court justices. The other amendment would add senate confirmation to the current selection process for all appellate judges (nominations from a nonpartisan committee, gubernatorial appointment, and then retention elections).

In Missouri, legislation was introduced to amend the state constitution to require the advice and consent of the Senate for appellate judgeships, reduce the term of office from 12 to five years for Supreme Court justices, and shift the standard for retention elections from a simple majority to two-thirds of the vote.

Relationships among the three branches of government will always be undergoing change. In 2005, the mostly unsuccessful legislative efforts in a number of states sought to revolutionize those relations. States need to return to what is sometimes termed the "flexible model" of separation of powers, one in which there is separateness but interdependence; autonomy but reciprocity. "In the flexible model, there can be a greater amount of give and take between the branches, but there are limits. First, no branch can arrogate to itself the core functions of a coordinate branch of government. Second no branch may deprive another branch of the powers and resources necessary to perform its core function."[13]

Courts and the Public

The ultimate implications of these efforts to politicize the judiciary rest with the public's response. On the one hand, once granted, the public resolutely refuses to give up its right to elect its judges.[14] On the other hand, an informed and vigilant public is the best available bulwark against efforts to politicize the judiciary.

One reading of the public mood was recorded in response to one of the most controversial court cases of 2005. In the *Schiavo* case, the public was emphatic in opposing Congressional tampering with court jurisdiction: 74 percent of Americans believed that Congress should not have involved itself in the matter. That preference was across the board: large majorities (more than two-thirds) of white evangelicals, conservatives and Republicans believed that Congress should have stayed out of the case.[15]

Several public opinion surveys in 2005 were particularly revealing about the public's image of the judicial branch of government and its relations to the other branches. Overall, when it comes to the role of the judiciary, the public is poor on details, but more solid on principles. In mid-year, the American Bar Association sponsored an opinion survey on civic education, concluding that the "majority of Americans could use a civics refresher course."

Among the findings, just over half (55 percent) of American adults can identify the three branches of government, and a more substantial two-thirds (64 percent) identify the principle of checks and balances.[16] Once explained, the public overwhelmingly believes the principle of checks and balances is very important (69 percent), and another 17 percent say it is important. The more people know about our political system, the more likely they are to feel checks and balances are important.

The public's views on checks and balances were further elaborated in another national survey conducted in July.[17] The researchers concluded that certain core American values underlie the opinions people hold about the judiciary across the nation: fairness, responsibility and preservation of one's rights. These core values were expressed in:

- A strong belief in the courts' role in protecting individual rights by upholding the Constitution;

- A priority given to guaranteeing access to justice for all Americans;

- A desire for the courts to be fair and impartial, which was defined in the survey as being free from political influence or pressure once a judge is on the bench; and

- The need for accountability to ensure that judges follow the law and Constitution, and not their own personal beliefs.

Even on a controversial topic such as gay marriage, the public's preference is that the courts be left to adjudicate disputes: 61 percent of Americans believe that "politicians should not prevent the courts from hearing (these) cases, because the purpose of the courts is to provide access to justice to everyone, even those with unpopular beliefs (See Table A).

Table A:
Public Views on the Role of the Courts in Controversial Cases

Key: With whom do you agree with more, those who say: (a) When judges make decisions that are outside the mainstream of American belief, such as legalizing gay marriage, Congress should stop the courts from hearing the cases, or (b) Politicians should not prevent the courts from hearing cases, because the purpose of the courts is to provide access to justice to everyone, even those with unpopular beliefs.

Congress should stop courts (a)		Congress should not stop courts (b)		
Strongly agree	Somewhat agree	Strongly agree	Somewhat agree	Don't know
23%	10%	43%	19%	6%

Source: Belden, Russonello and Stewart, *Speak to American Values*, Washington, D.C.: Justice at Stake, 2006 (unpublished data provided to the author).

Table B:
Public Views on the Need for Checks on the Courts

We need more congressional checks on the courts to reduce the power of the courts and individual judges

Strongly agree	Somewhat agree	Somewhat disagree	Strongly disagree	Don't know
23%	26%	22%	23%	5%

Source: Belden, Russonello and Stewart, *Speak to American Values*, Washington, D.C.: Justice at Stake, 2006 (unpublished data provided to the author).

As noted above, however, the American public also believes the courts must be accountable. Respondents in the "Speak to Values" survey were split evenly on whether more congressional checks on the courts are needed (Table B).

Accountability also was on the mind of the California public in another major opinion survey about the courts conducted in 2005.[18] Nearly one-half of the adults interviewed reported their expectation that the courts should report on their job performance to the public was not being met. That was the greatest unmet expectation to emerge from the survey, ahead of ensuring public safety and concluding cases in a timely manner.

These and other findings from the California 2005 survey are being explored in greater depth through a second round of opinion research. Focus groups of 10 to 12 citizens are being held around the state to hear what people have to say about judicial accountability and other topics. Nationally, the state court community has engaged in extensive discussion and preliminary testing of *CourTools*, a set of 10 performance measures for trial courts. Measures are offered in such areas as access and fairness, effective use of jurors, and cost per case.[19]

Ultimately, however, individual judges are accountable to the Constitution and to the law. As one chief justice put it in 2005:

> "Judges are accountable to uphold the rule of law through their decisions. This means that, just as juries are asked to set aside their personal beliefs and decide a case based on the law and the evidence, judges also must set aside their personal feelings, beliefs and attitudes and decide each case according to the facts and law in that case. Accountability to the law sometimes comes at a high price—a judge must follow the law even when doing so would be extremely unpopular."[20]

Such a formulation seems broadly consistent with the public's view of how judges should be held accountable.

In every state, appellate court review and independent judicial discipline bodies are the primary mechanism for ensuring that judges are accountable to the law. And in 39 states, some or all judges are accountable directly to the electorate.

Checks in Balance

Fair and impartial courts require that judges be treated differently from officials in the political branches of government. Legislators and governors, as well as other executive branch officials, represent the public and can take sides in disputes at any stage. Judges represent the law. Efforts to further politicize the judiciary threaten the checks and balances that underpin our system of government. In 2006 state judiciaries must work with legislators to rebuild a relationship of mutual respect, increase efforts to educate the public about the role of the judicial branch, both through renewed and innovative efforts to promote civics education and in their written decisions.

The state judiciaries have pledged to do their part. In July, the Conference of (State) Chief Justices and the Conference of State Court Administrators jointly resolved "to promote judicial governance and accountable state Judicial Branch institutions that provide the highest quality of service to the public" and noted that "judicial accountability can foster an environment where other branches of government and the public understand the judiciary's role and are less likely to interfere with the judiciary's ability to govern itself."[21]

Author's Note:

The views expressed in this article are those of the author and do not represent the views of the National Center for State Courts or any other organizaiton.

Notes

[1] Dan Baldwin, "Police: DNA from Lefkow Killings Matches Man who Committed Suicide," Associated Press, March 11, 2005.

[2] Jeffrey Rosen, "It's the Law, Not the Judge; But These Days the Bench is the Hot Seat," *Washington Post*, March 27, 2005, Outlook, B01. As the Florida Supreme Court noted in an earlier phase of the *Schiavo* proceedings, "As we recently explained, '[w]hat is in the Constitution always must prevail over emotion. Our oaths as judges require that this principle is our polestar, and it alone.'" *Bush v. Schiavo*, 885 So. 2d 321, 336 (Fla. 2004).

[3] *Republican Party v. White* (a/k/a/ *White II*) 416 F.3d 738, (2005) petition for cert denied 1/23/06; *Family Trust Foundation of Kentucky v. Wolnitzek*, 345 F. Supp. 2d 672 (2004); *North Dakota Family Alliance v. Bader*, 361 F. Supp. 1021 (2005); *Alaska Right to Life Political Action Committee v. Feldman*, 380 F. Supp. 2d 1080 (2005).

[4] The resolution, for now, is the selection of a Democrat to preside over the case, but one whose own political contributions amounted to only $450. Kelly Shannon, "DeLay Case Finally Gets Judge—A Democrat," Associated Press, November 4, 2005.

[5] The summits were funded by the Bureau of Justice Assistance, U.S. Department of Justice and co-sponsored by the National Center for State Courts and the National Sheriff Association.

[6] Erin McKean, editor of the *Oxford American Dictionary*, quoted in an interview by Steve Inskeep on NPR's Morning Edition, "New Words of 2005 and Beyond," December 30, 2005.

[7] Such legislation was often retaliation for court decisions that challenged popular pieces of legislation, as in Florida where the proposed legislative takeover of court rule-making came in response to a decision that allowed convicted more time to seek DNA testing.

[8] The Supreme Court ultimately reversed its decision but also ruled the law as unconstitutional since the legislature was assuming powers reserved for the courts. Esteban Parra, "Top Court to Revisit Sentencing," *News Journal* (New Castle), February 5, 2005.

[9] Tom Barnes. "Voters Reject Supreme Court Justice Nigro." *Pittsburgh Post Gazette*. November 9, 2005.

[10] David G. Savage, "Supreme Court Ruling Could Spur Partisan Judicial Campaigns." *L.A. Times*, January 24, 2006. The quote is by James Bopp Jr. after the U.S. Supreme Court denied Minnesota's petition to review the 8th Circuit's decision. The case was originally *White v. the Republican Party of Minnesota*; by 2005 it had become the *Dimick* case.

[11] Canon 5A(3)(d)(ii).

[12] C.J. Karamargin, "O'Connor, in Tucson, Blasts Moves to Alter how Ariz. Judges are Picked, " *Arizona Daily Star*, February 3, 2006.

[13] J. Clark Kelso, *A Manual for Judges and Court Managers about Judicial Involvement in Legislative Processes*, Capital Center for Government Law and Policy, University of the Pacific, McGeorge School of Law, 2002. See also the National Center for State Courts Web-resource on the topic at *http://www.ncsconline.org/projects_Initiatives/PTC/Public Trust7Wtr05.htm*.

[14] D. Rottman and R. Schotland, "2004 Judicial Elections," *Spectrum: The Journal of State Government* 78, 17–19 (Winter 2005).

[15] Findings reported are from surveys of 2,000 adults conducted by the Pew Research Center for the People and the Press, "Abortion and Rights of Terror Suspects Top Court Issues," August 3, 2005. Other surveys conducted at the time of Congressional action report very similar findings. See the summary provided in "Americans on the Terri Schiavo Situation in Review," available at *http://www.heartheissues.com/americanson-terrischiavoinreview-g.html*.

[16] Telephone interviews were completed with 1,000 randomly selected adults in late July 2005. "Civics Education," prepared for the American Bar Association, July 2005 by Harris Interactive.

[17] Some 1,300 American adults were interviewed. Belden, Russonello & Stewart, *Speak to American Values*, Washington, D.C.: Justice at Stake, 2006, available at *http://www.justiceatstake.org/files/SpeaktoAmericasValues2.pdf*.

[18] David Rottman, "Trust and Confidence in the California Courts," 2005 (Part I: Findings and Recommendations, San Francisco, Judicial Council of California, 2005) available at *http://www.courtinfo.ca.gov/reference/documents/4_37pubtrust1.pdf*.

[19] *CourTools* was developed by the National Center for State Courts and builds on the previous work of the Commission on Trial Court Performance Standards, which set out 20 standards that all trial courts should meet. See: *http://www.ncsconline.org/D_Research/CourTools/tcmp_courttools.htm*.

[20] Chief Justice Michael A. Wolff, "Missouri Judges are Accountable … to the Law." Supreme Court of Missouri, December 15, 2005.

[21] Resolution 14 (of 2005) in Support of Measuring Court Performance. *http://ccj.ncsc.dni.us/CourtAdminResolutions/resol14MeasuringCourtPerformance.html*.

About the Author

David Rottman is principal court research consultant at the National Center for State Courts, where he has worked since 1987. His current interests include judicial selection, public opinion on the courts, the evolution of court structure, and the pros and cons of problem-solving courts. He is the author of books on modern Ireland, social class, and community courts. Rottman has a Ph.D. in sociology from the University of Illinois at Urbana, and previously worked at the Economic and Social Institute in Dublin, Ireland.

Table 5.1
STATE COURTS OF LAST RESORT

State or other jurisdiction	Name of court	Justices chosen (a)		No. of judges (b)	Term (in years) (c)	Chief justice	
		At large	By district			Method of selection	Term of office for chief justice
Alabama	S.C.	★		9	6	Popular election	6 years
Alaska	S.C.	★		5	10	By court	3 years (d)
Arizona	S.C.	★		5	6	By court	5 years
Arkansas	S.C.	★		7	8	Popular election	8 years
California	S.C.	★		7	12	Appointed by governor	12 years
Colorado	S.C.	★		7	10	By court	Indefinite
Connecticut	S.C.	★		7	8	Legislative appointment (e)	8 years
Delaware	S.C.	★ (f)		5	12	Appointed by governor, with consent of Senate	12 years
Florida	S.C.	★		7	6	By court	2 years
Georgia	S.C.	★		7	6	By court	4 years
Hawaii	S.C.	★		5	10	Appointed by governor, with consent of Senate (g)	10 years
Idaho	S.C.	★		5	6	By court	4 years
Illinois	S.C.		★	7	10	By court	3 years
Indiana	S.C.	★		5	10 (h)	Judicial nominating commission appointment	5 years
Iowa	S.C.	★		7	8	By court	8 years
Kansas	S.C.	★		7	6	Rotation by seniority	Indefinite
Kentucky	S.C.		★	7	8	By court	4 years
Louisiana	S.C.		★	7	10	By seniority of service	Duration of service
Maine	S.J.C.	★		7	7	Appointed by governor	7 years
Maryland	C.A.		★	7	10	Appointed by governor	Indefinite
Massachusetts	S.J.C.	★		7	To age 70	Appointed by governor (j)	To age 70
Michigan	S.C.	★		7	8	By court	2 years
Minnesota	S.C.	★		7	6	Popular election	6 years
Mississippi	S.C.		★	9	8	By seniority of service	Duration of service
Missouri	S.C.	★		7	12	By court (k)	2 years
Montana	S.C.	★		7	8	Popular election	8 years
Nebraska	S.C.		★ (l)	7	6 (m)	Appointed by governor from Judicial Nominating Commission	Duration of service
Nevada	S.C.	★		5	6	Rotation	2 years
New Hampshire	S.C.	★		5	To age 70	Appointed by governor with approval of elected executive council	To age 70
New Jersey	S.C.	★		7	7 (n)	Appointed by governor, with consent of Senate	Duration of service
New Mexico	S.C.	★		5	8	By court	2 years
New York	C.A.	★		7	14	Appointed by governor from Judicial Nomination Commission	14 years
North Carolina	S.C.	★		7	8	Popular election	8 years
North Dakota	S.C.	★		5 (o)	10	By Supreme and district court judges	5 years (p)
Ohio	S.C.	★		7	6	Popular election	6 years
Oklahoma	S.C.		★	9	6	By court	2 years
	C.C.A.		★	5	6	By court	2 years
Oregon	S.C.	★		7	6	By court	6 years
Pennsylvania	S.C.	★		7	10	Rotation by seniority	Duration of term
Rhode Island	S.C.	★		5	Life	Appointed by seniority (i)	Life
South Carolina	S.C.	★		5	10	Legislative election	10 years

See footnotes at end of table.

STATE COURTS OF LAST RESORT—Continued

State or other jurisdiction	Name of court	Justices chosen (a)		No. of judges (b)	Term (in years) (c)	Chief justice	
		At large	By district			Method of selection	Term of office for chief justice
South Dakota	S.C.		★(g)	5	8	By court	4 years
Tennessee	S.C.	★		5	8	By court	4 years
Texas	S.C.	★		9	6	Partisan election	6 years
Texas	C.C.A.	★		9	6	Partisan election	6 years (r)
Utah	S.C.	★		5	10 (s)	By court	4 years
Vermont	S.C.	★		5	6	Appointed by governor from Judicial Nomination Commission, with consent of Senate	6 years
Virginia	S.C.	★		7	12	Seniority	Indefinite
Washington	S.C.	★		9	6	By court	4 years
West Virginia	S.C.A.		★	5	12	Rotation by seniority	1 year
Wisconsin	S.C.	★		7	10	Seniority	Until declined
Wyoming	S.C.	★		5	8	By court	At pleasure of court
Dist. of Columbia	C.A.	★		9	15	Judicial Nominating Commission appointment	4 years
Puerto Rico	S.C.	★		7	To age 70	Appointed by governor, with consent of Senate	To age 70

Source: National Center for State Courts, February 2006.

Key:
S.C. — Supreme Court
S.C.A. — Supreme Court of Appeals
S.J.C. — Supreme Judicial Court
C.A. — Court of Appeals
C.C.A. — Court of Criminal Appeals
H.C. — High Court

(a) See Chapter 5 table entitled, "Selection and Retention of Judges," for details.
(b) Number includes chief justice.
(c) The initial term may be shorter. See Chapter 5 table entitled, "Selection and Retention of Judges," for details.
(d) A justice may serve more than one term as chief justice, but may not serve consecutive terms in that position.
(e) Governor nominates from candidates submitted by Judicial Selection Commission.
(f) Regional (5), Statewide (2), Regional based on District of Appeal.
(g) Judicial Selection Commission nominates.

(h) Initial two years; retention 10 years.
(i) With House and Senate confirmation.
(j) Chief Justices are appointed, until age 70, by the Governor with the advice and consent of the Executive (Governor's) Council.
(k) Selection is typically rotated among the judges.
(l) Chief justice chosen statewide; associate judges chosen by district.
(m) More than three years for first election and every six years thereafter.
(n) Followed by tenure.
(o) A temporary court of appeals was established July 1, 1987 to exercise appellate and original jurisdiction was delegated by the supreme court. This court does not sit, has no assigned judges, has heard no appeals and is currently unfunded.
(p) Or expiration of term, whichever is first.
(q) Initially chosen by district; retention determined statewide.
(r) Presiding judge of Court of Criminal Appeals.
(s) Initial three years; retention 10 years.

Table 5.2
STATE INTERMEDIATE APPELLATE COURTS AND GENERAL TRIAL COURTS: NUMBER OF JUDGES AND TERMS

State or other jurisdiction	Intermediate appellate court			General trial court		
	Name of court	No. of judges	Term (years)	Name of court	No. of judges	Term (years)
Alabama	Court of Criminal Appeals	5	6	Circuit Court	142	6
	Court of Civil Appeals	5	6			
Alaska	Court of Appeals	3	8	Superior Court	34 (a)	6
Arizona	Court of Appeals	22	6	Superior Court	160	4
Arkansas	Court of Appeals	12	8	Chancery/Probate Court and Circuit Court	115	(b)
California	Court of Appeals	105	12	Superior Court	1,498 (c)	6
Colorado	Court of Appeals	16	8	District Court	132 (d)	6
Connecticut	Appellate Court	10	8	Superior Court	180	8
Delaware	...	...	...	Superior Court	19	12
				Court of Chancery	(e)	12
Florida	District Courts of Appeals	62	6	Circuit Court	527	6
Georgia	Court of Appeals	12	6	Superior Court	188	4
Hawaii	Intermediate Court of Appeals	4	10	Circuit Court	28 (f)	10
Idaho	Court of Appeals	3	6	District Court	39 (g)	4
Illinois	Appellate Court	54 (h)	10	Circuit Court	494 (i)	6 (j)
Indiana	Court of Appeals	15 (k)	10 (l)	Superior Court, Probate Court and Circuit Court	296	6
Iowa	Court of Appeals	9	6	District Court	179 (m)	6
Kansas	Court of Appeals	11	4	District Court	234 (n)	4
Kentucky	Court of Appeals	14	8	Circuit Court	129 (dd)	8
Louisiana	Court of Appeals	53	10	District Court	211 (o)	6
Maine	...	...	...	Superior Court	16	7
Maryland	Court of Special Appeals	13	10	Circuit Court	146	15
Massachusetts	Appeals Court	25	(p)	Superior Court	82	(p)
Michigan	Court of Appeals	28	6	Circuit Court	216	6
Minnesota	Court of Appeals	16	6	District Court	275	6
Mississippi	Court of Appeals	10	8	Circuit Court	49	4
Missouri	Court of Appeals	32	8	Circuit Court	136 (q)	6
Montana	...	...	...	District Court	402 (r)	6
Nebraska	Court of Appeals	6	12 (s)	District Court	55	6 (t)
Nevada	...	...	...	District Court	60	6
New Hampshire	...	...	...	Superior Court	27 (u)	(p)
New Jersey	Appellate Division of Superior Court	33	7 (v)	Superior Court	429 (w)	7 (x)
New Mexico	Court of Appeals	10	8	District Court	72	6
New York	Appellate Division of Supreme Court	56	5 (y)	Supreme Court	346 (ii)	(z)
	Appellate Terms of Supreme Court	15	5 (y)	County Court	128	(z)
North Carolina	Court of Appeals	15	8	Superior Court	106 (aa)	8
North Dakota	...	...	...	District Court	42 (ll)	6
Ohio	Court of Appeals	68	6	Court of Common Pleas	380	6

See footnotes at end of table.

STATE INTERMEDIATE APPELLATE COURTS AND GENERAL TRIAL COURTS: NUMBER OF JUDGES AND TERMS

State or other jurisdiction	Intermediate appellate court			General trial court		
	Name of court	No. of judges	Term (years)	Name of court	No. of judges	Term (years)
Oklahoma	Court of Appeals	12	6	District Court	221 (bb)	4
Oregon	Court of Appeals	10	6	Circuit Court	169	6
				Tax Court	1 (jj)	6
Pennsylvania	Superior Court	15	10	Court of Common Pleas	408	10
	Commonwealth Court	9	10			
Rhode Island	...	...	Life	Superior Court	22 (kk)	Life
South Carolina	Court of Appeals	9	Life	Circuit Court	46 (cc)	6
South Dakota	...	...	...	Circuit Court	38	8
Tennessee	Court of Appeals	12	8	Chancery Court	35	8
	Court of Criminal Appeals	12	8	Circuit Court	85	8
				Criminal Court	35	8
				Probate Court	2	(ee)
Texas	Court of Appeals	80	6	District Court	410	4
Utah	Court of Appeals	7	10 (ff)	District Court	70 (gg)	6
Vermont	...	...	...	Superior Court and District Court	32 (hh)	6
Virginia	Court of Appeals	11	8	Circuit Court	155	8
Washington	Court of Appeals	22	6	Superior Court	177	4
West Virginia	...	...	...	Circuit Court	65	8
Wisconsin	Court of Appeals	16	6	Circuit Court	241	6
Wyoming	...	...	...	District Court	19	6
Dist. of Columbia	...	...	...	Superior Court	59	15
Puerto Rico	Circuit Court of Appeals	39	16	Court of First Instance	328	12

Source: National Center for State Courts, February 2006.

Key:

... — Court does not exist in jurisdiction or not applicable.

(a) Plus nine masters.

(b) Circuit court judges serve four-year terms. Chancery probate court judges serve six-year terms. (Some judges serve both circuit and chancery courts.)

(c) Plus 417 commissioners and referees.

(d) Plus 12 Water Court judges.

(e) One chancellor and four vice-chancellors.

(f) Plus 17 family judges.

(g) Plus 83 full-time magistrate/judges.

(h) Plus nine circuit court judges assigned to the appellate court.

(i) Plus 356 associate judges.

(j) Associate judges, four years.

(k) Plus one tax court judge.

(l) Two years initial; 10 years retention.

(m) Plus 135 part-time magistrates, 12 associate juvenile judges, one associate probate judge, and six part-time alternate district associate judges.

(n) Includes 74 magistrates.

(o) Plus 11 commissioners.

(p) To age 70.

(q) Plus 136 associate circuit judges, 19 family court commissioners, 7 drug commissioners, 4 probate and 3 deputy probate commissioners.

(r) Plus five water judges and one workers' compensation judge.

(s) More than three years for first election and every six years thereafter.

(t) The initial term is for three years but not more than five years.

(u) Plus 10 full-time marital masters.

(v) Followed by tenure.

(w) Twenty-one are surrogates that also serve as deputy superior court clerks.

(x) On reapportionment until age 70.

(y) Or duration.

(z) Fourteen years for Supreme Court; 10 years for county court.

(aa) Includes 13 special judges and there in addition 100 clerks who hear uncontested probate.

(bb) This includes 71 district, 77 associate district and 73 special judges.

(cc) Plus 22 masters-in-equity.

(dd) Plus 59 domestic relations commissioners.

(ee) Locally determined.

(ff) Three years initial; six years retention.

(gg) Plus seven domestic court commissioners.

(hh) Plus five magistrates for Family Court.

(ii) Plus 50 acting supreme court judges and 12 quasi-judicial staff.

(jj) Plus six magistrates.

(kk) Plus five magistrates.

(ll) Plus 7.5 judicial referees.

Table 5.3
QUALIFICATIONS OF JUDGES OF STATE APPELLATE COURTS AND GENERAL TRIAL COURTS

State or other jurisdiction	Years of minimum residence				Minimum age		Legal credentials	
	In state		In district					
	A	T	A	T	A	T	A	T
Alabama	1	1	...	1	...	...	Licensed attorney	Licensed attorney
Alaska	5	5	...	...	...	...	8 years practice	5 years practice
Arizona	10 (a)	5	(b)	1	(ee)	30	(c)	(d)
Arkansas	2	2	(b)	...	30	28	8 years practice	6 years practice/bench
California	...	...	...	...	...	...	10 years state bar	10 years state bar
Colorado	★	★(e)	...	★	...	...	5 years state bar	5 years state bar
Connecticut	★	★	(f)	(f)	...	...	10 years state bar	Member of the bar
Delaware	★	★	(f)	(g)	...	...	"Learned in law"	"Learned in law"
Florida	★(h)	★	(i)	★(j)	...	...	10 years state bar	5 years state bar
Georgia	★	3	...	...	...	30	7 years state bar	7 years state bar
Hawaii	★	★	...	...	...	...	10 years state bar	10 years state bar
Idaho	2	1	...	...	30	...	10 years state bar	10 years state bar
Illinois	★	★	★	★	...	...	Licensed attorney	...
Indiana	...	1	(b)	★	...	...	10 years state bar (k)	...
Iowa	...	...	...	★	...	...	Licensed attorney	...
Kansas	...	...	...	★	30	...	10 years active and continuous practice (l)	5 years state bar
Kentucky	2	2	2	2	...	...	8 years state bar and licensed attorney	8 years state bar
Louisiana	2	2	2	2	...	...	5 years state bar	5 years state bar
Maine	...	...	...	...	...	...	"Learned in law"	"Learned in law"
Maryland	5	5	6 mos.	6 mos.	30	30	State bar member	State bar member
Massachusetts	...	...	...	...	...	...	...	No law degree required
Michigan	...	...	(b)	...	...	...	State bar member (m)	State bar member
Minnesota	...	...	(n)	...	...	...	State bar member	State bar member
Mississippi	5	5	...	...	30	26	5 years state bar	5 years practice
Missouri	(o)	(o)	(b)	★	30	30	State bar member	State bar member
Montana	2	2	...	...	...	...	5 years state bar	5 years state bar
Nebraska	3 (p)	...	★	★	30	30	5 years practice	5 years practice
Nevada	2	2	...	...	25	25	State bar member	...
New Hampshire	...	...	...	...	...	...	...	...
New Jersey	...	(q)	...	(q)	...	...	Admitted to practice in state for at least 10 years	10 years practice of law
New Mexico	3	3	...	★	35	35	10 years active practice (r)	6 years active practice
New York	★	★	(s)	(s)	...	18	10 years state bar	10 years state bar
North Carolina	...	N.A.	...	★	...	...	State bar member	State bar member
North Dakota	★(p)	...	...	★	...	...	License to practice law	State bar member
Ohio	★(p)	★	(t)	★	...	...	6 years practice	6 years practice
Oklahoma	...	(u)	1	★	30	...	5 years state bar	(v)
Oregon	3	3	...	(w)	...	...	State bar member	State bar member
Pennsylvania	1	1	(f)	★	...	...	State bar member	State bar member
Rhode Island	...	...	...	...	21	...	License to practice law	State bar member
South Carolina	5	5	...	...	32	32	8 years state bar	8 years state bar
South Dakota	★	★	★	★	...	...	State bar member	State bar member
Tennessee	5	5	★(x)	1	35	30	Qualified to practice law	Qualified to practice law
Texas	★	...	...	2	35	25	(y)	(z)
Utah	5 (aa)	3	...	★	30	25	State bar member	State bar member
Vermont	5	5	...	(bb)	...	...	5 years state bar	5 years state bar
Virginia	...	★	...	★	...	...	5 years state bar	5 years state bar
Washington	1	1	1	1	...	...	(cc)	State bar member
West Virginia	5	★	...	★	30	30	10 years state bar	5 years state bar
Wisconsin	10 days	10 days	10 days	10 days	...	...	5 years state bar	5 years state bar
Wyoming	3	2	...	...	30	28	9 years state bar	...
Dist. of Columbia	★	★	90 days	90 days	...	...	5 years state bar	5 years state bar (dd)
No. Mariana Islands	...	...	...	...	...	30	N.A.	N.A.
Puerto Rico	5	...	...	...	...	...	10 years state bar	7 years state bar

See footnotes at end of table.

QUALIFICATIONS OF JUDGES — Continued

Source: National Center for State Courts, February 2006.

Key:

A — Judges of courts of last resort and intermediate appellate courts.

T — Judges of general trial courts.

★ — Provision; length of time not specified.

. . . — No specific provision.

N.A.— Not applicable

(a) For court of appeals, five years.

(b) No local residency requirement stated for Supreme Court. Local residency required for Court of Appeals.

(c) Supreme Court–ten years state bar, Court of Appeals–five years state bar.

(d) Admitted to the practice of law in Arizona for five years.

(e) State residency requirement for District Court, no residency requirement stated for Denver Probate Court, Denver Juvenile Court or Water Court.

(f) Local residency not required.

(g) Court of Chancery does not have residency requirement, Superior Court requires residency.

(h) For District Courts of Appeal must reside within the territorial jurisdiction of the court.

(i) Initial appointment, must be resident of district at the time of original appointment.

(j) Circuit court judge must reside within the territorial jurisdiction of the court.

(k) In the Supreme Court and the Court of Appeals, five years service as a general jurisdiction judge may be substituted.

(l) Relevant legal experience, such as being a member of a law faculty or sitting as a judge, may qualify under the 10-year requirement.

(m) Supreme Court: state bar member and practice at least five years.

(n) No residency requirement stated for Supreme Court, Court of Appeals varies.

(o) At the appellate level must have been a state voter for nine years. At the general trial court level must have been a state voter for three years.

(p) No state residency requirement specified for Court of Appeals.

(q) For Superior Court: out of a total of 427 authorized judgeships (including 32 in the appellate division), there are restricted superior court judgeships that require residence within the particular county of assignment at time of appointment and reappointment; there are 142 unrestricted judgeships for which assignment of county is made by the chief justice.

(r) Supreme Court and Court of Appeals: and/or judgeship in any court of the state.

(s) No local residency requirement stated for Court of Appeals, local residency requirement for presiding judge of Supreme Court, Appellate Divisions.

(t) No local residency requirement for Supreme Court; Court of Appeals requires district residency.

(u) Six months if elected.

(v) District Court: judges must be a state bar member for four years or a judge of court record. Associate judges must be a state bar member for two years or a judge of a court of record.

(w) Local residency requirement for Circuit Court, no residency requirement stated for Tax Court.

(x) Supreme Court: one justice from each of three divisions and two seats at large. Court of Appeals and Court of Criminal Appeals: must reside in the grand division served.

(y) Ten years practicing law or a lawyer and judge of a court of record at least 10 years.

(z) District Court: judges must have been a practicing lawyer or a judge of a court in this state, or both combined, for four years.

(aa) Supreme Court is five; Court of Appeals is three.

(bb) No local residency requirement stated for Superior Court, District Court must reside in geographic unit.

(cc) Supreme Court: state bar member; Court of Appeals: five years state bar.

(dd) Superior Court: Judge must also be an active member of the unified District of Columbia bar and have been engaged, during the five years immediately preceding the judicial nomination, in the active practice of law as an attorney by the United States, of District of Columbia government.

(ee) Court of Appeals minimum age is 30.

Table 5.4
COMPENSATION OF JUDGES OF APPELLATE COURTS AND GENERAL TRIAL COURTS

State or other jurisdiction	Appellate courts						General trial courts	Salary
	Court of last resort	Chief Justice salaries	Associate Justice salaries	Intermediate appellate court	Chief/Presiding salaries	Judges salaries		
Alabama	Supreme Court	$153,000	$152,000	Court of Criminal Appeals	$152,000	$151,000	Circuit courts	$112,000
Alaska	Supreme Court	126,000	126,000	Court of Appeals	119,000	119,000	Superior courts	(e)
Arizona	Supreme Court	129,000	127,000	Court of Appeals	124,000	124,000	Superior courts	121,000
Arkansas	Supreme Court	142,000	132,000	Court of Appeals	129,000	127,000	Chancery courts	123,000
California	Supreme Court	199,000	182,000	Court of Appeals	178,000	171,000	Superior court	149,000
Colorado	Supreme Court	122,000	120,000	Court of Appeals	118,000	115,000	District courts	110,255
Connecticut	Supreme Court	166,000	154,000	Appellate Court	152,000	145,000	Superior courts	139,000
Delaware	Supreme Court	189,000	180,000	...	...	...	Superior courts	164,000
Florida	Supreme Court	160,000	160,000	District Court of Appeals	149,000	149,000	Circuit courts	139,000
Georgia	Supreme Court	158,000	158,000	Court of Appeals	157,000	157,000	Superior courts	(a)
Hawaii	Supreme Court	140,000	135,000	Intermediate Court	130,000	125,000	Circuit courts	122,000
Idaho	Supreme Court	106,000	104,000	Court of Appeals	103,000	103,000	District courts	99,000
Illinois	Supreme Court	177,000	177,000	Court of Appeals	167,000	167,000	Circuit courts	153,000
Indiana	Supreme Court	134,000	134,000	Court of Appeals	130,000	130,000	Circuit courts	110,000
Iowa	Supreme Court	133,000	128,000	Court of Appeals	128,000	123,000	District courts	117,000
Kansas	Supreme Court	124,000	121,000	Court of Appeals	120,000	117,000	District courts	106,000
Kentucky	Supreme Court	137,000	132,000	Court of Appeals	130,000	127,000	Circuit courts	121,000
Louisiana	Supreme Court	124,000	118,000	Court of Appeals	118,000	112,000	District courts	106,000
Maine	Supreme Judicial Court	125,000	108,000	...	...	...	Superior courts	102,000
Maryland	Court of Appeals	156,000	137,000	Court of Special Appeals	131,000	128,000	Circuit courts	123,000
Massachusetts	Supreme Judicial Court	132,000	127,000	Appellate Court	122,000	117,000	Superior courts	113,000
Michigan	Supreme Court	165,000	165,000	Court of Appeals	151,000	151,000	Circuit courts	140,000
Minnesota	Supreme Court	149,000	136,000	Court of Appeals	134,000	128,000	District courts	120,000
Mississippi	Supreme Court	115,000	113,000	Court of Appeals	108,000	105,000	Chancery courts	104,000
Missouri	Supreme Court	126,000	123,000	Court of Appeals	115,000	115,000	Circuit courts	108,000
Montana	Supreme Court	102,000	101,000	...	...	...	District courts	94,000
Nebraska	Supreme Court	123,000	123,000	Court of Appeals	117,000	117,000	District courts	114,000
Nevada	Supreme Court	(f)	(f)	...	...	...	District courts	(g)
New Hampshire	Supreme Court	132,000	128,000	...	...	...	Superior courts	120,000
New Jersey	Supreme Court	164,000	159,000	Appellate division of	...	150,000	Superior courts	141,000
New Mexico	Supreme Court	109,000	107,000	Court of Appeals	104,000	102,000	District courts	97,000
New York	Court of Appeals	156,000	151,000	Appellate divisions of	148,000	144,000	Supreme courts	137,000
North Carolina	Supreme Court	124,000	121,000	Court of Appeals	118,000	116,000	Superior courts	109,000
North Dakota	Supreme Court	106,000	103,000	...	...	...	District courts	94,000
Ohio	Supreme Court	144,000	135,000	Court of Appeals	126,000	126,000	Courts of common pleas	116,000
Oklahoma	Supreme Court	118,000	114,000	Court of Appeals	110,000	108,000	District courts	103,000
Oregon	Supreme Court	108,000	105,000	Court of Appeals	105,000	103,000	Circuit courts	96,000
Pennsylvania	Supreme Court	160,000	156,000	Superior Court	153,000	151,000	Courts of common pleas	135,000
Rhode Island	Supreme Court	158,000	144,000	...	...	...	Superior courts	129,000
South Carolina	Supreme Court	134,000	128,000	Court of Appeals	127,000	125,000	Circuit courts	122,000

See footnotes at end of table.

COMPENSATION OF JUDGES OF APPELLATE COURTS AND GENERAL TRIAL COURTS—Continued

State or other jurisdiction	Appellate courts						General trial courts	Salary
	Court of last resort	Chief Justice salaries	Associate Justice salaries	Intermediate appellate court	Chief/Presiding salaries	Judges salaries		
South Dakota.............	Supreme Court	110,000	108,000	...	...	...	Circuit courts	101,000
Tennessee................	Supreme Court	130,000	130,000	Court of Appeals	124,000	124,000	Chancery courts	119,000
Texas......................	Supreme Court	153,000	150,000	Court of Appeals	(b)	(b)	District courts	(c)
Utah.......................	Supreme Court	124,000	122,000	Court of Appeals	118,000	117,000	District courts	111,000
Vermont..................	Supreme Court	125,000	119,000	...	...	...	Superior/District/Family	113,000
Virginia...................	Supreme Court	159,000 (d)	149,000 (d)	Court of Appeals	142,000 (d)	141,000 (d)	Circuit courts	138,000
Washington..............	Supreme Court	141,000	141,000	Court of Appeals	135,000	135,000	Superior courts	128,000
West Virginia............	Supreme Court	121,000	121,000	...	...	...	Circuit courts	116,000
Wisconsin................	Supreme Court	134,000	126,000	Court of Appeals	119,000	119,000	Circuit courts	112,000
Wyoming.................	Supreme Court	111,000	111,000	...	...	...	District courts	106,000
Dist. of Columbia......	Court of Appeals	176,000	175,000	...	...	...	Superior courts	165,000
American Samoa.........	High Court	120,000	115,000	...	...	...	District courts	76,000
Guam	Supreme Court	(h)	(i)	...	...	...	Superior courts	(j)
No. Mariana Islands	Commonwealth Supreme Court	130,000	126,000	...	...	...	Superior courts	120,000
Puerto Rico..............	Supreme Court	125,000	120,000	Appellate Court	105,000	105,000	Superior courts	90,000
U.S. Virgin Islands	Territorial Court	145,000	135,000	...	...	...	...	...

Source: National Center for State Courts, *Survey of Judicial Salaries* Vol. 30 No. 2 (as of January 2006).

Note: Compensation is shown rounded to the nearest thousand, and is reported according to most recent legislation, even though laws may not yet have taken effect. There are other non-salary forms of judicial compensation that can be a significant part of a judge's compensation package. It should be noted that many of these can be important to judges or attorneys who might be interested in becoming judges or justices. These include retirement, disability, and death benefits, expense accounts, vacation, holiday, and sick leave and various forms of insurance coverage.

(a) Salary range is between $113,000 and $166,000.
(b) Salary range is between $138,000 and $145,000, based on local supplements.
(c) Salary range is between $125,000 and $133,000, Associates $76,000 and $83,000, based on local supplements.
(d) Plus $6,500 in lieu of travel, lodging and other expenses.
(e) Salary range is between $116,000 and $123,000, varies by location and cost of living.
(f) Salary range is between $140,000 and $171,000 and may include longevity pay.
(g) Salary range is between $130,000 and $159,000 and may include longevity pay and may be dependent on election cycle.
(h) Salary range is between $128,000 and $161,000.
(i) Salary range is between $126,000 and $154,000.
(j) Salary range is between $100,000 and $127,000.

Table 5.5
SELECTED DATA ON COURT ADMINISTRATIVE OFFICES

State or other jurisdiction	Title	Established	Appointed by (a)	Salary
Alabama	Administrative Director of Courts	1971	CJ (b)	$105,000
Alaska	Administrative Director	1959	CJ (b)	124,000
Arizona	Administrative Director of Courts	1960	SC	(g)
Arkansas	Director, Administrative Office of the Courts	1965	CJ (c)	97,000
California	Administrative Director of the Courts	1960	JC	(h)
Colorado	State Court Administrator	1959	SC	118,000
Connecticut	Chief Court Administrator (d)	1965	CJ	160,000
Delaware	Director, Administrative Office of the Courts	1971	CJ	122,000
Florida	State Courts Administrator	1972	SC	131,000
Georgia	Director, Administrative Office of the Courts	1973	JC	132,000
Hawaii	Administrative Director of the Courts	1959	CJ (b)	105,000
Idaho	Administrative Director of the Courts	1967	SC	99,000
Illinois	Administrative Director of the Courts	1959	SC	167,000
Indiana	Executive Director, Division of State Court Administration	1975	CJ	103,000
Iowa	Court Administrator	1971	SC	(i)
Kansas	Judicial Administrator	1965	CJ	106,000
Kentucky	Administrative Director of the Courts	1976	CJ	121,000
Louisiana	Judicial Administrator	1954	SC	112,000
Maine	Court Administrator	1975	CJ	102,000
Maryland	State Court Administrator	1955	CJ (b)	129,000
Massachusetts	Chief Justice for Administration & Management	1978	SC	122,000
Michigan	State Court Administrator	1952	SC	142,000
Minnesota	State Court Administrator	1963	SC	120,000
Mississippi	Court Administrator	1974	SC	69,000
Missouri	State Courts Administrator	1970	SC	115,000
Montana	State Court Administrator	1975	SC	90,000
Nebraska	State Court Administrator	1972	CJ	103,000
Nevada	Director, Office of Court Administration	1971	SC	112,000
New Hampshire	Director of the Administrative Office of the Court	1980	SC	98,000
New Jersey	Administrative Director of the Courts	1948	CJ	150,000
New Mexico	Director, Administrative Office of the Courts	1959	SC	105,000
New York	Chief Administrator of the Courts	1978	CJ	148,000
North Carolina	Director, Administrative Office of the Courts	1965	CJ	112,000
North Dakota	Court Administrator (h)	1971	CJ	82,500
Ohio	Administrative Director of the Courts	1955	SC	129,000
Oklahoma	Administrative Director of the Courts	1967	SC	108,000
Oregon	Court Administrator	1971	SC	119,000
Pennsylvania	Court Administrator	1968	SC	147,000
Rhode Island	State Court Administrator	1969	CJ	115,000
South Carolina	Director of Court Administration	1973	CJ	115,000
South Dakota	State Court Administrator	1974	SC	96,000
Tennessee	Director	1963	SC	120,000
Texas	Administrative Director of the Courts (i)	1977	SC	98,000
Utah	Court Administrator	1973	SC	111,000
Vermont	Court Administrator	1967	SC	113,000
Virginia	Executive Secretary to the Supreme Court	1952	SC	141,000
Washington	Administrator for the Courts	1957	SC (e)	122,000
West Virginia	Administrative Director of the Supreme Court of Appeals	1975	SC	105,000
Wisconsin	Director of State Courts	1978	SC	119,000
Wyoming	Court Coordinator	1974	SC	95,000
Dist. of Columbia	Executive Officer, Courts of D.C.	1971	(f)	165,200
American Samoa	Administrator/Comptroller	N.A.	N.A.	(j)
Guam	Administrative Director of Superior Court	N.A.	CJ (m)	90,000
No. Mariana Islands				70,000
Puerto Rico	Administrative Director of the Courts	1952	CJ	111,000
U.S. Virgin Islands	Court/Administrative Clerk	N.A.	N.A.	88,500

Source: Salary information was taken from National Center for State Courts, *Survey of Judicial Salaries* Vol. 30 No. 2 (as of January 2006).
Note: Compensation shown is rounded to the nearest thousand, and is reported according to most recent legislation, even though laws may not yet have taken effect. Other information from State Court Administrator Web sites.
Key:
SC — State court of last resort.
CJ — Chief justice or chief judge of court of last resort.
JC — Judicial council.
N.A. — Not available.

(a) Term of office for all court administrators is at pleasure of appointing authority.
(b) With approval of Supreme Court.
(c) With approval of Judicial Council.
(d) Administrator is an associate judge of the Supreme Court.
(e) Appointed from list of five submitted by governor.
(f) Joint Committee on Judicial Administration.
(g) Salary range is between $101,000 and $163,000.
(h) Salary range is between $ 168,000 and $185,000.
(i) Salary range is between $95,000 and $143,000.
(j) Salary range is between $29,000 and $63,000, plus $1,170/yr. increment.

Table 5.6
SELECTION AND RETENTION OF JUDGES

State or other jurisdiction	Court	Appointive systems — Merit (a)	Appointive systems — Gubernatorial or Legislative (b)	Elective systems — Non-partisan	Elective systems — Partisan	Initial term of office (years)	Method of retention (c)
Alabama	Supreme Court	. . .	. . .	. . .	★	6	Re-election (6 yr. term)
	Court of Civil App.	. . .	. . .	. . .	★	6	Re-election (6 yr. term)
	Court of Crim. App.	. . .	. . .	. . .	★	6	Re-election (6 yr. term)
	Circuit Court	. . .	. . .	. . .	★	6	Re-election (6 yr. term)
Alaska	Supreme Court	★	. . .	. . .	. . .	3	Retention election (10 yr. term)
	Court of Appeals	★	. . .	. . .	. . .	3	Retention election (8 yr. term)
	Superior Court	★	. . .	. . .	. . .	3	Retention election (6 yr. term)
Arizona	Supreme Court	★	. . .	. . .	. . .	2	Retention election (6 yr. term)
	Court of Appeals	★	. . .	. . .	. . .	2	Retention election (6 yr. term)
	Superior Court – county pop. greater than 250,000	★	. . .	. . .	. . .	2	Retention election (4 yr. term)
	Superior Court – county pop. less than 250,000	. . .	. . .	★	. . .	4	Re-election (4 yr. term)
Arkansas (d)	Supreme Court	. . .	. . .	★	. . .	8	Re-election for additional terms
	Court of Appeals	. . .	. . .	★	. . .	8	Re-election for additional terms
	Circuit Court	. . .	. . .	★	. . .	6	Re-election for additional terms
California	Supreme Court	. . .	G	. . .	. . .	12	Retention election (12 yr. term)
	Courts of Appeal	. . .	G	. . .	. . .	12	Retention election (12 yr. term)
	Superior Court (e)	. . .	. . .	★	. . .	6	Nonpartisan election (6 yr. term) (f)
Colorado	Supreme Court	★	. . .	. . .	. . .	2	Retention election (10 yr. term)
	Court of Appeals	★	. . .	. . .	. . .	2	Retention election (8 yr. term)
	District Court	★	. . .	. . .	. . .	2	Retention election (6 yr. term)
Connecticut	Supreme Court	★	. . .	. . .	. . .	8	(g)
	Appellate Court	★	. . .	. . .	. . .	8	(g)
	Superior Court	★	. . .	. . .	. . .	8	(g)
Delaware (h)	Supreme Court	★	. . .	. . .	. . .	12	(i)
	Court of Chancery	★	. . .	. . .	. . .	12	(i)
	Superior Court	★	. . .	. . .	. . .	12	(i)
Florida	Supreme Court	★	. . .	. . .	. . .	1	Retention election (6 yr. term)
	District Court of Appeal	★	. . .	. . .	. . .	1	Retention election (6 yr. term)
	Circuit Court	. . .	. . .	★	. . .	6	Re-election for additional terms
Georgia	Supreme Court	. . .	. . .	★	. . .	6	Re-election for additional terms
	Court of Appeals	. . .	. . .	★	. . .	6	Re-election for additional terms
	Superior Court	. . .	. . .	★	. . .	4	Re-election for additional terms
Hawaii	Supreme Court	★	. . .	. . .	. . .	10	Reappointed to subsequent term by Judicial Selection Comm. (10 yr. term)
	Intermediate Court of Appeals	★	. . .	. . .	. . .	10	Reappointed to subsequent term by Judicial Selection Comm. (10 yr. term)
	Circuit and Family Courts	★	. . .	. . .	. . .	10	Reappointed to subsequent term by Judicial Selection Comm. (10 yr. term)
Idaho	Supreme Court	. . .	. . .	★	. . .	6	Re-election for additional terms
	Court of Appeals	. . .	. . .	★	. . .	6	Re-election for additional terms
	District Court	. . .	. . .	★	. . .	4	Re-election for additional terms
Illinois	Supreme Court	. . .	. . .	. . .	★	10	Retention election (10 yr. term)
	Apellate Court	. . .	. . .	. . .	★	10	Retention election (10 yr. term)
	Circuit Court	. . .	. . .	. . .	★	6	Retention election (6 yr. term)
Indiana	Supreme Court	★	. . .	. . .	. . .	2	Retention election (10 yr. term)
	Court of Appeals	★	. . .	. . .	. . .	2	Retention election (10 yr. term)
	Circuit Court	. . .	. . .	. . .	★	6	Re-election for additional terms
	Circuit Court (Vanderburg Co.)	. . .	. . .	★	. . .	6	Re-election for additional terms
	Superior Court	. . .	. . .	. . .	★	6	Re-election for additional terms
	Superior Court (Allen Co.)	. . .	. . .	★	. . .	6	Re-election for additional terms
	Superior Court (Lake Co.)	★(j)	. . .	. . .	. . .	2	Retention election (6 yr. term)
	Superior Court (St. Joseph Co.)	★	. . .	. . .	. . .	2	Retention election (6 yr. term)
	Superior Court (Vanderburg Co.)	. . .	. . .	★	. . .	6	Re-election for additional terms

See footnotes at end of table.

SELECTION AND RETENTION OF JUDGES — Continued

State or other jurisdiction	Court	Methods of initial selection				Initial term of office (years)	Method of retention (c)
		Appointive systems		Elective systems			
		Merit (a)	Gubernatorial or Legislative (b)	Non-partisan	Partisan		
Iowa	Supreme Court	★	...	...	...	1	Retention election (8 yr. term)
	Court of Appeals	★	...	...	...	1	Retention election (6 yr. term)
	District Court	★	...	...	...	1	Retention election (6 yr. term)
Kansas	Supreme Court	★	...	...	...	1	Retention election (6 yr. term)
	Court of Appeals	★	...	...	...	1	Retention election (4 yr. term)
	District Court (17 districts)	★	...	...	...	1	Retention election (4 yr. term)
	District Court (14 districts)	...	...	...	★	4	Re-election for additional terms
Kentucky	Supreme Court	...	...	★	...	8	Re-election for additional terms
	Court of Appeals	...	...	★	...	8	Re-election for additional terms
	Circuit Court	...	...	★	...	8	Re-election for additional terms
Louisiana	Supreme Court	...	...	...	★(k)	10	Re-election for additional terms
	Court of Appeals	...	...	...	★(k)	10	Re-election for additional terms
	District Court	...	...	...	★(k)	6	Re-election for additional terms
Maine	Supreme Judicial Court	...	G	...	...	7	Reappointment by governor subject to legislative confirmation
	Superior Court	...	G	...	...	7	Reappointment by governor subject to legislative confirmation
Maryland (h)	Court of Appeals	★	...	...	...	(l)	Retention election (10 yr. term)
	Court of Special Appeals	★	...	...	...	(l)	Retention election (10 yr. term)
	Circuit Court	★	...	...	...	(l)	Nonpartisan election (15 yr. term) (m)
Massachusetts (h)	Supreme Judicial Court	★	...	...	...	to age 70	...
	Appeals Court	★	...	...	...	to age 70	...
	Trial Court of Massachusetts	★	...	...	...	to age 70	...
Michigan	Supreme Court	...	...	...	★(n)	8	Re-election for additional terms
	Court of Appeals	...	...	★	...	6	Re-election for additional terms
	District Court/ Circuit Court	...	...	★	...	6	Re-election for additional terms
Minnesota	Supreme Court	...	...	★	...	6	Re-election for additional terms
	Court of Appeals	...	...	★	...	6	Re-election for additional terms
	District Court	...	...	★	...	6	Re-election for additional terms
Mississippi	Supreme Court	...	...	★	...	8	Re-election for additional terms
	Court of Appeals	...	...	★	...	8	Re-election for additional terms
	Chancery Court	...	...	★	...	4	Re-election for additional terms
	Circuit Court	...	...	★	...	4	Re-election for additional terms
Missouri	Supreme Court	★	...	...	...	1	Retention election (12 yr. term)
	Court of Appeals	★	...	...	...	1	Retention election (12 yr. term)
	Circuit Court	...	...	...	★	6	Re-election for additional terms
	Circuit Court (Jackson, Clay, Platte, & Saint Louis Counties)	★	...	...	...	1	Retention election (6 yr. term)
Montana	Supreme Court	...	...	★	...	8	Re-election; unopposed judges run for retention
	District Court	...	...	★	...	6	Re-election; unopposed judges run for retention
Nebraska	Supreme Court	★	...	...	...	3	Retention election (6 yr. term)
	Court of Appeals	★	...	...	...	3	Retention election (6 yr. term)
	District Court	★	...	...	...	3	Retention election (6 yr. term)
Nevada	Supreme Court	...	...	★	...	6	Re-election for additional terms
	District Court	...	...	★	...	6	Re-election for additional terms
New Hampshire	Supreme Court	(w)	(w)	...	...	to age 70	...
	Superior Court	(w)	(w)	...	...	to age 70	...
New Jersey	Supreme Court	...	G	...	...	7	Reappointed by governor (to age 70) with advice & consent of the Senate
	Appellate Div. of Superior Court	...	G	...	...	7	Reappointed by governor (to age 70 with advice & consent of the Senate
	Superior Court	...	G	...	...	7	Reappointed by governor (to age 70) with advice & consent of the Senate

See footnotes at end of table.

SELECTION AND RETENTION OF JUDGES — Continued

State or other jurisdiction	Court	Methods of initial selection				Initial term of office (years)	Method of retention (c)
		Appointive systems		Elective systems			
		Merit (a)	Gubernatorial or Legislative (b)	Non-partisan	Partisan		
New Mexico	Supreme Court	★	...	...	...	(p)	(q)
	Court of Appeals	★	...	...	...	(p)	(q)
	District Court	★	...	...	...	(p)	(q)
New York	Court of Appeals	★	...	...	...	14	(i)
	Appellate Div. of Supreme Court	★	...	...	...	5	(r)
	Supreme Court	...	...	...	★	14	Re-election for additional terms
	County Court	...	...	...	★	10	Re-election for additional terms
North Carolina	Supreme Court	...	...	★	...	8	Re-election for additional terms
	Court of Appeals	...	...	★	...	8	Re-election for additional terms
	Superior Court	...	...	★	...	8	Re-election for additional terms
North Dakota................	Supreme Court	...	...	★	...	10	Re-election for additional terms
	District Court	...	...	★	...	6	Re-election for additional terms
Ohio	Supreme Court	...	...	...	★(t)	6	Re-election for additional terms
	Court of Appeals	...	...	...	★(t)	6	Re-election for additional terms
	Court of Common Pleas	...	...	...	★(t)	6	Re-election for additional terms
Oklahoma	Supreme Court	★	...	...	...	1	Retention election (6 yr. term)
	Court of Criminal Appeals	★	...	...	...	1	Retention election (6 yr. term)
	Court of Appeals	★	...	...	...	1	Retention election (6 yr. term)
	District Court	...	...	★	...	4	Re-election for additional terms
Oregon	Supreme Court	...	...	★	...	6	Re-election for additional terms
	Court of Appeals	...	...	★	...	6	Re-election for additional terms
	Circuit Court	...	...	★	...	6	Re-election for additional terms
	Tax Court	...	...	★	...	6	Re-election for additional terms
Pennsylvania	Supreme Court	...	...	...	★	10	Retention election (10 yr. term)
	Superior Court	...	...	...	★	10	Retention election (10 yr. term)
	Commonwealth Court	...	...	...	★	10	Retention election (10 yr. term)
	Court of Common Pleas	...	...	...	★	10	Retention election (10 yr. term)
Rhode Island	Supreme Court	★	...	...	...	Life	...
	Superior Court	★	...	...	...	Life	...
	Worker's Compensation Court	★	...	...	...	Life	...
South Carolina	Supreme Court	...	L (u)	...	...	10	Reappointment by legislature
	Court of Appeals	...	L (u)	...	...	6	Reappointment by legislature
	Circuit Court	...	L (u)	...	...	6	Reappointment by legislature
South Dakota................	Supreme Court	★	...	...	...	3	Retention election (8 yr. term)
	Circuit Court	...	...	★	...	8	Re-election for additional terms
Tennessee	Supreme Court	★	...	...	...	(v)	Retention election (8 yr. term)
	Court of Appeals	★	...	...	...	(v)	Retention election (8 yr. term)
	Court of Criminal Appeals	★	...	...	...	(v)	Retention election (8 yr. term)
	Chancery Court	...	...	...	★	8	Re-election for additional terms
	Criminal Court	...	...	...	★	8	Re-election for additional terms
	Circuit Court	...	...	...	★	8	Re-election for additional terms
Texas	Supreme Court	...	...	...	★	6	Re-election for additional terms
	Court of Criminal Appeals	...	...	...	★	6	Re-election for additional terms
	Court of Appeals	...	...	...	★	6	Re-election for additional terms
	District Court	...	...	...	★	4	Re-election for additional terms
Utah	Supreme Court	★	...	...	...	(s)	Retention election (10 yr. term)
	Court of Appeals	★	...	...	...	(s)	Retention election (6 yr. term)
	District Court	★	...	...	...	(s)	Retention election (6 yr. term)
	Juvenile Court	★	...	...	...	(s)	Retention election (6 yr. term)
Vermont	Supreme Court	★	...	...	...	6	Retained by vote of General Assembly (6 yr. term)
	Superior Court	★	...	...	...	6	Retained by vote of General Assembly (6 yr. term)
	District Court	★	...	...	...	6	Retained by vote of General Assembly (6 yr. term)
Virginia..........................	Supreme Court	...	L	...	...	12	Reappointment by the legislature
	Court of Appeals	...	L	...	...	8	Reappointment by the legislature
	Circuit Court	...	L	...	...	8	Reappointment by the legislature
Washington....................	Supreme Court	...	...	★	...	6	Re-election for additional terms
	Court of Appeals	...	...	★	...	6	Re-election for additional terms
	Superior Court	...	...	★	...	4	Re-election for additional terms

See footnotes at end of table.

SELECTION AND RETENTION OF JUDGES — Continued

State or other jurisdiction	Court	Methods of initial selection				Initial term of office (years)	Method of retention (c)
		Appointive systems		Elective systems			
		Merit (a)	Gubernatorial or Legislative (b)	Non-partisan	Partisan		
West Virginia...............	Supreme Court	...	...	...	★	12	Re-election for additional terms
	Circuit Court	...	...	...	★	8	Re-election for additional terms
Wisconsin.....................	Supreme Court	...	...	★	...	10	Re-election for additional terms
	Court of Appeals	...	...	★	...	6	Re-election for additional terms
	Circuit Court	...	...	★	...	6	Re-election for additional terms
Wyoming......................	Supreme Court	★	...	...	...	1	Retention election (8 yr. term)
	District Court	★	...	...	...	1	Retention election (6 yr. term)
Dist. of Columbia	Court of Appeals	★	...	...	...	15	Reappointment by judicial tenure commission (o)
	Superior Court	★	...	...	...	15	Reappointment by judicial tenure commission (o)

Source: American Judicature Society's *Judicial Selection in the States: Appellate and General Jurisdiction Courts*, March 2006.

Key:

★ — Yes

. . . — No

(a) Merit selection through nominating commission.

(b) Gubernatorial (G) or legislative (L) appointment without nominating commission.

(c) In a retention election, judges run unopposed on the basis of their record.

(d) In November 2000, Arkansas voters passed an amendment to the Arkansas constitution shifting judicial elections to a nonpartisan system.

(e) The California constitution provides that local electors may choose gubernatorial appointments instead of nonpartisan election to select superior court judges. As of September 2004, no counties have chosen gubernatorial appointments.

(f) If the election is uncontested, the incumbent's name does not appear on the ballot.

(g) Commission reviews incumbent's performance on noncompetitive basis; governor re-nominates and legislature confirms.

(h) Merit selection established by executive order in Delaware, Maryland, Massachusetts. In all other jurisdictions, merit selection established by constitutional or statutory provision.

(i) Incumbent reapplies to nominating commission and competes with other applicants for nomination to the governor. The governor may reappoint the incumbent or another nominee. The senate confirms the appointment.

(j) Three of the judges run in partisan elections for six-year terms then have to be re-elected for additional terms.

(k) Louisiana judicial elections are partisan in as much as the candidates' party affiliations appear on the ballot. However, two factors lend a somewhat nonpartisan character to these elections: (1) primaries are open to all candidates; and (2) judicial candidates generally do not solicit party support for their campaigns.

(l) Until the first general election following the expiration of one year from the date of the occurrence of the vacancy.

(m) May be challenged by other candidates.

(n) Although party affiliations for Supreme Court candidates are not listed on the general election ballot, candidates are nominated at party conventions.

(o) Initial appointment is made by the President of the United States and is confirmed by the Senate. Six months prior to the expiration of the term of office, the judge's performance is reviewed by the tenure commission. Those found "Well Qualified" are automatically reappointed. If a judge is found to be "Qualified", the President may nominate the judge for an additional term (subject to Senate confirmation). If the President does not wish to re-appoint the judge, the District of Columbia Nominating Commission compiles a new list of candidates.

(p) Until next general election.

(q) Partisan election at next general election after appointment for eight-year term for appellate judges, six-year term for district. The winner thereafter runs in a retention election for subsequent terms.

(r) Commission reviews and recommends for or against reappointment by governor.

(s) First general election three years after appointment.

(t) Although party affiliations for judicial candidates are not listed on the general election ballot, candidates are nominated in partisan party elections.

(u) South Carolina has a 10-member Judicial Merit Selection Commission that screens judicial candidates and reports the findings to the state's General Assembly. Since 1997, the Assembly is restricted to voting only on those candidates found qualified by the Judicial Merit Selection Commission. However, the nominating commission itself is not far removed from the ultimate appointing body, and cannot be considered to be nonpartisan as control over member nominations is vested in majority party leadership. Although most nominating commissions contain members appointed by the governor or legislature, no other commission actually contains the governor or current legislators who have final approval over the candidate as voting members of the commission. In contrast, the Judicial Merit Selection Commission in South Carolina contains six current members of the General Assembly appointed by the Speaker of the House of Representatives, the Chairman of the Senate Judiciary Committee, and the President Pro Tempore of the Senate. State legislators also choose the remaining four members of the Commission who are selected from the general public.

(v) Until next biennial general election.

(w) The New Hampshire Constitution states that judges are to be selected by the governor. By executive order 2005-2, Governor Lynch created a merit selection nominating commission. The commission is appointed by the governor and charged with screening judicial applicants and making recommendations to the governor for his appointment. The governor's appointee must be confirmed by the Executive Council.

Table 5.7
REMOVAL OF JUDGES

State or other jurisdiction	Methods of removal		
	Judicial conduct commissions, boards, councils	Impeachment	Recall	Gubernatorial, Supreme Court and/or legislature
Alabama..........	The Judicial Inquiry Commission investigates complaints against judges and files complaints with the Court of the Judiciary. The Court of the Judiciary may censure, suspend, or remove a judge. Decisions of the court of the judiciary may be appealed to the Supreme Court.	Judges may be impeached.	...	...
Alaska..........	Judges may be suspended, removed from office, retired, or censured by the Supreme Court upon the recommendation of the Commission on Judicial Conduct.	Judges may be impeached by two-thirds of the Senate and convicted by two-thirds of the House of Representatives.	...	...
Arizona..........	The Supreme Court may censure, suspend, remove, or retire a judge upon recommendation of the Commission on Judicial Content.	Judges may be impeached by a majority vote of the House of Representatives and convicted by a two-thirds vote of the Senate.	Judges are subject to recall election.	...
Arkansas..........	The Judicial Discipline and Disability Commission, which is responsible for enforcing the Arkansas Code of Judicial Conduct, has the authority to investigate, as well as to initiate, complaints concerning misconduct of judges. After notice and hearing, the Commission may, by majority vote of the membership, recommend to the Supreme Court that a judge be suspended or removed, and the Supreme Court sitting en banc may take such action.	Judges may be impeached by the House of Representatives and convicted by two-thirds of the Senate.	...	The Governor may remove judges for good cause upon the address of two-thirds of the members of both houses of the general assembly.
California..........	The Commission on Judicial Performance investigates complaints of judicial misconduct and incapacity and may privately admonish, suspend, censure, retire, or remove a judge. The Commission's decisions are subject to review by the Supreme Court.	Judges may be impeached by the Assembly and convicted by two-thirds of the Senate.	Judges are subject to recall election.	...
Colorado..........	On the recommendation of the Judicial Discipline Commission, the Supreme Court may remove, retire, suspend, censure, reprimand, or discipline a judge.	Judges may be impeached by a majority vote of the House of Representatives and convicted by a two-thirds vote of the Senate.	Judges are subject to recall election.	...
Connecticut..........	The Judicial Review Council investigates complaints of judicial misconduct. If the investigation indicated that there is probable cause that the judge is guilty of misconduct, the Council conducts a hearing and makes a recommendation to the Supreme Court. The Supreme Court may suspend or remove the judge.	Judges may be impeached by the House of Representatives and removed by two-thirds vote of the Senate.	...	Judges may be removed by the Governor on the address of two-thirds of the general assembly.
Delaware	Judges may be removed, retired, or disciplined by a two-thirds vote of the Court on the Judiciary.	Judges may be impeached by a majority of the House of Representatives and convicted by two-thirds of the Senate.	...	...
Florida..........	On the recommendation of the Judicial Qualifications Commission, the Supreme Court may discipline, retire, or remove a judge.	Judges may be impeached by a two-thirds vote of the House of Representatives and convicted by a two-thirds vote of the Senate.	...	...

See footnotes at end of table.

REMOVAL OF JUDGES — Continued

State or other jurisdiction	Judicial conduct commissions, boards, councils	Methods of removal		
		Impeachment	Recall	Gubernatorial, Supreme Court and/or legislature
Georgia............	The Judicial Qualifications Commission may discipline, retire, or remove a judge. Removal and retirement decisions must be reviewed by the Supreme Court.	Judges may be impeached by the House of Representatives and convicted by a two-thirds vote of the Senate.	...	...
Hawaii	The Commission on Judicial Conduct has the authority to investigate and conduct hearings concerning allegations of judicial misconduct or disability and to recommend to the Supreme Court that a judge be reprimanded, disciplined, suspended, retired, or retired.	...		...
Idaho............	The Idaho Judicial Council investigates complaints against Idaho judges and may recommend to the Supreme Court the discipline, removal, or retirement of judges. The Supreme Court may review the recommendation of the Judicial Council and take additional evidence. The court may then reject the recommendation of the Judicial Council, or order discipline, removal, of retirement of the judge.	Judges may be impeached by a majority vote of the House of Representatives and convicted by a two-thirds vote of the Senate.		...
Illinois............	The Judicial Inquiry Board files complaints with the courts Commission. After notice and hearing, the Commission may reprimand, censure, suspend, retire, or remove a judge.	Judges may be impeached by a majority vote of the House of Representatives and removed by two-thirds vote of the Senate.		...
Indiana............	On the recommendation of the Commission on Judicial Qualifications, the Supreme Court may discipline, suspend, retire, or remove a judge.	Judges may be impeached by the House of Representatives and convicted by the Senate.	...	Judges may be removed by joint resolution of the General Assembly, upon the agreement of two-thirds of each house.
Iowa............	The Commission on Judicial Qualifications has the authority to investigate complaints of Judicial misconduct and recommend to the Supreme Court that it retire, discipline, or remove a judge.	Judges may be impeached by a majority of the House of Representatives and convicted by two-thirds vote of the Senate.	...	...
Kansas............	Judges of the Court of Appeals and District Court may be removed by the Supreme Court on the recommendation of the Commission on Judicial Qualifications. The Commission on Judicial Qualifications is authorized to investigate allegations of misconduct and to recommend a formal hearing. If the charges are proven by clear and convincing evidence, the Commission may admonish the judge, issue a cease-and-decease order, or recommend to the Supreme Court public censure, suspension , removal or compulsory retirement.	Judges may be removed by impeachment and conviction, as prescribed in Article 2 of the Kansas Constitution.	...	Supreme Court justices are subject to retirement upon certification to the Governor (after a hearing by the Supreme Court Nominating Commission) that the justice is so incapacitated as to be unable to perform his duties.
Kentucky............	After notice and hearing the Judicial Conduct Commission may admonish, reprimand, censure, suspend, retire, or remove a judge. The commission's decisions are subject to review by the Supreme Court.	Judges may be impeached by the House of Representatives and convicted by two-thirds vote of the Senate.		...

See footnotes at end of table.

REMOVAL OF JUDGES — Continued

State or other jurisdiction	Methods of removal			
	Judicial conduct commissions, boards, councils	Impeachment	Recall	Gubernatorial, Supreme Court and/or legislature
Louisiana................	On recommendation of the Judiciary Commission, the Supreme Court may censure, suspend, remove, or retire judges.	Judges may be impeached by the House of Representatives and removed by a two-thirds vote of the Senate.	...	...
Maine....................	The Supreme Judicial Court may retire, remove, or discipline judges upon recommendation of the Committee on Judicial Responsibility and Disability.	Judges may be impeached by the House of Representatives and convicted by two-thirds vote of the Senate.	...	Judges may be removed upon the address by the Governor of both houses of the legislature.
Maryland	Judges may be removed or retired by the Court of Appeals on the recommendation of the Commission on Judicial Disabilities.	Judges may be impeached by a majority of the House of delegates and convicted by two-thirds of the Senate.	...	Judges may be removed by the Governor upon address of the General Assembly with the concurrence of two-thirds of the members of each House. Judges may also be retired by the General Assembly with a two-thirds vote of each House and the Governor's concurrence.
Massachusetts........	The Commission on Judicial Conduct investigates complaints of judicial misconduct. Following a formal hearing, the commission may recommend to the Supreme Judicial Court removal, retirement, or reprimand of a judge.	Judges may be impeached by the House of Representatives and convicted by the Senate.	...	The Governor, with consent of the Governor's Council, may remove judges upon the address of both Houses of the General Court. The Governor, with consent of the Governor's Council, may also retire judges because of advanced age or mental or physical disability.
Michigan	On the recommendation of the Judicial Tenure Commission, the Supreme Court may censure, suspend, retire, or remove a judge.	Judges may be impeached by a majority vote of the House of Representatives and convicted by a two-thirds vote of the Senate.	...	The Governor may remove a judge upon the concurrent resolution of two-thirds of the members of both Houses of the Legislature.
Minnesota.............	After a public hearing and on the recommendation of the Board on Judicial Standards, the Supreme Court may censure, retire, or remove a judge.	Judges may be impeached by a majority vote of the House of Representatives and convicted by a two-thirds vote of the Senate.	Judges are subject to recall election.	...
Mississippi............	On the recommendation of the Commission on Judicial Performance, the Supreme Court may censure, remove, or retire a judge.	Judges may be impeached by two-thirds vote of the House of Representatives and removed by the Senate.	...	Judges may be removed by the Governor on the joint address of two-thirds of both Houses of the Legislature.
Missouri	On the recommendation of the Commission on Retirement, Removal, and Discipline, the Supreme Court may suspend, discipline, reprimand, retire, or remove a judge.	Judges may be impeached by the House of Representatives. Impeachments are tried by the Supreme Court or by special commission in the case of impeachments of the Governor or a Supreme Court Justice. Convictions require the concurrence of five-sevenths of the court or commission.	...	...

See footnotes at end of table.

REMOVAL OF JUDGES—Continued

State or other jurisdiction	Judicial conduct commissions, boards, councils	Methods of removal		
		Impeachment	Recall	Gubernatorial, Supreme Court and/or legislature
Montana..............	On the recommendation of the Judicial Standards Commission, the Supreme Court may retire, censure, suspend, or remove a judge.	Judges may be impeached by a two-thirds vote of the House of Representatives and convicted by a two-thirds vote of the Senate.	...	...
Nebraska..............	Based on the recommendation of the judicial qualifications commission, the Supreme Court may reprimand, censure, discipline, suspend, retire, or remove a judge.	Judges may be impeached by majority vote of the legislature and removed with the concurrence of two-thirds of the members of the court of impeachment. The Supreme Court sits as the court of impeachment, unless a supreme court justice has been impeached. In that case, seven district court judges are selected to try the impeachment.	...	Judges may be impeached by majority vote of the legislature and removed with the concurrence of two-thirds of the members of the court of impeachment. The Supreme Court sits as the court of impeachment, unless a supreme court justice has been impeached. In that case, seven district court judges are selected to try the impeachment.
Nevada..............	The Commission on Judicial Discipline may discipline, censure, retire, or remove a judge. Commission decisions may be appealed to the Supreme Court.	Judges may be impeached by a majority vote of the Assembly and convicted by a two-thirds vote of the Senate.	Judges are subject to recall election	Judges may be removed by legislative resolution, passed by two-thirds of the members of both Houses.
New Hampshire..............	The Governor with the consent of the Executive Council, may remove judges for reasonable cause upon the joint address of both houses of the General Court.	Judges may be impeached by the House of Representatives and convicted by the Senate.	...	...
New Jersey..............	When the Supreme Court certifies to the Governor that a judge is so incapacitated that she/he cannot substantially perform his/her duties, a three-person commission is appointed to look into the matter. Upon the Commission's recommendation, the Governor may retire the judge from office.	Judges may be impeached by a majority vote of all members of the General Assembly and removed by a two-thirds vote of the Senate.	...	Removal proceedings may be instigated by a majority of either House, by the Governor filing a complaint with the Supreme Court, or by the Supreme Court on its own motion. The Supreme Court maintains an advisory committee on judicial conduct composed of private citizens appointed by the Court. The committee reviews all allegations of misconduct and either dismisses the charges or recommends a formal hearing. Based upon the hearing, judges may be reprimanded, censured and suspended without pay, or removed from office.
New Mexico..............	On the recommendation of the Judicial Standards Commission, the Supreme Court may discipline, retire, or remove a judge.	Judges may be impeached by a majority vote of the House of Representatives and removed by a two-thirds vote of the Senate.	...	...
New York..............	Judges may be admonished, censured, retired, or removed from office by the Commission on Judicial Conduct. The Commission's disciplinary actions are subject to review by the Court of Appeals.	Judges may be impeached by a majority vote of the Assembly and removed by a two-thirds vote of the Court for the Trial of Impeachments. The Court consists of the President of the Senate, the Senators, and the judges of the Court of Appeals.	...	Judges of the Courts of Appeals and justices of the Supreme Court may be removed by two-thirds vote of both houses of the legislature. Other judges may be removed by a two-thirds vote of the senate on the recommendation of the Governor.

See footnotes at end of table.

REMOVAL OF JUDGES—Continued

State or other jurisdiction	Judicial conduct commissions, boards, councils	Methods of removal		
		Impeachment	Recall	Gubernatorial, Supreme Court and/or legislature
North Carolina	On the recommendation of the Judicial Standards Commission, the Supreme Court may censure or remove a judge.	Judges may be impeached by the House of Representatives and convicted by a two-thirds vote of the Senate.	...	Judges may be removed for mental or physical incapacity by joint resolution of two-thirds of the members of each house of the General Assembly.
North Dakota	On the recommendation of the Commission on Judicial Conduct, the Supreme Court may discipline, censure, suspend, retire, or remove a judge.	Judges may be impeached by a majority vote of the House of Representatives and convicted by a two-thirds vote of the Senate.	Judges are subject to recall election.	...
Ohio	Complaints alleging judicial misconduct may be filed with the Disciplinary Council or with a certified grievance committee of the Board of Commissioners on Grievances and Discipline, both of which have the authority to investigate and file formal complaints with the Board. If two-thirds of the members of the board believe there is substantial credible evidence to support the complaint, the Supreme Court appoints a commission of five judges to determine whether retirement, removal, or suspension is warranted. The Commission's decision may be appealed to the Supreme Court.	...	...	Judges may be removed by a concurrent resolution of two-thirds of both Houses of the general Assembly.
Oklahoma	Judges are subject to removal from office, or to compulsory retirement, by proceedings in the Court on the Judiciary.	Judges may be impeached by the House of Representatives and convicted by two-thirds of the Senate.	...	...
Oregon	On the recommendation of the Commission on Judicial Fitness and Disability, the Supreme Court may censure, suspend, retire, or remove a judge.	...	Judges are subject to recall election.	...
Pennsylvania	The Judicial Conduct Board investigates complaints regarding judicial conduct filed by individuals or initiated by the board. The board determines whether probable cause exists to file formal charges, and presents its case to the court of judicial discipline. The court has the authority to impose sanctions, ranging from a reprimand to removal from office, if the formal charges are sustained.	Judges may be impeached by the House of Representatives and convicted by a two-thirds vote of the Senate.	...	...
Rhode Island	The Commission on Judicial Tenure and Discipline reviews complaints against judges. Following a formal hearing, the Commission either dismisses the complaint or recommends to the Supreme Court that the judge be reprimanded, censured, suspended, removed, or retired. The Commission may also recommend the retirement of a judge for physical or mental disability.	Judges may be impeached by a majority of the House of Representatives and convicted by a two-thirds vote of the Senate.	...	...

See footnotes at end of table.

REMOVAL OF JUDGES — Continued

State or other jurisdiction	Judicial conduct commissions, boards, councils	Methods of removal		
		Impeachment	Recall	Gubernatorial, Supreme Court and/or legislature
South Carolina..............	The Commission on Judicial Conduct is authorized to investigate complaints of judicial misconduct and incapacity. Disciplinary counsel appointed by the Supreme Court evaluates each complaint and either dismisses the complaint or conducts a preliminary investigation. If evidence supports the complaint, a full investigation is authorized. If the investigation supports the filing of formal charges, a hearing is conducted, after which recommendation is made to the Supreme Court for sanctions, dismissal, transfer to inactive status, retirement, or removal.	Judges may be impeached by a two-thirds vote of the House of Representatives and convicted by a two-thirds vote of the Senate.	. . .	Judges may be removed by the Governor upon the address of two-thirds of each house of the General Assembly.
South Dakota	On the recommendation of the Judicial Qualifications Commission, the Supreme Court, after a hearing, may censure, remove, or retire a judge.	Judges may be impeached by a majority of the House of Representatives and convicted by two-thirds vote of the Senate.	. . .	. . .
Tennessee....................	Upon recommendation by the Court of the Judiciary, the General Assembly may remove judges by a two-thirds vote of both Houses, with each House voting separately.	Judges may be impeached by the House of Representatives and convicted by two-thirds vote of the Senate.	. . .	. . .
Texas.........................	The State Commission on Judicial Conduct investigates, and if warranted, prosecutes allegations of misconduct. Upon a Commission recommendation of removal or retirement, the Supreme Court selects a review tribunal from among Court of Appeals judges to verify the findings and enter a judgment. Judges may appeal decisions of the review tribunal to the Supreme Court.	Judges may be impeached by the House of Representatives and removed by two-thirds vote of the Senate.	. . .	Judges may be removed by the Governor on address of two-thirds of the House and Senate. The Supreme Court may remove District Court judges from office.
Utah..........................	The Judicial Conduct Commission may reprimand, censure, suspend, retire, or remove a judge. The Commission's decisions are subject to review by the Supreme Court.	Judges may be impeached by a two-thirds vote of the House of Representatives and convicted by a two-thirds vote of the Senate.	. . .	. . .
Vermont......................	The Judicial Conduct Board investigates complaints of judicial misconduct of disability and recommends any necessary action to the Supreme Court. Possible disciplinary actions include public reprimand of the judge, suspension for a part or the remainder of the judge's term of office, or retirement of the judge if physically or mentally disabled.	Judges may be impeached by a two-thirds vote of the House of Representatives and convicted by a two-thirds vote of the Senate.	. . .	. . .
Virginia	The Judicial Inquiry and Review Commission investigates complaints of judicial misconduct or serious mental or physical disability that interferes with a judge's duties. The Commission may conduct hearings and gather evidence to determine whether the charges are substantial. If the Commission finds the charges to significant, a formal complaint is filed with the Supreme Court of West Virginia. The Supreme Court may dismiss the complaint or it may retire, censure, or remove the judge.	Judges may be impeached by the House of Delegates and removed by a two-thirds vote of the Senate.	. . .	. . .

See footnotes at end of table.

REMOVAL OF JUDGES — Continued

State or other jurisdiction	Judicial conduct commissions, boards, councils	Methods of removal		
		Impeachment	Recall	Gubernatorial, Supreme Court and/or legislature
Washington	The Commission on Judicial Conduct investigates complaints of judicial misconduct or disability and recommends to the Supreme Court that the judge be suspended, removed, or retired. The Supreme Court makes the final decision after reviewing the commission's record and hearing argument on the matter.	. . .	. . .	Judges may be removed from office by joint resolution of the legislature, in which three-fourths of the members of each house must concur.
West Virginia	The Judicial Hearing Board investigates complaints against judges and makes recommendations to the Supreme Court regarding the disposition of those complaints. The Court has the authority to censure, suspend, and retire judges.	Judges may be impeached by the House of Delegates and removed by a two-thirds vote of the Senate.	. . .	. . .
Wisconsin	On the recommendation of the Judicial Commission and after review, the Supreme Court may reprimand, censure, suspend, or remove a judge.	Judges may be impeached by a majority vote of the Assembly and convicted by a two-thirds vote of the Senate.	Judges are subject to recall election	Judges may be removed by address of both Houses of the Legislature with the concurrence of two-thirds of the members of each House.
Wyoming	The Supreme Court, on its own motion or on the recommendation of the Commission on Judicial Conduct and ethics, may censure, suspend, retire, or remove a judge.	Judges may be impeached by a majority of the House of Representatives and convicted by two-thirds of the Senate.	. . .	. . .
Dist. of Columbia	The Judicial Disabilities and Tenure Commission has the authority to suspend, involuntarily retire, or remove judges upon the filing of an order with the D.C. Court of Appeals.	. . .	. . .	. . .

Source: American Judicature Society's Judicial Selection in the States, March 2006. http://www.ajs.org.
Key:
. . . — No provision for method.
N.A. — Not available.

Chapter Six

ELECTIONS AND ETHICS

"State policymakers, like those in many other fields, are facing a crisis in leadership."

—Robert B. Denhardt and Janet V. Denhardt

"With ethics questions related to gifts and gratuities in the states and nationally continuing to unfold, there is no doubt that attention to, and reform of, the standards by which they are to be judged will continue as a leading ethics trend."

—David E. Freel

"Ballot proposition activity was muted in 2005, as usual for odd-year elections, but several high profile campaigns emerged across the country."

—John G. Matsusaka

Leadership for State Policymakers

By Robert B. Denhardt and Janet V. Denhardt

State policymakers, like those in many other fields, are facing a crisis in leadership. Recent studies of leadership recommend greater attention to shared leadership and a "values" perspective. But the most recent literature also recognizes leadership is an art rather than a science—an art that can be learned.

State policymakers, like those in many other fields, are facing a crisis in leadership. Trust in government and indeed trust in all major social institutions has declined dramatically in the past several decades. People are frustrated with the apparent lack of effective leadership in government, in corporations and throughout society. Some, including Warren Bennis, speak of a leadership crisis in this country and around the world. But that crisis is subtle and hard to identify (Bennis 1997, 21).

Certainly there have been some helpful contributions to improved leadership the last several decades. James MacGregor Burns' classic and Pulitzer Prize-winning book, *Leadership* (1978), began efforts to recast leadership in terms of values and transformation. In addition, important contributions to our understanding of leadership have recently been made by Lee Bolman and Terrence Deal (2003), Daniel Goleman (2002), Robert Greenleaf (1996), Ronald Heifetz (1994, 2002), Sally Helgesen (1995a, 1995b), James Kouzes and Barry Posner (2002), and James O'Toole (1996). While there are certainly variations in these and other significant works on leadership, there are also some common threads that tie these contributions together: an emphasis on shared leadership and a more intense connection between values and leadership.

Shared Leadership

First, most of these recent works emphasize the notion of shared leadership: the idea that people throughout groups and organizations must be involved in leading for the most creative and effective possibilities to be pursued. This idea has been proposed for several reasons. One is that more people want to participate in the decisions that affect them. People in organizations large and small, public and private, simply want a piece of the action. They want a say in changes that affect them. Moreover, clients and citizens want to participate, as they should. As Bennis correctly predicted some years ago, "leadership … will become an increasingly intricate process of multilateral brokerage.

… More and more decisions will be public decisions: that is, the people they affect will insist on being heard" (Bennis 1992, 311).

Shared leadership has also been advanced because having more people involved increases the creativity and flexibility of the group or organization. Today's problems are so complex that no individual could possibly be expected to have all the answers. Finding ways of sharing leadership generates more effective solutions in a fast-paced, rapidly changing world. Finally, shared leadership has been put forward because those who are involved in decisions are more likely to help in their implementation.

One implication of the shared leadership model is that leadership can no longer be thought of as a position but should be thought of as a function or process, something that happens throughout groups, organizations and societies. To understand leadership today and in the future we need to make an important shift from thinking about leadership only as something that happens at the top, to thinking of leading as a function or a process, a set of activities in which people throughout society can, do and should engage. Indeed, one important role of our top leaders is to encourage and support acts of leadership throughout their organizations and across their communities.

Values and Leadership

Recent literature on leadership has placed far more emphasis on the role of values in the act of leading than did earlier work. That is not to say that earlier writers failed to recognize the importance of such ideas as honesty, integrity and principle in leadership. What more recent studies have brought to the fore is the role leaders play in shaping and even defining human values in society. Leadership, in this view, deals with identifying and trying to achieve basic human purposes; it has to do with choices and opportunities, dreams and aspiration, and the application of reason to human intentions.

Previous studies of leadership assumed a close connection between leadership and power (the latter meaning the leader's capacity to carry out his or her will despite resistance). James Macgregor Burns, however, argued leadership involves a relationship between leaders and followers. Leaders act on their own motives and interests, but these must be connected to the motives and interests of followers. Leadership, Burns wrote, is exercised "when persons with certain motives and purposes, mobilize, in competition or conflict with others, institutional, political, psychological, and other resources so as to arouse, engage, and satisfy the motives of followers" (Burns 1978, 18). The difference between power and leadership is that power serves the interests of the one who seeks power, while leadership serves the interests of both the leader and the followers.

If leadership has not served the common moral purposes of both those who lead and those who follow, the requirements of transformational leadership have not been met. For example, there is the classic illustration of Adolf Hitler's leadership and the nagging question of the quality of his leadership. While Hitler certainly changed German society (and much beyond), his leadership clearly didn't advance notions of freedom, justice and equality. Since the purposes of his leadership were not purposes based in the common good of humanity, Burns would say his leadership was not transformational, if indeed it was real leadership at all.

Burns's work is classic, but more recent studies have thoughtfully pursued similar themes. James O'Toole, for example, has argued in *Leading Change* (1996) that leaders who attempt to impose their own will on followers, and even fail to consult or involve them, engage in "the ultimate disrespect for individuals" (O'Toole 1996, 12). In contrast, he argues, leaders must advance ideas that resonate with followers, indeed, ideas often generated through discussions with followers. People don't follow leaders just because they have power. They don't even follow leaders, O'Toole suggests, because they are right. Rather people are more likely to follow leaders who act with integrity and respect for others, who listen to the concerns of followers, and who act with their needs and interests in mind. And is that simply moral leadership or is it also the most effective? "If the goal is to bring about constructive change, values-based leadership is, yes, always more effective" (O'Toole 1996, 15).

Similarly, in *The New Public Service* (Denhardt and Denhardt, 2003), we argue that in the public sector, values-based leadership must be fundamentally grounded in democratic principles and norms. Public leaders must not only work to ensure that the goals being sought are consistent with shared val-

ues and followers' needs, but also that the process used to define those goals are consistent with the ideals of citizenship, justice and the public interest. It is no longer enough for public leaders to work only towards creating more efficient organizations. Rather, public leaders are called on to honor public service ideals and to facilitate engaged and responsible citizenship.

Another example of a values-oriented approach to leadership is Ronald Heifetz's book, *Leadership Without Easy Answers* (1994). Heifetz suggests that when we talk about leadership, we must inevitably confront issues of trust and responsibility within a community. These basic human values, and others like them, are always a part of the relationship between leaders and followers. Leaders challenge communities to face tough issues; they engage in "adaptive work"; that is, work that will "address conflicts in the values people hold, or … diminish the gap between the values people stand for and the reality they face" (Heifetz 1994, 22). Adaptive work helps people confront the values conflicts they face and move toward their resolution. Given this formulation, Heifetz, like Burns, finds Hitler a failed leader, in the sense that he did not help Germany adapt to the social and political realities of his time.

The Art of Leadership

A more recent development in leadership studies is the recognition by leadership scholars of what practitioners have always known—that leadership is an art rather than a science. Leaders in all fields agree there is something about leadership that defies rational or scientific explanation. And while they may have trouble describing exactly what the art of leadership involves, they clearly see its impact. It is the art, not the science, of leadership that enables leaders to connect with others in a way that stimulates them to act.

What is it leaders do that causes others to follow? In some cases, a potential leader will supply others with a rational explanation of why moving in a new direction might be in their interest. But providing an explanation is rarely enough for real leadership to occur. People can get interested in, even occasionally excited about, "explanations," but they are rarely "energized" in the absence of an emotional commitment. For this to happen, the leader must touch not only the "head" but also the "heart."

Connecting with the emotions is the work of art, and, for this reason, real-world leaders are absolutely correct when they say leadership is an art, not a science. It's not surprising then to find the following definition of leadership from one of the most significant public leaders of our time, Secretary of State Colin Powell: "Leadership is the art of accomplishing more than the science of management says is possible" (Harari 2002, 13). We may conclude that leadership is indeed an art.

In our book, *The Dance of Leadership* (2006), we explore the artistic elements of leadership, including issues such as rhythm and timing, improvisation, communicating in images, symbols and metaphors, and focus and concentration. Among those we interviewed for the book, several state government officials helped us understand how their leadership reflected artistic elements that go far beyond simple rationality.

As David Frohnmayer, president of the University of Oregon and former Oregon attorney general, said: "Leadership is a continuously creative act," one that is enhanced by an understanding of the rhythm of events that are unfolding around you. "I can see rhythm quite profoundly in the academic world, just because we are driven by a peculiar calendar that affects almost no one else in the world. The group will gear up in the fall, then to coincide with the rising sap and warmer weather, things come to fruition."

Daniel Evans, a former governor and senator, also helped us understand the connection between rhythm and timing, pointing out that a leader has to react to rhythm and understanding. With respect to timing, Evans offered what he called the "surfer's theory of politics."

Three things can happen when you get out there and you are waiting for a wave. You either can go too early and the wave crunches you. Or you can wait a little too long and the wave passes underneath you. Or you can catch the wave just right and ride it for a long way. It's the same way in the leadership of ideas. If you are too early you can get banged around pretty good. Or if you wait too late then times goes on and you can't catch up.

Finally, Arizona Gov. Jane Hull emphasized the importance of a leader being able to improvise, just like a jazz musician or dancer. In part, the need to improvise comes from the fact that you don't usually have a script. "Many times you have to think on your feet. When you've got that press corps looking at you and you're figuring out what question they are going to ask next, you have to think on your feet. Prioritize and say what's important to you." The capacity to improvise also comes because things change so rapidly. "In any given day in a governor's life, there are at least three unanticipated crises, little ones or big ones." A leader has to be able to quickly adapt to what's going on in the environment.

Conclusion

Understanding shared leadership, the role of values in leadership, and the artistic side of leadership is a significant challenge, but one that will be important as state policymakers attempt to address the crisis of leadership that they and others face today. There are certain skills leaders exercise that cause others to follow. Identifying these skills, many of which are artistic in nature, then learning to apply them more broadly will significantly improve the quality of leadership at the state level and throughout society.

References

Bennis, Warren. 1992. "The Artform of Leadership." in *Public administration in action: readings, profiles, and cases*, edited by Robert B. Denhardt, and Barry R. Hammond. Belmont, CA: Brooks/Cole.

Bennis, Warren G. 1997. *Managing people is like herding cats*. Provo, UT: Executive Excellence Publishing.

Bolman, Lee G., and Terrence E. Deal. 2003. *Reframing organizations: artistry, choice, and leadership*, 3rd ed. San Francisco: Jossey-Bass.

Burns, James MacGregor. 1978. *Leadership*, 1st ed. New York: Harper & Row.

Denhardt, Janet V. and Robert B. Denhardt. 2003. *The new public service*. Amonk, NY: M. E. Sharpe.

Denhardt, Robert B. and Janet V. Denhardt. 2006. *The dance of leadership*. Amonk, NY: M. E. Sharpe.

Goleman, Daniel, Richard E. Boyatzis, and Annie McKee. 2002. *Primal leadership: realizing the power of emotional intelligence*. Cambridge: Harvard Business School Press.

Greenleaf, Robert K., Don M. Frick, and Larry C. Spears. 1996. *On becoming a servant-leader*, 1st ed. San Francisco: Jossey-Bass Publishers.

Harari, Oren. 2002. *The leadership secrets of Colin Powell*, 1st ed. New York: McGraw-Hill.

Heifetz, Ronald A. 1994. *Leadership without easy answers*. Cambridge: Belknap Press of Harvard University Press.

Heifetz, Ronald A., and Marty Linsky. 2002. *Leadership on the line: staying alive through the dangers of leading*. Cambridge: Harvard Business School Press.

Helgesen, Sally. 1995a. *The female advantage: women's ways of leadership*, 1st Currency pbk. ed. New York: Doubleday Currency.

Helgesen, Sally. 1995b. *The web of inclusion: a new architecture for building great organizations*, 1st ed. New York: Currency/Doubleday.

Kouzes, James M., and Barry Z. Posner. 2002. *The leadership challenge*, 3rd ed. San Francisco: Jossey-Bass.

O'Toole, James. 1996. *Leading change: the argument for values-based leadership*. San Francisco: Jossey-Bass Publishers.

About the Authors

Robert and Janet Denhardt are faculty members in the School of Public Affairs at Arizona State University and the authors of several books on public service leadership, including *The Dance of Leadership*. They have conducted workshops on artistic leadership for a variety of public organizations.

Table 6.1
STATE EXECUTIVE BRANCH OFFICIALS TO BE ELECTED: 2006–2010

State or other jurisdiction	2006	2007	2008	2009	2010
Alabama	G,LG,AG,AR,A,SS,T				G,LG,AG,AR,A,SS,T
Alaska (a)	G,LG				G,LG
Arizona	G,AG,SS,SP,T (b)				G,AG,SS,SP,T (b)
Arkansas	G,LG,AG,A,SS,T (f)				G,LG,AG,A,SS,T (f)
California	G,LG,AG,SS,SP,T (c)(g)				G,LG,AG,SS,SP,T (c)(g)
Colorado	G,LG,AG,SS,T				G,LG,AG,SS,T
Connecticut	G,LG,AG,C,SS,T				G,LG,AG,C,SS,T
Delaware	AG,A,T		G,LG (d)		AG,A,T
Florida	G,LG,AG,AR,CFO				G,LG,AG,AR,CFO
Georgia	G,LG,AG,AR,C,SS,SP (e)				G,LG,AG,AR,C,SS,SP (e)
Hawaii	G,LG				G,LG
Idaho	G,LG,AG,C,SS,SP,T				G,LG,AG,C,SS,SP,T
Illinois	G,LG,AG,C,SS,T				G,LG,AG,C,SS,T
Indiana	A,SS,T		G,LG,AG,SP		A,SS,T
Iowa	G,LG,AG,AR,A,SS,T				G,LG,AG,AR,A,SS,T
Kansas	G,LG,AG,SS,T (d)				G,LG,AG,SS,T (d)
Kentucky		G,LG,AG,AR,A,SS,T			
Louisiana		G,LG,AG,AR,A,SS,T (d)			
Maine (h)	G				G
Maryland	G,LG,AG,C				G,LG,AG,C
Massachusetts	G,LG,AG,A,SS,T				G,LG,AG,A,SS,T
Michigan	G,LG,AG,SS (i)		(i)		G,LG,AG,SS (i)
Minnesota	G,LG,AG,A,SS				G,LG,AG,A,SS
Mississippi		G,LG,AG,AR,A,SS,T (d)			
Missouri	A		G,LG,AG,A,SS,T		A
Montana			G,LG,AG,A,SS,SP		G,LG,AG,A,SS,T
Nebraska	G,LG,AG,A,SS,T				G,LG,AG,A,SS,T
Nevada	G,LG,AG,SS,T (g)				G,LG,AG,SS,T (g)
New Hampshire	G		G		G
New Jersey				G,LG	LG
New Mexico	G,LG,AG,A,SS,T (k)				G,LG,AG,A,SS,T (k)
New York	G,LG,AG,C				G,LG,AG,C
North Carolina	SS,AG,AR (m)(j)		G,LG,AG,AR,A,SS,SP,T (l)		SS,AG,AR (m)(j)
North Dakota	G,LG,AG,A,SS,T		G,LG,A,T,SP (d)(m)		G,LG,AG,A,SS,T
Ohio					
Oklahoma	G,LG,AG,A,SP,T (n)		AG,SS,T		G,LG,AG,A,SP,T (n)
Oregon	G,SP (u)		AG,A,T		G,SP (u)
Pennsylvania	G,LG				G,LG
Rhode Island	G,LG,AG,SS,T				G,LG,AG,SS,T
South Carolina	G,LG,AG,AR,C,SS,SP,T (o)				G,LG,AG,AR,C,SS,SP,T (o)

See footnotes at end of table.

STATE EXECUTIVE BRANCH OFFICIALS TO BE ELECTED: 2006–2010—Continued

State or other jurisdiction	2006	2007	2008	2009	2010
South Dakota	G,LG,AG,A,SS,T (p)	...	(p)	...	G,LG,AG,A,SS,T (p)
Tennessee	G	...	...	...	G
Texas	G,LG,AG,AR,C (q)	...	(q)	...	G,LG,AG,AR,C (q)
Utah	...	...	G,LG,AG,A,T	...	...
Vermont	G,LG,AG,A,SS,T	...	G,LG,AG,A,SS,T	...	G,LG,AG,A,SS,T
Virginia	...	...	...	G,LG,AG	...
Washington	...	...	G,LG,AG,A,SS,SP,T (s)	...	...
West Virginia	...	...	G,AG,AR,A,SS,T	...	...
Wisconsin	G,LG,AG,SS,T	...	...	...	G,LG,AG,SS,T
Wyoming	G,A,SS,SP,T	...	...	SP	G,A,SS,SP
American Samoa	...	...	G, LG	...	...
Guam	G,LG,A,AG	...	...	...	G,LG,A,AG
No. Mariana Islands	...	...	...	G,LG	...
Puerto Rico	...	...	G (t)	...	...
U.S. Virgin Islands	G,LG	...	...	...	G,LG
Totals for year					
Governor	38	3	13	3	38
Lieutenant Governor	32	3	10	3	32
Attorney General	31	3	10	1	31
Agriculture	7	3	2	0	7
Auditor	16	2	8	0	16
Chief Financial Officer	1	0	0	0	1
Comptroller	8	0	0	0	8
Secretary of State	26	3	7	1	26
Supt. of Public Inst. (r)	8	0	5	1	8
Treasurer	24	3	9	0	24

Sources: The Council of State Governments' survey, September 2005 and state election administration offices and Web sites, January 2006.

Note: This table shows the executive branch officials up for election in a given year. Footnotes indicate other offices (e.g., commissioners of labor, insurance, public service, etc.) also up for election in a given year. The data contained in this table reflect information available at press time.

Key:
... — No regularly scheduled elections
G — Governor
LG — Lieutenant Governor
AG — Attorney General
AR — Agriculture
A — Auditor
C — Comptroller
CFO — Chief Financial Officer
SS — Secretary of State
SP — Superintendent of Public Instruction (r)
T — Treasurer

(a) Election of school boards established to maintain system of state dependent public school systems established in areas of the unorganized borough and military reservations not served by other public school systems. Elections are held annually on the first Tuesday in October.
(b) Corporation commissioners (5)–4-year terms, 2006–2 seats, 2008–3 seats. State Mine Inspector–4-year term, 2006 election.
(c) Insurance Commissioner and Board of Equalization.
(d) Commissioner of Insurance.
(e) Commissioner of Labor–4-year term, 2006 and 2010.
(f) Commissioner of State Lands.
(g) Controller.

(h) In Maine the legislature elects constitutional officers (AG,SS,T) in even-numbered years for 2-year terms; the auditor will be elected by the legislature in 2004 and will serve a 4-year term.
(i) Michigan State University trustees (8)–8-year terms, 2006–2, 2008–2, 2010–2, 2012–2; University of Michigan regents (8)–8-year terms, 2006–2, 2008–2, 2012–2; Wayne State University governors (8)–8-year terms, 2006–2, 2008–2, 2012–2; State Board of Education (8)–8-year terms, 2006–2, 2008–2, 2012–2.
(j) Tax Commissioner.
(k) Commissioner of Public Lands–4-year term, 2006.
(l) Commissioner of Labor and Commissioner of Insurance are elected in 2008.
(m) There are three Public Service Commissioners. One is up for election every two years. (3)–6-year terms, 2006–1, 2008–1, 2010–1; Commissioner of Insurance–4-year term; Commissioner of Labor–4-year term.
(n) Corporation Commissioner (3)–6-year terms, 2006–1, 2008–1, 2010–1; Commissioner of Insurance–4-year term.
(o) Adjutant General–4-year term.
(p) Commissioner of School and Public Lands, 2006; Public Utility Commissioners (3)–6-year terms, 2006–1, 2008–1, 2010–1.
(q) Commissioner of General Land Office–4-year term, 2006; Railroad Commissioners (3)–6-year terms, 2006–1, 2008–1, 2010–1; Board of Education (15)–4-year terms, 2004–8, 2006–7, 2008–8, 2010–7.
(r) Superintendent of Public Instruction or Commissioner of Education.
(s) Commissioner of Public Lands, 2008 and Insurance Commissioner, 2008.
(t) Resident Commissioner, 2008.
(u) Commissioner of Labor.

Table 6.2
STATE LEGISLATURE MEMBERS TO BE ELECTED: 2006–2010

State or other jurisdiction	Total legislators Senate	House/Assembly	2006 Senate	House/Assembly	2007 Senate	House/Assembly	2008 Senate	House/Assembly	2009 Senate	House/Assembly	2010 Senate	House/Assembly
Alabama	35	105	35	105	…	…	…	40	…	…	35	105
Alaska	20	40	10	40	…	…	10	60	…	…	10	40
Arizona	30	60	30	60	…	…	30	60	…	…	30	60
Arkansas	35	100	17	100	…	…	18	100	…	…	17	100
California	40	80	20	80	…	…	20	80	…	…	20	80
Colorado	35	65	17	65	…	…	18	65	…	…	17	65
Connecticut	36	151	36	151	…	…	36	151	…	…	36	151
Delaware	21	41			…	…	11	41	…	…		
Florida	40	120	20	120	…	…	20	120	…	…	20	120
Georgia	56	180	56	180	…	…	56	180	…	…	56	180
Hawaii	25	51	13	51	…	…	12	51	…	…	13	51
Idaho	35	70	35	70	…	…	35	70	…	…	35	70
Illinois	59 (a)	118	39	118	39	105	39	118	…	…	20	118
Indiana	50	100	25	100	…	…	25	100	…	…	25	100
Iowa	50	100	25 (c)	100	…	…	25 (b)	100	…	…	25 (c)	100
Kansas	40	125		125	…	…	40	125	…	…		
Kentucky	38	100	19	100	…	…	19	100	…	…	19	100
Louisiana	39	105			39	105	…	…	…	…		
Maine	35	151	35	151	…	…	35	151	…	…	35	151
Maryland	47	141	47	141	…	…	…	…	…	…	47	141
Massachusetts	40	160	40	160	…	…	40	160	…	…	40	160
Michigan	38	110	38	110	…	…		110	…	…	38	110
Minnesota	67	134	67	134	…	…		134	…	…	67	134
Mississippi	52	122			52	122	…	…	…	…		
Missouri	34	163	17	163	…	…	17	163	…	…	17	163
Montana	50	100	25	100	…	…	25	100	…	…	25	100
Nebraska	49	U	24	U	…	…	25	U	…	…	24	U
Nevada	21	42	11	42	…	…	10	42	…	…	11	42
New Hampshire	24	400	24	400	…	…	24	400	…	…	24	400
New Jersey	40	80		…	40	80	…	…	…	80	…	…
New Mexico	42	70		70	…	…	42	70	…	…		70
New York	62	150	62	150	…	…	62	150	…	…	62	150
North Carolina	50	120	50	120	…	…	50	120	…	…	50	120
North Dakota	47	94	24 (c)	48	…	…	23 (b)	46	…	…	24 (c)	48
Ohio	33	99	17	99	…	…	16	99	…	…	17	99
Oklahoma	48	101	24	101	…	…	24	101	…	…	24	101
Oregon	30	60	15	60	…	…	15	60	…	…	15	60
Pennsylvania	50	203	25	203	…	…	25	203	…	…	25	203
Rhode Island	38	75	38	75	…	…	38	75	…	…	38	75
South Carolina	46	124		124	…	…	46	124	…	…		124

See footnotes at end of table.

STATE LEGISLATURE MEMBERS TO BE ELECTED: 2006–2010—Continued

State or other jurisdiction	Total legislators		2006		2007		2008		2009		2010	
	Senate	House/Assembly	Senate	House/Assembly	Senate	House/Assembly	Senate	House/Assembly	Senate	House/Assembly	Senate	House/Assembly
South Dakota.............	35	70	35	70	…	…	35	70	…	…	35	70
Tennessee.................	33	99	17	99	…	…	16	99	…	…	17	99
Texas.......................	31	150	16	150	…	…	15	150	…	…	16	150
Utah.........................	29	75	15	75	…	…	14	75	…	…	15	75
Vermont....................	30	150	30	150	…	…	30	150	…	…	30	150
Virginia.....................	40	100	…	…	40	100	…	…	…	100	…	…
Washington...............	49	98	24	98	…	…	25	98	…	…	24	98
West Virginia............	34	100	17	100	…	…	17	100	…	…	17	100
Wisconsin.................	33	99	17	99	…	…	16	99	…	…	17	99
Wyoming...................	30	60	15	60	…	…	15	60	…	…	15	60
American Samoa.........	18	20	(e)	20	…	…	(d)	20	…	…	(e)	20
No. Mariana Islands ...	9	18	…	…	3	18	…	…	6	18	…	…
Puerto Rico (e)	28	51	…	…	…	…	28	51	…	…	…	…
U.S. Virgin Islands	15	U	15	U	…	…	15	U	…	…	15	U
State Totals................	1,971	5,411	1,166	4,917	171	407	1,114	4,710	0	180	1,147	4,792
Totals........................	2,041	5,500	1,181	4,937	174	425	1,157	4,781	6	198	1,162	4,812

Source: The Council of State Governments survey, December 2005.

Note: This table shows the number of legislative seats up for election in a given year. As a result of redistricting, states may adjust some elections. The data contained in this table reflect information available at press time. See the Chapter 3 table entitled, "The Legislators: Numbers, Terms, and Party Affiliations," for specific information on legislative terms.

Key:

… — No regularly scheduled elections

U — Unicameral legislature

(a) The entire Senate is up for election every 10 years, beginning in 1972. Senate districts are divided into three groups. One group of senators is elected for terms of four years, four years and two years; two years, four years and four years; four years, two years and four years.

(b) Even-numbered Senate districts.

(c) Odd-numbered Senate districts.

(d) In American Samoa, Senators are not elected by popular vote. They are selected by county councils of chiefs.

(e) If in the general election more than 2/3 of the members of either house are elected from one party or from a single ticket, as both are defined by law, the numbers shall be increased in accordance with Article III Section 7 of the Puerto Rico Constitution.

Table 6.3
METHODS OF NOMINATING CANDIDATES FOR STATE OFFICES

State or other jurisdiction	*Method(s) of nominating candidates*
Alabama	Primary election; however, the state executive committee or other governing body of any political party may choose instead to hold a state convention for the purpose of nominating candidates. Submitting a petition to run as an independent or third-party candidate.
Alaska	Primary election. Petition for no-party candidates.
Arizona	Candidates who are members of a recognized party are nominated by an open primary election. Candidates who are not members of a recognized political party may file petitions to appear on the general election ballot. A write-in option is also available.
Arkansas	Primary election, convention and petition.
California	Primary election or independent nomination procedure.
Colorado	Assembly/primary. Political parties hold state assemblies to nominate candidates for the primary ballot. A candidate is placed on the ballot if he/she receives 30 percent of the vote or, after two ballots, is one of the two candidates receiving the highest number of votes. Candidates (including those from major political parties) can also petition their name on the ballot. Each party's gubernatorial candidate selects a lieutenant governor candidate after the primary election.
Connecticut	Convention/primary election. Major political parties hold state conventions (convening not earlier than the 68th day and closing not later than the 50th day before the date of the primary) for the purpose of endorsing candidates. If no one challenges the endorsed candidate, no primary election is held. However, if anyone (who received at least 15 percent of the delegate vote on any roll call at the convention) challenges the endorsed candidate, a primary election is held to determine the party nominee for the general election.
Delaware	Primary election for Democrats and primary election and convention for Republicans.
Florida	Primary election. Minor parties may nominate their candidate in any manner they deem proper.
Georgia	Primary election.
Hawaii	Primary election.
Idaho	Primary election and convention. New political parties hold a convention nominating candidates to be placed on a general election ballot.
Illinois	Primary election.
Indiana	Primary election, convention and petition. The governor is chosen by a primary. All other state officers are chosen at a state convention, unless the candidate is an independent. Any party that obtains between 2 percent and 8 percent of the vote for secretary of state may hold a convention to select a candidate.
Iowa	Primary election, convention and petition. Candidates from minor parties do not run in the primary election.
Kansas	Candidates for the two major parties are nominated by primary election. Candidates for minor parties are nominated for the general election at state party conventions. Independent candidates are nominated for the general election by petition.
Kentucky	Primary election. A slate of candidates for governor and lieutenant governor that receives the highest number of its party's votes but which number is less than 40 percent of the votes cast for all slates of candidates of that party, shall be required to participate in a runoff primary with the slate of candidates of the same party receiving the second highest number of votes.
Louisiana	Candidates may qualify for any office they wish, regardless of party affiliation, by completing the qualifying document and paying the appropriate qualifying fee; or a candidate may file a nominating petition.
Maine	Primary election or non-party petition.
Maryland	Primary election, convention and petition. Unaffiliated candidates or candidates affiliated with non-recognized political parties may run for elective office by collecting the requisite number of signatures on a petition. The required number equals 1 percent of the number of registered voters eligible to vote for office. Only recognized non-principal political parties may nominate their candidates by a convention in accordance with their bylaws (at this time, Maryland has four non-principal parties: Libertarian, Green, Constitution and Populist).
Massachusetts	Primary election.
Michigan	Primary election held for governor, state senate and state house. State convention held to nominate candidates for lieutenant governor, secretary of state and attorney general.
Minnesota	Primary election. Candidates for minor parties or independent candidates are by petition. They must have the signatures of 2,000 people who will be eligible to vote in the next general election.
Mississippi	Primary election.
Missouri	Primary election.
Montana	Primary election.
Nebraska	Primary election.
Nevada	Primary election. Independent candidates are nominated by petition for the general election. Minor parties nominated by petition or by party.
New Hampshire	Primary election. Minor parties by petition.
New Jersey	Primary election. Independent candidates are nominated by petition for the general election.
New Mexico	Statewide candidates petition to go to convention and are nominated in a primary election. District and legislative candidates petition for primary ballot access.
New York	Primary election/petition.
North Carolina	Primary election. Newly recognized parties just granted access submit their first nominees by convention. All established parties use primaries.
North Dakota	Convention/primary election. Political parties hold state conventions for the purpose of endorsing candidates. Endorsed candidates are automatically placed on the primary election ballot, but other candidates may also petition their name on the ballot.
Ohio	Primary election.

See footnotes at end of table.

METHODS OF NOMINATING CANDIDATES FOR STATE OFFICES — Continued

State or other jurisdiction	Method(s) of nominating candidates
Oklahoma	Primary election.
Oregon	Primary election, convention and petition.
Pennsylvania	Primary election, and nomination papers for minor political parties and political bodies.
Rhode Island	Primary election.
South Carolina	Primary election for Republicans and Democrats; party conventions held for minor parties. Candidates can have name on ballot via petition.
South Dakota	Primary election, convention and petition. South Dakota has closed primary election. Lieutenant governor, secretary of state, attorney general, state auditor, state treasurer, commission of school and public lands and public utility commissioners are all nominated at their party convention. Governor, state legislators and U.S. House and Senate candidates are all nominated by petition.
Tennessee	Primary election/petition.
Texas	Primary election/convention. Minor parties without ballot access nominate candidates for the general election after qualifying for ballot access by petition.
Utah	Convention, primary election and petition. Parties generally nominate their candidates in a convention. If one candidate does not get a certain percentage of delegate votes, the top two candidates go to a primary. Candidates not affiliated with a party can gain ballot access by petition.
Vermont	Primary election. Major parties by primary, minor parties by convention, independents by petition.
Virginia	Primary election and petition.
Washington	Primary election; minor parties hold convention for nomination, to qualify and appear on the general election ballot.
West Virginia	Primary election for major parties. Convention is held for official parties that received less than 10 percent of the last gubernatorial vote total. Minor parties and independent candidates nominated by petition.
Wisconsin	Primary election/petition. Candidates must file nomination papers (petitions) containing the minimum number of signatures required by law. Candidates appear on the primary ballot for the party they represent. The candidate receiving the most votes in each party primary goes on the the November election.
Wyoming	Primary election.
Dist. of Columbia	Primary election. Independent and minor party candidates file by nominating petition.
American Samoa	Individual files petition for candidacy with the chief election officer. Petition must be signed by statutorily mandated number of qualified voters.
No. Mariana Islands	Candidates are all nominated by petition. Candidates seeking the endorsement of recognized political parties must also include in their petition submission a document signed by the recognized political parties' chairperson/president and secretary attesting to such nomination. Recognized political parties may, or may not, depending on their bylaws and party rules, conduct primaries separate from any state election agency participation.
Puerto Rico	Primary election and convention.
U.S. Virgin Islands	Primary election.

Source: The Council of State Governments' survey of state election administration offices, December 2005.

Note: The nominating methods described here are for state offices; procedures may vary for local candidates. Also, independent candidates may have to petition for nomination.

Table 6.4
ELECTION DATES FOR NATIONAL, STATE AND LOCAL ELECTIONS
(Formulas and dates of state elections)

State or other jurisdiction	National (a) Primary	National Runoff	National General	State (b) Primary	State Runoff	State General	Local Primary	Local Runoff	Local General
Alabama	June, 1st T / June 3, 2008	⋯	Nov.,★ / Nov. 4, 2008	June, 1st T / June 6, 2006	June, Last T / June 27, 2006	Nat. / Nov. 7, 2006	v	v	v
Alaska	Aug., 4th T / Aug. 26, 2008	⋯	Nov.,★ / Nov. 4, 2008	Nat. / Aug. 22, 2006	⋯	Nat. / Nov. 7, 2006	⋯	⋯	v
Arizona	Feb., 4th T / Feb. 26, 2008	⋯	Nov.,★ / Nov. 4, 2008	8th T Prior / Sept. 12, 2006	⋯	Nat. / Nov. 7, 2006	Mar., 2nd T / Mar. 14, 2006	May, 3rd T / May 16, 2006	8 T prior to Nat. or Nat. / Sept. 12, Nov. 7, 2006
Arkansas	Feb., 1st T / Feb. 4, 2008	⋯	Nov.,★ / Nov. 4, 2008	T 3 wks. prior to runoff / May 23, 2006	June, 2nd T / June 13, 2006	Nat. / Nov. 7, 2006	State / May 23, 2006	State / June 13, 2006	Nov. 7, 2006
California	(l) / June 3, 2008	⋯	Nov.,★ / Nov. 4, 2008	June ★ / June 6, 2006	⋯	Nat. / Nov. 7, 2006	⋯	⋯	Nat.
Colorado	(l) (m) / Date not set at press time.	⋯	Nov.,★ / Nov. 4, 2008	Aug., 2nd T / Aug. 8, 2006	⋯	Nat. / Nov. 7, 2006	v	⋯	v
Connecticut	Aug., 2nd T / Aug. 12, 2008	⋯	Nov.,★ / Nov. 4, 2008	Aug., 2nd T / Aug. 8, 2006	⋯	Nat. / Nov. 7, 2006	56th day preceding election	⋯	Nat. or May, 1st M (c)
Delaware	(l) / Feb. 2008	⋯	Nov.,★ / Nov. 4, 2008	Sept., 1st S After 1st M / Sept. 6, 2008	⋯	Nat. / Nov. 4, 2008	⋯ Sept. 2, 2006	⋯	(d)
Florida	T 9 wks. prior to General Election / Sept. 2, 2008	⋯	Nov.,★ / Nov. 4, 2008	9th T prior to General Election / Sept. 5, 2006	⋯ / Oct. 3, 2006	Nat. / Nov. 7, 2006	Varies	Varies	Varies
Georgia	⋯ / Mar. 4, 2008	⋯	Nov.,★ / Nov. 4, 2008	Nat. / July 18, 2006	Nat. / Aug. 8 or 15, 2006 (q)	Nat. / Nov. 7, 2006	Nat. / July 18, 2006	Nat. / Aug. 8 or 15, 2006 (q)	Nat. / Nov. 7, 2006
Hawaii	(l) (m) / Date not set at press time.	⋯	Nov.,★ / Nov. 4, 2008	Sept., 2nd Last S / Sept. 23, 2006	⋯	Nat. / Nov. 7, 2006	State	⋯	Nat.
Idaho	May, 4th T / May 27, 2008	⋯	Nov.,★ / Nov. 4, 2008	May, 4th T / May 23, 2006	⋯	Nat. / Nov. 7, 2006	State	⋯	Nat.
Illinois	Mar., 3rd T / Mar. 18, 2008	⋯	Nov.,★ / Nov. 4, 2008	3rd T in Mar. / Mar. 21, 2006	⋯	Nat. / Nov. 7, 2006	⋯	⋯	⋯
Indiana	May,★ / May 6, 2008	⋯	Nov.,★ / Nov. 4, 2008	Nat. / May 2, 2006	⋯	Nat. / Nov. 7, 2006	Nat. / May 2, 2006	⋯	Nat.
Iowa	(k) / Date not set at press time.	⋯	Nov.,★ / Nov. 4, 2008	June,★ / June 6, 2006	⋯	Nat. / Nov. 7, 2006	State / June 6, 2006	⋯	Nat. / Nov. 7, 2006
Kansas	Set by SS or defaults to 1st T in April / Date not set at press time.	⋯	Nov.,★ / Nov. 4, 2008	Aug., 1st T (d) / Aug. 1, 2006	⋯	Nat. (d) / Nov. 7, 2006	5 wks. prior to General in odd yrs.	⋯	Apr., 1st T in odd yrs.
Kentucky	May, 1st T after 3rd M / May 20, 2008	⋯	Nov.,★ / Nov. 4, 2008	Nat. / May 22, 2007	35 days AP	Nat. / Nov. 6, 2007	Nat. / May 16, 2006	⋯	Nat. / Nov. 7, 2006

See footnotes at end of table.

ELECTION DATES FOR NATIONAL, STATE AND LOCAL ELECTIONS — Continued
(Formulas and dates of state elections)

State or other jurisdiction	National (a) Primary	Runoff	General	State (b) Primary	Runoff	General	Local Primary	Runoff	General
Louisiana (f)	(l) Oct. 4, 2008 (r)	... Dec. 6, 2008 (r)	Nov.,★ Nov. 4, 2008	(l) Sept. 30, 2006 (r)	(l) Dec. 9, 2006 (r)	(r) Nov. 7, 2006 (r)	V Apr. 22, 2006	...	V Apr. 29, 2006
Maine	(l) (m) Date not set at press time.	...	Nov.,★ Nov. 4, 2008	June, 2nd T June 13, 2006	...	Nat. Nov. 7, 2006	...	...	V
Maryland	Mar., 1st T Mar. 4, 2008	...	Nov.,★ Nov. 4, 2008	2nd T after 1st Mon. in Sept. Sept. 12, 2006	...	Nat. Nov. 7, 2006	Same as state	...	Same as state
Massachusetts	(l) Date not set at press time.	...	Nov.,★ Nov. 4, 2008	7th T Prior Sept. 19, 2006	...	Nat. Nov. 7, 2006	V	...	V
Michigan	Feb., 4th T Feb. 26, 2008	...	Nov.,★ Nov. 4, 2008	Aug.,★ Aug. 8, 2006	...	Nat. Nov. 7, 2006	V	...	V
Minnesota	(l) (m) Date not set at press time.	...	Nov.,★ Nov. 4, 2008	Sept., 1st T after 2nd M Sept. 12, 2006	...	Nat. Nov. 7, 2006	State (d)	...	Nat. (d)
Mississippi	June, 1st T (g) June 3, 2008	...	Nov.,★ Nov. 4, 2008	June, 1st T (g) June 6, 2006	3rd T AP June 27, 2006	Nat. (d) Nov. 7, 2006	May, 1st T (d)	2nd T AP	June,★ (d)
Missouri	Feb.,★ Feb. 5, 2008	...	Nov.,★ Nov. 4, 2008	Aug.,★ Aug. 8, 2006	...	Nat. Nov. 7, 2006	State	...	Nat.
Montana	June,★ June 3, 2008	...	Nov.,★ Nov. 4, 2008	June,★ June 6, 2006	...	Nat. Nov. 4, 2008	Nat. June 6, 2006	...	Nat. Nov. 7, 2006
Nebraska	May, 1st T After 2nd M May 13, 2008	...	Nov.,★ Nov. 4, 2008	Nat. May 9, 2006	...	Nat. Nov. 7, 2006	Nat.	...	Nat. Nov. 7, 2006
Nevada	Sept., 1st T Sept. 2, 2008	...	Nov.,★ Nov. 4, 2008	3rd T Aug. Aug. 15, 2006	...	Nat. Nov. 7, 2006	Nat.	...	Nat. Nov. 7, 2006
New Hampshire	Set by SS ...	...	Nov.,★ Nov. 4, 2008	Nat. Sept. 12, 2006	...	Nat. Nov. 7, 2006	V	...	V
New Jersey	June,★ June 3, 2008	...	Nov.,★ Nov. 4, 2008	June,★ June 6, 2006	...	Nat. Nov. 7, 2006	June,★ June 6, 2006	...	Nat. Nov. 7, 2006
New Mexico	June, 1st T June 3, 2008	...	Nov.,★ Nov. 4, 2008	Nat. June 6, 2006	...	Nat. Nov. 7, 2006	Nat.	...	Nat. Nov. 7, 2006
New York	Mar., 1st T Mar. 4, 2008	...	Nov.,★ Nov. 4, 2008	Sept.,★ Sept. 12, 2006	...	Nat. Nov. 7, 2006	State	Sept., 2 wks AP (d)	Nat.
North Carolina	May,★ May 6, 2008	...	Nov.,★ Nov. 4, 2008	Nat. May 2, 2006	4 wks. AP May 30, 2006	Nat. Nov. 7, 2006	Nat. May 2, 2006	Nat. May 30, 2006	Nat. Nov. 7, 2006
North Dakota	(n) Date not set at press time.	...	Nov.,★ Nov. 4, 2008	June, 2nd T June 13, 2006	...	Nat. Nov. 7, 2006	June 13, 2006	...	June, 2nd T (e) Nov. 7, 2006
Ohio	Mar.,★ Mar. 4, 2008	...	Nov.,★ Nov. 4, 2008	Nat. May 2, 2006	...	Nat. Nov. 7, 2006	Nat. (d)	...	Nat. (d)
Oklahoma	July, last T (h) July 25, 2006	...	Nov.,★ Nov. 4, 2008	Nat. July 25, 2006	Aug., 4th T Aug. 22, 2006	Nat. Nov. 7, 2006	Nat.	Nat.	Nat.

See footnotes at end of table.

ELECTION DATES FOR NATIONAL, STATE AND LOCAL ELECTIONS—Continued
(Formulas and dates of state elections)

State or other jurisdiction	National (a)			State (b)			Local		
	Primary	Runoff	General	Primary	Runoff	General	Primary	Runoff	General
Oregon	May, 3rd T May 20, 2008	...	Nov.,★ Nov. 4, 2008	Nat. May 16, 2006	...	Nat. Nov. 7, 2006	Nat.	...	Nat.
Pennsylvania	Apr., 4th T Apr. 22, 2008	...	Nov.,★ Nov. 4, 2008	May, 3rd T May 16, 2006	...	Nat. Nov. 7, 2006	Nat.	...	Nat.
Rhode Island	(l) Date not set at press time.	...	Nov.,★ Nov. 4, 2008	Sept., 2nd T After 1st M Sept. 12, 2006	...	Nat. Nov. 7, 2006	State	...	Nat.
South Carolina	(s)	2nd T AP June 17, 2008	Nov.,★ Nov. 4, 2008	June, 2nd T June 13, 2006	2nd T AP June 27, 2006	Nat. Nov. 7, 2006	State (d)	State June 27, 2006	Nat. (d) Nov. 7, 2006
South Dakota	June,★ June 3, 2008	2nd T AP June 17, 2008	Nov.,★ Nov. 4, 2008	June,★ June 6, 2006	2nd T AP June 20, 2006	Nat. Nov. 7, 2006	State	...	Nat.
Tennessee	Feb., 2nd T Feb. 12, 2008	...	Nov.,★ Nov. 4, 2008	Aug., 1st TH Aug. 3, 2006	...	Nat. Nov. 7, 2006	Feb., 2nd T May, 1st T	...	Aug., 1st TH
Texas	Mar., 1st T Mar. 4, 2008	Apr., 2nd T Apr. 8, 2008	Nov.,★ Nov. 4, 2008	Nat. Mar. 7, 2006	Nat. Apr. 11, 2006	Nat. Nov. 7, 2006	Nat. Mar. 7, 2006	Nat. Apr. 11, 2006	Nat. Nov. 7, 2006
Utah	(l) (m)	...	Nov.,★ Nov. 4, 2008	June, 4th T June 27, 2006	...	Nat. Nov. 7, 2006	State	...	Nat.
Vermont (i)	1st T in Mar. Mar. 4, 2008	...	Nov.,★ Nov. 4, 2008	Sept., 2nd T Sept. 12, 2006	...	Nat. Nov. 7, 2006	...	...	(l)
Virginia	(l) Date not set at press time.	...	Nov.,★ Nov. 4, 2008	June, 2nd T June 13, 2006	...	Nat. Nov. 7, 2006	State or Feb., last T	...	Nat. or May, 1st T
Washington	Sept., 3rd T (m) Sept. 16, 2008	...	Nov.,★ Nov. 4, 2008	Sept., 3rd T (o) Sept. 19, 2008	...	Nat. Nov. 7, 2006	State Sept. 19, 2006	...	Nat.
West Virginia	May, 2nd T May 13, 2008	...	Nov.,★ Nov. 4, 2008	May, 2nd T May 9, 2006	...	Nat. Nov. 7, 2006	May, 2nd T May 9, 2006	...	Nat. Nov. 7, 2006
Wisconsin	Sept., 2nd T Sept. 9, 2008	...	Nov.,★ Nov. 4, 2008	(l) Sept. 12, 2006	...	Nat. Nov. 7, 2006	Feb., 3rd T Feb. 21, 2006	...	Apr., 1st T Apr. 4, 2006
Wyoming	(l) (m)	...	Nov.,★ Nov. 4, 2008	Aug., 1st T After 3rd M Aug. 22, 2006	...	Nat. Nov. 7, 2006	State	...	Nat.
Dist. of Columbia	(l) Date not set at press time.	...	Nov.,★ Nov. 4, 2008	Sept. 12, 2006	...	Nov. 7, 2006	Sept., 1st T after 2nd M	...	Nov.,★
American Samoa	(j)	14 days after General Nov. 21, 2008	Nov.,★ Nov. 4, 2008	(j)	14 days after General Nov. 18, 2008	Nov.,★ Nov. 4, 2008	(j)	...	(o)
Puerto Rico	...	...	...	(l) Mar. 9, 2008	...	Nov.,★ Nov. 4, 2008	...	...	...
U.S. Virgin Islands	...	...	...	Sept., 2nd S Sept. 11, 2006	14 days AP Sept. 25, 2006	Nat. Nov. 7, 2006	Sept., 2nd S Sept. 11, 2006	14 days AP Sept. 25, 2006	Nov., 1st T Nov. 7, 2006

See footnotes at end of table.

ELECTION DATES FOR NATIONAL, STATE AND LOCAL ELECTIONS — Continued

Sources: The Council of State Governments' survey of state election offices, December 2005 and state web sites, January 2006.

Note: This table describes the basic formulas for determining when national, state and local elections will be held. For specific information on a particular state, the reader is advised to contact the specific state election administration office. All dates provided are based on the state election formula.

Key:

★ — First Tuesday after first Monday.

. . . — No provision.

M — Monday

T — Tuesday

TH — Thursday

S — Saturday

Nat. — Same date as national elections.

State — Same date as state elections.

Prior — Prior to general election.

AP — After primary.

V — Varies

(a) National refers to presidential elections.

(b) State refers to election in which a state executive official or U.S. senator is to be elected. See Table 6.2, State Officials to be Elected.

(c) Unless that date conflicts with Passover, then first Tuesday following last day of Passover.

(d) In Delaware, elections are determined by city charter. In Iowa, partisan elections only. In Kansas, state and county elections. In Minnesota, county elections only. In Mississippi, state and county elections are held together; municipal elections are held in separate years. In Montana, municipalities only. In New York, runoff in New York City only. In Ohio, municipalities and towns in odd years and counties in even years. In South Carolina, school boards vary.

(e) Cities only.

(f) Louisiana has an open primary which requires all candidates, regardless of party affiliation, to appear on a single ballot. If a candidate receives over 50 percent of the vote in the primary, that candidate is elected to the office. If no candidate receives a majority vote, then a single election is held between the two candidates receiving the most votes. For national elections, the first vote is held on the first Saturday in October of even-numbered years with the general election held on the first Tuesday after the first Monday in November. For state

elections, the election is held on the second to last Saturday in October with the runoff being held on the fourth Saturday after first election. Local elections vary depending on the location and the year.

(g) Except in presidential election year when congressional races correspond to Super Tuesday.

(h) The primary election is held on the fourth Tuesday in August in each even-numbered year, including presidential election years. The presidential preferential primary is held on the first Tuesday in February during presidential election years.

(i) In Vermont, if there is a tie in a primary or general election (and a recount does not resolve the tie) the appropriate superior could order a recessed election, among the tied candidates only, within three weeks of the recount. In state primary runoffs, the runoff election must be proclaimed within seven days after primary; after proclamation, election is held 15–22 days later. Local elections are held by annual town meetings which may vary depending on town charter.

(j) American Samoa does not conduct primary elections. (In addition, elections are conducted for territory-wide offices. There are no local elections.)

(k) Eight days before any other nomination process.

(l) Formula not available at press time.

(m) State did not hold a presidential primary in 2004.

(n) On one designated day, following presidential nominating contests in the states of Iowa and New Hampshire and prior to the first Wednesday in March in every presidential election year, every political party entitled to a separate column may conduct a presidential preference caucus. Before August 15 of the odd-numbered year immediately preceding the presidential election year, the secretary of state shall designate the day after consulting with and taking recommendations from the two political parties casting the greatest vote for president of the United States at the most recent general elections when the office of president appeared on the ballot.

(o) Must be held on the third Tuesday of the preceding September or on the seventh Tuesday immediately preceding such general election, whichever occurs first.

(p) In Louisiana, a Congressional primary election is not held.

(q) Primary runoff in 2006 may be August 8 under current law. If a new law is approved by U.S. Justice Department, the primary runoff will be August 15, 2006.

(r) 2005 legislation is currently pending U.S. Justice Department approval that will enact these date changes.

(s) Determined by state party.

(t) Most local (i.e. town/municipal) officials in Vermont are elected at town meeting, either by traditional meeting or by Australian ballot. (County officials are elected in November of even-numbered years.)

Table 6.5
POLLING HOURS: GENERAL ELECTIONS

State or other jurisdiction	Polls open	Polls close	Notes on hours (a)
Alabama	7 a.m.	7 p.m.	
Alaska	7 a.m.	8 p.m.	
Arizona	6 a.m.	7 p.m.	
Arkansas	7:30 a.m.	7:30 p.m.	
California	7 a.m.	8 p.m.	
Colorado	7 a.m.	7 p.m.	
Connecticut	6 a.m.	8 p.m.	
Delaware	7 a.m.	8 p.m.	
Florida	7 a.m.	7 p.m.	
Georgia	7 a.m.	7 p.m.	
Hawaii	7 a.m.	6 p.m.	
Idaho	8 a.m.	8 p.m.	Clerk has the option of opening all polls at 7 a.m. Idaho is in two time zones—MST and PST.
Illinois	6 a.m.	7 p.m.	
Indiana	6 a.m.	6 p.m.	
Iowa	7 a.m.	9 p.m.	
Kansas	7 a.m.	7 p.m.	Counties may choose to open polls as early as 6 a.m. and close as late as 8 p.m. Several western counties are on Mountain Time.
Kentucky	6 a.m.	6 p.m.	
Louisiana	6 a.m.	8 p.m.	
Maine	Between 6 and 10 a.m.	8 p.m.	Applicable opening time depends on variables related to the size of the precinct. Anyone in line at 8 p.m. will be allowed to vote.
Maryland	7 a.m.	8 p.m.	
Massachusetts	7 a.m.	8 p.m.	
Michigan	7 a.m.	8 p.m.	
Minnesota	7 a.m.	8 p.m.	Towns outside of the twin cities metro area with less than 500 inhabitants may have a later time for the polls to open as long as it is not later than 10 a.m.
Mississippi	7 a.m.	7 p.m.	
Missouri	6 a.m.	7 p.m.	Those individuals in line at 7 p.m. will be allowed to vote.
Montana	7 a.m.	8 p.m.	Polling places with fewer than 200 registered electors must be open from noon until 8 p.m. or until all registered electors in any precinct have voted.
Nebraska	7 a.m. MST/8 a.m. CST	7 p.m. MST/8 p.m. CST	
Nevada	7 a.m.	7 p.m.	
New Hampshire	No later than 11 a.m.	No earlier than 7 p.m.	Polling hours vary from town to town. The hours of 11 a.m. to 7 p.m. are by statute.
New Jersey	6 a.m.	8 p.m.	
New Mexico	7 a.m.	7 p.m.	
New York	6 a.m.	9 p.m.	
North Carolina	6:30 a.m.	7:30 p.m.	
North Dakota	Between 7 and 9 a.m.	Between 7 and 9 p.m.	Counties must have polls open by 9 a.m., but can choose to open as early as 7 a.m. Polls must remain open until 7 p.m., but can be open as late as 9 p.m. The majority of polls in the state are open from 8 a.m. to 7 p.m. in their respective time zones (CST and MST).
Ohio	6:30 a.m.	7:30 p.m.	
Oklahoma	7 a.m.	7 p.m.	
Oregon	7 a.m.	8 p.m.	
Pennsylvania	7 a.m.	8 p.m.	
Rhode Island	7 a.m.	9 p.m.	
South Carolina	7 a.m.	7 p.m.	
South Dakota	7 a.m.	7 p.m.	
Tennessee	8 a.m.	7 p.m. CST/8 p.m. EST	Poll hours are set by each county election commission. Polling places shall be open a minimum of 10 hours but no more than 13 hours. All polling locations in the eastern time zone shall close at 8 p.m. and those in the central time zone shall close at 7 p.m.
Texas	7 a.m.	7 p.m.	
Utah	7 a.m.	8 p.m.	
Vermont	Between 7 and 10 a.m.	7 p.m.	The opening time for polls is set by local boards of civil authority.
Virginia	6 a.m.	7 p.m.	
Washington	7 a.m.	8 p.m.	
West Virginia	6:30 a.m.	7:30 p.m.	
Wisconsin	Between 7 and 9 a.m.	8 p.m.	In cities with a population of 10,000 or more, the polls must open at 7:00 a.m. In cities, towns and villages with populations of 10,000, the polls may open anytime between 7:00 a.m. and 9:00 a.m.
Wyoming	7 a.m.	7 p.m.	

See footnotes at end of table.

POLLING HOURS: GENERAL ELECTIONS — Continued

State or other jurisdiction	Polls open	Polls close	Notes on hours (a)
Dist. of Columbia	7 a.m.	8 p.m.	
American Samoa			Election proclamation issued by Chief Election Officer contains a statement of time and place for each territorial election.
Guam	8 a.m.	8 p.m.	
No. Mariana Islands	7 a.m.	7 p.m.	Elections are held on six separate islands. At the close of the polls, ballots are flown to Saipan where they are tabulated at election headquarters.
Puerto Rico...................	8 a.m.	3 p.m.	
U.S. Virgin Islands	7 a.m.	7 p.m.	

Sources: The Council of State Governments' survey, September 2005 and state election Web sites, October 2005.

Note: Hours for primary, municipal and special elections may differ from those noted.

(a) In all states, voters standing in line when the polls close are allowed to vote; however, provisions for handling those voters vary across jurisdictions.

Table 6.6
VOTER REGISTRATION INFORMATION

State or other jurisdiction	Closing date for registration before general election (days)	Persons eligible for absentee registration (a)	Absentee voting		Residency requirements	Registration in other places	Criminal status	Mental competency
			Cut-off for receiving absentee ballots	Absentee votes signed by witness or notary				
Alabama	10	M/O	Close of polls	N or 2W	S, C (m)	...	★	★
Alaska	30	A	10 days after election	N or 2W	...	★	★	★
Arizona	29	A	7 p.m. Election Day	...	S, C, 29	★	★	★
Arkansas..................	30	A	7:30 p.m. Election Day	...	(n)	★	★	...
California	15	A	8 p.m. Election Day	...	S	...	★	★
Colorado...................	29	A	7 p.m. Election Day	...	S, 30	...	★	...
Connecticut	14	A	8 p.m. Election Day	...	S, T	...	★	...
Delaware...................	20	A	12 p.m. day before election	N or W	S (o)	...	★	★
Florida	29	A	7 p.m. Election Day	W	S, C	...	★	★
Georgia	(b)	A	Close of polls	W (x)	S, C	...	★	★
Hawaii......................	30	A	Close of polls	W (x)	S	...	★	★
Idaho........................	25	A	8 p.m. Election Day	...	S, C, 30	...	★	...
Illinois......................	27 (z)	M/O	Close of polls	...	S, P, 30	★	★	...
Indiana.....................	29	C, D, E, M/O, O, P, T	12 p.m. day before election	...	P, 30	...	★	...
Iowa	10	M/O	Postmarked day before election	...	S (aa)	★	★	★
Kansas	15	A (bb)	(cc)	...	(dd)	★	★	★
Kentucky	29	A	Close of polls	...	S, C, 28	★	★	★
Louisiana	30	B, D, O, P, S, T (ee)	Election Day	N and 2W	S, 30 (ff)	★	★	★
Maine	Election Day	A	Tuesday before election	...	S, M	...	★	★
Maryland	21	B, C, D, O, S, T (gg)	Friday after election	...	S, 21 (hh)	...	★	★
Massachusetts...........	20	A	10 days after election	...	S	...	★	★
Michigan...................	30	A	8 p.m. Election Day	W (x)	S, T, 30 (p)	...	★	...
Minnesota	Election Day (d)	A	Election Day	N or W	S, 20	...	★	★
Mississippi	30	A	5 p.m. day before election	W	S, C, 30	...	★	★
Missouri	28	A	Close of polls	N	S	...	★	★
Montana	30	A	8 p.m. Election Day	...	S, C, D, M, P, T, 30	★	★	★
Nebraska...................	(f)	A	10 a.m. 2 days after election	W	S	...	★	★
Nevada	(k)	M/O	Close of polls	...	S, C, 30; P, 10 (t)	...	★	★
New Hampshire.........	Election Day (d)	B, D, E, O, R, S, T	(ii)	...	S	★	★	...
New Jersey................	29	A	8 p.m. Election Day	W or N	S, C, 30 (q)	...	★	...
New Mexico	28	T	7 p.m. Election Day	...	S	...	★	★
New York	25	A	Postmarked day before election	W (x)	S, C, 30 (r)	★	★	★
North Carolina	25	A (bb)	5 p.m. day before election	2W	S, C, D, M, P, T, 30	★	★	...
North Dakota............	(e)	(e)	2 days after election	...	S, C, D, M, P, T, 30	(e)	(e)	(e)
Ohio	30	A	Close of polls	...	S, 30	...	★	★
Oklahoma	25	A	7 p.m. Election Day	N or W	S	...	★	★
Oregon	21	A	8 p.m. Election Day	...	S	...	★	...
Pennsylvania	30	B, D, M/O, O, P, R, S, T	5 p.m. Friday before election	W (x)	S, P, 30	...	★	...
Rhode Island	30	D	9 p.m. Election Day	N or 2W	S, 30	...	★	★
South Carolina	30	B, C, D, O, S (i)	7 p.m. Election Day	W	S, C, D, M, P, T, 30	★	★	★
South Dakota............	15	A	Close of polls	(jj)	S, C, D, 1 (kk)	...	★	★
Tennessee	30	A	Close of polls	W (x)	S	...	★	★
Texas	30	A	Before close of polls	(y)	S, C	...	★	★
Utah	20	A (bb)	12 p.m. Monday after election	W (x)	S, 30	...	★	★
Vermont	8 (l)	A (bb)	7 p.m. Election Day	...	S, C (aa)	...	...	...
Virginia....................	29	(j)	Close of polls	W	S, P	...	★	★
Washington...............	15 (c)	A	(ll)	...	S, C, P, 30	★	★	★
West Virginia............	21	A	(x)	N	(w)	★	★	★
Wisconsin.................	Election Day (c)(u)	A	Close of polls	W	S, 10	...	★	★
Wyoming...................	Election Day (d)	A	7 p.m. Election Day	...	S (s)	...	★	★

See footnotes at end of table.

VOTER REGISTRATION INFORMATION—Continued

State or other jurisdiction	Closing date for registration before general election (days)	Persons eligible for absentee registration (a)	Cut-off for receiving absentee ballots	Absentee votes signed by witness or notary	Residency requirements	Registration in other places	Criminal status	Mental competency
			Absentee voting					
Dist. of Columbia	30	A	10 days after election	...	D, 30	★	★	★
American Samoa	30	A	1:30 p.m. Election Day	...	S, 30	N.A.	N.A.	N.A.
Guam	10	A	N.A.	N.A.	N.A.	N.A.	N.A.	N.A.
No. Mariana Islands..	50	B, D, E, O, R, S, T	14 days after election	N (v)	(h)	★	★	★
Puerto Rico	40 or 60	A	30 or 45 days after election	N.A.	S (g)	...	...	★
U.S. Virgin Islands	30	M/O	14 days before election	...	S, D 30	★	★	★

Sources: The Council of State Governments survey, December 2005; Federal Election Commission, http://www.fec.gov, October 2005; and Election Assistance Commission, October 2005.

Key:

★ — Column 6: state provision prohibiting registration or claiming the right to vote in another state or jurisdiction. Columns 7 and 8: state provision regarding criminal status or mental competency.

. . . — No state provision.

N.A. — Information not available.

Column 4: N — Notary, W — Witness. Numbers indicate the number of signatures required.

Column 5: S — State, C — County, D — District, M — Municipality, P — Precinct, T — Town. Numbers represent the number of days before an election for which one must be a resident.

Note: Previous editions of this chart contained a column for "Automatic cancellation of registration for failure to vote for ___ years". However, the National Voter Registration Act requires a confirmation notice prior to any cancellation and thus effectively bans any automatic cancellation of voter registration. In addition, all states and territories except Puerto Rico and the U.S. Virgin Islands allow mail-in registration.

(a) In this column: A — All of these; B — Absent on business; C — Senior citizen; D — Disabled person; E — Not absent, but prevented by employment from registering; M/O — No absentee registration except military and overseas citizens as required by federal law; O — Out of state; P — Out of precinct (or municipality in PA); R — Absent for religious reasons; S — Students; T — Temporarily out of jurisdiction.

(b) The 5th Monday before a general primary, general election, or presidential preference primary; the 5th day after the date of the call for all other special primaries and special elections.

(c) By mail: Washington, 30 days; Wisconsin, 13 days.

(d) Minnesota — delivered 21 days before an election or election-day registration at polling precincts; New Hampshire — Received by city or town clerk 10 days before election or election-day registration at precincts; Wyoming — delivered 30 days before or election-day registration at polling precincts.

(e) No voter registration.

(f) Received by the 2nd Friday before election or postmarked by the 3rd Friday before the election.

(g) According to Electoral Law, the voter must have a permanent residence in Puerto Rico to be a qualified elector.

(h) State/territory: 120 days; district, municipality, precinct: 50 days.

(i) In South Carolina, all the following are eligible for absentee registration in addition to those categories already listed: electors with a death in the family within 3 days before the election; overseas military, Red Cross, U.S.O. government employees, and their dependents and spouses residing with them; persons on vacation; persons admitted to the hospital as emergency patients 4 days prior to election; persons confined to jail or pretrial facility pending disposition of arrest/trial; and persons attending sick/disabled persons.

(j) In Virginia, the following temporarily out-of-jurisdiction persons are eligible for absentee registration: (1) uniformed services voters on active duty, merchant marine, and persons temporarily residing overseas by virtue of employment (and spouse/dependents of these persons residing with them), who are not normally absent from their locality, or have been absent and returned to reside within 28 days prior to an election, may register in person up to and including the day of the election; (2) members of uniformed services discharged from active duty during 60 days preceding election (and spouse/dependents) may register, if otherwise qualified, in person up to and including the day of the election.

(k) By 9 p.m. on the 5th Saturday preceding any primary or general election.

(l) Second Monday preceding election.

(m) At the time of registration.

(n) Must live in Arkansas at the address in Box 2 of your voter application.

(o) Must be a permanent state resident.

(p) Must be a resident of the town or city at least 30 days before election day.

(q) Must be a resident of the state and county at your address for 30 days before election.

(r) Must be a resident of the county or the City of New York at least 30 days before election.

(s) Must be "an actual and physically bona fide resident."

(t) Must have continuously resided in the state and county at least 30 days and in precinct at least 10 days before election. Must claim no other place as legal residence.

(u) Registration may be completed in the local voter registration office one day before the election.

(v) Notary public or commissioned officer authorized to administer oath for Armed Services personnel.

(w) A voter must be a resident for 30 days prior to the election. West Virginia poll books for each election require that the voters acknowledge that their address is current and that they have been at that location for 30 days prior to the election.

(x) The request deadline is 6 days before the election, to be mailed the next day; the receipt deadline is before canvass with election-day postmark, the day after the election with no postmark, and before canvass for military and overseas regardless of postmark.

(y) If unable to sign.

(z) Closing date for registration before general election is 27 days before. Illinois now has grace period registration which allows for registration of voters and change of address during a period from close of registration for a primary or election and until 14th day before the primary or election. If a voter who registers during this time period wishes to vote at that first election occurring after grace period, he/she must do so by grace period voting.

(aa) Iowa does not have a residency length of time requirement, but you must be a resident of the state and precinct. Vermont has no durational residency requirement.

(bb) No excuse required.

(cc) In person: 12 p.m. day before election. By mail: close of polls on election day.

(dd) Date of registration.

(ee) Must be in Handicapped Program.

(ff) A voter must be registered to vote 30 days before an election, and must be a resident in order to register.

(gg) Voter is eligible if they may be out of the county; students eligible if out of precinct.

(hh) State election law does not apply to municipal elections. Therefore, each municipality may have a separate requirement.

(ii) In person: day before election. By mail: day of election.

(jj) Absentee ballot applications (not absentee ballots) are required to be notarized or submitted with a copy of the voter's photo identification.

(kk) Municipality: at least 30 days during the year preceding the election. Town: 30 consecutive days each year.

(ll) Postmarked by Election Day, and received by date of certification.

Table 6.7
VOTING STATISTICS FOR GUBERNATORIAL ELECTIONS BY REGION: 2002–2005

State or other jurisdiction	Date of last election	Primary election					General election								
		Republican	Democrat	Independent	Other	Total votes	Republican	Percent	Democrat	Percent	Independent	Percent	Other	Percent	Total votes
Eastern Region															
Connecticut	2002	(b)					573,958	56.1	448,984	43.9	0	0.0	0	0.0	1,022,942
Delaware	2004	21,670	31,799	0	0	53,469	167,008	45.8	185,548	50.9	10,753	2.9	1,450	0.4	364,759
Maine	2002	78,783	71,735(d)	0	1,613	152,131	209,496	41.5	238,179	47.1	10,612	2.1	46,903	9.3	505,190
Massachusetts	2002	227,960(d)	746,190	0	2,752	976,902	1,091,988	49.8	985,981	44.9	15,335	0.7	100,875	4.6	2,194,179
New Hampshire	2004	246,266	207,284	0	0	453,550	326,007	47.7	339,773	49.7	0	0.0	13,028	1.9	683,672
New Jersey	2005	302,521	235,778	0	0	538,299	985,271	43.0	1,224,551	53.5	0	0.0	80,277	3.5	2,290,099
New York (c)	2002	20,936	633,078	18,598	0	672,612	2,262,255	49.4	1,534,064	33.5	654,016	14.3	128,743	2.8	4,579,078
Pennsylvania	2002	538,757(d)	1,242,236	0	0	1,780,993	1,589,408	44.4	1,913,235	53.4	0	0.0	79,346	2.2	3,581,989
Rhode Island	2002	26,824	122,535	0	399	149,758	181,827	54.8	150,229	45.2	0	0.0	0	0.0	332,056
Vermont	2004	27,673	83,116	0	0	112,327	181,540	58.7	117,327	37.9	2,431	0.7	7,782	2.9	309,285
Regional total		1,491,390	3,373,751	18,598	4,764	4,890,041	7,568,758	47.7	7,137,871	45.0	693,147	4.3	458,404	2.9	15,863,249
Midwestern Region															
Illinois	2002	917,828	1,252,516	0	0	2,170,345	1,594,960	45.1	1,847,040	52.2	23,089	0.7	73,794	2.1	3,538,883
Indiana	2004	505,758	283,924	0	0	789,682	1,302,912	53.2	1,113,900	45.4	0	0.0	31,684	1.3	2,448,498
Iowa	2002	206,138	97,079(d)	0	439	303,656	412,863	44.5	353,584	52.7	254,753	0.0	17,004	2.8	1,040,201
Kansas	2002	294,504	87,499(d)	0	0	382,003	376,830	45.1	441,858	52.9	0	0.0	17,004	2.0	835,692
Michigan	2002	583,391	1,046,680	0	0	1,630,071	1,506,104	47.4	1,633,796	51.4	0	0.0	37,665	1.2	3,177,565
Minnesota	2002	195,099	224,238	0	46,269	465,606	999,473	44.4	821,268	36.5	9,698	0.4	422,034	18.7	2,252,473
Nebraska	2002	147,718	61,312	0	36	209,066	330,349	68.7	132,348	27.5	0	0.0	18,294	3.8	480,991
North Dakota	2004	42,135	35,597	0	0	77,732	220,803	71.3	84,877	27.4	4,193	1.3	0	0.0	309,873
Ohio	2002	658,700(d)	585,615(d)	0	121,438	1,365,753	1,865,007	57.7	1,236,924	38.3	0	0.0	127,061	4.0	3,228,992
South Dakota	2002	111,264	68,037	0	0	179,301	189,920	56.8	140,263	41.9	2,393	0.7	1,983	0.6	340,407
Wisconsin	2002	230,232	553,634	741	18,831	803,439	734,779	41.4	800,515	45.2	8,123	0.5	229,566	12.9	1,775,349
Regional total		3,892,767	4,296,131	741	187,013	8,376,654	9,534,000	49.0	8,606,373	44.3	302,249	1.5	959,085	4.9	19,428,924
Southern Region															
Alabama	2002	357,497	435,310	0	0	792,807	672,225	49.2	669,105	48.9	0	0.0	25,723	1.9	1,367,053
Arkansas	2002	92,237	279,097	0	0	371,334	427,082	53.0	378,250	46.9	0	0.0	210	0.0	805,332
Florida	2002	(d)	1,357,381	0	0	1,357,381	2,856,845	56.0	2,201,427	43.1	42,039	0.8	370	0.0	5,100,681
Georgia	2002	533,936	565,778(d)	8,348	0	1,108,062	1,041,700	51.4	937,070	46.2	0	0.0	47,123	2.4	2,032,110
Kentucky	2003	160,050	298,082	0	0	458,341	596,284	55.0	487,159	45.0	0	0.0	0	0.0	1,083,443
Louisiana (a)	2003	351,371	871,198	172,158	0	1,394,727	368,698	48.0	871,715	52.0	175,228	0.0	0	0.0	1,415,641
Maryland	2002	247,566	543,607	2,953	71	841,395	879,592	51.2	813,422	47.4	1,619	0.1	11,546	0.3	1,717,068
Mississippi	2003	177,122	504,319	0	0	681,441	470,404	52.6	409,787	45.8	0	0.0	14,296	1.6	894,487
Missouri	2004	604,757	847,748	0	3,755	1,456,260	1,382,419	50.8	1,301,442	47.9	0	0.0	35,678	1.1	2,719,599
North Carolina	2004	364,420	444,559	0	0	808,979	1,495,021	42.8	1,939,154	55.6	0	0.0	52,513	1.1	3,486,688
Oklahoma	2002	205,876	350,389	0	0	556,265	441,277	42.6	448,143	43.3	146,200	14.1	0	0.0	1,035,620
South Carolina	2002	384,944	114,346	0	0	499,290	585,422	52.8	521,140	47.1	0	0.0	1,163	0.1	1,116,936
Tennessee	2002	534,824	539,018	0	809	1,074,651	786,803	47.6	837,284	50.6	28,704	1.7	376	0.2	1,653,167
Texas	2002	620,463	1,003,338(d)	0	(b)	1,623,851	2,632,591	57.8	1,819,798	40.0	0	0.0	101,538	2.2	4,553,927
Virginia	2005	175,170	(b)	(b)	0	175,170	912,327	46.0	1,025,942	52.0	43,953	2.0	1,556	0.1	1,983,778
West Virginia	2004	26,041	149,362	(b)	0	175,403	253,131	34.0	472,758	63.5	0	0.0	18,544	0.2	744,433
Regional total		4,836,274	8,303,532	183,459	4,635	13,375,357	15,801,821	49.8	15,133,596	47.7	437,743	1.3	310,636	0.9	31,709,963

See footnotes at end of table.

VOTING STATISTICS FOR GUBERNATORIAL ELECTIONS BY REGION: 2002–2005 — Continued

State or other jurisdiction	Date of last election	Primary election					General election								
		Republican	Democrat	Independent	Other	Total votes	Republican	Percent	Democrat	Percent	Independent	Percent	Other	Percent	Total votes
Western Region															
Alaska	2002	72,248	32,547	0	2,723	107,518	129,279	55.8	94,216	40.7	0	0.0	7,989	3.5	231,484
Arizona	2002	320,090	234,084	0	3,263	557,437	554,465	45.2	566,284	46.2	84,947	6.9	20,415	1.7	1,255,615
California	2002	2,328,937	2,402,077	56,268	493,473	5,286,204	3,169,801	42.4	3,533,490	47.3	0	0.0	773,020	10.3	7,476,311
Colorado	2002	189,705	98,897		0	288,602	884,583	62.6	475,373	33.7	0	0.0	52,646	3.7	1,412,602
Hawaii	2002	79,871	188,781		1,463	270,115	197,009	51.1	179,647	46.6	0	0.0	8,801	2.3	385,457
Idaho	2002	145,549	38,083		1,106	202,270	231,566	56.3	171,711	41.7	13	0.0	8,187	2.0	416,533
Montana	2004	110,198	94,795	0	0	204,993	205,313	46.0	225,016	50.4	0	0.0	15,817	3.5	456,096
Nevada	2002	117,474	88,974	0	0	206,448	344,001	68.2	110,935	22.0	0	0.0	49,143	9.7	504,079
New Mexico	2002	98,320	168,496	0	0	266,816	189,074	39.0	268,693	55.5	0	0.0	26,466	5.5	484,233
Oregon	2002	357,764	374,246	109,905	16,610	858,525	517,243	40.1	530,708	41.0	213,657	16.5	32,153	2.4	1,293,761
Utah	2004	----(b)----					524,816	57.8	373,670	41.2	0	0.0	8,220	0.9	906,706
Washington	2004	557,106	793,015	0	15,268	1,480,247	1,373,232	48.8	1,373,361	48.8	0	0.0	63,465	2.2	2,883,499
Wyoming	2002	90,685	36,799	0	0	127,484	88,873	47.9	92,662	50.0	0	0.0	3,924	2.1	185,459
Regional total		4,467,947	4,550,794	166,173	533,906	9,856,765	8,409,255	47.0	7,995,766	44.7	298,617	1.7	1,070,246	6.0	17,891,835
Regional total without California		2,139,010	2,148,717	109,905	40,433	4,570,455	5,239,454	50.0	4,462,276	42.8	298,617	2.9	297,226	2.8	10,415,524
U.S. Virgin Islands	2002	3,839	29,267	14,883	1,961	49,950	3,036	6.2	29,006	59.2	15,097	30.8	1,833	3.7	48,972
Puerto Rico	2004	N.A.	N.A.	N.A.	N.A.	N.A.	(e)	(e)	(e)	(e)	(e)	(e)	1,990,372	(e)	1,990,372

Sources: The Council of State Governments' survey of election administration offices, December 2005 and state elections web sites.

Key:
N.A. — Not applicable
(a) Louisiana has an open primary which requires all candidates, regardless of party affiliation, to appear on a single ballot. If a candidate receives over 50 percent of the vote in the primary, he is elected to the office.

If no candidate receives a majority vote, then a single election is held between the two candidates receiving the most votes.
(b) Candidate nominated by convention.
(c) Total includes the Conservative Party. Governor Pataki was the candidate for both parties.
(d) Candidate ran unopposed.
(e) Unavailable.

Table 6.8
VOTER TURNOUT FOR PRESIDENTIAL ELECTIONS BY REGION: 1996, 2000 AND 2004
(In thousands)

State or other jurisdiction	2004 Voting age population (a)	2004 Number registered	2004 Number voting (b)	2000 Voting age population (a)	2000 Number registered	2000 Number voting (b)	1996 Voting age population (a)	1996 Number registered	1996 Number voting (b)
U.S. Total	208,247	170,937	122,501	205,410	156,420	105,587	195,193	132,796	96,414
Eastern Region									
Connecticut	2,574	1,823	1,579	2,499	1,874	1,460	2,300	1,900	750
Delaware	594	554	376	582	505	328	547	(c)	271
Maine	1,042	957	741	968	882	652	934	1,001	606
Massachusetts	4,931	3,973	2,927	4,749	4,009	2,734	4,623	(c)	2,556
New Hampshire	991	856	684	911	857	569	860	755	514
New Jersey	6,669	5,009	3,612	6,245	4,711	3,187	6,124	(c)	3,076
New York	14,206	11,837	7,448	13,805	11,263	6,960	13,564	9,161	6,439
Pennsylvania	9,404	8,367	5,770	9,155	7,782	4,912	9,197	6,806	4,506
Rhode Island	803	709	437	753	655	409	751	603	390
Vermont	490	445	312	460	427	294	430	385	261
Regional total	41,704	34,530	23,886	40,127	32,965	21,505	39,330	20,611	19,369
Midwestern Region									
Illinois	9,519	7,499	5,274	8,983	7,129	4,742	11,431	6,663	4,418
Indiana	4,420	4,163	2,468	4,448	4,001	2,180	4,146	3,500	2,135
Iowa	2,212	2,107	1,522	2,165	1,841	1,314	2,138	1,776	1,252
Kansas	2,038	1,694	1,188	1,983	1,624	1,072	1,823	1,257	1,129
Michigan	7,541	7,164	4,839	7,358	6,861	4,233	7,072	6,677	3,849
Minnesota	3,823	2,977	2,828	3,547	3,265	2,439	3,412	2,730	2,211
Nebraska	1,257	1,160	778	1,234	1,085	697	1,208	1,015	677
North Dakota	487	(d)	316	477	(c)	288	437	(c)	272
Ohio	8,604	7,973	5,426	8,433	7,538	4,702	8,300	6,638	4,534
South Dakota	573	502	395	543	471	316	530	456	324
Wisconsin	4,119	2,957(d)	2,997	3,930	(d)	2,599	3,786	(d)	2,196
Regional total	44,593	38,196	28,031	43,101	33,815	24,582	44,283	30,712	22,997
Southern Region									
Alabama	3,252	2,597	1,883	3,333	2,529	1,666	3,220	2,471	1,534
Arkansas	1,951	1,686	1,055	1,929	1,556	922	1,873	1,369	884
Florida	12,539	10,301	7,610	11,774	8,753	5,963	11,043	8,078	5,444
Georgia	6,080	4,249	3,285	5,893	3,860	2,583	5,396	3,811	2,299
Kentucky	3,012	2,819	1,796	2,993	2,557	1,544	2,928	2,391	1,388
Louisiana	3,249	2,923	1,957	3,255	2,730	1,766	3,137	(c)	1,784
Maryland	3,922	3,070	2,396	3,925	2,715	2,024	3,811	2,577	1,794
Mississippi	2,014	1,865	1,140	2,047	1,740	994	1,961	1,826	894
Missouri	4,297	4,194	2,731	4,105	3,861	2,360	3,902	3,343	2,158
North Carolina	6,453	5,527	3,501	5,797	5,122	2,915	5,800	4,300	2,515
Oklahoma	2,515	2,143	1,464	2,531	2,234	1,234	2,419	1,823	1,206
South Carolina	3,214	2,315	1,618	2,977	2,157	1,386	2,872	1,814	1,203
Tennessee	4,284	3,532	2,437	4,221	3,181	2,076	3,660	3,056	1,894
Texas	16,071	13,098	7,411	14,479	12,365	6,408	13,698	10,541	5,612
Virginia	5,194	4,528	3,195	5,263	3,770	2,790	5,089	3,323	2,417
West Virginia	1,406	1,169	744	1,416	1,068	648	1,414	(c)	636
Regional total	79,453	66,016	44,223	75,938	60,198	37,279	72,223	50,723	33,662
Western Region									
Alaska	460	472	313	436	474	286	410	415	245
Arizona	3,800	2,643	2,038	3,625	2,173	1,532	3,233	2,245	1,404
California	22,075	16,557	12,589	21,461	15,707	11,142	19,526	15,662	10,263
Colorado	3,246	2,890	2,130	3,067	2,274	1,741	2,843	2,285	1,551
Hawaii	873	647	429	909	637	368	882	545	370
Idaho	996	798	613	921	728	502	858	700	492
Montana	680	596	450	668	698	411	647	590	417
Nevada	1,580	1,094	830	1,390	898	609	1,180	778	464
New Mexico	1,318	1,105	756	1,263	973	599	1,224	838	580
Oregon	2,665	2,120	1,837	2,530	1,944	1,534	2,344	1,962	1,399
Utah	1,522	1,278	928	1,465	1,123	771	1,322	1,050	691
Washington	4,596	3,508	2,883	4,368	3,336	2,487	4,122	3,078	2,294
Wyoming	370	246	244	358	220	214	343	241	216
Regional total	44,181	33,954	26,040	42,461	31,185	22,196	38,934	30,389	20,386
Regional total without California	22,106	17,397	13,451	21,000	15,478	11,054	19,408	14,727	10,123
Dist. of Columbia	435	384	228	411	354	202	422	361	186

Sources: 1996 data provided by Committee for the Study of the American Electorate, with update by the state election administration offices. U.S. Congress, Clerk of the House, Statistics of the Presidential and Congressional Election, 2004, U.S. Census Bureau, Current Population Survey, November 2002, released July 2004.

The Council of State Governments' survey of election officials, December 2005. 2000 data provided by the Federal Election Commission.

Key:
(a) Estimated population, 18 years old and over. Includes armed forces in each state, aliens, and institutional population.
(b) Number voting is number of ballots cast in presidential race.
(c) Information not available.
(d) No statewide registration required. Excluded from totals for persons registered.

2006 Ethics Trends and Issues
By David E. Freel

A continuing and leading trend in 2006 in state ethics issues is a fundamental re-examination of the core characteristics embodied within and mechanisms used to implement ethics oversight. In some states, this review emanates from the apparent absence of institutional processes to address public sector conduct widely viewed as unethical. In others, this reassessment of ethics adminis-tration standards, including agency independence and internal operation, accompanies executive and legislative consideration of additional measures for ethics reform. Significantly, all the state efforts appear directed at enhancing rather than diminishing ethics oversight.

Drawing accurate contrasts and identifying significant trends in ethics governance across the states can be challenging. Due to factors described in earlier editions of *The Book of States* by this author, generic comparisons among ethics agencies with different mandates and public policy obligations throughout the country are easily subject to unintended error.[1]

A continuing and leading trend in state ethics issues in 2006, however, is a fundamental re-exami-nation of core characteristics embodied within and mechanisms used to implement ethics oversight. In some states, this review emanates from the apparent absence of existing institutional processes to address public sector conduct widely viewed as unethical. In others, this reassessment of standards of eth-ics administration, including agency independence and internal operation, accompanies executive and legislative consideration of additional ethics reform measures. Significantly, all the state efforts appear directed at enhancing rather than diminishing over-sight. Rarely outcomes of routine or deliberative review of compliance measures, these reform efforts are instead public policy changes forged in the wake of real or perceived state ethics scandals.

Additional ethics trends in 2006 include a shift to mandatory, rather than voluntary, ethics education for public officials, either under statute or execu-tive order; creative and more efficient uses of the Internet in education and online service outreach; a resurgence in nepotism concerns in the public sector; and increased disclosure requirements or outright bans on gifts and gratuities from those with interests before government.

The East Coast Experience

As 2006 began, ethics scandals in New Jersey and Connecticut continue to precipitate several trends, the most significant of which is the fundamental re-examination of the core attributes of state ethics governance. These two states' experiences warrant further analysis, particularly for those who seek to enhance ethics compliance measures. However, they are not alone in their central focus for reform. Sev-eral others—including Tennessee, North Carolina, Wisconsin, Oregon and Michigan—closed 2005 and entered 2006 weighing core ethics administration and the independence and efficacy of ethics processes as integral elements of reform, while also exploring fur-ther accountability measures. These efforts come on the heels of new or restructured ethics governance in other states, including Illinois, Indiana and Nevada.

In New Jersey, the re-examination of key traits of ethics oversight and additional accountability mea-sures arises from public frustration over a series of "dismal ethics lapses," particularly apparent the past three years.[2] These lapses culminated with the resig-nation of former New Jersey Gov. James McGreevey due to ethics breaches in his administration, and the appointment by his successor, Richard J. Codey, of two Special Ethics Counsel in November 2004 to review state ethics oversight. While several cir-cumstances involving misconduct transpired in the absence of existing state regulation,[3] a number of situations involved alleged or since-proven receipt of improper gifts and gratuities by public officials, as well as their abuse of public position.[4]

The two Special Ethics Counsel—a retired New Jersey Supreme Court associate justice and a cur-rent Seton Hall law professor—submitted an exten-sive report March 14, 2005.[5] While the executive summary, and subsequent "Rutgers Law Review" description cited here provide insightful outlines of the report to policymakers, the full report and its citations should be required reading for those seri-ously studying ethics oversight improvements and meaningful public policy change. After conducting the most recent review of significant attributes of existing ethics governance in the country, and while recognizing and addressing ethics concerns prevalent in New Jersey, Special Counsel established 10 essential premises and a number of specific recommendations for ethics reform in New Jersey. The majority of concepts analyzed are germane to ethics review elsewhere.[6]

Significantly, counsel's first direct recommendation was reforming the New Jersey Executive Commission on Ethical Standards into an "entirely independent" State Ethics Commission. The commission would become "responsible for performing *meaningful* routine ethics audits, imposing *stringent* penalties for transgressions, and conducting mandatory ethics training for *all* state officials and employees."[7] The counsel's second recommendation, also significant, vested the commission with "much greater enforcement authority."[8]

New Jersey's existing commission was composed of executive branch employees charged with governance of the executive branch. Before recent changes, the commission had no public members.[9] Special Counsel's review determined that New Jersey did not reflect the national model for state ethics governance and lacked adequate and important authority. As such, New Jersey's commission is one of a handful of ethics agencies viewed as critically limited.[10] Counsel recommended an independent commission, composed of public members, with uniform executive and legislative oversight, and with state and local governance.[11]

Gov. Jon Corzine and the New Jersey legislature will critique the counsel's full recommendations and expansive ethics reform before implementation. Before assuming office, Corzine had formed an Ethics Advisory Group that includes one of the former Special Counsel to recommend ethics changes in 2006.[12] While developments are likely, the New Jersey legislature enacted significant ethics changes in other arenas in 2005. These changes came in the form of extensive "pay to play" legislation, touted as one of the nation's strongest. That legislation prohibits campaign contributions, in some instances, from businesses seeking or holding state contracts.[13]

Codey also issued a series of executive orders to implement portions of the recommendations in Special Counsel's report.[14] Required ethics education for members and employees of independent authorities, boards and commissions by Jan. 1, 2006, is part of the recommendations implemented to date. Funding for the New Jersey Commission to hire an ethics training officer, ethics compliance officer and support personnel was provided in FY06.[15] With a new state administration and more ethics legislation

being considered, trend-setting reform in New Jersey will likely continue.

New Jersey's experience is but one indicator that the independence and strength of ethics oversight continues to be central to state ethics reform. Connecticut also conducted a core examination of ethics principles and oversight structures in 2005, and significantly reorganized state ethics governance. This reform followed the resignation of former Gov. John G. Rowland, in a rare exercise of the legislative impeachment process, and the governor's ultimate criminal plea and incarceration on federal charges for the illegal receipt of gratuities from state contractors.[16]

Connecticut labored to restructure both the independence and mission of its lead ethics agency. Effective July 1, 2005, legislation replaced the Connecticut State Ethics Commission with the Office of State Ethics, containing a nine-member Citizens' Ethics Advisory Board with terms beginning Oct. 1, 2005. One interesting aspect of the transition was that all former State Ethics Commission staff members were transferred "in their current position, with existing funds allocated for such positions, to *other agencies* of the state." From July 1, 2005, to the end of the year, an interim executive director and staff oversaw the transition.[17] The legislature restructured appointments to the Citizens' Advisory Board, dividing them among executive and General Assembly leadership. The legislature also expanded and created divisional responsibilities for enforcement and legal advice within the Office of State Ethics.[18]

With these changes, Connecticut has the unique distinction not only of forcing the resignation of its chief executive for ethical misconduct, but also, in the aftermath, of forcibly dissolving the State Ethics Commission composed of the former governor's appointees and reassigning its staff. Ironically, this same board had earlier terminated its executive director who was responsible for leading the commission's ethics investigation into the former governor's conduct.[19]

Whether Connecticut's restructuring of ethics oversight, and resulting experience in 2006, will serve as a model for other states is yet to be determined. But, like its neighbor, Connecticut also enacted broad ethics changes in late 2005. In fact, Connecticut's ethics scandals led to a comprehensive campaign reform law that will establish full public financing of campaigns for all state offices, and bar campaign contributions from certain state contractors and lobbyists.[20] These significant ethics-related changes could become a model of reform.

Other States Examining Fundamental Ethics Reform

In 2005, in what was dubbed "Operation Tennessee Waltz," five members of the Tennessee General Assembly and campaign operatives were indicted—with several since convicted—for allegedly taking bribes in return for legislative favor. The massive FBI undercover investigation and public corruption sting produced tremendous public outrage and added Tennessee to the list of states examining ethics oversight.

Gov. Phil Bredesen responded to the ethics debacle by forming a 13-member Citizens' Advisory Group on Ethics in Government, co-chaired by a former Tennessee attorney general. The group recommended on Sept. 29, 2005, creation of an "independent ethics commission" in addition to or in lieu of the Tennessee Registry of Elections Finance Commission; the reduction of contribution limits; and stronger regulation of lobbyists.[21] Bredesen called a special legislative session for January 2006, to consider changes in a Comprehensive Governmental Ethics Reform Act proposed by a Special Joint Committee of the General Assembly, which incorporated portions of the Citizens' Advisory Group's recommendations.[22]

Several other states—including North Carolina, Wisconsin, Oregon and Michigan—are reviewing fundamental ethics oversight measures. In North Carolina, the speaker of the House created a 22-member House Select Committee on Ethics and Government Reform in 2005 to examine the governor's ethics proposals, including legislation to create a new ethics agency and lobbyist reporting requirements. North Carolina's ethics governance is a creature of executive order, unlike those in most states. Allegations of undisclosed conflicts of interest by officials administering a newly-created North Carolina Lottery, the extent of ethics governance over lottery officials, and the alleged conduct of two individuals connected to the House speaker involving potential lobbying law violations are central to reform activity.[23]

In response to an ethics scandal that has produced criminal convictions and pending charges against former members of the Wisconsin General Assembly, legislation is moving forward to merge the functions of the state ethics board with those of the state elections board into a new "Government Accountability Board."[24] The ethics scandal in a state not generally known for corruption has fostered the creation of an ethics oversight reform model that asserts a new tenacity in enforcement by incorporating an "Enforcement Division" into the new board. Funding for the division is independent of ordinary budget processes, and the board is given independent

prosecutorial power, after a right of first refusal to existing authorities.[25] As this plan and related legislation move forward, the structure Wisconsin has chosen provides another variation in the model of centralized ethics governance.

At least two other states are revising their ethics structures. In its 2005 session, the Oregon Legislative Assembly appropriated $224,000 to the Oregon Law Commission for a comprehensive review of existing ethics and lobbying laws and development of recommendations for possible legislative action in 2007. The review includes examination of the structure and operation of the Oregon Government Standards and Practices Commission, and consideration of assigning enforcement duties elsewhere.[26] In late 2005, Michigan Gov. Jennifer Granholm proposed significant reform for legislative consideration in 2006. Her proposals involve ethics and campaign finance disclosure law changes that would include new ethics oversight bodies for both the executive and legislative branches, tougher conflict of interest rules and restrictions on accepting gifts.[27]

Mandatory vs. Voluntary Ethics Education

New Jersey Special Counsel's recommendations, and the former governor's 2005 executive order, are examples of a movement by states to require ethics education or training of those in public service. While the majority of states provide voluntary ethics education programs, at least 13 states report some segment of those they regulate are subject to mandatory ethics training.[28]

For example, in 2005, the Hawaii Legislature passed a law requiring the State Ethics Commission to conduct mandatory training for high-ranking state officials, including the governor and lieutenant governor, state legislators and executive department heads and their deputies. These required sessions are repeated each year for those who have not attended the course.[29] In Illinois, with the creation of new state ethics oversight in 2004, mandatory training for elected officials, members of their personal staffs and senior administrative personnel is now required once every four years.[30] These states join Maryland, Massachusetts, Ohio and Texas, among others, in requiring certain officials to undergo training, either as a matter of executive order covering a governor's subordinates, or by statute.

Whether mandatory education will significantly improve the public sector ethics climate in the states, or is even capable of being measured in outcomes related to the actions of public officials, remains to be seen. Assuring citizens that those in public service will act with increased awareness of ethics, and demonstrating a state priority to ethics education, may well be a positive public policy endeavor.

Online and New Information and Education Strategies

Many states report much stronger reliance on information systems, and particularly on new online and Internet strategies, for service and education.[31] The availability of ethics information through Web page access and portals has largely ended arguments that those regulated had no way to learn more about ethics restrictions. Simply entering ethics agency identities in Internet search engines now easily links anyone, in most states, to ethics information, an increasing availability of online filing processes, educational materials and advice.

Delaware, Florida, Massachusetts, Maryland, Pennsylvania and Texas all report significant improvements in online mechanisms for required reporting and filing. Educational materials and model use of technology range from utilizing online modules like those in New Jersey, to quizzes or tests such as the Washington State "Ethics Challenge."[32] Wisconsin Ethics Board, now to be part of the Government Accountability Board, recently received a grant to create online financial disclosure, which follows successful implementation of online lobbying reporting that has been touted as a state model.[33]

Many state and local jurisdictions, such as Connecticut and Chicago, have created "clear language" guides or links easily found on their Web sites. These guides help those doing business with the state to understand and follow ethics restrictions.[34] This trend of innovative uses of the Web and information systems is likely to continue.

Nepotism Concerns

One common subject of ethics concern—issues involving the hiring or employment of a public official's family member—appears to be growing. Ethics agencies throughout the country have reported a resurgence of nepotism-related issues.[35] Oregon's Government Standards and Practices Commission reported an increase of family and public contracting issues in 2005. Louisiana continues to see a number of legislative bills pertaining to family hires, employment or supervision at both the state and local levels.

Massachusetts and Pennsylvania report recent cases involving nepotism and the alleged misuse of public position to benefit family.[36] New Jersey's recommendations for reform include strengthening prohibitions on nepotism.[37] The definition of those who may subject a public official to conflicting interests also appears to be expanding to include domestic partners.[38]

Gifts

The provision, receipt, disclosure and/or outright prohibition of gifts from those doing business with government present continuing ethics questions. Improper gifts from contractors, lobbyists or regulated parties to public officials have resulted in a wide range of scandals. Among the scandals: the criminal prosecutions of former governors of Illinois and Connecticut and senior administration officials in other states, including New Jersey and Kentucky; the conviction of legislators in Tennessee and Wisconsin, among others; and new investigations and indictments of federal lawmakers for allegedly accepting graft or favor.

The acceptance of cash, traditional gifts and other payments—such as exclusive golf outings, home improvements, loans, vacations or tuition—illustrates the ethical quandary to public governance. It also provides dramatic examples of influence-peddling and the weakness of human nature involving those in and around public power. These scandals offer evidence of public outrage at those controlling taxpayer funds, and weakened confidence in the positive and necessary efforts of government.

This level of public discontent and cynicism was noted by New Jersey's Special Ethics Counsel in the 2005 report setting forth reform based on a series of "dismal ethical lapses" that involved illegal or allegedly improper gifts. Notably, however, counsel found that New Jersey was not the only state in which citizens viewed their government as the "most corrupt" in the country.[39]

Federal and state prosecutions in 2005 demonstrate the varying impact that significant and different facts have on the collective judgment of wrongdoing, and the level of impropriety perceived, in gifts to public officials. Ethics restraints were designed to supplement rather than replace criminal bans on bribery and related illegal conduct. Ethics restraints involving gifts and gratuities often differ when the evidence does not explicitly demonstrate some illegal expectation in the source of a gift, or some improper action taken by the public official who accepts it.

Circumstances and public perception can make the demarcation of policy limits on those in government, and their sanctions, at times difficult. Occasionally, these restraints stand in stark contrast to what may be allowed in private employment, although recent reforms in the private sector have narrowed this disparity. Differences in state ethics restraints support the contention that varying ethical standards reflect the unique facts and public appearance of scandal in an individual jurisdiction preceding reform. We continue to be reminded by the adoption of remedies that all politics are local.

In 2005 many states reported significant enforcement issues and cases involving gifts and other things of value in violation of state laws or rules, and as noted, many have become the catalyst for ethics reform in 2006.[40]

In Ohio, a developing scandal involving gifts where quid pro quo was not evidenced involved both ethics prohibitions on the gift and state disclosure requirements. These events took place in the backdrop of an alleged loss of more than $200 million in the state's Bureau of Workers' Compensation (BWC) fund.

In August 2005, Gov. Bob Taft pleaded no contest to four first-degree criminal misdemeanor ethics charges for failing to identify in financial disclosure statements 19 different individuals as sources of 52 gifts totaling approximately $5,800. Notably, the Ohio Ethics Commission, which referred the governor's conduct for criminal prosecution, is composed of independent, but bipartisan, gubernatorial appointees.

The sources not identified in the governor's required filings paid an average of more than $110 for professional hockey and concert tickets and dinners, but primarily for golf with the governor at exclusive Ohio courses. Earlier dismissals of senior administration officials ordered by the governor's office, and criminal ethics charges brought against them for the acceptance and non-reporting of improper gifts, resonated in public and media perceptions of the governor's misconduct. Taft accepted full responsibility, received the maximum statutory fine of $1,000 on each count, and was ordered to apologize, via e-mail, to all state employees and, through the media, to the citizens of Ohio.[41]

Alleged wrongdoing in the BWC investment of public and private workers' compensation premiums into $50 million worth of rare and collectible coins was significant to actions taken against Taft and two former staff members in July 2005. The former staff members' conduct and Taft's activities and resulting charges, came under scrutiny because of alleged actions by Thomas Noe, who managed the coin venture, in the early stages of an ongoing joint task force criminal investigation involving Ohio's Ethics Commission, inspector general, highway patrol, and state and federal prosecutors. While Noe managed the BWC investment, he also served as chairman of two major state boards, the Board of Regents

and Ohio Turnpike Commission, and was a prolific political fundraiser. The revelation that the workers' compensation system had invested in coins became compounded by admissions of Noe's legal counsel that the coin investment was $12 million short.

Noe's alleged unrestricted investment of BWC funds led to questions about whether his expenditures and the source of payment for lavish entertainment could be workers' compensation money. The scrutinized expenditures included golf outings, some not reported by the governor, vacation trips to Key West homes and repeated expensive wining and dining, thousands of dollars in loans to the governor's former staff, and significant political contributions. A federal grand jury also indicted Noe in October 2005 on three counts of allegedly laundering money for President George W. Bush's re-election campaign. Allegedly in order to fulfill a pledge to raise $50,000 for a Bush-Cheney fundraiser, which the former chief of staff helped organize, Noe contributed $45,400 through 24 illegal "conduit" donors. These donors purportedly received money Noe gave them, but reported contributions to the campaign as their own donations. With alleged losses in the coin fund, and more than $200 million lost in other workers' compensation investments, the investigation into alleged misconduct of Noe and others may lead to further reform in Ohio and nationally.

Notably, Florida adopted widespread change in lobbying activities in late 2005, and has enacted reforms that reportedly exclude all gifts from lobbyists. Officials did so "to counter the public image that (legislators') cozy relationships with lobbyists were unseemly."[42] Federal officials also appear poised to address alleged gifts and gratuities from lobbyists.[43]

With ethics questions related to gifts and gratuities in the states and nationally continuing to unfold, there is no doubt that attention to, and reform of, the standards by which they are judged will continue as a leading ethics trend.

Additional Resources

There are additional resources for general assistance to those examining ethics trends. The Council on Governmental Ethics Laws (COGEL) conducts annual surveys on ethics, lobbying, campaign finance, public records and electronic filing. COGEL's membership includes those responsible for ethics administration in all three branches of government at the national, state, provincial and local level in the United States and Canada, as well as a growing number of other countries. It includes professionals, academics and individuals practicing or interested in ethics. The *COGEL Blue Book Ethics Updates* have been repeatedly cited, and the 2005 charts have been used here. The surveys summarize the authority and responsibility—as well as advisory, enforcement, litigative and legislative developments—of states and other jurisdictions.[44] Information is also available through The Council of State Governments, National Association of State Legislatures and Ethics Resource Center.

Notes

[1] David E. Freel, "Trends and Issues in State Ethics Agencies," *The Book of the States 2005*, (Lexington, KY: The Council of State Governments, 2005).

[2] Paula A. Franzese & Daniel J. O'Hern Sr., "Restoring the Public Trust: An Agenda for Ethics Reform of State Government and a Proposed Model for New Jersey," *Rutgers Law Review*, Vol. 57, No. 4, Summer 2005, 1175.

[3] Ibid., 1181.

[4] Ibid., 1181–83, notes 16–22 describe several of the "ethics transgressions" initiating ethics reform.

[5] Daniel O'Hern Sr. & Paula A. Franzese, Report of the Special Ethics Counsel to the Governor of the State of New Jersey, Ethics Reform Recommendations for the Executive Branch of New Jersey Government, March 14, 2005, *http://www.state.nj.us/ethics_report.pdf*.

[6] See note 2 above.

[7] Ibid., 1179, 1184–86.

[8] Ibid., 1186–89.

[9] The New Jersey Commission will add two public members in January of 2006, with four executive branch members and four public members, *COGEL Blue Book 2005 Ethics Update* (Council on Governmental Ethics Laws, 2005), 211; also see *COGEL Blue Book 2005 Ethics Update Charts* at end of this article.

[10] See note 2 above, 1185–89.

[11] Pending New Jersey legislation addresses portions of the Report's challenges, see *http://www.state.nj.us/lps/ethics/holiday2005.pdf*.

[12] *http://nj.gov/govelect/news/approved/051130.html*.

[13] *http://www.state.nj.us/cgi-bin/governor/njnewsline/view_article.pl?id=2427*; see also *http://www.commoncause.org/site/pp.asp?c=dkLNK1MQIwG&b=192884*.

[14] "The Time Is Now: Seizing the Opportunity to Advance the Cause of Ethics Reform," *Newark Star Ledger*, November 10, 2005; one of these Executive Orders received significant attention at the end of 2005 for imposing a bar on the presidents and governing boards of state colleges and universities from doing business with their institutions, see *http://www.dailytargum.com/media/paper168/news/2005/12/08/PageOne/Rcga-Demands.Zoffinger.Resign-1124800.shtml?norewrite&sourcedomain=www.dailytargum.com*.

[15] *http://www.state.nj.us/lps/ethics/holiday2005.pdf*.

[16] *http://www.courant.com/news/politics/hc-ap-ellef-tomasso-1220,0,7060867.story?coll=hc-headlines-politics-state*.

[17] *http://www.ct.gov/ethics/site/default.asp*; *http://www.ct.gov/governorrell/cwp/view.asp?Q=304048&A=1761*; *http://www.ct.gov/ethics/cwp/view.asp?a=2313&q=301954*.

[18] *http://www.ct.gov/ethics/cwp/view.asp?a=2306&q=301614*; *http://www.ct.gov/ethics/cwp/view.asp?a=2313&q=301954*.

[19] *http://select.nytimes.com/gst/abstract.html?res=FB0B16F6355D0C768EDDA00894DC404482&n=Top%2fRefer ence%2fTimes%20Topics%2fPeople%2fR%2fRowland%2c%20John%20G%2e*.

[20] *http://www.ct.gov/seec/cwp/view.asp?Q=308026&A=2357*.

[21] *http://tennessean.com/assets/pdf/DN12280119.pdf* and *http://www.tennessean.com/apps/pbcs.dll/article?AID=/20050930/NEWS0201/509300408&theme=arrest*.

[22] *http://www.state.tn.us/governor/viewArticleContent.do?id=693*.

[23] *http://www.myrtlebeachonline.com/mld/myrtlebeachonline/news/breaking_news/13304979.htm*.

[24] *http://www.legis.state.wi.us/2005/data/SB-1.pdf*.

[25] *http://badgerherald.com/news/2005/11/02/senate_approves_pane.php*. *http://www.thenorthwestern.com/apps/pbcs.dll/article?AID=/20051223/OSH06/512230419/1189*.

[26] *Council on Governmental Ethics Law (COGEL) Blue Book 2005 Ethics Update*, 257; see also *http://www.gazettetimes.com/articles/2005/10/04/news/oregon/tueore02.txt*.

[27] *http://www.detnews.com/apps/pbcs.dll/article?AID=/20051219/OPINION01/512190307/1007/METRO*; see also *http://www.michigan.gov/gov/0,1607,7-168--132111--,00.html*.

[28] *Council on Governmental Ethics Law (COGEL) Blue Book 2005 Ethics Update*; see accompanying Chart #3 at the end of this article that shows the majority of states have voluntary education, although 13 report some form of mandatory education, and required education is more prevalent in local ethics agencies, generally founded later.

[29] Ibid., 97.

[30] See note 2 above, 1191.

[31] *Council on Governmental Ethics Law (COGEL) Blue Book 2005 Ethics Update*.

[32] Ibid., 221 and 320.

[33] *http://wistechnology.com/article.php?id=1828*.

[34] *http://www.ct.gov/ethics/cwp/view.asp?a=2313&Q=301720&ethicsNav=/*.

[35] *Council on Governmental Ethics Law (COGEL) Blue Book 2005 Ethics Update*, note the comments of the Oregon Government Standards and Practices Commission, 257.

[36] Ibid., 176–81 and 261.

[37] See note 2 above, 1212.

[38] *Council on Governmental Ethics Law (COGEL) Blue Book 2005 Ethics Update*, see recent New York City Conflict of Interest Board Advisory Opinion 2004–3, 220.

[39] See note 2 above, 1183–84.

[40] *Council on Governmental Ethics Law (COGEL) Blue Book 2005 Ethics Update*.

[41] Ibid., 243–44; see also, Toledo Blade series at, *http://www.toledoblade.com/apps/pbcs.dll/section?Category=SRRARECOINS2*.

[42] *http://www.tallahassee.com/apps/pbcs.dll/article?AID=/20051209/NEWS02/512090347/1010/NEWS01*.

[43] Of note in Ohio, after a referral for criminal prosecution by the Ohio Ethics Commission, former Ohio Police and Fire Pension Fund Trustee David Harker plead guilty on June 21, 2005, to misdemeanor ethics counts alleging unlawful acceptance of meals, drinks, golf outings, and other entertainment, that also included a trip worth several thousand dollars to play golf in Scotland, from investment companies

employed by the fund. Harker was also convicted of failing to disclose these on annual financial disclosures filed with the Ethics Commission, see *Council on Governmental Ethics Law (COGEL) Blue Book 2005 Ethics Update*, 244.

[44] They are available on searchable CD, and include in the identification of the issue or development those questions that the ethics agency itself classifies as the year's most significant. Survey updates are available to members and to others at a relatively modest cost through COGEL's Web site at *www.cogel.org*.

About the Author

David Freel has been the executive director of the Ohio Ethics Commission since 1994. Before joining the Ethics Commission staff, he was a faculty member of the Ohio State University College of Law. Freel has written articles on Ohio's Ethics Law and given ethics presentations at seminars and conferences in the United States and Canada. He is a past president of the Council on Governmental Ethics Laws (COGEL) and was honored with the COGEL Service Award in 2002.

Table A
ETHICS AGENCIES: JURISDICTION

State or other jurisdiction	Agency	Executive branch employees	Judges	Judicial employees	Legislative employees	Legislators	Lobbyists	Local appointed officials	Local elected officials	Local employees	Private sector/vendors	State appointed officials	State elected officials	State employees	State colleges & universities
Alabama	Ethics Comm.	Y	Y	Y	Y	Y	Y	Y	Y	Y	Y	Y	Y	Y	Y
Alaska	Legisltv. Ethics Cmte.;	N	N	N	Y	Y	N	N	N	N	N	N	N	N	N
	Public Ofcs. Comm.	Y	N	N	Y	Y	Y	Y	Y	Y	Y	Y	N	N	Y
Arizona	Citizens Clean Elections Comm.	N	N	N	N	Y	N	N	N	N	Y	N	Y	N	N
Arkansas	Ethics Comm.	Y	Y	Y	Y	Y	Y	Y	Y	Y	N	Y	Y	Y	Y
California	Fair Political Practices Comm.;	Y	Y	Y	Y	Y	Y	Y	Y	Y	N	Y	Y	Y	Y
	L.A. Co. Metro. Transit Authority;	N	N	N	N	N	Y	Y	N	Y	Y	N	N	N	N
	L.A. Ethics Comm.;	Y	N	N	Y	Y	Y	Y	Y	Y	Y	N	N	N	N
	Oakland Public Ethics Comm.;	N	N	N	N	N	N	Y	N	Y	Y	N	N	Y	N
	San Diego Ethics Comm.;	N	N	N	N	N	Y	Y	Y	Y	Y	N	N	Y	N
	San Francisco Ethics Comm.	N	N	N	N	N	Y	Y	Y	Y	Y	N	N	N	N
Colorado	Denver Bd. of Ethics	N	N	N	N	N	N	Y	Y	Y	N	N	N	N	N
Connecticut	Freedom of Info. Comm.;	Y	Y	Y	Y	Y	Y	Y	Y	Y	Y	Y	N	Y	Y
	Ofc. of State Ethics	Y	N	Y	Y	Y	Y	N	N	N	Y	Y	Y	Y	Y
Delaware	New Castle Co. Ethics Comm.;	N	N	N	N	N	N	Y	Y	Y	N	N	N	N	N
	Public Integrity Comm.	Y	Y	Y	Y	Y	Y	Y	Y	Y	N	Y	Y	Y	Y
Florida	City of Jacksonville;	Y	N	N	Y	Y	Y	Y	Y	Y	Y	N	N	N	N
	City of Tampa;	Y	N	N	Y	N	Y	Y	Y	Y	Y	N	N	N	N
	Comm. on Ethics;	Y	N	Y	Y	Y	Y	Y	Y	Y	N	Y	Y	Y	Y
	Elections Comm.	N	N	N	N	N	N	Y	N	N	N	N	N	N	N
Georgia	Atlanta Bd. of Ethics;	Y	Y	Y	Y	N	Y	Y	Y	Y	Y	N	N	N	N
	State Ethics Comm.	N	Y	N	N	Y	Y	N	Y	N	Y	Y	Y	N	N
Hawaii	Campaign Spending Comm.;	N	N	N	N	N	N	Y	N	Y	N	N	Y	N	N
	Honolulu Ethics Comm.;	Y	N	N	N	N	N	Y	Y	Y	N	N	N	N	N
	Maui Co. Bd. of Ethics;	N	N	N	N	N	N	N	N	Y	N	N	N	N	N
	State Ethics Comm.	Y	N	Y	Y	Y	Y	N	N	N	N	Y	Y	Y	Y
Idaho	Secretary of State	N	N	N	N	Y	Y	N	N	N	N	N	N	N	N
Illinois	Chicago Bd. of Ethics;	Y	N	N	N	N	Y	Y	Y	Y	Y	N	N	N	N
	City of Champaign;	N	N	N	N	N	N	Y	N	N	Y	N	N	N	N
	Cook Co. Bd. of Ethics	N	N	N	N	N	Y	Y	Y	Y	N	N	N	N	N
Indiana	Public Access Counselor's Ofc.;	Y	Y	Y	Y	Y	Y	Y	Y	Y	Y	Y	N	Y	Y
	State Ethics Comm.	Y	N	N	N	Y	N	N	N	N	N	Y	Y	Y	N
Iowa	Ethics & Campaign Discl. Bd.	Y	N	N	N	Y	Y	N	N	N	N	Y	N	Y	Y
Kansas	Govtl. Ethics Comm.	Y	N	N	Y	Y	Y	Y	Y	Y	Y	Y	Y	Y	Y
Kentucky	Exec. Branch Ethics Comm.;	Y	N	Y	Y	N	N	N	N	N	Y	Y	Y	Y	N
	Legisltv. Ethics Comm.	N	N	N	N	Y	Y	N	N	N	N	N	N	N	N
Louisiana	Ethics Admin.	Y	N	Y	Y	Y	Y	Y	Y	Y	Y	Y	Y	Y	Y
Maine	Comm. on Govtl. Ethics & Election Practices	N	Y	Y	N	N	N	Y	N	N	Y	N	N	N	N
Maryland	Anne Arundel Co. Ethics Comm.;	Y	N	N	Y	Y	Y	Y	Y	Y	N	N	N	N	N
	Montgomery Co. Ethics Comm.;	Y	N	N	Y	Y	Y	Y	Y	Y	N	N	N	N	N
	State Ethics Comm.	Y	N	Y	N	N	Y	N	N	N	Y	Y	Y	Y	Y
Massachusetts	State Ethics Comm.	Y	Y	Y	Y	Y	Y	Y	Y	Y	Y	Y	Y	Y	Y
Michigan	Dept. of State;	N	Y	N	N	Y	Y	N	Y	Y	Y	Y	Y	N	N
	State Bd. of Ethics	Y	N	N	N	N	N	N	N	Y	N	Y	Y	N	N
Minnesota	Camp. Finance & Public Discl. Bd.	Y	Y	N	Y	Y	Y	Y	Y	Y	N	N	N	N	N
Mississippi	Ethics Comm.	N	N	N	N	N	N	N	N	N	N	N	N	N	N
Missouri	Ethics Comm.	Y	Y	Y	N	Y	Y	Y	Y	Y	N	Y	Y	Y	Y
Montana	Commr. of Political Practices	Y	Y	Y	Y	Y	Y	N	Y	N	N	Y	Y	Y	N
Nebraska	Accountability & Discl. Comm.	Y	N	N	Y	Y	Y	Y	Y	Y	Y	Y	Y	Y	Y
Nevada	Comm. on Ethics	Y	N	N	Y	N	Y	N	Y	Y	Y	Y	Y	Y	Y
New Hampshire	Attorney General's Ofc.	Y	N	N	Y	Y	N	N	N	N	N	Y	Y	Y	Y
New Jersey	Exec. Comm. on Ethical Stds.;	Y	N	N	N	N	N	N	N	N	N	N	N	Y	Y
	Jt. Leg. Cmte. on Ethical Stds.	N	N	N	Y	Y	N	N	N	N	N	N	N	N	N
New Mexico	Secretary of State, Bureau of Elections & Ethics Administration	Y	Y	Y	Y	Y	Y	Y	N	N	N	Y	N	N	N
New York	Buffalo Bd. of Ethics;	N	N	N	N	N	N	Y	N	Y	Y	N	N	Y	N
	NYC Conflicts of Interest Bd.;	N	N	N	N	N	N	Y	Y	Y	N	N	N	N	N
	State Ethics Comm.;	Y	N	N	N	N	N	N	N	N	N	Y	Y	Y	Y
	Suffolk Co. Camp. Finance Bd.;	N	N	N	N	N	N	N	Y	N	N	N	N	N	N
	Temp. State Comm. on Lobbying	N	N	N	N	N	Y	N	N	N	Y	N	N	N	N

See footnotes at end of table.

ETHICS AGENCIES: JURISDICTION — Continued

State or other jurisdiction	Agency	Executive branch employees	Judges	Judicial employees	Legislative employees	Legislators	Lobbyists	Local appointed officials	Local elected officials	Local employees	Private sector/vendors	State appointed officials	State elected officials	State employees	State colleges & universities
North Carolina	Bd. of Ethics	Y	N	N	N	N	N	N	N	N	N	N	N	N	N
North Dakota	Secretary of State	N	N	N	N	N	N	N	N	N	N	N	N	N	N
Ohio	Ethics Comm.;	Y	N	N	N	N	N	Y	Y	Y	Y	Y	Y	Y	Y
	Legisltv. Insp. Gen. Ofc.	N	N	N	Y	Y	Y	N	N	N	N	N	N	N	N
Oklahoma	Ethics Comm.	Y	Y	Y	Y	Y	Y	N	Y	Y	Y	Y	Y	Y	Y
Oregon	Govt. Standards & Practices Comm.	Y	Y	Y	Y	Y	Y	Y	Y	Y	Y	Y	Y	Y	Y
Pennsylvania	Ethics Comm.	Y	N	N	Y	Y	N	Y	Y	Y	N	Y	Y	Y	Y
Rhode Island	Ethics Comm.	Y	Y	Y	Y	Y	N	Y	Y	Y	Y	Y	Y	Y	Y
South Carolina	House Legisltv. Ethics Cmte.	N	N	N	N	N	N	N	N	N	Y	N	N	N	N
South Dakota	Secretary of State	N	N	N	N	N	N	N	N	N	N	N	N	N	N
Tennessee	....N.A..
Texas	Ethics Comm.;	Y	Y	Y	Y	Y	Y	N	N	N	Y	Y	N	N	Y
	San Antonio City Attorney's Ofc.;	N	N	N	N	N	Y	N	Y	Y	Y	N	N	N	N
	Univ. of Texas System, Ofc. of Gen. Counsel	Y	N	N	N	N	N	N	N	N	N	N	N	N	N
Utah	State Elections Ofc.	N	Y	Y	Y	Y	Y	N	N	N	Y	Y	N	N	N
Vermont	....N.A..
Virginia	State Bd. of Elections	N	Y	N	N	Y	N	Y	N	N	Y	N	N	N	N
Washington	Seattle Ethics & Elections Comm.;	N	N	Y	N	N	N	N	Y	Y	Y	N	N	N	N
	King Co. Bd. of Ethics;	Y	N	N	Y	N	N	Y	Y	Y	N	N	N	N	N
	King Co. Ofc. of Citizen Complaints;	N	N	Y	Y	N	N	Y	N	Y	Y	N	N	Y	N
	State Comm. on Judicial Conduct;	N	Y	Y	N	N	N	N	N	N	N	N	N	N	N
	State Exec. Ethics Bd.;	Y	N	N	N	N	N	N	N	N	N	Y	Y	Y	Y
	State Legisltv. Ethics Bd.;	N	N	N	Y	N	N	N	N	N	N	N	N	N	N
	State Public Discl. Comm.	N	Y	N	N	Y	Y	N	Y	Y	N	Y	Y	N	Y
West Virginia	Ethics Comm.	Y	Y	Y	Y	Y	Y	Y	Y	Y	Y	Y	Y	Y	Y
Wisconsin	Ethics Bd.	Y	Y	N	Y	Y	Y	N	N	N	N	Y	Y	Y	Y
Wyoming	....N.A..
Guam	Ethics Comm.	N	N	N	N	N	N	N	N	N	Y	N	N	N	N
Puerto Rico	Ofc. of Govt. Ethics	Y	N	N	N	N	N	Y	Y	Y	N	Y	Y	Y	Y
U.S. Virgin Islands	Dept. of Justice	N	N	N	N	N	N	N	N	N	Y	N	N	N	N

Source: The Council on Governmental Ethics Laws (COGEL) Blue Book 2005 Ethics Update.

Key:
Y — Yes
N — No
N.A. — Not available.

Table B
ETHICS AGENCIES: ADVISORY OPINIONS, INVESTIGATIONS & TRAINING

State or other jurisdiction	Agency	Advisory opinions			Investigations					Agency conducts training	Training		
		Authority to issue	Binding on requestor	Number per year	Authority to investigate				Number per year		Optional or required	Estimated number per year	Training methods
					On own initiative	For reimbursement	Anonymous complaints	Respond to complaint					
Alabama	State Ethics Comm.	Y	N	28	Y	Y	N	Y	277	Y	O	29	C
Alaska	Legislv. Ethics Cmte.;	Y	Y	3–5	Y	N	Y	Y	4–6	Y	O	2	C
	Public Ofcs. Comm.	Y	Y	5–25	Y	Y	Y	Y	5–30	Y	O	5–25	C, T, V, VT, CD, W
Arizona	Citizens Clean Elections Comm.	N	Y	2–3	Y	Y	N	Y	25	Y	R	30	C, CD, W
Arkansas	Ethics Comm.	Y	N	13	Y	N	N	Y	93	Y	O	12	C
California	Fair Political Practices Comm.;	Y	N	200–300	Y	Y	Y	Y	839	Y	B	52	C, W
	L.A. Co. Metro. Transit Authority;	Y	N	150	Y	Y	Y	Y	150	Y	B	52+	C, VT, CD
	L.A. Ethics Comm.;	Y	Y	12–15	Y	Y	Y	Y	150	Y	B	35–40	C
	Oakland Public Ethics Comm.;	Y	N	1–2	Y	Y	Y	Y	30–40	N	B	4	…
	San Diego Ethics Comm.;	Y	N	10	N	Y	Y	Y	55	Y	R	10–15	C, VT, CD, W
	San Francisco Ethics Comm.	Y	N	N.A.	Y	N	Y	Y	38	Y	O	20	…
Colorado	Denver Bd. of Ethics	Y	N	approx. 45	N	Y	N	Y	16 (a)	Y	R	500	C
Connecticut	Freedom of Info. Comm.;	Y	Y	700	Y	Y	Y	Y	N.A.	Y	O	70	C, T, V, VT, CD, W
	Ofc. of State Ethics	Y	Y	30	Y	Y	Y	Y	75	Y	B	35	C
Delaware	New Castle Co. Ethics Comm.;	Y	Y	21	Y	Y	Y	Y	2	Y	R	20	…
	Public Integrity Comm.	Y	N	60	Y	N	Y	Y	3–7	Y	O	15–20	C, VT
Florida	City of Jacksonville;	Y	N	0	Y	N	Y	Y	0	Y	R	30	C, T, VT, W
	City of Tampa;	Y	N	0	Y	N	Y	Y	0	Y	R	N.A.	…
	Comm. on Ethics;	Y	Y	23 (b)	N	Y	N	Y	150 (b)	Y	O	30	C, W
Georgia	Elections Comm.;	N	N	…	N	N	Y	Y	300 (g)	N	…	…	…
	Atlanta Bd. of Ethics;	Y	N	7	N	Y	Y	Y	6	N	O	18	C
	State Ethics Comm.	Y	N	1	Y	N	N	Y	100	Y	O	44	C
Hawaii	Campaign Spending Comm.;	Y	Y	12	Y	Y	Y	Y	20	Y	N.A.	5	C, T
	Honolulu Ethics Comm.;	N	N	5–10	Y	N	N	Y	20–30	Y	B	30	C, VT
	Maui Co. Bd. of Ethics;	Y	Y	10	N	N	N	Y	3	Y	N.A.	1	C, CD
	State Ethics Comm.	Y	Y	1–5	Y	N	Y	Y	10–20	Y	B	30–60	C, V
Idaho	Secretary of State	N	N	…	Y	N	N	N	…	N	N.A.	…	…
Illinois	Chicago Bd. of Ethics;	Y	N	30	Y	Y	Y	Y	25	Y	B	70	C, VT, W
	City of Champaign;	Y	N	20	N	N	Y	N	N.A.	N	O	1	C, T, V, VT, CD, W
	Cook Co. Bd. of Ethics	Y	N	15	Y	N	Y	Y	6	N	R	40	C
Indiana	Public Access Counselor's Ofc.;	Y	N	64	N	Y	Y	Y	N.A.	Y	O	29	C, T, V, VT, CD, W
	State Ethics Comm.	Y	N	15	Y	N	Y	Y	100	Y	R	35	C, VT, CD, W
Iowa	Ethics & Campaign Discl. Bd.	Y	N	12	Y	Y	Y	N	10	Y	N.A.	5	C, W
Kansas	Govtl. Ethics Comm.	Y	Y	25–30	Y	Y	Y	Y	5–10	Y	O	35–40	C
Kentucky	Exec. Branch Ethics Comm.;	Y	Y	50	Y	Y	Y	Y	34	Y	O	38	C
	Legislv. Ethics Comm.	Y	Y	5 formal	Y	N	N	Y	5–7	Y	B	2–4	C, VT
Louisiana	Ethics Admin.	Y	Y	390	Y	N	N	Y	165	Y	N.A.	68	C
Maine	Comm. on Govtl. Ethics & Election Practices	Y	Y	<6	Y	Y	Y	Y	<10	Y	R	(c)	…
Maryland	Anne Arundel Co. Ethics Comm.;	Y	Y	75+/-	Y	N	Y	Y	5–15	Y	O	10–15	C
	Montgomery Co. Ethics Comm.;	Y	Y	10+	Y	Y	Y	Y	4	N	O	N.A.	W
	State Ethics Comm.	Y	Y	3–5	Y	Y	Y	Y	about 100	Y	R	15	C

See footnotes at end of table.

ETHICS AGENCIES: ADVISORY OPINIONS, INVESTIGATIONS & TRAINING—Continued

State or other jurisdiction	Agency	Advisory opinions — Authority to issue	Binding on requestor	Number per year	Investigations — Authority to investigate — On own initiative	For reimbursement	Anonymous complaints	Respond to complaint	Number per year	Agency conducts training	Training — Optional or required	Estimated number per year	Training methods
Massachusetts	State Ethics Comm.	Y	Y	3 (d)	Y	Y	Y	Y	62 (e)	Y	B	101 (e)	C, CD
Michigan	Dept. of State;	Y	N	...	Y	Y	N	N	...	Y	O	6	...
	State Bd. of Ethics	Y	N	1–2	Y	N	N	N	0	N	...	...	...
Minnesota	Camp. Finance & Public Discl. Bd.	Y	N	10	N	Y	N	Y	2	N	...	...	...
Mississippi	Ethics Comm.	Y	N	...	N	Y	N	N	N.A.	N	...	...	...
Missouri	Ethics Comm.	Y	N	15	Y	N	Y	Y	180	Y	N.A.	25	...
Montana	Commr. of Political Practices	Y	N	50	N	N	N	Y	15–20	N	O	2	C
Nebraska	Accountability & Discl. Comm.	Y	N	9	Y	N	N	Y	30	Y	O	8	C
Nevada	Comm. on Ethics	Y	Y	20	Y	N	N	Y	100	Y	O	25	C
New Hampshire	Attorney General's Ofc.	N	N	...	Y	N	Y	Y	10+/-	Y	O	3–5	C
New Jersey	Exec. Comm. on Ethical Stds.;	Y	N	20	Y	N	N	Y	50	Y	B	50–60 (f)	C, CD, W
	Jt. Leg. Cmte. on Ethical Stds.	Y	N	varies	Y	N	Y	Y	varies	N	R	N.A.	W
New Mexico	Secretary of State, Bureau of Elections & Ethics Administration	N	N	...	Y	N	N	Y	10	Y	N.A.	3	C, VT, W
New York	Buffalo Bd. of Ethics;	Y	N	0	Y	Y	Y	Y	1–2	N	...	0	...
	NYC Conflicts of Interest Bd.;	Y	Y	470 (a)	Y	N	Y	Y	93 (a)	Y	O	288 (a)	C, VT, W
	State Ethics Comm.;	Y	Y	5–10	Y	Y	Y	Y	60+	Y	O	65	C, VT, W
	Suffolk Co. Camp. Finance Bd.;	Y	N	0	Y	N	N	Y	0	Y	O	2	...
	Temp. State Comm. on Lobbying	Y	Y	5–10	Y	N	N	Y	50	Y	N.A.	6	C, T, W
North Carolina	Bd. of Ethics	Y	N	10–15	Y	Y	Y	Y	5–10	Y	O	100+	...
North Dakota				N.A.			N.A.						
Ohio	Ethics Comm.;	Y	Y	162	Y	Y	Y	Y	100	Y	B	161	C
	Legisltv. Insp. Gen. Ofc.	Y	N	N.A.	Y	N	Y	Y	4	Y	N.A.	7	C, T
Oklahoma	Ethics Comm.	Y	Y	5–7	Y	N	Y	Y	over 10	Y	O	over 10	C, W
Oregon	Govt. Standards & Practices Comm.	Y	Y	25–30	Y	N	N	Y	50–100	Y	O	20–30	C
Pennsylvania	Ethics Comm.	Y	N	125–200	Y	Y	Y	Y	100	Y	O	50	C, VT, CD
Rhode Island	Ethics Comm.	Y	N	120	Y	Y	Y	N	30	Y	O	25	C, W
South Carolina	House Legisltv. Ethics Cmte.	Y	Y	2	N	Y	N	Y	3	Y	N.A.	1	...
South Dakota	Secretary of State	N	N	...	N	N	N.A.	N	0	Y	O	10	...
Tennessee	Ethics Comm.;	Y	Y	10	Y	Y	Y	Y	76	Y	B	40	C
Texas	San Antonio City Attorney's Ofc.;	Y	N	20	Y	N	N	Y	1–3	Y	B	30	C
	Univ. of Texas System, Ofc. of Gen. Counsel	N	N	...	Y	Y	Y	N	...	Y	R	N.A.	C, W
Utah	State Elections Ofc.	Y	N	3	Y	Y	Y	N	3	N	...	...	...
Vermont							N.A.						
Virginia													C, T, V, VT, CD, W
Washington	Seattle Ethics & Elections Comm.;	Y	Y	30	Y	Y	Y	Y	75	Y	O	25	C
	King Co. Bd. of Ethics;	Y	N	varies	Y	N	Y	Y	various	Y	B	94 (a)	C, VT
	King Co. Ofc. Of Citizen Complaints	N	N	...	Y	Y	Y	Y	10–20	Y	N.A.	3–5	C, T, V, VT, CD, W

See footnotes at end of table.

ETHICS AGENCIES: ADVISORY OPINIONS, INVESTIGATIONS & TRAINING—Continued

State or other jurisdiction	Agency	Advisory opinions			Investigations — Authority to investigate					Training			
		Authority to issue	Binding on requestor	Number per year	On own initiative	For reimbursement	Anonymous complaints	Respond to complaint	Number per year	Agency conducts training	Optional or required	Estimated number per year	Training methods
West Virginia.........							N.A.						
Wisconsin..........							N.A.						
Wyoming..........							N.A.						
Guam	Ethics Comm.	Y	N	...	N	Y	Y	N	N.A.	N	...	...	
Puerto Rico.........	Ofc. of Govt. Ethics	Y	Y	1,738	Y	Y	Y	Y	500	Y	R	400	C, T, V, VT, CD
U.S. Virgin Islands.......							N.A.						

Source: The Council on Governmental Ethics Laws (COGEL) Blue Book 2005 Ethics Update.

(a) In 2004.
(b) Three-year average.
(c) One biennially for new Legislature.
(d) Three formal advisory opinions in FY 05.
(e) In Fiscal Year 2005.
(f) In 2005.
(g) Estimated.

Key:
Y — Yes
N — No
B — Both
O — Optional
R — Required
N.A. — Not available
... — None

C — Classroom
T — Teleconference
V — Videoconference
VT — Video tape
CD — CDRom
W — Web-based

Table C
ETHICS AGENCIES: PERSONAL FINANCIAL DISCLOSURE STATEMENTS

State or other jurisdiction	Agency	Who must file with agency							Other	Number filed per year	File via web	File other electronic	FDS available via web site	Reviews or audits conducted	Reviews or audits available electronically
		Agency heads	Board or commission members	Judges	Legislators	Candidates for legislature	State elected officials	Candidates for statewide office							
Alabama	Ethics Comm.	Y	Y	Y	Y	Y	Y	Y	(a)(h)	31,749	N	N	Y	N	N
Alaska	Public Ofcs. Comm.	Y	Y	Y	Y	Y	Y	Y	(c)	2,000	Y	N	N	N	N
Arizona	Citizens Clean Elections Comm.	N	N	N	Y	Y	Y	Y	(z)	6	Y	Y	N	Y	N
Arkansas	Ethics Comm.			····(f)····			Y	Y		240 (f)	Y	N	N	Y	N
California	Fair Political Practices Comm.;	Y	Y	Y	Y	N	Y	Y	(a)	21,000	N	N	N	Y	N
	L.A. Co. Metro. Transit Authority;	Y	Y	N	N	N	N	N	(pp)	1,200	N	N	N	Y	N
	L.A. Ethics Comm.;	Y	Y	N	Y	Y	N	N	(c)(aa)	6,000	Y	Y	N	Y	N
	Oakland Public Ethics Comm.;	Y	Y	N	N	N	N	N	(c)(z)(bb)	750	Y	Y	N	Y	N
	San Diego Ethics Comm.;	Y	Y	N	N	N	N	N	(c)(z)	2,000	Y	Y	N	Y	N
	San Francisco Ethics Comm.	Y	Y	N	N	N	N	N	(gg)(kk)	650	Y	N	N	Y	N
Colorado	Denver Bd. of Ethics	N	N	N	N	N	N	n	(zz)	N.A.	Y	N	N	N	N
Connecticut	Freedom of Info. Comm.;	N	N	N	N	N	N	N	(zz)	N.A.	Y	N	N	N	N
	Ofc. of State Ethics	Y	Y	N	N	N	N	N	(i)(zz)	1,500	Y	Y	Y	Y	N
Delaware	New Castle Co. Ethics Comm.;	Y	N	N	N	N	N	N	(b)(mm)	300	N	N	N	Y	N
	Public Integrity Comm.	Y	Y	Y	Y	Y	Y	Y	(j)(zz)	300+	N	N	Y	Y	N
Florida	City of Jacksonville;	Y	Y	N	N	N	N	N	(a)(aaa)	250	N	N	N	N	N
	City of Tampa;	Y	Y	N	N	N	N	N	(c)	150	N	N	N	Y	N
	Comm. on Ethics	Y	N	Y	Y	Y	Y	N	(k)(zz)	30,000	Y	N	Y	Y	N
Georgia	Atlanta Bd. of Ethics;	Y	Y	N	N	N	N	N	(d)(yy)	1,250	Y	Y	Y	Y	N
	State Ethics Comm.	Y	Y	N	Y	Y	Y	Y	(a)(u)	7,000	Y	Y	Y	Y	N
Hawaii	Campaign Spending Comm.;	N	N	N	N	N	N	N	(ddd)	N.A.	Y	Y	Y	Y	N
	State Ethics Comm.;	Y	Y	N	Y	Y	Y	Y	(a)(v)	1,800+	Y	Y	Y	Y	N
	Honolulu Ethics Comm.;	Y	Y	N	N	N	N	N	(b)	575	N	N	N	Y	N
	Maui Co. Bd. of Ethics	Y	Y	N	N	N	N	N		100	Y	N	Y	Y	N
Idaho	Secretary of State	N	N	N	N	N	N	N	(ll)	1,090	Y	Y	N	N	N
Illinois	Chicago Bd. of Ethics;	Y	Y	N	N	N	N	N	(c)(ll)	9,300	Y	N	N	Y	N
	City of Champaign	N	N	N	N	N	N	N	(zz)	N.A.	N	N	N	Y	N
Indiana	Public Access Counselor's Ofc.;	N	N	N	N	N	N	N	(zz)	N.A.	Y	Y	Y	Y	N
	State Ethics Comm.	N	N	N	N	N	N	N		1,210	Y	Y	N	Y	N
Iowa	Ethics & Campaign Discl. Bd.	Y	Y	N	N	N	Y	Y	(zz)	600	N	N	Y	Y	N
Kansas	Govtl. Ethics Comm.	Y	Y	Y	Y	Y	Y	Y	(cc)(zz)	6,000	Y	N	N	Y	N
Kentucky	Exec. Branch Ethics Comm.;	Y	Y	N	N	N	Y	Y		1,300	Y	N	N	Y	N
	Legisltv. Ethics Comm.	N	N	Y	Y	Y	N	N	(oo)	150	N	N	N	Y	N
Louisiana	Ethics Admin.	N	N	N	Y	Y	Y	N	(e)(qq)	7,273	Y	Y	Y	Y	N
Maine	Comm. on Govtl. Ethics & Election Practices	N	Y	N	Y	Y	Y	Y	(zz)	<450	Y	Y	Y	Y	N
Maryland	Anne Arundel Co. Ethics Comm.;	Y	Y	N	N	N	N	N	(b)	200+	N	N	N	Y	N
	Montgomery Co. Ethics Comm.;	Y	Y	N	Y	Y	N	N	(b)(w)(zz)	1,400	Y	N	N	Y	Y
	State Ethics Comm.	Y	Y	Y	Y	N	Y	Y	(rr)(zz)	11,000	Y	N	N	Y	N
Massachusetts	State Ethics Comm.	Y	Y	N	Y	Y	Y	Y		4,386	Y	N	N	Y	N
Michigan	Dept. of State	N	N	Y	N	N	Y	Y		10,000	N	N	Y	Y	N
Minnesota	Camp. Finance & Public Discl. Bd.	Y	Y	N	Y	Y	Y	Y	(zz)	1,300	Y	N	Y	N	N
Mississippi	Ethics Comm.	N	N	N	N	N	N	N	(zz)	N.A.	Y	Y	N	N	N
Missouri	Ethics Comm.	Y	Y	N	Y	Y	Y	Y	(a)(m)(zz)	9,500	N	N	N	N	N

See footnotes at end of table.

ETHICS AGENCIES: PERSONAL FINANCIAL DISCLOSURE STATEMENTS — Continued

State or other jurisdiction	Agency	Who must file with agency — Agency heads	Board or commission members	Judges	Legislators	Candidates for legislature	State elected officials	Candidates for statewide office	Other	Number filed per year	File via web	File other electronic	FDS available via web site	Reviews or audits conducted	Reviews or audits available electronically
Montana	Commr. of Political Practices	Y	N	N	Y	Y	Y	N	(a)(n)	190	N	N	N	N	N
Nebraska	Accountability & Discl. Comm.	Y	Y	N	Y	Y	Y	Y	(ss)(zz)	2,500	N	N	N	N	N
Nevada	Comm. on Ethics	Y	Y	N	N	N	N	N	300	N	N	N	N	N
New Hampshire	Attorney General's Ofc.	Y	Y	N	Y	Y	Y	Y	(b)(bbb)	1,000–1,500	N	N	Y	N	N
New Jersey	Exec. Comm. on Ethical Stds.;	Y	Y	N	N	N	N	N	(o)(zz)	2,000	N	N	N	Y	N
	Jt. Leg. Cmte. on Ethical Stds.	N	N	N	Y	N	Y	N		120	N	N	Y	N	N
New Mexico	Secretary of State, Bureau of Elections & Ethics Administration	Y	Y	Y	Y	Y	Y	Y	(b)	3,000	N	N	Y	N	N
New York	Buffalo Bd. of Ethics;	Y	Y	N	N	N	N	N	(d)(zz)	550	Y	Y	N	Y	N
	NYC Conflicts of Interest Bd.;	Y	Y	N	N	N	N	N	(a)(dd)	8,000	N	Y	N	Y	N
	State Ethics Comm.;	Y	Y	N	N	N	Y	Y	(p)(zz)	18,000	Y	Y	N	Y	N
	Temp. State Comm. on Lobbying;	N	N	N	Y	Y	N	N	(ee)	apx. 20,000	Y	Y	Y	Y	N
	Suffolk Co. Camp. Finance Bd.	N	N	N	N	N	N	N	(b)(tt)	200	Y	Y	N	Y	N
North Carolina	Bd. of Ethics	Y	Y	N	N	N	N	Y	(q)	2,500+	N	N	N	Y	N
North Dakota	Secretary of State	N	N	Y	N	N	Y	Y		N.A.	N	N	N	N	N
Ohio	Ethics Comm.;	Y	Y	N	N	N	Y	Y	(a)(r)(zz)	10,500	N	Y	N	Y	N
	Legisltv. Insp. Gen. Ofc.	N	N	N	Y	Y	N	N	(s)	340	N	N	Y	Y	N
Oklahoma	Ethics Comm.	Y	Y	Y	Y	Y	Y	Y	(b)(ff)(zz)	6,000	N	N	N	Y	N
Oregon	Govt. Standards & Practices Comm.	Y	Y	Y	Y	Y	Y	Y	(b)(d)(uu)(zz)	4,200	N	Y	Y	Y	N
Pennsylvania	Ethics Comm.	Y	Y	N	Y	Y	Y	Y	(a)(hh)	150,000	Y	Y	Y	Y	N
Rhode Island	Ethics Comm.	Y	Y	Y	Y	Y	Y	N	(c)	6,500	Y	Y	N	Y	N
South Carolina	House Legisltv. Ethics Cmte.	N	Y	N	Y	Y	Y	N	(zz)	800	Y	Y	N	Y	Y
South Dakota	Secretary of State	N	N	N	Y	Y	Y	Y		N.A.	N	N	Y	N	N
Tennessee		N.A.	N.A.	N.A.	N.A.	N.A.	N.A.	N.A.							
Texas	Ethics Comm.;	Y	Y	N	Y	Y	Y	Y	(ii)(zz)	2,500	Y	Y	N	Y	N
	San Antonio City Attorney's Ofc.;	Y	Y	Y	N	N	N	N	(c)(vv)	700	N	N	N	N	N
	Univ. of Texas System, Ofc. of Gen. Counsel	Y	Y	N	N	N	N	N	(ccc)	N.A.	N	N	N	N	N
Utah		N.A.	N.A.	N.A.	N.A.	N.A.	N.A.	N.A.							
Vermont	State Elections Ofc.	N	N	N	Y	Y	Y	Y	(jj)	3,500	Y	Y	Y	Y	N
Virginia	State Bd. of Elections	N	N	N	N	N	N	N	(zz)	N.A.	Y	Y	N	N	N
Washington	Seattle Ethics & Elections Comm.;	Y	Y	Y	N	N	N	N	(c)(xx)	1,964	Y	Y	N	Y	N
	King Co. Bd. of Ethics;	Y	Y	N	N	N	N	N	(b)(t)	2,763 in 2004	N	N	N	Y	N
West Virginia	State Legisltv. Ethics Bd.;	N	N	N	N	N	N	N	(g)	N.A.	N	Y	N	N	N
	State Public Discl. Comm.	Y	Y	Y	Y	Y	Y	Y	(a)(zz)	6,500–8,500	Y	Y	N	Y	Y
Wisconsin	Ethics Comm.	Y	Y	Y	Y	Y	Y	Y	(b)	2,700	N	N	N	Y	N
Wyoming	Ethics Bd.	Y	Y	N	Y	Y	Y	Y	(ww)(zz)	2,400	N	N	N	Y	N
Guam	Ethics Comm.	N	N	N	N	N	N	N	(zz)	N.A.	Y	Y	N	N	N
Puerto Rico	Ethics Comm.	Y	Y	Y	Y	Y	Y	N	(d)(nn)(zz)	10,600	Y	Y	N	Y	Y
U.S. Virgin Islands	Dept. of Justice	N	N	N	N	N	N	N	(zz)	N.A.	Y	Y	N	N	N

See footnotes at end of table.

ETHICS AGENCIES: PERSONAL FINANCIAL DISCLOSURE STATEMENTS — Continued

Source: The Council on Governmental Ethics Laws (COGEL) Blue Book 2005 Ethics Update.

Key:
Y — Yes
N — No
N.A. — Not available
(a) City and county elected officials and candidates.
(b) County elected officials and candidates.
(c) City elected officials and candidates.
(d) City elected officials.
(e) City and county office candidates.
(f) Disclosures are filed with Secretary of State. Ballot and legislative question committees make their filings with the commission.
(g) Financial statements to be filed with Public Disclosure Commission, not ethics board.
(h) Certain other employees.
(i) Senior employees; Quasi-Public Agency members and senior employees.
(j) Division directors and their equivalents.
(k) Local officers and employees file with the supervisor of elections of the county in which they reside. Candidates file with the officer before whom they qualify. County elected officials.
(l) Aldermen must file with the city clerk. All city employees whose annual compensation rate is at or above an amount specified by the Board each year must file with the Board.
(m) Some political subdivisions have established their own method of disclosing conflicts of interest and therefore their candidates for office are not required to file the disclosure statement.
(n) City elected officials and candidates for same file if city falls within a certain population category. Members of certain boards file if duties fall within statutory criteria.
(o) Executive branch employees from assistant division director up; casino and gaming employees.
(p) Certain political party chairs, candidates for statewide elected office.
(q) High-level appointees and employees in the executive branch of state government, including gubernatorial appointees to non-advisory boards/commissions. By invitation, employees and appointees as designated by the nine elected heads of the Council of State Agencies, the Board of Governors of the 16-campus University system, the president pro tempore of the Senate and the Speaker of the House of Representatives.
(r) School board treasurers, superintendents and business managers. High-ranking state employees. Public university and college presidents must file.
(s) High-ranking legislative employees are also required to file. Also accept filings by other legislative employees as "voluntary filers."
(t) Local officials, candidates.
(u) State Board & Authority members, not Commission members. Do not file directly with agency: reports are filed with filing offices.
(v) Certain appointed officers and employees.
(w) County employees.
(y) Designated state and county employees in policymaking positions.
(z) Persons making independent expenditures exceeding $550.
(aa) Other employees and public officials designated in a Conflict of Interest Code adopted for any City of Los Angeles agency.
(bb) Filings made with the city clerk.
(cc) Any state employee designated by an agency head who is in a major policymaking position, responsible for contracting, purchasing or procurement, responsible for writing or drafting specifications for contracts, responsible for awarding grants, benefits or subsidies, or responsible for inspecting, licensing or regulating any person or entity.

(dd) Deputy and assistant agency heads, higher-level managers, policymakers; employees involved in negotiating, authorizing, or approving contracts, leases, franchises, revocable consents, or land use applications; compensated board and commission members.
(ee) Lobbyists and clients.
(ff) Employees of state educational institutions who make policy or spending decisions.
(gg) City and county elected officials.
(hh) Disclosure requirements also apply to many local and state employees.
(ii) State political chairs.
(jj) Political action committees, political issues committees, political parties, corporations.
(kk) Employees who are designated in the Campaign and Governmental Conduct Code file Statements of Economic Interests with their department heads.
(ll) Candidates for Supreme, Court of Appeals and District judicial office.
(mm) Specified county employees, nominees for county boards and commissions.
(nn) High-level position public servants, purchase officials, bid board members and public (government owned) Corporations Board.
(oo) Major management personnel of Legislative Research Commission, the staff of the General Assembly.
(pp) Board members and employees who make financial decisions including persons who participate or procurement source selection teams and consultants, file disclosure forms.
(qq) Lobbyists, in accordance with La R.S. 24:50 et seq. and La. R.S. 49:71 et seq.
(rr) All state employees who are determined by the State Ethics Commission to be "public officials" or who have procurement responsibilities for contracts in excess of $10,000 per year must file the financial disclosure statements.
(ss) The Nevada Secretary of State Elections Division is responsible for the financial disclosure statement filings of elected public officers (state, city, county and legislative) and candidates for public office. The NCOE accepts financial disclosure statements only for appointed public officers who are entitled to receive compensation of more than $6,000 per year of public service.
(tt) Political committees (including PACs) which support candidates for non-judicial county elected offices.
(uu) City and county chief executive officers; designated state agency directors and superintendents and business managers of public school districts.
(vv) Executive-level employees also file financial disclosure, e.g. the city manager and the assistant city managers; assistant department heads; members of police and fire departments involved in procurements; the city clerk; all executive secretaries. Also, "specified employees," i.e. higher-level employees who are not on executive staff file a shorter financial disclosure form reporting gifts.
(ww) Key administrators of state agencies, including the technical college and university systems.
(xx) City employees that fit criteria for filing.
(yy) Eighteen categories of employees and neighborhood planning unit officers.
(zz) State colleges and universities.
(aaa) Certain appointed officials.
(bbb) Reports are filed with the secretary of state, but reviewed and enforced by the attorney general.
(ccc) Employees who execute contracts or exercise discretion with regard to pecuniary transactions of government.
(ddd) In addition to state department directors, other state employees as provided by law, are also required to file financial disclosure statements. These employees include deputy directors, division chiefs, purchasing agents and fiscal officers, permanent employees of the legislature (other than clerical personnel), assistants in the office of the governor and the lt. governor (other than clerical personnel), and hearing officers. High-ranking state university officials, including the president, vice presidents, chancellors, and provosts, also must file financial disclosure statements.

2005 Initiatives and Referendums[1]

By John G. Matsusaka

Ballot proposition activity was muted in 2005, as usual for odd-year elections, but several high-profile campaigns emerged across the country. The number of citizen-initiated measures, 19, was a record high for an odd-year election, but only two of the initiatives were approved. All eight measures were defeated in California's special election, and Colorado voters approved a partial TABOR suspension.

Ballot proposition activity was muted in 2005, as usual for odd-year elections. A total of 45 statewide measures went before the voters in 12 states, compared to 174 in 35 states in 2004. Just over half—23 of 45—of the propositions were approved, well below the 67 percent approval rate in 2004. Table A summarizes the number of propositions by state, and the number that were approved. Table B lists the individual measures.[2]

Even though overall activity was modest, the number of citizen-initiated measures, 19, was a record high for an off-year election, eclipsing the previous high of seven. This continues the almost 30-year trend of growing initiative use that began with California's Proposition 13 in 1978. Of the 19 measures, 18 were initiatives and one was a referendum (a proposal to repeal a law passed by the legislature). Also remarkable, voters approved only two of the 19 measures, far below the historical passage rate for initiatives of 41 percent. The high rejection rate does not seem to signal a rejection of the idea of citizen lawmaking so much as distaste for the particular issues on the ballot. Opinion polls continue to show strong public support for direct democracy. For example, even as California voters rejected all eight initiatives that came before them, 78 percent agreed that initiatives brought up important issues that the governor and legislature did not adequately address, and 39 percent thought initiatives should have the most influence on policy, compared to 32 percent that chose the legislature and 18 percent that chose the governor.[3]

California's Special Election

Republican Gov. Arnold Schwarzenegger called a special election to advance his "reform agenda." His allies qualified four initiatives for the ballot: Proposition 74, which would have required public school teachers to wait longer before receiving tenure; Proposition 75, which would have made it more difficult for public employee unions to spend dues for

political purposes; Proposition 76, which would have limited state spending growth and given the governor more power to cut spending in a fiscal emergency; and Proposition 77, which would have taken redistricting out of the hands of the legislature and given it to a panel of judges and then voters in a referendum.

Public employee unions spent more than $100 million campaigning against the governor's measures, beginning in the summer. Union spending overwhelmed the $50 million spent by Schwarzenegger, including $7 million from his own pocket, and the governor's campaign seemed to start late and never got rolling. The advertising by opponents of Propositions 74–77 was considered by some observers to be among the most deceptive in memory,[4] but it had its desired effect, and all the governor's measures were rejected by voters. Four other initiatives on the ballot also went down to defeat, including two prescription drug measures that attracted $80 million from the pharmaceutical industry, and a law requiring parental notification before a minor could receive an abortion. Overall spending topped $250 million, apparently a record.

TABOR Suspension in Colorado

In 1992, Colorado voters approved, by a 54-46 margin, the Taxpayer Bill of Rights Act (TABOR), an amendment to the state constitution. TABOR is the toughest tax and expenditure limitation law in the country, restricting government revenue to the previous year's total plus an adjustment for inflation and population growth, requiring excess funds to be rebated to taxpayers, and requiring voter approval of any state or local tax increase. With the 2000–01 recession, state revenues plunged, requiring spending cuts. But when revenues began to recover recently, spending was held to the historically low recession level, the so-called "ratchet effect." At the same time, pressure for public spending was increased by passage of Amendment 23 in 2000 that required increases in education spending every year through

Table A: Initiatives and Referendums State-by-State Totals, 2005

State	Number of initiatives and referendums	Number of legislative measures	Notable issues
California	8 (0)	. . .	Union dues, redistricting, abortion, budget
Colorado	. . .	2 (1)	TABOR tax rebates
Kansas	. . .	1 (1)	Marriage
Maine	1 (0)	6 (5)	Gay rights, bonds
New Jersey	. . .	2 (2)	Hazardous waste
New York	. . .	2 (1)	Bonds, budget procedures
Ohio	4 (0)	1 (1)	Bonds, redistricting, campaign finance
Oklahoma	1 (0)	. . .	Gas tax
Texas	. . .	9 (8)	Marriage, term limits
Washington	5 (2)	1 (1)	Medical malpractice, gas tax, smoking
West Virginia	. . .	1 (0)	Pension bonds
Wisconsin	. . .	1 (1)	Term limits
Total	19 (2)	26 (21)	

Source: Initiative & Referendum Institute (www.iandrinstitute.org).
Note: The number of measures that were approved is reported in the parentheses. All entries under "initiatives and referendums" were initiatives, except for a single popular referendum in Maine.
Key:
. . . — None

2010, and by growing medical costs. Republican Gov. Bill Owens and the Democratic-controlled legislature placed on the ballot Referendum C, which asked voters to forego the tax rebates they were due over the next five years, an amount expected to be about $3.7 billion, and to eliminate the ratchet effect. Proponents argued that a yes vote was not a repeal of TABOR (indeed, some lauded TABOR's role in helping the state avoid the fiscal crises that afflicted other states), but a "tweaking" of the measure in light of new information. Opponents, including TABOR sponsor Douglas Bruce, argued that existing revenue would be adequate if the state cut back on wasteful spending. National anti-tax figures, including Dick Armey, former U.S. House majority leader from Texas, and Grover Norquist, president of Washington-based Americans for Tax Reform, joined the fray as well, arguing that a weakening of TABOR would undermine tax limitation efforts across the nation. Many state officials from both parties ended up campaigning for Referendum C. In the end, voters narrowly approved the TABOR suspension, 52-48 percent.

Election Reform in Ohio

Ohio was a pivotal state in the 2004 presidential election, and the spotlight on the state cast a harsh light on the state's election processes. Reform Ohio Now, a coalition of Democratic activists, placed four initiatives on the 2005 ballot that sought to remove what they saw as a corruption of the state's elections.

The initiatives would have made it easier for citizens to vote with absentee ballots, limited campaign contributions, created a nonpartisan commission to redistrict, and taken oversight of elections from the Secretary of State and given it to an independent commission. An ethics scandal involving Republican Gov. Bob Taft gave hope to the reform campaign even though it did not involve the issues on the ballot. The Ohio measures attracted national attention from Democratic groups and an e-mail campaign by *moveon.org* caused significant funds to pour into Ohio from John Kerry supporters across the nation. The $2 million raised by supporters included 3,300 contributions of less than $500 from citizens in 50 states. Opposition groups raised $2.2 million, mostly from business groups. Voters soundly rejected all four measures on Nov. 8.[5]

Emerging and Ongoing Trends

Due to the limited number of issue campaigns in 2005, there is a need for some caution in discussing trends. The critical issues tended to vary by state, and the politics often revolved around state-specific issues, but there were a few noticeable trends:

- **Failure of Election Reform.** Thoughtful observers continue to be concerned about the nature of elections in the country. In addition to the issue of campaign finance, attention has recently turned to the lack of competitiveness in legislative elections. In some states, reformers have attempted to increase competition by taking redistricting out

Table B:
Complete List of Statewide Ballot Propositions in 2005

State	Measure	Date	Type (a)	Description	Result
California	Prop. 73	Nov. 8	I, A	Required parental notification before minor receives abortion.	Failed 47-53
	Prop. 74	Nov. 8	I, S	Extended the period before teachers receive tenure from two to five years.	Failed 45-55
	Prop. 75	Nov. 8	I, S	Required member approval to use public employee union dues for politics.	Failed 47-53
	Prop. 76	Nov. 8	I, A	Capped spending growth, relaxed spending requirements for education.	Failed 38-62
	Prop. 77	Nov. 8	I, A	Nonpartisan redistricting with voter approval by referendum.	Failed 41-59
	Prop. 78	Nov. 8	I, S	Created voluntary state prescription drug discount program.	Failed 42-58
	Prop. 79	Nov. 8	I, S	Created mandatory state prescription drug discount program.	Failed 39-61
	Prop. 80	Nov. 8	I, S	Restricted competition among electricity suppliers.	Failed 34-66
Colorado	Referendum C	Nov. 1	L, S	Suspended TABOR provision requiring tax rebates.	Passed 52-48
	Referendum C	Nov. 1	L, S	$2.1 billion bonds for roads.	Failed 49-51
Kansas	Amendment	Apr. 5	L, A	Defined marriage as only between a man and a woman.	Passed 70-30
Maine	Question 1	Nov. 8	I, R	Repealed state law prohibiting discrimination against gays and lesbians.	Failed 45-55
	Question 2	Nov. 8	L, S	$33.1 million bonds for transportation.	Passed 67-33
	Question 3	Nov. 8	L, S	$8.9 million bonds for water systems.	Passed 58-42
	Question 4	Nov. 8	L, S	$20 million bonds to promote research.	Passed 58-42
	Question 5	Nov. 8	L, S	$12 million bonds for land conservation.	Passed 65-35
	Question 6	Nov. 8	L, S	$9 million bonds for higher education buildings.	Failed 49.7-50.3
	Question 7	Nov. 8	L, S	Lowered assessment of waterfront property used for fishing.	Passed 72-28
New Jersey	Public Question 1	Nov. 8	L, A	Created the office of lieutenant governor.	Passed 56-44
	Public Question 2	Nov. 8	L, A	Allowed hazardous waste funds to be used for air pollution.	Passed 56-44
New York	Proposal 1	Nov. 8	L, A	Appropriated funds at previous year's level is state budget late.	Failed 35-65
	Proposal 2	Nov. 8	L, S	$2.9 billion bonds for transportation.	Passed 55-45
Ohio	Issue 1	Nov. 8	L, S	$1.85 billion bonds for infrastructure and R&D.	Passed 54-46
	Issue 2	Nov. 8	I, A	Allowed absentee ballots for any reason.	Failed 37-63
	Issue 3	Nov. 8	I, A	Limited campaign contributions.	Failed 33-67
	Issue 4	Nov. 8	I, A	Created a nonpartisan redistricting commission.	Failed 30-70
	Issue 5	Nov. 8	I, A	Created an independent board to oversee elections.	Failed 30-70
Oklahoma	Question 723	Sep. 13	I, A	Raised gas tax for highways and bridges.	Failed 13-83
Texas	Prop. 1	Nov. 8	L, A	Established state fund for railway projects.	Passed 54-46
	Prop. 2	Nov. 8	L, A	Defined marriage as only between a man and a woman.	Passed 76-24
	Prop. 3	Nov. 8	L, A	Allowed local governments to borrow without voter approval.	Passed 52-48
	Prop. 4	Nov. 8	L, A	Gave judges more freedom to deny bail to criminal defendants.	Passed 85-15
	Prop. 5	Nov. 8	L, A	Removed interest rate limits on commercial loans.	Failed 43-57
	Prop. 6	Nov. 8	L, A	Expanded Judicial Conduct Commission.	Passed 63-37
	Prop. 7	Nov. 8	L, A	Allowed a variety of reverse mortgages.	Passed 60-40
	Prop. 8	Nov. 8	L, A	Relinquished state claim to certain land in two counties.	Passed 61-39
	Prop. 9	Nov. 8	L, A	Established term limits for local transportation boards.	Failed 47-53
Washington	I-330	Nov. 8	I, S	Limited pain and suffering awards.	Failed 48-52
	I-336	Nov. 8	I, S	Established state medical malpractice insurance program.	Failed 42-58
	I-900	Nov. 8	I, S	Required performance audits for state and local governments.	Passed 57-43
	I-901	Nov. 8	I, S	Banned indoor smoking in public places.	Passed 63-37
	I-912	Nov. 8	I, S	Repealed 9.5 gas tax increase enacted by legislature in 2005.	Failed 49-51
	SJR-8207	Nov. 8	L, A	Allowed municipal court judges on Judicial Conduct Commission.	Passed 66-34
West Virginia....	Amendment 1	Jun. 25	L, A	$5.5 billion bonds for public employee pensions.	Failed 46-54
Wisconsin..........	Referendum	Apr. 5	L, A	Term limits for certain county offices.	Passed 75-25

Source: Initiative & Referendum Institute (www.iandrinstitute.org).
Key:
(a) Types are indicated as I = initiative (new law placed on ballot by citizen petition), R = referendum (proposal to repeal existing law, placed on ballot by petition), L = legislative measure (placed on ballot by legislature), S = statute or bond authorization, A = constitutional amendment.

of the hands of elected officials who tend to draw safe districts for themselves, and place it in the hands of nonpartisan commissions. California and Ohio were the latest states to consider nonpartisan redistricting commissions, but both measures went down to defeat. Interestingly, the political parties took opposite positions in the two states, reflecting the partisan balance in the legislature: Democrats, the majority party in California, opposed reform, while Republicans, the majority party in Ohio, were the opponents. Ohio voters also rejected three other election reform measures. Despite the defeat of both measures, redistricting reform does not appear to be dead; California legislators began talking of reform as soon as the votes were counted.

- **Fiscal Liberalism.** As states put the fiscal crises of the recession behind them, voters were more willing to support government spending programs than in past years. Huge transportation bond issues were approved in New York ($2.9 billion) and Ohio ($1.85 billion), while Maine voters approved four of five bond issues (totaling $74 million). A $2.1 billion bond issue in Colorado narrowly failed. On the tax front, Washington voters declined to roll back the state gas tax; California voters rejected a proposal to limit the growth of state spending to the growth of state revenue; and in a Nov. 1 election, Colorado voters agreed to forego $3.7 billion of promised tax rebates over the next five years. However, there were also some notable reverses for bond and tax measures. West Virginia voters refused to authorize $5.5 billion in bonds for public employee pensions in a June election; and Oklahoma voters decisively rejected (with 83 percent against) a gas tax increase with funds dedicated for highways and bridges. Voters do not seem to want states to return to the free-spending ways of the late 1990s, but seem willing to let out the budget belt a few notches.

- **Gay Rights.** Gay marriage was one of the big stories of 2004. In February 2004, the Massachusetts Supreme Court ruled that the state's constitution contained a right to gay marriage. Shortly thereafter, the mayor of San Francisco authorized the city to issue marriage licenses to gay and lesbian couples, in defiance of a state initiative approved in 2000. Legislatures and citizens in 13 states responded by placing measures on the ballot amending their constitutions to define marriage as solely between a man and a woman. All 13 marriage amendments were approved in 2004, even in the "blue" states of Michigan and Oregon. Gay rights continued to be worked out in 2005. Kansas adopted a marriage amendment in April 2005, and Texas followed suit on Nov. 8. In better news for gay rights supporters, Maine voters declined to repeal a state law that prohibits discrimination on the basis of sexual orientation.

Notes

[1] This article uses referend*ums* instead of referend*a* as the plural of referendum following the *Oxford English Dictionary* and common practice.

[2] All current data provided by the Initiative and Referendum Institute at USC and available at *www. iandrinstitute. org*. Historical and legal information taken from *Initiative and Referendum Almanac*, by M. Dane Waters (Carolina Academic Publishers, 2003) and *For the Many or the Few: The Initiative, Public Policy, and American Democracy*, by John G. Matsusaka (University of Chicago Press, 2004).

[3] *PPIC Statewide Survey: Special Survey on Californians and the Initiative Process*, by Mark Baldassare, Public Policy Institute of California, San Francisco, September 2005, available at *www.ppic.org*.

[4] Daniel Weintraub, "The politicians are lying to you about Prop. 77," *Sacramento Bee*, November 3, 2005, page b7; *Union-Tribune* editorial, "Beyond shameless: Ad attacks on Prop. 76 are utterly dishonest," *San Diego Union-Tribune*, November 3, 2005.

[5] Contribution information from "Kerry supporters donate to Ohio law-change effort: Moveon.org helps promote Issues 2–5," by Carrie Spencer Ghose, *The Enquirer* (Cincinatti), November 4, 2005.

About the Author

John G. Matsusaka is a professor in the Marshall School of Business and School of Law, and president of the Initiative & Referendum Institute, all at the University of Southern California. He is the author of *For the Many or the Few: The Initiative, Public Policy, and American Democracy* (University of Chicago Press, 2004).

Table 6.9
STATE INITIATIVES & REFERENDUMS, 2005

State	Measure	Type of election	Type	Topics addressed by measure	Pass	Fail
Alabama (a)		(b)				
Alaska		(b)				
Arizona		(b)				
Arkansas		(b)				
California	Proposition 73	Special Election, Nov. 8, 2005	I	Abortion; Constitutional; Civil Law		★
	Proposition 74	Special Election, Nov. 8, 2005	I	Education; Teacher Tenure		★
	Proposition 75	Special Election, Nov. 8, 2005	I	Public Employees; Unions; Political Campaigns		★
	Proposition 76	Special Election, Nov. 8, 2005	I	State Spending Cap; Education		★
	Proposition 77	Special Election, Nov. 8, 2005	I	Redistricting Commission		★
	Proposition 78	Special Election, Nov. 8, 2005	I	Health; Prescription Drugs; Medi-Cal		★
	Proposition 79	Special Election, Nov. 8, 2005	I	Health; Prescription Drugs		★
	Proposition 80	Special Election, Nov. 8, 2005	I	Energy; Public Utilities; Renewable Energy		★
Colorado	Referendum C	General Election, Nov. 1, 2005	LR	Economic; TABOR; Taxes	★	
	Referendum D	General Election, Nov. 1, 2005	LR	Economic; Bonds; State Spending		★
Connecticut (a)		(b)				
Delaware (a)		(b)				
Florida		(b)				
Georgia (a)		(b)				
Hawaii (a)		(b)				
Idaho		(b)				
Illinois (d)		(b)				
Indiana (a)		(b)				
Iowa (a)		(b)				
Kansas (a)	Constitutional Amendment	General Election, April 5, 2005	LR	Marriage; Constitutional Law; Civil Law	★	
Kentucky (a)		(b)				
Louisiana (a)		(b)				
Maine	Question 1	General Election, Nov. 8, 2005	PR	People's Veto; Civil Rights; Civil Law		★
	Question 2	General Election, Nov. 8, 2005	I	Bond; Highways; Transportation	★	
	Question 3	General Election, Nov. 8, 2005	I	Bond; Agriculture/Environment	★	
	Question 4	General Election, Nov. 8, 2005	I	Bond; Economic Growth; Education	★	
	Question 5	General Election, Nov. 8, 2005	I	Bond; Environment/Natural Resources		
	Question 6	General Election, Nov. 8, 2005	I	Bond; Education		
	Question 7	General Election, Nov. 8, 2005	LR	Legislative; Taxes; Economic Development	★	
Maryland (a)		(b)				
Massachusetts		(b)				
Michigan		(b)				

See footnotes at end of table.

STATE INITIATIVES & REFERENDUMS, 2005 — Continued

State	Measure	Type of election	Type	Topics addressed by measure		Pass	Fail
Minnesota (a)			(b)				
Mississippi			(b)				
Missouri			(b)				
Montana			(b)				
Nebraska			(b)				
Nevada			(b)				
New Hampshire (a)(c)			(b)				
New Jersey (a)	Public Question No. 1	General Election, Nov. 8, 2005		Lieutenant Governor	Succession / State Government	★	
	Public Question No. 2	General Election, Nov. 8, 2005		Environment	Spending	★	
New Mexico (a)			(b)				
New York (a)	Proposal 1	General Election, Nov. 8, 2005	LR	Budget	Legislature		★
	Proposal 2	General Election, Nov. 8, 2005	LR	Bonds	Transportation	★	
North Carolina (a)			(b)				
North Dakota			(b)				
Ohio	Issue 1	General Election, Nov. 8, 2005	LR	Economic Development	Infrastructure	★	
	Issue 2	General Election, Nov. 8, 2005	I	Elections	Absentee Ballot		★
	Issue 3	General Election, Nov. 8, 2005	I	Political Campaigns	Contributions		★
	Issue 4	General Election, Nov. 8, 2005	I	Redistricting Commission	Public Disclosures		★
	Issue 5	General Election, Nov. 8, 2005	I	Election Administration			★
Oklahoma	Question 723	Special Election, Sept. 13, 2005	I	Gas Tax	Highways		★
Oregon			(b)				
Pennsylvania (a)			(b)				
Rhode Island (a)			(b)				
South Carolina (a)			(b)				
South Dakota			(b)				
Tennessee (a)			(b)				
Texas (a)	Proposition 1	General Election, Nov. 8, 2005	LR	Railways	Funds	★	
	Proposition 2	General Election, Nov. 8, 2005	LR	Marriage	Constitutional Law / Civil Law	★	
	Proposition 3	General Election, Nov. 8, 2005	LR	Economic Development	Economic Development	★	
	Proposition 4	General Election, Nov. 8, 2005	LR	Criminal Justice			★
	Proposition 5	General Election, Nov. 8, 2005	LR	Economic Development	Commercial Loans	★	
	Proposition 6	General Election, Nov. 8, 2005	LR	Judiciary	Judicial Conduct	★	
	Proposition 7	General Election, Nov. 8, 2005	LR	Reverse Mortgages		★	
	Proposition 8	General Election, Nov. 8, 2005	LR	Land Titles		★	
	Proposition 9	General Election, Nov. 8, 2005	LR	Terms of Office	Transportation Board		★

See footnotes at end of table.

STATE INITIATIVES & REFERENDUMS, 2005 — Continued

State	Measure	Type of election	Type	Topics addressed by measure		Pass	Fail
Utah					(b)		
Vermont (a)					(b)		
Virginia (a)					(b)		
Washington...............	Initiative 330	General Election, Nov. 8, 2005	I	Personal Injury Limits	Health Care		★
	Initiative 336	General Election, Nov. 8, 2005	I	Medical Malpractice			★
	Initiative 900	General Election, Nov. 8, 2005	I	Performance Audits	State Auditor	★	
	Initiative 901	General Election, Nov. 8, 2005	I	Smoking Prohibitions		★	
	Initiative 912	General Election, Nov. 8, 2005	I	Fuel Taxes	Transportation		★
	SJR 8207	General Election, Nov. 8, 2005	LR	Judiciary	Judicial Conduct	★	
West Virginia (a)	Amendment 1	Special Election, June 25, 2005	LR	Bonds	Public Employee Pensions	★	
Wisconsin (a)	Referendum	Spring General Election, April 5, 2005	LR	Terms of Office			★
Wyoming...............					(b)		

Source: The Council of State Governments' survey of election Web sites, November 2005.

Key:
LR — Legislative referendum
I — Initiative
PR — Popular referendum
O — Other
(a) State does not have an initiative process.
(b) State had no ballot measures in 2005.
(c) Requires 2/3 majority to pass.
(d) The state has an initiative process, but it is unusable.

Table 6.10
STATEWIDE INITIATIVE AND REFERENDUM

State or other jurisdiction	Changes to constitution			Changes to statutes			
	Initiative		Referendum	Initiative		Referendum	
	Direct (a)	Indirect (a)	Legislative (b)	Direct (c)	Indirect (c)	Legislative	Citizen petition (d)
Alabama	...	...	★	...	...	...	...
Alaska	★	...	★	★	...	...	★
Arizona	★	...	★	★	...	★	★
Arkansas	★	...	★	★	...	★	★
California	★	...	★	★	...	★	...
Colorado	★	...	★	★	...	...	...
Connecticut	...	...	★	...	...	...	...
Delaware	...	...	★	...	...	★	...
Florida	★	...	★	...	...	...	...
Georgia	...	...	★	...	...	★	...
Hawaii	...	...	★	...	...	...	...
Idaho	...	...	★	★	...	★	★
Illinois	★	...	★	★	...	★	...
Indiana	...	...	★	...	...	★	...
Iowa	...	...	★	...	...	...	...
Kansas	...	...	★	...	...	...	...
Kentucky	...	...	★	...	...	★	★
Louisiana	...	...	★	...	...	...	...
Maine	...	...	★	...	★	★	★
Maryland	...	...	★	...	...	...	★
Massachusetts	...	★	★	...	★	★	★
Michigan	★	...	★	...	★	★	★
Minnesota	...	...	★	...	...	...	...
Mississippi	★	...	★	...	★	...	★
Missouri	★	...	★	★	...	★	★
Montana	★	...	★	★	...	★	★
Nebraska	★	...	★	★	...	...	★
Nevada	★	...	★	★	★	...	★
New Hampshire	...	...	★	...	...	...	...
New Jersey	...	...	★	...	...	...	...
New Mexico	...	...	★	...	...	...	...
New York	...	...	★	...	...	★	...
North Carolina	...	...	★	...	...	...	...
North Dakota	★	...	★	★	...	★	...
Ohio	★	...	★	★	...	...	...
Oklahoma	★	...	★	★	...	★	★
Oregon	★	...	★	★	...	★	★
Pennsylvania	...	...	★	...	...	...	...
Rhode Island	...	...	★	...	...	...	...
South Carolina	...	...	★	...	...	...	...
South Dakota	★	...	★	★	...	...	★
Tennessee	...	...	★	...	...	★	...
Texas	...	...	...	...	...	...	...
Utah	...	...	★	★	...	★	★
Vermont	...	...	★	...	...	★(limited)	...
Virginia	...	...	★(e)	...	...	...	...
Washington	...	...	★	★	...	★	★
West Virginia	...	...	★	...	...	...	...
Wisconsin	...	...	★	...	...	...	...
Wyoming	...	...	★	...	★	...	★
American Samoa	...	...	★	...	...	...	...
No. Mariana Islands	★	★	★	★	★	★	★
Puerto Rico	...	...	★	...	...	★	...
U.S. Virgin Islands	...	...	★	★	...	★	...

Sources: The Council of State Governments' survey of state election administration offices, December 2005 and state Web sites.

Note: This table summarizes state provisions for initiatives and referenda. Initiatives may propose constitutional amendments or develop state legislation and may be formed either directly or indirectly. The direct initiative allows a proposed measure to be placed on the ballot after a specific number of signatures has been secured on a citizen petition. The indirect initiative must be submitted to the legislature for a decision after the required number of signatures has been secured on a petition and prior to placing the proposed measure on the ballot. Referendum refers to the process whereby a state law or constitutional amendment passed by the legislature may be referred to the voters before it goes into effect. Three forms of referenda exist: (1) citizen petition, whereby the people may petition for a referendum on legislation which has been considered by the legislature; (2) submission by the legislature (designated in table as "Legisla-tive"), whereby the legislature may voluntarily submit laws to the voters for their approval; and (3) constitutional requirement, whereby the state constitution may require that certain questions be submitted to the voters.

Key:
★ — State provision   . . . — No state provision
(a) See Table 1.3, "Constitutional Amendment Procedure: By Initiative," for more detail.
(b) See Table 1.2, "Constitutional Amendment Procedure: By the Legislature," for more detail.
(c) See Chapter 6 tables on State Initiatives, for more detail.
(d) See Chapter 6 tables on State Referendums, for more detail.
(e) In Virginia, voter approval is required for certain types of bonds issued by the Commonwealth.

Table 6.11
STATE INITIATIVES: REQUESTING PERMISSION TO CIRCULATE A PETITION

State or other jurisdiction	Applied to (a)		Signatures required to request a petition (b)		Request submitted to	Request form furnished by (c)	Restricted subject matter (d)	Individual responsible for petition		Financial contributions reported (e)	Deposits required (f)
	Const.amdt.	Statute	Const.amdt.	Statute				Title	Summary		
Alabama	...	...	...	...	...	...	...	...	...	...	...
Alaska	...	D	...	100	LG	ST	Y	LG	LG	Y	$100
Arizona	D	D	15% (g)	10% (g)	SS	SS	N	(s)	(s)	Y	...
Arkansas	D	D	10% (t)	8% (t)	AG	SS	Y	SP	...	Y	...
California	D	D	...	...	AG	...	Y	AG	AG	N (r)	$200 (r)
Colorado	D	D	...	...	...	SP	N	(h)	(h)	Y	N
Connecticut	...	...	...	...	...	...	...	...	...	...	...
Delaware	...	...	...	...	...	...	...	...	...	...	...
Florida	D	...	(u)	...	SS	SP	N	SP	SP	Y	N
Georgia	...	...	...	...	...	...	...	...	...	...	...
Hawaii	...	...	...	...	...	...	...	...	...	...	...
Idaho	...	D	...	20	SS	SP	N	AG	AG	Y	N
Illinois	D	...	...	...	SBE	...	...	P	...	Y	N
Indiana	...	...	...	...	...	...	...	...	...	...	...
Iowa	...	...	...	...	...	...	...	...	...	...	...
Kansas	...	...	...	...	...	...	...	...	...	...	...
Kentucky	...	...	...	...	...	...	...	...	...	...	...
Louisiana	...	...	...	...	...	...	...	...	...	...	...
Maine	...	I	...	5 (i)	SS	SS	Y	P	SS	Y	...
Maryland	...	...	...	3 (v)	SS (w)	SBE	Y	...	...	Y	N
Massachusetts	I	I	10	10	AG	SS	Y	AG	AG	Y	...
Michigan	...	...	...	...	...	...	Y	SP	SP	Y	N
Minnesota	...	...	...	...	...	...	...	...	...	...	...
Mississippi	I	...	...	...	SS	...	Y	AG	AG	Y	...
Missouri	D	D	...	...	SS	SP	Y	SS, AG	SS, AG	Y	N
Montana	D	D	10%	5%	(x)	SP	Y	AG	AG	Y	N
Nebraska	D	D	...	...	SS	SP	Y	SP	SP	Y	N
Nevada	...	...	...	...	SS	SS	Y	P, SP	P, SP	...	...
New Hampshire	...	...	...	...	...	...	...	...	...	...	...
New Jersey	...	...	...	...	...	...	...	...	...	...	...
New Mexico	...	...	...	...	...	...	...	...	...	...	...
New York	...	...	...	...	...	...	...	...	...	...	...
North Carolina	...	...	...	...	...	...	...	...	...	...	...
North Dakota	D	D	4% (j)	2% (j)	SS	SP	N	SS, AG	SS	Y (e)	N
Ohio	D	I	...	...	AG	SP	Y	...	AG	Y	...
Oklahoma	D	D	15%	8%	SS	O	N	P	P	Y	N
Oregon	D	D	25	25	SS	SS, SP	N	AG	AG	Y	N
Pennsylvania	...	...	...	...	...	...	...	...	...	...	...
Rhode Island	...	...	...	...	...	...	...	...	...	...	...
South Carolina	...	...	...	...	...	...	...	...	...	...	...
South Dakota	D	D	(y)	...	SS	SS, SP	N	SS	AG	Y	N
Tennessee	...	...	...	...	...	...	...	...	...	...	...
Texas	...	...	...	...	...	...	...	...	...	...	...
Utah	...	D	...	10% (m)	LG	ST	N	SP	SP	Y (k)	...
Vermont	...	...	...	...	...	...	...	...	...	...	...
Virginia	...	...	...	...	...	...	...	...	...	...	...
Washington	...	D	...	(q)	SS	SP	Y	AG	AG	Y	5
West Virginia	...	...	...	...	...	...	...	...	...	...	...
Wisconsin	...	...	...	...	...	...	...	...	...	...	...
Wyoming	...	I	...	100	SS	SS	Y	SS	SS, AG	Y	$500
American Samoa	...	...	...	...	...	...	...	...	...	...	...
No. Mariana Islands	D	I	50%	20%	AG	AG	Y	SP	SP	Y	N
Puerto Rico	...	D	...	(o)	SBE	(l)	N	(l)	(l)	Y	$500
U.S. Virgin Islands	...	D	41%	41%	SBE	(p)	N	P	(n)	N	N

See footnotes at end of table.

STATE INITIATIVES: REQUESTING PERMISSION TO CIRCULATE A PETITION — Continued

Source: The Council of State Governments' survey of state election administration offices, December 2005 and state Web sites.

Key:

. . . — Not applicable
D — Direct initiative
I — Indirect initiative
EV — Eligible voters
LG — Lieutenant Governor
SS — Secretary of State
SBE — State Board of Elections

AG — Attorney General
P — Proponent
ST — State
SP — Sponsor
Y — Yes
N — No

(a) An initiative may provide a constitutional amendment or develop a new statute, and may be formed either directly or indirectly. The direct initiative allows a proposed measure to be placed on the ballot after a specific number of signatures has been secured on a petition. The indirect initiative must first be submitted to the legislature for decision after the required number of signatures has been secured on a petition, prior to placing the proposed measure on the ballot.

(b) Prior to circulating a statewide petition, a request for permission to do so must first be submitted to a specified state officer.

(c) The form on which the request for petition is submitted may be the responsibility of the sponsor or may be furnished by the state.

(d) Restrictions may exist regarding the subject matter to which an initiative may be applied. The majority of these restrictions pertain to the dedication of state revenues and appropriations, and laws that maintain the preservation of public peace, safety, and health. In Illinois, amendments are restricted to "structural and procedural subjects contained in" the legislative article.

(e) In some states, a list of financial contributors and the amount of their contributions must be submitted to the specified state officer with whom the petition is filed. In North Dakota, must report any contributions and/or expenditures in excess of $100. Must also report the gross total of all contributions received and gross totals of all expenditures made. Must give total cash on hand in the filer's account at the start and close of a reporting period.

(f) A deposit may be required after permission to circulate a petition has been granted. This amount is refunded when the completed petition has been filed correctly.

(g) The number of signatures required to request permission to circulate a petition: constitutional amendment, 183,917; statute, 122,612.

(h) Title Setting Board—secretary of state, attorney general, director of legislative legal services.

(i) The name and address of five voters.

(j) Percentage of resident population of the state at the last federal decennial census.

(k) Must report if contributions exceed $750 or expenditures exceed $50.

(l) Office of the Supervisor of Elections Titling Board.

(m) Percentage of votes cast in last gubernatorial election and of all votes cast in 26 of 29 senate districts.

(n) Titling Board.

(o) Ten percent district and 41 percent territorial.

(p) Petitioner.

(q) Statute requires 224,880.

(r) No report required at time of filing request, but later if any money is raised, $200 deposit required.

(s) The proponent and sponsor are responsible for the title and summary.

(t) Signatures required for constitutional amendment: 10 percent times the votes cast for governor in preceding election. Statute: eight percent times votes cast for governor in preceding election.

(u) Eight percent of votes cast in last presidential election.

(v) Three percent of last vote for governor—at this time 51,185.

(w) Secretary of state accepts and turns over to State Board of Elections.

(x) First to Legislative Services; second Attorney General and Secretary of State.

(y) Number of signatures required to request a petition for a constitutional amendment, 33,456.

Table 6.12
STATE INITIATIVES: CIRCULATING THE PETITION

State or other jurisdiction	Basis for signatures (see key below)		Maximum time period allowed for petition circulation (a)	Can signatures be removed from petition (b)	Completed petition filed with	Days prior to election	
	Const. amdt.	Statute				Const. amdt.	Statute
Alabama...............	...	...	...	...	...	...	...
Alaska...................	15% EV	10% TV from 3/4 ED	1 yr.	Y	(c)	...	...
Arizona.................	10% VG	10% EV	2 yr.	Y	SS	4 mos.	4 mos.
Arkansas..............	10% VG	8% VG	...	N	SS	4 mos.	4 mos.
California.............	8% VG	5% VG	150 days	Y	(d)	131 days	131 days
Colorado..............	5% VSS	5% VSS	6 mos.	N	SS	3 mos.	3 mos.
Connecticut.........	...	...	...	...	...	...	...
Delaware..............	...	...	...	...	...	...	...
Florida..................	8% VEP, 8% from 1/2 CD	...	...	N	SS	Feb. 1 (t)	...
Georgia.................	...	...	...	...	...	...	...
Hawaii..................	...	...	...	...	...	...	...
Idaho....................	...	6% EV	(e)	Y	SS	...	4 mos.
Illinois.................	8% VG	...	2 yr.	Y	SBE	6 mos.	...
Indiana.................	...	...	...	...	...	...	...
Iowa.....................	...	...	...	...	...	...	...
Kansas..................	...	...	...	...	...	...	...
Kentucky..............	...	...	...	...	...	...	...
Louisiana.............	...	...	...	...	SS	...	(f)
Maine...................	...	10% VG	1 yr.	...	SS	...	...
Maryland..............	...	...	...	...	...	...	...
Massachusetts......	3% VG, no more than 25% from 1 county	3% VG, no more than 25% from 1 county (g)	From 1st Wed. in Sept. to 1st Wed. in Dec. (o)	Y (p)	SS (o)	(g)	(q)
Michigan..............	10% VG	8% VG	180 days	N (m)	SS	120 days	160 days
Minnesota............	...	...	...	...	...	...	...
Mississippi...........	12% VG	...	1 yr.	...	SS (d)	90 days prior to LS	...
Missouri...............	8% VG, 8% each from 2/3 CD	5% VG, 5% each from 2/3 CD	Approx. 18 mos.	Y	SS	6 mos.	6 mos.
Montana...............	10% VG	5% VG	(u)	Y	SS	(j)	(j)
Nebraska..............	10% EV	7% EV	...	Y	SS	4 mos.	4 mos.
Nevada.................	10% TV, 10% each from 3/4 counties	10% TV, 10% each from 3/4 counties	(k)	Y	SS	90 days	30 days prior to LS
New Hampshire.....	...	...	...	...	...	...	...
New Jersey............	...	...	...	...	...	...	...
New Mexico..........	...	...	...	...	...	...	...
New York..............	...	...	...	...	...	...	...
North Carolina.....	...	...	...	...	...	...	...
North Dakota.......	4% resident population	2% resident population	1 yr.	N	SS	90 days	90 days
Ohio.....................	10% VG, 5% each from 1/2 counties	3% VG, 1.5% each from 1/2 counties	...	Y (l)	SS	90 days	(h)

See footnotes at end of table.

STATE INITIATIVES: CIRCULATING THE PETITION — Continued

State or other jurisdiction	Basis for signatures (see key below)		Maximum time period allowed for petition circulation (a)	Can signatures be removed from petition (b)	Completed petition filed with	Days prior to election	
	Const. amdt.	Statute				Const. amdt.	Statute
Oklahoma	15% VH	8% VH	90 days	Y	SS	60 days	60 days
Oregon	8% VG	6% VG	2 yr.	N (m)	SS	4 mos.	4 mos.
Pennsylvania	. . .	. . .	. . .	. . .	. . .	. . .	. . .
Rhode Island	. . .	. . .	. . .	. . .	. . .	. . .	. . .
South Carolina	. . .	. . .	. . .	. . .	. . .	. . .	. . .
South Dakota	10% VG	5% VG	(i)	N	SS	1 yr.	6 mos.
Tennessee	. . .	. . .	. . .	. . .	. . .	. . .	. . .
Texas	. . .	. . .	. . .	. . .	. . .	. . .	. . .
Utah	10% VG, 10% each from 26 of 29 senate districts	. . .	1 yr.	Y	LG	. . .	June 1
Vermont	. . .	. . .	. . .	. . .	. . .	. . .	. . .
Virginia	. . .	. . .	. . .	. . .	. . .	. . .	. . .
Washington	. . .	8% VG	6 mos.	Y	SS	. . .	(n)
West Virginia	. . .	. . .	. . .	. . .	. . .	. . .	. . .
Wisconsin	. . .	. . .	. . .	. . .	. . .	. . .	. . .
Wyoming	15% TV, from 2/3 counties	15% TV, from 2/3 counties	18 mos.	Y	SS	. . .	120 days
American Samoa	. . .	. . .	(s)	Y	. . .	. . .	. . .
No. Mariana Islands	. . .	. . .	. . .	Y	. . .	. . .	. . .
Puerto Rico	. . .	. . .	. . .	. . .	. . .	. . .	. . .
U.S. Virgin Islands	. . .	10% ED	180 days	Y	(r)	. . .	6 mos.

Sources: The Council of State Governments' survey of state election administration offices and state Web sites, December 2005.

Key:
. . . — Not applicable
VG — Total votes cast for the position of governor in the last election
EV — Eligible voters
VH — Total votes cast for the office receiving the highest number of votes in last general election
TV — Total voters in last election
VSS — Total votes cast for all candidates for the office of secretary of state at the previous general election
VEP — Total votes cast in the state as a whole on the last presidential election
ED — Election district
CD — Congressional district
SBE — State Board of Elections
SLD — State legislative district
LG — Lieutenant Governor
SS — Secretary of State
LS — Legislative session
Y — Yes
N — No
T — Tuesday

(a) The petition circulation period begins when petition forms have been approved and provided to sponsors. Sponsors are individuals granted permission to circulate a petition, and are therefore responsible for the validity of each signature on a given petition.
(b) Should an individual wish to remove his/her name from a petition, a request to do so must be submitted in writing to the state officer with whom the petition is filed.
(c) Division of Elections.
(d) County elections officials.

(e) Eighteen months from receipt of ballot title or April 30 of year of election on initiative, whichever occurs first.
(f) To be placed on November ballot, petitions must be submitted to SS by 5:00 p.m. on 50th day after convening of Legislature in 1st regular session, or by 5:00 p.m. on 25th day in 2nd regular session.
(g) First Wednesday in December.
(h) Ten days prior to commencement of General Assembly session for initial filing; second petition must be filed within 90 days after General Assembly takes no action, fails to enact or pass amended form; the petition is filed with the secretary of state.
(i) Constitutional amendment—24 months preceding the election date designated on the petition. Statute: Initiated measure—18 months preceding the election date designated on the petition. Statute: Referred law—must be filed within 90 days from adjournment of the legislative session in which the measure was passed.
(j) Third Friday of the 4th month prior to the general election.
(k) Constitutional amendment—276 days; amend or create a statute—291 days.
(l) By request of signer or by circulator prior to filing.
(m) Not after petition has been filed.
(n) Within 10 months prior to the election in which they are to be submitted.
(o) Petitions first must be submitted to local municipal clerks for signature certification.
(p) Should an individual wish to remove his/her name from a petition, a request to do so must be submitted in writing to the local election official before the petition is submitted for certification of signatures.
(q) After legislative inaction, petitions must be filed no later than the 1st Wednesday in July, signed by not less than 1/2 of 1 percent of the last vote cast for governor.
(r) Supervisor of elections.
(s) Until 120 days before the date of the election.
(t) February 1 of the general election year.
(u) No maximum, but petitions may not be submitted to Secretary of State for review more than one year before final submission of signatures to county election offices.

Table 6.13
STATE INITIATIVES: PREPARING THE INITIATIVE TO BE PLACED ON THE BALLOT

State or other jurisdiction	Signatures verified by: (a)	Within how many days after filing	Number of days to amend/appeal a petition that is:		Penalty for falsifying petition (denotes fine, jail term)	Petition certified by: (d)
			Incomplete (b)	Not Accepted (c)		
Alabama	...	...	...	...	...	...
Alaska	Division of Elections	60 days	...	30 days	...	LG
Arizona	County recorder	10 days (i)	...	...	Class 1 misdemeanor	SS
Arkansas	SS	30 days	30 days	30 days	Class A misdemeanor	SS
California	County clerk	30 days	...	...	Felony or misdemeanor (depending on severity)	SS
Colorado	SS	30 days	15 days	15 days	(e)	SS
Connecticut	...	...	...	...	...	...
Delaware	...	...	...	...	...	...
Florida	Supervisor of elections	N.A.	N.A.	N.A.	First degree misdemeanor	SS
Georgia	...	...	...	...	...	...
Hawaii	...	...	...	...	...	...
Idaho	County clerk	60 days	...	10 days	$5,000, 2 yrs.	SS
Illinois	SBE	...	...	...	...	SBE
Indiana	...	...	...	...	...	...
Iowa	...	...	...	...	...	...
Kansas	...	...	...	...	...	...
Kentucky	...	...	...	...	...	...
Louisiana	...	...	...	...	...	...
Maine	Registrar of voters	...	...	...	...	SS
Maryland	...	...	...	...	...	...
Massachusetts	Local board of registrar	2 weeks	...	...	$1,000, 1 yr.	SS
Michigan	SS	Approx. 60 days	...	...	$500, 90 days	BSC
Minnesota	...	...	...	...	...	...
Mississippi	Circuit clerk	63 days	...	...	$1,000, 1 yr.	SS
Missouri	County clerk	...	...	10 days	Class A misdemeanor	SS
Montana	County clerk	4 weeks	...	...	$500, 6 mos.	SS
Nebraska	County clerk	40 days	...	...	...	SS
Nevada	County clerk	(l)	5 days (f)	...	...	SS
New Hampshire	...	...	...	...	...	...
New Jersey	...	...	...	...	...	...
New Mexico	...	...	...	...	...	...
New York	...	...	...	...	...	...
North Carolina	...	...	...	...	...	...
North Dakota	SS	35 days	...	...	(m)	SS
Ohio	County board of elections	10 days	10 days	20 days	5th degree felony	SS
Oklahoma	SS	...	10 days	...	$1,000, 1 yr.	SS
Oregon	SS, county clerk	...	10 days	...	Class C felony	SS
Pennsylvania	...	...	...	...	...	...
Rhode Island	...	30 days	...	...	...	...
South Carolina	...	...	...	...	...	...

See footnotes at end of table.

STATE INITIATIVES: PREPARING THE INITIATIVE TO BE PLACED ON THE BALLOT — Continued

State or other jurisdiction	Signatures verified by: (a)	Within how many days after filing	Number of days to amend/appeal a petition that is:		Penalty for falsifying petition (denotes fine, jail term)	Petition certified by: (d)
			Incomplete (b)	Not Accepted (c)		
South Dakota..............	SS	...	...	...	Class 1 misdemeanor	SS
Tennessee...................	...	...	...	...	...	...
Texas..........................	...	...	...	...	...	...
Utah...........................	County clerk	By July 1	...	By July 20	Class A misdemeanor	LG
Vermont......................	...	...	...	...	...	...
Virginia......................	...	...	...	...	...	...
Washington.................	SS	(g)	10	5	Fine or imprisonment	SS
West Virginia..............	...	...	...	...	...	...
Wisconsin...................	...	...	...	...	...	...
Wyoming.....................	SS	60 days	30 days	30 days	$1,000, 1 yr.	SS
American Samoa..........	Election Commission	...	...	...	...	AG
No. Mariana Islands	Office of the Supervisor of Elections	(h)	30 days (j)	119 days	(k)	SBE
Puerto Rico.................	...	15 days	3 days	...	...	...
U.S. Virgin Islands..............	Titling Board	180 days	...	...	...	SBE

Sources: The Council of State Governments' survey of state election administration offices, December 2005 and state Web sites.

Key:

... — Not applicable
SS — Secretary of State
LG — Lieutenant Governor
BSC — Board of State Canvassers
SBE — State Board of Elections

(a) The validity of the signatures, as well as the correct number of required signatures must be verified before the initiative is allowed on the ballot.

(b) If an insufficient number of signatures is submitted, sponsors may amend the original petition by filing additional signatures within a given number of days after filing. If the necessary number of signatures has not been submitted by this date, the petition is declared void.

(c) In some cases, the state officer will not accept a valid petition. In such a case, sponsors may appeal this decision to the Supreme Court, where the sufficiency of the petition will be determined. If the petition is determined to be sufficient, the initiative is required to be placed on the ballot.

(d) A petition is certified for the ballot when the required number of signatures has been submitted by the filing deadline, and are determined to be valid.

(e) No more than $500, one year in county jail, or both.

(f) In Nevada, appeal must be within 5 working days after SS determines the petition is not sufficient.

(g) Signatures filed not less than four months before next general statewide election.

(h) Within 90 days before the date of election.

(i) Removal of petition and ineligible signatures by Secretary of State's office 15 days (A.R.S. § 19-121.01), certification by County Recorder 10 days after receipt from Secretary of State's office (A.R.S. § 19-121.02).

(j) 30 days if submitted 150 days before the date of the election. No amendment/appeal if submitted 120 days before the date of election.

(k) Subject to statute governing fraud and perjury.

(l) 1. Within four days, county clerk totals the number of signatures and forwards to the secretary of state. 2. The secretary of state immediately notifies county clerks if they are to proceed or not proceed with the signature verification. 3. If ordered by the secretary of state, the county clerks verify signatures within nine days (excluding weekends and holidays).

(m) Any violations discovered will be reported to the attorney general for investigation and prosecution.

Table 6.14
STATE INITIATIVES: VOTING ON THE INITIATIVE

State or other jurisdiction	Ballot (a)		Election where initiative voted on	Effective date of approved initiative (b)		Days to contest election results (c)	Can an approved initiative be:			Can a defeated initiative be refiled?
	Title by:	Summary by:		Const. amdt.	Statute		Amended?	Vetoed?	Repealed?	
Alabama	...	...	...	...	...	...	...	...	...	...
Alaska	LG, AG	LG, AG	(d)	...	90 days (e)	10	Y (q)	N	N	Y
Arizona	SS, AG	LC	GE	...	IM (f)	5	(t)	N	N	Y
Arkansas....................	Other	AG	GE	30 days	...	60	Y	N	Y	Y
California	AG	AG	GE, PR or SP	1 day	IM	5 (e)	Y (h)	N	Y (h)	Y
Colorado....................	TB	TB	GE	30 days	30 days	10	N	N	N	Y
Connecticut	...	...	...	...	...	...	...	...	...	...
Delaware....................	...	...	...	...	...	...	...	...	...	...
Florida	SP	SP	GE	(i)	...	10	Y (u)	N	Y (u)	Y
Georgia	...	...	...	...	...	...	...	...	...	...
Hawaii.........................	...	...	...	...	...	...	...	...	...	...
Idaho..........................	AG	AG	GE	...	30 days	20	Y	N	Y	Y
Illinois.......................	LLS	LLS	GE	...	...	...	Y	N	Y	Y
Indiana.......................	...	...	...	...	...	...	...	...	...	...
Iowa	...	...	...	...	...	...	...	...	...	...
Kansas	...	...	...	...	...	...	...	...	...	...
Kentucky	...	...	...	...	...	...	...	...	...	...
Louisiana	...	...	...	...	...	...	...	...	...	...
Maine	Sponsor, SS	(p)	REG or SP	...	30 days (f)	5	Y	N	Y	...
Maryland	...	...	...	...	...	...	...	...	...	...
Massachusetts.............	AG	AG	GE	30 days	30 days	10	Y	Y	Y	after 2 biennial elections
Michigan.....................	BSC	BSC	GE	45 days	10 days	2 (j)	Y	N	Y	Y
Minnesota	...	...	...	...	...	...	...	...	...	...
Mississippi	AG	AG	GE	30 days	...	...	Y	N	Y	after 2 yrs.
Missouri	SS, AG	SS, AG	GE	30 days	IM	30 (j)	Y	N	Y	Y
Montana	AG	AG	GE	July 1	Oct. 1	1 yr.	Y	N	Y	Y
Nebraska.....................	AG	AG	GE	10 days	10 days	40	Y	N	Y	N (s)
Nevada	SS, AG	SS, AG	GE	(l)	(l)	14	(m)	(m)	(m)	Y
New Hampshire.........	...	...	...	...	...	...	...	...	...	...
New Jersey..................	...	...	...	...	...	...	...	...	...	...
New Mexico	...	...	...	...	...	...	...	...	...	...
New York	...	...	...	...	...	...	...	...	...	...
North Carolina...........	...	...	...	...	...	...	...	...	...	...
North Dakota..............	SS, AG	SS	PR or GE	30 days	30 days	14	(n)	N	(n)	Y
Ohio	Ohio Ballot Board	Ohio Ballot Board	GE	30 days	30 days	15	N	N	N	N
Oklahoma	AG	P	GE or SP	IM	IM	...	Y	Y	Y	after 3 yrs.
Oregon	AG	AG	GE	30 days	30 days	35	(g)	(g)	(g)	Y
Pennsylvania	...	...	...	...	...	...	...	...	...	...
Rhode Island	...	...	...	...	...	...	...	...	...	...
South Carolina	...	...	...	...	...	...	...	...	...	...
South Dakota..............	AG	AG	GE	1 day	1 day	10	Y	N	Y	Y
Tennessee	...	...	...	...	...	...	...	...	...	...
Texas	...	...	...	...	...	...	...	...	...	...
Utah	LC	LC	GE	...	5 days (o)	40	Y	N	Y	after 1 yr.
Vermont	...	...	...	...	...	...	...	...	...	...
Virginia......................	...	...	...	...	...	...	...	...	...	...
Washington.................	AG	AG	GE	...	30 days	...	Y (v)	...	Y (v)	Y
West Virginia..............	...	...	...	...	...	...	...	...	...	...
Wisconsin....................	...	...	...	...	...	...	...	...	...	...
Wyoming.....................	SS	SS, AG	GE 120 days after LS	...	90 days	15 after Canvass	Y	N	after 2 yrs.	after 5 yrs.
American Samoa	...	...	...	...	...	...	...	...	...	...
No. Mariana Islands...	AG	AG	GE	(k)	(k)	30	...	...	...	Y
Puerto Rico.................	LC	AG, LLS	GE	...	IM	...	Y	...	...	Y
U.S. Virgin Islands	(r)	(r)	GE	IM	IM	30	(m)	(m)	(m)	Y

See footnotes at end of table.

STATE INITIATIVES: VOTING ON THE INITIATIVE — Continued

Sources: The Council of State Governments' survey of state election administration offices, October 2005 and state Web sites.

Key:

. . . — Not applicable	GE — General election
LG — Lieutenant Governor	REG — Regular election
SS — Secretary of State	SP — Special election
AG — Attorney General	IM — Immediately
P — Proponent	LS — Legislative session
LC — Legislative Council	TB — Title Board
LLS — Legislative Legal Services	Y — Yes
BSC — Board of State Canvassers	N — No
SBE — State Board of Elections	w/i — Within
PR — Primary election	

(a) In some states, the ballot title and summary will differ from that on the petition.

(b) A majority of the popular vote is required to enact a measure. In Massachusetts and Nebraska, apart from satisfying the requisite majority vote, the measure must receive, respectively, 30% and 35% of the total votes cast in favor. An initiative approved by the voters may be put into effect immediately after the approving votes have been canvassed. In California and Nebraska, the measure may specify an enacting date. In Colorado, measures take effect from the date of proclamation by governor, but no later than 30 days after votes have been canvassed and certified by secretary of state. In Nebraska, 10 days after completion of canvass by the State Board of Canvassers.

(c) Individuals may contest the results of a vote on an initiative within a certain number of days after the election including the measure proposed.

(d) First statewide election at least 120 days after the legislative session.

(e) After certification of election.

(f) Upon governor's proclamation.

(g) Subject to court order.

(h) By vote only.

(i) It is effective the first Tuesday after the first Monday in January following election unless specified in the amendment.

(j) After election is certified.

(k) Effective upon approval by voters and certification of election result by Election Commission: usually 15 days after date of election or later if there is an election contest.

(l) Constitutional amendment—after passed twice by the voters it becomes effective upon the completion of the canvass of votes by the Supreme Court on the fourth Tuesday of November following the election. Statute—effective on the date approved by the governor or the canvass of the vote by the Supreme Court.

(m) It cannot be amended, vetoed or repealed within three years from the date it takes effect.

(n) A measure approved by the electors may not be amended or repealed by the legislative assembly for seven years from its effective date, except by a two-thirds vote of the members elected to each house.

(o) Effective date may be written in the initiative, otherwise it takes place within five days.

(p) Revisor of Statutes.

(q) Once it becomes law, the legislature may pass legislation changing the law.

(r) Supervisor of elections, attorney general and chief counsel of the Legislature.

(s) Not on next ballot.

(t) Initiative can be amended by three-fourths vote of the members of each house of the legislature (AZ Constitution Article 4, Part 1, Section 14).

(u) Amendments or repeal must be voted on by the voters.

(v) No act, law or bill approved by a majority of the electors voting thereon shall be amended or repealed by the legislature within a period of two years following such enactment. Such enactment may be amended or repealed at any general, regular or special election by direct vote of the people thereon.

Table 6.15
STATE REFERENDUMS: REQUESTING PERMISSION TO CIRCULATE A CITIZEN PETITION

State or other jurisdiction	Citizen petition (a)	Signatures required to request a petition (b)	Request submitted to:	Request forms furnished by: (c)	Restricted subject matter (d)	Individual responsible for petition		Financial contributions reported (e)	Deposit required (f)
						Title	Summary		
Alabama	...	...	...	...	...	...	...	...	...
Alaska	Y	100	LG	ST	Y	LG, AG	LG, AG	Y	Y
Arizona	Y	5% VG	SS	SS	Y	P	P	Y	N
Arkansas	Y	...	SS	SS	N	SP	AG	Y	N
California	Y	...	AG	...	Y	AG	AG	N	$200
Colorado	Y	...	...	SP	N	P (g)	P (g)	Y	N
Connecticut	...	...	...	...	...	...	...	...	...
Delaware	...	...	...	...	...	...	...	...	...
Florida	...	...	...	...	...	...	...	...	...
Georgia	...	...	...	...	...	...	...	...	...
Hawaii	...	...	...	...	...	...	...	...	...
Idaho	Y	20	SS	SP	N	AG	AG	Y	N
Illinois	Y	...	...	...	Y	...	...	...	...
Indiana	(k)	Varies	SS	SS	Y	Varies	...	...	...
Iowa	...	...	...	...	...	...	...	...	...
Kansas	...	...	...	...	...	...	...	...	...
Kentucky	Y	...	SS	...	Y	...	...	...	...
Louisiana	...	...	...	...	...	...	...	...	...
Maine	Y	5 (h)	SS	SS	Y	SP, SS	SS (j)	Y	...
Maryland	Y	(o)	...	...	Y	SP	SP	Y	N
Massachusetts	Y	10	SS	SS	Y	AG	AG	Y	N
Michigan	Y	...	...	...	Y	SP	SP	Y	...
Minnesota	...	...	...	...	...	...	...	...	...
Mississippi	...	...	...	...	...	...	...	...	...
Missouri	Y	...	...	SP	Y	SS, AG	(l)	Y	N
Montana	Y	5%	LS, SS, AG	SP	Y	AG	AG	Y	N
Nebraska	Y	...	SS	...	Y	SP	SP	Y	N
Nevada	Y	...	SS	SS	Y	P, SP	P, SP	Y	N
New Hampshire	...	...	...	...	...	...	...	...	...
New Jersey	...	...	...	...	...	...	...	...	...
New Mexico	...	...	...	...	...	...	...	...	...
New York	...	...	...	...	...	...	...	...	...
North Carolina	...	...	...	...	...	...	...	...	...
North Dakota	Y	(m)	SS	SP	N	SS, AG	SS	Y	N
Ohio	Y	...	SS	SP	Y	...	AG	Y	N
Oklahoma	Y	(i)	SS	(n)	N	P	P	Y	N
Oregon	Y	...	SS	SS, SP	N	AG	AG	Y	N
Pennsylvania	...	...	...	...	...	...	...	...	...
Rhode Island	...	...	...	...	...	...	...	...	...
South Carolina	...	...	...	...	...	...	...	...	...
South Dakota	Y	(p)	SS	SP	N	SS	AG	Y	N
Tennessee	...	...	...	...	...	...	...	...	...
Texas	...	...	...	...	...	...	...	...	...
Utah	Y	10% VG and 10% VG 1/2 counties	LG	ST	N	SP	SP	Y	...
Vermont	...	...	...	...	...	...	...	...	...
Virginia	...	...	...	...	...	...	...	...	...
Washington	Y	8% VG	SS	SP	Y	AG	AG	Y	Y
West Virginia	...	...	...	...	...	...	...	...	...
Wisconsin	...	...	...	...	...	...	...	...	...
Wyoming	Y	100	SS	SS	Y	SS	SS	Y	$500
American Samoa	...	...	...	...	...	...	...	...	...
No. Mariana Islands	Y	...	...	...	Y	SP	AG	Y	N
Puerto Rico	Y	10% district/ 41% territorial	Other	SBE	N	SP	Other	Y	N
U.S. Virgin Islands	...	...	...	...	...	...	...	...	...

See footnotes at end of table.

STATE REFERENDUMS: REQUESTING PERMISSION TO CIRCULATE A CITIZEN PETITION — Continued

Sources: The Council of State Governments' survey of state election administration offices, December 2005 and state Web sites.

Key:

. . . — Not applicable	SBE — State Board of Elections
EV — Eligible voters	AG — Attorney General
VG — Total votes cast for the position of governor in the last election	P — Proponent
	ST — State
LG — Lieutenant Governor	SP — Sponsor
LS — Legislative services	Y — Yes
SS — Secretary of State	N — No

(a) Three forms of referenda exist: citizen petition, submission by the legislature, and constitutional requirement. This table outlines the steps necessary to enact a citizen's petition.

(b) Prior to circulating a statewide petition, a request for permission to do so must first be submitted to a specified state officer. Some states require such signatures to only be those of eligible voters.

(c) The form on which the request for petition is submitted may be the responsibility of the sponsor or may be furnished by the state.

(d) Restrictions may exist regarding the subject matter to which a referendum may be applied. The majority of these restrictions pertain to the dedication of state revenues and appropriations, and laws that maintain the preservation of public peace, safety and health. In Kentucky, referenda are only permitted for the establishment of soil and water and watershed conservation districts.

(e) In some states, a list of individuals who contribute financially to the referendum campaign must be submitted to the specified state officer with whom the petition is filed.

(f) A deposit may be required after permission to circulate a petition has been granted. This amount is refunded when the completed petition has been filed correctly.

(g) Colorado secretary of state rule 23.

(h) The name and address of five voters.

(i) Five percent of legal voters based upon the total number of votes cast at the last general election for the state office receiving the highest number of votes at such election.

(j) Revisor of statutes.

(k) A referendum can only be placed on the ballot if authorized by a state law. As a result, a county or town election board cannot print any referendum on the ballot unless the legislature has already passed a law to permit the referendum. Therefore, each statute is different.

(l) State auditor writes the fiscal note.

(m) Two percent of resident population of state at the last federal decennial census.

(o) Petition sponsor may submit proposed petition summary for approval to State Administrator of Elections but a formal request to circulate a petition is not required.

(p) Current number of signatures required, 16,728.

Table 6.16
STATE REFERENDUMS: CIRCULATING THE CITIZEN PETITION

State or other jurisdiction	Basis for signatures	Maximum time period allowed for petition circulation (a)	Can signatures be removed from petition (b)	Completed petition filed: With	Completed petition filed: Days after legislative session
Alabama	...	...	...	...	...
Alaska	10% TV, from 3/4 ED	w/i 90 days of LS	Y	SBE	90 days after LS
Arizona	5% VG	w/i 90 days after LS	Y	SS	90 days
Arkansas	6% VG	...	N	SS	90 days
California	5% VG	90 days	Y	(d)	...
Colorado	5% VSS	90 days after LS	N	SS	90 days
Connecticut	...	...	...	...	...
Delaware	...	...	...	...	...
Florida	...	...	...	...	...
Georgia	...	...	...	...	...
Hawaii	...	...	...	...	...
Idaho	6% EV	w/i 60 days after LS	Y	SS	60 days
Illinois	10% EV	24 mos. prior to election	N	SBE	...
Indiana	...	...	...	...	...
Iowa	...	...	...	...	...
Kansas	...	...	...	...	...
Kentucky	5% VG	...	...	SS	4 mos.
Louisiana	...	...	...	...	...
Maine	10% VG	90 days of LS (c)	...	SS	90 days
Maryland	3% VG	(h)	Y	SS	...
Massachusetts	1.5% VG for emergency 2% or immediate suspension	90 days	Y (e)	SS	90 days after signed by governor
Michigan	5% VG	90 days after LS	N	SS	90 days
Minnesota	...	...	...	...	...
Mississippi	...	...	...	...	...
Missouri	5% VG, from 2/3 ED	w/i 90 days after LS	Y	SS	90 days
Montana	5% EV	(j)	Y	SS	6 mos.
Nebraska	5% EV	...	Y	SS	90 days
Nevada	10% EV last GE	(f)	Y	SS	120 prior to next GE
New Hampshire	...	...	...	...	...
New Jersey	...	...	...	...	...
New Mexico	...	...	...	...	...
New York	...	...	...	...	...
North Carolina	...	...	...	...	...
North Dakota	2% total population	90 days	N	SS	(i)
Ohio	6% VG, 3% each from 1/2 county	90 days	(g)	SS	90 days
Oklahoma	5% VH	w/i 90 days of LS	Y	SS	90 days
Oregon	4% VG	w/i 90 days of LS	N	SS	90 days
Pennsylvania	...	...	...	...	...
Rhode Island	...	...	...	...	...
South Carolina	...	...	...	...	...
South Dakota	5% VG	w/i 90 days of LS	N	SS	90 days
Tennessee	...	...	...	...	...
Texas	...	...	...	...	...
Utah	10% VG	40 days after LS	Y	LG	5 days
Vermont	...	...	...	...	...
Virginia	...	...	...	...	...
Washington	(k)	...	Y	SS	90 days
West Virginia	...	...	...	...	...
Wisconsin	...	...	...	...	...
Wyoming	15% TV, from 2/3 county	18 mos.	N	SS	90 days
American Samoa	...	...	...	...	...
No. Mariana Islands	...	Up to 120 days before election	Y	AG	...
Puerto Rico	...	...	...	...	...
U.S. Virgin Islands	...	...	...	...	...

See footnotes at end of table.

STATE REFERENDUMS: CIRCULATING THE CITIZEN PETITION — Continued

Sources: The Council of State Governments' survey of state election administration offices and state Web sites, December 2005.

Key:

. . . — Not applicable

VG — Total votes cast for the position of governor in the last election

EV — Eligible voters

TV — Total voters in the last general election

VH — Total votes cast for the office receiving the highest number of votes in last general election

VSS — Total votes cast for all candidates for the office of secretary of state at the previous general election

ED — Election district

GE — General election

LS — Legislative session

LG — Lieutenant governor

SBE — State Board of Elections

SS — Secretary of State

AG — Attorney General

Y — Yes

N — No

w/i — Within

(a) The petition circulation period begins when petition forms have been approved and provided to or by the sponsors. Sponsors are those individuals granted permission to circulate a petition, and are therefore responsible for the validity of each signature on a given petition.

(b) Should an individual wish to remove his/her name from a petition, a request to do so must first be submitted in writing to the state officer with whom the petition is filed.

(c) Request for petition must be submitted within 10 days of adjournment of legislative session.

(d) County elections office.

(e) Should an individual wish to remove his/her name from a petition, a request to do so must first be submitted in writing to the local election official prior to the petition being submitted for certification of signatures.

(f) Not later than the third Tuesday in May of even-numbered years.

(g) By request of signer or by circulator before filing.

(h) No signature may be collected until the final action of the General Assembly. Session ends the second Monday in April. One-third of the signatures must be submitted not later than May 31st. The remaining signatures are due no later than June 30th.

(i) Within 90 days after the legislation is filed in the Secretary of State's office.

(j) Not specified, but goes from end of the legislative session, usually in April to six months later.

(k) If any legal voter of the state, either individually or on behalf of an organization, desires to petition the legislature to enact a proposed measure, or submit a proposed initiative measure to the people, or order that referendum of all or part of any act, bill, or law, passed by the legislature be submitted to the people, he or she shall file with the secretary of state a legible copy of the measure proposed, or the act or part of such act on which a referendum is desired, accompanied by an affidavit that the sponsor is a legal voter and a filing fee prescribed under RCW 43.07.120.

Table 6.17
STATE REFERENDUMS: PREPARING THE CITIZEN PETITION REFERENDUM
TO BE PLACED ON THE BALLOT

State or other jurisdiction	Signatures verified by: (a)	Within how many days after filing	Number of days to amend/appeal a petition that is:		Penalty for falsifying petition (denotes fine, jail term)	Petition certified by: (d)
			Incomplete (b)	Not Accepted (c)		
Alabama	. . .	. . .	. . .	. . .	. . .	. . .
Alaska	Director of elections	60	10	. . .	. . .	LG
Arizona	County recorder	(f)	. . .	. . .	Class 1 misdemeanor	SS
Arkansas....................	SS	30	30	. . .	Class A misdemeanor	SS
California	County clerk	8	. . .	. . .	Felony or misdemeanor (depending on severity)	SS
Colorado	SS	30	15	. . .	(h)	SS
Connecticut	. . .	. . .	. . .	. . .	. . .	. . .
Delaware....................	. . .	. . .	. . .	. . .	. . .	. . .
Florida	. . .	. . .	. . .	. . .	. . .	. . .
Georgia	. . .	. . .	. . .	. . .	. . .	. . .
Hawaii.......................	. . .	. . .	. . .	. . .	. . .	. . .
Idaho........................	County clerk	. . .	. . .	. . .	$5,000, 2 yrs.	SS
Illinois......................	County clerk	Varies	. . .	. . .	. . .	SBE
Indiana......................	County clerk	. . .	. . .	. . .	. . .	. . .
Iowa	. . .	. . .	. . .	. . .	. . .	. . .
Kansas	. . .	. . .	. . .	. . .	. . .	. . .
Kentucky	. . .	. . .	. . .	. . .	. . .	. . .
Louisiana	. . .	. . .	. . .	. . .	. . .	. . .
Maine	Registrar of voters	30	. . .	. . .	. . .	SS
Maryland	Local Board of Elections	20	. . .	. . .	Misdemeanor (n)	SS, SBE
Massachusetts.............	Local boards of registrars	14	. . .	. . .	$1,000, 1 yr.	SS
Michigan....................	SS	Approx. 60	. . .	. . .	$500, 90 days	BSC
Minnesota	. . .	. . .	. . .	. . .	. . .	. . .
Mississippi	. . .	. . .	. . .	. . .	. . .	. . .
Missouri.....................	County clerk	(m)	. . .	10	Class A misdemeanor	SS
Montana	County clerk	28	. . .	. . .	$500, 6 mos. (o)	SS
Nebraska....................	County clerk	40	. . .	. . .	. . .	SS
Nevada	County clerk	(g)	5	. . .	. . .	SS
New Hampshire.........	. . .	. . .	. . .	. . .	. . .	. . .
New Jersey.................	. . .	. . .	. . .	. . .	. . .	. . .
New Mexico	. . .	. . .	. . .	. . .	. . .	. . .
New York	. . .	. . .	. . .	. . .	. . .	. . .
North Carolina..........	. . .	. . .	. . .	. . .	. . .	. . .
North Dakota.............	SS	35	. . .	20	(i)	SS
Ohio	County board of elections	10	10	. . .	5th degree felony	SS
Oklahoma	SS	. . .	10	. . .	$1,000, 1 yr.	SS
Oregon	SS, county clerk	30	. . .	. . .	Class C felony	SS
Pennsylvania	. . .	. . .	. . .	. . .	. . .	. . .
Rhode Island	. . .	. . .	. . .	. . .	. . .	. . .
South Carolina	. . .	. . .	. . .	. . .	. . .	. . .
South Dakota.............	SS	. . .	. . .	. . .	Class 1 misdemeanor	SS
Tennessee	. . .	. . .	. . .	. . .	. . .	. . .
Texas	. . .	. . .	. . .	. . .	. . .	. . .
Utah	County clerks	55 (l)		10	Class A misdemeanor	LG
Vermont.....................	. . .	. . .	. . .	. . .	. . .	. . .
Virginia.....................	. . .	. . .	. . .	. . .	. . .	. . .
Washington................	SS	(j)	. . .	10 (k)	Class C felony (possible)	SS
West Virginia.............	. . .	. . .	. . .	. . .	. . .	. . .
Wisconsin...................	. . .	. . .	. . .	. . .	. . .	. . .
Wyoming....................	SS	60	60	60	$1,000, 1 yr.	SS
American Samoa.......	. . .	. . .	. . .	. . .	. . .	. . .
No. Mariana Islands...	AG	. . .	(p)	(p)	. . .	AG
Puerto Rico...............	. . .	. . .	. . .	. . .	. . .	. . .
U.S. Virgin Islands....	. . .	. . .	. . .	. . .	. . .	. . .

See footnotes at end of table.

STATE REFERENDUMS: PREPARING THE CITIZEN PETITION REFERENDUM TO BE PLACED ON THE BALLOT — Continued

Sources: The Council of State Governments' survey of state election administration offices, December 2005 and state Web sites.

Key:

. . . — Not applicable

SS — Secretary of State

LG — Lieutenant Governor

BSC — Board of State Canvassers

SBE — State Board of Elections

(a) The validity of the signatures, as well as the correct number of required signatures must be verified before the referendum is allowed on the ballot.

(b) If an insufficient number of signatures are submitted, sponsors may amend the original petition by filing additional signatures within a given number of days after filing. If the necessary number of signatures have not been submitted by this date, the petition is declared void.

(c) In some cases, the state officer will not accept a valid petition. In such cases, sponsors may appeal this decision to the Supreme Court, where the sufficiency of the petition will be determined. If the petition is determined to be sufficient, the referendum is required to be placed on the ballot.

(d) A petition is certified for the ballot when the required number of signatures has been submitted by the filing deadline, and they are determined to be valid.

(e) If within 90 days of the legislative session.

(f) In Arizona, the secretary of state has 15 days to count signatures and to complete random sample; the county recorder then has 10 days to verify signatures.

(g) 1. Within four days, county clerks count total number of signatures and forward to the secretary of state. 2. The secretary of state immediately notifies county clerks if they are to proceed or not proceed with the signature verification. 3. If ordered by the secretary of state, the county clerks verify signatures within nine days (excluding weekends and holidays).

(h) Not more than $500 or one year in city jail, or both.

(i) Any violations discovered will be reported to the attorney general for investigation and prosecution.

(j) No specified time.

(k) In Washington, a petition that is not accepted may be appealed in 10 days.

(l) After the end of the legislative session.

(m) In Missouri, must be certified as sufficient or insufficient by the 13th Tuesday prior to the general election.

(n) Misdemeanor, punishable by a $10–$250 fine or 30 days–six months in jail, or both.

(o) Penalty for giving a false statement—$500 or six months in county jail or both. Penalty for tampering with public records—$10,000 or up to 10 years in state prison or both.

(p) Incomplete: 30 or more days if submitted 150 days before date of the election; none if submitted 120 days before date of election. Not Accepted: if submitted 119 days or less before the election.

(q) Subject to statute governing fraud or perjury.

Table 6.18
STATE REFERENDUMS: VOTING ON THE CITIZEN PETITION REFERENDUM

State or other jurisdiction	Ballot (a) Title by:	Ballot (a) Summary by:	Election where referendum voted on	Effective date of approved referendum (b)	Days to contest election results
Alabama	...	...	...	...	...
Alaska	LG, AG	LG, AG	1st statewide election 180 days after LS	30 days	10
Arizona	SS, AG	LC	GE	(i)	5
Arkansas	AG	AG	GE	30 days	60 (e)
California	AG	AG	GE or PR	1 day	5 (e)
Colorado	(h)	(h)	GE (d)	30 days	10
Connecticut	...	...	...	...	...
Delaware	...	...	...	...	...
Florida	...	...	...	...	...
Georgia	...	...	...	...	...
Hawaii	...	...	...	...	...
Idaho	AG	AG	GE	30 days	20 (e)
Illinois	...	...	GE	...	Varies
Indiana	...	...	...	...	...
Iowa	...	...	...	...	...
Kansas	...	...	...	...	...
Kentucky	...	...	GE or SP	IM	...
Louisiana	...	...	...	...	...
Maine	...	...	GE or statewide election more than 60 days after filing	30 days	5
Maryland	SS	LLS	GE	(j)	...
Massachusetts	SS, AG	AG	GE more than 60 days after filing	30 days	10
Michigan	BSC	BSC	GE	10 days	2 (e)
Minnesota	...	...	...	...	...
Mississippi	...	...	...	...	...
Missouri	SS, AG	SS	GE	IM	30
Montana	AG	AG	GE	(f)	1 yr.
Nebraska	AG	AG	GE	...	...
Nevada	SS, AG	SS, AG	GE	Nov., 4th Tues.	14
New Hampshire	...	...	...	...	...
New Jersey	...	...	...	...	...
New Mexico	...	...	...	...	...
New York	...	...	...	...	...
North Carolina	...	...	...	...	...
North Dakota	SS, AG	SS	PR	30 days	14 (e)
Ohio	...	...	GE	IM	15 (e)
Oklahoma	LLS, AG	LLS	GE or SP	...	...
Oregon	AG	AG	GE (g)	30 days	35
Pennsylvania	...	...	...	...	...
Rhode Island	...	...	...	...	...
South Carolina	...	...	...	...	...
South Dakota	AG	AG	GE	1 day	10
Tennessee	...	...	...	...	...
Texas	...	...	...	...	...
Utah	LC	LC	GE	5 days	40
Vermont	...	...	...	...	...
Virginia	...	...	...	...	...
Washington	AG	AG	GE	IM	3
West Virginia	...	...	...	...	...
Wisconsin	...	...	...	...	...
Wyoming	SS	SS, AG	GE more than 120 days after LS	90 days	15
American Samoa	...	...	...	...	...
No. Mariana Islands	AG	AG	GE or special election if specified	(k)	30 days
Puerto Rico	...	...	...	...	...
U.S. Virgin Islands	...	...	...	...	...

See footnotes at end of table.

STATE REFERENDUMS: VOTING ON THE CITIZEN PETITION REFERENDUM — Continued

Sources: The Council of State Governments' survey of state election administration offices, December 2005 and state Web sites.

Key:

. . . — Not applicable	SBE — State Board of Elections
LG — Lieutenant Governor	GE — General election
SS — Secretary of State	PR — Primary election
AG — Attorney General	REG — Regular election
BSC — Board of State Canvassers	SP — Special election
LC — Legislative Counsel	IM — Immediately
LLS — Legislative Legal Services	LS — Legislative session

(a) In some states, the ballot title and summary will differ from that on the petition.

(b) A majority of the popular vote is required to enact a measure in every state. In Arizona, a referendum approved by the voters becomes effective upon the governor's proclamation. In Nebraska, a referendum may be put into effect immediately after the approving votes have been canvassed by the Board of State Canvassers and upon the governor's proclamation. In Colorado, measures take effect from the date of proclamation by governor, but no later than 30 days after votes have been canvassed and certified by secretary of state. In Massachusetts, the measure must also receive at least 30 percent of the total ballots cast in the last election. In Oklahoma, put into effect upon certification of election results by state election board. In Utah, after proclamation by governor and date specified in petition.

(c) Individuals may contest the results of a vote on a referendum within a certain number of days after the election including this matter. In Alaska, five days to request recount with appeal to the court within five days after recount.

(d) Next general election that occurs at least three months after the referendum petition is filed with the Secretary of State.

(e) After election is certified.

(f) Date canvass is filed with Secretary of State. Generally, 20 days after November election.

(g) Special election can be held at the request of the Legislative Assembly.

(h) Proponent; Colorado Secretary of State Rule 23.

(i) Upon proclamation of the governor after the canvas. (AZ Const. Article 4, Part 1, Section 13.)

(j) After the certification of election results. Depends on date Board of State Canvassers meets. They must meet within 35 days after General Election.

(k) Upon approval by voters and certification of election results by Election Commission, usually 15 days after date of election if no contest.

Table 6.19
STATE RECALL PROVISIONS

State or other jurisdiction	Provision for recall	Officials subject to recall	Constitutional and statutory citations for recall of state officials	Constitutional or statutory language
Alabama	No			
Alaska	Yes	All (a)	Const. Art., 11 § 8; AS § 15.45.510–710, 15.60.010	All elected public officials in the State, except judicial officers, are subject to recall by the voters of the State or political subdivision from which elected. Procedures and grounds for recall shall be prescribed by the legislature.
Arizona	Yes	All	Const. Art. 8, § 1-6; ARS § 19-201–19-234	Every public officer in the state of Arizona, holding an elective office, either by election or appointment, is subject to recall from such office by the qualified electors of the electoral district from which candidates are elected to such office.
Arkansas	No			
California	Yes	All	Const. Art. 2, § 13–19; CA Election Code § 19-201–19-234	Recall is the power of the electors to remove an elective officer. Recall of a state officer is initiated by delivering to the Secretary of State a petition alleging reason for recall. Sufficiency of reason is not reviewable.
Colorado	Yes	All	Const. Art. 21, § 1; CRS § 1-12-101–1-12-122, 23-17-120.5, 31-4-501–505	Every elective public officer of the state of Colorado may be recalled from office at any time by the registered electors entitled to vote for a successor of such incumbent through the procedure and in the manner herein provided for, which procedure shall be known as the recall, and shall be in addition to and without excluding any other method of removal by law.
Connecticut	No			
Delaware	No			
Florida	No			
Georgia	Yes	All	Const. Art. 2, § 2.4; GA Code § 21-4-1 et seq.	The General Assembly is hereby authorized to provide by general law for the recall of public officials who hold elective office. The procedures, grounds, and all other matters relative to such recall shall be provided for in such law.
Hawaii	No			
Idaho	Yes	All (a)	Const. Art 6, § 6; ID Code § 34-1701–34-1715	Every public officer in the state of Idaho, excepting the judicial officers, is subject to recall by the legal voters of the state or of the electoral district from which he is elected. The legislature shall pass the necessary laws to carry this provision into effect.
Illinois	No			
Indiana	No			
Iowa	No			
Kansas	Yes	All (a)	Const. Art. 4, § 3; KSA § 25-4301–25-4331	All elected public officials in the State, except judicial officers, shall be subject to recall by voters of the state or political subdivision from which elected. Procedures and grounds for recall shall be prescribed by law.
Kentucky	No			
Louisiana	Yes	All (a)	Const. Art. 10, § 26; LRS § 18:1300.1–18:1300.17	The legislature shall provide by general law for the recall by election of any state, district, parochial, ward, or municipal officer except judges of the courts of record. The sole issue at a recall election shall be whether the official shall be recalled.
Maine	No			

See footnotes at end of table.

STATE RECALL PROVISIONS — Continued

State or other jurisdiction	Provision for recall	Officials subject to recall	Constitutional and statutory citations for recall of state officials	Constitutional or statutory language
Maryland................	No			
Massachusetts..........	No			
Michigan................	Yes	All (a)	Const. Art. 2, § 8; MCL § 168.951–168.975	Laws shall be enacted to provide for the recall of all elective officers except judges of courts of record upon petition of electors equal in number to 25 percent of the number of persons voting in the last preceding election for the office of governor in the electoral district of the officer sought to be recalled. The sufficiency of any statement of reasons or grounds procedurally required shall be a political rather than a judicial question.
Minnesota	Yes	(b)	Const. Art. 8, § 6; MS § 211C.01 et. seq.	A member of the senate or the house of representatives, an executive officer of the state identified in section 1 of article V of the constitution, or a judge of the supreme court, the court of appeals, or a district court is subject to recall from office by the voters.
Mississippi	No			
Missouri	No			
Montana	Yes	All	Mont. Code § 2-16-601–2-16-635	Every person holding a public office of the state or any of its political subdivisions, either by election or appointment, is subject to recall from such office.
Nebraska................	No			
Nevada	Yes	All	Const. Art. 2, § 9; NRS § 294A.006	Every public officer in the State of Nevada is subject, as herein provided, to recall from office by the registered voters of the state, or of the county, district, or municipality which he represents.
New Hampshire.........	No			
New Jersey..............	Yes	All	Const. Art. 1, § 2; NJRS § 19:27A-1–19:27A-18	The people reserve unto themselves the power to recall, after at least one year of service, any elected official in this State or representing this State in the Untied States Congress.
New Mexico.............	No			
New York................	No			
North Carolina.........	No			
North Dakota...........	Yes	All (c)	Const. Art. 3, § 1 and 10; ND Century Code § 16.1-01-09.1	Any elected official of the state, of any county or of any legislative or county commissioner district shall be subject to recall by petition of electors equal in number to twenty-five percent of those who voted at the preceding general election for the office of governor in the state, county, or district in which the official is to be recalled.
Ohio.....................	No			
Oklahoma...............	No			
Oregon	Yes	All (c)	Const. Art. 2, § 18; ORS § 249.865–249.880	Every public official in Oregon is subject, as herein provided, to recall by the electors of the state or of the electoral district from which the public official is elected.
Pennsylvania	No			
Rhode Island	Yes	(d)	Const. Art. 4, § 1	Recall is authorized in the case of a general officer who has been indicted or informed against for a felony, convicted of a misdemeanor, or against whom a finding of probable cause of violation of the code of ethics has been made by the ethics commission.
South Carolina.........				

See footnotes at end of table.

STATE RECALL PROVISIONS—Continued

State or other jurisdiction	Provision for recall	Officials subject to recall	Constitutional and statutory citations for recall of state officials	Constitutional or statutory language
South Dakota...............	No			
Tennessee	No			
Texas	No			
Utah	No			
Vermont....................	No			
Virginia....................	No			
Washington................	Yes	All (a)	Const. Art. 1, Sec. 33-34; WRC § 29.82-010–29.82.220	Every elective public officer of the state of Washington except judges of courts of record is subject to recall and discharge by the legal voters of the state, or of the political subdivision of the state, from which he was elected whenever a petition demanding his recall, . . . is filed with the officer with whom a petition for nomination, or certificate for nomination, to such office must be filed under the laws of this state, and the same officer shall call a special election as provided by the general election laws of this state, and the result determined as therein provided.
West Virginia..............				
Wisconsin...................	Yes	All	Const. Art. 13, § 12; Wisc. Stat. § 9.10	The qualified electors of the state, of any congressional, judicial or legislative district or of any county may petition for the recall of any incumbent elective officer after the first year of the term for which the incumbent was elected, by filing a petition with the filing officer with whom the nomination petition is filed, demanding the recall of the incumbent.
Wyoming....................	No			
No. Mariana Islands	Yes	All	N.A.	N.A.
Puerto Rico.................	Yes	All	N.A.	N.A.

Sources: The Council of State Governments, state constitutions and statutes, December 2005.

N.A. — Not available

(a) Except judicial.

(b) State executive officers, legislators, and judicial officers.

(c) Except for U.S. Congress.

(d) Governor, Lieutenant Governor, Secretary of State, and Treasurer.

Table 6.20
STATE RECALL PROVISIONS: APPLICABILITY TO STATE OFFICIALS AND PETITION CIRCULATION

State or other jurisdiction	Officers to whom recall is applicable (a)	No. of times recall can be attempted	Recall may be initiated after official has been in office	Recall may not be initiated with days remaining in term	Basis for signatures (b) (see key below) Statewide officers	Others	Maximum time allowed for petition circulation (c)
Alabama	...	...					...
Alaska	All state level officers	...	120 days	180	25% VO	25% VO	...
Arizona	All elected officials	1 (d)	6 mos./5 days legislators	...	25% VO (v)	25% VO (v)	120 days
Arkansas	...	...					160 days
California	All elected officials	(e)	90 days	6 mos.	12% VO, 1% from 5 counties	20% VO	60 days
Colorado	All elected officials	(f)	6 mos./5 days legislators	6 mos.	25% VO	25% VO	60 days
Connecticut	...	...					...
Delaware	...	...					...
Florida	...	...					...
Georgia	All state level officials, county and city elected officials	...	180 days	180	15% EV (g), 1/15 from each congressional district	30% EV (g)	(t)
Hawaii	...	...					...
Idaho	All but judicial officers	(d)	90 days	...	20% EVg	50% VO	60 days
Illinois	...	...					...
Indiana	...	...					...
Iowa	...	...					...
Kansas	All but judicial officers	1	120 days	180	40% VO	40% VO	90 days
Kentucky	...	...					...
Louisiana	All officers	(h)	1 day	6 mos.	33 1/3% EV (i)	33 1/3% EV (i)	180 days
Maine	...	...					...
Maryland	...	...					...
Massachusetts	...	...					...
Michigan	All but judicial officers	...	6 mos.	6 mos.	25% VG in district	25% VG in district	...
Minnesota	All state level officials	...	...	6 mos.	25% VO	25% VO	90 days
Mississippi	...	...					...
Missouri	...	...					...
Montana	All state level officers and elected officials	(w)	2 mos.	...	10% EV	(k)	3 mos.
Nebraska	Elected officials from political subdivisions	(u)	6 mos.	6 mos.		35–45% VO	...
Nevada	All officers	(d)	6 mos. (l)	...	25% VO in given jurisdiction	25% VO in given jurisdiction	90 days
New Hampshire	...	...					...
New Jersey	All elected officials	(p)	(q)	(r)	25% VO in given jurisdiction	25% VO in given jurisdiction	(s)
New Mexico	...	...					...
New York	...	...					...
North Carolina	...	...					...
North Dakota	All elected officials	1	...	190	25% EVg	25% EV	90 days
Ohio	...	...					...
Oklahoma	All officers	No limit	6 mos.	...	15% (m)	15% (m)	90 days
Oregon	All officers	No limit	6 mos.	...	15% (m)	15% (m)	90 days
Pennsylvania	...	...					...
Rhode Island	Gov., lt. gov., atty. gen., sec. of state, treasurer	...	6 mos.	...	15% VO	...	90 days
South Carolina	...	...					...

See footnotes at end of table.

STATE RECALL PROVISIONS: APPLICABILITY TO STATE OFFICIALS AND PETITION CIRCULATION — Continued

State or other jurisdiction	Officers to whom recall is applicable (a)	No. of times recall can be attempted	Recall may be initiated after official has been in office	Recall may not be initiated with days remaining in term	Basis for signatures (b) (see key below)		Maximum time allowed for petition circulation (c)
					Statewide officers	Others	
South Dakota	...	...	...	...	...	...	...
Tennessee	...	...	...	...	...	...	...
Texas	...	...	...	...	...	...	...
Utah	...	...	...	...	...	...	...
Vermont	...	...	...	...	...	...	...
Virginia	All but judges of courts of records	...	...	...	...	35% VO	...
Washington	...	...	IM	180	25% VO		(n)
West Virginia	...	...	...	...	...	...	...
Wisconsin	All elected officials	1	1 yr.	...	25% VG (o)	25% VG (o)	60 days
Wyoming	...	...	...	...	...	...	...
American Samoa	...	...	...	...	...	...	...
No. Mariana Islands	All elected officials	(x)	180 days	...	40% EV (y)	...	(z)
Puerto Rico	...	...	...	...	...	...	...
U.S. Virgin Islands	All elected officials	Unlimited	1 year	6 mos.	...	...	180 days

Sources: The Council of State Governments' survey of state election administration offices, December 2005 and state Web sites.

Key:
... — Not applicable
All — All elective officials
VO — Number of votes cast in the last election for the office or official being recalled
EVg — Number of eligible voters in the last general election for governor
EV — Eligible voters
VG — Total votes cast for the position of governor in the last election
VP — Total votes cast for position of president in the last presidential election
IM — Immediately

(a) An elective official may be recalled by qualified voters entitled to vote for the recalled official's successor. An appointed official may be recalled by qualified voters entitled to vote for the successor(s) of the elective officer(s) authorized to appoint an individual to the position.
(b) Signature requirements for recall of those other than state elective officials are based on votes in the jurisdiction to which the said official has been elected.
(c) The petition circulation period begins when petition forms have been approved and provided to sponsors. Sponsors are those individuals granted permission to circulate a petition, and are therefore responsible for the validity of each signature on a given petition.
(d) Additional recall attempts can be made, provided that the state treasury is reimbursed the cost of the previous recall attempt(s). The specific reason for recalling on one petition cannot be the basis for a second recall petition during the current term of office.
(e) Open ended.
(f) One attempt unless able to gather signatures at least equal in number to 50 percent of those voting for the office in the last general election.
(g) Eligible voters for office at last general election to fill office.
(h) Unlimited. Once every 18 months.
(i) Basis for signatures 33 1/3 percent if over 1,000 eligible voters; 40 percent if under 1,000 eligible voters.

(j) Forty-eight hours if certified on state level and six days if certified on county level.
(k) Fifteen percent to twenty percent of eligible voters, depending on the office.
(l) For legislators, anytime after 10 days from the beginning of the first legislative session after their election.
(m) Fifteen percent of the total number of votes cast in the public officer's electoral district for all candidates for governor at the last election at which a candidate for governor was elected to a full term.
(n) Statewide officials, 270 days; others, 180 days.
(o) At least 25 percent of the vote case for the office of governor at the last election within the same district or territory as that of the officeholder being recalled.
(p) An elected official sought to be recalled who is not recalled as the result of a recall election shall not again be subject to recall until after having served one year of a term calculated from the date of the recall election.
(q) The recall drive may not commence before the 50th day preceding the completion of the elected official's first year of the current term.
(r) No election to recall an elected official shall be held after the date occurring six months prior to the general election or regular election for that office, as appropriate, in the final year of the official's term.
(s) The maximum time allowed for petition circulation is 320 days for a governor or 160 days for other elected officials.
(t) For any statewide office, 90 days. Any officer holding an office other than statewide office and for whom no less than 5,000 signatures are required for the recall petition, 45 days. Any officer holding an office other than statewide office and for whom less than 5,000 are required, 30 days.
(u) If voted on, no recall for one year.
(v) Twenty-five percent of the number of votes cast at the preceding general election for all candidates for the office held by the officer, even if the officer was not elected at that election, divided by the number of offices that were being filled at that election. (A.R.S. § 19-201.)
(w) No limit specified in law.
(x) Not more than once a year or not during the first six months in office.
(y) Grounds for recall must be stated and must be signed by 40 percent of voters represented by the elected official.
(z) Until 120 days before the election.

Table 6.21
STATE RECALL PROVISIONS: PETITION REVIEW, APPEAL AND ELECTION

State or other jurisdiction	Signatures verified (a) by:	Days to amend/appeal a petition that is: Incomplete (b)	Not Accepted (c)	Penalty for falsifying petition (denotes fines, jail time)	Days allowed for petition to be certified (d)	Days to step down after certification (e)	Voting on the recall (f) Election held	Election type	Days to contest election results (g)
Alabama	...	...	...	...	...	...	...	...	...
Alaska	Director of elections	20	...	...	30	...	60–90 days after cert.	SP	10
Arizona	County recorder	...	...	Class 1 misdemeanor	70	1	(x)	(u)	5
Arkansas	...	...	...	...	...	5	...	...	...
California	County clerk/registrar of voters	10	10	...	10	(w)	60–80 days after cert.	GE	5
Colorado	SS	60 (r)	60 (r)	$1,000, 1 yr. or both	10	5	45–75 days after cert.	SP or GE	10
Connecticut	...	...	...	...	...	...	...	...	...
Delaware	...	...	...	...	...	...	...	...	...
Florida	...	...	...	...	...	...	...	...	...
Georgia	Registrar of voters	...	...	Misdemeanor	30–45	...	30–45 days after cert.	SP	5
Hawaii	...	...	...	...	...	...	...	...	...
Idaho	County clerk	30	...	$5,000, 2 yrs.	10	5	45+ days after cert. (h)	SP, PR, GE (h)	20 (i)
Illinois	...	...	...	...	...	...	...	...	...
Indiana	...	...	...	...	...	...	...	...	...
Iowa	...	...	...	...	...	...	...	...	...
Kansas	County clerk	...	...	Class B misdemeanor; up to $1,000, up to one year or both	30	Next day	60–90 days after cert.	SP	5 (i)
Kentucky	...	...	...	...	...	...	...	...	...
Louisiana	Registrar of voters	(v)	(v)	...	15–20	(y)	(j)	SP	(z)
Maine	...	...	...	...	...	...	...	...	...
Maryland	...	...	...	...	...	...	...	...	...
Massachusetts	...	...	...	...	...	...	...	...	...
Michigan	SS, local election officials (k)	...	...	$500, 90 days	35	IM	w/i 60 days after cert.	SP	2 (i)
Minnesota	SS	...	...	Misdemeanor	10	...	Not less than 15 days after cert.	GE	7
Mississippi	...	...	...	...	...	...	...	...	...
Missouri	...	...	...	...	...	...	...	...	...
Montana	County clerk	...	...	(aa)	90	5	Not specified	SP or GE	12 mos.
Nebraska	County clerk	...	...	...	15	5	30–45 days after cert.	SP	40
Nevada	County clerk, registrar of voters	5	...	Misdemeanor	(s)	5	(l)	SP	(t)
New Hampshire	...	...	...	...	...	...	...	...	...
New Jersey	Recall elections official	...	...	Crime of the 4th degree	10	5	(p)	SP or GE	(q)
New Mexico	...	...	...	...	...	...	...	...	...
New York	...	...	...	...	...	...	...	...	...
North Carolina	...	...	...	...	...	...	...	...	...
North Dakota	SS	...	...	...	30	10	50–60 days	SP	14 (m)
Ohio	...	...	...	...	...	...	...	...	...
Oklahoma	...	...	...	...	...	...	...	...	...
Oregon	SS or county clerk	...	...	Class C felony	10	5	40 days after cert.	SP	35
Pennsylvania	...	...	...	...	...	...	...	...	...
Rhode Island	SBE	w/i 90 days	...	Misdemeanor and/or felony	90	...	...	SP	...
South Carolina	...	...	...	...	...	...	...	...	...

See footnotes at end of table.

STATE RECALL PROVISIONS: PETITION REVIEW, APPEAL AND ELECTION — Continued

State or other jurisdiction	Signatures verified (a) by:	Days to amend/appeal a petition that is:		Penalty for falsifying petition (denotes fines, jail time)	Days allowed for petition to be certified (d)	Days to step down after certification (e)	Voting on the recall (f)		Days to contest election results (g)
		Incomplete (b)	Not Accepted (c)				Election held	Election type	
South Dakota............	...	...	...	...	...	...	...	...	...
Tennessee	...	...	...	...	...	...	...	...	...
Texas	...	...	...	...	...	...	...	...	...
Utah	...	...	...	...	...	...	...	...	...
Vermont	...	...	...	...	...	...	...	...	...
Virginia...................	...	...	...	...	...	...	...	...	3
Washington...............	SS, county auditor	10 (n)	...	Felony	Not specified	IM	45–60 days after cert.	SP	3
West Virginia	...	...	...	...	...	...	...	...	...
Wisconsin.................	SBE	...	...	Class 1 felony—$10,000, 3 yrs. prison or both	31	10	6 weeks after cert.	GE or PR	3 (o)
Wyoming..................	...	...	...	...	...	...	...	...	...
American Samoa	AG	...	...	...	...	...	(bb)	...	...
No. Mariana Islands ...	...	150 days	...	...	15	...	...	GE, SP	30
Puerto Rico...............	...	...	...	Statute governs fraud or perjury.	15	IM	...	...	...
U.S. Virgin Islands......	Other	3	...	N.A.	...	...	...	SP	...

Sources: The Council of State Governments' survey of state election administration offices, December 2005 and state Web sites.

Key:

... — Not applicable
SBE — State Board of Elections
SS — Secretary of State
SP — Special election
GE — General election
PR — Primary election
IM — Immediate and automatic removal from office
w/i — Within
N.A. — Information not available

(a) The validity of the signatures, as well as the correct number of required signatures must be verified before the recall is allowed on the ballot.

(b) If an insufficient number of signatures is submitted, sponsors may amend the original petition by filing additional signatures within a given number of days. If the necessary number of signatures have not been submitted by this date, the petition is declared void.

(c) In some cases, the state officer will not accept a valid petition. In such a case, sponsors may appeal this decision to the Supreme Court, where the sufficiency of the petition will be determined. When this is declared, the recall is not required to be placed on the ballot.

(d) A petition is certified for the ballot when the required number of signatures has been submitted by the filing deadline, and are determined to be valid.

(e) The official to whom a recall is proposed has a certain number of days to step down from his position before a recall election is initiated, if he desires to do so.

(f) A majority of the popular vote is required to recall an official in each state.

(g) Individuals may contest the results of a vote on a recall within a certain number of days after the results are certified. In Alaska, an appeal to courts must be filed within five days of the recount.

(h) In Idaho, the dates on which elections may be conducted are the first Tuesday in February, the fourth Tuesday in May, the first Tuesday in August, or the Tuesday following the first Monday in November. In addition, an emergency election may be called upon motion of the governing board of a political subdivision. Recall elections conducted by any political subdivision shall be held on the nearest of these dates which falls more than 45 days after the clerk of the political subdivision orders that the recall election shall be held.

(i) After election is certified. In Michigan, if a petition is filed against a local officer, a recount can be requested up to 6 days after certification of recall election.

(j) The local registrar of voters sends the original certified recall petition to the governor, who issues, within 15 days, a proclamation calling a special election, placing the special election on the next regularly scheduled election date.

(k) Secretary of state if filed on the state level; county or local clerks if filed on the county level.

(l) In Nevada, a recall election is held 10–20 days after the Secretary of State completes notification of the petition sufficiency unless a complaint is filed, the clerk shall issue a call for the election which is to be held within 30 days after the issuance of the call.

(m) Fourteen days after the canvass board has certified the results.

(n) In Washington, a petition that is not accepted may be appealed in 10 days.

(o) Business days.

(p) New Jersey Permanent Statutes, 19:27A-13. In the case of an office which is ordinarily filled at the general election, a recall election shall be held at the next general election occurring at least 55 days following the fifth business day after service of certification, unless it was indicated in the notice of intention to recall that the recall election shall be held at a special election in which case the recall election official shall order and fix the date for holding the recall election to be the next Tuesday occurring during the period beginning with the 55th day and ending on the 61st day following the fifth business day after service of the certification of the petition.

(q) New Jersey Permanent Statutes, 19:27A-16.

(r) Petitions may be amended once during the 60 days allowed for petition circulation.

(s) Within four days, county clerks count signature totals and forward to the Secretary of State. The Secretary of State immediately notifies the clerks if they are to proceed with signature verification.

(t) Five days after recount is completed or 14 days after the election if no recount is demanded.

(u) To be held on the next consolidated election date pursuant to § 16-204 that is 90 days or more after the order calling the election (A.R.S. § 19-209(A)).

(v) The Registrar of Voters shall honor the written request of any voter who either desires to have his handwritten signature stricken from or added to the petition at any time prior to certification of the petition, or within five days after receipt of such signed petition, whichever is earlier.

(w) Prior to election being called.

(x) The election order is issued within 15 days if the officer does not resign within five days after certification.

(y) Election returns are certified on the fifth day after the election, and the office is immediately vacant.

(z) Not later than 4:30 p.m. of the 30th day after the official promulgation of the results of the election. Promulgation is on or before the 12th day after the election.

(aa) Penalty for false statement—$500 or six months in county jail, or both. Penalty for tampering with public records—$10,000 or ten months in state prison, or both.

(bb) The election is held at the next regular general election or at a special election set forth in the recall petition.

Chapter Seven

STATE FINANCE

"Most state budgets were in very good shape at the end of fiscal year 2006, and election-year budgets for 2007 will lead to tax cuts."

—Don Boyd

State Finances: Solid Recovery but Challenges Ahead
By Don Boyd

Most state budgets were in very good shape at the end of fiscal year 2006, and election-year budgets for 2007 will lead to tax cuts. But beyond 2007 states will face challenges, including the need to fund or constrain rapid Medicaid growth, pressures to strengthen pension funding and begin financing newly disclosed liabilities for retiree health care, and the need to respond to large cuts in federal grants.

States responded to the sharp fiscal crisis of 2001 differently than to several previous crises. They raised taxes by less than before and cut employment and spending by much more. Despite renewed rapid growth, tax revenue adjusted for inflation and population growth remains below the pre-recession peak and, similarly adjusted, the "bread and butter" operations of state government other than Medicaid are smaller in a majority of states than when the crisis hit.

Most state budgets were in very good shape at the end of fiscal year 2006, and election-year budgets for 2007 will lead to tax cuts. But beyond 2007 states will face challenges, including the need to fund or constrain rapid Medicaid growth, pressures to strengthen pension funding and begin financing newly disclosed liabilities for retiree health care, and the need to respond to large cuts in federal grants.

The Recovery in State Tax Revenue and State Budgets
State budget conditions have improved dramatically

State tax revenue grew 8.2 percent in fiscal year 2004 and 11 percent in 2005. Personal income taxes were up 12 percent in 2005, sales taxes were up 7 percent, and corporate income taxes were up an astounding 33 percent.[1] Strong growth continued at the start of fiscal year 2006, with 9.2 percent growth in the initial quarter.[2] The rapid tax growth has been driven by a rebound in financial markets and moderate economic recovery, with assistance from state tax increases.

Most states have participated in this good news. Those that rely heavily on income taxes benefited from a surge early in 2005 when taxpayers filed tax returns reflecting the strong stock market in 2004. The few states that rely meaningfully on corporate

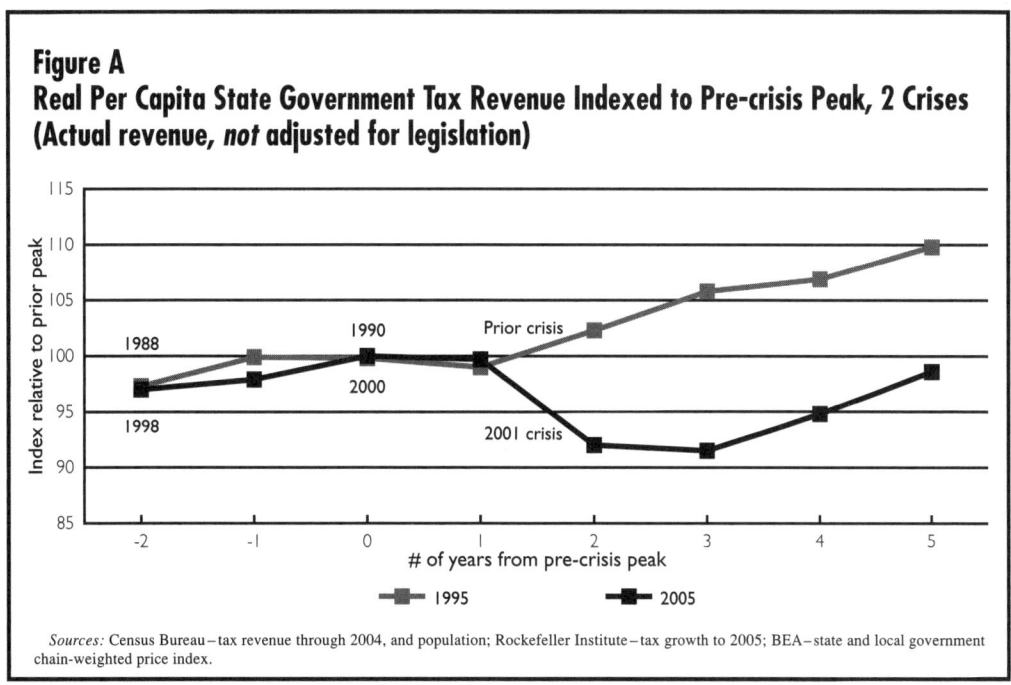

Figure A
Real Per Capita State Government Tax Revenue Indexed to Pre-crisis Peak, 2 Crises
(Actual revenue, *not* adjusted for legislation)

Sources: Census Bureau – tax revenue through 2004, and population; Rockefeller Institute – tax growth to 2005; BEA – state and local government chain-weighted price index.

Table A
Real Per Capita State Tax Revenue
Percent Change FY 2000 to FY 2005

State	Percent change FY 2000 to FY 2005
Alabama	0.4%
Alaska	4.3
Arizona	6.1
Arkansas	3.1
California	-4.2
Colorado	-14.5
Connecticut	-7.3
Delaware	-2.8
Florida	10.3
Georgia	-9.5
Hawaii	9.9
Idaho	-2.7
Illinois	-1.4
Indiana	5.8
Iowa	-11.1
Kansas	-1.4
Kentucky	-0.8
Louisiana	17.0
Maine	-5.9
Maryland	9.3
Massachusetts	-6.2
Michigan	-9.1
Minnesota	-2.6
Mississippi	-4.1
Missouri	-7.1
Montana	6.3
Nebraska	14.0
Nevada	6.3
New Hampshire	0.9
New Jersey	8.5
New Mexico	-0.2
New York	2.9
North Carolina	-4.7
North Dakota	5.4
Ohio	4.1
Oklahoma	-4.1
Oregon	-10.3
Pennsylvania	2.6
Rhode Island	7.4
South Carolina	-6.7
South Dakota	0.1
Tennessee	6.0
Texas	-5.1
Utah	-7.0
Vermont	19.0
Virginia	4.6
Washington	-5.0
West Virginia	8.6
Wisconsin	-11.5
Wyoming	51.2

Sources: Census Bureau–tax revenue through 2004, and population; Rockefeller Institute–tax growth to 2005; BEA–state and local government chain-weighted price index.

through fiscal year 2006, 42 states reported revenue collections were above forecasts.[5] Even California, which has deep structural problems, is getting a boost from rapid revenue growth, with revenue that may exceed the governor's budgeted amounts by more than $2 billion over two years.[6]

There are relatively few significant exceptions. Michigan and Ohio have suffered from weakness in auto manufacturing. More recently, Louisiana's revenue has been devastated by Hurricanes Katrina and Rita and Mississippi has been hurt to a lesser extent. Rhode Island has experienced revenue shortfalls and structural budget difficulties. New Jersey, while benefiting from strong revenue growth, is still working its way out of budget problems.

The positive revenue trend has been abetted by easing spending pressures, with only 19 states reporting spending overruns in 2006, down from 23 in 2005. As happens almost every year, Medicaid was the program most frequently over budget.[7]

As a result, only six states made midyear budget cuts in 2005, down from 37 in 2003. After drawing year-end fund balances down from 10.4 percent of expenditures in 2000 to 3.2 percent in 2003, states rebuilt them to 6.9 percent at the end of 2005—not enough to cushion a modest recession, but an improvement nonetheless. The number of states with fund balances of at least 5 percent rose from 12 at the end of 2003 to 33 at year-end 2005.[8] Finally, states have begun to cut taxes again; fiscal year 2005 was the first year of net tax cuts since 2000.[9]

State tax revenue is still below the pre-crisis peak

Despite rapid growth, state tax revenue in 2005 remained below the pre-recession peak, adjusting for inflation and population growth. In other words, state taxes still cannot finance the level of services they could before the fiscal crisis. As Figure A shows, this is a marked difference from the previous recovery.

Table B
State Tax Increases in Three Recessions

Recession	Cumulative tax increases as a percent of tax revenue
1980–82 recessions	9.9%
1990–91 recession	9.8
2001 recession	3.7

Sources: Tax increases are from *Fiscal Survey of the States*, December 2005.

Tax revenue is from the Census Bureau. Based on the three largest tax-increase years associated with each recession.

income taxes benefited from double-digit growth in 11 of 12 recent quarters.[3] States that rely on oil and natural gas taxes—especially Alaska, New Mexico, North Dakota, Oklahoma and Wyoming—experienced a surge due to rising energy prices.[4] Partway

This phenomenon is common—by fiscal year 2005, real per capita tax revenue was below the 2000 peak in 25 states (Table A).

This reflects three factors. First, tax revenue fell far more sharply in the recent crisis than in the previous one, as Table A shows, so that more growth is required to reach the prior peak. Second, the economic recovery has been modest. Finally, states enacted smaller tax increases in this recession, as Table B shows.

State Spending Restraint

Instead of raising taxes significantly, states trimmed payrolls and cut spending more deeply.

Employment cuts

Private sector employment usually contracts sharply during recessions, while state and local government employment is stable, partly because demand for government services rarely diminishes and often increases during recessions. In the three recessions before 2001, state government employment either did not decline, or declined only briefly.

The response to the 2001 recession has been different. While state government *education* employment has increased (largely in institutions of higher education), non-education employment declined more

than 2 percentage points before resuming its rise. As Figure B shows, nearly six years after the recession began, state government non-education employment remained below its pre-recession level.

State government employment declines have been widespread. Figure C shows the percentage change in state government employment per 1,000 population from the final quarter of 2001 to the final quarter of 2005. For the nation as a whole this share declined by 1 percent. It fell in 33 states, declining by more than 5 percent in 15 states. It rose by more than 5 percent in only four. Most of the states that increased government employment had strong tax revenue growth.

Spending reductions

Recently released state fiscal data show state efforts at restraining spending. Between fiscal year 2002, when states began responding to recession-induced tax revenue declines, and 2004, state real per capita spending rose by only 1.2 percent, a sharp slowdown from earlier years.[10] More telling was the way spending was distributed: After adjusting for inflation and population growth, medical vendor payments (which correspond closely to Medicaid) rose by 16.5 percent while all other state government spending actually fell by 2 percent, suggesting that Medicaid spending "crowded out" other spending.[11]

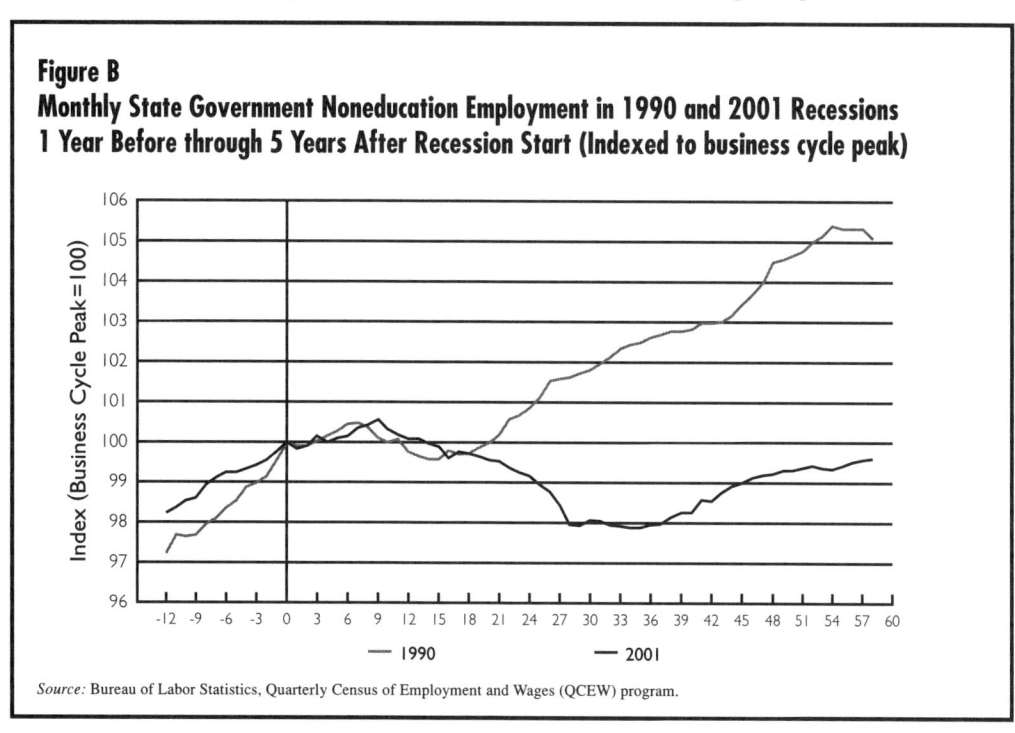

Figure B
Monthly State Government Noneducation Employment in 1990 and 2001 Recessions
1 Year Before through 5 Years After Recession Start (Indexed to business cycle peak)

Source: Bureau of Labor Statistics, Quarterly Census of Employment and Wages (QCEW) program.

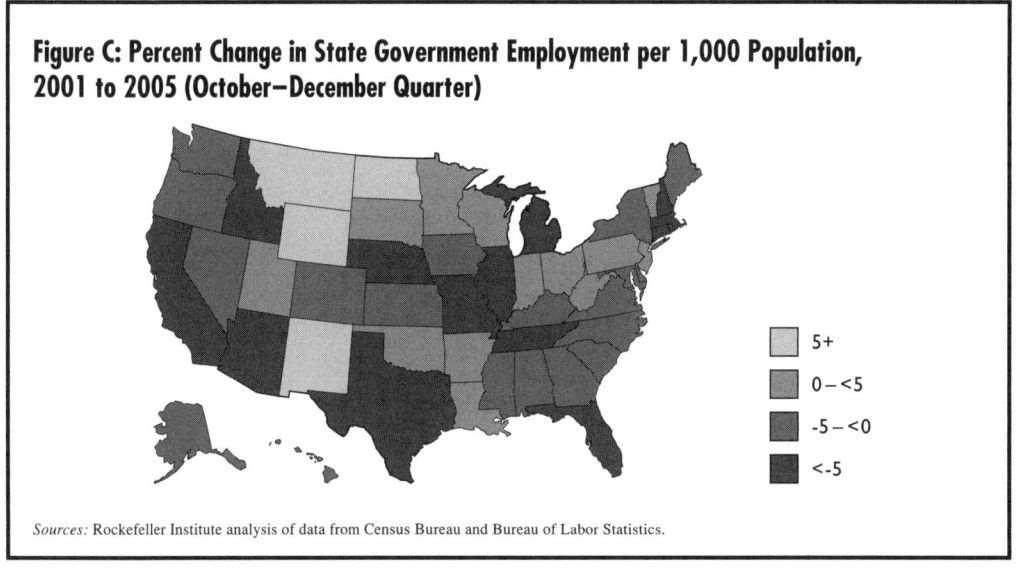

Figure C: Percent Change in State Government Employment per 1,000 Population, 2001 to 2005 (October–December Quarter)

Legend:
- 5+
- 0 – <5
- -5 – <0
- <-5

Sources: Rockefeller Institute analysis of data from Census Bureau and Bureau of Labor Statistics.

Elementary and secondary education rose the fastest of the large spending categories. Higher education spending also rose, supported by very substantial tuition increases that offset cuts in state appropriations.[12] (See Table C.) All other spending in aggregate declined.

Medical vendor payments rose in virtually all states, while 33 states cut other spending, with western states far more likely to cut than eastern states. (See Figures D and E.)

Spending reductions hit many areas of the budget. More than half the states reduced spending on libraries (a relatively small spending area) by more than 10 percent, and nearly as many reduced spending on legislative operations and staff quite significantly.

Many other areas were reduced by a majority of states, often quite significantly. (See Table D.)

Finally, Table E shows how recent changes fit into longer-term trends. When viewed over the period from 1999 to 2004 (the right-most column), state spending in all major categories (and in most smaller functional areas, not shown on the table) has increased, despite the declines between 2002 and 2004, and increases over longer periods are more significant. The table also shows the dominating effect of Medicaid on state budgets over the last 20 years.

In sum, states' initial response to the fiscal crisis of 2001 included widespread cuts throughout the nation and across spending categories. Many cuts were sig-

Table C
State Government Expenditures in 2002 and 2004 Fiscal Years, Real Per Capita

	Real per capita, 2004 dollars			
	2002	*2004*	*Change*	*Percent change*
General expenditures	$4,119.8	$4,167.5	$47.7	1.2%
Medical vendor payments (mostly Medicaid)	704.4	820.9	116.5	16.5
Other state government expenditures (excluding medical vendor payments)	3415.4	3346.5	(68.8)	-2.0
Elementary and secondary education	823.0	842.8	19.7	2.4
Higher education (including tuition-supported spending)	519.0	526.4	7.4	1.4
Public welfare (excluding medical vendor payments)	361.6	348.5	(13.1)	-3.6
Highways, and transit subsidies	336.8	319.0	(17.8)	-5.3
All other state government expenditures	1375.0	1309.8	(65.1)	-4.7

Sources: Census Bureau for finance and population data; Bureau of Economic Analysis for price index. Inflation measured by the state and local government chain-weighted price index.

Note: Census data on higher education include spending from tuition funds. State government support for higher education actually declined between 2002 and 2004.

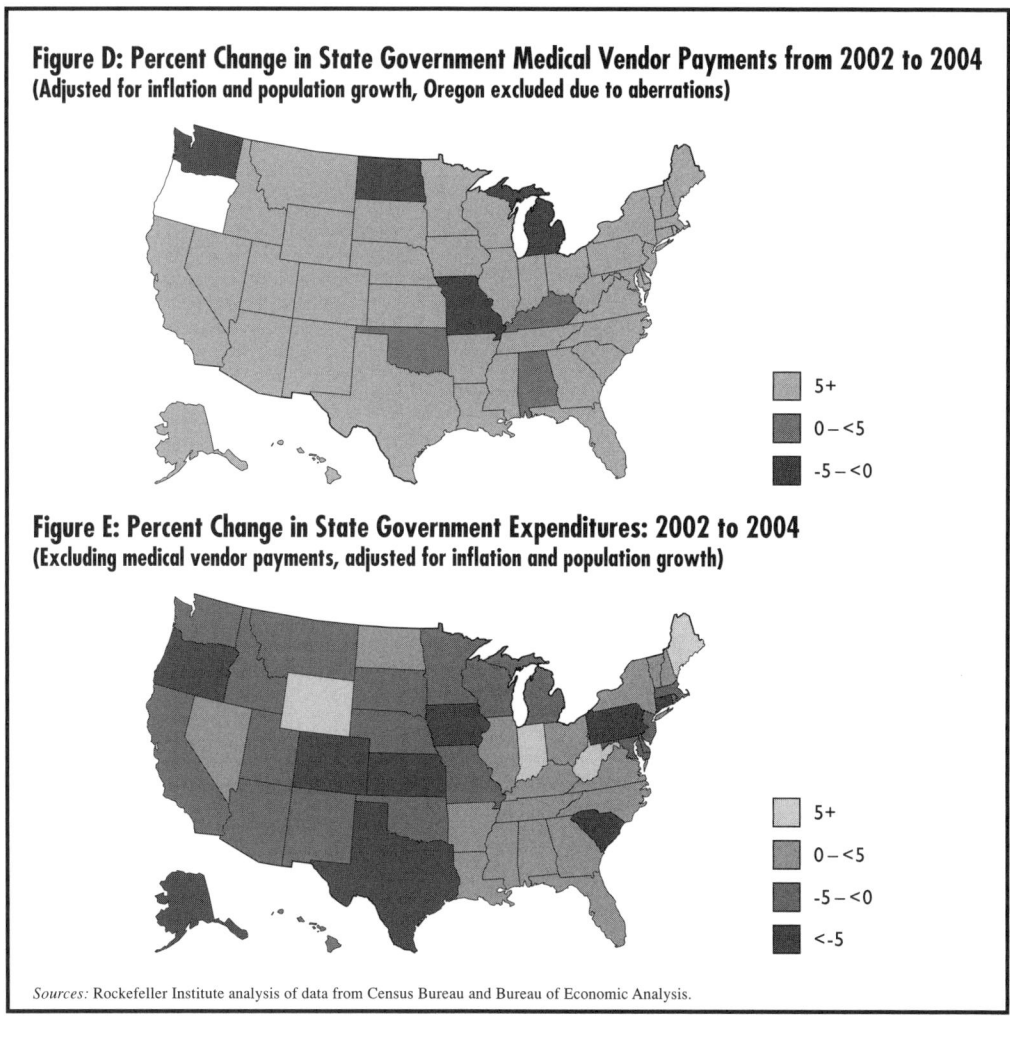

Figure D: Percent Change in State Government Medical Vendor Payments from 2002 to 2004
(Adjusted for inflation and population growth, Oregon excluded due to aberrations)

5+
0 – <5
-5 – <0

Figure E: Percent Change in State Government Expenditures: 2002 to 2004
(Excluding medical vendor payments, adjusted for inflation and population growth)

5+
0 – <5
-5 – <0
<-5

Sources: Rockefeller Institute analysis of data from Census Bureau and Bureau of Economic Analysis.

nificant relative to two years earlier, but aggregate cuts were modest when viewed in historical context.

Short-term Outlook: Tax Cuts and Spending Increases

Even-numbered years often are election years, and gubernatorial seats in 36 states are up for election in 2006, as are more than 80 percent of state legislative seats. Strong revenue growth combined with election-year pressures can create an environment conducive to tax cuts and spending increases.

At this writing, many Republican and Democratic governors alike have proposed or promised tax cuts for their 2006–07 budgets, including the following: Alabama Gov. Bob Riley (R) is again seeking to reduce taxes on low-income families, Arizona Gov.

Janet Napolitano (D) proposed $100 million of tax cuts, New York Gov. George Pataki (R) has proposed a package of individual and business tax cuts, and Wisconsin Gov. Jim Doyle (D) is proposing a "living wage" tax credit.[13]

Spending increases also will be common, particularly in elementary and secondary education and in higher education.[14] Napolitano proposed a 17 percent increase for elementary and secondary education, Gov. Arnold Schwarzenegger (R) in California proposed an 11 percent increase in general fund support for schools, and Gov. Robert L. Ehrlich (R) of Maryland proposed a 12 percent increase. Higher education also is faring well in most states.

Tax increases will be rare, often limited to the recent "go-to" source—cigarette taxes—and in the

Table D: State Government Real Per Capita Spending, Fiscal Year 2002 to 2004
(Prevalence of reductions and increases, selected expenditure areas)

| | Number of state with: | | | | |
| | Reductions of: | | Increases of: | | |
	More than 10 percent	0 to 10 percent	0 to 10 percent	More than 10 percent	Median percent change
General expenditures	1	16	31	2	0.7%
Medical vendor payments (mostly Medicaid)	1	4	11	34	16.5
Other state government expenditures (excluding medical vendor payments)	2	31	16	1	-1.1
Libraries	26	12	3	8	-11.3
Legislative	25	18	3	4	-10.3
Parks	19	14	7	10	-4.2
General capital outlay	18	15	8	9	-5.0
Natural resources	17	12	10	11	-3.1
Health (other than medical vendor payments)	16	13	11	10	-2.2
Corrections	11	25	10	4	-6.2
Public welfare (other than medical vendor payments)	11	14	10	15	-0.2
Elementary and secondary education	2	24	17	7	0.0
Higher education (including tuition supported spending)	1	16	26	7	2.0

Sources: Census Bureau for finance and population data; Bureau of Economic Analysis for price index. Inflation measured by the state and local government chain-weighted price index.

Note: Census data on higher education include spending from tuition funds. State government support for higher education actually declined between 2002 and 2004.

context of budgets that cut taxes in other areas. Govs. Mitch Daniels (R) of Indiana, Thomas Vilsack (D) of Iowa, and Pataki of New York have all proposed cigarette tax increases.[15]

Widespread tax cuts and some spending increases seem a near certainty for 2006–07. Over the longer term, however, these will have to compete with other challenges states will face.

Challenges Ahead
Medicaid

Medicaid, the federal-state program that finances health care for the poor and medically needy, is the largest item in the majority of state budgets when funding from all sources is considered.[16]

Medicaid will continue to grow rapidly, reflecting expensive new technologies and drugs, the general

lack of incentives for consumers to limit care, and the impending growth of the elderly population. Health-finance analysts project that Medicaid spending will grow about 8.6 percent annually over the decade ahead, outpacing population growth plus general price inflation by an average of 5.1 percentage points annually—faster than state tax systems are likely to grow.[17]

The federal government finances about 57 percent of Medicaid costs. Congress adopted legislation in early 2006 intended to reduce federal Medicaid spending by $5 billion over five years, and the president's fiscal year 2007 budget would reduce federal spending by $14 billion over five years, in part by shifting some costs to states.[18] Federal actions to constrain Medicaid spending growth to date have been modest relative to the program's size, although

Table E: Percentage Change in Real Per Capita State Government Expenditures

| | Five-year time periods | | | |
	1984 to 1989	1989 to 1994	1994 to 1999	1999 to 2004
General expenditures	22.1%	18.3%	9.7%	10.9%
Elementary and secondary education	24.2	6.1	20.8	6.3
Medical vendor payments (mostly Medicaid)	29.3	88.3	4.6	40.5
Higher education	14.6	10.6	10.3	13.4
All other expenditures	21.9	11.9	7.0	3.1

Sources: Census Bureau for finance and population data; Bureau of Economic Analysis for price index. Inflation measured by the state and local government chain-weighted price index.

Note: Census data on higher education include spending from tuition funds. State government support for higher education actually declined between 2002 and 2004.

Table F: Federal Grants to State and Local Governments: Federal Fiscal Year 2006 (OMB) Estimates

	Amount ($billions)	Share of total
Medicaid	$192.3	42.8
State Children's Health Program (SCHIP)	5.8	1.3
Other health programs	12.5	2.8
Health total	210.6	46.9
Temporary Assistance to Needy Families (TANF)	17.4	3.9
Housing and urban development	31.3	7.0
Other income security	45.0	10.0
Income security total	93.7	20.9
Education, training, employment and social services	60.3	13.4
Highway aid from the Highway Trust Fund	32.6	7.3
Other transportation aid	14.1	3.1
Transportation total	46.7	10.4
Community and regional development	22.3	5.0
Other federal grants	15.6	3.5
Total federal grant outlays	449.3	100.0

Source: Federal Budget for Fiscal Year 2007, historical table 12.3.

some cuts have affected many beneficiaries. Given projected deficits that cumulatively exceed $1 trillion over the next five years, pressure for more and deeper federal cuts is likely.

The federal budget

State and local governments depend on federal aid to implement many federally funded programs. When the federal government cuts grants in aid it is felt in statehouses throughout the nation.

Federal grants to state and local governments amount to about 17 percent of the federal budget. Nearly 90 percent of these grants go directly to state governments, and account for almost 30 percent of state general revenue. Medicaid is by far the largest, accounting for more than 40 percent of federal grants. Income security (such as housing assistance and nutrition programs for children and pregnant women), education and training, and transportation are the other large categories, as Table F shows.

Table G: Proposed Federal Outlays for Grants to State and Local Governments, Real Per Capita President's Budget for FY 2007

	Real per capita, 2006 dollars			
	2005	2011	Change	Percent change
Medicaid	$627.3	$762.8	$135.6	21.6%
Transportation	149.7	156.6	6.9	4.6
Other grants	694.4	548.3	(146.0)	-21.0
Income security	313.7	274.0	(39.8)	-12.7
Community and regional development	69.6	30.8	(38.8)	-55.7
Education, training, employment and social services	197.6	159.0	(38.6)	-19.6
Administration of justice	16.5	6.7	(9.8)	-59.2
Non-Medicaid health	55.7	48.5	(7.2)	-12.9
Natural resources and environment	20.2	14.4	(5.8)	-28.6
General government	15.1	10.0	(5.1)	-33.6
All other	5.9	4.9	(1.1)	-17.9
Total outlays for grants to state and local governments	1471.4	1467.8	(3.6)	-0.2

Sources: Federal Budget for 2007 historical table 12.1 and budget tables 1.2 and 25-13; Census Bureau population data for 2005; plus assumed population growth of 0.85% annually.

Note: 2005 is used as comparison year, rather than 2006, to ensure that the base year is not boosted by temporary payments related to Hurricane Katrina, which would overstate the size of cuts.

The president's 2007 budget proposed to cut most grants substantially, particularly after the initial budget year. After adjusting for inflation and population growth, reductions in most categories are proposed to be 20 percent or more by 2011, relative to 2005 (the most recently completed year). (See Table G.) The two major exceptions are Medicaid and transportation. Real per capita Medicaid expenditures are projected to grow by 21.6 percent, driven by forces affecting both private and public health care spending. (The president's budget proposes cuts that would reduce the growth of Medicaid spending, as the previous section noted.) Transportation grants are expected to grow by 4.6 percent, reflecting revenue projected in the federal Highway Trust Fund. All other categories, on average, are proposed to be cut by 21.6 percent, with all major categories facing large cuts.

The net cuts in non-Medicaid grants would be equivalent to about 4.4 percent of total state government tax revenue—about half as large as the falloff in state tax revenue in the last fiscal crisis and several times larger than in the previous one. The reduction would not be as sudden, giving states opportunity to plan, but it would undoubtedly be more enduring. States can reasonably expect taxes to surge after the worst of a recession is over, but they should not expect a resurgence of federal grant revenue after cuts take effect.

Will these cuts come to pass? Not in the short term, if we take guidance from press reports pronouncing the budget "dead on arrival," or from the 2006 federal budget, when enacted cuts were far smaller than those proposed. But over the longer term, state and local governments should expect significant cuts. Federal budget pressures are likely to be greater than those implied in the proposed budget, which does not include funding to "fix" unintended effects of the alternative minimum tax or funds for the war in Iraq beyond fiscal year 2007, both of which could create additional demands on the federal budget.[19]

In the mid- and late-1990s, many states knew the tax revenue boom would end and eventually reverse, but they did not know when. They face a similar risk now. Absent a federal tax increase, significant cuts in federal grants are likely, but there is no obvious way to predict when that will occur.

Pensions

Pension benefits are a significant and rising obligation that state and local governments have to their current and former workers. State government pension contributions amounted to about 3.7 percent of tax revenue in 2004 in the typical state, and local

government contributions were an estimated 5.5 percent of local tax revenue.[20]

In the short run, state and local government budgets are affected not by the size of pension benefits or pension fund investment returns, but through contribution requirements that can be set a year or more in advance. In any single year these contributions may be only loosely connected to benefits and returns. Over the long run, these contributions will change in a lagging and usually smooth manner in relation to changes in benefits, investment returns and work force demographics.

State and local government pension plans have large holdings of corporate stock, and when the stock market booms as it did in the late 1990s, pension assets soar. States cannot "withdraw" money from these plans if they have extraordinary stock market earnings, but they have many ways to share in that benefit, generally with a short lag. Some fiscal benefit occurs automatically. For example, when the value of plan assets increases, the unfunded liability (if there is one) goes down, reducing what governments must pay to amortize that liability. Governments and pension plans also can take explicit action to reduce contributions, including raising estimates of future investment returns, or declaring "contribution holidays" (skipping or drastically reducing contributions for a year or two).

Between 1994 and 2002, two-thirds of state governments reduced pension contributions relative to tax revenue, and many declines were quite significant. Ten states reduced contributions by more than 3 percentage points (relative to tax revenue); by contrast, only two states increased contributions by more than 3 percentage points. Figure F shows five state governments with very large declines in pension contributions. In several states, contributions have recently begun to rise.

State and local governments now face pressures that have begun driving pension contributions upward. The stock market decline of 2000–2002 has begun causing contributions to rise (some of this will be dampened by the strong stock market of 2003 and 2004, but the net effect will be upward). Changes in actuarial assumptions can cause contributions to rise—some plans have lowered assumed investment returns based on recent experience. Demographic assumptions also can cause contributions to rise—if, for example, retirees live longer than previously assumed, or if the work force salary base grows less quickly than expected (reducing projected pension plan revenue from future employee contributions), government contributions may have to rise. Also,

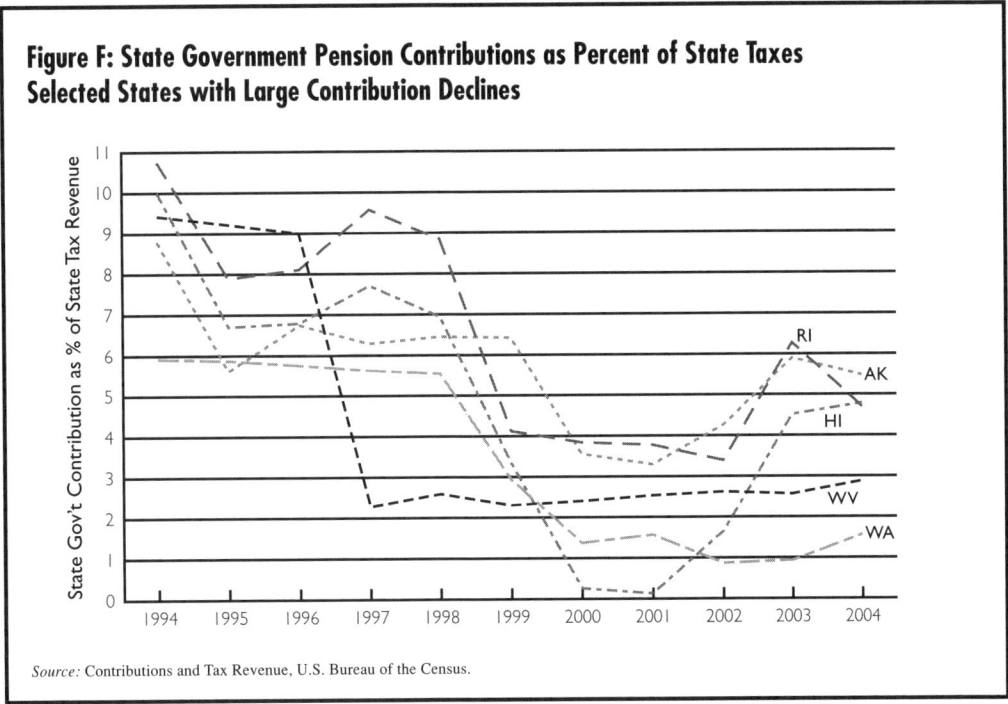

**Figure F: State Government Pension Contributions as Percent of State Taxes
Selected States with Large Contribution Declines**

Source: Contributions and Tax Revenue, U.S. Bureau of the Census.

many governments enriched pension benefits during the fiscal boom, and those increases drive unfunded liabilities and their amortization upward. Finally, states that reduced their contributions to artificially low levels during the boom years will see contributions rise, and this has already begun.

In which states will pension contributions have to rise the most? Analysts use several indicators to draw conclusions about the potential budget implications of state and local government pension plans. One is the ratio of plan assets to plan liabilities. A recent Standard and Poor's report noted that the average funded ratio of large state-sponsored plans exceeded 100 percent in 2000, reflecting the strong stock market, but fell to about 84 percent by 2004 and was below 100 percent in all but three states. The aggregate unfunded liability was estimated to be $284 billion. However, it is not unusual for the funded ratio to drop substantially following recessions and rise afterward. State pension plans, in aggregate, have far higher funding ratios than they did in the 1960s and 1970s. A second measure is the ratio of employer contributions to the "actuarial required contribution" (the amount a government *should* pay to meet the plan's funding requirements).

Each measure has flaws as a guide to pressures faced by governments participating in a plan. A plan could be underfunded (its funded ratio is less than 100 percent), but a participating government's current payments might already be large enough to amortize the unfunded liability. If a government is making payments below the actuarially required amount, it might not necessarily face a sharp rise in future contributions if, for example, the plan is overfunded. Despite these and other flaws, these measures are the best readily available indicators of pension plan health.

Table H shows both measures for the largest state employee pension plan in several states that appear significantly underfunded or that have low contribution rates. It also shows the extent to which these state governments reduced their contributions between 1994 and 2002 when many governments were reducing contributions.[21] The table cannot tell us how much contributions might have to rise, but the magnitude of the drop suggests that contribution increases might be substantial. For reference, a rise equal to 4 percent of tax revenue is larger than the typical tax increase following the 2001 recession. Hawaii's contributions already have increased substantially from their 2002 level.

Even when governments are paying the full actuarial required contribution, substantial increases may be necessary. First, the funding method alone

Table H: Pension Plan Funding Measures, Selected States

	Reported funding status of state employees plan		Change in state government contributions to all plans as percent of state tax revenue, 1994 to 2002
	Funded ratio: actuarial assets as percent of actuarial liabilities	Employer contribution as percent of actuarial required contribution	
Alaska	72.8%	52.7%	(4.6%)
Colorado	70.1	51.0	(1.5)
Hawaii..................................	71.7	100.0	(8.4)
Illinois.................................	54.4	58.8	N.A.
Kentucky	73.6	58.7	(1.7)
Oklahoma	72.0	52.5	0.6
Rhode Island	65.5	100.0	(7.4)
Washington..........................	77.2	7.0	(5.1)
West Virginia......................	73.1	104.5	(6.9)

Sources: Funding status based upon most recent available Comprehensive Financial Report, Schedule of Funding Progress and Schedule of Employer Contributions.

can require sharp contribution increases. Second, the actuarial required contribution is based on assumptions that may prove wrong. A good example is Rhode Island, where employers were paying 100 percent of required contributions. The Rhode Island employees retirement system recently revised its actuarial assumptions to reflect younger-than-expected retirement ages, which lengthened the period over which benefits would be paid, and rising average benefits. As a result of these and other assumption changes, the state's actuarial consulting firm projected that employer contributions would have to more than double between fiscal years 2005 and 2008.[22]

As this discussion shows, readily available measures do not provide good information on the pressures that pension underfunding will place on state budgets. The funded ratio is helpful but is dependent on embedded economic and demographic assumptions that vary considerably across states and over time, and it can be misleading for technical reasons as well. Although the ratio of actual contributions to required contributions can provide insight, the Rhode Island example shows this measure has weaknesses as well.

Perhaps the best way to understand the pressures state-local pension systems will place on government finances in the near term is to project the annual contributions that would be required under several scenarios (different economic, demographic and funding assumptions), and compare those potential contributions with current contributions and the size of government budgets. Such an analysis is beyond the scope of this article.

Given weaknesses in available measures, what do we know? The vast majority of states have underfunded pension systems. In aggregate this underfunding is not large relative to long-run experience.

However, some states clearly have serious underfunding problems, and contributions will need to rise substantially, although it is difficult to predict precisely when. Many states that took contribution holidays in the 1990s may have to raise contributions substantially just to get back to where they were. Predicting which states will face the greatest pressure in the near term would take analysis that goes beyond the measures currently examined by most analysts, and analyzes underlying actuarial assumptions and how they may change.

Retiree health care and related benefits

State and local governments often provide health care and other "post-employment benefits" to retirees. As with pensions, employees earn these benefits during working years but don't receive them until retirement. The aging government work force, rapidly rising health care costs and increasing life spans of retirees are conspiring to create huge liabilities for the future health care costs of current and retired workers, which one analyst estimates could approach $1 trillion.[23]

Unlike pensions, governments have not been required to report their obligations for these benefits (dubbed "other post-employment benefits," or OPEB, by accountants), and most do not set aside reserves to cover those future costs. As a result, governments have had an incentive to provide compensation in the form of future benefits rather than current wages.

New accounting rules will change this. Beginning with 2007–08 financial statements, states and large local governments will be required to estimate their "actuarial liability" for these post-employment benefits and amortize the unfunded liability over 30 years.[24] The new rules will NOT require governments to set aside reserves, but those that continue

Table I: How Three Early-Reporting Governments Could be Affected if They Fully Funded Retiree Health Benefits

	Los Angeles Unified School District ($millions)	Delaware State Government ($millions)	Maryland State Government ($millions)
Actuarially required annual contribution, including amortization of unfunded liability (i.e. full funding)	$529	$286	$1,959
Less: Current annual contribution (pay as you go)	172	101	311
Equals: Increase in annual payments needed for full funding	357	185	1,648
Government own-source revenue	2,499	4,972	18,968
Increase needed for full funding, as % of own source revenue	14.3%	3.7%	8.7%
Full funding amount divided by current amount	3.1	2.8	6.3

Sources and notes: Current and actuarially required contributions based on valuation analyses prepared for each government (see endnote). Fiscal year for each government year used in its own analysis: LAUSD (2005–06), DE (2007–08), MD (2006–07). Government own-source revenue for MD and DE: Census Bureau data for 2004 plus 5 percent annual growth. Government own-source revenue for LAUSD: local revenue plus transfers; Superintendent's Final Budget for 2005–06.

on a "pay-as-you-go" basis generally will report a rapidly growing liability.

The amounts are large and can dwarf unfunded pension liabilities. Maryland, which analyzed its liability early, estimated an unfunded retiree health care liability of $23 billion, compared with an unfunded pension liability of $4.6 billion. One important issue is how annual budgets might be affected if governments choose to fund benefits more fully. Table I shows relevant information for three early-reporting governments—Delaware, Maryland and the Los Angeles school district. In each case the full funding amount is several times the current payments, and the increase would be large relative to revenue raised from own sources (taxes, fees and charges)—ranging from 3.7 percent of revenue in Delaware to more than 14 percent in the Los Angeles school district.

The amounts will vary dramatically depending upon the generosity of the retiree health care package, the age and health of the work force, actuarial assumptions and other factors.

Whether and how governments will respond is a decision for elected officials. Options include:

- *Do nothing:* Governments that continue on a pay-as-you-go basis will still face increased costs as their work force ages, retirements increase and health costs rise. Outlays may rise less rapidly initially under a do-nothing strategy than if they begin to prefund, but far more rapidly in later years. Judging by the responses of many governments so far, "do nothing" is not an option that many will consider seriously.
- *Raise taxes, cut other spending or use surplus funds to begin prefunding existing liabilities:* The governments of Fairfax County, Va., and the District of Columbia each have made modest contributions to

reserve funds. New York Mayor Michael Bloomberg proposed using $2 billion of unanticipated revenue to "establish a trust to fund a portion of its liability for the benefits of its current and future retirees. … Deposits into the trust are irrevocable and all money deposited into the trust must be used to pay the costs of retiree health care benefits in future years."[25]

- *Issue bonds to prefund existing liabilities:* Gainesville, Fla., has already done this, and investment banks are marketing this option to governments.[26]
- *Scale back benefits:* Governments have many options, including restricting eligibility for benefits, increasing the time it takes to vest in full benefits, and increasing co-payments and deductibles. They may consider tiered approaches that make benefits for future retirees less generous than those for current retirees, and benefits for future hires less generous than those for current workers. A panel examining New Jersey's funding obligations to retirees recommended that the state consider requiring all employees to contribute to retiree health care costs (the state now pays 100 percent of the cost).[27] They will have to weigh the impact these choices may have on worker recruitment and retention.

These choices are likely to play out over the next several years as more governments conduct the actuarial valuations required by the new accounting rules and debate their options.

Other issues

States face many other issues that will place pressure on budgets, including:

- The general long-term decline in state sales tax bases. This may be mitigated eventually if Congress adopts legislation to give states greater authority to collect taxes from out of state vendors, in response to state streamlining of sales tax systems.

- Litigation that requires states to increase funding in low-spending school districts, or creates pressures for them to do so. At least eight states are in the midst of complying with or responding to recent successful challenges.[28]
- Property tax revolts in New Jersey and some other states, which can create pressure for state-financed property tax relief.
- Continuing efforts in some states to impose constitutional tax and expenditure limitations on legislators and governors. These efforts largely have been unsuccessful in recent years but remain a potential source of fiscal tension.

Conclusions

The recovery in state finances has been solid and widespread, with only a few exceptions. Most states raised taxes by very little in the recent fiscal crisis, and have cut employment and spending relative to their economies. Most state budgets were in good shape at the end of fiscal year 2006, and election-year budgets for 2007 will lead to tax cuts. But beyond 2007 states will face challenges, including the need to fund or constrain rapid Medicaid growth, pressures to strengthen pension funding and begin financing newly disclosed liabilities for retiree health care, and the need to respond to large cuts in federal grants.

Notes

[1] Nicholas W. Jenny, "Strong Revenue Growth Continues in Most States," *State Revenue Report,* No. 61, Rockefeller Institute of Government, (September 2005).

[2] Nicholas W. Jenny, "State Tax Revenue Off to a Flying Start for Fiscal Year 2006," *State Revenue Report,* No. 62, Rockefeller Institute of Government, (December 2005).

[3] Ibid.

[4] Judy Zelio, *State Energy Revenues Gushing,* National Conference of State Legislatures, (January 2006).

[5] Out of 49 that reported results—*State Budget Update: November 2005,* National Conference of State Legislatures, Washington, D.C.

[6] California Legislative Analyst's Office, Analysis of the 2006–07 Budget Bill: Perspectives and Issues, February 22, 2006.

[7] National Conference of State Legislatures, *State Budget Update: November 2005,* 2.

[8] *The Fiscal Survey of the States,* National Governors Association and National Association of State Budget Officers, (Washington D.C., December 2005 and April 2004).

[9] Nicholas W. Jenny, "2005 Tax and Budget Review," *State Fiscal Brief,* No. 74, Rockefeller Institute of Government, (January 2006).

[10] It would be preferable to examine combined state and local spending over this time period, because it is possible that some changes in state government spending reflect shifts in responsibilities between state and local spending, but local government finance data for 2004 are not yet available from the Bureau of the Census.

[11] See Kane, Thomas, Peter Orszag, and David Gunter, *State Fiscal Constraints and Higher Education Spending: The Role of Medicaid and the Business Cycle.* The Urban-Brookings Tax Policy Center, Discussion Paper No. 11. May 2003, for an analysis of the tendency of Medicaid to crowd out spending on higher education and other areas.

[12] The Census Bureau data used here do not allow us to look easily at net state support for higher education (excluding tuition funds).

[13] See Brian T. Stenson, *Governors' Budgets Reflect Strong Revenue Growth,* Rockefeller Institute of Government, (February 2006).

[14] See Brian T. Stenson, *Governors' Budgets Reflect Strong Revenue Growth,* Rockefeller Institute of Government, (February 2006); and Peterson, Kavan, "State surpluses a boon to education," *Stateline.org,* February 22, 2006.

[15] Kathleen Hunter, "Rising revenues spur tax cuts, spending," *Stateline.org,* January 31, 2006, plus individual state budget documents.

[16] *State Expenditure Report 2004,* National Association of State Budget Officers, December 2005, Table 5.

[17] Christin Borger, Sheila Smith, Christopher Truffer, Sean Keehan, Andrea Sisko, John Poisal, and M. Kent Clemens, "Health Spending Projections Through 2015: Changes On The Horizon," Health Affairs–Web Exclusive, 22 February 2006.

[18] See Andy Schneider, Leighton Ku, and Judith Solomon, *The Administration's Medicaid Proposals Would Shift Federal Costs to States,* Center on Budget and Policy Priorities, February 14, 2006, for analysis of these cuts. The Center on Budget and Policy Priorities opposes most of these cuts.

[19] See Leonard E. Burman, William G. Gale and Jeffrey Rohaly, *The Expanding Reach of the Individual Alternative Minimum Tax,* The Urban-Brookings Tax Policy Center, Updated May 2005, for analysis of the Alternative Minimum Tax and reform options.

[20] Based on median contributions for the 50 states. State share based upon Census Bureau data on retirement contributions and tax revenue. Local share based upon Census Bureau data on retirement contributions and on author's estimates of local tax revenue.

[21] The data for each plan was obtained from its most recent comprehensive annual financial report—in most cases for 2005. In the case of West Virginia, which is widely regarded as one of the poorest-funded plans in the nation, the most recent report was for 2003 and it appears to be unaudited. Standard and Poor's recently issued a report showing funding ratios for the two largest plans combined in the 50 states, and the funded ratio for West Virginia for these plans was 43.9 percent (see Young, Parry, Robin Prunty and Ben Cutler, *Rising U.S. State Unfunded Pension Liabilities Are Causing Budgetary Stress,* Standard and Poor's Corporation, February 22, 2006).

[22] State of Rhode Island Pension Review Team, *ESRI Evaluation Report*, (February 2005), 42.

[23] Steven McElhaney, actuary and principal at Mercer Consulting, as cited in Freudenheim, Milt and Mary Williams Wash, "The Next Retirement Time Bomb," *New York Times*, December 11, 2005.

[24] These rules are set forth in Statements 43 and 45 of the Governmental Accounting Standards Board (GASB).

[25] "MAYOR BLOOMBERG PRESENTS $52.2 BILLION FY 2007 PRELIMINARY BUDGET," PR- 033-06, January 31, 2006.

[26] See presentation by UBS to the Michigan Task Force on Local Government Services and Fiscal Stability: Revenue and Fiscal Constraint Work Group, "Financing Unfunded Legacy Costs," December 1, 2005.

[27] Benefits Review Task Force, "The Report of the Benefits Review Task Force to Acting Governor Richard J. Codey," December 1, 2005.

[28] Based on information provided at *www.schoolfunding. info/litigation/litigation.php3*.

About the Author

Don Boyd is the director of fiscal studies at the Rockefeller Institute of Government of the State University of New York. His past positions include director of the economic and revenue staff for New York state's budget office, and director of the tax staff for New York's Assembly Ways and Means Committee. Boyd holds a Ph.D. in managerial economics from Rensselaer Polytechnic Institute.

Table 7.1
FISCAL 2005 STATE GENERAL FUND, PRELIMINARY ACTUAL, BY REGION
(In millions of dollars)

State or other jurisdiction	Beginning balance	Revenues	Adjustments	Resources	Expenditures	Adjustments	Ending balance	Budget stabilization fund
U.S. total	$18,866	$568,294	. . .	$594,796	$557,052	. . .	$32,170	$14,855
Eastern Region								
Connecticut (e)	0	14,212	0	14,212	13,909	0	303	606
Delaware*......................	646	2,878	0	3,524	2,822	0	701	148
Maine (m).......................	15	2,791	12	2,818	2,784	0	34	47
Massachusetts* (o)........	756	24,373	0	25,129	23,779	0	1,955	1,728
New Hampshire	15	1,392	0	1,407	1,325	0	82	17
New Jersey*...................	834	27,429	-13	28,250	27,612	0	638	288
New York* (u)	1,077	43,760	0	44,837	43,619	0	1,218	872
Pennsylvania (aa)..........	77	23,309	98	23,483	23,105	14	365	330
Rhode Island (bb)	35	3,033	-61	3,007	2,966	0	41	92
Vermont (hh).................	0	1,035	48	1,083	1,038	45	0	46
Regional totals	3,455	144,212	. . .	147,750	142,959	. . .	5,337	4,174
Midwestern Region								
Illinois (g).....................	182	23,647	2,513	26,342	22,187	3,658	497	276
Indiana (h)	0	11,488	158	11,647	11,800	-272	119	317
Iowa (i).........................	0	4,826	0	4,826	4,590	160	76	226
Kansas (j).......................	328	4,841	2	5,171	4,690	0	481	0
Michigan (p).................	0	8,260	395	8,655	8,655	0	0	0
Minnesota (q)................	1,269	14,330	0	15,598	14,595	0	1,003	1,003
Nebraska (t)...................	177	3,032	-84	3,124	2,720	0	403	177
North Dakota (w)..........	77	997	0	1,074	906	100	69	100
Ohio (x)	158	25,551	0	25,708	24,831	739	138	575
South Dakota (dd).........	0	958	33	991	989	2	0	134
Wisconsin* (jj)	105	11,779	5	11,889	11,758	125	6	0
Regional totals	2,296	109,709	. . .	115,025	107,721	. . .	2,792	2,808
Southern Region								
Alabama (a)	347	6,273	78	6,697	6,030	-8	675	157
Arkansas	0	3,630	0	3,630	3,630	0	0	0
Florida	2,457	25,254	0	27,711	24,808	0	2,903	988
Georgia*........................	869	16,789	0	17,657	16,429	0	1,228	223
Kentucky (k).................	250	7,559	279	8,087	7,735	98	255	29
Louisiana (l)	0	7,164	76	7,240	7,241	-20	19	452
Maryland (n).................	453	11,548	438	12,438	11,264	0	1,174	521
Mississippi (r)...............	3	3,941	0	3,945	3,632	-261	52	52
Missouri (s)...................	488	6,933	0	7,421	7,121	0	300	232
North Carolina (v)	289	16,327	0	16,616	15,798	324	493	313
Oklahoma (y)................	67	5,377	-301	5,142	4,945	188	10	461
South Carolina (cc).......	55	5,591	0	5,646	5,073	105	468	75
Tennessee (ee)...............	545	9,374	-16	9,904	9,373	88	443	275
Texas (ff)	1,448	32,655	295	35,398	29,695	1,003	3,700	7
Virginia.........................	274	14,168	0	14,442	13,879	0	563	482
West Virginia	291	3,505	8	3,803	3,410	32	361	79
Regional totals	7,836	176,088	. . .	185,777	170,063	. . .	12,644	4,346
Western Region								
Alaska...........................	0	3,055	0	3,055	3,046	0	9	2,274
Arizona* (b)	360	7,786	158	8,304	7,661	0	643	165
California* (c)	3,489	81,947	3,791	89,227	81,728	0	7,499	0
Colorado* (d)...............	224	6,397	-257	6,363	6,211	0	152	0
Hawaii	185	4,486	0	4,671	4,185	0	486	53
Idaho (f)........................	100	2,268	-43	2,325	2,110	0	215	16
Montana........................	135	1,529	0	1,664	1,367	0	297	0
Nevada..........................	221	2,992	0	3,213	3,076	0	137	0
New Mexico*	447	4,969	0	4,969	4,748	13	682	682
Oregon (z).....................	-443	5,516	0	5,073	4,777	0	296	0
Utah (gg)	54	3,921	2	3,978	3,978	0	0	146
Washington (ii)	500	12,225	471	13,196	12,220	0	977	0
Wyoming (kk)...............	10	1,197	0	1,207	1,202	0	5	70
Regional totals	5,282	138,288	. . .	147,245	136,309	. . .	11,398	3,406
Regional totals without California......	1,793	56,341	. . .	58,018	54,581	. . .	3,899	3,406

See footnotes at end of table.

FISCAL 2005 STATE GENERAL FUND, PRELIMINARY ACTUAL, BY REGION — Continued
(In millions of dollars)

Source: National Association of State Budget Officers, *The Fiscal Survey of the States* (December 2005).

Note: For all states unless otherwise noted, transfers into budget stabilization funds are counted as expenditures and transfers from budget stabilization funds are counted as revenues.

Key:

* — In these states, the ending balance includes the balance in the budget stabilization fund.

(a) Revenue adjustments reflect a $17 million Finance Authority excess, an $18 million supersedeas bond, a $9.5 million surplus in board/commission accounts, $21.4 million in unrealized capital gains, and $12 million from the demutualization of insurance companies. Expenditure adjustments reflect $53 million of transfers to the Education Trust Fund Rainy Day Fund. -$15 million of estimated revisions, reducing debt service payments from the Capital Improvement Trust Fund and the General Fund by -$21.2 million, and -$24 million of supplemental appropriations.

(b) Revenue adjustments represent fund transfers, a withholding adjustment to compensate for federal withholding changes, and a judicial collections program.

(c) Revenue adjustments reflect an adjustment to the fiscal 2005 beginning balance of $3,789.8 million.

(d) Revenue adjustment includes diversions to the Older Coloradan's Program and State Education Fund.

(e) Expenditures include $639.8 million of surplus funds.

(f) Revenue adjustments include $1.7 million in transfers from other funds and $44.8 million in transfers to other funds, $21 million of which was to the Budget Stabilization Fund. Fiscal 2005 revenue came in $112 million higher than the estimate used during the 2006 legislative session. This will undoubtedly result in revising the fiscal 2006 revenue estimate upward.

(g) Revenue adjustments include $2,513 million of transfers into general funds. Expenditure adjustments include transfers-out of $3,163 million and $495 million to repay the Pension Obligation Bond debt service.

(h) Revenue adjustments represent one-time transfers from dedicated funds and transfers to the Rainy Day Fund. Expenditure adjustments represent one-time capital reversions from prior biennia and one-time property tax relief reversions. In addition to the ending and Rainy Day Fund balances noted, Indiana reserves a portion of the General Fund to tuition support payments for K–12 education. In fiscal 2005 that amount was $290.5 million. The ending General Fund balance does not reflect that amount.

(i) Expenditure adjustments reflect an appropriation from the General Fund ending balance to the property tax credit fund to pay for property tax credits in fiscal 2006.

(j) Revenues have been adjusted for released encumbrances.

(k) Revenue includes $109 million in Tobacco Settlement funds. Revenue adjustments include fund transfers ($159 million), and the Reserve for Continuing Appropriations ($120 million). Expenditure adjustments include funds reserved for continued appropriations.

(l) Revenue adjustments reflect carry forwards of $22.8 million, the use of prior year surpluses of $32.9 million, other fund balances of $2.7 million, and $17.3 million of non-recurring payments for capital outlay. Expenditure adjustments reflect the three-year average of revisions, which is $19.5 million. Actual expenditures will not be available until the CAFR is prepared.

(m) Revenue adjustments reflect legislative and statutory authorized transfers. These include $14.2 million of unbudgeted lapsed balances, -$37.6 million of statutory year-end transfers from unappropriated surplus, $31.8 million of transfers and $4 million of prior period and other accounting adjustments.

(n) Revenue adjustments reflect a $91 million transfer from the Rainy Day Fund and $385.5 million transfer from other funds. Both are offset by a $37 million reduction to prior year revenues.

(o) Figures include operating fund balances. The ending balance includes $304.8 million in the Transportation Escrow Fund. Those funds are available for appropriation through June 30, 2006. At that time any remaining balance will be transferred to the Stabilization Fund (Rainy Day Fund).

(p) Revenue adjustments include federal and state law changes (-$266.2 million); a revenue sharing freeze ($324 million); suspension of county revenue sharing payments ($182.3 million); escheats enforcement revenue ($2.5 million); a freeze on interfund borrowing rates ($20 million); deposits from state restricted funds ($33.4 million); other revenue adjustments ($3.1 million); and several pending actions including the sale of properties ($12.5 million) and a Rainy Day Fund withdrawal ($83.1 million). The estimated ending balance will likely be expended by fiscal year-end close.

(q) The ending balance includes a budget reserve of $653 million and a cash flow account of $350 million.

(r) Expenditure adjustments reflect transfers to the Rainy Day Fund, transfers to the Budget Contingency Fund, and aid to municipalities.

(s) Revenues are net of refunds. Refunds for fiscal 2005 totaled $1,071.3 million. Revenues include $175.9 million transferred to the General Revenue Fund and $45.2 million from bond proceeds for capital improvement projects.

(t) Revenue adjustments are transfers between the General Fund and other

funds. Per Nebraska law, this includes a transfer to the Cash Reserve Fund (Rainy Day Fund) of the amount the prior year's net General Fund receipts exceeded the official forecast.

(u) The ending balance includes $872 million in the tax stabilization reserve fund (Rainy Day Fund), $325 million in the Community Projects Fund and $21 million in reserve funds for litigation risks.

(v) Expenditure adjustments include $199.1 million allocated to the Rainy Day Fund and $125 million allocated to the Repair and Renovation Reserve.

(w) Expenditure adjustments reflect a transfer from the General Fund to the stabilization fund.

(x) Federal reimbursements for Medicaid and other human services programs are included in the general revenue fund. Beginning balances are undesignated, unreserved fund balances. The actual cash balances would be higher by the amount reserved for encumbrances and designated transfers from the general revenue fund. Expenditures for fiscal 2005 do not include encumbrances outstanding at the end of the year. Ohio reports expenditures based on disbursements for the general revenue fund. Expenditure adjustments reflect a transfer to the Budget Stabilization Fund of $394.2 million and miscellaneous transfers-out of $195.3 million. These transfers-out are adjusted for an anticipated net change in encumbrances from fiscal 2004 levels of $151 million.

(y) Revenue adjustments reflect the subtraction out of the Rainy Day Fund deposit of $243 million and an increase into the Cash Flow Reserve Fund from fiscal 2005 to fiscal 2006. Expenditure adjustments include law changes from the 2005 session. HB1193 created the Taxpayer Relief Fund and Oklahoma Dynamic Economy and Budget Security Fund. The bill directed any excess revenue over the amount needed to reach the 10 percent cap in the Rainy Day Fund to the funds. Each fund receives 50 percent of the excess revenue. For fiscal 2005, there was $188 million in excess over the amount needed ($243 million) to reach the 10 percent cap in the Rainy Day Fund.

(z) Oregon budgets on a biennial basis. The constitution requires the state to be balanced at the end of each biennium.

(aa) Revenue adjustments include $97.2 million in prior year relapses and a -$0.7 million adjustment to the beginning balance. Expenditure adjustments reflect current year lapses of $50.9 million and the transfer of 15 percent of the ending balance to the budget stabilization fund (Rainy Day Fund).

(bb) Revenue adjustments reflect a contribution to the budget stabilization fund.

(cc) Expenditure adjustments reflect the correction of prior year's accounting errors.

(dd) Revenue adjustments reflect $7.4 million from one-time receipts, $24.6 million transferred from the Property Tax Reduction Fund to cover the budget shortfall and $1.2 million transferred to the Budget Reserve Fund from the prior year's obligated cash and $0.8 million of obligated cash to the Budget Reserve Fund.

(ee) Revenue adjustments reflect a $42.7 million transfer from debt service unexpended appropriations and a -$58.4 million transfer to the Rainy Day Fund. Expenditure adjustments reflect a $21.6 million transfer to the Transportation Equity Fund, a $58.9 million transfer to the capital outlay projects fund, and $7 million for dedicated revenue appropriations.

(ff) The beginning balance is from Comptroller's January 2005 Biennial Revenue Estimate. Revenues are from the Comptroller's monthly collections report through August 2005. Revenue adjustments reflect the actual change in dedicated account balances. Total expenditures are preliminary 2005 budgeted, as reported by the Legislative Budget Board. Expenditure adjustments include $905 million reserved for transfer to the Rainy Day Fund and other adjustments to reconcile the ending balance.

(gg) Revenue adjustments include a $107.2 million reserve from the prior fiscal year, $11.7 million of transfers from miscellaneous restricted accounts, $5 million of lapsing balances, a $4.4 million industrial assistance fund reserve transfer to the Rainy Day Fund, and -$117.6 million held in reserve for the following fiscal year.

(hh) Revenue adjustments reflect -$2 million for Vermont Economic Development Authority debt forgiveness; $20.6 million in direct applications and transfers-in; a $13.8 million increase in property transfer tax revenue (estimated); and $15.6 million from the General Fund Surplus Reserve. Expenditure adjustments include $4.8 million to the Transportation Fund; $1.7 million from the General Bond Fund; $14.3 million to the Health Access Trust Fund; $3.7 million to the Internal Service Funds; $3.1 million to miscellaneous other funds; $1.3 million to the Budget Stabilization Reserve; and $19.6 million to the General Fund Surplus Reserve.

(ii) Revenue adjustments represent transfers from other accounts to the General Fund.

(jj) Revenue adjustments include Indian Gaming ($5.1 million). Expenditures include the compensation transfer ($163 million). Expenditure adjustments include a transfer to the Medical Assistance Trust Fund ($125 million).

(kk) The state budgets on a biennial basis. To complete the survey using annual figures, certain assumptions and estimates were required. Caution is advised when drawing conclusions or making projections using this information.

Table 7.2
FISCAL 2006 STATE GENERAL FUND, APPROPRIATED, BY REGION
(In millions of dollars)

State or other jurisdiction	Beginning balance	Revenues	Adjustments	Resources	Expenditures	Adjustments	Ending balance	Budget stabilization fund
Eastern Region								
Connecticut..................	$0	$14,134	$0	$14,134	$14,132	$0	$2	$0
Delaware (a)(e).............	701	3,020	0	3,721	3,244	0	477	161
Maine (m)......................	34	2,743	41	2,818	2,811	0	7	0
Massachusetts (o)	442	25,342	0	25,784	25,576	0	208	2,241
New Hampshire.............	31	1,295	0	1,325	1,309	0	16	31
New Jersey (a)..............	638	27,331	0	27,968	27,368	0	600	288
New York (a)(v)............	1,218	46,799	0	48,017	46,205	0	1,812	872
Pennsylvania (y)...........	365	23,915	0	24,280	24,278	1	2	337
Rhode Island (z)............	41	3,166	-64	3,142	3,142	0	0	96
Vermont (ee).................	0	1,059	39	1,098	1,054	44	0	52
Regional totals..............	3,470	148,804	...	152,287	149,119	...	3,124	4,078
Midwestern Region								
Illinois (h).....................	497	24,492	2,179	27,168	23,854	2,806	508	276
Indiana (i)	119	11,987	0	12,106	12,066	0	40	328
Iowa (j).........................	0	4,988	2	4,990	4,926	0	64	302
Kansas	481	4,937	0	5,418	5,150	0	268	0
Michigan (p)..................	0	8,449	529	8,978	8,977	0	0	0
Minnesota (a)(q)..........	1,003	15,033	0	16,036	15,020	0	1,016	1,003
Nebraska......................	403	3,186	-266	3,324	2,972	110	241	274
North Dakota	69	957	0	1,026	975	0	51	100
Ohio (w)	138	25,626	0	25,765	25,531	-215	449	577
South Dakota (aa)	0	1,002	17	1,019	1,019	0	0	115
Wisconsin (a)(gg)	6	12,632	119	12,756	12,456	236	65	0
Regional totals..............	2,716	113,289	...	118,586	112,946	...	2,702	2,975
Southern Region								
Alabama (b)...................	675	6,223	47	6,945	6,619	237	89	350
Arkansas	0	3,825	0	3,825	3,825	0	0	0
Florida	2,903	25,053	0	27,956	26,565	0	1,391	1,080
Georgia (a)(f)................	1,228	17,415	0	18,643	17,406	9	1,228	223
Kentucky (k)..................	255	7,934	232	8,421	8,369	47	4	29
Louisiana (l)	0	7,272	-10	7,262	7,260	0	2	636
Maryland (n).................	1,174	11,459	139	12,772	12,169	0	603	753
Mississippi (r)...............	52	4,014	0	4,066	3,910	-127	30	0
Missouri (s)..................	300	6,972	0	7,273	7,220	0	52	240
North Carolina..............	479	16,816	0	17,295	17,181	0	113	313
Oklahoma	10	5,620	0	5,629	5,355	0	275	0
South Carolina..............	468	5,617	0	6,085	5,969	0	116	154
Tennessee (bb)	443	9,562	-49	9,956	9,761	137	58	325
Texas (cc)	3,700	31,901	108	35,709	32,107	450	3,152	165
Virginia........................	563	14,192	0	14,755	14,745	0	10	664
West Virginia	361	3,287	28	3,676	3,614	45	17	124
Regional totals..............	12,611	177,162	...	190,268	182,075	...	7,140	5,056
Western Region								
Alaska..........................	0	3,078	0	3,078	3,038	0	40	2,308
Arizona (a)(c)	643	7,900	16	8,560	8,214	0	345	170
California (a)	7,499	84,471	0	91,970	90,026	0	1,944	0
Colorado (d)	152	6,682	-84	6,750	6,666	0	84	0
Hawaii	486	4,665	0	5,151	4,612	0	539	63
Idaho (g)......................	215	2,082	14	2,311	2,181	0	130	16
Montana (t)..................	297	1,421	0	1,718	1,473	0	245	0
Nevada (u)....................	137	2,936	0	3,073	2,905	0	168	159
New Mexico (a)............	682	5,281	0	5,281	4,760	6	1,210	1,210
Oregon (x)	296	5,545	0	5,842	5,731	0	111	0
Utah (dd)	0	4,060	126	4,186	4,176	0	10	170
Washington (ff).............	977	12,296	132	13,405	12,769	0	636	0
Wyoming (hh)...............	5	1,202	0	1,207	1,197	0	10	70
Regional totals..............	11,389	141,619	...	152,532	147,748	...	5,472	4,166
Regional totals.............. without California......	3,890	57,148	...	60,562	57,722	...	3,528	4,166

See footnotes at end of table.

FISCAL 2006 STATE GENERAL FUND, APPROPRIATED, BY REGION — Continued
(In millions of dollars)

Source: National Association of State Budget Officers, *The Fiscal Survey of the States* (December 2005).

Note: For all states, unless otherwise noted, transfers into budget stabilization funds are counted as expenditures and transfers from budget stabilization funds are counted as revenues.

Key:

N.A. — Not available.

(a) In these states, the ending balance includes the balance in the budget stabilization fund.

(b) Revenue adjustments reflect a $47.2 million transfer of tobacco revenue balances to the General Fund. Expenditure adjustments reflect $13 million of preliminary supplemental appropriations, $192.7 million of transfers to the Rainy Day Fund, and a $31.5 million cost-of-living adjustment for state employees.

(c) Revenue adjustments represent fund transfers and a change in the lottery distribution.

(d) Revenue adjustments include diversions to the Older Coloradan's Program and State Education Fund.

(e) Figures reflect the September 2005 meeting of the Delaware Economic and Financial Advisory Council.

(f) Expenditure adjustments reflect the governor's veto.

(g) Revenue adjustments include $21.3 million in transfers from other funds and $7.6 million in transfers to other funds. The revenue estimate incorporates a $170 million reduction caused by the phase-out of a two-year temporary sales tax increase.

(h) Revenue adjustments include $2,179 million of transfers into general funds. Expenditure adjustments include $431 million to repay Pension Obligation Bond debt service and transfers-out from general funds of $2,375 million.

(i) In addition to the ending and Rainy Day Fund balances noted, Indiana reserves a portion of the General Fund for tuition support payments for K–12 education. In fiscal 2006, that amount is $290.5 million. The ending General Fund balance does not reflect that amount.

(j) Revenue adjustments reflect tax credits and various minimal adjustments in fees, fines and miscellaneous receipts.

(k) Revenue includes $109 million in Tobacco Settlement funds. Revenue adjustments include fund transfers ($184 million) and the Reserve for Continuing Appropriations ($47 million). Expenditure adjustments include funds reserved for continued appropriations.

(l) Revenue adjustments consist of an increased statutory dedication due to Act 398.

(m) Revenue adjustments reflect $41.2 million in legislative and statutory authorized transfers.

(n) Revenue adjustments reflect transfers from other (special) funds.

(o) Figures include budgeted operating fund balances. The Rainy Day Fund balance assumes that no Transitional Escrow Funds are appropriated.

(p) Revenue adjustments include federal and state law changes (-$236.2 million); a revenue sharing freeze ($377.8 million); suspension of county revenue sharing payments ($182.3 million); escheats enforcement revenue ($10 million); a freeze on interfund borrowing rates ($20 million); enhanced tax enforcement revenue ($24.6 million); deposits from state restricted funds ($59.1 million); and several pending actions including the sale of properties ($60 million); and interest from the securitization of a portion of the Tobacco Settlement proceeds ($31 million).

(q) The ending balance includes a budget reserve of $653 million and a cash flow account of $350 million.

(r) Expenditure adjustments reflect a transfer to the Budget Contingency Fund.

(s) Revenues are net of refunds. Estimated refunds for fiscal 2006 total $1,184.2 million. Revenues include $178.2 million transferred to the General Revenue Fund.

(t) The revenues included are those projected by the Legislature during session. General Fund revenues appear stronger than anticipated during the

legislative session. A higher ending fund balance is anticipated at this time. In fiscal 2006, $46 million of the expenditures are one-time only and will not impact the long-term obligations of the state.

(u) Revenue adjustments are transfers between the General Fund and other funds. Per Nebraska law, this includes a transfer to the Cash Reserve Fund (Rainy Day Fund) of the amount the prior year's net General Fund receipts exceeded the official forecast. Expenditure adjustments are carryover appropriations from the prior fiscal year and a small amount reserved for supplemental/ deficit appropriations.

(v) The ending balance includes $872 million in the tax stabilization reserve fund (Rainy Day Fund), $601 million in the fiscal stability reserve fund, $316 million in the Community Projects Fund and $21 million in reserve funds for litigation risks.

(w) Federal reimbursements for Medicaid and other human services programs are included in the general revenue fund. Beginning balances are undesignated, unreserved fund balances. The actual cash balances would be higher by the amount reserved for encumbrances and designated transfers from the general revenue fund. Expenditures for fiscal 2005 do not include encumbrances outstanding at the end of the year. Ohio reports expenditures based on disbursements for the general revenue fund. Expenditure adjustments reflect projected miscellaneous transfers-out of $49.6 million. These transfers-out are adjusted for an anticipated net change in encumbrances from fiscal 2005 levels of negative $265 million dollars.

(x) Oregon budgets on a biennial basis. The constitution requires the state to be balanced at the end of each biennium.

(y) Expenditure adjustment reflects the transfer of 25 percent of the ending balance to the budget stabilization (Rainy Day) fund.

(z) Revenue adjustments reflect a contribution to the budget stabilization fund.

(aa) Revenue adjustments reflect a $17.4 million transfer from the property tax reduction fund to cover the anticipated budget shortfall.

(bb) Revenue adjustments reflect a -$49.3 million transfer to the Rainy Day Fund. Expenditure adjustments reflect a $23.5 million transfer to the Transportation Equity Fund, a $68.8 million transfer to the Capital Outlay Projects Fund, a $7.8 million transfer to the debt service fund, a $10 million transfer to the highway fund, a $20 million transfer to the local government fund (state-shared taxes), and a $7 million transfer to dedicated revenue appropriations.

(cc) The beginning balance is a preliminary estimate. Estimated revenues are from Comptroller's June 20, 2005 and August 12, 2005 certification worksheets. Total expenditures are preliminary 2006 appropriated, as reported by the Legislative Budget Board. Expenditure adjustments of $449.7 million reflect the estimated reserve for transfer to the Rainy Day Fund.

(dd) Revenue adjustments reflect $117.6 million held in reserve from the previous fiscal year, the $25 million repayment of an emergency loan to Washington County, $7 million of one-time revenue from implementing double-weighted sales tax reform, $0.2 million from the miscellaneous revenue sources, and a -$24 million transfer to the Rainy Day Fund.

(ee) Revenue adjustments reflect $7.7 million in direct applications and transfers-in; a $11.5 million increase in property transfer tax revenue (estimated); and $19.6 million from the General Fund Surplus Reserve. Expenditure adjustments include $1.3 million from the Capital Services Caseload Reserve; $6.1 million to the Budget Stabilization Reserve; and $39.1 million to the Capital General Fund Surplus Reserve.

(ff) Revenue adjustments represent transfers from other accounts to the General Fund.

(gg) Revenue adjustments include Indian Gaming ($118.6 million). Expenditures include the compensation reserve ($90 million). Expenditure adjustments include transfer to the Medical Assistance Trust Fund ($235 million).

(hh) The state budgets on a biennial basis. To complete the survey using annual figures, certain assumptions were required. Caution is advised when drawing conclusions or making projections using this information.

Table 7.3
FISCAL 2005 STATE TAX COLLECTIONS COMPARED WITH PROJECTIONS
USED IN ADOPTING FISCAL 2005 BUDGETS, BY REGION
(In millions of dollars)

State or other jurisdiction	Sales tax		Personal income tax		Corporate income tax		Total revenue collection
	Original estimate	Current estimate	Original estimate	Current estimate	Original estimate	Current estimate	
U.S. total	$186,548	$188,829	$206,602	$218,400	$30,664	$34,217	...
Eastern Region							
Connecticut....................	3,320	3,290	5,131	5,571	502	679	H
Delaware........................	N.A.	N.A.	824	883	96	114	H
Maine............................	944	941	1,260	1,270	123	136	H
Massachusetts	3,803	3,886	7,572	9,690	1,067	1,063	H
New Hampshire	N.A.	N.A.	N.A.	N.A.	N.A.	N.A.	H
New Jersey	6,600	6,520	8,855	9,550	2,632	2,403	H
New York (a)	10,492	10,587	26,738	28,100	1,751	1,858	H
Pennsylvania..................	8,001	8,000	8,595	8,748	1,951	1,921	T
Rhode Island.................	849	N.A.	981	N.A.	112	N.A.	T
Vermont	195	207	448	501	41	60	H
Regional totals	34,204	33,431	60,404	64,313	8,275	8,234	...
Midwestern Region							
Illinois	6,431	6,595	7,565	7,979	858	1,172	H
Indiana..........................	5,122	4,960	4,033	4,213	578	825	H
Iowa.............................	1,767	1,798	2,620	2,750	185	254	H
Kansas	1,892	1,892	2,040	2,051	205	226	H
Michigan (b)	6,801	6,625	6,022	6,016	1,918	1,886	T
Minnesota	4,226	4,239	6,176	6,359	829	827	H
Nebraska.......................	1,173	1,231	1,263	1,400	149	198	H
North Dakota	418	442	223	240	46	63	H
Ohio (c)	7,866	7,827	8,103	8,599	900	1,052	H
South Dakota	534	534	N.A.	N.A.	N.A.	N.A.	T
Wisconsin	4,107	4,039	5,796	5,700	554	764	T
Regional totals	40,337	40,182	43,841	45,307	6,222	7,267	...
Southern Region							
Alabama........................	1,726	1,796	2,100	2,306	250	300	H
Arkansas	1,886	1,945	1,726	1,875	180	264	H
Florida	16,491	17,622	N.A.	N.A.	1,435	1,730	H
Georgia	5,249	5,216	7,242	7,276	536	730	H
Kentucky	2,577	2,577	2,947	2,947	398	398	H
Louisiana	N.A.	N.A.	N.A.	N.A.	N.A.	N.A.	H
Maryland	2,954	3,129	5,292	5,661	339	512	H
Mississippi	1,493	1,544	1,062	1,100	316	321	H
Missouri........................	1,922	1,913	4,016	4,107	261	328	H
North Carolina	4,359	4,477	8,106	8,409	881	1,194	H
Oklahoma	1,545	1,556	2,271	2,499	134	184	H
South Carolina	2,250	2,319	1,979	2,215	120	186	H
Tennessee......................	6,097	6,094	142	155	1,146	1,367	H
Texas............................	15,432	16,248	N.A.	N.A.	N.A.	N.A.	H
Virginia.........................	2,852	2,946	7,774	9,587	408	617	H
West Virginia	946	960	1,101	1,170	173	281	H
Regional totals	67,779	70,342	45,758	49,307	6,577	8,412	...
Western Region							
Alaska...........................	N.A.	N.A.	N.A.	N.A.	250	436	H
Arizona.........................	3,627	3,661	2,665	2,967	691	702	H
California.......................	25,146	25,233	38,974	42,032	7,573	7,674	H
Colorado	1,862	1,855	3,553	3,712	251	315	H
Hawaii	1,950	2,131	1,233	1,381	35	86	H
Idaho............................	903	951	954	1,036	116	140	H
Montana........................	11	13	578	706	69	96	H
Nevada..........................	791	914	N.A.	N.A.	N.A.	N.A.	H
New Mexico	1,514	1,557	1,023	1,086	123	243	H
Oregon..........................	N.A.	N.A.	4,906	4,723	296	323	H
Utah.............................	1,497	1,590	1,713	1,830	184	190	H
Washington	6,577	6,618	N.A.	N.A.	N.A.	N.A.	T
Wyoming	351	351	N.A.	N.A.	N.A.	N.A.	H
Regional totals	44,229	44,874	55,599	59,473	9,588	10,205	...
Regional totals without California	19,803	19,641	16,625	17,441	2,015	2,531	...

See footnotes at end of table.

FISCAL 2005 STATE TAX COLLECTIONS COMPARED WITH PROJECTIONS USED IN ADOPTING FISCAL 2005 BUDGETS, BY REGION — Continued
(In millions of dollars)

Source: National Association of State Budget Officers, *The Fiscal Survey of the States* (December 2005).

Note: Unless otherwise noted, original estimates reflect the figures used when the fiscal 2004 budget was adopted, and current estimates reflect preliminary actual tax collections.

Key:

H — Revenues higher than expected.

T — Revenues on target.

N.A. — Indicates data are not available because, in most cases, these states do not have this type of tax.

(a) Reported personal income tax collections include dedicated personal income tax receipts that flow through the revenue bond tax fund. Reported sales tax collections include dedicated sales tax receipts that flow through the Local Government Assistance Corporation.

(b) The original fiscal 2005 budget has been modified and is based on the special August 2005 consensus estimates and is net of all enacted tax changes. Tax estimates represent total tax collections. Sales tax collections are for the Michigan sales tax only and do not include collections from Michigan use tax. Michigan does not have a Corporate income tax; estimates are for Michigan's Single Business Tax.

(c) Revenue estimates for fiscal 2005 were revised in July 2004.

Table 7.4
FISCAL 2005 STATE TAX COLLECTIONS COMPARED WITH PROJECTIONS
USED IN ADOPTING FISCAL 2006 BUDGETS, BY REGION
(In millions of dollars)

State or other jurisdiction	Sales tax		Personal income tax		Corporate income tax	
	Fiscal 2005	Fiscal 2006	Fiscal 2005	Fiscal 2006	Fiscal 2005	Fiscal 2006
U.S. total	$188,829	$196,321	$218,321	$224,598	$34,217	$34,896
Eastern Region						
Connecticut....................	3,290	3,432	5,571	5,786	679	646
Delaware........................	N.A.	N.A.	883	953	114	131
Maine............................	941	1,011	1,260	1,166	136	119
Massachusetts................	3,886	4,066	9,690	9,787	1,063	1,156
New Hampshire	N.A.	N.A.	N.A.	N.A.	N.A.	N.A.
New Jersey	6,520	6,850	9,550	10,275	2,403	2,502
New York (a)	10,587	10,611	28,100	30,345	1,858	2,024
Pennsylvania.................	8,000	8,269	8,748	9,182	1,921	2,059
Rhode Island.................	N.A.	888	N.A.	1,034	N.A.	110
Vermont	207	211	501	491	60	46
Regional totals..............	33,431	35,338	64,303	69,019	8,234	8,793
Midwestern Region						
Illinois	6,595	6,873	7,979	8,235	1,172	1,266
Indiana..........................	4,960	5,187	4,213	4,309	825	755
Iowa..............................	1,798	1,850	2,750	2,791	254	296
Kansas	1,892	1,950	2,051	2,130	226	210
Michigan.......................	6,625	6,905	6,016	6,176	1,886	1,914
Minnesota	4,239	4,395	6,359	6,566	927	768
Nebraska.......................	1,231	1,252	1,400	1,440	198	186
North Dakota	442	432	240	227	63	42
Ohio..............................	7,827	7,481	8,599	8,674	1,052	953
South Dakota	534	565	N.A.	N.A.	N.A.	N.A.
Wisconsin	4,039	4,139	5,700	6,141	764	683
Regional totals..............	40,182	41,029	45,307	46,689	7,367	7,073
Southern Region						
Alabama........................	1,796	1,873	2,306	2,405	300	314
Arkansas	1,945	1,999	1,875	1,879	264	271
Florida	17,622	18,642	N.A.	N.A.	1,730	1,841
Georgia	5,216	5,637	7,276	7,748	730	564
Kentucky	2,577	2,717	2,947	3,089	398	331
Louisiana	N.A.	N.A.	N.A.	N.A.	N.A.	N.A.
Maryland	3,129	3,109	5,661	5,416	512	451
Mississippi....................	1,544	1,558	1,100	1,100	321	341
Missouri........................	1,913	1,948	4,107	4,184	328	342
North Carolina	4,477	4,693	8,409	8,840	1,194	906
Oklahoma.....................	1,556	1,624	2,499	2,486	184	183
South Carolina	2,319	2,396	2,215	2,158	186	143
Tennessee......................	6,094	6,346	155	162	1,367	1,359
Texas............................	16,248	16,558	N.A.	N.A.	N.A.	N.A.
Virginia.........................	2,946	2,828	9,587	8,335	617	508
West Virginia	960	972	1,170	1,153	281	245
Regional totals..............	70,342	72,900	49,307	48,955	8,412	7,799
Western Region						
Alaska...........................	N.A.	N.A.	N.A.	N.A.	436	329
Arizona.........................	3,661	3,866	2,967	2,875	702	820
California.......................	25,233	26,951	42,032	42,230	7,674	8,822
Colorado	1,855	1,955	3,712	3,884	315	305
Hawaii	2,131	2,144	1,381	1,400	86	71
Idaho............................	951	784	1,036	1,046	140	134
Montana........................	13	13	706	607	96	81
Nevada..........................	914	926	N.A.	N.A.	N.A.	N.A.
New Mexico	1,557	1,597	1,086	1,012	243	210
Oregon..........................	N.A.	N.A.	4,723	4,942	323	261
Utah	1,590	1,614	1,830	1,940	190	203
Washington	6,618	6,851	N.A.	N.A.	N.A.	N.A.
Wyoming	351	353	N.A.	N.A.	N.A.	N.A.
Regional totals..............	44,874	47,054	59,473	59,936	10,205	11,236
Regional totals without California......	19,641	20,103	17,441	17,706	2,531	2,414

Source: National Association of State Budget Officers, *The Fiscal Survey of the States* (December 2005).

Note: Unless otherwise noted, fiscal 2005 figures reflect preliminary actual tax collection estimates as shown in Table 7.3, and fiscal 2006 figures reflect the estimates used in enacted budgets.

Key:

N.A. — Indicates data are not available because, in most cases, these states do not have this type of tax.

(a) Reported personal income tax collections include dedicated personal income tax receipts that flow through the revenue bond tax fund. Reported sales tax collections include dedicated sales tax receipts that flow through the Local Government Assistance Corporation.

Table 7.5
TOTAL STATE EXPENDITURES: CAPITAL INCLUSIVE, BY REGION
(In millions of dollars)

State or other jurisdiction	Actual fiscal 2003					Actual fiscal 2004					Estimated fiscal 2006				
	General fund	Federal funds	Other state funds	Bonds	Total	General fund	Federal funds	Other state funds	Bonds	Total	General fund	Federal funds	Other state funds	Bonds	Total
U.S. total	$492,994	$325,102	$275,361	$33,804	$1,127,261	$507,913	$347,107	$292,424	$29,844	$1,777,288	$535,654	$371,075	$315,435	$38,009	$1,260,173
Eastern Region															
Connecticut (b)	12,092	3,344	2,899	1,631	19,966	12,547	3,502	3,240	1,025	20,314	13,361	3,603	3,567	201	20,732
Delaware	2,454	945	653	486	4,538	2,454	1,000	744	488	4,686	2,883	1,093	807	590	5,373
Maine	2,533	1,996	1,434	101	6,064	2,584	2,346	1,502	117	6,549	2,710	2,545	1,526	172	6,953
Massachusetts	19,412	4,260	812	1,579	26,063	18,311	4,710	1,314	1,348	25,683	19,311	4,849	691	1,834	26,685
New Hampshire	1,244	1,237	1,499	91	4,071	1,265	1,381	1,602	69	4,317	1,293	1,439	1,551	68	4,351
New Jersey (u)	23,172	7,451	4,231	899	35,753	24,180	8,006	3,937	908	37,031	27,177	8,581	4,309	910	40,977
New York (i)	37,612	33,303	16,209	1,931	89,055	42,066	35,995	17,329	1,938	97,328	43,619	36,697	18,561	1,791	100,668
Pennsylvania	20,400	14,576	11,015	1,216	47,207	21,885	16,075	9,439	623	48,022	23,031	17,950	11,118	400	52,499
Rhode Island	2,690	1,601	1,141	111	5,543	2,729	1,760	1,187	84	5,760	2,963	1,932	1,181	170	6,246
Vermont	588	893	1,533	41	3,055	561	1,007	1,604	41	3,213	673	972	1,972	53	3,670
Regional totals	122,197	69,606	41,426	8,086	241,315	128,582	75,782	41,898	6,641	252,903	137,021	79,661	45,283	6,189	268,154
Midwestern Region															
Illinois (c)	18,128	7,549	13,142	2,059	40,878	17,436	9,126	21,737	2,037	50,336	17,743	8,220	19,671	1,255	46,889
Indiana (d)	10,235	5,766	3,054	233	19,288	11,652	6,908	2,761	174	21,495	11,723	6,758	2,666	139	21,286
Iowa	4,526	3,760	4,683	164	13,133	4,510	4,236	4,573	137	13,456	4,519	4,107	5,400	151	14,177
Kansas	4,137	2,997	2,800	148	10,082	4,316	2,945	2,714	222	10,197	4,680	2,987	2,987	159	10,813
Michigan	9,000	10,142	20,155	557	39,854	8,723	10,868	19,798	368	39,757	8,498	12,710	19,098	312	40,618
Minnesota	14,216	5,155	4,068	478	23,917	14,087	5,533	3,479	438	23,537	15,145	5,805	3,747	450	25,147
Nebraska (g)	2,619	2,053	2,137	0	6,809	2,575	2,250	2,278	0	7,103	2,854	2,705	2,884	0	8,443
North Dakota	860	1,102	842	20	2,824	894	1,164	832	35	2,925	920	1,335	996	115	3,366
Ohio (j)	22,653	6,923	15,780	1,443	46,799	23,839	7,294	15,622	1,399	48,154	25,020	9,147	19,154	1,718	55,039
South Dakota	866	1,014	637	8	2,525	847	1,173	633	9	2,662	971	1,233	703	25	2,932
Wisconsin	11,033	6,492	14,245	0	31,770	10,660	6,408	15,843	0	32,911	11,860	6,976	13,033	0	31,869
Regional totals	98,273	52,953	81,543	5,110	237,879	99,539	57,905	90,270	4,819	252,533	103,933	61,983	90,339	4,324	260,579
Southern Region															
Alabama	5,467	5,870	4,115	250	15,702	5,513	5,980	4,219	370	16,082	6,075	7,276	5,070	236	18,657
Arkansas	3,238	3,797	5,543	53	12,631	3,505	4,234	5,869	66	13,674	3,689	5,277	6,895	339	16,200
Florida	20,257	13,997	13,115	1,197	48,566	21,119	16,016	12,869	1,834	51,838	24,392	18,035	14,810	1,342	58,579
Georgia	14,929	11,955	848	249	27,981	14,449	12,840	857	524	28,670	14,633	13,992	933	810	30,368
Kentucky	7,047	5,966	5,355	0	18,368	7,206	6,344	5,457	0	19,007	7,640	6,795	5,802	0	20,237
Louisiana	6,670	5,937	5,865	354	18,826	6,501	6,967	6,399	350	20,217	6,865	6,468	11,070	352	24,755
Maryland	7,176	4,366	3,429	77	15,048	7,486	4,790	4,364	262	16,902	8,294	5,060	4,878	236	18,468
Mississippi	3,255	3,821	2,939	0	10,015	3,262	4,230	3,307	0	10,799	3,490	4,358	3,687	0	11,535
Missouri (e)	6,379	5,619	5,171	291	17,460	6,660	5,060	5,861	364	17,945	7,172	5,972	5,848	54	19,046
North Carolina	13,856	8,337	5,875	712	28,780	14,704	9,506	6,224	1,662	32,096	15,918	8,967	4,847	1,079	30,811
Oklahoma	4,409	4,151	4,330	32	12,922	4,116	4,596	4,099	258	13,069	5,027	5,153	3,694	336	14,210
South Carolina	4,995	5,570	4,882	477	15,924	4,901	5,649	5,148	171	15,869	4,996	5,726	5,229	0	15,951
Tennessee (k)	8,150	7,933	3,941	47	20,071	8,432	8,796	4,257	210	21,695	9,758	9,685	4,774	494	24,711
Texas (l)	29,911	19,691	9,692	1,465	60,759	29,360	21,654	10,472	1,934	63,420	29,015	21,851	11,955	2,344	65,165
Virginia	10,974	5,129	10,325	497	26,925	11,238	5,740	10,609	644	28,231	12,328	5,682	12,887	816	31,713
West Virginia	2,936	3,027	9,449	335	15,747	3,012	3,411	9,996	250	16,669	3,165	3,471	9,843	223	16,702
Regional totals	149,649	115,166	94,874	6,036	365,725	151,464	125,813	100,007	8,899	386,183	162,457	133,768	112,222	8,661	417,108

See footnotes at end of table.

TOTAL STATE EXPENDITURES: CAPITAL INCLUSIVE, BY REGION—Continued
(In millions of dollars)

State or other jurisdiction	Actual fiscal 2003					Actual fiscal 2004					Estimated fiscal 2006				
	General fund	Federal funds	Other state funds	Bonds	Total	General fund	Federal funds	Other state funds	Bonds	Total	General fund	Federal funds	Other state funds	Bonds	Total
Western Region															
Alaska	2,540	2,482	1,043	594	6,659	2,413	2,805	2,432	0	7,650	2,383	3,409	3,929	66	9,787
Arizona (a)	5,955	6,169	6,235	394	18,753	7,589	6,857	6,684	599	21,729	7,486	7,737	6,993	569	22,785
California	77,482	54,733	18,282	11,015	161,512	78,345	52,420	18,892	6,986	156,643	80,283	56,686	22,091	15,116	174,176
Colorado	5,483	3,018	4,824	301	13,626	5,594	3,222	4,757	60	13,633	5,799	3,227	4,771	0	13,797
Hawaii	3,336	1,181	2,221	477	7,215	3,840	1,416	2,344	349	7,949	4,166	1,678	2,388	775	9,007
Idaho	1,926	1,548	880	5	4,359	1,988	1,719	873	4	4,584	2,114	1,965	1,069	10	5,158
Montana (f)	1,264	1,442	943	0	3,649	1,269	1,491	1,181	0	3,941	1,351	1,804	1,377	0	4,532
Nevada	1,952	1,880	2,302	100	6,234	2,268	1,986	2,243	272	6,769	2,721	1,794	2,726	283	7,524
New Mexico	3,851	3,282	1,711	440	9,284	4,032	3,492	1,727	340	9,591	4,417	3,894	1,849	874	11,034
Oregon	3,467	3,622	9,094	0	16,183	5,214	3,731	8,189	0	17,134	4,995	4,564	8,973	0	18,532
Utah	3,536	1,934	1,720	343	7,533	3,574	2,076	2,002	253	7,905	3,978	2,179	2,253	5	8,415
Washington	11,334	5,530	7,371	903	25,138	11,452	5,858	8,034	622	25,966	11,788	6,188	8,271	1,137	27,384
Wyoming	749	556	892	0	2,197	750	534	891	0	2,175	762	538	901	0	2,201
Regional totals	122,875	87,377	57,518	14,572	282,342	128,328	87,607	60,249	9,485	285,669	132,243	95,663	67,591	18,835	314,332
Regional totals without California	45,393	32,644	39,236	3,557	120,830	49,983	35,187	41,357	2,499	129,026	51,960	38,977	45,500	3,719	140,156

Source: National Association of State Budget Officers, *State Expenditure Report* (2005).

Note: State funds refers to general funds plus other state fund spending. State spending from bonds is excluded. Total funds refers to funding from all sources; general fund, federal funds, other state funds and bonds.

Key:

(a) Federal funds are generally excluded from the General Fund. In fiscal 2004 and 2005 Arizona received approximately $87 million (each year) which was not earmarked for any program, grant or any other stipulation and was subsequently deposited into the General Fund.

(b) Fiscal 2004 actual and fiscal 2005 estimated bond fund data are unavailable due to problems associated with the implementation of a new accounting system.

(c) General Funds do not include federal receipts. Federal receipts were added to federal funds. This presentation differs from NASBO's *Fiscal Survey of States.*

(d) Figures reflect funding in support of pre–K–12 education and the operation of the Pennsylvania Department of Education.

(e) Total expenditures exclude refunds. Fiscal 2003 expenditures exclude refunds of $1,210 million, including $1,166 million general revenue. Fiscal 2004 estimates exclude refunds of $1,118 million, including $1,075 million general revenue. Fiscal 2005 estimates exclude refunds of $1,330 million, including $1,287 million general revenue. Other funds include federal reimbursements received by the Department of Highways and Transportation received by the Department of Conservation which have constitutionally created funds. Federal and other funds for fiscal 2005 represent appropriations available to state agencies. These appropriations are often established at higher levels to provide agencies with appropriation authority in the event that revenues are aviable for various programs. Final expenditures will be lower.

(f) Principal and interest payments on bonds are included in total expenditures.

(g) Fiscal 2004–2005 amounts shown are equal to appropriations for the year and do not reflect an estimate of expenditures.

(h) Figures include pension, post retirement medical debt service on pension bonds, payroll taxes, and health

benefits expenditures which total $988 million in general funds in fiscal 2004 and $1.1 billion in fiscal 2005, spread across education, corrections, transportation and all other.

(i) New York budgets most employer contributions to employees' benefits and pensions centrally. The portion of employer contributions to employees' benefits not distributed to an expenditure category has been included in the all other expenditures category.

(j) Certain federal reimbursements and block grants for certain human services programs are deposited into the state's General Revenue Fund. Expenditures of these federal funds are contained in the General Fund number in this table to be consistent with other portrayals of Ohio's General Fund. This amounts to $4,972.4 million in fiscal 2003 and $5,516.4 million in fiscal 2004. This has an impact on percentage of total General Fund expenditure calculations as well as on comparisons of Ohio's federal funding levels. Also, inherent in Ohio's budgetary accounting environment are significant overstatements of total spending due to two phenomena. First, fiduciary fund expenditures represent the distribution of funds collected by the state on behalf of other entities. These are not operating, program, or subsidy expenditures for the state. These expenditures total $5,613.1 million in fiscal 2003 and $5,569.0 million in fiscal 2004. Additionally, "double counting" of revenue and expenditures related to intrastate transactions overstates overall state expenditure activity. The overstatement is primarily found in general services. Expenditure activity from these funds totals $1,186.1 million in fiscal 2003 and $1,295.2 million in fiscal 2004. This results in Ohio's "All Other" expenditures as a percentage of the total being overstated, and consequently other areas being understated departmental revenues. Ohio appropriates capital appropriations on a biennial basis rather than an annual basis; therefore, the amounts shown for fiscal 2005 are estimates.

(k) Tennessee collects personal income tax on income from dividends on stocks and interest on certain bonds. Tax revenue estimates do not include federal funds and other departmental revenues. However, federal funds and other departmental revenues are included in the budget as funding sources for the General Fund, along with state tax revenues.

(l) Fiscal 2005 does not include the supplemental funds that are expected to be necessary to complete the fiscal year. Supplemental funds have not yet been appropriated.

Table 7.6
ELEMENTARY AND SECONDARY EDUCATION EXPENDITURES, BY REGION
(In millions of dollars)

State or other jurisdiction	Actual fiscal 2003					Actual fiscal 2004					Estimated fiscal 2006				
	General fund	Federal funds	Other state funds	Bonds	Total	General fund	Federal funds	Other state funds	Bonds	Total	General fund	Federal funds	Other state funds	Bonds	Total
U.S. total	$176,281	$34,426	$25,275	$9,578	$245,560	$181,393	$39,501	$25,398	$5,820	$252,112	$192,476	$42,851	$27,164	$12,960	
Eastern Region															
Connecticut	1,990	360	5	488	2,843	2,000	368	4	0	2,372	2,102	391	4	0	2,497
Delaware	840	103	362	131	1,436	857	121	402	135	1,515	915	135	446	152	1,648
Maine	919	145	7	4	1,075	925	168	12	10	1,115	975	148	15	8	1,146
Massachusetts	4,103	687	0	0	4,790	4,225	839	0	0	5,064	4,030	916	0	500	5,446
New Hampshire	83	121	905	6	1,115	63	140	848	9	1,060	62	153	750	6	971
New Jersey	7,505	703	24	0	8,232	8,299	770	24	0	9,093	9,091	825	32	0	9,948
New York (a)	13,664	2,429	1,936	54	18,083	13,677	3,176	1,934	41	18,828	14,171	3,321	2,317	71	19,880
Pennsylvania	6,965	1,561	15	0	8,541	7,282	1,696	16	0	8,994	7,867	1,724	2	0	9,593
Rhode Island	742	128	1	11	882	777	148	2	0	927	795	169	5	0	969
Vermont	14	91	858	13	976	13	103	894	6	1,016	14	106	1,180	4	1,304
Regional totals	36,825	6,328	4,113	707	47,973	38,118	7,529	4,136	201	49,984	40,022	7,888	4,751	741	53,402
Midwestern Region															
Illinois	6,135	1,675	96	568	8,474	6,288	1,710	40	474	8,512	6,713	1,833	52	288	8,886
Indiana	4,193	552	34	0	4,779	4,211	692	12	0	4,915	4,291	750	18	0	5,059
Iowa	1,913	311	80	0	2,304	1,971	367	9	0	2,347	2,075	383	18	0	2,476
Kansas	2,113	316	81	0	2,510	2,175	352	100	0	2,627	2,316	369	80	0	2,765
Michigan	412	1,216	10,899	0	12,527	407	1,353	10,686	0	12,446	195	1,479	11,035	0	12,709
Minnesota	5,528	515	32	31	6,106	5,716	557	29	17	6,319	6,329	595	32	4	6,960
Nebraska	834	198	5	0	1,037	819	222	4	0	1,045	829	248	4	0	1,081
North Dakota	300	100	41	0	441	309	118	36	0	463	317	87	38	0	442
Ohio	6,263	1,141	988	507	8,899	6,523	1,354	981	465	9,323	6,632	1,485	1,284	536	9,937
South Dakota	322	110	0	0	433	281	174	0	0	455	342	139	3	0	484
Wisconsin	5,234	530	57	0	5,821	5,268	591	99	0	5,958	5,298	612	125	0	6,035
Regional totals	33,247	6,664	12,313	1,106	53,331	33,968	7,490	11,996	956	54,410	35,337	7,980	12,689	828	56,834
Southern Region															
Alabama	2,921	664	123	0	3,708	2,901	712	143	0	3,756	3,148	951	159	0	4,258
Arkansas	1,592	352	246	0	2,190	1,627	384	222	0	2,233	1,655	528	671	0	2,854
Florida	7,559	1,865	491	0	9,915	8,038	2,014	624	0	10,676	8,783	2,357	647	0	11,787
Georgia	5,749	1,374	283	0	7,406	5,484	1,677	290	174	7,625	5,483	1,792	306	176	7,757
Kentucky	3,044	480	18	0	3,542	3,053	609	15	0	3,677	3,302	626	16	0	3,944
Louisiana	2,582	719	325	0	3,626	2,530	916	295	0	3,741	2,678	693	303	0	3,674
Maryland	3,146	670	125	0	3,941	3,383	698	3	0	4,084	3,702	710	2	0	4,414
Mississippi	1,502	469	352	0	2,323	1,503	529	508	0	2,540	1,687	556	420	0	2,663
Missouri	2,324	725	1,314	0	4,363	2,447	787	1,163	0	4,397	2,566	995	1,214	0	4,775
North Carolina	5,873	821	49	0	6,743	6,167	940	119	0	7,226	6,157	915	47	0	7,119
Oklahoma	1,447	424	952	0	2,823	1,427	484	1,082	0	2,993	2,065	615	533	0	3,213
South Carolina	1,795	502	642	103	3,042	1,738	579	702	74	3,093	1,839	524	612	0	2,975
Tennessee	2,696	600	22	0	3,318	2,799	722	11	0	3,532	3,016	856	21	0	3,893
Texas	12,824	2,872	1,057	0	16,753	12,116	3,584	1,418	0	17,118	11,674	3,857	1,435	0	16,966
Virginia	4,010	419	118	0	4,547	4,154	485	123	0	4,762	4,758	522	137	0	5,417
West Virginia	1,521	255	51	132	1,959	1,563	270	50	76	1,959	1,614	393	52	89	2,148
Regional totals	60,585	13,211	6,168	235	80,199	60,930	15,390	6,757	324	83,412	64,127	16,890	6,575	265	87,857

See footnotes at end of table.

ELEMENTARY AND SECONDARY EDUCATION EXPENDITURES, BY REGION—Continued
(In millions of dollars)

State or other jurisdiction	Actual fiscal 2003					Actual fiscal 2004					Estimated fiscal 2006				
	General fund	Federal funds	Other state funds	Bonds	Total	General fund	Federal funds	Other state funds	Bonds	Total	General fund	Federal funds	Other state funds	Bonds	Total
Western Region															
Alaska	801	151	52	0	1,004	740	162	87	0	989	823	170	102	0	1,095
Arizona	2,598	638	413	0	3,649	2,959	680	446	0	4,085	3,184	769	524	0	4,477
California	26,517	4,980	67	7,268	38,832	27,283	5,388	56	4,152	36,879	31,285	6,100	59	10,626	48,070
Colorado	2,312	339	434	0	3,085	2,417	406	461	0	3,284	2,540	471	472	0	3,483
Hawaii	1,282	160	31	232	1,705	1,467	223	44	144	1,878	1,555	230	50	234	2,069
Idaho	942	154	63	0	1,159	966	172	64	0	1,202	988	182	63	0	1,233
Montana	525	120	53	0	698	518	135	49	0	702	519	153	56	0	728
Nevada	690	191	148	0	1,029	776	225	141	0	1,142	896	221	147	0	1,264
New Mexico	1,892	240	26	30	2,188	1,975	309	30	43	2,357	2,097	266	30	266	2,659
Oregon	1,425	350	527	0	2,302	2,554	408	126	0	3,088	2,150	478	548	0	3,176
Utah	1,648	288	-2	0	1,934	1,679	311	24	0	2,014	1,788	315	44	0	2,147
Washington	4,970	524	428	0	5,922	5,021	585	530	0	6,136	5,141	648	612	0	6,401
Wyoming	22	88	440	0	550	22	88	440	0	550	24	90	442	0	556
Regional totals	45,624	8,223	2,680	7,530	64,057	48,377	9,092	2,498	4,339	64,306	52,990	10,093	3,149	11,126	77,358
Regional totals without California	19,107	3,243	2,613	262	25,225	21,094	3,704	2,442	187	27,427	21,705	3,993	3,090	500	29,288

Source: National Association of State Budget Officers, *State Expenditure Report* (2005).

Note: For this table, 10 states wholly or partially excluded employer contributions to teacher pensions and 14 states wholly or partially excluded contributions to health benefits. See the National Association of Budget Officers' *2004 State Expenditure Report* for additional details.

Key:

(a) State appropriations to school districts for operational costs include funding intended to be expended by school districts for contributions to current employee's pensions, employee health benefits, and for operational costs of libraries.

(b) Figures reflect K–12 education, the Michigan Department of Education, adult education and pre-school. Employer contributions to current employees' pensions and health benefits are reported for Department of Education employees.

(c) "Double counting" of revenue and expenditures related to intrastate transactions overstates overall state expenditure activity.

(d) Figures reflect funding in support of pre-K–12 education and the operation of the Pennsylvania Department of Education.

(e) South Dakota received $50 million in fiscal relief payments from the Federal Jobs and Growth Tax Relief Reconciliation Act of 2003 in fiscal 2004. These funds were used to fund a portion of state aid to K–12 education and resulted in a decrease in General Fund expenditures and an increase in federal fund expenditures of $50 million for fiscal 2004.

(f) Included in the General Fund are school funds (income tax revenue) which in Utah are restricted by the state constitution for the sole use of public and higher education. Public education in Utah is organized to include the Utah State Office of Rehabilitation (USOR). The numbers reflected in this report for public education include USOR. The USOR amounts are as follows: for fiscal 2003, $18 million in general funds, $30 million in federal funds, and $1 million in other state funds; for fiscal 2004, $18 million in general funds, $33 million in federal funds, and $1 million in other state funds; for fiscal 2005, $19 million in general funds, $33 million in federal funds, and $1 million in other state funds.

Table 7.7
MEDICAID EXPENDITURES BY STATE AND REGION
(In millions of dollars)

State or other jurisdiction	Actual fiscal 2003				Actual fiscal 2004				Estimated fiscal 2006			
	General fund	Federal funds	Other state funds	Total	General fund	Federal funds	Other state funds	Total	General fund	Federal funds	Other state funds	Total
U.S. total	$84,737	$142,251	$20,625	$247,613	$85,906	$154,585	$22,070	$262,561	$96,199	$161,906	$25,611	$283,716
Eastern Region												
Connecticut (b)	2,758	1,857	649	5,264	2,849	1,938	692	5,479	3,027	1,992	740	5,759
Delaware	346	357	0	703	346	384	0	730	397	429	0	826
Maine	513	1,177	40	1,730	529	1,454	64	2,047	576	1,579	157	2,312
Massachusetts	2,712	2,712	0	5,424	2,908	2,908	0	5,816	3,093	3,093	0	6,186
New Hampshire	292	449	144	885	374	599	168	1,141	438	612	169	1,219
New Jersey	3,831	3,994	48	7,873	3,556	4,023	50	7,629	3,759	4,080	50	7,889
New York (g)	5,952	16,902	2,462	25,316	6,061	18,729	2,772	27,562	6,953	19,778	2,624	29,355
Pennsylvania (i)	4,179	7,633	2,254	14,066	5,054	8,441	1,553	15,048	5,415	8,857	2,594	16,866
Rhode Island	631	819	0	1,450	592	845	0	1,437	657	844	0	1,501
Vermont	133	410	110	653	60	439	191	690	69	499	185	753
Regional totals	21,347	36,310	5,707	63,364	22,329	39,760	5,490	67,579	24,384	41,763	6,519	72,666
Midwestern Region												
Illinois	3,618	4,583	1,468	9,669	3,277	5,539	1,684	10,500	3,655	5,858	2,447	11,960
Indiana (d)	1,495	2,451	11	3,957	1,488	2,808	11	4,307	1,697	2,878	0	4,575
Iowa	419	1,471	511	2,401	332	1,509	556	2,397	353	1,308	475	2,136
Kansas	607	1,083	87	1,777	549	1,103	80	1,732	703	1,240	90	2,033
Michigan (e)	1,665	4,560	1,730	7,955	1,960	4,803	1,492	8,255	1,827	4,803	1,852	8,482
Minnesota	2,327	2,473	0	4,800	2,341	2,831	0	5,172	2,284	2,775	0	5,059
Nebraska	453	823	13	1,289	457	895	25	1,377	556	891	18	1,465
North Dakota	109	336	2	447	136	356	0	492	171	369	0	540
Ohio (h)	8,377	1,620	822	10,819	9,858	1,702	934	12,494	9,575	2,060	1,100	12,735
South Dakota (j)	170	362	0	532	169	410	0	579	193	426	0	619
Wisconsin	1,456	2,483	55	3,994	778	2,728	1,291	4,797	1,529	2,759	268	4,556
Regional totals	20,696	22,245	4,699	47,640	21,345	24,684	6,073	52,102	22,543	25,367	6,250	54,160
Southern Region												
Alabama	289	2,645	764	3,698	326	2,731	716	3,773	436	2,760	676	3,872
Arkansas	368	1,823	276	2,467	459	2,101	150	2,710	533	2,291	258	3,082
Florida (c)	3,700	7,115	817	11,632	3,711	8,330	1,038	13,079	4,530	8,761	1,047	14,338
Georgia	1,609	3,533	18	5,160	1,716	3,669	53	5,438	1,816	3,946	53	5,815
Kentucky	732	2,691	392	3,815	740	3,003	377	4,120	834	2,949	448	4,231
Louisiana	789	3,241	420	4,450	723	3,614	541	4,878	714	3,767	625	5,106
Maryland	1,984	2,086	0	4,070	2,142	2,432	0	4,574	2,544	2,548	0	5,092
Mississippi	237	2,402	474	3,113	258	2,674	541	3,473	247	2,709	788	3,744
Missouri (f)	1,190	3,529	974	5,693	1,097	3,691	957	5,745	1,385	4,029	1,147	6,561
North Carolina	2,039	4,381	320	6,740	1,983	5,163	235	7,381	2,360	5,096	432	7,888
Oklahoma	543	1,664	168	2,375	596	1,852	125	2,573	637	1,913	164	2,714
South Carolina	449	2,590	620	3,659	487	2,868	602	3,957	641	2,954	595	4,190
Tennessee (k)	2,057	4,483	324	6,864	2,108	4,857	666	7,631	2,540	5,297	853	8,690
Texas (l)	5,773	9,245	0	15,018	5,811	9,631	0	15,442	6,003	9,254	0	15,257
Virginia	1,737	1,836	71	3,644	1,812	1,977	37	3,826	2,147	2,091	71	4,309
West Virginia	179	1,321	239	1,739	228	1,554	211	1,993	298	1,549	212	2,059
Regional totals	23,675	54,585	5,877	84,137	24,197	60,147	6,249	90,593	27,665	61,914	7,369	96,948

See footnotes at end of table.

MEDICAID EXPENDITURES BY STATE AND REGION—Continued
(In millions of dollars)

State or other jurisdiction	Actual fiscal 2003				Actual fiscal 2004				Estimated fiscal 2006			
	General fund	Federal funds	Other state funds	Total	General fund	Federal funds	Other state funds	Total	General fund	Federal funds	Other state funds	Total
Western Region												
Alaska	212	574	58	844	230	669	83	982	225	673	78	976
Arizona	589	2,345	344	3,278	674	2,781	359	3,814	914	3,142	387	4,443
California (a)	11,983	15,981	2,984	30,948	11,009	15,459	3,018	29,486	13,635	17,599	3,959	35,193
Colorado	989	1,202	165	2,356	1,127	1,442	148	2,717	1,259	1,422	194	2,875
Hawaii	309	456	10	775	322	530	8	860	363	529	10	902
Idaho	224	569	60	853	225	650	77	952	288	696	77	1,061
Montana	124	435	11	570	127	493	20	640	149	499	28	676
Nevada	490	560	110	1,160	524	624	86	1,234	532	653	89	1,274
New Mexico	428	1,595	25	2,048	418	1,886	34	2,338	490	1,892	42	2,424
Oregon	734	1,686	442	2,862	731	1,731	262	2,724	751	1,872	425	3,048
Utah (m)	199	764	133	1,096	192	915	163	1,270	253	996	184	1,433
Washington	2,702	2,880	0	5,582	2,420	2,750	0	5,170	2,708	2,829	0	5,537
Wyoming	36	64	0	100	36	64	0	100	40	60	0	100
Regional totals	19,019	29,111	4,342	52,472	18,035	29,994	4,258	52,287	21,607	32,862	5,473	59,942
Regional totals without California	7,036	13,130	1,358	21,524	7,026	14,535	1,240	22,801	7,972	15,263	1,514	24,749

Source: National Association of State Budget Officers, *State Expenditure Report* (2005).

Note: States were asked to report Medicaid expenditures as follows: General funds: all general funds appropriated to the Medicaid agency and any other agency which are used for direct Medicaid matching purposes under Title XIX. Other state funds: other funds and revenue sources used as Medicaid match, such as local funds and provider taxes, fees, donations, assessments (as defined by the Health Care Finance Administration). Federal funds: all federal matching funds provided pursuant to Title XIX.

As noted above, the figures reported as Other State Funds reflect the amounts reported as provider taxes, fees, donations, assessments and local funds by states. State Medicaid agencies report these amounts to the Health Care Finance Administration (HCFA) on form 37, as defined by the Medicaid Voluntary Contribution and Provider-specific Tax Amendments of 1991 (RL. I 02-234). However some state budget offices are unable to align their financial reporting to separate these costs for the NASBO *State Expenditure Report*. Thus this report does not capture 100 percent of state provider taxes, fees, donations, assessments and local funds. Small dollar amounts, when rounded, cause an aberration in the percentage increase. In these instances, the actual dollar amounts should be consulted to determine the exact percentage increase. The states were asked to separately detail the amount of provider taxes, fees, donations, assessments and local funds reported as other state funds.

Key:

(a) Other State Funds includes local government matching funds for Disproportionate Share Hospitals, Voluntary Governmental Transfers, Targeted Case Management, Local Education Agencies, Medi-Cal Administrative Activities, Los Angeles Co. Medicaid Demonstration Project, Hospital Outpatient Supplemental Payments,Teaching Hospitals, mental health services, and personal care services. Medi-Cal changed from accrual to cash-based budgeting in fiscal 2003–2004.

(b) Medicaid appropriations are "gross funded": federal funds are deposited directly to the State Treasury.

(c) For fiscal 2003, Other State Funds include provider assessments of $275 million, cigarette taxes of $109 million, tobacco settlement funds of $50 million, tobacco non-general funds transferred for matching funds of $71 million, other non-general funds transferred as matching funds of $2 million, state recoupments of $22 million, and local county funds of $287 million. For fiscal 2004, Other State Funds include provider assessments of $268 million, cigarette taxes of $113 million, tobacco settlement funds of $72 million, tobacco

non-general funds transferred for matching funds of $28 million, state recoupments of $21 million, and local county funds of $536 million. The decrease from the previous year in tobacco non-general funds transferred for matching funds is due to a shortfall in tobacco settlement funds. The increase in local county funds from the previous year is due to a funding increase at the local level. For fiscal 2005, Other State Funds include provider assessments of $295 million, cigarette taxes of $113 million, tobacco settlement funds of $82 million, tobacco non-general funds transferred for matching funds of $33 million, state recoupments of $18 million, and local county funds of $506 million.

(d) Indiana received $130.9 million from the Federal Jobs & Growth Tax Relief Reconciliation Act of 2003 in fiscal 2004. This enhanced match understates General Fund expenditures and overstates Federal expenditures by $130.9 million for fiscal 2004.

(e) Other State Funds include local funds of $38.3 million and provider taxes of $169.6 million for fiscal 2003; local funds of $38.3 million and provider taxes of $324.2 million for fiscal 2004; and local funds of $40.5 million and provider taxes of $486.4 million for fiscal 2005. Public health and community and institutional care for mentally and developmentally disabled persons are partially reported in the Medicaid totals.

(f) Medicaid and CHIP data are from the CMS 64 Report used for federal reporting of Medicaid expenditures. The split between the General Revenue Fund and Other Funds is an estimate. Medicaid does not track the General Revenue Fund versus Other State/Local Funds in its reporting. Other Funds include estimated local funds of $389 million for fiscal 2003, $415 million for fiscal 2004, and $418 million for fiscal 2005.

(g) Medicaid spending does not include administrative costs or local government shares.

(h) Federal funds deposited to the state General Fund and shown as General Fund expenditures for Medicaid amount to $4,710.4 million in fiscal 2003 and $5,270.2 million in fiscal 2004. See General Notes for Ohio on this issue. Local dollars are used as state match for Medicaid services and administration. Dollars that are generated at the local level that are then used to draw down federal match are not included in Ohio's numbers for purposes of making the numbers reported here consistent with other reports for Ohio General Fund and All Fund spending.

(i) Intergovernmental transfer (IGT) funds are included in the Other State Funds category and total in $1,902 billion in 2003, $1,432 billion in 2004, and $1.009 billion in 2005. State expenditures for Medicaid match are

MEDICAID EXPENDITURES BY STATE AND REGION — Continued
(In millions of dollars)

not accounted for separately from the state's overall medical assistance program. Therefore, the state match has been derived based upon federal reimbursement rates for individual clients who do not qualify under Title XIX. A portion of the IGT funds provides the 10 percent local match required by Pennsylvania law for Medicaid clients in nursing homes. Other local funds used as match are not included in this report.

(j) The enhanced FMAP from the Federal Jobs & Growth Tax Relief Reconciliation Act of 2003 resulted in a decrease in general fund expenditures of $16.3 million and an increase in federal fund expenditures by the same amount for fiscal 2004.

(k) Regarding premium revenue: fiscal 2003 totals $53 million, fiscal 2004 totals $65 million and fiscal 2005 totals $65 million. Regarding Certified Public Expenditures Local Fund from Hospitals: fiscal 2003 totals $248 million, fiscal 2004 totals $236 million and fiscal 2005 totals $207 million. Regarding Nursing Home Tax:

fiscal 2003 totals $87 million, fiscal 2004 totals $85 million and fiscal 2005 totals $85 million. Regarding the ICF/MR 6 Percent Gross Receipts Tax: fiscal 2003 totals $15 million, fiscal 2004 totals $15 million and fiscal 2005 totals $15 million. Regarding Intergovernmental Transfers: fiscal 2003 totals $57 million, fiscal 2004 totals $52 million and fiscal 2005 totals $50 million.

(l) Medicaid expenditures are reported from the Medicaid History Report (11/2004), which does not distinguish other funds from state funds.

(m) The slight reduction in state General Fund between fiscal 2003 and fiscal 2004 is a result of the temporary increase in federal sharing in the Medicaid program funded in the Jobs & Growth Tax Relief Reconciliation Act of 2003.

Table 7.8
ALLOWABLE INVESTMENTS

State or other jurisdiction	CDs within state	CDs nationally	State and local government obligations	U.S. Treasury obligations	U.S. agency obligations	Other time deposits	Bankers' acceptances	Commercial paper	Corporate notes/bonds	Mortgage backed securities	Mutual/ Money Market funds	Derivatives	Real estate	Repurchase agreements	Venture capital/ Private equity	Corporate stocks (foreign)	Corporate stocks (domestic)	Other
Alabama	★		★	★	★					★				★				(a)
Alaska	★	★	★	★	★	★	★	★		★	★			★			★	
Arizona	★		★	★	★	★	★	★	★		★			★				(b)
Arkansas	★	★	★	★	★	★	★	★	★	★				★				
California	★	★	★	★	★	★	★	★	★	★	★			★			★	(c)
Colorado	★			★	★			★	★	★	★			★				
Connecticut	★	★	★	★	★	★	★	★	★	★	★			★				(d)
Delaware	★		★	★	★		★	★	★	★	★	★		★				(d)
Florida	★		★	★	★		★	★	★	★	★			★				
Georgia	★	★	★	★	★	★	★	★		★				★				
Hawaii	★	★		★	★	★	★	★	★	★	★			★				
Idaho	★		★	★	★		★	★	★	★	★			★				
Illinois	★	★	★	★	★	★	★	★	★	★	★			★				
Indiana	★		★	★	★	★		★	★		★			★				
Iowa	★			★	★	★	★	★	★	★	★			★				
Kansas	★	★	★	★	★	★	★	★		★	★			★				(e)
Kentucky	★	★	★	★	★	★	★	★	★	★	★	★		★			★	
Louisiana	★		★	★	★		★	★	★	★	★			★				
Maine	★			★	★	★		★	★		★			★			★	
Maryland	★	★	★	★	★	★	★	★	★	★	★		★	★	★	★	★	
Massachusetts	★		★	★	★	★		★		★				★		★	★	(f)
Michigan	★		★	★	★			★ (h)	★	★	★			★		★	★	(g)
Minnesota		★		★	★	★	★	★	★	★	★			★			★	
Mississippi	★			★	★		★	★	★		★			★				
Missouri	★		★	★	★	★	★	★	★		★	★	★	★			★	
Montana	★	★	★	★	★	★	★	★	★	★	★			★			★	
Nebraska	★		★	★	★	★		★	★	★	★		★	★			★	
Nevada	★			★	★		★	★	★	★	★	★		★				
New Hampshire	★		★	★	★	★	★	★	★	★	★		★	★			★	
New Jersey	★			★	★			★		★	(i)			★				
New Mexico	★		★	★	★	★	★	★	★	★	★			★			★	
New York	★		★	★	★	★	★	★	★	★	★			★				
North Carolina	★			★	★			★	★	★	★		★	★		★	★	
North Dakota	★	★	★	★	★	★	★	★	★	★	★			★				
Ohio	★		★	★	★		★	★	★	★	★			★				

See footnotes at end of table.

ALLOWABLE INVESTMENTS — Continued

State or other jurisdiction	CDs within state	CDs nationally	State and local government obligations	U.S. Treasury obligations	U.S. agency obligations	Other time deposits	Bankers' acceptances	Commercial paper	Corporate notes/bonds	Mortgage backed securities	Mutual/Money Market funds	Derivatives	Real estate	Repurchase agreements	Venture capital/Private equity	Corporate stocks (foreign)	Corporate stocks (domestic)	Other
Oklahoma	★	★	★	★	★	...	★	★	...	...	★	...	...	★	...	...	...	...
Oregon	★	...	★	★	★	★	★	★	★	★	...	★	...	★	...	...	...	(j)
Pennsylvania	★	★	★	★	★	★	★	★	★	★	★	...	...	★	...	...	★	...
Rhode Island	★	★	...	★	★	★	...	★	★	★	★	...	★	★	...	★	★	...
South Carolina	★	...	★	★	★	...	...	★	★	...	...	...	...	★	...	...	...	...
South Dakota	★	★	...	★	★	★	★	★	★	★	★	...	★	★	...	★	★	...
Tennessee	★	...	...	★	★	...	★	★	★	★	★	★	★	★	(k)	★	★	...
Texas	...	★	★	★	★	★	★	★	★	★	★	...	...	★	...	★	(l)	...
Utah	★	...	...	★	★	★	★	...	...	...	★	...	★	★	...	...	...	...
Vermont	★	★	★	★	★	...	★	...	...	...	★	...	...	★	...	...	...	(m)
Virginia	★	★	★	★	★	★	★	★	★	★	★	...	...	★	...	...	...	...
Washington	★	...	★	★	★	...	★	★	★	...	...	★	...	★	...	...	...	...
West Virginia	★	★	★	★	★	★	★	★	★	★	★	★	★	★	...	★	★	(n)
Wisconsin	★	★	★	★	★	★	...	...	...	★	...	...	...	★	★	★	★	...
Wyoming	★	★	★	★	...	★	★	★	★	...	★	...	★	★	★	★	★	...
District of Columbia	★	★	★	★	★	★	★	★	★	★	★	...	★	★	...	...	★	...

Source: The National Association of State Treasurers, January 2006.

Key:
★ — Yes
... — No

(a) Nothing is restricted by statute. Commission is subject to prudent investor rule.
(b) Small Business Administration guaranteed loans.
(c) Asset backed securities.
(d) Convertible Bonds.
(e) Collateralized Mortgage Obligations and Other Mortgages; Assets Banking.
(f) Massachusetts Municipal Depository Trust; Chapter 29 Section 38A.

(g) Emergency loans to municipalities within the state.
(h) Time deposits within state.
(i) Money market funds.
(j) Reverse repurchase agreements.
(k) Private Equity.
(l) Trust funds only.
(m) For certain non-pension trust funds identified by statute, equities and corporate bonds/notes are permitted investments.
(n) Economic Development Loans.

Table 7.9
CASH FLOW MANAGEMENT: FORECASTING AND DISTRIBUTION OF DEMAND DEPOSITS

State or other jurisdiction	Development of cash flow forecasting method	Forecasting		Distribution of demand deposits			
		Float analysis in collection and disbursement processes	Automated system for cash flow forecasting	Used as depositories		Number of	
				Banks	Savings and loans	Banks in state	Savings and loans in state
Alabama	...	...	...	171	0	175	...
Alaska	In-house	...	★	4	0	3	0
Arizona	In-house	★	...	7	0	61	4
Arkansas	...	...	...	...	...	...	...
California	In-house	★	★	7	0	268	33
Colorado	...	...	...	3	0	...	...
Connecticut	In-house	★	★	...	...	...	...
Delaware	In-house	★	...	4	0	36	14
Florida	In-house	...	★	5	0	254	29
Georgia	In-house	★	...	(a)	0	340+	0
Hawaii	...	...	...	...	...	...	...
Idaho	In-house	★	...	11	0	30	5
Illinois	...	...	...	9	0	5	0
Indiana	In-house	★	...	232	37	300	55
Iowa	In-house	★	...	80	0	...	...
Kansas	In-house	...	...	2	0	354	16
Kentucky	In-house	★	★	(b)	(c)	...	...
Louisiana	In-house	★	...	15	0	120	9
Maine	...	...	...	14	0	...	...
Maryland	In-house	★	...	12	...	62	...
Massachusetts	In-house	★	...	19	0	270	...
Michigan	In-house	★	...	61	0	139	5
Minnesota	In-house	★	...	200	0	463	22
Mississippi	In-house	...	...	...	...	...	...
Missouri	In-house	...	...	80	2	300	6
Montana	In-house	★	...	62	...	267	...
Nebraska	In-house	★	...	...	...	...	...
Nevada	In-house	★	...	3	0	41	1
New Hampshire	In-house	★	...	5	...	42	...
New Jersey	In-house	★	...	45	4	110	74
New Mexico	In-house	★	...	44	6	48	9
New York	In-house	★	...	100+	N.A.	...	...
North Carolina	In-house	★	★	87	9	93	16
North Dakota	In-house	★	...	(d)	0	1	0
Ohio	In-house	...	...	137	...	...	...
Oklahoma	In-house	★	★	190	2	325	20
Oregon	In-house	...	...	20	0	55	4
Pennsylvania	Outsourced	★	★	96	15	96	15
Rhode Island	In-house	...	★	5	0	17	...
South Carolina	In-house	★	...	30	...	...	...
South Dakota	...	...	...	...	...	...	...
Tennessee	In-house	★	★	50	...	...	...
Texas	In-house	★	...	363	8	661	20
Utah	In-house	★	...	13	...	38	4
Vermont	In-house	★	...	13	0	24	1
Virginia	In-house	★	★	60	0	150	8
Washington	In-house	★	★	46	2	86	16
West Virginia	In-house	★	...	51	0	68	6
Wisconsin	...	...	...	...	...	...	...
Wyoming	In-house	★	...	1	...	47	3
District of Columbia	In-house	★	★	10	4	21	6

Source: The National Association of State Treasurers, January 2006.
Key:
★ — Yes
... — No
N.A. — Not applicable

(a) 7 primary plus 100s of others.
(b) 1 Primary Depository.
(c) 0 – 100 + Interest + Local Receipt Accounts.
(d) 1 State-owned bank.

Table 7.10
UTILIZATION OF CASH MANAGEMENT

State or other jurisdiction	Collection services	Lock boxes	Wire transfers	Federal reserve wire transfer	Bank wire transfer	Depository transfer checks	Zero balance accounts	Bank drafts	Controlled disbursement programs	Information systems	Account reconciliation services	Data transfer services	Business services	Automated clearinghouse
Alabama	N	Y	Y	Y	Y	Y	Y	Y	Y	Y	Y	Y	N	Y
Alaska	Y	Y	Y	N	Y	Y	Y	Y	Y	Y	N	Y	N	Y
Arizona	N	N	Y	Y	Y	Y	Y	Y	N	Y	Y	Y	N	Y
Arkansas	N	Y	Y	N	Y	N	Y	N	N	Y	Y	Y	Y	Y
California	Y	Y	Y	Y	Y	Y	Y	N	N	Y	Y	Y	Y	Y
Colorado	N	Y	Y	Y	Y	Y	Y	Y	Y	Y	Y	Y	N	Y
Connecticut	Y	Y	Y	Y	Y	N	Y	Y	Y	Y	Y	Y	N	Y
Delaware	Y	Y	Y	Y	Y	N	N	N	Y	Y	Y	Y	N	Y
Florida	N	Y	Y	Y	Y	N	N	N	Y	N	Y	N	N	Y
Georgia	N	Y	Y	N	Y	N	N	N	Y	N	Y	N	N	Y
Hawaii	:	:	:	:	:	:	:	:	:	:	:	:	:	:
Idaho	N	N	Y	Y	Y	N	Y	N	N	N	N	N	N	Y
Illinois	N	Y	Y	Y	Y	Y	Y	N	N	Y	Y	Y	N	Y
Indiana	Y	Y	Y	Y	Y	Y	Y	N	N	N	N	N	N	Y
Iowa	Y	Y	Y	Y	Y	N	Y	Y	Y	Y	Y	N	N	Y
Kansas	N	Y	Y	Y	Y	N	Y	N	N	Y	Y	Y	N	Y
Kentucky	Y	N	Y	Y	Y	N	Y	N	Y	Y	Y	Y	N	Y
Louisiana	Y	Y	Y	Y	N	Y	Y	N	Y	Y	Y	Y	N	Y
Maine	Y	N	Y	N	N	Y	Y	N	Y	N	Y	Y	Y	Y
Maryland	N	Y	Y	Y	Y	N	Y	Y	Y	Y	Y	Y	N	Y
Massachusetts	Y	Y	Y	Y	Y	N	Y	N	Y	Y	Y	Y	N	Y
Michigan	N	Y	Y	Y	Y	N	Y	N	N	N	Y	N	N	Y
Minnesota	N	Y	Y	Y	Y	N	Y	N	N	Y	Y	Y	N	Y
Mississippi	N	N	Y	Y	N	Y	N	N	N	Y	N	N	N	Y
Missouri	Y	Y	Y	Y	Y	N	Y	Y	Y	Y	Y	Y	N	Y
Montana	N	N	Y	N	N	N	N	N	N	Y	N	N	N	Y
Nebraska	Y	Y	Y	Y	Y	N	Y	N	N	Y	Y	Y	N	Y
Nevada	Y	N	Y	Y	Y	N	Y	N	Y	Y	Y	Y	N	Y
New Hampshire	N	N	Y	N	N	N	Y	N	Y	Y	N	N	N	Y
New Jersey	Y	Y	Y	Y	Y	N	Y	N	Y	Y	Y	Y	Y	Y
New Mexico	Y	Y	Y	Y	Y	Y	Y	Y	Y	Y	N	N	N	Y
New York	N	Y	Y	Y	N	N	Y	N	Y	Y	Y	Y	N	Y
North Carolina	Y	Y	Y	Y	Y	N	Y	Y	Y	Y	Y	Y	N	Y
North Dakota	N	N	Y	Y	Y	N	Y	N	N	N	Y	N	N	Y
Ohio	Y	Y	Y	Y	Y	N	Y	N	N	Y	Y	Y	N	Y

See footnotes at end of table.

UTILIZATION OF CASH MANAGEMENT — Continued

State or other jurisdiction	Collection services	Lock boxes	Wire transfers	Federal reserve wire transfer	Bank wire transfer	Depository transfer checks	Zero balance accounts	Bank drafts	Controlled disbursement programs	Information systems	Account reconciliation services	Data transfer services	Business services	Automated clearinghouse
Oklahoma	N	Y	Y	N	Y	Y	Y	N	N	N	N	N	N	Y
Oregon	Y	Y	Y	Y	Y	N	Y	Y	Y	Y	Y	Y	N	Y
Pennsylvania	Y	Y	Y	Y	Y	N	Y	N	Y	Y	Y	Y	N	Y
Rhode Island	Y	Y	Y	Y	Y	Y	Y	N	Y	Y	Y	N	N	Y
South Carolina	N	Y	Y	Y	Y	Y	Y	Y	N	Y	Y	Y	N	Y
South Dakota	Y	Y	Y	Y	Y	Y	Y	Y	Y	N	Y	N	N	Y
Tennessee	Y	Y	Y	Y	N	N	Y	Y	Y	Y	Y	Y	N	Y
Texas	N	Y	Y	Y	Y	N	Y	Y	Y	Y	Y	N	N	Y
Utah	N	Y	N	Y	N	N	Y	N	N	Y	Y	N	N	Y
Vermont	Y	Y	Y	Y	Y	Y	Y	N	Y	Y	Y	Y	Y	Y
Virginia	N	Y	Y	Y	Y	N	Y	N	Y	Y	Y	Y	N	Y
Washington	N	Y	Y	Y	Y	N	Y	N	N	Y	N	Y	N	Y
West Virginia	N	Y	N	N	Y	N	N	N	Y	Y	Y	N	N	Y
Wisconsin	N	Y	Y	N	N	N	Y	N	Y	Y	Y	Y	N	Y
Wyoming	N	N	Y	Y	Y	Y	Y	N	Y	Y	Y	Y	N	Y
District of Columbia	Y	Y	Y	Y	Y	N	Y	N	Y	Y	Y	Y	N	Y

Source: The National Association of State Treasurers, March 2006.

Key:
Y — Utilized
N — Not utilized
. . . — No response

Table 7.11
BOND AUTHORIZATION

State or other jurisdiction	Central agency overseeing debt issuance	Party which holds issuance authority					Authority to issue foreign currency denominated debt
		General obligation bonds	Revenue bonds	Taxable bonds	Taxable debt	Short-term debt	
Alabama	No Central Agency	R, L, C	L, C	...	...	...	...
Alaska		...	...	...	...	...	...
Arizona	State does not issue debt	...	...	...	...	...	...
Arkansas		...	...	...	...	...	...
California	California State Treasurer's Office	R (a)	B	...	...	(RANS)	No
Colorado	No Central Agency						No
Connecticut	Debt Management Division, Office of the Treasurer	L, C, T	L, G, C, T	L, C, T	L, C, T	L, G, C, T	No
Delaware	Department of Finance	L	L			L	No
Florida	Division of Bond Finance	L, B	L, B	L, B	L, B	L, B	Yes
Georgia	Georgia State Financing and Investment Commission	L, C	L, C	L, C	L, C	L, C	No
Hawaii	No Central Agency	...	...	...	...	B	...
Idaho	Public Finance Officer	L, G	L, G, B	...	...	R, L, G	No
Illinois							No
Indiana	(b)	(b)	(b)	(b)	(b)	(b)	...
Iowa	Treasury	R, L, G	L, G, B	L, G, B	...	G, TR	No
Kansas	Kansas Development Finance Authority	R	R, B	R	R, B	R, B	Yes
Kentucky	Office of Financial Management	L, C	R		R	R	Yes (c)
Louisiana	State Bond Commission	R, L, G, TR	L, C	L, C	R, L, G, TR	L, C	No
Maine	Office of the State Treasurer		L, G			TR, Other	No
Maryland	General Obligation Debt – State Treasurer	L, B	L	L, B		B, TR	No
Massachusetts	Financial Advisory Board	L, G	L, G	L, G	L, G	L, G	No
Michigan	State Administrative Board	R, L, B, TR	L, B, TR	L, B, TR	L, B, TR	L, B, TR	No
Minnesota	Department of Finance (d)	L	L	L	L	L	No
Mississippi	State Treasury/OFA – Bond Advisory Division	L, C	L, C	L, C	L, C	L, C	No
Missouri	Office of Administration	R, L, B	L, B				No
Montana	No Central Agency	L, B, TR	L, B, TR	L, B, TR	L, B, TR	B, TR	No
Nebraska	State does not issue debt						
Nevada	No Central Agency	L, B	L, B	L, B	L, B	L, B	No
New Hampshire	Treasury	L				L, B	No
New Jersey	Treasury, Office of Public Finance	R, L	L, G, B	R		L, G, B	No
New Mexico	State Board of Finance	R, L, G	L, G (f)	L, G (f)	L, G (f)	L, B, T	No
New York	(e)	Comptroller issues	L, G (f)	L, G (f)	L, G (f)	L, G (f)	No
North Carolina	State and Local Government Finance Division, Dept. of State Treasurer	R, L	L	L	L	L	No
North Dakota	No Central Agency	...	...	...	...	...	...
Ohio	Office of Budget and Management	...	...	...	...	...	No

See footnotes at end of table.

BOND AUTHORIZATION — Continued

State or other jurisdiction	Central agency overseeing debt issuance	Party which holds issuance authority					Authority to issue foreign currency denominated debt
		General obligation bonds	Revenue bonds	Taxable bonds	Taxable debt	Short-term debt	
Oklahoma..............	State Bond Advisor's Office	R	L, B, C	B, C	B, C	B, C	No
Oregon..................	Oregon State Treasury Debt Management Division	L, G, TR	L, G, TR	...	L, G, TR	L, G, TR	No
Pennsylvania........	Office of Budget	R, L	L, B, C	Not authorized	Not authorized	L	No
Rhode Island........	Budget Office & Treasury	R, G	...	...	...	L	No
South Carolina	...	...	...	...	...	...	...
South Dakota........	State does not issue debt	L, C	...	...	...	...	...
Tennessee	Comptroller's Office – Division of Bond Finance	R, L, B, C	...	C	C	C	No
Texas	Texas Bond Review Board	L	L, B, C	L, B, C	L, B, C	L, B, C	No
Utah	Treasurer	L	L	L	L	TR	Yes (g)
Vermont................	Office of the State Treasurer	L	L	L	...	TR	No
Virginia................	Department of the Treasury	R, L, G	L, G, B, TR	...	...	...	No
Washington...........	Division of Debt Management	R, L	R, L	R, L	R, L	R, L	No
West Virginia........	No Central Agency	R, L, G, TR, AG	L, B, C	L, G, B, C	L, G, B, C	L, G	No
Wisconsin..............	State does not issue debt	...	...	...	...	...	...
Wyoming...............	No Central Agency	Not authorized	...	L, C	Not authorized	L, G, C, T	No
District of Columbia.........	Office of the Chief Financial Officer	L, TR, A, (h)	L (h)	N.A.	N.A.	L, TR (h)	No

Source: The National Association of State Treasurers, January 2006.

Key:
AG — Auditor General
B — Board
C — Commission
G — Governor
L — Legislation
R — Referendum
TR — Treasurer
... — Does not perform function

(a) Committee.
(b) Indiana by statute cannot issue debt, so quasi-agencies are set up to do so.
(c) Requires legislative approval. Previously issued debt in Yen.
(d) Only for general obligation debt or for reporting purposes.
(e) No, the Office of the State Comptroller approves terms and conditions for certain negotiated bond deals of public authorities and local governments and issues State General Obligation bonds and LGAC bonds. Various State Public Authorities issue State-supported debt.
(f) Taxable debt may be issued for general obligation as well as revenue bonds. If general obligation, referendum is needed.
(g) Requires entering into a foreign exchange agreement with a AA or higher rated institution when bonds are issued to hedge the currency risk.
(h) Mayor.

Table 7.12
AGENCIES ADMINISTERING MAJOR STATE TAXES

State or other jurisdiction	Income	Sales	Gasoline	Motor vehicle
Alabama	Dept. of Revenue	Dept. of Revenue	Dept. of Revenue	Dept. of Revenue
Alaska	Dept. of Revenue	. . .	Dept. of Revenue	Dept. of Public Safety
Arizona	Dept. of Revenue	Dept. of Revenue	Dept. of Transportation	Dept. of Transportation
Arkansas	Dept. of Fin. & Admin.	Dept. of Fin. & Admin.	Dept. of Fin. & Admin.	Dept. of Fin. & Admin.
California	Franchise Tax Bd.	Bd. of Equalization	Bd. of Equalization	Dept. of Motor Vehicles
Colorado	Dept. of Revenue	Dept. of Revenue	Dept. of Revenue	Dept. of Revenue
Connecticut	Dept. of Revenue Serv.	Dept. of Revenue Serv.	Dept. of Revenue Serv.	Dept. of Motor Vehicles
Delaware	Div. of Revenue	. . .	Dept. of Transportation	Dept. of Public Safety
Florida	Dept. of Revenue	Dept. of Revenue	Dept. of Revenue	Dept. of Motor Vehicles
Georgia	Dept. of Revenue	Dept. of Revenue	Dept. of Revenue	Dept. of Revenue
Hawaii	Dept. of Taxation	Dept. of Taxation	Dept. of Taxation	County Treasurer
Idaho	Tax Comm.	Tax Comm.	Tax Comm.	Dept. of Transportation
Illinois	Dept. of Revenue	Dept. of Revenue	Dept. of Revenue	Secretary of State
Indiana	Dept. of Revenue	Dept. of Revenue	Dept. of Revenue	Bur. of Motor Vehicles
Iowa	Dept. of Revenue	Dept. of Revenue	Dept. of Revenue	Local
Kansas	Dept. of Revenue	Dept. of Revenue	Dept. of Revenue	Local (a)
Kentucky	Dept. of Revenue	Dept. of Revenue	Dept. of Revenue	Transportation Cabinet
Louisiana	Dept. of Revenue	Dept. of Revenue	Dept. of Revenue	Dept. of Public Safety
Maine	Revenue Services	Revenue Services	Revenue Services	Secretary of State
Maryland	Comptroller	Comptroller	Comptroller	Dept. of Transportation
Massachusetts	Dept. of Revenue	Dept. of Revenue	Dept. of Revenue	Reg. of Motor Vehicles
Michigan	Dept. of Treasury	Dept. of Treasury	Dept. of Treasury	Secretary of State
Minnesota	Dept. of Revenue	Dept. of Revenue	Dept. of Revenue	Dept. of Public Safety
Mississippi	Tax Comm.	Tax Comm.	Tax Comm.	Tax Comm.
Missouri	Dept. of Revenue	Dept. of Revenue	Dept. of Revenue	Dept. of Revenue
Montana	Dept. of Revenue	. . .	Dept. of Transportation	Local
Nebraska	Dept. of Revenue	Dept. of Revenue	Dept. of Revenue	Dept. of Motor Vehicles
Nevada	. . .	Dept. of Taxation	Dept. of Motor Vehicles	Dept. of Motor Vehicles
New Hampshire	Dept. of Revenue Admin.	. . .	Dept. of Safety	Dept. of Safety
New Jersey	Dept. of Treasury	Dept. of Treasury	Dept. of Treasury	Dept. of Law & Public Safety
New Mexico	Tax. & Revenue Dept.	Tax. & Revenue Dept.	Tax. & Revenue Dept.	Tax. & Revenue Dept.
New York	Dept. of Tax. & Finance	Dept. of Tax. & Finance	Dept. of Tax. & Finance	Dept. of Motor Vehicles
North Carolina	Dept. of Revenue	Dept. of Revenue	Dept. of Revenue	Dept. of Transportation
North Dakota	Tax Commr.	Tax Commr.	Tax Commr.	Dept. of Transportation
Ohio	Dept. of Taxation	Dept. of Taxation	Dept. of Taxation	Bur. of Motor Vehicles
Oklahoma	Tax Comm.	Tax Comm.	Tax Comm.	Tax Comm.
Oregon	Dept. of Revenue	. . .	Dept. of Transportation	Dept. of Transportation
Pennsylvania	Dept. of Revenue	Dept. of Revenue	Dept. of Revenue	Dept. of Transportation
Rhode Island	Dept. of Administration	Dept. of Administration	Dept. of Administration	Dept. of Administration
South Carolina	Dept. of Revenue	Dept. of Revenue	Dept. of Revenue	Dept. of Public Safety
South Dakota	. . .	Dept. of Revenue & Reg.	Dept. of Revenue & Reg.	Dept. of Revenue & Reg.
Tennessee	Dept. of Revenue	Dept. of Revenue	Dept. of Revenue	Dept. of Safety
Texas	. . .	Comptroller	Comptroller	Dept. of Transportation
Utah	Tax Comm.	Tax Comm.	Tax Comm.	Tax Comm.
Vermont	Dept. of Taxes	Dept. of Taxes	Commr. of Motor Vehicles	Commr. of Motor Vehicles
Virginia	Dept. of Taxation	Dept. of Taxation	Dept. of Motor Vehicles	Dept. of Motor Vehicles
Washington	. . .	Dept. of Revenue	Dept. of Licensing	Dept. of Licensing
West Virginia	Dept. of Revenue	Dept. of Revenue	Dept. of Revenue	Div. of Motor Vehicles
Wisconsin	Dept. of Revenue	Dept. of Revenue	Dept. of Revenue	Dept. of Transportation
Wyoming	. . .	Dept. of Revenue	Dept. of Revenue	Dept. of Transportation
Dist. of Columbia	Office of Tax & Rev.	Office of Tax & Rev.	Office of Tax & Rev.	Office of Tax & Rev.

See footnotes at end of table.

AGENCIES ADMINISTERING MAJOR STATE TAXES — Continued

State or other jurisdiction	Tobacco	Death	Alcoholic beverage	Number of agencies administering taxes
Alabama	Dept. of Revenue	Dept. of Revenue	Alcoh. Bev. Control Bd.	2
Alaska	Dept. of Revenue	Dept. of Revenue	Dept. of Revenue	2
Arizona	Dept. of Revenue	Dept. of Revenue	Dept. of Revenue	2
Arkansas	Dept. of Fin. & Admin.	Dept. of Fin. & Admin.	Dept. of Fin. & Admin.	1
California	Bd. of Equalization	Controller	Bd. of Equalization	4
Colorado	Dept. of Revenue	Dept. of Revenue	Dept. of Revenue	1
Connecticut	Dept. of Revenue Serv.	Dept. of Revenue Serv.	Dept. of Revenue Serv.	2
Delaware	Div. of Revenue	Div. of Revenue	Dept. of Public Safety	3
Florida	Dept. of Business Reg.	Dept. of Revenue	Dept. of Business Reg.	3
Georgia	Dept. of Revenue	Dept. of Revenue	Dept. of Revenue	1
Hawaii	Dept. of Taxation	Dept. of Taxation	Dept. of Taxation	2
Idaho	Tax Comm.	Tax Comm.	Tax Comm.	2
Illinois	Dept. of Revenue	Attorney General	Dept. of Revenue	3
Indiana	Dept. of Revenue	Dept. of Revenue	Dept. of Revenue	2
Iowa	Dept. of Revenue	Dept. of Revenue	Dept. of Revenue	2
Kansas	Dept. of Revenue	Dept. of Revenue	Dept. of Revenue	2
Kentucky	Dept. of Revenue	Dept. of Revenue	Dept. of Revenue	2
Louisiana	Dept. of Revenue	Dept. of Revenue	Dept. of Revenue	2
Maine	Revenue Services	Revenue Services	Bur. of Liquor Enf.	3
Maryland	Comptroller	Local	Comptroller	3
Massachusetts	Dept. of Revenue	Dept. of Revenue	Dept. of Revenue	2
Michigan	Dept. of Treasury	Dept. of Treasury	Liquor Control Comm.	3
Minnesota	Dept. of Revenue	Dept. of Revenue	Dept. of Revenue	2
Mississippi	Tax Comm.	Tax Comm.	Tax Comm.	1
Missouri	Dept. of Revenue	Dept. of Revenue	Dept. of Revenue	1
Montana	Dept. of Revenue	Dept. of Revenue	Dept. of Revenue	3
Nebraska	Dept. of Revenue	Dept. of Revenue	Liquor Control Comm.	3
Nevada	Dept. of Taxation	Dept. of Taxation	Dept. of Taxation	2
New Hampshire	Dept. of Revenue Admin.	Dept. of Revenue Admin.	Liquor Comm.	3
New Jersey	Dept. of Treasury	Dept. of Treasury	Dept. of Treasury	2
New Mexico	Tax. & Revenue Dept.	Tax. & Revenue Dept.	Tax. & Revenue Dept.	1
New York	Dept. of Tax. & Finance	Dept. of Tax. & Finance	Dept. of Tax. & Finance	2
North Carolina	Dept. of Revenue	Dept. of Revenue	Dept. of Revenue	2
North Dakota	Tax Commr.	Tax Commr.	Treasurer	3
Ohio	Dept. of Taxation	Dept. of Taxation	State Treasurer	3
Oklahoma	Tax Comm.	Tax Comm.	Tax Comm.	1
Oregon	Dept. of Revenue	Dept. of Revenue	Liquor Control Comm.	3
Pennsylvania	Dept. of Revenue	Dept. of Revenue	Dept. of Revenue	2
Rhode Island	Dept. of Administration	Dept. of Administration	Dept. of Administration	1
South Carolina	Dept. of Revenue	Dept. of Revenue	Dept. of Revenue	2
South Dakota	Dept. of Revenue & Reg.	Dept. of Revenue & Reg.	Dept. of Revenue & Reg.	1
Tennessee	Dept. of Revenue	Dept. of Revenue	Dept. of Revenue	2
Texas	Comptroller	Comptroller	Comptroller	2
Utah	Tax Comm.	Tax Comm.	Tax Comm.	1
Vermont	Dept. of Taxes	Dept. of Taxes	Dept. of Taxes	2
Virginia	Dept. of Taxation	Dept. of Taxation	Alcoh. Bev. Control	3
Washington	Dept. of Revenue	Dept. of Revenue	Liquor Control Bd.	3
West Virginia	Dept. of Revenue	Dept. of Revenue	Dept. of Revenue	2
Wisconsin	Dept. of Revenue	Dept. of Revenue	Dept. of Revenue	2
Wyoming	Dept. of Revenue	Dept. of Revenue	Dept. of Revenue	2
Dist. of Columbia	Office of Tax & Rev.	Office of Tax & Rev.	Office of Tax & Rev.	1

Source: The Federation of Tax Administrators, January 2006.
Key:
. . . — Not applicable
(a) Joint state and local administration. State-level functions are performed by the Department of Revenue in Kansas.

Table 7.13
STATE TAX AMNESTY PROGRAMS
1982—2006

State or other jurisdiction	Amnesty period	Legislative authorization	Major taxes covered	Accounts receivable included	Collections ($millions) (a)	Installment arrangements permitted (b)
Alabama	1/20/84–4/1/84	No (c)	All	No	3.2	No
Arizona	11/22/82–1/20/83	No (c)	All	No	6.0	Yes
	1/1/02–2/28/02	Yes	Individual income	No	N.A.	No
	9/1/03–10/31/03	Yes	All (t)	N.A.	73.0	Yes
Arkansas.......................	9/1/87–11/30/87	Yes	All	No	1.7	Yes
California	12/10/84–3/15/85	Yes	Individual income	Yes	154.0	Yes
		Yes	Sales	No	43.0	Yes
	2/1/05–3/31/05	Yes	Income, Franchise, Sales	N.A.	N.A.	Yes
Colorado	9/16/85–11/15/85	Yes	All	No	6.4	Yes
	6/1/03–6/30/03	N.A.	All	N.A.	18.4	Yes
Connecticut	9/1/90–11/30/90	Yes	All	Yes	54.0	Yes
	9/1/95–11/30/95	Yes	All	Yes	46.2	Yes
	9/1/02–12/2/02	N.A.	All	N.A.	109	N.A.
Florida	1/1/87–6/30/87	Yes	Intangibles	No	13.0	No
	1/1/88–6/30/88	Yes (d)	All	No	8.4 (d)	No
	7/1/03–10/31/03	Yes	All	N.A.	80	N.A.
Georgia	10/1/92–12/5/92	Yes	All	Yes	51.3	No
Idaho............................	5/20/83–8/30/83	No (c)	Individual income	No	0.3	No
Illinois..........................	10/1/84–11/30/84	Yes	All (u)	Yes	160.5	No
	10/1/03–11/17/03	Yes	All	N.A.	532	N.A.
Indiana.........................	9/15/05–11/15/05	N.A.	All	N.A.	255	Yes
Iowa	9/2/86–10/31/86	Yes	All	Yes	35.1	N.A.
Kansas	7/1/84–9/30/84	Yes	All	No	0.6	No
	10/1/03–11/30/03	Yes	All	Yes	53.7	N.A.
Kentucky	9/15/88–9/30/88	Yes (c)	All	No	100	No
	8/1/02–9/30/02	Yes (c)	All	No	100	No
Louisiana	10/1/85–12/31/85	Yes	All	No	1.2	Yes (f)
	10/1/87–12/15/87	Yes	All	No	0.3	Yes (f)
	10/1/98–12/31/98	Yes	All	No (q)	1.3	No
	9/1/01–10/30/01	Yes	All	Yes	173.1	No
Maine	11/1/90–12/31/90	Yes	All	Yes	29.0	Yes
	9/1/03–11/30/03	Yes	All	N.A.	37.6	N.A.
Maryland	9/1/87–11/2/87	Yes	All	Yes	34.6 (g)	No
	9/1/01–10/31/01	Yes	All	Yes	39.2	No
Massachusetts...............	10/17/83–1/17/84	Yes	All	Yes	86.5	Yes (h)
	10/1/02–11/30/02	Yes	All	Yes	96.1	Yes
	1/1/03–2/28/03	Yes	All	Yes	N.A.	N.A.
Michigan.......................	5/12/86–6/30/86	Yes	All	Yes	109.8	No
	5/15/02–6/30/02	Yes	All	Yes	N.A.	N.A.
Minnesota	8/1/84–10/31/84	Yes	All	Yes	12.1	No
Mississippi	9/1/86–11/30/86	Yes	All	No	1.0	No
	9/1/04–12/31/04	Yes	All	No	7.9	No
Missouri	9/1/83–10/31/83	No (c)	All	No	0.9	No
	8/1/02–10/31/02	Yes	All	Yes	76.4	N.A.
	8/1/03–10/31/03	Yes	All	Yes	20	N.A.
Nebraska.......................	8/1/04–10/31/04	Yes	All	No	7.5	No
Nevada	2/1/02–6/30/02	N.A.	All	N.A.	7.3	N.A.
New Hampshire............	12/1/97–2/17/98	Yes	All	Yes	13.5	No
	12/1/01–2/15/02	Yes	All	Yes	13.5	N.A.
New Jersey....................	9/10/87–12/8/87	Yes	All	Yes	186.5	Yes
	3/15/96–6/1/96	Yes	All	Yes	359.0	No
	4/15/02–6/10/02	Yes	All	Yes	276.9	N.A.
New Mexico	8/15/85–11/13/85	Yes	All (i)	No	13.6	Yes
	8/16/99–11/12/99	Yes	All	Yes	45	Yes

See footnotes at end of table.

STATE TAX AMNESTY PROGRAMS — Continued
1982 – 2006

State or other jurisdiction	Amnesty period	Legislative authorization	Major taxes covered	Accounts receivable included	Collections ($millions) (a)	Installment arrangements permitted (b)
New York	11/1/85 – 1/31/86	Yes	All (j)	Yes	401.3	Yes
	11/1/96 – 1/31/97	Yes	All	Yes	253.4	Yes (o)
	11/18/02 – 1/31/03	Yes	All	Yes	582.7	Yes (s)
North Carolina	9/1/89 – 12/1/89	Yes	All (k)	Yes	37.6	No
North Dakota	9/1/83 – 11/30/83	No (c)	All	No	0.2	Yes
	10/1/03 – 1/31/04	Yes	N.A.	N.A.	6.9	N.A.
Ohio	10/15/01 – 1/15/02	Yes	All	No	48.5	No
	1/1/06 – 2/15/06	Yes	All	No	N.A.	No
Oklahoma	7/1/84 – 12/31/84	Yes	Income, Sales	Yes	13.9	No (l)
	8/15/02 – 11/15/02	N.A.	All (r)	Yes	N.A.	N.A.
Pennsylvania	10/13/95 – 1/10/96	Yes	All	Yes	N.A.	No
Rhode Island	10/15/86 – 1/12/87	Yes	All	No	0.7	Yes
	4/15/96 – 6/28/96	Yes	All	Yes	7.9	Yes
South Carolina	9/1/85 – 11/30/85	Yes	All	Yes	7.1	Yes
	10/15/02 – 12/2/02	Yes	All	Yes	66.2	N.A.
South Dakota	4/1/99 – 5/15/99	Yes	All	Yes	0.5	N.A.
Texas	2/1/84 – 2/29/84	No (c)	All (m)	No	0.5	No
	3/11/04 – 3/31/04	No (c)	All (m)	No	N.A.	No
Vermont	5/15/90 – 6/25/90	Yes	All	Yes	1.0 (e)	No
Virginia	2/1/90 – 3/31/90	Yes	All	Yes	32.2	No
	9/2/03 – 11/3/03	Yes	All	Yes	98.3	N.A.
West Virginia	10/1/86 – 12/31/86	Yes	All	Yes	15.9	Yes
	9/1/04 – 10/31/04	Yes	All	N.A.	10.4	Yes
Wisconsin	9/15/85 – 11/22/85	Yes	All	Yes (n)	27.3	Yes
	6/15/98 – 8/14/98	Yes	All	Yes	30.9	N.A.
Dist. of Columbia	7/1/87 – 9/30/87	Yes	All	Yes	24.3	Yes
	7/10/95 – 8/31/95	Yes	All (p)	Yes	19.5	Yes (p)

Source: The Federation of Tax Administrators, January 2006.
Key:
N.A. — Not available.
(a) Where applicable, figure indicates local portions of certain taxes collected under the state tax amnesty program.
(b) "No" indicates requirement of full payment by the expiration of the amnesty period. "Yes" indicates allowance of full payment after the expiration of the amnesty period.
(c) Authority for amnesty derived from pre-existing statutory powers permitting the waiver of tax penalties.
(d) Does not include intangibles tax and drug taxes. Gross collections totaled $22.1 million, with $13.7 million in penalties withdrawn.
(e) Preliminary figure.
(f) Amnesty taxpayers were billed for the interest owed, with payment due within 30 days of notification.
(g) Figure includes $1.1 million for the separate program conducted by the Department of Natural Resources for the boat excise tax.
(h) The amnesty statute was construed to extend the amnesty to those who applied to the department before the end of the amnesty period, and permitted them to file overdue returns and pay back taxes and interest at a later date.
(i) The severance taxes, including the six oil and gas severance taxes, the resources excise tax, the corporate franchise tax, and the special fuels tax were not subject to amnesty.

(j) Availability of amnesty for the corporation tax, the oil company taxes, the transportation and transmissions companies tax, the gross receipts oil tax and the unincorporated business tax restricted to entities with 500 or fewer employees in the United States on the date of application. In addition, a taxpayer principally engaged in aviation, or a utility subject to the supervision of the State Department of Public Service was also ineligible.
(k) Local taxes and real property taxes were not included.
(l) Full payment of tax liability required before the end of the amnesty period to avoid civil penalties.
(m) Texas does not impose a corporate or individual income tax. In practical effect, the amnesty was limited to the sales tax and other excises.
(n) Waiver terms varied depending upon the date the tax liability was assessed.
(o) Installment arrangements were permitted if applicant demonstrated that payment would present a severe financial hardship.
(p) Does not include real property taxes. All interest was waived on tax payments made before July 31, 1995. After this date, only 50 percent of the interest was waived.
(q) Exception for individuals who owed $500 or less.
(r) Except for property and motor fuel taxes.
(s) Multiple payments can be made so long as the required balance is paid in full no later than March 15, 2003.
(t) All taxes except property, estate and unclaimed property.
(u) Does not include the motor fuel use tax.

Table 7.14
STATE EXCISE TAX RATES
(As of January 1, 2006)

State or other jurisdiction	General sales and gross receipts tax (percent)	Cigarettes (cents per pack of 20)	Distilled spirits ($ per gallon)	Motor fuel excise tax rates (cents per gallon) (c)		
				Gasoline	Diesel	Gasohol
Alabama	4.0	42.5 (d)	(g)	18.0 (j)(c)	19.0 (j)(c)	18.0 (j)(c)
Alaska	. . .	160	12.80 (i)	8.0	8.0	. . .
Arizona	5.6	118	3.00	18.0 (l)	18.0 (l)	18.0 (l)
Arkansas	6	59 (e)	2.50 (i)	21.5	22.5	21.5
California	7.25 (b)(r)	87	3.30 (i)	18.0 (q)	18.0 (q)	18.0 (q)
Colorado	2.9	84	2.28	22.0	20.5	22.0
Connecticut	6.0	151	4.50 (i)	25.0	26.0	25.0
Delaware	. . .	55	5.46 (i)	23.0 (t)(n)	22.0 (t)(n)	23.0 (t)(n)
Florida	6.0	33.9	6.50 (i)	14.9 (k)(q)	27.7 (k)(q)	14.9 (k)(q)
Georgia	4.0	37	3.79 (i)	15.3 (q)	16.5 (q)	15.3 (q)
Hawaii	4.0	140	5.98	16.0 (j)(q)	16.0 (j)(q)	16.0 (j)(q)
Idaho	5.0	57	(g)	25.0 (p)	25.0 (p)	22.5 (p)
Illinois	6.25 (r)	98 (d)	4.50 (i)	20.1 (j)(l)(q)	22.6 (l)(q)	20.1 (l)(q)
Indiana	6.0	55.5	2.68 (i)	18.0 (l)(q)	16.0 (l)(q)	18.0 (l)(q)
Iowa	5.0	36	(g)	20.7	22.5	19.0
Kansas	5.3	79	2.50 (i)	24.0	26.0	24.0
Kentucky	6.0	30 (e)	1.92 (h)(i)	18.5 (l)(m)(q)	15.5 (l)(m)(q)	18.5 (l)(m)(q)
Louisiana	4.0	36	2.50 (i)	20.0	20.0	20.0
Maine	5.0	200	(g)	25.9 (n)	27.0 (n)	25.9 (n)
Maryland	5.0	100	1.50	23.5	24.25	23.5
Massachusetts	5.0	151	4.05 (h)(i)	21.0	21.0	21.0
Michigan	6.0	200	(g)	19.0 (q)	15.0 (q)	19.0 (q)
Minnesota	6.5	123 (u)	5.03 (i)	20.0	20.0	20.0
Mississippi	7.0	18	(g)	18.4 (q)	18.4 (q)	18.4 (q)
Missouri	4.225	17 (d)	2.00	17.55 (q)	17.55 (q)	17.55 (q)
Montana	. . .	170	(g)	27.0	27.75	27.0
Nebraska	5.5	64	3.75	27.0 (i)(n)	27.0 (i)(n)	27.0 (i)(n)
Nevada	6.5	80	3.60 (i)	24.805 (j)(q)	27.75 (j)(q)	24.805 (j)(q)
New Hampshire	. . .	80	(g)	19.625 (q)	19.625 (q)	19.625 (q)
New Jersey	6.0	240	4.40	14.5 (q)	17.5 (q)	14.5 (q)
New Mexico	5.0	91	6.06	18.9 (q)	22.9 (q)	18.9 (q)
New York	4.0	150 (d)	6.44 (i)	23.9 (q)	22.15 (q)	23.9 (q)
North Carolina	4.5	30 (s)	(g)(h)	30.15 (m)(q)	30.15 (m)(q)	30.15 (m)(q)
North Dakota	5.0	44	2.50 (i)	23.0	23.0	23.0
Ohio	5.5	125	(g)	28.0 (q)	28.0 (q)	28.0 (q)
Oklahoma	4.5	103	5.56 (i)	17.0 (q)	14.0 (q)	17.0 (q)
Oregon	. . .	118	(g)	24.0 (j)	24.0 (j)	24.0 (j)
Pennsylvania	6.0	135	(g)	31.2 (q)	38.1 (q)	31.2 (q)
Rhode Island	7.0	246	3.75	31.0 (q)	31.0 (q)	31.0 (q)
South Carolina	5.0	7	2.72 (i)	16.0	16.0	16.0
South Dakota	4.0	53	3.93 (i)	22.0 (j)	22.0 (j)	20.0 (j)
Tennessee	7.0	20 (d)(e)	4.40 (i)	21.4 (j)(q)	18.4 (j)(q)	21.4 (j)(q)
Texas	6.25	41	2.40 (i)	20.0	20.0	20.0
Utah	4.75	69.5	(g)	24.5	24.5	24.5
Vermont	6.0	119	(f)(g)	20.0 (q)	26.0 (q)	20.0 (q)
Virginia	5.0 (r)	30 (d)	(g)	17.5 (j)(o)	16.0 (j)(o)	17.5 (j)(o)
Washington	6.5	202.5	(g)(h)	31.0 (a)(q)	31.0 (a)(q)	31.0 (a)(q)
West Virginia	6.0	55	(g)	27.0 (q)	27.0 (q)	27.0 (q)
Wisconsin	5.0	77	3.25	32.9 (n)(q)	32.9 (n)(q)	32.9 (n)(q)
Wyoming	4.0 (b)	60	(g)	14.0 (q)	14.0 (q)	14.0 (q)
Dist. of Columbia	5.75	100	1.50 (i)	22.5	22.5	22.5

See footnotes at end of table.

STATE EXCISE TAX RATES — Continued
(As of January 1, 2006)

Source: Compiled by The Federation of Tax Administrators from various sources, January 2006.

Key:

... — Tax is not applicable.

(a) Tax rate scheduled to increase to 34 cents on July 1, 2006.

(b) Tax rate may be adjusted annually according to a formaula based on balances in the unappropriated general fund and the school foundation fund.

(c) Inspection fee.

(d) Counties and cities may impose an additional tax on a pack of cigarettes in Alabama, 1–6 cents; Illinois, 10–15 cents; Missouri, 4–7 cents; New York City, $1.50; Tennessee, 1 cent; and Virginia, 2–15 cents.

(e) Dealers pay an additional enforcement and administrative fee of 0.1 cents per pack in Kentucky and 0.05 cents in Tennessee. In Arkansas, a fee of $1.25/1,000 cigarette fee is imposed.

(f) 10 percent on-premise sales tax.

(g) In 18 states, the government directly controls the sales of distilled spirits. Revenue in these states is generated from various taxes, fees and net liquor profits.

(h) Sales tax is applied to on-premise sales only.

(i) Other taxes in addition to excise taxes for the following states: Alaska, under 21 percent – $2.50/gallon; Arkansas, under 5 percent – $0.50/gallon, under 21 percent – $1.00/gallon, $0.20/case and 3 percent off – 14 percent on-premise retail taxes; California, over 50 percent – $6.60/gallon; Connecticut, under 7 percent – $2.05/gallon; Delaware, under 25 percent – $3.64/gallon; Florida, under 17.259 percent – $2.25/gallon, over 55.780 percent – $9.53/gallon, 6.67 cents/ounce on-premise retail tax; Georgia, $0.83/gallon local tax; Illinois, under 20 percent – $0.73/gallon, $1.845/gallon in Chicago and $2.00/gallon in Cook County; Indiana, under 15 percent – $0.47/gallon; Kansas, 8 percent off- and 10 percent on-premise retail tax; Kentucky, under 6 percent – $0.25/gallon, $0.05/case and 11 percent wholesale tax; Louisiana, under 6 percent – $0.32/gallon; Massachusetts, under 15 percent – $1.10/gallon, over 50 percent alcohol – $4.05/proof gallon, 0.57 percent on private club sales; Minnesota, $0.01/bottle (except miniatures) and 9 percent sales tax; Nebraska, petroleum fee; Nevada, under 14 percent – $0.70/gallon and under 21 percent – $1.30/gallon; New York, under 24 percent – $2.54/gallon, $1.00/gallon New York City; North Dakota, 7 percent state sales tax; Oklahoma, 13.5 percent on-premise; South Carolina, $5.36/case and 9 percent surtax; South Dakota, under 14 percent – $0.93/gallon, 2 percent wholesale tax; Tennessee, $0.15/case and 15 percent on-premise, under 7 percent – $1.21/gallon; Texas, 14

percent on-premise and $0.05/drink on airline sales; and District of Columbia, 8 percent off- and 10 percent on-premise sales tax.

(j) Tax rates do not include local option taxes. In Alabama, 1–3 cents and inspection fee; Hawaii, 8.8–18 cents; Illinois, 5 cents in Chicago and 6 cents in Cook County (gasoline only); Nevada 4.0–9.0 cents; Oregon, 1–3 cents; South Dakota, 1 cent; Tennessee, 1 cent; and Virginia, 2 percent.

(k) Local taxes for gasoline and gasohol vary from 9.7 cents to 17.7 cents. Plus a 2.07 cents/gallon pollution tax.

(l) Carriers pay an additional surcharge equal to Arizona, 8 cents; Illinois, 6.3 cents (gasoline) and 6.0 cents (diesel); Indiana, 11 cents; Kentucky, 2 percent (gasoline) and 4.7 percent (diesel).

(m) Tax rate is based on the average wholesale price and is adjusted quarterly. The actual rates are: Kentucky, 9 percent; and North Carolina, 17.5 cents plus 7 percent.

(n) A portion of the rate is adjustable based on maintenance costs, sales volume, or inflation.

(o) Large trucks pay an additional 3.5 cents.

(p) Tax rate is reduced by the percentage of ethanol used in blending (reported rate assumes the maximum 10 percent ethanol).

(q) Other taxes and fees; California – sales tax applicable; Florida – sales tax added to excise; Georgia – sales tax added to excise; Hawaii – sales tax applicable; Illinois – sales tax applicable, environmental fee and leaking underground storage tax (LUST); Indiana – sales tax applicable; Kentucky – environmental fee; Michigan – sales tax applicable; Mississippi – environmental fee; Missouri – inspection fee; Nebraska – petroleum fee; Nevada – inspection and cleanup fee; New Hampshire – oil discharge cleanup fee; New Jersey – petroleum fee; New Mexico – petroleum loading fee; New York – sales tax applicable and petroleum tax; North Carolina – inspection tax; Ohio – plus 3 cents commercial; Oklahoma – environmental fee; Pennsylvania – oil franchise tax; Rhode Island – leaking underground storage tank tax (LUST); Tennessee – petroleum tax and environmental fee; Vermont – petroleum cleanup fee; Washington – $0.5 percent privilege tax; West Virginia – sales tax added to excise; Wisconsin – petroleum inspection fee; Wyoming – license tax.

(r) Includes statewide local tax of 1.0 percent in California, Illinois and Virginia.

(s) Tax rate is scheduled to increase to 35 cents per pack on July 1, 2006.

(t) Plus 0.5 percent GRT.

(u) Plus an additional 25.5 cent sales tax is added to the wholesale price of a tax stamp (total $1.485).

Table 7.15
FOOD AND DRUG SALES TAX EXEMPTIONS
(As of January 1, 2006)

State or other jurisdiction	Tax rate (percentage)	Exemptions		
		Food (a)	Prescription drugs	Nonprescription drugs
Alabama	4	. . .	★	. . .
Alaska	none	. . .	★	. . .
Arizona	5.6	★	★	. . .
Arkansas	6	. . .	★	. . .
California (c)	7.25 (b)	★	★	. . .
Colorado	2.9	★	★	. . .
Connecticut	6	★	★	★
Delaware	none	. . .	. . .	. . .
Florida	6	★	★	★
Georgia	4	★(d)	★	. . .
Hawaii	4	. . .	★	. . .
Idaho	5	. . .	★	. . .
Illinois (b)	6.25	1 percent	1 percent	1 percent
Indiana	6	★	★	. . .
Iowa	5	★	★	. . .
Kansas	5.3	. . .	★	. . .
Kentucky	6	★	★	. . .
Louisiana	4	★(d)	★	. . .
Maine	5	★	★	. . .
Maryland	5	★	★	★
Massachusetts	5	★	★	. . .
Michigan	6	★	★	. . .
Minnesota	6.5	★	★	★
Mississippi	7	. . .	★	. . .
Missouri	4.225	1.225 percent	★	. . .
Montana	none	. . .	. . .	. . .
Nebraska	5.5	★	★	. . .
Nevada	6.5	★	★	. . .
New Hampshire	none	. . .	. . .	. . .
New Jersey	6	★	★	★
New Mexico	5	★	★	. . .
New York	4	★	★	★
North Carolina (f)	4.5	★(d)	★	. . .
North Dakota	5	★	★	. . .
Ohio	5.5	★	★	. . .
Oklahoma	4.5	. . .	★	. . .
Oregon	none	. . .	. . .	. . .
Pennsylvania	6	★	★	★
Rhode Island	7	★	★	★
South Carolina	5	. . .	★	. . .
South Dakota	4	. . .	★	. . .
Tennessee	7	6 percent	★	. . .
Texas	6.25	★	★	★
Utah	4.75	. . .	★	. . .
Vermont	6	★	★	★
Virginia (b)	5 (b)	2.5 percent (b)	★	★
Washington	6.5	★	★	. . .
West Virginia	6	5 percent	★	. . .
Wisconsin	5	★	★	. . .
Wyoming (c)	4	. . .	★	. . .
Dist. of Columbia	5.75	★	★	★

Source: The Federation of Tax Administrators, January 2006.
Key:
★ — Yes, exempt from tax.
. . . — Subject to general sales tax.
(a) Some states tax food, but allow an (income) tax credit to compensate poor households. They are: Hawaii, Idaho, Kansas, South Dakota and Wyoming.

(b) Includes statewide local tax of 1.0 percent in California and 1 percent in Virginia.
(c) The tax rate may be adjusted annually according to a formula based on balances in the unappropriated general fund and the school foundation fund.
(d) Food sales are subject to local sales tax.

Table 7.16
STATE INDIVIDUAL INCOME TAXES
(Tax rates for the tax year 2006 — as of January 1, 2006)

State or other jurisdiction	Tax rate range (in percents) Low	High	Number of brackets	Income brackets Low	High	Personal exemptions Single	Married	Dependents	Federal income tax deductible
Alabama	2.0 –	5.0	3	500 (b) –	3,000 (b)	1,500	3,000	300	★
Alaska	-----------			-(x)------					...
Arizona	2.87 –	5.04	5	10,000 (b) –	150,000 (b)	2,100	4,200	2,300	...
Arkansas (a)	1.0 –	7.0 (e)	6	3,999 –	28,500	20 (c)	40 (c)	20 (c)	...
California (a)	1.0 –	9.3 (z)	6	6,139 (b) –	41,477 (b)	87 (c)	174 (c)	272 (c)	...
Colorado	4.63		1	-----------Flat rate-----------		--------------------None--------------------			...
Connecticut	3.0 –	5.0	2	10,000 (b) –	10,000 (b)	12,750 (f)	24,500 (f)	0	...
Delaware	2.2 –	5.95	6	5,000 –	60,000	110 (c)	220 (c)	110 (c)	...
Florida	-----------			-(x)------					...
Georgia	1.0 –	6.0	6	750 (g) –	7,000 (g)	2,700	5,400	3,000	...
Hawaii	1.4 –	8.25	9	2,000 (b) –	40,000 (b)	1,040	2,080	1,040	...
Idaho (a)	1.6 –	7.8	8	1,159 (h) –	23,000 (h)	3,300 (d)	6,600 (d)	3,300 (d)	...
Illinois	3.0		1	-----------Flat rate-----------		2,000	4,000	2,000	...
Indiana	3.4		1	-----------Flat rate-----------		1,000	2,000	1,000	...
Iowa (a)	0.36 –	8.98	9	1,269 –	51,106	40 (c)	80 (c)	40 (c)	★
Kansas	3.5 –	6.45	3	15,000 (b) –	30,000 (b)	2,250	4,500	2,250	...
Kentucky	2.0 –	6.0	6	3,000 –	75,000	20 (c)	40 (c)	20 (c)	...
Louisiana	2.0 –	6.0	3	12,500 (b) –	25,000 (b)	4,500 (i)	9,000 (i)	1,000 (i)	★
Maine (a)	2.0 –	8.5	4	4,550 (b) –	18,250 (b)	2,850	5,700	2,850	...
Maryland	2.0 –	4.75	4	1,000 –	3,000	2,400	4,800	2,400	...
Massachusetts	5.3		1	-----------Flat rate-----------		3,575	7,150	1,000	...
Michigan (a)	3.9		1	-----------Flat rate-----------		3,100	6,200	3,100	...
Minnesota (a)	5.35 –	7.85	3	20,510 (j) –	67,360 (j)	3,300 (d)	6,600 (d)	3,300 (d)	...
Mississippi	3.0 –	5.0	3	5,000 –	10,000	6,000	12,000	1,500	...
Missouri	1.5 –	6.0	10	1,000 –	9,000	2,100	4,200	2,100	★(s)
Montana (a)	2.0 –	6.9	7	2,300 –	13,900	1,900	3,800	1,900	★
Nebraska (a)	2.56 –	6.84	4	2,400 (k) –	26,500 (k)	103 (c)	206 (c)	103 (c)	...
Nevada	-----------			-(x)------					...
New Hampshire	-----------			-(y)------					...
New Jersey	1.4 –	8.97	6	20,000 (l) –	500,000 (l)	1,000	2,000	1,500	...
New Mexico	1.7 –	5.3	4	5,500 (m) –	16,000 (m)	3,300 (d)	6,600 (d)	3,300 (d)	...
New York	4.0 –	7.7	7	8,000 (n) –	500,000 (n)	0	0	1,000	...
North Carolina (o)	6.0 –	8.25	4	12,750 (o) –	120,000 (o)	3,300 (d)	6,600 (d)	3,300 (d)	...
North Dakota	2.1 –	5.54 (p)	5	29,700 (p) –	326,450 (p)	3,300 (d)	6,600 (d)	3,300 (d)	...
Ohio (a)	0.712–	7.185	9	5,000 –	200,000	1,300 (q)	2,600 (q)	1,300 (q)	...
Oklahoma	0.5 –	6.25 (r)	8	1,000 (b) –	10,000 (b)	1,000	2,000	1,000	★(r)
Oregon (a)	5.0 –	9.0	3	2,650 (b) –	6,550 (b)	159 (c)	318 (c)	159 (c)	★(s)
Pennsylvania	3.07		1	-----------Flat rate-----------		--------------------None--------------------			...
Rhode Island	-----------			-(t)------					...
South Carolina (a)	2.5 –	7.0	6	2,570 –	12,850	3,300 (d)	6,600 (d)	3,300 (d)	...
South Dakota	-----------			-(x)------					...
Tennessee	-----------			-(y)------					...
Texas	-----------			-(x)------					...
Utah (a)	2.3 –	7.0	6	863 (b) –	4,313 (b)	2,475 (d)	4,950 (d)	2,475 (d)	★(u)
Vermont (a)	3.6 –	9.5	5	29,900 (v) –	326,450 (v)	3,300 (d)	6,600 (d)	3,300 (d)	...
Virginia	2.0 –	5.75	4	3,000 –	17,000	900	1,800	900	...
Washington	-----------			-(x)------					...
West Virginia	3.0 –	6.5	5	10,000 –	60,000	2,000	4,000	2,000	...
Wisconsin	4.6 –	6.75	4	8,840 (w) –	132,580 (w)	700	1,400	400	...
Wyoming	-----------			-(x)------					...
Dist. of Columbia	4.5 –	9.0	3	10,000 –	30,000	1,370	2,740	1,370	...

See footnotes at end of table.

STATE INDIVIDUAL INCOME TAXES — Continued
(Tax rates for the tax year 2006 — as of January 1, 2006)

Source: The Federation of Tax Administrators from various sources, January 2006.

★ — Yes

. . . — No

(a) Fifteen states have statutory provision for automatic adjustment of tax brackets, personal exemption or standard deductions to the rate of inflation. Massachusetts, Michigan, Nebraska and Ohio index the personal exemption amounts only.

(b) For joint returns, the taxes are twice the tax imposed on half the income.

(c) Tax credits.

(d) These states allow personal exemption or standard deductions as provided in the Internal Revenue Code. Utah allows a personal exemption equal to three-fourths the federal exemptions.

(e) A special tax table is available for low income taxpayers reducing their tax payments.

(f) Combined personal exemptions and standard deduction. An additional tax credit is allowed ranging from 75 percent to 0 percent based on state adjusted gross income. Exemption amounts are phased out for higher income taxpayers until they are eliminated for households earning over $56,500.

(g) The tax brackets reported are for single individuals. For married households filing separately, the same rates apply to income brackets ranging from $500 to $5,000; and the income brackets range from $1,000 to $10,000 for joint filers.

(h) For joint returns, the tax is twice the tax imposed on half of the income. A $10 filing tax is charged for each return and a $15 credit is allowed for each exemption.

(i) Combined personal exemption and standard deduction.

(j) The tax brackets reported are for single individuals. For married couples filing jointly, the same rates apply for income under $29,980 to over $119,100.

(k) The tax brackets reported are for single individuals. For married couples filing jointly, the same rates apply for income under $4,000 to over $46,750.

(l) The tax brackets reported are for single individuals. For married individuals filing jointly, the tax rates range from 1.4 percent to 8.97 percent (with 7 income brackets) applying to income brackets from $20,000 to over $500,000.

(m) The tax brackets reported are for single individuals. For married couples filing jointly, the same rates apply for income under $8,000 to over $24,000. Married households filing separately pay the tax imposed on half the income.

(n) The tax brackets reported are for single individuals. For married taxpayers, the same rates apply to income brackets ranging from $16,000 to $500,000.

(o) The tax brackets reported are for single individuals. For married taxpayers, the same rates apply to income brackets ranging from $21,250 to $200,000. Lower exemption amounts allowed for high income taxpayers. Tax rates scheduled to decrease after year 2007.

(p) The tax brackets reported are for single individuals. For married taxpayers, the same rates apply to income brackets ranging from $49,600 to $326,450. An additional $300 personal exemption is allowed for joint returns or unmarried heads of households.

(q) Plus an additional $20 per exemption tax credit.

(r) The rate range reported is for single persons not deducting federal income tax. For married persons filing jointly, the same rates apply to income brackets that are twice the dollar amounts. Separate schedules, with rates ranging from 0.5 percent to 10 percent, apply to taxpayers deducting federal income taxes.

(s) Deduction is limited to $10,000 for joint returns and $5,000 for individuals in Missouri and to $5,000 in Oregon.

(t) Twenty-five percent federal tax liability. Federal income tax liability prior to the enactment of the Economic Growth and Tax Relief Act of 2001.

(u) One-half of the federal income taxes are deductible.

(v) The tax brackets reported are for single individuals. For married couples filing jointly, the same rates apply for income under $49,650 to over $326,450.

(w) The tax brackets reported are for single individuals. For married taxpayers, the same rates apply to income brackets ranging from $11,780 to $176,770. An additional $250 exemption is provided for each taxpayer or spouse age 65 or over.

(x) No state income tax.

(y) State income tax is limited to dividends and interest income only.

(z) An additional 1 percent tax is imposed on taxable income over $1 million.

Table 7.17
STATE PERSONAL INCOME TAXES: FEDERAL STARTING POINTS
(As of January 1, 2006)

State or other jurisdiction	Relation to Internal Revenue Code	Tax base
Alabama	. . .	. . .
Alaska	(a)	(a)
Arizona	1/2/2009	Federal adjusted gross income
Arkansas	. . .	. . .
California	1/2/2009	Federal adjusted gross income
Colorado	Current	Federal taxable income
Connecticut	Current	Federal adjusted gross income
Delaware	Current	Federal adjusted gross income
Florida	(a)	(a)
Georgia	1/2/2009	Federal adjusted gross income
Hawaii	1/1/2009	Federal taxable income
Idaho	1/2/2009	Federal taxable income
Illinois	Current	Federal adjusted gross income
Indiana	1/2/2009	Federal adjusted gross income
Iowa	2/1/2009	Federal adjusted gross income
Kansas	Current	Federal adjusted gross income
Kentucky	1/1/2009	Federal adjusted gross income
Louisiana	Current	Federal adjusted gross income
Maine	5/29/2007	Federal adjusted gross income
Maryland	Current	Federal adjusted gross income
Massachusetts	Current	Federal adjusted gross income
Michigan	Current (b)	Federal adjusted gross income
Minnesota	3/16/2006	Federal taxable income
Mississippi	. . .	. . .
Missouri	Current	Federal adjusted gross income
Montana	Current	Federal adjusted gross income
Nebraska	4/16/2008	Federal adjusted gross income
Nevada	(a)	(a)
New Hampshire	(c)	(c)
New Jersey	. . .	. . .
New Mexico	Current	Federal adjusted gross income
New York	Current	Federal adjusted gross income
North Carolina	1/2/2009	Federal taxable income
North Dakota	Current	Federal taxable income
Ohio	Current	Federal adjusted gross income
Oklahoma	Current	Federal adjusted gross income
Oregon	Current	Federal taxable income
Pennsylvania	. . .	. . .
Rhode Island	6/4/2005	Federal adjusted gross income
South Carolina	1/1/2007	Federal taxable income
South Dakota	(a)	(a)
Tennessee	(c)	(c)
Texas	(a)	(a)
Utah	Current	Federal taxable income
Vermont	1/2/2006	Federal taxable income
Virginia	1/8/2009	Federal adjusted gross income
Washington	(a)	(a)
West Virginia	1/1/2004	Federal adjusted gross income
Wisconsin	1/1/2007	Federal adjusted gross income
Wyoming	(a)	(a)
Dist. of Columbia	Current	Federal adjusted gross income

Source: Compiled by the Federation of Tax Administrators from various sources, January 2006.

Key:
. . . — State does not employ a Federal starting point.
Current — Indicates state has adopted the Internal Revenue Code as currently in effect. Dates indicate state has adopted the IRC as amended to that date.

(a) No state income tax.
(b) Or 1/1/1999, taxpayer's option.
(c) On interest and dividends only.

Table 7.18
RANGE OF STATE CORPORATE INCOME TAX RATES
(For tax year 2006—as of January 1, 2006)

State or other jurisdiction	Tax rate (percent)	Tax brackets Lowest	Tax brackets Highest	Number of brackets	Tax rate (a) (percent) financial institution	Federal income tax deductible
Alabama	6.5	-------Flat Rate-------		1	6.5	★
Alaska	1.0–9.4	10,000	90,000	10	1.0–9.4	...
Arizona	6.968 (b)	-------Flat Rate-------		1	6.968	...
Arkansas	1.0–6.5	3,000	100,000	6	1.0–6.5	...
California	8.84 (c)	-------Flat Rate-------		1	10.84 (c)	...
Colorado	4.63	-------Flat Rate-------		1	4.63	...
Connecticut	7.5 (d)	-------Flat Rate-------		1	7.5 (d)	...
Delaware	8.7	-------Flat Rate-------		1	8.7–1.7 (e)	...
Florida	5.5 (f)	-------Flat Rate-------		1	5.5 (f)	...
Georgia	6.0	-------Flat Rate-------		1	6.0	...
Hawaii	4.4–6.4 (g)	25,000	100,000	3	7.92 (g)	...
Idaho	7.6 (h)	-------Flat Rate-------		1	7.6 (h)	...
Illinois	7.3 (i)	-------Flat Rate-------		1	7.3 (i)	...
Indiana	8.5	-------Flat Rate-------		1	8.5	...
Iowa	6.0–12.0	25,000	250,000	4	5.0	★(k)
Kansas	4.0 (l)	-------Flat Rate-------		1	2.25 (l)	...
Kentucky	4.0–7.0 (m)	50,000	100,000	3	(a)	...
Louisiana	4.0–8.0	25,000	200,000	5	(a)	★
Maine	3.5–8.93 (n)	25,000	250,000	4	1.0	...
Maryland	7.0	-------Flat Rate-------		1	7.0	...
Massachusetts	9.5 (o)	-------Flat Rate-------		1	10.5 (o)	...
Michigan	--------See Note--------					
Minnesota	9.8 (p)	-------Flat Rate-------		1	9.8 (p)	...
Mississippi	3.0–5.0	5,000	10,000	3	3.0–5.0	...
Missouri	6.25	-------Flat Rate-------		1	7.0	★(k)
Montana	6.75 (q)	-------Flat Rate-------		1	6.75 (q)	...
Nebraska	5.58–7.81	50,000		2	(a)	...
Nevada	--------See Note--------					
New Hampshire	8.5 (r)	-------Flat Rate-------		1	8.5 (r)	...
New Jersey	9.0 (s)	-------Flat Rate-------		1	9.0 (s)	...
New Mexico	4.8–7.6	500,000	1 million	3	4.8–7.6	...
New York	7.5 (t)	-------Flat Rate-------		1	7.5 (t)	...
North Carolina	6.9 (u)	-------Flat Rate-------		1	6.9 (u)	...
North Dakota	2.6–7.0	3,000	30,000	5	7.0 (b)	★
Ohio	5.1–8.5 (v)	50,000		2	(v)	...
Oklahoma	6.0	-------Flat Rate-------		1	6.0	...
Oregon	6.6 (b)	-------Flat Rate-------		1	6.6 (b)	...
Pennsylvania	9.99	-------Flat Rate-------		1	(a)	...
Rhode Island	9.0 (b)	-------Flat Rate-------		1	9.0 (w)	...
South Carolina	5.0	-------Flat Rate-------		1	4.5 (x)	...
South Dakota	...	...		...	6.0–0.25% (b)	...
Tennessee	6.5	-------Flat Rate-------		1	6.5	...
Texas	--------See Note--------					
Utah	5.0 (b)	-------Flat Rate-------		...	5.0 (b)	...
Vermont	7.0–9.75 (b)	10,000	250,000	4	7.0–9.75 (b)	...
Virginia	6.0	-------Flat Rate-------		1	6.0 (y)	...
Washington	--------See Note--------					
West Virginia	9.0	-------Flat Rate-------		1	9.0	...
Wisconsin	7.9	-------Flat Rate-------		1	7.9	...
Wyoming	--------See Note--------					
Dist. of Columbia	9.975 (z)	-------Flat Rate-------		...	9.975 (z)	...

See footnotes at end of table.

RANGE OF STATE CORPORATE INCOME TAX RATES — Continued
(For tax year 2006 — as of January 1, 2006)

Source: Compiled by the Federation of Tax Administrators from various sources January 2006.

Key:

★ — Yes

. . . — No

Note: Michigan imposes a single business tax (sometimes described as a business activities tax or value added tax) of 1.9% on the sum of federal taxable income of the business, compensation paid to employees, dividends, interest, royalties paid and other items. Similarly, Texas imposes a franchise tax of 4.5% of earned surplus or 2.5 mills of net worth. Nevada, Washington, and Wyoming do not have state corporate income taxes.

(a) Rates listed include the corporate tax rate applied to financial institutions or excise taxes based on income. Some states have other taxes based upon the value of deposits or shares.

(b) Minimum tax is $50 in Arizona, $50 in North Dakota (banks), $10 in Oregon, $250 in Rhode Island, $500 per location in South Dakota (banks), $100 in Utah, $250 in Vermont.

(c) Minimum tax is $800. The tax rate on S-corporations is 1.5% (3.5% for banks).

(d) Or 3.1 mills per dollar of capital stock and surplus (maximum tax $1 million) or $250. A 25% surcharge applies to corporations with liability greater than $250.

(e) The marginal rate decreases over 4 brackets ranging from $20 to $650 million in taxable income. Building and loan associations are taxed at a flat 8.7%.

(f) Or 3.3% Alternative Minimum Tax. An exemption of $5,000 is allowed.

(g) Capital gains are taxed at 4%. There is also an alternative tax of 0.5% of gross annual sales.

(h) Minimum tax is $20. An additional tax of $10 is imposed on each return.

(i) Includes a 2.5% personal property replacement tax.

(k) Fifty percent of the federal income tax is deductible.

(l) Plus a surtax of 3.35% (2.125% for banks) taxable income in excess of $50,000 ($25,000).

(m) Minimum tax of $175. Or, the alternative minimum tax equal to 0.095% of gross sales in the state or 0.75% of state gross profits.

(n) Or the Maine Alternative Minimum Tax.

(o) Rate includes a 14% surtax, as does the following: an additional tax of $7.00 per $1,000 on taxable tangible property (or net worth allocable to state, for intangible property corporations); minimum tax of $456.

(p) Plus a 5.8% tax on any Alternative Minimum Taxable Income over the base tax.

(q) A 7% tax on taxpayers using water's edge combination. Minimum tax is $50.

(r) Plus a 0.50 percent tax on the enterprise base (total compensation, interest and dividends paid). Business profits tax imposed on both corporations and unincorporated associations.

(s) The rate reported in the table is the corporation business franchise tax rate. The minimum tax is $500. An Alternative Minimum Assessment based on Gross Receipts applies if greater than corporate franchise tax. Corporations not subject to the franchise tax are subject to a 7.25% income tax. Banking and financial corporations are subject to the franchise tax. Corporations with net income under $100,000 are taxed at 6.5%. The tax on S-corporations is being phased out through 2007. The tax rate on a New Jersey S-corporation that has entire net income not subject to federal corporate income tax in excess of $100,000 will remain at 1.33% for privilege periods ending on or before June 30, 2006. The rate will be 0.67% for privilege periods ending on or after July 1, 2006, but on or before June 30, 2007; and there will be no tax imposed for privilege periods ending on or after July 1, 2007. The tax on S-corporations with entire net income not subject to federal corporate income tax of $100,000 or less is eliminated for privilege periods ending on or after July 1, 2007.

(t) Or 1.78 mills per dollar of capital (up to $350,000); or a 2.5% alternative minimum tax; or a minimum tax of $10,000 to $100 depending on payroll size; if any of these is greater than the tax computed on net income. Small corporations with income under $290,000 are subject to lower rates of tax on net income. An additional tax of 0.9 mills per dollar of subsidiary capital is imposed on corporations. For banks, the alternative bases of tax are 3% of alternative net income; or up to 1/50th mill of taxable assets; or a minimum tax of $250.

(u) Financial institutions are also subject to a tax equal to $30 per one million in assets.

(v) Rates shown are for the Franchise tax, which is being phased out through 2010 and replaced with the CAT. Current rates apply to 80% of the liability, or 80% of 4 mills times the value of the taxpayer's issued and outstanding share of stock with a maximum payment of $150,000; or $50 to $1,000 minimum tax, depending on worldwide gross receipts. The Commercial Activity Tax (CAT) equals $150 for gross receipts between $150,000 and $1 million, plus 0.26% of gross receipts over $1 million. The CAT applies to 23% of receipts through March 31, and 40% for the remainder of the year. Banks will pay the Franchise tax. An additional litter tax is imposed equal to 0.11% on the first $50,000 of taxable income, 0.22% on income over $50,000; or 0.14 mills on net worth.

(w) For banks, the alternative tax is $2.50 per $10,000 of capital stock ($100 minimum).

(x) Savings and Loans are taxed at a 6% rate.

(y) State and national banks subject to the state's franchise tax on net capital are exempt from the income tax.

(z) Minimum tax is $100. Includes surtax.

Table 7.19
STATE SEVERANCE TAXES: 2005–2006

State	Title and application of tax (a)	Rate
Alabama	Iron Ore Mining Tax	$.03/ton
	Forest Products Severance Tax	Varies by species and ultimate use.
	Oil and Gas Conservation & Regulation of Production Tax	2% of gross value at point of production, of all oil and gas produced. 1% of the gross value (for a 5-year period from the date production begins) for well, for which the initial permit issued by the Oil and Gas Board is dated on or after July 1, 1996, and before July 1, 2002, except a replacement well for which the initial permit was dated before July 1, 1996.
	Oil and Gas Privilege Tax on Production	8% of gross value at point of production; 4% of gross value at point of incremental production resulting from a qualified enhanced recovery project; 4% if wells produce 25 bbl. or less oil per day or 200,000 cu. ft. or less gas per day; 6% of gross value at point of production for certain onshore and offshore wells. A 50% rate reduction for wells permitted by the oil and gas board on or after July 1, 1996, and before July 1, 2002, for 5 years from initial production, except for replacement wells for which the initial permit was dated before July 1, 1996. Under Act 2004-635 a temporary tax is levied (July 1, 2004 through June 30, 2005) of 1% of offshore production ond 0.5% of onshore production.
	Coal Severance Tax	$.135/ton
	Coal and Lignite Severance Tax	$.20/ton in addition to coal severance tax.
Alaska	Fisheries Business Tax	1% to 5% of fish value based on type of fish and processing.
	Fishery Resource Landing Tax	3% of the value of the fishery resource at the place of landing for an established commercial fish species; 1% of the value of the fishery resource at the place of landing for a developing commercial fish species.
	Seafood Marketing Assessment	.03% on all commercial fish species.
	Oil and Gas Properties Production Tax	(Oil) The greater of either $0.80/bbl. for old crude oil or 15% of gross value at the production point for oil fields in production more than five years and 12.25 percent for oil fields in production less than 5 years, multiplied by the Economic Limit Factor for oil; (Gas) The greater of either $0.64/1,000 cu. ft. of gas or 10% of gross value at the production point, multiplied by the Economic Limit Factor for Gas; and conservation surcharges of $.03 cents per barrel, with an additional $.02 cents per barrel as needed to maintain a $50 million balance in the oil and hazardous substance response fund.
	Salmon Marketing Tax	1% of the value of salmon that is removed or transferred.
Arizona	Severance Tax (b)	2.5% of net severance base for mining; $1.50/1,000 board ft. ($2.13 for ponderosa pine) for timbering.
Arkansas	Natural Resources Severance Tax	Separate rate for each substance.
	Oil and Gas Conservation Tax	Natural gas 0.3 of $.01 cent per MCF; crude oil 4% to 5% depending on production levels.
	Oil and Gas Conservation Assessment	Maximum 43 mills/bbl. of oil and 9 mills per MCF produced of gas.
California	Oil and Gas Production Assessment	Rate determined annually by Department of Conservation. (d)
Colorado	Severance Tax (e)	Taxable years commencing prior to July 1, 1999, 2.25% of gross income exceeding $11 million for metallic minerals and taxable years commencing after July 1,1999, 2.25% of gross income exceeding $19 million for metallic minerals; on or after July 1,1999, $.05/ton for each ton exceeding 625,000 tons each quarter for molybdenum ore; 2% to 5% based on gross income for oil, gas, CO2, and coalbed methane; after July 1,1999, $.36/ton adjusted by the producers' prices index for each ton exceeding 300,000 tons each quarter for coal; and 4% of gross proceeds on production exceeding 15,000 tons per day for oil shale.
	Oil and Gas Conservation Levy	Maximum 1.5 mills/$1 of market value at wellhead. (f)
Florida	Oil, Gas and Sulfur Production Tax	5% of gross value for small well oil, and 8% of gross value for all other, and an additional 12.5% for escaped oil; the gas base rate times the gas base rate adjustment rate each fiscal year for gas; and the sulfur base rate times the sulfur base rate adjustment each fiscal year for sulfur.
	Solid Minerals Tax (g)	8% of the value of the minerals severed, except phosphate rock (rate computed annually at $1.69/ton times the changes in the producer price index) and heavy minerals (rate computed annually at a base rate of $2.93/ton times the base rate adjustment).
Idaho	Ore Severance Tax	1% of net value.
	Oil and Gas Production Tax	Maximum of 5 mills/bbl. of oil and 5 mills/50,000 cu. ft. of gas. (c)
	Additional Oil and Gas Production Tax	2% of market value at site of production.
Illinois	Timber Fee	4% of purchase price (h)

See footnotes at end of table.

STATE SEVERANCE TAXES — Continued

State	Title and application of tax (a)	Rate
Indiana	Petroleum Production Tax (i)	1% of value or $.24 per barrel for oil or $.03 per 1,000 cu. ft. of gas, whichever is greater.
Kansas	Severance Tax (j)	8% of gross value of oil and gas, less property tax credit of 3.67%; $1/ton of coal.
	Oil and Gas Conservation Tax	54.7 mills/bbl. crude oil or petroleum marketed or used each month; 9.13 mills/1,000 cu. ft. of gas sold or marketed each month.
Kentucky	Mined-Land Conservation & Reclamation Tax	$50, plus per ton fee of between $.03 and $.10.
	Oil Production Tax	4.5% of market value.
	Coal Severance Tax	4.5% of gross value, less transportation expenses.
	Natural Resource Severance Tax (k)	4.5% of gross value, less transportation expenses.
Louisiana	Natural Resources Severance Tax	Rate varies according to substance.
	Oil Field Site Restoration Fee	Rate varies according to type of well and production.
	Freshwater Mussel Tax	5% of revenues from the sale of whole freshwater mussels, at the point of first sale.
Maine	Mining Excise Tax	The greater of a tax on facilities and equipment or a tax on gross proceeds.
Maryland	Mine Reclamation Surcharge	$.17/ton of coal removed by open-pit, strip or deep mine methods. Of the $.15, $.06 is remitted to the county from which the coal was removed.
Michigan	Gas and Oil Severance Tax	5% (gas), 6.6% (oil) and 4% (oil from stripper wells and marginal properties) of gross cash market value of the total production. Maximum additional fee of 1% of gross cash market value on all oil and gas produced in state in previous year.
Minnesota	Taconite and Iron Sulfides	$2.137 per ton of concentrates or pellets.
	Direct Reduced Iron (l)	$2.137 per ton of concentrates plus an additional $.03 per ton for each 1% that the iron content exceeds 72%.
Mississippi	Oil and Gas Severance Tax	6% of value at point of gas production; 3.5% of gross value of occluded natural gas from coal seams at point of production for well's first five years; also, maximum 35 mills/bbl. oil or 4 mills/1,000 cu. ft. gas (Oil and Gas Board maintenance tax). 6% of value at point of oil production; 3% of value at production when enhanced oil recovery method used.
	Timber Severance Tax	Varies depending on type of wood and ultimate use.
	Salt Severance Tax	3% of value of entire production in state.
Montana	Coal Severance Tax	Varies from 3% to 15% depending on quality of coal and type of mine.
	Metalliferous Mines License Tax (m)	Progressive rate, taxed on amounts in excess of $250,000. For concentrate shipped to smelter, mill or reduction work, 1.81%. Gold, silver or any platinum group metal shipped to refinery, 1.6%.
	Oil or Gas Conservation Tax	Maximum 0.3% on the market value of each barrel of crude petroleum oil or 10,000 cu. ft. of natural gas produced, saved and marketed or stored within or exported from the state. (n)
	Oil and Natural Gas Production Tax	Varies from 0.5% to 14.8% according to the type of well and type of production.
	Micaceous Minerals License Tax	$.05/ton
	Cement License Tax (o)	$.22/ton of cement, $.05/ton of cement, plaster, gypsum or gypsum products.
	Mineral Mining Tax	$25 plus 0.5% of gross value greater than $5,000. For talc, $25 plus 4% of gross value greater than $625. For coal, $25 plus 0.40% of gross value greater than $6,250. For vermiculite, $25 plus 2% of gross value greater than $1,250. For limestone, $25 plus 10% of gross value greater than $250. For industrial garnets, $25 plus 1% of gross value greater than $2,500.00.
Nebraska	Oil and Gas Severance Tax	3% of value of nonstripper oil and natural gas; 2% of value of stripper oil.
	Oil and Gas Conservation Tax	Maximum 15 mills/$1 of value at wellhead, as of January 1, 2000. (c)
	Uranium Tax	2% of gross value over $5 million. The value of the uranium severed subject to tax is the gross value less transportation and processing costs.
Nevada	Minerals Extraction Tax	Between 2% and 5% of net proceeds of each geographically separate extractive operation, based on ratio of net proceeds to gross proceeds of whole operation.
	Oil and Gas Conservation Tax	$50/mills/bbl. of oil and 50 mills/50,000 cu. ft. of gas.

See footnotes at end of table.

STATE SEVERANCE TAXES — Continued

State	Title and application of tax (a)	Rate
New Hampshire	Refined Petroleum Products Tax Excavation Tax Timber Tax	0.1% of fair market value. $.02 per cubic yard of earth excavated. 10% of stumpage value at the time of cutting.
New Mexico	Resources Excise Tax (p) Severance Tax (p) Oil and Gas Severance Tax Oil and Gas Emergency School Tax Natural Gas Processor's Tax Oil and Gas Ad Valorem Production Tax Oil and Gas Conservation Tax (q)	Potash .5%, molybdenum .125%, copper .25%, all others .75% of value. Potash 2.5%, copper .5%, timber .125% of value. Pumice, gypsum, sand, gravel, clay, fluospar and other non-metallic minerals, .125% of value. Gold, silver .20%; Lead, zinc, thorium, molybdenum, manganese, rare earth and other .125% of value. 3.75% of value of oil, other liquid hydrocarbons, natural gas and carbon dioxide. 3.15% of value of oil, other liquid hydrocarbons and carbon dioxide. 4% of value of natural gas. $0.0220/Mmbtu tax on volume. Varies, based on property tax in district of production. 0.19% of value.
North Carolina	Oil and Gas Conservation Tax Primary Forest Product Assessment Tax	Maximum 5 mills/barrel of oil and 0.5 mill/1,000 cu. ft. of gas. $.50/1,000 board ft. for softwood sawtimber, $.40/1,000 board ft. for hardwood sawtimber, $.20/cord for softwood pulpwood, $.12/cord hardwood pulpwood.
North Dakota	Oil Gross Production Tax Gas Gross Production Tax Coal Severance Tax Oil Extraction Tax	5% of gross value at well. $.04/1,000 cu.ft. of gas produced (the rate is subject to a gas rate adjustment each fiscal year). For FY 05, the rate was 10.37 cents per mcf. $.375/ton plus $.02/ton. (r) 6.5% of gross value at well (with exceptions due to production volumes and production incentives for enhanced recovery projects).
Ohio	Resource Severance Tax	$.10/bbl. of oil; $.025/1,000 cu. ft. of natural gas; $.04/ton of salt; $.02/ton of sand, gravel, limestone and dolomite; $.09/ton of coal; and $0.01/ton of clay, sandstone or conglomerate, shale, gypsum or quartzite.
Oklahoma	Oil, Gas and Mineral Gross Production Tax and Petroleum Excise Tax (s)	Rate: 0.75% levied on asphalt and metals. 7% (if greater than $2.10 mcf) 4% (if greater than $1.75 mcf, but less than $2.10 mcf) 1% (if less than $1.75 mcf) casinghead gas and natural gas, as well as 0.95% being levied on crude oil, casinghead gas and natural gas. Oil Gross Production Tax is now a variable rate tax, beginning with January 1999 production, at the following rates based on the average price of Oklahoma oil: a) If the average price equals or exceeds $17/bbl., the tax shall be 7%; b) If the average price is less than $17/bbl., but is equal to or exceeds $14/bbl., the tax shall be 4%; c) If the average price is less than $14/bbl., the tax shall be 1%.
Oregon	Forest Products Harvest Tax Oil and Gas Production Tax STF Severance Tax – Eastern Oregon Forestland Option STF Severance Tax – Western Oregon Forestland Option	$2.85/1,000 board ft. harvested from public and private land (rate is for 2005 harvests). 6% of gross value at well. $3.12/1,000 board ft. harvested from land under the Small Tract Forestland Option. $4.00/1,000 board ft. harvested from land under the Small Tract Forestland Option.
South Carolina	Forest Renewal Tax	Softwood products: 20 cents per 1,000 board feet or 25 cents per cord. Hardwood products: 25 cents per 1,000 board feet or 7 cents per cord.
South Dakota	Precious Metals Severance Tax Energy Minerals Severance Tax (t) Conservation Tax	$4 per ounce of gold severed plus additional tax depending on price of gold; 10% on net profits or royalties from sale of precious metals, and 8% of royalty value. 4.5% of taxable value of any energy minerals. 2.4 mills of taxable value of any energy minerals.
Tennessee	Oil and Gas Severance Tax Coal Severance Tax (u)	3% of sales price $.20/ton
Texas	Gas Production Tax Oil Production Tax Sulphur Production Tax Cement Production Tax Oil-Field Cleanup Regulatory Fees	7.5% of market value. The greater of 4.6% of market value or $.046/bbl. 2.3% of market value for oil produced from qualified enhanced recovery projects. $1.03/long ton or fraction thereof. $.0275/100 lbs. or fraction thereof. 5/8 of $.01/barrel; 1/15 of $.01/1,000 cubic feet of gas. (v)

See footnotes at end of table.

STATE SEVERANCE TAXES — Continued

State	Title and application of tax (a)	Rate
Utah	Mining Severance Tax	2.6% of taxable value for metals or metalliferous minerals sold or otherwise disposed of.
	Oil and Gas Severance Tax	3% of value for the first $13 per barrel of oil, 5% from $13.01 and above; 3% of value for first $1.50/mcf, 5% from $1.51 and above; and 4% of taxable value of natural gas liquids.
	Oil and Gas Conservation Fee	.2% of market value at wellhead.
Virginia	Forest Products Tax	Varies by species and ultimate use.
	Coal Surface Mining Reclamation Tax	Varies depending on balance of Coal Surface Mining Reclamation Fund.
Washington	Uranium and Thorium Milling Tax	$0.05/per pound.
	Enhanced Food Fish Tax	0.09% to 5.62% of value (depending on species) at point of landing.
	Timber Excise Tax	5% of stumpage value for harvests on public and private lands.
West Virginia	Natural Resource Severance Taxes	Coal: state rate is greater of 5% or $.75 per ton (4.65% for state purposes and .35% for distribution to local governments). Special state rates for coal from new low seam mines. For seams between 37" and 45" the rate is greater of 2% or $.75/ton (1.65% for state purposes and .35% for distribution to local governments). For seams less than 37" the rate is greater of 1% or $.75/ton (.65% for state purposes and .35% for distribution to local governments). For coal from gob, refuse piles, or other sources of waste coal, the rate is 2.5% (distributed to local governments). Additional tax for workers' compensation debt reduction is $.56/ton. Two special reclamation taxes at $.14/clean ton and $.02/clean ton. Limestone or sandstone, quarried or mined, and other natural resources: 5% of gross value. Natural gas: 5% of gross value (10% of net tax distributed to local governments), additional tax for workers' compensation debt reduction is $.047/mcf of natural gas prodcued. Oil: 5% of gross value (10% of net tax distributed to local governments). Timber: 3.22%, additional tax for workers' compensation debt reduction is 2.78%.
Wisconsin	Mining Net Proceeds Tax	Progressive net proceeds tax ranging from 3% to 15% is imposed on the net proceeds from mining metalliferous minerals. The tax brackets are annually adjusted for inflation based on the change in the GNP deflator.
	Oil and Gas Severance Tax	7% of market value of oil or gas at the mouth of the well. There are no wells in the state.
Wyoming	Severance Tax	Severance Tax is defined as an excise tax imposed on the present and continuing privilege of removing, extracting, severing or producing any mineral in this state. Except as otherwise provided by W.S. 39-14-205 (Tax Exemptions), the total severance tax on crude oil, lease condensate or natural gas shall be six percent (6%), comprising one and one-half percent (1.5%) imposed by the Wyoming constitution article 15, section 19 and four and one-half percent (4.5%) imposed by Wyoming statute. The tax shall be distributed as provided in W.S. 39-14-211 and is imposed as follows: i. One and one-half percent (1.5%); plus ii. One-half percent (.5%); plus iii. Two percent (2%); plus iv. Two percent (2%). Severance Tax is applied to the taxable value of crude oil, lease condensate or natural gas. The taxable value is the gross sales value of the product less Federal, State or Tribal Royalties paid and less allowable transportation deductions. If the product produced is natural gas, an additional deduction is allowed for processing. Rates vary from 1.50% to 6.0% on different grades of oil. Taxes on coal and other minerals vary from 2% to 7%.

See footnotes at end of table.

STATE SEVERANCE TAXES — Continued

Sources: The Council of State Governments' survey, October 2005, and state Web sites, January 2006.

Key:

(a) Application of tax is same as that of title unless otherwise indicated by a footnote.

(b) Timber, metalliferous minerals.

(c) Actual rate set by administrative actions. Idaho – Current conservation rate is 5 mills (.005); Nebraska – Current conservation rate is 4 mills (.004).

(d) For 2005–06, $0.050898/bbl. of oil or 10,000 cu. ft. of natural gas.

(e) Metallic minerals, molybdenum ore, coal, oil shale, oil, gas, CO2, and coalbed methane.

(f) As of July 1, 2004, set at .0005 mill/$1.

(g) Clay, gravel, phosphate rock, lime, shells, stone, sand, heavy minerals and rare earths.

(h) Buyer deducts amount from payment to grower; amount forwarded to Department of Conservation.

(i) Petroleum, oil, gas and other hydrocarbons.

(j) Coal, oil and gas.

(k) Coal and oil excepted.

(l) Production is considered commercial when it exceeds 50,000 tons annually. There is a six-year phase-in of the tax. In years one and two, the rate is zero. In year three, it is 25% of the statutory rate and 50% and 75% in years four and five respectively. An Aggregate Materials Tax is imposed by resolution of county boards. It is not required that any county impose the tax, which is $.10/cubic yard or $.07/ton on materials produced in the county.

(m) Metals, precious and semi-precious stones and gems.

(n) The maxiumum rate of 0.3% is split between the Oil or Gas Conservation Tax and the Oil, Gas and Coal Natural Resource Account Fund. Currently the Oil or Gas Conservation Tax is .18% and the Oil, Gas and Coal Natural Resource Account fund tax rate is .08%.

(o) Cement and gypsum or allied products.

(p) Natural resources except oil, natural gas, liquid hydrocarbons or carbon dioxide.

(q) Oil, coal, gas, liquid hydrocarbons, geothermal energy, carbon dioxide and uranium.

(r) Rate reduced by 50 percent if burned in cogeneration facility using renewable resources as fuel to generate at least 10 percent of its energy output. Coal shipped out of state is subject to the $.02/ton tax and 30% of the $.375/ton tax. The coal may be subject to up to the $.375/ton tax at the option of the county in which the coal is mined.

(s) Asphalt and ores bearing lead, zinc, jack, gold, silver, copper or petroleum or other crude oil or other mineral oil, natural gas or casinghead gas and uranium ore.

(t) Any mineral fuel used in the production of energy, including coal, lignite, petroleum, oil, natural gas, uranium and thorium.

(u) Counties and municipalities also authorized to levy severance taxes on sand, gravel, sandstone, chert and limestone at a rate up to $.15/ton.

(v) Fees will not be collected when Oil-Field Cleanup Fund reaches $20 million, but will again be collected when fund falls below $10 million.

Table 7.20
STATE GOVERNMENT TAX REVENUE, BY TYPE OF TAX: 2004
(In thousands of dollars)

State	Total taxes	Sales and gross receipts	Licenses	Individual income	Corporation net income	Severance	Property taxes	Death and gift	Documentary and stock transfer	Other
United States*	$593,821,649	$293,776,038	$39,626,991	$197,878,965	$30,896,860	$6,362,179	$11,425,114	$5,738,697	$7,889,382	$227,423
Alabama	7,018,242	3,675,562	397,429	2,243,537	292,051	113,646	221,470	29,467	45,080	N.A.
Alaska	1,338,707	168,392	83,738	N.A.	339,564	697,394	47,368	2,251	N.A.	N.A.
Arizona	9,606,318	6,070,737	289,803	2,315,865	525,650	15,544	346,427	42,292	N.A.	N.A.
Arkansas	5,580,678	2,934,030	187,876	1,685,585	181,830	15,840	520,324	21,394	25,972	7,827
California	85,721,483	33,984,188	5,744,089	36,398,983	6,925,916	14,471	2,079,326	574,510	N.A.	N.A.
Colorado	7,051,457	2,894,035	337,911	3,413,891	239,591	115,884	N.A.	50,145	N.A.	N.A.
Connecticut	10,291,289	4,900,376	385,265	4,319,546	379,822	N.A.	N.A.	130,464	175,816	N.A.
Delaware	2,375,482	383,383	882,389	781,212	217,768	N.A.	N.A.	11,725	98,556	449
Florida	30,534,283	23,409,406	1,774,881	N.A.	1,441,338	48,651	276,786	386,767	3,196,454	N.A.
Georgia	14,570,573	6,468,785	617,663	6,830,486	494,701	N.A.	65,118	66,018	420	27,382
Hawaii	3,849,135	2,470,299	123,257	1,169,205	58,119	N.A.	N.A.	9,829	18,426	N.A.
Idaho	2,647,790	1,403,155	220,800	907,795	103,784	2,568	N.A.	7,418	N.A.	2,270
Illinois	25,490,593	12,526,542	2,385,596	8,139,558	2,068,574	349	57,084	221,733	91,157	N.A.
Indiana	11,957,470	6,906,954	448,387	3,807,861	644,787	563	8,923	139,995	N.A.	N.A.
Iowa	5,143,126	2,437,323	575,515	1,958,697	89,826	N.A.	N.A.	67,896	13,869	N.A.
Kansas	5,283,676	2,723,152	274,619	1,915,530	166,609	98,148	57,554	48,064	N.A.	N.A.
Kentucky	8,463,400	4,006,307	542,480	2,819,393	381,538	187,109	455,460	67,679	3,434	N.A.
Louisiana	8,030,495	4,610,512	429,068	2,192,038	236,745	476,609	39,739	45,784	N.A.	N.A.
Maine	2,896,759	1,360,152	158,199	1,160,028	111,616	N.A.	45,308	32,076	29,380	N.A.
Maryland	12,314,799	5,212,424	511,559	5,277,844	447,487	N.A.	478,796	152,251	183,189	51,249
Massachusetts	16,839,243	5,602,614	664,556	8,830,334	1,301,076	N.A.	51	194,706	245,906	N.A.
Michigan	24,061,065	10,844,250	1,545,457	6,576,065	1,841,010	58,220	2,803,017	75,543	317,480	23
Minnesota	14,734,921	6,384,318	941,783	5,709,584	637,183	14,814	607,863	87,022	352,354	N.A.
Mississippi	5,124,730	3,391,202	318,488	1,061,704	243,846	53,809	40,241	15,440	N.A.	N.A.
Missouri	9,119,664	4,468,508	605,590	3,720,749	224,366	53	22,763	69,657	7,940	38
Montana	1,625,692	437,051	233,372	605,582	67,723	83,503	183,937	11,431	N.A.	3,093
Nebraska	3,639,811	1,988,078	201,921	1,242,603	167,429	1,806	2,336	26,423	9,215	N.A.
Nevada	4,738,877	3,824,602	623,400	N.A.	N.A.	37,155	132,468	24,548	96,704	N.A.
New Hampshire	2,005,389	674,354	199,170	54,769	407,603	1,894	493,589	30,536	145,368	N.A.
New Jersey	20,981,428	9,740,284	1,177,242	7,400,733	1,896,998	N.A.	3,660	516,008	246,503	N.A.
New Mexico	4,001,780	2,038,440	169,805	1,007,248	138,196	587,625	53,074	7,392	N.A.	N.A.
New York	45,826,429	16,478,965	1,193,019	24,647,225	2,044,504	N.A.	N.A.	736,004	726,712	N.A.
North Carolina	16,836,454	7,269,201	1,017,247	7,510,978	837,085	1,894	N.A.	145,110	54,939	N.A.
North Dakota	1,228,890	666,738	118,377	213,982	49,807	175,625	1,478	2,883	N.A.	N.A.
Ohio	22,475,528	10,783,304	1,813,479	8,705,161	1,060,594	8,112	40,636	64,242	N.A.	N.A.
Oklahoma	6,426,713	2,339,028	840,421	2,319,123	133,309	655,051	N.A.	111,143	12,048	16,590
Oregon	6,103,071	748,882	651,016	4,270,740	320,065	16,603	15,865	73,608	6,292	N.A.
Pennsylvania	25,346,879	12,529,651	2,547,850	7,323,364	1,677,998	N.A.	68,389	708,588	470,790	20,249
Rhode Island	2,408,861	1,305,374	94,481	899,939	69,479	N.A.	1,532	25,313	12,645	98
South Carolina	6,803,568	3,689,986	383,505	2,438,712	196,510	N.A.	11,597	32,765	50,493	N.A.

See footnotes at end of table.

STATE GOVERNMENT TAX REVENUE, BY TYPE OF TAX: 2004
(In thousands of dollars) — Continued

State	Total taxes	Sales and gross receipts	Licenses	Individual income	Corporation net income	Severance	Property taxes	Death and gift	Documentary and stock transfer	Other
South Dakota	1,062,722	865,262	138,877	N.A.	47,108	2,012	N.A.	9,322	141	N.A.
Tennessee	9,529,171	7,344,662	1,045,665	139,991	694,798	1,061	N.A.	96,534	174,206	32,254
Texas	30,751,860	24,620,778	4,083,148	N.A.	N.A.	1,896,803	N.A.	151,131	N.A.	N.A.
Utah	4,195,962	2,142,240	156,999	1,692,035	145,005	50,009	N.A.	9,674	N.A.	N.A.
Vermont	1,766,719	687,595	98,758	429,817	62,228	N.A.	448,203	14,712	20,762	4,644
Virginia	14,233,065	5,212,063	613,910	7,422,071	422,119	1,680	20,778	149,647	340,591	50,206
Washington	13,895,346	10,864,600	686,564	N.A.	N.A.	37,624	1,526,617	139,855	640,086	N.A.
West Virginia	3,749,013	2,093,253	179,107	1,068,212	181,515	181,515	3,370	9,301	10,129	N.A.
Wisconsin	12,638,266	5,621,037	811,548	5,251,190	681,990	4,610	104,158	86,357	66,325	11,051
Wyoming	1,504,777	574,004	101,712	N.A.	N.A.	683,208	139,809	6,044	N.A.	N.A.

Source: Population Division, U.S. Census Bureau, released December 22, 2005.
Key:
N.A.—not applicable
* U.S. Totals, includes the 50 state governments and does not include the District of Columbia or any local government.

Table 7.21
STATE GOVERNMENT SALES AND GROSS RECEIPT TAXES: 2004
(In thousands of dollars)

State	Sales and gross receipts total	General sales and gross receipts	Selective sales taxes total	Selective sales taxes							
				Alcoholic beverages	Amusements	Insurance premiums	Motor fuels	Pari-mutuels	Public utilities	Tobacco products	Other selective sales
United States	$293,776,038	$198,208,985	$95,567,053	$4,615,463	$4,990,713	$13,914,196	$33,708,933	$301,878	$10,608,630	$12,303,265	$15,123,975
Alabama	3,675,562	1,892,560	1,783,002	137,222	97	245,577	535,493	3,226	600,558	93,270	167,559
Alaska	168,392	N.A.	168,392	28,262	2,413	49,873	40,660	N.A.	3,962	43,222	N.A.
Arizona	6,070,737	4,719,642	1,351,095	55,954	625	312,852	671,765	566	34,617	274,716	N.A.
Arkansas	2,934,030	2,149,527	784,503	41,240	N.A.	91,330	453,148	4,574	N.A.	146,485	47,726
California	33,984,188	26,506,911	7,477,277	312,826	N.A.	2,114,980	3,324,883	42,143	520,589	1,081,588	80,268
Colorado	2,894,035	1,909,246	984,789	31,317	99,145	177,782	597,558	4,504	9,339	65,144	N.A.
Connecticut	4,900,376	3,127,221	1,773,155	44,026	435,061	218,202	456,805	10,660	195,646	277,333	135,422
Delaware	383,383	N.A.	383,383	13,385	N.A.	68,009	112,435	188	35,536	75,479	78,351
Florida	23,409,406	17,128,515	6,280,891	591,682	N.A.	711,145	2,021,677	26,747	1,712,380	449,360	767,900
Georgia	6,468,785	4,921,337	1,547,448	149,801	N.A.	317,463	755,994	N.A.	N.A.	227,348	96,842
Hawaii	2,470,299	1,900,377	569,922	41,250	N.A.	81,916	84,378	N.A.	99,504	79,387	183,487
Idaho	1,403,155	1,036,924	366,231	6,609	N.A.	82,283	218,019	N.A.	1,827	52,271	5,222
Illinois	12,526,542	6,922,587	5,603,955	147,883	785,922	378,517	1,421,927	12,042	1,704,655	760,226	392,783
Indiana	6,906,954	4,759,445	2,147,509	38,509	765,707	178,303	802,168	4,762	10,573	338,716	8,771
Iowa	2,437,323	1,617,505	819,818	12,709	213,522	138,229	357,835	3,241	N.A.	94,282	N.A.
Kansas	2,723,152	1,932,927	790,225	87,637	651	121,827	428,985	3,531	740	124,586	22,268
Kentucky	4,006,307	2,466,033	1,540,274	79,104	232	331,903	476,605	15,466	N.A.	20,627	616,337
Louisiana	4,610,512	2,680,716	1,929,796	53,422	524,119	342,353	560,769	20,420	7,467	101,040	320,206
Maine	1,360,152	917,248	442,904	39,279	N.A.	77,770	220,410	4,509	8,310	92,626	N.A.
Maryland	5,212,424	2,945,060	2,267,364	26,863	10,432	279,089	746,044	3,028	137,373	272,066	792,469
Massachusetts	5,602,614	3,743,204	1,859,410	68,522	5,255	399,764	684,242	5,697	N.A.	425,421	270,509
Michigan	10,844,250	7,894,458	2,949,792	149,424	99,455	230,272	1,081,259	11,825	28,561	992,793	356,203
Minnesota	6,384,318	4,066,790	2,317,528	69,497	55,784	265,970	648,428	1,489	50	190,116	1,086,194
Mississippi	3,391,202	2,482,908	908,294	39,793	167,327	161,201	464,748	N.A.	12,067	55,587	7,571
Missouri	4,468,508	2,950,055	1,518,453	28,026	307,062	304,848	726,705	N.A.	N.A.	109,653	42,159
Montana	437,051	N.A.	437,051	20,570	50,496	61,063	197,605	97	28,169	45,209	33,842
Nebraska	1,988,078	1,524,591	463,487	23,159	6,136	38,460	302,899	296	3,107	71,220	18,210
Nevada	3,824,602	2,264,749	1,559,853	33,867	861,511	194,228	293,595	N.A.	9,651	129,055	37,946
New Hampshire	674,354	N.A.	674,354	12,239	1,777	79,450	129,913	4,115	65,581	100,014	281,265
New Jersey	9,740,284	6,261,700	3,478,584	87,357	468,072	417,873	546,952	N.A.	942,744	777,512	238,074
New Mexico	2,038,440	1,443,300	595,140	37,503	38,543	87,448	210,863	1,188	18,141	52,718	148,736
New York	16,478,965	10,050,291	6,428,674	191,128	570	833,073	518,557	36,067	821,911	1,009,595	3,017,773
North Carolina	7,269,201	4,351,822	2,917,379	212,224	11,503	432,975	1,272,612	N.A.	319,730	43,733	624,602
North Dakota	666,738	367,304	299,434	5,910	10,079	30,928	118,744	2,585	34,098	21,167	75,923
Ohio	10,783,304	7,881,510	2,901,794	88,267	N.A.	423,078	1,541,151	15,918	275,811	557,569	N.A.
Oklahoma	2,339,028	1,594,246	744,782	68,420	5,356	144,186	415,318	2,822	21,172	63,398	24,110
Oregon	748,882	N.A.	748,882	13,306	84	52,167	404,547	2,893	10,537	265,348	N.A.
Pennsylvania	12,529,651	7,773,133	4,756,518	221,410	566	639,578	1,785,201	26,617	1,016,640	981,254	85,252
Rhode Island	1,305,374	804,647	500,727	10,607	N.A.	43,350	133,415	4,651	88,640	115,503	104,561
South Carolina	3,689,986	2,726,657	963,329	146,658	39,627	106,643	489,322	N.A.	45,071	29,742	106,266

See footnotes at end of table.

STATE GOVERNMENT SALES AND GROSS RECEIPT TAXES: 2004
(In thousands of dollars) — Continued

State	Sales and gross receipts total	General sales and gross receipts	Selective sales taxes total	Selective sales taxes							
				Alcoholic beverages	Amusements	Insurance premiums	Motor fuels	Pari-mutuels	Public utilities	Tobacco products	Other selective sales
South Dakota............	865,262	586,389	278,873	12,435	26	55,339	126,017	880	1,949	27,644	54,583
Tennessee..................	7,344,662	5,845,206	1,499,456	92,062	N.A.	351,111	832,168	N.A.	4,761	119,482	99,872
Texas.........................	24,620,778	15,460,221	9,160,557	601,841	23,086	1,130,499	2,918,842	11,793	793,107	534,577	3,146,812
Utah...........................	2,142,240	1,560,902	581,338	28,700	N.A.	106,776	341,885	N.A.	13,845	61,663	28,469
Vermont.....................	687,595	256,958	430,637	16,894	N.A.	49,018	85,994	N.A.	10,769	51,182	216,780
Virginia......................	5,212,063	2,977,401	2,234,662	146,019	50	351,278	909,468	N.A.	128,815	16,199	682,833
Washington................	10,864,600	8,423,160	2,441,440	192,618	60	345,614	925,723	1,770	353,136	352,527	269,992
West Virginia.............	2,093,253	1,021,365	1,071,888	8,624	N.A.	102,181	309,274	9,537	188,412	107,609	346,251
Wisconsin..................	5,621,037	3,899,395	1,721,642	48,071	362	138,388	935,953	1,804	286,063	307,425	3,576
Wyoming....................	574,004	462,842	111,162	1,332	N.A.	18,034	69,975	227	3,016	18,578	N.A.

Source: Population Division, U.S. Census Bureau, released December 22, 2005.
Key:
N.A.—not applicable
* U.S. Totals, includes the 50 state governments and does not include the District of Columbia or any local government.

Table 7.22
STATE GOVERNMENT LICENSE TAX REVENUE: 2004
(In thousands of dollars)

State	Total license revenue	Alcoholic beverages	Amusements	Corporation	Hunting and fishing	Motor vehicle operators	Motor vehicle	Public utility	Occupation and business, NEC	Other licenses
United States	39,626,991	385,659	232,062	6,339,371	1,233,754	17,299,372	1,982,746	510,213	10,881,425	762,389
Alabama	397,429	2,491	N.A.	73,183	14,700	172,815	16,712	10,344	107,177	7
Alaska	83,738	1,829	1	1,319	23,713	43,782	N.A.	281	9,090	3,723
Arizona	289,803	3,732	28	14,048	18,253	161,398	16,069	N.A.	63,308	12,967
Arkansas	187,876	1,652	2,162	8,595	21,246	109,831	15,875	2,271	20,779	5,465
California	5,744,089	43,841	5,191	70,580	83,013	2,155,042	187,395	124,000	3,062,827	12,200
Colorado	337,911	5,632	752	7,232	66,073	192,923	14,293	N.A.	50,297	709
Connecticut	385,265	6,092	66	15,747	4,049	197,418	38,204	311	118,424	4,954
Delaware	882,389	614	380	568,190	1,036	33,592	205	4,046	220,992	53,334
Florida	1,774,881	34,492	4,583	161,423	14,520	1,124,851	151,774	27,727	255,501	10
Georgia	617,663	2,331	N.A.	53,227	24,020	279,991	36,907	N.A.	117,376	103,811
Hawaii	123,257	N.A.	N.A.	2,114	275	89,268	189	10,450	19,484	1,477
Idaho	220,800	1,309	398	1,754	29,455	107,269	7,042	28,350	42,094	3,129
Illinois	2,385,596	10,838	2,163	169,444	30,025	1,370,405	77,409	N.A.	718,979	6,328
Indiana	448,387	9,648	4,049	5,298	17,119	158,542	211,999	N.A.	40,284	1,448
Iowa	575,515	8,710	17,401	38,999	24,693	377,672	19,100	10,951	75,977	2,012
Kansas	274,619	2,460	219	47,170	18,241	161,497	14,841	4,914	22,510	2,767
Kentucky	542,480	5,104	3,828	198,245	21,345	205,314	11,205	8,192	85,419	3,828
Louisiana	429,068	N.A.	N.A.	186,912	27,507	114,090	11,236	8,726	76,956	3,641
Maine	158,199	3,090	775	3,600	12,144	81,740	7,109	N.A.	49,464	277
Maryland	511,559	960	31	53,264	11,920	282,167	29,065	N.A.	131,948	2,204
Massachusetts	664,556	2,937	445	25,575	6,686	292,688	90,605	N.A.	140,493	105,127
Michigan	1,545,457	13,079	N.A.	19,344	48,304	1,064,774	66,634	15,389	171,844	146,089
Minnesota	941,783	1,039	727	6,814	56,535	517,447	37,952	N.A.	283,517	37,752
Mississippi	318,488	2,346	3,825	89,763	12,833	117,892	22,763	N.A.	59,525	9,541
Missouri	605,590	3,885	62	90,862	30,349	254,740	16,559	19,990	135,328	53,814
Montana	233,372	1,975	4,884	1,112	37,208	144,651	5,082	5	37,855	599
Nebraska	201,921	285	N.A.	6,731	13,770	88,780	8,210	N.A.	63,980	20,165
Nevada	623,400	N.A.	95,668	52,760	7,171	139,467	14,546	N.A.	308,850	4,938
New Hampshire	199,170	17,514	354	4,041	9,031	84,431	13,051	6,510	61,597	2,641
New Jersey	1,177,242	3,960	66,430	249,862	12,162	398,691	34,669	621	407,712	3,028
New Mexico	169,805	963	258	2,651	17,126	121,246	5,855	55	21,575	76
New York	1,193,019	46,000	47	57,682	4,293	679,515	227,424	23,081	146,388	8,589
North Carolina	1,017,247	13,796	N.A.	337,741	14,891	440,180	75,371	N.A.	131,728	3,540
North Dakota	118,377	259	452	N.A.	12,838	54,707	3,889	6	46,226	N.A.
Ohio	1,813,479	29,843	N.A.	297,031	30,826	713,149	67,504	3,169	666,510	5,447
Oklahoma	840,421	5,204	4,731	41,960	21,571	552,799	14,039	3	199,713	401
Oregon	651,016	2,610	798	4,257	39,882	418,903	31,752	12,010	131,592	9,212
Pennsylvania	2,547,850	14,765	101	787,502	64,809	792,430	60,210	50,762	763,240	14,031
Rhode Island	94,481	99	403	3,982	1,881	56,986	577	N.A.	30,031	522
South Carolina	383,505	8,076	2,198	72,898	19,275	122,056	36,094	N.A.	113,236	9,672

See footnotes at end of table.

STATE GOVERNMENT LICENSE TAX REVENUE: 2004
(In thousands of dollars) — Continued

State	Total license revenue	Alcoholic beverages	Amusements	Corporation	Hunting and fishing	Motor vehicle operators	Motor vehicle	Public utility	Occupation and business, NEC	Other licenses
South Dakota.............	138,877	296	134	2,718	22,129	42,167	1,875	892	57,993	10,673
Tennessee.................	1,045,665	2,444	785	506,776	24,997	255,137	41,737	6,221	203,248	4,320
Texas	4,083,148	38,515	6,923	1,896,287	79,988	1,232,494	96,199	17,343	681,645	33,754
Utah	156,999	1,147	N.A.	2,628	20,674	92,802	9,233	N.A.	27,232	3,283
Vermont...................	98,758	520	143	4,604	6,105	62,566	4,175	N.A.	18,873	1,772
Virginia....................	613,910	8,209	57	46,342	20,145	340,085	45,826	N.A.	147,815	5,431
Washington..............	686,564	10,045	75	18,616	30,399	334,244	47,812	14,848	190,476	40,049
West Virginia...........	179,107	10,489	12	8,033	15,933	83,663	3,808	17,158	39,790	221
Wisconsin.................	811,548	527	523	14,016	60,795	330,291	30,759	81,587	289,639	3,411
Wyoming..................	101,712	5	N.A.	6,327	27,801	50,784	1,907	N.A.	14,888	N.A.

Source: Population Division, U.S. Census Bureau, released December 22, 2005.
Key:
N.A.—not applicable
* U.S. Totals, includes the 50 state governments and does not include the District of Columbia or any local government.

Table 7.23
FISCAL YEAR, POPULATION AND PERSONAL INCOME, BY STATE

State	Date of close of fiscal year in 2003	Total population (excluding armed forces overseas) (in thousands)			Personal income, calendar year 2003		Personal income, calendar year 2002	
		July 1, 2003	July 1, 2002	July 1, 2001	Amount (in millions)	Per capita (in dollars)	Amount (in millions)	Per capita (in dollars)
United States		290,231	287,405	284,533	$9,124,680	$31,439	$8,873,371	$30,874
Alabama	September 30	4,504	4,479	4,468	119,373	26,504	114,428	25,548
Alaska	June 30	648	641	632	21,531	33,227	21,040	32,824
Arizona	June 30	5,579	5,441	5,297	151,933	27,233	143,429	26,361
Arkansas..............	June 30	2,728	2,706	2,692	66,515	24,382	63,750	23,559
California	June 30	35,463	35,002	34,532	1,184,997	33,415	1,154,685	32,989
Colorado..............	June 30	4,548	4,501	4,427	157,171	34,558	151,790	33,724
Connecticut	June 30	3,487	3,459	3,433	149,843	42,972	146,881	42,463
Delaware..............	June 30	818	806	796	27,981	34,207	25,862	32,087
Florida	June 30	16,999	16,692	16,354	511,641	30,098	496,706	29,757
Georgia	June 30	8,676	8,544	8,391	251,621	29,002	246,247	28,821
Hawaii.................	June 30	1,249	1,241	1,222	38,013	30,435	37,064	29,866
Idaho...................	June 30	1,367	1,343	1,321	35,409	25,903	34,217	25,478
Illinois.................	June 30	12,649	12,586	12,518	416,978	32,965	416,018	33,054
Indiana................	June 30	6,200	6,157	6,128	178,786	28,836	172,592	28,032
Iowa	June 30	2,942	2,936	2,932	83,375	28,340	82,465	28,088
Kansas	June 30	2,725	2,712	2,701	80,213	29,436	78,382	28,902
Kentucky	June 30	4,118	4,090	4,068	109,442	26,576	104,264	25,492
Louisiana	June 30	4,494	4,476	4,467	118,236	26,310	113,231	25,297
Maine	June 30	1,309	1,295	1,287	38,181	29,168	36,307	28,036
Maryland..............	June 30	5,512	5,451	5,379	206,412	37,448	197,869	36,300
Massachusetts.......	June 30	6,420	6,422	6,395	253,632	39,507	250,994	39,083
Michigan..............	September 30	10,082	10,043	10,005	314,346	31,179	299,449	29,817
Minnesota	June 30	5,064	5,025	4,986	172,337	34,032	167,434	33,320
Mississippi	June 30	2,883	2,867	2,858	67,643	23,463	64,645	22,548
Missouri...............	June 30	5,719	5,670	5,643	168,512	29,465	161,648	28,509
Montana	June 30	918	910	906	23,327	25,411	22,606	24,842
Nebraska..............	June 30	1,737	1,728	1,719	52,436	30,188	50,414	29,175
Nevada	June 30	2,242	2,167	2,095	71,549	31,913	66,235	30,565
New Hampshire....	June 30	1,289	1,274	1,259	45,286	35,133	43,310	33,995
New Jersey............	June 30	8,642	8,575	8,506	342,040	39,579	338,388	39,462
New Mexico	June 30	1,879	1,852	1,832	46,955	24,989	45,974	24,824
New York	March 31	19,212	19,134	19,086	693,791	36,112	685,110	35,806
North Carolina......	June 30	8,421	8,306	8,198	236,391	28,072	230,777	27,784
North Dakota........	June 30	633	634	636	18,319	28,940	17,022	26,849
Ohio	June 30	11,438	11,409	11,388	344,603	30,128	333,079	29,194
Oklahoma	June 30	3,506	3,490	3,467	93,691	26,723	90,508	25,934
Oregon	June 30	3,564	3,520	3,474	102,419	28,737	101,359	28,795
Pennsylvania	June 30	12,371	12,329	12,298	394,761	31,910	383,618	31,115
Rhode Island	June 30	1,076	1,068	1,059	34,476	32,041	32,967	30,868
South Carolina	June 30	4,149	4,104	4,061	108,463	26,142	104,653	25,500
South Dakota........	June 30	765	760	758	22,072	28,852	20,507	26,983
Tennessee	June 30	5,845	5,790	5,748	167,415	28,642	159,865	27,611
Texas	August 31	22,103	21,737	21,335	642,630	29,074	631,208	29,038
Utah	June 30	2,352	2,319	2,281	59,761	25,409	57,134	24,637
Vermont	June 30	619	616	613	19,131	30,906	18,347	29,784
Virginia................	June 30	7,365	7,288	7,186	248,432	33,731	238,991	32,792
Washington..........	June 30	6,131	6,067	5,993	203,890	33,256	198,018	32,639
West Virginia........	June 30	1,811	1,805	1,802	44,456	24,548	42,945	23,792
Wisconsin.............	June 30	5,474	5,440	5,406	167,979	30,687	163,464	30,049
Wyoming..............	June 30	502	499	494	16,285	32,440	15,474	31,010

Source: Population Estimates Program, Population Division, U.S. Bureau of the Census, Washington, D.C. 20233. Personal Income from Survey of Current Business (Oct 2003), BEA

Contact: Statistical Information Staff, Population Division, U.S. Bureau of the Census, (301) 457-2422.
Key:
. . . — Not applicable

Table 7.24
SUMMARY OF FINANCIAL AGGREGATES, BY STATE: 2003
(In millions of dollars)

State	Revenue Total	Revenue General	Revenue Utilities and liquor store	Revenue Insurance trust	Expenditure Total	Expenditure General	Expenditure Utilities and liquor store	Expenditure Insurance trust	Total debt outstanding at end of fiscal year	Total cash and security holdings at end of fiscal year
United States	$1,296,701	$1,113,391	$17,036	$166,274	$1,358,965	$1,163,885	$26,101	$168,979	$697,929	$2,594,116
Alabama	19,099	16,575	168	2,356	18,471	17,010	173	1,288	6,285	28,661
Alaska	6,924	6,099	16	810	8,122	7,112	62	948	5,830	42,721
Arizona	17,927	16,890	25	1,012	19,606	17,503	29	2,074	5,554	34,307
Arkansas.................	11,805	10,731	0	1,075	12,085	11,081	0	1,004	3,295	17,000
California	195,545	147,998	4,603	42,944	204,439	173,158	5,126	26,155	95,210	382,874
Colorado	13,806	13,999	9	-202	17,691	14,793	12	2,887	8,921	39,820
Connecticut	18,241	16,217	22	2,002	20,721	17,885	309	2,527	22,490	31,425
Delaware.................	5,041	4,721	9	310	4,858	4,376	87	395	4,358	10,615
Florida	55,213	49,584	18	5,610	56,317	50,218	58	6,041	21,993	138,711
Georgia	29,874	26,320	0	3,554	32,527	29,291	0	3,236	8,890	61,859
Hawaii.....................	6,808	6,378	0	431	7,611	6,852	0	759	5,653	13,312
Idaho......................	5,493	4,617	69	807	5,415	4,760	54	602	2,603	10,509
Illinois....................	44,423	40,816	0	3,607	51,291	43,954	0	7,337	46,689	87,545
Indiana....................	24,553	21,675	0	2,879	23,090	21,295	31	1,764	11,854	33,491
Iowa	12,973	11,097	123	1,753	13,088	11,715	85	1,289	4,279	25,148
Kansas	10,402	9,752	0	650	10,954	9,843	0	1,111	2,472	12,194
Kentucky	18,377	16,526	0	1,852	19,117	16,858	0	2,259	7,109	32,922
Louisiana	19,438	18,276	5	1,157	18,681	16,323	9	2,350	9,773	36,969
Maine......................	6,801	6,093	86	622	6,706	6,072	60	574	4,418	11,980
Maryland.................	21,801	20,539	98	1,165	24,592	21,789	487	2,316	12,951	40,694
Massachusetts.........	30,371	27,012	121	3,238	32,710	27,871	289	4,551	48,479	59,207
Michigan.................	50,077	43,010	638	6,428	51,016	44,522	521	5,973	22,479	65,432
Minnesota	25,596	23,073	0	2,524	28,899	25,384	112	3,403	7,150	50,296
Mississippi	13,393	11,873	184	1,336	13,503	12,095	149	1,259	4,167	22,100
Missouri..................	22,024	19,135	0	2,889	21,566	19,137	0	2,429	13,855	49,559
Montana	4,608	3,968	47	593	4,437	3,917	40	480	2,879	9,802
Nebraska.................	7,285	6,750	0	535	6,824	6,494	0	330	2,136	8,610
Nevada....................	8,351	6,549	146	1,657	7,817	6,706	150	961	3,604	19,162
New Hampshire.......	5,207	4,566	347	293	5,277	4,592	299	386	5,594	8,837
New Jersey..............	46,078	38,820	580	6,679	44,948	34,860	2,370	7,718	33,609	84,401
New Mexico.............	9,848	9,007	0	840	10,673	9,714	0	959	4,601	29,827
New York	118,275	98,842	5,499	13,934	127,475	101,825	11,559	14,091	91,635	229,311
North Carolina	30,043	30,171	0	-128	34,361	30,428	20	3,913	12,142	65,592
North Dakota..........	4,402	4,078	0	324	4,268	4,044	0	224	1,599	6,805
Ohio	49,905	42,422	545	6,937	56,392	44,614	350	11,429	21,054	143,620
Oklahoma	14,919	12,903	316	1,699	15,125	13,306	298	1,521	6,747	24,654
Oregon	19,252	13,283	270	5,700	18,006	14,130	141	3,734	7,464	50,893
Pennsylvania	49,459	46,905	1,014	1,541	57,429	48,253	990	8,186	24,330	93,430
Rhode Island	5,856	5,172	18	666	5,977	5,027	100	850	6,189	10,762
South Carolina	19,669	15,409	1,033	3,227	21,040	17,685	1,193	2,162	10,990	28,498
South Dakota..........	3,000	2,683	0	317	2,898	2,663	0	235	2,567	8,593
Tennessee	20,564	19,278	0	1,286	21,022	19,387	6	1,630	3,496	28,066
Texas	82,621	66,458	0	16,164	76,386	66,804	0	9,583	14,616	181,581
Utah	11,534	8,759	134	2,642	9,022	7,946	100	976	5,064	16,919
Vermont	3,639	3,352	35	252	3,859	3,594	43	222	2,532	4,917
Virginia...................	28,185	25,528	368	2,290	29,129	26,289	336	2,504	13,530	50,836
Washington.............	29,661	24,134	384	5,144	32,600	26,021	357	6,222	14,621	59,772
West Virginia..........	9,766	8,317	56	1,394	10,004	7,998	56	1,950	4,261	10,381
Wisconsin................	25,165	23,433	0	1,732	27,658	23,813	0	3,845	14,801	69,017
Wyoming.................	3,403	3,603	52	-252	3,264	2,881	46	337	1,111	10,480

Source: U.S. Department of Commerce, Bureau of the Census, January 2003. Released March 2006.

Note: Detail may not add to total due to rounding. Data presented are statistical in nature and do not represent an accounting statement. Therefore, a difference between an individual government's total revenue and expenditure does not necessarily indicate a budget surplus or deficit.

Table 7.25
NATIONAL TOTALS OF STATE GOVERNMENT FINANCES FOR SELECTED YEARS: 2001–2003

Item	2003	2002	2001	Per capita 2003	Per capita 2002	Per capita 2000	Percent change 2002–2003	Percent change 2001–2002
Population (in thousands)...............	290,231	287,405	284,744					
Revenue total	$1,295,658,820	$1,096,347,277	$1,180,305,168	$4,464	$3,820	$4,486	12.4	-4.8
General revenue.............................	1,112,349,024	1,060,822,965	1,049,297,849	3,833	3,697	3,504	22.8	17.2
Taxes	548,990,867	534,063,430	559,679,125	1,892	1,863	1,920	9.8	7.1
Intergovernmental revenue	361,617,049	335,422,978	305,620,837	1,246	1,167	977	42.5	32.2
From Federal Government	343,307,800	317,581,354	288,308,607	1,183	1,105	922	43.7	32.9
Public welfare	196,954,235	181,516,646	165,800,087	679	632	525	45.6	34.2
Education	56,361,735	51,103,376	45,760,336	194	178	150	45.5	31.9
Highways	29,481,357	29,641,477	27,894,263	102	103	83	41.2	42.0
Employment security administration	5,026,880	4,168,288	3,645,033	17	15	14	27.5	5.7
Other	55,483,593	51,151,567	45,208,888	191	178	150	38.3	27.5
From local government	18,309,249	17,841,624	17,312,230	63	62	55	24.1	21.0
Charges and miscellaneous revenue	201,741,108	191,336,557	183,997,887	695	667	607	32.3	25.7
Liquor stores revenue	4,517,992	4,287,846	4,091,986	16	15	14	25.5	19.1
Utility revenue	12,517,945	11,935,400	6,930,060	43	42	16	187.3	174.0
Insurance trust revenue..................	166,273,859	19,301,066	119,985,273	573	67	953	-30.4	-91.9
Employee retirement	110,838,528	-25,244,197	79,526,570	382	-88	820	-45.0	-112.5
Unemployment compensation	35,190,504	26,959,673	23,221,445	121	94	83	59.0	21.8
Worker compensation..................	16,122,680	13,624,173	13,103,030	56	47	42	24.8	5.5
Other.....................................	4,122,147	3,961,417	4,134,228	14	14	8	79.9	72.9
Expenditure and debt redemption	1,426,714,871	1,335,230,625	1,235,568,426	4,916	4,645	4,028	36.4	27.6
Debt redemption..........................	67,666,492	54,820,936	49,460,012	233	190	172	41.4	14.2
Expenditure total	1,359,048,379	1,280,409,689	1,186,108,414	4,683	4,455	3,856	36.1	28.2
General expenditure.......................	1,163,968,202	1,109,346,913	1,045,296,043	4,010	3,860	3,432	30.9	24.7
Education.....................................	411,093,625	389,390,099	374,443,539	1,416	1,355	1,238	29.0	22.2
Intergovernmental expenditure...	240,408,489	227,336,087	222,092,587	828	791	742	24.9	18.1
State institutions of higher education	145,941,224	139,745,935	131,679,610	503	486	432	32.9	27.3
Other education........................	265,152,401	249,644,164	242,763,929	914	869	805	27.0	19.6
Public welfare.............................	314,406,504	287,015,523	262,346,226	1,083	999	850	42.2	29.8
Intergovernmental expenditure	49,301,258	47,112,496	41,926,990	170	164	144	26.6	21.0
Cash assistance, categorical program...............	9,487,944	9,233,827	9,903,374	33	32	35	-12.5	-14.8
Cash assistance, other	1,993,148	1,417,080	1,322,567	7	5	5	52.6	8.5
Other public welfare	302,925,412	276,364,616	251,120,285	1,044	962	809	44.9	32.2
Highways....................................	85,726,099	84,197,951	78,785,864	295	293	264	25.5	23.2
Intergovernmental expenditure	13,271,218	12,949,850	12,350,136	46	45	44	9.9	7.2
Regular state highway facilities	78,142,687	77,295,568	72,726,624	269	269	245	22.3	21.0
State toll highways/facilities......	7,583,412	6,902,383	6,059,240	26	24	19	70.9	55.6
Health and hospitals	88,615,522	87,685,190	78,270,107	305	305	266	30.3	28.9
State hospitals and institutions for handicapped	37,874,685	36,864,020	34,031,665	130	128	114	28.6	25.2
Other	520,199	528,621	506,735	2	2	2	-5.1	-3.6
Natural resources...........................	18,576,793	17,821,117	17,308,799	64	62	57	28.3	23.1
Corrections	39,187,839	38,918,307	38,164,541	135	135	125	19.3	18.5
Financial administration...............	20,805,632	19,193,207	17,297,856	72	66	58	34.0	22.9
Employment security administration	5,258,083	5,072,948	4,354,992	18	18	15	27.5	23.0
Police protection..........................	11,144,395	10,705,936	10,144,976	38	37	35	26.7	21.7
Interest on general debt	31,294,763	31,426,313	30,451,772	108	109	104	12.6	13.1
Veterans' services	1,016,563	361,190	336,520	4	1	1	258.9	27.5
Utility expenditure.........................	22,404,931	20,278,852	18,632,043	77	71	38	155.2	131.0
Insurance trust expenditure.............	168,978,731	147,285,899	118,833,109	582	513	375	73.9	51.6
Employee retirement	103,048,619	91,971,465	83,770,450	355	320	271	53.0	36.6
Unemployment compensation......	51,410,604	42,016,889	22,920,255	177	146	66	168.3	119.3
Other......................................	14,519,508	13,297,545	12,142,404	50	46	30	36.6	25.1

NATIONAL TOTALS OF STATE GOVERNMENT FINANCES FOR SELECTED YEARS: 2001–2003—Continued

Item	2003	2002	2001	Per capita 2003	Per capita 2002	Per capita 2000	Percent change 2002–2003	Percent change 2001–2002
Total expenditure by character								
and object....................................	1,359,048,379	1,280,409,689	1,186,108,414	4,683	$4,455	$3,856	36.1	28.2
Direct expenditure	976,851,809	915,620,209	835,781,868	3,366	3,186	2,690	40.9	32.0
Current operation	656,989,385	620,882,668	580,373,943	2,264	2,160	1,858	37.7	30.1
Capital outlay	91,942,748	89,918,425	81,881,058	317	313	270	34.2	31.3
Construction............................	72,374,446	71,034,814	64,668,030	249	247	213	34.4	31.9
Other capital outlay structures	19,568,302	18,883,611	17,213,028	67	66	57	33.6	28.9
Assistance and subsidies	25,900,969	24,313,447	23,495,900	89	85	79	16.5	9.4
Interest on debt............................	33,039,976	33,219,770	31,197,858	114	116	107	15.6	16.2
Insurance benefits								
and repayments	168,978,731	147,285,899	118,833,109	582	513	375	73.9	51.6
Intergovernmental expenditure.......	382,196,570	364,789,480	350,326,546	1,317	1,269	1,167	25.3	19.6
Cash and security holdings								
at end of fiscal year.....................	2,594,215,994	2,534,028,608	2,537,722,111	8,938	8,818	8,972	14.5	11.8
Insurance trust................................	1,859,116,896	1,841,239,368	1,857,741,551	6,406	6,407	6,638	12.2	11.1
Unemployment fund balance	28,795,978	44,546,198	52,164,412	99	155	195	-40.4	-7.7
Debt offsets....................................	315,588,433	305,728,839	285,380,813	1,087	1,064	980	22.2	18.3

Source: U.S. Department of Commerce, Bureau of the Census, January 2002. Released March 2006.

Table 7.26
STATE GENERAL REVENUE, BY SOURCE AND BY STATE: 2003 (In thousands of dollars)

State	Total general revenue (a)	Taxes Total	Sales and gross receipts Total (b)	General	Motor fuels	Licenses Total (b)	Motor vehicle	Individual income	Corporation net income	Intergovernmental revenue	Charges and miscellaneous general revenue
United States	$1,113,391,406	$548,990,867	$273,811,221	$184,596,707	$32,269,077	$35,863,173	$16,009,467	$181,932,513	$28,384,474	$362,519,737	$201,880,802
Alabama	16,574,756	6,416,251	3,350,223	1,764,557	516,858	399,871	184,196	2,035,538	242,411	6,668,784	3,489,621
Alaska	6,098,669	1,120,133	152,132	0	37,353	70,107	31,419	0	207,075	1,997,175	2,981,361
Arizona	16,890,346	8,691,761	5,511,479	4,332,982	642,050	271,023	155,124	2,102,361	389,406	6,092,557	2,106,028
Arkansas	10,730,541	5,145,554	2,657,867	1,951,630	431,449	206,286	119,535	1,528,231	176,875	3,685,249	1,899,738
California	147,998,249	79,198,255	31,914,035	24,899,025	3,202,511	4,916,856	1,827,556	32,709,761	6,803,559	48,245,951	20,554,043
Colorado	13,998,588	6,636,190	2,793,901	1,833,200	578,754	315,096	181,149	3,235,796	199,853	4,178,537	3,183,861
Connecticut	16,216,542	9,508,645	4,790,870	3,065,486	450,330	387,546	216,705	3,639,362	344,684	4,020,036	2,687,861
Delaware	4,721,118	2,116,458	326,552	0	107,268	755,354	31,707	710,304	208,283	994,952	1,609,708
Florida	49,584,279	26,993,487	20,575,312	14,963,444	1,909,506	1,756,585	1,085,628	0	1,226,980	12,850,982	9,739,810
Georgia	26,320,141	13,411,632	6,027,411	4,770,869	678,115	452,513	222,207	6,271,374	484,139	9,028,114	3,880,395
Hawaii	6,377,451	3,569,824	2,349,595	1,792,698	80,194	124,430	87,245	1,037,854	30,603	1,537,997	1,269,630
Idaho	4,616,599	2,344,344	1,167,477	842,006	211,278	221,200	106,080	843,780	93,490	1,455,705	816,550
Illinois	40,815,713	22,211,693	11,385,175	6,558,746	1,388,323	1,845,165	1,262,085	7,340,982	1,293,188	12,027,338	6,576,682
Indiana	21,674,754	11,216,456	6,224,623	4,210,262	750,089	415,373	140,574	3,644,159	729,164	6,346,679	4,111,619
Iowa	11,096,904	4,922,455	2,368,986	1,589,917	348,520	537,574	366,609	1,791,129	140,031	3,534,400	2,640,049
Kansas	9,752,078	5,008,411	2,664,383	1,888,543	411,458	256,372	155,959	1,776,884	124,519	3,266,719	1,476,948
Kentucky	16,525,770	8,318,707	3,883,845	2,387,206	469,944	536,797	186,500	2,813,947	369,572	5,330,212	2,876,851
Louisiana	18,276,111	7,449,507	4,374,737	2,488,627	555,621	426,741	112,287	1,867,150	198,716	6,501,978	4,324,626
Maine	6,093,384	2,697,275	1,281,442	857,495	194,472	150,171	79,001	1,074,826	91,188	2,062,560	1,333,549
Maryland	20,538,540	10,980,324	4,864,474	2,720,162	716,686	440,705	260,438	4,681,860	379,020	5,829,817	3,728,399
Massachusetts	27,012,438	15,608,027	5,410,920	3,708,069	676,426	597,079	307,874	8,026,149	1,184,610	5,130,127	6,274,284
Michigan	43,010,240	22,748,159	10,194,232	7,685,308	1,100,931	1,339,579	905,923	6,519,643	1,843,072	12,221,555	8,040,526
Minnesota	23,072,489	13,981,287	6,065,761	3,903,717	638,722	909,927	513,330	5,374,550	596,584	5,982,225	3,108,977
Mississippi	11,873,033	4,999,144	3,304,878	2,459,984	416,277	314,482	117,185	1,020,028	288,778	5,086,417	1,787,472
Missouri	19,135,079	8,627,396	4,226,396	2,819,814	705,019	562,934	246,371	3,519,844	205,729	7,172,806	3,334,877
Montana	3,967,788	1,487,019	385,840	0	192,770	207,449	130,830	535,830	44,137	1,582,665	898,104
Nebraska	6,749,800	3,347,700	1,886,726	1,426,914	307,181	199,584	87,405	1,122,893	111,597	2,139,810	1,262,290
Nevada	6,548,496	4,129,137	3,501,965	2,192,321	265,846	449,224	130,064	0	0	1,498,008	921,351
New Hampshire	4,566,307	1,959,211	632,757	0	125,614	192,420	81,188	55,118	396,162	1,464,454	1,142,642
New Jersey	38,819,455	19,935,266	9,021,440	5,936,057	530,957	1,169,923	410,037	6,735,282	2,397,043	9,064,614	9,818,575
New Mexico	9,007,272	3,607,156	1,873,420	1,368,200	207,094	152,092	114,543	923,113	101,546	3,220,765	2,179,351
New York	98,842,100	42,253,291	15,145,453	8,841,872	546,846	1,043,227	685,740	22,648,364	2,089,104	43,442,351	13,146,458
North Carolina	30,171,034	15,848,650	6,752,122	4,005,124	1,156,905	937,372	416,199	7,089,142	898,369	10,278,725	4,043,659
North Dakota	4,077,908	1,177,727	649,606	360,831	114,409	102,750	52,712	199,390	55,989	2,030,717	869,464
Ohio	42,422,137	20,651,597	10,091,149	6,761,515	1,456,148	1,701,782	617,089	7,916,410	794,645	14,058,065	7,712,475

See footnotes at end of table.

STATE GENERAL REVENUE, BY SOURCE AND BY STATE: 2003 (In thousands of dollars)—Continued

State	Total general revenue (a)	Taxes Total	Sales and gross receipts Total (b)	General	Motor fuels	Licenses Total (b)	Motor vehicle	Individual income	Corporation net income	Intergovernmental revenue	Charges and miscellaneous general revenue
Oklahoma	12,903,184	5,905,884	2,238,817	1,480,137	406,052	785,044	522,798	2,113,947	104,448	4,255,172	2,742,128
Oregon	13,282,526	5,701,691	746,272	0	419,329	576,207	366,380	4,023,579	225,501	4,215,696	3,365,139
Pennsylvania	46,904,770	23,187,302	11,972,007	7,561,149	1,767,817	2,213,875	788,763	6,661,780	1,189,314	14,466,919	9,250,549
Rhode Island	5,171,932	2,256,654	1,233,877	764,217	138,781	93,032	53,439	824,870	67,118	1,855,350	1,059,928
South Carolina	15,408,525	6,353,115	3,431,009	2,555,851	373,814	325,511	103,447	2,334,066	173,886	5,738,966	3,316,444
South Dakota	2,682,852	1,012,955	811,176	539,396	131,133	127,683	40,860	0	43,976	1,111,450	558,447
Tennessee	19,278,302	8,811,612	6,860,749	5,414,674	815,210	953,999	240,933	115,593	612,943	8,292,209	2,174,481
Texas	66,457,732	29,098,584	23,360,935	14,347,144	2,839,858	3,980,083	1,016,922	0	0	24,349,595	13,009,553
Utah	8,758,929	3,954,815	2,014,484	1,485,977	333,161	148,835	88,229	1,572,512	148,218	2,493,503	2,310,611
Vermont	3,352,248	1,558,712	547,462	220,827	72,164	102,721	57,651	411,343	41,641	1,152,305	641,231
Virginia	25,528,061	12,969,177	4,762,982	2,692,151	865,248	588,665	340,399	6,775,746	328,444	5,679,471	6,879,413
Washington	24,133,548	12,960,220	10,103,404	8,007,337	752,392	671,917	330,421	0	0	7,012,389	4,160,939
West Virginia	8,316,567	3,593,993	1,953,313	978,022	286,018	186,386	88,967	1,055,523	182,364	2,975,382	1,747,192
Wisconsin	23,433,155	12,089,770	5,450,900	3,738,000	884,738	645,311	292,042	5,252,500	526,500	7,094,092	4,249,293
Wyoming	3,602,966	1,217,154	516,650	425,244	61,438	98,315	49,722	0	0	1,798,192	587,620

Source: U.S. Department of Commerce, Bureau of the Census, January 2003. Released March 2006

Note: Detail may not add to total due to rounding.

(a) Total general revenue equals total taxes plus intergovernmental revenue plus charges and miscellaneous revenue.
(b) Total includes other taxes not shown separately in this table.

Table 7.27
STATE EXPENDITURE, BY CHARACTER AND OBJECT AND BY STATE: 2003 (In thousands of dollars)

State	Intergovernmental expenditures	Total	Direct expenditures Current operation	Capital outlay Total	Capital outlay Construction	Capital outlay Other	Assistance and subsidies	Interest on debt	Insurance benefits and repayments	Exhibit: Total salaries and wages
United States	$382,781,397	$976,183,468	$656,089,768	$92,186,403	$72,609,708	$19,576,695	$25,888,450	$33,040,116	$168,978,731	$183,385,651
Alabama	4,074,005	14,397,105	10,379,978	1,473,974	1,192,193	281,781	1,002,597	252,401	1,288,155	3,299,406
Alaska	1,091,391	7,030,149	4,733,293	934,820	826,656	108,164	149,123	265,237	947,676	1,165,806
Arizona	6,936,753	12,669,264	8,825,995	1,241,058	1,019,327	221,731	331,701	196,092	2,074,418	2,632,816
Arkansas	3,210,582	8,874,236	6,563,752	954,604	858,642	95,962	237,342	115,076	1,003,462	1,489,802
California	84,468,847	119,969,614	81,879,249	6,091,850	4,524,255	1,567,595	1,842,062	4,001,753	26,154,700	20,385,549
Colorado	4,666,350	13,024,575	8,333,398	1,209,265	1,086,321	122,944	170,852	424,283	2,886,777	2,841,045
Connecticut	3,030,485	17,690,709	11,923,834	1,585,401	1,271,988	313,413	413,465	1,240,680	2,527,329	3,056,867
Delaware	903,476	3,954,425	2,761,452	471,112	360,107	111,005	73,892	253,383	394,586	1,750,026
Florida	14,460,722	41,856,609	28,408,648	5,227,276	4,001,068	1,226,208	1,163,059	1,016,285	6,041,341	6,719,508
Georgia	9,016,458	23,510,366	16,188,708	2,752,260	2,268,991	483,269	903,832	429,906	3,235,660	4,072,334
Hawaii	125,434	7,485,852	5,599,621	654,432	559,078	95,354	118,970	353,448	759,381	1,972,441
Idaho	1,449,076	3,966,062	2,653,561	449,761	377,584	72,177	118,952	141,690	602,098	806,729
Illinois	13,369,662	37,921,428	23,627,136	3,637,228	3,168,897	468,331	1,248,491	2,071,586	7,336,987	5,492,804
Indiana	6,760,945	16,328,995	12,176,868	1,534,104	1,297,702	236,402	406,708	447,431	1,763,884	3,335,114
Iowa	3,442,552	9,645,448	6,887,136	1,074,918	944,049	130,869	272,050	122,471	1,288,873	2,440,167
Kansas	2,925,220	8,028,791	5,663,264	869,012	756,823	112,189	256,911	128,976	1,110,628	1,605,346
Kentucky	3,693,634	15,423,182	10,564,278	1,706,778	1,413,254	293,524	456,684	436,241	2,259,201	3,034,764
Louisiana	4,329,053	14,352,261	9,375,738	1,469,143	1,102,941	366,202	586,638	570,949	2,349,793	3,683,276
Maine	1,051,164	5,654,952	4,264,824	384,445	310,022	74,423	197,322	233,917	574,444	796,528
Maryland	5,358,342	19,233,786	13,588,358	1,801,019	1,544,862	256,157	668,085	860,049	2,316,275	4,072,059
Massachusetts	6,435,841	26,274,594	15,374,587	3,218,802	2,890,529	328,273	599,566	2,530,478	4,551,161	4,143,111
Michigan	19,851,778	31,164,502	21,540,679	1,828,224	1,309,912	518,312	777,955	1,044,621	5,973,023	6,745,547
Minnesota	9,618,471	19,280,043	13,352,931	1,374,433	991,298	383,135	763,675	385,954	3,403,050	3,938,713
Mississippi	3,665,580	9,837,305	7,263,115	951,104	768,473	182,631	164,132	199,916	1,259,038	1,819,086
Missouri	5,159,094	16,407,103	11,063,929	1,712,778	1,298,247	414,531	596,467	604,950	2,428,979	3,078,519
Montana	938,000	3,498,890	2,349,347	468,124	409,826	58,298	76,440	125,218	479,761	716,005
Nebraska	1,784,749	5,039,100	3,887,592	594,969	516,427	78,542	119,341	107,132	330,066	1,819,583
Nevada	2,648,660	5,167,821	3,481,697	488,663	415,969	72,694	99,343	136,806	961,312	1,220,624
New Hampshire	1,283,091	3,993,375	2,846,144	348,795	254,553	94,242	102,268	310,212	385,956	746,377
New Jersey	8,997,417	35,950,181	22,852,847	3,815,532	2,946,561	868,971	405,566	1,157,886	7,718,350	3,006,554
New Mexico	2,951,328	7,721,275	5,853,821	432,775	325,390	107,385	300,597	175,261	958,821	1,694,661
New York	40,874,514	86,600,719	56,424,800	10,405,974	6,220,985	4,184,989	1,174,490	4,504,681	14,090,774	14,726,908
North Carolina	10,356,152	24,004,825	16,677,794	2,462,686	1,954,805	507,881	504,697	446,717	3,912,931	5,762,164
North Dakota	1,190,923	3,077,116	2,205,024	537,225	490,571	46,654	25,679	85,335	223,853	520,385
Ohio	15,249,395	41,142,829	23,774,544	3,307,861	2,942,159	365,702	1,484,488	1,146,890	11,429,046	6,480,500

See footnotes at end of table.

STATE EXPENDITURE, BY CHARACTER AND OBJECT AND BY STATE: 2003 (In thousands of dollars) — Continued

State	Intergovernmental expenditures	Total	Current operation	Capital outlay Total	Capital outlay Construction	Other	Assistance and subsidies	Interest on debt	Insurance benefits and repayments	Exhibit: Total salaries and wages
Oklahoma................	3,395,494	11,729,596	8,249,232	1,398,395	1,169,764	228,631	199,982	361,080	1,520,907	2,054,127
Oregon....................	4,071,501	13,934,272	8,556,101	863,664	640,475	223,189	494,889	285,327	3,734,291	3,097,945
Pennsylvania...........	11,943,470	45,484,996	31,144,060	3,735,390	3,414,059	321,331	1,332,146	1,087,130	8,186,270	7,168,728
Rhode Island...........	828,198	5,148,312	3,532,564	313,585	243,345	70,240	201,048	251,321	849,794	1,074,358
South Carolina........	4,155,920	16,883,832	11,533,662	2,081,357	1,736,802	344,555	612,270	494,440	2,162,103	3,009,070
South Dakota..........	514,949	2,383,095	1,594,554	391,640	316,899	74,741	48,783	113,155	234,963	455,357
Tennessee...............	4,952,923	16,068,994	12,398,856	1,309,757	1,141,354	168,403	543,432	187,328	1,629,621	2,858,757
Texas......................	17,332,957	59,053,086	40,150,860	6,858,775	4,809,917	2,048,858	1,509,538	951,418	9,582,495	15,077,936
Utah........................	2,165,151	6,856,716	4,573,743	842,179	707,505	134,674	274,611	190,363	975,820	1,595,731
Vermont..................	938,085	2,920,872	2,260,239	180,957	138,411	42,546	116,023	141,884	221,769	589,570
Virginia..................	8,352,635	20,776,501	14,973,244	1,672,483	1,198,880	473,603	978,980	647,384	2,504,410	4,961,010
Washington.............	6,785,341	25,814,995	15,552,519	2,320,037	2,081,455	238,582	992,998	727,208	6,222,233	5,228,336
West Virginia..........	1,544,758	8,458,971	5,344,698	811,852	668,206	143,646	145,135	207,095	1,950,191	1,472,413
Wisconsin...............	9,478,166	18,180,009	11,420,567	1,521,182	1,356,970	164,212	587,739	805,769	3,844,752	3,194,515
Wyoming.................	952,705	2,311,734	1,456,927	414,745	365,201	49,544	37,436	65,303	337,323	476,674

Source: U.S. Department of Commerce, Bureau of the Census, January 2003. Released March 2006.
Note: Detail may not add to total due to rounding.

Table 7.28
STATE GENERAL EXPENDITURE, BY FUNCTION AND BY STATE: 2003 (In thousands of dollars)

State	Total general expenditures (a)	Education	Public welfare	Highways	Hospitals	Natural resources	Health	Corrections	Financial administration	Employment security administration	Police
United States	$1,163,884,688	$411,531,528	$313,230,417	$86,104,257	$38,394,884	$18,623,901	$50,270,775	$39,226,109	$20,830,863	$5,262,701	$11,158,200
Alabama	17,009,944	7,053,792	4,531,802	1,163,904	1,211,084	225,308	762,009	356,928	171,876	84,209	129,591
Alaska	7,111,497	1,693,672	1,312,794	810,807	35,437	256,006	168,955	182,046	150,255	30,383	83,961
Arizona	17,503,052	6,419,012	4,482,224	1,839,644	53,792	231,187	845,027	731,041	231,281	54,635	172,512
Arkansas	11,081,356	4,529,282	2,705,341	1,098,172	543,347	190,638	292,724	305,803	250,004	46,327	69,422
California	173,158,060	61,457,162	48,472,281	7,158,608	5,025,205	3,487,188	9,291,005	5,690,346	4,556,897	410,817	1,443,127
Colorado	14,792,539	6,133,704	3,442,625	1,378,238	297,784	198,642	708,767	723,572	183,868	68,121	105,653
Connecticut	17,885,021	4,794,156	3,785,383	693,891	1,431,533	138,336	585,249	615,670	408,883	92,562	169,501
Delaware	4,376,306	1,594,007	748,059	345,859	56,325	63,032	282,530	206,085	95,204	12,252	78,549
Florida	50,217,755	16,326,315	13,399,713	4,943,244	224,631	1,697,840	2,902,463	2,141,271	670,616	117,360	415,772
Georgia	29,291,099	12,748,724	8,059,442	1,842,562	686,804	498,380	884,198	1,271,565	372,437	142,778	263,366
Hawaii	6,851,905	2,331,771	1,216,609	259,303	214,517	109,274	448,818	135,034	72,743	44,864	10,349
Idaho	4,759,455	1,886,421	1,092,616	521,746	45,747	162,831	116,088	164,813	103,501	42,692	40,953
Illinois	43,954,103	14,118,807	11,478,589	3,834,256	958,446	422,712	2,569,793	1,369,510	890,688	258,579	407,932
Indiana	21,295,408	8,639,690	5,377,805	1,712,840	282,438	277,385	545,088	654,475	292,751	132,509	196,066
Iowa	11,714,669	4,589,923	2,795,400	1,356,482	759,789	243,227	241,311	294,911	210,965	107,509	86,332
Kansas	9,843,383	4,210,861	1,905,638	1,094,228	102,323	184,607	524,233	336,268	266,891	47,738	72,321
Kentucky	16,857,615	6,096,709	4,964,095	1,816,167	523,447	316,167	519,701	474,334	227,653	52,605	188,584
Louisiana	16,323,015	6,235,015	2,800,278	1,142,621	1,507,432	393,305	418,057	619,414	316,192	101,087	262,317
Maine	6,072,093	1,574,270	1,990,470	492,304	50,970	156,234	400,804	107,345	99,707	27,296	68,212
Maryland	21,789,034	7,271,618	5,051,914	1,715,935	411,021	429,907	1,507,476	1,050,389	344,941	46,548	397,090
Massachusetts	27,870,663	6,774,160	5,292,878	2,429,436	507,129	266,116	1,878,337	1,049,512	434,762	134,395	424,923
Michigan	44,522,173	19,262,143	9,138,181	2,786,999	1,672,783	489,925	3,748,496	1,678,957	351,684	230,281	320,612
Minnesota	25,383,926	9,727,645	7,890,539	1,839,550	204,374	531,913	560,327	403,527	247,056	131,335	225,726
Mississippi	12,094,517	4,028,841	3,712,507	974,381	667,307	214,849	285,729	295,629	69,221	83,038	68,338
Missouri	19,137,212	6,732,710	5,591,971	1,854,329	893,540	290,176	585,878	656,273	262,573	22,884	162,920
Montana	3,917,125	1,372,442	663,613	495,515	42,815	187,761	262,645	103,384	149,095	14,159	45,678
Nebraska	6,493,783	2,233,120	1,809,391	557,869	191,539	164,263	391,150	182,378	87,182	50,238	69,707
Nevada	6,705,536	2,666,071	1,190,018	705,996	128,511	109,909	198,602	216,356	75,383	63,509	58,925
New Hampshire	4,591,789	1,635,389	1,185,850	374,780	48,940	70,642	175,661	95,637	65,847	29,522	41,749
New Jersey	34,859,788	11,215,395	7,005,033	2,559,450	1,402,133	371,247	882,500	1,294,773	520,621	472,670	390,817
New Mexico	9,713,782	3,677,414	2,410,880	818,750	446,538	179,821	290,949	264,845	142,981	55,308	109,352
New York	101,825,036	27,209,154	38,893,504	3,881,359	3,646,135	390,580	5,026,482	2,535,996	1,738,026	347,391	587,382
North Carolina	30,428,323	12,376,047	7,813,094	2,722,986	1,052,927	563,816	1,026,171	942,711	232,271	124,434	359,016
North Dakota	4,044,186	1,429,254	574,908	743,440	43,184	176,877	99,563	82,796	79,080	10,395	26,450
Ohio	44,613,676	16,327,787	12,527,978	3,183,792	1,367,067	383,998	2,022,067	1,686,179	1,366,618	272,425	278,653

See footnotes at end of table.

STATE GENERAL EXPENDITURE, BY FUNCTION AND BY STATE: 2003 (In thousands of dollars) — Continued

State	Total general expenditures (a)	Education	Public welfare	Highways	Hospitals	Health	Natural resources	Corrections	Financial administration	Employment security administration	Police
Oklahoma	13,305,832	5,564,983	3,177,322	1,283,363	181,208	460,187	212,083	486,313	328,105	71,226	92,508
Oregon	14,130,154	4,815,553	3,818,049	1,126,861	741,215	256,379	426,280	533,090	638,902	72,304	180,957
Pennsylvania	48,252,480	14,838,088	16,085,269	5,032,532	1,945,368	1,495,004	579,003	1,359,531	823,057	177,280	1,026,678
Rhode Island	5,026,490	1,385,449	1,803,847	228,646	108,890	190,225	42,396	159,095	119,979	6,034	50,475
South Carolina	17,684,894	6,037,317	4,775,314	1,341,643	1,112,095	698,202	190,004	426,300	483,410	91,230	243,452
South Dakota	2,663,081	838,579	621,617	420,985	44,658	90,008	114,037	79,858	58,059	18,044	26,076
Tennessee	19,386,815	6,169,486	7,634,185	1,576,290	348,111	881,367	211,306	558,669	165,233	84,105	144,177
Texas	66,803,548	26,995,012	18,498,427	5,265,805	2,833,200	1,401,878	789,999	3,201,068	761,470	276,065	430,531
Utah	7,946,241	4,189,768	658,734	771,231	532,586	247,222	189,195	261,283	177,978	14,872	82,771
Vermont	3,593,817	1,442,926	913,772	300,353	13,024	78,710	92,995	81,767	81,663	2,881	59,903
Virginia	26,289,267	9,776,565	5,234,986	2,588,474	1,886,966	682,070	175,851	1,194,241	564,266	164,731	552,064
Washington	26,020,778	10,696,522	6,250,197	1,906,430	1,073,482	1,374,328	696,612	786,781	349,992	126,675	245,281
West Virginia	7,997,646	2,759,464	2,230,629	961,586	105,211	232,084	184,606	182,064	271,986	30,387	53,903
Wisconsin	23,813,423	8,664,093	5,769,188	1,708,811	697,378	607,032	451,004	906,725	218,853	129,257	109,852
Wyoming	2,881,398	955,240	445,458	441,804	34,498	126,226	194,431	89,551	48,157	34,755	27,714

Source: U.S. Department of Commerce, Bureau of the Census, January 2003. Released March 2006.
Note: Detail may not add to total due to rounding.

(a) Does not represent sum of state figures because total includes miscellaneous expenditures not shown.

Table 7.29
STATE DEBT OUTSTANDING AT END OF FISCAL YEAR, BY STATE: 2003
(In thousands of dollars, per capita in dollars)

State	Total	Per capita	Long-term Total	Long-term Full faith and credit	Long-term Nonguaranteed	Short-term	Net long-term (a) Total	Net long-term (a) Full faith and credit
United States	$697,929,028	$2,404.7	$681,795,872	$179,372,361	$502,423,511	$16,133,156	$366,207,439	$170,136,870
Alabama	6,284,640	1,395.3	6,263,020	1,932,831	4,330,189	21,620	4,295,404	1,932,831
Alaska	5,829,798	8,996.6	5,679,798	1,091,096	4,588,702	150,000	1,861,576	1,062,310
Arizona	5,554,020	995.5	5,530,996	757,656	4,773,340	23,024	4,429,459	757,656
Arkansas..............	3,295,143	1,207.9	3,261,623	853,757	2,407,866	33,520	1,518,232	853,757
California	95,209,988	2,684.8	84,244,988	27,586,960	56,658,028	10,965,000	52,762,077	27,212,479
Colorado..............	8,921,416	1,961.6	8,911,782	1,642	8,910,140	9,634	2,538,823	1,642
Connecticut	22,490,115	6,449.7	22,489,565	12,820,492	9,669,073	550	11,975,757	11,020,147
Delaware..............	4,358,281	5,328.0	4,349,302	829,603	3,519,699	8,979	1,788,996	829,603
Florida	21,993,221	1,293.8	21,980,643	314,390	21,666,253	12,578	17,675,404	233,117
Georgia	8,890,184	1,024.7	8,890,184	6,864,720	2,025,464	0	7,049,842	6,817,544
Hawaii..................	5,652,531	4,525.6	5,652,531	3,648,368	2,004,163	0	4,540,474	3,646,616
Idaho...................	2,602,620	1,903.9	2,598,287	0	2,598,287	4,333	377,969	0
Illinois.................	46,688,761	3,691.1	46,677,953	22,607,763	24,070,190	10,808	23,682,192	21,377,107
Indiana.................	11,853,847	1,911.9	11,809,255	0	11,809,255	44,592	4,113,425	0
Iowa	4,279,448	1,454.6	4,279,448	0	4,279,448	0	1,647,030	0
Kansas.................	2,471,939	907.1	2,456,776	0	2,456,776	15,163	2,374,791	0
Kentucky	7,108,634	1,726.2	7,096,536	0	7,096,536	12,098	3,641,722	-6,074
Louisiana	9,773,279	2,174.7	9,766,978	2,311,853	7,455,125	6,301	4,368,022	1,775,520
Maine	4,417,481	3,374.7	4,398,361	358,410	4,039,951	19,120	743,529	358,410
Maryland	12,950,949	2,349.6	12,791,455	3,400,602	9,390,853	159,494	5,315,137	3,376,726
Massachusetts......	48,478,722	7,551.2	48,442,222	20,857,043	27,585,179	36,500	23,619,457	20,455,128
Michigan..............	22,478,857	2,229.6	21,706,068	2,726,400	18,979,668	772,789	7,101,166	2,726,400
Minnesota	7,150,401	1,412.0	6,691,245	3,382,010	3,309,235	459,156	3,378,500	2,516,655
Mississippi	4,166,614	1,445.2	4,158,474	2,872,649	1,285,825	8,140	3,213,137	2,768,591
Missouri	13,855,016	2,422.6	13,848,155	900,745	12,947,410	6,861	2,643,141	793,194
Montana	2,879,317	3,136.5	2,870,531	229,913	2,640,618	8,786	504,577	227,625
Nebraska..............	2,135,502	1,229.4	2,134,037	24,659	2,109,378	1,465	342,034	24,659
Nevada	3,604,272	1,607.6	3,604,186	2,164,878	1,439,308	86	2,406,283	2,164,878
New Hampshire....	5,594,078	4,339.9	5,544,078	635,640	4,908,438	50,000	1,066,046	556,957
New Jersey...........	33,608,678	3,889.0	33,586,856	3,385,874	30,200,982	21,822	21,035,005	3,385,874
New Mexico	4,601,117	2,448.7	4,567,622	1,221,622	3,346,000	33,495	2,267,663	1,221,622
New York	91,634,857	4,769.7	90,831,207	8,915,455	81,915,752	803,650	52,256,579	6,340,455
North Carolina	12,141,890	1,441.9	12,122,540	5,366,796	6,755,744	19,350	6,445,970	5,366,796
North Dakota.......	1,599,233	2,526.4	1,596,689	0	1,596,689	2,544	210,745	0
Ohio	21,054,220	1,840.7	20,664,206	6,447,965	14,216,241	390,014	12,010,200	6,323,596
Oklahoma	6,747,020	1,924.4	6,715,948	531,185	6,184,763	31,072	3,611,866	531,185
Oregon	7,463,722	2,094.2	7,463,722	2,250,123	5,213,599	0	4,493,720	1,698,898
Pennsylvania	24,330,327	1,966.7	23,431,423	6,771,793	16,659,630	898,904	10,951,824	6,738,000
Rhode Island	6,189,389	5,752.2	6,182,240	881,459	5,300,781	7,149	2,142,440	881,459
South Carolina	10,990,201	2,648.9	10,687,024	3,911,754	6,775,270	303,177	8,996,348	3,911,754
South Dakota........	2,566,542	3,355.0	2,565,724	0	2,565,724	818	563,274	0
Tennessee	3,496,139	598.1	3,371,344	1,096,814	2,274,530	124,795	1,370,234	1,066,325
Texas	14,616,237	661.3	14,023,112	3,373,543	10,649,569	593,125	11,349,750	3,213,143
Utah	5,064,112	2,153.1	5,038,131	1,623,680	3,414,451	25,981	2,365,987	1,577,865
Vermont	2,532,071	4,090.6	2,520,571	489,355	2,031,216	11,500	719,951	489,355
Virginia	13,530,190	1,837.1	13,530,190	603,251	12,926,939	0	5,963,597	603,251
Washington..........	14,620,855	2,384.7	14,611,861	8,547,841	6,064,020	8,994	9,384,329	8,524,043
West Virginia........	4,260,461	2,352.5	4,260,461	801,179	3,459,282	0	1,846,011	801,179
Wisconsin.............	14,801,308	2,703.9	14,785,139	3,978,592	10,806,547	16,169	7,100,337	3,978,592
Wyoming..............	1,111,385	2,213.9	1,111,385	0	1,111,385	0	147,407	0

Source: U.S. Department of Commerce, Bureau of the Census, January 2003. Released March 2006.

Note: Detail may not add to total due to rounding.
(a) Long-term debt outstanding minus long-term debt offsets.

Table 7.30
MEMBERSHIP AND BENEFIT OPERATIONS OF STATE-ADMINISTERED EMPLOYEE RETIREMENT SYSTEMS: LAST MONTH OF FISCAL YEAR: MARCH 2002–2003

State	Beneficiaries receiving periodic benefit payments				Periodic benefit payment for the month (in thousands of dollars)			
	Total membership	Total (a)	Retired by service	Retired on disability	Survivors	Total (a)	Retired by service	Retired on disability	Survivors
United States	15,788,945	5,420,937	4,642,902	342,286	435,749	$7,852,487,401	$7,013,919,983	$462,604,657	$375,962,761
Alabama	240,255	86,384	74,348	6,135	5,901	114,777,439	105,330,442	5,142,580	4,304,417
Alaska	67,450	27,226	24,479	558	2,189	46,841,362	43,770,450	933,249	2,137,663
Arizona	354,446	79,257	72,434	5,562	1,261	112,615,009	103,532,281	6,777,887	2,304,841
Arkansas	125,684	40,912	34,552	3,207	3,153	54,256,565	49,016,813	3,458,470	1,781,282
California	1,710,072	687,683	528,124	79,130	80,429	1,066,744,721	912,660,799	112,877,244	41,206,678
Colorado	291,013	66,262	56,126	7,966	2,170	136,173,243	109,171,966	15,952,577	11,048,700
Connecticut	129,200	61,527	53,602	3,519	4,406	129,964,827	119,701,392	5,738,667	4,524,768
Delaware	39,482	18,862	13,763	2,155	2,944	20,449,406	17,007,439	1,785,283	1,656,684
Florida	685,075	206,679	186,427	12,211	8,041	220,088,992	204,896,128	9,191,932	6,000,932
Georgia	499,672	102,705	82,871	8,957	10,877	185,005,535	158,841,854	11,945,269	14,218,412
Hawaii	66,442	31,389	28,546	1,184	1,659	47,593,000	45,176,000	909,000	1,508,000
Idaho	70,396	25,629	23,397	418	1,814	25,180,154	22,927,532	502,548	1,750,074
Illinois	700,053	232,764	194,008	3,343	35,413	360,750,666	336,019,694	4,561,654	20,169,318
Indiana	276,811	91,169	71,522	6,638	13,009	75,380,476	53,229,211	4,890,277	17,260,988
Iowa	203,415	78,236	76,145	1,086	1,005	66,220,845	62,970,043	2,269,380	981,422
Kansas	187,698	61,183	57,307	316	3,560	50,295,283	49,168,020	177,140	950,123
Kentucky	274,795	95,337	91,006	2,427	1,904	139,349,596	131,306,236	5,176,360	2,867,000
Louisiana	261,126	109,872	89,479	6,475	13,918	178,354,604	160,313,695	7,845,731	10,195,178
Maine	56,904	30,774	24,533	1,853	4,388	34,754,091	27,705,962	2,092,196	4,955,933
Maryland	238,826	91,821	75,235	5,585	11,001	103,350,670	84,682,451	6,286,145	12,382,074
Massachusetts	213,772	91,851	82,891	2,962	5,998	143,058,311	127,217,954	8,590,223	7,250,134
Michigan	423,004	200,557	169,774	9,360	21,423	294,835,479	252,938,921	12,599,222	29,297,336
Minnesota	466,285	120,072	108,171	4,178	7,723	189,722,058	173,952,630	5,606,590	10,162,838
Mississippi	268,288	60,131	48,277	3,986	7,868	57,145,106	49,405,763	3,436,235	4,303,108
Missouri	288,924	94,188	81,824	2,057	10,307	134,118,192	124,327,499	1,816,393	7,974,300
Montana	77,066	26,754	25,267	688	799	25,035,941	24,025,609	460,025	550,307
Nebraska	59,450	11,683	10,962	342	379	13,201,362	12,548,949	422,968	229,445
Nevada	85,311	27,312	23,814	1,329	2,169	50,592,674	47,083,208	1,077,436	2,432,030
New Hampshire	57,479	17,005	13,958	1,261	1,786	20,470,083	17,537,833	1,728,250	1,204,000
New Jersey	504,083	201,104	182,084	0	19,020	354,601,304	323,291,873	0	31,309,431
New Mexico	146,089	42,217	38,066	1,414	2,737	65,679,482	61,434,397	1,821,310	2,423,775
New York	901,514	431,904	376,664	24,722	30,518	652,158,001	603,229,096	29,267,349	19,661,556
North Carolina	535,042	162,733	135,947	12,589	14,197	206,107,171	178,339,106	16,170,337	11,597,728
North Dakota	32,774	10,673	9,327	387	959	9,896,905	9,045,937	195,360	655,608
Ohio	1,198,625	332,598	268,914	34,704	28,980	514,740,621	434,247,785	57,952,065	22,540,771
Oklahoma	153,088	71,382	60,716	5,955	4,711	87,072,882	77,088,894	5,247,228	4,736,760
Oregon	213,584	96,684	91,526	5,158	0	184,602,124	177,552,344	7,049,780	0
Pennsylvania	443,085	239,214	210,478	12,662	16,074	309,959,996	287,565,039	12,943,842	9,451,115
Rhode Island	32,470	19,348	16,737	1,569	1,042	36,015,082	31,154,871	2,920,594	1,939,617
South Carolina	349,726	92,991	74,958	10,559	7,474	120,156,232	104,728,432	9,726,378	5,701,422

See footnotes at end of table.

MEMBERSHIP AND BENEFIT OPERATIONS OF STATE-ADMINISTERED EMPLOYEE RETIREMENT SYSTEMS: LAST MONTH OF FISCAL YEAR: MARCH 2002–2003—Continued

State	Total membership	Beneficiaries receiving periodic benefit payments				Periodic benefit payment for the month (in thousands of dollars)			
		Total (a)	Retired by service	Retired on disability	Survivors	Total (a)	Retired by service	Retired on disability	Survivors
South Dakota...........	47,493	16,441	13,546	394	2,501	15,977,083	14,250,385	339,051	1,387,647
Tennessee...............	221,075	83,121	71,595	4,227	7,299	76,720,000	69,550,000	2,256,000	4,914,000
Texas.....................	1,311,269	324,345	293,784	14,984	15,577	496,621,797	450,815,452	30,593,711	15,212,634
Utah......................	118,113	31,982	31,982	0	0	42,311,610	42,311,610	0	0
Vermont.................	31,520	9,515	8,193	623	699	8,847,449	7,982,581	436,569	428,299
Virginia..................	396,038	108,758	91,583	15,609	1,566	132,228,706	112,118,000	19,108,000	1,002,706
Washington.............	246,254	110,105	93,165	5,027	11,913	148,256,556	127,574,483	5,639,167	15,042,906
West Virginia..........	78,755	28,416	28,416	0	0	37,556,750	37,556,750	0	0
Wisconsin...............	370,532	116,287	108,292	6,572	1,423	241,267,880	223,631,200	16,357,961	1,278,719
Wyoming................	39,422	15,895	14,087	243	1,565	15,384,080	13,984,974	329,024	1,070,082

Source: U.S. Department of Commerce, Bureau of the Census, January 2003.
(a) Detail may not add to totals due to rounding.

Table 7.31
FINANCES OF STATE-ADMINISTERED EMPLOYEE RETIREMENT SYSTEMS, BY STATE: FISCAL YEAR 2003
(In thousands of dollars)

		Receipts during fiscal year				Payments during fiscal year			
			Government contributions						
State	Total	Employee contributions	From states	From local governments	Earnings on investments	Total	Benefits	Withdrawals	Other
United States	147,747,004	28,843,747	19,567,749	26,644,538	72,690,968	134,844,916	122,306,460	4,891,041	7,647,415
Alabama	2,368,807	412,888	324,616	76,463	1,554,840	954,055	867,816	51,905	34,334
Alaska	709,481	168,237	65,741	99,381	376,122	816,998	767,212	16,865	32,921
Arizona	394,040	244,980	43,091	153,395	-47,426	1,478,911	1,337,494	72,191	69,226
Arkansas...............	906,320	86,912	128,782	203,982	486,644	714,522	620,164	5,389	88,969
California	31,451,306	4,602,041	2,309,259	2,714,476	21,825,530	15,332,902	12,790,610	476,404	2,065,888
Colorado	-1,056,710	479,416	168,291	325,764	-2,030,181	1,905,703	1,633,157	119,213	153,333
Connecticut	1,687,551	301,839	517,811	16,809	851,092	1,606,163	1,588,426	13,091	4,646
Delaware...............	295,121	40,211	84,419	7,106	163,385	266,361	244,067	3,092	19,202
Florida	4,984,754	27,000	502,030	1,458,765	2,996,959	4,747,443	4,045,849	422,879	278,715
Georgia	3,763,207	499,830	803,879	233,706	2,225,792	2,260,508	2,144,740	46,710	69,058
Hawaii...................	417,924	57,214	158,858	31,728	170,124	636,176	602,805	2,606	30,765
Idaho....................	584,680	131,528	72,551	146,089	234,512	333,488	302,240	1	31,247
Illinois..................	4,231,532	1,543,840	1,918,882	386,487	382,323	4,559,121	4,254,831	148,279	156,011
Indiana.................	2,532,482	271,062	111,423	824,313	1,325,684	1,097,848	1,000,508	39,521	57,819
Iowa	1,456,585	205,364	68,942	257,836	924,443	921,712	824,519	36,527	60,666
Kansas	486,658	224,746	167,238	64,227	30,447	717,041	653,542	39,609	23,890
Kentucky	1,691,327	514,750	356,968	27,498	792,111	1,643,720	1,576,870	31,183	35,667
Louisiana	1,603,056	554,685	787,405	140,582	120,384	2,136,195	1,930,058	74,308	131,829
Maine	793,269	136,971	295,370	0	360,928	450,326	417,181	13,834	19,311
Maryland	1,068,487	206,177	617,370	52,706	192,234	1,554,449	1,488,422	13,233	52,794
Massachusetts.......	2,999,901	908,273	1,146,180	100,030	845,418	2,074,897	1,757,761	238,424	78,712
Michigan...............	5,036,305	644,014	363,855	604,891	3,423,545	3,705,545	3,567,929	17,572	120,044
Minnesota	1,936,705	517,024	145,978	411,481	862,222	2,393,734	2,275,101	35,769	82,864
Mississippi............	1,295,099	334,893	172,202	282,105	505,899	1,085,943	967,710	62,024	56,209
Missouri................	3,045,599	435,227	634,361	485,546	1,490,465	1,758,845	1,666,850	38,695	53,300
Montana	424,986	122,363	56,690	82,337	163,596	318,319	295,685	17,967	4,667
Nebraska...............	436,899	94,955	25,380	92,123	224,441	200,682	170,677	10,433	19,572
Nevada	1,463,564	55,477	119,683	604,525	683,879	652,466	592,151	11,112	49,203
New Hampshire.....	246,790	117,412	26,283	32,888	70,207	286,907	244,725	15,223	26,959
New Jersey............	4,168,057	880,860	27,283	137,998	3,121,916	4,773,885	4,647,571	86,212	40,102
New Mexico	979,902	294,377	253,070	131,867	300,588	823,033	751,023	54,324	17,686
New York	8,622,715	387,062	365,655	232,720	7,637,278	8,845,383	8,459,068	60,709	325,606
North Carolina	-1,034,313	908,810	123,063	200,179	-2,266,365	2,512,327	2,385,986	115,946	10,395
North Dakota........	153,494	34,902	13,762	46,484	58,346	130,882	115,778	4,458	10,646
Ohio	5,819,217	2,386,862	1,715,282	1,938,987	-221,914	8,080,220	7,523,072	298,015	259,133
Oklahoma	1,605,257	306,190	339,546	285,777	673,744	1,248,939	1,097,307	84,285	67,347
Oregon	4,756,827	467,369	670,106	1,951,731	1,667,621	2,261,428	2,001,280	42,640	217,508
Pennsylvania	-1,130,909	1,069,982	51,456	49,302	-2,301,649	4,986,264	4,544,574	24,170	417,520
Rhode Island	423,085	129,365	140,527	0	153,193	467,056	432,181	5,277	29,598
South Carolina	2,951,847	465,709	228,934	378,565	1,878,639	1,526,803	1,421,675	71,657	33,471
South Dakota......	320,930	81,093	26,894	44,955	167,988	216,161	181,275	19,338	15,548
Tennessee..............	950,336	197,711	264,320	134,014	354,291	926,732	881,232	26,631	18,869
Texas	15,670,690	2,278,461	1,577,664	832,685	10,981,880	6,976,781	6,473,803	358,078	144,900
Utah	2,582,581	31,482	352,562	0	2,198,537	521,923	488,489	9,008	24,426
Vermont................	209,222	35,992	30,102	38,007	105,121	121,312	96,953	3,845	20,514
Virginia.................	2,108,453	129,149	252,393	660,293	1,066,618	1,786,217	1,597,735	72,150	116,332
Washington...........	1,854,550	214,732	109,916	702	1,529,200	2,633,997	1,779,125	743,915	110,957
West Virginia........	719,703	108,143	84,495	324,087	202,978	509,481	479,396	11,481	18,604
Wisconsin..............	1,294,022	28,237	316,348	851,889	97,548	2,922,456	2,671,699	37,898	212,859
Wyoming...............	59,988	53,905	11,225	42,329	-47,471	196,465	177,315	8,886	10,264

Source: U.S. department of Commerce, Bureau of the Census, January 2003.

Table 7.32
NUMBER, MEMBERSHIP, AND MONTHLY BENEFIT PAYMENTS
OF STATE-ADMINISTERED EMPLOYEE RETIREMENT SYSTEMS: 2001–2002 TO 2002–2003

Item	2002–2003	2001–2002
	$7,852,487,401	$7,116,489,779
Number of systems..	218	219
Membership last month of fiscal year:		
Total Membership..	15,788,945	15,394,714
Active members	12,538,604	12,407,222
Inactive members...	3,250,341	2,987,492
Percent distribution..	100.0	100.0
Active members	79.4	80.6
Other...	20.6	19.4
Beneficiaries receiving periodic benefits...		
Total number retired or survivors...	5,420,937	5,180,415
Former active members, retired service	4,642,902	4,453,077
Former active members, retired disability	342,286	321,346
Survivors of former active members..	435,749	405,992
Percent distribution..	100.0	100.0
Percent former active members, retired service	85.6	86.0
Percent former active members, retired disability	6.3	6.2
Percent survivors of former active members................................	8.1	7.8
Recurrent benefit payments for last month of fiscal year..................		
Total amount of benefit for retired/survivors..............................	$7,852,487,401	$7,116,489,779
Amount former active members, retired service............................	$7,013,919,983	$6,351,351,225
Amount former active members, retired disability...........................	$462,604,657	$435,866,540
Amount survivors of former active members	$375,962,761	$329,272,014
Percent distribution..	100.0	100.0
Percent former active members, retired service	89.3	89.2
Percent former active members, retired disability	5.8	6.1
Percent survivors of former active members................................	5	4.6
Average monthly payment for beneficiaries:.......................................		
Average for all beneficiaries (in dollars).....................................	$1,448	$1,374
For former active members, retired service...................................	$1,510	$1,426
For former active members retired disibility.................................	$1,351	$1,356

Source: U. S. Department of Commerce, U. S. Census Bureau, March 2004
Detail may not add to totals due to rounding.

Table 7.33
NATIONAL SUMMARY OF FINANCES OF STATE-ADMINISTERED EMPLOYEE RETIREMENT SYSTEMS: SELECTED YEARS, 2001–2003

	Amount (in millions of dollars)			Percentage distribution		
	2002–03	2001–02	2000–01	2002–03	2001–02	2000–01
Total Receipts..	$147,747,004	-$6,120,528	$106,023,718	100.0	...	100.0
Employee contributions	28,843,747	27,544,022	22,100,169	19.5	...	20.8
Government contributions..................	46,212,289	38,792,031	32,181,984	31.3	...	30.4
From State Government	19,567,749	17,182,861	16,806,868	13.2	...	15.9
From Local Government	26,644,540	21,609,170	15,375,116	18.0	...	14.5
Earnings on investments	72,690,968	-72,456,581	51,741,565	49.2	...	48.8
Total Payments......................................	134,844,916	121,980,231	88,708,288	100.0	100.0	100.0
Benefits paid	122,306,460	110,128,411	79,671,054	90.7	90.3	89.8
Withdrawals	4,891,041	4,079,492	3,479,630	3.6	3.3	3.9
Other payments	7,647,415	7,772,328	5,557,604	5.7	6.4	6.3
Total cash and investment .... holdings at end of fiscal year	2,172,001,788	2,157,990,956	1,789,565,105	100.0	100.0	100.0
Cash and short-term investments	99,812,059	109,762,677	93,836,486	4.6	5.0	5.2
Total Securities......................................	1,891,957,833	1,875,395,501	1,546,748,279	87.1	86.9	86.4
Government securities........................	222,534,967	225,584,917	197,270,659	10.3	10.5	11.0
Federal government............................	221,684,160	224,762,717	196,550,168	10.2	10.4	11.0
United States Treasury	161,289,726	153,870,084	136,506,409	7.4	7.1	7.6
Federal agency	60,394,434	70,892,633	60,043,759	2.8	3.3	3.4
State and local government	850,807	822,200	720,491	0.0	0.0	0.0
Nongovernment securities	1,669,422,866	1,649,810,584	1,349,477,620	76.9	76.5	75.4
Corporate bonds................................	317,074,720	352,193,553	312,819,028	14.6	16.3	17.5
Corporate stocks................................	811,107,881	814,835,143	632,627,096	37.3	37.8	35.4
Mortgages	22,795,540	20,765,586	21,557,692	1.1	1.0	1.2
Funds held in trust............................	67,250,825	70,422,530	NA	3.1	3.3	NA
Foreign and international	266,812,023	254,662,228	228,590,532	12.3	11.8	12.8
Other nongovernmental......................	184,381,877	136,931,544	153,883,272	8.5	6.4	8.6
Other investments	180,231,896	172,832,778	148,980,340	8.3	8.0	8.3
Real property......................................	46,766,729	42,908,542	35,995,896	2.2	2.0	2.0
Miscellaneous investments..................	133,465,167	129,924,236	112,984,444	6.1	6.0	6.3

Source: U.S. Department of Commerce, Bureau of the Census, March 2003.
Key:
. . . —Not available.

Chapter Eight

STATE MANAGEMENT AND ADMINISTRATION

"*The use of 311 and similar mechanisms of non-emergency call management systems has emerged as a viable alternative for increasing citizen access to government, and improving government responses to the issues of greatest concern to citizens.*"

—Marc Holzer, Richard Schwester, Angie McGuire and Kathryn Kloby

"*Clearly, there are distinctive and substantial differences across the 50 states in the extent to which women have sought and gained access to elected legislative posts and top appointed administrative positions in state government.*"

—Christine Kelleher, Cynthia Bowling, Jennifer Jones and Deil S. Wright

"*Savings generated from strategic sourcing initiatives have reportedly been substantial.*"

—John Adler, Dugan Petty and Rebecca Randall

"*Under the right conditions, states can greatly benefit from outsourcing certain IT functions and business processes.*"

—Mary Gay Whitmer

"*State legislatures show signs of departing from their customary professional licensing approach as new professions gain state licensure without initiation by a profession or the public.*"

—Pam Brinegar

State-level 311 Systems: Leveraging Service Enhancement and Performance Measurement at the State Level

By Marc Holzer, Richard Schwester, Angie McGuire and Kathryn Kloby

The use of 311 and similar mechanisms of non-emergency call management systems has emerged as a viable alternative for increasing citizen access to government, and improving government responses to the issues of greatest concern to citizens. This article describes the state of best practices for 311 systems and suggests ways to extend those successes throughout state and local government. Improving technology allows the exploration of widespread adoption and integration with other systems. Challenges and alternatives of designing and offering a 311 system are provided as recommendations to assist public managers in decision-making.

Introduction

Government responsiveness is a foundational concern of elected officials, public managers, citizens, the media and watchdog organizations. Finding appropriate ways to monitor government performance, provide mechanisms for citizen feedback and complaints, and document government responsiveness has a long history. Measuring public sector performance efforts, for example, has been defined and shaped by the Good Government model, Planning-Programming-Budgeting System, Total Quality Management, service scorecards, measurement of efficiency and effectiveness, and other strategies geared toward promoting productivity and performance improvement. More recent calls for "doing more with less," promoting a public sector that is results-oriented, and boosting public trust through accountability and responsiveness have reinforced interest in performance measurement systems at all government levels.

Technology is accelerating the use of mechanisms that can open the lines of communication between citizens and their governments. The use of 311 and similar mechanisms for non-emergency call management systems provides a viable alternative for increasing citizen access to government and improving government response to issues that are most important to citizens. The integration of Web-based services into 311 systems can enhance the responsiveness, effectiveness and efficiency of government entities endeavoring to provide citizens with better services.

In addition, new applications of technology support integration of existing systems and the Web. That integration provides opportunities for the consideration of statewide 311 system deployment across jurisdictional boundaries to accomplish fiscal and scheduling efficiencies for smaller municipalities and government entities.

This article addresses the widespread implementation of 311 systems in the context of government performance improvement, with examples of best practices throughout the United States. Highlighting successful applications of 311 in large cities and presenting modified versions of 311 at the state level, we demonstrate that this mechanism offers citizens a convenient way to contact government for information and services and provides government managers with performance measures to assure that problems are resolved in a timely manner. Challenges and alternatives for state implementation are presented to assist public managers and elected officials with adoption and implementation decisions.

The Origins of 311

By 1996, non-emergency calls to 911 had reached a level that required national attention. President Clinton challenged the Department of Justice (DOJ) to relieve the 911 systems of congestion resulting from unnecessary calls. The White House and the Office of Community Oriented Policing Services (COPS Office) of the DOJ sought corrective action. The COPS Office requested that the Federal Communications Commission (FCC) set aside 311 for use as a national help number for non-emergencies (Solomon and Uchida, 2005). In 1997, the FCC established the abbreviated telephone number 311 for non-emergency local government services (Moving Oakland Forward, 2002). A 311 system is operated either by the police department in order to reduce the frequency of non-emergency 911 calls, or by a municipality or county to address non-emergency calls regarding service delivery. (See Figure A.)

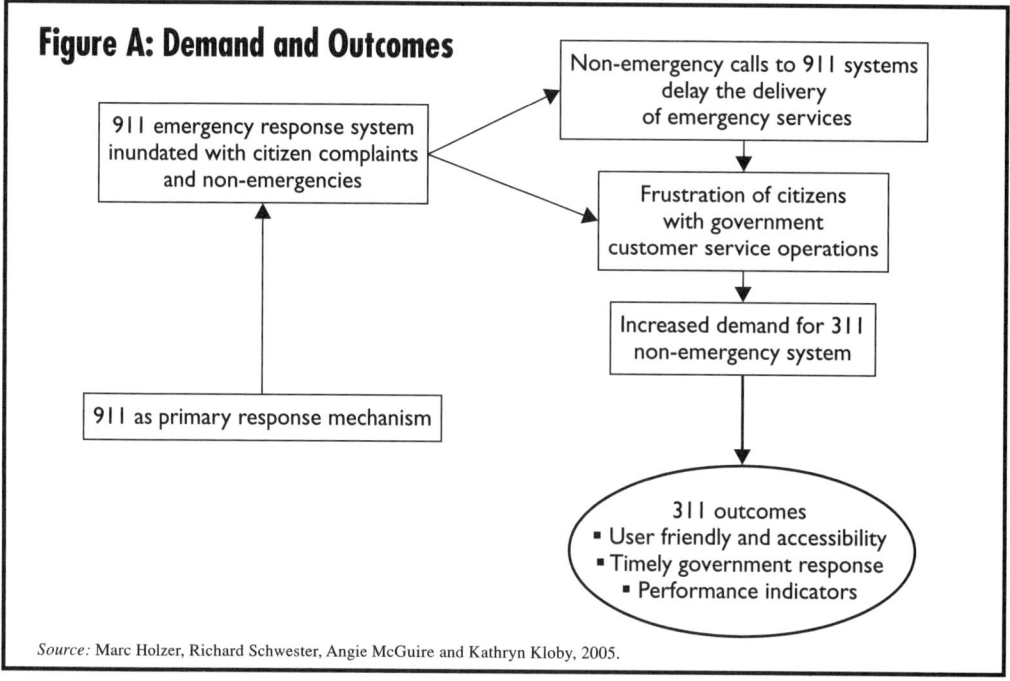

Figure A: Demand and Outcomes

Source: Marc Holzer, Richard Schwester, Angie McGuire and Kathryn Kloby, 2005.

311 Systems as Performance Improvement Tools

In addition to alleviating bottlenecks caused by non-emergency calls made to 911 systems, 311 systems have emerged as a means of enhancing citizen access to government services, expanding the traditional "police non-emergency" role. This service approach for 311 reflects the nation's move toward community-oriented government. Typically, 311 systems have the potential to support community-oriented government by establishing a direct, citizen-driven link to government service agencies (Harris, 2005). Responding to the increasing demand for quality customer service, municipal and county governments across the United States are implementing 311 customer call centers.

According to Martin (2004), 311 systems could potentially enhance government efficiency by centralizing the point of contact between government and citizens. That is, 311 systems have been characterized as "proactive management tools" that allow government officials to monitor the volume and types of calls received via that system. Data from incoming calls can then be tracked and reviewed using customer relationship management (CRM) software.

Such 311 systems allow government departments and agencies to more effectively address their core functions. That is, such systems minimize instances where a government worker must take time to answer a citizen's general query or transfer that citizen to the appropriate government department or agency. All too often, government workers must act as switchboard operators, constantly transferring citizens to other departments. Experience suggests that 311 decreases such instances.

Practice indicates that 311 systems are ideal in terms of gathering performance data relevant to government service delivery. Data collected via 311 may be fed into CRM systems, thereby allowing city officials to utilize that data to make better-informed strategic decisions on how city resources should be deployed and how services could be more effectively managed. An added benefit of 311 systems is the capture and strategic use of data as a tool to allow government officials to measure average response time. Categorizing the types of calls and requests, along with response times, allows government to set performance standards within a department or agency and provide citizens with realistic expectations as to when a complaint will be addressed, a problem solved, or a service rendered.

311 Models and Outcomes

Several large cities have successfully deployed 311 systems. Offloading workload from 911 systems and improving the response time to citizens in an array of service areas are key outcomes of implementation.

The following examples highlight successful applications of 311 in large cities as well as 311 modifications for implementation in states.

Baltimore

Baltimore was the first city to implement a 311 system in October 1996. The 311 system was specifically designed to siphon calls from the 911 system and create more opportunities for police officers to engage in community- and problem-oriented policing activities (Mazerolle et al., 2003). The Baltimore Police Department recorded the following improvements subsequent to launching 311 (Harris, 2005):

- Average answer time for 911 calls decreased by 50 percent.
- Percentage of abandoned 911 calls decreased by 50 percent.
- Average time between incoming 911 calls increased from 70 to 143 seconds.
- Percentage of 911 calls receiving a recorded message decreased from 18 to 4 percent.
- Average "total position busy" time decreased by 169 hours each month and the percentage of time operators were occupied with calls decreased from 59 to 41 percent.
- From September 1996–September 1999, the number of police calls dispatched to field units decreased by 12 percent.

New York City

Launched in March 2003 at a cost of $21 million, New York City's 311 system averages 1 million calls monthly. It is the largest 311 system in the country. Citizens previously had to navigate an 11-page directory of city government phone numbers and often found it challenging to determine which government agency to contact about a specific matter. From January 2004 to February 2005, the system had logged nearly 13 million calls, more than double the number of calls annually to city departments and agencies prior to the consolidation to a single 311 help line. This 24-hour, seven-days-a-week service handles more volume and reduces waiting time for callers to register complaints and receive action. Under the old system, New Yorkers in need were forced to navigate a labyrinth of city hotlines, departments and agency phone numbers (Taylor, 2005).

Dallas

In December 1997, the city of Dallas implemented a holistic non-emergency call system. The city consolidated 28 customer service numbers and seven call-taking centers under the fire department to accept citizen requests for the vast majority of city services. While Baltimore's non-emergency call system was designed to specifically reduce non-emergency calls to the police, the Dallas non-emergency system was implemented to provide citizens with easier and more efficient access to a wide range of city services (Mazerolle et al., 2003). The consolidated non-emergency call center allowed citizens to call 311 for the following city services: animal control (e.g. animal cruelty, unrestrained animal, noisy animal); sanitation (e.g. missed garbage, illegal dumping); streets (e.g. street and shoulder repair, drainage repair, storm drain cleaning); public works and transportation (e.g. illegal parking, street lighting, traffic signals); code compliance (e.g. junk auto, high weeds, property damage, litter, graffiti); economic development (e.g. building permits, motor repairs); parks (e.g. tree trimming, park maintenance); environmental and health services (e.g. noise pollution, air pollution); city controller (e.g. cable television, electric); housing (e.g. human services, housing programs); and water (e.g. main break, sewer leak, burst pipe). The Dallas non-emergency call system was designed to provide citizens with accurate information about city services, eliminate bureaucratic red tape and provide citizens with the city services they need in a timely and efficient manner.

Chicago

Chicago implemented the 311 system in January 1999 in an effort to create a "one stop shopping" center for access to all city and non-emergency police services, which eliminated the need for a number of smaller call centers. In May 1999, Chicago replaced its outdated mainframe system with a modern PC-based system that would improve communication among departments, reduce response time regarding resident requests, and generate management reports to ensure a more efficient service delivery system for all departments. The system is fully transparent and gives residents the ability to track the progress of their complaints. Thus, 311 City Services has given Chicago residents a direct link to city services and information (Gorecki, 2004).

Houston

In August 2001, the 311 Houston Service Helpline successfully met the challenge of operating an advanced technological call center that consolidated staff and responsibilities from the Citizens' Assistance Division, City Switchboard, Municipal Courts Administration, Public Works and Engineering and

Solid Waste Management departments. The 311 Houston Service Helpline provides a single point for customers to contact the city departments and agencies for a variety of needs, including service requests, trouble reports and answers to frequently asked questions (City of Houston, 2003).

State-level Applications

The promising use of technology to serve a broad range of citizen interests is already being explored. Transportation systems and social services access are joining 311 systems as viable tools for improving government service, streamlining operations and strategically using data. The FCC has established 211 dialing for use by government agencies providing social services, and 511 dialing for transportation networks. These systems may well serve as templates for statewide mobilization of resources in the integration of phone- and Web-based 311 services.

The state of New Jersey, for example, established a 211 system to provide "all residents of New Jersey with a single, easy to use system for information and assistance" (United Ways of New Jersey, 2005). On Oct. 3, 2002, the New Jersey Board of Public Utilities approved the use of 211 dialing for community information and referral purposes and recognized the NJ 211 Partnership as the sole administrator of 211 in New Jersey. Working with nonprofit service providers, counties and state agencies, the New Jersey 211 Partnership hopes to create a virtual response center through an alliance of information providers and referral services. Those organizations have joined to design and implement a comprehensive statewide database so every New Jersey resident has immediate access to health, human and community services information (United Ways of New Jersey, 2005). Call specialists for 211 provide comprehensive information and referral services to callers about a variety of issues, including basic human needs resources, physical and mental health resources, children's health insurance programs, and more.

Some departments of transportation are now implementing 511 traveler information numbers, which are currently in use in 14 states. At the request of the U.S. Department of Transportation and a host of transportation planning organizations, the FCC designated 511 as the national travel information number on July 21, 2000. This easy-to-remember number permits travelers to call a single number, from any location in the United States, to learn local traffic and transit conditions. These systems also incorporate automatic toll-payment transponders equipped in some areas to monitor the time between

toll booths and thus provide an automated measure of traffic flow. The FCC did not mandate the dedicated use of 511 as a telephone number for travel information, but it did reserve this number for transportation agency use, which has spawned several 511 systems across the country.

The 511 system serves as a portal to a variety of travel-related information systems in the state of Washington. Developed by the Washington State Department of Transportation (WSDOT), the main dialog menu prompts callers to select from the following: real-time traffic for the central Puget Sound area, roadway conditions and construction information, road restrictions and conditions of mountain passes, ferry information and other information such as public transit phone numbers, passenger rail phone numbers, airline telephone numbers, and adjacent states and provinces (WSDOT, 2005). Current Washington State highway hotline call volumes average 387,000 per month, with the capacity to address a call volume of more than 500,000 per month (WSDOT, 2005).

Challenges and Alternatives

With the success of 311 system deployments at the city level, broader jurisdictional applications are being considered. Alternative forms of 311 are being considered for state and regionalized federal services. The existing large city models may provide the needed insight to accomplish this goal. For example, the scope of New York City's system encompasses departments and agencies covering a broad geographical area and multiple purposes. Other cases highlighted above can also serve as a template for assessing system capacity to address statewide functions and call handling.

In addition to offering citizens a convenient way to contact state and local government for information and services, a 311 center integrated with Web-based services has the potential to provide government managers with performance benchmarks to assure that problems are resolved on time. A statewide 311 system that integrates municipalities over a number of jurisdictions would underscore the emphasis on customer service. It would function as a proactive management tool to highlight the volume and types of calls, and the length of time it takes to deal with them. Information and data based on incoming calls could be tracked and reviewed with the software tools already in use in several cities. Such information provides actionable measures of performance and problem identification for public managers.

There is growing consensus of the benefits to be gained from statewide 311 system deployment. As promising practices are evaluated and considered, several issues are being addressed:

1. Integrating Technology: Statewide systems need to handle a myriad of requests from a large number of jurisdictions and departments. Integrating Web requests into phone service responses will be critical to ensuring response times at an efficient price point. Integrating access and responses will also provide the opportunity for better data management and the creation of databases to be used by government at all levels for assessing performance.

2. Integrating Existing Systems: The deployment of 211 and 511 systems provides both a challenge and an opportunity. Integrating call handling operations potentially provides an efficient use of deployed capital and trained call management workers. A review of existing call centers and information sources in a state may yield alternatives to creating parallel operations.

3. Jurisdictional Boundaries: Each state operates with a subset of jurisdictions at the county, city and even "authority" level, such as water districts with separate independent authority status. Ensuring the sharing of information and accountability for response times is the basis of an effective 311 system. Large city deployments in New York, Los Angeles and Dallas can provide insight to typical challenges and potential solutions.

Scale and leverage brought about by a statewide effort to integrate call management with Web access provides the opportunity for speed and financial savings. An enhanced 311 system spanning jurisdictions and integrating phone and Web-based technology can illustrate a new model for state collaborations with communities. The creative application of e-commerce technologies to traditional government functions can then enhance the abilities of states and communities to better serve their constituents. Although the technology has rapidly evolved and is commercially available, design and deployment deficiencies, as well as investment and human resource constraints, are often barriers to implementation.

References

City of Houston. (2003). 311 Houston Service Helpline, FY 03 Performance Report. Retrieved December 12, 2005 from *http://www.houstontx.gov/311/fy03.pdf.*

Gorecki, S. (2004). City of Chicago's Award Winning 311 System Focal Point of International Symposium. Press Release, Motorola, Inc. retrieved December 12, 2005 from *http://www.motorola.com/mediacenter/news/detail/0,,4185_3540_23,00.html.*

Harris, E. (2005). COPS Fact Sheet: 311 for Non-Emergencies. Retrieved June 20, 2005 *from http://www.cops.us doj.gov/default.asp?Item=510.*

Martin, E.W. (2004). Point of Contact. Public CIO. Retrieved December 11, 2005 from *http://www.public-cio. com/story.print.php?id=90220.*

Mazerolle, L., D. Rogan, J. Frank, C. Famega, & J.E. Eck. (2003). Managing Citizen Calls to the Police: An Assessment of Non-Emergency Call Systems. Retrieved May 10, 2005 from *http://www.ncjrs.org/pdffiles1/nij/206256.pdf.*

Moving Oakland Forward. (2002). City Manager SummitRecommendations. Retrieved May 10, 2005 from: *http://www.oaklandnet.com/movingforward/8CRecommen dationsDetailed.pdf.*

Solomon, S.E. & C.D. Uchida. (2005). Building a 3-1-1 System for Non-Emergency Calls: A Process and Impact Evaluation. Retrieved on December 12, 2005 from *http:// www.cops.usdoj.gov/default.asp?Item=1275.*

Taylor, C.L. (2005). "NYers are Using 311 More Than Ever." *New York News Day.*

United Ways of New Jersey. (2005). About the NJ 2-1-1 Partnership. Retrieved October 10, 2005 from *http://www. nj211.org/content/aboutnj211.htm.*

WSDOT. (2005). WSDOT 511 Details. Retrieved November 9, 2005 from: *http://www.wsdot.wa.gov/Traffic/511/ details.htm.*

About the Authors

Marc Holzer is professor and chair of the Graduate Department of Public Administration. Since 1975 he has directed the National Center for Public Productivity, and he is the founder and editor in chief of the *Public Performance & Management Review.* His recent publications include the *Public Productivity Handbook* (edited, second edition in press, 2004). He is a past president of the American Society for Public Administration and a fellow of the National Academy of Public Administration.

Richard W. Schwester received his doctorate from the Graduate Department of Public Administration, Rutgers University-Newark. Schwester's research interests include citizen participation, e-government, and urban revitalization projects. Schwester is a senior research associate for the National Center for Public Productivity (NCPP) at Rutgers-Newark, assistant editor of *Public Performance & Management Review* and associate editor for the *Journal of Public Management and Social Policy.*

Angie McGuire is a doctoral candidate in the Graduate Department of Public Administration at Rutgers University-Newark Campus. As a senior research associate for the National Center for Public Productivity, she works to develop outreach mechanisms, fundraising initiatives, and partnerships with organizations with similar interests and goals.

Kathryn Kloby is a doctoral candidate in the Graduate Department of Public Administration at Rutgers University-Newark Campus. As a researcher and project coordinator for the National Center for Public Productivity, she works to deliver online classes to public managers in Public Performance Measurement and design performance measurement systems in New Jersey Municipalities.

Women in State Governments: Trends and Issues

By Christine Kelleher, Cynthia Bowling, Jennifer Jones and Deil S. Wright

This article focuses on the representation of women as leaders of state administrative agencies and a comparison of women within state legislatures. We begin with aggregate trends in representation from 1970 to 2004. We then classify trends on a state-by-state basis. Finally, we compare state government to other private and public sectors of American society.

More than a half-century ago, a prominent political scientist contended that the national civil service (or bureaucracy) was more representative than the Congress. He referred to representation not only:

"with respect to the class structure of the country but, equally significantly, with respect to the learned groups, skills, economic interests, races, nationalities, and religions. The rich diversity that makes up the United States is better represented in its civil service than anywhere else."[1]

This argument can be extended to the 50 states and applied specifically to gender representation. American political and economic institutions are often examined in isolation. Examples include women in the bureaucracy in general, in leadership positions or as candidates for, or members of, state legislatures.[2] Although few studies have examined gender issues through cross-branch comparisons, a recent piece on elected and appointed state officials in multiple branches pointed to a slowed progress of women in statewide elected offices.[3]

This essay focuses on trends in the representation of women as leaders of state administrative agencies and within state legislatures across three decades (and into a fourth). We rely primarily on data from three sources. First is the documentation of women state legislators from the Center for American Women in Politics (1971–2003).[4] The second relies on a 50 percent sample of individual names of persons (women and men) heading 125 types of state administrative agencies from listings by The Council of State Governments, 1970–2004.[5] We call this the ANS or Agency Name Sample. The third source is data from responses to mail questionnaires sent to state agency heads twice each decade by the American State Administrators Project (ASAP).[6] Additionally, we supplement our analyses by comparisons with other public and private sectors to explore the representation of men versus women in varied arenas of American society. In particular, we address the following two research questions:

1. How do increases in women heading state administrative agencies compare with the rising levels of representation of women in state legislatures? Beyond comparative trends aggregated for all 50 states, what do state-by-state gender proportions reveal when comparisons are made between legislative and administrative representativeness?

2. How does the rise in the proportion of women heading state agencies compare with proportionate representation in other governmental jurisdictions and with proportions in non-profit and for-profit organizations?

It should be noted that "state agency heads" include both elected and appointed administrators. Elected agency heads, however, are a small proportion (4–8 percent) of the ANS and ASAP datasets. Furthermore, governors directly appoint less than 50 percent of the agency heads in the ANS and ASAP groupings.

Gender Representation in State Legislatures and State Administrative Agencies

Figure A shows that increased representation of women in state legislatures and administrative agencies has roughly progressed in tandem. The number of female legislators increased at a slightly higher rate than agency heads across the 1970s, although both sectors had less than or about 10 percent women. Growth occurred at an even pace through the 1980s but the proportion of female administrators increased more rapidly in the 1990s. By 2004, on an aggregate basis, women occupied 30 percent of agency head positions compared to 22 percent women legislators. Riccucci and Saidel found that in most cases women were not well represented in top policymaking positions in state government across the country.[7] That finding is subject to revision and is not uniformly true in all states. Aggregate counts tell only part of the story; the numbers vary considerably across the 50 states.

Table A displays percentages for each of the 50 states for the two institutions.[8] In the 1990s, women

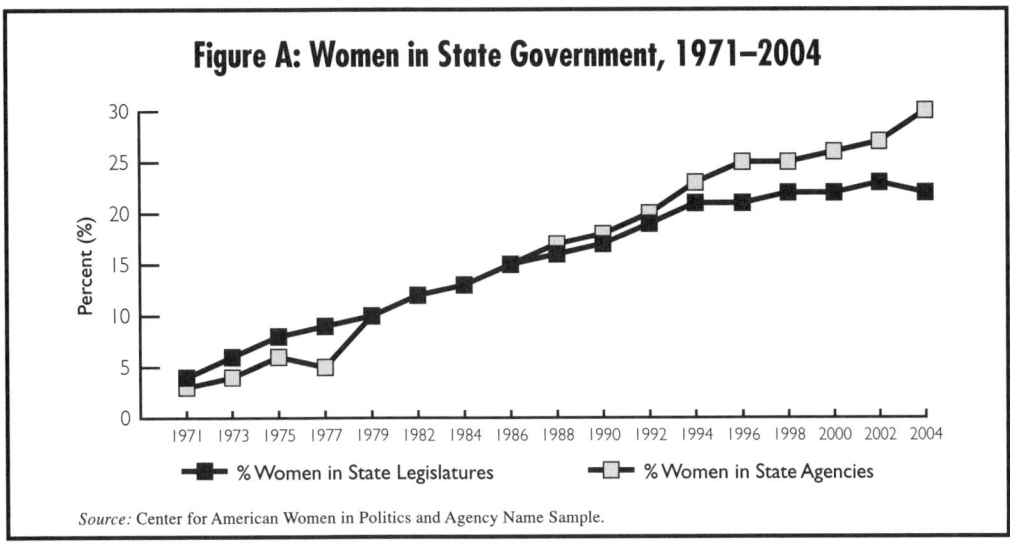

Figure A: Women in State Government, 1971–2004

Percent (%)

1971 1973 1975 1977 1979 1982 1984 1986 1988 1990 1992 1994 1996 1998 2000 2002 2004

—■— % Women in State Legislatures   —□— % Women in State Agencies

Source: Center for American Women in Politics and Agency Name Sample.

constituted 25 percent (or more) of state agency heads in 19 states. Relying on percentages from only three points in time in the current decade (2000, 2002 and 2004), the number of states with more than 25 percent of agencies headed by women increased to 29 (see Table A). Overall, the differences in gender representation in the legislature and in state agency head positions were not great; in most cases through the 1990s less than 10 percentage points separate the proportions between the two institutions. Table A classifies patterns of female legislative and administrative representation in the American states into three groups: (a) Dominant Administrative (DA), (b) Dominant Legislative (DL) and (c) Parallel (roughly equal) Representation (PR). These three groups are identified based on differences in female proportions in the legislature and agencies for the 1990s. It remains to be seen whether differences will continue to change or remain the same throughout the first decade of this century. For example, some of the Dominant Legislative states' recent figures show shifts occurring toward greater representation of women leading state agencies than serving in the legislature.

These categories reflect the recent balance of women in the legislature and agency head positions as well as the trends since 1970. By the 1990s, 16 states in the Dominant Administrative category showed a consistent and substantially higher proportion of women agency heads than state legislators. Six of these states were in the southern region(s) of the nation where female representation in legislative bodies has tended to be lower than in other sections

of the country. Eight states (Arizona, Colorado, Connecticut, Kansas, Maine, New Hampshire, Vermont and Washington) were identified as Dominant Legislative, where legislatures have consistently higher percentages of women than found in top agency positions. In the remaining half of the states (26), women attained Parallel Representation in executive and legislative posts in roughly the same proportions. By the 2000s, however, some of the states in this final category shifted toward greater representation of women in state agencies than in state legislatures. It will be interesting to watch whether these trends persist as the decade continues.

Over the past three decades, researchers have devoted important attention to explanations for these patterns. While Sigelman was relatively unsuccessful in determining why differences existed in female bureaucratic representation across the states,[9] more recently, Riccucci and Saidel identified Democratic and female governors as sources for appointed women policy leaders.[10] Brewer and Selden found that external or state-level predictors (region, unemployment rates, gross state products and policy liberalism) were helpful in understanding female employment success in the states.[11] Additionally, female representation in the state legislatures has been linked to legislative professionalism, region, liberalism, partisanship and party attributes.[12]

We now turn to a substantively different but related issue—the comparative presence of women in other public and private sectors of society. We investigate whether state government is a leader or follower with respect to equal female representation.

Table A: Female Representation in State Legislatures and Administrative Agencies by State and Across Four Decades (percent)

State	Group (a)	1970s		1980s		1990s		2000, 2002 and 2004	
		Legislatures	ANS and ASAP average	Legislatures	ANS and ASAP average	Legislatures	ANS and ASAP average	Legislatures	ANS and ASAP average
Alabama	DA	1	6	5	9	5	12	4	14
Alaska	DA	10	6	16	21	20	29	15	28
Arizona	DL	16	6	21	12	33	20	24	28
Arkansas..............	PR	2	6	6	12	12	14	7	9
California	PR	4	10	12	13	21	19	12	30
Colorado	DL	13	7	26	13	33	22	24	34
Connecticut	DL	14	10	22	17	26	21	21	32
Delaware..............	DA	12	11	16	24	19	25	16	39
Florida	PR	8	4	18	14	20	23	15	31
Georgia	PR	3	3	9	14	16	18	10	20
Hawaii..................	DA	10	7	20	15	23	28	18	29
Idaho....................	PR	8	10	18	10	27	25	18	23
Illinois..................	PR	6	4	16	16	22	26	15	17
Indiana.................	DA	6	3	12	15	18	25	12	37
Iowa	DA	8	4	13	12	18	30	13	35
Kansas	DL	5	5	17	12	29	17	17	28
Kentucky	DA	4	8	6	13	8	13	6	22
Louisiana	DA	1	12	3	14	9	29	4	21
Maine....................	DL	13	6	15	14	29	22	22	26
Maryland..............	PR	10	4	19	14	26	29	18	22
Massachusetts.......	PR	5	5	15	10	22	24	14	31
Michigan	PR	5	10	12	16	20	15	13	36
Minnesota	PR	4	6	14	21	25	26	15	34
Mississippi	DA	2	5	3	15	10	14	5	16
Missouri	PR	7	4	14	8	19	24	13	36
Montana	PR	7	6	14	18	22	25	14	41
Nebraska...............	PR	4	4	15	12	23	21	14	14
Nevada	PR	10	6	14	18	29	30	17	29
New Hampshire....	DL	23	4	31	16	31	19	28	24
New Jersey............	DA	7	7	6	21	14	25	10	40
New Mexico	PR	4	5	6	22	20	22	11	40
New York	PR	4	9	10	17	17	14	10	40
North Carolina.....	PR	8	7	13	9	16	16	13	24
North Dakota........	PR	9	3	12	8	16	13	12	19
Ohio	DA	5	2	10	23	20	26	12	20
Oklahoma	DA	4	1	8	13	10	19	7	24
Oregon	PR	11	10	20	16	26	32	19	36
Pennsylvania	DA	4	4	5	10	11	22	6	21
Rhode Island	PR	5	4	14	18	22	20	14	32
South Carolina	PR	4	2	7	11	12	16	8	20
South Dakota........	PR	7	10	16	12	19	21	14	23
Tennessee..............	DA	2	8	8	18	13	18	9	23
Texas	PR	4	2	8	7	16	19	9	26
Utah	DA	6	4	8	16	15	23	10	22
Vermont................	DL	14	9	23	20	32	27	23	36
Virginia................	DA	4	4	8	16	13	30	8	30
Washington...........	DL	12	4	23	17	37	35	24	36
West Virginia........	PR	8	1	15	14	17	22	13	28
Wisconsin..............	PR	7	8	19	18	25	25	17	33
Wyoming...............	PR	8	8	22	15	22	18	18	16
Unweighted average..............		7	6	13	15	20	22	14	28

Sources: The ANS (Agency Name Sample) is a 50-percent sample of the listings of individuals (women and men) heading 125 types of state administrative agencies from The Council of State Governments, 1970–2000. The ASAP data (American State Administrators Project) includes responses to mail questionnaires, six surveys of state agency heads at six junctures in the past three decades (1974, 1978, 1984, 1988, 1994 and 1998). In this table, the ASAP and ANS percentages were averaged for each decade for simplicity of presentation.

Key:
(a) DA — Dominant Administrative (States with higher gender representation in agency head positions in the 1990s).

DL — Dominant Legislative (States with consistently higher gender representation in the legislature through the 1990s).

PR — Parallel Representation (States that, by the 1990s, had about equal gender representation in the legislature and agency head positions or no dominant pattern).

Gender Representation: Inter-Sector Comparisons

The question of women in higher-level positions of state government administration takes on greater relevance when compared to their presence as executives or administrators in other sectors. How are women represented in other parts of the public sector, including the national and local governments? How are they represented in the non-profit and private sectors? Among these sectors, where are women better represented? We have already established a growing female presence in both state legislatures and administrative agencies. In Table B, we present the proportions of women in additional sectors of American society, in years ranging from 2000 through 2005, depending on data availability.

Early in this decade, women in the Senior Executive Service (SES) of the national government occupied a status comparable to top-level state administrators. A GAO study (2001) reported that women in the SES rose from 10 percent in 1990 to 22 percent by 1999.[13] By 2003, this number reached 26 percent,[14] while the percent of women state administrators hovered around 29 percent. However, when comparing women in top posts of state government and the SES, the 10 percent figure in 1990 for the Senior Executive Service marks a decade-long lag. In positions of state agency leadership, women exceeded the 10 percent figure by 1980. In 2002 (the 107th Congress), women in the United States Congress at 14–15 percent lagged behind both state governments and the Senior Executive Service.

It is possible to identify female representation by broad functional groups at both the national and state levels for comparative purposes. In 2002, the percent of women in the Social Security Administration was 34 percent, a figure that approximates the ASAP Income Security functional category at 39 percent. Also at the national level, the Department of Health and Human Services had 38 percent women, a proportion similar to the 33 percent of women heading state health agencies. It is noteworthy that female representation among national agencies most closely matches the representation of women in top posts at the state level. These types of agencies (human/social services) are also where women have attained greater access to top positions.

Does administrative gender representation in local governments match proportions at the state level? The simple answer is, no. In 1998, women in U.S. local governments comprised less than 5 percent of the top management positions. In state government (both executive and legislative branches), women

Table B: Women in Administrative Leadership Positions: Inter-Sectoral Comparisons of Female Representation at the Turn of the Century, 2000–2005

Sector	Percentage
State Government	
ANS (2004)	30%
ASAP (2004)	27
Governors (2004)	16
National Government	
U.S. Senate (2005)	14
U.S. House (2005)	15
Senior executive service (2002)	26
Local Government	
City councils (2003)	28
Mayors (population > 100,000) (2005)	16
City managers (2000)	12
Local government managers (2005)	10
Higher Education	
University presidents (2003)	21
For-Profit	
Fortune 500 CEOs (2003)	2
Fortune 500 executive vice presidents (2003)	8
Fortune 500 officers (2003)	16
Non-Profit	
CEOs/executive directors (2005)	36

Source: Multiple publications.

exceeded 20 percent.[15] Although the percentage of women in local government increased to 12 percent in 2000, this figure was far short of bureaucratic representation at the national and state levels.[16] In 2005, the aggregate percentage for managers at all levels of local government (city, county, township, etc.) reached 10 percent.[17] The percentage of female mayors is also lagging. In 2005, women occupied this office in only 13 percent of the nations' 100 largest cities and 16 percent of cities with populations over 100,000.[18] These figures depart notably from state administrators and legislatures. However, a slightly different finding emerged for women on city councils. Here, representation paralleled state legislatures and agencies more directly, with women accounting for approximately 28 percent of all positions in 2003.[19]

The proportions of women in high-level positions in the private sector provide further contrast from findings about the representation of women in state government. As of 2002, only 16 percent of officers in Fortune 500 companies were female and women held barely 2 percent of chief executive officer (CEO) positions, the highest-ranking positions in corporations.[20] Additionally, in 2003, women in Fortune 500 companies held only 8 percent of the executive vice-president positions. A sector that more closely parallels trends in state government is higher education where, in 2003, 21 percent of all college/university presidents were female.

The non-profit sector adds a further dimension to the representation of women. Despite the preponderance of women volunteers and employees in most non-profit organizations (approximately 70 percent),[21] research indicates that women are less present in executive positions. For example, in 2005, approximately 36 percent of non-profit CEOs/executive directors were women.[22] Additionally, as the size of the organization's budget increases, the proportion of women in positions of leadership decreases. For example, in agencies with budgets less than $250,000, 55 percent of CEOs or executive directors were women. However, in agencies with budgets greater than $50 million, only 14 percent were women. While aggregate trends show that the proportion of women leading non-profits is greater than leadership in the other previously discussed sectors of society—both governmental and nongovernmental—when considerations are made for the size of agency budgets, a slightly different picture emerges.

A comparison of the earnings of men and women across these sectors yields interesting and important findings. We begin by noting the remarkable equity that exists between the salaries of men and women state administrators. In the 1994 and 1998 ASAP surveys, women administrators reported earning 93 and 95 percent of the salaries of men, on average. A comparison of their median salaries reveals even greater near-equality, with women earning 96 and 98 percent of men, respectively, in the two years. In 2004, the mean percentage of the relative earnings of women to men was slightly lower at 92 percent, but the median salaries reveal near equity, with women earning 97 percent of the salary of male counterparts. Additionally, in earlier survey years, the amount of variation in women's salaries was also much greater; over time, the range from highest to lowest salaries has become more compressed.

The approximate salary equality between men and women state administrators is even more notable when considered in light of sharp pay differentials in the private sector. According to the Current Population Survey (2004), the median salary for women executives in management occupations was 72 percent of men.[23] Additionally, a recent GAO study (2002) reported female communications managers in the private sector earning only 73 cents to the dollar earned by male managers in 2000—a figure that had dropped from 86 cents in 1995.[24] These findings for state agencies differ markedly from trends in other sectors. A private sector study by Koretz (2000) found that women CEOs earned about 45 percent less than their male counterparts. (This equates to approximately $900,000 for women as compared to $1.3 million for men.)

A notable salary gap also plagues the non-profit sector. According to a 2001 report, the average female CEO earned about $33,000 compared to the $42,000 paid to the average male CEO.[25] Additionally, across all job categories in non-profits for FY 2002, women earned 28 percent less than their male counterparts.[26] This 80 percent salary ratio for women CEOs in non-profits is in marked contrast with the salary parity women state executives achieved years earlier.

In all sectors/arenas discussed in this essay, the representation of women is largest in the non-profit sector. While female proportions of state agency heads and SES administrators are roughly comparable, lagging far behind are city managers with about 10 percent females and corporate CEOs with only 2 percent women. Yet, the administrative establishment of state government is near the forefront among various employment sectors in access by women and equality in terms of compensation. This adds to the significance and importance of deeper probes into gender representation at the top levels of state administration.

Concluding Observations and Issues

This essay documents and compares female representation in state administrative agencies and legislatures, noting aggregate similarities in overall growth from the 1970s through the 1990s and into the 21st century. It identifies administrative and legislative representation patterns within and between the 50 states and classifies them according to three possible categories—Dominant Administrative, Dominant Legislative or Parallel Representation. The respective number of states in each category is 16, eight, and 26. Clearly, there are distinctive and substantial differences across the 50 states in the extent to which women have sought and gained access to elected legislative posts and top appointed administrative positions in state government. These differences as well as similarities merit further careful and systematic examination.

While growth in state administrative leadership roughly parallels the increases in female legislators and is now about equal to the proportion of women in the senior executive service of the national government, it far outpaces the number of women in either private sector or local government leadership positions. These contrasting trends of representation are notable because they highlight the importance of state governments in offering a model for cracking the "glass ceiling" of women's access to and achievements in the executive workplace.[27] Among the most exceptional feature of our findings is the gender salary equality present among state agency heads. Seldom, if ever, has such a commonality been documented among a substantial cohort of administrators. Our findings provide exploratory and previously undocumented comparisons that lay the foundation for future work investigating the progress toward greater balance and adequate representation for women in all sectors of American society.

Authors' Note:

We gratefully acknowledge the support of the Earhart Foundation of Ann Arbor, Michigan, Auburn University Center for Governmental Services and Department of Political Science, and the Odum Institute for Research in the Social Services at the University of North Carolina at Chapel Hill.

Notes

[1] Norton E. Long, "Bureaucracy and Constitutionalism," *American Political Science Review*, Vol. 46, (September 1952): 814.

[2] Lee Sigelman, "The Curious Case of Women in State and Local Government," *Social Science Quarterly*, Vol. 57, (March 1976): 591–604.

Angela M. Bullard and Deil S. Wright, "Circumventing the Glass Ceiling: Women Executives in American State Governments," *Public Administration Review*, Vol. 53, (May/June 1993): 189–202.

Norma Riccucci and Judith Saidel, "The Representativeness of State-Level Leaders: A Missing Piece of the Representative Bureaucracy Puzzle." *Public Administration Review*, Vol. 57, (1997): 423–30.

Norma Riccucci and Judith Saidel, "The Demographics of Gubernatorial Appointees: Toward an Explanation of Variation," *Policy Studies Journal*, Vol. 29, (2001): 11–22.

Peverill Squire, "Legislative Professionalization and Membership Diversity in State Legislatures," *Legislative Studies Quarterly*, Vol. 17, (1992): 69–79.

Gary F. Montcrief, Peverill Squire, and Malcolm E. Jewell, *Who Runs for the Legislature?* Upper Saddle River, (NJ: Prentice Hall, 2001).

Kira Sanbanmatsu, "Political Parties and the Recruit-

ment of Women to State Legislatures," *Journal of Politics*, Vol. 64, (2002): 791–810.

Judith Saidel and Norma Riccucci, "Women State Agency Heads and Their Leadership," *Spectrum: The Journal of State Government*, Volume 75, Issue 1, (2002): 18–19.

Susan J. Carrol, "The Impact of Term Limits on Women," *Spectrum: The Journal of State Government*, Volume 74, Issue 4, (2001): 19–21.

[3] Susan J. Carroll, "Women in State Government: Historical Overview and Current Trends," in *The Book of the States* (Lexington, KY: The Council of State Governments, 2004): 389–398.

[4] For more information, see the following Web site: *http://www.cawp.rutgers.edu/*.

[5] The Agency Name Sample (ANS) lists all agency heads in 67 agencies biennially from 1970 to 2000. The agencies are representative of all types and functions of administrative activities in the American states. Names were recorded from the *State Leadership Directory, Directory III: Administrative Officials*, published by the Council of State Governments. Each name was coded male or female, and androgynous names with no gender identifiers were omitted. This methodology resulted in a sample of 36,759 names from 15 time points. For additional information, see Cynthia Bowling and Jinhwa Hong, "Women Leading State Agencies: Breaking the Glass Ceiling to Provide Policy Representation." This paper was presented at the Annual Conference of the Midwest Political Science Association in Chicago, IL, April 25–28, 2002. Two additional years of data were added to this sample (2002 and 2004). Those years are slightly different because of changed information in the directory from The Council of State Governments. Because data for the listings include a smaller subset of agencies (approximately 50), these figures may be slightly biased (although conservatively so) toward "older" agencies as opposed to more recently created ones. However, comparisons with other sources, including the ASAP survey results and the entire population of ASAP survey targets, does not reveal large or problematic differences. Therefore we are quite confident in the reliability of our results.

[6] Cynthia J. Bowling and Deil S. Wright, "Change and Continuity in State Administration: Administrative Leadership Across Four Decades," *Public Administration Review*, Vol. 58, (1998): 429–94.

Jeffrey L. Brudney and Deil S. Wright, "Revisiting Administrative Reform in the American States: The Status of Reinventing Government in the 1990s," *Public Administration Review*, Vol. 62, (2001): 353–61.

Chung-Lae Cho, Yoo-Sung Choi and Deil S. Wright, "Characteristics and Qualities of Top-Level Administrators in the American States," in *The Book of the States* (Lexington, KY: The Council of State Governments, 2002): 370–79.

[7] Riccucci and Saidel, op. cit., 1997.

[8] In this table, we average the percentages of state agency heads from the ANS and ASAP datasets for clarity of presentation. These two variables are positively correlated, across all years, at approximately 0.7.

[9] Sigelman, n. 2 above.

[10] Riccucci and Saidel, 2001, n. 2 above.

[11] Gene A. Brewer and Sally Coleman Selden, "Bureaucratic Representation in U.S. State Governments: Determinants of Minority and Female Employment Success," Paper presented at the Annual Meeting of the American Political Science Association in Philadelphia, PA, (August 28–31, 2003).

[12] Sanbanmatsu; Squire, n. 2 above.

[13] GAO, "Senior Executive Service: Diversity Increased in the Past Decade (GAO-01-377)," (Washington, D.C.: United States General Accounting Office, March 2001).

[14] The Office of Personnel Management. *http://www.opm.gov/feddata/factbook/2004/factbook.pdf*. Retrieved on September 11, 2005.

[15] Robert A. Schumann and Richard L. Fox, "Women Chief Administrative Officers: Perceptions of Their Role in Government," in *Municipal Year Book 1998.* (Washington: 1998): 16–22.

[16] Tari Renner, "The Local Government Profession at Century's End," *The Municipal Yearbook* (Washington, D.C.: International City/County Management Association, 2001): 35–46.

[17] Avon Pagon, International City/County Management Association, e-mail contact, 3 February 2005.

[18] Center for American Women and Politics. *http:/www.cawp.rutgers.edu.*

[19] James H. Svara, "Two Decades of Continuity and Change in American City Councils," Report commissioned by the National League of Cities (2003). *http://www.nlc.org/content/Files/RMPcitycouncilrpt.pdf.* Retrieved on February 1, 2005.

[20] Patricia Sellers, "Power: Do Women Really Want It?" *Fortune,* (New York, 2003): 80–100.

[21] Murray S. Weitzman and Nadine T. Jalandoni, *The New Nonprofit Almanac and Desk Reference* (Urban Institute/Jossey Bass, 2002).

[22] GuideStar, *Nonprofit Compensation Report,* (2005).

[23] *http://www.bls.gov/cps/cpsaat39.pdf.* Retrieved September 11, 2005.

[24] GAO, "Women in Management: Analysis of Selected Data from the Current Population Survey Data (GAO-02-156)," (Washington, D.C.: United States General Accounting Office, October 2001).

Shannon Henry, "The Widening Pay Gap," (Washington, D.C.: *The Washington Post,* February 3, 2002).

[25] GuideStar, *Nonprofit Compensation Report,* (2001).

[26] GuideStar, *Nonprofit Compensation Report,* (2004).

[27] Cynthia J. Bowling, Christine A. Kelleher, Jennifer Jones, and Deil S. Wright, "Glass Ceilings, Flexible Floors, and Porous Walls: Gender Representation in the Bureaucracies of American State Governments from 1970 to 2000," *Public Administration Review* (Forthcoming).

interests include public administration, public finance and budgeting, and state and local government.

Jennifer Jones is a graduate of the Master of Public Administration Program at the University of North Carolina-Chapel Hill. She currently works as a performance analyst for the Texas state budgeting agency, the Legislative Budget Board.

Deil S. Wright is an Alumni Distinguished Professor of Political Science and Public Administration at the University of North Carolina at Chapel Hill. His research focuses on various dimensions of public administration, state and local government, federalism and intergovernmental relations.

About the Authors

Christine Kelleher is an assistant professor of political science at the University of Michigan-Dearborn. Her research interests include state and local government, welfare policy and women in politics.

Cynthia Bowling is an associate professor in the Department of Political Science at Auburn University. Her research

Table 8.1
THE OFFICE OF STATE PERSONNEL EXECUTIVE:
SELECTION, PLACEMENT AND STRUCTURE

State	Method of selection	Reports to: Governor	Reports to: Personnel board	Reports to: Department head	Reports to: Other	Directs departmental employees	Legal basis for personnel department	Organizational status: Separate agency	Organizational status: Part of a larger agency
Alabama	B	...	★	...	...	★	S	★	...
Alaska	D	...	...	★	...	★	C, S	...	★
Arizona	D	...	...	★	...	★	C, S	...	★
Arkansas	D	★	...	★	...	★	S	...	...
California	B	...	★	...	...	★	C	★	...
Colorado	D	...	...	★	...	...	C	...	★
Connecticut	G	★	...	...	...	★	S	...	★
Delaware	D	...	...	★	...	★	S	...	★
Florida	D	...	...	★	...	★(a)	C, S	...	★
Georgia	G	★	...	...	...	★	C, S, E	★	...
Hawaii	D, G	★	...	...	...	...	S	★	...
Idaho	G	★	...	...	...	★	S	...	★
Illinois	D	...	...	★	...	★	S	...	★
Indiana	G	★	...	...	...	★	S	★	...
Iowa	D	...	...	★	...	★	S	...	★
Kansas	(j)	...	...	...	★(i)	★	S	...	★
Kentucky	G	★	...	...	...	★	S	★	...
Louisiana	B	...	★	...	...	★	C	★	...
Maine	D	...	...	★	...	...	S	...	★
Maryland	D	...	...	★	...	★	S	...	★
Massachusetts	G (k)	...	...	...	★(j)	★	S	★	...
Michigan	(b)	...	...	...	★(b)	★	C, S (c)	★	...
Minnesota	G	★	...	...	...	★	S	★	...
Mississippi	B	...	★	...	...	★	S	★	...
Missouri	G	...	...	★	...	★	C, S	...	★
Montana	D	...	...	★	...	★	S	...	★
Nebraska	D	...	...	★	...	★	S	...	★
Nevada	G	★	...	...	...	...	S	★	...
New Hampshire	(d)	...	...	★	...	★	S	...	★
New Jersey	G (e)	★	...	...	...	★	C, S	★	...
New Mexico	B	★	★	...	...	...	S	★	...
New York	G	★	...	...	...	★	C, S	★	...
North Carolina	G	★	...	...	...	★	S	...	★
North Dakota	(f)	...	...	...	★(f)	★	S	...	★
Ohio	D	...	...	★	...	(l)	S	...	★
Oklahoma	G	★	...	...	...	★	S	★	...
Oregon	D	...	...	★	...	...	S	...	★
Pennsylvania	D (i)	...	...	★	★(h)	★	E	...	★(m)
Rhode Island	D	...	...	★	...	...	S	...	★
South Carolina	(g)	...	...	...	★(g)	★	S	...	★
South Dakota	G	★	...	...	...	...	S	★	...
Tennessee	G	★	...	...	...	★	S	★	...
Texas	(k)	...	...	...	★(k)	...	S	...	★
Utah	G	★	...	...	...	★	S	★	...
Vermont	G	...	...	...	★(h)	...	S	...	★
Virginia	G	...	...	...	★(h)	★	S	★	...
Washington	G	★	...	...	...	★	S	★	...
West Virginia	G	...	...	★	...	...	S	★	...
Wisconsin	G	★	...	...	...	★	S	★	...
Wyoming	D	...	...	★	...	...	S	...	★

See footnotes at end of table.

THE OFFICE OF STATE PERSONNEL EXECUTIVE:
SELECTION, PLACEMENT AND STRUCTURE — Continued

Source: The Council of State Governments' survey of state personnel offices, October 2005.

Key:

★ — Yes

. . . — No

B — Appointment by personnel board.

D — Appointment by department head.

G — Appointment by governor.

C — Constitution.

S — Statute.

E — Executive order.

R — Rules.

(a) The director of human resource management directs the employees of the Division of Human Resource Management (HRM). HRM administers and manages the policies and programs of the state personnel system, which is comprised of Career Service, Selected Exempt Service and Senior Management Service pay plans.

(b) Civil Service Commission. This commission is a bipartisan unit appointed by the governor(s) at staggered intervals.

(c) The Civil Service Commission and the state personnel director are constitutionally established. The Department of Civil Service was statutorily created.

(d) Governor, department head. Nominated by commissioner of administrative services and appointed by the governor and council.

(e) Confirmed by the Senate.

(f) Office of Management and Budget director.

(g) Budget and Control Board chief of staff.

(h) Secretary of Administration.

(i) Cabinet secretary.

(j) Nominated by the secretary of administration and finance. Reports to the secretary of administration and finance and the governor.

(k) Appointed by the state auditor and subject to approval by the Legislative Audit Committee. Reports to state auditor.

(l) Directs employees of the Human Resource Division.

(m) The Office of Human Resources and Management exists as a separate department within the Governor's Office of Administration.

Table 8.2
STATE PERSONNEL ADMINISTRATION: FUNCTIONS

State	Administers merit testing	Establishes qualifications	Provides human resource information system	Human resource planning	Classification	Position allocation	Compensation	Recruitment	Selection	Performance evaluation	Position audits	Other personnel function audits	Employee promotion	Employee assistance & counseling	Human resource development
Alabama	CPA	CPA	SR	SR	CPA	CPA	CPA	SR	DA	SR	CPA	CPA	SR	DA	SR
Alaska	N.A.	CPA	CPA	SR	CPA	CPA	CPA	CPA	SR	SR	CPA	CPA	SR	CPA	SR
Arizona	CPA	SR	SR	CPA	CPA	CPA	CPA	SR	DA	DA	CPA	CPA	DA	SR	SR
Arkansas	CPA	CPA	CPA	SR	CPA	CPA	CPA	DA	DA	DA	DA	DA	DA	DA	SR
California	CPA	CPA	CPA	CPA	SR	SR	SR	SR	CPA	SR	SR	SR	DA	DA	SR
Colorado	DA	CPA, DA	CPA	CPA	CPA	DA	CPA	DA	DA	DA	DA	CPA	DA	CPA	CPA
Connecticut	CPA	CPA	O	SR	CPA	O	CPA	SR	CPA	DA	CPA	N.A.	SR	DA	SR
Delaware	CPA	CPA	CPA	CPA	CPA	CPA	CPA	SR	SR	DA	CPA	N.A.	DA	SR	SR
Florida	N.A.	DA	CPA	SR	CPA	DA	CPA	DA	DA	SR	CPA	DA	DA	DA	DA
Georgia	SR	SR	SR	SR	SR	DA	SR	SR	SR	SR	DA	DA	DA	SR	SR
Hawaii	CPA	CPA	CPA	CPA, SR	CPA, O	O	CPA	CPA, O, SR	O, SR	SR	CPA	CPA	O	SR	SR
Idaho	CPA	CPA	SR	SR	CPA	O	SR	SR	SR	DA	CPA	...	SR	SR	SR
Illinois	CPA	CPA	SR	SR	CPA	SR	CPA	SR	SR	DA	CPA	CPA	DA	SR	SR
Indiana	SR	SR	CPA	SR	CPA	SR	CPA	SR	DA	DA	SR	SR	DA	DA	SR
Iowa	CPA	CPA	CPA, O	SR	CPA	CPA	CPA	DA	SR	SR	CPA	N.A.	DA	O	SR
Kansas	DA	SR	CPA	SR	SR	SR	CPA	SR	DA	DA	SR	SR	DA	SR	SR
Kentucky	CPA	CPA	CPA	CPA	CPA	CPA	CPA	SR	CPA	SR	CPA	CPA	SR	CPA	SR
Louisiana	SR	CPA	CPA	SR	SR	SR	SR	SR	DA	DA	SR	CPA	SR	DA	SR
Maine	SR	SR	SR	SR	CPA	SR	SR	SR	DA	DA	SR	N.A.	SR	DA	SR
Maryland	SR	CPA	CPA	CPA	SR	O	CPA	SR	DA	DA	CPA	SR	SR	CPA	SR
Massachusetts	CPA	CPA, DA	SR, CPA	SR	SR	DA	CPA	DA	SR, CPA	SR, CPA	CPA	CPA	DA	O	SR
Michigan	CPA	CPA	SR	SR	CPA	CPA	CPA	SR	SR	SR	CPA	SR	DA	CPA	SR
Minnesota	SR	SR	CPA	SR	SR	SR	SR	SR	SR	DA	SR	CPA	SR	CPA	SR
Mississippi	N.A.	CPA	CPA	SR	CPA	SR	SR	SR	SR	DA	SR	SR	DA	DA	DA
Missouri	SR	CPA	SR	CPA, DA	CPA	CPA	CPA	SR	SR	DA	CPA	SR	DA	O	CPA, DA
Montana	DA	DA	CPA	DA	SR	DA	SR	DA	DA	DA	DA	CPA	DA	CPA	DA
Nebraska	N.A.	SR	SR	CPA	CPA	SR	CPA	CPA	O	O	CPA	CPA	O	O	SR
Nevada	SR	CPA	SR	SR	SR	SR	SR	SR	DA	SR	SR	SR	DA	SR	SR
New Hampshire	CPA	CPA	CPA	SR	CPA	SR	CPA	SR	SR	SR	CPA	CPA	SR	SR	SR
New Jersey	CPA	CPA	CPA	SR	CPA	O	CPA	SR	SR	DA	CPA	CPA	DA	CPA	SR
New Mexico	N.A.	CPA	O	SR	CPA	CPA	CPA	CPA	SR	DA	CPA	O	SR	DA	SR
New York	CPA	SR	SR	DA	CPA	DA	SR	SR	DA	DA	CPA	CPA	DA	DA	SR
North Carolina	N.A.	SR	CPA	SR	CPA	N.A.	SR	DA	DA	SR	CPA	CPA	DA	SR	SR
North Dakota	SR	CPA	SR	DA	CPA	N.A.	SR	SR	DA	DA	CPA	SR	DA	N.A.	SR
Ohio	SR	SR	CPA	DA	SR	SR	CPA	SR	DA	DA	CPA	N.A.	DA	O	SR

See footnotes at end of table.

STATE PERSONNEL ADMINISTRATION: FUNCTIONS — Continued

State	Administers merit testing	Establishes qualifications	Provides human resource information system	Human resource planning	Classification	Position allocation	Compensation	Recruitment	Selection	Performance evaluation	Position audits	Other personnel function audits	Employee promotion	Employee assistance & counseling	Human resource development
Oklahoma	CPA	CPA	CPA	SR	CPA	SR	CPA	SR	SR	SR	SR	CPA	SR	SR	SR
Oregon	SR	CPA	CPA	SR	CPA	DA	CPA	SR	SR	DA	CPA	CPA	DA	SR	SR
Pennsylvania (b)	O	CPA	CPA	SR	SR	SR	SR	SR	DA	SR	SR	+ SR	DA	SR	SR
Rhode Island	CPA	CPA	CPA, DA	CPA, DA	CPA	CPA, O	CPA	CPA, DA	CPA, DA	DA (e)	CPA	DA	CPA	CPA	CPA
South Carolina	DA	CPA, DA	CPA	CPA, DA	CPA	CPA	CPA, DA	CPA, DA	DA	DA	CPA, DA	CPA, DA	DA	CPA, DA, O	CPA, DA
South Dakota	N.A.	CPA	CPA	CPA	CPA	CPA	CPA	SR	SR	CPA	CPA	N.A.	SR	⋮	CPA
Tennessee	CPA	CPA	CPA	SR	CPA	CPA	CPA	DA	CPA	DA	CPA	CPA	CPA	O	SR
Texas	N.A.	DA	DA	DA	CPA	N.A.	CPA	DA	DA	DA	CPA	DA	DA	DA	DA
Utah	DA	SR	CPA	SR	SR	SR	CPA	DA	DA	DA	SR	SR	SR	DA	SR
Vermont	CPA	CPA	CPA	CPA	CPA	CPA	CPA	CPA	O	O	CPA	O	O	O (c)	CPA
Virginia	N.A.	SR	CPA	SR	SR	SR	SR	SR	DA	SR	SR	SR	DA	SR	SR
Washington	⋮	DA	CPA	SR	CPA	DA	CPA	SR	DA	DA	SR	CPA	DA	CPA	SR
West Virginia	CPA	CPA	SR	SR	CPA	CPA	CPA	SR	SR	DA	CPA	SR	SR	DA	SR
Wisconsin	SR	SR	CPA	SR	SR	SR	CPA	SR	DA	DA	SR	SR	SR	DA	SR
Wyoming	N.A.	CPA	SR	CPA	SR	CPA	SR	SR	DA	CPA	CPA	N.A.	DA	N.A.	CPA

See footnotes at end of table.

STATE PERSONNEL ADMINISTRATION: FUNCTIONS — Continued

State	Training	Employee health & wellness programs	Affirmative action	Labor & employee relations	Retirement	Employee incentive	Productivity system	Customer surveys	Child care/elder care	Workers compensation	Group health insurance	Deferred compensation	Drug testing	Budget recommendations to legislature	Cafeteria benefits
Alabama	SR	O	DA	SR	O	N.A.	DA	DA	N.A.	O	O	O	DA	DA	O
Alaska	CPA	SR	CPA	SR	O	SR	N.A.	N.A.	N.A.	SR	O	O	SR	SR	O
Arizona	SR	CPA	DA	SR	SR	SR	CPA	CPA	CPA	O	CPA	O	DA	CPA	N.A.
Arkansas	CPA, SR	CPA, SR	DA	CPA	DA	CPA, DA	CPA, DA	CPA, DA	CPA, DA	DA	CPA	CPA	DA	CPA	CPA
California	SR	CPA, SR	CPA, SR	CPA, SR	CPA	CPA	CPA	SR	CPA	CPA, SR	CPA	CPA	CPA, SR	SR	CPA
Colorado	CPA, DA	CPA	N.A.	CPA	CPA, O	CPA, DA	CPA	CPA, DA	CPA, DA	CPA	CPA	CPA	CPA, DA	CPA	N.A.
Connecticut	DA	DA	O	O	O	N.A.	N.A.	DA	CPA, DA	O	O	O	O	O	N.A.
Delaware	SR	CPA	SR	SR	CPA	DA	DA	DA	N.A.	CPA	CPA	O	DA	DA	N.A.
Florida	DA	DA	DA	SR	O	DA	DA	DA	SR	CPA	O	O	DA	DA	N.A.
Georgia	SR	SR	SR	SR	O	SR	SR	SR	O	O	O	CPA	CPA	CPA	CPA
Hawaii	SR	N.A.	DA	SR	O	N.A.	N.A.	N.A.	N.A.	CPA	O	O	SR	O	SR
Idaho	SR	SR	SR	SR	O	DA	DA	SR	N.A.	O	CPA	O	DA	CPA	O
Illinois	SR	SR	SR	SR	O	CPA	SR	SR	CPA	SR	CPA	SR	SR	O	CPA
Indiana	DA	SR	SR	SR	SR	CPA	SR	DA	SR	CPA	CPA	SR	SR	SR	CPA
Iowa	SR	SR	SR	CPA	O	CPA	O	CPA	DA	CPA	O	CPA	DA	CPA	CPA
Kansas	SR	CPA	SR	SR	N.A.	SR	SR	SR	N.A.	CPA	CPA	CPA	CPA	CPA	CPA
Kentucky	SR	CPA	CPA	SR	SR	SR	SR	SR	SR	CPA	CPA	O	N.A.	SR	N.A.
Louisiana	SR	DA	SR	SR	O	SR	SR	DA	DA	O	O	O	DA	O	O
Maine	SR	SR	SR	DA	O	N.A.	N.A.	CPA	N.A.	SR	CPA	CPA	SR	SR	N.A.
Maryland	SR	SR	SR	SR	O	SR	N.A.	N.A.	DA	O	CPA	CPA	DA	CPA	CPA
Massachusetts	SR	O	SR	SR	O	N.A.	N.A.	DA	N.A.	SR	O	O	DA	DA	DA
Michigan	SR	CPA	SR	SR	O	N.A.	N.A.	SR	N.A.	SR	CPA	CPA	CPA	SR	CPA
Minnesota	SR	SR	SR	SR	CPA	SR	SR	SR	SR	SR	O	SR	DA	SR	N.A.
Mississippi	SR	DA	N.A.	DA	DA	DA	CPA	DA	N.A.	O	CPA	CPA	DA	CPA	O
Missouri	CPA, DA	DA	SR	SR	O	N.A.	N.A.	CPA, DA	N.A.	O	CPA	CPA	N.A.	O	O
Montana	SR	CPA	SR	CPA	O	DA	DA	DA	CPA	O	CPA	O	DA	CPA	CPA
Nebraska	SR	SR	CPA	CPA	O	N.A.	N.A.	SR	O	O	CPA	CPA	SR	SR	N.A.
Nevada	SR	O	SR	SR	O	SR	DA	SR	N.A.	O	O	SR	DA	O	N.A.
New Hampshire	SR	SR	SR	CPA	DA	SR	SR	SR	...	CPA	O	CPA	SR	CPA	...
New Jersey	SR	SR	SR	SR	O	DA	N.A.	N.A.	O	O	O	O	DA	O	O
New Mexico	SR	O	O	O	O	SR	N.A.	N.A.	O	O	O	DA	DA	SR	N.A.
New York	SR	O	SR	DA, O	DA, O	DA	DA	DA	DA, O	O	CPA	CPA	SR	DA	DA, O
North Carolina	SR	DA	SR	SR	O	CPA	N.A.	SR	N.A.	CPA	O	O	DA	SR	N.A.
North Dakota	SR	O	DA	...	O	DA	N.A.	N.A.	N.A.	O	O	O	DA	SR	N.A.
Ohio	SR	SR	O	SR	O	DA	DA	SR	N.A.	O	CPA	N.A.	CPA (a)	DA	CPA

See footnotes at end of table.

STATE PERSONNEL ADMINISTRATION: FUNCTIONS — Continued

State	Training	Employee health & wellness programs	Affirmative action	Labor & employee relations	Retirement	Employee incentive	Productivity system	Customer surveys	Child care/elder care	Workers compensation	Group health insurance	Deferred compensation	Drug testing	Budget recommendations to legislature	Cafeteria benefits
Oklahoma	SR	SR	SR	N.A.	O	SR	SR	SR	N.A.	O	O	O	N.A.	CPA	O
Oregon	SR	DA	SR	CPA	SR	N.A.	SR	SR	N.A.	DA	CPA	CPA	SR	CPA	CPA
Pennsylvania (b)	SR	DA	SR	SR	O	DA	DA	DA	CPA	CPA	CPA	CPA	SR	O	N.A.
Rhode Island	CPA, DA	CPA	CPA, DA	CPA, DA	CPA	CPA	CPA	CPA	CPA	CPA	CPA	CPA	CPA	CPA	CPA
South Carolina	CPA, DA	CPA, DA	DA, O	CPA, DA	CPA	DA	DA	CPA, DA	DA	O	CPA	CPA	DA	O	CPA
South Dakota	CPA	CPA	CPA	CPA	O	CPA	…	…	N.A.	CPA	O	O	CPA	…	CPA
Tennessee	SR	O	SR	SR	O	SR	…	CPA	O	O	O	O	O (d)	SR	SR
Texas	DA	DA	DA	DA	O	DA	DA	DA	DA	O	O	DA	DA	DA	O
Utah	SR	DA	SR	SR	O	DA	DA	SR	N.A.	O	O	O	DA	DA	N.A.
Vermont	SR	CPA	CPA	CPA	CPA	SR	N.A.	SR	O	O	CPA	O	N.A.	SR	N.A.
Virginia	SR	SR	SR	SR	SR	SR	N.A.	SR	DA	SR	CPA	CPA	DA	CPA	N.A.
Washington	SR	SR	SR	SR	O	N.A.	N.A.	SR	CPA	O	O	O	DA	SR	O
West Virginia	SR	O	O	SR	O	SR	DA	O	N.A.	O	O	O	DA	DA	O
Wisconsin	SR	O	SR	SR	O	N.A.	N.A.	N.A.	N.A.	O	O	O	DA	SR	N.A.
Wyoming	SR	CPA	DA	CPA	DA	N.A.	N.A.	CPA	N.A.	DA	CPA	DA	DA	CPA	CPA

Source: The Council of State Governments' survey of state personnel offices, October 2005.

Key:

CPA — Functions performed in centralized personnel agency.
DA — Functions performed in a decentralized agency.
O — Functions performed by other agency.
SR — Functions are a shared responsibility.
N.A. — Not applicable.
… — State did not provide an answer.

(a) Drug tests are not conducted by a state agency, but they are coordinated by a centralized personnel agency.
(b) The Office of Human Resources and Management establishes policy and administers requirements for most of these functions. Daily HR operations are decentralized to 34 agencies under the governor's jurisdiction. The Pennsylvania State Civil Service Commission performs civil service testing for state government agencies under the governor's jurisdiction.
(c) External vendor.
(d) May apply to specific state agencies.
(e) In selected cases only.

Table 8.3
CLASSIFICATION AND COMPENSATION PLANS

State	Legal basis for classification and compensation plan	Current number of classifications in state	State merit system*		Number of "at will" employees (both full- and part-time)	Date of most recent comprehensive review of classification	Requirement for periodic comprehensive classification review plan	Basis for compensation plan	Compensation schedules determined by:
			Number of full-time employees	Number of part-time employees					
Alabama	S	1,308	29,308	389	3,278	(ii)	★	J, M, S	P, L (o)
Alaska	C, S, R, CB (q)	959	14,140	147	1,171	(a)	...	J, G, V, S	P, L, GV, CB
Arizona	S, R	1,086	29,188	999	6,446	(e)	...	J, M	P
Arkansas	S	3,309 (kk)	26,210	...	26,210	1991	...	J, M	L
California	C, S, CB	3,500	191,055	4,943	2,857	(a)	...	J, M, G, V, S	P, CB
Colorado	C, S, R	527	29,028	2,317	N.A.	(f)	★	J, M, F, S	P
Connecticut	S, CB	2,450	35,707	3,868	35,981	(n)	...	J, S	P, CB
Delaware	S (r)	900	12,218	124 (nm)	1,202	(oo)	...	S	P, L, GV, CB
Florida	S	(c)	83,948	1,012	19,659	2002	★	S	P, L, GV
Georgia	S, R, EO	4,086	20,137	198	64,063	1996	...	S	P, L, GV
Hawaii	S	1,604	19,131	1,469	2,039	(s)	...	J, M, G, F, V (t)	GV, CB
Idaho	S	1,140	12,037	707	5,356	1993	...	S, J, M, F	P, L
Illinois	S, R	954	51,602	1,041	1,983	(d)	...	J, M, G, F, V, S	P, L, GV, CB
Indiana	S	1,170	20,410	98	1,515	(h)	...	(m)	P
Iowa	S	760	17,080	231	2,240	1971	...	J, M, F, V, S	P, CB
Kansas	S	561	21,781	285 (pp)	17,117	(bb)	...	J, M, G, S	GV (u)
Kentucky	S	1,440	34,789	899	4,590	(dd)	...	J, M, S	GV, P, L
Louisiana	C	2,490	62,256	530	36,419	1987	...	(v)	GV, P
Maine	S	1,107	13,520	1,105	348	1977 (d)	...	J, M, F, S	CB
Maryland	S, R	2,468	43,884	1,366	2,582	N.A.	...	J, S	P, L, GV, CB
Massachusetts	S, CB	200–250	14,000	N.A.	3,500	1997 (d)(w)	...	J, M, G, F, V, S (ee)	P, L, GV, CB (ff)
Michigan	C	(gg)	52,373	1,532	165	(d)	...	(b)	(b)
Minnesota	S	1,946	30,418 (qq)	4,756 (qq)	21,371 (qq)	2004	...	J, F, V, S	L, CB
Mississippi	S	2,052	22,664	676 (rr)	7,877	(d)	...	S	P
Missouri	S, R	1,033	41,854	N.A.	N.A.	(d)	...	S	GV, CB (o)
Montana	S	4,400	10,800	1,780	955	2002	...	J, M, F, V, S	GV, CB, L (cc)
Nebraska	S, R	1,250	13,833 (ss)	605 (ss)	1,986	1999	...	J, M, V, CB	P, CB, L
Nevada	S, CB	1,153	15,658	688	N.A.	(d)	...	S	GV, L (p)
New Hampshire	S	1,000	10,000	3,000	...	(i)	...	J, M, CB	P, L, CB
New Jersey	S	(jj)	81,715 (tt)	2,235 (tt)	7,573	N.A.	...	S	P, CB (x)
New Mexico	S, R	(hh)	18,399	431	N.A.	2002	...	J, M	P
New York	S, R	3,763	146,642 (uu)	17,824 (uu)	4,411 (uu)	(d)	...	J, M, G	P
North Carolina	S	3,000	85,977	1,611	535 (mm)	(a)	...	J, M, F	P, L
North Dakota	S	940	6,413	About 200	899	(d)	...	J, M, F, S	L, P
Ohio	S, CB	2,500	30,713 (ccc)	857 (ccc)	12,450	1986	...	S, V	L, CB
Oklahoma	S	375	27,000	N.A.	9,000	1999	...	J, M, F, V, S (y)	P
Oregon	S, CB	732	32,944	7,425	820	1990	...	M, S, CB	P, L, CB
Pennsylvania	S	2,828	57,654	2,542	29,449 (vv)	(d)(e)	...	J, M, V	L, GV, CB
Rhode Island	S	(ll)	9,936	152	2,475	2003	...	J, M	P
South Carolina	S, R	500	(eee)	(eee)	9,943 (fff)	1996 (d)	...	J, M, G, F, S	P

See footnotes at end of table.

CLASSIFICATION AND COMPENSATION PLANS — Continued

State	Legal basis for classification and compensation plan	Current number of classifications in state	State merit system* Number of full-time employees	Number of part-time employees	Number of "at will" employees (both full- and part-time)	Requirement for periodic comprehensive classification review plan	Date of most recent comprehensive review of classification	Basis for compensation plan	Compensation schedules determined by:
South Dakota	S	450	6,223 (ww)	302 (ww)	1,599 (ww)	...	2001	S	P, GV
Tennessee	S	1,800	39,558 (xx)	0	8,951 (xx)	...	(d)	J, M	P
Texas	S	950	(ddd)	(ddd)	142,394	★	2002	M, G, F	(z)
Utah	S	940	N.A.	N.A.	N.A.	...	2002	J, M, V, S	P, L
Vermont	S	1,400	7,342	286	951	...	2000	J, V, S	L, CB
Virginia	S	300	71,819	616	149	★	2001	J, M, G, F	GV, P, L
Washington	S	1,354	50,816	4,209	6,943	...	(d)	M, G, V, S	P (k)
West Virginia	S, R	1,040	21,049 (yy)	N.A.	3,655 (yy)	...	1994 (zz)	M, S	P, GV (aaa)
Wisconsin	S, R	1,840	38,644	N.A.	254	...	(g)(d)	J, M, V, S	P, L, CB
Wyoming	R	500	7,580	400	(bbb)	...	(l)	J, M, S	P

Source: The Council of State Governments' survey of state personnel offices, October 2005.

*Note: Survey questions—
How many full-time employees are covered by the merit system?
How many part-time employees are covered by the merit system?
Provide the numer of "at-will" employees. Those employes who may be hired or fired at the will of the state.

Key:
★ — Yes
. . . — No; or state did not respond to survey.
C — Constitution
F — Performance
G — Geographic
J — Job Analysis
L — Legislature
M — Market
P — Personnel Department
S — Statute
R — Regulation
V — Longevity/Seniority
CB — Collective Bargaining
GV — Governor
EO — Executive Order
N.A. — Not available.
(a) Date not known.
(b) In Michigan, the civil service commission, appointed by the governor, must approve collective bargaining agreements for exclusively represented employers. The employee relations board makes recommendations for non-exclusively represented employers.
(c) Florida has a broadband classification system comprised of 23 job families, 38 occupational groups, 236 occupations (classifications) and 148 broadband levels.
(d) Continually or ongoing. Washington's review began June 1, 2005.
(e) Classes reviewed on a case-by-case basis as the need arises.
(f) System was completely redesigned as of January 1, 1995. Have been performing consolidation studies on nine occupational groups since. Perform studies of specific classes or class series as needed.
(g) Recently completed a review of one-tenth of classified employees. Future focus likely to be on classification simplification/consolidation.
(h) Periodically.

(i) Every 5–10 years.
(j) Periodically, based on need, review specific occupational categories.
(k) State Personnel Board; determined by the directory of the Department of Personnel.
(l) Last total review of all positions was in 1987. Since that time, the state reviews by occupational grouping on a rotating basis.
(m) Equitable distribution of funds allocated by the legislature.
(n) The calendar for job classification reviews for the majority of Connecticut's job classifications (i.e., bargaining unit classifications) has been set by agreement.
(o) State Personnel Board.
(p) Personnel commission.
(q) State or federal employment laws have impact when their provisions supercede normal classification or compensation rules.
(r) State merit rules.
(s) Reviews are done in segments, not overall.
(t) Salary schedules are negotiated. They cover pay rates for each pay grade including steps recognizing length of satisfactory service. Market and geographic differentials may be approved for positions in labor market shortages. Variable pay increases for managers recognize performance.
(u) Personnel recommends to governor for approval.
(v) Civil service rules.
(w) Applies to non-management positions. Review for management positions will occur in 2005–2006.
(x) Modified Hay System.
(y) Statute provides use of several optional "Pay Movement Mechanisms" that include pay-for-performance, skill-based pay, market adjustments and equity adjustments. All state employees with two years service or more receive statutorily established lump-sum longevity payments that increase with each two years of service.
(z) State Classification Office.
(aa) Last complete review during the late 1980s. Classification review of clerical occupational series undertaken in September and November 2003.
(bb) Phased review – last phase completed in 1994. Currently underway with a comprehensive review of all job classes.
(cc) Legislature sets statewide pay plan ranges; governor sets broadband pay ranges, and union pay plans are collectively bargained.
(dd) None in over 20 years.
(ee) Only a limited number of titles have salary determined by geography or by statute. Only a couple of bargaining units have longevity pay. Non-management schedules have steps whereby an employee advances to the next step based on 12 months of satisfactory performance. Management pay is primarily performance-based.

CLASSIFICATION AND COMPENSATION PLANS — Continued

(ff) Legislature and governor approves annual management salary schedules. Legislature and governor must approve any collective bargaining contracts/increases before they are implemented.

(gg) 607 classifications; 1,953 classifications including levels within the classification series.

(hh) 245 technical occupation groups and five manager categories.

(ii) Twenty percent per year are reviewed.

(jj) New Jersey reports 7,848 classifications. This includes 4,389 state titles, 3,270 county or municipal titles and 189 common titles.

(kk) Includes classified and unclassified positions.

(ll) Rhode Island reports total classifications of 3,412. Classified service – 1,835; Unclassified service – 1,491, this classification includes elected officials and support staff, members of boards and commissions appointed by the governor, directors of state departments, and judges; Non-classified – 86, this classification includes the state educational system, either the Department of Elementary and Secondary Education or the Department of Higher Education.

(mm) This number includes "at will" employees that are subject to the State Personnel Act. It does not include employees totally exempt from the Act.

(nn) Less than 30 hours and not hourly.

(oo) 1987 was the last time that all classifications were reviewed at one time. However, many classes have had a comprehensive review since that time.

(pp) Part-time was defined at FTE .50 and below.

(qq) These numbers do not include members of the legislative branch as our payroll records are separate. It includes only executive and judicial branches, plus members of the legislative auditor and Legislative Coordinating Commission. The "at will" employees column are unclassified positions. The large number reflects the high number of academic employees in the state college and university system, as well as judicial branch employees.

(rr) Part-time employees, those who work less than 40 hours per week or 12 months per year, are also considered "at will."

(ss) Nebraska does not have a merit system. Full-time includes classified/code and non-code only and excludes legislature and courts. Part-time includes classified and non-classified employees. At will includes all "N" code employees except patient workers, student workers, per diem and board members.

(tt) In addition to the state employees who fall under the merit system, there are also approximately 4,000 state college employees and more than 112,000 local employees who fall under the system.

(uu) All offices and positions in the civil service not included in the unclassified service or "other service"; divided into four jurisdictional classes: competitive, non-competitive, labor and exempt. Some of the at will employees are included in the numbers for full-time and part-time employees.

(vv) This number includes collective bargaining covered employees who are not in the merit system.

(ww) Excludes higher education.

(xx) Full-time employees are career service and at will employees are executive service.

(yy) This does not include employees of higher education merit system, elected, judiciary and legislature.

(zz) Complete review of one agency in 2004 (800 employees) and more are planned.

(aaa) Developed by personnel department, approved by personnel board and governor.

(bbb) There are 140 executives and 450 at will employment contract employees.

(ccc) For full-time and part-time employees, this number is the classified count. The provisional count (merit, if no test given for two years after hire date) is 10,839 full-time and 1,098 part-time.

(ddd) Texas does not have a merit system. All employees are at will.

(eee) No merit system. 52,329 employees are covered under the Employee Grievance Act.

(fff) This includes faculty at higher education institutions who may be covered by their institution's faculty grievance procedure.

Table 8.4
SELECTED EMPLOYEE LEAVE POLICIES

State	Annual leave			Sick leave		Other types of leave reimbursed (c)	Child care offered on state property
	Accrual 1st year (in days/year)	Accrual 5th year (in days/year)	Employees reimbursed for unused annual leave	Accrual 1st year (in days/year)	Employees reimbursed for unused sick leave		
Alabama	13	16.25	★ (a)	13	(b)	C	...
Alaska	24 (x)	27 (x)	★	(x)	(x)	(i)	...
Arizona	12	15	(a)	12	(b)	V, C	★
Arkansas	12	15	★	12	(b)	A	...
California	16.5	18	★ (a)	12	(b)	...	★(n)
Colorado	12	12	★ (a)	10	(b)	C	★(n)
Connecticut	15	15	★ (a)	15	★(b)	...	...
Delaware	15	15	★	15	★(b)	C	...
Florida	13	15.5	★ (a)	13	★(b)	C (j)	★
Georgia	15	18	★ (a)	15	(b)	(k)	★
Hawaii	21	21	(a)	21	...	C	...
Idaho	12	15	★ (a)	12	(b)	C	...
Illinois	10	10	★	12	(b)	(z)	★
Indiana	15 (r)	18 (s)	★ (a)	9	(b)	...	★
Iowa	(h)	(h)	★ (a)	18	★(b)	C	...
Kansas	12	15	(a)	12	(b)	C (t)	★(w)
Kentucky	12	15	★ (a)	12	(b)	C	...
Louisiana	12	15	★ (a)	12	(b)	C	★(n)
Maine	12	15	★ (a)	12	(b)	C	...
Maryland	10	15	★ (a)	15	(b)	...	...
Massachusetts	10 (u)	15	★ (a)	15	(b)	P, C (v)	★(n)
Michigan	14 (d)	17.9 (d)	★	13	(b)	A	...
Minnesota	13	16.25	★	13	(b)	V	...
Mississippi	18	21	★ (a)	12	...	A, C	...
Missouri	15	15	...	15	(b)	A, C	...
Montana	15	15	★	12	★(b)	...	(aa)
Nebraska	12	12	★ (a)	12	★(b)	...	★(n)
Nevada	15	15	★	15	★	C	...
New Hampshire	12	15	★	15	★	A (l)(m)	...
New Jersey	12	15	(a)	12	★(b)	C (bb)	★(n)
New Mexico	10	12	★ (a)	12	★(b)	...	...
New York	13	13	★ (a)	(q)	(b)	P (o)	★
North Carolina	11.75	16.75	(a)	12	(b)	...	...
North Dakota	12	15	★	12	(b)	C	...
Ohio	14	20	★ (a)	10	★(b)	C (p)	★
Oklahoma	15	18	★ (a)	15	...	C (y)	...
Oregon	12	15	★ (a)	12	...	P	...
Pennsylvania	7 (e)	15	★ (a)	13	★(b)	C, P (cc)	★(n)
Rhode Island	10	15	★ (a)	15	(b)	...	★
South Carolina	15	15	★ (a)	15	(b)	C	★(n)
South Dakota	15	15	★	14	★(b)	...	...
Tennessee	12 (f)	18 (f)	★	12	...	A, C	...
Texas	12	15	(a)	12	...	...	★
Utah	13	16.25	...	13	...	C	...
Vermont	12	15	★ (a)	12	(b)	C	...
Virginia	4 hours (g)	5 hours (g)	★(g)	15	(b)	C	★(n)
Washington	12	15	★ (a)	12	★(b)	C	★
West Virginia	15	15	★ (a)	18	(b)	C	★(n)
Wisconsin	15	20	(a)	16.25	★(b)	...	...
Wyoming	12	15	★ (a)	12	★(b)	...	★(n)

See footnotes at end of table.

SELECTED EMPLOYEE LEAVE POLICIES — Continued

Source: The Council of State Governments' survey of state personnel offices, October 2005.

Key:

★ — Yes

. . . — No

A — Annual leave

C — Compensatory leave

P — Personal leave

V — Vacation leave

(a) Alabama – Up to 480 hours upon separation.

Arizona – Covered employees may accrue up to 240 hours; reimbursement may occur when transferring to another agency, upon leaving state service, or when management approves payment for excesses beyond 240 hours.

California – Reimbursement at time of separation.

Colorado – Payout for unused leave is up to the maximum accrual rate and at the time of separation.

Connecticut – Upon leaving state service.

Florida – Civil service can receive payment up to 240 hours of unused annual leave. The 240-hour cap is over an employee's entire career with the state. Selected Exempt Service and Senior Management Service employees may receive payment up to 480 hours of unused annual leave. The lifetime cap provision does not apply.

Georgia – Employees forfeit annual leave after accruing 360 hours. On separation from state employment, employees are paid for all accrued leave and all forfeited leave. Employees may also use accrued and forfeited leave as service credit toward retirement.

Hawaii – Unused leave is paid upon separation from employment.

Idaho – Upon separation.

Indiana – Up to 30 days vacation (unused at time of separation and up to $5,000 at 50 percent conversion rate on retirement).

Iowa – At time employment terminates.

Kansas – Employees can convert up to 40 hours of annual leave in excess of the maximum accumulation allowed to sick leave. Annual leave balances are paid out at the time of employee separation.

Kentucky – If separated by proper resignation or retirement, but shall not exceed the maximum amounts established by regulation.

Louisiana – Up to 300 hours annual leave upon separation.

Maine – Reimbursement limited to 240 hours upon termination for most employees.

Maryland – A maximum of 50 days of annual leave may be carried into a new calendar year. An employee who separates from state employment shall be paid for any unused, accumulated annual leave at a rate equal to the last hourly rate times the number of hours of annual leave up to 400 hours.

Massachusetts – Departments can request permission from the Human Resources Division to allow a higher accrual rate for newly hired managers which is commensurate with their years of comparable experience.

Mississippi – Employees reimbursed for a maximum of 240 hours of unused annual leave upon separation from state employment.

Nebraska – Balanced to 35 days on December 31 each year.

New Jersey – Employees who do not use their allotted vacation leave during a single year may roll it over to the following calendar year. But employees may not have more than two years worth of unused vacation leave at any time.

New Mexico – Employees may be reimbursed up to a maximum of 240 hours at their current hourly rate.

New York – Although there is no lump-sum payment for unused sick leave at time of separation, a specified number of days of unused sick leave may be applied at retirement toward health insurance premiums and counted as additional retirement service credit.

North Carolina – Receive pay when separated up to 30 days.

Ohio – Up to 40 hours. Personal leave may be cashed out annually at 100 percent of base rate of pay. Unused vacation leave is reimbursed only if such leave was denied during the past 12 months and the employee is at the maximum accrual limit.

Oklahoma – Separating employees will be reimbursed for unused annual leave up to 480-hour maximum.

Oregon – Up to 250 hours upon separation.

Pennsylvania – Unused annual leave may be carried over to maximum of 45 days. Annual leave in excess of 45 days is converted to sick leave after seven pay periods, not to exceed a 300 sick days balance. Unused leave is paid on separation from service.

Rhode Island – Upon retirement or termination.

South Carolina – One additional bonus day of leave is rewarded for each service year above 10 years, to a maximum of 30 days. Forty-five days may be carried forward to the next calendar year. Employees are paid for unused leave only upon termination or retirement.

Texas – Hours in excess of maximum allowable carryover limits are credited to employee's sick leave balance.

Vermont – Accumulation cap of annual days based upon years of service. Annual leave carries over from year to year as long as it doesn't go over the accumulation cap. When an employee separates from service, up to 60 hours of annual leave accrued is paid.

Washington – When employee who has completed six continuous months of employment separates, for any one of several reasons, the employee is entitled to a lump-sum payment of unused annual leave.

West Virginia – Depending on date of hire, paid on any type of separation or may be used to "purchase" additional service credit or insurance coverage when retiring from active employment.

Wisconsin – State employees with 15 or more years of state service may elect to receive up to 40 hours of their leave as a cash payment.

Wyoming – Only on termination or retirement.

(b) Alabama – May be paid for one-half upon retirement.

Arizona – Sick leave in excess of 500 hours is reimbursed on a partial basis at retirement.

Arkansas – As of July 1, 1999, sick leave not used is reimbursed upon retirement.

California – Service credit given at time of retirement.

Colorado – Employees who retire are paid one-fourth of their unused sick leave, up to the maximum accrual rate.

Connecticut – At retirement, with limitations.

Delaware – Reimbursed for retirement or if laid off up to a maximum of 337.5 hours. If upon death, also up to maximum of 675 hours.

Florida – Employees may receive payment upon separation of employment if they have 10 years of service. Twenty-five percent of sick leave is paid up to 480 hours.

Georgia – Employees forfeit sick leave after accruing 720 hours. Forfeited sick leave may be restored to employees in the event of extended illness. Forfeited sick leave counts as service credit towards retirement.

Illinois – Only sick leave accrued between January 1, 1984, and December 31, 1997, is subject to reimbursement at 50 percent of pay at separation from state service.

Idaho – Partial reimbursement at retirement for health insurance premiums.

Indiana – No, except as covered by the 50 percent conversion rate at retirement.

Iowa – After at least 240 hours of sick leave is accrued, employees may elect to accrue additional vacation in lieu of the normal sick leave accrual at the rate of one hour of vacation for three hours of sick leave. At the time of retirement, some employees can receive compensation for up to $2,000 of unused sick leave. As of July 1, 2006, a new sick leave conversion program will be available to executive branch state employees. Under this program, accrued sick leave will be converted first to $2,000 cash payment and the remainder will go into a bank for the purpose of paying the state's share of health insurance after retirement. The employee share of the premium will continue to be paid by retired employee. The conversion of sick leave will be according to the following: Sick leave balance of 0–750 hours will accrue at rate of 18 days per year, and conversion rate of 60 percent of value. Sick leave balance of 750–1500 hours will accrue at 12 days per year, and conversion rate of 80 percent of value. Sick leave balance over 1500 hours will accrue at 6 days per year and conversion rate of 100 percent.

Kansas – Upon retirement, employees who have met length of service and sick leave accumulation requirements are reimbursed for a portion of their unused sick leave.

Kentucky – However, upon retirement if unused sick leave amounts to a month, then the months are used for final compensation for retirement.

Louisiana – At retirement unused balance is applied toward additional service credit.

Maine – Up to 30 days may be credited toward service time for retirement benefit calculations.

Maryland – Not if separation is for reasons other than retirement, in which case the employee's sick leave is added on a day-for-day basis to their service credit for calculation of retirement benefit amount.

Massachusetts – Employees who are retiring can cash out 20 percent of their sick leave balance.

Michigan – Only employees hired prior to October 1, 1980 are reimbursed for unused sick leave in increments up to 50 percent based upon the number of accumulated hours. Employees hired prior to October 1, 1980 are paid 50 percent of their sick leave upon retirement or death.

Minnesota – Eligible employees who meet separation criteria.

Missouri – Unused sick leave is creditable toward retirement.

Montana – Reimbursed for one-fourth of value.

Nebraska – Balanced to 1440 hours on December 31 each year.

New Jersey – Sick leave may be carried over from year to year. At the time

SELECTED EMPLOYEE LEAVE POLICIES — Continued

of retirement, eligible employees can receive supplemental compensation on retirement (SCOR). The maximum amount is $15,000. SCOR is computed at the rate of one-half the employee's daily rate of pay for each day of earned and unused accumulated sick leave at the effective date of retirement.

New Mexico – In accordance with the provisions of NMSA 1978, Section 10-7-10, employees who have accumulated 600 hours of unused sick leave are entitled to be paid for unused sick leave in excess of 600 hours at a rate equal to 50 percent of their hourly rate of pay for up to 120 hours of sick leave. Payment for unused sick leave may be made only once per fiscal year on either the payday immediately following the first full pay period in January or the first full pay period in July. Immediately prior to retirement from the classified service, employees who have accumulated 600 hours of unused sick leave are entitled to be paid for unused sick leave in excess of 600 hours at a rate equal to 50 percent of their hourly rate for up to 400 hours of sick leave.

New York – Upon separation from state service, employees may receive a lump-sum payment for accrued and unused vacation credits up to a maximum of 30 days if they meet eligibility requirements for that payment. Certain bargaining units can exchange up to five days of accumulated credits of annual leave for an equivalent amount of cash. Employees must have 35 or more days of such credits during an annual election period.

North Carolina – May apply unused leave toward retirement.

North Dakota – Upon termination, an employee with 10 years of continuous service is eligible for 10 percent payout of accrued sick leave.

Ohio – Reimbursed up to 75 percent of base rate of pay.

Pennsylvania – Unused sick leave may be carried over to a maximum of 300 days. Unused sick leave is paid on retirement (but not other separations) on a sliding scale from 30 percent to 50 percent based on years of service.

Rhode Island – Upon retirement only. A formula is used for percentage payout.

South Carolina – Ninety days of unused sick leave may be credited as service credit upon retirement.

South Dakota – One-fourth after seven years of service.

Vermont – No limit placed on the total accumulation of earned sick leave, carries over from year to year.

Virginia – Twenty-five percent up to $5,000 upon separation.

Washington – In January of each year, an employee whose sick leave balance at the end of the previous year exceeds 480 hours may elect to convert the sick leave hours earned in the previous calendar year, minus those hours used during the year, to monetary compensation. Monetary compensation for converted hours is paid at the rate of 25 percent, based on the employee's current salary. All converted hours are deducted from employee's sick leave balance. Also, employees who separate from state service because of retirement or death are compensated for their total unused sick leave accumulation at the rate of 25 percent.

West Virginia – Depending on employee's date of hire, may be used to "purchase" additional service credit or insurance coverage when retiring from active employment.

Wisconsin – Under sick leave plan, employees can be reimbursed for hours when they retire by converting to a pool of money to pay for health insurance.

Wyoming – Only on termination to a maximum of 480 hours (or one-half of total hours accumulated).

(c) For information on the specific methods of reimbursement, state personnel departments should be consulted.

(d) Includes 16 hours of personal leave that all employees receive on October 1 of each year.

(e) In Pennsylvania, management gets 10 days.

(f) In Tennessee, annual leave can be carried over according to the fol-

lowing: 1–5 years, 30 days; 5–10 years, 36 days; 10–20 years, 39 days; and 20+ years, 42 days.

(g) Annual leave can be carried over according to the following: 1–5 years, 24 days; 5–9 years, 30 days; 10–14 years, 36 days; 15–19 years, 42 days; 20–24 years, 48 days; and 25+ years, 54 days.

(h) In first year – 10 vacation days, plus two unscheduled holidays. In fifth year – 15 vacation days, plus two unscheduled holidays.

(i) Some collective bargaining agreements provide special leave terms such as educational leave.

(j) Special compensatory time.

(k) Employees may convert up to 24 hours of unused sick leave to personal leave each year.

(l) Floating holidays.

(m) Bonus.

(n) At some facilities.

(o) Pregnancy or childbirth, adoption, childcare leave, workers' compensation, civil service examinations, jury duty, civil defense duty, ordered military duty, bone marrow and organ donation, and professional examinations and meetings (at discretion of agency).

(p) Overtime eligible employees are paid for compensatory time not used within 180 days.

(q) The amount of sick leave that can be accrued varies by bargaining unit. A new full-time, annual-salaried employee is credited with 6.5 days of vacation after 13 biweekly pay periods with no break in service of more than one year. After that, the employee accumulates vacation at the rate of one-half day per pay period during each year of service through the first seven years. An M/C employee earns bonus vacation days on anniversary date. The number of bonus days earned equals the employee's completed years of continuous service.

(r) In Indiana, 12 vacation days, 3 personal days.

(s) In Indiana, 12 vacation days, 3 bonus vacation days, 3 personal days.

(t) Holiday compensatory time.

(u) Twelve days for managers and confidentials.

(v) Organ donation leave, bereavement leave and blood donation leave.

(w) Child care is offered on state property in some very limited instances. The state of Kansas also allows new parents to bring infants to work with them until the infant is six months old.

(x) Leave provisions exist in statute, but most employees in the executive branch receive leave in accordance with terms of the applicable collective bargaining agreement. The statute provides personal leave (the usual type in collective bargaining agreements as well). The statutory amount for personal leave is listed in the annual leave section. The amount is about the same as the amount available in the collective bargaining agreement covering the largest group of employees in the classified service.

(y) Employees may use a maximum of 10 days of "enforced leave" for family illnesses or emergencies per year; however, this leave is charged against sick leave balance. Agencies may elect to compensate overtime with compensatory time.

(z) Employees typically receive three personal leave days each year; however, beginning in 1995, one additional personal day is granted if no sick leave was used during the prior calendar year.

(aa) State pays lease fees for private day care facility in the capitol city.

(bb) Military leave, family leave, and convention leave for approved organizations.

(cc) Compensatory leave is reimbursed if not taken within 90 days of date earned. Earned unused personal leave is paid on termination of Commonwealth employment or transfer to an unqualified entity.

Table 8.5
STATE EMPLOYEES: PAID HOLIDAYS**

State	Major holidays (a)	Martin Luther King's Birthday (b)	Lincoln's Birthday	President's Day (c)	Washington's Birthday (c)	Good Friday	Memorial Day (d)	Columbus Day (e)	Veteran's Day	Day after Thanksgiving	Day before or after Christmas	Day before or after New Year's	Election Day (f)	Other (g)
Alabama	★	★			★(i)			★	★	(k)	(k)			★
Alaska	★	★		★			★		★	(k)	(k)			★
Arizona	★	★		★	★		★	★	★	(k)				
Arkansas	★	★		★			★		★	★	Before			★
California	★	★	★	★			★	★	★	★	Before			★
Colorado	★	★		★			★	★	★					
Connecticut	★	★	★	★		★	★	★	★					
Delaware	★	★		★		★	★	★	★	★				★
Florida	★	★					★		★				★	★
Georgia	★	★		★	(l)		★		★	(l)	(l)			★
Hawaii	★			★			★		★				★	
Idaho	★	★					★	★	★	★				★
Illinois	★	★(h)	★	★			★	★	★				★	
Indiana	★	★	(m)		(m)		★	★	★	(m)	(m)		★	
Iowa	★	★					★		★					★
Kansas	★	★					★		★					
Kentucky	★	★				★(n)	★		★	★	★		★(t)	★
Louisiana	★	★			★	★	★	★	★	★			★(u)	★
Maine	★	★		★			★	★	★					
Maryland	★	★		★			★	★	★				★	★
Massachusetts	★	★		★			★	★	★					
Michigan	★	★		★			★		★		★			★
Minnesota	★	★		★			★		★	(k)	★	★	★(z)	★
Mississippi	★	★					★(v)		★	(k)	(k)			★
Missouri	★	★	★	★	★		★	★	★	(k)				★
Montana	★	★		★			★		★	★				
Nebraska	★	★		★			★		★	★			★	★
Nevada	★	★		★			★		★	★				
New Hampshire	★	★					★		★	★				★
New Jersey	★	★	★	★	★	★	★	★	★	★				★
New Mexico	★	★		(o)			★	★	★	(o)			★(w)	
New York	★	★	(j)	★			★	★	★				(j)	★
North Carolina	★	★			★		★		★	★	(x)			
North Dakota	★	★		★		★	★		★		(p)			
Ohio	★	★		★		★	★	★	★					
Oklahoma	★	★		★			★		★	(k)	(k)			
Oregon	★	★		★	★		★		★	★	(k)			
Pennsylvania	★	★		★			★	★	★	★			★	
Rhode Island	★	★		★			★	★	★		(k)	(k)		★
South Carolina	★	★		★			★		★	★	★		★	★

See footnotes at end of table.

STATE EMPLOYEES: PAID HOLIDAYS** — Continued

State	Major holidays (a)	Martin Luther King's Birthday (b)	Lincoln's Birthday	President's Day (c)	Washington's Birthday (c)	Good Friday	Memorial Day (d)	Columbus Day (e)	Veteran's Day	Day after Thanksgiving	Day before or after Christmas	Day before or after New Year's	Election Day (f)	Other (g)
South Dakota	★	★	…	★	…	(k)	★	(y)	★	(k)	(k)	…	…	…
Tennessee	★	★	…	★	…	★	★	(q)	★	(q)	(k)	…	…	…
Texas	★	★	…	★	…	(r)	★	★	★	★	★	★	…	★
Utah	★	★	…	★	★	…	★	★	★	…	…	…	…	★
Vermont	★	★	…	★	★	…	★	★	★	…	…	…	…	…
Virginia	★	★	…	…	…	…	★	…	★	★	…	…	…	★
Washington	★	★	…	…	…	…	★	…	★	★	…	…	…	★
West Virginia	★	★	★	★	…	…	★	★	★	(k)	(s)	(s)	…	★
Wisconsin	★	★	…	★	…	…	★	★	(aa)	…	★	★	(bb)	…
Wyoming	★	★	…	…	…	…	★	…	★	…	★	…	…	…

**Holidays in addition to any other authorized paid personal leave granted state employees.

Source: The Council of State Governments' survey of state personnel offices, October 2005.

Note: In some states, the governor may proclaim additional holidays or select from a number of holidays for observance by state employees. In some states, the list of paid holidays is determined by the personnel department at the beginning of each year; as a result, the number of holidays may change from year to year. Number of paid holidays may also vary across some employee classifications. If a holiday falls on a weekend, generally employees get the day preceding or following.

Key:

★ — Paid holiday granted.

… — Paid holiday not granted.

(a) New Year's Day, Independence Day, Labor Day, Thanksgiving Day and Christmas Day.

(b) Third Monday in January.

(c) Generally, third Monday in February; Washington's Birthday or President's Day. In some states the holiday is called President's Day or Washington-Lincoln Day. Most frequently, this day recognizes George Washington and Abraham Lincoln.

(d) Last Monday in May in all states indicated, except Vermont where holiday is observed on May 30. Generally, states follow the federal government's observance (last Monday in May) rather than the traditional Memorial Day (May 30).

(e) Second Monday in October.

(f) General election day only, unless otherwise indicated. In Indiana, primary and general election days.

(g) Additional holidays: Alabama—Mardi Gras Day (fourth Monday in April), Jefferson Davis Day (or personal leave day)(Tuesday before Ash Wednesday), Jefferson Davis' Birthday (first Monday in June).

Confederate Memorial Day (fourth Monday in April), Jefferson Davis Day (or personal leave day)(Tuesday before Ash Wednesday),

Alaska—Seward's Day (last Monday in March), Alaska Day (October 18).

Arkansas—Employee's birthday.

California—One personal holiday.

Delaware—Return Day, after noon (Thursday after a general election) in Sussex County only.

Florida—One personal day is granted every July 1. This personal day does not accrue.

Georgia—Confederate Memorial Day (fourth Monday in April).

Hawaii—Admission Day (third Friday in August), Prince Kuhio Day (March 26), King Kamehameha Day (June 11).

Iowa—Two additional floating holidays are prorated and accrued biweekly as vacation.

Kansas—One discretionary holiday that can be used any time during the calendar year.

Louisiana—Mardi Gras Day (Tuesday before Ash Wednesday), Inauguration Day (every four years, in Baton Rouge only).

Maine—Patriot's Day (third Monday in April).

Massachusetts—Patriot's Day (third Monday in April), Evacuation Day (June 17—Suffolk County only), Bunker Hill Day (March 17—Suffolk County only).

Minnesota—One floating holiday.

Mississippi—Confederate Memorial Day (last Monday in April).

Missouri—Harry Truman's Birthday (May 8).

Nebraska—Arbor Day (last Friday in April).

Nevada—Nevada Day (last Friday in October).

Rhode Island—Victory Day (second Monday in August).

South Carolina—Confederate Memorial Day (May 10).

Texas—The following are partial staffing state holidays where state offices are scheduled to be open: Confederate Heroes Day (January 19), Texas Independence Day (March 2), San Jacinto Day (April 21), Emancipation Day (June 19) and Lyndon Johnson's Birthday (August 27). The following are optional holidays that a state employee may observe in lieu of any state holiday on which the employee's agency is required to be open: Rosh Hashanah, Yom Kippur, Good Friday and Cesar Chavez Day (March 31).

Utah—Pioneer Day (July 24).

Virginia—Lee-Jackson Day (Friday preceding the third Monday in January).

Washington—One floating holiday.

West Virginia—West Virginia Day.

(h) Celebrated as Robert E. Lee's Birthday.

(i) Celebrated as George Washington's and Thomas Jefferson's Birthday.

(j) Floating holiday; employee may choose either to work on that day or to take it off. If an employee works on the floating holiday, they may take another day off at any time within one year with supervisory approval.

(k) At the discretion of the governor. In South Carolina, the day after Christmas is an established holiday.

(l) In Georgia, Robert E. Lee's Birthday is observed on the day after Thanksgiving, and Washington's Birthday is observed on the day after Christmas.

(m) In Indiana, Lincoln's Birthday is observed on the day after Thanksgiving, and Washington's Birthday is observed the day before Christmas.

(n) In Kentucky, half day.

(o) In New Mexico, President's Day is observed on the day after Thanksgiving.

STATE EMPLOYEES: PAID HOLIDAYS** — Continued

(p) In North Dakota, offices close at noon on December 24th, but it is not considered a holiday.

(q) In Tennessee, state employees have been selected by ballot to observe Columbus Day on the day after Thanksgiving during the past few years.

(r) In Texas, a state employee may observe Good Friday in lieu of any state holiday on which the employee's agency is required to be open.

(s) Half day on Christmas Eve and New Year's Eve if they fall on Monday, Tuesday, Wednesday or Thursday. West Virginia – includes Friday.

(t) Up to four hours.

(u) Every two years.

(v) Also for Jefferson Davis' Birthday.

(w) Employees are allowed up to two hours paid administrative leave to vote.

(x) Three days when Christmas Day falls on Tuesday, Wednesday or Thursday; two days when Christmas Day falls on Friday or Monday.

(y) Celebrated as Native Americans Day.

(z) Election Day approved beginning in 2006 (even years only) with the exception of employees who work in 24/7 shifts. Those employees receive four hours of annual leave each year in lieu of the paid Election Day.

(aa) Also receive day for primary election during even years.

Table 8.6
ALTERNATIVE WORKING ARRANGEMENTS FOR STATE EMPLOYEES

State	Flextime	Share leave	Telecommute	Job sharing	Incentives/credits for not using sick leave
Alabama (n)	★	...	...	★	...
Alaska (b)	★	★	★	★	...
Arizona	★	★	★	★	★
Arkansas	★	...	★	★	★
California	★	★	★	★	...
Colorado	★	★	★	★	★(c)
Connecticut	★	★	★	...	...
Delaware	★		★	★	★(r)
Florida	★	★(l)	★	★	...
Georgia	★	★	★	★	...
Hawaii	★	★	★	...	★
Idaho	★	★	★	★	★
Illinois	★	★	★	★	★
Indiana	★	...	★	★	...
Iowa	★	...	★	...	★
Kansas (d)	★	★	★	★	★
Kentucky	★	★	★	...	★(a)
Louisiana	★	★	★	★	★(e)
Maine	★	★	...	★	...
Maryland	★	...	★	...	...
Massachusetts	★	★(f)	★	★	...
Michigan (g)	★	★	★	★	...
Minnesota	★	...	★	★	★(s)
Mississippi	...	...	...	...	...
Missouri	★	★	★(limited)	★(limited)	...
Montana	★	★	...	★	★(m)
Nebraska	★	★	★	★	...
Nevada	★	★	★	★	★
New Hampshire	★	...	...	★	★
New Jersey	★	★(h)	★	...	★(h)
New Mexico	★(n)	...	★(n)	★(n)	★
New York	★	★	★	★	★
North Carolina	★	★	★	★	...
North Dakota	★	★	★	★	...
Ohio	★	...	...	...	★(o)
Oklahoma	★	★	★	...	...
Oregon	★	★	★	★	...
Pennsylvania	...	...	★(p)	★	★(q)
Rhode Island	★	...	★	★	★
South Carolina	★	★(i)	★	★	...
South Dakota	★	...	★	★	...
Tennessee	★	★	★	★	...
Texas	★	...	★	★	...
Utah	★	★	★	★	★
Vermont	★	...	★(limited)	★	★
Virginia	★	★	★	★	★
Washington	★	★	★	★	...
West Virginia (j)	★	★(k)	★	★	...
Wisconsin	★	...	★	★	★
Wyoming	★	★	★	★	...

See footnotes at end of table.

ALTERNATIVE WORKING ARRANGEMENTS FOR STATE EMPLOYEES — Continued

Source: The Council of State Governments' survey of state personnel offices, October 2005.

Key:

★ — Yes

. . . — No

N.A.— Not applicable

(a) Unused sick leave converts to service credit upon retirement.

(b) The arrangements checked, most of which are not in general use, may be available in collective bargaining agreements. The terms of these vary and are subject to change when successor agreements are negotiated.

(c) One-fourth unused sick leave is paid out at retirement.

(d) The shared leave program is managed by a central committee made up of representatives from agencies. The opther options listed here are at the agencies' discretion.

(e) A small number of agencies offer rewards for not using leave through a rewards and recognition program.

(f) Collective extended illness sick leave bank for all employees for personal illness only; no direct allowed to specific employees unless legislation is passed on behalf of a particular employee.

(g) Each department establishes their own work rules governing these options. Only the Department of Corrections provides incentives for not using sick leave.

(h) Share leave: the state has a donated leave program which allows employees to donate their leave time to other employees who suffer from a catastrophic health condition or injury or who provide care to a member of the employee's immediate family who is suffering from a catastrophic health condition or injury; or require absence from work due to the donation of an organ. Incentives/credits: At the time of retirement, eligible employees can receive supplemental compensation on retirement (SCOR). The maximum amount is $15,000. SCOR is computed at the rate of one-half the employee's daily rate of pay for each day of earned and unused accumulated sick leave at the effective date of retirement.

(i) The state administers a leave pool which allows employees to draw upon unused sick leave donated by employees to be used in emergency situations.

(j) Alternative working arrangements are at the discretion of each agency/department director.

(k) Annual leave donation program established by statute and implemented by rule.

(l) Agency optional programs: sick leave pool – requires employees to have one year of state service and have a minimum of 64 hours of accrued sick leave. Sick leave transfer plan – agencies may adopt intra- or interagency sick leave transfer plans to be requested by and donated to employees who have exhausted all of their leave.

(m) Payout at one-fourth of unused leave.

(n) Utilized by some, not all, state agencies.

(o) When 40.1 through 80 hours of sick leave are used within a 12-month period, it is paid at 70 percent of base rate of pay (versus being paid at 100 percent for hours used less than 40.1 or more than 80).

(p) Telecommuting may be approved on a temporary basis for those employees whose work is critical to the agency and cannot be performed by others.

(q) Incentives/credits for not using sick leave include employee compensation upon retirement for a percentage of unused sick leave balances which exceed 100 days.

(r) Senate Bill 178, which became law on July 1, 2004, allows sick leave to be used concurrently to supplement short-term disability. A short-term and long-term disability program is being offered to employees beginning calendar year 2006. This same bill allows unused sick leave to be utilized toward extra creditable pension time for those otherwise eligible (21 days equals one month of pension).

(s) Severance pay for eligible employees is calculated as a percentage of unused sick leave.

Table 8.7
PERFORMANCE EVALUATIONS

State	Mandatory by law	Annual evaluation	Separate evaluation for managers and employees	Agency heads allowed customization in evaluation
Alabama	★	★	...	...
Alaska	★	★(a)	...	★
Arizona	...	★	...	★
Arkansas	★	★	...	★
California	★	★	★	★
Colorado (b)	★	★	...	...
Connecticut (c)	...	...	...	...
Delaware	★	★	...	★
Florida	★	★	...	★
Georgia	★	★	...	...
Hawaii	★	★	★	(d)
Idaho	★	★	★	★
Illinois	...	★	★	★
Indiana	★	★	★	★
Iowa	★	★	...	★(e)
Kansas (o)	★	★	...	★
Kentucky	★	★	★	...
Louisiana	★	★	★	★
Maine	★	★	...	...
Maryland	★	★	★(p)	★
Massachusetts	★	★	★	...
Michigan	★	★	★	★
Minnesota	★	★	★	★
Mississippi	★	★	...	...
Missouri (f)	...	★	★	★
Montana	...	★(g)	...	★
Nebraska	...	★	...	★
Nevada	★	★	...	★
New Hampshire	....N.A..			
New Jersey	★	★	★	★
New Mexico	★	★	...	...
New York (h)	...	★	★	★
North Carolina	★	★	...	★
North Dakota	★(i)	★	...	★
Ohio (j)	★	★	★	...
Oklahoma	★	★	...	...
Oregon	★	★	★	★
Pennsylvania	...	★	(k)	(l)
Rhode Island	...	...	...	...
South Carolina	....N.A..			
South Dakota	...	★	...	...
Tennessee	...	★	★	★(q)
Texas	...	...	...	★
Utah	...	★	...	★(m)
Vermont	...	...	...	...
Virginia	★	★	...	★
Washington	★	★	★	★(r)
West Virginia	★	★(g)	★(n)	★
Wisconsin	★	★	...	★
Wyoming	...	★	...	...

See footnotes at end of table.

Source: The Council of State Governments' survey of state personnel offices, October 2005.

Key:

★ — Yes

. . . — No

N.A. — Did not respond.

(a) Regulations and various collective bargaining agreements generally refer to the evaluations being done on a merit anniversary date rather than annually, but the interval is still about once a year in general.

(b) Agencies must use the statewide core competencies and number of rating levels. Agencies develop their own forms and descriptive labels for the ratings levels. They develop performance objectives and additional competencies if desired.

(c) Managers are covered by statute, labor units are covered by the separate bargaining agreements.

(d) Generally no, unless customization/changes are needed for special circumstances (e.g. to meet hospital accreditation requirements).

(e) To customize, agencies must first have alternative system reviewed by the Department of Management for adherence to the state's Accountable Government Act. The Highway Patrol Division and the Division of Criminal Investigation of the Department of Public Safety have received such approval. Department directors and staff of the governor are reviewed on different systems also.

(f) Missouri has begun the transition from performance evaluation, which looks back at performance; to performance management, which is a more forward outlook that incorporates planning for individual and organizational success, based on effective communication, shared knowledge of organizational objectives, performance expectations and development opportunities.

(g) By rule.

(h) In accordance with state policy, employee performance is evaluated regularly. While each bargaining unit has its own performance evaluation program, each one generally involves the development of a performance plan by an employee with his or her supervisor, a review of employee performance, recognition of positive employee accomplishments, and suggestions for further improving the employee's contribution to the organization. Such reviews are usually conducted annually for each state employee.

(i) Administrative rule.

(j) Ohio uses standard evaluation forms that vary by nine classification groupings (e.g. clerical, trades/technical, professional/paraprofessional).

(k) Managers and supervisors are rated on an additional supervision criteria.

(l) Agencies typically do not customize evaluations; however, attorneys, senior management service, Integrated Enterprise System staff, and PA Liquor Control Board Wine and Spirits shop employees have separate evaluation forms.

(m) DHRM sets statewide policy that gives agencies flexibility to adopt a variety of approaches to performance evaluation.

(n) Additional evaluation criteria provided for managers.

(o) Agencies are authorized to adopt an evaluation system that best supports their operational needs. All systems convert to three levels of official rating for system-wide consistency.

(p) Only for employees in the Executive Pay Plan.

(q) A variety of forms are used for the different types of performance evaluations.

(r) Agency heads may develop alternate procedures and forms which must be approved by the director of the Department of Personnel.

Table 8.8
CIVIL SERVICE REFORM

State	Comprehensive (wholesale) civil service reform	Extent of civil service reform	Incremental civil service reform	Functional areas where reform has taken place
		Has your state implemented a comprehensive (wholesale) or incremental civil service reform in the past five years?		
Alabama	...		...	
Alaska	...		(a)	
Arizona	...		★(b)	
Arkansas..................	...		...	
California	...		...	
Colorado..................	...	Referendum to change Constitution in general election, Nov. 2004, failed.	★	B, CL, CO, E, M, P, R, S, T
Connecticut	...		★	M, S
Delaware..................	★	Simplify and streamline Merit Rules – Jan. 1, 2004.	...	
Florida	★		...	
Georgia	★	Effective July 1, 1996, all classification, selection and salary admin-istration authority was decentralized to agencies. Final authority for resolution of grievances and adverse actions was also decentralized to agencies on this date. Employees hired before July 1, 1996, who remain on classified positions still have appeal rights to the State Personnel Board.	...	
Hawaii......................	★	Replacement of seven-member Civil Service Commission with a three-member Merit Appeals Board. Redefined the merit principle as the selection of persons based on their fitness and ability for public employ-ment and the retention of employees based on their demonstrated appropriate conduct and productive performance. Clarified that layoffs, suspensions, discharges, and demotions shall be in accordance with procedures negotiated under Chapter 89 or determined under Chapter 89C, HRS. Authorized drug testing for all prospective employees.	...	
Idaho........................	...		★	CL, CO, P, T
Illinois......................	...		...	
Indiana.....................	...		★	B, E, P, R, S
Iowa	★	A complete review of our predecessor agency, the Dept. of Personnel, by our new director was made in 1999 at the behest of the governor, resulting in the 100-day Plan and a major reorganization of the depart-ment. On July 1, 2003, IDOP was merged into the new Department of Administrative Services. Human resource functions previously assigned to IDOP were retained in the Human Resources unit. Administrative/support functions were transferred to the new combined units in these areas within the new department. Fee-for-service billing established by a customer council was also implemented along with a marketplace (competative) funding approach for training and development functions.	...	
Kansas	★	Working in partnership, the central and field HR agencies evaluated all aspects of the state's HR operations and acted to: 1. Streamline systems, system requirements and processes; 2. Determine the most effective and efficient balance of centralized and decentralized author-ities, decentralizing a number of HR functions; 3. Create and act upon shared services philosophy that shares resources, responsibilities and authorities; 4. Build the capacity of the work force and HR operations; and 5. Change the state's HR regulations to support the above efforts. All of these efforts are ongoing.	...	
Kentucky	...		★	B, CL, CO, E, M, P, R, S, T
Louisiana	...		★(c)	CL, CO, M, P, R, S, T
Maine.......................	...		★(d)	CL, CO, M, P, R, S, T
Maryland	...		...	
Massachusetts..........	...		★(e)	CL, M, R, S
Michigan..................	★	There have been no legal mandates or citizens review committee rec-ommendations to mandate change, however, the Department of Civil Service has undergone changes in virtually all areas of its responsibility within the last five years. The DCS worked collaboratively with all human resource directors and the state employer to centralize and standardize HR functions. The project, called HR Optimization, was implemented in 2004 and created a central point of contact (the MI HR Service Center) to process routine HR transactions. We continue to seek additional areas to centralize/standardize, and are in the process of consolidating training, compensation adjustments, position actions, and other HR transactions.	★	B, CL, CO, E, M, P, R, S, T
Minnesota	...		★(f)	M, R, S
Mississippi	...		★(g)	M, P, R, S
Missouri...................	...		...	

See footnotes at end of table.

CIVIL SERVICE REFORM — Continued

State	Comprehensive (wholesale) civil service reform	Extent of civil service reform	Incremental civil service reform	Functional areas where reform has taken place
		Has your state implemented a comprehensive (wholesale) or incremental civil service reform in the past five years?		
Montana	...		★	CL, CO
Nebraska..................	...		...	
Nevada	...		★(h)	M, P, R, S
New Hampshire.......	....N.A..			
New Jersey..............	...		★	P
New Mexico	...		★	CL, CO
New York	★	The Department of Civil Service has transformed the state's 120 year-old civil service system from an inflexible relic of declining relevance into a dynamic and progressive practitioner of quality merit system and human resources management. The department has achieved a multitude of improvements which have benefited state and local management, government employees and the taxpaying public. Quality standards include: new interagency transfer provision, effective testing of professionals, annual promotion testing, prompt test results, enhanced hiring flexibility, targeted title control, superlative customer services, comprehensive outreach network, and advanced information sytems.	★	CL, CO, E, M, R, S, T
North Carolina.......				
North Dakota...........	...		...	
Ohio	...		...	
Oklahoma	★	Classification and Compensation Act of 1999 consolidated approximately 2,000 classifications into approximately 370 job families. Central office retains assignment of job family to positions, but the level within the job family is the responsibility of each agency appointing authority. Old 13-step salary schedule was replaced with wide salary bands and agencies given greater flexibility over pay within appropriate salary band. New pay movement mechanisms give agencies more latitutde on pay as well. New performance management process adopted tying performance to accountabilities of the job and all agencies required to use OPM official form for performance appraisals.	★(i)	
Oregon	...		★	B, CL, CO, M, P, R, S
Pennsylvania	...		★(j)	M, R, S
Rhode Island	...		★	M (o), R
South Carolina	...		★(k)	B, E, P, R, T
South Dakota...........	...		★(l)	S
Tennessee	...		...	
Texas	...		...	
Utah	...		★(m)	CL
Vermont	...		...	
Virginia	...		★	CL, CO, P
Washington..............	★	New civil service rules developed and collective bargaining (wages, hours and other terms and conditions of employment) implemented 7/1/05. Ongoing comprehensive review of classifications.	...	
West Virginia...........	...		★	CO, S, T
Wisconsin.................	...		★	B, CL, CO, S
Wyoming..................	...		★(n)	CL, CO

Source: The Council of State Governments' survey of state personnel offices, October 2005.

Key:
★ — Yes
... — No
N.A. — Did not respond.
B — Benefit
CL — Classification
CO — Compensation
E — Employee relations
M — Merit testing
P — Performance evaluation
R — Recruitment
S — Selection/hiring
T — Training

(a) The state has not implemented a civil service reform, but it did centralize all human resource services into one division creating a shared service model for service delivery.

(b) A Personnel Rules Review Committee was established to help guide incremental reform.

(c) Work force planning.

(d) Reform limited to high-level civil service managers who are not covered

by collective bargaining agreements – the Maine Management Service was created several years ago and civil service policies were reformed for those employees at that time.

(e) Essential Functions Study, study of current classifications and identification of essential functions and classification reforms resulting in consolidation of a number of classifications.

(f) Went to a skills matching selection system using Resumix Software and Web-based tools.

(g) Currently piloting a competency-based performance evaluation system; considering certifying all eligible candidates to the hiring agency instead of the top 10 as is now the practice; recently published a comprehensive recruitment handbook; discontinued written and proficiency testing, effective Oct. 2003; and as part of our Total Workforce Initiative Project, we continuously seek improvements to our civil service components, particularly those involving the selection component.

(h) Performance evaluation form and rating scale revised; regulations revised to make evaluation more flexible and responsive to agency needs.

(i) "Incremental" reform is ongoing. Primary features of this reform are delegation of HR processes, i.e. allocation of positions and certification of qualification of applicants for promotion to individual agencies through delegation of agreements.

(j) During the past few years, the Pennsylvania State Civil Service Commission has pursued several administrative enhancements to include online applications, computerized examinations, the electronic posting of available jobs on a centralized Web site, and allowing non-civil service employees to be appointed from promotion lists as opposed to employment lists.

(k) The areas of classification, compensation and merit testing were part of the 1996 system reforms. While merit testing was completely decentralized, all other areas noted above are constantly monitored for needed and potential revision.

(l) Moved from training and experience rating to evaluation of knowledge, skills and abilities.

(m) Last year we implemented a title reduction project reducing over 2,500 classification titles to 940.

(n) Implemented broad banding in January 1998 and decentralized compensation at the same time.

(o) Efforts have been made to improve test updates and testing methods.

We are attempting to link testing to department/agency hiring needs because the state is mandated by law to research, develop and administer examinations to qualified state employees and jobseekers for the classified service. Types of examination methods include written, oral or education/experience rating, which can be used independently or in combination, whichever is deemed to be the most effective method of determining the capacity of the examinees to perform the duties of the tested classification. In partnership with departmental human resource managers, a retrospective analysis of state hiring as well as forecasted staffing needs was conducted and revealed 50 classifications that were most utilized by the departments and agencies. These most utilized classification titles are the focus of testing to ensure that active civil service lists comprised of qualified candidates are continuously available for department and agency usage. Additionally, the examination unit is required by statute to provide consultation services to cities and towns to assist them in their examination and testing programs.

Table 8.9
SUMMARY OF STATE GOVERNMENT EMPLOYMENT: 1953–2004

| Year (October) | Employment (in thousands) | | | | | | Monthly payrolls (in millions of dollars) | | | Average monthly earnings of full-time employees | | |
| | Total, full-time and part-time | | | Full-time equivalent | | | | | | | | |
	All	Education	Other	All	Education	Other	All	Education	Other	All	Education	Other
1953	1,082	294	788	966	211	755	$278.6	$73.5	$205.1	$289	$320	$278
1954	1,149	310	839	1,024	222	802	300.7	78.9	221.8	294	325	283
1955	1,199	333	866	1,081	244	837	325.9	88.5	237.4	302	334	290
1956	1,268	353	915	1,136	250	886	366.5	108.8	257.7	321	358	309
1957 (April)	1,300	375	925	1,153	257	896	372.5	106.1	266.4	320	355	309
1958	1,408	406	1,002	1,259	284	975	446.5	123.4	323.1	355	416	333
1959	1,454	443	1,011	1,302	318	984	485.4	136.0	349.4	373	427	352
1960	1,527	474	1,053	1,353	332	1,021	524.1	167.7	356.4	386	439	365
1961	1,625	518	1,107	1,435	367	1,068	586.2	192.4	393.8	409	482	383
1962	1,680	555	1,126	1,478	389	1,088	634.6	201.8	432.8	429	518	397
1963	1,775	602	1,173	1,558	422	1,136	696.4	230.1	466.3	447	545	410
1964	1,873	656	1,217	1,639	460	1,179	761.1	257.5	503.6	464	560	427
1965	2,028	739	1,289	1,751	508	1,243	849.2	290.1	559.1	484	571	450
1966	2,211	866	1,344	1,864	575	1,289	975.2	353.0	622.2	522	614	483
1967	2,335	940	1,395	1,946	620	1,326	1,105.5	406.3	699.3	567	666	526
1968	2,495	1,037	1,458	2,085	694	1,391	1,256.7	477.1	779.6	602	687	544
1969	2,614	1,112	1,501	2,179	746	1,433	1,430.5	554.5	876.1	655	743	597
1970	2,755	1,182	1,573	2,302	803	1,499	1,612.2	630.3	981.9	700	797	605
1971	2,832	1,223	1,609	2,384	841	1,544	1,741.7	681.5	1,060.2	731	826	686
1972	2,957	1,267	1,690	2,487	867	1,619	1,936.6	746.9	1,189.7	778	871	734
1973	3,013	1,280	1,733	2,547	887	1,660	2,158.2	822.2	1,336.0	843	952	805
1974	3,155	1,357	1,798	2,653	929	1,725	2,409.5	932.7	1,476.9	906	1,023	855
1975	3,271	1,400	1,870	2,744	952	1,792	2,652.7	1,021.7	1,631.1	964	1,080	909
1976	3,343	1,434	1,910	2,799	973	1,827	2,893.7	1,111.5	1,782.1	1,031	1,163	975
1977	3,491	1,484	2,007	2,903	1,005	1,898	3,194.6	1,234.4	1,960.1	1,096	1,237	1,031
1978	3,539	1,508	2,032	2,966	1,016	1,950	3,483.0	1,332.9	2,150.2	1,167	1,311	1,102
1979	3,699	1,577	2,122	3,072	1,046	2,026	3,869.3	1,451.4	2,417.9	1,257	1,399	1,193
1980	3,753	1,599	2,154	3,106	1,063	2,044	4,284.7	1,608.0	2,676.6	1,373	1,523	1,305
1981	3,726	1,603	2,123	3,087	1,063	2,024	4,667.5	1,768.0	2,899.5	1,507	1,671	1,432
1982	3,747	1,616	2,131	3,083	1,051	2,032	5,027.7	1,874.0	3,153.7	1,625	1,789	1,551
1983	3,816	1,666	2,150	3,116	1,072	2,044	5,345.5	1,989.0	3,357.0	1,711	1,850	1,640
1984	3,898	1,708	2,190	3,177	1,091	2,086	5,814.9	2,178.0	3,637.0	1,825	1,991	1,740
1985	3,984	1,764	2,220	2,990	945	2,046	6,328.6	2,433.7	3,884.9	1,935	2,155	1,834
1986	4,068	1,800	2,267	3,437	1,256	2,181	6,801.4	2,583.4	4,226.9	2,052	2,263	1,956
1987	4,115	1,804	2,310	3,491	1,264	2,227	7,297.8	2,758.3	4,539.5	2,161	2,396	2,056
1988	4,236	1,854	2,381	3,606	1,309	2,297	7,842.3	2,928.6	4,913.7	2,260	2,490	2,158
1989	4,365	1,925	2,440	3,709	1,360	2,349	8,443.1	3,175.0	5,268.1	2,372	2,627	2,259
1990	4,503	1,984	2,519	3,840	1,418	2,432	9,083.0	3,426.0	5,657.0	2,472	2,732	2,359
1991	4,521	1,999	2,522	3,829	1,375	2,454	9,437.0	3,550.0	5,887.0	2,479	2,530	2,433
1992	4,595	2,050	2,545	3,856	1,384	2,472	9,828.0	3,774.0	6,054.0	2,562	2,607	2,521
1993	4,673	2,112	2,562	3,891	1,436	2,455	10,288.2	3,999.3	6,288.9	2,722	3,034	2,578
1994	4694	2115	2579	3,917	1,442	2,475	10,666.3	4,176.8	6,489.3	2,776	3,073	2,640
1995	4,719	2,120	2,598	3,971	1,469	2,502	10,926.5	4,173.3	6,753.2	2,854	3,138	2,725
1996	(a)	(a)	(a)	(a)	(a)	(a)	(a)	(a)	(a)	(a)	(a)	(a)
1997 (March)	4,733	2,114	2,619	3,987	1,484	2,503	11,413.1	4,372.0	7,041.1	2,968	3,251	2,838
1998 (March)	4,758	2,173	2,585	3,985	1,511	2,474	11,845.2	4,632.1	7,213.1	3,088	3,382	2,947
1999 (March)	4,818	2,229	2,588	4,034	1,541	2,493	12,564.1	4,957.0	7,607.7	3,236	3,544	3,087
2000 (March)	4,877	2,259	2,618	4,083	1,563	2,520	13,279.1	5,255.3	8,023.8	3,374	3,692	3,219
2001 (March)	4,985	2,329	2,656	4,173	1,615	2,559	14,136.3	5,620.7	8,515.6	3,521	3,842	3,362
2002 (March)	5,072	2,414	2,658	4,223	1,659	2,564	14,837.8	5,996.6	8,841.2	3,657	4,007	3,479
2003 (March)	5,042	2,413	2,629	4,190	1,656	2,534	15,116.4	6,154.3	8,962.0	3,646		
2004 (March)	5,041	2,432	2,608	4,187	1,672	2,514	15,477.5	6,411.7	9,065.7	3,635		

Source: U.S. Department of Commerce, Bureau of the Census, January 2004. Internet release date June 2005.

Note: Detail may not add to totals due to rounding.

Key:

. . . —Not applicable.

(a) Due to a change in the reference period, from October to March, the October 1996 Annual Survey of Government Employment and Payroll was not concluded. This change incollection period was effective, beginning with the March 1997 survey.

Table 8.10
EMPLOYMENT AND PAYROLLS OF STATE AND LOCAL GOVERNMENTS, BY FUNCTION: MARCH 2004

Functions	All employees, full-time and part-time (in thousands)			March payrolls (in millions of dollars)			Average March earnings of full-time employees
	Total	State government	Local government	Total	State government	Local government	
All functions	18,760	5,041	13,719	$55,914,919	$15,477,521	$40,437,397	$3,667
Education:							
Higher education	2,830	2,274	557	7,091,321	5,897,811	1,193,511	4,268
Instructional personnel only...	1,006	736	269	3,318,132	2,676,665	641,467	5,818
Elementary/Secondary schools..	7,541	63	7,477	21,456,188	191,291	21,264,896	3,430
Instructional personnel only...	5,083	45	5,039	16,864,616	154,046	16,710,570	3,852
Libraries..	182	1	181	346,659	1,584	345,075	3,094
Other Education..............................	95	95	0	322,679	322,679	0	3,635
Selected functions:							
Streets and Highways................	564	244	320	1,827,948	851,456	976,492	3,394
Public Welfare	523	229	294	1,596,848	719,855	876,993	3,241
Hospitals	987	424	564	3,196,090	1,352,923	1,843,167	3,528
Police protection........................	960	105	855	3,796,512	440,786	3,355,726	4,339
Police Officers........................	689	63	626	3,054,554	295,226	2,759,328	4,645
Fire protection	431	0	431	1,484,543	0	1,484,543	4,809
Firefighters only	395	0	395	1,383,333	0	1,383,333	4,874
Natural Resources	208	162	47	638,875	509,308	129,568	3,558
Correction...................................	714	465	249	2,405,275	1,553,829	851,446	3,440
Social Insurance	93	93	0	314,894	314,894	0	3,574
Financial Admin.	428	173	255	1,375,676	602,997	772,679	3,595
Judicial and Legal	436	168	268	1,657,663	703,839	953,824	4,083
Other Government Admin.	462	58	403	1,014,742	202,075	812,667	3,742
Utilities.......................................	505	38	466	2,013,506	185,759	1,827,748	4,223
State Liquor stores	9	9	0	19,012	19,012	0	2,878
Other and unallocable...............	1,791	441	1,350	5,356,489	1,607,426	3,749,063	3,606

Source: U.S. Department of Commerce, Bureau of the Census, January 2005.

Table 8.11
STATE AND LOCAL GOVERNMENT EMPLOYMENT, BY STATE: MARCH 2004

| State or other jurisdiction | All employees (full-time and part-time) | | | Full-time equivalent employment | | | | | | 2004 Population |
| | | | | Number | | | Number per 10,000 population | | | |
	Total	State	Local	Total	State	Local	Total	State	Local	
United States	18,759,692	5,041,143	13,718,549	15,788,784	4,187,648	11,601,136	538	143	395	293,655
Alabama	307,602	101,161	206,441	270,632	85,647	184,985	597	189	408	4,530
Alaska	60,537	28,121	32,416	50,841	24,657	26,184	776	376	400	655
Arizona	319,554	82,357	237,197	270,719	66,026	204,693	471	115	356	5,744
Arkansas...............	179,035	63,677	115,358	151,938	54,005	97,933	552	196	356	2,753
California	2,153,632	473,840	1,679,792	1,776,132	393,057	1,383,075	495	110	385	35,894
Colorado	301,331	83,100	218,231	248,404	65,652	182,752	540	143	397	4,601
Connecticut	215,019	70,923	144,096	181,617	58,648	122,969	518	167	351	3,504
Delaware..............	54,794	29,025	25,769	47,879	24,254	23,625	577	292	285	830
Florida	930,620	208,624	721,996	824,337	183,265	641,072	474	105	368	17,397
Georgia	558,937	145,024	413,913	500,305	121,526	378,779	567	138	429	8,829
Hawaii..................	86,883	71,506	15,377	70,932	56,540	14,392	562	448	114	1,263
Idaho....................	99,997	29,715	70,282	78,310	23,198	55,112	562	167	396	1,393
Illinois.................	785,161	160,408	624,753	635,760	133,672	502,088	500	105	395	12,714
Indiana.................	393,189	110,228	282,961	329,581	90,404	239,177	528	145	383	6,238
Iowa	235,534	65,897	169,637	184,552	53,291	131,261	625	180	444	2,954
Kansas	228,859	55,735	173,124	179,546	43,787	135,759	656	160	496	2,736
Kentucky	273,069	94,629	178,440	237,217	79,481	157,736	572	192	380	4,146
Louisiana	322,271	108,676	213,595	282,311	90,600	191,711	625	201	425	4,516
Maine	99,887	26,033	73,854	77,055	21,720	55,335	585	165	420	1,317
Maryland	321,166	96,786	224,380	282,362	90,682	191,680	508	163	345	5,558
Massachusetts.......	384,617	107,011	277,606	323,067	88,051	235,016	503	137	366	6,417
Michigan..............	647,918	168,707	479,211	504,272	132,825	371,447	499	131	367	10,113
Minnesota	359,143	91,392	267,751	275,067	74,543	200,524	539	146	393	5,101
Mississippi	216,156	65,381	150,775	188,369	56,968	131,401	649	196	453	2,903
Missouri................	369,768	106,550	263,218	311,206	90,730	220,476	541	158	383	5,755
Montana	70,468	24,990	45,478	54,272	18,571	35,701	585	200	385	927
Nebraska...............	142,351	39,062	103,289	114,767	33,662	81,105	657	193	464	1,747
Nevada	116,627	32,990	83,637	96,376	25,279	71,097	413	108	304	2,335
New Hampshire....	85,398	25,120	60,278	68,484	19,955	48,529	527	154	373	1,300
New Jersey............	580,190	170,729	409,461	495,189	149,374	345,815	569	172	398	8,699
New Mexico	144,082	59,823	84,259	124,642	49,286	75,356	655	259	396	1,903
New York	1,342,095	273,860	1,068,235	1,184,394	246,385	938,009	616	128	488	19,227
North Carolina.....	536,951	156,142	380,809	453,940	132,110	321,830	531	155	377	8,541
North Dakota........	62,027	22,922	39,105	40,884	17,754	23,130	645	280	365	634
Ohio	763,132	177,196	585,936	623,226	136,041	487,185	544	119	425	11,459
Oklahoma	238,861	80,314	158,547	200,939	64,094	136,845	570	182	388	3,524
Oregon	234,168	74,705	159,463	179,817	57,423	122,394	500	160	340	3,595
Pennsylvania	670,340	192,458	477,882	570,379	161,089	409,290	460	130	330	12,406
Rhode Island	57,533	24,507	33,026	50,521	20,158	30,363	467	186	281	1,081
South Carolina	274,187	88,381	185,806	243,004	75,603	167,401	579	180	399	4,198
South Dakota........	61,000	16,233	44,767	43,549	13,201	30,348	565	171	394	771
Tennessee	361,645	97,418	264,227	317,514	81,905	235,609	538	139	399	5,901
Texas	1,417,912	313,426	1,104,486	1,271,164	268,172	1,002,992	565	119	446	22,490
Utah	163,138	61,352	101,786	127,595	48,900	78,695	534	205	329	2,389
Vermont	46,968	15,479	31,489	38,149	13,922	24,227	614	224	390	621
Virginia	489,924	148,765	341,159	410,885	119,317	291,568	551	160	391	7,460
Washington...........	401,739	145,840	255,899	322,991	112,738	210,253	521	182	339	6,204
West Virginia........	112,241	44,039	68,202	98,232	37,583	60,649	541	207	334	1,815
Wisconsin.............	382,992	96,385	286,607	287,256	69,834	217,422	521	127	395	5,509
Wyoming...............	53,231	14,501	38,730	43,533	12,063	31,470	859	238	621	507
District of Columbia	45,813	0	45,813	44,671	0	44,671	806	0	806	554

Source: U.S. Department of Commerce, Bureau of the Census, Internet release date, June 2005.

Note: Statistics for local governments are estimates subject to sampling variation. Detail may not add to totals due to rounding.

Table 8.12
STATE AND LOCAL GOVERNMENT PAYROLLS AND AVERAGE EARNINGS
OF FULL-TIME EMPLOYEES, BY STATE: MARCH 2004

State or other jurisdiction	Amount of payroll (in thousands of dollars)			Percentage of March payroll		Average earnings of full-time state and local government employees (dollars)		
	Total	State government	Local governments	State government	Local government	All	Education employees	Other
United States	51,339,082	13,976,251	37,362,831	27	73	3,667	3,589	3,748
Alabama	727,440	256,614	470,826	35	65	2,969	2,958	2,980
Alaska	188,472	93,685	94,788	50	50	4,129	3,863	4,370
Arizona	832,552	192,573	639,979	23	77	3,499	3,332	3,668
Arkansas...............	383,232	154,243	228,989	40	60	2,709	2,779	2,618
California	7,396,450	1,670,278	5,726,171	23	77	4,867	4,698	5,008
Colorado	800,703	217,929	582,774	27	73	3,820	3,639	4,005
Connecticut	707,503	242,795	464,708	34	66	4,432	4,410	4,460
Delaware..............	157,204	78,943	78,261	50	50	3,655	3,807	3,507
Florida	2,521,796	567,802	1,953,994	23	77	3,371	3,152	3,545
Georgia	1,392,770	355,837	1,036,933	26	74	3,048	3,131	2,944
Hawaii..................	225,110	171,676	53,434	76	24	3,520	3,387	3,633
Idaho....................	199,772	62,118	137,654	31	69	3,003	2,867	3,155
Illinois	2,137,526	461,826	1,675,700	22	78	3,850	3,665	4,059
Indiana.................	902,341	254,893	647,448	28	72	3,167	3,343	2,951
Iowa	510,856	180,746	330,110	35	65	3,336	3,257	3,436
Kansas	482,931	132,040	350,891	27	73	3,028	3,047	3,003
Kentucky	635,586	237,782	397,804	37	63	2,949	2,886	3,038
Louisiana	725,109	271,233	453,876	37	63	2,775	2,706	2,843
Maine	199,311	67,238	132,074	34	66	3,034	2,874	3,274
Maryland	1,012,418	321,627	690,792	32	68	4,007	4,213	3,791
Massachusetts.......	1,188,576	337,596	850,981	28	72	4,098	3,927	4,301
Michigan...............	1,645,060	457,295	1,187,765	28	72	3,980	4,089	3,831
Minnesota	890,595	275,244	615,352	31	69	3,912	3,811	4,036
Mississippi	454,425	153,539	300,886	34	66	2,631	2,696	2,558
Missouri	825,621	240,712	584,909	29	71	2,929	2,947	2,910
Montana	133,998	50,845	83,153	38	62	2,887	2,799	2,984
Nebraska...............	314,637	86,053	228,584	27	73	3,155	3,057	3,253
Nevada.................	346,632	84,669	261,963	24	76	4,064	3,468	4,525
New Hampshire....	188,501	56,216	132,284	30	70	3,265	3,118	3,468
New Jersey............	2,060,173	642,687	1,417,486	31	69	4,569	4,704	4,418
New Mexico	318,362	126,636	191,727	40	60	2,826	2,679	2,995
New York	4,780,246	1,024,532	3,755,714	21	79	4,460	4,359	4,540
North Carolina	1,311,829	392,987	918,843	30	70	3,146	3,332	2,968
North Dakota........	107,468	44,595	62,873	41	59	3,205	3,475	2,896
Ohio	1,923,050	432,012	1,491,039	22	78	3,545	3,519	3,573
Oklahoma	495,584	175,770	319,815	35	65	2,703	2,607	2,821
Oregon	560,402	181,873	378,530	32	68	3,668	3,502	3,811
Pennsylvania	1,929,242	541,970	1,387,272	28	72	3,788	4,001	3,550
Rhode Island	194,340	76,194	118,146	39	61	4,200	4,259	4,137
South Carolina	656,313	210,177	446,136	32	68	2,923	2,955	2,889
South Dakota........	109,439	35,283	74,157	32	68	2,843	2,819	2,877
Tennessee	861,215	224,647	636,568	26	74	2,948	2,957	2,939
Texas	3,633,989	837,655	2,796,334	23	77	3,068	2,992	3,177
Utah	344,937	143,773	201,165	42	58	3,243	3,176	3,320
Vermont	109,519	47,266	62,253	43	57	3,260	3,146	3,455
Virginia.................	1,219,916	358,373	861,543	29	71	3,327	3,272	3,396
Washington...........	1,117,293	371,701	745,592	33	67	4,249	4,192	4,288
West Virginia........	259,095	103,998	155,097	40	60	2,851	3,087	2,577
Wisconsin..............	907,314	234,118	673,196	26	74	3,726	3,765	3,678
Wyoming..............	116,298	35,959	80,339	31	69	3,127	3,155	3,103
District of Columbia	195,928	0	195,928	0	100	4,732	4,552	4,783

Source: U.S. Department of Commerce, Bureau of the Census, Internet release date June 2005.

Note: Statistics for local governments are estimates subject to sampling variation. Detail may not add to totals due to rounding.

Table 8.13
STATE GOVERNMENT EMPLOYMENT (FULL-TIME EQUIVALENT) FOR SELECTED FUNCTIONS, BY STATE: MARCH 2004

State	All functions	Education: Higher education (a)	Education: Other education (b)	Highways	Public welfare	Hospitals	Corrections	Police protection	Natural resources	Financial and other governmental administration	Judicial and legal administration
United States	4,187,648	1,532,627	140,128	239,638	225,569	399,170	460,368	102,951	146,799	220,987	163,474
Alabama	85,647	37,964	2,692	4,300	4,344	11,412	4,715	1,231	2,184	3,171	2,980
Alaska	24,657	4,782	3,622	2,962	1,764	264	1,775	476	2,297	1,574	1,215
Arizona	66,026	25,892	2,869	2,875	5,349	748	9,895	2,014	2,888	4,352	1,300
Arkansas..............	54,005	20,905	1,333	3,559	3,719	4,321	4,476	1,057	1,957	2,528	1,305
California	393,057	146,031	4,497	20,820	3,683	38,962	49,696	13,515	13,776	25,452	4,171
Colorado	65,652	37,049	1,282	3,132	1,939	3,520	6,257	1,180	1,400	2,656	3,415
Connecticut	58,648	15,659	2,335	2,827	4,296	10,561	7,473	1,991	681	3,415	4,324
Delaware..............	24,254	7,265	366	1,605	1,533	1,839	2,839	925	472	976	1,491
Florida	183,265	54,068	3,464	7,773	11,730	4,806	27,443	4,347	10,379	9,459	18,013
Georgia	121,526	47,815	3,009	5,831	8,785	8,158	19,530	2,209	4,405	5,512	2,535
Hawaii..................	56,540	8,512	26,752	879	960	3,975	2,376	0	1,091	1,341	2,267
Idaho....................	23,198	8,714	538	1,761	1,791	899	1,746	462	1,946	1,759	445
Illinois	133,672	55,674	2,381	7,748	10,549	11,962	14,468	3,665	3,835	7,254	3,018
Indiana..................	90,404	52,790	1,207	4,318	5,506	4,171	8,194	1,940	2,616	3,235	1,279
Iowa	53,291	26,070	1,196	2,531	2,759	6,774	3,223	873	1,607	1,931	2,281
Kansas	43,787	19,213	586	3,593	2,676	2,345	3,571	1,101	864	2,697	2,100
Kentucky	79,481	31,089	2,895	5,097	6,859	5,631	3,731	2,187	3,819	4,295	4,962
Louisiana	90,600	29,849	3,370	5,355	5,032	17,088	7,823	1,654	5,016	4,111	1,723
Maine	21,720	7,316	318	2,531	2,014	667	1,348	562	1,249	1,765	741
Maryland	90,682	26,357	2,055	4,702	6,796	5,208	11,943	2,500	2,064	5,130	4,550
Massachusetts.......	88,051	25,516	1,179	3,839	6,623	6,804	6,672	5,572	1,166	6,089	8,933
Michigan..............	132,825	64,638	2,273	2,775	10,500	11,472	17,626	2,662	4,613	6,088	1,864
Minnesota	74,543	33,485	4,083	4,685	2,674	4,722	3,787	911	3,153	3,766	2,683
Mississippi	56,968	18,826	1,589	3,295	2,801	12,155	4,172	1,170	3,315	1,689	658
Missouri	90,730	28,412	2,176	6,544	7,842	12,331	11,605	2,221	2,785	3,612	4,074
Montana	18,571	6,553	421	2,161	1,510	551	1,100	437	1,370	1,301	470
Nebraska................	33,662	12,271	550	2,159	2,769	5,090	2,530	757	2,170	865	678
Nevada..................	25,279	8,802	133	1,714	1,482	1,033	3,274	780	1,207	2,260	611
New Hampshire......	19,955	7,141	327	1,873	1,402	776	1,369	421	576	1,184	931
New Jersey............	149,374	31,372	22,324	7,274	6,627	17,186	10,082	4,111	2,661	7,596	14,422
New Mexico	49,286	17,657	1,091	2,301	1,562	9,922	4,106	633	1,784	2,071	2,685
New York	246,385	47,026	4,673	12,360	6,404	41,999	33,292	6,299	3,594	17,785	22,521
North Carolina	132,110	49,713	2,711	11,401	1,851	16,534	19,291	3,319	3,911	4,970	5,920
North Dakota.......	17,754	8,064	280	993	469	984	656	204	1,639	853	519
Ohio......................	136,041	66,797	2,518	7,142	2,813	11,436	16,082	2,663	3,457	9,111	2,732
Oklahoma	64,094	26,007	1,869	2,889	5,674	2,434	5,509	1,876	1,980	2,534	2,565
Oregon	57,423	18,592	952	3,378	5,505	4,804	4,725	1,179	2,875	5,403	2,969
Pennsylvania	161,089	57,779	3,797	13,730	12,714	12,619	17,319	5,955	6,685	10,873	3,024
Rhode Island	20,158	5,628	1,221	846	1,474	1,226	1,716	281	500	1,628	1,153
South Carolina	75,603	27,573	2,708	4,826	4,367	8,031	7,570	2,953	1,954	2,706	673
South Dakota........	13,201	4,831	397	976	1,024	930	792	274	850	719	576
Tennessee	81,905	34,527	1,982	4,452	5,996	8,097	6,959	1,956	3,596	3,573	2,018
Texas	268,172	95,599	4,836	15,087	18,581	30,426	46,892	4,046	11,043	11,408	5,316
Utah	48,900	23,255	1,077	1,720	3,332	5,691	3,152	778	1,147	1,977	1,524
Vermont	13,922	4,643	567	1,071	1,183	213	1,112	390	577	1,242	602
Virginia..................	119,317	48,787	2,768	9,997	2,360	13,267	13,997	2,864	3,162	5,232	3,558
Washington............	112,738	47,808	2,120	6,894	8,715	8,861	9,069	2,210	4,960	4,126	1,825
West Virginia........	37,583	11,003	1,398	5,403	3,113	1,657	3,040	966	2,273	2,870	1,351
Wisconsin..............	69,834	34,020	1,118	1,813	1,346	3,787	9,405	921	2,422	4,091	2,019
Wyoming................	12,063	3,288	223	1,841	772	821	945	253	828	752	485

Source: U.S. Department of Commerce, Bureau of the Census, January 2004.
 (a) Includes instructional and other personnel.
 (b) Includes instructional and other personnel in elementary and secondary schools.

Table 8.14
STATE GOVERNMENT PAYROLLS FOR SELECTED FUNCTIONS, BY STATE: MARCH 2004
(In thousands of dollars)

| | | Education | | | Selected functions | | | | | | |
State	All functions	Higher education (a)	Other education (b)	Highways	Public welfare	Hospitals	Corrections	Police protection	Natural resources	Financial and other governmental administration	Judicial and legal administration
United States	$15,477,521	$5,897,811	$513,970	$851,456	$719,855	$1,352,923	$1,553,829	$440,786	$509,308	$805,073	$703,839
Alabama	284,979	135,318	8,754	11,704	12,914	35,446	14,968	4,589	6,873	11,014	12,094
Alaska	99,339	19,259	12,361	13,092	6,114	1,050	7,162	2,313	9,131	6,401	5,397
Arizona	216,009	92,118	7,904	9,157	14,142	2,375	28,072	8,012	10,564	13,442	6,083
Arkansas...............	164,061	72,609	4,008	10,680	9,564	12,063	10,614	3,329	5,057	7,616	3,792
California	1,890,811	689,243	19,109	117,092	15,841	176,238	235,513	69,729	60,497	102,715	24,973
Colorado..............	266,516	149,989	4,923	12,611	7,847	12,502	24,098	5,266	6,413	11,159	14,964
Connecticut	270,629	72,782	10,882	12,284	19,449	52,512	33,863	10,011	3,070	15,013	17,690
Delaware..............	86,929	29,138	1,686	4,936	4,713	5,543	9,356	4,496	1,590	3,475	5,109
Florida.................	613,716	218,602	9,777	27,818	32,085	13,369	76,041	14,808	29,063	32,809	67,125
Georgia	391,417	181,919	10,576	15,762	23,066	20,299	48,573	7,374	12,745	18,709	11,616
Hawaii..................	191,080	33,774	82,876	3,218	3,218	13,555	8,652	0	4,193	4,666	8,478
Idaho....................	72,917	27,089	1,665	5,406	5,110	2,479	4,885	1,629	6,306	5,980	2,358
Illinois.................	504,647	187,446	9,547	31,505	42,953	42,981	57,264	18,678	12,799	27,543	19,159
Indiana.................	286,111	174,942	3,773	11,491	14,278	10,696	22,390	7,513	8,503	10,012	6,488
Iowa	213,163	106,489	4,734	9,805	9,817	26,302	12,095	3,803	6,120	7,715	9,730
Kansas..................	146,063	74,592	1,916	10,368	6,722	5,991	9,370	3,904	2,772	7,857	7,050
Kentucky	260,019	106,905	10,661	16,503	19,998	18,412	9,891	7,605	11,246	15,155	16,111
Louisiana	289,111	105,255	11,007	16,017	13,909	49,363	22,378	5,121	15,491	12,983	7,291
Maine...................	74,919	25,024	1,084	8,630	6,130	2,339	4,474	2,400	4,532	5,911	2,929
Maryland..............	346,871	113,768	8,136	17,532	22,452	17,466	39,362	11,068	8,593	20,511	15,488
Massachusetts.......	373,002	100,802	5,515	17,767	27,933	23,736	29,422	28,499	5,532	25,265	39,631
Michigan..............	520,648	261,775	8,420	11,133	37,018	40,077	67,286	10,288	17,489	24,713	9,491
Minnesota.............	309,849	141,741	16,336	19,750	8,908	17,409	14,291	4,261	12,773	15,101	13,405
Mississippi............	164,643	65,543	4,557	8,260	6,186	29,856	9,075	3,358	8,520	5,485	3,534
Missouri...............	259,789	95,125	6,071	19,497	17,951	31,639	26,110	6,600	7,677	9,670	14,081
Montana	57,591	20,604	1,238	7,163	4,327	1,440	3,130	1,378	4,340	3,796	1,755
Nebraska...............	95,149	37,034	1,937	4,660	6,692	13,452	6,858	2,573	5,697	2,727	2,749
Nevada.................	93,456	28,605	557	6,742	5,096	4,253	12,564	3,401	4,504	8,306	3,271
New Hampshire....	64,719	23,563	1,067	5,953	4,117	2,458	4,593	1,673	1,812	3,941	3,360
New Jersey............	675,359	153,387	106,583	31,332	27,254	61,650	46,407	23,756	11,718	30,395	66,735
New Mexico..........	146,757	48,171	3,490	6,664	4,310	31,298	12,562	2,410	5,698	6,907	9,282
New York..............	1,080,559	200,445	19,085	46,021	26,313	168,446	152,024	34,634	14,754	67,956	111,835
North Carolina......	430,231	187,502	8,760	24,137	6,134	51,252	50,162	12,180	11,783	14,697	22,191
North Dakota.......	51,916	24,913	853	3,002	1,215	1,896	1,642	623	4,185	2,443	1,813
Ohio.....................	495,367	222,879	10,787	28,525	13,014	34,644	62,680	12,105	11,853	38,826	12,154
Oklahoma.............	193,697	82,623	5,567	8,054	14,109	6,396	15,529	5,888	5,456	8,039	9,385
Oregon	208,384	70,697	3,509	12,915	18,598	18,121	16,565	4,715	9,318	17,795	10,424
Pennsylvania	608,193	236,820	14,358	44,316	45,054	37,692	61,770	27,757	27,576	39,135	14,572
Rhode Island	81,780	45,009	5,009	3,602	6,908	5,127	7,950	1,702	2,145	6,266	5,186
South Carolina	226,910	94,160	8,345	12,712	11,022	16,954	18,224	8,099	5,833	9,078	2,810
South Dakota........	40,050	16,009	1,077	2,824	2,738	2,300	2,025	919	2,482	2,290	1,995
Tennessee..............	245,996	111,635	5,962	11,354	14,871	22,015	18,335	6,243	10,348	12,050	8,685
Texas	919,721	396,940	16,473	49,107	49,999	98,420	113,402	13,228	39,346	38,645	22,501
Utah	158,969	79,263	3,280	6,191	9,974	16,219	9,205	2,640	3,768	6,395	5,421
Vermont................	50,707	17,383	2,131	3,758	4,140	664	3,691	1,948	2,320	4,146	2,345
Virginia................	404,881	182,604	9,866	31,384	7,731	39,076	37,547	10,426	10,130	17,545	14,216
Washington...........	424,844	173,787	7,941	29,618	33,849	36,934	30,051	10,143	18,462	16,075	9,476
West Virginia.......	111,413	38,384	4,423	15,982	7,215	3,814	6,434	2,955	6,985	8,194	4,452
Wisconsin.............	275,465	138,176	4,582	7,513	4,568	12,781	32,743	3,727	8,646	15,955	11,301
Wyoming...............	38,169	11,040	815	5,908	2,293	1,923	2,535	1,011	2,602	2,551	1,864

Source: U.S. Department of Commerce, Bureau of the Census, Internet release date June 2005.

(a) Includes instructional and other personnel.

(b) Includes instructional and other personnel in elementary and secondary schools.

Public Procurement: Past, Present and Future

By John Adler, Dugan Petty and Rebecca Randall

While the past few years have held a tremendous amount of change for state procurement officials, 2005 demonstrated that the role of the procurement official has become more complex. The procurement official is now expected to be a leader in the charge to streamline the procurement process and eliminate procedures that are perceived as adding delay and cost without any commensurate benefit. These demands for change are occurring at a time that government's reliance on purchased services and commodities is increasing; the services and commodities are less routine; and the role that public procurement plays within the executive branch is becoming more important to the success of essential government programs.

Introduction

Governments in the United States spend between $1.3 trillion and $1.6 trillion annually for goods and services.[1] Government procurement is being transformed at all levels—federal, state and local. No longer viewed as a technical exercise, public procurement is evolving into a strategic business process throughout government. This transformation of government procurement is a reflection of the overall changing nature of government. Today's government processes are much more complex, reflecting the desire to provide faster, more cost-effective services to citizens and members of the business community. This article provides a brief history of the evolution of public procurement as well as an insight into trends we believe will continue for several years to come.

The Last Five Years

State governments entered the 21st century with serious revenue shortfalls and increasing expenditures. According to the National Association of State Budget Officers, states experienced some of the largest budget deficits in history over the course of the past five years.[2] After implementing traditional budget-cutting measures, several state government executives began to explore more innovative cost-cutting measures and increasingly relied on state procurement directors for implementation of potential savings opportunities. Through the use of private sector enterprises introducing business supply chain management techniques, several states launched groundbreaking spend management and strategic sourcing projects to generate considerable savings on common purchases.

Other procurement innovations were also borne from the budget crises. Seeking greater efficiency in the delivery of traditional government services, executives began to explore a savings method long used in the private sector—outsourcing, or more specifically, privatization. Procurement officers were called on to develop, negotiate and administer complex outsourcing contracts for technology, data centers, telecommunications and other government services traditionally performed in-house. Many of these contracts were performance-based and some included unique revenue and risk-shared funding mechanisms. Examples include:

- shared savings from reduced energy consumption in public buildings;
- self-funded Web portals;
- shared revenue from tax system technology upgrades; and
- shared savings cost recovery audit contracts; and
- performance fees based on generation of additional federal cost reimbursement.

While state executives relied more and more on their procurement professionals, traditional budget-cutting measures downsized state procurement offices. Layoffs ensued and many procurement offices migrated from general-funded programs to a more diversified self-funded environment. A variety of revenue-generating methods were developed, such as collecting transaction fees, industrial fees and consulting fees, and performing agency assessments. Procurement offices also faced the migration of staff to private sector and local government jobs paying higher wages. Faced with the reality of fewer staff and the increasing demand for more complex contracts and savings targets, state procurement officials continued to explore and initiate a number of innovations, many borrowed from the private sector. Procurement card programs were developed for small purchases, bid thresholds were increased and procurement officials relied more on cooperative purchasing programs such as the Minnesota multi-state contract for drugs and pharmaceuticals and the Western States Contracting Alliance (WSCA) contracts to maintain service levels. State directors also turned to e-procurement systems to streamline back office processes and consulting services for strategic sourcing initiatives. During this time a handful of major e-procurement projects concluded with varying degrees of success.

With the trend toward increased bid thresholds and expanded agency purchasing delegations, procurement officials also recognized that training is essential to maintain effective, accountable and relevant procurement programs. Several states followed Virginia's groundbreaking program that addressed both traditional procurement practices and emerging best practices. Alaska, Arizona, Arkansas, Florida, Oregon, Massachusetts and Texas developed formal training programs delivered by professional procure-

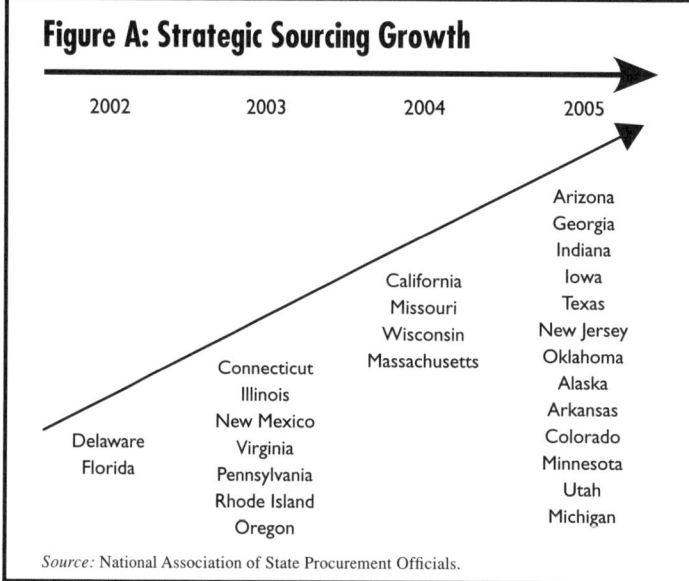

Figure A: Strategic Sourcing Growth

2002	2003	2004	2005
			Arizona
			Georgia
			Indiana
		California	Iowa
		Missouri	Texas
		Wisconsin	New Jersey
	Connecticut	Massachusetts	Oklahoma
	Illinois		Alaska
	New Mexico		Arkansas
Delaware	Virginia		Colorado
Florida	Pennsylvania		Minnesota
	Rhode Island		Utah
	Oregon		Michigan

Source: National Association of State Procurement Officials.

ment training officers. As a way of strengthening competency, states also increased their focus on more professional certifications based on a body of knowledge, including the Universal Public Purchasing Certification Council (UPPCC), Certified Public Procurement Officer (CPPO) and Certified Public Procurement Buyer (CPPB), Institute of Supply Management, National Contract Management Association and other designations. Some states, such as Arkansas, require certification for all state procurement officers.

State Procurement Today

While most state economies are improving, many state procurement directors are finding themselves with smaller staffs and increased project demands. Deferred capital, construction and information technology acquisitions are being moved from the back burner to the procurement office for swift action. These complex contracts, along with continuing privatization efforts and performance-based contracting trends, are piling more intricate projects into the realm of the procurement directors, while staff continues to decrease in number and experience.

Strategic Sourcing— Today's Most Significant Trend

The federal Office of Management and Budget defines strategic sourcing as the "collaborative and structured process of critically analyzing an organization's spending and using this information to make business decisions about acquiring commodities and services more effectively and efficiently."[3] Strategic sourcing involves a systematic analysis of the requirements, suppliers, market, environment and other factors to locate and capture, track and document savings. During the last three years, more than 20 states have embarked or are planning to initiate some form of strategic sourcing (see Figure A).

Savings generated from strategic sourcing initiatives have reportedly been substantial. Delaware, Virginia, Illinois and Pennsylvania reported generating millions of dollars in savings by employing strategic sourcing techniques for computers, office supplies, furniture and other high-volume common-use commodities. Additionally, strategic sourcing assisted states in other areas such as improvements in quality and service delivery. Attracted by savings, other states adopted strategic sourcing programs as a way of improving performance and reducing the overall cost of operations.

States that have completed the first phase of strategic sourcing are now faced with challenges of how to integrate strategic sourcing into their ongoing procurement business protocols. These next phases will involve significant staff training as well as changes within the procurement office organizational structure. Rather than a traditional transaction-based work flow, different structures that empower responsive decision-making and cross functional work teams will be needed to support a variety of sourcing team activities. Massachusetts, Illinois, Pennsylvania and Virginia have all made gains in this area of organizational transformation.

Although achieving savings within the future phases of strategic sourcing could prove more difficult, states are expected to continue to reap benefits from strategic sourcing.

The Future of State Procurement

More state procurement directors will build and enhance training programs and require professional certification

While statute and administrative law, policies, procedures and organizational structure combine to provide the mechanism for public purchasing, only people can ensure its functionality. Training and certification will become critical as state procurement continues to evolve from tactical to strategic, and procurement requirements and contracts become more complex. Procurement training programs will extend far beyond the traditional buying and bidding processes to better develop skills within the areas of communication, negotiation, strategic sourcing, technology and others essential for the modern contracting officer.

To prepare procurement officers for this dynamic environment, the National Institute of Governmental Purchasing is upgrading its training program through its LEAP initiative.[4] States are also implementing or upgrading training programs and turning to private sector consultants to provide strategic sourcing, performance-based contracting and other current best practice training programs.

Procurement directors are preparing for recruitment and retention of professional staff

Most state procurement offices are emerging from revenue deficits with smaller staffs and are now preparing for increased turnover resulting from worker retirements and increased job competition. As with most other state government workers, procurement salaries have traditionally lagged behind the private sector and local governments, creating a significant wage disparity. For example, the state of Arizona estimates that state salaries are now 21 percent below market. While some states are already experiencing

high turnover, many states may lose as many as 50 percent of existing staff to retirement and other higher paying job opportunities. The state of Arkansas predicts that it could lose up to 67 percent of its senior procurement staff in the next five years; and the Arizona Enterprise Procurement Services Office has already experienced nearly 100 percent turnover of its procurement staff in the last two years.

To counter this trend, state procurement offices will need to offer more competitive salaries and benefits, and develop more innovative recruitment, training and career progression programs. Procurement directors may face resistance from state executives and legislators as well as competition from other programs for budget increases. It may be necessary to explore alternative funding sources such as cooperative purchasing.

The shift of buying goods to buying services

It is essential to recognize that the future role of government will continue to shift from its historic mission of being a "provider" of goods and services to the role of one who "manages the providers." While government will continue to buy goods, internal procurement offices will continue to face the challenge of a broadening range of contracts for services. When buying services, the role of government shifts from a generalist to one that must specify and develop outcome and performance measures in relation to a specified need. Service contracts also require much more intensive administration to ensure that the intended outcomes are achieved. At times this may require procurement offices to contract with knowledge workers as consultants to augment knowledge gaps in existing staff. The role of internal procurement staff will broaden and become more valuable as they manage and tailor deliverables into a public contracting vehicle that optimizes outcomes for the state agency and complies with public procurement statutes.

Programs will continue to take advantage of e-procurement innovations

The primary advantage of electronic procurement is that it allows government to buy goods more quickly, efficiently and at a reduced cost. State governments are realizing that in order to take full advantage of the potential offered by electronic commerce, they must transform their acquisition process. The existence of an electronic procurement system provides many options to government buyers and suppliers. The implementation of e-commerce, especially in the logistics area, provides dramatic improvements in timeliness, responsiveness, performance, fairness, visibility and cost reductions. E-procurement initiatives already adopted by many states include the use of electronic signatures, posting solicitation, bid and award documents online and reverse auctions.

Despite a decade of interest in and various approaches to e-procurement systems, there is no single silver bullet solution. Future e-procurement systems are likely to take one of two paths. States will continue to assess the feasibility of enterprise resource planning (ERP) systems with applications deployed within various state functions including procurement. ERP systems based on commercial manufacturing industry models can present challenges when attempting to fit to public procurement processes driven by public policy. Other states will launch e-procurement systems using discrete point-to-point modules for which business cases support funding the improvement. These more manageable bite-sized components will streamline processes such as contract management, online bidding, reverse auctions, and contract search and online ordering. Systems deployed incrementally in modules that can be interconnected and modified to keep pace with changing business processes and technology will continue to be launched, but on a smaller scale than the e-procurement launches of the 1990s.

Environmentally preferred purchases

Environmentally preferred and sustainable purchasing will continue to emerge as a value consideration in state purchasing. This movement is already well-established in Massachusetts, Minnesota, Washington, Oregon and California and can be expected to expand. The number of contracts providing environmentally-preferred products is also expected to increase. Purchases aimed at reducing fuel consumption and greenhouse gas emissions are likely to expand commensurate with fuel and environmental concerns. California, Oregon and Washington, for example, are teaming to collaborate on purchases of low rolling resistance tires and other efforts to reduce energy consumption and greenhouse gas emissions.

Procurement takes on a more strategic role

As state executives have turned to state procurement to generate savings through strategic sourcing, program efficiencies and other initiatives to develop innovative and complex contracts, state procurement has assumed a much higher profile in state government enterprise decisions. Where state procurement officials were often relegated to a tactical role of buying what the customer wanted, now state procurement is involved in and often leads the strategic procurement planning process for major initiatives such as strategic sourcing and cross organization projects. As a result, the value added and the profile of state procurement in government enterprise planning is increasing.

Today procurement offices are called on to participate and lead many strategic efforts to support state government. As these efforts succeed, procurement offices can expect to assume more responsibility. Examples include:

- leadership roles in complex procurements designed to provide enterprise wide services and delivery systems;
- strategic sourcing;
- project and contract management;
- business process improvements within the supply chain and statewide distribution channels;
- managed service provider contracts that provide a menu of choices for agencies to select a variety of professional services; and
- procurement policy development designed to support socioeconomic values ranging from minority and women-owned businesses contracting to sustainability.

As in the private sector, procurement offices are ideally suited to lead strategic efforts related to state business transactions and supplier relationships. Procurement organizations that fulfill this role will transition from a reactive status using traditional transactional approaches to a more proactive strategy seeking system-oriented results that are designed to reduce costs in government operations, streamline processes and optimize contract outcomes.

Cooperative purchasing will continue to grow

With declining resources and increasing workloads, governments are relying more on cooperative contracts. Cooperative contracts offer state government quick and convenient access to many common products and services as well as savings from the economies of scale of combined governments. State procurement offices typically act as gatekeepers for state and local access to these contracts and must consider local statutes, rules and policies before participating. Many states require local advertising of the contracts to ensure local small businesses have an opportunity to participate, or weigh the impact on local small businesses before agreeing to participate in cooperative contracts.

State and local government cooperative programs, as well as regional and national programs such as WSCA, U.S. Communities and the limited General Service Administration (GSA) schedules serve nearly every county, city and school district. Recent trends are especially important to government procurement. According to a 2004 National Association of State Procurement Officials (NASPO) survey, 43 states now serve local governments with cooperative purchasing programs.

The E-Government Act now gives state and local governments access to thousands of GSA Schedule 70 contracts. In 2004, 27 states had laws permitting use of GSA schedules. While most state governments have been slow in adopting the GSA contracts, GSA is stepping up its marketing and training programs and steady growth is anticipated.

States will continue with their procurement process efficiency efforts

Nearly every state streamlined its procurement process and improved value for customers through use of e-procurement technology, reverse auctions, purchasing cards, strategic sourcing or other tools during and since the 1990s. State directors leveraged these improvements to move from a tactical perspective to a more strategic one and to improve customer service and program efficiency.

There is, however, a growing concern among some procurement officials that recent headlines about federal emergency contracting practices and federal and local contracting scandals may tip the regulatory pendulum toward less flexibility. Many of the state procurement reforms in the past five years provide procurement offices with the ability to achieve more effective results by relaxing the constraints of acquisition systems that are Invitation to Bid-based only. As Steven Kelman of Harvard University, a leading procurement reformer in the federal government from 1993 through 1997, has observed, "An organization exists for its goals. It does not exist for its constraints."[5] More and more, procurement offices today are trying to help state organizations achieve their goals with procurement system-driven results while ensuring that the system boundaries or constraints established in law are met. Procurement reform that emphasizes constraints at the expense of eliminating the organization's ability to deliver effective business solutions will move procurement offices in a direction that limits their ability to improve on delivering timely and cost-effective contracting outcomes within their states.

Conclusion

An effective procurement program reduces the cost of government and inspires public confidence. It improves the quality and timeliness of services rendered by program departments and agencies. During the past five years, most procurement offices were asked to assume greater roles in reducing the cost of government operations at a time when their own budgets were reduced. Responding to these pressures, procurement offices employed innovative and strategic thinking to help manage expenses across the state government enterprise. Through the use of cooperative purchasing contracts, procurement officials are learning how to leverage limited staffs with competitive pricing. Procurement offices moved in a more strategic direction with reverse auctions, strategic sourcing and enterprise-wide contract solutions to support better outcomes. Staff recruitment and retention of skilled and knowledgeable staff in a changing business environment will continue to challenge procurement offices.

Procurement offices are government's link to the business community and a comprehensive channel of intergovernmental operations. The ability to continue delivering cost-effective solutions that advance state agency goals is linked to the procurement office's ability to establish a strategic role within state governments that provide fresh, knowledgeable and responsive support.

Notes

[1] Khi V. Thai, "Public Procurement Re-Examined," *Journal of Public Procurement* (2001).

[2] National Association of State Budget Officers, *The Fiscal Survey of the States*, June 2005.

[3] Executive Office of the President, Office of Management and Budget, Memorandum May 2005. *http://www.white house.gov/omb/procurement/comp_src/implementing_stra tegic_sourcing.pdf.*

[4] For more information on NIGP's LEAP program, please visit *http://www.nigp.org/educate/LEAPInfo.htm.*

[5] Steve Kelman, August 30, 2005, Annual Conference National Association of State Procurement Officials Annual Meeting.

About the Authors

John Adler is the state procurement administrator for the state of Arizona and past president (2004–2005) of the National Association of State Procurement Officials (NASPO).

Dugan Petty, CPPO is the deputy administrator, State Services Division, Oregon Department of Administrative Services, and a current life member and past president (1998–1999) of NASPO.

Rebecca Randall is a senior project coordinator for NASPO with responsibility for coordinating association activities, policy research and analysis, and promoting information exchange between states on procurement issues.

IT Outsourcing in the States: An Increasingly Popular and Evolving Option

By Mary Gay Whitmer

Hiring private sector contractors to perform functions and services that would otherwise be performed by government employees—now called "outsourcing"—is not new to state government, especially for Information Technology (IT). Many states have outsourced key IT functions and services, including all or part of their networks, since the 1990s. In fact, as early as 1999, the National Association of State Chief Information Officers (NASCIO) gave recognition awards to states with outstanding public-private partnerships. What has changed for states are (1) the increased importance of using IT outsourcing in ways that tangibly enhance efficiency and cost-effectiveness; and (2) emphasis on successfully managing the outsourced IT function.

Hiring private sector contractors to perform functions and services that would otherwise be performed by government employees—now called "outsourcing"—is not new to state government, especially for Information Technology (IT). Many states have outsourced key IT functions and services, including all or part of their networks, since the 1990s. In fact, as early as 1999, the National Association of State Chief Information Officers (NASCIO) gave recognition awards to states with outstanding public-private partnerships. What has changed for states are (1) the increased importance of using IT outsourcing in ways that tangibly enhance efficiency and cost-effectiveness; and (2) emphasis on successfully managing the outsourced IT function. Many states now are viewing their relationships with private sector firms as partnerships instead of merely contractual arrangements. Moreover, states are not choosing to outsource only IT functions, but business processes, such as training and Medicaid claims processing, as well. Greater dependence on IT systems and networks and heightened infrastructure security concerns have also contributed to the evolution of IT outsourcing.

Under the right conditions, states can greatly benefit from outsourcing certain IT functions and business processes, including data centers, physical networks, telecommunications, Medicaid claims processing, Web portals, network and desktop management, and training. Potential benefits include:

- Access to advanced technology;
- Greater ability to meet the demand for skilled IT personnel;
- Quick deployment;
- Flexibility in the choice of technology and modules; and
- Cost savings.[1]

Another potential benefit of outsourcing is that private sector firms may have more flexibility to use innovative funding models to finance outsourcing projects.

However, IT outsourcing can involve one or more of the following risks or costs:

- Loss of control over service quality;
- Possibility of compromised security (for example, data breaches);
- Potential service disruption due to the instability of vendors;
- Increased complexity of managing and monitoring the outsourcing contract;
- Prolonged procurement process; and
- Union pressure and budgetary uncertainty.[2]

Trends in State IT Outsourcing

Spending on state government outsourcing continues to increase, but the rate of increase has slowed somewhat in recent years. Reported figures indicate that state and local IT outsourcing spending grew slightly from 2003 to 2004 to $11.3 billion. The decreased growth rate has been explained, at least in part, by controversies surrounding the outsourcing of IT functions to private sector organizations that conduct all or part of the outsourced functions outside the United States,[3] although tight state fiscal conditions during that time also played a role. The debate has centered on security concerns that could be created by permitting sensitive IT functions or data to be handled outside the United States in countries such as India, China, Russia and Mexico, and the creation of IT jobs overseas instead of in the United States. Special concerns with offshore IT outsourcing are addressed in more detail in the next section.

In 2004, according to NASCIO, approximately one-third of states reported utilizing a mix of direct, in-house service provision with partial outsourcing. This marked a slight increase in state IT outsourcing and is consistent with the fact that many states were still reorganizing their IT governance structures in 2003 following the gubernatorial and legislative elections of 2002. Typical services at least partially outsourced in 2004 included application development, IT architecture, desktop configuration, project management, telecommunications, telephone/voice-related services, training and Web site/portals. However, fewer than 10 percent of states reported outsourcing a service in its entirety. Multimedia products, training, videoconferencing facilities, and Web site portals had higher rates of being entirely outsourced.[4] States may also outsource a service or business process to multiple firms to avoid potential service disruptions.

State IT outsourcing is likely to increase substantially in the next five years. As state fiscal conditions improve, pent-up demand will contribute to increased outsourcing, as will better metrics to measure the performance of private sector outsourcing firms. An increase in IT outsourcing from $10 billion in 2005 to $18 billion in 2010, a 75 percent increase, has been predicted. The primary drivers will be the need for IT expertise as state IT employees retire at higher rates and the need to replace aging legacy systems. Forecasts predict states will use outsourcing for application management, platform operations and desktop services.[5]

Emerging Issues Associated with State IT Offshoring

As previously mentioned, IT offshoring has been controversial in the last few years. According to a recent U.S. Government Accountability Office (GAO) report, IT offshoring refers to a state's purchase of goods or services, previously produced in the U.S., from abroad.[6] There are two main scenarios in which a state may procure offshore services or goods:

- The services or goods may be produced by a company not based in the United States; or

- A company may be based in the United States, but may produce products or perform services abroad (or even contract with another company that provides the services or goods abroad).

In either case, government leaders have raised concerns that include potential impacts on:

- The average U.S. standard of living;

- Employment and job displacement;

- Income distribution; and

- National security and consumer privacy.

While the GAO report said "traditional economic theory predicts that offshoring is likely to benefit the overall economy," many unresolved questions remain, and the report recommended additional research be conducted to gauge potential impacts on U.S. workers, their privacy and the nation's security.[7]

In response to IT offshoring concerns, many state legislatures have become actively involved in the issue. Bills have centered on either restricting a state's ability to outsource to companies that provide services abroad, or creating incentives to ensure services are provided domestically. In 2003, only four states attempted to address outsourcing abroad. However, 2004 heralded a very large increase with more than 200 bills introduced in 40 states to restrict offshoring. Five of those bills became laws. Other states issued executive orders or procurement policies to address the issue. The number of bills introduced by October 2005 decreased to 127. However, seven of those bills became law. Also in 2005, three states enacted laws requiring studies or creating commissions to examine the potential impacts of IT offshoring.[8]

Although there appears to be ongoing concerns with offshore outsourcing in general, the Information Technology Association of America (ITAA) anticipates that "(s)pending for global sourcing of computer software and services is expected to grow at a compound annual rate of just over 20 percent, increasing from approximately $15 billion in 2005 to $38 billion in 2010." ITAA also predicts that "total savings from the use of offshore resources are estimated to grow from $8.7 billion to $20.4 billion." To combat potential concerns over displaced workers, ITAA recommends that the U.S. focus on training programs for displaced workers and encourage investment in technology research and development.[9]

State IT Outsourcing—An Evolving Process

In developing an overall strategy for determining where outsourcing would be most cost-effective, states will likely start by identifying the areas in which they may need expertise from external sources versus areas in which they already have a sufficient amount of expertise. To focus on a specific set of in-house core competencies, states may decide to outsource only those functions in which they require additional expertise.

As the IT work force ages and retirements of key in-house IT experts become more prevalent, states will seek opportunities that are ripe for outsourcing. Heightened security concerns and demands for e-government applications will also drive the quest for successful IT outsourcing opportunities. As states actively pursue this path, they will find that outsourcing is shifting from a simple procurement and contract management model to a more complex service and relationship management model. There also will be a greater emphasis on the security and information privacy measures that a private sector firm can provide in performing IT services for the state.[10]

To increase the odds of long-term success in IT outsourcing, states should focus more on managing the relationship with the private sector provider even after the contract is signed. This involves a greater emphasis on selecting outsourcing opportunities that are aligned with a state's overall, long-term IT objectives. It will also require states to place more time and resources toward managing the transitioning of IT functions to a private sector firm and thereafter managing the firm's performance. By adopting a model of this nature, it may be easier for states to work through unanticipated contingencies that often occur during a complex IT outsourcing project. In addition, states should also examine and address security throughout every phase of the outsourcing life cycle, instead of addressing it as an afterthought.[11] Critical success factors for this evolving model of IT outsourcing include:

- Top management support and involvement;

- Ample time and resource input;

- Strong procurement and relationship management skills;

- Continual learning and service benchmarking; and

- Frequent communication between agencies and their service providers.

The Future

As with state Web portals, many of which are now outsourced, the involvement of private sector firms in providing IT functions and services for states will be virtually transparent to citizens. Moreover, with the anticipated growth of state IT outsourcing well into this decade and beyond, new ways of using IT outsourcing will occur. For example, Virginia recently became the first state to outsource the bulk of its IT operations to one private sector firm. Outsourced functions include the state's mainframe, server, desktop, voice and data networks. In doing so, Virginia has had to determine how best to handle issues involving the state IT work force and eco-

nomic development.[12] While there is potential for substantial benefits, dealing with the complexity of larger efforts such as Virginia's can pose a daunting challenge. Large IT outsourcing initiatives in Florida and Connecticut that were ultimately curtailed stand as examples of why state government officials must use careful consideration in initiating and proceeding with large-scale IT outsourcing.

Given the challenges associated with larger initiatives, some states are turning to outsourcing for smaller projects and testing the waters before pursuing larger-scale projects. In the coming years, states will begin to experiment more with IT outsourcing. Questions that are currently unresolved—such as the success of large-scale efforts like Virginia's and IT offshoring's impact on the domestic IT work force—will act as forces that will shape the future of state IT outsourcing in addition to its current drivers, including the aging IT work force and increased security requirements.

Notes

[1] Yu-Che Chen and James L. Perry, IBM Endowment for The Business of Government, (February 2003).

[2] Ibid.

[3] Doug Beizer, "State and local spending on outsourcing levels off," *gcn.com*, December 28, 2004.

[4] "2004–2005 NASCIO Compendium of Digital Government in the States," NASCIO, (2004).

[5] "State and Local IT Outsourcing Spending to Grow 75 Percent by FY2010," INPUT, January 23, 2006.

[6] "Offshoring of Services: An Overview of the Issues," U.S. Government Accountability Office (GAO), Report to Congressional Committee, GAO-06-5, (November 2005).

[7] Ibid.

[8] National Foundation for American Policy, 2005.

[9] "Executive Summary: The Comprehensive Impact of Offshore Software and IT Services Outsourcing on the U.S. Economy and the IT Industry," Information Technology Association of America (ITAA) and Global Insight (USA), Inc., (October 2005).

[10] Yu-Che Chen and James L. Perry, "IT Outsourcing: A Primer for Public Managers," IBM Endowment for The Business of Government, New Ways to Manage Series, (February 2003).

[11] Ibid.

[12] Pat McDougall, "Virginia Is For Outsourcing," *Informationweek*, November 21, 2005.

About the Author

Mary Gay Whitmer, JD, CIPP/G is an issues coordinator for the National Association of State Chief Information Officers (NASCIO) with responsibility for coordinating association activities in the areas IT procurement and privacy.

Professional and Occupational Regulation
By Pam Brinegar

State legislatures show signs of departing from their customary professional licensing approach as new professions gain state licensure without initiation by a profession or the public. Unprecedented measures are being enacted, some on behalf of the licensees. Agencies in many states are focusing on emergency preparedness for displaced professional populations.

U.S. Licensing System

Professional and occupational regulation is largely a state function[1] exercised and protected under Article X of the U.S. Constitution. Article X grants states the authority to regulate activities affecting the health, safety and welfare of their citizens. Practitioner disciplinary matters follow each state's administrative procedures act.[2] Exceptions to this state oversight are the expanding areas of municipal-level licensing[3] and professionals employed by the federal government to work within state borders.

Renewed Economist Interest

The occasional economist has long been intrigued by the occupational and professional licensing industry, perhaps most notably in the United States, beginning with Milton Friedman.

Friedman established himself in 1945 with *Income from Independent Professional Practice*, coauthored with Simon Kuznets. In it he argued that state licensing procedures limited entry into the medical profession, thereby allowing doctors to charge higher fees than if competition were more open.[4]

This focus on the medical profession as self- rather than public-serving was subsequently taken to be an accurate description of every profession. During the past decade several economists have expressed a renewed interest in studying licensing and its largely hidden, yet pervasive, costs. Economist Morris Kleiner estimates that more than 20 percent of the U.S. work force is covered by state licensing laws, as well as federal, county and city regulations. He suggests that the benefits of state licensing may not justify the substantial cost passed on to the consumer in the form of higher professional fees. "One result of occupational regulation has been that prices in regulated occupations have increased more—and the earnings of practitioners have become higher—than in comparable occupations with similar levels of human capital investments and experience."[5]

Reed Neil Olsen posits that regulation's very existence can be explained as a reflection of defined interests, either those of the professional, the public or both:

(1) the capture theory, which assumes the professionals 'capture' regulation and use it to deter entry and increase their incomes; (2) the public interest theory, which assumes that professional licensure is used in the public interest in order to insure the quality of professional services; and (3) the political economy theory, which assumes that both professional interests and public interests may simultaneously have an impact upon the existence and nature of licensing...[6]

The popularity of the capture theory[7] may be yielding to the political economy theory that looks at the interrelationship of the political and economic systems. Olsen points out that so far, very few studies have tested hypotheses designed to consider the possibility that licensure has a more complex explanation than any of the three interest-reflection theories.

Federal Trade Commission

Despite a ruling by the U.S. Supreme Court that it is not good for the public if the "learned professions" are permitted to function freely in the market system, the Federal Trade Commission stands by its position adopted following several antitrust cases involving the professions:

"We conclude that the major economic issues are now settled: There are no good reasons, either from a theoretical or an empirical vantage point, for concern about the effects of competition in the professions. To the contrary, the evidence supports the conclusion that competition yields major benefits to consumers in the form of lower prices, without adverse effects on quality. The concerns articulated by the Supreme Court are not supported by current economic understanding."[8]

Emerging/Expanding Professions

A Pattern Repeated?

In 1952, The Council of State Governments (CSG) identified "the problem of licensing occupations" as the rate at which new professions were being regulated by the states.[9] The book identified 75 state-regulated professions of which 14 were regulated by all of the then 48 states. The number of state-regulated professions ultimately grew to more than 1,100, fewer than 60 of which are regulated by every state (see Tables A and B for selected professions). Concerned about the high costs of regulation and armed with a recently published evaluation framework,[10] state houses by the early 1980s were consistently refusing regulation to emerging professions.

Sunset reviews,[11] intended to weed out unnecessary licensing, did not result in professional deregulation. On the other hand, sunrise analyses, intended to place the burden of demonstrating the necessity of licensure on the profession, have served as a deterrent to the extraordinary growth in state professional regulation. For a sunrise report currently under review, see "Genetic Counselor Draft Sunrise Review," Washington State Department of Health.[12]

As a result of the difficulty of obtaining state licensure, new professions began to certify practitioners through private sector voluntary credentialing organizations. Some of these voluntary membership groups, once they had sufficient resources to do so, demonstrated to states that it could be cost-effective to license a new profession. There is some evidence that the larger a professional association's budgetary and membership resources, the greater the probability of state licensure for the profession.[13] Legislatures can simply adopt an association's examination, ethical standards, etc. without trying to recapture development costs from licensing fees.

One group making such progress is paralegals, whose National Federation of Paralegal Associations has a Model Act for Paralegal Licensure ready for adoption by legislatures.[14] Sometimes the national association encounters resistance beyond that offered by legislators. In Florida, the state bar association wants to create a new membership section for paralegals in lieu of state licensure, but the legislature is prepared to reconsider regulating paralegals, and there is strong support for the measure.[15] Other emerging groups include home inspectors, who have gained regulation in 30 states during the past decade, and payday lenders, although state laws vary regarding whether the business, the individual lender, or both, are licensed.

State oversight of a profession is difficult to abolish once it has been granted. The Louisiana legislature has repeatedly declined to do away with its 65-year-old florist licensing law. Unsuccessful candidates recently sued to have the law set aside, but a federal judge upheld the state's right to determine citizen protection needs. A state's authority to regulate matters concerning its citizens continues to be upheld. The U.S. Supreme Court declined to consider the question of whether an Oklahoma state law requiring licensed funeral directors to handle casket sales is constitutionally discriminatory. This refusal upholds a 10th Circuit Court of Appeals decision that it is not a judge's job to "second-guess" laws designed to protect consumers.

Limited State Initiatives

There is some evidence that states have once again started defining and regulating professions in a singular fashion. The conclusion of all early work was that the public was rarely, if ever, involved in the licensing of a new profession, while the professional association was always instrumental. The three growth areas for state licensure in the past 20 years are allied health, construction and environmental (e.g., genetic counselors, home inspectors, mold remediators), all with strong association backing.

What is unusual about some current measures is that the request for regulation is not coming from the professionals or their associations. One impetus may be states' concern for missed revenue opportunities. An example of this new category is online auctioning. States are beginning to require auctioneer or gallery licenses for individuals who sell items on behalf of others through such venues as eBay.

Other Recent Extraordinary Items

Illinois has enacted a law that will allow nurses from only Puerto Rico and other U.S. territories to work for up to one year in Illinois before they pass the licensure exam. Those nurses must be licensed in their home territory, be proficient in English, and be under the direct supervision of a nurse licensed in Illinois.[16]

There is a movement among licensed pharmacists seeking authorization from legislatures to permit their conscience, rather than physician prescriptions for a controlled substance, to act as their guide when filling prescriptions. Some states (e.g., Illinois and Wisconsin) favor requiring their licensees to function under current statutes, while others (e.g., Arkansas, Mississippi, South Dakota) have sided with the pharmacists. At least a dozen states will consider whether to enact "conscience clauses" during upcoming sessions.

New Jersey has enacted a law requiring the state's lawyers, and many doctors, to pay $75 a year for three years to help doctors in high-risk specialties pay for malpractice insurance. Lawyers are challenging the law because of their presumed role in increasing insurance premiums through litigious activity.

In Florida, designated licensees, including architects, contractors, cosmetologists and veterinarians, whose licenses expire due to hardship or circumstances beyond a licensee's control, may have their licenses restored without having to meet the qualifications for initial licensure.

Following New Mexico's lead, some Louisiana psychologists are prescribing drugs. The fight to win prescriptive privileges was high profile, but the actual implementation once the Louisiana law passed was hardly noticed. In both states, prescribing certifications are only issued to licensed psychologists who complete specialized training and pass a national examination.

The speaker of the House in Connecticut has called for licensing of hypnotists (they are currently registered in California and Colorado), and there is a bill in Washington that seeks licensure of Christmas tree growers.

Technology

Licensing agencies continue to increase their reliance on technology to support their examination, licensing and professional discipline activities. Candidates for licensure and renewal are taking increasing advantage of online applications and renewals. Some states now offer live scan fingerprinting for licensing applicants on whom background checks are required.

States continue to make licensee information, including disciplinary actions, available to the public, although there may be challenges to doing so. A licensed nurse in Alaska has filed a class-action lawsuit against the state for providing her address on its Division of Occupational Licensing Web site.[17]

Emergency Preparedness

In 1992, Hurricane Andrew's impact made apparent a need to allow licensed personnel from other jurisdictions to practice in a disaster area. The result was the Emergency Management Assistance Compact, which says in part: "Persons holding licenses, certificates, or other permits ... shall be deemed licensed, certified, or permitted by the state requesting assistance."[18]

In 2005, Hurricanes Katrina and Rita revealed an additional need: providing for emergency licensing of professional populations displaced during a disaster. Within hours after the hurricanes, numerous health care practitioners were transported out of the Gulf Coast states to provide client care en route to other jurisdictions. Upon arrival, they could no longer provide client care (unless they were also licensed in the new jurisdiction) and were unable to return to their home areas. The situation intensified as thousands of licensed professionals were displaced without credentials or certainty of when they could obtain them. Many licensing agencies were caught completely unprepared to provide assistance, while some, such as the South Carolina Department of Labor, Licensing and Regulation, were far more prepared to move quickly, partly as a result of their own experience with natural disasters.

A preliminary report, *Licensing Agencies and Emergency Preparedness*,[19] is a first step toward understanding this new situation and helping licensing agencies prepare for future disasters. At least five states (Maine, Missouri, South Carolina, Tennessee and Virginia[20]) issued post-hurricane executive orders addressing displaced licensed personnel. Numerous agencies and associations also took emergency action, and many of these efforts are identified.

The report provides a brief outline of the necessary emergency capacity an agency should have in place for disasters of any kind:

- authority to issue temporary licenses
- authority to waive fees
- immunity from civil action
- flexibility in scopes of practice (such as smallpox vaccinations by dentists)

Regulatory agencies in disaster areas also have challenges dealing with unlicensed practice. Florida is now struggling with enormous problems caused by charlatan practitioners of construction-related industries who have often left the state before they could be disciplined.

Federal Activity

Congress passed H.R. 2862[21] "to permit certain health professionals who are displaced by Hurricane Katrina to provide health-related services under the Medicare, Medicaid, SCHIP, and Indian Health Service programs in states to which such professionals relocate."

The federal government is slowly increasing its efforts to provide health services to underserved, rural areas. Despite opposition from the American Dental Association and the Alaska Dental Society, and amid congressional equivocation, dental aides have begun work in rural Alaska under the existing Community Health Aide Program authorized by the federal government and operated by Alaska tribal health programs.[22]

Notes

[1] Licensure, the most restrictive form of state regulation, specifies that it is illegal to perform any of the activities specified in a scope-of-practice act without meeting state-defined standards, minimally specified educational and additional examination requirements. Certification, also known as title protection, may also have restrictive requirements, but does not prevent individuals from performing the tasks associated with the profession as long as they do not use the regulated title. The term certification is widely used in the private sector with varying definitions, which is a source of considerable confusion not only for consumers, but for those involved with state and voluntary certification programs as well. Registration, the least restrictive form of state regulation, requires individuals to file their names, addresses and qualifications with a designated state agency before performing the duties of the occupation. A useful primer on the U.S. professional licensing system is K. Schmitt, and B. Shimberg, *Demystifying Occupational and Professional Regulation: Answers to Questions You May Have Been Afraid to Ask*, (Lexington, KY: The Council on Licensure, Enforcement and Regulation, 1996).

[2] The National Conference of Commissioners on Uniform State Laws is currently revising its Model State Administrative Procedures Act. For the October 2005 draft, see *http://www.law.upenn.edu/bll/ulc/msapa/2005OctMtgDraft.htm.*

[3] For example, The Bedford Massachusetts County Health Department has begun licensing massage therapists and will continue the program until there is a state law in place to regulate the profession.

[4] *http://www.econlib.org/library/Enc/bios/Friedman.html.*

[5] M. Kleiner, "Our Guild-Ridden Economy," *Wall Street Journal*, Saturday October 15, 2005, Opinion A7.

[6] R.O. Olsen, "The Regulation of Medical Professions," 1999, *http://encyclo.findlaw.com/5870book.pdf.*

[7] G. Stigler's "capture theory" suggested that regulations seldom protect the consumer as intended, but rather industries, by inhibiting new competition (*http://www.econlib.org/library/Enc/bios/Stigler.html*).

[8] J. Kwoka, *The Federal Trade Commission and the Professions: A Quarter Century of Accomplishments and Some New Challenges*, American Antitrust Institute Working Paper 04-04, *http://www.antitrustinstitute.org/recent2/354.pdf.*

[9] *Occupational Licensing Legislation in the States*, (Chicago: The Council of State Governments, 1952).

[10] B. Shimberg and D. Roederer, *Questions a Legislator Should Ask*. 2d., K. Schmitt, ed., (Lexington, KY, The Council on Licensure, Enforcement and Regulation), 1994 [orig. 1978]. This influential pamphlet said that regulation should meet a public need, provide the minimum amount of oversight to meet that need, avoid overlap with other regulated services, provide for continued competence and professional discipline, and involve the public in the process. In other words, it educated legislators to understand that the only valid reason to regulate a profession is to protect consumers from any harm they may experience as a result of practice of the profession or occupation. It also pointed out that no consumer group has ever sought licensing for regulation, but that the push for regulation comes from the practitioners of a profession.

[11] Sunset is the automatic termination of regulatory boards and agencies unless legislative action is taken to reinstate them. Sunrise is a process under which an occupation or profession wishing to receive state certification or licensure must propose the components of the legislation, along with cost and benefit estimates of the proposed regulation. What is more common at this time is the statutory inclusion of sunset provisions in new laws as well as the periodic examination of agencies through performance audits, also known as legislative or evaluation audits. See "Sunset, Sunrise and Agency Audits," *http://www.clearhq.org/sunset.htm.*

[12] *http://www.doh.wa.gov/hsqa/sunrise/gen_couns_draft_sunrise.doc.*

[13] Charles J. Whelan, "Politics or Public Interest?," *Perspectives on Work*, Winter 2005.

[14] *http://www.paralegals.org/displaycommon.cfm?an=1&subarticlenbr=341.*

[15] *http://www.floridabar.org/DIVCOM/JN/jnnews01.nsf/8c9f13012b96736985256aa900624829/9851c792032bd9bf852570c7004ea6b5?OpenDocument.*

[16] "History Made in Nursing Legislation," Illinois Nurses Association, *www.illinoisnurses.org/files/INA_newsletter.pdf.*

[17] *http://www.commerce.state.ak.us/occ/.*

[18] Emergency Management Assistance Compact: *http://www.emacweb.org/.*

[19] Emergency Preparedness Working Group, CLEAR, November 2005, *http://www.clearhq.org/draft_report.htm.*

[20] Excerpted from Virginia's Executive Order 97, as revised September 23, 2005: During the next 120 days, the Director of the Department of Health Professions shall issue temporary licenses, registrations, and certifications to practice in the Commonwealth, for a period not to exceed one year, to qualified health care practitioners who are displaced residents of Hurricane Katrina or Rita-affected states, who hold their unrestricted licenses, registrations, or certifications in their resident states, and who may be unable to furnish or have furnished on their behalf complete documentation of their credentials and license status as otherwise required by Virginia law or regulation. The Director shall also have authority to defer the payment of licensing fees. Any license, registration or certification so issued may be revoked for cause without a hearing by the Director. Source: *http://www.governor.virginia.gov/Press_Policy/Executive_Orders/html/EO_97.html.*

[21] *http://www.clearhq.org/hr2862.htm.*

[22] Alaska Dental Health Aide Program Brief, The Center for the Health Professions, University of California San Francisco, September 2005, *http://www.ucsf.edu/dphtalk/powerpoint/AK%20Dental%20Health%20Aide%20Program_white%20paper%209-05.pdf.* The dental aides program has three levels of aides, the most basic of which provides prevention education. The second level practitioner works with a dentist, cleaning and filling teeth. The third, called dental health aide therapists, can perform some tasks usually reserved for dentists, such as extracting teeth and preparing teeth for fillings. Licensed dentists must give permission for the therapists to perform any procedure.

About the Author

Pam Brinegar is executive director of The Council on Licensure, Enforcement and Regulation (CLEAR), which provides educational programs for professional licensing officials.

Table A
STATE REGULATION OF SELECTED NON-HEALTH OCCUPATIONS AND PROFESSIONS: DECEMBER 2005

State or other jurisdiction	Accountant, certified public	Agriculture inspector	Architect	Auctioneer	Barber	Cosmetologist	Embalmer (a)	Engineer, professional (b)	Environmental science & protection tech.	Forester	Funeral director	Geologist	Hazardous materials removal worker	Insurance agent	Insurance broker	Landscape architect	Polygraph examiner	Real estate agent	Real estate broker	Surveyor, land	Water & liquid waste treatment plant/ system operator
Alabama	L	…	L	L	L	L	L	L	…	L	L	L	L	L	L	L	L	L	L	L	L
Alaska	L	…	L	…	L	L	L	L	…	…	L	L	L	L	L	L	…	L	L	L	L
Arizona	L	…	L	L	L	L	L	L	…	…	L	L	…	L	L	L	…	L	L	L	…
Arkansas	L	L	L	L	L	L	L	L	L	L	L	L	L	L	L	L	L	L	L	L	L
California	L	L	L	…	L	L	L	L	L	L	L	L	…	L	L	L	…	L	L	L	L
Colorado	L	…	L	…	L	L	…	L	…	…	…	…	L	L	…	L	…	L	L	L	…
Connecticut	L	…	L	…	L	L	L	L	L	L	L	…	L	L	L	L	…	L	L	L	L
Delaware	L	…	L	L	L	L	…	…	…	L	L	L	L	L	…	L	…	L	L	L	L
Florida	L	…	L	L	L	L	L	L	…	…	L	L	L	L	L	L	…	L	L	L	L
Georgia	L	…	L	L	L	L	L	L	…	L	L	…	L	L	L	L	…	L	L	L	L
Hawaii	L	…	L	…	L	L	L	L	…	…	L	…	…	L	L	L	…	L	L	L	…
Idaho	L	…	L	…	L	L	L	L	…	…	L	L	…	L	L	L	…	L	L	L	…
Illinois	L	…	L	L	L	L	L	L	…	…	L	L	…	L	…	L	L	L	L	L	L
Indiana	L	…	L	L	L	L	L	L	…	…	L	…	L	L	…	L	L	L	L	L	L
Iowa	L	…	L	…	L	L	…	…	…	…	L	…	L	L	…	L	L	L	L	L	L
Kansas	L	…	L	…	L	L	L	L	…	…	L	L	…	L	L	L	…	L	L	L	…
Kentucky	L	…	L	L	L	L	L	L	…	…	L	L	…	L	L	L	L	L	L	L	L
Louisiana	L	L	L	L	L	L	L	L	…	…	L	L	…	L	L	L	…	L	L	L	…
Maine	L	…	L	L	L	L	L	L	…	L	L	L	…	L	L	L	L	L	L	L	L
Maryland	L	…	L	…	L	L	…	…	…	L	L	…	L	L	L	L	…	L	L	L	L
Massachusetts	L	…	L	L	L	L	L	…	…	…	L	…	L	L	L	L	L	L	L	L	L
Michigan	L	L	L	…	L	L	L	…	…	L	L	…	L	L	L	L	L	L	L	L	L
Minnesota	L	…	L	L	L	L	…	L	…	…	L	L	L	L	L	L	…	L	L	L	L
Mississippi	L	…	L	L	L	L	L	…	…	…	L	…	L	L	L	L	…	L	L	L	L
Missouri	L	…	L	L	L	L	L	L	…	…	L	…	L	L	L	L	…	L	L	L	…
Montana	L	…	L	…	L	L	L	…	…	…	L	…	L	L	…	L	…	L	L	L	L
Nebraska	L	…	L	…	L	L	L	L	L	…	L	…	L	L	L	L	L	L	L	L	L
Nevada	L	…	L	L	L	L	L	L	…	…	L	…	L	L	L	L	L	L	L	L	L
New Hampshire	L	…	L	L	L	L	L	L	…	L	L	L	L	L	L	…	…	L	L	L	L
New Jersey	L	…	…	L	L	L	…	L	L	…	L	…	L	…	L	…	…	L	L	L	L
New Mexico	L	…	L	…	L	L	L	L	L	…	L	…	L	L	L	L	L	L	L	L	L
New York	L	…	L	…	L	L	L	L	L	…	L	…	L	L	L	L	…	L	L	L	L
North Carolina	L	L	L	L	L	L	L	L	…	L	L	L	L	L	L	L	L	L	L	L	L
North Dakota	L	…	L	L	L	L	L	L	…	…	L	…	L	L	L	L	L	L	L	L	L
Ohio	L	…	L	L	L	L	L	L	…	…	L	…	L	L	L	L	L	L	L	L	…
Oklahoma	L	…	L	…	L	L	L	L	…	…	L	…	L	L	L	L	L	L	L	L	L
Oregon	L	…	L	…	L	L	L	L	L	…	L	L	L	L	L	…	L	L	L	L	L
Pennsylvania	L	…	L	L	L	L	…	L	L	…	L	L	…	L	L	L	…	L	L	L	…
Rhode Island	L	…	L	L	L	L	L	L	L	…	L	L	…	L	L	L	L	L	L	L	…
South Carolina	L	…	L	L	L	L	L	L	…	L	L	…	L	L	L	L	L	L	L	L	…
South Dakota	L	L	L	…	L	L	…	…	L	…	L	…	L	L	L	L	…	L	L	L	L
Tennessee	L	…	L	L	L	L	L	L	…	L	L	…	L	L	L	L	…	L	L	L	L
Texas	L	…	L	L	L	L	L	L	…	…	L	L	…	L	L	L	…	L	L	L	L
Utah	L	…	L	…	L	L	L	L	…	…	L	…	L	L	L	L	L	L	L	L	L
Vermont	L	…	L	L	L	L	L	L	…	…	L	…	L	L	L	L	…	L	L	L	L
Virginia	L	L	L	L	L	L	L	L	…	…	L	L	…	L	…	L	C	L	L	L	L
Washington	L	…	L	L	L	L	L	L	…	…	L	…	L	L	L	L	…	L	L	L	L
West Virginia	L	…	L	L	L	L	L	L	…	L	L	…	L	L	L	L	L	L	L	L	L
Wisconsin	L	L	L	L	L	L	…	L	L	…	L	L	L	L	L	…	L	L	L	L	L
Wyoming	L	…	L	…	L	L	L	L	…	L	L	…	L	L	L	L	L	L	L	L	L
Dist. of Columbia	L	…	L	L	L	L	…	L	…	…	L	…	…	L	L	…	…	L	L	L	…

Sources: Council on Licensure, Enforcement and Regulation, December 2005 and various national associations of state boards.

Key:
C — Certification.
L — Licensure.
R — Registration.

(a) In some states, embalmers are not licensed separately from funeral directors; embalming is part of the funeral director's job.

(b) In addition to licensing professional engineers, some states regulate engineers by specific areas of expertise, such as civil engineers.

Table B
STATE REGULATION OF HEALTH OCCUPATIONS AND PROFESSIONS: DECEMBER 2005

State or other jurisdiction	Acupuncturist	Chiropractor	Counselor, professional (a)	Counselor, alcohol & drug	Counselor, pastoral	Counselor, substance abuse (b)	Dentist	Dental assistant (c)	Dental hygienist	Denturist	Dietitian	Emergency medical technician (d)	Hearing aid dealer & fitter
Alabama	...	L	L	...	...	...	L	...	L	...	L	L	L
Alaska	L	L	L	...	...	...	L	...	L	...	L	L	L
Arizona	L	L	L	...	...	L	L	C	L	L	...	L	L
Arkansas	L	L	L	...	L	...	L	R	L	...	L	L	L
California	L	L	L	...	...	...	L	L	L	...	R	L	L
Colorado	L	L	L	...	...	C, L	L	...	L	...	...	L	L
Connecticut	L	L	L	C, L	...	...	L	...	L	...	L	L	L
Delaware	...	L	L	...	...	L	L	...	L	...	C	L	L
Florida	L	L	L	...	...	...	L	C	L	...	L	L	L
Georgia	L	L	L	...	...	...	L	...	L	...	L	L	L
Hawaii	L	L	...	...	...	C	L	...	L	...	C	L	L
Idaho	L	L	L	...	...	...	L	C	L	L	L	L	L
Illinois	L	L	L	...	...	...	L	...	L	...	L	L	L
Indiana	L	L	...	...	...	...	L	...	L	...	C	L	L
Iowa	L	L	L	...	...	...	L	R	L	...	L	L	L
Kansas	...	L	L	...	...	...	L	...	L	...	L	L	L
Kentucky	...	L	L	C	L (e)	...	L	...	L	...	L	L	L
Louisiana	L	L	L	...	...	C	L	...	L	...	L	L	L
Maine	L	L	L	L	L	L	L	L	L	L	L	L	L
Maryland	L	L	L	C, L	...	...	L	L	L	...	L	L	L
Massachusetts	L	L	L	...	...	...	L	...	L	...	L	L	L
Michigan	...	L	L	...	...	...	L	L	L	...	...	L	L
Minnesota	L	L	L	L	...	...	L	L	L	...	L	L	L
Mississippi	...	L	L	...	...	...	L	L	L	...	L	L	L
Missouri	L	L	L	...	...	C	L	...	L	...	L	L	L
Montana	L	L	L	...	...	L	L	...	L	L	L	L	L
Nebraska	L	L	L	L	...	...	L	...	L	...	L	L	L
Nevada	L	L	...	...	...	C, L	L	...	L	...	C	L	L
New Hampshire	L	L	L	L	L	L	L	...	L	...	L	L	L
New Jersey	L	L	L	C, L	...	...	L	L	L	...	...	L	L
New Mexico	L	L	L	L	...	L	L	C	L	...	L	L	L
New York	L	L	L	C	...	C	L	L	L	...	C	L	L
North Carolina	L	L	L	...	L	C	L	...	L	...	L	L	L
North Dakota	...	L	L	...	...	L	L	L	L	...	L	L	L
Ohio	L	L	L	...	...	C, L	L	...	L	...	L	L	L
Oklahoma	...	L	L	C, L	...	...	L	C	L	...	L	L	L
Oregon	L	L	L	C	...	...	L	C	L	L	L	L	L
Pennsylvania	R	L	L (f)	C	...	...	L	C	L	...	C	L	L
Rhode Island	L	L	L	...	...	L	L	...	L	...	L	L	L
South Carolina	L	L	L	...	...	...	L	...	L	...	...	L	L
South Dakota	...	L	L	...	...	C	L	L	L	...	L	L	L
Tennessee	L	L	L	L	L	...	L	L	L	...	L	L	L
Texas	L	L	L	...	...	L	L	...	L	...	L	L	L
Utah	L	L	L	...	...	L	L	...	L	...	L	L	L
Vermont	L	L	L	L	...	...	L	L	L	...	L	L	L
Virginia	L	L	L	...	...	C, L	L	...	L	...	C	L	L
Washington	L	L	L	...	...	C	L	...	L	L	L	L	L
West Virginia	L	L	L	...	...	...	L	...	L	...	L	L	L
Wisconsin	L	L	L	...	...	C	L	...	L	...	C	L	L
Wyoming	...	L	L	...	...	L	L	...	L	...	...	L	L
Dist. of Columbia	L	L	L	...	...	R	L	...	L	...	L	L	...

Key:
C — Certification.
L — Licensure.
R — Registration.
. . . — Not regulated.
See footnotes at end of table.

STATE REGULATION OF HEALTH OCCUPATIONS AND PROFESSIONS: DECEMBER 2005 — Continued

State or other jurisdiction	Homeopath	Massage therapist	Nurse, licensed practical (g)	Nurse midwife (g)	Nurse, practitioner (g)	Nurse, registered (g)	Nursing home administrator	Occupational therapist	Occupational therapy assistant	Optician (h)	Optometrist	Osteopath	Pharmacist	Physical therapist
Alabama	...	L	L	L	L	L	L	L	L	...	L	L	L	L
Alaska	...	...	L	L	L	L	L	L	L	L	L	L	L	L
Arizona	L	L	L	L	L	L	L	L	L	L	L	L	L	L
Arkansas	...	L	L	L	L	L	L	L	L	L	L	L	L	L
California	...	...	L	L	L	L	L	L	C	L	L	L	L	L
Colorado	...	...	L	L	L	L	L	...	...	...	L	L	L	L
Connecticut	L	L	L	L	L	L	L	L	L	L	L	L	L	L
Delaware	...	L	L	L	L	L	L	L	L	...	L	L	L	L
Florida	...	L	L	L	L	L	L	L	L	L	L	L	L	L
Georgia	...	...	L	L	L	L	L	L	L	L	L	L	L	L
Hawaii	...	L	L	L	L	L	L	L	...	L	L	L	L	L
Idaho	...	...	L	L	L	L	L	L	L	L	L	L	L	L
Illinois	...	L	L	L	...	L	L	L	L	...	L	L	L	L
Indiana	...	...	L	L	L	L	L (i)	L	C	...	L	L	L	L
Iowa	...	L	L	L	L	L	L	L	L	...	L	L	L	L
Kansas	...	...	L	L	L	L	L	L	L	L	L	L	L	L
Kentucky	...	L	L	L	L	L	L	L	L	L	L	L	L	L
Louisiana	...	L	L	L	C	L	L	L	L	...	L	L	L	L
Maine	...	L	L	L	L	L	L	L	L	...	L	L	L	L
Maryland	...	C	L	L	L	L	L	L	L	...	L	L	L	L
Massachusetts	...	...	L	L	L	L	L	L	L	L	L	L	L	L
Michigan	...	...	L	L	C	L	L	R	R	...	L	L	L	L
Minnesota	...	...	L	L	L	L	L	L	L	...	L	L	L	L
Mississippi	...	L	L	L	L	L	L	L	L	L	L	L	L	L
Missouri	...	L	L	L	...	L	L	L	L	...	L	L	L	L
Montana	...	...	L	L	L	L	L	L	L	...	L	L	L	L
Nebraska	...	L	L	L	L	L	L	L	L	...	L	L	L	L
Nevada	L	...	L	L	L	L	L	L	L	L	L	L	L	L
New Hampshire	...	L	L	L	L	L	L	L	L	L	L	L	L	L
New Jersey	...	C	L	L	L	L	L	L	L	L	L	L	L	L
New Mexico	...	L	L	L	...	L	L	L	L	...	L	L	L	L
New York	...	L	L	L	L	L	L	L	L	L	L	L	L	L
North Carolina	...	L	L	L	L	L	L	L	L	L	L	L	L	L
North Dakota	...	L	L	L	L	L	L	L	L	...	L	L	L	L
Ohio	...	L	L	L	L	L	L	L	L	L	L	L	L	L
Oklahoma	...	...	L	L	C	L	L	L	L	...	L	L	L	L
Oregon	...	L	L	L	L	L	L	L	L	...	L	L	L	L
Pennsylvania	...	...	L	L	L	L	L	L	L	...	L	L	L	L
Rhode Island	...	L	L	L	L	L	L	L	L	L	L	L	L	L
South Carolina	...	L	L	L	L	L	L	L	L	L	L	L	L	L
South Dakota	...	L	L	L	L	L	L	L	L	...	L	L	L	L
Tennessee	...	L	L	L	L	L	L	L	L	L	L	L	L	L
Texas	...	R	L	L	L	L	L	L	L	L	L	L	L	L
Utah	...	L	L	L	L	L	L (i)	L	L	...	L	L	L	L
Vermont	...	...	L	L	L	L	L	L	L	L	L	L	L	L
Virginia	...	C	L	L	L	L	L	L	...	L	L	L	L	L
Washington	...	L	L	L	L	L	L	L	L	L	L	L	L	L
West Virginia	...	L	L	L	L	L	L	L	L	...	L	L	L	L
Wisconsin	...	C	L	L	C	L	L	L	L	...	L	L	L	L
Wyoming	...	...	L	L	L	L	L	L	L	...	L	L	L	L
Dist. of Columbia	...	L	L	L	C	L	L	L	L	...	L	L	L	L

Sources: Council on Licensure, Enforcement and Regulation, December 2005 and various national associations of state boards.

Key:
C — Certification.
L — Licensure.
R — Registration.
. . . — Not regulated.
See footnotes at end of table.

STATE REGULATION OF HEALTH OCCUPATIONS AND PROFESSIONS: DECEMBER 2005 — Continued

State or other jurisdiction	Physical therapy assistant	Physician	Physician assistant	Podiatrist	Psychologist	Radiologic technologist/ technician	Radiation therapist	Respiratory therapist	Sanitarian	Social worker (j)	Speech-language pathologist & aud.	Therapist, marriage & family	Veterinarian	Veterinary technician
Alabama	L	L	L	L	L	...	...	L	...	L	L	L	L	L
Alaska	L	L	L	L	L	...	...	...	...	...	L	L	L	L
Arizona	L	L	L	L	L	L	L	L	R	L	L	L	L	L
Arkansas	L	L	L	L	L	L	L	L	R	L	L	L	L	L
California	L	L	L	L	L	C	L	L	...	L	L	L	L	R
Colorado	...	L	C	L	L	...	...	L	...	L	L	L	L	C
Connecticut	R	L	L	L	L	L	...	L	L	L	L	L	L	R
Delaware	L	L	L	L	L	L	L	L	...	L	L	...	L	...
Florida	L	L	L	L	L	L	L	L	...	L	L	L	L	R
Georgia	L	L	L	L	L	...	...	L	...	L	L	L	L	L
Hawaii	...	L	L	L	L	L	L	...	L	L	L	L	L	R
Idaho	L	L	L	L	L	...	...	L	L	L	...	L	L	R
Illinois	L	L	L	L	L	L	L	L	...	L	L	L	L	L
Indiana	L	L	C	L	L	C	...	C	R	L	L	L	L	L
Iowa	L	L	L	L	L	L	L	L	...	L	L	L	L	L
Kansas	L	L	L	L	L	...	...	L	...	L	L	L	L	L
Kentucky	L	L	L	L	L	L	...	L	L	L	L	L	L	L
Louisiana	L	L	L	L	L	L	L	L	L	L	L	L	L	R
Maine	L	L	L	L	L	L	L	L	...	L	L	L	L	L
Maryland	L	L	L	L	L	L	L	L	L	L	L	C, L	L	L
Massachusetts	L	L	L	L	L	L	L	L	L	L	L	L	L	R
Michigan	...	L	L	L	L	...	...	L	R	L	...	L	L	L
Minnesota	...	L	L	L	L	L	L	R	R	L	L	L	L	L
Mississippi	L	L	L	L	L	L	L	L	L	L	L	L	L	R
Missouri	L	L	L	L	L	...	...	L	C	L	L	L	L	L
Montana	L	L	L	L	L	L	...	L	...	L	L	...	L	...
Nebraska	C	L	L	L	L	C	L	L	R	L	L	C	L	L
Nevada	L	L	L	L	L	...	...	L	R	L	L	L	L	L
New Hampshire	L	L	L	L	L	...	...	L	...	C, L	L	L	L	...
New Jersey	L	L	L	L	L	L	L	L	L	L	L	L	L	R
New Mexico	L	L	L	L	L	C	L	L	...	L	L	L	L	L
New York	L	L	L	L	L	L	L	L	...	C, L	L	L	L	L
North Carolina	L	L	L	L	L	...	...	L	L	L	L	L	L	L
North Dakota	L	L	L	L	L	L	...	L	L	L	L	L	L	L
Ohio	L	L	L	L	L	L	L	L	L	L	L	L	L	L
Oklahoma	L	L	L	L	L	...	...	L	L	L	L	L	L	L
Oregon	L	L	L	L	L	L	L	L	L	L	L	L	L	L
Pennsylvania	R	L	C	L	L	...	...	L	...	L (f)	L	L (f)	L	R
Rhode Island	L	L	L	L	L	L	L	L	L	L	L	L	L	R
South Carolina	L	L	L	L	L	C	C	L	R	L	L	L	L	L
South Dakota	L	L	L	L	L	L	...	L	...	L	L	L	L	L
Tennessee	L	L	L	L	L	L	L	L	C	L	L	L	L	L
Texas	L	L	L	L	L	L	L	L	L	L	L	L	L	R
Utah	...	L	L	L	L	L	L	L	L	L	L	L	L	...
Vermont	L	L	C	L	L	L	L	L	...	L	L	L	L	R
Virginia	L	L	L	L	L	L	...	L	...	L	L	L	L	L
Washington	...	L	L	L	L	C	L	L	...	L	L	L	L	L
West Virginia	L	L	L	L	L	L	L	L	L	L	L	...	L	L
Wisconsin	L	L	L	L	L	...	...	L	L	C, L	L	L	L	L
Wyoming	L	L	L	L	L	L	L	L	...	L	L	L	L	R
Dist. of Columbia	L	L	L	L	L	...	...	L	...	L	...	...	L	...

Sources: Council on Licensure, Enforcement and Regulation, December 2005 and various national associations of state boards.

Key:
C — Certification.
L — Licensure.
R — Registration.
. . . — Not regulated.

(a) In some states, professional counselors can practice without a license as long as they do not use the title "licensed professional counselor."

(b) In some states, substance abuse counselors use the title "addiction counselor/therapist," "chemical dependency professional," or "substance abuse treatment practitioner." Most states do not distinguish between alcohol and drug counselor and substance abuse counselor.

(c) In some states, certification is only required for dental assistants to perform expanded functions and take x-rays.

(d) There are eight categories of emergency medical technicians, from basic to paramedic to task-specific certifications. No state regulates all categories, but every state regulates at least one category.

(e) In Kentucky, pastoral counselors must be certified only if their practice is fee-based.

(f) In Pennsylvania, professional counselors, social workers, and marriage and family therapists do not need a license to practice unless they hold themselves out to be licensed.

(g) Some states recognize various categories of advanced practice nurses (e.g., geriatric, school health, and women's health).

(h) In many states, opticians are not licensed separately from optometrists; making and selling eyeglasses is part of the optometrist's job.

(i) In Indiana and Utah, nursing home administrators are not licensed as such, but they are licensed more broadly as health facility administrators.

(j) In some states, social work practice is regulated at one or more of the following levels: basic, intermediate, advanced, and clinical. Certification may be required for practice at the lower levels and licensure required for practice at the higher levels.

Chapter Nine

SELECTED STATE POLICIES AND PROGRAMS

"Hurricane Katrina shone a bright light on the nation's level of preparedness and revealed serious gaps in the country's ability to respond to another terrorist attack."

—Beverly Bell

"How NCLB's ambitions fare through implementation, court challenges and state resistance will have much to say about the feasibility of its authors' hopes."

—Frederick M. Hess

"Direct funding of public higher education institutions from state sources has not kept pace with rising overall costs, so that states are now providing a smaller percentage of institutional revenues than ever before."

—John W. Curtis

"A modernized Medicaid system will give states greater flexibility with reduced administrative burden."

—Dennis G. Smith, Lyn R. Killman, Susan N. Hill and Janet G. Freeze

"Whether the country is experiencing an economic downturn or moving toward recuperation, states are driven to retain jobs and create revenue."

—Jeffrey A. Finkle

"The clash over cash to corporate projects is headed to the country's highest court, and is also the subject of a new bill in Congress."

—Adam Bruns

Chapter Nine — Continued

“*Congress reauthorized the nation's welfare bill along with the Deficit Reduction Act of 2005…. The new participation requirement will present a challenge to many states.*”

—Sheila R. Zedlewski and Meghan Williamson

“*There can be no doubt that the interest shown by Canadian subnational government representatives in developing ties with the United States is far greater than the interest in Canada manifested by U.S. state or municipal leaders.*”

—Earl H. Fry

State Emergency Management and Homeland Security: More Changes Ahead After Hurricane Katrina
By Beverly Bell

Similar to the attacks of Sept. 11, 2001, Hurricane Katrina shone a bright light on the nation's level of preparedness and revealed serious gaps in the country's ability to respond to another terrorist attack. Debate continues on whether the federal government's focus on preparing for a terrorism incident has overlooked the more common threat of natural disasters. Adequate funding for all-hazards is a major concern for all state and local emergency managers, particularly since federal mandates in preparedness and response increase regularly, without matching federal funding.

Introduction

The events of 2005 served as a wake-up call that Mother Nature remains a serious threat to the nation's security. Hurricanes Katrina and Rita required the largest deployment of federal, state and interstate resources in this country's history. It will take years for the Gulf Coast to fully recover. Yet, since 2001, terrorism prevention has been the main focus of the federal government. Homeland security activities have been funded, often at the expense of all-hazards planning and day-to-day public safety programs. Additional federal initiatives such as the National Preparedness Goal, the National Incident Management System and the National Response Plan have been created in an attempt to bring uniformity and consistency to preparedness and response efforts.

It is not known if the natural disasters of 2005 will change the federal government's focus on terrorism. All that is known is that the new national priority of homeland security has created a dynamic and complex interaction of local, state and federal governments, the private sector and the international community.

Emergency Management's Purpose and Structure

The main responsibilities of state emergency management agencies include the following:
- All facets of preparation such as the development of emergency operation plans and procedures for disasters and emergencies; as well as conducting training, drills and exercises.
- During a disaster, coordinating emergency response such as the facilitation of resources and supplemental assistance to local governments when events exceed their capabilities; managing transportation and evacuation; overseeing the emergency operation center and acting as the lead in incident management.

- During and after a disaster, assisting the governor's office by 1) providing accurate and realistic information for crisis communication, 2) activating mutual aid agreements, 3) providing damage assessments and estimates; coordinating public information and warnings, and 4) managing resources and logistics; facilitating sheltering and mass care; coordinating local volunteer organizations.

The organization of state emergency management agencies varies widely. In 13 states,[1] the emergency management agency is located within the department of public safety; in 17 states it is located within the military department under the auspices of the adjutant general; and in 13 states, it is located within the governor's office. Regardless of agencies' organizational structure for daily operations, emergency management ranks high among governors' priorities. In 32 states, the emergency management director is appointed by the governor. The position is appointed by the adjutant general in nine states and by the secretary of public safety in six states.

Emergency Management-Homeland Security Relationship and Structure

Three and a half years after a National Strategy for Homeland Security was developed, many states still face the challenge of assimilating homeland security into their emergency management and response systems. Even as this integration takes place, the relationship between the two is still being defined. Does emergency management with its long-standing focus on preparedness, mitigation, response and recovery encompass homeland security? Or is emergency management a discipline within the objective of homeland security?

While questions remain, all states have moved forward in their homeland security structures. Each

Table A: State Emergency Management: Agency Structure, Budget and Staffing

State or other jurisdiction	Position appointed	Appointed/ selected by	Reports to	Organizational structure	Agency operating budget FY 2006	Full-time employee positions
Alabama	★	G	G	Department of Emergency Management	$ 900,000	89
Alaska	★	G	ADJ	Adjutant General/Military Affairs	2,330,500	44.5
Arizona	★	G	G	Governor's Office	1,340,000	61
Arkansas	★	G	G	Department of Emergency Management	1,146,000	78
California	★	G	G	Governor's Office	37,694,000	473
Colorado	. . .	CS	ED	Department of Local Affairs	600,000	27
Connecticut	★	G	C	Emergency Management/Homeland Security	1,500,000	75
Delaware	★	G	HSD	Dept. of Safety & Homeland Security	650,000	35
Florida	★	G	G	Department of Community Affairs	28,865,000	132
Georgia	★	G	G	Governor's Office	3,200,000	101 (a)
Hawaii	★	ADJ	ADJ	Department of Defense	1,500,000	40
Idaho	★	ADJ	ADJ	Adjutant General/Military Department	1,300,000	48 (a)
Illinois	★	G	G	Governor's Office	30,000,000	267
Indiana	★	G	G	Department of Homeland Security	942,718	261
Iowa	★	G	ADJ	Department of Public Defense	2,740,000	42.14
Kansas	. . .	ADJ	ADJ	Adjutant General/Military Department	600,000	37 (a)
Kentucky	★	G	ADJ	Adjutant General/Military Department	3,200,000	81
Louisiana	★	G	G	Governor's Office	980,000	64
Maine	★	ADJ	ADJ	Adjutant General/Military Department	986,281	22
Maryland	★	G	ADJ	Adjutant General/Military Department	2,511,481	67
Massachusetts	★	G	PSS	Public Safety	3,600,000	75
Michigan	. . .	CS	SPS	State Police	4,500,000	77
Minnesota	★	G	PSS	Public Safety	4,952,000	53 (a)
Mississippi	★	G	G	Governor's Office	2,377,906	64
Missouri	★	ADJ	ADJ	Adjutant General/Military Department	3,000,000	58
Montana	. . .	CS	ADJ	Adjutant General/Military Department	454,000	21
Nebraska	★	ADJ	ADJ	Adjutant General/Military Department	885,793	32
Nevada	★	PSS	PSS	Public Safety	680,000	24
New Hampshire	★	PSS	PSS	Public Safety	3,208,726	46
New Jersey	★	G	AG	State Police	3,409,000	366
New Mexico	. . .	G	G	Public Safety	1,070,000	39
New York	★	G	G	Public Safety	6,100,000	123
North Carolina	★	G	PSS	Public Safety	2,500,000	175
North Dakota	★	ADJ	ADJ	Adjutant General/Military Department	470,000	54
Ohio	★	PSS	PSS	Public Safety	4,164,697	101
Oklahoma	★	G	G	Governor's Office	680,000	32
Oregon	★	HS	HS	Governor's Office	1,800,000	34
Pennsylvania	★	G	G	Governor's Office	8,000,000	162
Rhode Island	★	G	ADJ	Adjutant General/Military Department	572,000	26
South Carolina	★	ADJ	ADJ	Adjutant General/Military Department	922,000	50
South Dakota	★	PSS	PSS	Public Safety	2,860,987	16
Tennessee	★	G	ADJ	Adjutant General/Military Department	3,475,100	108
Texas	★	SPS	HS	Governor's Office	1,200,000	65
Utah	★	PSS	PSS	Public Safety	797,500	65
Vermont	★	PSS	PSS	Public Safety	3,700,000	20
Virginia	★	G	PSS	Public Safety	11,300,000	108
Washington	★	ADJ	ADJ	Adjutant General/Military Department	3,879,470	104.8
West Virginia	★	G	ADJ	Military Affairs & Public Safety	1,269,496	43
Wisconsin	★	G	ADJ	Adjutant General/Military Department	2,996,089	49.25
Wyoming				......(b)......		
Dist. of Columbia	★	M	DM	Public Safety	3,100,000	39
Guam	. . .	CS	HSD	Governor's Office	598,000	10
No. Mariana Islands	★	G	G	Governor's Office	1,487,000	36
				(Continuing Resolution) No budget yet		
Puerto Rico	★	G	G	Governor's Office	7,314,000	150
U.S. Virgin Islands	★	G	ADJ	Adjutant General/Military Department	569,970	20

Source: The National Emergency Management Association, September 2005.

Key:

★ — Yes   . . . — No
G — Governor
GO — Governor's Office
ADJ — Adjutant General
AG — Attorney General
ED — Executive Director
M — Mayor
C — Commissioner

HSD — Homeland Security Director/Secretary
DM — Deputy Mayor
PSS — Public Safety Secretary/Commissioner/Director
SPS — State Police Superintendent/Commissioner
CS — Civil Service
PS — Public Safety
HS — Homeland Security
SP — State Police
(a) Homeland security and emergency management share positions.
(b) Wyoming is not a member of NEMA, and therefore is not represented in the survey data.

state has a designated homeland security point of contact. This position has become a critical component of a governor's staff and one that has an enormous responsibility to the public for preparing citizens, businesses and governments for the next emergency or large-scale disaster. To date, 22 states have established a unique position of *homeland security advisor* or *homeland security director*. In 11 states, the emergency management director is the primary point of contact, and in seven states it is the adjutant general. Seven public safety secretaries/commissioners also serve in the position.

Increasingly, the homeland security director is becoming less of a political appointment in the governor's office and more institutionalized in the organizational structure of state government. Currently, 39 states have authorized their homeland security offices, departments or agencies through either executive order or state statute. The majority of funding for these state homeland security offices comes from the federal government in the form of grants. In fact, 39 states receive at least 60 percent of their homeland security funding from federal monies. Of these 39 states, 21 receive 100 percent from federal funding. The number of state personnel dedicated to homeland security activities ranges from one person to 1,160 people.

Many states continue to modify the structure of their homeland security office. Fifteen states house the day-to-day operations in the governor's office while seven run it out of the adjutant general/military affairs department. Ten states have the homeland security function in their emergency management office, while another 11 operate out of their public safety department. The remaining states have other structures in place.

Lack of Commitment to Key Funding

For the past several years, Congress and the federal government have provided billions of dollars to build a national capacity for domestic preparedness. Funding was provided through states for distribution to local governments in support of objectives identified in the statewide homeland security strategies required by the U.S. Department of Homeland Security. Congress requires that 80 percent of all funding be passed through to local governments, leaving a much smaller amount for use by the state to coordinate the state strategy. Three years into the funding cycle, homeland security money was diverted from states to major metropolitan cities. This is creating isolated pockets of capability, rather than a coordinated statewide or regional approach.

In addition, key funding for emergency management specifically is not adequate. State and local emergency management rely on federal funds to prepare for, respond to and recover from a disaster. The Emergency Management Performance Grant (EMPG) is the only source of federal funding to state and local governments for planning, training exercises and personnel for all-hazards. EMPG is a pass-through program for states to distribute funds to local governments. It provides the foundation for basic emergency management capabilities. States are not required to pass through a set amount, but most allocate more than half their funding to local jurisdictions. At the federal level, funding is allocated in a .75 percent base plus population formula.

For FY 2006, Congress appropriated an additional $5 million for EMPG, but this didn't address the $246 million shortfall identified in 2004. In an October 2005 survey,[2] state emergency management officials outlined how important EMPG is to their sustained, all-hazards efforts. For example, EMPG funds 1,566 full-time and 83 part-time state emergency management personnel, an average of 31 staff members per state. The program pays for 3,246 full-time and part-time local emergency management professionals. The grant also trains and provides exercises for more than 7,000 volunteers. Volunteers far outnumber the full-time professional staff in state and local emergency management programs. Finally, while EMPG is intended to be a 50-50 matching program, state and local governments are overmatching by $96 million annually.

There is a significant need for federal assistance to increase the local capacity in coordination with the states. Since local personnel are the first responders to any disaster, this inadequate emergency management capacity could seriously compromise the safety of local citizens and property.

Strong Local and State Emergency Response Capabilities Needed

Money remains in the pipeline for such programs as bioterrorism preparedness, law enforcement prevention activities and terrorism response equipment purchase, but funding for traditional programs such as the Predisaster Mitigation Program and the Hazard Mitigation Grant Program (HMGP) continues its decline. These programs provide long-term, critical operational funding for emergency management and the proven, successful programs that minimize the risk to property and life before a disaster occurs.

HMGP, for example, is used to rebuild structures at a higher building code level, purchase repetitive loss properties and institute projects that will prevent or

Table B: Homeland Security Structures

State or other jurisdiction	State homeland security advisor		Homeland security organizations	
	Designated contact	Operates under authority of	Day-to-day operations under	Full-time employee positions
Alabama	Homeland Security Director	SS	Homeland Security Department	12
Alaska	EM Director	SS	Adjutant General/Military Affairs	13.5
Arizona	EM Director	EAO	Governor's Office	13
Arkansas	EM Director	GA	Emergency Management	8
California	Homeland Security Director	EAO	Governor's Office	53
Colorado	Public Safety Dir./Sec.	GA	Public Safety	15
Connecticut	Commissioner/EM/HS	SS	Emergency Management/Homeland Security	35
Delaware	Homeland Security Dir./Adv.	GA	Department of Safety and Homeland Security	35
Florida	Domestic Security Oversight Council	SS	Law Enforcement Dep. Comm.	(a)
Georgia	EM Director	EAO	Governor's Office	101 (b)
Hawaii	Adjutant General	GA	Department of Defense	5
Idaho	Adjutant General	EAO	Adjutant General/Military Affairs	48 (b)
Illinois	Governor's Office	GA	Emergency Management	8
Indiana	Homeland Security Dir./Adv.	EAO	Homeland Security Department	279
Iowa	EM Director	GA/SS	Department of Public Defense	25
Kansas	Adjutant General	GA	Emergency Management	37 (b)
Kentucky	Homeland Security Dir./Adv.	EAO	Governor's Office	20
Louisiana	Homeland Security Dir./Adv.	SS	Governor's Office	10
Maine	EM Director	EAO	Adjutant General/Military Affairs	4
Maryland	Homeland Security Dir./Adv.	EAO	Governor's Office	4
Massachusetts	Public Safety Dir./Sec.	EAO	Public Safety	9
Michigan	EM Director	EAO	Emergency Management	10
Minnesota	Public Safety Dir./Sec.	EAO	Public Safety	53 (b)
Mississippi	Homeland Security Dir./Adv.	EAO	Public Safety	12
Missouri	Homeland Security Dir./Adv.	EAO	Public Safety	13
Montana	EM Director	SS	Emergency Management	4
Nebraska	Lieutenant Governor	GA	Emergency Management	6
Nevada	EM Director	GA	Public Safety	5
New Hampshire	EM Director	SS	Public Safety	1
New Jersey	Governor's Office	EAO	Attorney General	1,160
New Mexico	Homeland Security Dir./Adv.	EAO	Governor's Office	2
New York	Homeland Security Dir./Adv.	SS	Governor's Office	86
North Carolina	Public Safety Dir./Sec.	GA	Emergency Management	15
North Dakota	EM Director	SS	Adjutant General/Military Affairs	7
Ohio	Public Safety Dir./Sec.	SS	Public Safety	23
Oklahoma	Homeland Security Dir./Adv.	EAO	Public Safety	12
Oregon	Homeland Security Dir./Adv.	EAO	Homeland Security Department	2
Pennsylvania	Homeland Security Dir./Adv.	EAO	Governor's Office	3
Rhode Island	Adjutant General	EAO	Emergency Management	6
South Carolina	State Police Superintendent	SS	State Police	10 (c)
South Dakota	Homeland Security Dir./Adv.	GA	Public Safety	3
Tennessee	Homeland Security Dir./Adv.	EAO	Governor's Office	28
Texas	Homeland Security Dir./Adv.	EAO	Governor's Office	6
Utah	Public Safety Dir./Sec.	GA	Homeland Security Department	100
Vermont	Homeland Security Dir./Adv.	EAO	Public Safety	5
Virginia	Homeland Security Dir./Adv.	EAO	Governor's Office	3
Washington	Adjutant General	EAO	Adjutant General/Military Affairs	25
West Virginia	Homeland Security Dir./Adv.	EAO	Governor's Office	4
Wisconsin	Adjutant General	EAO	Adjutant General/Military Affairs	(a)
Wyoming			(d)	
Dist. of Columbia	Deputy Mayor, Public Safety	GA	Mayor's Office	(a)
Guam	Homeland Security Dir./Adv.	EAO	Emergency Management	8
No. Mariana Islands	Special Assistant for Homeland Security	SS	Governor's Office	3
Puerto Rico	Homeland Security Dir./Adv.	GA	Governor's Office	10
U.S. Virgin Islands	Adjutant General	GA	Adjutant General/Military Affairs	12

Source: The National Emergency Management Association, September 2005.

Key:
GA — Governor's verbal authority
EAO — Executive/Administrative order
SS — State statute

(a) Data not available.
(b) Homeland security and emergency management share positions.
(c) Five of the 10 FTEs are permanent and five are temporary positions.
(d) Wyoming is not a member of NEMA, and therefore is not represented in the survey data.

minimize the next disaster. All mitigation lessons are particularly important to put into practice after Hurricanes Katrina and Rita. With less available funding, disaster victims have a harder time recovering economically, and remain vulnerable to future disasters.

Lessons Learned from Katrina

From the importance of mutual aid to addressing interoperability, Hurricane Katrina provided many lessons in preparedness, response and recovery. Federal, state and local jurisdictions alike are evaluating plans, procedures and systems so that the country is better prepared the next time a major disaster occurs.

The Critical Role of Mutual Aid

Hurricane Katrina required the largest disaster response in the country's history. Coordinating and deploying much of the help was the Emergency Management Assistance Compact (EMAC), a national interstate mutual aid agreement that allows support across state lines when a disaster occurs.

By the end of 2005, the compact had deployed $829 million in equipment and personnel, with 49 states sending approximately 66,000 people in response to both Hurricanes Katrina and Rita. The largest EMAC response previously was during the 2004 hurricane season when four hurricanes hit the United States during a six-week period, requiring 800 personnel from 38 states.

The compact's significant role in the Katrina response underscores why the federal government considers mutual aid a cornerstone in preparing the country for either a natural or man-made disaster. No government—local, state or federal—has all the resources to respond to all disasters.

Mutual aid compacts help bridge the gap. States can capitalize on existing capabilities, years of experience and lessons learned from past disasters, which can be readily applied to all types of events, including domestic terrorist attacks. As a result, both the National Preparedness Goal and the National Incident Management System (NIMS) emphasize the importance of regional cooperation and collaboration. In fact, the National Preparedness Goal, a document which identifies capabilities the United States should have to prevent, respond to and recover from a major disaster, cites expanding regional collaboration as a national priority. All state and local governments are required to have mutual aid agreements in place by the end of fiscal year 2006 to be eligible for federal funding in the future.

EMAC was formed in 1992 after the devastation of Hurricane Andrew. When it was signed into law

(Public Law 104-321) in 1996, EMAC became the first national disaster-relief agreement ratified by Congress since the Civil Defense Compact of 1950. Currently, 49 states, the District of Columbia, Puerto Rico and the Virgin Islands are members. Each member state is required to secure state legislative approval to become part of EMAC. Administered by the National Emergency Management Association, the compact includes key provisions on reimbursement, liability and workers compensation.

The Importance of FEMA

FEMA received serious criticism for its response to Hurricane Katrina, and as a result, has suffered major credibility issues. This contrasts with the agency's reputation in the mid- to late-1990s, when it was considered knowledgeable, adept and responsive.

There are several factors explaining FEMA's decline. With the creation of DHS and FEMA's absorption into that department, the agency lost clout and influence. Its funding was also reduced. In FY 2006, FEMA has $63 million less for programmatic preparedness, mitigation, response and recovery funding compared to FY 2000, as authorized by the Congress in Appropriations legislation. Grant programs that addressed traditional all-hazards missions were transferred from the department to other DHS agencies not related to direct disaster preparedness and response.

FEMA also lost expertise. Due to a mandatory hiring freeze, the agency is understaffed at the regional and federal levels. Regional offices are the direct line of communication for state and local governments to tap into federal resources. This lack of personnel has negatively impacted the relationship between states and their federal partners.

As mandated by law under the Stafford Act, FEMA is the only federal agency authorized to carry out disaster-relief duties on behalf of the president. State emergency management has offered several strategies to restore the agency's effectiveness and credibility. These include making the FEMA director position a fixed-term appointment for not less than five years; having the FEMA director report directly to the president; and selecting a director with demonstrated leadership skills and extensive emergency management experience at an executive level.

Military Response in a Disaster

As a result of Hurricane Katrina, it has been suggested that the military take a leadership role in disaster response. This same issue was raised following Hurricane Andrew in 1992.

States do not agree with the proposal. Governors have direct and legal responsibility for the protection and safety of their citizens. In addition, disaster response is typically a layered system, beginning on the local level. When local resources and capabilities are overwhelmed, the state becomes the second responder. Federal emergency management is the third responder, providing support while coordinating assets with state and local government. Finally, the National Response Plan identifies the U.S. Department of Defense as a support agency only.

A report[3] released by the National Academy of Public Administration in 1993 concurs with the governors' position. It says that the primary mission for the Armed Forces is to prepare for war and to fight if necessary. States do agree that procedures allowing civilian authorities to request assistance and support, when the magnitude of the event deems it necessary, should be improved.

Better Evacuation Planning

Hurricane Katrina raised serious concerns about the adequacy of evacuation plans. States and many local communities are reviewing their procedures, including the following components: scenarios, authority and enforcement of mandatory evacuations; a state's legal authority in reversing interstate or state roadways; elderly and low-income evacuations; school evacuations; private hospital and nursing home evacuation requirements; the availability of fuel and car assistance during an evacuation; the availability of public vehicles; and pet evacuations.

States and local jurisdictions have learned that planning is key to effective evacuation procedures. This includes the integration of all elements of the population during the evacuation and looking at the issue from the perspective of an evacuated state and one receiving evacuees.

Interoperability Remains a Problem

Hurricane Katrina revealed that the issue of interoperability—the ability of various emergency responders to talk to each other through both voice and data systems—still has not been resolved.

The Category 4 storm knocked down cell phone towers, as well as electricity and phone lines. In many areas, hand-held radios were the only options, but some of these were incompatible, making communication difficult, if not impossible.

Since the 2001 terrorist attacks, DHS has invested an estimated $11 billion in grants to improve communications systems. Larger cities have been able to take advantage of Urban Area Security Initiative Program

(UASI) grants to enhance their systems. However, less populous states or those with smaller to midsize communities that don't qualify for these programs, face a distinct disadvantage. Comprehensive interoperable communication is expensive and requires long-term financial investments. The results of a 2004 survey, representing 192 cities, illustrate the problem. Thirty-four percent of the respondents said they did not have basic interoperability across police, fire and EMS.[4]

More Changes Coming

Hurricane Katrina after-action reports from both houses of Congress and the White House will result in additional changes for emergency management. This could include all areas of operations and organization structure on both the state and federal level.

An Ever-changing Environment

Increasing mandates from the federal government and inadequate funding continue to put more pressure on state and local governments. The changing structure of DHS also prohibits the agency from developing strong relationships with its state and local partners.

Changes in Funding Allocation Formulas

Congress is considering legislation that would change the funding allocation formula for states to receive federal homeland security grants, placing greater emphasis on risk and critical infrastructure vulnerability as opposed to the current approach of allocating dollars on a percentage plus population basis. Changes in funding allocations will have major impacts on smaller rural states that cannot take the necessary terrorism-preparedness steps without federal support.

The terrorism response equipment purchased by states and localities, along with the planning efforts and training conducted for thousands of state and local emergency response personnel, are characterized as a national security effort. These require long-term support from the federal government. Among states and emergency response disciplines, there is a common concern regarding long-term sustainable federal funding for homeland security.

States require a minimum level of funding to build state and local capacity for preparedness. Because of unique needs in addressing their specific homeland security preparedness, states and localities have requested greater flexibility on the use of federal homeland security funds.

Pandemic/Avian Flu Preparation

Federal and state governments are taking numerous steps to protect citizens and control the spread of the avian flu, which had resulted in approximately 70 deaths worldwide by the end of 2005. Most of these deaths occurred in Asia. To date, there has been no transmission of the avian flu from human to human, only from infected birds in close contact with humans. One of the main defenses in this country is to continue to safeguard the U.S. poultry industry, estimated at $23.9 billion in 2004. State emergency management agencies expect to play a key support role in pandemic/avian flu preparedness and response, and are actively engaged in planning with their public health counterparts..

Notes

[1] In this context, states refer to all 50 states, the territories and the District of Columbia.

[2] National Emergency Management Association, *States Report Need for Special EMPG Allocation to Address Gaps Identified by Recent Disasters*, (October 2005).

[3] National Academy for Public Administration, *Coping With Catastrophe, Building an Emergency Management System to Meet People's Needs in Natural and Manmade Disasters*, (1993).

[4] U.S. Conference of Mayors Interoperability Survey, June 2004.

About the Author

Beverly Bell is the policy analyst for the National Emergency Management Association, an affiliate of The Council of State Governments. In her position, she coordinates and conducts research, interacts with the states on changing federal policy, and acts as an information clearinghouse for emergency management and homeland security issues

No Child Left Behind: Trends and Issues
By Frederick M. Hess

The No Child Left Behind Act is the most ambitious piece of educational legislation ever enacted by Congress. Designed to promote accountability and prod states to address educational inequities, NCLB included significant new provisions regarding assessment, sanctions for low-performing schools and districts, teacher quality, and standards for educational research.

On January 8, 2002, surrounded by smiling members of the Democratic and Republican congressional leadership, President George W. Bush signed No Child Left Behind (NCLB) into law. NCLB is arguably the nation's most significant piece of federal legislation on K–12 schooling adopted since the Elementary and Secondary Education Act (ESEA) of 1965, and it is undoubtedly the most ambitious federal intervention in a domain long regarded as the preserve of state and local government. With its sweeping changes to ESEA, NCLB marked both a bold embrace of proposals that dated back a decade or more and a dramatic departure from the traditional federal role in schooling.[1]

Enacted just months after the September 11, 2001 terrorist attacks, NCLB was approved amid a wave of national unity. It was backed by large, bipartisan majorities in Congress. The U.S. Senate supported the new law 87–10, and the House of Representatives endorsed it 381–41.[2] Emerging from an exhaustive year of negotiations, NCLB refashioned federal education policy in the areas of testing, accountability, and teacher quality. More than anything else, NCLB amounted to a roar of frustration from Washington, D.C. policymakers demanding that state and local officials stop making excuses and do something about low-performing schools.

From ESEA to NCLB

Enacted in 1965 as a pillar of President Lyndon Johnson's "Great Society," the original ESEA included five titles. The heart of the law was a program of aid for the education of disadvantaged children. This provision, Title I, claimed the lion's share of ESEA funding. Over time, critics both left and right expressed concerns about the failure of Title I to improve achievement visibly among low-income students.[3]

By the early 1990s, Republican and Democratic leaders largely agreed that school improvement required more than targeted assistance, new texts, and better curricula. The Washington-driven rem-

edies urged by Presidents George H.W. Bush and Bill Clinton shared a commitment to higher standards, educational accountability, measuring student achievement, and increasing school choice. Where Bush had termed his 1990 package of education proposals "America 2000," Clinton termed his 1994 initiative "Goals 2000"—but few outside the federal bureaucracy saw major differences between the two. President Bill Clinton sought to use the 1994 ESEA reauthorization and his companion "Goals 2000" legislation to require every state to establish academic standards and assess whether students had mastered them.[4]

Sympathetic observers regarded the 1994 ESEA's requirement that all states create performance-based accountability systems for schools by 2000 as a radical advance. Given the law's voluntary cast and the federal government's lack of meaningful enforcement authority, however, most states failed to comply.[5] In 1999, ESEA was again due for reauthorization but proposals to build on the 1994 law's testing and accountability provisions died a quiet death in the face of the approaching Presidential election.

NCLB Standards and Assessment

The heart of NCLB is its language on standards and assessment. NCLB aggressively supersized the tentative standards and testing requirements embodied in the 1994 ESEA. Eager to support a Republican president after two terms under a Democratic White House, conservatives on Capitol Hill quelled their complaints and accepted requirements regarding standards, testing, and accountability that dwarfed those put forward in 1994 and 1999.

The NCLB accountability system requires that states develop challenging content standards for what students should know and be able to do, create state assessments that reflect these, and annually test students to measure competency in the "core subjects" of reading and math. By 2013–14, all states are to ensure that 100 percent of students attain proficiency in accord with state reading and math standards. While the law requires states to develop standards, it is silent on the content or rigor these are to entail.[6]

NCLB requires states to set academic standards that define three levels of achievement: basic, proficient and advanced. The expectation embodied in NCLB is that all students will reach at least the proficient level. For each assessment, each state must establish its own determination of basic, proficient, and advanced performance and then develop corresponding tests in reading and math. These assessments are to be administered every year in grades third through eighth and at least once in high school. States also are required to design and administer a science assessment by 2007–08 and must test students at least once in grades third through fifth, sixth through ninth, and tenth through twelfth.

Adequate yearly progress (AYP) is the metric used to evaluate school and district performance under NCLB. The expectation is that all schools and districts will "make AYP." The concept of "making AYP" can be compared to schools and districts jumping over a bar. The bar is the percentage of children that must score "proficient" on the math and reading assessments. Over time, states must raise the bar so that, by 2013–14, it is set at 100 percent. For instance, a state could deem a school to be making AYP if 50 percent of its students were "proficient" in reading in 2007, and 70 percent in 2009, so long as expectations were stepped up to 100 percent by 2013–14.

Calculating AYP is not as simple as measuring the percentage of students that meet the proficiency standard. Instead, NCLB requires that states hold schools accountable for various subpopulations as well. Since accountability focused on aggregate performance can mask poor performance by poor or disadvantaged children, NCLB requires schools and districts to calculate AYP for each of a variety of subgroups. Each state is required to analyze the achievement of the following subgroups within each school: all racial/ethnic groups (white, African-American, Latino, Native American, and so on); low-income students; students with disabilities; and students with limited English proficiency. In order for schools or districts to make AYP, each subgroup must clear the AYP bar in reading and in math. Obviously, some subgroups will be quite small. To protect student confidentiality and heighten statistical reliability, states are allowed to establish a minimum size for subgroups to be counted. To date, states have adopted minimums for subgroups that range from a low of five to a high of 100.

NCLB's testing requirements pose a number of challenges, and the legislation and subsequent guidance from the U.S. Department of Education have tried, with mixed success, to anticipate and address these. The law stipulates that schools must test 95 percent of their enrolled students or be deemed to have failed to make AYP, regardless of the results. It also includes a "safe harbor" provision that allows schools that miss the AYP bar to still make AYP if they increase the percentage of students who are proficient at a rapid enough rate and permits schools and districts to exclude from AYP calculations a small portion of special needs students.

NCLB Sanctions

The standards and testing provisions themselves constitute only the first two-thirds of the NCLB accountability system. To put teeth in these measures, NCLB seeks to link test results to consequences for schools and school districts. Under NCLB, schools that fail to make AYP are subject to a series of cascading remedies, sanctions, and interventions that are designed to compel the schools to improve and to grant additional options to children in those schools. These interventions become increasingly intense if the school or district continues to fail for consecutive years, eventually resulting in major changes in school status, governance, staffing, or all of the above.

If a school fails to make AYP two years in a row, it enters "in need of improvement" status. Once in improvement status, district and school officials must develop a school improvement plan, as well as explain to parents what the label signifies and what the school is doing to improve its rating. In addition to these school improvement activities, schools that fail to make AYP for two consecutive years must offer students the option of transferring to a district school that is making AYP. Schools that fail to improve for a third straight year must provide supplemental education services, or free tutoring, to needy students. A fourth year of failure prompts what the law terms "corrective action," which could entail staffing changes, curriculum reform, or the extension of the school day and year. Finally, if a school fails to make AYP for a fifth year, the district must "restructure" that school, either by converting it to a charter school, replacing the majority of the staff, hiring an educational management company, turning it over to the state, or through imposing another serious remedy at the state's choosing. The sanctions for districts are similar in intent to those for schools but different in the particulars. When applying AYP, NCLB basically treats districts as if they were one big school.

Districts that fail to make AYP for multiple years are eventually subject to restructuring, including the possibility of state takeover.[7]

Highly Qualified Teachers

Beyond its accountability and choice provisions, the other radical development adopted by NCLB was the federal mandate that all children be taught by a "highly qualified teacher" by the end of the 2005–06 school year (during 2005, the Department of Education pushed back the effective date to 2006–07). Unlike the testing and accountability provisions, the highly qualified teacher (HQT) language focuses less on outcomes than on "inputs"—it seeks to ensure that all schools have quality teachers. The provision was designed to stop local school districts from hiring unqualified teachers and push states to place a higher priority on teacher subject matter knowledge.

Under NCLB's regulations, all teachers of core academic subjects like mathematics, science and history must be highly qualified by 2005–06 (now 2006–07). To be "highly qualified," a teacher must have attained a bachelor's degree, have passed the state teacher licensing examination or obtained a state teaching certification, and have demonstrated knowledge of the subject that he or she teaches. Again, as with state standards and assessments, the law allows states to determine what all this means in practice.[8]

Research and Reading First

Despite their import, NCLB's accountability and teacher quality provisions comprise only a small portion of the sprawling legislation. The law encompasses 10 separate titles authorizing more than 50 federal education programs. Noteworthy is NCLB's emphasis on "scientifically based research" (SBR), a phrase that appears more than 100 times throughout NCLB and is applied to everything from reading programs, to teacher training, to school safety. SBR is defined as "the application of rigorous, systematic, and objective procedures to obtain reliable and valid knowledge relevant to education activities and programs." The focus on scientifically based research has potentially far-reaching consequences for both daily classroom practice and academic research.[9]

SBR is best illustrated by the law's Reading First program. Reading First marked a dramatic departure for federal policy by favoring particular approaches to reading instruction. Based on the conclusions of the National Reading Panel, convened in 1997 at Congress's request, Reading First requires schools seeking federal funds to implement a classroom-based reading program that includes the elements of scientifically based instruction.

Debating NCLB

NCLB has been a subject of fierce debate. Critics have attacked the system for encouraging states to engage in gamesmanship, promoting a fixation on testing, failing to acknowledge the different burdens borne by different schools, and setting unrealistic goals.[10] Meanwhile, supporters like officials at the U.S. Department of Education and at the Education Trust have applauded the focus on results, the attention AYP has brought to performance disparities, and the insistence on uniform expectations for all students.

This mixed assessment is reflected in public opinion. Like most pieces of sweeping and compromise-filled legislation, NCLB elicits mixed reactions. Parents and voters tend to endorse its goals while expressing concerns about its means. In fall 2005, the Educational Testing Service (ETS) reported that public awareness of the law had doubled since 2001, but that still just 61 percent of adults had heard about NCLB. Of those who had a view of the law, ETS reported that 45 percent were favorable and 38 percent unfavorable.[11]

Emerging Trends

Perhaps the fiercest dispute over NCLB implementation has revolved around funding. Funding for the education programs in NCLB increased after the law's passage, especially for Title I, rising nearly 58 percent between 2001 and 2004. The General Accounting Office ruled in 2003 that the federal aid fully covered the mandated expenses.[12] Meanwhile, critics have responded that, through 2005, the federal funds fell $36 billion short of the amount promised by the law's authorization. Many states have argued that the actions necessitated by NCLB cost billions more than the law provides.[13] What effect such pleas will have in a tight fiscal environment remains to be seen.

State reaction to the law has been mixed, with press coverage highlighting vocal resistance to the law in states like Connecticut and Utah. This resistance has been newsworthy because states have the right to opt out of the law by forfeiting their federal NCLB funding. Responding to state resistance, U.S. Department of Education officials have reaffirmed their commitment to NCLB's accountability goals while accepting modifications regarding the testing, sanctions, and teacher quality provisions. The goal has been to give states enough leeway so that none will opt out of the law without abandoning the principles of the statute. This is playing out against a backdrop of lawsuits in which the National Education Association and several states have gone to court—unsuccessfully, as of late 2005—seeking to have NCLB declared an impermissible unfunded mandate or an unconstitutional violation of 10th Amendment limits on the federal government.[14]

One widely discussed modification to NCLB accountability is the effort to focus it less on the level at which a school's students are performing and more on their rate of improvement.[15] State interest in such "value-added" accountability is motivated by the concern that many schools serving disadvantaged populations will otherwise be deemed "in need of improvement" even though students are making respectable achievement gains. In November 2005, Secretary Margaret Spellings allowed a handful of states to experiment with "value-added" approaches.[16] Meanwhile, there is accumulating research suggesting that states have incentives to "game" the NCLB accountability system by setting lax standards.[17]

As states anticipate the reauthorization of NCLB, scheduled for 2007 but ultimately likely to take place in 2008 or 2009, these issues will deserve much scrutiny. How NCLB's ambitions fare through implementation, court challenges, and state resistance will have much to say about the feasibility of its authors' hopes.

Notes

[1] Chester E. Finn, Jr. and Frederick M. Hess, "On Leaving No Child Behind," *The Public Interest* 157 (Fall 2004): 35–56.

[2] Andrew Rudalevige, "No Child Left Behind: Forging a Congressional Compromise," in Paul E. Peterson and Martin R. West, eds., *No Child Left Behind? The Politics and Practice of School Accountability* (Washington, D.C.: Brookings Institution Press, 2003), 23–54.

[3] Diane Ravitch, "A Historical Perspective on a Historic Piece of Legislation," in John Chubb, ed., *Within Our Reach: How America Can Educate Every Child* (New York: Rowman & Littlefield, 2005), 35–51.

[4] Finn and Hess, 35–56.

[5] See former United States Secretary of Education Richard W. Riley's statement before the United States House of Representatives Committee on Education and the Workforce on the Reauthorization of the Elementary and Secondary Education Act of 1965, 11 February 1999.

[6] Detailed information on the mechanics of No Child Left Behind is available at the United States Department of Education Web site, <*http://www.ed.gov/nclb/landing.jhtml?src=pb*> (30 November 2005).

[7] See Education Commission of the States, "No Child Left Behind: State Requirements Under NCLB," June 2005, <*http://www.ecs.org/clearinghouse/44/27/4427.pdf*> (30 November 2005).

[8] Terry M. Moe, "A Highly Qualified Teacher in Every Classroom," in John E. Chubb, ed., *Within Our Reach: How America Can Educate Every Child* (Lanham, Md.: Rowman & Littlefield, 2005), 173–99.

[9] Detailed information on what the scientifically based research language entails is available at the United States Department of Education Web site, <*http://www.ed.gov/nclb/landing.jhtml?src=pb*> (30 November 2005).

[10] Linda Darling-Hammond, "From 'Separate but Equal' to 'No Child Left Behind': The Collision of New Standards and Old Inequalities," in Deborah Meier and George Wood, eds., *Many Children Left Behind: How the No Child Left Behind Act Is Damaging Our Children and Our Schools* (Boston: Beacon Press, 2004), 3–32.

[11] Peter D. Hart and David Winston, "Ready for the Real World? Americans Speak on High School Reform" (Washington, D.C.: Educational Testing Service, 2005).

[12] United States General Accounting Office, "Title I: Characteristics of Tests Will Influence Expenses; Information Sharing May Help States Realize Efficiencies," May 2003, <*http://www.nasbe.org/Archives/testcosts5-03.pdf*> (30 November 2005).

[13] William J. Mathis, "The Cost of Implementing the Federal No Child Left Behind Act: Different Assumptions, Different Answers," *Peabody Journal of Education* 80, no. 2 (2005): 90–119.

[14] Michael Janofsky, "Judge Rejects Challenge to Bush Education Law," *The New York Times*, 24 November 2005, sec. A, p. 22.

[15] John Chubb et al., "Do We Need to Repair the Monument? Debating the Future of No Child Left Behind," *Education Next* 5, no. 2 (Spring 2005): 8–19.

[16] United States Department of Education Press Release, "Secretary Spellings Announces Growth Model Pilot, Addresses Chief State School Officers' Annual Policy Forum in Richmond," 18 November 2005, <*http://www.ed.gov/news/pressreleases/2005/11/11182005.html*> (30 November 2005).

[17] Thomas B. Fordham Foundation Press Release, "Has a 'Race to the Bottom' Begun? Gains on State Reading Tests Evaporate on NAEP," 19 October 2005, <*http://www.edexcellence.net/foundation/about/press_release.cfm?id=19*> (30 November 2005).

About the Author

Frederick M. Hess is director of education policy studies at the American Enterprise Institute and executive editor of *Education Next*. His many books include *Common Sense School Reform*, *No Child Left Behind: A Primer*, and *Spinning Wheels*. A former high school teacher, he holds a Ph.D. in Government from Harvard University.

Table 9.1
PUBLIC ELEMENTARY AND SECONDARY STUDENTS AND TEACHERS: 2003–2004

State or other jurisdiction	Number of schools having membership	Total student membership	Number of teachers	Student/ teacher ratio	Number of public high school completers (d)
United States total (a)	92,816	48,540,725	3,048,549	15.9	2,946,487
Alabama	1,389	731,220	58,070	12.6	43,366
Alaska	500	133,933	7,808	17.2	8,382
Arizona	1,931	1,012,068	47,507	21.3	53,516
Arkansas	1,128	454,523	30,876	14.7	30,840
California	9,222	6,413,862 (b)	304,311 (b)	21.1	350,148
Colorado	1,658	757,693	44,904	16.9	47,000
Connecticut	1,099	577,203	42,370	13.6	34,859
Delaware	200	117,668	7,749	15.2	7,075
Florida	3,427	2,587,628	144,955	17.9	147,971
Georgia	2,032	1,522,611	97,150	15.7	82,692
Hawaii	284	183,609	11,129	16.5	10,878
Idaho	664	252,120	14,049	17.9	17,511
Illinois	4,267	2,100,961	127,669	16.5	123,713
Indiana	1,911	1,011,130	59,924	16.9	64,227
Iowa	1,491	481,226	34,791	13.8	36,647
Kansas	1,410	470,490	32,589	14.4	32,048
Kentucky	1,370	663,885	41,201	16.1	41,822
Louisiana	1,519	727,709	50,495	14.4	42,468
Maine	662	202,084	17,621	11.5	14,058
Maryland	1,366	869,113	55,140	15.8	55,149
Massachusetts	1,860	980,459	72,062	13.6	60,953
Michigan	3,869	1,757,604	97,014 (c)	18.1	106,196
Minnesota	2,187	842,654	51,611	16.3	62,146
Mississippi	897	493,540	32,591	15.1	29,157
Missouri	2,260	905,941	65,169	13.9	60,436
Montana	858	148,356	10,301	14.4	11,944
Nebraska	1,228	285,542	20,921	13.6	21,474
Nevada	545	385,401	20,234	19.0	19,178
New Hampshire	473	207,417	15,112	13.7	13,902
New Jersey	2,428	1,380,753	109,177	12.7	83,553
New Mexico	814	323,066	21,569	15.0	19,514
New York	4,514	2,864,775	216,116	13.3	159,696
North Carolina	2,260	1,360,209	89,988	15.1	74,993
North Dakota	517	102,233	8,037	12.7	8,689
Ohio	3,836	1,845,428	121,735	15.2	119,755
Oklahoma	1,786	626,160	39,253	16.0	39,666
Oregon	1,225	551,273	26,732	20.6	40,239
Pennsylvania	3,189	1,821,146	119,889	15.2	126,187
Rhode Island	328	159,375	11,918 (c)	13.4	9,878
South Carolina	1,091	699,198	45,830	15.3	37,642
South Dakota	734	125,537	9,245	13.6	9,648
Tennessee	1,644	936,681 (b)	59,584	15.7	53,887
Texas	7,843	4,331,751	289,481	15.0	252,811
Utah	886	495,981	22,147	22.4	32,166
Vermont	358	99,103	8,749	11.3	7,460
Virginia	1,856	1,192,092	90,573	13.2	80,223
Washington	2,241	1,021,349	52,824	19.3	65,922
West Virginia	755	281,215	20,202	14.0	18,962
Wisconsin	2,218	880,031	58,216	15.1	6,3272 (e)
Wyoming	380	87,462	6,567	13.3	6,607
Dist. of Columbia	206	78,057	5,676	13.8	3,160
American Samoa	31	15,893	988	16.1	840
Guam	37	31,572	1,760	17.9	1,524
No. Mariana Islands	32	11,244	550	20.4	431
Puerto Rico	1,508	584,916	42,444	13.8	31,408 (e)
U.S. Virgin Islands	34	17,716	1,512	12.0	931

Source: Hoffman, L., and Sable, J. (2006). *Public Elementary and Secondary Students, Staff, Schools and School Districts: School Year 2003–2004* (NCES 2006-307). U.S. Department of Education. Washington D.C.: National Center for Education Statistics.

Key:
(a) U.S. totals include the 50 states and the District of Columbia.

(b) Kindergarten data were imputed based on current year (fall 2003 data).
(c) All teacher data were imputed for Michigan and Rhode Island.
(d) Figure includes individuals who receive certificates of attendance or some other credential in lieu of diplomas and individuals 19 or younger who met the passing score on the General Education Development test.
(e) Figure includes diploma recipients only.

Table 9.2
NUMBER OF STAFF EMPLOYED BY PUBLIC ELEMENTARY AND SECONDARY SCHOOL SYSTEMS; SCHOOL YEAR 2003–2004

State or other jurisdiction	Total staff	Number of teachers	Instructional aides	Instructional coordinators and supervisors	Guidance counselors	Librarians	Student/other support staff (a)	School administrators	School district administrators	Administrative support staff (b)
United States total (a)	5,948,475	3,048,549	685,242	44,076	99,395	54,351	1,363,629	165,531	63,561	424,141
Alabama	100,592	58,070	6,240	698	1,682	1,388	24,216	3,452	1,345	3,501
Alaska	16,550	7,808	2,118	160	274	152	3,548	675	413	1,402
Arizona	96,341	47,507	13,438	183	1,292	802	23,476	2,240	424	6,979
Arkansas	64,693	30,876	6,623	621	1,218	934	19,075	1,552	682	3,112
California	572,835	304,311 (b)	69,201	6,589	6,640	1,218	113,514	13,340	2,766	55,256
Colorado	89,530	44,904	10,216	963	1,371	845	21,374	2,382	974	6,501
Connecticut	85,367	42,370	11,567	367	1,327	789	20,723	2,193	1,333	4,698
Delaware	14,587	7,749	1,361	188	262	129	3,461	370	288	779
Florida	295,775	144,955	29,616	696	5,772	2,710	73,998	6,946	1,819	29,263
Georgia	200,512	97,150	24,111	1,376	3,338	2,170	55,021	5,063	1,913	10,370
Hawaii	21,113	11,129	2,640	511	648	290	3,892	504	188	1,311
Idaho	25,133	14,049	2,637	268	575	170	5,239	726	116	1,353
Illinois	253,924	127,669	33,302	833	3,049	2,200	58,858	6,422	4,061	17,530
Indiana	130,532	59,924	18,289	1,662	1,804	1,004	36,060	2,985	1,080	7,724
Iowa	68,137	34,791	9,095	472	1,180	589	14,917	2,111	928	4,054
Kansas	63,778	32,589	7,085	118	1,118	923	15,955	1,709	1,239	3,042
Kentucky	95,926	41,201	13,769	877	1,471	1,147	24,627	2,527	1,011	9,296
Louisiana	102,990	50,495	11,398	1,387	3,155	1,233	26,217	2,694	330	6,081
Maine	35,866	17,621	5,952	297	627	251	7,493	967	625	2,033
Maryland	102,525	55,140	9,878	1,195	2,241	1,118	24,289	3,149	836	4,679
Massachusetts	134,414	72,062	18,272	1,115	2,118	946	24,783	3,666	1,751	9,701
Michigan	206,034	97,014 (c)	25,170	3,457	2,708	1,405	53,652	4,937	3,304	14,387
Minnesota	103,744	51,611	14,036	467	1,064	942	21,969	2,190	1,030	9,835
Mississippi	68,377	32,591	8,603	671	1,009	969	17,778	1,757	986	4,013
Missouri	125,783	65,169	10,906	952	2,608	1,621	31,219	3,044	1,308	8,956
Montana	18,641	10,301	1,870	182	431	357	3,614	504	145	1,237
Nebraska	40,573	20,921	4,722	427	757	557	9,548	998	574	2,069
Nevada	34,059	20,234	2,438	524	719	324	6,168	1,079	263	2,310
New Hampshire	30,830	15,112	6,380	185	772	296	5,771	537	538	1,239
New Jersey	204,038	109,177	24,010	1,466	3,673	1,871	40,725	4,917	1,832	16,467
New Mexico	44,841	21,569	5,243	724	769	298	10,873	995	858	3,512
New York	394,178	216,116	53,423	2,083	6,440	3,318	70,466	7,823	2,844	31,665
North Carolina	172,193	89,988	27,852	852	3,444	2,335	31,589	4,777	1,609	9,747
North Dakota	15,066	8,037	1,811	134	278	198	3,295	395	436	482
Ohio	242,520	121,735	18,274	500	3,694	1,669	56,962	6,499	6,214	26,973
Oklahoma	71,313	39,253	6,049	248	1,495	996	15,481	1,932	710	5,149
Oregon	54,272	26,732	8,466	406	1,114	461	10,330	1,539	613	4,611
Pennsylvania	233,269	119,889	24,897	1,424	4,344	2,217	58,248	4,630	1,667	15,953
Rhode Island	19,892	11,918 (c)	2,526	190	380	215	2,674	557	164	1,268
South Carolina	62,910	45,830	2,311	678	1,699	1,135	1,900	3,224	299	5,834

See footnotes at end of table.

NUMBER OF STAFF EMPLOYED BY PUBLIC ELEMENTARY AND SECONDARY SCHOOL SYSTEMS; SCHOOL YEAR 2003–2004—Continued

State or other jurisdiction	Total staff	Number of teachers	Instructional aides	Instructional coordinators and supervisors	Guidance counselors	Librarians	Student/other support staff (a)	School administrators	School district administrators	Administrative support staff (b)
South Dakota...............	19,039	9,245	3,337	380	328	146	3,955	402	445	801
Tennessee.................	116,118	59,584	14,430	1,130	1,918	1,545	23,940	5,080	1,239	7,252
Texas	596,330	289,481	58,741	1,238	9,937	4,864	164,991	29,621	7,833	29,624
Utah	41,545	22,147	5,911	711	683	279	7,821	1,012	156	2,825
Vermont....................	18,701	8,749	4,208	318	426	226	3,168	441	147	1,018
Virginia....................	166,578	90,573	15,287	1,525	2,564	1,986	38,058	3,924	1,556	11,105
Washington...............	109,294	52,824	10,051	546	1,955	1,309	32,326	2,747	915	6,621
West Virginia............	37,957	20,202	3,113	335	660	386	9,827	1,044	421	2,151
Wisconsin.................	104,531	58,216	10,632	1,527	1,910	1,247	20,596	2,512	932	6,959
Wyoming...................	14,121	6,567	1,868	152	394	131	3,390	333	305	981
Dist. of Columbia.......	10,608	5,676	1,269	68	60	40	2,559	408	96	432
American Samoa.........	1,771	988	116	45	49	6	276	73	39	179
Guam	3,466	1,760	704	104	54	23	310	58	18	435
No. Mariana Islands	1,155	550	250	12	18	1	157	32	7	128
Puerto Rico................	74,697	42,444	237	312	1,009	1,080	21,888	1,512	1,611	4,604
U.S. Virgin Islands......	2,896	1,512	326	19	81	38	570	84	67	199

Source: Hoffman, L., and Sable, J. (2006). *Public Elementary and Secondary Students, Staff, Schools and School Districts: School Year 2003–2004* (NCES 2006-307). U.S. Department of Education. Washington D.C.: National Center for Education Statistics.

Key:
(a) Student/other support services include library support staff, student support services staff, and all other non-administrative support staff.
(b) Administrative support staff includes district and school level administrative support staff.

Issues in Faculty Salaries and Higher Education Financing

By John W. Curtis

The article provides an overview of several systematic factors contributing to the variation in faculty salaries. Institutional type is the most significant factor in determining faculty salaries overall; faculty members are also compared according to academic rank. Two other important factors are gender and region, and several individual factors are also identified. The article also discusses several policy issues related to the decline in state funding for higher education.

Faculty salaries, like much of American higher education, vary widely based on several factors. The most significant sources of variation are institutional type, including both the level of degree offered and institutional affiliation, and academic rank. Two other important factors affecting salaries are gender and regional location. Finally, a number of factors affecting the salaries of individual faculty members are specific to each situation, even though commonalities can be observed across the spectrum. These individual factors include the faculty member's discipline, record of publications and scholarship, the presence of collective bargaining, and race or ethnicity. This article provides an overview of the most salient differences in faculty salaries, as identified above, and points to trends which should be of particular interest to policymakers. In addition, it situates the consideration of faculty salaries within the context of broader issues in public higher education.

The source of primary data presented here is the annual Faculty Compensation Survey conducted by the American Association of University Professors (AAUP). The AAUP survey includes accredited institutions at all levels, both public and private. AAUP has collected and published faculty salary data in its "Annual Report on the Economic Status of the Profession" for nearly six decades. Table B reports average faculty salary at four-year institutions for academic year 2004–05 by state, level and control of institution, and academic rank. (The AAUP collects data from associate degree colleges as well, but the survey response for 2004–05 did not provide sufficient cases for an accurate breakdown by state.)

In comparing faculty salaries between states, the most important factor—and perhaps the most significant source of variation in faculty salaries overall—is institutional type. Institutional type can be divided into two components: the level of institution, categorized in the AAUP survey by highest degree; and the control of the institution, generally distinguishing between public and private. Table A shows the variation in national average faculty salary by these two components of institutional type.

Approximately 70 percent of full-time faculty members in the United States are employed at public institutions. However, as Table A indicates, faculty salaries at private-independent four-year institutions are 9 to 29 percent higher than those at public institutions. (Private-independent associate degree institutions, by contrast, are few in number and tend to compensate their faculty at lower levels.) Table A distinguishes between two categories of institutions that are often lumped together as "private"—those that are independent and those that are affiliated with a religious denomination. Faculty salaries at institutions in the latter category are generally lower, although the average for church-related doctoral institutions is pushed up by a relatively small group of large research universities

Table A
Average Full-Time Faculty Salary 2004–05, by Institutional Category and Control

	Public		Private-Independent		Church-Related	
	Average salary 2004–05	*Percent increase over 2003–04*	*Average salary 2004–05*	*Percent increase over 2003–04*	*Average salary 2004–05*	*Percent increase over 2003–04*
Doctoral	73,960	3.0%	95,299	3.7%	79,041	2.3%
Master's	59,874	2.1	65,073	2.9	59,800	2.1
Baccalaureate	55,376	3.2	65,520	3.6	51,931	2.9
Associate	51,573	1.2	50,029	n.d.	35,097	n.d.

Source: American Association of University Professors, Faculty Compensation Survey.
Notes: Includes all full-time primarily instructional faculty, with or without academic rank. Figures are weighted average (mean) salaries; salaries of faculty members on 12-month contracts have been adjusted to an academic year (9-month) equivalent.
n.d. = no data. There were too few responding institutions for meaningful analysis.

that pay higher salaries. By contrast, the average salaries for private baccalaureate colleges in some states
are depressed by combining private-independent and
church-related colleges into one category (Table B).
This occurs since the proportion of church-related colleges is much larger in some states and most church-
related colleges are in the baccalaureate category.

Tables A and B give an indication for the most
current year of the issue of primary interest to state
policymakers: the divergence of faculty salaries
between public and private sectors. At the national
level, and in most states, faculty at public institutions
receive lower salaries on average than do faculty at
comparable private institutions. But this situation is
not static. The AAUP annual report has followed the
trend of public/private differentials for many years.
As Ronald G. Ehrenberg summarized in a recent
AAUP report:

> Several researchers have used AAUP data to docu-
> ment the decrease in the average salary of faculty
> members at public academic institutions relative to
> that of their peers at private institutions that took
> place between 1978–79 and 2001–02. Most of the
> decline occurred before the mid-1990s; the relative
> salaries of faculty in the public and private sectors
> remained roughly constant between 1996–97 and
> 2001–02. … [H]owever, average salaries in public
> institutions of higher education dropped this past
> year relative to those in private institutions.[1]

The public/private salary gap continued to widen
in 2004–05, as Table A indicates. The table shows the
increase in average salary levels by institutional type
from 2003–04. Overall, faculty salary levels at public
institutions increased below the rate of inflation (measured at 3.3 percent from December 2003 to December 2004), while salary levels at private-independent
institutions rose at higher rates. Although these differences for a single year are small, the cumulative
effect over time is stark: During the 1970–71 academic year, the average full professor at a private-
independent doctoral university earned 10 percent
more than his or her counterpart at a public doctoral
university; by 2004–05, that gap was 30 percent.

Although average faculty salary alone is not a
sufficient indicator of institutional quality, it seems
self-evident to observe that, given substantial and
widening differences in pay over time, public colleges and universities will have difficulty attracting
and keeping the most productive and innovative
scholars and teachers. This becomes a public policy
issue if we wish to make high-quality higher education accessible to large segments of the public, and

not only to those who can pay the cost of, and gain
admission to, private universities and colleges.

For the comparison of average faculty salaries
between states, Table B also shows the important distinction between senior faculty members (holding the
rank of professor) and entry-level faculty (assistant
professors). Differences between states in average
salary at either rank could indicate a disadvantage
in attracting highly-qualified faculty, whether they
are established scholars who bring immediate pres-
tige and assume leadership of both scholarly projects
and collegiate governance structures, or entry-level
faculty who represent the potential for developing
research and teaching.

A number of researchers have investigated the
continuing salary differences between male and
female faculty, which cut across institutional type
and academic rank. The AAUP has collected institu-
tion-level data on average salaries by gender since
the mid-1970s. An analysis of those data indicates a
remarkably persistent salary disadvantage for female
faculty over more than a quarter century. When faculty members of the same rank are compared, average salaries for women are 7 to 12 percent lower
than those of men. The greatest differences are at
the rank of full professor. There are some variations
in this comparison by institutional type, as average
salaries are more equal in baccalaureate and associate colleges, and are generally more equal at public
colleges and universities. However, it is also the case
that female faculty are more likely to hold positions
that have lower salaries on average: they are more
likely than men to be at public community colleges;
they are less likely to achieve the rank of professor;
and they are less likely to have tenure. (Women are
also more likely than men to hold part-time faculty
positions, but the AAUP survey includes salary data
only for full-time faculty.) As a result, when the
weighted average salaries of all full-time female faculty members are compared with all full-time men,
women receive only about 80 percent of the salary
of men. The AAUP data indicate that this has been
the case since the late 1970s, with surprisingly little
change in the overall figure.

The AAUP data allow only for comparisons of
institutional averages. Other investigators have utilized individual-level data to attempt to determine
whether gender differences in salary can be attributed to differences in the distribution of female faculty according to other professional characteristics. A
recent analysis of 1998 data by the U.S. Department
of Education considered some 13 factors that might
contribute to the salary difference between male

and female faculty.[2] It concluded that, even when all those factors are controlled in the analysis, men still earn 9.4 percent more on average than women. Toutkoushian and Conley, in a recent comprehensive review and extension of various analytical models developed during the 1990s, found that progress appeared to have been made in narrowing the "unexplained" salary gap between male and female faculty but that the gap remains at between 4 and 6 percent.

As they point out, "[t]hese unexplained wage gaps are not only statistically significant, but are large in a practical sense especially when compounded over a woman's career. These inequities persist across most institution types and fields, and thus we should not lose focus on the fact that more improvement in the situation for women is needed."[3] What many statistical analyses fail to investigate, however, are the reasons that women continue to be overrepresented in the situations that result in lower average salary, as noted above. That, too, is a critical policy issue that remains to be addressed if women are to participate fully in the academic profession.

Faculty salaries also vary by geographic region. The AAUP data, divided into nine regions, indicate that the highest overall average faculty salaries are found in New England,[4] a region dominated by private higher education institutions, and the Pacific,[5] heavily influenced by relatively high salaries in California. An analysis of regional salary trends over time indicates that the regional differences have also been widening. Growth in average salaries over the last 25 years has been most rapid in New England and in the South Atlantic,[6] with salaries in the latter region falling generally into the middle range nationally. Salary growth in the Middle Atlantic region[7] has also generally kept pace, while faculty salaries in the East North Central[8] and, especially, East South Central[9] regions have fallen further behind. The latter two regions are characterized by more public institutions, especially at the doctoral level, reflecting the public/private salary disparities discussed above.

In addition to the broad differences in faculty salaries by categories previously discussed, salaries for individual faculty members also vary according to a number of specific aspects of the individual situation. In recent years, salary differences between faculty members in different disciplines have emerged as a recurring topic for discussion, with the influence of "the market" often cited as the force driving widening disparities even within the same institution. Faculty in fields such as business, engineering or computer technologies, whose skills have been in demand in the private sector, have frequently been able to secure higher salaries than their colleagues in the humanities and social sciences. Analyses such as the two individual-level studies cited previously have also concluded that faculty members with a more substantial record of publications and scholarship earn higher salaries, even when other factors are taken into account. This likely reflects the continuing premium accorded to research among the several roles of faculty, an emphasis that appears to apply to faculty even in predominantly teaching institutions. Finally, the existence of systematic differences in faculty salary by race or ethnicity is a controversial topic, on which there is not conclusive evidence. The U.S. Department of Education analysis referenced above concluded that "… some racial/ethnic differences (in salary) existed in 1998. Compared with White faculty, Asian/Pacific Islander faculty had higher average salaries, were more likely to hold advanced degrees, and had greater representation at public doctoral, research, and medical institutions. Black faculty had lower average salaries and were less likely to have advanced degrees or attain tenure or full professorship than White faculty."[10] However, the analysis concluded that when all factors were considered simultaneously, racial or ethnic category did not represent a statistically significant source of differences in faculty salaries.

In recent years, the issue of faculty compensation has increasingly been linked to other trends in higher education financing. Although space does not allow for a full consideration of these issues here, it is important to include them in order to place faculty salaries in their proper context.

The fundamental challenge facing higher education in the last few years has been a withdrawal of public funding. This has happened both directly and indirectly, and at state and federal levels. Direct funding of public higher education institutions from state sources has not kept pace with rising overall costs, so that states are now providing a smaller percentage of institutional revenues than ever before. According to figures compiled by the U.S. Department of Education, in Fiscal Year 2003 state and local governments supplied 37 percent of total revenues for public higher education institutions, down from 49 percent only 20 years before.[11] And this figure is much lower at large research universities, where the proportion of state support now frequently falls below 20 percent.

Faced with a decline in state revenues, public institutions have raised tuition at an accelerated pace. Some observers have portrayed this as a shift to a "high tuition/high aid" model, in which rising tuition prices would be met with increased levels of financial aid so that students with financial need would not be denied access to college. It does not appear that student financial aid has kept pace with increased tuition prices, however. The largest federal source of student financial aid is the Pell Grant program. The maximum Pell award has remained flat for several years, so that needy students must find additional sources for more of their tuition bills. At the same time, many states and institutions have shifted funding for student aid programs from need-based to merit-based awards. As Donald E. Heller notes, merit-based awards increased from 9 percent of state grants awarded without consideration of need in 1981 to nearly 25 percent of those awards in 2001. And at the same time, non-need-based aid increased to 44 percent of all grant aid.[12] Thus, rising tuition prices threaten the ability of low-income students to afford higher education, because need-based financial aid has not kept pace with tuition increases.

Nor have tuition revenues fueled higher faculty salaries. As reported in the AAUP's 2004–05 "Annual Report on the Economic Status of the Profession," average faculty salaries have not kept pace with increasing tuition rates over the last 25 years. The report compared faculty salary data from the AAUP annual survey with figures on tuition from the College Board's annual report *Trends in College Pricing*. It concluded:

> The bottom line is that although faculty and staff salary increases obviously contribute to increases in tuition, other factors have played more important roles during the last quarter century. These factors include the escalating costs of benefits for all employees, reductions in state support of public institutions, growing institutional financial-aid costs, expansion of the science and research infrastructure at research universities, and the increasing costs of information technology. If tuition and fee increases had been held to the rate of average faculty salary increases during this period, average tuition and fees would be substantially lower today in both the public and private sectors.[13]

Viewed in this broader context, rising tuition rates are a consequence of the trend also producing increased disparities in faculty salaries between public and private institutions: a withdrawal of public funding. This article has provided an overview of the key factors differentiating faculty salaries. It has also identified critical issues facing state government policymakers with regard to their public higher education sectors: the long-term decline in faculty salaries at public institutions, relative to those at private institutions; disadvantages for female faculty; and the con-

sequences of a withdrawal of state funding for both quality and accessibility at public colleges and universities. States look to their higher education institutions to provide high-quality education in a range of rapidly changing fields of endeavor, as centers of innovation in science and technology, and as sources of solutions to pressing social needs. As enrollments continue to grow and the need for expanded access to high-quality higher education becomes increasingly apparent, state policymakers must identify sufficient

Notes

[1] Ronald G. Ehrenberg, "Unequal Progress: The Annual Report on the Economic Status of the Profession," *Academe* 89, no. 2 (March–April 2003): 26.

[2] U.S. Department of Education, National Center for Education Statistics. *The Condition of Education 2002*. (NCES 2002-025) Washington, D.C.: 103.

[3] Robert K. Toutkoushian and Valerie Martin Conley. "Progress for Women in Academe, Yet Inequities Persist: Evidence from NSOPF:99." *Research in Higher Education* 46, no. 1 (February 2005): 1–28.

[4] New England: Connecticut, Maine, Massachusetts, New Hampshire, Vermont and Rhode Island.

[5] Pacific: Alaska, California, Guam, Hawaii, Oregon and Washington.

[6] South Atlantic: Delaware, District of Columbia, Florida, Georgia, Maryland, North Carolina, Puerto Rico, South Carolina, Virginia and West Virginia.

[7] Middle Atlantic: New Jersey, New York and Pennsylvania.

[8] East North Central: Illinois, Indiana, Michigan, Ohio and Wisconsin.

[9] East South Central: Alabama, Kentucky, Mississippi and Tennessee.

[10] *Condition of Education 2002*, 103.

[11] Figure for FY 2003 from U.S. Department of Education, National Center for Education Statistics. *Enrollment in Postsecondary Institutions, Fall 2003; Graduation Rates 1997 & 2000 Cohorts; and Financial Statistics, Fiscal Year 2003* (NCES 2005-177) Washington, D.C.: 9–10. Figure for FY 1981 from U.S. Department of Education, National Center for Education Statistics. *Digest of Education Statistics 2003*. (Available online at *http://www.nces.ed.gov/programs/digest/d03_tf.asp*) Table 334.

[12] Donald E. Heller, "The Changing Nature of Financial Aid," *Academe* 90, no. 4 (July–August 2004): 36–38.

[13] Ronald G. Ehrenberg, "Don't Blame Faculty for High Tuition: The Annual Report on the Economic Status of the Profession," *Academe* 90, no. 2 (March–April 2004): 30.

About the Author

John W. Curtis is director of research at the American Association of University Professors in Washington, D.C. He holds a Ph.D. in sociology from Johns Hopkins University, and has worked at colleges and universities in the United States, Germany, and Kenya. Opinions expressed in this article are those of the author, and not of the AAUP.

Table B
AVERAGE FULL-TIME FACULTY SALARY IN FOUR-YEAR INSTITUTIONS 2004–05,
BY STATE, INSTITUTIONAL CONTROL, INSTITUTION CATEGORY, AND ACADEMIC RANK

| | Public | | | | | | | | | | | |
| State or other jurisdiction | Doctoral | | | | Master's | | | | Baccalaureate | | | |
	Prof.	Assoc.	Asst.	All	Prof.	Assoc.	Asst.	All	Prof.	Assoc.	Asst.	All
United States	97,837	68,533	58,249	73,960	76,533	60,839	51,218	59,874	71,048	57,980	48,138	55,376
Alabama	90,461	64,794	54,557	69,056	67,574	54,584	46,704	52,416	...	...	...	...
Alaska	76,776	59,934	50,061	58,053	74,457	58,576	50,363	56,968	...	...	...	...
Arizona	95,195	65,480	57,880	73,606	88,825	70,815	54,836	63,758	...	...	...	...
Arkansas..............	84,505	63,032	54,560	66,496	68,204	58,369	48,086	52,363	62,457	53,027	43,815	47,886
California	112,059	73,523	62,935	90,062	83,472	67,257	55,642	69,644	87,401	75,606	67,618	68,110
Colorado	91,897	67,904	58,698	73,530	80,100	61,223	54,371	59,033	64,424	53,913	45,375	49,991
Connecticut	110,922	78,961	63,824	85,960	81,803	63,751	52,590	66,757	...	...	...	...
Delaware..............	109,631	76,053	61,455	81,793	...	...	...	...	...	...	...	...
Florida	90,769	65,251	56,883	68,029	77,630	60,851	52,333	57,910	75,601	59,265	45,854	58,436
Georgia	102,859	69,438	60,940	76,728	69,721	55,796	47,259	53,027	67,640	56,508	45,404	50,563
Hawaii.................	90,455	67,971	58,113	72,535	...	...	...	...	68,805	58,190	49,962	56,776
Idaho..................	71,840	57,563	48,614	58,709	66,696	54,741	46,716	50,859	55,370	45,631	38,959	47,402
Illinois................	98,003	67,794	58,910	73,695	75,359	60,677	50,156	56,806	...	...	...	...
Indiana................	95,022	67,289	56,523	72,101	77,416	61,762	51,267	57,466	70,535	57,889	45,864	52,414
Iowa	98,146	69,847	60,504	76,887	80,693	62,387	52,927	62,920	...	...	...	...
Kansas	86,187	63,896	54,083	67,101	70,056	55,685	46,639	53,770	...	...	...	...
Kentucky	89,189	64,866	54,800	70,277	71,878	57,235	49,650	53,808	...	...	...	...
Louisiana	86,936	64,593	54,924	63,328	64,390	53,689	45,726	49,272	65,410	51,893	43,789	46,071
Maine..................	74,152	63,021	47,836	60,938	78,683	60,616	48,300	61,133	58,454	47,585	39,922	48,330
Maryland	110,694	75,847	67,873	83,719	79,930	63,562	52,759	59,516	98,374	75,064	60,611	80,004
Massachusetts.......	101,957	81,453	63,704	82,192	79,257	63,308	53,159	65,470	65,186	54,955	43,662	56,524
Michigan..............	103,114	72,680	59,823	76,500	76,722	61,197	51,598	59,670	...	...	...	...
Minnesota	105,362	70,676	62,525	85,788	75,748	59,678	51,089	61,091	72,678	57,603	47,968	58,057
Mississippi	78,893	61,983	52,513	59,773	...	...	...	...	55,683	50,323	44,055	45,814
Missouri...............	93,490	65,645	54,450	70,402	65,971	53,388	45,692	52,539	65,972	51,410	44,481	50,819
Montana	69,205	54,597	47,555	55,195	59,061	48,120	46,481	47,184	57,350	47,648	44,113	48,167
Nebraska..............	93,929	68,119	57,572	75,112	69,897	58,121	49,620	56,541	60,443	45,119	41,380	49,866
Nevada	100,556	74,330	59,811	75,537	...	...	...	...	...	...	...	...
New Hampshire....	95,416	71,581	60,197	78,606	73,318	59,734	49,364	60,891	...	...	...	...
New Jersey...........	114,614	81,028	65,377	88,309	95,798	74,726	59,834	76,211	94,016	72,749	54,025	72,394
New Mexico	82,184	61,476	53,677	65,123	59,029	49,926	44,487	47,992	...	...	...	...
New York	104,580	75,241	62,299	81,424	85,045	66,094	54,486	66,432	84,869	64,901	53,709	65,062
North Carolina	100,875	71,113	61,418	75,450	79,500	62,632	54,984	60,695	70,075	56,878	52,034	56,570
North Dakota.......	70,685	57,237	50,967	54,798	...	...	...	...	...	...	...	...
Ohio	94,253	66,750	54,911	70,114	78,921	63,032	52,792	65,920	70,636	58,064	47,089	55,065
Oklahoma	84,676	61,934	52,681	64,062	63,912	54,635	47,235	51,249	49,054	42,820	36,798	42,537
Oregon	80,046	60,588	52,646	60,472	58,540	47,809	39,987	47,551	55,426	47,731	40,643	45,975
Pennsylvania	108,149	74,833	62,108	76,842	86,113	69,478	55,959	66,937	76,635	63,187	53,831	56,009
Rhode Island	85,412	62,313	55,308	73,697	64,907	54,910	48,228	57,413	...	...	...	...
South Carolina	91,356	66,366	59,663	71,419	68,472	58,282	46,895	55,696	63,316	54,642	46,115	50,991
South Dakota.......	72,964	56,787	47,106	54,625	69,213	56,512	49,827	55,754	61,270	55,604	45,323	49,454
Tennessee	89,064	66,573	56,142	67,424	69,428	56,044	46,792	55,623	...	...	...	...
Texas	99,347	67,475	59,661	72,906	74,088	59,744	51,597	56,717	72,173	58,524	50,268	53,552
Utah	86,934	61,841	55,597	64,868	63,481	50,928	44,587	50,832	...	...	...	...
Vermont	86,858	65,314	55,259	63,295	...	...	...	...	54,456	44,648	36,577	48,150
Virginia................	103,621	71,034	58,694	76,515	70,393	59,694	49,480	57,494	78,404	61,015	48,170	59,860
Washington...........	93,656	66,952	61,462	73,151	66,757	54,580	46,908	53,619	...	...	...	...
West Virginia.......	76,302	59,762	49,140	61,029	63,200	51,787	42,603	53,145	58,182	50,356	41,666	46,048
Wisconsin.............	94,736	68,936	60,471	77,619	67,139	55,193	47,697	56,549	...	...	...	...
Wyoming..............	82,531	62,381	58,932	65,047	...	...	...	...	...	...	...	...
District of Columbia	...	...	...	...	72,207	57,075	45,773	61,779	...	...	...	...
Guam	...	...	...	...	...	...	...	...	70,952	56,727	45,138	54,304
Puerto Rico..........	...	...	...	...	...	...	...	...	56,447	47,262	37,272	46,735

See footnotes at end of table.

AVERAGE FULL-TIME FACULTY SALARY IN FOUR-YEAR INSTITUTIONS 2004–05, BY STATE, INSTITUTIONAL CONTROL, INSTITUTION CATEGORY, AND ACADEMIC RANK — Continued

State or other jurisdiction	Private											
	Doctoral				Master's				Baccalaureate			
	Prof.	Assoc.	Asst.	All	Prof.	Assoc.	Asst.	All	Prof.	Assoc.	Asst.	All
United States	123,016	79,637	68,006	91,280	81,187	62,827	51,747	62,658	75,112	57,259	47,678	58,618
Alabama	...	...	...	...	71,187	55,616	49,309	56,713	68,837	55,748	43,551	56,501
Alaska	...	...	...	...	...	...	...	...	...	...	...	...
Arizona	...	...	...	...	...	...	...	...	67,018	63,861	48,937	56,470
Arkansas					...	...	...	...	59,338	49,345	41,072	49,239
California	128,091	85,038	73,818	100,265	92,692	69,852	58,206	72,544	94,518	68,330	55,913	75,269
Colorado	92,393	68,820	57,218	69,686	33,373	29,647	26,572	29,581	94,645	65,858	53,147	72,369
Connecticut	145,550	82,142	69,402	106,577	93,452	68,854	57,042	71,384	94,288	69,818	55,054	72,590
Delaware	...	...	...	...	60,557	58,100	52,953	55,437	60,968	51,914	42,463	51,478
Florida	103,029	68,335	62,706	73,229	79,339	59,998	50,042	61,065	66,054	55,429	48,528	54,008
Georgia	131,898	84,309	74,471	101,351	80,643	60,147	50,628	60,564	65,173	53,772	43,496	51,663
Hawaii	...	...	...	...	...	...	...	...	70,176	56,385	47,703	54,526
Idaho	...	...	...	...	...	...	...	...	53,261	45,045	38,910	43,592
Illinois	130,095	81,095	67,366	94,189	69,508	59,358	47,942	57,488	66,397	54,627	45,290	53,897
Indiana	118,670	78,750	67,677	94,675	76,488	57,976	48,661	57,537	67,063	52,726	46,901	54,987
Iowa	...	...	...	...	82,985	60,077	49,607	62,239	63,231	52,156	44,445	52,193
Kansas	...	...	...	...	55,178	50,772	47,407	48,919	47,585	40,367	35,262	39,832
Kentucky	...	...	...	...	68,861	56,956	46,305	57,082	59,366	49,463	42,091	49,551
Louisiana	102,827	73,450	61,263	74,245	92,514	64,385	52,058	66,787	56,717	48,254	40,678	48,472
Maine	...	...	...	...	68,727	58,443	47,253	53,178	97,772	70,553	56,753	76,478
Maryland	115,540	79,520	65,025	85,016	81,532	64,241	52,855	62,403	71,469	57,537	48,825	58,816
Massachusetts	136,455	84,593	74,677	102,785	94,683	71,437	60,062	71,572	98,136	68,771	56,052	76,001
Michigan	...	...	...	...	74,636	59,136	49,176	57,912	66,524	54,440	45,801	55,680
Minnesota	80,055	67,136	56,746	66,535	64,859	53,029	45,275	51,824	75,974	57,346	49,319	59,520
Mississippi	...	...	...	...	63,453	52,390	44,260	49,946	73,155	54,347	46,783	54,480
Missouri	115,501	72,942	62,249	85,078	68,951	55,162	47,704	55,737	57,090	50,388	42,956	47,438
Montana	...	...	...	...	...	...	...	...	53,568	42,210	37,795	45,886
Nebraska	...	...	...	...	80,522	60,348	48,893	58,033	59,473	48,207	42,307	47,684
Nevada	...	...	...	...	...	...	...	...	...	...	...	...
New Hampshire	124,496	86,010	68,957	99,513	79,856	63,571	47,647	65,055	67,610	55,825	45,707	54,700
New Jersey	138,953	78,217	66,809	101,355	83,909	70,763	54,443	66,526	68,728	57,531	48,283	58,291
New Mexico	...	...	...	...	...	...	...	...	64,717	52,309	45,925	58,091
New York	121,874	81,231	68,034	90,119	84,946	65,806	54,764	65,582	87,414	64,878	51,980	66,654
North Carolina	131,246	89,481	75,460	106,709	79,836	63,189	47,921	62,129	62,368	49,383	42,894	49,640
North Dakota	...	...	...	...	...	...	...	...	48,848	43,000	40,233	42,351
Ohio	109,616	79,079	68,518	86,252	76,967	57,478	49,905	58,303	70,671	56,642	46,664	56,827
Oklahoma	...	...	...	...	77,956	56,814	47,777	58,152	...	...	...	37,292
Oregon	...	...	...	...	76,542	58,194	49,082	59,075	79,353	56,758	48,158	61,965
Pennsylvania	124,658	85,105	77,824	97,253	86,435	66,405	53,082	64,167	78,695	60,515	49,212	59,435
Rhode Island	123,090	78,370	69,725	99,013	77,639	60,112	51,054	56,968	97,816	75,920	65,304	82,229
South Carolina	...	...	...	...	...	...	...	...	69,360	52,286	44,523	54,064
South Dakota	...	...	...	...	...	...	...	...	56,364	49,080	42,544	46,488
Tennessee	123,905	79,043	65,009	90,957	63,865	54,692	46,069	53,757	60,982	48,947	43,592	49,817
Texas	104,504	72,236	65,410	76,063	74,963	57,175	47,829	58,859	59,042	51,670	42,695	49,215
Utah	...	...	...	...	...	...	...	...	66,842	58,699	50,544	56,803
Vermont	...	...	...	...	69,280	55,999	44,893	58,710	94,521	64,751	55,305	70,132
Virginia	64,555	56,567	50,222	55,904	60,975	49,964	43,652	50,123	77,526	60,448	49,305	61,290
Washington	...	...	...	...	74,245	61,935	50,471	59,555	68,246	54,107	47,095	56,046
West Virginia	...	...	...	...	65,130	52,367	44,742	49,566	52,314	46,229	35,802	43,480
Wisconsin	94,143	69,729	59,696	69,431	62,146	49,907	42,741	46,903	64,112	53,490	44,950	52,566
Wyoming	...	...	...	...	...	...	...	...	...	...	...	...
District of Columbia	108,647	75,502	60,989	80,990	102,981	75,922	58,134	82,482	63,736	51,776	43,573	51,082
Guam	...	...	...	...	...	...	...	...	...	...	...	...
Puerto Rico	...	...	...	...	40,314	36,525	31,833	34,803	41,052	31,676	29,091	30,679

Source: American Association of University Professors, Faculty Compensation Survey. More extensive tables and complete definitions are in "The Annual Report on the Economic Status of the Profession 2004–05" *Academe* 91, no. 2 (March/April 2005).

Notes:

. . . — Indicates no responses in that category.

"Prof."= Professor; "Assoc."= Associate Professor; "Asst."= Assistant Professor; "All" includes all full-time faculty, with or without academic rank.

Data include full-time primarily instructional faculty only.

Figures are weighted average (mean) salaries; salaries of faculty members on 12-month contracts have been adjusted to an academic year (9-month) equivalent.

Table 9.3

ESTIMATED UNDERGRADUATE TUITION AND FEES AND ROOM AND BOARD RATES IN INSTITUTIONS OF HIGHER EDUCATION, BY CONTROL OF INSTITUTION AND STATE: 2002–2003 AND 2003–2004

State or other jurisdiction	Public 4-year 2002–2003		Public 4-year 2003–2004 (a)				Private 4-year 2002–2003		Private 4-year 2003–2004 (a)				Public 2-year tuition only (in-state)	
	Total	Tuition (in-state)	Total	Tuition (in-state)	Room	Board	Total	Tuition	Total	Tuition	Room	Board	2002–2003	2003–2004 (a)
United States	$9,787	$4,046	$10,720	$4,630	$3,212	$2,877	$23,787	$16,826	$25,204	$17,902	$3,948	$3,355	$1,483	$1,670
Alabama	7,903	3,511	8,983	3,977	2,401	2,605	15,726	10,528	16,452	10,980	2,690	2,782	2,128	2,479
Alaska	9,459	3,163	10,118	3,423	3,302	3,393	15,638	11,107	17,941	11,856	2,742	3,342	1,789	1,943
Arizona	8,728	2,587	10,140	3,586	3,643	2,911	17,258	11,829	19,035	12,358	3,454	3,223	1,029	1,140
Arkansas	7,740	3,690	8,349	4,010	2,277	2,062	15,094	10,445	16,001	11,098	2,330	2,573	1,507	1,641
California	10,812	2,786	12,275	3,785	4,296	4,194	26,435	18,357	28,222	19,645	4,676	3,901	316	486
Colorado	9,150	3,104	9,751	3,447	2,971	3,333	24,464	16,501	26,260	17,684	4,244	4,332	1,727	1,784
Connecticut	11,803	5,154	12,772	5,761	3,743	3,269	30,586	22,220	32,383	23,489	5,391	3,504	2,008	2,307
Delaware	11,461	5,432	12,496	6,176	3,542	2,778	15,586	9,336	16,408	9,796	3,350	3,263	1,878	1,992
Florida	8,714	2,591	9,207	2,773	3,502	2,931	21,213	14,695	22,723	15,775	3,669	3,280	1,493	1,576
Georgia	8,784	2,929	9,090	3,239	3,445	2,407	21,921	15,066	23,309	16,145	4,113	3,050	1,363	1,411
Hawaii	8,184	3,134	8,760	3,239	2,949	2,573	17,151	8,720	18,041	9,243	3,655	5,143	1,069	1,118
Idaho	7,560	3,033	8,091	3,323	2,097	2,671	10,279	5,231	10,905	5,163	2,261	3,481	1,541	1,658
Illinois	10,984	5,171	11,804	5,653	2,965	3,186	24,313	17,094	25,666	18,180	4,305	3,181	1,660	1,783
Indiana	10,595	4,614	11,637	5,384	2,865	3,387	23,657	17,719	25,151	18,884	3,106	3,161	2,363	2,483
Iowa	9,190	4,141	10,878	4,991	2,883	3,004	21,092	15,922	22,121	16,758	2,484	2,879	2,555	2,686
Kansas	7,751	3,168	8,604	3,686	2,405	2,512	17,586	12,658	18,607	13,429	2,288	2,889	1,639	1,792
Kentucky	7,673	3,409	8,521	3,868	2,434	2,218	15,332	10,410	18,142	12,698	2,617	2,826	1,867	2,264
Louisiana	6,905	2,885	7,494	3,208	2,161	2,124	24,233	17,244	25,677	18,416	3,987	3,274	1,062	1,285
Maine	10,322	4,623	11,010	5,011	2,977	3,022	25,750	18,935	27,131	19,903	3,564	3,665	2,764	2,772
Maryland	12,283	5,402	13,419	6,230	4,015	3,174	27,413	19,950	28,961	21,148	4,449	3,365	2,354	2,601
Massachusetts	10,764	4,951	12,250	6,080	3,489	2,681	32,000	23,244	33,719	24,591	5,133	3,995	2,347	2,725
Michigan	11,357	5,487	12,208	6,015	3,075	3,118	17,450	11,832	18,232	12,491	2,897	2,844	1,813	1,868
Minnesota	9,957	5,030	10,845	5,754	2,869	2,222	23,414	17,822	24,635	18,712	3,033	2,890	2,866	3,414
Mississippi	8,008	3,715	8,547	3,754	2,389	2,403	15,113	10,539	15,973	11,113	2,422	2,438	1,453	1,392
Missouri	9,407	4,627	10,320	5,367	2,841	2,112	19,682	13,690	20,837	14,646	3,169	3,021	1,789	1,940
Montana	8,941	3,928	9,348	4,155	2,376	2,817	15,669	10,650	16,635	11,354	2,403	2,878	2,313	2,580
Nebraska	8,413	3,610	9,620	4,238	2,470	2,912	17,768	12,814	19,207	13,895	2,644	2,669	1,566	1,678
Nevada	8,973	2,531	10,333	2,724	4,400	3,210	17,295	10,518	18,354	10,941	3,880	3,533	1,456	1,507
New Hampshire	9,416	3,535	13,852	7,623	3,774	2,454	27,200	19,674	28,410	20,573	4,469	3,369	4,481	4,828
New Jersey	13,903	6,698	15,109	7,266	4,991	2,851	26,652	18,426	28,011	19,519	4,514	3,978	2,315	2,444
New Mexico	7,951	3,013	8,238	3,161	2,435	2,641	17,375	11,787	18,501	12,330	3,027	3,145	942	997
New York	10,916	4,205	12,002	4,885	4,009	3,108	27,669	19,185	29,294	20,444	5,123	3,726	2,728	2,949
North Carolina	8,305	3,086	8,805	3,251	2,966	2,589	22,006	15,891	23,169	16,981	3,060	3,128	1,112	1,166
North Dakota	7,369	3,387	8,028	3,835	1,634	2,558	12,526	8,923	13,476	9,483	1,772	2,220	2,229	2,419
Ohio	12,216	5,882	13,319	6,561	3,828	2,931	23,128	17,018	24,354	17,975	3,200	3,180	2,595	2,793

See footnotes at end of table.

ESTIMATED UNDERGRADUATE TUITION AND FEES AND ROOM AND BOARD RATES IN INSTITUTIONS OF HIGHER EDUCATION, BY CONTROL OF INSTITUTION AND STATE: 2002–2003 AND 2003–2004 — Continued

State or other jurisdiction	Public 4-year 2002–2003		Public 4-year 2003–2004 (a)				Private 4-year 2002–2003		Private 4-year 2003–2004 (a)				Public 2-year tuition only (in-state)	
	Total	Tuition (in-state)	Total	Tuition (in-state)	Room	Board	Total	Tuition	Total	Tuition	Room	Board	2002–2003	2003–2004 (a)
Oklahoma	6,828	2,613	7,901	3,200	2,197	2,504	16,739	11,579	17,999	12,445	2,620	2,934	1,290	1,650
Oregon	10,510	4,017	11,626	4,677	3,660	3,288	25,066	18,608	26,074	19,546	3,245	3,283	1,968	2,421
Pennsylvania	12,899	7,071	13,754	7,633	3,366	2,756	27,429	19,942	29,050	21,209	4,240	3,601	2,384	2,514
Rhode Island	12,231	5,082	12,763	5,387	3,910	3,467	27,782	19,986	29,376	21,188	4,454	3,734	2,014	2,120
South Carolina	11,024	6,224	12,710	7,482	2,982	2,246	18,973	13,735	20,189	14,621	2,800	2,769	2,174	2,635
South Dakota	7,682	3,965	8,379	4,441	1,721	2,217	16,268	11,772	17,001	12,324	2,282	2,395	3,166	2,812
Tennessee	8,298	3,585	8,936	4,043	2,434	2,459	20,004	14,309	21,170	15,233	3,192	2,746	1,751	2,076
Texas	8,636	3,313	9,202	3,579	3,014	2,610	19,589	13,862	20,892	14,849	3,111	2,933	1,031	1,171
Utah	7,367	2,635	7,865	2,902	1,993	2,970	9,206	4,278	9,993	4,460	2,754	2,779	1,804	1,946
Vermont	13,969	7,744	14,766	8,260	4,110	2,396	24,219	17,287	25,567	18,277	4,156	3,134	3,652	3,604
Virginia	9,516	4,083	10,900	5,069	3,137	2,694	21,589	15,765	22,628	16,522	3,112	2,994	1,272	1,799
Washington	10,723	4,286	11,353	4,630	3,196	3,526	23,639	17,230	24,767	18,300	3,371	3,096	2,097	2,230
West Virginia	8,175	2,898	8,751	3,172	2,842	2,737	17,807	12,441	19,029	13,311	2,765	2,953	1,743	1,754
Wisconsin	8,157	3,965	9,066	4,675	2,569	1,822	22,155	16,514	23,340	17,399	3,031	2,910	2,557	2,583
Wyoming	7,977	2,997	8,485	3,090	2,372	3,023	(b)	(b)	(b)	(b)	(b)	(b)	1,561	1,613
Dist. of Columbia	(b)	2,070	(b)	2,070	(b)	(b)	27,914	19,494	29,509	20,587	5,700	3,222	(b)	(b)

Source: U.S. Department of Education, National Center for Education Statistics, 2002–2003 and 2003–2004; Integrated Postsecondary Education Data System (IPEDS), Fall 2002, Fall 2003 and Spring 2003. (This table was prepared March 2005).

Note: Data are for the entire academic year and are average charges. Tuition and fees were weighted by the number of full-time equivalent undergraduates in 2002, but are not adjusted to reflect student residency. Room and board are based on full-time students. Some data revised from previously published figures. Detail may not sum to totals due to rounding.

Key:
(a) Preliminary data based on fall 2002 enrollments.
(b) Not applicable.

Table 9.4
DEGREE GRANTING INSTITUTIONS AND BRANCHES, BY TYPE AND CONTROL OF INSTITUTION, 2003–2004

State or other jurisdiction	Total	All public institutions	Public 4-year					Public 2-year	All private institutions	Private 4-year					Private 2-year
			Total	Doctoral extensive (a)	Master's (b)	Baccalaureate (c)	Other (d)			Total	Doctoral extensive (a)	Master's (b)	Baccalaureate (c)	Other (d)	
United States	4,236	1,720	634	165	281	103	85	1,086	2,516	1,896	96	363	545	892	620
Alabama	75	46	17	6	10	1	0	29	29	23	0	4	9	10	6
Alaska	8	5	3	1	2	0	0	2	3	3	0	1	1	1	0
Arizona	74	25	5	3	1	0	1	20	49	30	0	6	1	23	19
Arkansas	47	33	11	2	5	2	2	22	14	12	0	1	8	3	2
California	401	144	34	10	20	2	2	110	257	194	13	31	27	123	63
Colorado	74	28	13	4	3	4	2	15	46	30	1	5	3	21	16
Connecticut	45	22	10	1	7	1	1	12	23	19	4	5	4	6	4
Delaware	10	5	2	1	1	0	0	3	5	4	1	0	2	1	1
Florida	169	40	15	6	4	1	4	25	129	90	5	20	24	41	39
Georgia	126	74	22	3	13	1	5	52	52	43	2	5	15	21	9
Hawaii	20	10	3	1	0	2	0	7	10	8	0	3	1	4	2
Idaho	14	7	4	2	1	1	0	3	7	6	0	1	1	4	1
Illinois	173	60	12	5	7	0	0	48	113	98	6	15	20	57	15
Indiana	101	29	14	5	6	3	0	15	72	48	1	8	22	17	24
Iowa	63	19	3	2	1	0	0	16	44	41	0	4	22	15	3
Kansas	63	36	9	3	4	0	2	27	27	23	0	8	10	5	4
Kentucky	77	34	8	2	6	0	0	26	43	28	1	4	16	7	15
Louisiana	90	62	16	4	9	0	3	46	28	13	0	4	3	6	15
Maine	30	15	8	1	1	5	1	7	15	12	0	3	5	4	3
Maryland	62	29	13	3	9	1	0	16	33	28	1	5	6	16	5
Massachusetts	122	31	15	3	7	1	4	16	91	82	9	15	21	37	9
Michigan	110	45	15	7	8	0	0	30	65	60	1	9	22	28	5
Minnesota	113	52	12	1	7	3	1	40	61	49	3	6	14	26	12
Mississippi	40	26	9	4	3	1	1	17	14	11	0	2	5	4	3
Missouri	123	34	14	1	6	2	2	20	89	68	2	11	14	41	21
Montana	23	18	6	2	2	1	1	12	5	4	0	1	2	1	1
Nebraska	39	15	7	1	5	0	1	8	24	16	0	4	8	4	8
Nevada	17	7	4	2	0	1	1	3	10	6	0	1	2	3	4
New Hampshire	25	9	5	1	2	2	0	4	16	15	2	2	5	6	1
New Jersey	58	33	14	3	8	2	1	19	25	23	3	6	6	8	2
New Mexico	42	27	7	3	3	0	1	20	15	13	0	1	6	6	2
New York	307	78	43	6	20	7	10	35	229	175	16	32	35	92	54
North Carolina	130	75	16	4	8	3	1	59	55	49	2	7	26	14	6
North Dakota	21	15	7	2	1	3	1	8	6	4	0	1	1	2	2
Ohio	187	61	25	10	1	6	8	36	126	76	3	15	25	33	50
Oklahoma	53	29	15	2	7	3	3	14	24	20	1	5	7	7	4
Oregon	59	26	9	3	3	1	2	17	33	29	0	6	9	14	4
Pennsylvania	262	65	44	4	17	20	3	21	197	107	6	28	34	39	90
Rhode Island	13	3	2	1	1	0	0	1	10	10	1	1	1	7	0
South Carolina	63	33	12	3	5	3	1	21	30	25	0	3	15	7	5

See footnotes at end of table.

DEGREE GRANTING INSTITUTIONS AND BRANCHES, BY TYPE AND CONTROL OF INSTITUTION, 2003–2004—Continued

State or other jurisdiction	Total	All public institutions	Public 4-year					Public 2-year	All private institutions	Private 4-year					Private 2-year
			Total	Doctoral extensive (a)	Master's (b)	Baccalaureate (c)	Other (d)			Total	Doctoral extensive (a)	Master's (b)	Baccalaureate (c)	Other (d)	
South Dakota	26	14	9	2	2	2	3	5	12	11	0	2	5	4	1
Tennessee	95	22	9	5	4	0	0	13	73	56	1	11	16	28	17
Texas	208	111	42	12	20	2	8	69	97	61	4	14	20	23	36
Utah	28	13	7	2	2	2	1	6	15	8	1	2	1	4	7
Vermont	27	6	5	1	2	1	1	1	21	19	0	6	9	4	2
Virginia	104	39	15	6	6	3	0	24	65	55	0	9	17	29	10
Washington	81	46	11	2	8	1	0	35	35	32	0	11	4	17	3
West Virginia	40	18	12	1	2	9	0	6	22	10	0	2	7	1	12
Wisconsin	68	31	13	2	11	0	0	18	37	35	1	8	10	16	2
Wyoming	9	8	1	0	1	0	0	7	1	0	0	0	0	0	1
Dist. of Columbia	16	2	2	0	0	1	1	0	14	14	5	4	1	4	0

Source: U.S. Department of Education, National Center for Education Statistics, 2003–04 Integrated Postsecondary Education Data System (IPEDS), Fall 2003. (This table was prepared March 2005).

Note: New institutions which do not have sufficient data to report by detailed level are included under "other 4-year" or 2-year depending on the level reported by the institution.

Key:

(a) Doctoral, extensive institutions are committed to graduate education through the doctorate, and award 50 or more doctor's degrees per year across at least 15 disciplines. Doctoral, intensive institutions are committed to education through the doctorate and award at least 10 doctor's degrees per year across three or more disciplines or at least 20 doctor's degrees overall.

(b) Master's institutions offer a full range of baccalaureate programs and are committed to education through the master's degree. They award at least 20 master's degrees per year.

(c) Baccalaureate institutions primarily emphasize undergraduate education.

(d) Other specialized 4-year institutions award degrees primarily in single fields of study, such as medicine, business, fine arts, theology and engineering. Includes some institutions which have 4-year programs, but have not reported sufficient data to identify program category. Also, includes institutions classified as 4-year under the IPEDS system, which had been classified as 2-year in the Carnegie classification system because they primarily award associate's degrees.

The Future of Medicaid

By Dennis G. Smith, Janet G. Freeze, Susan N. Hill and Lyn R. Killman

A modernized Medicaid system will give states greater flexibility with reduced administrative burden. The Deficit Reduction Act of 2005 gives states additional flexibility to provide health insurance coverage among low-income but healthy children and families that reflect the 21st century dynamics in health insurance and increased options for community alternatives rather than being stuck in the assumptions that are now 40 years behind the times.

Introduction

As it has over the past four decades, the future of Medicaid will reflect changes both inside and outside the program, including changes in Medicare and our health insurance system as a whole. The Medicaid mission statement, clearly and boldly provided by Section 1901 is, "[f]or the purpose of enabling each State, as far as practicable under the conditions in such State, to furnish (1) medical assistance on behalf of families with dependent children and of aged, blind, or disabled individuals, whose income and resources are insufficient to meet the costs of necessary medical services, and (2) rehabilitation and other services to help such families and individuals attain or retain capability for independence or self-care. ..."

Medicaid is a jointly funded, cooperative agreement between federal and state governments through the authority of Title XIX of the Social Security Act—Grants to States for Medical Assistance Programs. Within the overall federal framework, federal dollars generally follow state decisions regarding eligibility, benefits, provider reimbursement. However, the federal government still retains its authority to determine whether it is appropriate to match state (or local government) dollars.

Medicaid was created nearly 40 years ago to provide access to health care for individuals on welfare, *based on the assumptions and the health care system available at the time.* Forty years ago, less than one-fourth of the civilian population had major medical insurance. Of the $28 billion in private national health expenditures, $18 billion came from out-of-pocket payments and only $10 billion came from insurance payments. The majority of public funds ($10.6 billion) came from state and local government sources ($5.8 billion). Access to health care truly was on a cash basis for most American families, not just those on welfare. But with an average daily hospital cost of $40, access was still affordable to working families. Medicaid eligibility was strictly tied to populations on welfare.

Today, only a minority of Medicaid eligibles are on welfare. Two-thirds of Medicaid enrollees live in families in the work force and the majority (56 percent) have family income above the poverty level.

Between 2000 and 2003, the U.S. population grew by 3 percent, while Medicaid eligibles grew 25 percent nationally (Table C). The majority of the 55 million people served by Medicaid today are healthy

Table A: 2003 Medicaid Beneficiaries and Payment by Basis of Eligibility (State detail Tables D and E)

Eligibility category (a)	Percentage of enrollment	Percentages of expenditures	Per capita eligible (b)	Per capita beneficiary (c)
Aged	8%	24%	$10,832	$13,664
Blind/disabled	15	44	12,129	13,294
Children (d)	48	17	1,331	1,462
Adults	23	11	1,861	2,285
Other (e)	7	4	N.A.	N.A.

Source: FY 2003 Medicaid Beneficiaries Per Capita Expenditures for Eligibles and Beneficiaries by Basis of Eligibility; CMS, MSIS State Summary, October 27, 2005.
Key:
N.A. — Not available.
(a) Category definitions: Disabled–Unable to engage in any substantial gainful activity because of a medically determinable physical or mental impairment expected to last less than 12 months. Blind–Central visual acuity of 20/200 or less with the use of a correcting lens. Adults–Non-disabled and ages

19 through 64 who have dependent children in their care. Children–Non-disabled individuals under age 18 or 19, or at state option, 20 or 21. BCCA–Women under age 65, and need treatment for breast or cervical cancer.
(b) Eligible–Enrolled in their state's Medicaid program.
(c) Beneficiary–Enrolled and had a service reimbursed for them during the fiscal year.
(d) Children is inclusive of foster children.
(e) Other includes breast and cervical cancer eligibles and categorically unknown beneficiaries.

Table B: Summary Premium Cost-sharing as a Percent of Income
Private Employer Based Coverage

Low income family of four with employer based health coverage average annual cost-sharing expenditures

Federal poverty level (a)	Family of four income 2005 FPL levels	Total average annual PPO premium (b)	Employee share of annual premium	Additional employee cost-sharing	Employee cost-sharing as percent of income
150%	$29,025	$11,090	$2,641	$679	11.4%
200%	38,700	11,090	2,641	679	8.5

Sources: The Kaiser Family Foundation Health Research and Education Trust Employer Health Benefits 2005 Summary of Findings, pages 2 and 3; Column 1 source: Federal Register, Vol. 70, No. 33, (February 2005), 8373–75, www.aspe.hhs.gov/poverty.html.

Key: (a) 2005 federal poverty level for family of four equals $19,350 (HHS Poverty Guidelines).
(b) Preferred provider organizations (PPOs) cover a majority of covered workers.

---

children and adults. The growth cannot be explained simply by general population growth and economic trends. Dynamics both inside and outside Medicaid are influencing its course.

Medicaid Spending

Medicaid spending is quite disproportionate to its categorical enrollment. Even though children make up 48 percent of Medicaid enrollment, spending on children is just 17 percent of the funds. Moreover, 23 percent of Medicaid beneficiaries are elderly and disabled, and their spending accounts for 68 percent of Medicaid costs.[1] The services and supports required among the different groups vary drastically, and different reform solutions are required for each population.

The Deficit Reduction Act of 2005— Transformation of Medicaid at all Points

The Medicaid provisions in the Deficit Reduction Act of 2005 (DRA) reflect the bipartisan recommendations of the National Governors Association, the experience of the successful State Children's Health Insurance Program (SCHIP), and state Medicaid waivers requested by Republican and Democratic governors alike. Many of the reform measures are aligned and encompass prescription drug reimbursement reform, cost-sharing options, assets transfer reform, finance reform, tax credits, Health Savings Accounts (HSA) and private insurance subsidies, personal accountability, long-term care reforms including expanded home and community-based programs, long-term care partnerships and innovation through health care technology.

As states consider new options to administer Medicaid programs under the DRA, the provisions on benefit flexibility and cost-sharing are likely to be widely debated. These options reflect mainstream thinking and recognize that Medicaid now serves families in the work force. In the Commonwealth Fund's October 2005 Health Care Opinion Leaders Survey, 61 percent of those surveyed on the Future of Medicaid favored an option that provides flexibility in benefit designs for beneficiaries with incomes above 100 percent of the federal poverty level. In addition, survey participants favored an option that includes premium or cost-sharing provisions that do not exceed 5 percent of the family income. The DRA caps co-payments and premiums for all family members at income levels over 100 percent at 5 percent, and provides flexibility in benefit design based on SCHIP.

Moreover, in a recent report to Congress on SCHIP, researchers from Mathematica Policy Research Inc. and The Urban Institute report: "In most of the study states, case study respondents reported that cost-sharing was viewed as a positive feature of SCHIP constituencies—including advocates for families. Consistently, case study respondents, who were interviewed between May 2001 and January 2002, described premium and co-payment amounts as reasonable and affordable."

According to the Center for Studying Health System Change, more than 40 percent of low-income families (less than 200 percent FPL) pay for private health insurance. The 2005 Kaiser Employer Health Benefits Survey reported the annual premium a health insurer charges an employer for a PPO health plan covering a family of four averages $11,090, of which the employee shares $2,641. In addition to premium payments, 56 percent of employees in employer sponsored plans pay deductibles and co-payments. The average cost-sharing for a PPO plan (in which most people are enrolled) is $679 for family coverage.

This table shows that an aggregate cap of 5 percent of income is well below what the average low-income family currently pays for health insurance. But it also shows the importance of ensuring access to affordable health insurance for our working families so they are not priced out of the health insurance market. Part of Medicaid's future will depend on making health care more affordable. Potential solutions include the administration's proposals on tax credits, incentives to small businesses, purchasing pools and Health Savings Accounts (HSAs).

With the benefit flexibility provisions of DRA, states will have new options to serve the healthy but low-income Medicaid parents and children. Families will gain continuity in coverage as family members move together from Medicaid to SCHIP to, eventually, private coverage. Today, one child may be in Medicaid, another in SCHIP and the parent in private coverage. With new flexibility, families can be together in the same plan. Administrative simplification can help retention in the program and give families experience with insurance coverage, which will become important when income rises above Medicaid and SCHIP eligibility levels. Building on the success of SCHIP, states will be able to offer "benchmark" plans that will allow them to take greater advantage of marketplace dynamics.

LTC—The Call for Community-based Alternatives Is Heard

Congress answered the call from state officials, individuals with disabilities and older people for reform of our nation's long-term support system. This groundbreaking legislation recognizes that every American—young and old—should have the choice to live in the community and Medicaid policies should support their choice.

It renews the promise of freedom for every individual with a disability or long-term illness. It is a long-awaited commitment to independence, choice and dignity for countless Americans who want to have control of their lives.

The DRA gives states many of the tools they need to "rebalance" their long-term support programs so individuals with disabilities and older people can live meaningful lives in the community while sustaining the integrity and viability of the Medicaid program for those in the greatest need.

The law bolsters state efforts to:

1. Increase access to community supports so that individuals have true choice of a range of quality options;

2. Promote personal responsibility, independence and choice by helping individuals take control of their long-term support needs, including planning for the future;

3. Sustain the integrity and viability of the Medicaid program so that the program is there for those who rely on it for critical life supports.

Increasing Access to Community Supports

The Money Follows the Person Rebalancing Demonstration (MFP) supports state efforts to "rebalance" their long-term support systems by providing over five years $1.75 billion in competitive grants to states. With this critical assistance, states will be able to make targeted reforms to shore up the community-based infrastructure so individuals have a choice of where they live and receive services.

Specifically, the federal government will give states an MFP-enhanced FMAP rate for a period of one year for each person the state transitions from an institution to the community. Demonstration grants will be awarded from Jan. 1, 2007, through Sept. 30, 2011. CMS anticipates inviting proposals that illustrate the state's plan to "rebalance" its long-term support programs.

Beginning Jan. 1, 2007, home and community-based services can be offered as a state plan option without waivers. This significant step toward ending the "institutional bias" allows states to offer community-based services to individuals regardless of their need for institutional care. The fundamental shift in the program recognizes that not everyone wants or needs institutional care. Individuals will be provided individualized care plans based on an assessment of needs and may be offered the option of self-directing their care.

States will be able to establish the number of individuals served under the home and community-based state plan option and thus will have necessary control over the development and growth of their systems so they can ensure the success of the programs. At the same time, states will be able to tighten the standard for admission to the institutional and home and community-based waiver services without having to request an 1115 waiver and demonstrate budget neutrality.

This provision will require a simple state plan amendment. Interim guidance is being developed to assist states with submitting the plan amendment prior to the Jan. 1, 2007 effective date.

The DHHS secretary will develop a system of performance measures, including client satisfaction, and will make best practices available to states.

The demonstration projects regarding home and community-based alternatives to psychiatric residential treatment facilities for children support state efforts to keep families together by expanding the availability of home and community-based services to children under age 21 with serious emotional disturbances. These children would otherwise be removed from their families and placed in a psychiatric residential treatment facility to receive needed services.

In the past, states were unable to develop home and community-based waiver programs as an alternative to this institutional care because the law only permitted such waivers as an alternative to care in a hospital, nursing facility or intermediate care facility for the mentally retarded.

The secretary is now authorized to conduct five-year demonstration projects in up to 10 states during the period from FY 2007 through FY 2011. The proposal appropriates $218 million for the project period, and includes $1 million for required interim and final evaluations and reports. CMS anticipates inviting proposals in late summer 2006.

As of Jan. 1, 2007, states may choose to allow families (up to 300 percent of the federal poverty level) to buy Medicaid coverage for their disabled children. This flexibility allows states to help hard-working families have access to the critical supports Medicaid provides without additional financial strain. States can extend this critical lifeline to families struggling to make ends meet by charging a sliding-scale premium based on family income.

CMS will issue guidance regarding the implementation of these new coverage provisions near the end of 2006.

Promoting Personal Responsibility, Independence and Choice

The expansion of the State Long-term Care Partnership Program encourages individuals to take more responsibility in planning for and financing their future long-term care needs by purchasing long-term care insurance. The program allows an individual who purchased a qualified policy, but who eventually uses all its benefits, to apply for Medicaid without first having to spend most of his or her assets. Specifically, an individual will be able to qualify for Medicaid while retaining assets in the amount of insurance benefit payments made on their behalf under their insurance policy. These newly protected assets will also be exempted from Medicaid estate recovery provisions.

A National Clearinghouse demonstration (FY 2006–2010) will help individuals and their caregivers navigate the labyrinth of long-term support options available to them. The clearinghouse will empower individuals with information about which long-term care services Medicare and Medicaid do and do not cover, and will help them to plan ahead for long-term care, including the possible purchase of long-term care insurance.

States that are now ready to change their state plans by submitting an amendment should contact their regional office to begin a dialog to assist in submitting that amendment. States can offer a state plan benefit for self-directed personal care services without a waiver. In the past, self-directed personal care services were provided through waiver programs. With this new option, self-directed personal care services, including services provided by family members, can be provided under the state plan. States will also be able to provide items that increase independence or substitute for human assistance to the extent that expenditures would otherwise be made for such human assistance. Thus, states become allies with individuals and their families, friends and health care professionals in creating individualized plans and budgets that will give individuals control of their lives. The person's preferences, choices and abilities drive how they receive services.

Prior to Jan. 1, 2007, CMS will develop a user-friendly template to assist states in electing this option in their plans.

Sustaining the Integrity and Viability of the Medicaid Program

Various reforms of asset transfer rules give states new tools to maintain the integrity of the Medicaid program. The provisions curtail the growing practice of individuals artificially impoverishing themselves by sheltering their assets to become eligible for Medicaid. For example, the period during which states can look back to see if assets have been transferred is extended to 60 months. The rules about when the period begins during which Medicaid will not pay for a person's nursing home care because assets were transferred has been changed to make it harder to avoid such a penalty. Rules concerning how annuities are treated under Medicaid have been tightened.

Although most of these provisions are effective upon enactment, some states may need to enact legislation. All states will have to submit amendments to their state plans to implement at least some of the provisions. States that are now ready to change their state plan by submitting an amendment should contact their regional office to begin a dialog to assist in submitting that amendment.

A Modernized Medicaid System

A modernized Medicaid system will give states greater flexibility with reduced administrative burden. The DRA gives states additional flexibility to provide health insurance coverage among low-income but healthy children and families that reflect the 21st century dynamics in health insurance rather than being stuck in the assumptions that are now 40 years behind the times. With long-term care accounting for one-third of Medicaid expenditures, new options will also allow states to choose new ways to improve consumer direction and home and community-based programs for those individuals requiring long-term care.[2]

It is also clear that the long-term sustainability of the program requires changes outside Medicaid, including expanded access to affordable health insurance and greater preparation for one's own long-term care in retirement, and the DRA provides individuals the tools to do so.

Notes

[1] FY 2003 Medicaid Beneficiaries and Payment by Basis of Eligibility; Source CMS, MSIS State Summary, November 2, 2005.

[2] Justification of Estimates for Appropriations Committees, Fiscal Year 2006, Centers for Medicare and Medicaid Services, Department of Health and Human Services, 89.

About the Authors

Dennis G. Smith has been the director of the Center for Medicaid and State Operations (CMSO) since July 2001. Prior to his appointment as director, he served on the Bush-Cheney transition team as chief liaison to the U.S. Department of Health and Human Services. Smith has a master's degree in Public Administration from George Mason University.

Janet G. Freeze is a health insurance specialist in the Finance Systems and Budget Group at the Center for Medicaid and State Operations.

Susan N. Hill is a health insurance specialist in the Disabled and Elderly Health Programs Group at the Center for Medicaid and State Operations.

Lyn R. Killman is a health insurance specialist in the Division of Quality Evaluation and Health Outcomes at the Center for Medicaid and State Operations.

Table C
TOTAL MEDICAID ELIGIBLES WITH PERCENT CHANGE OVER TIME
AND PERCENT CHANGE IN CENSUS POPULATION 2000–2003

State or other jurisdiction	2000	2001	2002	2003	Percent change (2000–2003)	Percent change in census population (2000–2003)
Total	44,261,683	47,167,031	51,746,795	55,362,297	25%	3%
Alabama	665,767	780,431	845,125	893,115	34	1
Alaska	109,457	115,996	121,400	126,587	16	3
Arizona	683,223	808,377	1,053,602	1,278,894	87	9
Arkansas......................	504,297	550,668	608,017	675,552	34	2
California	8,063,710	8,495,216	9,336,447	10,047,498	25	5
Colorado	377,671	410,304	438,670	473,880	25	6
Connecticut	416,930	444,250	487,989	502,265	20	2
Delaware......................	124,327	133,078	147,197	156,721	26	4
Florida	2,237,597	2,462,162	2,691,502	2,841,305	27	6
Georgia	1,238,809	1,328,466	1,459,631	1,640,500	32	6
Hawaii.........................	191,137	189,928	195,684	420,690	120	3
Idaho...........................	150,817	172,348	196,406	208,748	38	6
Illinois.........................	1,736,185	1,796,811	2,076,146	2,177,724	25	2
Indiana........................	755,502	825,583	884,942	945,267	25	2
Iowa	316,425	331,025	358,708	378,708	20	1
Kansas	263,440	281,058	305,110	325,177	23	1
Kentucky	709,168	747,127	769,826	810,159	14	2
Louisiana	827,856	886,819	990,286	1,054,455	27	1
Maine..........................	208,158	277,843	346,449	378,346	82	3
Maryland.....................	720,877	704,625	752,065	825,493	15	4
Massachusetts..............	1,102,790	1,124,833	1,204,312	1,193,533	8	1
Michigan......................	1,363,060	1,430,543	1,527,627	1,572,356	15	1
Minnesota	594,452	658,199	680,627	730,195	23	3
Mississippi	595,824	681,213	707,986	730,995	23	1
Missouri.......................	991,428	1,032,316	1,098,525	1,157,231	17	2
Montana	97,176	101,970	106,229	110,549	14	2
Nebraska......................	238,883	249,721	266,245	269,331	13	2
Nevada	158,526	168,069	203,251	236,211	49	12
New Hampshire............	110,154	108,561	115,517	129,685	18	4
New Jersey...................	855,630	923,309	982,676	974,601	14	3
New Mexico	398,497	423,542	462,878	492,830	24	3
New York	3,401,448	3,548,626	4,387,453	4,583,362	35	1
North Carolina.............	1,226,986	1,375,846	1,389,445	1,450,218	18	5
North Dakota................	62,222	64,968	71,619	76,677	23	-1
Ohio	1,420,385	1,690,520	1,754,379	1,938,785	36	1
Oklahoma	584,620	631,995	677,788	666,529	14	2
Oregon	560,731	594,666	637,140	625,704	12	4
Pennsylvania	1,767,856	1,647,439	1,710,999	1,787,059	1	1
Rhode Island	182,149	193,885	204,789	211,136	16	3
South Carolina	772,043	871,642	895,963	992,090	29	3
South Dakota...............	98,740	106,254	113,925	119,693	21	1
Tennessee	1,535,121	1,603,304	1,700,384	1,651,486	8	3
Texas	2,714,736	2,884,707	3,202,171	3,661,162	35	6
Utah	203,751	214,620	233,156	278,232	37	5
Vermont	147,720	152,099	156,958	159,701	8	2
Virginia.......................	681,292	700,710	727,784	736,672	8	4
Washington..................	917,383	1,005,424	1,104,813	1,160,614	27	4
West Virginia...............	354,326	351,489	362,264	366,787	4	0
Wisconsin.....................	619,128	673,537	776,638	903,902	46	2
Wyoming......................	52,470	58,013	69,802	76,786	46	2
Dist. of Columbia	150,802	152,596	151,340	157,101	4	-3

Sources: MSIS State Summary Data FY 2000; created Nov. 8, 2005. The data in the column "Percent change in census population" was derived from the U.S. Census Bureau's "Annual Estimates of the Population for the United States and State, and for Puerto Rico: April 1, 2000 to July 1, 2005

(NST-EST2005-01)" (available on the Web at *http://www.census.gov/popest/states/NST-ann-est.html*). The data for the column "Percent change in census population (2000–2003)" was derived from MSIS State Summary data for FY 2000–2003.

Table D
FY 2003 MEDICAID BENEFICIARIES AND PAYMENT BY BASIS OF ELIGIBILITY

State or other jurisdiction	All BOE		Aged				Blind/disabled				All children (a)			
	Total Medicaid paid amount	Number of beneficiaries	Medicaid paid amount	Number of benes.	Percent of Medicaid payments	Percent of benes.	Medicaid paid amount	Number of benes.	Percent of Medicaid payments	Percent of benes.	Medicaid paid amount	Number of benes.	Percent of Medicaid payments	Percent of benes.
Alabama	$3,471,319,724	780,617	$739,295,461	60,923	21%	8%	$1,195,700,995	176,058	34%	23%	$698,456,500	421,546	20%	54%
Alaska	835,515,131	116,211	125,219,729	6,373	15	5	298,852,035	12,294	36	11	276,972,989	67,506	33	58
Arizona	3,285,364,385	1,014,813	497,680,316	38,197	15	4	1,223,565,495	105,387	37	10	857,742,556	567,484	26	56
Arkansas	2,211,952,987	702,064	554,988,891	45,125	25	6	998,137,559	107,672	45	15	479,808,573	324,422	22	46
California	25,812,495,569	9,319,148	5,335,095,155	645,049	21	7	11,667,891,084	1,011,069	45	11	4,743,242,067	3,381,832	18	36
Colorado	2,268,794,322	459,207	600,883,857	42,746	28	9	916,590,485	61,625	40	13	416,086,478	247,649	18	54
Connecticut	3,359,497,127	496,680	1,291,738,558	52,076	39	10	1,282,135,823	57,208	38	12	516,634,604	259,965	15	52
Delaware	750,252,370	149,864	170,533,927	8,676	23	6	288,040,472	17,604	38	12	132,724,356	66,434	18	44
Florida	11,104,376,050	2,743,368	2,098,204,755	223,315	19	8	5,513,050,645	464,796	50	17	1,696,540,186	1,353,721	15	49
Georgia	5,357,550,685	1,732,120	1,048,884,651	100,703	20	6	1,999,829,241	233,042	37	13	1,226,689,364	872,626	23	50
Hawaii	1,506,926,856	417,790	402,366,777	36,478	27	9	463,858,415	44,483	31	11	276,841,851	189,746	18	45
Idaho	867,160,476	193,302	187,402,733	12,038	22	6	421,046,250	26,474	49	14	164,918,266	119,851	19	62
Illinois	9,391,357,857	1,830,233	1,252,639,010	109,691	13	6	4,000,108,210	274,824	43	15	1,594,387,370	1,002,394	17	55
Indiana	3,950,802,203	895,973	999,618,031	66,237	25	7	1,698,587,979	113,730	43	13	786,562,094	522,004	20	58
Iowa	1,996,207,221	361,760	626,207,889	35,604	31	10	850,991,665	58,901	43	16	306,611,511	182,537	15	50
Kansas	1,614,744,381	316,411	458,521,303	28,080	28	9	730,035,966	48,388	45	15	276,378,896	168,399	17	53
Kentucky	3,557,820,183	847,943	716,048,775	58,738	20	9	1,746,970,969	205,698	49	24	730,505,211	389,419	21	46
Louisiana	3,614,909,979	995,362	835,477,317	48,485	23	8	1,677,725,917	161,260	46	16	581,817,335	544,023	16	55
Maine	2,074,246,677	307,279	377,887,425	54,971	18	18	904,286,804	53,556	44	17	457,882,561	110,152	22	26
Maryland	4,398,301,341	725,820	910,379,388	48,083	21	7	2,137,761,270	114,781	49	16	871,539,125	435,124	20	60
Massachusetts	6,391,977,781	1,042,123	1,762,043,506	90,463	28	9	3,257,283,641	240,532	51	23	766,589,795	394,477	12	38
Michigan	6,479,009,763	1,589,501	1,315,793,772	91,594	20	6	3,093,142,126	287,226	48	18	913,654,885	842,763	14	53
Minnesota	4,701,612,364	667,500	1,239,733,121	61,531	26	9	2,164,975,399	92,824	46	14	836,485,867	344,777	18	52
Mississippi	2,569,776,154	717,435	642,643,840	70,229	25	10	1,181,364,075	154,752	46	22	486,999,852	352,056	19	49
Missouri	4,406,852,103	1,081,496	1,143,672,894	87,687	26	8	1,791,293,565	148,423	41	14	969,090,103	583,045	22	54
Montana	536,372,686	110,403	140,512,245	8,865	26	8	196,134,377	16,717	37	15	111,683,798	54,570	21	49
Nebraska	1,282,568,106	253,728	354,328,273	21,241	28	8	409,351,439	29,070	32	11	290,956,462	151,946	23	60
Nevada	881,323,024	220,417	160,250,795	15,104	18	7	376,540,325	28,236	43	13	179,208,293	109,735	20	50
New Hampshire	786,014,720	112,044	250,292,571	11,823	32	11	302,832,461	15,015	39	13	182,891,786	66,745	23	60
New Jersey	6,029,601,253	949,741	1,614,914,219	86,401	37	9	3,013,580,661	163,495	50	17	843,221,307	461,779	14	49
New Mexico	2,033,470,195	452,120	270,457,015	21,122	13	5	807,915,064	52,675	40	12	578,921,825	282,420	28	62
New York	35,206,760,472	4,449,939	9,295,916,378	352,338	26	8	16,674,169,265	652,536	47	15	3,823,062,476	1,721,575	11	39
North Carolina	6,521,288,060	1,416,912	1,687,387,669	149,824	26	11	2,832,620,867	226,547	43	16	1,157,105,321	722,725	18	51
North Dakota	444,803,367	76,754	170,673,120	8,495	38	11	172,593,901	8,998	39	12	56,749,891	33,817	13	44
Ohio	10,235,239,405	1,778,325	3,143,570,019	135,291	31	8	4,633,554,067	282,529	45	16	1,407,772,769	927,489	14	52
Oklahoma	2,128,524,455	625,875	574,489,081	52,330	27	8	830,691,498	75,720	39	12	561,507,335	400,520	26	64
Oregon	2,115,608,505	598,110	480,576,701	42,211	23	7	756,167,570	70,807	36	12	422,801,466	246,234	20	41
Pennsylvania	9,450,026,724	1,721,707	3,143,134,958	178,460	33	10	3,989,630,470	385,363	42	22	1,531,165,495	815,581	16	47
Rhode Island	1,338,212,632	201,875	343,257,642	16,338	26	8	655,631,139	36,362	49	18	208,275,147	92,591	16	46
South Carolina	3,541,714,949	861,216	654,374,273	96,507	18	11	1,240,501,808	120,897	34	14	703,876,410	443,119	19	51

See footnotes at end of table.

FY 2003 MEDICAID BENEFICIARIES AND PAYMENT BY BASIS OF ELIGIBILITY — Continued

State or other jurisdiction	All BOE		Aged				Blind/disabled				All children (a)			
	Total Medicaid paid amount	Number of beneficiaries	Medicaid paid amount	Number of benes.	Percent of Medicaid payments	Percent of benes.	Medicaid paid amount	Number of benes.	Percent of Medicaid payments	Percent of benes.	Medicaid paid amount	Number of benes.	Percent of Medicaid payments	Percent of benes.
South Dakota............	541,910,489	123,590	131,033,456	10,275	24	8	227,974,433	16,854	42	14	123,880,176	73,151	23	59
Tennessee................	5,459,293,763	1,729,589	885,130,831	88,908	16	5	2,354,835,526	326,168	43	19	842,300,736	707,819	15	41
Texas	12,524,526,333	3,339,796	3,114,427,406	271,486	25	8	4,471,325,415	344,265	36	10	3,327,501,027	2,065,998	27	62
Utah	1,200,789,944	285,370	133,897,319	11,623	11	4	415,047,995	28,449	35	10	243,015,672	149,131	20	52
Vermont	641,738,944	154,664	151,820,352	17,789	24	12	251,771,276	18,933	39	12	144,491,473	64,278	23	42
Virginia...................	3,180,990,089	709,488	884,797,753	80,232	28	11	1,446,657,396	124,473	45	18	564,603,598	375,486	18	53
Washington..............	4,524,032,645	1,077,070	766,408,811	71,065	17	7	1,248,440,754	139,354	28	13	652,109,072	584,219	14	54
West Virginia............	1,829,967,627	373,154	390,586,860	27,313	21	7	833,680,609	87,394	46	23	277,036,943	164,001	15	44
Wisconsin................	3,921,363,613	829,287	1,089,237,882	111,609	28	13	1,908,437,926	133,936	49	16	419,815,535	351,663	11	42
Wyoming.................	324,630,777	66,605	71,534,687	4,276	22	6	142,746,652	7,487	44	11	71,690,428	39,799	22	60
Dist. of Columbia	1,199,837,436	158,179	212,921,941	8,581	18	5	546,642,885	25,820	46	16	217,922,929	75,025	18	47
Total........................	233,959,453,418	52,180,158	55,454,893,338	4,058,419	24	8	102,242,701,831	7,690,707	44	15	40,008,730,065	24,925,568	17	48

See footnotes at end of table.

FY 2003 MEDICAID BENEFICIARIES AND PAYMENT BY BASIS OF ELIGIBILITY — Continued

State or other jurisdiction	All adults				Unknown				BCCA women			
	Medicaid paid amount	Number of benes.	Percent of Medicaid payments	Percent of benes.	Medicaid paid amount	Number of benes.	Percent of Medicaid payments	Percent of benes.	Medicaid paid amount	Number of benes.	Percent of Medicaid payments	Percent of benes.
Alabama	$148,033,794	99,551	4%	13%	$687,367,071	22,276	20%	3%	$2,465,903	263	0.07%	0.03%
Alaska	122,653,258	23,785	15	20	10,701,854	6,164	1	5	1,115,266	89	0.13	0.08
Arizona	649,914,748	257,372	20	25	56,461,270	46,373	2	5	0		0.00	0.00
Arkansas	139,935,542	110,869	6	16	39,082,422	113,976	2	16	0		0.00	0.00
California	3,565,542,160	3,224,684	14	35	469,395,862	1,052,228	2	11	31,329,241	4,286	0.12	0.05
Colorado	242,826,730	93,424	11	20	90,310,302	13,639	4	3	2,096,470	124	0.09	0.03
Connecticut	245,994,685	103,737	7	21	15,396,197	23,568	0	5	1,597,260	126	0.05	0.03
Delaware	153,690,084	52,733	20	35	4,972,423	4,372	1	3	291,108	45	0.04	0.03
Florida	981,629,106	474,929	9	17	813,214,744	226,445	7	8	1,736,614	162	0.02	0.01
Georgia	740,880,454	250,337	14	14	319,129,451	273,490	6	16	22,137,497	1,922	0.41	0.11
Hawaii	297,843,316	131,247	20	31	65,874,836	15,988	4	4	141,664	28	0.01	0.01
Idaho	86,521,744	26,740	10	10	7,271,483	8,199	1	4	0		0.00	0.00
Illinois	885,605,655	316,249	9	17	1,655,300,022	126,695	18	7	3,317,590	380	0.04	0.02
Indiana	376,989,086	150,525	10	17	87,028,843	43,201	2	5	2,016,170	276	0.05	0.03
Iowa	177,351,029	69,802	9	19	35,045,127	14,916	2	4	0		0.00	0.00
Kansas	113,609,400	48,485	7	15	35,337,608	22,984	2	7	861,208	75	0.05	0.02
Kentucky	320,548,779	117,743	9	14	42,106,149	76,098	1	9	1,640,300	247	0.05	0.03
Louisiana	315,908,545	108,501	9	11	199,344,895	36,826	6	10	4,635,970	267	0.30	0.03
Maine	319,932,497	81,567	15	27	12,409,441	7,101	1	2	1,847,949	112	0.09	0.04
Maryland	437,756,072	108,000	10	15	40,865,486	19,832	1	3	0		0.00	0.00
Massachusetts	555,141,537	256,170	9	25	50,919,302	60,481	1	6	0		0.00	0.00
Michigan	558,937,423	261,421	9	16	597,501,557	106,497	9	7	0		0.00	0.00
Minnesota	413,209,037	149,759	9	22	46,342,212	18,401	1	3	866,728	208	0.02	0.03
Mississippi	243,786,672	83,764	9	12	14,981,715	56,634	1	8	0		0.00	0.00
Missouri	474,910,578	235,399	11	22	27,884,963	26,942	1	2	0		0.00	0.00
Montana	66,741,500	21,051	12	19	20,415,278	9,098	4	8	885,488	102	0.17	0.09
Nebraska	111,667,617	43,604	9	17	114,958,770	7,727	9	3	1,305,545	140	0.10	0.06
Nevada	108,713,491	45,935	12	21	56,610,120	21,407	6	10	0		0.00	0.00
New Hampshire	47,128,604	14,811	6	13	2,869,328	3,450	0	3	0		0.00	0.00
New Jersey	464,093,388	187,607	8	20	91,163,562	50,321	2	5	2,628,116	138	0.04	0.01
New Mexico	235,979,233	83,187	12	18	138,259,653	12,530	7	3	1,937,405	186	0.10	0.04
New York	4,968,658,742	1,256,818	14	28	442,916,018	466,389	1	10	2,037,593	283	0.01	0.01
North Carolina	794,579,673	256,610	12	18	49,594,230	61,206	1	4	0		0.00	0.00
North Dakota	36,898,173	17,453	8	23	7,888,282	7,991	2	10	0		0.00	0.00
Ohio	1,022,172,178	378,325	10	21	28,170,372	54,691	0	3	0		0.00	0.00
Oklahoma	147,233,558	82,552	7	13	14,602,983	14,753	1	2			0.00	0.00
Oregon	434,141,895	206,996	21	35	20,520,368	31,738	1	5	1,400,505	124	0.07	0.02
Pennsylvania	746,947,001	271,033	8	16	34,432,405	70,699	0	4	4,716,395	571	0.05	0.03
Rhode Island	123,026,853	51,497	9	26	6,700,535	4,835	1	2	1,321,316	252	0.10	0.12
South Carolina	351,583,405	182,960	10	21	589,527,246	17,600	19	2	1,851,807	133	0.05	0.02

See footnotes at end of table.

FY 2003 MEDICAID BENEFICIARIES AND PAYMENT BY BASIS OF ELIGIBILITY — Continued

State or other jurisdiction	All adults				Unknown				BCCA women			
	Medicaid paid amount	Number of benes.	Percent of Medicaid payments	Percent of benes.	Medicaid paid amount	Number of benes.	Percent of Medicaid payments	Percent of benes.	Medicaid paid amount	Number of benes.	Percent of Medicaid payments	Percent of benes.
South Dakota..........	50,029,397	19,155	9	15	8,641,374	4,128	2	3	357,653	26	0.07	0.02
Tennessee..............	1,339,391,041	496,185	25	29	37,635,629	110,508	1	6	0		0.00	0.00
Texas....................	1,426,401,554	513,867	11	15	179,520,437	143,748	1	4	5,350,494	432	0.04	0.01
Utah.....................	116,448,694	71,685	10	25	2,905,444,766	24,276	24	9	1,835,041	206	0.15	0.07
Vermont................	88,362,067	47,451	14	31	5,010,438	6,182	1	4	283,338	31	0.04	0.02
Virginia.................	227,137,553	89,330	7	13	55,192,174	39,757	2	6	2,601,615	210	0.08	0.03
Washington............	575,143,956	249,200	13	23	1,281,930,052	33,232	28	3	0		0.00	0.00
West Virginia..........	131,452,245	54,999	7	15	195,062,251	39,079	11	10	2,148,719	368	0.12	0.10
Wisconsin..............	484,014,670	215,614	12	26	18,293,816	16,313	0	2	1,563,784	152	0.04	0.02
Wyoming...............	38,037,078	11,398	12	17	621,932	3,645	0	5	0		0.00	0.00
Dist. of Columbia	125,424,657	35,380	10	22	96,925,024	13,373	8	8	0		0.00	0.00
Total.....................	26,830,554,154	11,741,458	11	23	9,312,252,278	3,752,002	4	7	110,321,752	11,964	0.05	0.02

Source: MSIS State Summary Data, created Nov. 15, 2005.
Key:
(a) All children is inclusive of foster children.

Table E
FY 2003 MEDICAID PER CAPITA EXPENDITURES FOR ELIGIBLES AND BENEFICIARIES BY BASIS OF ELIGIBILITY

State or other jurisdiction	All BOE		Aged		Blind/disabled		Children	
	Per capita eligibles	Per capita beneficiaries	Per capita eligibles	Per capita beneficiaries	Per capita eligibles	Per capita beneficiaries	Per capita eligibles	Per capita beneficiaries
Total	$4,226	$4,484	$10,832	$13,664	$12,129	$13,294	$1,331	$1,462
Alabama	3,887	4,447	7,038	12,135	6,067	6,792	1,411	1,468
Alaska	6,660	7,190	18,336	19,684	22,980	24,309	3,346	3,924
Arizona	2,569	3,237	7,673	13,029	10,583	11,610	1,440	1,509
Arkansas	3,274	3,151	10,956	12,299	8,171	9,270	1,300	1,377
California	2,569	2,770	7,619	8,271	11,203	11,540	1,109	1,291
Colorado	4,788	4,941	12,348	14,057	13,867	14,874	1,089	1,144
Connecticut	6,689	6,764	20,385	24,920	20,856	22,412	1,890	1,957
Delaware	4,787	5,006	14,861	19,656	15,520	16,362	1,701	1,773
Florida	3,908	4,048	7,435	9,369	10,653	11,861	1,068	1,154
Georgia	3,266	3,093	7,528	10,416	7,324	8,581	1,239	1,337
Hawaii	3,582	3,605	10,083	11,030	9,511	10,428	1,382	1,421
Idaho	4,154	4,486	14,422	15,568	14,743	15,904	1,179	1,331
Illinois	4,312	5,131	3,763	11,420	13,034	14,555	1,211	1,402
Indiana	4,180	4,410	12,377	15,092	12,834	14,935	1,339	1,437
Iowa	5,271	5,518	15,107	17,588	13,506	14,448	1,357	1,483
Kansas	4,966	5,103	14,048	16,329	13,812	15,087	1,187	1,301
Kentucky	4,392	4,196	9,953	12,191	7,910	8,493	1,630	1,658
Louisiana	3,428	3,632	7,605	9,889	9,148	10,404	881	1,034
Maine	5,482	6,750	5,106	6,897	9,054	16,885	3,125	3,275
Maryland	5,328	6,060	13,997	18,933	17,035	18,625	1,770	1,851
Massachusetts	5,356	6,134	15,052	19,478	12,727	13,542	1,591	1,941
Michigan	4,121	4,076	12,502	14,366	10,240	10,769	976	1,026
Minnesota	6,439	7,044	17,353	20,148	21,550	23,323	2,113	2,275
Mississippi	3,515	3,582	8,470	9,151	7,109	7,634	1,208	1,364
Missouri	3,808	4,075	11,412	13,043	10,673	12,069	1,350	1,446
Montana	4,852	4,858	14,165	15,850	10,793	11,733	1,537	1,667
Nebraska	4,762	5,055	15,155	16,681	13,410	14,082	1,378	1,492
Nevada	3,731	3,998	7,501	10,610	10,803	13,335	1,075	1,241
New Hampshire	6,061	7,015	17,472	21,170	17,323	20,169	1,941	2,322
New Jersey	6,187	6,349	14,466	18,691	16,477	18,432	1,332	1,381
New Mexico	4,126	4,498	11,158	12,805	14,298	15,338	1,803	1,936
New York	7,681	7,912	23,061	26,384	23,838	25,553	1,737	2,049
North Carolina	4,497	4,602	9,480	11,262	11,554	12,503	1,400	1,455
North Dakota	5,801	5,795	16,977	20,091	17,160	19,181	1,208	1,319
Ohio	5,279	5,756	21,077	23,236	14,498	16,400	1,302	1,451
Oklahoma	3,193	3,401	9,277	10,978	9,482	10,971	1,117	1,185
Oregon	3,381	3,537	9,888	11,385	10,216	10,679	1,313	1,411
Pennsylvania	5,288	5,489	14,482	17,613	9,752	10,353	1,656	1,745
Rhode Island	6,338	6,629	16,540	21,010	16,028	18,031	1,474	1,516
South Carolina	3,671	4,229	4,889	6,781	9,242	10,261	1,291	1,444

See footnotes at end of table.

FY 2003 MEDICAID PER CAPITA EXPENDITURES FOR ELIGIBLES AND BENEFICIARIES BY BASIS OF ELIGIBILITY — Continued

State or other jurisdiction	All BOE		Aged		Blind/disabled		Children	
	Per capita eligibles	Per capita beneficiaries	Per capita eligibles	Per capita beneficiaries	Per capita eligibles	Per capita beneficiaries	Per capita eligibles	Per capita beneficiaries
South Dakota..........	4,528	4,385	12,741	12,753	13,522	13,526	1,585	1,589
Tennessee..............	3,306	3,156	9,367	9,956	7,131	7,220	1,030	1,054
Texas	3,421	3,750	7,840	11,472	10,580	12,988	1,387	1,512
Utah	4,316	4,208	10,290	11,520	13,892	14,589	1,328	1,361
Vermont	4,018	4,149	7,806	8,535	12,743	13,298	1,622	1,743
Virginia.................	4,318	4,484	9,097	11,028	10,529	11,622	1,251	1,347
Washington...........	3,898	4,200	9,369	10,785	8,212	8,959	1,029	1,090
West Virginia.........	4,989	4,904	13,021	14,300	8,648	9,539	1,245	1,360
Wisconsin..............	4,338	4,729	8,484	9,759	13,149	14,249	972	1,076
Wyoming...............	4,228	4,374	13,135	16,729	16,455	19,066	1,356	1,605
Dist. of Columbia	7,637	7,585	19,998	24,813	18,419	21,171	1,991	2,079

See footnotes at end of table.

FY 2003 MEDICAID PER CAPITA EXPENDITURES FOR ELIGIBLES AND BENEFICIARIES BY BASIS OF ELIGIBILITY — Continued

State or other jurisdiction	Adults		Foster care children		BOE unknown		BCCA women	
	Per capita eligibles	Per capita beneficiaries	Per capita eligibles	Per capita beneficiaries	Per capita eligibles	Per capita beneficiaries	Per capita eligibles	Per capita beneficiaries
Total	$1,861	$2,285	$5,191	$5,680	$8,233,645	$2,482	$8,268	$9,221
Alabama	972	1,487	13,171	13,477		30,857	8,387	9,376
Alaska	4,443	5,157	9,229	10,160		1,736	11,153	12,531
Arizona	1,290	2,525	1,647	1,647		1,218		
Arkansas	879	1,262	6,714	6,889	953,230	343	6,538	7,310
California	814	1,106	3,633	3,881	78,232,644	446		
Colorado	2,448	2,599	8,494	8,735	799,206	6,621	15,882	16,907
Connecticut	2,281	2,371	3,084	3,172		653	12,287	12,677
Delaware	2,675	2,914	9,715	9,804		1,137	6,065	6,469
Florida	1,697	2,067	3,995	4,355		3,591	9,924	10,720
Georgia	2,607	2,960	4,061	4,544	319,129,451	1,167	10,757	11,518
Hawaii	2,177	2,269	1,933	1,991		4,120	4,885	5,059
Idaho	2,702	3,236	3,593	3,865	1,829,857	887		
Illinois	2,359	2,800	3,590	4,219		13,065	8,052	8,731
Indiana	2,206	2,504	4,006	4,532		2,015	6,504	7,305
Iowa	2,358	2,541	4,699	4,934		2,349		
Kansas	2,058	2,343	5,746	6,248		1,537	10,252	11,483
Kentucky	2,651	2,722	9,710	10,057		553	6,382	6,641
Louisiana	2,572	2,912	2,981	3,291		2,059	14,265	17,363
Maine	3,604	3,922	28,018	30,337		1,748	15,931	16,500
Maryland	2,429	4,053	5,590	5,778	40,865,486	2,061		
Massachusetts	1,636	2,167	2,890	3,560		842		
Michigan	1,993	2,138	2,235	2,265	3,643,302	5,611		
Minnesota	2,211	2,759	7,848	8,415		2,518	3,439	4,167
Mississippi	2,673	2,910	3,216	3,697	325,689	265		
Missouri	1,794	2,017	6,262	6,680		1,035		
Montana	2,877	3,170	6,918	7,444		2,244	7,441	8,681
Nebraska	2,225	2,561	7,336	7,935	226,743	14,878	7,680	9,325
Nevada	2,058	2,367	8,139	10,174	11,322,024	2,644		
New Hampshire	2,606	3,182	12,351	13,257		832	18,508	19,044
New Jersey	2,345	2,474	9,629	11,476		1,812		
New Mexico	2,179	2,837	10,033	11,844	138,259,653	11,034	9,591	10,416
New York	3,419	3,953	5,984	6,665		950	5,507	7,200
North Carolina	2,884	2,096	7,580	8,052		810		
North Dakota	1,879	2,114	7,701	8,387		987		
Ohio	2,365	2,702	2,840	3,627		515		
Oklahoma	1,609	1,784	6,402	7,065		990	9,933	11,294
Oregon	1,820	2,097	6,174	6,481	102,091	647	6,374	8,260
Pennsylvania	2,491	2,756	3,768	4,047		487	4,876	5,243
Rhode Island	2,302	2,389	13,690	15,471		1,386		
South Carolina	1,539	1,922	8,151	8,980		39,178	13,322	13,923

See footnotes at end of table.

FY 2003 MEDICAID PER CAPITA EXPENDITURES FOR ELIGIBLES AND BENEFICIARIES BY BASIS OF ELIGIBILITY — Continued

State or other jurisdiction	Adults		Foster care children		BOE unknown		BCCA women	
	Per capita eligibles	Per capita beneficiaries	Per capita eligibles	Per capita beneficiaries	Per capita eligibles	Per capita beneficiaries	Per capita eligibles	Per capita beneficiaries
South Dakota.............	2,603	2,611	5,306	5,326	8,641,374	2,093	13,756	13,756
Tennessee................	2,665	2,699	7,228	7,336	7,527,126	341		
Texas......................	2,420	2,776	6,884	7,334		1,249	11,312	12,385
Utah	1,413	1,624	7,096	7,150		11,968	8,738	8,908
Vermont..................	1,716	1,862	14,066	14,497		810	7,265	9,140
Virginia...................	2,354	2,543	5,473	6,280	55,192,174	1,388	11,614	12,389
Washington..............	1,881	2,308	1,807	2,185	640,965,026	38,575		
West Virginia...........	2,166	2,390	9,271	10,363		4,991	5,481	5,839
Wisconsin................	2,014	2,245	3,369	3,838		1,121	9,092	10,288
Wyoming.................	2,468	3,337	4,444	5,620		171		
Dist. of Columbia	3,280	3,545	14,865	16,212		7,248		

Source: MSIS State Summary Data FY 2003, created Oct. 27, 2005.

Table F
FY 2003 MEDICAID ELIGIBLES, BENEFICIARIES AND PAYMENTS BY BASIS OF ELIGIBILITY

State or other jurisdiction	All BOE			Aged			Blind/disabled			Children		
	Eligibles	Beneficiaries	Medicaid payments	Eligibles	Beneficiaries	Medicaid payments	Eligibles	Beneficiaries	Medicaid payments	Eligibles	Beneficiaries	Medicaid payments
Total	55,362,297	52,180,158	$233,959,453,418	5,119,618	4,058,419	$55,454,893,338	8,429,855	7,690,707	$102,242,701,831	26,456,564	24,079,881	$35,205,148,359
Alabama	893,115	780,617	3,471,319,724	105,048	60,923	739,295,461	197,087	176,058	1,195,700,995	431,577	414,916	609,105,175
Alaska	126,587	116,211	835,515,131	6,829	6,373	125,219,729	13,005	12,294	298,852,035	76,918	65,574	257,343,172
Arizona	1,278,894	1,014,813	3,285,364,385	64,862	38,197	497,680,316	115,615	105,387	1,223,565,495	585,992	559,010	843,788,427
Arkansas	675,552	702,064	2,211,952,987	50,654	45,125	554,988,891	122,160	107,672	998,137,559	337,428	318,447	438,649,280
California	10,047,498	9,319,148	25,812,495,569	700,243	645,249	5,335,095,155	1,041,513	1,011,069	11,667,891,084	3,764,945	3,235,980	4,177,156,299
Colorado	473,880	459,207	2,268,794,322	48,662	42,746	600,883,857	66,101	61,625	916,590,485	241,678	230,157	263,296,667
Connecticut	502,265	496,680	3,359,497,127	63,663	52,076	1,297,738,558	61,476	57,208	1,282,135,823	262,458	253,456	498,990,581
Delaware	156,721	149,864	750,252,370	11,475	8,676	170,533,927	18,559	17,604	288,040,472	67,300	64,572	114,469,125
Florida	2,841,305	2,743,368	11,104,376,050	282,213	223,315	2,098,204,755	517,489	464,796	5,513,050,645	1,417,109	1,311,792	1,513,946,575
Georgia	1,640,500	1,732,120	5,357,550,658	139,339	100,703	1,048,884,651	273,064	233,042	1,999,829,241	920,863	853,845	1,141,356,199
Hawaii	420,690	417,970	1,506,926,856	39,904	36,478	402,366,777	48,770	44,483	463,858,412	182,136	177,139	251,738,814
Idaho	208,748	193,302	867,160,476	12,994	12,038	187,402,733	28,560	26,474	421,046,250	132,879	117,722	156,690,729
Illinois	2,177,724	1,830,233	9,391,357,857	332,849	109,691	1,252,639,010	306,897	274,824	4,000,108,210	1,083,466	935,457	1,311,959,895
Indiana	945,267	895,973	3,950,802,203	80,763	66,237	999,618,031	132,350	113,730	1,698,587,979	547,706	510,267	733,373,467
Iowa	378,708	361,760	1,996,207,221	41,451	35,604	626,207,889	63,008	58,901	850,991,665	188,110	172,142	255,317,704
Kansas	325,177	316,411	1,614,744,381	32,639	28,080	458,521,303	52,856	48,388	730,035,966	171,792	156,806	203,945,216
Kentucky	810,159	847,943	3,557,820,183	71,942	58,738	716,048,775	220,868	205,698	1,746,970,969	385,715	379,308	628,822,054
Louisiana	1,054,455	995,362	3,614,909,979	109,866	84,485	835,477,317	183,396	161,260	1,677,725,917	628,621	535,484	553,716,835
Maine	378,346	307,229	2,074,246,677	74,004	54,791	377,887,425	99,876	53,556	904,286,804	111,704	106,564	349,034,445
Maryland	825,493	725,820	4,398,301,341	65,039	48,083	910,379,388	125,492	114,781	2,137,761,270	437,377	418,297	774,315,231
Massachusetts	1,193,533	1,042,123	6,391,977,781	117,067	90,463	1,762,043,506	255,925	240,532	3,257,283,641	480,537	393,934	764,656,473
Michigan	1,572,356	1,589,501	6,479,029,769	105,249	91,594	1,315,793,772	302,074	287,226	3,093,142,126	844,079	802,945	823,454,423
Minnesota	730,195	667,500	4,701,612,364	71,442	61,531	1,239,733,121	100,461	92,824	2,164,975,399	362,023	336,290	765,070,679
Mississippi	730,995	717,435	2,569,776,154	75,869	70,229	642,643,840	166,169	154,752	1,181,364,075	394,359	349,136	476,204,347
Missouri	1,157,231	1,081,496	4,406,852,103	100,220	87,687	1,143,672,894	167,827	148,423	1,791,293,565	598,712	558,929	807,993,897
Montana	110,549	110,403	536,372,686	9,920	8,865	140,512,245	18,172	16,717	196,134,377	55,283	50,985	84,995,702
Nebraska	269,331	253,728	1,282,568,106	23,380	21,241	354,328,273	30,525	29,070	409,351,439	153,772	141,978	211,857,601
Nevada	236,211	220,417	881,323,024	21,364	15,104	160,250,795	34,855	28,236	376,540,325	121,157	104,922	130,238,571
New Hampshire	129,685	112,044	786,014,720	14,325	11,823	250,292,571	17,482	15,015	302,832,431	77,099	64,437	149,642,070
New Jersey	974,601	949,741	6,029,601,253	111,637	96,401	1,614,914,219	182,900	163,495	3,013,580,661	457,769	441,440	609,817,002
New Mexico	492,830	452,120	2,033,470,195	24,239	21,122	270,457,015	56,505	52,675	807,915,064	299,696	279,168	540,404,002
New York	4,586,362	4,449,939	35,206,760,472	403,101	352,338	9,295,916,378	699,479	652,536	16,674,169,265	1,955,958	1,657,628	3,396,858,398
North Carolina	1,450,218	1,416,912	6,521,288,060	177,992	149,824	167,387,669	245,171	226,547	2,832,620,867	734,480	706,682	1,027,935,373
North Dakota	76,677	76,754	444,803,367	10,053	8,495	170,673,120	10,058	8,998	172,593,901	35,054	32,098	42,332,794
Ohio	1,938,785	1,778,325	10,235,239,405	149,145	135,291	3,143,570,019	319,592	282,529	4,633,554,067	1,001,316	898,937	1,304,201,683
Oklahoma	666,529	625,875	2,128,524,455	61,923	52,330	574,489,081	87,603	75,720	830,691,498	409,229	385,763	457,248,295
Oregon	625,704	598,110	2,115,608,505	48,604	42,211	480,576,701	74,019	70,807	756,164,570	248,606	231,373	326,486,376
Pennsylvania	1,787,059	1,721,707	9,450,026,724	217,044	178,460	3,143,134,958	409,097	385,363	3,989,630,470	809,934	768,661	1,341,287,830
Rhode Island	211,136	201,875	1,338,212,632	20,753	16,338	343,257,642	40,906	36,362	655,631,139	90,271	87,727	133,022,394
South Carolina	992,090	861,216	3,641,714,949	133,834	96,507	654,374,273	134,227	120,897	1,240,501,808	485,999	434,612	627,484,689

See footnotes at end of table.

FY 2003 MEDICAID ELIGIBLES, BENEFICIARIES AND PAYMENTS BY BASIS OF ELIGIBILITY — Continued

State or other jurisdiction	All BOE			Aged			Blind/disabled			Children		
	Eligibles	Beneficiaries	Medicaid payments	Eligibles	Beneficiaries	Medicaid payments	Eligibles	Beneficiaries	Medicaid payments	Eligibles	Beneficiaries	Medicaid payments
South Dakota..........	119,693	123,590	541,910,489	10,284	10,275	131,033,456	16,859	16,854	227,974,433	71,246	71,098	112,945,430
Tennessee.............	1,651,486	1,729,589	5,459,293,763	94,493	88,908	885,130,831	330,246	326,168	2,354,835,526	708,468	692,450	729,551,275
Texas...................	3,661,162	3,339,796	12,524,526,333	397,251	271,486	3,114,427,406	422,619	344,265	4,471,325,415	2,214,113	2,030,929	3,070,293,430
Utah	278,232	285,370	1,200,789,487	13,012	11,623	133,897,319	29,877	28,449	415,047,995	145,734	142,218	193,585,813
Vermont	159,701	154,664	641,738,944	19,449	17,789	151,820,352	19,757	18,933	251,771,276	66,343	61,735	107,624,807
Virginia.................	736,672	709,488	3,180,990,089	97,260	80,232	884,797,753	137,395	124,473	1,466,657,396	391,602	363,561	489,713,489
Washington............	1,160,614	1,077,070	4,524,032,645	81,800	71,065	766,408,811	152,019	139,354	1,248,440,754	603,911	570,116	621,293,209
West Virginia..........	366,787	373,154	1,829,967,627	29,996	27,313	390,586,860	96,397	87,394	833,680,609	172,616	158,010	214,949,909
Wisconsin..............	903,902	829,287	3,921,363,613	128,380	111,609	1,089,237,882	145,143	133,936	1,908,437,926	372,872	336,688	362,345,995
Wyoming...............	76,786	66,605	324,630,777	5,446	4,276	71,534,687	8,675	7,487	142,746,652	44,793	37,853	60,753,801
Dist. of Columbia	157,101	158,179	1,199,837,436	10,647	8,581	212,921,941	29,679	25,820	546,642,885	73,762	70,643	146,882,712

See footnotes at end of table.

FY 2003 MEDICAID ELIGIBLES, BENEFICIARIES AND PAYMENTS BY BASIS OF ELIGIBILITY — Continued

State or other jurisdiction	Adults			Foster care children			BOE unknown			BCCA women		
	Eligibles	Beneficiaries	Medicaid payments	Eligibles	Beneficiaries	Medicaid payments	Eligibles	Beneficiaries	Medicaid payments	Eligibles	Beneficiaries	Medicaid payments
Total...............	14,416,492	11,741,498	$26,830,554,154	925,293	845,687	$4,803,581,706	1,131	3,752,002	$9,312,252,278	13,344	11,964	$110,321,752
Alabama..............	152,325	99,551	148,033,794	6,784	6,630	89,351,325	0	22,276	687,367,071	294	263	2,465,903
Alaska................	27,608	23,785	122,653,258	2,127	1,932	19,629,817	0	6,164	10,701,854	100	89	1,115,266
Arizona...............	503,951	257,372	649,914,748	8,474	8,474	13,954,129	0	46,373	56,461,270	0	0	0
Arkansas.............	159,139	110,869	139,935,542	6,130	5,975	41,159,293	41	113,976	39,082,422	0	0	0
California............	4,380,161	3,224,684	3,565,542,160	155,838	145,852	566,085,768	6	1,052,228	469,395,862	4,792	4,286	31,329,241
Colorado..............	99,205	93,424	242,826,730	17,989	17,492	152,789,811	113	13,639	90,310,302	132	124	2,096,470
Connecticut	107,845	103,737	245,994,685	6,693	6,509	20,644,023	0	23,568	15,396,197	130	126	1,597,260
Delaware..............	57,460	52,733	156,690,084	1,879	1,862	18,255,231	0	4,372	4,975,423	48	45	291,108
Florida	578,619	474,929	981,629,106	45,700	41,929	182,593,611	0	226,445	813,214,744	175	162	1,736,614
Georgia	284,163	250,337	740,880,454	21,012	18,781	85,333,165	1	273,490	319,129,451	2,058	1,922	22,137,497
Hawaii.................	136,827	131,247	297,843,316	12,988	12,607	25,103,037	36	15,988	65,974,936	29	28	141,664
Idaho..................	32,025	26,740	86,521,744	2,290	2,129	8,227,537	0	8,199	7,271,483	0	0	0
Illinois................	375,431	316,249	885,605,655	78,669	66,937	282,427,475	0	126,695	1,655,300,022	412	380	3,317,590
Indiana...............	170,861	150,525	376,989,086	13,277	11,737	53,188,627	0	43,201	87,028,843	310	276	2,016,170
Iowa...................	75,222	69,802	177,351,029	10,917	10,395	51,293,807	0	14,916	35,045,127	0	0	0
Kansas................	55,200	48,485	113,609,400	12,606	11,593	72,433,680	0	22,984	35,337,608	84	75	861,208
Kentucky	120,905	117,743	320,548,779	10,472	10,111	101,683,157	0	76,098	42,106,149	257	247	1,640,300
Louisiana	122,822	108,501	315,908,545	9,425	8,539	28,100,500	0	96,826	199,344,895	325	267	4,635,970
Maine	88,761	81,567	319,932,497	3,885	3,588	108,848,116	0	7,101	12,409,441	116	112	1,847,949
Maryland..............	180,192	108,000	437,756,072	17,392	16,827	97,223,894	1	19,832	40,865,486	0	0	0
Massachusetts.......	339,338	256,170	555,141,537	669	543	1,933,322	0	60,481	50,919,302	0	0	0
Michigan..............	280,423	261,421	558,937,423	40,367	39,818	90,200,462	164	106,497	597,501,557	0	0	0
Minnesota............	186,917	149,759	413,209,037	9,100	8,487	71,415,188	0	18,401	46,342,212	252	208	866,728
Mississippi...........	91,195	83,764	243,786,672	3,357	2,920	10,795,505	46	56,634	14,981,715	0	0	0
Missouri...............	264,744	235,399	474,910,578	25,728	24,116	161,096,206	0	26,942	27,884,963	0	0	0
Montana...............	23,197	21,051	66,741,500	3,858	3,585	26,688,096	0	9,098	20,415,278	119	102	885,488
Nebraska..............	50,194	43,604	111,667,617	10,783	9,968	79,098,861	507	7,727	114,958,770	170	140	1,305,545
Nevada................	52,813	45,935	108,719,491	6,017	4,813	48,969,722	5	21,407	56,610,120	0	0	0
New Hampshire......	18,087	14,811	47,128,604	2,692	2,508	33,249,716	3	3,450	2,869,328	0	0	0
New Jersey............	197,914	187,607	464,093,388	24,239	20,339	233,404,305	0	50,321	91,163,562	142	138	2,628,116
New Mexico...........	108,348	83,187	235,979,233	3,839	3,252	38,517,823	1	12,530	138,259,653	202	186	1,937,405
New York..............	1,453,232	1,256,818	4,968,658,742	71,222	63,947	426,204,078	0	466,389	442,916,018	370	283	2,037,593
North Carolina.......	275,533	256,610	794,579,673	17,042	16,043	129,170,248	0	61,206	49,594,230	0	0	0
North Dakota.........	19,640	17,453	36,898,173	1,872	1,719	14,417,097	0	7,991	7,888,282	0	0	0
Ohio...................	432,260	378,325	1,022,172,178	36,472	28,552	103,571,086	0	54,691	28,170,372	0	0	0
Oklahoma.............	91,489	82,522	147,233,558	16,285	14,757	104,259,040	0	14,753	14,602,983	0	0	0
Oregon	238,528	206,996	434,141,895	15,605	14,861	96,315,090	201	31,738	20,520,368	141	124	1,400,505
Pennsylvania	299,857	271,033	746,947,001	50,387	46,920	189,877,665	0	70,699	34,432,405	740	571	4,716,395
Rhode Island	53,438	51,497	123,026,853	5,497	4,864	75,252,753	0	4,835	6,700,535	271	252	1,321,316
South Carolina.......	228,519	182,960	351,583,405	9,372	8,507	76,391,721	0	17,600	689,527,246	139	133	1,851,807

See footnotes at end of table.

FY 2003 MEDICAID ELIGIBLES, BENEFICIARIES AND PAYMENTS BY BASIS OF ELIGIBILITY — Continued

State or other jurisdiction	Adults			Foster care children			BOE unknown			BCCA women		
	Eligibles	Beneficiaries	Medicaid payments	Eligibles	Beneficiaries	Medicaid payments	Eligibles	Beneficiaries	Medicaid payments	Eligibles	Beneficiaries	Medicaid payments
South Dakota..........	19,216	19,156	50,023,397	2,061	2,053	10,934,746	1	4,128	8,641,374	26	26	357,653
Tennessee................	502,674	496,186	1,339,391,041	15,600	15,369	112,749,461	5	110,508	37,635,629	0	0	0
Texas	589,342	513,867	1,426,401,554	37,364	35,069	257,207,597	0	143,748	179,520,437	473	432	5,350,494
Utah	82,433	71,685	116,448,694	6,966	6,913	49,429,859	0	24,276	290,544,766	210	206	1,835,041
Vermont	51,492	47,451	88,362,067	2,621	2,543	36,866,666	0	6,182	5,010,438	39	31	283,338
Virginia...................	96,506	89,330	227,137,553	13,684	11,925	74,890,109	1	39,757	55,192,174	224	210	2,601,615
Washington..............	305,831	249,200	575,143,956	17,051	14,103	30,815,863	2	33,232	1,281,930,052	0	0	0
West Virginia...........	60,689	54,999	131,452,245	6,697	5,991	62,087,034	0	39,079	195,062,251	392	368	2,148,719
Wisconsin.................	240,276	215,614	484,014,670	17,059	14,975	57,469,540	0	16,313	18,293,816	172	152	1,563,784
Wyoming..................	15,411	11,398	38,037,078	2,461	1,946	10,936,627	0	3,645	621,932	0	0	0
Dist. of Columbia	38,234	35,380	125,424,657	4,779	4,382	71,040,217	0	13,373	96,925,024	0	0	0

Source: MSIS State Summary Data FY 2003, created Oct. 27, 2005.

Table 9.5
HEALTH INSURANCE COVERAGE STATUS BY STATE FOR ALL PEOPLE: 2004
(In thousands)

| State or other jurisdiction | Total | Covered and not covered by health insurance during the year | | | |
		Covered	Percent	Not covered	Percent
United States	291,155	245,335	84.3%	45,820	15.7%
Alabama	4,511	3,902	86.5	609	13.5
Alaska	648	538	83.0	110	17.0
Arizona	5,767	4,778	82.9	989	17.1
Arkansas	2,731	2,282	83.6	448	16.4
California	35,850	29,140	81.3	6,710	18.7
Colorado	4,523	3,756	83.0	767	17.0
Connecticut	3,493	3,086	88.4	407	11.6
Delaware	827	707	85.5	120	14.5
Florida	17,467	13,987	80.1	3,479	19.9
Georgia	8,705	7,193	82.6	1,513	17.4
Hawaii	1,250	1,130	90.4	120	9.6
Idaho	1,376	1,164	84.6	212	15.4
Illinois	12,595	10,832	86.0	1,764	14.0
Indiana	6,137	5,264	85.8	872	14.2
Iowa	2,906	2,629	90.5	277	9.5
Kansas	2,674	2,377	88.9	297	11.1
Kentucky	4,074	3,492	85.7	582	14.3
Louisiana	4,422	3,661	82.8	761	17.2
Maine	1,294	1,164	90.0	130	10.0
Maryland	5,549	4,739	85.4	810	14.6
Massachusetts	6,373	5,625	88.3	748	11.7
Michigan	9,972	8,816	88.4	1,156	11.6
Minnesota	5,125	4,677	91.1	458	8.9
Mississippi	2,868	2,379	82.9	489	17.1
Missouri	5,615	4,908	87.4	707	12.6
Montana	912	737	80.9	174	19.1
Nebraska	1,728	1,531	88.6	197	11.4
Nevada	2,390	1,947	81.5	443	18.5
New Hampshire	1,293	1,142	88.3	152	11.7
New Jersey	8,665	7,343	84.7	1,322	15.3
New Mexico	1,902	1,504	79.0	399	21.0
New York	19,049	16,345	85.8	2,705	14.2
North Carolina	8,431	7,110	84.3	1,322	15.7
North Dakota	627	557	88.8	70	11.2
Ohio	11,270	9,987	88.6	1,282	11.4
Oklahoma	3,445	2,760	80.1	685	19.9
Oregon	3,582	2,991	83.5	591	16.5
Pennsylvania	12,178	10,724	88.1	1,454	11.9
Rhode Island	1,057	937	88.6	120	11.4
South Carolina	4,123	3,518	85.3	605	14.7
South Dakota	754	663	88.0	90	12.0
Tennessee	5,857	5,030	85.9	828	14.1
Texas	22,323	16,741	75.0	5,583	25.0
Utah	2,394	2,056	85.9	337	14.1
Vermont	617	548	88.8	69	11.2
Virginia	7,387	6,326	85.6	1,061	14.4
Washington	6,116	5,323	87.0	793	13.0
West Virginia	1,793	1,499	83.6	294	16.4
Wisconsin	5,465	4,898	89.6	566	10.4
Wyoming	498	428	86.0	70	14.0
Dist. of Columbia	547	474	86.7	73	13.3

Source: U.S. Census Bureau, Current Population Survey, 2005 Annual Social and Economic Supplement. Revised July 19, 2005.

Table 9.6
NUMBER AND PERCENT OF CHILDREN UNDER 19 YEARS OF AGE, AT OR BELOW
200 PERCENT OF POVERTY, BY STATE: THREE-YEAR AVERAGES FOR 2002, 2003 AND 2004
(In thousands)

State or other jurisdiction	Total children under 19 years, all income levels	At or below 200 percent of poverty		At or below 200 percent of poverty without health insurance	
		Number	Percent	Number	Percent
United States	76,978	29,704	38.6%	5,641	7.3%
Alabama	1,156	487	42.1	66	5.7
Alaska	199	67	33.9	12	5.9
Arizona	1,577	685	43.4	163	10.3
Arkansas.............................	711	352	49.6	38	5.4
California	10,017	4,218	42.1	848	8.5
Colorado	1,206	396	32.8	114	9.5
Connecticut	899	220	24.5	36	4.0
Delaware............................	207	66	32.0	11	5.5
Florida	4,146	1,678	40.5	393	9.5
Georgia	2,385	954	39.9	194	8.1
Hawaii	319	103	32.2	10	3.1
Idaho.................................	394	169	43.0	30	7.7
Illinois..............................	3,416	1,256	36.8	243	7.1
Indiana..............................	1,673	603	36.0	100	6.0
Iowa	745	244	32.7	37	5.0
Kansas	733	247	33.8	38	5.2
Kentucky	1,031	456	44.2	78	7.6
Louisiana	1,233	603	48.9	106	8.6
Maine	295	107	36.4	11	3.6
Maryland	1,444	373	25.8	69	4.8
Massachusetts.....................	1,567	434	27.7	53	3.4
Michigan	2,660	957	36.0	107	4.0
Minnesota	1,311	311	23.8	51	3.9
Mississippi	802	404	50.3	70	8.7
Missouri	1,462	500	34.2	57	3.9
Montana	227	105	46.3	23	10.0
Nebraska............................	465	156	33.5	18	3.9
Nevada	616	246	40.0	72	11.7
New Hampshire...................	323	66	20.4	8	2.6
New Jersey.........................	2,270	549	24.2	121	5.3
New Mexico	519	269	51.9	51	9.8
New York	4,842	1,974	40.8	271	5.6
North Carolina	2,178	940	43.2	184	8.5
North Dakota......................	155	55	35.7	9	5.9
Ohio	3,019	1,034	34.3	156	5.2
Oklahoma	912	412	45.1	86	9.4
Oregon	881	344	39.1	62	7.0
Pennsylvania	2,997	1,034	34.5	195	6.5
Rhode Island	262	91	34.7	9	3.4
South Carolina	1,073	446	41.6	62	5.7
South Dakota......................	204	73	35.9	8	4.1
Tennessee...........................	1,457	601	41.2	94	6.4
Texas	6,493	3,193	49.2	967	14.9
Utah	803	285	35.5	47	5.9
Vermont.............................	144	42	29.3	3	2.1
Virginia.............................	1,897	557	29.4	100	5.3
Washington........................	1,594	567	35.6	68	4.3
West Virginia.....................	413	197	47.7	24	5.8
Wisconsin..........................	1,405	472	33.6	53	3.8
Wyoming...........................	125	45	35.6	8	6.3
Dist. of Columbia	117	61	52.7	7	5.9

Source: U.S. Census Bureau, Current Population Survey, 2002, 2003 and 2004 Annual Social and Economic Supplements.
Note: Average of the three years' percentages: not average 'number' divided by average total children. Results may differ slightly based on the method used.

State Economic Development Strategies: Trends and Issues
By Jeffrey A. Finkle

While the national economy began to ease its way out of the recession two years after economists declared an end to the debilitating condition, state economic development organizations continued their ardent efforts to further economic development in 2005 as though the recession was still nipping at the nation's heels. States' ardent drive for local economic advancement expanded in several areas, from increased efforts to lure filmmakers to developing comprehensive information Web site portals for businesses seeking to relocate.

Economists are saying it. Politicians are saying it. The national economy is on the mend—leaving behind the ramifications of a recession that began an about-face two years ago—and the numbers tell the story. A statement issued in December by Kathleen P. Utgoff, the commissioner of the U.S. Department of Labor's Bureau of Labor Statistics, reported the unemployment rate in November was 5 percent, having held steady from October. Between 2003 and 2005, unemployment peaked at 6.3 percent in June 2003 and reached its lowest point over the three-year period at 4.9 percent in August 2005. Additionally, according to the U.S. Bureau of Economic Analysis, the annual rate of economic growth was 4.3 percent in the third quarter of 2005, a full percentage point over the second quarter figure. The positive numbers, however, have provided no cause for relaxation in the economic development community.

While the country's economy ventures down the road to recovery, the push to foster economic development from coast to coast is no less pressing than it was when the country was in the throes of its most recent recession. Certain factors, however, pervade in both conditions. Although the unemployment rate is on the decline, a plethora of low-wage jobs continue to be shipped overseas, and at the other end of the spectrum, mid-level technology positions are being filled abroad as well.

Whether the country is experiencing an economic downturn or moving toward recuperation, states are driven to retain jobs and create revenue. There is no boiling point, especially since the nation is not immune to economic relapse. In 2005, the contest among states to spur economic development continues at an intense level as companies in industries ranging from information technology to bioscience continue to seek the consummate business-friendly environment. These environments provide a substantial suitably educated work force, low taxes, cost-effective real estate options, and any number of other enticing incentives that an area's economic developers and government entities are willing to offer up in the name of competition. Every year, state economic development organizations fine-tune and expand their economic development efforts as a means of cultivating avenues to economic achievement, maintaining previous accomplishments or, in some cases, recovering from debilitating conditions that have created a chokehold on progress. In 2005, the tried and true methods of playing off certain weaknesses of neighboring states continued to prove successful through new programs, while the need to quickly fabricate means of troubleshooting newly emerged hurdles—such as those faced in California due to energy issues and in the Gulf region as a result of Hurricane Katrina—also yielded a variety of new economic development endeavors. All the while, more state organizations hopped on the portal bandwagon, creating one-stop-shopping Web sites that provide businesses considering relocation with a single location for information; and organizations also stepped up efforts in what has been an increasing source of revenue—the movie industry's pursuit of film location sites.

One State's Burden...

Economic development is a boundless pursuit in the United States. In California that pursuit from the state level took a blow during a government leadership change two years ago that left the economic development engine in disarray. Operations were divided into a handful of departments, and for the most part, landed in the Business, Transportation & Housing Agency (BTH). Taking another step to re-centralize economic development, this year BTH created the Commerce and Economic Development Program (CEDP). "California is struggling because, once upon a time, we had the California Technology, Trade and Commerce Agency, but that was abolished in 2003," said Yolanda Benson, BTH deputy secretary, Economic Development. "CEDP is not creating new government. We put together a single team that includes private, local and regional organizations to leverage what we do at the state level."

Structural organization challenges and developments notwithstanding, California made strides in confronting a new flight issue. For all its economic development successes over the years, partially due to its perennially agreeable climate and proximity to a major port, California has lost some of its luster in the eyes of some state-based businesses. The culprit is the current energy crisis. With companies seeking to escape the state's increasingly high utility costs, the crisis has paved the way for a small but indisputable exodus, of sorts, among the business population. The most glaring example of business loss due to high business costs involves frozen organic foods processor Amy's Kitchen. Although its headquarters are located in Santa Rosa, Calif., the company announced in late 2004 that it would develop its new production and distribution plant in Medford, Ore. The 135,000-square foot facility will ultimately create as many as 250 new jobs.[1] But California fought back last year with the California Public Utilities Commission's (PUC) passage of the five-year Economic Development Rate (EDR) program.[2] The program adopted economic development electricity rates for Pacific Gas and Electric Co. (PG&E) and Southern California Edison specifically, Benson says, "to help decrease the burden of high utility costs on businesses in the hopes of retaining financially hobbling companies and attracting new ones." The five-year program provides eligible businesses with discounts, beginning with 25 percent in the first year, decreasing 5 percent each year until the end of the program. PG&E had filed for emergency rate relief for Amy's Kitchen, but withdrew in December upon the company's decision to expand in Oregon.[3] EDR was devised with an eye on preventing such losses in the future.

Like Oregon, California's neighbor, Nevada, has benefited from touting its proximity to the Golden State, with a similarly desirable climate and lower costs of doing business. "Our geographical presence gives us a leg up because businesses can still do business in California but they don't have the same costs," said Tim Rubald, interim executive director for the Nevada Commission on Economic Development (NCED). "Last year we generated a lot of interest with companies looking to get out of California."

Much of that interest was in no small part due to the "Nevada to the Rescue" campaign created by the Nevada Economic Development Partnership, which

consists of the Nevada Commission on Economic Development, the Nevada Development Authority, the Economic Development Authority of Western Nevada, the Northern Nevada Development Authority and Sierra Pacific Power Company. The yearlong "Nevada to the Rescue" marketing program, which started in 2004, was formulated to catch the eye of company heads in major California cities and consisted of ads with the question—"Will Your Business be Terminated?"—adorning images of visibly worn and defeated businesspeople. The issues of California's rising utility costs were targeted, as were the state's rising workers' compensation costs and its supplement of state employee-friendly laws to the Federal Family Medical Leave Act.[4] The cost of the campaign, Ribald says, was only $600,000 in 2004. It is not feasible to measure the impact this campaign had on relocations. However, a poll released in January by the Chief Executive Group put the state in the number two spot on the list of the best states in which to do business, beating out California, which was ranked as the worst state for business.[5]

While much attention continued to be given to competition among the states, economic development organizations also continued to pursue programs that highlighted attributes not found abroad. In mid-2005, Washington Gov. Christine Gregoire established the Global Competitiveness Council, which is charged with isolating issues and developing programs to further the state's status as a leading business location within the global business world.[6] "We are uniquely positioned for global competition because of our quality products, sources and quality of life," says Juli Wilkerson, director, Washington State Department of Community, Trade & Economic Development. "We are known internationally for companies located here like Boeing, Starbucks and Nordstrom's. We're known for the quality of our agricultural products such as cherries, apples and potatoes. And wine industry people are well aware of our wines."

In addition to the presence of large companies and the proliferation of desirable products serving as a draw for international companies, the state's geographic location has also proved to be a great attraction. "We're in a terrific position to trade with internationally," Wilkerson adds. "We are the most trade dependent state in the nation."

Competing with the Unexpected

The Gulf Coast was presented with a colossal challenge in the guise of the economic devastation left in the wake of Hurricane Katrina, which swept across the region Aug. 29, 2005. Despite the shock of having to contend with the loss or damage of 25,200 businesses and 484,000 housing units, loss of homes, etc., economic development officials in Louisiana, Mississippi and Alabama took immediate steps to begin the process of rebuilding.[7] One of Louisiana's first acts was the establishment of the Louisiana Bridge Loan Program to assist small businesses in immediate need of funds in order to get their companies back in operation. "This was gap funding to help businesses awaiting funds from insurance companies or for federal assistance in meeting payroll and replacing equipment," said Lana Sonnier of Louisiana Economic Development. "We had $10 million and we expended it in three weeks. We were able to issue 407 loans, at an average of about $25,000 each. What we were able to do with a small amount of time and with a limited amount of funds was better than what the Small Business Association could do, because we were able to use the framework that already existed with local banks." In addition to relying on the local infrastructure, LED was able to call on the assistance of fellow economic development organizations beyond the Gulf region. Florida and New York economic development organizations provided guidance, based on their experiences in handling their respective devastating occurrences, and Florida's history with hurricanes.

"This is a tragedy that affects the whole nation and our economic development partners understand that," Sonnier notes. "Our ports, gas and oil industries are invaluable to the national economy." While the state has had to focus much of its attention on recovery, projects in unaffected areas and previous economic development endeavors in both damaged and undamaged regions have not been put on the back burner. Those pursuits are part of economic developers' new mantra—getting back to business. "We were impacted by the storm, but it increased our resolve to move forward," says Sonnier. "We're greeted with tremendous new opportunities as part of rebuilding."

Mississippi, too, wasted little time in planning for post-Katrina rebuilding. In October, the Governor's Commission on Recovery, Rebuilding and Renewal put together a charette (a strong effort to solve an architectural problem within a short amount of time) consisting of 100 architects from across the country with Mississippi architects in order to craft detailed plans for redeveloping areas that suffered the most extensive damage.[8] "A key part of redevelopment on the coast is how it will be rebuilt," says Scott Hamilton of the Mississippi Development Author-

ity (MDA). Through the new Mississippi Renewal Forum at *www.MississippiRenewal.com*, the community is able to have input into what shape their new community will take. "It's a once in a lifetime opportunity to help redevelop the Coast," Hamilton adds. Additionally, MDA put together a six-point plan to address immediate demands and to lay the groundwork for the state's future. The first part of the plan was to get out the message that "we're still in business and that we'll rebuild Mississippi better than it was before," says Hamilton.

The next three steps involved reaching out. Existing industries in the state were contacted to assess immediate needs and offer assistance. Plans were made to relocate conventions that had been scheduled to take place in various locations. Global partners were called and informed that the state is still interested in pursuing previously discussed projects. The fifth step in the multifaceted recovery plan targeted small businesses with the creation of programs to help business owners navigate the system of programs available for recovery assistance. The final part of MDA's plan was not Katrina-centric, but involved continuing promotion of the rest of the state. Hamilton said 85 percent of Mississippi was not affected by the hurricane. "It was an incredibly disruptive event, but from an overall standpoint, it really doesn't affect the state's outlook," he said. "New economic activity equals rebuilding and it will be of great benefit to people in trades such as plumbing and construction; there shouldn't be an unemployed construction worker in America—especially between Texas, Alabama, Mississippi and Louisiana."

Emerging Trends

California is the movie capital of the world, but other states have long held an interest for moviemakers seeking locations. State economic developers are capitalizing on that interest with the expansion and development of film departments, and the creation of new incentives. New Mexico passed the Filmmakers Tax Credit, which became available Jan. 1, 2005, and provides eligible film production companies with a 5 percent tax credit on certain production expenditures for television programs made in New Mexico that, among other stipulations, employ a below-the-line crew that includes a minimum of 60 percent of New Mexico residents.[9] Toward the end of 2005, Massachusetts Gov. Mitt Romney signed a bill that went into effect for seven years beginning Jan. 1, 2006, and will provide filmmakers with a 20 percent tax credit for productions using Massachusetts labor, and a sales tax credit for those movie industry companies that spend an annual $250,000 in the state.[10] Massachusetts' film office just reopened after having been shut down due to budget constraints in 2002.[11]

States also hopped on another bandwagon, one which has proved successful for those that started the trend. The development of state Web site portals increased in 2005 as economic development leaders realized the value of providing businesses with a single location for acquiring all necessary information for issues ranging from state incentives for relocation to details on the state's social climate. "We're working collaboratively; we're trying to be a conduit so we're working on the same page," BTH's Benson says of new endeavors of the recently developed CEDP. "One of the projects is the creation of the increasingly popular online portal, which will serve as a virtual CEDP, condensing any range of information on the state's offerings and business procedures—culled from various organizations—for new, relocating and expanding businesses." The State of Washington began developing a comprehensive Web portal in 2005.

2005 will go down in history as a year that can only be best described as a mixed bag. While evidence of a national economic recovery finally began to emerge two years after economists declared the end of the nation's most recent recession, economic development leaders were, perhaps, as zealous as ever in continuing and crafting programs to fuel their respective economies. In addition to reacting to this post-recession climate, economic developers also faced unforeseen challenges, reaped the rewards of new and existing programs, and embarked on new roads to further success.

Notes

[1] Greg Stiles, "Time to Dig in at Amy's," *Mail Tribune*, August 20, 2005.

[2] "PUC Adopts New Electricity Rate Plan for PG&E and Edison to Promote California's Economy," (California Public Utilities Commission, September 8, 2005).

[3] "Assigned Commissioner's Ruling Granting the Request of Pacific Gas and Electric Company to Withdraw Its Motion for an Interim Decision Related to Amy's Kitchen," (California Public Utilities Commission, June 14, 2004).

[4] "First Year Anniversary for California's Paid Leave Program," (California Employment Development Department, July 1, 2005).

[5] "Texas Tops List of Business-Friendly States," Chief Executive Group, Jan./Feb. 2005.

[6] "Gov. Gregoire Appoints CTED Director, Creates Global Competitive Council and Names Fitzsimmons Permanent Chief of Staff," Office of Governor Christine Gregoire, June 1, 2005.

[7] *Overview of Comparative Damage from Hurricane Katrina*, Louisiana Recovery Authority, December 9, 2005.

[8] Andrea Oppenheimer Dean, "Mississippi Charette Report is Complete," *Architectural Record*, November 30, 2005.

[9] Application for New Mexico Filmmaker Tax Credit, State of New Mexico–Taxation and Revenue Department.

[10] "'Lights, Camera, Action!' in Massachusetts!," The Commonwealth of Massachusetts Executive Department, November 23, 2005.

[11] Fiscal Year 2006 Budget, Massachusetts Senate, May 23, 2005; Gayle Fee and Laura Raposa, "State's Film Feud Fades to Black with New Agency," Boston Herald, June 28, 2005.

Reference Sources

http://www.cpuc.ca.gov/word_pdf/RULINGS/42290.pdf

http://www.amys.com/news/050820_mail_tribune.php

http://www.cpuc.ca.gov/word_pdf/NEWS_RELEASE/49396.pdf

http://www.edd.ca.gov/nwsrel05-36.pdf

http://www.chiefexecutive.net/ME2/dirmod.asp?sid=&nm=&type=Publishing&mod=Publications%3A%3AArticle&mid=8F3A7027421841978F18BE895F87F791&tier=4&id=0F75E4210E1642E88DFE205A747BEAD4

http://www.governor.wa.gov/news/news-view.asp?pressRelease=95&newsType=1

http://lra.louisiana.gov/assets/120905_Katrina_Impact.ppt

http://archrecord.construction.com/news/daily/archives/051130report.asp

http://www.state.nm.us/tax/forms/year03/rpd41303.pdf

http://www.mass.gov/portal/site/massgovportal/menuitem.b6302844a78a31c14db4a11030468a0c/?pageID=pressreleases&agId=Agov2&prModName=gov2pressrelease&prFile=gov_pr_051123_film.xml

http://www.mass.gov/legis/journal/sj052305.htm

http://thetrack.bostonherald.com/moreTrack/view.bg?articleid=91842&format=text

About the Author

Jeffrey A. Finkle, CEcD, is the president and CEO of the Washington, D.C.-based International Economic Development Council. He is a 20-year veteran in the world of economic development, Finkle, who earned a Bachelor of Science degree in communications from Ohio University and studied business administration at the graduate level at Ohio State University, also has a history in the public sector, having served as deputy assistant secretary of community planning and development for program management with the U.S. Department of Housing and Urban Development.

State Business Incentives:
Some Companies 'More Equal' Than Others
By Adam Bruns

The clash over cash to corporate projects is headed to the country's highest court, and is also the subject of a new bill in Congress. What emerges from those two branches of the federal government may go a long way toward solving state and corporate uncertainty about incentive programs. Details of a case in North Carolina may offer some guidance as to what lies ahead.

In economic development circles, the "takings" power may have taken over the headlines in 2005, but good ol' incentives were still hot as a firecracker. Upcoming 2006 decisions and debate by the U.S. judicial and legislative branches will heat things up more—and perhaps provide some clarity for both states and corporations.

Court decisions will continue to figure prominently in legislative chamber decisions. Some have pointed to property rights as the most significant subject of cases before the U.S. Supreme Court in 2005–2006. That includes the decision by that court to consider the *Cuno v. DaimlerChrysler* case. A U.S. Sixth Circuit panel in 2004 found certain tax incentives for the DaimlerChrysler expansions in Toledo, Ohio, to be unconstitutional, and refused to hear an appeal in early 2005. On Sept. 27, 2005, the case officially made its way onto the Supreme Court's docket.

A national measure seeking to affirm the rights of states to offer their own investment tax incentives for economic development was expected to be heard before a Senate committee in the fall of 2005. But it is now expected to stay in that committee until after the Supreme Court decision is handed down, despite chief sponsor Sen. George Voinovich's pleas to the contrary in September 2005:

"I believe that the Congress must pass The Economic Development Act of 2005 this year regardless of how the Supreme Court decides the *Cuno* case," he said of his measure, which is backed by every senator within the Sixth Circuit's jurisdiction, several governors, the National League of Cities, the National Association of Manufacturers, the Federation of Tax Administrators and the International Brotherhood of Teamsters. A House version of the bill, also referred to committee, has some 50 sponsors.

"State governments and businesses shouldn't have to litigate cases all the way to the Supreme Court in order to find out whether or not a tax incentive is constitutional," Voinovich continued. "The Economic Development Act is a long-term legislative solution

that would once and for all clarify the constitutionality of state tax incentives … I can assure you that China and India aren't going to stop using tax incentives."

Then again, those are nations, not states. And in an interview with *Site Selection* in mid-2005, one of the chief opponents of "corporate welfare" said a national incentives policy would be all right with him.

As Lawsuit Simmers, Dell Gets to Work

The US $279 million that Dell is slated to receive from state and local governments for building a new assembly plant in Winston-Salem was challenged in Wake County Superior Court in the summer of 2005 by former North Carolina Supreme Court Justice Robert Orr, now executive director and senior counsel for the North Carolina Institute for Constitutional Law.

Orr and the seven property-owning plaintiffs from five counties around the state are not just challenging that package. They want the whole kit 'n' caboodle stricken from the proverbial economic development toolbox on the grounds that paying corporations to come is unconstitutional. The defendants range from James T. Fain III, secretary of the N.C. Department of Commerce, to local economic developers and Dell itself.

At issue is the passage of special legislation on Nov. 4, 2004, to award Dell $242 million in state incentives. The language in the complaint will seem familiar to those in the industry, as it echoes the Sixth Circuit's *Cuno* decision:

"The Dell legislation discriminates in favor of instate economic activity and against interstate commerce thereby violating the Commerce Clause of the United States Constitution and otherwise violates the U.S. Constitution and various provisions of the North Carolina Constitution," states the lawsuit. In other words, inducing companies to locate in North Carolina via the specific tax breaks and other incentives outlined in the suit is no more legal than it was in Ohio. Oddly enough, the amounts are nearly equivalent.

"The tax credits provided to Dell are very similar to those at issue in *Cuno*, and we believe are unconstitutional under the Sixth Circuit's holding in *Cuno*," states the NCICL's Web site.

Similarly, claim the plaintiffs, the $37 million to be doled out by Winston-Salem and Forsyth County violates the state constitution.

One policy under the microscope is the William S. Lee Quality Jobs and Business Expansion Act (Bill Lee Act), which allows for both the granting of subsidies and the designation of economic distress rankings to counties for the provision of additional aid.

At issue here is the notion that Forsyth County, which for 10 years has been among the lowest-distress counties in the state according to the state's own rankings, has, for the purposes of the Dell credit program, been given the equivalent of a high-distress ranking. The lawsuit calls the legislative language allowing such shifting "arbitrary and irrational."

The complaint goes on to note that both the new law and the Bill Lee Act also violate the Equal Protection Clause of the U.S. Constitution by not allowing the plaintiffs similar access to such benefits. Other clauses violated? The N.C. Constitution's Separation of Powers Clause (by allowing the secretary of commerce and executive branch such power over taxing authority), Exclusive Emoluments Provision ("Dell is provided a special tax benefit merely for operating its own private business"), Public Purpose Clause and Uniformity of Taxation Clause. Finally, in Count 15, the suit calls the new manufacturing credit "impermissibly vague and ambiguous" because of the latitude it affords the secretary of commerce in determining tax credit eligibility.

Just the suit itself caused enough consternation among the parties involved that their contract with the computer maker was changed: while the incentives offered by Winston-Salem and Forsyth County will still add up to the same dollar amount, Dell is now paying for the land instead of receiving it as a gift.

The suit came on the heels of another one, by the N.C. Press Association, that earlier in the year caused the release of 4,000 pages of documents relating the intimate details of the deal's negotiations. According to published accounts of the notes in the *Raleigh News & Observer*, the frank bargaining between Dell Corp.'s Kip Thompson, vice president, worldwide facility management and corporate real estate, and state officials included references to patriotism, gratitude for 2,000 new jobs and threats to take the project to Tennessee or elsewhere.

In 2000, in the pages of *Site Selection*, Thompson said, "We have a mantra in Dell corporate real estate:

Set unrealistic expectations … and then exceed them." He also said, " 'No' simply means that you don't yet have enough information."

The context of those comments was the internal workings of Dell's then-12-person corporate real estate department, on the heels of a big new project in Nashville. But the nature of expectations and the primacy of information were also at the heart of the company's unfolding project in Winston-Salem.

The negotiation details have sparked further conversation in the state about incentives' worthiness and confidentiality. Such open records debates are also now taking place in Virginia and other states, including Georgia, where in November 2005 a lawyer for Ford Motor Co. told a judge that releasing documents related to its negotiations with the state over keeping open its Hapeville plant might seriously jeopardize those negotiations.

In North Carolina, Commerce Secretary Jim Fain did the bulk of negotiating on the Dell deal, with Gov. Mike Easley meeting with Dell officials in July 2004 and a special legislative session in November 2004 approving $242 million in tax breaks and other incentives—a 40-percent jump from the $166 million the company garnered for its Nashville plant. Many in North Carolina wanted the process to be more open, but others were concerned that could potentially blow the entire deal, at a time when the state—and the Triad region especially—could use a big-jobs project in the wake of textile, tobacco and other industry cutbacks.

Where to tread the thin line between transparency and economic development effectiveness is the subject of separate proposed legislation to change North Carolina's open government statutes.

Asked at what exact point he thinks details of business attraction negotiations should be made public, Dell's Kip Thompson told *Site Selection*, "It depends on the community. Clearly there is a need for information to flow, that does not compromise companies being able to do their business. There is a need for the public sector to have information available as well. What that point is would be, in the abstract, a hard line to draw."

Let's Get Specific

In an interview with *Site Selection*, Orr said that *Kelo v. New London*, the recent U.S. Supreme Court ruling on eminent domain's legality in serving a "public purpose," actually gives his side more momentum, not less. It comes not so much from a legal perspective (it's a state constitution's public purpose in the Dell case) as it does from a public policy perspective.

"The immediate negative reaction to the *Kelo* decision ... plays into the public policy argument we're trying to make," said Orr. Only with incentives, he said, the sense of violation is even greater.

"With eminent domain, you take somebody's property and give it to a private developer—at least in taking physical property, you're entitled to just compensation for that taking," he explained. "In the incentives game, the government uses the power of taxation to take the money you've earned and turn around and give it to a private corporation. Arguably, the taxpayer gets little if any in return. In Dell's case, the money ultimately helps benefit Dell's bottom line. I think when the public and politicians start recognizing that what is happening in the incentives game is even more egregious than what happened in *Kelo*, we'll see a greater interest in trying to make changes in the incentives practice."

Extension of the Lee Act, due to expire at the end of 2005, was signed into law by North Carolina Gov. Mike Easley in late July 2005, thereby extending the act's benefits through 2007. In a nod to critics, the extension legislation created an oversight committee that is due to report its recommendations to the 2006 legislature. The extension also freed several notable projects from the bounds of uncertainty: among the projects taking advantage of JDIG in the latter part of the year were investments from Smiths Aerospace Components ($44 million investment in West Jefferson) and Lenovo, which is making an $84 million investment in an R&D center in Morrisville. And not insignificantly, Dell started up on schedule in Winston-Salem. According to the state, since 2003, JDIG is responsible for bringing more than $2 billion in investment and 10,000 jobs to North Carolina.

In an interesting sidelight to the legal action, Orr's opponent in court, representing Dell, will be a fellow former State Supreme Court Justice, Burley Mitchell, whose view was opposed to Orr's on the topic back when their court ruled on the legality of incentives in a 1996 case that determined economic development served a public purpose.

Visitors to the NCICL Web site may glimpse the lawsuit in full detail, as well as a copy of a draft agreement between Dell and various local and state economic development entities. In October 2005, Dell asked a state court to toss out the suit for lack of merit.

Take It to the Feds

Of course, other states don't have to follow North Carolina's example, which would put the Tarheel State at a distinct disadvantage should the plaintiffs prevail. The case is expected to take about a year to reach a decision—which should be long enough for the Congressional measures, the U.S. Supreme Court decision or both to provide some direction to every state.

In introducing the Economic Development Act of 2005, Sen. Voinovich noted that he had enacted the now-nullified machinery and equipment tax incentive when he was governor of Ohio. (Oddly enough, almost simultaneously with the act's introduction in the spring of 2005, current Ohio Gov. Bob Taft was doing away with the provision entirely by signing a comprehensive tax reform package.) Voinovich noted the pall that the *Cuno* decision had cast over deals in all 50 states, as they endeavor to compete on a truly global stage.

"As a former governor who had to compete against Japan, Canada, China and Europe for new business projects, I know just how important a role tax incentives can play in attracting new businesses," he said. He went on to note the high rankings in new plants and expansions for Ohio in *Site Selection* between 1993 and 1997, earned in part by the state's expanded incentives programs.

In fact, a look back at *Site Selection*'s coverage shows that Ohio did indeed lead the way, but nipping on its heels was ... North Carolina, which won the Governor's Cup title outright in 1996. That was the same year that Justice Orr issued a dissent in the *Maready v. City of Winston-Salem et al.* case that found incentives constitutional. The *Maready* case quickly became a case study, available online, at the John F. Kennedy School of Government at Harvard University.

The Voinovich measure's simple goal: to authorize states to provide tax incentives for economic development purposes. In his critique of the Sixth Circuit's action, Voinovich noted "a little legal fiction present in the *Cuno* decision. The court states that Ohio could have provided a direct subsidy to companies that undertook investment in the State. Because Ohio decided to structure the program as a tax credit, however, the court said that it ran afoul of the Commerce Clause. I do not see how a direct subsidy does not violate the dormant Commerce Clause, but a tax credit does. They are economically the same."

While a *Cuno* override would help manufacturers in sore need of it, said Voinovich, the ultimate reason the decision needs revisiting is that it "sets a bad precedent that, if not checked, could upset our carefully balanced federal system. One of the most ingenious aspects of the U.S. Constitution is that it leaves a great deal of power with the States. ... My legislation will guarantee that the States remain our engines of innovation."

In conclusion, Voinovich noted that the U.S. Supreme Court itself had described its dormant Commerce Clause jurisprudence as a "quagmire." And he quoted a statement from Supreme Court Justice Felix Frankfurter:

"At best, this Court can only act negatively; it can determine whether a specific state tax is imposed in violation of the Commerce Clause. Such decisions must necessarily depend on the application of rough and ready legal concepts. We cannot make a detailed inquiry into the incidence of diverse economic burdens in order to determine the extent to which such burdens conflict with the necessities of national economic life. Neither can we devise appropriate standards for dividing up national revenue on the basis of more or less abstract principles of constitutional law, which cannot be responsive to the subtleties of the interrelated economies of nation and state.

The problem calls for solution by devising a congressional policy. Congress alone can provide for a full and thorough canvassing of the multitudinous and intricate factors which compose the problem of the taxing freedom of the States and the needed limits on such state taxing power. Congressional committees can make studies and give the claims of the individual States adequate hearing before the ultimate legislative formulation of policy is made by the representatives of all the States. … Congress alone can formulate policies founded upon economic realities."

Gaming the System
May Be the Real System

To many, the incentives game is an economic reality. But Orr and his allies think reality bites, and equate the incentives game to an addiction. He calls the Voinovich effort "misguided," especially in its attempts to link the need for incentives to keeping jobs in the United States.

"This has nothing to do with losing jobs overseas—what we're concerned about is the practice of [states] outbidding each other to move companies," Orr said.

Asked about the reality of some corporate location short lists involving U.S. cities pitted against foreign cities, Orr said the "occasional circumstance" may involve moving to Mexico versus staying in the United States, but that the business decisions are made with regard to other factors than incentives. He quoted from a recent U.S. Supreme Court decision, *Granholm vs. Heald*, that referred to the challenges the Constitu-

tion's framers faced with the prospect of "economic balkanization" in the new union of colonies.

"What we have now is economic balkanization," said Orr. "North Carolina is looking out for North Carolina, Virginia is looking out for Virginia, Ohio for Ohio. Companies recognize this and are able to exploit it."

So, should there be a federal policy on incentives? Barring a better idea, yes, says Orr.

"If you're going to have a trade policy that addresses concerns with jobs being lost overseas, then the Congress needs to be doing that, not the individual states," he said. "If the issue is 'What do we do to keep the textile and furniture industries?' the solution needs to be at a national level. That's why we have international trade treaties and the WTO. And let it apply equally among the 50 states."

In other words, as is being played out right now on the WTO stage with the U.S. vs. Europe over Airbus and Boeing, let the countries battle it out. Meanwhile, Orr thinks anybody involved with incentives will say it's out of hand and they need to be "outlawed, stricken, prohibited on a national basis."

In fact, in an informal Web poll conducted on *Site Selection* Web portal SiteNet, when asked "Which statement best reflects your opinion on economic development incentives?," 63 percent of 127 respondents picked "They are necessary and helpful." Just 15 percent picked "States are giving away too much money." But 22 percent picked "All incentives programs should cease."

He hopes his state will return to an across-the-board economic development package that isn't so slanted toward "the wealthiest corporations," but benefits "everybody that's in the business of job creation and economic development."

Orr had the opportunity to discuss the topic at the annual conference of North Carolina economic developers.

"When I talked about the system being gamed, there were a lot of heads nodding in agreement," he says. "They understand something is wrong with the system, they just don't know how to get out of the system."

About the Author

Adam Bruns is managing editor of *Site Selection*, a business publication published by Norcross, Ga.-based Conway Data Inc. since 1954. *Site Selection* offers national and international coverage of corporate real estate and economic development through industry reports and geographic spotlights, highlighted by exclusive corporate interviews and proprietary research.

Table A
FINANCIAL ASSISTANCE FOR INDUSTRY

State or other jurisdiction	State sponsored industrial development authority	Privately sponsored development credit corporation	State authority or agency revenue bond financing	State authority or agency general obligation bond financing	City and/or county revenue bond financing	City and/or County General obligation bond financing	State loans for building construction	State loans for equipment, machinery	City and/or county loans for building construction	City and/or county loans for equipment, machinery	State loan guarantees for building construction	State loan guarantees for equipment, machinery	City and/or county loan guarantees for building construction	City and/or county loan guarantees for equipment, machinery	State financing aid for existing plant expansion	State matching funds for city and/or county industrial financing programs	State incentive for establishing industrial plants in areas of high unemployment	City and/or county incentive for establishing industrial plants in areas of high unemployment
Alabama	★	★	★		★	★	★	★	★	★	★	★			★		★	★
Alaska	★				★		★	★		★	★	★			★	★	★	★
Arizona		★	★	★	★				★	★					★		★	★
Arkansas	★	★	★		★	★	★	★	★	★	★	★	★	★	★	★	★	★
California	★	★			★	★	★	★	★	★			★	★	★		★	★
Colorado	★	★	★		★	★	★	★	★	★					★		★	★
Connecticut	★		★	★	★	★	★	★	★	★	★	★			★	★	★	★
Delaware		★	★		★	★	★	★	★	★	★	★			★		★	★
Florida	★	★	★		★	★	★	★	★	★	★	★	★	★	★	★	★	★
Georgia	★		★		★		★	★	★	★					★		★	★
Hawaii	★	★	★	★	★	★	★	★						★	★	★	★	★
Idaho		★			★		★	★	★	★							★	★
Illinois	★	★	★	★	★	★	★	★	★	★	★	★	★	★	★	★	★	★
Indiana	★		★	★	★	★			★	★					★	★	★	★
Iowa	★	★	★		★		★	★	★	★	★	★			★		★	★
Kansas	★	★	★		★	★	★	★	★	★	★	★	★	★	★	★	★	★
Kentucky		★	★	★	★	★	★	★	★	★	★	★	★	★	★	★	★	★
Louisiana	★	★	★	★	★	★	★	★	★	★	★	★			★	★	★	★
Maine	★	★	★	★	★	★	★	★	★	★	★	★	★	★	★	★	★	★
Maryland	★	★	★	★	★		★	★	★	★	★	★			★	★	★	★
Massachusetts	★	★	★	★	★	★	★	★	★	★	★	★	★	★	★	★	★	★
Michigan	★	★	★	★	★	★	★	★	★	★	★	★	★	★	★	★	★	★
Minnesota	★	★	★		★	★	★	★	★	★	★	★	★	★	★	★	★	★
Mississippi	★		★	★	★	★	★	★	★	★	★	★	★	★	★	★	★	★
Missouri	★	★	★	★	★		★	★	★	★					★		★	★
Montana	★		★	★	★	★	★	★	★	★	★	★			★	★	★	★
Nebraska	★	★	★	★	★	★	★	★	★	★			★	★	★	★	★	★
Nevada	★		★		★	★	★	★	★	★			★	★	★		★	★
New Hampshire		★	★	★	★	★	★	★	★	★	★	★	★	★	★	★	★	★
New Jersey	★	★	★	★	★		★	★	★	★	★	★	★	★	★	★	★	★
New Mexico	★	★	★	★	★	★	★	★	★	★			★	★	★		★	★
New York	★	★	★	★	★	★	★	★	★	★	★	★	★	★	★		★	★
North Carolina	★		★	★	★	★	★	★	★	★	★	★			★		★	
North Dakota		★	★	★	★		★	★	★	★			★	★	★	★	★	★
Ohio	★		★	★	★		★	★	★	★					★	★	★	★

See footnotes at end of table.

FINANCIAL ASSISTANCE FOR INDUSTRY — Continued

State or other jurisdiction	State sponsored industrial development authority	Privately sponsored development credit corporation	State authority or agency revenue bond financing	State authority or agency general obligation bond financing	City and/or county revenue bond financing	City and/or County General obligation bond financing	State loans for building construction	State loans for equipment, machinery	City and/or county loans for building construction	City and/or county loans for equipment, machinery	State loan guarantees for building construction	State loan guarantees for equipment, machinery	City and/or county loan guarantees for building construction	City and/or county loan guarantees for equipment, machinery	State financing aid for existing plant expansion	State matching funds for city and/or county industrial financing programs	State incentive for establishing industrial plants in areas of high unemployment	City and/or county incentive for establishing industrial plants in areas of high unemployment
Oklahoma	★	…	★	★	★	★	★	★	★	★	★	★	★	★	★	★	★	★
Oregon	★	★	★	★	★	★	★	★	★	★	★	★	★	★	★	★	★	★
Pennsylvania	★	★	★	★	★	★	★	★	★	★	★	★	★	★	★	★	★	★
Rhode Island	★	★	★	★	★	…	★	★	★	★	★	★	…	…	★	★	★	★
South Carolina	…	★	★	…	★	★	★	★	★	★	…	…	★	★	★	…	★	★
South Dakota	★	…	★	★	★	★	★	★	★	★	…	…	…	…	★	★	…	…
Tennessee	…	★	★	★	★	★	★	★	★	★	★	★	…	…	★	★	★	…
Texas	★	★	★	★	★	★	★	★	★	★	★	…	★	…	…	★	★	★
Utah	★	★	…	…	★	★	…	…	★	★	…	★	…	★	★	…	★	…
Vermont	…	…	★	…	★	★	…	…	★	★	★	…	…	…	…	★	…	…
Virginia	★	★	★	…	★	★	★	★	…	★	…	★	★	★	★	★	★	★
Washington	★	★	★	…	★	…	★	★	★	★	…	★	…	…	★	★	★	…
West Virginia	★	★	★	…	★	…	★	★	★	★	★	★	…	…	…	★	…	…
Wisconsin	★	…	★	…	★	★	★	★	★	★	…	…	★	★	★	…	★	…
Wyoming	★	★	…	★	★	★	★	★	★	★	…	★	…	…	★	★	…	…
Puerto Rico	★	★	★	…	★	★	★	★	★	…	★	★	…	…	★	★	★	★

Source: *Site Selection*, November 2005.
Note: A significant number of footnotes are published with these charts in the November 2004 issue of *Site Selection* Magazine. For more information or to obtain a set of the footnotes, contact editor Adam Bruns at adam.bruns@conway.com.

Key:
★ — Yes
… — No; or state/jurisdiction did not respond to survey.

Table B
TAX INCENTIVES FOR INDUSTRY

State or other jurisdiction	Corporate income tax exemption	Personal income tax exemption	Excise tax exemption	Tax exemption or moratorium on land, capital improvements	Tax exemption or moratorium on equipment, machinery	Inventory tax exemption on goods in transit (freeport)	Tax exemption on manufacturers' inventories	Sales/use tax exemption on new equipment	Tax exemption on raw materials used in manufacturing	Tax incentive for creation of jobs	Tax incentive for industrial investment	Tax credits for use of specified state products	Tax stabilization agreements for specified industries	Tax exemption to encourage research and development	Accelerated depreciation of industrial equipment
State totals............	41	37	28	40	44	49	47	49	50	45	45	8	12	42	41
Alabama.................	★	★	★	★	★	★	★	★	★	★	★			★	★
Alaska...................		★	★	★	★			★	★						
Arizona.................	★	★		★	★	★	★	★	★	★	★	★		★	★
Arkansas................	★	★	★	★	★	★	★	★	★	★	★	★		★	★
California..............			★	★	★	★	★	★	★	★	★				★
Colorado...............	★		★	★	★	★	★	★	★	★	★			★	★
Connecticut............	★	★	★	★	★	★	★	★	★	★	★		★	★	★
Delaware...............	★	★	★	★	★	★	★	★	★	★	★			★	★
Florida.................	★	★		★	★	★	★	★	★	★	★			★	★
Georgia.................	★		★	★	★	★	★	★	★	★	★		★	★	★
Hawaii..................	★	★	★	★	★	★	★	★	★	★	★			★	★
Idaho...................	★	★		★	★	★	★	★	★	★	★			★	★
Illinois................	★	★	★	★	★	★	★	★	★	★	★			★	★
Indiana.................	★	★	★	★	★	★	★	★	★	★	★			★	★
Iowa....................	★	★	★	★	★	★	★	★	★	★	★		★	★	★
Kansas..................	★	★		★	★	★	★	★	★	★	★			★	★
Kentucky................	★	★	★	★	★	★	★	★	★	★	★	★		★	★
Louisiana...............	★	★	★	★	★	★	★	★	★	★	★		★	★	★
Maine...................	★	★		★	★	★	★	★	★	★	★			★	★
Maryland................	★	★	★	★	★	★	★	★	★	★	★			★	★
Massachusetts...........	★	★	★	★	★	★	★	★	★	★	★		★	★	★
Michigan................	★	★	★	★	★	★	★	★	★	★	★		★	★	★
Minnesota...............	★	★	★	★	★	★	★	★	★	★	★		★	★	★
Mississippi.............	★	★	★	★	★	★	★	★	★	★	★		★	★	★
Missouri................	★	★	★	★	★	★	★	★	★	★	★			★	★
Montana.................	★	★		★	★	★	★	★	★	★	★		★	★	★
Nebraska................	★	★	★	★	★	★	★	★	★	★	★			★	★
Nevada..................				★	★	★	★	★	★	★	★	★	★	★	★
New Hampshire...........	★		★	★	★	★	★	★	★	★	★				
New Jersey..............	★			★	★	★	★	★	★	★	★			★	★
New Mexico..............	★	★	★	★	★	★	★	★	★	★	★			★	★
New York................	★	★	★	★	★	★	★	★	★	★	★			★	★
North Carolina.........	★	★	★	★	★	★	★	★	★	★	★			★	★
North Dakota...........	★	★	★	★	★	★	★	★	★	★	★			★	★
Ohio....................	★	★		★	★	★	★	★	★	★	★			★	★

See footnotes at end of table.

TAX INCENTIVES FOR INDUSTRY — Continued

State or other jurisdiction	Corporate income tax exemption	Personal income tax exemption	Excise tax exemption	Tax exemption or moratorium on land, capital improvements	Tax exemption or moratorium on equipment, machinery	Inventory tax exemption on goods in transit (freeport)	Tax exemption on manufacturers' inventories	Sales/use tax exemption on new equipment	Tax exemption on raw materials used in manufacturing	Tax incentive for creation of jobs	Tax incentive for industrial investment	Tax credits for use of specified state products	Tax stabilization agreements for specified industries	Tax exemption to encourage research and development	Accelerated depreciation of industrial equipment
Oklahoma	★	★	★	★	★	★	★	★	★	★	★	★	★	★	★
Oregon	…	…	★	★	★	★	★	★	★	…	★	…	…	★	★
Pennsylvania	★	★	★	★	★	★	★	★	★	★	★	★	★	★	★
Rhode Island	★	…	…	★	★	★	★	★	★	★	★	★	★	★	★
South Carolina	★	★	…	★	…	…	…	★	★	★	★	…	★	★	★
South Dakota	★	★	★	★	…	★	★	★	★	★	★	…	…	★	★
Tennessee	★	★	★	★	★	★	★	★	★	★	★	…	…	★	★
Texas	…	…	…	…	★	★	…	★	★	★	★	…	…	★	…
Utah	…	…	…	…	…	★	★	★	★	★	…	…	…	…	★
Vermont	…	…	…	…	…	★	…	★	★	★	…	★	★	…	★
Virginia	★	★	…	★	★	★	…	★	★	★	★	★	★	★	★
Washington	★	★	★	…	★	★	★	★	★	★	★	…	…	★	…
West Virginia	★	★	★	★	★	★	★	★	★	★	★	★	…	★	★
Wisconsin	★	★	…	…	★	★	…	★	★	★	★	…	…	★	★
Wyoming	…	★	…	…	…	★	★	…	★	★	★	…	…	…	…
Puerto Rico	★	★	★	★	★	★	★	…	★	★	★	★	★	★	★

Source: Site Selection, November 2005.

Note: A significant number of footnotes are published with these charts in the November issue of *Site Selection* Magazine. For more information or to obtain a set of the footnotes, contact Editor Adam Bruns at adam.bruns@ conway.com.

Key:
★ — Yes
… — No; or state/jurisdiction did not respond to survey.

Table 9.7
STATE REVENUES USED FOR HIGHWAYS, BY REGION: 2003
(In thousands of dollars)

| State or other jurisdiction | Beginning balance total (a) | Highway-user revenues (b) | | | | Appropriations from general funds (c) | Other state imposts | Miscellaneous | Bond proceeds (d) | Payments from other governments | | | Total receipts |
| | | Motor-fuel taxes | Motor-vehicle and motor-carrier taxes | Road and crossing tolls | Total | | | | | Federal funds | | Local government | |
										Federal Hwy. Administration	Other agencies		
United States	$39,280,834	$27,873,913	$15,848,125	$5,012,705	$48,734,743	$3,399,724	$3,382,232	$2,748,979	$17,088,988	$28,383,735	$796,715	$1,658,684	$106,193,800
Eastern Region													
Connecticut..............	813,943	297,362	149,595	155	447,112	107,735	65,529	89,661	646,007	407,569	9,471	5,632	1,778,716
Delaware..................	269,384	108,699	99,678	165,057	373,434	104,085	0	30,154	562,873	110,788	456	0	1,181,790
Maine......................	121,052	199,294	50,184	64,203	313,681	2,541	0	16,952	51,000	171,126	1,944	0	557,244
Massachusetts	1,108,360	662,316	310,422	226,739	1,199,477	636,957	0	192,635	916,474	508,637	9,084	0	3,463,264
New Hampshire	252,201	142,966	90,632	65,059	298,657	10,253	0	9,802	8,855	143,228	825	8,879	480,499
New Jersey	2,408,051	337,060	330,671	533,950	1,201,681	0	0	133,665	3,700,825	734,476	6,819	0	5,777,466
New York	-243,590	949,062	609,998	964,839	2,523,899	304,687	0	88,674	2,255,068	1,316,564	20,903	17,511	6,527,306
Pennsylvania	2,087,583	1,218,188	554,745	478,893	2,251,826	527,101	0	316,715	447,798	1,361,855	33,304	32,867	4,971,466
Rhode Island	43,498	78,015	3,772	11,725	93,512	0	3,454	17,297	51,211	137,563	3,133	0	302,716
Vermont...................	68,880	80,664	106,731	0	187,395	2,041	0	7,808	1,656	108,163	2,306	2,465	315,288
Regional average	692,936	407,363	230,643	251,062	889,067	169,540	6,898	90,336	864,177	499,997	8,825	6,735	2,535,576
Midwestern Region													
Illinois....................	1,783,219	1,108,047	1,016,620	387,014	2,511,681	54,048	0	31,665	601,491	836,519	14,406	45,217	4,095,027
Indiana....................	511,813	1,073,868	222,331	83,420	1,379,619	2,669	0	9,876	445,000	597,252	18,112	0	2,452,528
Iowa........................	45,362	394,917	358,586	0	753,503	60,077	245,731	7,441	0	343,791	5,893	0	1,416,436
Kansas.....................	984,409	383,753	128,989	67,971	580,713	11,206	89,854	44,915	529,450	330,931	3,676	20,683	1,611,428
Michigan..................	1,156,371	944,893	801,482	30,487	1,776,862	165,999	0	67,227	0	592,450	13,270	31,237	2,647,045
Minnesota	1,036,796	612,674	504,394	0	1,117,068	16,128	184,957	74,976	28,477	330,300	7,188	22,218	1,781,312
Nebraska	105,555	288,916	68,240	0	357,156	33,614	135,315	27,981	0	210,107	1,282	58,753	824,208
North Dakota	46,529	103,880	50,185	0	154,065	11,875	5,711	382	0	198,301	3,959	12,501	386,794
Ohio........................	1,217,871	1,360,444	562,959	182,317	2,105,720	39,033	0	85,232	291,168	888,290	14,170	57,507	3,481,120
South Dakota............	57,552	106,173	55,100	0	161,273	351	55,793	22,677	0	198,098	2,583	14,024	454,799
Wisconsin.................	325,522	773,714	345,015	0	1,118,729	0	0	31,913	213,182	563,295	9,775	87,136	2,024,030
Regional average	661,000	650,116	373,991	68,292	1,092,399	35,909	65,215	36,753	191,706	462,667	8,574	31,752	1,924,975
Southern Region													
Alabama...................	440,789	531,569	229,606	0	761,175	62,657	5,710	4,104	200,000	587,033	8,849	50,000	1,679,528
Arkansas..................	231,291	421,719	133,383	0	555,102	28,732	1,339	26,705	225,728	437,083	8,323	1,970	1,284,982
Florida....................	1,219,577	1,610,528	608,135	723,768	2,942,431	193,339	95,821	113,245	1,881,269	1,695,189	15,482	149,871	7,086,647
Georgia....................	1,305,174	373,499	281,662	21,176	676,337	203,744	217,296	90,067	0	792,804	11,767	0	1,992,015
Kentucky..................	1,103,023	453,169	601,480	0	1,054,649	192,527	0	56,585	0	513,357	10,450	0	1,827,568
Louisiana.................	644,603	572,462	129,789	35,582	737,833	101,176	36,012	25,334	352,244	483,710	7,875	0	1,744,184
Maryland..................	721,913	390,541	343,161	87,508	821,210	0	113,552	33,010	321,735	496,292	9,264	0	1,795,063
Mississippi...............	496,131	366,323	129,326	0	495,649	0	44,815	12,701	0	411,567	6,470	13,707	984,909
Missouri..................	632,212	665,441	233,752	0	899,193	19,705	217,095	26,562	0	732,290	8,067	13,162	1,916,074
North Carolina..........	972,506	982,013	375,423	2,425	1,359,861	0	383,485	81,721	0	791,500	13,078	10,424	2,640,069
Oklahoma.................	548,337	286,691	197,651	171,990	656,332	10,518	53,649	39,492	99,597	394,602	5,010	8,309	1,267,509
South Carolina..........	412,731	327,184	116,467	8,341	451,992	0	0	26,484	46,505	426,764	20,535	10,544	982,824
Tennessee.................	1,045,728	712,364	235,959	23	948,346	23,653	39,038	42,168	0	538,661	11,403	31,675	1,634,944
Texas.......................	3,154,647	2,039,526	1,253,373	150,034	3,442,933	33,510	30,942	171,707	481,105	2,494,149	30,966	322,273	7,007,585
Virginia...................	1,192,845	610,106	527,563	89,641	1,227,310	101,978	411,991	77,307	1,107,396	656,374	19,537	39,685	3,641,578
West Virginia............	252,324	285,658	257,234	46,133	589,025	14,995	0	9,186	62,696	407,254	15,787	0	1,098,943
Regional average	14,373,831	10,628,793	5,653,964	1,336,621	17,619,378	986,534	1,650,745	836,378	4,778,275	11,858,629	202,863	651,620	38,584,422

See footnotes at end of table.

STATE REVENUES USED FOR HIGHWAYS, BY REGION: 2003—Continued
(In thousands of dollars)

| State or other jurisdiction | Beginning balance total (a) | Highway-user revenues (b) | | | | Appropriations from general funds (c) | Other state imposts | Miscellaneous | Bond proceeds (d) | Payments from other governments | | | Total receipts |
| | | Motor-fuel taxes | Motor-vehicle and motor-carrier taxes | Road and crossing tolls | Total | | | | | Federal funds | | Local government | |
										Federal Hwy. Administration	Other agencies		
Western Region													
Alaska.............	0	27,279	26,839	19,188	73,306	83,244	0	23,456	113,866	398,917	4,257	0	697,046
Arizona............	736,846	600,951	249,846	0	850,797	43,533	579,148	1,995	452,217	447,986	11,127	41,967	2,428,770
California..........	6,403,743	2,284,272	1,480,933	274,525	4,039,730	5,411	264,838	283,379	0	2,481,325	76,051	513,258	7,663,992
Colorado...........	897,530	526,022	640,960	0	1,166,982	28,740	1,010	131,963	105,859	427,569	15,973	2,170	1,880,266
Hawaii.............	418,363	70,460	77,019	0	147,479	14,415	2,079	15,691	44,940	135,085	259	0	359,948
Idaho..............	206,268	199,898	129,432	0	329,330	0	0	0	0	207,684	16,257	2,413	555,684
Montana............	101,374	177,721	69,987	0	247,708	0	0	2,807	0	307,434	13,852	625	572,426
Nevada.............	237,954	402,589	182,288	210	585,087	4,213	0	6,977	199,483	203,431	963	0	1,000,154
New Mexico.........	408,030	216,103	152,332	0	368,435	0	2,317	16,513	16,699	269,258	30,671	0	703,893
Oregon.............	342,594	384,652	258,718	0	643,370	37,215	9,745	15,246	0	366,640	111,578	0	1,183,794
Utah...............	442,817	318,892	86,583	206	405,681	69,708	38,031	40,484	161,597	223,395	20,721	0	959,617
Washington.........	417,312	699,220	277,494	120,126	1,096,840	10,474	27	59,490	441,985	587,235	30,266	25,073	2,251,390
Wyoming............	32,665	85,407	47,337	0	132,744	0	11,301	6,011	0	226,448	77,385	4,928	458,817
Regional average...	818,884	461,036	283,059	31,866	7,759,761	22,843	69,884	46,462	118,204	483,262	31,489	45,418	1,593,523
Regional average without California...	353,479	309,100	183,236	11,644	503,980	24,295	53,638	26,719	128,054	316,757	27,776	6,431	1,087,650
Dist. of Columbia	61,146	26,749	94,064	0	120,813	25,837	36,647	941	23,532	153,396	1,933		363,099

Source: U.S. Department of Transportation, Federal Highway Administration, *Highway Statistics, 2003* (October 2004).
Note: Detail may not add to totals due to rounding.
This table was compiled from reports of state authorities.
Key:
(a) Amount includes reserves for current highway work and reserves for debt service. Any differences between beginning balances and the closing balances on last year's information are the result of accounting adjustments, inclusion of funds not previously reported, etc.

(b) Amounts shown represent only those highway-user revenues that were expended on state or local roads.
(c) Amounts shown represent gross general fund appropriations for highways reduced by the amount of highway-user revenues placed in the State General Fund.
(d) Amount shown represents original and refunding issues.

Table 9.8
STATE DISBURSEMENTS FOR HIGHWAYS, BY REGION: 2003
(In thousands of dollars)

State or other jurisdiction	Capital outlay — State administered highways (a)	Capital outlay — Locally administered roads	Total	Maintenance and highway service expenditures (b)	Administration, research and planning	Highway law enforcement and safety	Interest	Bond retirement (c)	Grants-in-aid to local governments	Total disbursements	Total year-end balances (d)
United States	49,239,801	$2,975,521	$52,215,322	$14,359,544	$6,524,559	$7,149,255	$3,926,813	$11,764,607	$13,456,582	$109,396,682	$36,077,952
Eastern Region											
Connecticut	603,613	11,798	615,411	111,434	79,479	117,822	160,246	640,164	18,672	1,743,228	849,431
Delaware	248,387	0	248,387	99,177	175,003	44,954	75,293	286,032	0	928,846	522,328
Maine	264,597	914	265,511	153,415	25,553	71,873	17,897	22,540	21,895	578,684	99,612
Massachusetts	1,429,522	104,234	1,533,756	259,788	210,863	190,622	499,357	726,999	125,140	3,546,525	1,025,099
New Hampshire	144,486	10,236	154,722	133,243	35,078	56,258	20,300	26,118	27,012	452,731	279,969
New Jersey	1,943,706	13,109	1,956,815	302,592	231,499	204,819	520,679	2,873,172	274,253	6,363,829	1,821,688
New York	2,233,467	285,850	2,519,317	1,136,696	248,493	306,640	595,971	1,520,644	264,408	6,592,169	-308,453
Pennsylvania	2,835,396	0	2,835,396	750,960	282,304	461,140	173,609	546,141	208,245	5,257,795	1,801,254
Rhode Island	121,100	11,486	132,586	66,998	29,856	16,993	15,237	37,414	0	299,084	47,130
Vermont	115,799	20,743	136,542	51,107	41,351	46,130	506	2,954	33,073	311,663	72,505
Regional average	994,007	45,837	1,039,844	306,541	163,009	151,725	207,910	668,218	97,270	2,607,455	621,056
Midwestern Region											
Illinois	1,907,846	605,027	2,512,873	478,131	189,785	227,340	157,819	370,547	658,930	4,595,425	1,282,821
Indiana	927,522	186,874	1,114,396	318,346	109,545	203,115	90,649	31,925	576,844	2,444,820	519,521
Iowa	620,041	0	620,041	105,405	43,749	80,309	0	0	569,970	1,419,474	42,324
Kansas	697,771	95,891	793,662	131,542	72,449	56,398	78,528	612,345	146,454	1,891,378	704,459
Michigan	1,094,807	103,492	1,198,299	245,353	92,693	228,512	37,741	25,628	970,581	2,798,807	1,004,609
Minnesota	678,085	0	678,085	434,738	74,863	94,300	4,266	16,240	666,830	1,969,322	848,786
Nebraska	344,330	12,308	356,638	150,653	61,261	58,719	0	0	211,409	838,680	91,083
North Dakota	211,443	12,177	223,620	43,450	25,698	20,698	0	0	65,549	379,015	54,308
Ohio	1,347,514	268,587	1,616,101	419,904	214,477	238,473	101,760	201,905	867,588	3,660,208	1,038,783
South Dakota	267,191	19,537	286,728	46,283	35,014	31,584	0	0	41,613	441,222	71,129
Wisconsin	843,522	156,645	1,000,167	163,601	172,158	72,823	66,033	45,557	383,465	1,903,804	445,748
Regional average	812,734	132,776	945,510	230,673	106,139	119,297	48,800	118,559	469,021	2,031,105	554,870
Southern Region											
Alabama	958,803	0	958,803	134,540	105,590	103,400	384	13,600	255,822	1,572,139	548,178
Arkansas	745,458	9,519	754,977	154,110	26,355	55,168	23,996	0	161,558	1,176,164	340,109
Florida	3,481,552	117,029	3,598,581	714,002	199,039	279,648	286,376	1,399,768	186,199	6,663,613	1,642,611
Georgia	1,148,379	102,382	1,250,761	144,106	96,639	293,316	78,313	86,099	570	1,949,804	1,347,385
Kentucky	1,101,898	34,679	1,136,577	450,634	187,527	57,476	60,162	121,090	138,680	2,152,146	778,445
Louisiana	803,432	0	803,432	273,280	43,717	137,442	38,407	147,776	53,773	1,497,827	890,960
Maryland	794,873	25,149	820,022	223,190	69,101	151,289	46,467	143,153	431,450	1,884,672	632,304
Mississippi	559,095	112,542	671,637	80,960	51,110	47,632	17,937	38,210	106,571	1,014,057	466,983
Missouri	1,181,263	77,568	1,258,831	366,202	69,409	124,997	28,041	15,935	256,441	2,119,856	428,430
North Carolina	1,834,157	0	1,834,157	569,994	169,367	283,596	8,681	16,675	130,206	3,012,676	599,899
Oklahoma	530,351	32,328	562,679	172,133	117,658	79,922	85,377	137,511	223,487	1,378,767	437,079
South Carolina	628,619	0	628,619	229,711	75,984	114,275	39,896	61,600	40,823	1,190,908	204,647
Tennessee	817,176	33,029	850,205	302,167	135,242	90,417	0	0	282,474	1,660,505	1,020,167
Texas	4,042,753	0	4,042,753	1,134,762	383,190	462,826	42,937	253,395	437,718	6,757,581	3,404,651
Virginia	1,245,921	0	1,245,921	926,846	191,273	143,476	132,511	526,091	253,034	3,419,152	1,415,271
West Virginia	612,529	0	612,529	302,217	88,831	41,565	35,621	87,824	0	1,168,587	182,680
Regional average	1,282,689	34,014	1,314,405	350,134	127,756	154,153	57,819	190,545	184,925	2,413,653	896,237

See footnotes at end of table.

HIGHWAYS

STATE DISBURSEMENTS FOR HIGHWAYS, BY REGION: 2003 — Continued
(In thousands of dollars)

State or other jurisdiction	Capital outlay — State administered highways (a)	Capital outlay — Locally administered roads	Capital outlay — Total	Maintenance and highway service expenditures (b)	Administration, research and planning	Highway law enforcement and safety	Interest	Bond retirement (c)	Grants in-aid to local governments	Total disbursements	Total year-end balances (d)
Western Region											
Alaska	401,540	0	401,540	143,742	42,440	26,268	0	0	4,087	618,077	78,969
Arizona	949,937	28,336	978,273	98,324	175,074	149,816	86,855	351,100	613,725	2,453,167	712,449
California	4,130,309	75,114	4,205,423	708,201	1,156,616	1,141,513	0	0	2,137,241	9,348,994	4,718,741
Colorado	825,201	2,170	827,371	453,789	82,950	113,052	70,102	0	240,446	1,787,710	990,086
Hawaii	151,891	0	151,891	33,622	53,956	4,837	22,651	65,797	42,140	374,894	403,417
Idaho	267,703	40,919	308,622	60,290	23,629	22,371	0	0	131,859	546,771	215,181
Montana	322,101	0	322,101	78,691	51,393	43,179	515	13,095	69,015	577,989	95,811
Nevada	373,456	0	373,456	75,080	118,059	63,157	5,996	8,430	162,386	806,564	431,544
New Mexico	443,459	13	443,472	149,147	71,098	12,671	50,792	69,780	64,677	861,637	250,286
Oregon	419,163	83,226	502,389	214,488	65,419	52,722	13,368	26,860	107,919	983,165	543,223
Utah	451,097	0	451,097	107,064	62,396	36,845	51,609	35,550	134,255	878,816	523,618
Washington	855,960	31,556	887,516	303,246	90,015	162,161	76,885	147,030	621,574	2,288,427	380,275
Wyoming	281,580	0	281,580	81,642	43,066	24,696	0	0	36,521	467,505	23,977
Regional average	799,318	20,103	779,595	192,871	159,838	142,561	29,136	55,203	335,834	1,691,824	720,583
Regional average without California	496,501	15,518	494,109	149,927	69,221	59,315	31,564	59,804	185,717	1,053,727	387,403
Dist. of Columbia	0	251,054	251,054	70,548	27,245	0	7,043	11,913	0	367,803	56,442

Source: U.S. Department of Transportation, Federal Highway Administration, *Highway Statistics, 2003* (November 2004).

Note: This table is compiled from reports provided by state authorities.

(a) Includes expenditures for local roads and streets under state control. Most local roads are under state control in Delaware, North Carolina, Virginia and West Virginia.

(b) Includes disbursements for state administered highways and local roads and streets.

(c) Bond retirement includes current revenues or sinking funds and refunding bonds.

(d) Total year-end balances include reserves for current highway work and debt reserve.

Table 9.9
TOTAL ROAD AND STREET MILEAGE: 2003
(Classified by jurisdiction)

State or other jurisdiction	Rural mileage						Urban mileage						Total rural & urban mileage
	Under state control	Under county control	Town, township & municipal control (a)	Other jurisdictions (b)	Under federal control (c)	Total rural roads	Under state control	Under county control	Town, township & municipal control (a)	Other jurisdictions (b)	Under federal control (c)	Total urban mileage	
United States	652,522	1,623,786	580,825	55,792	120,208	3,033,133	120,033	156,598	647,448	13,331	3,560	940,970	3,974,103
Eastern Region													
Connecticut	1,288	0	4,572	243	17	6,120	2,430	0	12,452	37	50	14,969	21,089
Delaware	3,587	0	271	1	6	3,865	1,593	0	435	0	0	2,028	5,893
Maine	7,634	0	12,099	159	168	20,060	771	0	1,816	41	4	2,632	22,692
Massachusetts	704	0	6,769	408	28	7,909	2,131	4	25,114	350	82	27,681	35,590
New Hampshire	3,674	0	8,834	0	85	12,593	440	0	2,578	0	16	3,034	15,627
New Jersey	453	2,467	3,639	582	268	7,409	1,860	4,868	24,282	443	89	31,542	38,951
New York	11,003	16,864	43,412	674	27	71,980	4,030	3,513	32,836	699	68	41,146	113,126
Pennsylvania	29,558	12	48,998	3,420	745	82,733	10,335	274	26,656	336	88	37,689	120,422
Rhode Island	317	0	896	0	10	1,223	786	0	4,386	3	18	5,193	6,416
Vermont	2,453	0	10,165	210	149	12,977	177	0	1,182	0	24	1,383	14,360
Regional total	6,067	1,934	13,966	570	150	22,687	2,455	866	13,174	191	44	16,730	39,417
Midwestern Region													
Illinois	11,619	14,614	74,639	419	227	101,518	4,542	1,837	30,342	261	25	37,007	138,525
Indiana	9,534	61,113	3,351	0	0	73,998	1,652	5,618	13,329	0	0	20,599	94,597
Iowa	7,920	88,740	5,693	359	100	102,812	961	1,106	8,450	170	19	10,706	113,518
Kansas	9,755	111,373	5	2,786	499	124,418	623	0	2,442	7,529	0	10,594	135,012
Michigan	7,145	75,145	3,063	37	1,744	87,134	2,596	14,709	17,782	0	0	35,087	122,221
Minnesota	10,806	43,252	58,312	1,311	2,003	115,684	1,123	1,958	13,122	5	0	16,208	131,892
Nebraska	9,650	61,241	16,081	296	162	87,430	336	563	4,867	0	0	5,766	93,196
North Dakota	7,177	9,996	66,209	23	1,542	84,947	205	0	1,630	0	0	1,835	86,782
Ohio	14,264	25,825	36,572	3,168	430	80,259	5,027	3,318	34,839	73	5	43,262	123,521
South Dakota	7,652	35,993	35,712	113	1,954	81,424	188	160	1,877	37	1	2,263	83,687
Wisconsin	10,000	19,370	62,757	11	839	92,977	1,772	1,230	17,233	57	0	20,292	113,269
Regional total	9,593	49,697	32,945	775	864	93,873	1,730	2,773	13,265	739	5	18,511	112,384
Southern Region													
Alabama	8,959	58,464	5,072	169	812	73,476	1,933	298	18,153	0	574	20,958	94,434
Arkansas	15,027	65,580	4,970	1	2,154	87,732	1,355	476	8,806	0	170	10,807	98,539
Florida	7,058	40,553	2,342	0	1,944	51,897	4,994	30,537	32,807	0	141	68,479	120,376
Georgia	14,859	67,658	4,005	368	1,085	87,975	3,013	15,307	9,768	427	43	28,558	116,533
Kentucky	24,995	36,969	2,060	237	767	65,028	2,503	1,579	7,697	47	157	11,983	77,011
Louisiana	14,654	29,107	2,601	3	622	46,987	2,039	3,321	8,576	14	0	13,950	60,937
Maryland	3,099	10,249	377	139	43	13,907	2,037	10,335	4,168	125	115	16,780	30,687
Mississippi	9,583	50,570	2,490	30	770	63,443	1,330	2,313	6,956	6	57	10,662	74,105

See footnotes at end of table.

TOTAL ROAD AND STREET MILEAGE: 2003—Continued
(Classified by jurisdiction)

State or other jurisdiction	Rural mileage						Urban mileage						Total rural & urban mileage
	Under state control	Under county control	Town, township & municipal control (a)	Other jurisdictions (b)	Under federal control (c)	Total rural roads	Under state control	Under county control	Town, township & municipal control (a)	Other jurisdictions (b)	Under federal control (c)	Total urban mileage	
Southern Region													
Missouri (d)	30,682	69,810	5,586	1	1,031	107,110	1,766	1,797	14,013	0	0	17,576	124,686
North Carolina	69,350	0	4,572	748	3,079	77,749	9,291	0	14,978	0	142	24,411	102,160
Oklahoma	11,077	78,509	6,838	1,107	54	97,585	1,186	2,142	11,551	112	0	14,991	112,576
South Carolina	34,524	18,098	490	191	2,243	55,546	6,951	2,104	1,631	0	0	10,686	66,232
Tennessee	10,945	52,623	3,697	531	304	68,100	2,848	3,950	13,604	11	7	20,420	88,520
Texas	68,373	136,412	13,060	23	833	218,701	11,121	6,412	65,625	130	0	83,288	301,989
Virginia	47,932	28	602	24	1,645	50,231	9,391	1,582	9,812	15	212	21,012	71,243
West Virginia	32,444	0	609	73	677	33,803	1,455	0	1,721	14	0	3,190	36,993
Regional total	25,223	44,664	3,711	228	1,129	74,954	3,951	5,135	14,367	56	101	23,609	98,564
Western Region													
Alaska	5,060	2,214	1,861	736	2,289	12,160	565	1,477	24	3	0	2,069	14,229
Arizona	5,869	16,459	1,880	152	11,269	35,629	917	3,088	17,306	151	438	21,900	57,529
California	11,414	53,745	1,875	3,018	13,875	83,927	3,811	11,772	69,350	47	641	85,621	169,548
Colorado	7,693	50,437	2,155	1,283	7,125	68,693	1,420	4,571	12,077	25	35	18,128	86,821
Hawaii	675	1,357	0	48	101	2,181	260	1,842	0	8	17	2,127	4,308
Idaho	4,655	15,080	159	14,401	8,223	42,518	301	105	2,244	1,750	11	4,411	46,929
Montana	7,684	43,702	1,203	374	13,735	66,698	196	42	2,514	0	0	2,752	69,450
Nevada	4,900	20,277	564	689	1,820	28,250	549	1,551	3,626	0	0	5,726	33,976
New Mexico	10,593	36,037	2,196	145	8,168	57,139	814	2,648	3,352	0	0	6,814	63,953
Oregon	6,813	31,676	1,790	4,638	9,967	54,884	732	1,822	8,390	100	23	11,067	65,951
Utah	5,083	22,812	2,643	10	3,979	34,527	769	905	6,386	0	131	8,191	42,718
Washington	5,978	35,281	2,430	11,866	7,252	62,807	1,071	5,073	13,221	94	0	19,459	82,266
Wyoming	6,351	14,074	649	567	3,339	24,980	409	391	1,442	192	69	2,503	27,483
Regional total	6,367	26,396	1,493	2,917	7,011	44,184	909	2,714	10,764	182	105	14,674	58,859
Regional total without California	5,946	24,117	1,461	2,909	6,439	40,872	667	1,960	5,882	194	60	8,762	49,634
Dist. of Columbia	0	0	0	0	0	0	1,428	0	0	19	88	1,535	1,535
Puerto Rico	1,061	0	2,072	0	22	3,155	3,494	0	9,082	0	7	12,583	15,738

Source: U.S. Department of Transportation, Federal Highway Administration, *Highway Statistics, 2003* (October 2004).

Key:

. . . — Not applicable.

(a) Prior to 1999, municipal was included with other jurisdictions.

(b) Includes state park, state toll, other state agency and other local agency and other roadways not identified by ownership.

(c) Roadways in federal parks, forests, and reservations that are not part of the state and local highway systems.

(d) 2002 data used.

Table 9.10
APPORTIONMENT OF FEDERAL-AID HIGHWAY FUNDS BY REGION: FISCAL YEAR 2004
(In thousands of dollars)

State or other jurisdiction	Interstate maintenance	National highway system	Surface transportation program	Bridge program	Congestion mitigation & air quality improvement	Appalachian development highway system	Recreation trails	Metropolitan planning	Minimum guarantee	Special minimum guarantee	Total (a)
United States	$4,623,245	$5,646,868	$6,612,124	$3,970,589	$1,618,091	$512,506	$57,657	$238,584	$7,252,725	$2,744,973	$33,277,362
Eastern Region											
Connecticut	47,666	44,141	61,695	76,807	32,211	0	675	3,375	169,814	47,878	484,262
Delaware	7,753	43,249	32,811	12,943	8,005	0	611	1,193	31,022	3,489	141,076
Maine	26,172	30,636	36,097	28,913	8,201	0	878	1,193	29,565	6,176	167,830
Massachusetts	81,299	81,467	115,571	146,159	62,270	0	937	6,677	73,260	26,702	594,342
New Hampshire	18,491	33,596	33,509	22,341	8,175	0	762	1,193	34,024	12,552	164,641
New Jersey	87,633	132,594	151,628	198,083	94,503	0	966	9,188	138,366	83,455	896,417
New York	163,828	190,396	254,640	396,669	149,873	12,174	1,377	18,373	325,707	133,314	1,646,351
Pennsylvania	173,369	190,915	237,435	402,417	84,589	140,113	1,403	9,730	214,245	136,617	1,590,833
Rhode Island	10,398	40,822	32,951	49,759	9,155	0	609	1,193	38,538	6,568	189,993
Vermont	15,639	36,015	33,230	25,478	8,107	0	704	1,193	20,952	4,509	145,827
Regional average	63,225	82,383	98,957	135,957	46,509	15,229	892	5,331	107,549	46,126	602,157
Midwestern Region											
Illinois	208,122	183,295	245,517	142,326	84,029	0	1,465	11,539	139,812	62,341	1,078,445
Indiana	120,463	126,487	155,990	41,893	15,085	0	959	4,042	219,994	67,280	752,191
Iowa	63,533	92,215	96,612	63,612	8,249	0	997	1,321	39,116	17,647	383,302
Kansas	60,363	83,602	106,243	59,404	8,261	0	992	1,431	35,568	17,775	373,640
Michigan	137,949	167,442	231,937	117,596	34,034	0	1,781	7,795	241,430	68,478	1,008,443
Minnesota	86,279	104,887	134,145	30,502	17,140	0	1,372	3,213	58,742	41,828	478,108
Nebraska	41,152	72,017	67,306	30,969	8,261	0	834	1,193	24,980	1,000	247,712
North Dakota	26,833	75,478	40,679	9,766	7,969	0	716	1,193	38,565	7,769	208,967
Ohio	193,760	178,737	230,364	121,892	52,020	25,241	1,367	8,664	214,907	110,305	1,137,257
South Dakota	31,841	62,878	44,819	14,040	7,957	0	724	1,193	47,630	16,890	227,972
Wisconsin	77,407	124,565	138,115	33,294	19,425	0	1,318	3,368	196,184	41,420	635,096
Regional average	95,246	115,600	135,612	60,481	23,857	2,295	1,139	4,087	114,266	41,158	593,739
Southern Region											
Alabama	90,138	102,254	131,709	77,780	8,106	56,582	1,128	2,300	134,649	41,705	646,352
Arkansas	63,041	77,596	90,170	46,637	7,904	0	934	1,193	94,920	38,983	421,378
Florida	180,339	256,640	305,847	65,166	40,416	0	1,932	15,962	608,741	151,046	1,626,091
Georgia	174,984	169,772	232,403	61,997	32,939	22,339	1,488	5,937	378,331	121,179	1,201,369
Kentucky	92,837	103,276	112,549	64,030	9,728	52,092	920	1,857	98,389	18,070	553,748
Louisiana	77,042	75,566	103,017	101,617	7,891	0	1,176	3,005	97,546	47,243	514,102
Maryland	80,288	88,116	108,096	73,558	48,435	8,953	820	5,096	95,174	48,538	557,073
Mississippi	58,674	81,598	93,153	51,596	7,991	6,255	1,151	1,193	63,834	30,536	395,981
Missouri	124,585	129,784	166,105	133,738	20,721	0	1,162	3,662	112,539	60,755	753,052
North Carolina	122,458	146,303	182,797	98,474	17,023	33,096	1,389	4,457	254,630	57,187	917,813
Oklahoma	85,188	106,299	131,582	94,797	8,247	0	1,071	1,758	49,936	50,231	529,111
South Carolina	80,662	81,370	113,715	54,805	7,871	2,692	879	2,220	160,233	48,459	552,907
Tennessee	118,259	121,609	146,120	66,485	14,224	62,438	1,082	3,513	131,744	64,448	729,925
Texas	360,453	456,184	545,406	153,547	96,045	0	2,534	17,533	803,010	308,890	2,743,602
Virginia	129,956	127,199	170,635	81,596	32,151	13,071	1,031	5,585	201,370	104,421	867,016
West Virginia	40,878	41,793	50,665	59,270	7,981	77,458	835	1,193	35,469	45,407	360,948
Regional average	117,486	135,335	167,748	80,318	22,980	20,936	1,221	4,779	207,532	77,319	835,654

See footnotes at end of table.

APPORTIONMENT OF FEDERAL-AID HIGHWAY FUNDS BY REGION: FISCAL YEAR 2004—Continued
(In thousands of dollars)

State or other jurisdiction	Interstate maintenance	National highway system	Surface transportation program	Bridge program	Congestion mitigation & air quality improvement	Appalachian development highway system	Recreation trails	Metropolitan planning	Minimum guarantee	Special minimum guarantee	Total (a)
Western Region											
Alaska	21,293	26,820	30,123	10,622	7,349	0	789	1,193	233,076	48,690	379,954
Arizona	92,543	100,206	113,571	11,412	33,173	0	1,245	4,631	181,799	56,372	594,953
California	412,855	529,273	646,100	319,659	352,511	0	4,024	35,573	548,626	252,160	3,100,780
Colorado	73,691	95,162	100,853	24,955	20,263	0	1,437	3,807	80,514	43,290	443,973
Hawaii	8,363	44,164	33,792	22,475	8,244	0	640	1,193	37,679	8,537	165,088
Idaho	35,315	47,121	40,470	15,207	8,023	0	958	1,193	70,811	27,020	246,117
Montana	46,785	64,508	39,511	13,292	7,590	0	959	1,193	119,029	23,755	316,623
Nevada	39,854	45,533	45,145	9,907	13,683	0	783	1,986	65,048	9,188	231,129
New Mexico	63,877	70,841	56,533	12,271	7,881	0	1,002	1,193	75,955	25,636	315,188
Oregon	61,688	80,058	87,190	49,970	11,464	0	990	2,342	59,574	35,224	388,500
Utah	65,224	47,390	55,829	27,137	10,822	0	990	2,071	27,795	16,806	254,063
Washington	91,963	102,415	131,087	109,705	25,635	0	1,373	5,100	70,241	32,492	570,011
Wyoming	47,205	81,573	31,999	9,567	7,807	0	891	1,193	28,410	13,014	221,658
Regional average	81,589	102,697	108,631	48,937	39,573	0	1,237	4,821	122,966	45,553	556,003
Regional average without California	53,983	67,149	63,842	26,377	13,495	0	1,005	2,258	87,494	28,335	343,938
Dist. of Columbia	2,857	51,013	34,656	24,457	8,455	0	594	1,193	1,231	1,695	126,152
American Samoa	0	0	3,015	0	0	0	0	0	0	0	3,015
Guam	0	0	9,592	0	0	0	0	0	0	0	9,592
No. Mariana Islands	0	0	3,015	0	0	0	0	0	0	0	3,015
Puerto Rico (b)	0	0	0	0	0	0	0	0	0	0	0
U.S. Virgin Islands	0	0	12,062	0	0	0	0	0	0	0	12,062

Source: U.S. Department of Transportation, Federal Highway Administration, *Highway Statistics, 2003* (November 2004).

Note: Apportioned pursuant to the Transportation Efficiency Act of 1998 (TEA-21) as amended by the TEA-21 Restoration Act. Does not include funds from the Mass Transit Account of the Highway Trust Fund.

(a) Does not include funds from the following programs: emergency relief, Federal lands highway programs, Commonwealth of Puerto Rico highway programs, high priority projects, Woodrow Wilson Bridge, National Byways, construction of ferry boats and ferry terminal facilities, and intelligent vehicle-system, among others. These funds are allocated from the Highway Trust Fund.

(b) Under several extensions of TEA-21, Puerto Rico received a stand-alone authorization of $72,974,214 for FY 2004.

Table 9.11
TRENDS IN STATE PRISON POPULATION BY REGION, 2003–2004

State or other jurisdiction	Total population June 30, 2004	Total population December 31, 2003	Total population June 30, 2003	Percent change from - June 30, 2003 to June 30, 2004	Percent change from - December 31, 2003 to June 30, 2004	Incarceration rate June 30, 2004 (a)
United States	1,494,216	1,468,530	1,464,197	2.1%	1.7%	486
Federal.................................	179,210	173,059	170,461	5.1	3.6	53
State....................................	1,315,006	1,295,471	1,293,736	1.6	1.5	433
Eastern Region						
Connecticut (b)	20,018	19,846	20,525	-2.5	0.9	379
Delaware (b)	6,973	6,794	6,879	1.4	2.6	487
Maine..................................	2,014	2,013	2,009	0.2	0.0	149
Massachusetts (c).................	10,365	10,232	10,511	-1.4	1.3	234
New Hampshire	2,441	2,434	2,483	-1.7	0.3	188
New Jersey (d)	28,107	27,246	28,213	-0.4	3.2	323
New York..............................	64,596	65,198	65,914	-2.0	-0.9	336
Pennsylvania........................	40,692	40,890	40,545	0.4	-0.5	328
Rhode Island (b)	3,701	3,527	3,569	3.7	4.9	187
Vermont (b)..........................	2,033	1,944	1,984	2.5	4.6	236
Regional total	180,940	180,124	182,632	-0.9	-1.4	...
Midwestern Region						
Illinois (d)............................	44,379	43,418	43,186	2.8	2.2	349
Indiana................................	23,760	23,069	22,576	5.2	3.0	380
Iowa	8,611	8,546	8,395	2.6	0.8	292
Kansas (d)............................	9,152	9,132	9,009	1.6	0.2	335
Michigan..............................	48,591	49,358	49,524	-1.9	-1.6	480
Minnesota............................	8,613	7,865	7,612	13.2	9.5	169
Nebraska..............................	4,042	4,040	4,103	-1.5	0.0	227
North Dakota	1,266	1,239	1,168	8.4	2.2	189
Ohio (d)	44,770	44,778	45,831	-2.3	0.0	391
South Dakota	3,101	3,026	3,059	1.4	2.5	402
Wisconsin	22,905	22,614	22,352	2.5	1.3	394
Regional total	219,190	217,085	216,815	1.1	0.1	...
Southern Region						
Alabama...............................	26,521	27,913	28,440	-6.7	-5.0	554
Arkansas..............................	13,477	13,084	12,378	8.9	3.0	487
Florida	84,733	82,012	80,352	5.5	3.3	489
Georgia (e)...........................	48,625	47,208	47,004	3.4	3.0	551
Kentucky	17,763	16,622	16,377	8.5	6.9	413
Louisiana	36,745	36,047	36,091	1.8	1.9	814
Maryland.............................	23,727	23,791	24,186	-1.9	-0.3	416
Mississippi...........................	20,429	20,589	20,542	-0.6	-0.8	682
Missouri...............................	30,775	30,303	30,649	0.4	1.6	536
North Carolina	34,917	33,560	33,334	4.7	4.0	358
Oklahoma (d).......................	24,767	22,821	23,004	7.7	8.5	684
South Carolina.....................	24,173	23,719	24,247	-0.3	1.9	555
Tennessee............................	25,834	25,403	25,409	1.7	1.7	439
Texas....................................	169,110	166,911	167,532	0.9	1.3	704
Virginia...............................	35,472	35,067	34,733	2.1	1.2	474
West Virginia	4,980	4,758	4,703	5.9	4.7	272
Regional total	622,048	609,808	608,981	2.2	0.1	...
Western Region						
Alaska (b)	4,515	4,527	4,431	1.9	-0.3	367
Arizona (e)...........................	31,631	31,170	30,741	2.9	1.5	506
California.............................	166,053	164,487	163,361	1.6	1.0	457
Colorado (d)	19,756	19,671	19,085	3.5	0.4	429
Hawaii (b)............................	5,946	5,828	5,635	5.5	2.0	320
Idaho...................................	6,312	5,887	5,825	8.4	7.2	454
Montana...............................	3,800	3,620	3,440	10.5	5.0	410
Nevada.................................	10,971	10,543	10,527	4.2	4.1	468
New Mexico	6,341	6,223	6,145	3.2	1.9	319
Oregon.................................	13,219	12,715	12,422	6.4	4.0	366
Utah....................................	5,802	5,763	5,603	3.6	0.7	239
Washington	16,559	16,148	16,284	1.7	2.5	264
Wyoming	1,923	1,872	1,809	6.3	2.7	382
Regional total	292,828	288,454	285,308	2.6	1.5	...
Regional total without California...........	126,775	123,967	121,947	4.0	1.7	...

Source: U.S. Department of Justice, Bureau of Justice Statistics, *Bulletin, Prisoners and Jail Inmates at Midyear 2004* (April 2005).

Key:
. . . — Not available.

(a) The number of prisoners with sentences of more than one year per 100,000 residents.

(b) Prisons and jails form one integrated system. Data include total jail and prison population.

(c) The incarceration rate includes an estimated 6,200 inmates sentenced to more than 1 year but held in local jails or houses of corrections.

(d) "Sentenced to more than 1 year" includes some inmates "sentenced to 1 year or less."

(e) Population figures are based on custody counts.

Table 9.12
NUMBER OF SENTENCED PRISONERS ADMITTED AND RELEASED, BY REGION: 2000, and 2002–2003

State or other jurisdiction	Admissions (a)				Releases (a)			
	2003	2002	2000	Percent change 2000–2003	2003	2002	2000	Percent change 2000–2003
United States	686,437	661,082	625,219	9.8%	656,384	630,176	604,858	8.5%
Federal..................................	52,288	48,144	43,732	19.6	44,199	42,339	35,259	25.4
State.....................................	634,149	612,938	581,487	9.1	612,185	587,837	569,599	7.5
Eastern Region								
Connecticut	6,571	7,169	6,185	6.2	6,890	6,209	5,918	16.4
Delaware (b)	2,212	. . .	2,709	-18.3	2,129	. . .	2,260	-5.8
Maine...................................	931	1,026	751	24.0	782	799	677	15.5
Massachusetts.....................	2,185	1,833	2,062	6.0	2,302	2,290	2,889	-20.3
New Hampshire	1,139	1,113	1,051	8.4	1,188	1,052	1,044	13.8
New Jersey	14,398	14,576	13,653	5.5	15,043	14,827	15,362	-2.1
New York.............................	26,040	26,216	27,601	-5.7	27,467	26,829	28,828	-4.7
Pennsylvania.......................	14,039	13,401	11,777	19.2	13,268	10,628	11,759	12.8
Rhode Island	3,881	3,760	3,701	4.9	3,684	3,312	3,223	14.3
Vermont (b).........................	1,987	1,785	984	101.9	1,985	1,857	946	109.8
Regional total	73,383	70,879	70,474	4.1	74,738	67,803	72,906	2.5
Midwestern Region								
Illinois	36,063	34,467	29,344	22.9	35,372	36,162	28,876	22.5
Indiana................................	15,615	14,001	11,876	31.5	14,146	13,337	11,053	28.0
Iowa....................................	5,545	5,516	4,656	19.1	6,074	5,748	4,379	38.7
Kansas	4,605	4,881	5,002	-7.9	4,405	4,524	5,231	-15.8
Michigan.............................	12,659	14,411	12,169	4.0	13,910	12,771	10,874	27.9
Minnesota	5,914	5,265	4,406	34.2	5,437	4,706	4,244	28.1
Nebraska	1,959	1,934	1,688	16.1	1,953	1,840	1,503	29.9
North Dakota	992	768	605	64.0	870	770	598	45.5
Ohio	26,506	25,689	23,780	11.5	27,369	25,322	24,793	10.4
South Dakota	1,915	1,819	1,400	36.8	1,980	1,797	1,327	49.2
Wisconsin	8,000	7,990	8,396	-4.7	8,107	7,699	8,158	-0.6
Regional total	119,773	116,741	103,322	16.0	119,623	114,676	101,036	18.4
Southern Region								
Alabama...............................	9,524	7,033	6,296	51.3	10,167	7,472	7,136	42.5
Arkansas	7,132	7,080	6,941	2.8	7,120	7,640	6,308	12.9
Florida	39,500	36,500	35,683	10.7	34,679	33,728	33,994	2.0
Georgia	17,575	18,078	17,373	1.2	17,333	16,608	14,797	17.1
Kentucky	9,595	8,731	8,116	18.2	9,208	8,313	7,733	19.1
Louisiana	15,353	15,079	15,735	-2.4	13,841	14,847	14,536	-4.8
Maryland.............................	10,170	10,027	10,327	-1.5	10,207	9,617	10,004	2.0
Mississippi..........................	8,421	5,655	5,796	45.3	7,679	5,592	4,940	55.4
Missouri..............................	17,151	16,637	14,454	18.7	16,967	15,127	13,346	27.1
North Carolina	9,494	9,661	9,848	-3.6	9,116	8,606	9,687	-5.9
Oklahoma	8,139	8,269	7,426	9.6	8,164	8,375	6,628	23.2
South Carolina	9,934	9,834	8,460	17.4	9,829	8,604	8,676	13.3
Tennessee	13,059	15,022	13,675	-4.5	13,768	13,541	13,893	-0.9
Texas...................................	69,921	63,446	58,197	20.1	65,169	64,720	59,776	9.0
Virginia...............................	11,700	11,392	9,791	19.5	11,606	10,033	9,148	26.9
West Virginia	2,097	2,161	1,577	33.0	1,881	1,807	1,261	49.2
Regional total	258,765	244,605	229,695	12.7	246,734	234,630	221,863	11.2
Western Region								
Alaska	2,805	2,315	2,427	15.6	2,736	2,230	2,599	5.3
Arizona	11,957	11,468	9,560	25.1	10,391	10,056	9,100	14.2
California.............................	125,312	124,179	129,640	-3.3	118,646	119,683	129,621	-8.5
Colorado	7,998	7,953	7,036	13.7	7,113	6,588	5,881	20.9
Hawaii	1,832	1,892	1,594	14.9	1,504	1,735	1,379	9.1
Idaho...................................	3,168	3,049	3,386	-6.4	3,033	2,855	2,697	12.5
Montana..............................	1,910	1,510	1,202	58.	1,642	1,518	1,031	59.3
Nevada................................	4,865	4,844	4,929	-1.3	4,800	4,734	4,374	9.7
New Mexico	4,160	4,009	3,161	31.6	3,943	3,809	3,383	16.6
Oregon	5,095	5,041	4,059	25.5	4,483	4,339	3,371	33.0
Utah	3,301	3,064	3,270	0.9	3,088	2,864	2,897	6.6
Washington (b)	9,034	8,305	7,094	. . .	9,067	7,401	6,764	. . .
Wyoming	791	769	638	24.0	644	686	697	-7.6
Regional total	182,228	178,398	177,996	2.4	171,090	168,498	173,794	-1.6
Regional total without California...........	56,916	54,219	48,356	17.7	52,444	48,815	44,173	18.7

Source: U.S. Department of Justice, Bureau of Justice Statistics, *Bulletin, Prisoners and Jail Inmates at Midyear 2004* (April 2005).
Note: Excludes escapes, AWOL's and transfers to and from other jurisdictions.
Key:
. . . — Data not reported and percent change not calculated.

(a) Based on inmates under jurisdiction with a sentence of more than one year.
(b) Data not comparable from year to year due to changes in reporting methods.

Table 9.13
STATE PRISON CAPACITIES, BY REGION: 2003

State or other jurisdiction	Rated capacity	Operational capacity	Design capacity	Population as a percent of capacity: (a) Highest capacity	Lowest capacity
Federal................................	106,046	...	...	139%	139%
Eastern Region					
Connecticut..........................	...	...	...	...	...
Delaware..............................	...	5,359	4,223	124	157
Maine...................................	1,779	1,779	1,779	109	109
Massachusetts......................	...	...	7,721	127	127
New Hampshire	2,419	2,238	2,213	100	110
New Jersey	...	26,536	...	87	87
New York.............................	60,392	62,568	53,601	105	122
Pennsylvania........................	34,240	34,240	26,493	118	152
Rhode Island........................	3,922	3,922	4,085	88	91
Vermont	1,636	1,636	1,474	91	101
Midwestern Region					
Illinois	31,434	31,434	27,339	138	159
Indiana................................	16,755	22,871	...	90	124
Iowa....................................	6,772	6,772	6,772	126	126
Kansas	9,244	...	...	99	99
Michigan..............................	...	50,103	...	98	98
Minnesota	...	7,595	...	99	99
Nebraska..............................	...	3,799	3,039	107	134
North Dakota	1,005	952	1,005	109	116
Ohio....................................	36,526	...	...	116	116
South Dakota	3,209	...	...	93	93
Wisconsin	...	15,951	...	127	127
Southern Region					
Alabama...............................	...	24,998	12,388	104	209
Arkansas (b)	12,866	12,649	11,976	94	101
Florida	...	80,942	60,000	98	133
Georgia	...	47,252	...	100	100
Kentucky	...	12,275	...	82	82
Louisiana	19,498	20,030	...	97	100
Maryland	...	23,745	...	100	100
Mississippi (b)	...	21,737	...	73	73
Missouri..............................	...	31,500	...	95	95
North Carolina	30,261	...	...	112	112
Oklahoma (b).......................	23,856	...	...	95	95
South Carolina	...	23,946	...	96	96
Tennessee (b)	20,122	19,670	...	95	97
Texas (b).............................	159,087	155,351	159,087	86	88
Virginia...............................	31,074	...	...	94	94
West Virginia	3,398	3,880	3,398	98	112
Western Region					
Alaska..................................	...	3,098	3,098	100	100
Arizona................................	26,940	30,626	25,346	94	113
California.............................	...	157,070	80,487	103	201
Colorado	...	14,069	12,611	116	130
Hawaii	...	3,487	2,451	115	164
Idaho...................................	5,871	5,544	4,564	75	96
Montana..............................	...	2,590	...	77	77
Nevada (b)	11,122	10,639	8,320	95	127
New Mexico (b)...................	6,391	6,385	5,985	97	104
Oregon................................	...	12,246	12,246	100	100
Utah....................................	...	4,536	4,752	97	102
Washington	12,507	14,824	14,824	109	130
Wyoming	1,190	1,146	1,161	96	99

Source: U.S. Department of Justice, Bureau of Justice Statistics, *Prisoners in 2003* (November 2004).

Key:

... — Not available.

(a) Population counts are based on the number of inmates held in facilities operated by the jurisdiction. Excludes inmates held in local jails, in other states, or in private facilities.

(b) Includes capacity of private and contract facilities and inmates housed in them.

Table 9.14
ADULTS ON PROBATION BY REGION, 2004

State or other jurisdiction	1/1/04	Probation population 2004 Entries	Exits	12/31/04	Percent change during 2004	Number on probation on 12/31/04 per 100,000 adult residents
United States (a)..............	4,144,782	2,217,900	2,210,400	4,151,125	0.2%	1,884
Federal..............................	30,601	12,780	14,895	28,346	-7.4	13
State..................................	4,087,012	1,957,306	1,951,231	4,122,779	. . .	. . .
Eastern Region						
Connecticut.........................	52,192	15,656	15,756	52,092	-0.2	1,955
Delaware............................	18,921	15,083	15,279	18,725	-1.0	2,940
Maine................................	9,855	5,676	6,209	9,322	-5.4	901
Massachusetts (b)(c)............	166,464	76,800	79,800	163,471	-1.8	3,301
New Hampshire (d).............	3,987	1,595	1,297	4,285	7.5	431
New Jersey	130,303	45,166	32,154	143,315	10	2,190
New York............................	126,138	38,647	42,758	122,027	-3.3	833
Pennsylvania (a)(c)..............	137,206	4,157	3,476	167,180	. . .	1,747
Rhode Island......................	25,929	6,279	6,123	26,085	0.6	3,117
Vermont	9,810	4,919	4,998	9,731	-0.8	2,000
Regional total	680,805	213,978	207,850	716,233	5.0	19,415
Midwestern Region						
Illinois	144,454	62,354	62,937	143,871	-0.4	1,518
Indiana...............................	118,773	93,918	96,260	116,431	-2	2,511
Iowa..................................	21,413	15,080	13,679	22,832	6.6	1,004
Kansas	14,740	19,577	20,008	14,309	-2.9	697
Michigan (b)(d)...................	179,486	124,000	127,400	176,083	-1.9	2,323
Minnesota	110,046	66,775	62,595	114,226	3.8	2,959
Nebraska............................	18,412	15,282	15,700	17,994	-2.3	1,371
North Dakota	3,566	2,525	2,404	3,687	3.4	744
Ohio (b)(d).........................	218,239	140,800	131,100	227,891	4.4	2,626
South Dakota	5,236	3,310	3,243	5,372	2.6	926
Wisconsin	54,118	24,929	24,077	54,970	1.6	1,308
Regional total	888,483	568,550	559,403	897,666	1.0	17,987
Southern Region						
Alabama (b)........................	39,660	14,700	17,500	36,795	-7.2	1,071
Arkansas	28,164	8,388	7,424	29,128	3.4	1,403
Florida (b)(d)	286,769	246,200	251,800	281,170	-2.0	2,099
Georgia (b)(d)(f).................	402,694	217,100	200,400	419,350	. . .	. . .
Kentucky (b).......................	28,869	20,200	15,800	33,286	15.3	1,051
Louisiana	36,813	14,350	12,693	38,470	4.5	1,148
Maryland	77,875	40,018	41,217	76,676	-1.5	1,842
Mississippi (c)(f)	19,116	8,483	6,275	21,324	11.6	990
Missouri (d)	54,543	25,105	25,816	53,832	-1.3	1,232
North Carolina	113,161	60,069	61,693	111,537	-1.4	1,737
Oklahoma (d)......................	28,326	14,044	13,935	28,435	0.4	1,068
South Carolina	40,354	13,972	15,470	38,856	-3.7	1,224
Tennessee (b)......................	44,359	25,700	21,400	47,392	6.8	1,051
Texas.................................	431,981	198,130	201,338	428,773	-0.7	2,643
Virginia..............................	41,663	25,409	23,602	43,470	4.3	769
West Virginia (b).................	6,864	3,300	3,200	6,977	1.6	488
Regional total	1,681,211	935,168	919,563	1,695,471	0.8	19,816
Western Region						
Alaska................................	5,406	998	857	5,547	2.6	1,187
Arizona (d)	65,554	43,660	39,871	69,343	5.8	1,652
California (d)	374,701	177,896	167,745	384,852	2.7	1,463
Colorado (b)(d)...................	55,297	29,400	26,500	58,108	5.1	1,698
Hawaii	20,165	8,541	7,260	21,446	6.4	2,224
Idaho (d)(g)........................	42,375	36,762	34,930	44,580	. . .	. . .
Montana (b)	6,914	4,000	3,700	7,221	4.4	1,005
Nevada...............................	12,159	6,755	6,393	12,521	3	723
New Mexico	15,899	8,414	6,588	17,725	11.5	1,256
Oregon...............................	43,415	17,183	16,163	44,435	2.3	1,620
Utah..................................	10,339	5,490	5,585	10,244	-0.9	621
Washington (b)(d)...............	172,511	75,300	122,600	125,222	-27.4	2,654
Wyoming	4,662	1,846	2,090	4,418	-5.2	1,134
Regional total	829,397	416,200	440,300	805,662	-2.9	1,620
Regional total without California...........	454,696	238,349	272,537	420,810	-8.0	15,774
Dist. of Columbia (d)..........	7,116	6,944	6,313	7,747	8.9	1,745

See footnotes at end of table.

ADULTS ON PROBATION BY REGION, 2004—Continued

Source: U.S. Department of Justice, Bureau of Justice Statistics, *Probation and Parole in the United States, 2004*, (November 2005).

Note: Because of incomplete data, the population for some jurisdictions on December 31, 2004, does not equal the population on January 1, 2004, plus entries, minus exits.

Key:

. . . — Not calculated.

(a) Due to a change in reporting, January 1, 2004 county probation counts for Pennsylvania were estimated. The comparable total was 164,375. Because of nonreporting, total entries (68,400) and exits (65,600) were estimated to include county probationers.

(b) Data for entries and exits were estimated for nonreporting agencies.

(c) Data are for June 30, 2003, and 2004. Some data for June 30, 2003, are estimated. Due to a change in reporting criteria, data are not comparable to previous reports.

(d) Some or all data were estimated.

(e) Reported data for entries and exits include only state probationers.

(f) Counts include private agency cases and may overstate the number under supervision.

(g) Counts include estimates for misdemeanors based on admissions.

Table 9.15
ADULTS ON PAROLE BY REGION, 2004

State or other jurisdiction	1/1/04	Parole population 2004 Entries	Parole population 2004 Exits	12/31/04	Percent change during 2004	Number on parole on 12/31/04 per 100,000 adult residents
United States (a)...............	745,125	503,200	483,000	765,355	2.7%	347
Federal.............................	86,567	37,712	34,149	89,821	3.8	41
State (reported).................	685,745	450,632	434,642	675,534	. . .	. . .
State (estimated)(a)...........	658,558	465,500	448,800	675,534	2.6	307
Eastern Region (b)						
Connecticut........................	2,343	2,857	2,648	2,552	8.9	96
Delaware............................	529	269	259	539	1.9	85
Maine..............................	32	0	0	32	0	3
Massachusetts....................	3,597	4,862	4,605	3,854	7.1	78
New Hampshire (c).............	1,199	766	753	1,212	1.1	122
New Jersey	13,248	11,030	10,098	14,180	7	217
New York..........................	55,853	23,715	25,044	54,524	-2.4	372
Pennsylvania (a)(d).............	102,244	10,083	8,665	77,175	. . .	806
Rhode Island.....................	363	403	398	368	1.4	44
Vermont	796	546	420	922	15.8	190
Regional total	153,017	69,369	67,059	155,358	1.5	2,013
Midwestern Region						
Illinois	35,008	35,260	35,991	34,277	-2.1	362
Indiana..............................	7,019	7,028	6,548	7,499	6.8	162
Iowa (e)	2,974	2,839	2,496	3,317	11.5	146
Kansas (e)..........................	4,145	4,542	4,162	4,525	9.2	221
Michigan............................	20,233	11,330	10,639	20,924	3.4	276
Minnesota..........................	3,596	4,770	4,494	3,872	7.7	100
Nebraska............................	648	1,112	955	805	24.2	61
North Dakota	225	650	636	239	6.2	48
Ohio..................................	18,427	11,724	11,269	18,882	2.5	218
South Dakota	1,944	1,865	1,592	2,217	14	382
Wisconsin	12,629	7,479	6,225	13,883	9.9	330
Regional total	106,848	88,599	85,007	110,440	3.2	2,306
Southern Region						
Alabama (c)	6,950	3,999	3,204	7,745	11.4	225
Arkansas	13,180	7,182	5,518	14,844	12.6	715
Florida	5,098	5,540	5,750	4,888	-4.1	36
Georgia.............................	21,161	13,178	10,995	23,344	10.3	359
Kentucky (e)	7,744	4,083	3,821	8,006	3.4	253
Louisiana	23,743	13,517	12,873	24,387	2.7	728
Maryland	13,742	8,145	7,536	14,351	4.4	345
Mississippi (d)	1,816	1,056	893	1,979	9	92
Missouri (c)	15,830	13,299	11,729	17,400	9.9	398
North Carolina	2,677	3,411	3,206	2,882	7.7	45
Oklahoma (c)......................	4,047	1,926	1,644	4,329	7	163
South Carolina	3,242	1,313	1,263	3,292	1.5	104
Tennessee..........................	7,957	3,394	2,660	8,410	5.7	186
Texas (c)	102,271	33,463	33,662	102,072	-0.2	629
Virginia (c)	4,834	2,601	3,043	4,392	-9.1	78
West Virginia	1,143	779	706	1,216	6.4	85
Regional total	235,435	116,886	108,503	243,537	3.3	4,441
Western Region						
Alaska (e)	927	630	606	951	2.6	204
Arizona..............................	5,367	8,211	7,907	5,671	5.7	135
California (c)	110,338	154,402	155,046	110,261	-0.1	419
Colorado............................	6,559	6,094	5,270	7,383	12.6	216
Hawaii	2,240	831	775	2,296	3	238
Idaho.................................	2,329	1,578	1,537	2,370	1.8	232
Montana (e)	815	648	653	810	-0.6	113
Nevada..............................	4,126	2,422	2,938	3,610	-12.5	209
New Mexico	2,328	2,062	1,714	2,676	14.9	190
Oregon..............................	19,456	8,919	7,517	20,858	7.2	761
Utah.................................	3,229	2,289	2,206	3,312	2.6	201
Washington (c)....................	105	48	33	120	14.3	3
Wyoming	578	279	294	563	-2.6	145
Regional total	158,397	188,413	186,496	160,881	1.6	324
Regional total without California...........	48,059	34,011	31,450	50,629	5.0	2,647
Dist. of Columbia (c)	4,861	2,203	1746.0	5,318	9.4	1,198

Source: U.S. Department of Justice, Bureau of Justice Statistics, *Probation and Parole in the United States, 2004* (November 2005).

Note: Because of incomplete data, the December 31, 2004 total does not equal the January 1 total, plus entries, minus exits.

Key:

. . . — Number not calculated.

(a) Due to a change in reporting, January 1, 2004 county counts for Pennsyl-

vania were estimated. The comparable total was 75,057. Total entries (24,900) and exits (22,800) were estimated to include county counts.

(b) Data for entries and exits were estimated for nonreporting agencies.

(c) All data were estimated.

(d) Reported data for entries and exits include only state parolees.

(e) Excludes parolees in one of the following categories: absconder, out of state, or inactive.

Table 9.16
CAPITAL PUNISHMENT (as of December 2004)

State or other jurisdiction	Capital offenses	Minimum age	Prisoners under sentence of death	Method of execution
Alabama	Intentional murder with 18 aggravating factors.	16	193	Electrocution or lethal injection
Alaska	. . .	. . .	. . .	. . .
Arizona (q)	First-degree murder accompanied by at least 1 of 10 aggravating factors.	(l)	105	Lethal gas or lethal injection (a)
Arkansas (q)	Capital murder with a finding of at least 1 of 10 aggravating circumstances; treason.	14 (m)	39	Lethal injection or electrocution (b)
California (q)	First-degree murder with special circumstances; train-wrecking; treason; perjury causing execution.	18	637	Lethal gas or lethal injection
Colorado (q)	First-degree murder with at least 1 of 17 aggravating factors; treason.	18	3	Lethal injection
Connecticut (q)	Capital felony with 8 forms of aggravated homicide. Capital sentencing excludes persons determined to be mentally retarded.	18 (n)	7	Lethal injection
Delaware (q)	First-degree murder with aggravating circumstances.	16	17	Hanging or lethal injection (c)
Florida (q)	First-degree murder; felony murder; capital drug-trafficking; capital sexual battery.	17	364	Electrocution or lethal injection
Georgia (q)	Murder; kidnapping with bodily injury or ransom when the victim dies; aircraft hijacking; treason.	17	109	Lethal injection
Hawaii	. . .	. . .	. . .	. . .
Idaho (q)	First-degree murder with aggravating factors; aggravated kidnapping, perjury resulting in death.	(l)	22	Firing Squad or lethal injection
Illinois (q)	First-degree murder with 1 of 21 aggravating circumstances.	18	6	Lethal injection
Indiana (q)	Murder with 16 aggravating circumstances.	18	27	Lethal injection
Iowa	. . .	. . .	. . .	. . .
Kansas (q)	Capital murder with 8 aggravating circumstances.	18	0	Lethal injection
Kentucky (q)	Murder with aggravating factors; kidnapping with aggravating factors.	16	34	Electrocution or lethal injection (d)
Louisiana (q)	First-degree murder; aggravated rape of victim under age 12; treason.	(l)	87	Lethal injection
Maine	. . .	. . .	. . .	. . .
Maryland (q)	First-degree murder, either premeditated or during the commission of a felony, provided that certain death eligibility requirements are satisfied.	18	9	Lethal injection
Massachusetts	. . .	. . .	. . .	. . .
Michigan	. . .	. . .	. . .	. . .
Minnesota	. . .	. . .	. . .	. . .
Mississippi	Capital murder; aircraft piracy.	16 (o)	70	Lethal injection
Missouri (q)	First-degree murder.	18 (r)	52	Lethal injection or lethal gas
Montana	Capital murder with 1 of 9 aggravating circumstances; capital sexual assault.	(p)	4	Lethal injection
Nebraska (q)	First-degree murder with a finding of at least 1 statutorily-defined aggravating circumstance.	18	8	Electrocution
Nevada (q)	First-degree murder with at least 1 of 15 aggravating circumstances.	16	83	Lethal injection
New Hampshire	Six categories of capital murder.	17	0	Lethal injection or hanging (e)
New Jersey	Murder by one's own conduct; committed in furtherance of a narcotics conspiracy, or during the commission of the crime of terrorism.	18	11	Lethal injection
New Mexico (q)	First-degree murder with at least 1 of 7 statutorily-defined aggravating circumstances.	18	2	Lethal injection
New York (q)	First-degree murder with 1 of 13 aggravating factors.	18	2	Lethal injection
North Carolina (q)	First-degree murder.	17 (f)	181	Lethal injection
North Dakota	. . .	. . .	. . .	. . .

See footnotes at end of table.

State or other jurisdiction	Capital offenses	Minimum age	Prisoners under sentence of death	Method of execution
Ohio	Aggravated murder with at least 1 of 10 aggravating circumstances.	18	201	Lethal injection
Oklahoma	First-degree murder in conjunction with a finding of at least 1 of 8 statutorily-defined aggravating circumstances.	16	91	Lethal injection, electrocution or firing squad (g)
Oregon	Aggravated murder.	18	30	Lethal injection
Pennsylvania	First-degree murder with 18 aggravating circumstances.	(l)	222	Lethal injection
Rhode Island	. . .	. . .	. . .	. . .
South Carolina (q)	Murder with 1 of 11 aggravating circumstances.	(l)	71	Electrocution or lethal injection
South Dakota (q)	First-degree murder with 1 of 10 aggravating circumstances; aggravated kidnapping.	18	4	Lethal injection
Tennessee (q)	First-degree murder with 1 of 15 aggravating circumstances.	18	99	Lethal injection or electrocution (h)
Texas	Criminal homicide with 1 of 8 aggravating circumstances.	17	446	Lethal injection
Utah (q)	Aggravated murder.	14 (j)	10	Lethal injection or firing squad (k)
Vermont	. . .	. . .	. . .	. . .
Virginia (q)	First-degree murder with 1 of 13 aggravating circumstances.	14 (j)	23	Electrocution or lethal injection
Washington (q)	Aggravated first-degree murder.	18	10	Lethal injection or hanging
West Virginia	. . .	. . .	. . .	. . .
Wisconsin	. . .	. . .	. . .	. . .
Wyoming	First-degree murder.	18	2	Lethal injection or lethal gas (i)
Dist. of Columbia	. . .	. . .	. . .	. . .

Sources: U.S. Department of Justice, Bureau of Statistics, *Capital Punishment, 2004* (November 2005).

Key:

. . . — No capital punishment statute.

(a) Arizona authorizes lethal injection for persons whose capital sentence was received after 11/15/92; for those sentenced before that date, the condemned may select lethal injection or lethal gas.

(b) Arkansas authorizes lethal injection for those whose capital offense occurred on or after 7/4/83; for those whose offense occurred before that date, the condemned may select lethal injection or electrocution.

(c) Delaware authorizes lethal injection for those whose capital offense occurred after 6/13/86; for those whose offense occurred before that date, the condemned may select lethal injection or hanging.

(d) Kentucky authorizes lethal injection for persons whose capital sentence was received on or after 3/31/98; for those sentenced before that date, the condemned may select lethal injection or electrocution.

(e) New Hampshire authorizes hanging only if lethal injection cannot be given.

(f) The age required is 17 unless the murderer was incarcerated for murder when a subsequent murder occurred; then the age may be 14.

(g) Oklahoma authorizes electrocution if lethal injection is ever held to be unconstitutional, and firing squad if both lethal injection and electrocution are held unconstitutional.

(h) Tennessee authorizes lethal injection for those whose capital offense occurred after 12/31/98; those whose offense occurred before that date may select electrocution.

(i) Wyoming authorizes lethal gas if lethal injection is ever held to be unconstitutional.

(j) The minimum age for transfer to adult court by statute is 14, but the effective age is 16 based on interpretation of U.S. Supreme Court decisions by the state attorney general's office.

(k) Authorizes firing squad if lethal injection is held unconstitutional.

(l) No age specified.

(m) See Arkansas Code Ann. 9-27-318(c)(2)(Supp. 2001).

(n) See Connecticut Gen. Stat. 53a-46a(g)(1).

(o) The minimum age defined by statute is 13, but the effective age is 16 based on interpretation of U.S. Supreme Court decisions by the Mississippi Supreme Court.

(p) Montana law specifies that offenders tried under the capital sexual assault statute be 18 or older. Age may be a mitigating factor for other capital crimes.

(q) As of December 31, 2004, 26 states excluded mentally retarded persons from capital sentencing: Arizona, Arkansas, California, Colorado, Connecticut, Delaware, Florida, Georgia, Idaho, Illinois, Indiana, Kansas, Kentucky, Louisiana, Maryland, Missouri, Nebraska, Nevada, New Mexico, New York, North Carolina, South Dakota, Tennessee, Utah, Virginia, and Washington. Mental retardation is a mitigating factor in South Carolina.

(r) The minimum age defined by statute is 16, but the effective age is 18 based on interpretation of the 8th Amendment of the U.S. Constitution by the Missouri Supreme Court.

Trends in Welfare Programs
By Sheila R. Zedlewski and Meghan Williamson

Congress reauthorized the nation's welfare bill along with the Deficit Reduction Act of 2005. The legislation substantially changes TANF's work participation requirements. States will need to meet a 50 percent participation rate for all families receiving assistance, including those in separate state-funded programs. The rate will be adjusted downward for any caseload decline occurring after 2005. The new participation requirement will present a challenge to many states. Current work participation rates generally fall substantially below the new requirement. Also, many states have depleted their TANF reserve funds, leaving them little flexibility to develop new strategies to increase work among caseload participants.

Recent Caseload Experience

Nationwide, Temporary Assistance for Needy Families (TANF) caseloads declined by 5 percent between the end of fiscal year 2003 and March 2005, reaching their lowest level in more than 30 years (Table A). Recent modest caseload declines contrast with the dramatic drops that followed the 1996 passage of welfare reform. Caseloads were cut in half in response to new reforms and an unusually strong economy between 1996 and 2000.

The recent national trends also mask important differences across the states. Since the end of federal fiscal year 2003, caseloads increased in 18 states (Table A); and four states experienced increases of 10 percent or more (Colorado, Idaho, Kansas and Pennsylvania). On the other hand, caseloads in 12 states (Arkansas, Georgia, Louisiana, Mississippi, Montana, Nevada, Oklahoma, South Carolina, Texas, Virginia, West Virginia and Wyoming) declined by more than 20 percent.

Caseload trends during the recent economic cycle have stumped many scholars. Most would have predicted caseload increases during periods of higher unemployment and decreases after a recovery (caseloads have traditionally lagged behind unemployment rates). Instead we observe continued caseload decline throughout the business cycle, and many of the states with substantial caseload declines during 2004 and early 2005 had higher than average unemployment rates. For example, state unemployment during 2004 exceeded the national average in five of the 12 states with the steepest caseload decline and fell below the national average in seven of the states with caseload increases.[1]

States' TANF programs also affect caseload trends. Some TANF programs discourage entry through diversion and work requirements, and sanctions and time limits cause some families to lose eligibility. Research has shown that new program rules have reduced entry rates making TANF less sensitive to unemployment rate changes.[2] Also, more families have reached their five-year federal time limit and lost benefit eligibility.[3]

Another factor at play may be the use of other safety net programs to tide former and potential welfare recipients over when jobs are scarce. In contrast to welfare, food stamp caseloads increased by about 40 percent between 2000 and 2004.[4] Recent research shows families are now more likely to receive these benefits after leaving welfare than they were during the early phase of welfare reform. Changes in states' administrative procedures that keep food stamp cases open after families leave welfare, new rules liberalizing the vehicle limits and recertification procedures, and more education about food stamp eligibility have increased food stamp enrollment among former welfare recipients.[5]

Caseload Work Participation

The closely watched performance measure for TANF—work participation rates—has continued to decline. Only 32 percent of the TANF caseload engaged in work in 2004 (the latest data available), compared with 38 percent in 1999. The reductions in caseload work participation reflect the general, slow decline in employment among single parents (Figure A). One study estimated that the recent economic downturn contributed to a decrease in the full-time employment rate among single-parent families of almost 13 percent between 2000 and 2003.[6]

Work participation rates in 2004 varied from less than 20 percent in the District of Columbia, Maryland, Missouri, Pennsylvania and West Virginia to more than 80 percent in Kansas and Montana (Table A). While the federal work participation target was

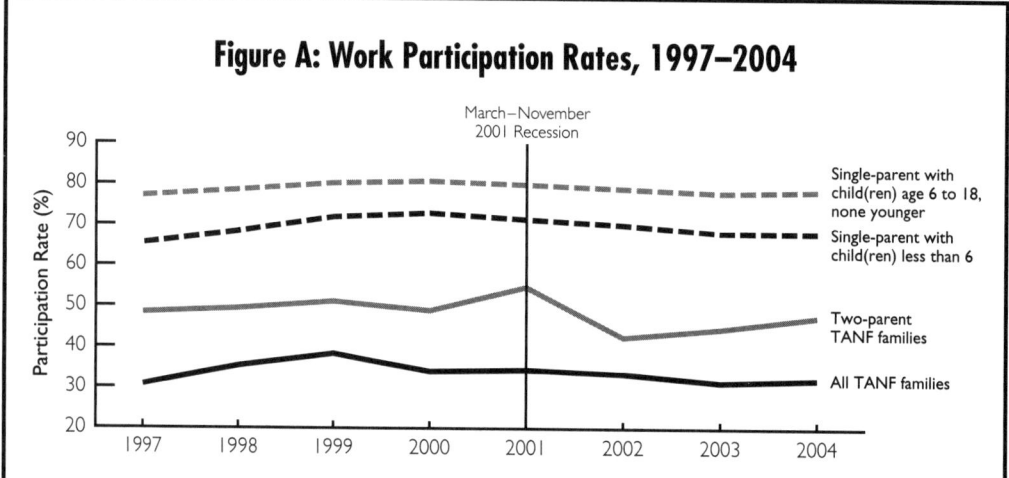

Figure A: Work Participation Rates, 1997–2004

March–November 2001 Recession

Single-parent with child(ren) age 6 to 18, none younger

Single-parent with child(ren) less than 6

Two-parent TANF families

All TANF families

Note: Participation rates among TANF families is reported for each federal fiscal year. Participation rates among all single-parent families is based on calendar year reporting.

Sources: U.S. Department of Health and Human Services, Administration for Children and Families, "TANF Work Participation Rates" Fiscal Years 1997–2003, downloaded from *http://www.acf.hhs.gov//programs/ofa/particip/indexparticip.htm*, November 30, 2005.

U.S. Department of Labor, Bureau of Labor Statistics, "Employment Characteristics of Families" 1997–2004, downloaded from *http://www.bls. gov*, November 30, 2005.

50 percent in 2004, all states except Indiana and Mississippi met the target because of the caseload reduction credit.[7] After accounting for the credit, states only had to meet an average work participation rate of 9 percent, and only five states (Idaho, Indiana, Kansas, Nebraska and Nevada) had to meet a work participation rate greater than 25 percent. Overall, states achieved substantially more than required by the 2004 federal rules, but many will face new challenges with the change in the caseload reduction credit under TANF reauthorization.

Also, comparisons of work participation rates across the states can be somewhat misleading because the meaning of the rate varies by state. For example, some states exclude families with a child younger than 1-year-old from work activities and the work participation rate calculation. Also, four states still had waivers approved before 1996 that affected participation rate calculations for 2004. In other words, some states exclude recipients not subject to work requirements from their rate calculations; work participation rates shown in Table A would be lower if these recipients were included.

TANF Spending

Total TANF-related spending was more than $28 billion in 2004 (Table B). Total spending fell below spending in 2003 ($29 billion) as states had fewer reserve funds to spend. Seventeen states had spent all their reserves by the end of 2004, and many

more states had very few reserves left. Nonetheless, reserve fund spending accounted for almost 10 percent of total 2004 expenditures.

Most states continued to spend considerably less than half their total expenditures on basic assistance in 2004.[8] Only a few states spent less than 15 percent of their resources on basic assistance (Idaho, Illinois and Wyoming), and six spent more than half on basic assistance (Arizona, California, Hawaii, Maine, Nebraska and New Hampshire). Child care remained a significant TANF expenditure for many states. Nationwide, states spent more than $5 billion for child care in 2004 (18 percent of all TANF dollars). Eight states (Alaska, Delaware, Florida, Illinois, Massachusetts, North Carolina, Oklahoma and Wisconsin) and the District of Columbia devoted at least 30 percent of their TANF dollars to this type of work support.

Limited funds for child care and diminished reserves raise concerns over states' abilities to meet new caseload needs. About half the states (24) had waiting lists or had frozen intake for child care subsidies in 2004.[9] Also, state TANF innovations have slowed in recent years as spending flexibility has declined.[10] As numerous studies have shown, many TANF recipients need intensive services before they can move into self-sustaining jobs. Nearly four in 10 recipients lack a high school diploma or GED and more than one-third have serious mental or physical challenges.[11] Under the new, tougher work partici-

Table A: Trends in TANF Caseload, 1996–2005

State or other jurisdiction	TANF family caseload March 2005 (a)	Percent change from FY 1996 to 2000 (b)	Percent change from FY 2000 to 2003 (b)	Percent change from FY 2003 to March 2005	Work participation rates FY 2004 (c)
Alabama	20,214	-55.0%	-1.3%	7.3%	37.9%
Alaska	4,814	-40.0	-27.4	-9.7	43.6
Arizona	43,223	-46.8	41.7	-9.6	25.5
Arkansas	8,660	-45.7	-9.6	-22.4	27.3
California	466,074	-44.4	-9.8	3.7	23.1
Colorado	15,903	-68.5	21.3	17.5	34.7
Connecticut	19,608	-51.7	-25.2	-6.7	24.3
Delaware	5,531	-41.7	-7.6	-1.2	22.1
Florida	59,761	-67.9	-13.7	2.8	40.4
Georgia	41,155	-59.4	5.7	-26.4	24.8
Hawaii	8,169	-34.3	-32.3	-16.4	70.5
Idaho	1,919	-85.8	31.8	14.2	41.0
Illinois	38,887	-62.6	-54.8	2.6	46.1
Indiana	48,389	-32.2	46.9	-8.2	30.0
Iowa	17,738	-38.9	-0.3	-11.2	50.0
Kansas	17,399	-50.0	21.6	13.7	88.0
Kentucky	34,864	-46.3	-9.4	-0.2	38.1
Louisiana	15,979	-60.6	-17.9	-30.0	35.4
Maine	9,729	-46.9	-15.8	6.3	32.1
Maryland	23,091	-60.4	-10.8	-11.6	16.0
Massachusetts	48,837	-50.0	11.7	-1.1	60.0
Michigan	81,329	-58.3	1.2	8.3	24.5
Minnesota	29,301	-33.0	-6.5	-19.7	26.8
Mississippi	15,763	-68.8	32.4	-20.5	21.0
Missouri	40,529	-43.5	-12.7	-0.8	19.5
Montana	4,861	-58.0	35.4	-21.2	92.7
Nebraska	9,787	-34.5	14.8	-10.6	34.5
Nevada	6,794	-57.7	69.5	-36.1	34.5
New Hampshire	6,209	-38.8	4.1	2.1	30.2
New Jersey	42,935	-51.1	-17.8	1.2	34.6
New Mexico	17,364	-30.1	-29.7	4.4	46.2
New York	141,446	-40.1	-42.5	-4.9	37.8
North Carolina	33,201	-59.6	-11.6	-17.9	31.4
North Dakota	2,832	-40.7	16.4	-16.1	25.3
Ohio	82,897	-52.6	-14.0	-1.7	65.2
Oklahoma	11,630	-63.1	5.1	-22.7	33.2
Oregon	20,240	-49.0	9.7	8.2	32.1
Pennsylvania	96,800	-52.8	-10.1	19.7	7.1
Rhode Island	10,763	-23.1	-18.2	-19.4	23.7
South Carolina	15,506	-61.8	23.3	-28.2	53.7
South Dakota	2,744	-53.3	-0.4	-1.7	54.8
Tennessee	70,379	-43.3	22.3	2.5	50.6
Texas	85,092	-49.8	4.2	-36.1	34.2
Utah	9,164	-43.1	1.5	7.3	26.2
Vermont	4,561	-33.3	-18.8	-7.1	24.9
Virginia	9,869	-50.9	-20.8	-60.9	50.1
Washington	58,311	-42.4	-4.1	6.6	35.4
West Virginia	11,963	-66.8	30.3	-24.4	11.7
Wisconsin	20,293	-72.2	22.4	-0.8	61.3
Wyoming	311	-87.2	-32.5	-23.8	77.8
Dist. of Columbia	16,905	-32.2	-4.9	1.9	18.2
United States	1,909,273	-50.3	-9.9	-5.0	32.0

Sources: U.S. Department of Health and Human Services, Administration for Children and Families, "Caseload Data as of 8/20/2005," downloaded from *http://www.acf.hhs.gov//programs/ofa/caseload/caseloadindex.htm*, November 30, 2005.

U.S. Department of Health and Human Services, Administration for Children and Families, "TANF Work Participation Rates Fiscal Year 2004," downloaded from *http://www.acf.hhs.gov/programs/ofa/particip/indexparticip.htm*, February 18, 2006.

Key:
(a) Average monthly caseload for FY 2005 not available at time of publication. Most recent 2005 data included here.
(b) Percent changes are based on the average monthly caseloads during the two relevant fiscal years.
(c) Work participation rates for all families, including two-parent families.

Table B: TANF Spending: Combined Federal and State, FY 2004

State or other jurisdiction	Total expenditures (federal and state) (a)	Percent basic assistance	Percent work-related activities	Percent child care (b)	Percent other	Federal funds in reserve (c)
Alabama	$ 144,752,676	31%	12%	11%	47%	16%
Alaska	95,116,599	46	13	30	12	12
Arizona	327,668,058	56	5	3	36	0
Arkansas	60,397,456	28	8	29	35	142
California	6,545,424,399	50	6	17	27	0
Colorado	254,884,850	26	0	12	63	0
Connecticut	461,555,688	27	7	3	63	0
Delaware	60,005,267	34	0	41	25	7
Florida	1,061,889,475	23	8	33	36	0
Georgia	548,493,594	30	20	6	44	29
Hawaii	145,179,669	60	7	14	18	78
Idaho	51,802,551	14	15	15	56	0
Illinois	1,015,145,153	11	10	37	42	0
Indiana	320,039,932	38	3	6	53	0
Iowa	202,679,788	39	10	17	34	10
Kansas	181,855,401	34	1	16	50	3
Kentucky	242,753,836	44	11	28	17	26
Louisiana	290,486,358	22	8	10	60	0
Maine	136,068,400	56	1	23	20	20
Maryland	391,762,105	28	12	11	49	17
Massachusetts	819,025,332	42	1	33	24	1
Michigan	1,308,006,810	31	4	26	40	9
Minnesota	431,587,903	39	13	22	26	16
Mississippi	115,399,285	28	6	20	46	2
Missouri	347,055,127	40	8	23	30	0
Montana	47,886,492	44	21	6	29	43
Nebraska	97,944,672	66	13	16	6	0
Nevada	69,101,107	47	3	4	46	22
New Hampshire	60,200,822	57	9	8	26	79
New Jersey	941,074,851	28	7	8	57	10
New Mexico	167,638,466	44	7	22	28	8
New York	4,725,899,100	34	5	11	51	5
North Carolina	528,022,699	23	12	35	31	0
North Dakota	34,473,275	36	8	5	51	36
Ohio	909,563,534	35	7	19	39	37
Oklahoma	238,875,407	18	0	42	40	8
Oregon	242,993,015	35	12	10	44	0
Pennsylvania	1,357,854,175	28	13	20	38	11
Rhode Island	168,684,072	47	5	27	22	0
South Carolina	38,174,709	47	(d)	10	(d)	4
South Dakota	31,183,844	36	10	3	51	71
Tennessee	290,295,689	41	10	25	24	6
Texas	767,925,783	28	10	3	60	0
Utah	115,227,837	40	27	8	25	15
Vermont	82,483,186	43	1	20	36	0
Virginia	311,177,014	36	27	13	25	0
Washington	694,778,008	46	15	24	15	1
West Virginia	157,270,102	44	4	14	38	2
Wisconsin	571,353,691	24	6	44	27	4
Wyoming	41,684,882	13	1	4	82	99
Dist. of Columbia	191,061,848	37	12	32	19	25
United States	28,441,863,992	37	8	18	38	7

Source: U.S. Department of Health and Human Services, Administration for Children and Families, "Fiscal Year 2004 TANF Financial Data," downloaded from *http://www.acf.hhs.gov/programs/ofs/data/tanf_2004.html*, November 30, 2005.

Key:

(a) Includes transfers to the Child Care Development Fund (CCDF) and the Social Services Block Grant (SSBG).

(b) Includes the CCDF transfer.

(c) Listed as a percentage of fiscal year 2004 expenditures. Excludes transfers to the CCDF and the SSBG and unliquidated obligations in the reserve.

(d) In 2004, South Carolina reported a negative expenditure on work-related activities in order to correct over-reporting of work-related expenditures in prior fiscal years.

pation requirements, many states will need to spend more for child care and support services in order to increase work participation among their caseloads.

Finally, the recent hurricane disasters show how unexpected demands can affect states' TANF programs. Some parents who lost their jobs as a result of the disaster have turned to state welfare programs for help. The Emergency Response and Relief Act provides additional TANF funding of up to 20 percent of basic block grants in the form of loans to three states affected by Hurricane Katrina (Alabama, Louisiana and Mississippi). Additionally, all states can apply for federal reimbursement for short-term, nonrecurrent cash benefits paid to affected families. States can apply for up to 20 percent of the monthly value of their basic TANF grant each month, until the $1.9 billion TANF contingency fund is exhausted.[12] The three states hit by Katrina, already fiscally strained states with essentially no TANF reserves, will potentially have TANF loans to repay among their recovery debts.

Reauthorization

The TANF reauthorization passed in the Deficit Reduction Act of 2005 represents a major breakthrough. The original legislation ended in federal fiscal year 2001, and states have been operating their TANF programs through continuing resolutions since then. The legislation also represents a significant compromise compared with earlier House and Senate Finance Committee reauthorization proposals. Under the new legislation, the work participation rate will remain fixed at 50 percent; original House and Senate Finance proposals would have increased the work participation rates to 70 percent by 2010.[13] The new legislation retains the existing 30 hour per week work requirement and existing categories of work participation (although the federal government must issue regulations no later than June 30, 2006 to define those work activities, uniform methods for reporting hours of work, the type of documentation required to verify reported hours of work, and who must be included in the work participation rates). The original House and Senate Finance proposals, in contrast, would have increased the required hours of work activity to 40 and 34, respectively, and the House proposal would have mandated more paid work activity.[14]

Despite the continued 30 hours workweek and 50 percent participation standard, states will face much stricter participation standards under reauthorization. Beginning in October 2006, the caseload reduction credit will only reflect decreases in the caseload since fiscal year 2005, raising the effective participation rate far above the current average of 9 percent.

Additionally, the participation standards will apply to state-only programs that were previously exempt from the federal standard. This will primarily affect the 26 states currently covering two-parent families with state-only funds. States are subject to a much higher participation standard (90 percent) for two-parent families. Many states will face an especially tough challenge in meeting the work participation rate requirement for two-parent families under the new rules. States that do not meet the participation rate targets can face penalties up to 5 percent of their federal block grants and higher maintenance of effort requirements.

The final bill includes $200 million more per year in additional state matching funds for child care. This amount falls far short of the Senate Finance Committee's request for $1.2 billion per year, but is double the House's request for $100 million per year in additional child care funds. It remains to be seen whether states will have sufficient funds to subsidize child care for the greater share of TANF recipients they must move into work activities without reducing child care subsidies for non-welfare low-income families.

Congress did not include the controversial "superwaivers" in the final bill. Previous attempts to reauthorize TANF would have allowed states to apply for waivers to redirect federal dollars from a variety of programs (including child care, TANF, and social services) to low-income families. The House and Senate Finance proposals, however, differed in how inclusive the proposed waivers would be.

The final bill does include grants for states to develop Healthy Marriage and responsible fatherhood initiatives. It also reduces federal funding for child support collections, allows states to increase the amount of child support that can be passed through to current and former welfare recipients, and mandates that states adjust child support orders of families on TANF every three years.

Conclusion

States' TANF caseloads continued to decline in 2004 relative to the prior year, although caseload trends varied considerably across the states. Work participation among TANF recipients also continued to decline, generally following employment trends for all single parents. States' TANF expenditures declined relative to 2003, as reserve funds continued to shrink.

Congress reauthorized TANF through the 2005 Deficit Reduction Act. Work participation rates will be higher, and more recipients must be included in these calculators. Many states will need to change their TANF programs to meet the new participation rates. Some states will need to shift more of their TANF spending toward work-related activities and child care for recipients.

The new legislation continues to freeze states' basic block grants at levels established in 1996. The recent Katrina disaster highlighted the constraints of this fixed block grant welfare program. When families' needs for cash assistance increase abruptly, states must depend on the federal government to pass emergency legislation to cover new state costs. While the federal government authorized contingency fund spending, it will cover some Katrinia-related costs through loans to the most affected states. Loan payments in turn represent an obligation that could reduce future TANF resources available in affected states.[15] Katrina demonstrates that states must plan for unexpected increases in families' needs.

Notes

[1] Bureau of Labor Statistics, U.S. Department of Labor, "Over-the-Year Change in Unemployment Rates for States," downloaded from *www.bls.gov*, November 30, 2005.

[2] Greg Acs, Katherin Ross Phillips, and Sandi Nelson, "The Road Not Taken: Changes in Welfare Entry During the 1990s," (Washington, D.C.: The Urban Institute, December 2003).

[3] Unfortunately, national statistics on the number of families ineligible for assistance due to time limits are not available.

[4] Food and Nutrition Service, U.S. Department of Agriculture, "Program Data: Annual State Level Data," downloaded from *http://www.fns.usda.gov/pd/fspmain.htm*, December 2, 2005.

[5] See Sheila Zedlewski and Kelly Rader, "Have Food Stamp Program Changes Increased Participation?" (*Social Service Review*, 537–61, September 2005).

[6] Greg Acs, Harry Holzer, and Austin Nichols, "How Have Households with Children Faired in the Job Market Downturn?" (Washington, D.C.: The Urban Institute, April 2005).

[7] The current caseload reduction credit allows states to reduce participation rates by one percentage point for each percentage point decline in the caseload since fiscal year 1995 that is not attributable to changes in eligibility policy.

[8] Note that these shares for basic assistance, child care, and work-related activities include funds spent for these types of assistance under state-only programs.

[9] David Edie, "Toward a New Child Care Policy," University of Wisconsin–Child Care Research Partnership, prepared for the Urban Institute "New Steps in the Working Families Agenda," (May 2005).

[10] Jack Tweedie, "Dollars Make a Difference," in *State Legislatures*, (February 2005).

[11] Sheila Zedlewski, "Work and Barriers to Work among Welfare Recipients in 2002," Assessing the New Federalism Snapshots3 of America's Families, Number 3, (August 2003).

[12] Mark Greenberg, "New TANF Law Provides Additional Funds for Katrina Relief: Key Improvements Still Needed," (Washington, D.C.: Center for Law and Social Policy, September 2005).

[13] The discussion reflects the bills passed by Senate Finance Committee in March 2005 and the welfare reauthorization rules passed by the House as part of its budget reconciliation bill in November 2005.

[14] Gene Falk, Melinda Gish, Carmen Solomon-Fears, and Emilie Stoltzfus, "Welfare Reauthorization: A Side-By-Side Comparison of Current Law, Senate Committee-Approved and House Budget Reconciliation Bill Provisions," (Washington, D.C.: Congressional Research Service, RL33157, November 2005).

[15] HHS has issued guidance, however, indicating that states will not be penalized for failing to pay interest or repay the loan through October 2007.

About the Authors

Sheila R. Zedlewski is the director of the Income and Benefits Policy Center at the Urban Institute, a nonpartisan think tank located in Washington, D.C. Her recent work focuses on understanding low-income family participation in government programs. She has written extensively about the TANF program with a focus on families unable to move from welfare to work.

Meghan Williamson is a research assistant in the Income and Benefits Policy Center at the Urban Institute. Since completing her B.A. at the College of William and Mary in 2004, she has focused on issues related to the TANF program.

U.S.-Canada Economic Relations: Interactions among the States and Provinces[1]

By Earl H. Fry

The United States and Canada have the largest and most diverse bilateral economic relationship in the world. Even though the national governments establish the broad policy parameters in their respective federal systems, state, provincial, and municipal governments are becoming more actively involved in cross-border relations. This proliferation of trans-border linkages among subnational governments can be expected to accelerate in the future.

Canada and the United States share a 4,000-mile border along the 49th parallel and another 1,500-mile border separating Alaska from British Columbia and the Yukon. The evolving cross-border relationship which affects 32 million Canadians and 297 million Americans is as complex and diverse as any in the world. In particular, the relationship goes far beyond the national governments in Washington, D.C. and Ottawa. Currently, Canada is the principal export destination for companies in 39 states, and businesses in each of Canada's 10 provinces now export more to the United States than anywhere else in the world, including to the other provinces in Canada.

In economic terms, the United States and Canada maintain the largest bilateral trading relationship in the world, with two-way trade in goods and services in the range of $1.2 billion per day, up more than 150 percent since 1988, the year before the Canada-U.S. Free Trade Agreement (FTA) went into effect (Figure A). U.S. foreign direct investment in Canada, a type of investment which provides Americans with control over the management of companies operating in Canada, surpassed $216 billion in 2004, with U.S.-owned companies accounting for over 10 percent of Canada's gross domestic product (GDP) and providing more than one million jobs for Canadian workers.[2] Canadian foreign direct investment in

the United States stood at $134 billion at the end of 2004, with 473,000 Americans working for Canadian "majority-owned non-bank enterprises" (Figure B).[3]

Americans also account for more than 90 percent of all foreign visitors to Canada, and Canadians rank number one in terms of international arrivals to the United States (Figure C). Many Canadian and American families also have relatives on the other side of the border; 821,000 U.S. residents were born in Canada, according to the 2000 U.S. Census, and 238,000 residents in Canada come from the United States, according to the 2001 Canadian Census.

This represents only the tip of the iceberg, because for most of the history of these two nations, the border was completely open for people to move north or south without any interaction with immigration officers or census takers. Even today, with elaborate and time-consuming border checks, there are more than 200 million human crossings annually across the shared border.

The bilateral relationship is certainly asymmetrical in a number of ways. Canada's economic well-being is linked inextricably to its neighbor to the south. Exports represent more than 40 percent of the nation's GDP and four-fifths of these exports go to a single foreign market: the United States. The U.S. has nine times more people, an economy which

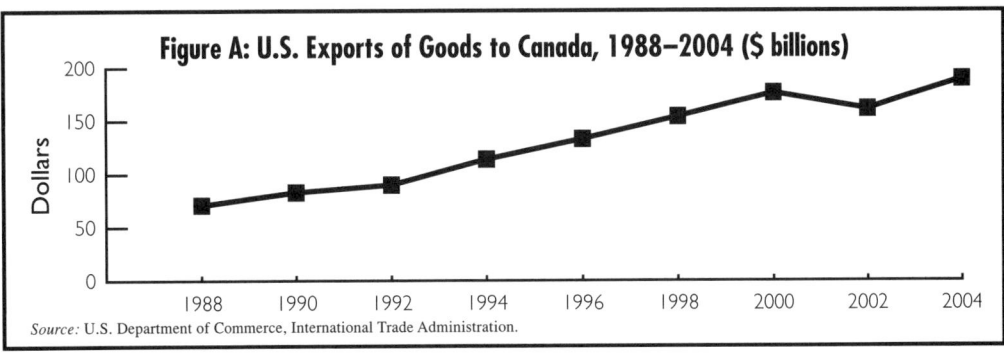

Figure A: U.S. Exports of Goods to Canada, 1988–2004 ($ billions)

Source: U.S. Department of Commerce, International Trade Administration.

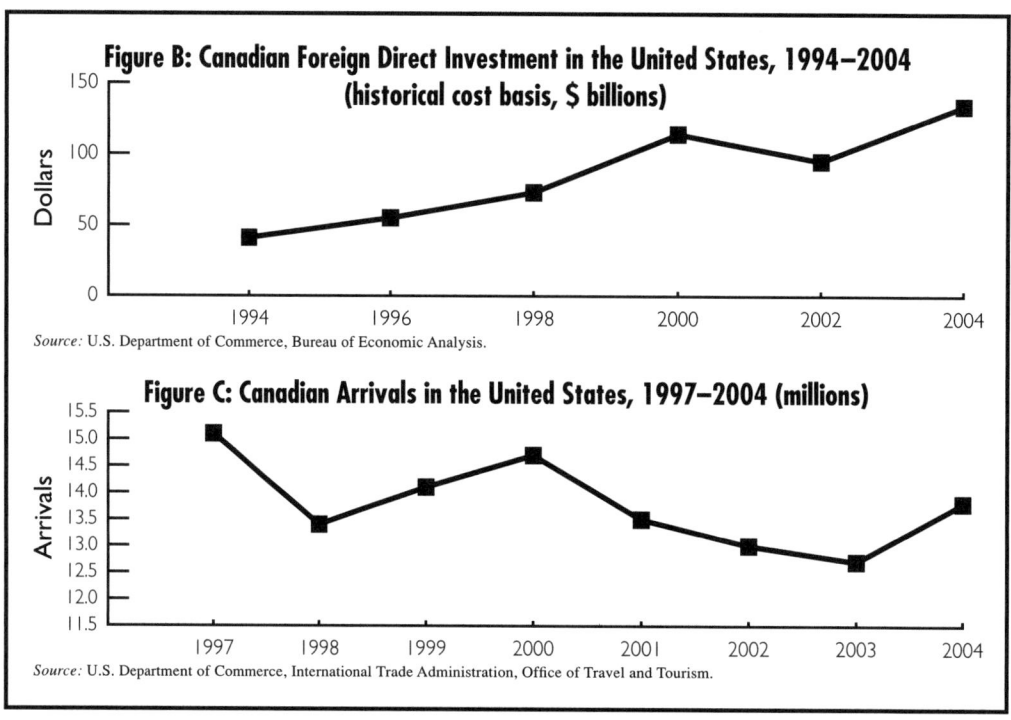

Figure B: Canadian Foreign Direct Investment in the United States, 1994–2004 (historical cost basis, $ billions)

Source: U.S. Department of Commerce, Bureau of Economic Analysis.

Figure C: Canadian Arrivals in the United States, 1997–2004 (millions)

Source: U.S. Department of Commerce, International Trade Administration, Office of Travel and Tourism.

is at least a dozen times larger, and expends almost half of what the entire world is spending annually in the defense sector. Yet, Canada remains of vital importance to the United States' security and economic growth. The 5,500 mile border could never be defended adequately by the United States without the active and persistent cooperation of Canadian authorities at all levels of government.

In addition, more than two million U.S. jobs are directly linked to exports to Canada, with the United States actually exporting more to Canada in 2004 than to the 25 members of the European Union which have a combined population of 456 million people.[4] Canada is also the leading foreign supplier of petroleum products to the United States and supplies 94 percent of U.S. natural gas imports, 35 percent of uranium imports utilized for U.S. nuclear power generation, and nearly 100 percent of U.S. hydroelectricity imports.

The Transgovernmental Dimension— States, Provinces, and Cities

Roughly two dozen of the 200 or so nation-states in the world today maintain federal systems of government, meaning that they divide governmental authority constitutionally between a national government and regional governments. All three members

of the North America Free Trade Area (NAFTA), the United States, Canada and Mexico, are among the relatively few governments worldwide which maintain federal systems.[5] The U.S. Constitution, which went into effect in 1789, provides the national government with authority over many aspects of foreign affairs, including making treaties and conducting foreign commerce, although the 10th Amendment to the Constitution stipulates that what is not explicitly assigned to the national government is reserved to the state governments and to the people.

Canada's constitutions of 1867 and 1982 provide the reserved or residual powers to Ottawa, although a series of court decisions and intergovernmental agreements actually provide the provincial governments with some discretionary authority in the arena of international relations. The newly created Council of the Federation, consisting of the 10 provinces and three territories, includes the following wording in its preamble dated December 5, 2003: "Under the Constitution, Canada's two orders of government are of equal status, neither subordinate to the other, sovereign within their own areas of jurisdiction and accordingly, they should have adequate resources to meet their responsibilities."

All provincial and many state governments understand the importance of their neighboring nation to the economic well-being of their respective constituents. Canadian exports to the United States are now almost twice as large as trade within Canada itself. All provinces now export more internationally than they dispatch to other parts of Canada, with the great bulk of all of their exports headed directly south of the border (Table A).

Table A
Percentage of Provincial International Merchandise Exports to the United States, 2003

Province	Percentage
Newfoundland and Labrador	67.1%
Prince Edward Island	88.8
Nova Scotia	80.8
New Brunswick	88.9
Quebec	82.9
Ontario	91.4
Manitoba	76.3
Saskatchewan	63.8
Alberta	90.0
British Columbia	66.0

Source: Statistics Canada, *Provincial Pocket Facts: Canada's Merchandise Trade*, 2004.

In comparative perspectives, the state and provincial governments are by themselves powerful economic entities. The United States and Canada currently rank as the largest and ninth largest economies in the world, and Canada's economic performance has actually surpassed that of any other major Western nation over the past half decade in terms of GDP growth, the rate of job creation, and balancing government budgets. In 2004 three U.S. states could have been inserted among the top 10 nation-states in the world in terms of the annual production of goods and services, 14 states among the top 25 nation-states, 36 among the top 50, and all 50 plus the District of Columbia among the top 72.[6]

Because of the growing pressures linked to globalization and the necessity of protecting and enhancing the economic prospects of their local populations, provincial and state governments are increasingly reaching beyond national borders and engaging in international affairs. At the end of 2002, 37 states and Puerto Rico had 243 foreign offices or foreign-based representatives, up from just four states with foreign operations in 1980. Most governors or lieutenant governors lead international trade missions every year and about 1,000 state employees devote

their time to international pursuits. Total expenditures for international programs were $190 million in 2002, excluding hundreds of millions of dollars provided annually in incentives by state and local governments to foreign companies willing to locate facilities within their respective areas of jurisdiction.[7] Because of budgetary problems earlier in this decade, some state facilities abroad have recently been reduced in size or even eliminated, with California abandoning all of its foreign offices under Gov. Arnold Schwarzenegger.

Twelve of the state foreign offices are situated in Canada. Many governors, and not just those found in border states, have directed trade missions to Canada. For example, in July 2004, Gov. Jeb Bush led a delegation from Florida to Quebec. His main objectives were to meet with government officials in Quebec, convince Quebec business leaders to invest more in Florida, and to encourage average Quebecers to vacation more often and for longer periods in Florida, especially at a time when the Canadian dollar has strengthened dramatically against the U.S. currency. Reportedly, 10 percent of Quebec's population spends at least some part of each winter in Florida, so Bush had carefully targeted his audience.

The Canadian provincial governments are much more engaged internationally than their U.S. counterparts; Quebec, Ontario, Alberta, and British Columbia, which would each rank among the 40 largest nation-states in the world in terms of GDP, are the dominant Canadian players. Quebec alone has almost as many employees working on international programs and spends about half as much as the 50 U.S. state governments combined. Currently, Quebec maintains 25 offices in 17 different foreign countries, and has hired three business agents in two additional countries. Quebec's U.S. offices are located in Atlanta, Boston, Chicago, Los Angeles, Miami, New York City and Washington, D.C. Premier Jean Charest has met with more than a dozen governors during his term in office and has signed cooperative agreements with the states which border Quebec, placing special emphasis on regular consultations with Gov. George Pataki of New York.[8]

Ontario has 230 employees working on international programs and has focused on the United States as its prime international target, a priority which is not too surprising because Ontario alone is responsible for 53 percent of total Canadian merchandise exports to the United States and is the recipient of 74 percent of total U.S. exports to Canada.[9] Alberta maintains nine foreign offices and has recently opened a tenth within the Canadian Embassy in Washington, D.C.

Premier Ralph Klein has met several governors and has also been accorded two tête-à-tête sessions with Vice President Dick Cheney to directly discuss future energy cooperation between Alberta and the United States. Among the provinces, Alberta is the dominant supplier of energy products to the United States, especially natural gas. British Columbia's provincial government has about 100 employees who work on international issues, and the U.S. is clearly its foremost area of interest.

At most times of the year, at least one Canadian provincial delegation will be visiting some part of the United States. Even more important, however, is the fact that many of the provincial governments have institutionalized their linkages to U.S. state governments through the creation of bilateral or regional cross-border organizations and the signing of hundreds of memoranda, accords, or agreements with the U.S. states.[10] Table B lists some of the cross-border organizations which meet on a regular basis. The major provincial governments have also become associate members of large U.S. state government associations. For example, Alberta and British Columbia are associate members of The Council of State Governments—*West* (CSG-*West*) and Ontario and Quebec are associate members of the Council of Great Lakes Governors. Quebec and Ontario are also international partners of the 50-state organization, The Council of State Governments (CSG) and the government of Quebec actually hosted the annual meeting of CSG in Quebec City in 1999. These memberships provide provincial representatives with direct access to executive and legislative leaders within the states and allow them to articulate issues of prime concern to the individual provinces. Such contacts helped convince the legislatures of Washington, Oregon, Idaho and Alaska to pass resolutions in support of Vancouver's bid for the 2010 Winter Olympics, even though a successful bid may have diminished the chances of New York City being accorded the Summer Olympics in 2012 because of the International Olympic Committee's unwritten rule prohibiting any continent from hosting back-to-back Olympic games.[11]

Canada and the United States are also heavily urbanized nations with 80 percent of their respective populations living in municipalities. In Canada, over half of the population is concentrated in only four major urban regions—Toronto, Montreal, Vancouver, and the Calgary-Edmonton corridor. In the United States, three-quarters of the population reside in metropolitan areas with at least 250,000 people. Some municipal officials have begun to engender their own cross-border ties, although most are found in border states and provinces. The development of trade corridors between Canada, the United States and Mexico has also prompted cities along the corridors to meet on a periodic basis to pursue their common commercial interests. Representatives from the Federation of Canadian Municipalities, the U.S. National League of Cities, and the U.S. Conference of Mayors also meet occasionally and sponsor joint projects of interest to their municipal constituents on both sides of the border.

Future Prospects

There can be no doubt that the interest shown by Canadian subnational government representatives in developing ties with the United States is far greater than the interest in Canada manifested by U.S. state or municipal leaders. This is logical for a couple

---

Table B
Border Commissions and Groups

Alberta Bilateral Advisory Councils and Task Forces with Alaska, Idaho and Montana

Council of Great Lakes Governors
Illinois, Indiana, Michigan, Minnesota, New York, Ohio, Pennsylvania, Wisconsin; Ontario and Quebec (associate members)

The Council of State Governments *West*
13 Western states; Alberta and British Columbia (associate members)

New England Governors and Eastern Canadian Premiers
Connecticut, Maine, Massachusets, New Hampshire, Rhode Island, Vermont; New Brunswick, Newfoundland and Labrador, Nova Scotia, Prince Edward Island, Quebec

Northeast Regional Homeland Security Directors Group
Connecticut, Delaware, Maine, Massachusetts, New Hampshire, New York, Pennsylvania, Rhode Island, Vermont; Ontario, Quebec, New Brunswick, Nova Scotia

Pacific Northwest Economic Region (PNWER)
Alaska, Idaho, Montana, Oregon, Washington; Alberta, British Columbia, Yukon Territory

Western Canadian Premiers and Western Governors Association
4 provinces and 21 states which send designated representatives to each other's annual meetings

of reasons. First of all, even though Canada is the second largest nation in the world in territorial size, two-thirds of its residents live within 100 miles of the U.S. border and three-quarters within 200 miles. In contrast, only one American in four lives in a state which shares a common border or waterway with Canada. Secondly, the economic prosperity of Canada is highly dependent on maintaining relatively open access to the U.S. marketplace, whereas most of America's GDP is still generated from domestic trade flows.

Nonetheless, in spite of economic dependency which has been strengthened by the FTA and then NAFTA, the border still matters. As John Helliwell and others have pointed out, trade among Canadians, adjusted for population and distance, is still probably 10 times greater than trade between Canada and the United States.[12] Canadian and American attitudes on a wide variety of issues still differ quite dramatically, including issues linked to health care, cradle-to-grave security programs, gun control, legalization of drugs, gay marriage, religiosity, unilateralism vs. multilateralism, and the government's overall role in the economic sector.

However, in spite of some differences in outlook among the citizens of the two neighboring countries, one should anticipate that transgovernmental linkages involving provincial, state, and municipal governments will continue to proliferate, a direct result of the thick and expanding network of cross-border interdependence. Decisions made in Ottawa and Washington, D.C. will establish the major parameters of the relationship, but much of the future texture and substance of cross-border ties will be determined by the activities of subnational governments and private sector actors such as corporations and civic groups. In this respect, the work plan of the new Council of the Federation emphasizes that economic relations with the United States should be further strengthened, but the effort must involve a coordinated international strategy among federal, provincial, and territorial representatives in Canada.

As for the United States, most state governments can do much more to build linkages with Canadian provincial governments and to encourage their business communities to export to Canada. Canada has one of the largest national economies in the world and is located right on America's doorstep. NAFTA will also be fully implemented in 2008 and American companies can take advantage of free-trade arrangements in most economic sectors. Direct state-provincial linkages can also pay economic dividends, especially when one takes into account that Ontario

produces almost as much as Russia each year, Quebec as much as Denmark, Alberta as much as Portugal, and British Columbia as much as Ireland. A few cross-border irritants still exist in the areas of softwood lumber and certain other natural resources, but the world's largest bilateral trading relationship will most likely continue to grow and result in more job opportunities on both sides of the border.

Notes

[1] This article is adapted in part from Earl H. Fry, "Federalism and the Evolving Cross-Border Role of Provincial, State, and Municipal Governments," *International Journal* 60 (Spring 2005): 471–82. Permission to use this material was provided by the Canadian Institute of International Affairs, publisher of the *International Journal*.

[2] "U.S. Direct Investment Abroad," *Survey of Current Business*, September 2005, 136, and Raymond J. Mataloni, Jr., "U.S. Multinational Companies: Operations in 2003," *Survey of Current Business*, July 2005, 25.

[3] "Foreign Direct Investment in the United States," *Survey of Current Business*, September 2005, 116, and William J. Zeile, "U.S. Affiliates of Foreign Companies: Operations in 2003," *Survey of Current Business*, August 2005, 213.

[4] Department of Foreign Affairs and International Trade, "Canada's Relationship with the United States," at *http://www.dfait-maeci.gc.ca/can-am/*.

[5] In 1994, NAFTA superseded the FTA between the United States and Canada.

[6] Data derived from the World Bank for nation-states, and the U.S. Department of Commerce for states.

[7] Adrienne T. Edisis, "Global Activities by U.S. States: Findings of a Survey of State Government International Activities," paper prepared for the Elliott School of International Affairs, George Washington University, July 2003.

[8] *Le Soleil*, 4 October 2004.

[9] Department of Foreign Affairs and International Trade, *Annual Report of Canada's State of Trade* (Ottawa: Minister of Public Works and Government Services Canada, 2004), 29.

[10] The broad range of contacts between all levels of government in Canada and the United States is highlighted in Jeff Heynen and John Higginbotham, *Advancing Canadian Interests in the United States: A Practical Guide for Canadian Public Officials* (Ottawa: Canada School of Public Service, 2005).

[11] *New York Times*, 7 May 2003.

[12] John F. Helliwell, *How Much Do National Borders Matter?* (Washington, D.C.: Brookings Institution, 1998).

About the Author

Earl H. Fry is professor of Political Science and Endowed Professor of Canadian Studies at Brigham Young University. He has written extensively on Canada-U.S. relations over the past three decades and is the author of *The Expanding Role of State and Local Governments in U.S. Foreign Affairs* (Council on Foreign Relations, 1998).

Chapter Ten

STATE PAGES

Table 10.1
OFFICIAL NAMES OF STATES AND JURISDICTIONS, CAPITALS, ZIP CODES AND CENTRAL SWITCHBOARDS

State or other jurisdiction	Name of state capitol (a)	Capital	Zip code	Area code	Central switchboard
Alabama, State of	State House	Montgomery	36130	334	242-7000
Alaska, State of	State Capitol	Juneau	99801	907	465-4648
Arizona, State of	State Capitol	Phoenix	85007	602	542-4900
Arkansas, State of	State Capitol	Little Rock	72201	501	682-3000
California, State of	State Capitol	Sacramento	95814	916	322-9900
Colorado, State of	State Capitol	Denver	80203	303	866-5000
Connecticut, State of	State Capitol	Hartford	06106	860	240-0100
Delaware, State of	Legislative Hall	Dover	19903	302	744-4114
Florida, State of	The Capitol	Tallahassee	32399	850	487-0801
Georgia, State of	State Capitol	Atlanta	30334	404	656-2000
Hawaii, State of	State Capitol	Honolulu	96813	808	587-0221
Idaho, State of	State Capitol	Boise	83720	208	332-1000
Illinois, State of	State House	Springfield	62706	217	782-2000
Indiana, State of	State House	Indianapolis	46204	317	232-1000
Iowa, State of	State Capitol	Des Moines	50319	515	281-5011
Kansas, State of	Statehouse	Topeka	66612	785	296-0111
Kentucky, Commonwealth of	State Capitol	Frankfort	40601	502	564-1000
Louisiana, State of	State Capitol	Baton Rouge	70804	225	324-6600
Maine, State of	State House Station	Augusta	04333	207	287-6826
Maryland, State of	State House	Annapolis	21401	410	946-5400
Massachusetts, Commonwealth of	State House	Boston	02133	617	722-2000
Michigan, State of	State Capitol	Lansing	48909	517	373-0184
Minnesota, State of	State Capitol	St. Paul	55155	651	296-3962
Mississippi, State of	State Capitol	Jackson	39215	601	359-3770
Missouri, State of	State Capitol	Jefferson City	65101	573	751-2000
Montana, State of	State Capitol	Helena	59620	406	444-2511
Nebraska, State of	State Capitol	Lincoln	68509	402	471-2311
Nevada, State of	State Capitol	Carson City	89701	775	684-5670
New Hampshire, State of	State House	Concord	03301	603	271-1110
New Jersey, State of	State House	Trenton	08625	609	292-6000
New Mexico, State of	State Capitol	Santa Fe	87501	505	986-4600
New York, State of	State Capitol	Albany	12224	518	474-8390
North Carolina, State of	State Capitol	Raleigh	27601	919	733-4111
North Dakota, State of	State Capitol	Bismarck	58505	701	328-2000
Ohio, State of	Statehouse	Columbus	43215	614	466-2000
Oklahoma, State of	State Capitol	Oklahoma City	73105	405	521-2011
Oregon, State of	State Capitol	Salem	97310	503	986-1848
Pennsylvania, Commonwealth of	Main Capitol Building	Harrisburg	17120	717	787-2121
Rhode Island and Providence Plantations, State of	State House	Providence	02903	401	222-2653
South Carolina, State of	State House	Columbia	29211	803	896-0000
South Dakota, State of	State Capitol	Pierre	57501	605	773-3011
Tennessee, State of	State Capitol	Nashville	37243	615	741-2001
Texas, State of	State Capitol	Austin	78701	512	463-4630
Utah, State of	State Capitol	Salt Lake City	84114	801	538-3000
Vermont, State of	State House	Montpelier	05633	802	828-2231
Virginia, Commonwealth of	State Capitol	Richmond	23219	804	698-7410
Washington, State of	Legislative Building	Olympia	98504	360	735-5000
West Virginia, State of	State Capitol	Charleston	25305	304	558-3456
Wisconsin, State of	State Capitol	Madison	53702	608	266-0382
Wyoming, State of	State Capitol	Cheyenne	82002	307	777-7434
District of Columbia	District Building	. . .	20004	202	724-8000
American Samoa, Territory of	Maota Fono	Pago Pago	96799	684	633-4116
Guam, Territory of	Congress Building	Hagatna	96932	671	472-8931
No. Mariana Islands, Commonwealth of	Civic Center Building	Saipan	96950	670	664-0992
Puerto Rico, Commonwealth of	The Capitol	San Juan	00902	787	721-7000
U.S. Virgin Islands, Territory of	Capitol Building	Charlotte Amalie, St. Thomas	00804	340	774-0001

(a) In some instances the name is not official.

Table 10.2
HISTORICAL DATA ON THE STATES

State or other jurisdiction	Source of state lands	Date organized as territory	Date admitted to Union	Chronological order of admission to Union
Alabama	Mississippi Territory, 1798 (a)	March 3, 1817	Dec. 14, 1819	22
Alaska	Purchased from Russia, 1867	Aug. 24, 1912	Jan. 3, 1959	49
Arizona	Ceded by Mexico, 1848 (b)	Feb. 24, 1863	Feb. 14, 1912	48
Arkansas	Louisiana Purchase, 1803	March 2, 1819	June 15, 1836	25
California	Ceded by Mexico, 1848	(c)	Sept. 9, 1850	31
Colorado	Louisiana Purchase, 1803 (d)	Feb. 28, 1861	Aug. 1, 1876	38
Connecticut	Fundamental Orders, Jan. 14, 1638; Royal charter, April 23, 1662	(e)	Jan. 9, 1788 (f)	5
Delaware	Swedish charter, 1638; English charter, 1638	(e)	Dec. 7, 1787 (f)	1
Florida	Ceded by Spain, 1819	March 30, 1822	March 3, 1845	27
Georgia	Charter, 1732, from George II to Trustees for Establishing the Colony of Georgia	(e)	Jan. 2, 1788 (f)	4
Hawaii	Annexed, 1898	June 14, 1900	Aug. 21, 1959	50
Idaho	Treaty with Britain, 1846	March 4, 1863	July 3, 1890	43
Illinois	Northwest Territory, 1787	Feb. 3, 1809	Dec. 3, 1818	21
Indiana	Northwest Territory, 1787	May 7, 1800	Dec. 11, 1816	19
Iowa	Louisiana Purchase, 1803	June 12, 1838	Dec. 28, 1846	29
Kansas	Louisiana Purchase, 1803 (d)	May 30, 1854	Jan. 29, 1861	34
Kentucky	Part of Virginia until admitted as state	(c)	June 1, 1792	15
Louisiana	Louisiana Purchase, 1803 (g)	March 26, 1804	April 30, 1812	18
Maine	Part of Massachusetts until admitted as state	(c)	March 15, 1820	23
Maryland	Charter, 1632, from Charles I to Calvert	(e)	April 28, 1788 (f)	7
Massachusetts	Charter to Massachusetts Bay Company, 1629	(e)	Feb. 6, 1788 (f)	6
Michigan	Northwest Territory, 1787	Jan. 11, 1805	Jan. 26, 1837	26
Minnesota	Northwest Territory, 1787 (h)	March 3, 1849	May 11, 1858	32
Mississippi	Mississippi Territory (i)	April 7, 1798	Dec. 10, 1817	20
Missouri	Louisiana Purchase, 1803	June 4, 1812	Aug. 10, 1821	24
Montana	Louisiana Purchase, 1803 (j)	May 26, 1864	Nov. 8, 1889	41
Nebraska	Louisiana Purchase, 1803	May 30, 1854	March 1, 1867	37
Nevada	Ceded by Mexico, 1848	March 2, 1861	Oct. 31, 1864	36
New Hampshire	Grants from Council for New England, 1622 and 1629; made Royal province, 1679	(e)	June 21, 1788 (f)	9
New Jersey	Dutch settlement, 1618; English charter, 1664	(e)	Dec. 18, 1787 (f)	3
New Mexico	Ceded by Mexico, 1848 (b)	Sept. 9, 1850	Jan. 6, 1912	47
New York	Dutch settlement, 1623; English control, 1664	(e)	July 26, 1788 (f)	11
North Carolina	Charter, 1663, from Charles II	(e)	Nov. 21, 1789 (f)	12
North Dakota	Louisiana Purchase, 1803 (k)	March 2, 1861	Nov. 2, 1889	39
Ohio	Northwest Territory, 1787	May 7, 1800	March 1, 1803	17
Oklahoma	Louisiana Purchase, 1803	May 2, 1890	Nov. 16, 1907	46
Oregon	Settlement and treaty with Britain, 1846	Aug. 14, 1848	Feb. 14, 1859	33
Pennsylvania	Grant from Charles II to William Penn, 1681	(e)	Dec. 12, 1787 (f)	2
Rhode Island	Charter, 1663, from Charles II	(e)	May 29, 1790 (f)	13
South Carolina	Charter, 1663, from Charles II	(e)	May 23, 1788 (f)	8
South Dakota	Louisiana Purchase, 1803	March 2, 1861	Nov. 2, 1889	40
Tennessee	Part of North Carolina until land ceded to U.S. in 1789	June 8, 1790 (l)	June 1, 1796	16
Texas	Republic of Texas, 1845	(c)	Dec. 29, 1845	28
Utah	Ceded by Mexico, 1848	Sept. 9, 1850	Jan. 4, 1896	45
Vermont	From lands of New Hampshire and New York	(c)	March 4, 1791	14
Virginia	Charter, 1609, from James I to London Company	(e)	June 25, 1788 (f)	10
Washington	Oregon Territory, 1848	March 2, 1853	Nov. 11, 1889	42
West Virginia	Part of Virginia until admitted as state	(c)	June 20, 1863	35
Wisconsin	Northwest Territory, 1787	April 20, 1836	May 29, 1848	30
Wyoming	Louisiana Purchase, 1803 (d)(j)	July 25, 1868	July 10, 1890	44
Dist. of Columbia	Maryland (m)	. . .	. . .	. . .
American Samoa	---Became a territory, 1900---			
Guam	Ceded by Spain, 1898	Aug. 1, 1950	. . .	. . .
No. Mariana Islands	March 24, 1976	. . .	. . .	. . .
Puerto Rico	Ceded by Spain, 1898	. . .	July 25, 1952 (n)	. . .
U.S. Virgin Islands	---Purchased from Denmark, March 31, 1917---			

See footnotes at end of table.

HISTORICAL DATA ON THE STATES — Continued

Key:

(a) By the Treaty of Paris, 1783, England gave up claim to the 13 original Colonies, and to all land within an area extending along the present Canadian to the Lake of the Woods, down the Mississippi River to the 31st parallel, east to the Chattahoochee, down that river to the mouth of the Flint, border east to the source of the St. Mary's down that river to the ocean. The major part of Alabama was acquired by the Treaty of Paris, and the lower portion from Spain in 1813.

(b) Portion of land obtained by Gadsden Purchase, 1853.

(c) No territorial status before admission to Union.

(d) Portion of land ceded by Mexico, 1848.

(e) One of the original 13 Colonies.

(f) Date of ratification of U.S. Constitution.

(g) West Feliciana District (Baton Rouge) acquired from Spain, 1810; added to Louisiana, 1812.

(h) Portion of land obtained by Louisiana Purchase, 1803.

(i) See footnote (a). The lower portion of Mississippi also was acquired from Spain in 1813.

(j) Portion of land obtained from Oregon Territory, 1848.

(k) The northern portion of the Red River Valley was acquired by treaty with Great Britain in 1818.

(l) Date Southwest Territory (identical boundary as Tennessee's) was created.

(m) Area was originally 100 square miles, taken from Virginia and Maryland. Virginia's portion south of the Potomac was given back to that state in 1846. Site chosen in 1790, city incorporated 1802.

(n) On this date, Puerto Rico became a self-governing commonwealth by compact approved by the U.S. Congress and the voters of Puerto Rico as provided in U.S. Public Law 600 of 1950.

Table 10.3
STATE STATISTICS

State or other jurisdiction	Land area		Population (e)		Percentage change 2004 to 2005	Density per square mile	Number of Representatives in Congress	Capital	Population (d)(f)	Largest city	Rank in state	Population (d)(f)
	In square miles	Rank in nation	Size	Rank in nation								
Alabama	50,744	28	4,557,808	23	0.7	87.6	7	Montgomery	201,425	Birmingham	2	236,620
Alaska	571,951	1	663,661	47	0.9	1.1	1	Juneau	31,187	Anchorage	2	270,951
Arizona	113,635	6	5,939,292	18	3.5	45.2	8	Phoenix	1,388,416	Phoenix	1	1,388,416
Arkansas	52,068	27	2,779,154	32	1.1	51.3	4	Little Rock	184,053	Little Rock	1	184,053
California	155,959	3	36,132,147	1	0.8	217.2	53	Sacramento	445,335	Los Angeles	7	3,819,951
Colorado	103,718	8	4,665,177	22	1.4	41.5	7	Denver	557,478	Denver	1	557,478
Connecticut	4,845	48	3,510,297	29	0.3	702.9	5	Hartford	124,387	Bridgeport	3	139,664
Delaware	1,954	49	843,524	45	1.6	401.1	1	Dover	32,808	Wilmington	1	72,051
Florida	53,927	26	17,789,864	4	2.3	296.4	25	Tallahassee	153,938	Jacksonville	8	773,781
Georgia	57,906	21	9,072,576	9	1.7	141.4	13	Atlanta	423,019	Atlanta	1	423,019
Hawaii	6,423	47	1,275,194	42	1.0	188.6	2	Honolulu	380,149	Honolulu	1	380,149
Idaho	82,747	11	1,429,096	39	2.4	15.6	2	Boise	190,117	Boise	1	190,117
Illinois	55,584	24	12,763,371	5	0.4	223.4	19	Springfield	113,586	Chicago	6	2,869,121
Indiana	35,867	38	6,271,973	14	0.7	169.5	9	Indianapolis	783,438	Indianapolis	1	783,438
Iowa	55,869	23	2,966,334	30	0.5	52.4	5	Des Moines	196,093	Des Moines	1	196,093
Kansas	81,815	13	2,744,687	33	0.4	32.9	4	Topeka	122,008	Wichita	4	354,617
Kentucky	39,728	36	4,173,405	26	0.8	101.7	6	Frankfort	27,408	Louisville-Jefferson (b)	7	700,030
Louisiana	43,562	33	4,523,628	24	0.4	102.6	7	Baton Rouge	225,090	New Orleans	2	469,032
Maine	30,862	39	1,321,505	40	0.5	41.3	2	Augusta	18,560	Portland	9	63,635
Maryland	9,774	42	5,600,388	19	0.7	541.9	8	Annapolis	36,178	Baltimore	7	628,670
Massachusetts	7,840	45	6,398,743	13	-0.1	809.8	10	Boston	581,606	Boston	1	581,616
Michigan	56,804	22	10,120,860	8	0.2	175.0	15	Lansing	118,379	Detroit	6	911,402
Minnesota	79,610	14	5,132,799	21	0.7	61.8	8	St. Paul	280,404	Minneapolis	2	373,188
Mississippi	46,907	31	2,921,088	31	0.7	60.6	4	Jackson	179,599	Jackson	1	179,599
Missouri	68,886	18	5,800,310	17	0.7	81.2	9	Jefferson City	37,550	Kansas City	15	442,768
Montana	145,552	4	935,670	44	0.9	6.2	1	Helena	26,718	Billings	6	95,220
Nebraska	76,872	15	1,758,787	38	0.6	22.3	3	Lincoln	235,594	Omaha	2	404,267
Nevada	109,826	7	2,414,807	35	3.5	18.2	3	Carson City	55,311	Las Vegas	6	517,017
New Hampshire	8,968	44	1,309,940	41	0.8	137.8	2	Concord	41,823	Manchester	1	108,871
New Jersey	7,417	46	8,717,925	10	0.4	1,134.4	13	Trenton	85,314	Newark	9	277,911
New Mexico	121,356	5	1,928,384	36	1.3	15.0	3	Santa Fe	66,476	Albuquerque	3	471,856
New York	47,214	30	19,254,630	3	-0.1	401.9	29	Albany	93,919	New York City	6	8,085,742
North Carolina	48,711	29	8,683,242	11	1.7	165.2	13	Raleigh	316,802	Charlotte	2	584,658
North Dakota	68,976	17	636,677	48	0.1	9.3	1	Bismarck	56,344	Fargo	2	91,484
Ohio	40,948	35	11,464,042	7	0.1	277.3	18	Columbus	728,432	Columbus	1	728,432
Oklahoma	68,667	19	3,547,884	28	0.7	50.3	5	Oklahoma City	523,303	Oklahoma City	1	523,303
Oregon	95,997	10	3,641,056	27	1.4	35.6	5	Salem	142,914	Portland	3	538,544
Pennsylvania	44,817	32	12,429,616	6	0.3	274.0	19	Harrisburg	48,322	Philadelphia	13	1,479,339
Rhode Island	1,045	50	1,076,189	43	-0.3	1,003.2	2	Providence	176,365	Providence	1	176,365
South Carolina	30,110	40	4,255,083	25	1.4	133.2	6	Columbia	117,357	Columbia	1	117,357

See footnotes at end of table.

STATE STATISTICS — Continued

State or other jurisdiction	Land area In square miles	Land area Rank in nation	Population (e) Size	Population (e) Rank in nation	Percentage change 2004 to 2005	Density per square mile	Number of Representatives in Congress	Capital	Population (d)(f)	Rank in state	Largest city	Population (d)(f)
South Dakota............	75,885	16	775,933	46	0.7	9.9	1	Pierre	13,876	7	Sioux Falls	133,834
Tennessee...............	41,217	34	5,962,959	16	1.2	138.0	9	Nashville	544,765 (c)	2	Memphis	645,978
Texas	261,797	2	22,859,968	2	1.7	79.6	32	Austin	672,011	4	Houston	2,009,690
Utah	82,144	12	2,469,585	34	2.0	27.2	3	Salt Lake City	179,894	1	Salt Lake City	179,894
Vermont	9,250	43	623,050	49	0.3	65.8	1	Montpelier	8,035	13	Burlington	39,148
Virginia..................	39,594	37	7,567,465	12	1.2	178.8	11	Richmond	194,729	4	Virginia Beach	439,467
Washington..............	66,544	20	6,287,759	15	1.3	88.6	9	Olympia	43,963	18	Seattle	569,101
West Virginia...........	24,078	41	1,816,856	37	0.2	75.1	3	Charleston	51,394	1	Charleston	51,394
Wisconsin................	54,310	25	5,536,201	20	0.6	98.8	8	Madison	218,432	2	Milwaukee	586,941
Wyoming.................	97,100	9	509,294	51	0.7	5.1	1	Cheyenne	54,374	1	Cheyenne	54,374
Dist. of Columbia	63	...	550,521	50	-0.7	9,316.4	1 (a)	...	...	...	...	...
American Samoa (d)	77	...	57,291	...	22.0	...	1 (a)	Pago Pago	4,278	3	Tafuna	8,409
Guam (d)	210	...	154,805	...	...	...	1 (a)	Hagatna	1,100	18	Dededo	42,980
No. Mariana Islands (d)	181	...	69,221	...	...	...	...	Saipan	62,392	1	Saipan	62,392
Puerto Rico (d)	3,427	...	3,878,523	...	0.5	1,131.8	1 (a)	San Juan	421,958	1	San Juan	421,958
U.S. Virgin Islands (d) .	134	...	108,612	...	...	...	1 (a)	Charlotte Amalie, St. Thomas	11,004	1	Charlotte Amalie, St. Thomas	11,004

Source: U.S. Census Bureau, February 2006.
Key:
. . .—Not applicable
(a) Delegate with privileges to vote in committees and the Committee of the Whole.
(b) Coextensive with Jefferson County.
(c) This city is part of a consolidated city-county government and is coextensive with Davidson County.
(d) Information for territories and cities with a population under 100,000 is from the U.S. Census Bureau, Census 2000.
(e) 2004 Census Bureau estimate.
(f) 2003 Cencus Bureau estimate.

Alabama

Nickname... The Heart of Dixie
Motto .... *Aldemus Jura Nostra Defendere*
(We Dare Defend Our Rights)
Flower...Camellia
Bird.. Yellowhammer
Tree...Southern (Longleaf) Pine
Song.. *Alabama*
Entered the Union .... December 14, 1819
Capital .... Montgomery

STATISTICS

Land Area (square miles)... 50,744
   Rank in Nation...28th
Population... 4,557,808
   Rank in Nation...23rd
   Density per square mile..87.6
Capital City .... Montgomery
   Population 201,425
   Rank in State...2nd
Largest City .... Birmingham
   Population 236,620
Number of Representatives in Congress 7
Number of Counties...67
Number of Municipal Governments....................................451
Number of 2008 Electoral Votes 9
Number of School Districts 130
Number of Special Districts...525

LEGISLATIVE BRANCH

Legislative Body.. Legislature

President of the Senate.. Lt. Gov. Lucy Baxley
President Pro Tem of the Senate .... Lowell Ray Barron
Secretary of the Senate .... McDowell Lee

Speaker of the House .... Seth Hammett
Speaker Pro Tem of the House........................... Demetrius C. Newton
Clerk of the House... William G. Pappas

2006 Regular Session.................................. Jan. 10 – April 24
Number of Senatorial Districts 35
Number of Representative Districts 105

EXECUTIVE BRANCH

Governor..Bob Riley
Lieutenant Governor... Lucy Baxley
Secretary of State... Nancy Worley
Attorney General ....Troy King
Treasurer... Kay Ivey
Auditor .... Beth Chapman
Comptroller .... Robert Childree

Governor's Present Term .... 1/03 – 1/07
Number of Elected Officials in the Executive Branch...............7
Number of Members in the Cabinet 29

JUDICIAL BRANCH

Highest Court...Supreme Court
Supreme Court Chief Justice .... Drayton Nabers Jr.
Number of Supreme Court Judges 9
Number of Intermediate Appellate Court Judges 10
Number of U.S. Court Districts 3
U.S. Circuit Court... 11th Circuit

STATE INTERNET ADDRESSES

Official State Website ....http://www.alabama.gov
Governor's Website ....http://www.governor.state.al.us
State Legislative Website .... http://www.legislature.state.al.us
State Judicial Website ....http://www.judicial.state.al.us

Alaska

Nickname... The Last Frontier
Motto .... *North to the Future*
Flower...Forget-Me-Not
Bird... Willow Ptarmigan
Tree..Sitka Spruce
Song.. *Alaska's Flag*
Entered the Union... January 3, 1959
Capital .... Juneau

STATISTICS

Land Area (square miles)... 571,951
   Rank in Nation... 1st
Population... 663,661
   Rank in Nation...47th
   Density per square mile.. 1.1
Capital City .... Juneau
   Population 31,187
   Rank in State...2nd
Largest City .... Anchorage
   Population 270,951
Number of Representatives in Congress 1
Number of Counties...27
Number of Municipal Governments....................................149
Number of 2008 Electoral Votes 3
Number of School Districts 53
Number of Special Districts...14

LEGISLATIVE BRANCH

Legislative Body..Legislature

President of the Senate.. Ben Stevens
Secretary of the Senate .... Kirsten Waid

Speaker of the House .... John Harris
Chief Clerk of the House .... Suzanne Lowell

2006 Regular Session .... Jan. 9 – May 9
Number of Senatorial Districts 20
Number of Representative Districts 40

EXECUTIVE BRANCH

Governor.. Frank Murkowski
Lieutenant Governor.. Loren Leman
Attorney General .... David W. Marquez
Treasurer .... Tom Boutin
Auditor .... Pat Davidson
Comptroller .... Kim Gamero

Governor's Present Term .... 12/02 – 12/06
Number of Elected Officials in the Executive Branch...........................2
Number of Members in the Cabinet 18

JUDICIAL BRANCH

Highest Court... Supreme Court
Supreme Court Chief Justice .... Alexander O. Bryner
Number of Supreme Court Judges 5
Number of Intermediate Appellate Court Judges 3
Number of U.S. Court Districts 1
U.S. Circuit Court... 9th Circuit

STATE INTERNET ADDRESSES

Official State Website ....http://www.state.ak.us
Governor's Website .... http://www.gov.state.ak.us
State Legislative Website ....http://www.legis.state.ak.us
State Judicial Website .... http://www.state.ak.us/courts

Arizona

Nickname...The Grand Canyon State
Motto .... *Ditat Deus (God Enriches)*
Flower...Blossom of the Saguaro Cactus
Bird...Cactus Wren
Tree...Palo Verde
Songs .... *Arizona March Song* and *Arizona*
Entered the Union...February 14, 1912
Capital .... Phoenix

STATISTICS

Land Area (square miles)... 113,635
    Rank in Nation...6th
Population..5,939,292
    Rank in Nation..18th
    Density per square mile...49.1
Capital City...Phoenix
    Population..1,388,416
    Rank in State 1st
Largest City ....Phoenix
Number Representatives in Congress.....................................8
Number of Counties...15
Number of Municipal Governments.....................................87
Number of 2008 Electoral Votes 10
Number of School Districts 313
Number of Special Districts..305

LEGISLATIVE BRANCH

Legislative Body.. Legislature

President of the Senate...Ken Bennett
President Pro Tem of the Senate .... Marilyn Jarrett
Secretary of the Senate .... Charmion Billington

Speaker of the House .... James P. Weiers
Speaker Pro Tem of the House .... Bob Robson
Chief Clerk of the House .... Norman L. Moore

2006 Regular Session ....Jan. 9, 2006–TBD
Number of Senatorial Districts 30
Number of Representative Districts 30

EXECUTIVE BRANCH

Governor.. Janet Napolitano
Secretary of State...Jan Brewer
Attorney General ....Terry Goddard
Treasurer...David Petersen
Auditor .... Debra K. Davenport
Comptroller .... D. Clark Partridge

Governor's Present Term 1/03–1/07
Number of Elected Officials in the Executive Branch......................... 11
Number of Members in the Cabinet 38

JUDICIAL BRANCH

Highest Court.. Supreme Court
Supreme Court Chief Justice .... Ruth V. McGregor
Number of Supreme Court Judges 5
Number of Intermediate Appellate Court Judges 22
Number of U.S. Court Districts 1
U.S. Circuit Court..9th Circuit

STATE INTERNET ADDRESSES

Official State Website ....http://www.az.gov
Governor's Website .... http://www.governor.state.az.us
State Legislative Website ....http://www.azleg.state.az.us
State Judicial Website ....http://www.supreme.state.az.us

Arkansas

Nickname... The Natural State
Motto .... *Regnat Populus* (The People Rule)
Flower.. Apple Blossom
Bird.. Mockingbird
Tree... Pine
Song..*Arkansas*
Entered the Union .... June 15, 1836
Capital .... Little Rock

STATISTICS

Land Area (square miles)... 52,068
    Rank in Nation 27th
Population... 2,779,154
    Rank in Nation..32nd
    Density per square mile...51.3
Capital City..Little Rock
    Population...184,053
    Rank in State 1st
Largest City ....Little Rock
Number of Representatives in Congress 4
Number of Counties..75
Number of Municipal Governments......................................499
Number of 2008 Electoral Votes 6
Number of School Districts 309
Number of Special Districts..704

LEGISLATIVE BRANCH

Legislative Body..General Assembly

President of the Senate............................Lt. Gov. Winthrop Rockefeller
President Pro Tem of the Senate .... Jim Ague
Secretary of the Senate .... Ann Cornwell

Speaker of the House .... Bill H. Stovall III
Speaker Pro Tem of the House .... Jay Bradford
Chief Clerk of the House .... Jo Renshaw

2006 Regular Session .... No regular session in 2006
Number of Senatorial Districts 35
Number of Representative Districts 100

EXECUTIVE BRANCH

Governor.. Mike Huckabee
Lieutenant Governor......................................Winthrop Rockefeller
Secretary of State.. Charlie Daniels
Attorney General .... Mike Beebe
Treasurer.. Gus Wingfield
Auditor .... Jim Wood
Comptroller .... Richard Weiss

Governor's Present Term 1/03–1/07
Number of Elected Officials in the Executive Branch.........................7
Number of Members in the Cabinet 46

JUDICIAL BRANCH

Highest Court..Supreme Court
Supreme Court Chief Justice ....Jim Hannah
Number of Supreme Court Judges 7
Number of Intermediate Appellate Court Judges 12
Number of U.S. Court Districts 2
U.S. Circuit Court..8th Circuit

STATE INTERNET ADDRESSES

Official State Website ....http://www.state.ar.us
Governor's Website ....http://www.state.ar.us/governor
State Legislative Website ....http://www.arkleg.state.ar.us
State Judicial Website .... http://courts.state.ar.us

California

Nickname..The Golden State
Motto.. *Eureka* (I Have Found It)
Flower..Golden Poppy
Bird.. California Valley Quail
Tree...California Redwood
Song.. *I Love You, California*
Entered the Union.. September 9, 1850
Capital ....Sacramento

STATISTICS

Land Area (square miles)...155,959
   Rank in Nation...3rd
Population..36,132,147
   Rank in Nation..1st
   Density per Square Mile..217.2
Capital City...Sacramento
   Population..445,335
   Rank in State..7th
Largest City .... Los Angeles
   Population...3,819,951
Number of Representatives in Congress 53
Number of Counties..58
Number of Municipal Governments...475
Number of 2008 Electoral Votes 55
Number of School Districts..989
Number of Special Districts..2,830

LEGISLATIVE BRANCH

Legislative Body..Legislature

President of the Senate............................... Lt. Gov. Cruz Bustamante
President Pro Tem of the Senate .... Don Perata
Secretary of the Senate...Gregory Schmidt

Speaker of the Assembly......................................Fabian Núñez
Speaker Pro Tem of the Assembly .... Leland Yee
Chief Clerk of the Assembly.......................................E. Dotson Wilson

2006 Regular Session ....Jan. 4–Aug. 31, 2006
Number of Senatorial Districts 40
Number of Representative Districts 80

EXECUTIVE BRANCH

Governor..Arnold Schwarzenegger
Lieutenant Governor.. Cruz M. Bustamante
Secretary of State..Bruce McPherson
Attorney General ....Bill Lockyer
Treasurer..Philip Angelides
Auditor .... Elaine M. Howle
Controller .... Steve Westly

Governor's Present Term 11/03–1/07
Number of Elected Officials in the Executive Branch............................8
Number of Members in the Cabinet..11

JUDICIAL BRANCH

Highest Court... Supreme Court
Supreme Court Chief Justice ....Ronald M. George
Number of Supreme Court Judges 7
Number of Intermediate Appellate Court Judges 105
Number of U.S. Court Districts 4
U.S. Circuit Court..9th Circuit

STATE INTERNET ADDRESSES

Official State Website ....http://www.ca.gov
Governor's Website ....http://www.governor.ca.gov
State Legislative Website ....http://www.leginfo.ca.gov
State Judicial Website ....http://www.courtinfo.ca.gov

Colorado

Nickname.. The Centennial State
Motto .... *Nil Sine Numine*
(Nothing Without Providence)
Flower.. Columbine
Bird.. Lark Bunting
Tree.. Blue Spruce
Song..*Where the Columbines Grow*
Entered the Union... August 1, 1876
Capital .... Denver

STATISTICS

Land Area (square miles).. 103,718
   Rank in Nation..8th
Population... 4,665,177
   Rank in Nation...22nd
   Density per square mile..41.5
Capital City... Denver
   Population.. 557,478
   Rank in State.. 1st
Largest City .... Denver
Number of Representatives in Congress 7
Number of Counties..63
Number of Municipal Governments..270
Number of 2008 Electoral Votes 9
Number of School Districts..178
Number of Special Districts..1,414

LEGISLATIVE BRANCH

Legislative Body.......................................General Assembly

President of the Senate.. Joan Fitz-Gerald
President Pro Tem of the Senate .... Peter C. Groff
Secretary of the Senate..Karen Goldman

Speaker of the House .... Andrew Romanoff
Speaker Pro Tem of the House.......................................Cheri Jahn
Chief Clerk of the House .... Marilyn Eddins

2006 Regular Session ....Jan. 11–May 10, 2006
Number of Senatorial Districts 35
Number of Representative Districts 65

EXECUTIVE BRANCH

Governor... Bill Owens
Lieutenant Governor.. Jane Norton
Secretary of State..Gigi Dennis
Attorney General .... John W. Suthers
Treasurer.. Mark Hillman
Auditor .... Joanne Hill
Controller .... Leslie Shenefelt

Governor's Present Term 1/03–1/07
Number of Elected Officials in the Executive Branch.........................5
Number of Members in the Cabinet..21

JUDICIAL BRANCH

Highest Court... Supreme Court
Supreme Court Chief Justice... Mary Mullarkey
Number of Supreme Court Judges 7
Number of Intermediate Appellate Court Judges 16
Number of U.S. Court Districts 1
U.S. Circuit Court.. 10th Circuit

STATE INTERNET ADDRESSES

Official State Website ....http://www.state.co.us
Governor's Website..http://www.state.co.us/gov_dir/governor_office.html
State Legislative Website ....http://www.leg.state.co.us
State Judicial Website ....http://www.courts.state.co.us

Connecticut

Nickname	The Constitution State
Motto	*Qui Transtulit Sustinet*
	(He Who Transplanted Still Sustains)
Flower	Mountain Laurel
Bird	American Robin
Tree	White Oak
Song	*Yankee Doodle*
Entered the Union	January 9, 1788
Capital	Hartford

STATISTICS

Land Area (square miles)	4,845
Rank in Nation	48th
Population	3,510,297
Rank in Nation	29th
Density per square mile	702.97190
Capital City	Hartford
Population	124,387
Rank in State	3rd
Largest City	Bridgeport
Population	139,664
Number of Representatives in Congress	5
Number of Counties	8
Number of Municipal Governments	30
Number of 2008 Electoral Votes	7
Number of School Districts	166
Number of Special Districts	384

LEGISLATIVE BRANCH

Legislative Body	General Assembly
President of the Senate	Kevin Sullivan
President Pro Tem of the Senate	Donald E. Williams
Clerk of the Senate	Thomas P. Sheridan
Speaker of the House	James A. Amann
Deputy Speakers	
of the House	Emil Altobello, Mary G. Fritz, Bob Godfrey,
	Marie Kirkley-Bey
Clerk of the House	Garey E. Coleman
2006 Regular Session	Feb. 8 – May 3, 2006
Number of Senatorial Districts	36
Number of Representative Districts	151

EXECUTIVE BRANCH

Governor	M. Jodi Rell
Lieutenant Governor	Kevin Sullivan
Secretary of State	Susan Bysiewicz
Attorney General	Richard Blumenthal
Treasurer	Denise Nappier
Auditor	Robert Jaekle and Kevin P. Johnston
Comptroller	Nancy Wyman
Governor's Present Term	1/03 – 1/07
Number of Elected Officials in the Executive Branch	6
Number of Members in the Cabinet	27

JUDICIAL BRANCH

Highest Court	Supreme Court
Supreme Court Chief Justice	William J. Sullivan
Number of Supreme Court Judges	7
Number of Intermediate Appellate Court Judges	9
Number of U.S. Court Districts	1
U.S. Circuit Court	2nd Circuit

STATE INTERNET ADDRESSES

Official State Website	http://www.state.ct.us
Governor's Website	http://www.state.ct.us/governor
State Legislative Website	http://www.cga.state.ct.us
State Judicial Website	http://www.jud.state.ct.us

Delaware

Nickname	The First State
Motto	*Liberty and Independence*
Flower	Peach Blossom
Bird	Blue Hen Chicken
Tree	American Holly
Song	*Our Delaware*
Entered the Union	December 7, 1787
Capital	Dover

STATISTICS

Land Area (square miles)	1,954
Rank in Nation	49th
Population	843,524
Rank in Nation	45th
Density per square mile	401.1
Capital City	Dover
Population	32,808
Rank in State	2nd
Largest City	Wilmington
Population	72,051
Number of Representatives in Congress	1
Number of Counties	3
Number of Municipal Governments	57
Number of 2008 Electoral Votes	3
Number of School Districts	19
Number of Special Districts	260

LEGISLATIVE BRANCH

Legislative Body	General Assembly
President of the Senate	Lt. Gov. John Carney Jr.
President Pro Tem of the Senate	Thurman Adams Jr.
Secretary of the Senate	Bernard J. Brady
Speaker of the House	Terry R. Spence
Clerk of the House	JoAnn M. Hedrick
2006 Regular Session	Jan. 10 – June 30, 2006
Number of Senatorial Districts	21
Number of Representative Districts	41

EXECUTIVE BRANCH

Governor	Ruth Ann Minner
Lieutenant Governor	John Carney Jr.
Secretary of State	Harriet Smith Windsor
Attorney General	Craig Danberg
Treasurer	Jack Markell
Auditor	Thomas Wagner
Comptroller	Richard S. Cordrey
Governor's Present Term	1/01 – 1/09
Number of Elected Officials in the Executive Branch	5
Number of Members in the Cabinet	19

JUDICIAL BRANCH

Highest Court	Supreme Court
Supreme Court Chief Justice	Myron T. Steele
Number of Supreme Court Judges	5
Number of Intermediate Appellate Court Judges	0
Number of U.S. Court Districts	1
U.S. Circuit Court	3rd Circuit

STATE INTERNET ADDRESSES

Official State Website	http://delaware.gov
Governor's Website	http://www.state.de.us/governor
State Legislative Website	http://www.legis.state.de.us
State Judicial Website	http://courts.state.de.us

Florida

Nickname	The Sunshine State
Motto	*In God We Trust*
Flower	Orange Blossom
Bird	Mockingbird
Tree	Sabal Palmetto Palm
Song	*The Swannee River (Old Folks at Home)*
Entered the Union	March 3, 1845
Capital	Tallahassee

STATISTICS

Land Area (square miles)	53,927
Rank in Nation	26th
Population	17,789,864
Rank in Nation	4th
Density per square mile	296.4
Capital City	Tallahassee
Population	153,938
Rank in State	8th
Largest City	Jacksonville
Population	773,781
Number of Representatives in Congress	25
Number of Counties	67
Number of Municipal Governments	404
Number of 2008 Electoral Votes	27
Number of School Districts	67
Number of Special Districts	626

LEGISLATIVE BRANCH

Legislative Body	Legislature
President of the Senate	Tom Lee
President Pro Tem of the Senate	Charlie Clary
Secretary of the Senate	Faye W. Blanton
Speaker of the House	Allan G. Bense
Speaker Pro Tem of the House	Leslie Waters
Clerk of the House	John B. Phelps
2006 Regular Session	March 7 – May 5, 2006
Number of Senatorial Districts	40
Number of Representative Districts	120

EXECUTIVE BRANCH

Governor	Jeb Bush
Lieutenant Governor	Toni Jennings
Secretary of State	Sue Cobb
Attorney General	Charlie Crist
Chief Financial Officer	Tom Gallagher
Auditor	William O. Monroe
Governor's Present Term	1/03 – 1/07
Number of Elected Officials in the Executive Branch	5
Number of Members in the Cabinet	4

JUDICIAL BRANCH

Highest Court	Supreme Court
Supreme Court Chief Justice	Barbara J. Pariente
Number of Supreme Court Judges	7
Number of Intermediate Appellate Court Judges	62
Number of U.S. Court Districts	3
U.S. Circuit Court	11th Circuit

STATE INTERNET ADDRESSES

Official State Website	http://www.myflorida.com
Governor's Website	http://www.state.fl.us/eog
State Legislative Website	http://www.leg.state.fl.us
State Judicial Website	http://www.flcourts.org

Georgia

Nickname	The Empire State of the South
Motto	*Wisdom, Justice and Moderation*
Flower	Cherokee Rose
Bird	Brown Thrasher
Tree	Live Oak
Song	*Georgia on My Mind*
Entered the Union	January 2, 1788
Capital	Atlanta

STATISTICS

Land Area (square miles)	57,906
Rank in Nation	21st
Population	9,072,576
Rank in Nation	9th
Density per square mile	141.4
Capital City	Atlanta
Population	423,019
Rank in State	1st
Largest City	Atlanta
Number of Representatives in Congress	13
Number of Counties	159
Number of Municipal Governments	531
Number of 2008 Electoral Votes	15
Number of School Districts	180
Number of Special Districts	581

LEGISLATIVE BRANCH

Legislative Body	General Assembly
President of the Senate	Lt. Gov. Mark Taylor
President Pro Tem of the Senate	Eric Johnson
Secretary of the Senate	Frank Eldridge Jr.
Speaker of the House	Glenn Richardson
Speaker Pro Tem of the House	Mark Burkhalter
Clerk of the House	Robert E. Rivers Jr.
2006 Regular Session	Jan. 9 – TBD
Number of Senatorial Districts	56
Number of Representative Districts	180

EXECUTIVE BRANCH

Governor	Sonny Perdue
Lieutenant Governor	Mark Taylor
Secretary of State	Cathy Cox
Attorney General	Thurbert E. Baker
Treasurer	W. Daniel Ebersole
Auditor	Russell W. Hinton
Governor's Present Term	1/03 – 1/07
Number of Elected Officials in the Executive Branch	13
Number of Members in the Cabinet	No formal cabinet system

JUDICIAL BRANCH

Highest Court	Supreme Court
Supreme Court Chief Justice	Norman S. Fletcher
Number of Supreme Court Judges	7
Number of Intermediate Appellate Court Judges	12
Number of U.S. Court Districts	3
U.S. Circuit Court	11th Circuit

STATE INTERNET ADDRESSES

Official State Website	http://www.state.ga.us
Governor's Website	http://gov.state.ga.us/
State Legislative Website	http://www.legis.state.ga.us
State Judicial Website	http://www.georgiacourts.org

Hawaii

Nickname..The Aloha State
Motto ....*Ua Mau Ke Ea O Ka Aina I Ka Pono*
(The Life of the Land Is Perpetuated in Righteousness)
Flower...Native Yellow Hibiscus
Bird...Hawaiian Goose (Nene)
Tree...Kukue Tree (Candlenut)
Song..*Hawaii Ponoi*
Entered the Union...August 21, 1959
Capital ....Honolulu

STATISTICS

Land Area (square miles)...6,423
  Rank in Nation...47th
Population..1,275,194
  Rank in Nation..42nd
  Density per square mile...188.6
Capital City...Honolulu
  Population...380,149
  Rank in State..1st
Largest City ....Honolulu
Number of Representatives in Congress 2
Number of Counties...5
Number of Municipal Governments....................................1
Number of 2008 Electoral Votes 4
Number of School Districts 1
Number of Special Districts...15

LEGISLATIVE BRANCH

Legislative Body...Legislature

President of the Senate.....................................Robert Bunda
Vice President of the Senate ....Donna Mercado Kim
Chief Clerk of the Senate ....Paul T. Kawaguchi

Speaker of the House .... Calvin K.Y. Say
Vice Speaker of the House................................K. Mark Takai
Chief Clerk of the House .... Patricia A. Mau-Shimizu

2006 Regular Session ....Jan. 18 – May 3, 2006
Number of Senatorial Districts 25
Number of Representative Districts 51

EXECUTIVE BRANCH

Governor...Linda Lingle
Lieutenant Governor......................................James Aiona
Attorney General ....Mark J. Bennett
Treasurer..Georgina Kawamura
Auditor .... Marion M. Higa
Comptroller ....Russ K. Saito

Governor's Present Term .... 12/02 – 12/06
Number of Elected Officials in the Executive Branch...........................2
Number of Members in the Cabinet....................................25

JUDICIAL BRANCH

Highest Court...Supreme Court
Supreme Court Chief Justice.........................Ronald T.Y. Moon
Number of Supreme Court Judges 5
Number of Intermediate Appellate Court Judges 4
Number of U.S. Court Districts 1
U.S. Circuit Court...9th Circuit

STATE INTERNET ADDRESSES

Official State Website ....http://www.hawaii.gov
Governor's Website ....http://gov.state.hi.us
State Legislative Website......................http://www.capitol.hawaii.gov
State Judicial Website ....http://www.courts.hi.us

Idaho

Nickname... The Gem State
Motto ....*Esto Perpetua* (Let It Be Perpetual)
Flower...Syringa
Bird..Mountain Bluebird
Tree...Western White Pine
Song..*Here We Have Idaho*
Entered the Union... July 3, 1890
Capital ....Boise

STATISTICS

Land Area (square miles)..82,747
  Rank in Nation...11th
Population..1,429,096
  Rank in Nation..39th
  Density per square mile...15.6
Capital City..Boise
  Population...190,117
  Rank in State..1st
Largest City ....Boise
Number of Representatives in Congress 2
Number of Counties...44
Number of Municipal Governments................................200
Number of 2008 Electoral Votes 4
Number of School Districts 114
Number of Special Districts...798

LEGISLATIVE BRANCH

Legislative Body...Legislature

President of the Senate.............................Lt. Gov. Jim Risch
President Pro Tem of the Senate ....Robert L. Geddes
Secretary of the Senate .... Jeannine Wood

Speaker of the House .... Bruce Newcomb
Chief Clerk of the House .... Pamm Juker

2006 Regular Session .... Jan. 9 – TBD
Number of Senatorial Districts 35
Number of Representative Districts 35

EXECUTIVE BRANCH

Governor.. Dirk Kempthorne
Lieutenant Governor... Jim Risch
Secretary of State.. Ben Ysursa
Attorney General ....Lawrence Wasden
Treasurer...Ron Crane
Controller .... Keith Johnson

Governor's Present Term .... 1/03 – 1/07
Number of Elected Officials in the Executive Branch...........................7
Number of Members in the Cabinet....................................22

JUDICIAL BRANCH

Highest Court.. Supreme Court
Supreme Court Chief Justice...................................Gerald F. Schroeder
Number of Supreme Court Judges 5
Number of Intermediate Appellate Court Judges 3
Number of U.S. Court Districts 1
U.S. Circuit Court...9th Circuit

STATE INTERNET ADDRESSES

Official State Website ....http://www.state.id.us
Governor's Website http://www2.state.id.us/gov
State Legislative Website......................http://www2.state.id.us/legislat
State Judicial Website http://www2.state.id.us/judicial

Illinois

Nickname..The Prairie State
Motto..*State Sovereignty-National Union*
Flower...Native Violet
Bird.. Cardinal
Tree...White Oak
Song...*Illinois*
Entered the Union....................................... December 3, 1818
Capital .... Springfield

STATISTICS

Land Area (square miles)..55,584
   Rank in Nation..24th
Population... 12,763,371
   Rank in Nation...5th
   Density per square mile...223.4
Capital City... Springfield
   Population 113,586
   Rank in State...6th
Largest City ....Chicago
   Population...2,869,121
Number of Representatives in Congress 19
Number of Counties.. 102
Number of Municipal Governments...............................1,291
Number of 2008 Electoral Votes 21
Number of School Districts 887
Number of Special Districts..3,145

LEGISLATIVE BRANCH

Legislative Body.....................................General Assembly

President of the Senate......................................Emil Jones Jr.
Secretary of the Senate .... Linda Hawker

Speaker of the House .... Michael J. Madigan
House Chief Clerk .... Mark Mahoney

2006 Regular Session ....Jan. 11 – Dec. 31, 2006
Number of Senatorial Districts 59
Number of Representative Districts 118

EXECUTIVE BRANCH

Governor... Rod Blagojevich
Lieutenant Governor...Patrick Quinn
Secretary of State .... Jesse White
Attorney General .... Lisa Madigan
Treasurer... Judy Baar Topinka
Auditor .... William G. Holland
Comptroller .... Daniel Hynes

Governor's Present Term .... 1/03 – 1/07
Number of Elected Officials in the Executive Branch...........................6
Number of Members in the Cabinet 18

JUDICIAL BRANCH

Highest Court.. Supreme Court
Supreme Court Chief Justice....................... Robert R. Thomas
Number of Supreme Court Judges 7
Number of Intermediate Appellate Court Judges 52
Number of U.S. Court Districts 3
U.S. Circuit Court..7th Circuit

STATE INTERNET ADDRESSES

Official State Website .... http://www.state.il.us
Governor's Website .... http://www.state.il.us/gov
State Legislative Website ....http://www.legis.state.il.us
State Judicial Website .... http://www.state.il.us/court

Indiana

Nickname..The Hoosier State
Motto...*Crossroads of America*
Flower.. Peony
Bird.. Cardinal
Tree.. Tulip Poplar
Song................................... *On the Banks of the Wabash, Far Away*
Entered the Union.................................... December 11, 1816
Capital .... Indianapolis

STATISTICS

Land Area (square miles)... 35,867
   Rank in Nation..38th
Population...6,271,973
   Rank in Nation...14th
   Density per square mile...169.5
Capital City... Indianapolis
   Population 783,438
   Rank in State...1st
Largest City .... Indianapolis
Number of Representatives in Congress 9
Number of Counties.. 92
Number of Municipal Governments...............................567
Number of 2008 Electoral Votes 11
Number of School Districts 294
Number of Special Districts..1,125

LEGISLATIVE BRANCH

Legislative Body.....................................General Assembly

President of the Senate................................... Lt. Gov. Becky Skillman
President Pro Tem of the Senate .... Robert D. Garton
Principal Secretary of the Senate .... Mary C. Mendel

Speaker of the House .... Brian C. Bosma
Speaker Pro Tem of the House ....P. Eric Turner
Principal Clerk of the House ....Carolyn Spotts

2006 Regular Session ....Jan. 4 – March 14, 2006
Number of Senatorial Districts 50
Number of Representative Districts 100

EXECUTIVE BRANCH

Governor.. Mitch Daniels
Lieutenant Governor....................................... Becky Skillman
Secretary of State .... Todd Rokita
Attorney General .... Steve Carter
Treasurer..Tim Berry
Auditor .... Bruce Hartman

Governor's Present Term .... 1/05 – 1/09
Number of Elected Officials in the Executive Branch...........................7
Number of Members in the Cabinet 16

JUDICIAL BRANCH

Highest Court.. Supreme Court
Supreme Court Chief Justice.....................Randall T. Shepard
Number of Supreme Court Judges 5
Number of Intermediate Appellate Court Judges 16
Number of U.S. Court Districts 2
U.S. Circuit Court..7th Circuit

STATE INTERNET ADDRESSES

Official State Website ....http://www.state.in.us
Governor's Website .... http://www.in.gov/gov
State Legislative Website .... http://www.in.gov/legislative
State Judicial Website .... http://www.in.gov/judiciary

Iowa

Nickname	The Hawkeye State
Motto	*Our Liberties We Prize and Our Rights We Will Maintain*
Flower	Wild Rose
Bird	Eastern Goldfinch
Tree	Oak
Song	*The Song of Iowa*
Entered the Union	December 28, 1846
Capital	Des Moines

STATISTICS

Land Area (square miles)	55,869
Rank in Nation	23rd
Population	2,966,334
Rank in Nation	30th
Density per square mile	52.4
Capital City	Des Moines
Population	196,093
Rank in State	1st
Largest City	Des Moines
Number of Representatives in Congress	5
Number of Counties	99
Number of Municipal Governments	948
Number of 2008 Electoral Votes	7
Number of School Districts	370
Number of Special Districts	542

LEGISLATIVE BRANCH

Legislative Body	General Assembly
President of the Senate	John P. Kibbie
President Pro Tem of the Senate	Robert E. Dvorsky
Secretary of the Senate	Michael E. Marshall
Speaker of the House	Christopher Rants
Speaker Pro Tem of the House	Danny Carroll
Chief Clerk of the House	Margaret A. Thomson
2006 Regular Session	Jan. 9 – TBD
Number of Senatorial Districts	50
Number of Representative Districts	100

EXECUTIVE BRANCH

Governor	Thomas Vilsack
Lieutenant Governor	Sally Pederson
Secretary of State	Chet Culver
Attorney General	Thomas Miller
Treasurer	Michael Fitzgerald
Auditor	David A. Vaudt
Chief Operating Officer	Calvin McKelvogue
Governor's Present Term	1/03 – 1/07
Number of Elected Officials in the Executive Branch	7
Number of Members in the Cabinet	32

JUDICIAL BRANCH

Highest Court	Supreme Court
Supreme Court Chief Justice	Lewis A. Lavarato
Number of Supreme Court Judges	7
Number of Intermediate Appellate Court Judges	9
Number of U.S. Court Districts	2
U.S. Circuit Court	8th Circuit

STATE INTERNET ADDRESSES

Official State Website	http://www.state.ia.us
Governor's Website	http://www.governor.state.ia.us/
State Legislative Website	http://www.legis.state.ia.us
State Judicial Website	http://www.judicial.state.ia.us

Kansas

Nickname	The Sunflower State
Motto	*Ad Astra per Aspera* (To the Stars through Difficulties)
Flower	Wild Native Sunflower
Bird	Western Meadowlark
Tree	Cottonwood
Song	*Home on the Range*
Entered the Union	January 29, 1861
Capital	Topeka

STATISTICS

Land Area (square miles)	81,815
Rank in Nation	13th
Population	2,744,687
Rank in Nation	33rd
Density per square mile	32.9
Capital City	Topeka
Population	122,008
Rank in State	4th
Largest City	Wichita
Population	354,617
Number of Representatives in Congress	4
Number of Counties	105
Number of Municipal Governments	627
Number of 2008 Electoral Votes	6
Number of School Districts	302
Number of Special Districts	1,533

LEGISLATIVE BRANCH

Legislative Body	Legislature
President of the Senate	Stephen Morris
Secretary of the Senate	Derek Schmidt
Speaker of the House	Doug Mays
Speaker Pro tem of the House	Ray Merrick
Chief Clerk of the House	Janet E. Jones
2006 Regular Session	Jan. 9 – TBD
Number of Senatorial Districts	40
Number of Representative Districts	125

EXECUTIVE BRANCH

Governor	Kathleen Sebelius
Lieutenant Governor	John Moore
Secretary of State	Ron Thornburgh
Attorney General	Phill Kline
Treasurer	Lynn Jenkins
Auditor	Barbara J. Hinton
Director, Division of Accounts & Reports	Robert Mackey
Governor's Present Term	1/03 – 1/07
Number of Elected Officials in the Executive Branch	6
Number of Members in the Cabinet	14

JUDICIAL BRANCH

Highest Court	Supreme Court
Supreme Court Chief Justice	Kay McFarland
Number of Supreme Court Judges	7
Number of Intermediate Appellate Court Judges	10
Number of U.S. Court Districts	1
U.S. Circuit Court	10th Circuit

STATE INTERNET ADDRESSES

Official State Website	http://www.accesskansas.org
Governor's Website	http://www.ksgovernor.org
State Legislative Website	http://www.kslegislature.org
State Judicial Website	http://www.kscourts.org

Kentucky

Nickname...The Bluegrass State
Motto .... *United We Stand, Divided We Fall*
Flower...Goldenrod
Bird...Cardinal
Tree...Tulip Poplar
Song ....*My Old Kentucky Home*
Entered the Union .... June 1, 1792
Capital ....Frankfort

STATISTICS

Land Area (square miles)...39,728
    Rank in Nation...36th
Population...4,173,405
    Rank in Nation...26th
    Density per square mile...101.7
Capital City...Frankfort
    Population...227,408
    Rank in State..7th
Largest City ....Louisville-Jefferson Co.
    Population...700,030
Number of Representatives in Congress 6
Number of Counties...120
Number of Municipal Governments...................................424
Number of 2008 Electoral Votes 8
Number of School Districts...176
Number of Special Districts...720

LEGISLATIVE BRANCH

Legislative Body...General Assembly

President of the Senate.. David L. Williams
President Pro Tem of the Senate .... Katie Kratz Stine
Secretary of the Senate .... Jay Hartz

Speaker of the House .... Jody Richards
Speaker Pro Tem of the House.................................... Larry Clark
Chief Clerk of the House .... Lois Pulliam

2006 Regular Session .... Jan. 3–April 15
Number of Senatorial Districts 38
Number of Representative Districts 100

EXECUTIVE BRANCH

Governor.. Ernest L. Fletcher
Lieutenant Governor...Stephen Pence
Secretary of State .... Trey Grayson
Attorney General ....Gregory D. Stumbo
Treasurer..Jonathan Miller
Auditor ....Crit Luallen
Controller ....Ed Ross

Governor's Present Term 12/03–12/07
Number of Elected Officials in the Executive Branch............................7
Number of Members in the Cabinet 10

JUDICIAL BRANCH

Highest Court...Supreme Court
Supreme Court Chief Justice.................................. Joseph E. Lambert
Number of Supreme Court Judges 7
Number of Intermediate Appellate Court Judges 14
Number of U.S. Court Districts 2
U.S. Circuit Court ....6th Circuit

STATE INTERNET ADDRESSES

Official State Website ....http://kentucky.gov
Governor's Website ....http://governor.ky.gov/
Legislative Website...http://www.lrc.state.ky.us
Judicial Website ....http://www.kycourts.net

Louisiana

Nickname.. The Pelican State
Motto ....*Union, Justice and Confidence*
Flower..Magnolia
Bird..Eastern Brown Pelican
Tree...Bald Cypress
Songs ....*Give Me Louisiana* and
You Are My Sunshine
Entered the Union ....April 30, 1812
Capital .... Baton Rouge

STATISTICS

Land Area (square miles)...43,562
    Rank in Nation...33rd
Population...4,523,628
    Rank in Nation...24th
    Density per square mile...102.6
Capital City.. Baton Rouge
    Population...225,090
    Rank in State...2nd
Largest City .... New Orleans
    Population...469,032
Number of Representatives in Congress 7
Number of Parishes...64
Number of Municipal Governments...................................302
Number of 2008 Electoral Votes 9
Number of School Districts...68
Number of Special Districts...45

LEGISLATIVE BRANCH

Legislative Body.. Legislature

President of the Senate.. Donald E. Hines, M.D.
President Pro Tem of the Senate ....Diana E. Bajoie
Secretary of Senate ....Glenn Koepp

Speaker of the House .... Joe R. Salter
Speaker Pro Tem of the House......................................Yvonne Dorsey
Clerk of the House and Chief of Staff........................... Alfred W. Speer

2006 Regular Session ....March 27–June 19, 2006
Number of Senatorial Districts 39
Number of Representative Districts 105

EXECUTIVE BRANCH

Governor..Kathleen B. Blanco
Lieutenant Governor... Mitch Landrieu
Secretary of State .... Al Ater
Attorney General ....Charles C. Foti
Treasurer... John Neely Kennedy
Comptroller .... Jerry Luke LeBlanc

Governor's Present Term 1/04–1/08
Number of Elected Officials in the Executive Branch............................8
Number of Members in the Cabinet 14

JUDICIAL BRANCH

Highest Court...Supreme Court
Supreme Court Chief Justice...............................Pascal F. Calogero Jr.
Number of Supreme Court Judges 7
Number of Intermediate Appellate Court Judges 55
Number of U.S. Court Districts 3
U.S. Circuit Court ....5th Circuit

STATE INTERNET ADDRESSES

Official State Website ....http://www.state.la.us
Governor's Website .... http://www.gov.state.la.us
Legislative Website... http://www.legis.state.la.us
Judicial Website .... http://www.state.la.us/gov_judicial.htm

Maine

Nickname...The Pine Tree State
Motto .... *Dirigo* (I Direct or I Lead)
Flower...White Pine Cone and Tassel
Bird...Chickadee
Tree...White Pine
Song... *State of Maine Song*
Entered the Union..March 15, 1820
Capital ....Augusta

STATISTICS

Land Area (square miles)...30,862
 Rank in Nation 39th
Population...1,321,505
 Rank in Nation 40th
 Density per square mile...41.3
Capital City...Augusta
 Population 18,560
 Rank in State...9th
Largest City ....Portland
 Population 63,635
Number of Representatives in Congress 2
Number of Counties...16
Number of Municipal Governments....................................22
Number of 2008 Electoral Votes 4
Number of School Districts 283
Number of Special Districts...222

LEGISLATIVE BRANCH

Legislative Body..Legislature

President of the Senate.................................... Beth Edmonds
Secretary of the Senate .... Joy J. O'Brien

Speaker of the House .... John Richardson
Clerk of the House.................................... Millicent M. MacFarland

2006 Regular Session ....Jan. 4–April 19, 2006
Number of Senatorial Districts 35
Number of Representative Districts 151

EXECUTIVE BRANCH

Governor... John E. Baldacci
Secretary of State... Matthew Dunlap
Attorney General .... G. Steven Rowe
Treasurer... David Lemoine
Auditor .... Neria R. Douglas
Controller .... Edward Karass

Governor's Present Term 1/03–1/07
Number of Elected Officials in the Executive Branch............................1
Number of Members in the Cabinet......................................21

JUDICIAL BRANCH

Highest Court..Supreme Judicial Court
Supreme Court Chief Justice.................................. Leigh Ingalls Saufley
Number of Supreme Court Judges 7
Number of Intermediate Appellate Court Judges 0
Number of U.S. Court Districts 1
U.S. Circuit Court.. 1st Circuit

STATE INTERNET ADDRESSES

Official State Website ....http://www.state.me.us
Governor's Website ....http://www.state.me.us/governor
Legislative Website....................................http://janus.state.me.us/legis
Judicial Website .... http://www.courts.state.me.us

Maryland

Nicknames ....The Old Line State and Free State
Motto .... *Fatti Maschii, Parole Femine*
 (Manly Deeds, Womanly Words)
Flower..Black-eyed Susan
Bird.. Baltimore Oriole
Tree...White Oak
Song.. *Maryland, My Maryland*
Entered the Union..April 28, 1788
Capital ....Annapolis

STATISTICS

Land Area (square miles)...9,774
 Rank in Nation 42nd
Population...5,600,388
 Rank in Nation 19th
 Density per square mile...541.9
Capital City..Annapolis
 Population 36,178
 Rank in State...7th
Largest City .... Baltimore
 Population 628,670
Number of Representatives in Congress 8
Number of Counties...24
Number of Municipal Governments....................................157
Number of 2008 Electoral Votes 10
Number of School Districts 24
Number of Special Districts...85

LEGISLATIVE BRANCH

Legislative Body..General Assembly

President of the Senate....................................Thomas V. Mike Miller Jr.
President Pro Tem of the Senate ....Ida G. Ruben
Secretary of the Senate .... William B.C. Addison Jr.

Speaker of the House .... Michael Erin Busch
Speaker Pro Tem of the House .... Adrienne A. Jones
Clerk of the House.. Mary Monahan

2006 Regular Session .... Jan. 11–April 10, 2006
Number of Senatorial Districts 47
Number of Representative Districts 47

EXECUTIVE BRANCH

Governor...Robert Ehrlich Jr.
Lieutenant Governor.. Michael Steele
Secretary of State.. Mary Kane
Attorney General .... J. Joseph Curran Jr.
Treasurer... Nancy K. Kopp
Auditor .... Bruce A. Myers
Comptroller .... William Schaefer

Governor's Present Term 1/03–1/07
Number of Elected Officials in the Executive Branch............................4
Number of Members in the Cabinet......................................28

JUDICIAL BRANCH

Highest Court..Court of Appeals
Court of Appeals Chief Judge .... Robert M. Bell
Number of Court of Appeals Judges 7
Number of Intermediate Appellate Court Judges 13
Number of U.S. Court Districts 1
U.S. Circuit Court...4th Circuit

STATE INTERNET ADDRESSES

Official State Website ....http://www.marlyand.gov
Governor's Website ....http://www.gov.state.md.us
Legislative Website......................................http://www.mlis.state.md.us
Judicial Website ....http://www.courts.state.md.us/

Massachusetts

Nickname..The Bay State
Motto .... *Ense Petit Placidam Sub Libertate Quietem*
(By the Sword We Seek Peace,
but Peace Only under Liberty)
Flower...Mayflower
Bird...Chickadee
Tree...American Elm
Song.. *All Hail to Massachusetts*
Entered the Union.......................................February 6, 1788
Capital ....Boston

STATISTICS

Land Area (square miles)... 7,840
  Rank in Nation..45th
Population.. 6,398,743
  Rank in Nation..13th
  Density per square mile.. 809.8
Capital City...Boston
  Population...581,606
  Rank in State.. 1st
Largest City...Boston
Number of Representatives in Congress 10
Number of Counties... 14
Number of Municipal Governments.................................... 45
Number of 2008 Electoral Votes 12
Number of School Districts 350
Number of Special Districts.. 403

LEGISLATIVE BRANCH

Legislative Body.. General Court

President of the Senate... Robert E. Travaglini
President Pro Tem of the Senate .... Stanley C. Rosenberg
Clerk of the Senate ....William F. Welch

Speaker of the House... Salvatore F. DiMasi
Clerk of the House....................................... Steven T. James

2006 Regular Session .... Jan. 4 – TBD
Number of Senatorial Districts 40
Number of Representative Districts 160

EXECUTIVE BRANCH

Governor...Mitt Romney
Lieutenant Governor.. Kerry Healey
Secretary of the Commonwealth ....William F. Galvin
Attorney General ....Thomas Reilly
Treasurer & Receiver General..Timothy Cahill
Auditor .... Joseph DeNucci
Comptroller ....Martin J. Benison

Governor's Present Term .... 1/03 – 1/07
Number of Elected Officials in the Executive Branch............................6
Number of Members in the Cabinet 10

JUDICIAL BRANCH

Highest Court..Supreme Judicial Court
Supreme Judicial Court Chief Justice ....Margaret H. Marshall
Number of Supreme Judicial Court Judges 7
Number of Intermediate Appellate Court Judges 25
Number of U.S. Court Districts 1
U.S. Circuit Court... 1st Circuit

STATE INTERNET ADDRESSES

Official State Website ....http://www.mass.gov
Governor's Website ....http://www.state.ma.us/gov
Legislative Website..................................... http://www.state.ma.us/legis
Judicial Website .... http://www.state.ma.us/courts

Michigan

Nickname..The Wolverine State
Motto .... *Si Quaeris Peninsulam Amoenam Circumspice*
(If You Seek a Pleasant Peninsula, Look About You)
Flower.. Apple Blossom
Bird.. Robin
Tree... White Pine
Song.. *Michigan, My Michigan*
Entered the Union .... January 26, 1837
Capital .... Lansing

STATISTICS

Land Area (square miles)... 56,804
  Rank in Nation..22nd
Population.. 10,120,860
  Rank in Nation..8th
  Density per square mile.. 175.0
Capital City.. Lansing
  Population...118,379
  Rank in State..6th
Largest City.. Detroit
  Population...911,402
Number of Representatives in Congress 15
Number of Counties... 83
Number of Municipal Governments.................................... 533
Number of 2008 Electoral Votes 17
Number of School Districts 553
Number of Special Districts.. 366

LEGISLATIVE BRANCH

Legislative Body.. Legislature

President of the Senate... Lt. Gov. John Cherry
President Pro Tem of the Senate .... Patricia Birkholz
Secretary of the Senate .... Carol Morey Viventi

Speaker of the House... Craig DeRoche
Speaker Pro Tem of the House .... Jerry Kooiman
Clerk of the House....................................... Gary L. Randall

2006 Regular Session .... Jan. 11 – Dec. 31, 2006
Number of Senatorial Districts 38
Number of Representative Districts 110

EXECUTIVE BRANCH

Governor.. Jennifer Granholm
Lieutenant Governor.. John Cherry
Secretary of State... Terri Lynn Land
Attorney General .... Mike Cox
Treasurer.. Robert J. Kleine
Auditor ....Thomas McTavish
Director, Office of Financial Management................. Michael J. Moody

Governor's Present Term .... 1/03 – 1/07
Number of Elected Officials in the Executive Branch............................4
Number of Members in the Cabinet 24

JUDICIAL BRANCH

Highest Court.. Supreme Court
Supreme Court Chief Justice.......................................Clifford W. Taylor
Number of Supreme Court Judges 7
Number of Intermediate Appellate Court Judges 28
Number of U.S. Court Districts 2
U.S. Circuit Court... 6th Circuit

STATE INTERNET ADDRESSES

Official State Website ....http://www.michigan.gov
Governor's Website ....http://www.michigan.gov/gov
Legislative Website........................ http://www.michiganlegislature.org
Judicial Website .... http://www.courts.michigan.gov

Minnesota

Nickname	The North Star State
Motto	*L'Etoile du Nord* (The North Star)
Flower	Pink and White Lady-Slipper
Bird	Common Loon
Tree	Red Pine
Song	*Hail! Minnesota*
Entered the Union	May 11, 1858
Capital	St. Paul

STATISTICS

Land Area (square miles)	79,610
Rank in Nation	14th
Population	5,132,799
Rank in Nation	21st
Density per square mile	61.8
Capital City	St. Paul
Population	280,404
Rank in State	2nd
Largest City	Minneapolis
Population	373,188
Number of Representatives in Congress	8
Number of Counties	87
Number of Municipal Governments	854
Number of 2008 Electoral Votes	10
Number of School Districts	348
Number of Special Districts	403

LEGISLATIVE BRANCH

Legislative Body	Legislature
President of the Senate	James Metzen
Secretary of the Senate	Patrick E. Flahaven
Speaker of the House	Steven A. Sviggum
Speaker Pro Tem of the House	Ron Abrams, Gregory M. Davids
Chief Clerk of the House	Al Mathiowetz
2006 Regular Session	March 1 – May 22, 2006
Number of Senatorial Districts	67
Number of Representative Districts	67

EXECUTIVE BRANCH

Governor	Tim Pawlenty
Lieutenant Governor	Carol Molnau
Secretary of State	Mary Kiffmeyer
Attorney General	Mike Hatch
Commissioner of Finance	Peggy Ingison
Auditor	Patricia Anderson Awanda
Governor's Present Term	1/03 – 1/07
Number of Elected Officials in the Executive Branch	5
Number of Members in the Cabinet	25

JUDICIAL BRANCH

Highest Court	Supreme Court
Supreme Court Chief Justice	Kathleen A. Blatz
Number of Supreme Court Judges	7
Number of Intermediate Appellate Court Judges	16
Number of U.S. Court Districts	1
U.S. Circuit Court	8th Circuit

STATE INTERNET ADDRESSES

Official State Website	http://www.state.mn.us
Governor's Website	http://www.governor.state.mn.us
Legislative Website	http://www.leg.state.mn.us
Judicial Website	http://www.courts.state.mn.us/home/

Mississippi

Nickname	The Magnolia State
Motto	*Virtute et Armis* (By Valor and Arms)
Flower	Magnolia
Bird	Mockingbird
Tree	Magnolia
Song	*Go, Mississippi*
Entered the Union	December 10, 1817
Capital	Jackson

STATISTICS

Land Area (square miles)	46,907
Rank in Nation	31st
Population	2,921,088
Rank in Nation	31st
Density per square mile	60.6
Capital City	Jackson
Population	179,599
Rank in State	1st
Largest City	Jackson
Number of Representatives in Congress	4
Number of Counties	82
Number of Municipal Governments	296
Number of 2008 Electoral Votes	6
Number of School Districts	152
Number of Special Districts	458

LEGISLATIVE BRANCH

Legislative Body	Legislature
President of the Senate	Lt. Gov. Amy Tuck
President Pro Tem of the Senate	Travis Little
Secretary of the Senate	John O. Gilbert
Speaker of the House	William J. McCoy
Speaker Pro Tem of the House	J.P. Compretta
Clerk of the House	Don Richardson
2006 Regular Session	Jan. 3 – April 2, 2006
Number of Senatorial Districts	52
Number of Representative Districts	122

EXECUTIVE BRANCH

Governor	Haley Barbour
Lieutenant Governor	Amy Tuck
Secretary of State	Eric Clark
Attorney General	Jim Hood
Treasurer	Tate Reeves
Auditor	Phil Bryant
State Fiscal Officer	J.K. Stringer Jr.
Governor's Present Term	1/04 – 1/08
Number of Elected Officials in the Executive Branch	8
Number of Members in the Cabinet	No formal cabinet system

JUDICIAL BRANCH

Highest Court	Supreme Court
Supreme Court Chief Justice	James W. Smith Jr.
Number of Supreme Court Judges	9
Number of Intermediate Appellate Court Judges	10
Number of U.S. Court Districts	2
U.S. Circuit Court	5th Circuit

STATE INTERNET ADDRESSES

Official State Website	http://www.ms.gov
Governor's Website	http://www.governor.state.ms.us
Legislative Website	http://www.ls.state.ms.us
Judicial Website	http://www.mssc.state.ms.us

Missouri

Nickname..The Show Me State
Motto .... *Salus Populi Suprema Lex Esto*
    (The Welfare of the People Shall Be the Supreme Law)
Flower.. White Hawthorn Blossom
Bird...Bluebird
Tree .... Flowering Dogwood
Song... *Missouri Waltz*
Entered the Union ....August 10, 1821
Capital .... Jefferson City

STATISTICS

Land Area (square miles)... 68,886
    Rank in Nation 18th
Population... 5,800,310
    Rank in Nation 17th
    Density per square mile.. 81.2
Capital City.. Jefferson City
    Population... 37,550
    Rank in State 15th
Largest City .... Kansas City
    Population... 442,768
Number of Representatives in Congress 9
Number of Counties.. 115
Number of Municipal Governments........................... 946
Number of 2008 Electoral Votes 11
Number of School Districts 524
Number of Special Districts..................................... 1,514

LEGISLATIVE BRANCH

Legislative Body.................................Legislative Assembly

President of the Senate.........................Lt. Gov. Peter Kinder
President Pro Tem of the Senate .... Michael Gibbons
Secretary of the Senate ....Terry L. Spieler

Speaker of the House...Rod Jetton
Speaker Pro Tem of the House ....Carl Bearden
Clerk of the House ....Stephen S. Davis

2006 Regular Session .... Jan. 4 – May 30, 2006
Number of Senatorial Districts 34
Number of Representative Districts 163

EXECUTIVE BRANCH

Governor.. Matt Blunt
Lieutenant Governor.. Peter Kinder
Secretary of State .... Robin Carnahan
Attorney General .... Jeremiah W. Nixon
Treasurer.. Sarah Steelman
Auditor .... Claire McCaskill
Director, Division of Accounting .... Thomas Sadowski

Governor's Present Term .... 1/05 – 1/09
Number of Elected Officials in the Executive Branch...........................6
Number of Members in the Cabinet 17

JUDICIAL BRANCH

Highest Court..Supreme Court
Supreme Court Chief Justice........................ Michael A. Wolff
Number of Supreme Court Judges 7
Number of Intermediate Appellate Court Judges 32
Number of U.S. Court Districts 2
U.S. Circuit Court..8th Circuit

STATE INTERNET ADDRESSES

Official State Website ....http://www.state.mo.us
Governor's Website ....http://www.gov.state.mo.us
Legislative Website....................... http://www.moga.state.mo.us
Judicial Website ....http://www.osca.state.mo.us

Montana

Nickname... The Treasure State
Motto ....*Oro y Plata* (Gold and Silver)
Flower... Bitterroot
Bird...Western Meadowlark
Tree .... Ponderosa Pine
Song... *Montana*
Entered the Union .... November 8, 1889
Capital .... Helena

STATISTICS

Land Area (square miles)... 145,552
    Rank in Nation 4th
Population... 935,670
    Rank in Nation 44th
    Density per square mile.. 6.2
Capital City.. Helena
    Population... 26,718
    Rank in State 6th
Largest City .... Billings
    Population... 95,220
Number of Representatives in Congress 1
Number of Counties.. 56
Number of Municipal Governments........................... 129
Number of 2008 Electoral Votes 3
Number of School Districts 438
Number of Special Districts..................................... 592

LEGISLATIVE BRANCH

Legislative Body.................................Legislature

President of the Senate..John Tester
President Pro Tem of the Senate .... Dan W. Harrington
Secretary of the Senate .... Bill Lombardi

Speaker of the House .... Gary Matthews
Chief Clerk of the House ....Marilyn Miller

2006 Regular Session .... No regular session in 2006
Number of Senatorial Districts 50
Number of Representative Districts 100

EXECUTIVE BRANCH

Governor.. Brian Schweitzer
Lieutenant Governor.................................... John Bohlinger
Secretary of State .... Brad Johnson
Attorney General .... Mike McGrath
Treasurer.. Janet Kelly
Auditor .... John Morrison
Administrator, State Accounting .... Paul Christoferson

Governor's Present Term .... 1/05 – 1/09
Number of Elected Officials in the Executive Branch...........................6
Number of Members in the Cabinet 17

JUDICIAL BRANCH

Highest Court..Supreme Court
Supreme Court Chief Justice........................ Karla M. Gray
Number of Supreme Court Judges 7
Number of Intermediate Appellate Court Judges 0
Number of U.S. Court Districts 1
U.S. Circuit Court..9th Circuit

STATE INTERNET ADDRESSES

Official State Website ....http://www.state.mt.us
Governor's Website http://www.discoveringmontana.com/gov2
Legislative Website..............................http://leg.state.mt.us
Judicial Website ....http://www.lawlibrary.state.mt.us

Nebraska

Nickname..The Cornhusker State
Motto.. *Equality Before the Law*
Flower..Goldenrod
Bird..Western Meadowlark
Tree..Western Cottonwood
Song...*Beautiful Nebraska*
Entered the Union..March 1, 1867
Capital ....Lincoln

STATISTICS

Land Area (square miles)................................... 76,872
   Rank in Nation...15th
Population.. 1,758,787
   Rank in Nation...38th
   Density per square mile..22.3
Capital City..Lincoln
   Population.. 235,594
   Rank in State..2nd
Largest City..Omaha
   Population.. 404,267
Number of Representatives in Congress 3
Number of Counties..93
Number of Municipal Governments....................................531
Number of 2008 Electoral Votes 5
Number of School Districts..518
Number of Special Districts.. 1,146

LEGISLATIVE BRANCH

Legislative Body..Unicameral Legislature

President of the Legislature ....Lt. Gov. Kermit A. Brashear
Clerk of the Legislature ....Patrick J. O'Donnell

2006 Regular Session ....Jan. 4 – TBD
Number of Legislative Districts..49

EXECUTIVE BRANCH

Governor..David Heineman
Lieutenant Governor.......................................Rick Sheehy
Secretary of State...John Gale
Attorney General ....Jon Bruning
Treasurer ....Ron Ross
Auditor ....Kate Witek
State Accounting Administrator ....Paul Carlson

Governor's Present Term 1/03–1/07
Number of Elected Officials in the Executive Branch............................6
Number of Members in the Cabinet.....................................29

JUDICIAL BRANCH

Highest Court..Supreme Court
Supreme Court Chief Justice...........................John V. Hendry
Number of Supreme Court Judges 7
Number of Intermediate Appellate Court Judges 6
Number of U.S. Court Districts 1
U.S. Circuit Court...8th Circuit

STATE INTERNET ADDRESSES

Official State Website ....http://www.state.ne.us
Governor's Website ....http://gov.nol.org
Legislative Website.................http://www.unicam.state.ne.us
Judicial Website.......................................http://court.nol.org

Nevada

Nickname..The Silver State
Motto.. *All for Our Country*
Flower..Sagebrush
Bird.. Mountain Bluebird
Tree..Bristlecone Pine and Single-leaf Piñon
Song...*Home Means Nevada*
Entered the Union .... October 31, 1864
Capital ....Carson City

STATISTICS

Land Area (square miles)....................................... 109,826
   Rank in Nation..7th
Population.. 2,414,807
   Rank in Nation...35th
   Density per square mile..18.2
Capital City...Carson City
   Population.. 55,311
   Rank in State..6th
Largest City .... Las Vegas
   Population.. 517,017
Number of Representatives in Congress 3
Number of Counties..17
Number of Municipal Governments....................................19
Number of 2008 Electoral Votes 5
Number of School Districts 17
Number of Special Districts...158

LEGISLATIVE BRANCH

Legislative Body...Legislature

President of the Senate.......................Lt. Gov. Lorraine Hunt
President Pro Tem of the Senate ....Mark Amodei
Secretary of the Senate ....Claire Clift

Speaker of the Assembly................................Richard Perkins
Speaker Pro Tem of the Assembly ....Chris Giunchigliani
Chief Clerk of the Assembly...........................Nancy Tribble

2006 Regular Session ....No regular session in 2006
Number of Senatorial Districts...21
Number of Representative Districts.....................................42

EXECUTIVE BRANCH

Governor.. Kenny Guinn
Lieutenant Governor......................................Lorraine Hunt
Secretary of State... Dean Heller
Attorney General ....George J. Chanos
Treasurer ....Brian Krolicki
Auditor .... Paul V. Townsend
Controller ....Kathy Augustine

Governor's Present Term 1/03–1/07
Number of Elected Officials in the Executive Branch...........................6
Number of Members in the Cabinet............... No formal cabinet system

JUDICIAL BRANCH

Highest Court...Supreme Court
Supreme Court Chief Justice.......................Nancy A. Becker
Number of Supreme Court Judges 7
Number of Intermediate Appellate Court Judges 0
Number of U.S. Court Districts 1
U.S. Circuit Court...9th Circuit

STATE INTERNET ADDRESSES

Official State Website ....http://www.nv.gov
Governor's Website .... http://www.gov.state.nv.us
Legislative Website.......................... http://www.leg.state.nv.us
Judicial Website...................... http://silver.state.nv.us/elec_judicial.htm

New Hampshire

Nickname	The Granite State
Motto	*Live Free or Die*
Flower	Purple Lilac
Bird	Purple Finch
Tree	White Birch
Song	*Old New Hampshire*
Entered the Union	June 21, 1788
Capital	Concord

STATISTICS

Land Area (square miles)	8,968
Rank in Nation	44th
Population	1,309,940
Rank in Nation	41st
Density per square mile	137.8
Capital City	Concord
Population	41,823
Rank in State	3rd
Largest City	Manchester
Population	108,871
Number of Representatives in Congress	2
Number of Counties	10
Number of Municipal Governments	13
Number of 2008 Electoral Votes	4
Number of School Districts	178
Number of Special Districts	148

LEGISLATIVE BRANCH

Legislative Body	General Court
President of the Senate	Theodore Gatsas
President Pro Tem of the Senate	Carl R. Johnson
Clerk of the Senate	Tammy L. Wright
Speaker of the House	W. Douglas Scamman
Clerk of the House	Karen O. Wadsworth
2006 Regular Session	Jan. 4–July 1, 2006
Number of Senatorial Districts	24
Number of Representative Districts	103

EXECUTIVE BRANCH

Governor	John Lynch
Secretary of State	William M. Gardner
Attorney General	Kelly Ayotte
Treasurer	Michael A. Ablowich
Auditor	Michael Buckley
Comptroller	Sheri Rockburn
Governor's Present Term	1/05–1/07
Number of Elected Officials in the Executive Branch	1
Number of Members in the Cabinet	No formal cabinet system

JUDICIAL BRANCH

Highest Court	Supreme Court
Supreme Court Chief Justice	John T. Broderick Jr.
Number of Supreme Court Judges	5
Number of Intermediate Appellate Court Judges	0
Number of U.S. Court Districts	1
U.S. Circuit Court	1st Circuit

STATE INTERNET ADDRESSES

Official State Website	http://www.state.nh.us
Governor's Website	http://www.nh.gov/governor/
Legislative Website	http://www.gencourt.state.nh.us
Judicial Website	http://www.courts.state.nh.us/

New Jersey

Nickname	The Garden State
Motto	*Liberty and Prosperity*
Flower	Violet
Bird	Eastern Goldfinch
Tree	Red Oak
Song	*I'm From New Jersey*
Entered the Union	December 18, 1787
Capital	Trenton

STATISTICS

Land Area (square miles)	7,417
Rank in Nation	46th
Population	8,717,925
Rank in Nation	10th
Density per square mile	1,134.4
Capital City	Trenton
Population	85,314
Rank in State	9th
Largest City	Newark
Population	277,911
Number of Representatives in Congress	13
Number of Counties	21
Number of Municipal Governments	324
Number of 2008 Electoral Votes	15
Number of School Districts	598
Number of Special Districts	276

LEGISLATIVE BRANCH

Legislative Body	Legislature
President of the Senate	Richard J. Codey
President Pro Tem of the Senate	Shirley K. Turner
Secretary of the Senate	Ellen M. Davenport
Speaker of the Assembly	Joseph J. Roberts Jr.
Speaker Pro Tem of the Assembly	Wilfredo Caraballo
Clerk of the General Assembly	Dana M. Burley
2006 Regular Session	Jan. 10–Dec. 31, 2006
Number of Senatorial Districts	40
Number of Representative Districts	40

EXECUTIVE BRANCH

Governor	Jon Corzine
Secretary of State	Nina Mitchell Wells
Attorney General	Zulima Farber
Treasurer	Bradley I. Abelow
Auditor	Richard L. Fair
Controller	Charlene Holzbaur
Governor's Present Term	1/06–1/10
Number of Elected Officials in the Executive Branch	1
Number of Members in the Cabinet	19

JUDICIAL BRANCH

Highest Court	Supreme Court
Supreme Court Chief Justice	Deborah T. Poritz
Number of Supreme Court Judges	7
Number of Intermediate Appellate Court Judges	32
Number of U.S. Court Districts	1
U.S. Circuit Court	3rd Circuit

STATE INTERNET ADDRESSES

Official State Website	http://www.state.nj.us
Governor's Website	http://www.state.nj.us/governor
Legislative Website	http://www.njleg.state.nj.us
Judicial Website	http://www.judiciary.state.nj.us

New Mexico

Nickname..The Land of Enchantment
Motto...................................... *Crescit Eundo* (It Grows As It Goes)
Flower...Yucca (Our Lord's Candles)
Bird... Chaparral Bird
Tree... Piñon
Songs.. *Asi es Nuevo Mexico* and
O, Fair New Mexico
Entered the Union... January 6, 1912
Capital .... Santa Fe

STATISTICS

Land Area (square miles)................................... 121,356
  Rank in Nation..5th
Population.. 1,928,384
  Rank in Nation...36th
  Density per square mile.................................... 15.0
Capital City... Santa Fe
  Population.. 66,476
  Rank in State 3rd
Largest City .... Albuquerque
  Population.. 471,856
Number of Representatives in Congress 3
Number of Counties...33
Number of Municipal Governments...................................101
Number of 2008 Electoral Votes..5
Number of School Districts 89
Number of Special Districts..628

LEGISLATIVE BRANCH

Legislative Body... Legislature

President of the Senate....................... Lt. Gov. Diane Denish
President Pro Tem of the Senate .... Ben D. Altamirano
Chief Clerk of the Senate....................... Margaret Larragoite

Speaker of the House .... Ben Lujan
Chief Clerk of the House .... Stephen R. Arias

2006 Regular Session..................................Jan. 17–Feb. 16, 2006
Number of Senatorial Districts 42
Number of Representative Districts 70

EXECUTIVE BRANCH

Governor... Bill Richardson
Lieutenant Governor.............................. Diane Denish
Secretary of State................................. Rebecca Vigil-Giron
Attorney General .... Patricia Madrid
Treasurer.. Douglas Brown
Auditor .... Domingo P. Martinez
Controller .... Anthony Armijo

Governor's Present Term 1/03–1/07
Number of Elected Officials in the Executive Branch...........5
Number of Members in the Cabinet....................................17

JUDICIAL BRANCH

Highest Court.....................................Supreme Court
Supreme Court Chief Justice.................... Richard C. Bosson
Number of Supreme Court Judges 5
Number of Intermediate Appellate Court Judges 10
Number of U.S. Court Districts 1
U.S. Circuit Court................................. 10th Circuit

STATE INTERNET ADDRESSES

Official State Website ....http://www.state.nm.us
Governor's Website ....http://www.governor.state.nm.us
Legislative Website............................. http://legis.state.nm.us
Judicial Website.............................. http://www.nmcourts.com

New York

Nickname... The Empire State
Motto .... *Excelsior* (Ever Upward)
Flower..Rose
Bird.. Bluebird
Tree... Sugar Maple
Song .... *I Love New York*
Entered the Union....................................... July 26, 1788
Capital .... Albany

STATISTICS

Land Area (square miles)...................................47,214
  Rank in Nation...30th
Population.. 19,254,630
  Rank in Nation.. 3rd
  Density per square mile....................................401.9
Capital City... Albany
  Population.. 93,919
  Rank in State 6th
Largest City .... New York City
  Population.. 8,085,742
Number of Representatives in Congress 29
Number of Counties...62
Number of Municipal Governments...................................616
Number of 2008 Electoral Votes.......................................31
Number of School Districts 726
Number of Special Districts..1,135

LEGISLATIVE BRANCH

Legislative Body... Legislature

President of the Senate..................... Lt. Gov. Mary Donohue
President Pro Tem and Majority Leader of the Senate ...Joseph L. Bruno
Secretary of the Senate .... Steven M. Boggess

Speaker of the Assembly........................... Sheldon Silver
Speaker Pro Tem of the Assembly .... Aurelia Greene
Clerk of the Assembly........................... June Egeland

2006 Regular Session .... Jan. 4–Dec. 31, 2006
Number of Senatorial Districts 62
Number of Representative Districts 150

EXECUTIVE BRANCH

Governor... George Pataki
Lieutenant Governor.............................. Mary Donohue
Secretary of State................................. Frank P. Milano
Attorney General .... Eliot Spitzer
Treasurer.. Aida Brewer
Comptroller .... Alan G. Hevesi

Governor's Present Term 1/03–1/07
Number of Elected Officials in the Executive Branch...........4
Number of Members in the Cabinet....................................75

JUDICIAL BRANCH

Highest Court.....................................Court of Appeals
Court of Appeals Chief Justice....................... Judith S. Kaye
Number of Court of Appeals Judges 7
Number of Intermediate Appellate Court Judges 70
Number of U.S. Court Districts 4
U.S. Circuit Court................................. 2nd Circuit

STATE INTERNET ADDRESSES

Official State Website ....http://www.state.ny.us
Governor's Website ....http://www.state.ny.us/governor
Senate Website........................... http://www.senate.state.ny.us
Assembly Website........................... http://assembly.state.ny.us
Judicial Website.............................. http://www.courts.state.ny.us

North Carolina

Nickname................................The Tar Heel State and Old North State
Motto .... *Esse Quam Videri*
(To Be Rather Than to Seem)
Flower... Dogwood
Bird.. Cardinal
Tree.. Long Leaf Pine
Song... *The Old North State*
Entered the United States.. November 21, 1789
Capital .... Raleigh

STATISTICS

Land Area (square miles)... 48,711
    Rank in Nation 29th
Population.. 8,683,242
    Rank in Nation 11th
    Density per square mile.. 165.2
Capital City.. Raleigh
    Population 316,802
    Rank in State 2nd
Largest City .... Charlotte
    Population 584,658
Number of Representatives in Congress 13
Number of Counties.. 100
Number of Municipal Governments.................................... 541
Number of 2008 Electoral Votes 15
Number of School Districts 117
Number of Special Districts... 319

LEGISLATIVE BRANCH

Legislative Body... General Assembly

President of the Senate..................................... Lt. Gov. Beverly Perdue
President Pro Tem of the Senate .... Marc Basnight
Principal Clerk of the Senate .... Janet Pruitt

Democratic Speaker of the House .... James B. Black
Republican Speaker of the House .... Richard T. Morgan
Principal Clerk of the House... Denise Weeks

2006 Regular Session .... Jan. 9 – TBD
Number of Senatorial Districts 50
Number of Representative Districts 120

EXECUTIVE BRANCH

Governor.. Michael Easley
Lieutenant Governor.. Beverly Perdue
Secretary of State...Elaine Marshall
Attorney General .... Roy A. Cooper III
Treasurer... Richard H. Moore
Auditor .... Leslie W. Merritt Jr.
Controller .... Robert Powell

Governor's Present Term .... 1/01 – 1/09
Number of Elected Officials in the Executive Branch.......................... 10
Number of Members in the Cabinet..................................... 10

JUDICIAL BRANCH

Highest Court..Supreme Court
Supreme Court Chief Justice.. I.B. Lake Jr.
Number of Supreme Court Judges 7
Number of Intermediate Appellate Court Judges 12
Number of U.S. Court Districts 3
U.S. Circuit Court...4th Circuit

STATE INTERNET ADDRESSES

Official State Website .... http://www.ncgov.com
Governor's Website .... http://www.governor.state.nc.us
Legislative Website.. http://www.ncleg.net
Judicial Website .... http://www.nccourts.org

North Dakota

Nickname.. Peace Garden State
Motto .... *Liberty and Union, Now and Forever,*
One and Inseparable
Flower...Wild Prairie Rose
Bird...Western Meadowlark
Tree..American Elm
Song .... *North Dakota Hymn*
Entered the Union.. November 2, 1889
Capital ....Bismarck

STATISTICS

Land Area (square miles)... 68,976
    Rank in Nation 17th
Population.. 636,677
    Rank in Nation 48th
    Density per square mile..9.3
Capital City...Bismarck
    Population 56,344
    Rank in State 2nd
Largest City .... Fargo
    Population 91,484
Number of Representatives in Congress 1
Number of Counties.. 53
Number of Municipal Governments................................... 360
Number of 2008 Electoral Votes 3
Number of School Districts 213
Number of Special Districts.. 764

LEGISLATIVE BRANCH

Legislative Body... Legislative Assembly

President of the Senate..................................... Lt. Gov. Jack Dalrymple
President Pro Tem of the Senate .... John M. Andrist
Secretary of the Senate ....William R. Horton

Speaker of the House .... Matthew M, Klein
Clerk of the House... Brad Faye

2006 Regular Session .... No regular session in 2006
Number of Senatorial Districts 47
Number of Representative Districts 47

EXECUTIVE BRANCH

Governor.. John Hoeven
Lieutenant Governor... Jack Dalrymple
Secretary of State..Alvin Jaeger
Attorney General .... Wayne Stenehjem
Treasurer.. Kelly Schmidt
Auditor .... Robert R. Peterson

Governor's Present Term .... 12/00 – 12/08
Number of Elected Officials in the Executive Branch......................... 10
Number of Members in the Cabinet...................................... 18

JUDICIAL BRANCH

Highest Court..Supreme Court
Supreme Court Chief Justice............................. Gerald W. VandeWalle
Number of Supreme Court Judges 5
Number of Intermediate Appellate Court Judges 0
Number of U.S. Court Districts 1
U.S. Circuit Court..8th Circuit

STATE INTERNET ADDRESSES

Official State Website ....http://discovernd.com
Governor's Website ....http://www.governor.state.nd.us
Legislative Website... http://www.state.nd.us/lr
Judicial Website ....http://www.court.state.nd.us

Ohio

Nickname.. The Buckeye State
Motto .... *With God, All Things Are Possible*
Flower .... Scarlet Carnation
Bird .... Cardinal
Tree .... Buckeye
Song .... *Beautiful Ohio*
Entered the Union .... March 1, 1803
Capital .... Columbus

STATISTICS

Land Area (square miles) 40,948
   Rank in Nation 35th
Population 11,464,042
   Rank in Nation 7th
   Density per square mile 277.3
Capital City .... Columbus
   Population 728,432
   Rank in State 1st
Largest City .... Columbus
Number of Representatives in Congress 18
Number of Counties 88
Number of Municipal Governments 942
Number of 2008 Electoral Votes 20
Number of School Districts 613
Number of Special Districts 631

LEGISLATIVE BRANCH

Legislative Body .... General Assembly

President of the Senate .... Bill Harris
President Pro Tem of the Senate .... Jeff Jacobson
Clerk of the Senate .... David Battocletti

Speaker of the House .... Jon Husted
Speaker Pro Tem of the House .... Charles Blasdel
Legislative Clerk of the House .... Laura P. Clemens

2006 Regular Session .... Jan. 2 – Dec. 31, 2006
Number of Senatorial Districts 33
Number of Representative Districts 99

EXECUTIVE BRANCH

Governor .... Bob Taft
Lieutenant Governor .... Bruce Johnson
Secretary of State .... J. Kenneth Blackwell
Attorney General .... Jim Petro
Treasurer .... Jennette Bradley
Auditor .... Betty D. Montgomery
Director, Office of Management & Budget .... Thomas W. Johnson

Governor's Present Term 1/03–1/07
Number of Elected Officials in the Executive Branch 6
Number of Members in the Cabinet 24

JUDICIAL BRANCH

Highest Court .... Supreme Court
Supreme Court Chief Justice .... Thomas J. Moyer
Number of Supreme Court Judges 7
Number of Intermediate Appellate Court Judges 68
Number of U.S. Court Districts 2
U.S. Circuit Court .... 6th Circuit

STATE INTERNET ADDRESSES

Official State Website .... http://www.state.oh.us
Governor's Website .... http://governor.ohio.gov/
Legislative Website .... http://www.ohio.gov/ohio/GovState.stm#ohleg
Judicial Website .... http://www.sconet.state.oh.us

Oklahoma

Nickname .... The Sooner State
Motto .... *Labor Omnia Vincit* (Labor Conquers All Things)
Flower .... Mistletoe
Bird .... Scissor-tailed Flycatcher
Tree .... Redbud
Song .... *Oklahoma*
Entered the Union .... November 16, 1907
Capital .... Oklahoma City

STATISTICS

Land Area (square miles) 68,667
   Rank in Nation 19th
Population 3,547,884
   Rank in Nation 28th
   Density per square mile 50.3
Capital City .... Oklahoma City
   Population 523,303
   Rank in State 1st
Largest City .... Oklahoma City
Number of Representatives in Congress 5
Number of Counties 77
Number of Municipal Governments 590
Number of 2008 Electoral Votes 7
Number of School Districts 541
Number of Special Districts 560

LEGISLATIVE BRANCH

Legislative Body .... Legislature

President of the Senate .... Lt. Gov. Mary Fallin
President Pro Tem of the Senate .... Mike Morgan
Secretary of the Senate .... Michael Clingman

Speaker of the House .... Todd Hiett
Speaker Pro Tem of the House .... Susan Winchester
Chief Clerk/Administrator of the House .... Joel Kintsel

2006 Regular Session .... Feb. 6 – May 26, 2006
Number of Senatorial Districts 50
Number of Representative Districts 101

EXECUTIVE BRANCH

Governor .... Brad Henry
Lieutenant Governor .... Mary Fallin
Secretary of State .... Susan Savage
Attorney General .... W.A. Drew Edmondson
Treasurer .... Scott Meacham
Auditor .... Jeff McMahan
Comptroller .... Brenda Bolander

Governor's Present Term 1/03–1/07
Number of Elected Officials in the Executive Branch 8
Number of Members in the Cabinet 10–15

JUDICIAL BRANCH

Highest Court .... Supreme Court
Supreme Court Chief Justice .... Joseph M. Watt
Number of Supreme Court Judges 9
Number of Intermediate Appellate Court Judges 12
Number of U.S. Court Districts 3
U.S. Circuit Court .... 10th Circuit

STATE INTERNET ADDRESSES

Official State Website .... http://www.state.ok.us
Governor's Website .... http://www.governor.state.ok.us/
Legislative Website .... http://www.lsb.state.ok.us
Judicial Website .... http://www.oscn.net

Oregon

Nickname	The Beaver State
Motto	*She Flies with Her Own Wings*
Flower	Oregon Grape
Bird	Western Meadowlark
Tree	Douglas Fir
Song	*Oregon, My Oregon*
Entered the Union	February 14, 1859
Capital	Salem

STATISTICS

Land Area (square miles)	95,997
Rank in Nation	10th
Population	3,641,056
Rank in Nation	27th
Density per square mile	35.6
Capital City	Salem
Population	142,914
Rank in State	3rd
Largest City	Portland
Population	538,544
Number of Representatives in Congress	5
Number of Counties	36
Number of Municipal Governments	240
Number of 2008 Electoral Votes	7
Number of School Districts	199
Number of Special Districts	927

LEGISLATIVE BRANCH

Legislative Body	Legislative Assembly
President of the Senate	Peter Courtney
President Pro Tem of the Senate	Margaret Carter
Secretary of the Senate	Judy Hall
Speaker of the House	Karen Minnis
Chief Clerk of the House	Ramona Kenady
2006 Regular Session	No regular session in 2006
Number of Senatorial Districts	30
Number of Representative Districts	60

EXECUTIVE BRANCH

Governor	Ted Kulongoski
Secretary of State	Bill Bradbury
Attorney General	Hardy Myers
Treasurer	Randall Edwards
Auditor	Catherine Pollino
Controller	John Radford
Governor's Present Term	1/03–1/07
Number of Elected Officials in the Executive Branch	6
Number of Members in the Cabinet	No formal cabinet system

JUDICIAL BRANCH

Highest Court	Supreme Court
Supreme Court Chief Justice	Wallace P. Carson Jr.
Number of Supreme Court Judges	7
Number of Intermediate Appellate Court Judges	10
Number of U.S. Court Districts	1
U.S. Circuit Court	9th Circuit

STATE INTERNET ADDRESSES

Official State Website	http://www.oregon.gov
Governor's Website	http://www.governor.state.or.us
Legislative Website	http://www.leg.state.or.us
Judicial Website	http://www.ojd.state.or.us

Pennsylvania

Nickname	The Keystone State
Motto	*Virtue, Liberty and Independence*
Animal	White-tailed Deer
Flower	Mountain Laurel
Tree	Hemlock
Song	*Pennsylvania*
Entered the Union	December 12, 1787
Capital	Harrisburg

STATISTICS

Land Area (square miles)	44,817
Rank in Nation	32nd
Population	12,429,616
Rank in Nation	6th
Density per square mile	274.0
Capital City	Harrisburg
Population	48,322
Rank in State	13th
Largest City	Philadelphia
Population	1,479,339
Number of Representatives in Congress	19
Number of Counties	67
Number of Municipal Governments	1,018
Number of 2008 Electoral Votes	21
Number of School Districts	501
Number of Special Districts	1,885

LEGISLATIVE BRANCH

Legislative Body	General Assembly
President of the Senate	Lt. Gov. Catherine Baker Knoll
President Pro Tem of the Senate	Robert C. Jubelirer
Secretary-Parliamentarian of the Senate	Mark R. Corrigan
Speaker of the House	John M. Perzel
Chief Clerk of the House	Roger Nick
2006 Regular Session	Jan. 3–TBD
Number of Senatorial Districts	50
Number of Representative Districts	203

EXECUTIVE BRANCH

Governor	Ed Rendell
Lieutenant Governor	Catherine Baker Knoll
Secretary of State	Pedro A. Cortes
Attorney General	Tom Corbett
Treasurer	Robert Casey Jr.
Comptroller	Harvey Eckert
Governor's Present Term	1/03–1/07
Number of Elected Officials in the Executive Branch	5
Number of Members in the Cabinet	19

JUDICIAL BRANCH

Highest Court	Supreme Court
Supreme Court Chief Justice	Ralph J. Cappy
Number of Supreme Court Judges	7
Number of Intermediate Appellate Court Judges	24
Number of U.S. Court Districts	3
U.S. Circuit Court	3rd Circuit

STATE INTERNET ADDRESSES

Official State Website	http://www.state.pa.us
Governor's Website	http://www.governor.state.pa.us/
Legislative Website	http://www.legis.state.pa.us
Judicial Website	http://www.courts.state.pa.us

Rhode Island

Nicknames .... Little Rhody and Ocean State
Motto .... Hope
Flower .... Violet
Bird .... Rhode Island Red
Tree .... Red Maple
Song .... *Rhode Island*
Entered the Union .... May 29, 1790
Capital .... Providence

STATISTICS

Land Area (square miles) 1,045
   Rank in Nation 50th
Population 1,076,189
   Rank in Nation 43rd
   Density per square mile 1,003.2
Capital City .... Providence
   Population 176,365
   Rank in State 1st
Largest City .... Providence
Number of Representatives in Congress 2
Number of Counties 5
Number of Municipal Governments 8
Number of 2008 Electoral Votes 4
Number of School Districts 38
Number of Special Districts 75

LEGISLATIVE BRANCH

Legislative Body .... General Assembly

President of the Senate .... Lt. Gov. Joseph A. Montalbano
President Pro Tem of the Senate .... John C. Revens Jr.
Clerk of the Senate .... Raymond T. Hoyas Jr.

Speaker of the House .... William J. Murphy
Speaker Pro Tem of the House .... Charlene Lima
Clerk of the House .... Frank McCabe

2006 Regular Session .... Jan. 3 – TBD
Number of Senatorial Districts 38
Number of Representative Districts 75

EXECUTIVE BRANCH

Governor .... Don Carcieri
Lieutenant Governor .... Charles J. Fogarty
Secretary of State .... Matthew Brown
Attorney General .... Patrick Lynch
Treasurer .... Paul J. Tavares
Auditor .... Ernest A. Almonte
Controller .... Lawrence Franklin

Governor's Present Term .... 1/03 – 1/07
Number of Elected Officials in the Executive Branch 5
Number of Members in the Cabinet 14

JUDICIAL BRANCH

Highest Court .... Supreme Court
Supreme Court Chief Justice .... Frank J. Williams
Number of Supreme Court Judges 5
Number of Intermediate Appellate Court Judges 0
Number of U.S. Court Districts 1
U.S. Circuit Court .... 1st Circuit

STATE INTERNET ADDRESSES

Official State Website .... http://www.state.ri.us
Governor's Website .... http://www.governor.state.ri.us
Legislative Website .... http://www.rilin.state.ri.us
Judicial Website .... http://www.courts.state.ri.us

South Carolina

Nickname .... The Palmetto State
Motto .... *Animis Opibusque Parati*
(Prepared in Mind and Resources) and
Dum Spiro Spero (While I breathe, I Hope)
Flower .... Yellow Jessamine
Bird .... Carolina Wren
Tree .... Palmetto
Songs .... *Carolina* and *South Carolina on My Mind*
Entered the Union .... May 23, 1788
Capital .... Columbia

STATISTICS

Land Area (square miles) 30,110
   Rank in Nation 40th
Population 4,255,083
   Rank in Nation 25th
   Density per square mile 133.2
Capital City .... Columbia
   Population 117,357
   Rank in State 1st
Largest City .... Columbia
Number of Representatives in Congress 6
Number of Counties 46
Number of Municipal Governments 269
Number of 2008 Electoral Votes 8
Number of School Districts 89
Number of Special Districts 301

LEGISLATIVE BRANCH

Legislative Body .... General Assembly

President of the Senate .... Lt. Gov. Andre Bauer
President Pro Tem of the Senate .... Glenn F. McConnell
Clerk and Director of Senate Research .... Jeffrey S. Gossett

Speaker of the House .... Robert W. Harrell Jr.
Speaker Pro Tem of the House .... W. Douglas Smith
Clerk of the House .... Charles Reid

2006 Regular Session .... Jan. 10 – June 1, 2006
Number of Senatorial Districts 46
Number of Representative Districts 124

EXECUTIVE BRANCH

Governor .... Mark Sanford
Lieutenant Governor .... R. Andre Bauer
Secretary of State .... Mark Hammond
Attorney General .... Henry McMaster
Treasurer .... Grady L. Patterson Jr.
Auditor .... Thomas L. Wagner Jr.
Comptroller .... Richard Eckstrom

Governor's Present Term .... 1/03 – 1/07
Number of Elected Officials in the Executive Branch 9
Number of Members in the Cabinet 15

JUDICIAL BRANCH

Highest Court .... Supreme Court
Supreme Court Chief Justice .... Jean Hoefer Toal
Number of Supreme Court Judges 5
Number of Intermediate Appellate Court Judges 91
Number of U.S. Court Districts 1
U.S. Circuit Court .... 4th Circuit

STATE INTERNET ADDRESSES

Official State Website .... http://www.myscgov.com
Governor's Website .... http://www.scgovernor.com/
Legislative Website .... http://www.scstatehouse.net
Judicial Website .... http://www.judicial.state.sc.us

South Dakota

Nicknames .... The Mt. Rushmore State
Motto .... *Under God the People Rule*
Flower.. American Pasque
Bird.. Chinese Ring-necked Pheasant
Tree.. Black Hills Spruce
Song... *Hail, South Dakota*
Entered the Union .... November 2, 1889
Capital .... Pierre

STATISTICS

Land Area (square miles)... 75,885
  Rank in Nation 16th
Population... 775,933
  Rank in Nation 46th
  Density per square mile.. 9.9
Capital City .... Pierre
  Population 13,876
  Rank in State... 7th
Largest City .... Sioux Falls
  Population 133,834
Number of Representatives in Congress 1
Number of Counties.. 66
Number of Municipal Governments................................ 308
Number of 2008 Electoral Votes 3
Number of School Districts 172
Number of Special Districts.. 376

LEGISLATIVE BRANCH

Legislative Body.. Legislature

President of the Senate................................... Lt. Gov. Dennis Daugaard
President Pro Tem of the Senate .... Lee Schoenbeck
Secretary of the Senate .... Patricia Adam

Speaker of the House .... Matthew Michels
Speaker Pro Tem of the House ....Thomas J. Deadrick
Chief Clerk of the House .... Karen Gerdes

2006 Regular Session .... Jan. 10 – TBD
Number of Senatorial Districts 35
Number of Representative Districts 35

EXECUTIVE BRANCH

Governor... Mike Rounds
Lieutenant Governor................................... Dennis Daugaard
Secretary of State.. Chris Nelson
Attorney General .... Larry Long
Treasurer... Vernon L. Larson
Auditor .... Martin Guindon

Governor's Present Term .... 1/03 – 1/07
Number of Elected Officials in the Executive Branch........................... 7
Number of Members in the Cabinet 19

JUDICIAL BRANCH

Highest Court...Supreme Court
Supreme Court Chief Justice................................... David E. Gilbertson
Number of Supreme Court Judges 5
Number of Intermediate Appellate Court Judges 0
Number of U.S. Court Districts 1
U.S. Circuit Court... 8th Circuit

STATE INTERNET ADDRESSES

Official State Website .... http://www.state.sd.us
Governor's Website ....http://www.state.sd.us/governor
Legislative Website....................................http://legis.state.sd.us
Judicial Website .... http://www.sdjudicial.com

Tennessee

Nickname..The Volunteer State
Motto .... *Agriculture and Commerce*
Flower.. Iris
Bird.. Mockingbird
Tree.. Tulip Poplar
Songs .... *When It's Iris Time in Tennessee*;
    The Tennessee Waltz; *My Homeland, Tennessee*;
    My Tennessee; and *Rocky Top*
Entered the Union .... June 1, 1796
Capital .... Nashville

STATISTICS

Land Area (square miles)... 41,217
  Rank in Nation 34th
Population... 5,962,959
  Rank in Nation 16th
  Density per square mile.. 138.0
Capital City .... Nashville
  Population 544,765
  Rank in State... 2nd
Largest City .... Memphis
  Population 645,978
Number of Representatives in Congress 9
Number of Counties.. 95
Number of Municipal Governments................................ 349
Number of 2008 Electoral Votes 11
Number of School Districts 136
Number of Special Districts.. 475

LEGISLATIVE BRANCH

Legislative Body...General Assembly

Speaker of the Senate... Lt. Gov. John S. Wilder
Speaker Pro Tem of the Senate .... Michael R. Williams
Chief Clerk of the Senate... Russell Humphrey

Speaker of the House .... James O. Naifeh
Speaker Pro Tem of the House ....Lois M. DeBerry
Chief Clerk of the House .... Burney T. Durham

2006 Regular Session .... Jan. 10 – TBD
Number of Senatorial Districts 33
Number of Representative Districts 99

EXECUTIVE BRANCH

Governor... Phil Bredesen
Lieutenant Governor..................................... John S. Wilder
Secretary of State... Riley Darnell
Attorney General .... Paul G. Summers
Treasurer... Dale Sims
Auditor .... Art Hayes
Comptroller of the Treasury.. John Morgan

Governor's Present Term .... 1/03 – 1/07
Number of Elected Officials in the Executive Branch........................... 1
Number of Members in the Cabinet 28

JUDICIAL BRANCH

Highest Court...Supreme Court
Supreme Court Chief Justice................................... William M. Barker
Number of Supreme Court Judges 5
Number of Intermediate Appellate Court Judges 24
Number of U.S. Court Districts 3
U.S. Circuit Court... 6th Circuit

STATE INTERNET ADDRESSES

Official State Website ....http://www.state.tn.us
Governor's Website ....http://www.state.tn.us/governor
Legislative Website.......................... http://www.legislature.state.tn.us
Judicial Website .... http://www.tsc.state.tn.us

Texas

Nickname	The Lone Star State
Motto	*Friendship*
Flower	Bluebonnet (Buffalo Clover, Wolf Flower)
Bird	Mockingbird
Tree	Pecan
Song	*Texas, Our Texas*
Entered the Union	December 29, 1845
Capital	Austin

STATISTICS

Land Area (square miles)	261,797
Rank in Nation	2nd
Population	22,859,968
Rank in Nation	2nd
Density per square mile	79.6
Capital City	Austin
Population	672,011
Rank in State	4th
Largest City	Houston
Population	2,009,690
Number of Representatives in Congress	32
Number of Counties	254
Number of Municipal Governments	1,196
Number of 2008 Electoral Votes	34
Number of School Districts	1,040
Number of Special Districts	2,245

LEGISLATIVE BRANCH

Legislative Body	Legislature
President of the Senate	Lt. Gov. David Dewhurst
President Pro Tem of the Senate	Florence Shapiro
Secretary of the Senate	Patsy Spaw
Speaker of the House	Tom Craddick
Speaker Pro Tem of the House	Sylvester Turner
Chief Clerk of the House	Robert Haney
2006 Regular Session	No regular session in 2006
Number of Senatorial Districts	31
Number of Representative Districts	150

EXECUTIVE BRANCH

Governor	Rick Perry
Lieutenant Governor	David Dewhurst
Secretary of State	Roger Williams
Attorney General	Greg Abbott
Comptroller of Public Accounts	Carole Keeton Strayhorn
Auditor	John Keel
Governor's Present Term	1/03–1/07
Number of Elected Officials in the Executive Branch	9
Number of Members in the Cabinet	No formal cabinet system

JUDICIAL BRANCH

Highest Court	Supreme Court
Supreme Court Chief Justice	Wallace B. Jefferson
Number of Supreme Court Judges	9
Number of Intermediate Appellate Court Judges	80
Number of U.S. Court Districts	4
U.S. Circuit Court	5th Circuit

STATE INTERNET ADDRESSES

Official State Website	http://www.state.tx.us
Governor's Website	http://www.governor.state.tx.us
Legislative Website	http://www.capitol.state.tx.us
Judicial Website	http://www.courts.state.tx.us

Utah

Nickname	The Beehive State
Motto	*Industry*
Flower	Sego Lily
Bird	California Seagull
Tree	Blue Spruce
Song	*Utah, We Love Thee*
Entered the Union	January 4, 1896
Capital	Salt Lake City

STATISTICS

Land Area (square miles)	82,144
Rank in Nation	12th
Population	2,469,585
Rank in Nation	34th
Density per square mile	27.2
Capital City	Salt Lake City
Population	179,894
Rank in State	1st
Largest City	Salt Lake City
Number of Representatives in Congress	3
Number of Counties	29
Number of Municipal Governments	236
Number of 2008 Electoral Votes	5
Number of School Districts	40
Number of Special Districts	300

LEGISLATIVE BRANCH

Legislative Body	Legislature
President of the Senate	John L. Valentine
Secretary of the Senate	Annette B. Moore
Speaker of the House	Greg Curtis
Chief Clerk of the House	Sandy Tenney
2006 Regular Session	Jan. 16–March 1, 2006
Number of Senatorial Districts	29
Number of Representative Districts	75

EXECUTIVE BRANCH

Governor	Jon M. Huntsman Jr.
Lieutenant Governor	Gary Herbert
Attorney General	Mark L. Shurtleff
Treasurer	Edward T. Alter
Auditor	Auston G. Johnson
Governor's Present Term	1/05–1/09
Number of Elected Officials in the Executive Branch	5
Number of Members in the Cabinet	31

JUDICIAL BRANCH

Highest Court	Supreme Court
Supreme Court Chief Justice	Christine M. Durham
Number of Supreme Court Judges	5
Number of Intermediate Appellate Court Judges	7
Number of U.S. Court Districts	1
U.S. Circuit Court	10th Circuit

STATE INTERNET ADDRESSES

Official State Website	http://www.utah.gov
Governor's Website	http://www.utah.gov/governor/
Legislative Website	http://www.le.state.ut.us
Judicial Website	http://utcourts.gov

Vermont

Nickname... The Green Mountain State
Motto .... *Freedom and Unity*
Flower...Red Clover
Bird...Hermit Thrush
Tree...Sugar Maple
Song.. *Hail, Vermont!*
Entered the Union ....March 4, 1791
Capital .... Montpelier

STATISTICS

Land Area (square miles)... 9,250
   Rank in Nation 43rd
Population... 623,050
   Rank in Nation 49th
   Density per square mile...65.8
Capital City... Montpelier
   Population..8,035
   Rank in State...13th
Largest City ....Burlington
   Population 39,184
Number of Representatives in Congress 1
Number of Counties...14
Number of Municipal Governments...............................47
Number of 2008 Electoral Votes 3
Number of School Districts 299
Number of Special Districts 152

LEGISLATIVE BRANCH

Legislative Body.......................................General Assembly

President of the Senate.. Lt. Gov. Brian Dubie
President Pro Tem of the Senate .... Peter Welch
Secretary of the Senate .... David A. Gibson

Speaker of the House..Gaye R. Symington
Clerk of the House.. Donald G. Milne

2006 Regular Session .... Jan. 3–TBD
Number of Senatorial Districts 13
Number of Representative Districts 106

EXECUTIVE BRANCH

Governor..James Douglas
Lieutenant Governor.. Brian Dubie
Secretary of State..Deborah Markowitz
Attorney General ....William H. Sorrell
Treasurer.. Jeb Spaulding
Auditor ....Randy Brock

Governor's Present Term 1/03–1/07
Number of Elected Officials in the Executive Branch...........................6
Number of Members in the Cabinet 7

JUDICIAL BRANCH

Highest Court...Supreme Court
Supreme Court Chief Justice...........................Paul L. Reiber
Number of Supreme Court Judges 5
Total Number of Appellant Court Judges..............................0
Number of U.S. Court Districts 1
U.S. Circuit Court.. 2nd Circuit

STATE INTERNET ADDRESSES

Official State Website ....http://vermont.gov
Governor's Website ....http://www.vermont.gov/governor/
Legislative Website................................http://www.leg.state.vt.us
Judicial Website....................................http://www.vermontjudiciary.org

Virginia

Nickname.. The Old Dominion
Motto ....*Sic Semper Tyrannis* (Thus Always to Tyrants)
Flower... Dogwood
Bird... Cardinal
Tree... Dogwood
Song.. *Carry Me Back to Old Virginia*
Entered the Union .... June 25, 1788
Capital .... Richmond

STATISTICS

Land Area (square miles)..39,594
   Rank in Nation 37th
Population... 7,567,465
   Rank in Nation 12th
   Density per square miles 178.8
Capital City... Richmond
   Population..194,729
   Rank in State...4th
Largest City ....Virginia Beach
   Population 439,467
Number of Representatives in Congress 11
Number of Counties...135
Number of Municipal Governments...............................229
Number of 2008 Electoral Votes 13
Number of School Districts 134
Number of Special Districts 196

LEGISLATIVE BRANCH

Legislative Body.......................................General Assembly

President of the Senate.. Lt. Gov. Bill Bolling
President Pro Tem of the Senate .... John H. Chichester
Clerk of the Senate .... Susan Clarke Schaar

Speaker of the House..William J. Howell
Clerk of the House.. Bruce F. Jamerson

2006 Regular Session Jan.11–March 11, 2006
Number of Senatorial Districts 40
Number of Representative Districts 100

EXECUTIVE BRANCH

Governor.. Tim Kaine
Lieutenant Governor.. William T. Bolling
Secretary of the Commonwealth ....Katherine K. Hanley
Attorney General ....Robert F. McDonnell
Treasurer.. Braxton Powell
Auditor ....Walter J. Kucharski
Comptroller .... David Von Moll

Governor's Present Term 1/02–1/06
Number of Elected Officials in the Executive Branch...........................3
Number of Members in the Cabinet 13

JUDICIAL BRANCH

Highest Court...Supreme Court
Supreme Court Chief Justice...........................Leroy R. Hassell Sr.
Number of Supreme Court Judges 7
Total Number of Appellant Court Judges..............................11
Number of U.S. Court Districts 2
U.S. Circuit Court.. 4th Circuit

STATE INTERNET ADDRESSES

Official State Website ....http://www.virginia.gov
Governor's Website ....http://www.governor.state.va.us
Legislative Website................................http://legis.state.va.us
Judicial Website....................................http://www.courts.state.va.us

Washington

Nickname...The Evergreen State
Motto............................*Alki* (Chinook Indian word meaning By and By)
Flower.. Coast Rhododendron
Bird...Willow Goldfinch
Tree..Western Hemlock
Song... *Washington, My Home*
Entered the Union... November 11, 1889
Capital ....Olympia

STATISTICS

Land Area (square miles)..66,544
   Rank in Nation..20th
Population...6,267,759
   Rank in Nation..15th
   Density per square mile..88.6
Capital City..Olympia
   Population..43,963
   Rank in State..18th
Largest City ....Seattle
   Population..569,101
Number of Representatives in Congress 9
Number of Counties...39
Number of Municipal Governments..279
Number of 2008 Electoral Votes 11
Number of School Districts 296
Number of Special Districts..1,173

LEGISLATIVE BRANCH

Legislative Body..Legislature

President of the Senate...Lt. Gov. Brad Owen
President Pro Tem of the Senate ....Rosa Franklin
Secretary of the Senate ....Tom Hoemann

Speaker of the House ....Frank Chopp
Speaker Pro Tem of the House..John Lovick
Chief Clerk of the House ....Rich Nafziger

2006 Regular Session ....Jan. 9–March 9, 2006
Number of Senatorial Districts 49
Number of Representative Districts 49

EXECUTIVE BRANCH

Governor...Christine O. Gregoire
Lieutenant Governor..Brad Owen
Secretary of State..Sam Reed
Attorney General ....Rob McKenna
Treasurer..Michael J. Murphy
Auditor ....Brian Sonntag
Director of Office of Financial Management ....Victor Moore

Governor's Present Term 1/05–1/09
Number of Elected Officials in the Executive Branch...........................9
Number of Members in the Cabinet...28

JUDICIAL BRANCH

Highest Court..Supreme Court
Supreme Court Chief Justice.....................................Gerry L. Alexander
Number of Supreme Court Judges...9
Total Number of Appellant Court Judges...22
Number of U.S. Court Districts 2
U.S. Circuit Court..9th Circuit

STATE INTERNET ADDRESSES

Official State Website ....http://access.wa.gov
Governor's Website ....http://www.governor.wa.gov
Legislative Website...http://www.leg.wa.gov
Judicial Website...http://www.courts.wa.gov

West Virginia

Nickname..The Mountain State
Motto .... *Montani Semper Liberi*
(Mountaineers Are Always Free)
Flower.. Rhododendron
Bird.. Cardinal
Tree.. Sugar Maple
Songs... *West Virginia, My Home Sweet Home*;
The West Virginia Hills;
and *This is My West Virginia*
Entered the Union.. June 20, 1863
Capital ....Charleston

STATISTICS

Land Area (square miles)... 24,078
   Rank in Nation..41st
Population...1,816,856
   Rank in Nation..37th
   Density per square mile..75.1
Capital City...Charleston
   Population..51,394
   Rank in State..1st
Largest City ....Charleston
Number of Representatives in Congress 3
Number of Counties...55
Number of Municipal Governments..234
Number of 2008 Electoral Votes 5
Number of School Districts...55
Number of Special Districts..342

LEGISLATIVE BRANCH

Legislative Body..Legislature

President of the Senate... Earl Ray Tomblin
President Pro Tem of the Senate ....William R. Sharpe Jr.
Clerk of the Senate ....Darrell E. Holmes

Speaker of the House of Delegates ....Robert S. Kiss
Speaker Pro Tem of the House of Delegates ....John Pino
Clerk of the House of Delegates ....Gregory M. Gray

2006 Regular Session ....Jan. 11–March 11, 2006
Number of Senatorial Districts 17
Number of Representative Districts 58

EXECUTIVE BRANCH

Governor... Joe Manchin III
Lieutenant Governor... Earl Ray Tomblin
Secretary of State.. Betty Ireland
Attorney General ....Darrell V. McGraw Jr.
Treasurer... John D. Perdue
Auditor .... Glen B. Gainer III

Governor's Present Term 1/05–1/09
Number of Elected Officials in the Executive Branch...........................6
Number of Members in the Cabinet...10

JUDICIAL BRANCH

Highest Court..Supreme Court of Appeals
Supreme Court of Appeals Chief Justice...................Joseph P. Albright
Number of Supreme Court of Appeals Judges 5
Total Number of Appellant Court Judges...0
Number of U.S. Court Districts 2
U.S. Circuit Court..4th Circuit

STATE INTERNET ADDRESSES

Official State Website ....http://www.wv.gov/
Governor's Website ....http://www.state.wv.us/governor
Legislative Website................http://www.legis.state.wv.us/legishp.html
Judicial Website.......................................http://www.state.wv.us/wvsca

Wisconsin

Nickname*	The Badger State
Motto	*Forward*
Flower	Wood Violet
Bird	Robin
Tree	Sugar Maple
Song	*On, Wisconsin!*
Entered the Union	May 29, 1848
Capitol	Madison

STATISTICS

Land Area (square miles)	54,310
Rank in Nation	25th
Population	5,536,201
Rank in Nation	20th
Density per square mile	98.8
Capital City	Madison
Population	218,432
Rank in State	2nd
Largest City	Milwaukee
Population	586,941
Number of Representatives in Congress	8
Number of Counties	72
Number of Municipal Governments	585
Number of 2008 Electoral Votes	10
Number of School Districts	437
Number of Special Districts	684

LEGISLATIVE BRANCH

Legislative Body	Legislature
President of the Senate	Alan J. Lasee
President Pro Tem of the Senate	David A. Zien
Chief Clerk of the Senate	Robert J. Marchant
Speaker of the Assembly	John Gard
Speaker Pro Tem of the Assembly	Stephen J. Freese
Chief Clerk of the Assembly	Patrick Fuller
2006 Regular Session	Jan. 17 – TBD
Number of Senatorial Districts	33
Number of Representative Districts	99

EXECUTIVE BRANCH

Governor	James Doyle
Lieutenant Governor	Barbara Lawton
Secretary of State	Douglas LaFollette
Attorney General	Peg Lautenschlager
Treasurer	Jack C. Voight
Auditor	Janice L Mueller
Controller	William J. Rafferty
Governor's Present Term	1/03 – 1/07
Number of Elected Officials in the Executive Branch	6
Number of Members in the Cabinet	16

JUDICIAL BRANCH

Highest Court	Supreme Court
Supreme Court Chief Justice	Shirley S. Abrahamson
Number of Supreme Court Judges	7
Total Number of Appellant Court Judges	16
Number of U.S. Court Districts	2
U.S. Circuit Court	7th Circuit

STATE INTERNET ADDRESSES

Official State Website	http://www.wisconsin.gov
Governor's Website	http://www.wisgov.state.wi.us
Legislative Website	http://www.legis.state.wi.us
Judicial Website	http://www.courts.state.wi.us

*unofficial

Wyoming

Nicknames	The Equality State and The Cowboy State
Motto	*Equal Rights*
Flower	Indian Paintbrush
Bird	Western Meadowlark
Tree	Cottonwood
Song	*Wyoming*
Entered the Union	July 10, 1890
Capital	Cheyenne

STATISTICS

Land Area (square miles)	97,100
Rank in Nation	9th
Population	509,294
Rank in Nation	51st
Density per square mile	5.1
Capital City	Cheyenne
Population	54,374
Rank in State	1st
Largest City	Cheyenne
Number of Representatives in Congress	1
Number of Counties	23
Number of Municipal Governments	98
Number of 2008 Electoral Votes	3
Number of School Districts	48
Number of Special Districts	546

LEGISLATIVE BRANCH

Legislative Body	Legislature
President of the Senate	Grant C. Larson
Vice President of the Senate	John J. Hines
Chief Clerk of the Senate	Diane Harvey
Speaker of the House	Randall B. Luthi
Speaker Pro Tem of the House	Colin M. Simpson
Chief Clerk of the House	Patricia Benskin
2006 Regular Session	Feb. 13 – TBD
Number of Senatorial Districts	30
Number of Representative Districts	60

EXECUTIVE BRANCH

Governor	Dave Freudenthal
Secretary of State	Joe Meyer
Attorney General	Pat Crank
Treasurer	Cynthia M. Lummis
Auditor	Max Maxfield
Governor's Present Term	1/03 – 1/07
Number of Elected Officials in the Executive Branch	5
Number of Members in the Cabinet	20

JUDICIAL BRANCH

Highest Court	Supreme Court
Supreme Court Chief Justice	William U. Hill
Number of Supreme Court Judges	5
Total Number of Appellant Court Judges	0
Number of U.S. Court Districts	1
U.S. Circuit Court	10th Circuit

STATE INTERNET ADDRESSES

Official State Website	http://www.state.wy.us
Governor's Website	http://www.state.wy.us/governor/governor_home.asp
Legislative Website	http://legisweb.state.wy.us
Judicial Website	http://www.courts.state.wy.us

District of Columbia

Motto	*Justitia Omnibus* (Justice to All)
Flower	American Beauty Rose
Bird	Wood Thrush
Tree	Scarlet Oak
Became U.S. Capital	December 1, 1800

STATISTICS

Land Area (square miles)	63
Population	550,521
Density per square mile	9316.4
Delegate to Congress*	1
Number of Municipal Governments	1
Number of 2008 Electoral Votes	3
Number of School Districts	2
Number of Special Districts	1

*Committee voting privileges only.

LEGISLATIVE BRANCH

Legislative Body	Council of the District of Columbia
Chair	Linda W. Cropp
Chair Pro Tem	Jack Evans
Secretary to the Council	Ira Stohlman
2006 Regular Session	Jan. 2 – Dec. 31, 2006

EXECUTIVE BRANCH

Mayor	Anthony Williams
Secretary of the District of Columbia	Patricia Elwood
Corporation Counsel	Robert Spanoletti
Chief Financial Officer	Lasana Mack
Auditor	Deborah Nichols
Mayor's Present Term	1/01 – 1/07
Number of Elected Officials in the Executive Branch	10
Number of Members in the Cabinet	10

JUDICIAL BRANCH

Highest Court	D.C. Court of Appeals
Court of Appeals Chief Justice	Eric Washington
Number of Court of Appeals Judges	9
Number of U.S. Court Districts	1

INTERNET ADDRESSES

Official Website	http://www.washingtondc.gov
Mayor's Website	http://dc.gov/mayor/index.shtm
Legislative Website	http://www.dccouncil.washington.dc.us
Judicial Website	http://www.dcbar.org

American Samoa

Motto	*Samoa-Maumua le Atua* (Samoa, God Is First)
Flower	Paogo (Ula-fala)
Plant	Ava
Song	*Amerika Samoa*
Became a Territory of the United States	1900
Capital	Pago Pago

STATISTICS

Land Area (square miles)	77
Population	57,291
Density per square mile	744.0
Capital City	Pago Pago
Population	4,100
Rank in Territory	3rd
Largest City	Tafuna
Population	8,409
Delegate to Congress	1
Number of School Districts	1

LEGISLATIVE BRANCH

Legislative Body	Legislature
President of the Senate	Lola M. Moliga
President Pro Tem of the Senate	Faiivae A. Galea'l
Secretary of the Senate	Leo'o V. Ma'o
Speaker of the House	Matagi Mailo Ray McMoore
Vice Speaker	Savali Talavou Ale
Chief Clerk of the House	Fialupe Lutu
2006 Regular Session	Jan. 9 – TBD
Number of Senatorial Districts	12
Number of Representative Districts	17

EXECUTIVE BRANCH

Governor	Togiola T.A. Tulafono
Lieutenant Governor	Ipulasi Aitofele Sunia
Attorney General	Malaetasi M. Togafau
Treasurer	Belega Savali Jr.
Governor's Present Term	4/03 – 1/09
Number of Members in the Cabinet	16

JUDICIAL BRANCH

Highest Court	High Court
High Court Chief Justice	F. Michael Kruse
Number of High Court Judges	6

INTERNET ADDRESSES

Official Website	http://www.asg-gov.com/
Governor's Website	http://www.asg-/gov.com
Legislative Website	http://www.government.as/legislative.htm
Judicial Website	http://www.government.as/highcourt.htm

Guam

Nickname	Hub of the Pacific
Flower	Puti Tai Nobio (Bougainvillea)
Bird	Toto (Fruit Dove)
Tree	Ifit (Intsiabijuga)
Song	*Stand Ye Guamanians*
Stone	Latte
Animal	Iguana
Ceded to the United States by Spain	December 10, 1898
Became a Territory	August 1, 1950
Request to become a Commonwealth Plebiscite	November 1987
Capital	Hagatna

STATISTICS

Land Area (square miles)	210
Population	154,805
Density per square mile	737.1
Capital	Hagatna
Population	1,100
Rank in Territory	18th
Largest City	Dededo
Population	42,980
Delegate to Congress	1
Number of School Districts	1

LEGISLATIVE BRANCH

Legislative Body	Legislature
Speaker	Mark Forbes
Vice Speaker	Joanne M.S. Brown
Clerk of the Legislature	Edward J.B. Calvo
2006 Regular Session	Jan. 9, 2006 – TBD
Number of Senatorial Districts	15

EXECUTIVE BRANCH

Governor	Felix Camacho
Lieutenant Governor	Kaleo Moylan
Attorney General	Douglas Moylan
Treasurer	Y'Asela A. Pereira
Auditor	Doris Flores Brooks
Governor's Present Term	1/03 – 1/07
Number of Elected Officials in the Executive Branch	10
Number of Members in the Cabinet	55

JUDICIAL BRANCH

Highest Court	Supreme Court
Supreme Court Chief Justice	F. Philip Cabullido
Number of Supreme Court Judges	3

INTERNET ADDRESSES

Official Website	http://ns.gov.gu
Governor's Website	http://ns.gov.gu/webtax/govoff.html
Legislative Website	http://www.guam.net/gov/senate
Judicial Website	http://www.justice.gov.gu

Northern Mariana Islands

Flower	Plumeria
Bird	Marianas Fruit Dove
Tree	Flame Tree
Song	*Gi TaloGi Halom Tasi*
Administered by the United States a trusteeship for the United Nations	July 18, 1947
Voters approved a proposed constitution	June 1975
U.S. president signed covenant agreeing to commonwealth status for the islands	March 24, 1976
Became a self-governing Commonwealth	January 9, 1978
Capital	Saipan

STATISTICS

Land Area (square miles)	181
Population	69,221
Density per square mile	382.4
Capital City	Saipan
Population	62,392
Largest City	Saipan
Delegate to Congress	1
Number of School Districts	1

LEGISLATIVE BRANCH

Legislative Body	Legislature
President of the Senate	Joseph Mendiola
Vice President of the Senate	Pete R. Reyes
Clerk of the Senate	Doris Bermudes
Speaker of the House	Oscar M. Babauta
Vice Speaker of the House	Justo S. Quitugua
Clerk of the House	Evelyn C. Fleming
2006 Regular Session	Not Available
Number of Senatorial Districts	9
Number of Representative Districts	18

EXECUTIVE BRANCH

Governor	Benigno Fitial
Lieutenant Governor	Timothy Villagomez
Attorney General	Matt Gregory
Treasurer	Antoinette S. Calvo
Governor's Present Term	1/06 – 1/10
Number of Elected Officials in the Executive Branch	10
Number of Members in the Cabinet	16

JUDICIAL BRANCH

Highest Court	Commonwealth Supreme Court
Commonwealth Supreme Court Chief Justice	Miguel S. Demapan
Number of Commonwealth Supreme Court Judges	3

INTERNET ADDRESSES

Official Website	http://www.saipan.com/gov
Governor's Website	http://www.mariana-islands.gov.mp
Legislative Website	http://www.saipan.com/gov/branches/senate
Judicial Website	http://cnmilaw.org/htmlpage/hpg34.htm

Puerto Rico

Nickname... Island of Enchantment
Motto ....*Joannes Est Nomen Ejus*
(John is Thy Name)
Flower.. Maga
Bird.. Reinita
Tree... Ceiba
Song..*La Borinquena*
Became a Territory of the
   United States.. December 10, 1898
Became a self-governing Commonwealth........................ July 25, 1952
Capital .... San Juan

STATISTICS

Land Area (square miles)... 3,427
Population.. 3,878,523
   Density per square mile.. 1,111.8
Capital City... San Juan
   Population 421,958
Largest City .... San Juan
Delegate to Congress* 1
Number of School Districts 1

*Committee voting privileges only.

LEGISLATIVE BRANCH

Legislative Body.................................Legislative Assembly
President of the Senate....................... Kenneth D. McClintock
Vice President
   of the Senate .... Orlando Parga Figueroa
Secretary of the Senate .... Manuel A. Torres Nieves

Speaker of the House .... Jose Aponte Hernandez
Speaker Pro Tem.................................Epifanio Jimenez Cruz
Clerk of the House ....Nester Duprey-Salgado

2006 Regular Session .... Jan. 9 – June 30, 2006

EXECUTIVE BRANCH

Governor... Anibal Acevedo-Villa
Secretary of State................................... Fernando J. Bonilla
Attorney General .... Roberto J. Sanchez-Ramos
Treasurer.................................... Juan Carlos Mendez Torres
Controller .... Manuel Diaz-Saldana

Governor's Present Term ....1/05 – 1/09
Number of Elected Officials in the Executive Branch.......................... 10
Number of Members in the Cabinet...................................... 18

JUDICIAL BRANCH

Highest Court.. Supreme Court
Supreme Court Chief Justice................... Frederico Hernandez-Denton
Number of Supreme Court Judges 7

INTERNET ADDRESSES

Official State Website .... http://www.puertorico.pr
Governor's Website .... http://www.fortaleza.gobierno.pr
Senate Website................... http://www.camaradepuertorico.org
House Website .... http://www.camaradepuertorico.org
Judicial Website................................http://www.tribunalpr.org

U.S. Virgin Islands

Nickname.. The American Paradise
Motto ....*United in Pride and Hope*
Flower.. The Yellow Cedar
Bird.. Yellow Breast or Banana Quit
Song..*Virgin Islands March*
Purchased from Denmark... March 31, 1917
Capital .... Charlotte Amalie, St. Thomas

STATISTICS

Land Area (square miles)*... 134
Population.. 108,612
   Density per square mile.. 810.5
Capital City................................. Charlotte Amalie, St. Thomas
   Population.. 11,004
Largest City .... Charlotte Amalie, St. Thomas
Delegate to Congress** 1
Number of School Districts 1

*The U.S. Virgin Islands is comprised of three large islands (St. Croix, St. John, and St. Thomas) and 50 smaller islands and cays.

**Committee voting privileges only.

LEGISLATIVE BRANCH

Legislative Body... Legislature

President ....Lorraine L. Berry
Vice President..Ronald Russell
Legislative Secretary of the Senate .... Juan Figueroa-Serville

2006 Regular Session .... Jan. 9 – TBD

EXECUTIVE BRANCH

Governor...Charles W. Turnbull
Lieutenant Governor................................... Vargrave Richards
Attorney General .... Kerry Drue
Treasurer .... Bernice A. Turnbull

Governor's Present Term ....1/03 – 1/07
Number of Elected Officials in the Executive Branch.......................... 10
Number of Members in the Cabinet...................................... 21

JUDICIAL BRANCH

Highest Court...Territorial Court
Territorial Court Chief Justice .... Maria M. Cabret
Number of Territorial Court Judges 3
U.S. Circuit Court 3rd

INTERNET ADDRESSES

Official Website ....http://www.usvi.org
Governor's Website ....http://www.usvi.org
Legislative Website..........................http://www.senate.gov.vi
Judicial Website .... http://www.vid.uscourts.gov

Index

—H—